Accounting Trends & Techniques

Presenting and Analyzing Financial Reporting Practices

D1470974

10819-341

SIXTY-FOURTH EDITION

03262368

1 2 3 4 5 6 7 8 9 0 AAP 1 9 8 7 6 5 4 3 2 1 0

ISSN 1531-4340

ISBN 978-0-87051-927-7

Notice to readers: This book does not represent an official position of the American Institute of Certified Public Accountants, and it is distributed with the understanding that the authors and publisher are not rendering legal, accounting, or other professional services via this publication.

Publisher: Amy M. Stainken
Director, Accounting & Auditing Publications: Amy Eubanks
Senior Technical Manager: Doug Bowman
Developmental Editor: David Cohen
Project Manager: M. Donovan Scott

The 2010 edition of *Accounting Trends & Techniques* was developed by

Matthew C. Calderisi
Senior Editor

Doug Bowman
Senior Technical Manager
AICPA Accounting and Auditing Publications

David Cohen
Developmental Editor
AICPA Professional Product Development

Special acknowledgment and sincere thanks are due to the following individuals for their efforts and without whom this book would not be possible:

J. Richard Chaplin
Lisa Hopson
Peggy Hughes
Kathleen V. Karatas

Gene P. Leporiere
Toni Monier
Richard V. Rikert
Karen Venturini

About This Edition of *Accounting Trends & Techniques*

Accounting Trends & Techniques (*Trends*) compiles annual reporting and disclosure data and examples from a survey of the annual reports of publicly traded entities. *Trends* provides accounting professionals with an invaluable resource for incorporating new and existing accounting and reporting guidance into financial statements using presentation techniques adopted by some of the most recognized entities headquartered in the United States. This 2010 edition of *Trends* surveyed annual reports of 500 carefully selected industrial, merchandising, technology, and service entities for fiscal periods ending between January and December 2009.

To provide you with the most useful and comprehensive look at current financial reporting techniques and methods, *Trends* is organized by financial statement disclosure and offers guidance about reporting requirements, statistical tables that track reporting trends, excerpts from the surveyed annual reports showing reporting techniques, and detailed indexes.

Guidance

Trends offers thorough discussions of the significant U.S. generally accepted accounting principles (GAAP) financial statement reporting requirements for each type of disclosure. This guidance also provides the related authoritative sources for each requirement.

Trend Tables

Statistical tables that follow the guidance track significant disclosure and reporting trends, providing a comparison of current survey findings with those of prior years. These tables show trends in such diverse reporting matters as financial statement format and terminology and the treatment of transactions and events reflected in the financial statements. Note that some prior-year comparisons might be affected by the change in sample size to 500 entities from 600 entities in the previous edition.

Excerpts Showing Technique

Trends presents carefully selected excerpts from the annual reports of the survey entities to illustrate current reporting techniques and various presentation practices already subjected to the audit requirements mandated by the Public Company Accounting Oversight Board (PCAOB). Every edition of *Trends* includes all new annual report excerpts that were chosen to be particularly relevant and useful to financial statement preparers in illustrating current reporting practices.

Indexes

Indexes in this edition include the "Appendix of 500 Entities," which alphabetically lists each of the 500 survey entities included in the current edition and notes where in the text excerpts from their annual reports can be found; the "Pronouncement Index," which provides for easy cross-referencing of pronouncements to the applicable descriptive narratives; and a detailed "Subject Index," which is fully cross-referenced to all significant topics included throughout the narratives.

FASB Accounting Standards Codification™

Because Financial Accounting Standards Board (FASB) *Accounting Standards Codification*™ (ASC) is the source of authoritative U.S. GAAP for nongovernmental entities, in addition to guidance issued by the SEC, the guidance within *Trends* refers only to the appropriate FASB ASC reference for all standards and other authoritative guidance codified therein. This edition of *Trends* includes a number of financial statement reporting examples that do not reference FASB ASC either because it was not effective as of the end of the annual reporting period of the respective survey entity from which the examples were derived or because the survey entity chose not to include FASB ASC references.

Recent Guidance

Note that the effective dates of recently released guidance affect the timing of its inclusion in the financial statements of the survey entities, thereby affecting the availability of illustrative excerpts for potential inclusion in each edition of *Trends*. This 2010 edition of *Trends* includes survey entities having fiscal years ending within calendar year 2009. Recently issued technical guidance for which this edition supplies illustrative annual report excerpts include SFAS No. 141R, *Business Combinations* (FASB ASC 805, *Business Combinations*), SFAS No. 165, *Subsequent Events* (FASB ASC 855, *Subsequent Events*), SFAS No. 161, *Disclosures about Derivative Instruments and Hedging Activities—an amendment of FASB Statement No. 133* (FASB ASC 815, *Derivatives and Hedging*), and SFAS No. 160, *Noncontrolling Interests in Consolidated Financial Statements—an amendment of ARB No. 51* (FASB ASC 810, *Consolidation*), among other recently issued guidance.

Related Publications

Trends presents and analyzes financial reporting information for public, non-regulated entities across the industrial, merchandising, technology, and service sectors. To see a similar presentation and analysis for International Financial Reporting Standards, employee benefit plans, not-for-profit entities, and state and local governments, please see the related publications in AICPA's *Accounting Trends & Techniques* series:

IFRS Accounting Trends & Techniques

Employee Benefit Plans Accounting Trends & Techniques

Not-for-Profit Entities Accounting Trends & Techniques

State and Local Governments Accounting Trends & Techniques

Feedback

We hope that you find this year's edition of *Trends* to be informative and useful. Please let us know! What features do you like? What do you think can be improved or added? We encourage you to give us your comments and questions about all aspects of *Trends*. Please direct your feedback to David Cohen, using the following contact information. All feedback is greatly appreciated and kept strictly confidential.

David Cohen—Professional Publications
AMERICAN INSTITUTE OF CERTIFIED PUBLIC ACCOUNTANTS
220 Leigh Farm Road
Durham, NC 27707-8110
Telephone: 919-402-4030
E-mail: dcohen@aicpa.org

You can also contact the Accounting and Auditing Publications team of the AICPA directly via e-mail:

A&Apublications@aicpa.org

TABLE OF CONTENTS

Section   **Paragraph**

Section   **Paragraph**

Section			**Paragraph**

Section		Paragraph

LIST OF TABLES

Table	Paragraph

Table	Paragraph

Section 1: General

ENTITIES SELECTED FOR SURVEY

1.01 This section is concerned with general information about the 500 entities selected for the survey and with certain accounting information usually disclosed in notes accompanying the basic financial statements. In years prior to fiscal 2008, 600 entities were used in the survey. All tables of significant accounting trends will be based on a survey of 500 entities for the current and preceding year and 600 entities for the years prior to fiscal year 2008.

1.02 All 500 entities included in the survey are registered with the Securities and Exchange Commission (SEC). Many of the survey entities have securities traded on one of the major stock exchanges—81% on the New York and less than 1% on the American. The remaining entities were traded on NASDAQ or the "over-the-counter" exchanges.

1.03 Each year, entities are selected from the latest Fortune 1000 listing to replace those entities that were deleted from the survey (see the *Appendix of 500 Entities* for a comprehensive listing of the 500 entities as well as those that were added and removed in this edition). Generally, entities are deleted from the survey when they have either been acquired, become privately held (and are, therefore, no longer registered with the SEC), failed to timely issue a report, or ceased operations.

1.04

TABLE 1-1: INDUSTRY CLASSIFICATIONS OF SURVEY ENTITIES

	2009	2008
Advertising, marketing	4	4
Aerospace	14	14
Apparel	12	10
Beverages	8	8
Building materials, glass	9	8
Chemicals	25	25
Computer peripherals	5	5
Computer software	11	10
Computers, office equipment	9	8
Diversified outsourcing services	11	11
Electronics, electrical equipment	28	28
Engineering, construction	9	9
Entertainment	10	10
Food	22	21
Food and drug stores	13	14
Food services	10	9
Forest and paper products	11	10
Furniture	9	9
General merchandisers	11	11
Health care	6	11
Homebuilders	9	9
Hotels, casinos, resorts	5	5
Household and personal products	8	8
Industrial and farm equipment	26	26
Information technology services	12	12
Mail, package and freight delivery	2	2
Medical products and equipment	11	10
Metal products	8	9
Metals	12	12
Mining, crude-oil production	12	12
Miscellaneous	2	1
Motor vehicles and parts	13	15
Network communications	5	4
Packaging, containers	8	8
Petroleum refining	12	12
Pharmaceuticals	8	10
Publishing, printing	12	12
Rubber and plastic products	4	4
Scientific, photographic, and control equipment	15	13
Semiconductors	11	11
Soaps, cosmetics	6	5
Specialty retailers	19	20
Telecommunications	9	10
Temporary help	4	5
Textiles	2	2
Tobacco	4	4
Toys, sporting goods	2	2
Transportation equipment	4	4
Trucking, truck leasing	4	4
Waste management	2	2
Wholesalers	12	12
Total Entities	**500**	**500**

1.05   Table 1-2 indicates the relative size of the survey entities as measured by dollar amount of revenue.

1.06

TABLE 1-2: SIZE OF SURVEY ENTITIES BY AMOUNT OF REVENUE

	2009	2008	2007	2006
Less than $100,000,000	3	3	12	17
Between $100,000,000 and $500,000,000	13	10	30	30
Between $500,000,000 and $1,000,000,000	19	8	29	33
Between $1,000,000,000 and $2,000,000,000	75	53	81	82
Between $2,000,000,000 and $3,000,000,000	67	65	90	86
Between $3,000,000,000 and $4,000,000,000	44	53	42	55
Between $4,000,000,000 and $5,000,000,000	42	37	42	34
Between $5,000,000,000 and $10,000,000,000	93	105	116	108
More than $10,000,000,000	144	166	158	155
Total Entities	**500**	**500**	**600**	**600**

2008–2009 based on 500 entities surveyed; 2006–2007 based on 600 entities surveyed.

INFORMATION REQUIRED BY RULE 14a-3 TO BE INCLUDED IN ANNUAL REPORTS TO STOCKHOLDERS

1.07   Rule 14a-3, *Information to Be Furnished to Security Holders*, of the Securities Exchange Act of 1934, states that annual reports furnished to stockholders in connection with the annual meetings of stockholders should include audited financial statements—balance sheets as of the 2 most recent fiscal years, and statements of income and of cash flows for each of the 3 most recent fiscal years. *Rule 14a-3* also states that the following information, as specified in Securities and Exchange Commission (SEC) Regulation S-K, *Standard Instructions for Filing Forms Under the Securities Act of 1933, Securities Exchange Act of 1934 and Energy Policy and Conservation Act of 1975*, should be included in the annual report to stockholders:

1. Selected quarterly financial data.
2. Disagreements with accountants on accounting and financial disclosure.
3. Summary of selected financial data for the last 5 years.
4. Description of business activities.
5. Segment information.
6. Listing of company directors and executive officers.
7. Market price of company's common stock for each quarterly period within the two most recent fiscal years.

8. Management's discussion and analysis of financial condition and results of operations.
9. Quantitative and qualitative disclosures about market risk.

1.08   Examples of items 1, 3, 8, and 9 follow. Included with the item 8 examples are excerpts from management's discussion and analysis as to forward looking information, liquidity and capital resources, new accounting standards, and critical accounting policies.

1.09   Examples of segment information disclosures are presented under "Segment Information" in this section.

Quarterly Financial Data

1.10

CVS CAREMARK CORPORATION (DEC)

NOTES TO CONSOLIDATED FINANCIAL STATEMENTS

15. Quarterly Financial Information (Unaudited)

(In millions, except per share amounts)	First Quarter	Second Quarter	Third Quarter	Fourth Quarter	Fiscal Year
2009:					
Net revenues	$ 23,394	$ 24,871	$ 24,642	$ 25,822	$ 98,729
Gross profit	4,748	5,052	5,012	5,568	20,380
Operating profit	1,377	1,600	1,566	1,895	6,438
Income from continuing operations	743	889	1,023	1,053	3,708
Loss from discontinued operations, net of income tax benefit	(5)	(3)	(2)	(2)	(12)
Net income	738	886	1,021	1,051	3,696
Earnings per share from continuing operations, basic	$ 0.51	$ 0.61	$ 0.72	$ 0.75	$ 2.59
Loss per common share from discontinued operations	—	—	(0.01)	—	(0.01)
Net earnings per common share, basic	$ 0.51	$ 0.61	$ 0.71	$ 0.75	$ 2.58
Earnings per common share from continuing operations, diluted	$ 0.51	$ 0.60	$ 0.71	$ 0.74	$ 2.56
Loss per common share from discontinued operations	(0.01)	—	—	—	(0.01)
Net earnings per common share, diluted	$ 0.50	$ 0.60	$ 0.71	$ 0.74	$ 2.55
Dividends per common share	$0.07625	$0.07625	$0.07625	$0.07625	$0.30500
Stock price: (New York Stock Exchange)					
High	$ 30.47	$ 34.22	$ 37.75	$ 38.27	$ 38.27
Low	$ 23.74	$ 27.08	$ 30.58	$ 27.38	$ 23.74
2008[1]:					
Net revenues	$ 21,326	$ 21,140	$ 20,863	$ 24,143	$ 87,472
Gross profit	4,293	4,373	4,401	5,223	18,290
Operating profit	1,370	1,478	1,466	1,732	6,046
Income from continuing operations	749	824	819	952	3,344
Loss from discontinued operations, net of income tax benefit	—	(49)	(83)	—	(132)
Net income	749	775	736	952	3,212
Earnings per share from continuing operations, basic	$ 0.52	$ 0.57	$ 0.57	$ 0.66	$ 2.32
Loss per common share from discontinued operations	—	(0.03)	(0.06)	—	(0.09)
Net earnings per common share, basic	$ 0.52	$ 0.54	$ 0.51	$ 0.66	$ 2.23
Earnings per common share from continuing operations, diluted	$ 0.51	$ 0.56	$ 0.56	$ 0.65	$ 2.27
Loss per common share from discontinued operations	—	(0.03)	(0.06)	—	(0.09)
Net earnings per common share, diluted	$ 0.51	$ 0.53	$ 0.50	$ 0.65	$ 2.18
Dividends per common share	$0.06000	$0.06000	$0.06900	$0.06900	$0.25800
Stock price: (New York Stock Exchange)					
High	$ 41.53	$ 44.29	$ 40.14	$ 34.90	$ 44.29
Low	$ 34.91	$ 39.02	$ 31.81	$ 23.19	$ 23.19

[1] On December 23, 2008, our Board of Directors approved a change in our fiscal year-end from the Saturday nearest December 31 of each year to December 31 of each year to better reflect our position in the health care, rather than the retail, industry. The fiscal year change was effective beginning with the fourth quarter of fiscal 2008.

1.11

MERCK & CO., INC. (DEC)

SUPPLEMENTARY DATA

Selected quarterly financial data for 2009 and 2008 are contained in the Condensed Interim Financial Data table below.

Condensed Interim Financial Data (Unaudited)

($ in millions except per share amounts)	4th Q[1],[2],[3]	3rd Q[3],[4]	2nd Q[3],[5]	1st Q[3],[6]
2009[7]				
Sales	$10,093.5	$6,049.7	$5,899.9	$5,385.2
Materials and production costs	4,900.8	1,430.3	1,353.9	1,333.8
Marketing and administrative expenses	3,455.2	1,725.5	1,729.5	1,632.9
Research and development expenses	1,971.5	1,254.0	1,395.3	1,224.2
Restructuring costs	1,489.8	42.4	37.4	64.3
Equity income from affiliates	(373.8)	(688.2)	(587.1)	(585.8)
Other (income) expense, net	(7,814.8)	(2,791.1)	3.6	(67.2)
Income before taxes	6,464.8	5,076.8	1,967.3	1,783.0
Net income available to common shareholders	6,493.6	3,424.3	1,556.3	1,425.0
Basic earnings per common share available to common shareholders	$ 2.36	$ 1.62	$ 0.74	$ 0.67
Earnings per common share assuming dilution available to common shareholders	$ 2.35	$ 1.61	$ 0.74	$ 0.67
2008[7]				
Sales	$ 6,032.4	$5,943.9	$6,051.8	$5,822.1
Materials and production costs	1,470.0	1,477.9	1,396.5	1,238.1
Marketing and administrative expenses	1,862.1	1,730.3	1,930.2	1,854.4
Research and development expenses	1,386.6	1,171.1	1,169.3	1,078.3
Restructuring costs	103.1	757.5	102.2	69.7
Equity income from affiliates	(720.0)	(665.6)	(523.0)	(652.1)
Other (income) expense, net	(26.8)	30.6	(112.8)	(2,209.2)
Income before taxes	1,957.4	1,442.1	2,089.4	4,442.9
Net income available to common shareholders	1,644.8	1,092.7	1,768.3	3,302.6
Basic earnings per common share available to common shareholders	$ 0.78	$ 0.51	$ 0.82	$ 1.52
Earnings per common share assuming dilution available to common shareholders	$ 0.78	$ 0.51	$ 0.82	$ 1.52

[1] Amounts for 2009 include a gain on the fair value adjustment to Merck's previously held interest in the MSP Partnership.

[2] The fourth quarter 2008 tax provision reflects the favorable impact of foreign exchange rate changes and a benefit relating to the U.S. research and development tax credit.

[3] Amounts for third and fourth quarter 2009 and fourth quarter 2008 include the impact of additional Vioxx legal defense reserves. Amounts for third quarter and second quarter 2009 and first quarter 2008 include the impact of additional Fosamax legal defense reserves.

[4] Amounts for 2009 include a gain on the sale of Old Merck's interest in Merial Limited.

[5] Amounts for 2008 reflect the favorable impact of tax settlements.

[6] Amounts for 2008 include a gain on distribution from AstraZeneca LP, a gain related to the sale of the remaining worldwide rights to Aggrastat, the realization of foreign tax credits and an expense for a contribution to the Merck Company Foundation.

[7] Amounts for 2009 include the impacts of the Merger, including amortization of intangible assets and merger-related costs. Amounts for 2009 and 2008 include the impact of restructuring actions.

Selected Information for Five Years

1.12

INTERNATIONAL FLAVORS & FRAGRANCES INC.
(DEC)

FIVE-YEAR SUMMARY

(Dollars in thousands except per share amounts)	2009	2008	2007	2006	2005
Consolidated statement of income data					
Net sales	$2,326,158	$2,389,372	$2,276,638	$2,095,390	$1,993,393
Cost of goods sold[b]	1,391,032	1,418,738	1,324,424	1,211,259	1,168,992
Research and development expenses[b][g]	193,843	209,295	196,893	183,512	179,812
Selling and administrative expenses[b]	376,541	381,841	375,287	351,923	339,323
Amortization of intangibles	6,153	6,153	12,878	14,843	15,071
Curtailment loss	—	—	5,943	—	—
Restructuring and other charges, net[a]	18,301	18,212	—	2,680	23,319
Interest expense	61,818	74,008	41,535	25,549	23,956
Other (income) expense, net	1,921	(2,797)	(11,136)	(9,838)	(3,268)
	2,049,609	2,105,450	1,945,824	1,779,928	1,747,205
Income before taxes	276,549	283,922	330,814	315,462	246,188
Taxes on income[g]	81,023	54,294	83,686	88,962	53,122
Net income	$ 195,526	$ 229,628	$ 247,128	$ 226,500	$ 193,066
Percentage of net sales	8.4	9.6	10.9	10.8	9.7
Percentage of average shareholders' equity	28.9	38.0	32.0	24.6	20.9
Net income per share—basic	$ 2.48	$ 2.89	$ 2.84	$ 2.50	$ 2.06
Net income per share—diluted	$ 2.46	$ 2.86	$ 2.81	$ 2.48	$ 2.04
Average number of shares (thousands)	78,403	79,032	86,541	90,443	93,584
Consolidated balance sheet data					
Cash and cash equivalents	$ 80,135	$ 178,467	$ 151,471	$ 114,508	$ 272,545
Receivables, net	444,265	400,971	400,527	357,155	304,823
Inventories	444,977	479,567	484,222	446,606	430,794
Property, plant and equipment, net	501,293	496,856	508,820	495,124	499,145
Goodwill and intangible assets, net	720,530	726,683	732,836	745,716	772,651
Total assets[d]	2,644,774	2,749,913	2,726,314	2,478,904	2,638,196
Bank borrowings, overdrafts and current portion of long-term debt	76,780	101,982	152,473	15,897	819,392
Long-term debt	934,749	1,153,672	1,060,168	791,443	131,281
Total Shareholders' equity[b] [c] [d] [f]	771,910	580,642	626,359	916,056	925,808
Other data					
Current ratio[e]	2.3	2.6	2.1	2.4	1.0
Gross additions to property, plant and equipment	$ 66,819	$ 85,395	$ 65,614	$ 58,282	$ 93,433
Depreciation and amortization expense	78,525	75,986	82,788	89,733	91,928
Cash dividends declared	78,962	75,902	76,465	68,956	68,397
Per share	$ 1.00	$ 0.96	$ 0.88	$ 0.765	$ 0.73
Number of shareholders of record at year-end	3,004	3,167	3,248	3,393	3,207
Number of employees at year-end	5,377	5,338	5,315	5,087	5,160

[a] Restructuring and other charges ($14,763 after tax) in 2009, ($12,583 after tax) in 2008, ($1,982 after tax) in 2006, and ($15,857 after tax) in 2005, were the result of various restructuring and reorganization programs of the Company.

[b] 2006–2009 amounts include equity compensation expense in accordance with ASC 718 "Compensation—Stock Compensation."

[c] The 2006 amounts reflect adoption of ASC 715 "Compensation—Retirement Benefits."

[d] The 2007 amounts reflect adoption of ASC 740 "Income Taxes."

[e] Current ratio is equal to current assets divided by current liabilities.

[f] Includes noncontrolling interests for all periods presented.

[g] The 2005–2008 periods have been revised to properly recognize R&D expense, net of R&D credits. Previously, these credits were reflected as a reduction of tax expense.

1.13

NIKE, INC. (MAY)

SELECTED FINANCIAL DATA

| (In millions, except per share data and financial ratios)[1] | Financial History | | | | |
	2009	2008	2007	2006	2005
Year ended May 31,					
Revenues	$19,176.1	$18,627.0	$16,325.9	$14,954.9	$13,739.7
Gross margin	8,604.4	8,387.4	7,160.5	6,587.0	6,115.4
Gross margin %	44.9%	45.0%	43.9%	44.0%	44.5%
Restructuring charges	195.0	—	—	—	—
Goodwill impairment	199.3	—	—	—	—
Intangible and other asset impairment	202.0	—	—	—	—
Net income	1,486.7	1,883.4	1,491.5	1,392.0	1,211.6
Basic earnings per common share	3.07	3.80	2.96	2.69	2.31
Diluted earnings per common share	3.03	3.74	2.93	2.64	2.24
Weighted average common shares outstanding	484.9	495.6	503.8	518.0	525.2
Diluted weighted average common shares outstanding	490.7	504.1	509.9	527.6	540.6
Cash dividends declared per common share	0.98	0.875	0.71	0.59	0.475
Cash flow from operations	1,736.1	1,936.3	1,878.7	1,667.9	1,570.7
Price range of common stock					
High	70.28	70.60	57.12	45.77	46.22
Low	38.24	51.50	37.76	38.27	34.31
At May 31,					
Cash and equivalents	$ 2,291.1	$ 2,133.9	$ 1,856.7	$ 954.2	$ 1,388.1
Short-term investments	1,164.0	642.2	990.3	1,348.8	436.6
Inventories	2,357.0	2,438.4	2,121.9	2,076.7	1,811.1
Working capital	6,457.0	5,517.8	5,492.5	4,733.6	4,339.7
Total assets	13,249.6	12,442.7	10,688.3	9,869.6	8,793.6
Long-term debt	437.2	441.1	409.9	410.7	687.3
Redeemable preferred stock	0.3	0.3	0.3	0.3	0.3
Shareholders' equity	8,693.1	7,825.3	7,025.4	6,285.2	5,644.2
Year-end stock price	57.05	68.37	56.75	40.16	41.10
Market capitalization	27,697.8	33,576.5	28,472.3	20,564.5	21,462.3
Financial ratios:					
Return on equity	18.0%	25.4%	22.4%	23.3%	23.2%
Return on assets	11.6%	16.3%	14.5%	14.9%	14.5%
Inventory turns	4.4	4.5	4.4	4.3	4.4
Current ratio at May 31	3.0	2.7	3.1	2.8	3.2
Price/earnings ratio at May 31	18.8	18.3	19.4	15.2	18.3

[1] All share and per share information has been restated to reflect a two-for-one stock split affected in the form of a 100% common stock dividend distributed on April 2, 2007.

Management's Discussion and Analysis of Financial Condition and Results of Operations

1.14

ALBERTO-CULVER COMPANY (SEP)

MANAGEMENT'S DISCUSSION AND ANALYSIS OF FINANCIAL CONDITION AND RESULTS OF OPERATIONS

Description of Business

Alberto Culver Company (the company or New Alberto Culver) develops, manufactures, distributes and markets beauty care products as well as food and household products in the United States and more than 100 other countries. The company is organized into two reportable business segments—United States and International.

Overview

Discontinued Operations

Unless otherwise noted, all financial information in the accompanying consolidated financial statements and related notes, as well as all discussion in Management's Discussion and Analysis of Financial Condition and Results of Operations (MD&A), reflects only continuing operations.

Cederroth International

Prior to July 31, 2008, the company also owned and operated the Cederroth International (Cederroth) business which manufactured, marketed and distributed beauty, health care and household products throughout Scandinavia and in certain other parts of Europe. On May 18, 2008, the company entered into an agreement to sell its Cederroth business to CapMan, a Nordic based private equity firm. Pursuant to the transaction agreement, on July 31, 2008 Cederroth Intressenter AB, a company owned by two funds controlled by CapMan, purchased all of the issued and outstanding shares of Cederroth International AB in exchange for 159.5 million Euros, from Alberto Culver AB, a wholly-owned Swedish subsidiary of the company. The Euros were immediately converted into $243.8 million based on the deal contingent Euro forward contract entered into by the company in connection with the transaction. The purchase price was adjusted in fiscal year 2009, resulting in cash payments of $1.5 million from Alberto Culver AB to CapMan. These adjustments resulted from differences between the final, agreed-upon balances of cash, debt and working capital as of the July 31, 2008 closing date and the estimates assumed in the transaction agreement.

In accordance with the provisions of the Financial Accounting Standards Board's (FASB) Accounting Standards Codification (ASC) Subtopic 205-20, "Discontinued Operations," the results of operations and cash flows related to the Cederroth business are reported as discontinued operations for all periods presented.

As noted above, the company entered into a deal contingent forward contract to sell the Euros it expected to receive in exchange for U.S. dollars. In connection with the closing of the transaction on July 31, 2008, the company recognized a pre-tax loss of $5.1 million related to the settlement of the forward contract which partially offset the gain on the sale of Cederroth in 2008. Additionally, the company incurred trans-

action costs (primarily investment banking, legal and other professional service fees) of $8.4 million during fiscal years 2009 and 2008, most of which are not expected to give rise to an income tax benefit. These costs were expensed in the periods incurred and recorded as part of the gain (loss) on the sale of Cederroth.

In fiscal year 2008, Cederroth's discontinued operations results include special pre-tax charges of $1.5 million recognized in the fourth quarter in connection with the sale transaction, primarily related to compensation for key employees of the Cederroth business. During fiscal year 2007, Cederroth recognized pre-tax charges of $1.5 million that were previously classified as "restructuring and other" in the consolidated statement of earnings. These charges include $731,000 of severance and other exit costs related to the company's reorganization following the Separation. In addition, Cederroth's discontinued operations results include an $815,000 non-cash charge related to the acceleration of vesting of stock options and restricted shares that occurred in connection with the Separation (as more fully described in the *Sally Holdings, Inc.* section below). This charge reflects the amount of future compensation expense as of November 16, 2006, the closing date of the Separation, that would have been recognized in subsequent periods as the stock options and restricted shares for Cederroth employees vested over the original vesting periods.

Sally Holdings, Inc.

Prior to November 16, 2006, the company also operated a beauty supply distribution business which included two segments: (1) Sally Beauty Supply, a domestic and international chain of cash-and-carry stores offering professional beauty supplies to both salon professionals and retail consumers, and (2) Beauty Systems Group, a full-service beauty supply distributor offering professional brands directly to salons through its own sales force and professional-only stores in exclusive geographical territories in North America and Europe. These two segments comprised Sally Holdings, Inc. (Sally Holdings), a wholly-owned subsidiary of the company.

On June 19, 2006, the company announced a plan to split Sally Holdings from the consumer products business. Pursuant to an Investment Agreement, on November 16, 2006:

- The company separated into two publicly-traded companies: New Alberto Culver, which owns and operates the consumer products business, and Sally Beauty Holdings, Inc. (New Sally), which owns and operates Sally Holdings' beauty supply distribution business;
- CDRS Acquisition LLC (Investor), a limited liability company organized by Clayton, Dubilier & Rice Fund VII, L.P., invested $575 million in New Sally in exchange for an equity interest representing approximately 47.55% of New Sally common stock on a fully diluted basis, and Sally Holdings incurred approximately $1.85 billion of indebtedness; and
- The company's shareholders received, for each share of common stock then owned, (i) one share of common stock of New Alberto Culver, (ii) one share of common stock of New Sally and (iii) a $25.00 per share special cash dividend.

To accomplish the results described above, the parties engaged in a number of transactions including:

- A holding company merger, after which the company was a direct, wholly-owned subsidiary of New Sally and each share of the company's common stock converted into one share of New Sally common stock.

- New Sally, using a substantial portion of the proceeds of the investment by Investor and the debt incurrence, paid a $25.00 per share special cash dividend to New Sally shareholders (formerly the company's shareholders) other than Investor. New Sally then contributed the company to New Alberto Culver and proceeded to spin off New Alberto Culver by distributing one share of New Alberto Culver common stock for each share of New Sally common stock.

Notwithstanding the legal form of the November 16, 2006 transactions, because of the substance of the transactions, New Alberto Culver was considered the divesting entity and treated as the "accounting successor" to the company, and New Sally was considered the "accounting spinnee" for financial reporting purposes.

The separation of the company into New Alberto Culver and New Sally involving Clayton, Dubilier & Rice (CD&R) is referred to herein as the "Separation." For purposes of describing the events related to the Separation, as well as other events, transactions and financial results of Alberto Culver Company related to periods prior to November 16, 2006, the term "the company" refers to New Alberto Culver's accounting predecessor, or Old Alberto Culver.

In accordance with the provisions of the FASB ASC Subtopic 205-20, the results of operations and cash flows related to Sally Holdings' beauty supply distribution business are reported as discontinued operations for all periods presented.

In accordance with the Investment Agreement, upon the closing of the Separation, New Sally paid (i) all of Investor's transaction expenses and a transaction fee in the amount of $30 million to CD&R, (ii) $20 million to the company covering certain of the combined transaction expenses of Sally Holdings and the company and (iii) certain other expenses of the company. The transaction expenses that New Sally paid on behalf of Investor and the transaction fee paid to CD&R, along with other costs incurred by New Sally directly related to its issuance of new equity and debt in connection with the Separation, were capitalized as equity and debt issuance costs on New Sally's balance sheet. The transaction expenses of the company, including Sally Holdings' portion, were expensed by the company as incurred through the date of completion of the Separation and are included in discontinued operations. Approximately $18.7 million of transaction expenses were incurred in fiscal year 2007.

The company treated the Separation as though it constituted a change in control for purposes of the company's stock option and restricted stock plans. As a result, in accordance with the terms of these plans, all outstanding stock options and restricted shares of the company became fully vested upon completion of the Separation on November 16, 2006. Included in Sally Holdings' discontinued operations in fiscal year 2007 is a $5.3 million charge which reflects the amount of future compensation expense that would have been recognized in subsequent periods as the stock options and restricted shares for Sally Holdings employees vested over the original vesting periods.

In connection with the Separation, Michael H. Renzulli, the former Chairman of Sally Holdings, terminated his employment with the company and received certain contractual benefits totaling $4.0 million, which is included in discontinued operations in fiscal year 2007.

Non-GAAP Financial Measure

To supplement the company's financial results presented in accordance with U.S. generally accepted accounting principles (GAAP), the company discloses "organic sales growth" which measures the growth in net sales excluding the effects of foreign currency fluctuations, acquisitions and divestitures. This measure is a "non-GAAP financial measure" as defined by Regulation G of the Securities and Exchange Commission (SEC). This non-GAAP financial measure is not intended to be, and should not be, considered separately from or as an alternative to the most directly comparable GAAP financial measure of "net sales growth." This specific non-GAAP financial measure is presented in MD&A with the intent of providing greater transparency to supplemental financial information used by management and the company's board of directors in their financial and operational decision-making. This non-GAAP financial measure is among the primary indicators that management and the board of directors use as a basis for budgeting, making operating and strategic decisions and evaluating performance of the company and management as it provides meaningful supplemental information regarding the normal ongoing operations of the company and its core businesses. This amount is disclosed so that the reader has the same financial data that management uses with the belief that it will assist investors and other readers in making comparisons to the company's historical operating results and analyzing the underlying performance of the company's normal ongoing operations for the periods presented. Management believes that the presentation of this non-GAAP financial measure, when considered along with the company's GAAP financial measure and the reconciliation to the corresponding GAAP financial measure, provides the reader with a more complete understanding of the factors and trends affecting the company than could be obtained absent this disclosure. It is important for the reader to note that the non-GAAP financial measure used by the company may be calculated differently from, and therefore may not be comparable to, a similarly titled measure used by other companies. A reconciliation of this measure to its most directly comparable GAAP financial measure is provided in the "Reconciliation of Non-GAAP Financial Measure" section of MD&A and should be carefully evaluated by the reader.

Restructuring and Other

Restructuring and other expenses during the fiscal years ended September 30, 2009, 2008 and 2007 consist of the following:

(In thousands)	2009	2008	2007
Severance and other exit costs	$3,146	$ 6,196	$15,825
Impairment and other property, plant and equipment charges	3,552	6,265	500
Gain on sale of assets	(73)	(1,808)	(5,894)
Non-cash charges related to the acceleration of vesting of stock options and restricted shares in connection with the Separation	—	—	11,383
Contractual termination benefits for the former President and Chief Executive Officer in connection with the Separation	—	—	9,888
Non-cash charges for the recognition of foreign currency translation losses in connection with the liquidation of foreign legal entities	37	324	1,355
Legal fees and other expenses incurred to assign the company's trademarks following the closing of the Separation	114	208	42
	$6,776	$11,185	$33,099

Severance and Other Exit Costs

In November 2006, the company committed to a plan to terminate employees as part of a reorganization following the Separation. In connection with this reorganization plan, on December 1, 2006 the company announced that it was going to close its manufacturing facility in Dallas, Texas. The company's worldwide workforce has been reduced by approximately 215 employees as a result of the reorganization plan, including 125 employees from the Dallas, Texas manufacturing facility. Through September 30, 2009, the company has recorded cumulative charges related to this plan of $15.0 million for severance, $254,000 for contract termination costs and $1.4 million for other exit costs.

In October 2007, the company committed to a plan primarily related to the closure of its manufacturing facility in Toronto, Canada. As part of the plan, the company's workforce has been reduced by approximately 125 employees. Through September 30, 2009, the company has recorded cumulative charges related to this plan of $2.5 million for severance and $425,000 for other exit costs.

In May 2008, the company committed to a plan to close its manufacturing facility, reduce its headcount and relocate to a smaller commercial office in Puerto Rico. As part of the plan, the company's workforce has been reduced by approximately 100 employees. Through September 30, 2009, the company has recorded cumulative charges related to this plan of $1.7 million for severance, $8,000 for contract termination costs and $1.2 million for other exit costs.

The following table reflects the activity related to the three aforementioned restructuring plans during the fiscal year ended September 30, 2009:

(In thousands)	Liability at September 30, 2008	New Charges & Adjustments	Cash Payments & Other	Liability at September 30, 2009
Severance	$1,008	$(126)	$ (554)	$328
Contract termination costs	—	13	(13)	—
Other	551	407	(888)	70
	$1,559	$ 294*	$(1,455)	$398

In June 2009, the company committed to a plan primarily related to the downsizing of its manufacturing facility and the consolidation of its warehouse and office facilities in Chatsworth, California. As noted in the "Subsequent Event" section below, in November 2009 the company committed to a plan to cease all manufacturing activities at the Chatsworth facility. As part of the initial downsizing plan, the company's workforce will be reduced by approximately 160 employees. The following table reflects the activity related to this restructuring plan during the fiscal year ended September 30, 2009:

(In thousands)	Initial Charges	Cash Payments & Other	Liability at September 30, 2009
Severance	$2,107	$(144)	$1,963
Other	745	(313)	432
	$2,852*	$(457)	$2,395

* The sum of these amounts from the tables above represents the $3.1 million of total charges for severance and other exit costs recorded during fiscal year 2009.

Cash payments related to these plans are expected to be substantially completed by the third quarter of fiscal year 2010.

Impairment and Other Property, Plant and Equipment Charges

During fiscal year 2009, the company recorded fixed asset charges of $3.6 million, primarily related to the write-off of certain manufacturing equipment in connection with the downsizing of the company's manufacturing facility in Chatsworth, California. During fiscal year 2008, the company recorded total impairment and other fixed asset charges of $6.3 million. This amount includes impairments of $648,000 related to the building and certain manufacturing equipment in connection with the closure of the Dallas, Texas manufacturing facility, $1.3 million related to manufacturing equipment in connection with the closure of the Toronto, Canada manufacturing facility and $1.6 million related to the building and certain manufacturing equipment in connection with the closure of the Puerto Rico manufacturing facility. In each case, the fair value of the assets was determined using prices for similar assets in the respective markets as determined by management using data from external sources. In addition to the impairments, the company recognized $2.8 million of other fixed asset charges related to the closure of the Dallas, Texas, Toronto, Canada and Puerto Rico manufacturing facilities during fiscal year 2008.

Gain on Sale of Assets—Including Related Party Transactions

The company closed on the sale of its manufacturing facility in Puerto Rico on December 19, 2008. The company received net cash proceeds of $722,000 and recognized a pre-tax gain of $73,000 in fiscal year 2009 as a result of the sale. The company closed on the sale of its manufacturing facility in Toronto, Canada on May 30, 2008. The company received net cash proceeds of $7.5 million and recognized a pre-tax gain of $2.0 million in fiscal year 2008 as a result of the sale. The company closed on the sale of its manufacturing facility in Dallas, Texas on March 26, 2008. The company received net cash proceeds of $3.1 million and recognized a pre-tax loss of $226,000 in fiscal year 2008 as a result of the sale.

On December 21, 2006, the company entered into an agreement with 18000 LLC, a limited liability company controlled by Howard B. Bernick, NJI Sales, Inc., NetJets International, Inc. and NetJets Services, Inc. to assign 50% of the company's 1/8th interest in a fractional-ownership airplane to 18000 LLC in exchange for $1.2 million. Mr. Bernick, a former director and the former President and Chief Executive Officer of the company, was the husband of Carol Lavin Bernick, Executive Chairman of the Board of Directors of the company. The company recognized a pre-tax gain of $386,000 as a result of the sale, which closed on December 22, 2006. This transaction was approved by the audit committee of the board of directors of the company, consisting solely of independent directors.

On January 10, 2007, the Leonard H. Lavin Trust u/a/d 12/18/87, a trust for the benefit of Leonard H. Lavin (the Lavin Trust), purchased all of the membership units of Eighteen, LLC, an Oregon limited liability company and subsidiary of the company, pursuant to a Membership Interest Purchase Agreement dated January 10, 2007 among the Lavin Trust, Eighteen, LLC and the company. The trustees of the Lavin Trust are Leonard H. Lavin, a director of the company, and Ms. Bernick. The primary asset of Eighteen, LLC was a Gulfstream IV-SP airplane. The purchase price for the membership interests of Eighteen, LLC was $25.0 million and was paid on January 10, 2007. The company recognized a pre-tax gain of $5.1 million as a result of the sale. This transaction was approved by the audit committee of the board of directors of the company, consisting solely of independent directors.

On January 30, 2007, the company entered into an agreement with NJI Sales, Inc., NetJets International, Inc. and NetJets Services, Inc. to sell the remaining 50% of its 1/8th interest in a fractional-ownership airplane back to NetJets for $1.2 million. The company recognized a pre-tax gain of $389,000 as a result of the sale.

Acceleration of Vesting of Stock Options and Restricted Shares

As previously discussed, the company treated the Separation as though it constituted a change in control for purposes of the company's stock option and restricted stock plans. As a result, in accordance with the terms of these plans, all outstanding stock options and restricted shares of the company became fully vested upon completion of the Separation on November 16, 2006. The $11.4 million charge recorded by the company in fiscal year 2007 is equal to the amount of future compensation expense that would have been recognized in subsequent periods as the stock options and restricted shares vested over the original vesting periods.

Contractual Termination Benefits

In connection with the Separation, Howard B. Bernick, the former President and Chief Executive Officer of the company, terminated his employment with the company and received certain contractual benefits primarily consisting of a lump sum cash payment of $9.7 million plus applicable employer payroll taxes.

Foreign Currency Translation Loss

The company substantially completed the liquidation of two foreign legal entities in connection with its reorganization plan and is therefore recognizing in restructuring and other expenses the accumulated foreign currency translation losses related to the entities which resulted in charges of $37,000, $324,000 and $1.4 million during fiscal years 2009, 2008 and 2007, respectively.

Trademark Legal Fees and Other Expenses

Due to the series of transactions affecting the company's legal structure as part of the closing of the Separation, the company completed a process to assign many of its existing trademarks in various countries around the world. In connection with this effort, the company incurred legal fees and other expenses of $114,000, $208,000 and $42,000 in fiscal years 2009, 2008 and 2007, respectively.

Subsequent Event

In November 2009, the company committed to a plan primarily related to ceasing all manufacturing activities at its facility in Chatsworth, California. This plan is in addition to the company's initial plan to downsize the Chatsworth manufacturing facility, which was announced in June 2009. As part of this new plan, the company's workforce will be further reduced by approximately 110 employees. The company estimates that additional pre-tax restructuring and other related charges of approximately $8.0 million will be recognized during fiscal year 2010 related to this new plan, with approximately $5.0 million of the additional amount expected to be recognized in the first quarter.

Expected Savings

The company's first three reorganization and restructuring plans have been fully implemented as of September 30, 2009, and the reported financial results reflect the savings realized during those periods. As a result of the newest restructuring plans announced in June 2009 and November 2009 primarily related to the Chatsworth, California facilities, the company expects to recognize additional cost savings of approximately $12 million on an annualized basis. The additional cost savings will affect advertising, marketing, selling and administrative expense and gross profit on the consolidated statement of earnings.

Auction Rate Securities

Prior to the second quarter of fiscal year 2008, the company regularly invested in auction rate securities (ARS) which typically are bonds with long-term maturities that have interest rates which reset at intervals of up to 35 days through an auction process. These investments are considered available for sale in accordance with FASB ASC Topic 320, "Debt and Equity Securities." All of the company's remaining investments in ARS at September 30, 2009 represent interests in pools of student loans and have AAA/Aaa credit ratings. In addition, all of these securities carry an indirect guarantee by the U.S. federal government of at least 97% of the par value through the Federal Family Education Loan Program (FFELP). Based on these factors and the credit worthiness of the underlying assets, the company does not believe that it has significant principal risk with regard to these investments.

Historically, the periodic auctions for these ARS investments have provided a liquid market for these securities. As a result, the company carried its investments at par value, which approximated fair value, and classified them as short-term in the consolidated balance sheets. Starting in the second quarter of fiscal year 2008, each of the company's remaining ARS investments has experienced multiple failed auctions, meaning that there have been insufficient bidders to match the supply of securities submitted for sale. During fiscal year 2009, the company did not redeem any ARS investments as a result of successful auctions as all auctions for the company's remaining ARS investments continued to fail during the period. In addition, the company did not recognize any realized gains or losses from the sale of ARS investments in its statement of earnings. During the fourth quarter of fiscal year 2009, one security matured and the company received the full par value of $8.5 million. The company continues to earn interest on its investments at the maximum contractual rate and continues to collect the interest in accordance with the stated terms of the securities. At September 30, 2009, the company's outstanding ARS investments carried a weighted average tax exempt interest rate of 0.7%.

At September 30, 2009, the company has ARS investments with a total par value of $61.3 million. The company has recorded these investments on its consolidated balance sheet at an estimated fair value of $58.4 million and recorded an unrealized loss of $2.9 million in accumulated other comprehensive income (loss), reflecting the decline in the estimated fair value. The unrealized loss has been recorded in accumulated other comprehensive income (loss) and not the statement of earnings as the company has concluded at September 30, 2009 that no other-than-temporary impairment losses have occurred because its investments continue to be of high credit quality and the company does not have the intent to sell these investments, nor is it more likely than not that the company will be required to sell these investments until the anticipated recovery in market value occurs. The company will continue to analyze its ARS in future periods for impairment and may be required to record a charge in its statement of earnings in future periods if the decline in fair value is determined to be other-than-temporary. The fair value of these securities has been estimated by management using unobservable input data from external sources. Because there is no active market for these securities, management utilized a discounted cash flow valuation model to estimate the fair value of each individual security, with the key assumptions in the model being the expected holding period for the ARS, the expected coupon rate over the holding period and the required rate of return by market participants (discount rate), adjusted to reflect the current illiquidity in the market. For each of the company's existing securities, the model calculates an expected periodic coupon rate using regression analysis and a market required rate of return that includes a risk-free interest rate and a credit spread. At September 30, 2009, the estimated required rate of return was adjusted by a spread of 150 basis points to reflect the illiquidity in the market. The model then discounts the expected coupon rate at the adjusted discount rate to arrive at the fair value price. At September 30, 2009, the assumed holding period for the ARS was three years and the weighted average expected coupon rate and adjusted discount rate used in the valuation model were 5.1% and 3.2%, respectively.

All of the company's outstanding ARS investments have been classified as long-term on the September 30, 2009 balance sheet as the company cannot be certain that they will settle within the next twelve months. The company's outstanding ARS investments have scheduled maturities ranging from 2029 to 2042. It is management's intent to hold these investments until the company is able to recover the full par value, either through issuer calls, refinancings or other refunding initiatives, the recovery of the auction market or the emergence of a new secondary market. Management's assumption used in the current fair value estimates is that this will occur within the next three years.

Results of Operations

Comparison of the Years Ended September 30, 2009 and 2008

Net sales for the fiscal year ended September 30, 2009 were $1.43 billion, a decrease of 0.7% compared to the prior year. Organic sales, which exclude the effect of foreign currency fluctuations (an adverse impact of 8.1%), the net sales of Noxzema products in fiscal year 2009 (a positive impact of 2.5%) and the divestiture of the BDM Grange distribution business in New Zealand (an adverse impact of 0.1%), grew 5.0% during fiscal year 2009.

Earnings from continuing operations were $117.8 million for the fiscal year ended September 30, 2009 versus $106.0 million in the prior year. Diluted earnings per share from continuing operations were $1.19 in fiscal year 2009 compared to $1.05 in fiscal year 2008. In fiscal year 2009, the company recognized income tax expense related to discrete tax items which reduced earnings from continuing operations by $6.8 million and diluted earnings per share from continuing operations by 7 cents. In addition, restructuring and other expenses in fiscal year 2009 reduced earnings from continuing operations by $4.2 million and diluted earnings per share from continuing operations by 4 cents and the company incurred costs related to a dispute with a supplier which reduced earnings from continuing operations by $1.9 million and diluted earnings per share from continuing operations by 2 cents. In fiscal year 2008, discrete tax items decreased earnings from continuing operations by $8.5 million and diluted earnings per share from continuing operations by 8 cents, while restructuring and other expenses reduced earnings from continuing operations by $7.2 million and diluted earnings per share from continuing operations by 8 cents. In addition, in fiscal year 2008 the company benefited from the reversal of a contingent liability which increased earnings from continuing operations by $2.6 million and diluted earnings per share for continuing operations by 3 cents.

Net sales for the United States segment in fiscal year 2009 increased 6.3% to $917.0 million from $863.0 million in 2008. The 2009 sales increase was principally due to higher sales of TRESemmé hair care products (3.6%) and Nexxus products (1.1%). In addition, the acquisition of Noxzema in October 2008 added approximately 3.8% to sales for fiscal year 2009. These increases were partially offset by lower sales from other brands including Alberto VO5 and St. Ives, as well as certain multicultural brands.

Net sales for the International segment decreased to $517.0 million in fiscal year 2009 compared to $580.5 million in fiscal year 2008. This sales decrease of 10.9% was attributable to the effect of foreign currency fluctuations (20.0%), partially offset by higher sales of TRESemmé hair care products (5.7%) including the effect of the launch in Spain in the third quarter of 2008 and the Nordic region of Europe in the fourth quarter of 2009, as well as St. Ives (1.2%). The launch of Nexxus in Canada also contributed to the segment's organic growth during the period.

Gross profit decreased $22.1 million or 2.9% to $735.2 million in fiscal year 2009 compared to the prior year. Gross profit, as a percentage of net sales, was 51.3% for fiscal year 2009 compared to 52.5% for fiscal year 2008. Gross profit in the United States in fiscal year 2009 increased $15.5 million or 3.4% from the prior year.

As a percentage of net sales, United States' gross profit was 51.3% during fiscal year 2009 compared to 52.7% in the prior year. The decrease in gross profit margin in the United States was primarily attributable to higher raw material costs due to cost pressures resulting from higher oil prices, as well as higher prices for other materials such as tin plate and chemicals, partially offset by favorable product mix and decreased use of special packaging for promotions. Gross profit for the International segment decreased $37.6 million or 12.4% in fiscal year 2009 versus the prior year. As a percentage of net sales, International's gross profit was 51.2% in fiscal year 2009 compared to 52.1% in the prior year. The gross profit margin for International was also affected by higher raw material costs, as noted above, as well as negative effects from foreign currency fluctuations in certain markets where significant raw material purchases are made in U.S. dollars. In the International segment, these effects were partially offset by favorable product mix, driven by the TRESemmé launch in Spain in the third quarter of 2008, decreased use of special packaging for promotions and improved manufacturing efficiencies.

Advertising, marketing, selling and administrative expenses in fiscal year 2009 decreased $39.6 million or 6.8% compared to the prior year. This overall decrease consists of lower advertising and marketing expenses (4.4%) and selling and administrative expenses (2.4%).

Advertising and marketing expenditures decreased 9.6% to $239.5 million (16.7% of net sales) in fiscal year 2009 compared to $265.0 million (18.4% of net sales) in the prior year primarily due to the effect of foreign exchange rates, which accounted for 6.7 percentage points of the decrease, the timing of certain brand initiatives, media efficiencies in several markets and a shift to higher trade promotion spending. Advertising and marketing expenditures in the United States decreased 10.4% in fiscal year 2009 compared to the prior year. The decrease was primarily due to lower advertising and marketing expenditures for St. Ives (9.6%) and Alberto VO5 (7.2%) as a result of significant expenditures in fiscal year 2008 to support the Elements and Extreme Styling launches, respectively, partially offset by higher advertising and marketing expenditures for TRESemmé (3.2%) and Nexxus (1.9%), as well as expenditures in 2009 related to Noxzema (2.7%). Advertising and marketing expenditures for the International segment decreased 8.3% in fiscal year 2009 compared to the prior year, primarily due to the effect of foreign currency fluctuations (18.0%), partially offset by higher advertising and marketing expenditures for Nexxus (6.4%) to support the launch in Canada and TRESemmé (6.3%) due in part to the launches in Spain in the third quarter of 2008 and the Nordic region of Europe in the fourth quarter of 2009.

Selling and administrative expenses decreased 4.4% to $305.8 million in fiscal year 2009 from $319.9 million in fiscal year 2008. Selling and administrative expenses, as a percentage of net sales, decreased to 21.3% in fiscal year 2009 from 22.2% in the prior year. Selling and administrative expenses in the United States increased 0.9% for fiscal year 2009 compared to the prior year. This increase was primarily due to the effects of the $2.9 million of costs incurred in fiscal year 2009 related to a dispute with a supplier and the $3.9 million of benefit from the reversal of a contingent liability in the prior year. These increases in selling and administrative expenses were partially offset by lower selling and freight costs in 2009. International's selling and administrative expenses decreased 12.8% in fiscal year 2009 compared to the prior year primarily due to the effect of foreign currency fluctuations. Selling and administrative expenses for both reportable segments were also positively impacted by cost savings initiatives implemented by the company. Stock option expense, which is included in selling and administrative expenses but is not allocated to the company's reportable segments, was $7.8 million in fiscal year 2009 compared to $4.6 million in fiscal year 2008.

The company recorded net interest income of $2.7 million in fiscal year 2009 and $9.6 million in the prior year. Interest income was $3.3 million in fiscal year 2009 and $15.0 million in fiscal year 2008. The decrease in interest income was principally due to significantly lower interest rates in fiscal year 2009 compared to last year. Interest expense was $660,000 and $5.4 million in fiscal years 2009 and 2008, respectively. The decrease in interest expense is primarily due to the repayment of the company's $120 million of debentures in June 2008.

The provision for income taxes as a percentage of earnings from continuing operations before income taxes was 36.6% and 37.9% in fiscal years 2009 and 2008, respectively. The provision for income taxes in fiscal years 2009 and 2008 includes net expense of $6.8 million and $8.5 million, respectively, from discrete tax items. The net discrete tax items include taxes of approximately $7.1 million and $11.0 million, respectively, related to local currency gains on U.S. dollar denominated cash equivalents held by Alberto Culver AB in Sweden following the sale of Cederroth. On October 31, 2008, the remaining proceeds from the Cederroth sale were transferred to a newly formed, wholly-owned subsidiary in the Netherlands, and further exchange rate changes with respect to these proceeds are not expected to result in taxable income for the company. In addition, the effective tax rates in both 2009 and 2008 reflect discrete tax items related to reductions in tax contingency reserves for certain foreign entities due to the expiration of statutes of limitations and benefits from changes in certain estimates related to the previous years' tax provisions. The net discrete tax items resulted in 3.7 and 5.0 percentage point increases in the effective tax rates in fiscal years 2009 and 2008, respectively.

Comparison of the Years Ended September 30, 2008 and 2007

Net sales for the fiscal year ended September 30, 2008 were $1.44 billion, an increase of 9.7% over the prior year. Organic sales, which exclude the effects of foreign currency fluctuations (a positive impact of 1.0%), grew 8.7% in fiscal year 2008. Organic sales growth includes the effect of net sales to Sally Holdings after the November 16, 2006 closing of the Separation (0.4%). In fiscal year 2007, all transactions with Sally Holdings prior to November 16, 2006 were considered intercompany and the elimination of these intercompany sales is classified as part of continuing operations.

Earnings from continuing operations of $106.0 million increased 46.1% from the prior year's earnings from continuing operations of $72.6 million. Diluted earnings per share from continuing operations were $1.05 in fiscal year 2008 and 74 cents in fiscal year 2007. In fiscal year 2008, discrete tax items decreased earnings from continuing operations by $8.5 million and diluted earnings per share from continuing operations by 8 cents, while restructuring and other expenses reduced earnings from continuing operations by $7.2 million and diluted earnings per share from continuing operations by 8 cents. In addition, in fiscal year 2008 the company benefited from the reversal of a contingent liability which increased earnings from continuing operations by $2.6 million and diluted earnings per share from continuing operations by 3 cents. In fiscal year 2007, restructuring and other expenses reduced earnings from continuing operations by $21.8 million and diluted earnings per share from continuing operations by 22 cents, while discrete tax items increased earnings from continuing operations by $4.9 million and diluted earnings per share from continuing operations by 5 cents.

Net sales for the United States segment in fiscal year 2008 increased 5.0% to $863.0 million from $821.6 million in 2007. The 2008 sales increase was principally due to higher sales of TRESemmé hair care products (4.3%) and multicultural brands (0.7%).

Net sales for the International segment increased to $580.5 million in fiscal year 2008 compared to $498.1 million in 2007. This sales increase of 16.5% was primarily attributable to higher sales of TRESemmé hair care products (11.0%), St. Ives products (0.9%) and the effect of foreign currency fluctuations (2.8%).

Gross profit increased $84.0 million or 12.5% to $757.3 million in fiscal year 2008 compared to fiscal year 2007. Gross profit, as a percentage of net sales, was 52.5% for fiscal year 2008 compared to 51.2% for continuing operations in the prior year. Gross profit in the United States in fiscal year 2008 increased $28.7 million or 6.7% from the prior year. As a percentage of net sales, United States' gross profit was 52.7% during fiscal year 2008 compared to 51.9% in 2007. The gross profit margin improvement in the United States was primarily attributable to more effective inventory management and manufacturing efficiencies, partially offset by higher raw material and other input costs. Gross profit for the International segment increased $55.3 million or 22.4% in fiscal year 2008 versus fiscal year 2007. As a percentage of net sales, International's gross profit was 52.1% in fiscal year 2008 compared to 49.6% in the prior year. The increase in gross profit margin for the International segment was also due to more effective inventory management and improved manufacturing efficiencies, partially due to the closures of the Toronto, Canada and Puerto Rico manufacturing facilities.

Advertising, marketing, selling and administrative expenses in fiscal year 2008 increased $41.6 million or 7.6%. This overall increase consists of higher advertising and marketing expenses (3.1%) and selling and administrative expenses (4.5%).

Advertising and marketing expenditures increased 6.9% to $265.0 million (18.4% of net sales) in 2008 compared to $247.8 million (18.8% of net sales) in 2007. Advertising and marketing expenditures in the United States increased 2.1% in fiscal year 2008 compared to 2007. The increase was primarily due to higher advertising and marketing expenditures for TRESemmé (8.2%), partially offset by decreased advertising and marketing expenditures for Nexxus (5.1%). Advertising and marketing expenditures for the International segment increased 16.2% in fiscal year 2008 compared to the prior year, primarily due to higher advertising and marketing expenditures for TRESemmé (14.2%) due in part to the launch in Spain in the third quarter of 2008, and the effect of foreign exchange rates (2.5%).

Selling and administrative expenses increased 8.3% to $319.9 million from $295.5 million in the prior year. Selling and administrative expenses, as a percentage of net sales, decreased to 22.2% in fiscal year 2008 from 22.5% in 2007. Selling and administrative expenses in the United States increased 6.2% for fiscal year 2008 compared to 2007. International's selling and administrative expenses increased 10.1% in fiscal year 2008 compared to the prior year. Each of these increases was primarily due to higher incentive compensation costs, higher expenditures related to the implementation of a new worldwide ERP system and costs associated with the start-up of the company's Jonesboro, Arkansas manufacturing facility. The increase in the United States was partially offset by the reversal of a $3.9 million contingent liability that was favorably settled in 2008. Stock option expense, which is included in selling and administrative expenses but is not allocated to the company's reportable segments, was $4.6 million in fiscal year 2008 compared to $3.5 million in 2007.

The company recorded net interest income of $9.6 million in fiscal year 2008 and $3.9 million in 2007. Interest income was $15.0 million in fiscal year 2008 and $12.3 million in fiscal year 2007. The increase in interest income was principally due to higher cash and investment balances in fiscal year 2008. Interest expense was $5.4 million in fiscal year 2008 and $8.4 million for fiscal year 2007. The decrease in interest expense is primarily due to the repayment of the company's $120 million of debentures in June 2008 and higher interest capitalization in 2008.

The provision for income taxes as a percentage of earnings from continuing operations before income taxes was 37.9% and 28.0% in fiscal years 2008 and 2007, respectively. The provision for income taxes in fiscal year 2008 includes a net expense of $8.5 million from discrete tax items, while the 2007 provision is partially offset by a net income tax benefit of $4.9 million from discrete tax items. In fiscal year 2008, the net discrete tax items include taxes of approximately $11.0 million related to the local currency gain on U.S. dollar denominated cash held by Alberto Culver AB in Sweden following the sale of Cederroth. The effective tax rates in both 2008 and 2007 reflect discrete tax items related to reductions in income tax accruals for certain foreign entities following the expiration of various statutes of limitations and benefits from changes in certain estimates related to previous years' tax provisions, as well as other discrete tax items recognized in each period. The net discrete tax items resulted in a 5.0 percentage point increase in the 2008 effective tax rate and a 4.9 percentage point decrease in the 2007 effective tax rate. For both fiscal year periods, the effective tax rates were also affected by the varying tax rates in the jurisdictions in which the company's restructuring charges were recorded.

Financial Condition

Working capital at September 30, 2009 was $589.8 million, a decrease of $8.6 million from working capital of $598.4 million at September 30, 2008. The September 30, 2009 ratio of current assets to current liabilities of 3.14 to 1.00 increased from last year end's ratio of 3.10 to 1.00.

Cash, cash equivalents and investments, including short-term and long-term, increased $17.0 million to $528.2 million compared to last fiscal year end, primarily due to cash flows provided by operating activities ($208.1 million), partially offset by payments for acquisitions including the Noxzema business ($98.2 million), capital expenditures ($65.2 million) and cash dividends ($28.5 million). Total investments, including short-term and long-term, were $58.4 million at September 30, 2009 compared to $65.8 million at September 30, 2008.

Receivables, less allowance for doubtful accounts, decreased 6.3% to $229.0 million from $244.3 million at September 30, 2008 primarily due to the effect of foreign currency fluctuations and the sale of the company's subsidiaries in New Zealand, including the BDM Grange distribution business.

Inventories decreased $22.7 million or 15.2% from last fiscal year end to $126.8 million, principally due to inventory reduction initiatives implemented by the company, improved supply chain management, the sale of the company's subsidiaries in New Zealand, including the BDM Grange distribution business, and the effect of foreign currency fluctuations.

Net property, plant and equipment increased $28.2 million during fiscal year 2009 to $249.9 million at September 30, 2009. The increase resulted primarily from expenditures for the new Jonesboro, Arkansas manufacturing facility and the implementation of a new worldwide ERP system, partially offset by depreciation during the fiscal year as well as the effect of foreign currency fluctuations.

Goodwill and trade names of $314.0 million increased $79.9 million compared to last fiscal year end primarily due to the Noxzema acquisition, additional purchase price recorded related to the Nexxus acquisition and the acquisition of the remaining 49% minority interest in the company's subsidiary in Chile. These increases were partially offset by the sale of the company's subsidiaries in New Zealand, including the BDM Grange distribution business, and the effect of foreign currency fluctuations.

Retained earnings increased from $702.4 million at September 30, 2008 to $792.2 million at September 30, 2009 due to net earnings for fiscal year 2009, partially offset by the payment of $28.5 million of cash dividends.

Accumulated other comprehensive loss was $58.4 million at September 30, 2009 compared to $37.0 million at September 30, 2008. This change was primarily a result of the strengthening of the U.S. dollar versus the foreign currencies in which the company does significant business, particularly the British pound and Mexican peso.

Liquidity and Capital Resources

Cash Provided by Operating Activities

Net cash provided by operating activities was $208.1 million and $170.9 million for fiscal years 2009 and 2008, respectively. The most significant changes in comparing the 2009 operating cash flows to 2008 include lower inventories as discussed in the "Financial Condition" section of MD&A, as well as higher earnings from continuing operations and improved collections of receivables. Additionally, in November 2008 the company paid a tax obligation in Sweden related to foreign currency gains on U.S. dollar investments, which resulted in a cash outflow of $14.1 million. Net cash provided by operating activities increased by $82.1 million in fiscal year 2008 from $88.8 million in fiscal year 2007 due to significantly higher cash flows resulting from increased earnings from continuing operations, as well as an improvement in cash generated from overall working capital. In addition, cash flows from operating activities in 2007 were affected by the payment of significant income tax obligations in connection with the sale of the corporate airplane and higher payments in connection with the company's restructuring plans, primarily related to severance.

Cash Provided (Used) by Investing Activities

Net cash used by investing activities was $150.9 million and $188.0 million for fiscal years 2009 and 2007, respectively. In fiscal year 2008, net cash provided by investing activities was $360.0 million. Capital expenditures were $65.2 million, $64.1 million and $53.8 million in fiscal years 2009, 2008 and 2007, respectively. All three fiscal years were also affected by payments for additional purchase price related to the Nexxus acquisition, which totaled $7.6 million, $7.1 million and $6.3 million in fiscal years 2009, 2008 and 2007, respectively. Net cash used by investing activities in fiscal year 2009 included $83.6 million of payments related to the purchase of the Noxzema business and $7.0 million of payments related to the purchase of the remaining 49% minority interest in the company's subsidiary in Chile. In fiscal year 2009, the company received net cash proceeds of $6.2 million from the sale of its New Zealand subsidiaries, including the BDM Grange distribution business, and made payments of $3.2 million related to the sale of Cederroth. In addition, during the fourth quarter of fiscal year 2009, one ARS investment matured and the company received the full par value of $8.5 million. The net cash provided by investing activities in fiscal year 2008 includes $234.3 million of proceeds from the sale of Cederroth, net of direct selling costs incurred and Cederroth's ending cash balance that was transferred to CapMan. In fiscal year 2008, the company also generated cash of $185.8 million from net sales of investments as the company liquidated a significant portion of its ARS investments and transferred the cash to institutional money market funds and other cash equivalents. Proceeds from disposals of assets in fiscal year 2008 include $10.7 million related to the sales of the company's manufacturing facilities in Toronto, Canada and Dallas, Texas. In fiscal year 2007, proceeds from disposals of assets includes $27.4 million related to the sales of the corporate airplane and the company's 1/8th interest in a fractional-ownership of NetJets airplane. Also in fiscal year 2007, the company had net purchases of investments of $156.1 million.

Cash Provided (Used) by Financing Activities

Net cash used by financing activities was $27.4 million and $183.4 million for fiscal years 2009 and 2008, respectively. In fiscal year 2007, net cash provided by financing activities was $62.4 million. The company paid cash dividends of $28.5 million, $24.8 million and $16.0 million in fiscal years 2009, 2008 and 2007, respectively. Proceeds from the exercise of stock options were $3.9 million, $60.5 million and $70.9 million in fiscal years 2009, 2008 and 2007, respectively. In addition, during fiscal years 2009 and 2008 the company purchased shares of its common stock in the open market for an aggregate purchase price of $1.4 million and $109.5 million, respectively. In June 2008, the company repaid its $120 million of debentures because all the holders exercised their one-time put option. Net cash provided (used) by financing activities was also affected by the excess tax benefit from stock option exercises and changes in the book cash overdraft balance in each fiscal year.

Cash dividends paid on common stock were $.29 and $.25 per share in fiscal years 2009 and 2008, respectively. In connection with the Separation, the company's shareholders received a $25.00 per share special cash dividend for each share of common stock owned as of November 16, 2006. This special cash dividend in 2007 is included in net cash used by financing activities of discontinued operations. In addition to the special cash dividend, the company paid cash dividends on common stock of $.165 per share in fiscal year 2007.

At September 30, 2009, the company has ARS investments with a total par value of $61.3 million. All of these investments represent interests in pools of student loans and have AAA/Aaa credit ratings. In addition, all of these securities carry an indirect guarantee by the U.S. federal government of at least 97% of the par value through the Federal Family Education Loan Program (FFELP). However, starting in the second quarter of fiscal year 2008, each of the company's remaining ARS investments has experienced multiple failed auctions. During fiscal year 2009, the company did not redeem any ARS investments as a result of successful auctions as all auctions for the company's remaining ARS investments continued to fail during the period. In addition, the company did not recognize any realized gains or losses from the sale of ARS investments in its statement of earnings. During the fourth quarter of fiscal year 2009, one security matured and the company received the full par value of $8.5 million. The company has recorded these remaining investments on its consolidated balance sheet at an estimated fair value of $58.4 million and recorded an unrealized loss of $2.9 million in accumulated other comprehensive income (loss), reflecting the decline in the estimated fair value. All of the company's outstanding ARS investments have been classified as long-term on the September 30, 2009 balance sheet as the company cannot be certain that they will settle within the next twelve months. The company's outstanding ARS investments have scheduled maturities ranging from 2029 to 2042. It is currently management's intent to hold these investments until the company is able to recover the full par value, either through issuer calls, refinancings or other refunding initiatives, the recovery of the auction market or the emergence of a new secondary market. Management's assumption used in the current fair value estimates is that this will occur within the next three years.

The company anticipates that its cash and cash equivalents balance of $469.8 million as of September 30, 2009, along with cash flows from operations and available credit, will be sufficient to fund operating requirements in future years. During fiscal year 2010, the company expects that cash will continue to be used for capital expenditures, new product development, market expansion, dividend payments, payments related to restructuring plans and, if applicable, acquisitions. In addition, in the first quarter of fiscal year 2010 (through November 23, 2009) the company has purchased 494,131 shares of common stock in the open market for an aggregate purchase price of $13.5 million. The company may continue to purchase additional shares of its common stock in fiscal year 2010 depending on market conditions.

During the fourth quarter of fiscal year 2009, the company purchased 54,339 shares of common stock in the open market for an aggregate purchase price of $1.4 million. At September 30, 2009, the company has authorization remaining to purchase a total of 5,779,879 shares. On November 12, 2006, the board of directors authorized the company to purchase up to 5 million shares of common stock. During the third and fourth quarters of fiscal year 2008, the company purchased 4,165,782 common shares in the open market under this authorization for an aggregate purchase price of $109.5 million. On July 24, 2008, the board of directors authorized the company to purchase an additional 5 million shares of common stock.

In the past, the company has obtained long-term financing as needed to fund acquisitions and other growth opportunities. Funds may be obtained prior to their actual need in order to take advantage of opportunities in the debt markets. The company has a $300 million revolving credit facility which expires November 13, 2011. There were no borrowings outstanding on the revolving credit facility at September 30, 2009 or 2008. The facility may be drawn in U.S. dollars or certain foreign currencies. Under debt covenants, the company has sufficient flexibility to incur additional borrowings as needed. The current facility includes a covenant that limits the company's ability to purchase its common stock or pay dividends if the cumulative stock repurchases plus cash dividends exceeds $250 million plus 50% of "consolidated net income" (as defined in the credit agreement) commencing January 1, 2007.

The company is in compliance with the covenants and other requirements of its revolving credit agreement. Additionally, the revolving credit agreement does not include credit rating triggers or subjective clauses that would accelerate maturity dates.

The following table is a summary of contractual cash obligations and commitments outstanding by future payment dates at September 30, 2009:

| | Payments Due by Period | | | | |
(In thousands)	Less Than 1 Year	1–3 Years	3–5 Years	More Than 5 Years	Total
Long-term debt, including capital lease and interest obligations	$ 214	$ 383	$ 89	$ —	$ 686
Operating leases[1]	7,361	11,870	3,524	1,065	23,820
Other long-term obligations[2]	9,997	3,440	1,459	21,665	36,561
Total	$17,572	$15,693	$5,072	$22,730	$61,067

[1] In accordance with GAAP, these obligations are not reflected in the accompanying consolidated balance sheets.

[2] Other long-term obligations principally represent commitments under various deferred compensation arrangements, as well as commitments under the company's restructuring plans. These obligations are included in accrued expenses and other liabilities in the accompanying consolidated balance sheets. The above amounts do not include additional consideration of up to $29.0 million that may be paid over the next six years based on a percentage of sales of Nexxus branded products in accordance with the Nexxus purchase agreement. The above amounts also do not include the company's $11.4 million liability for unrecognized tax benefits, as management is unable to reliably estimate the timing of the expected payments for these obligations.

Off-Balance Sheet Financing Arrangements

At September 30, 2009 and 2008, the company had no off-balance sheet financing arrangements other than operating leases incurred in the ordinary course of business as disclosed in note 12 to the consolidated financial statements and outstanding standby letters of credit primarily related to various insurance programs which totaled $14.4 million and $18.9 million, respectively, at September 30, 2009 and 2008. The company does not have significant other unconditional purchase obligations or commercial commitments.

Inflation

The company was not significantly affected by inflation during the past three years. Management attempts to counteract the effects of inflation through productivity improvements, cost reduction programs, price increases and the introduction of higher margin products within the constraints of the highly competitive markets in which the company operates.

Quantitative and Qualitative Disclosures About Market Risk

As a multinational corporation that manufactures and markets products in countries throughout the world, the company is subject to certain market risks including foreign currency fluctuations, interest rates and government actions. The company considers a variety of practices to manage these market risks, including, when deemed appropriate, the use of derivative financial instruments. The company uses derivative financial instruments only for risk management and does not use them for trading or speculative purposes. The company only enters into derivative instruments with highly rated counterparties based in the United States, and does not believe that it has significant counterparty credit risk with regard to its current arrangements.

The company is exposed to potential gains or losses from foreign currency fluctuations affecting net investments and earnings denominated in foreign currencies. The company's primary exposures are to changes in exchange rates for the U.S. dollar versus the British pound, Canadian dollar, Euro, Australian dollar, Mexican peso, Argentine peso, Chilean peso and South African rand. The company's various currency exposures at times offset each other providing a natural hedge against currency risk.

Starting in the second quarter of fiscal year 2009, certain of the company's foreign subsidiaries entered into foreign currency forward contracts in an attempt to minimize the impact of short-term currency fluctuations on the forecasted sales and inventory purchases denominated in currencies other than their functional currencies. These contracts are designated as cash flow hedging instruments in accordance with FASB ASC Topic 815, "Derivatives and Hedging." As a result, unrealized gains and losses on these contracts are recorded to accumulated other comprehensive income (loss) until the underlying hedged items are recognized through operations. The ineffective portion of a contract's change in fair value is immediately recognized through operations. At September 30, 2009, the notional amount of these outstanding foreign currency forward contracts in U.S. dollars was $30.2 million and the contracts settle or mature within the next twelve months.

In addition, starting in the second quarter of fiscal year 2009, certain of the company's foreign subsidiaries entered into a series of foreign currency forward contracts to hedge their net balance sheet exposure for amounts designated in currencies other than their functional currencies. These contracts are not designated as hedging instruments and therefore do not qualify for hedge accounting treatment under FASB ASC Topic 815. As a result, gains and losses on these contracts are recorded directly to the statement of earnings and serve to offset the related exchange gains or losses on the underlying exposures. At September 30, 2009, the notional amount of these outstanding foreign currency forward contracts in U.S. dollars was $43.7 million and the contracts settle or mature within the next two months.

The foreign currency relationships covered by these foreign currency forward contracts are principally the British pound and Euro, the British pound and Swedish krona, the Mexican peso and U.S. dollar, the Canadian dollar and the U.S. dollar and the Chilean peso and U.S. dollar.

In May 2008, in connection with entering into an agreement to sell its Cederroth business, the company entered into a deal contingent forward contract to sell the Euros it expected to receive in exchange for U.S. dollars. In connection with the closing of the transaction on July 31, 2008, the company recognized a pre-tax loss of $5.1 million related to the settlement of the forward contract which partially offset the gain on the sale of Cederroth in discontinued operations.

The company considers combinations of fixed rate and variable rate debt, along with varying maturities, in its management of interest rate risk. At September 30, 2009, the company had no long-term debt outstanding other than capital lease obligations.

The company has occasionally used interest rate swaps to manage interest rate risk on debt securities. These instruments allow the company to exchange fixed rate debt into variable rate or variable rate debt into fixed rate. Interest rate differentials paid or received on these arrangements are recognized as adjustments to interest expense over the life of the agreement. At September 30, 2009, the company had no interest rate swaps outstanding.

The company is exposed to credit risk on certain assets, primarily cash equivalents, investments and accounts receivable. The credit risk associated with cash equivalents and investments is mitigated by the company's policy of investing in a diversified portfolio of securities with high credit ratings.

The company's investments in ARS are discussed further in the "Overview—Auction Rate Securities" section of MD&A.

The company provides credit to customers in the ordinary course of business and performs ongoing credit evaluations. The company's exposure to concentrations of credit risk with respect to trade receivables is mitigated by the company's broad customer base. The company's largest customer, Wal-Mart Stores, Inc. and its affiliated companies, accounted for approximately 25% of net sales during fiscal year 2009 and 24% during fiscal years 2008 and 2007. The company believes its allowance for doubtful accounts is sufficient to cover customer credit risks.

New Accounting Pronouncement

In December, 2007, the FASB issued new accounting guidance on business combinations. The new guidance, which is included in FASB ASC Topic 805 "Business Combinations," significantly changes the accounting for business combinations in a number of areas including the treatment of contingent consideration, preacquisition contingencies and transaction costs. In addition, FASB ASC Topic 805 also requires certain financial statement disclosures to enable users to evaluate and understand the nature and financial effects of the business combination. The new provisions of FASB ASC Topic 805 are effective for fiscal years beginning after December 15, 2008 and earlier application is prohibited. Accordingly, the company will apply these new provisions prospectively to business combinations that are consummated beginning in the first quarter of fiscal year 2010.

Critical Accounting Policies

The preparation of financial statements in conformity with GAAP requires management to make estimates and assumptions that affect the reported amounts of assets, liabilities, revenues and expenses in the financial statements. Actual results may differ from these estimates. Management believes these estimates and assumptions are reasonable.

Accounting policies are considered critical when they require management to make assumptions about matters that are highly uncertain at the time the accounting estimate is made and when different estimates that management reasonably could have used have a material impact on the presentation of the company's financial condition, changes in financial condition or results of operations.

The company's critical accounting policies relate to the calculation and treatment of sales incentives, allowance for doubtful accounts, valuation of inventories, income taxes, stock-based compensation and goodwill impairment.

Sales Incentives

Sales incentives primarily include consumer coupons and trade promotion activities such as advertising allowances, off-shelf displays, customer specific coupons, new item distribution allowances, and temporary price reductions. The company records accruals for sales incentives based on estimates of the ultimate cost of each program. The company tracks its commitments for sales incentive programs and, using historical experience, records an accrual at the end of each period for the estimated incurred, but unpaid costs of these programs. Actual costs differing from estimated costs could significantly affect these estimates and the related accruals. For example, if the company's estimate of incurred, but unpaid costs was to change by 10%, the impact to the sales incentive accrual as of September 30, 2009 would be approximately $4.5 million.

Allowance for Doubtful Accounts

The allowance for doubtful accounts requires management to estimate future collections of trade accounts receivable. Management records allowances for doubtful accounts based on historical collection statistics and current customer credit information. These estimates could be significantly affected as a result of actual collections differing from historical statistics or changes in a customer's credit status. As of September 30, 2009, the company's allowance for doubtful accounts was $2.0 million.

Valuation of Inventories

When necessary, the company provides allowances to adjust the carrying value of inventories to the lower of cost or market, including costs to sell or dispose. Estimates of the future demand for the company's products, anticipated product relaunches, changes in formulas and packaging and reductions in stock-keeping units are among the factors used by management in assessing the net realizable value of inventories. Actual results differing from these estimates could significantly affect the company's inventories and cost of products sold. As of September 30, 2009, the company's inventory allowances were $8.9 million.

Income Taxes

The company records tax provisions in its consolidated financial statements based on an estimation of current income tax liabilities. The development of these provisions requires judgments about tax issues, potential outcomes and timing.

The company's liability for unrecognized tax benefits at September 30, 2009 was $11.4 million, of which $5.8 million represented tax benefits that, if recognized, would favorably impact the effective tax rates for either continuing or discontinued operations.

The company recognizes accrued interest and penalties related to unrecognized tax benefits as a component of the income tax provision in the consolidated statements of earnings. At September 30, 2009, the company's long-term income tax liabilities include accrued interest and penalties of $1.5 million. The total amount of interest and penalties recognized in the consolidated statement of earnings for fiscal year 2009 was $272,000.

The company files a consolidated U.S. federal income tax return, as well as income tax returns in various states and foreign jurisdictions. With some exceptions, the company is no longer subject to examinations by tax authorities in the United States for fiscal years ending before 2006 and in its major international markets for fiscal years ending before 2002.

In the next twelve months, the company's effective tax rate and the amount of unrecognized tax benefits could be affected positively or negatively by the resolution of ongoing tax audits and the expiration of certain statutes of limitations. The company is unable to project the potential range of tax impacts at this time.

Deferred income taxes are recognized for the future tax consequences attributable to differences between the financial statement carrying amounts of assets and liabilities and their respective tax bases. Deferred tax assets and liabilities are measured using enacted tax rates expected to apply to taxable income in the years in which temporary differences are estimated to be recovered or settled. Management believes that it is more likely than not that results of future operations will generate sufficient taxable income to realize the company's deferred tax assets, net of the valuation allowance currently recorded. In the future, if the company determines that certain deferred tax assets will not be realizable, the related adjustments could significantly affect the company's effective tax rate at that time.

Stock-Based Compensation

The company recognizes compensation expense for stock options on a straight-line basis over the vesting period or to the date a participant becomes eligible for retirement, if earlier. The company recorded stock option expense in fiscal year 2009 of $7.8 million related to continuing operations. At September 30, 2009, the company had $11.2 million of unrecognized compensation cost related to stock options that will be recorded over a weighted average period of 2.3 years. The fair value of each stock option grant was estimated on the date of grant using the Black-Scholes option pricing model with the following assumptions:

	2009
Expected life	3.5–4 years
Expected volatility	30.8%
Risk-free interest rate	1.4%–2.5%
Dividend yield	1.0%

The expected life of stock options represents the period of time that the stock options granted are expected to be outstanding. The company estimates the expected life based on historical exercise trends. The company estimates expected volatility based primarily on the historical volatility of the company's common stock. For stock option grants following the Separation, the company's estimate of expected volatility also takes into consideration the company's implied volatility and the historical volatility of a group of peer companies. The estimate of the risk-free interest rate is based on the U.S. Treasury rate for the expected life of the stock options. The dividend yield represents the company's anticipated cash dividend over the expected life of the stock options. The amount of stock option expense recorded is significantly affected by these estimates. Changes in the company's estimates and assumptions used in the option pricing model would impact the fair value of future stock option grants but not those previously issued.

The weighted average grant date fair value of stock options granted to employees in fiscal year 2009 was $6.87. A one year increase in the expected life assumption would result in a higher weighted average fair value by approximately 11% for fiscal year 2009. A 1% increase in the expected volatility assumption would result in a higher weighted average fair value by approximately 3% for fiscal year 2009.

In addition, the company records stock option expense based on an estimate of the total number of stock options expected to vest, which requires the company to estimate future forfeitures. The company uses historical forfeiture experience as a basis for this estimate. Actual forfeitures differing from these estimates could significantly affect the timing of the recognition of stock option expense. During fiscal year 2009, the company has not recorded significant adjustments to stock option expense as a result of adjustments to estimated forfeiture rates.

Goodwill Impairment

In accordance with FASB ASC Topic 350, "Intangibles—Goodwill and Other," the company's goodwill is tested for impairment annually or more frequently if significant events or changes indicate possible impairment. The company's policy is to perform the annual goodwill impairment analysis during the second quarter of each fiscal year. Goodwill is evaluated using a two-step impairment test for each of the company's reporting units, as defined in FASB ASC Topic 350. The first step compares the carrying value of a reporting unit, including goodwill, with its fair value, which is generally estimated based on the company's best estimate of the present value of expected future cash flows. If the carrying value of a reporting unit exceeds its estimated fair value, the company would be required to complete the second step of the analysis. This step requires management to allocate the estimated fair value of the reporting unit to all of the assets and liabilities other than goodwill in order to determine an implied fair value of the reporting unit's goodwill. The amount of impairment loss to be recorded, if any, would be equal to the excess of the carrying value of the goodwill over its implied fair value.

The determination of the fair value of the company's reporting units requires management to consider changes in economic conditions and other factors to make assumptions regarding estimated future cash flows and long-term growth rates. These assumptions are highly subjective judgments based on the company's experience and knowledge of its operations, are based on the best available market information and are consistent with the company's internal forecasts and operating plans. These estimates can be significantly impacted by many factors including competition, changes in U.S. or global economic conditions, increasing operating costs and inflation rates and other factors discussed in the "Forward—Looking Statements" and "Risk Factors" sections of this Annual Report on Form 10-K. If the company's estimates or underlying assumptions change in the future, the company may be required to record goodwill impairment charges.

The company's annual goodwill impairment analysis completed in the second quarter of fiscal year 2009 resulted in no impairment. As of September 30, 2009, the company's total goodwill balance was $224.3 million.

Reconciliation of Non-GAAP Financial Measures

A reconciliation of "organic sales growth" to its most directly comparable financial measure under GAAP for the fiscal years ended September 30, 2009 and 2008 is as follows:

	2009	2008
Net sales growth (decline), as reported	(0.7)%	9.7%
Effect of foreign currency fluctuations	8.1	(1.0)
Effect of acquisition	(2.5)	—
Effect of divestiture	0.1	—
Organic sales growth	5.0%	8.7%

Forward-Looking Information Excerpt

1.15

AT&T INC. (DEC)

FORWARD-LOOKING STATEMENTS

Information set forth in this report contains forward-looking statements that are subject to risks and uncertainties, and actual results could differ materially. Many of these factors are discussed in more detail in the "Risk Factors" section. We claim the protection of the safe harbor for forward-looking statements provided by the Private Securities Litigation Reform Act of 1995.

The following factors could cause our future results to differ materially from those expressed in the forward-looking statements:

- Adverse economic and/or capital access changes in the markets served by us or in countries in which we have significant investments, including the impact on customer demand and our ability and our suppliers' ability to access financial markets.
- Changes in available technology and the effects of such changes, including product substitutions and deployment costs.
- Increases in our benefit plans' costs, including increases due to adverse changes in the U.S. and foreign securities markets, resulting in worse-than-assumed investment returns and discount rates, and adverse medical cost trends and unfavorable health care legislation and regulations.
- The final outcome of Federal Communications Commission and other federal agency proceedings and reopenings of such proceedings and judicial review, if any, of such proceedings, including issues relating to access charges, broadband deployment, E911 services, competition, net neutrality, unbundled loop and transport elements, wireless license awards and renewals and wireless services.
- The final outcome of regulatory proceedings in the states in which we operate and reopenings of such proceedings and judicial review, if any, of such proceedings, including proceedings relating to Interconnection terms, access charges, universal service, unbundled network elements and resale and wholesale rates, broadband deployment including our U-verse services, net neutrality, performance measurement plans, service standards and traffic compensation.
- Enactment of additional state, federal and/or foreign regulatory and tax laws and regulations pertaining to our subsidiaries and foreign investments, including laws and regulations that reduce our incentive to invest in our networks, resulting in lower revenue growth and/or higher operating costs.
- Our ability to absorb revenue losses caused by increasing competition, including offerings that use alternative technologies (e.g., cable, wireless and VoIP) and our ability to maintain capital expenditures.
- The extent of competition and the resulting pressure on access line totals and wireline and wireless operating margins.

- Our ability to develop attractive and profitable product/service offerings to offset increasing competition in our wireless and wireline markets.
- The ability of our competitors to offer product/service offerings at lower prices due to lower cost structures and regulatory and legislative actions adverse to us, including state regulatory proceedings relating to unbundled network elements and nonregulation of comparable alternative technologies (e.g., VoIP).
- The timing, extent and cost of deployment of our U-verse services; the development of attractive and profitable service offerings; the extent to which regulatory, franchise fees and build-out requirements apply to this initiative; and the availability, cost and/or reliability of the various technologies and/or content required to provide such offerings.
- Our continued ability to attract and offer a diverse portfolio of devices, some on an exclusive basis.
- The availability and cost of additional wireless spectrum and regulations relating to licensing and technical standards and deployment and usage, including network management rules.
- Our ability to manage growth in wireless data services, including network quality.
- The outcome of pending or threatened litigation, including patent and product safety claims by or against third parties.
- The impact on our networks and business of major equipment failures, our inability to obtain equipment/software or have equipment/software serviced in a timely and cost-effective manner from suppliers, severe weather conditions, natural disasters, pandemics or terrorist attacks.
- Our ability to successfully negotiate new collective bargaining contracts and the terms of those contracts.
- The issuance by the Financial Accounting Standards Board or other accounting oversight bodies of new accounting standards or changes to existing standards.
- The issuance by the Internal Revenue Service and/or state tax authorities of new tax regulations or changes to existing standards and actions by federal, state or local tax agencies and judicial authorities with respect to applying applicable tax laws and regulations and the resolution of disputes with any taxing jurisdictions.
- Our ability to adequately fund our wireless operations, including payment for additional spectrum; network upgrades and technological advancements.
- Changes in our corporate strategies, such as changing network requirements or acquisitions and dispositions, to respond to competition and regulatory, legislative and technological developments.

Readers are cautioned that other factors discussed in this report, although not enumerated here, also could materially affect our future earnings.

Liquidity and Capital Resources Excerpt

1.16

HESS CORPORATION (DEC)

LIQUIDITY AND CAPITAL RESOURCES

The following table sets forth certain relevant measures of the Corporation's liquidity and capital resources as of December 31:

(Millions of dollars)	2009	2008
Cash and cash equivalents	$ 1,362	$ 908
Current portion of long-term debt	$ 148	$ 143
Total debt	$ 4,467	$ 3,955
Total equity	$13,528	$12,391
Debt to capitalization ratio*	24.8%	24.2%

* Total debt as a percentage of the sum of total debt plus equity.

Cash Flows

The following table sets forth a summary of the Corporation's cash flows:

(Millions of dollars)	2009	2008	2007
Net cash provided by (used in):			
Operating activities	$ 3,046	$ 4,688	$ 3,627
Investing activities	(2,924)	(4,444)	(3,474)
Financing activities	332	57	71
Net increase in cash and cash equivalents	$ 454	$ 301	$ 224

Operating Activities

Net cash provided by operating activities, including changes in operating assets and liabilities, was $3,046 million in 2009 compared with $4,688 million in 2008, reflecting lower earnings. Operating cash flow increased to $4,688 million in 2008 from $3,627 million in 2007, primarily reflecting increased earnings. The Corporation received cash distributions from HOVENSA of $50 million in 2008 and $300 million in 2007.

Investing Activities

The following table summarizes the Corporation's capital expenditures:

(Millions of dollars)	2009	2008	2007
Exploration and production			
Exploration	$ 611	$ 744	$ 371
Production and development	1,927	2,523	2,605
Acquisitions (including leaseholds)	262	984	462
	2,800	4,251	3,438
Marketing, refining and corporate	118	187	140
Total	$2,918	$4,438	$3,578

Capital expenditures in 2009 include acquisitions of $188 million for unproved leaseholds and $74 million for a 50% interest in blocks PM301 and PM302 in Malaysia, which are adjacent to Block A-18 of the JDA. Capital expenditures in 2008 include $600 million for leasehold acquisitions in the United States and $210 million for the acquisition of the remaining 22.5% interest in the Corporation's Gabonese subsidiary. In 2008, the Corporation also selectively expanded its energy marketing business by acquiring fuel oil, natural gas, and electricity customer accounts, and a terminal and related assets, for an aggregate of approximately $100 million. In 2007, capital expenditures include the acquisition of a 28% interest in the Genghis Khan Field in the deepwater Gulf of Mexico for $371 million.

In 2007, the Corporation received proceeds of $93 million for the sale of its interests in the Scott and Telford fields located in the United Kingdom.

Financing Activities

During 2009, net proceeds from borrowings were $447 million. In February 2009, the Corporation issued $250 million of 5 year senior unsecured notes with a coupon of 7% and $1 billion of 10 year senior unsecured notes with a coupon of 8.125%. The majority of the proceeds were used to repay debt under the revolving credit facility and outstanding borrowings on other credit facilities. In December 2009, the Corporation issued $750 million of 30 year bonds with a coupon of 6% and tendered for the $662 million of bonds due in August 2011. The Corporation completed the repurchase of $546 million of the 2011 bonds in December 2009. The remaining $116 million of 2011 bonds, classified as Current

maturities of long term debt at December 31, 2009, was redeemed in January 2010, resulting in a charge of approximately $11 million ($7 million after income taxes). During 2008, net repayments of debt were $32 million, compared with net borrowings of $208 million in 2007.

Total common stock dividends paid were $131 million, $130 million and $127 million in 2009, 2008 and 2007, respectively. The Corporation received net proceeds from the exercise of stock options, including related income tax benefits, of $18 million, $340 million and $111 million in 2009, 2008 and 2007, respectively.

Future Capital Requirements and Resources

The Corporation anticipates investing a total of approximately $4.1 billion in capital and exploratory expenditures during 2010, substantially all of which is targeted for E&P operations. In the Corporation's M&R operations, refining margins are currently weak, which have adversely affected HOVENSA's liquidity position. The Corporation intends to provide its share of any necessary financial support for HOVENSA. The Corporation expects to fund its 2010 operations, including capital expenditures, dividends, pension contributions and required debt repayments and any necessary financial support for HOVENSA, with existing cash on-hand, cash flow from operations and its available credit facilities. Crude oil prices, natural gas prices and refining margins are volatile and difficult to predict. In addition, unplanned increases in the Corporation's capital expenditure program could occur. If conditions were to change, such as a significant decrease in commodity prices or an unexpected increase in capital expenditures, the Corporation would take steps to protect its financial flexibility and may pursue other sources of liquidity, including the issuance of debt securities, the issuance of equity securities, and/or asset sales.

The table below summarizes the capacity, usage, and available capacity of the Corporation's borrowing and letter of credit facilities at December 31, 2009 (in millions):

	Expiration Date	Capacity	Borrowings	Letters of Credit Issued	Total Used	Available Capacity
Revolving credit facility	May 2012[a]	$3,000	$—	$ —	$ —	$3,000
Asset backed credit facility	July 2010[b]	741	—	500	500	241
Committed lines	Various[c]	2,115	—	1,155	1,155	960
Uncommitted lines	Various[c]	1,192	—	1,192	1,192	—
Total		$7,048	$—	$2,847	$2,847	$4,201

[a] $75 million expires in May 2011.
[b] Total capacity of $1.0 billion subject to the amount of eligible receivables posted as collateral.
[c] Committed and uncommitted lines have expiration dates primarily through 2010.

The Corporation maintains a $3.0 billion syndicated, revolving credit facility (the facility), of which $2,925 million is committed through May 2012. The facility can be used for borrowings and letters of credit. At December 31, 2009, available capacity under the facility was $3.0 billion. The Corporation has a 364 day asset-backed credit facility securitized by certain accounts receivable from its M&R operations. At December 31, 2009, under the terms of this financing arrangement, the Corporation has the ability to borrow or issue letters of credit of up to $1.0 billion, subject to the availability of sufficient levels of eligible receivables. At December 31, 2009, outstanding letters of credit under this facility were collateralized by a total of $1,326 million of accounts receivable, which are held by a wholly owned subsidiary. These receiv-

ables are only available to pay the general obligations of the Corporation after satisfaction of the outstanding obligations under the asset backed facility.

The Corporation also has a shelf registration under which it may issue additional debt securities, warrants, common stock or preferred stock.

A loan agreement covenant based on the Corporation's debt to capitalization ratio allows the Corporation to borrow up to an additional $18.1 billion for the construction or acquisition of assets at December 31, 2009. The Corporation has the ability to borrow up to an additional $3.7 billion of secured debt at December 31, 2009 under the loan agreement covenants.

The Corporation's $2,847 million in letters of credit outstanding at December 31, 2009 were primarily issued to satisfy margin requirements. See also Note 14, Risk Management and Trading Activities.

Credit Ratings

There are three major credit rating agencies that rate the Corporation's debt. All three agencies have currently assigned an investment grade rating to the Corporation's debt. The interest rates and facility fees charged on some of the Corporation's credit facilities, as well as margin requirements from risk management and trading counterparties, are subject to adjustment if the Corporation's credit rating changes.

Contractual Obligations and Contingencies

Following is a table showing aggregated information about certain contractual obligations at December 31, 2009:

| | | | Payments Due by Period | | |
| | | | 2011 and | 2013 and | |
(Millions of dollars)	Total	2010	2012	2014	Thereafter
Long-term debt[1]	$ 4,467	$ 148	$ 66	$ 370	$3,883
Operating leases	3,282	482	695	677	1,428
Purchase obligations					
Supply commitments[2]	37,870	13,158	12,546	12,118	48
Capital expenditures	939	745	191	2	1
Operating expenses	937	457	276	70	134
Other long-term liabilities	$ 2,095	$ 145	$ 366	$ 199	$1,385

[1] At December 31, 2009, the Corporation's debt bears interest at a weighted average rate of 7.3%.
[2] The Corporation intends to continue purchasing refined product supply from HOVENSA. Estimated future purchases amount to approximately $6.0 billion annually using year-end 2009 prices, which have been included in the table through 2014.

In the preceding table, the Corporation's supply commitments include its estimated purchases of 50% of HOVENSA's production of refined products, after anticipated sales by HOVENSA to unaffiliated parties. The value of future supply commitments will fluctuate based on prevailing market prices at the time of purchase, the actual output from HOVENSA, and the level of sales to unaffiliated parties. Also included are term purchase agreements at market prices for additional gasoline necessary to supply the Corporation's retail marketing system and feedstocks for the Port Reading refining facility. In addition, the Corporation has commitments to purchase refined products, natural gas and electricity to supply contracted customers in its energy marketing business. These commitments were computed based predominately on year-end market prices.

The table also reflects future capital expenditures, including the portion of the Corporation's planned $4.1 billion capital investment program for 2010 that is contractually committed at December 31, 2009. Obligations for operating expenses include commitments for transportation, seismic purchases, oil and gas production expenses and other normal business expenses. Other long-term liabilities reflect contractually committed obligations on the balance sheet at December 31, 2009, including asset retirement obligations, pension plan liabilities and anticipated obligations for uncertain income tax positions.

The Corporation and certain of its subsidiaries lease gasoline stations, drilling rigs, tankers, office space and other assets for varying periods under leases accounted for as operating leases. The Corporation entered into a lease agreement for a new drillship and related support services for use in its global deepwater exploration and development activities. The total payments under this five year contract are expected to be approximately $950 million. The Corporation took delivery of the drillship in the fourth quarter of 2009.

The Corporation has a contingent purchase obligation, expiring in April 2012, to acquire the remaining interest in WilcoHess, a retail gasoline station joint venture, for approximately $184 million as of December 31, 2009.

The Corporation guarantees the payment of up to 50% of HOVENSA's crude oil purchases from certain suppliers other than PDVSA. The amount of the Corporation's guarantee fluctuates based on the volume of crude oil purchased and related prices and at December 31, 2009 it amounted to $121 million. In addition, the Corporation has agreed to provide funding up to a maximum of $15 million to the extent HOVENSA does not have funds to meet its senior debt obligations.

The Corporation is contingently liable under letters of credit and under guarantees of the debt of other entities directly related to its business at December 31, 2009 as shown below:

(Millions of dollars)	Total
Letters of credit	$100
Guarantees	136
	$236

Off-Balance Sheet Arrangements

The Corporation has leveraged leases not included in its balance sheet, primarily related to retail gasoline stations that the Corporation operates. The net present value of these leases is $412 million at December 31, 2009 compared with $491 million at December 31, 2008. The Corporation's December 31, 2009 debt to capitalization ratio would increase from 24.8% to 26.5% if these leases were included as debt.

New Accounting Standards Excerpt

1.17

OLIN CORPORATION (DEC)

NEW ACCOUNTING PRONOUNCEMENTS

In January 2010, the FASB issued Accounting Standards Update (ASU) 2010-06 "Improving Disclosures About Fair Value Measurements" (ASU 2010-06), which amends ASC 820 "Fair Value Measurements and Disclosures" (ASC 820). This update adds new fair value disclosure requirements about transfers into and out of Level 1 and 2 and separate disclosures about purchases, sales, issuances, and settlements related to Level 3 measurements. This update expands disclosures on valuation techniques and inputs used to measure fair value. This update is effective for fiscal years beginning after December 15, 2009, except for the requirement to provide the Level 3 activity of purchases, sales, issuances, and settlements, which will be effective for fiscal years beginning after December 15, 2010. We will adopt the provisions of ASU 2010-06 in 2010, except for the requirement to provide the additional Level 3 activity, which will be adopted in 2011. This update will require additional disclosure in our first quarter 2010 condensed financial statements. The adoption of this update will not have a material effect on our consolidated financial statements.

In July 2009, the FASB issued SFAS No. 168, "The FASB Accounting Standards Codification™ and the Hierarchy of Generally Accepted Accounting Principles," (the Codification), which was incorporated into ASC 105 "Generally Accepted Accounting Principles" (ASC 105). The Codification will be the single source of authoritative U.S. generally accepted accounting principles. The Codification does not change generally accepted accounting principles, but is intended to make it easier to find and research issues. The Codification introduces a new structure that takes accounting pronouncements and organizes them by approximately 90 accounting topics. The Codification was effective for interim and fiscal years ending after September 15, 2009. We adopted the Codification on July 1, 2009. The adoption of this statement did not have a material effect on our consolidated financial statements but changed our reference to generally accepted accounting principles beginning in the third quarter of 2009.

In June 2009, the FASB issued SFAS No. 166, "Accounting for Transfers of Financial Assets" (SFAS No. 166), which was incorporated into ASC 860 "Transfers and Servicing" (ASC 860) and SFAS No. 167, "Amendments to FASB Interpretation No. 46(R)" (SFAS No. 167), which was incorporated into ASC 810 "Consolidation" (ASC 810). These state-

ments changed the way entities account for securitizations and special-purpose entities. The new standards eliminate existing exceptions, strengthen the standards relating to securitizations and special-purpose entities, and enhance disclosure requirements. Both of these statements are effective for fiscal years beginning after November 15, 2009. The adoption of these statements will not have a material effect on our consolidated financial statements.

In May 2009, the FASB issued SFAS No. 165, "Subsequent Events" (SFAS No. 165), which was incorporated into ASC 855 "Subsequent Events" (ASC 855). ASC 855 provides guidance on management's assessment of subsequent events. The statement is not expected to significantly change practice because its guidance is similar to that in American Institute of Certified Public Accountants Professional Standards U.S. Auditing Standards Section 560, "Subsequent Events," with some modifications. This statement became effective for us on June 15, 2009. The adoption of this statement did not have a material effect on our consolidated financial statements.

In April 2009, the FASB issued three Staff Positions (FSP) intended to provide additional application guidance and enhance disclosures regarding fair value measurements and impairments of securities. FSP SFAS No. 157-4, "Determining Fair Value When the Volume and Level of Activity for the Asset or Liability Have Significantly Decreased and Identifying Transactions That Are Not Orderly" (SFAS No. 157-4) provided guidelines for making fair value measurements more consistent with the principles presented in ASC 820. FSP SFAS No. 107-1 and APB 28-1, "Interim Disclosures about Fair Value of Financial Instruments" (SFAS No. 107-1 and APB 28-1), which were incorporated into ASC 825 "Financial Instruments" (ASC 825), enhanced consistency in financial reporting by increasing the frequency of fair value disclosures. FSP SFAS No. 115-2 and SFAS No. 124-2, "Recognition and Presentation of Other-Than-Temporary Impairments" (SFAS No. 115-2 and SFAS No. 124-2), which were incorporated into ASC 320 "Investments—Debt and Equity Securities" (ASC 320), provided additional guidance designed to create greater clarity and consistency in accounting for and presenting impairment losses on securities.

The position updating ASC 820 related to determining fair values when there is no active market or where the price inputs being used represent distressed sales. This position stated that the objective of fair value measurement is to reflect how much an asset would be sold for in an orderly transaction (as opposed to a distressed or forced transaction) at the date of the financial statements under current market conditions.

The position updating ASC 825 related to fair value disclosures for any financial instruments that are not currently reflected on the balance sheet at fair value. Prior to issuing this position, fair values for these assets and liabilities were only disclosed once a year. This position required these disclosures on a quarterly basis, providing qualitative and quantitative information about fair value estimates for all those financial instruments not measured on the balance sheet at fair value.

The position updating ASC 320 on other-than-temporary impairments is intended to bring greater consistency to the timing of impairment recognition, and provide greater clarity to investors about the credit and noncredit components of impaired debt securities that are not expected to be sold. The measure of impairment in comprehensive income remains fair value. This position also required increased and more timely disclosures sought by investors regarding expected cash flows, credit losses, and an aging of securities with unrealized losses.

These positions became effective for interim and fiscal years ending after June 15, 2009, with early adoption permitted. We adopted these positions as of March 31, 2009. The adoption of these positions did not have a material effect on our consolidated financial statements.

In December 2008, the FASB issued FSP SFAS No. 132R-1, "Employers' Disclosures about Postretirement Benefit Plan Assets," (SFAS No. 132R-1), an amendment of SFAS No. 132 (revised 2003), "Employers' Disclosures about Pensions and Other Postretirement Benefits," (SFAS No. 132R), which were both incorporated into ASC 715. This position required more detailed disclosures regarding defined benefit pension plan assets including investment policies and strategies, major categories of plan assets, valuation techniques used to measure the fair value of plan assets and significant concentrations of risk within plan assets. This position became effective for fiscal years ending after December 15, 2009. Upon initial application, the provisions of this position were not required for earlier periods that are presented for comparative purposes. The adoption of this statement did not have a material impact on our consolidated financial statements.

In March 2008, the FASB issued SFAS No. 161, "Disclosures about Derivative Instruments and Hedging Activities," (SFAS No. 161), an amendment to SFAS No. 133, "Accounting for Derivative Instruments and Hedging Activities," (SFAS No. 133), which were both incorporated into ASC 815 "Derivatives and Hedging" (ASC 815). The statement required enhanced disclosures that expand the previous disclosure requirements about an entity's derivative instruments and hedging activities. It required more robust qualitative disclosures and expanded quantitative disclosures. This statement became effective for financial statements issued for fiscal years and interim periods beginning after November 15, 2008, with early application encouraged. We adopted the provisions of this statement on January 1, 2009, which required additional disclosure in our 2009 financial statements. The adoption of this statement did not have a material impact on our consolidated financial statements.

In December 2007, the FASB issued SFAS No. 141R, "Business Combinations," (SFAS No. 141R), which was incorporated into ASC 805 "Business Combinations" (ASC 805). This statement required the acquiring entity in a business combination to recognize all (and only) the assets acquired and liabilities assumed in the transaction, established the acquisition-date fair value as the measurement objective for all assets acquired and liabilities assumed, and required additional disclosures by the acquirer. Under this statement, all business combinations are accounted for by applying the acquisition method. This statement became effective for us on January 1, 2009. Earlier application was prohibited. The effect of the adoption of this statement on our consolidated financial statements will be on adjustments made to pre-acquisition Pioneer income tax contingencies, which will no longer be reflected as an adjustment to goodwill but recognized through income tax expense.

In December 2007, the FASB issued SFAS No. 160, "Noncontrolling Interests in Consolidated Financial Statements," (SFAS No. 160), which was incorporated into ASC 810. This statement required noncontrolling interests (previously referred to as minority interests) to be treated as a separate component of equity, not as a liability or other item outside of permanent equity. The statement applied to the accounting for noncontrolling interests and transactions with noncontrolling interest holders in consolidated financial statements. This statement became effective for us on January 1, 2009. Earlier application was prohibited. This statement was applied prospectively to all noncontrolling interests, including any that arose before the effective date except that comparative period information must be recast to classify noncontrolling interests in equity, attribute net income and other comprehensive income to noncontrolling interests, and provide additional required disclosures. The adoption of this statement did not have a material effect on our consolidated financial statements.

In September 2006, the FASB issued SFAS No. 157, "Fair Value Measurements," (SFAS No. 157), which was incorporated into ASC 820. This statement did not require any new fair value measurements, but rather, it provided enhanced guidance to other pronouncements that require or permit assets or liabilities to be measured at fair value. The changes to current practice resulting from the application of this statement related to the definition of fair value, the methods used to estimate fair value, and the requirement for expanded disclosures about estimates of fair value. This statement became effective for fiscal years beginning after November 15, 2007, and interim periods within those fiscal years. The effective date for this statement for all nonfinancial assets and nonfinancial liabilities, except for items that are recognized or disclosed at fair value in the financial statements on a recurring basis was delayed by one year. Nonfinancial assets and nonfinancial liabilities that were impacted by this deferral included assets and liabilities initially measured at fair value in a business combination, and intangible assets and goodwill tested annually for impairment. We adopted the provisions of this statement related to financial assets and financial liabilities on January 1, 2008, which required additional disclosure in our financial statements. The partial adoption of this statement did not have a material impact on our consolidated financial statements. We adopted the remaining provisions of this statement related to nonfinancial assets and nonfinancial liabilities on January 1, 2009. The adoption of the remaining provisions of this statement did not have a material impact on our consolidated financial statements.

Market Risk Information Excerpt

1.18

AUTOMATIC DATA PROCESSING, INC. (JUN)

MARKET RISK

Our overall investment portfolio is comprised of corporate investments (cash and cash equivalents, short-term marketable securities, and long-term marketable securities) and client funds assets (funds that have been collected from clients but not yet remitted to the applicable tax authorities or client employees).

Our corporate investments are invested in cash equivalents and highly liquid, investment-grade securities. These assets are available for repurchases of common stock for treasury and/or acquisitions, as well as other corporate operating purposes. All of our short-term and long-term fixed-income securities are classified as available-for-sale securities.

Our client funds assets are invested with safety of principal, liquidity, and diversification as the primary goals. Consistent with those goals, we also seek to maximize interest income and to minimize the volatility of interest income. Client funds assets are invested in highly liquid, investment-grade marketable securities with a maximum maturity of 10 years at time of purchase and money market securities and other cash equivalents. At June 30, 2009, approximately 85% of the available-for-sale securities categorized as U.S. Treasury and direct obligations of U.S. government agencies were invested in senior, unsecured, non-callable debt directly issued by the Federal Home Loan Banks, Fannie Mae and Freddie Mac.

We utilize a strategy by which we extend the maturities of our investment portfolio for funds held for clients and employ short-term financing arrangements to satisfy our short-term funding requirements related to client funds obligations. Our client funds investment strategy is structured to allow us to average our way through an interest rate cycle by laddering investments out to five years (in the case of the extended portfolio) and out to ten years (in the case of the long portfolio). As part of our client funds investment strategy, we use the daily collection of funds from our clients to satisfy other unrelated client fund obligations, rather than liquidating previously-collected client funds that have already been invested in available-for-sale securities. We minimize the risk of not having funds collected from a client available at the time such client's obligation becomes due by impounding, in virtually all instances, the client's funds in advance of the timing of payment of such client's obligation. As a result of this practice, we have consistently maintained the required

level of client fund assets to satisfy all of our client funds obligations.

There are inherent risks and uncertainties involving our investment strategy relating to our client fund assets. Such risks include liquidity risk, including the risk associated with our ability to liquidate, if necessary, our available-for-sale securities in a timely manner in order to satisfy our client funds obligations. However, our investments are made with the safety of principal, liquidity and diversification as the primary goals to minimize the risk of not having sufficient funds to satisfy all of our client funds obligations. We also believe we have significantly reduced the risk of not having sufficient funds to satisfy our client funds obligations by consistently maintaining access to other sources of liquidity, including our corporate cash balances, available borrowings under our $6 billion commercial paper program (rated A-1+ by Standard & Poor's and Prime-1 by Moody's, the highest possible credit rating), our ability to execute reverse repurchase transactions and available borrowings under our $6 billion committed revolving credit facilities. However, the availability of financing during periods of economic turmoil, even to borrowers with the highest credit ratings, may limit our flexibility to access short-term debt markets to meet the liquidity needs of our business. In addition to liquidity risk, our investments are subject to interest rate risk and credit risk, as discussed below.

We have established credit quality, maturity, and exposure limits for our investments. The minimum allowed credit rating at time of purchase for corporate bonds is BBB and for asset-backed and commercial mortgage-backed securities is AAA. The maximum maturity at time of purchase for BBB rated securities is 5 years, for single A rated securities is 7 years, and for AA rated and AAA rated securities is 10 years. Commercial paper must be rated A1/P1 and, for time deposits, banks must have a Financial Strength Rating of C or better.

Details regarding our overall investment portfolio are as follows:

(Dollars in millions)	2009	2008	2007
Average investment balances at cost:			
Corporate investments	$ 3,744.7	$ 3,387.0	$ 3,556.8
Funds held for clients	15,162.4	15,654.3	14,682.9
Total	$18,907.1	$19,041.3	$18,239.7
Average interest rates earned exclusive of realized gains/(losses) on:			
Corporate investments	3.6%	4.4%	4.6%
Funds held for clients	4.0%	4.4%	4.5%
Total	3.9%	4.4%	4.5%
Realized gains on available-for-sale securities	$ 11.4	$ 10.1	$ 20.8
Realized losses on available-for-sale securities	(23.8)	(11.4)	(12.5)
Net realized (losses)/gains on available-for-sale securities	$ (12.4)	$ (1.3)	$ 8.3
As of June 30:			
Net unrealized pre-tax gains/(losses) on available-for-sale securities	$ 436.6	$ 142.1	$ (184.9)
Total available-for-sale securities at fair value	$14,730.2	$15,066.4	$13,369.4

Our laddering strategy exposes us to interest rate risk in relation to securities that mature, as the proceeds from maturing securities are reinvested. Factors that influence the earnings impact of the interest rate changes include, among others, the amount of invested funds and the overall portfolio mix between short-term and long-term investments. This mix varies during the fiscal year and is impacted by daily interest rate changes. The annualized interest rates earned on our entire portfolio decreased by 50 basis points, from 4.4% for fiscal 2008 to 3.9% for fiscal 2009. A hypothetical change in both short-term interest rates (e.g., overnight interest rates or the federal funds rate) and intermediate-term interest rates of 25 basis points applied to the estimated average investment balances and any related short-term borrowings would result in approximately a $6 million impact to earnings before income taxes over the ensuing twelve-month period ending June 30, 2010. A hypothetical change in only short-term interest rates of 25 basis points applied to the estimated average short-term investment balances and any related short-term borrowings would result in approximately a $3 million impact to earnings before income taxes over the ensuing twelve-month period ending June 30, 2010.

We are exposed to credit risk in connection with our available-for-sale securities through the possible inability of the borrowers to meet the terms of the securities. We limit credit risk by investing in investment-grade securities, primarily AAA and AA rated securities, as rated by Moody's, Standard & Poor's, and for Canadian securities, Dominion Bond Rating Service. At June 30, 2009, approximately 83% of our available-for-sale securities held an AAA or AA rating. In addition, we limit amounts that can be invested in any security other than US and Canadian government or government agency securities.

We are exposed to market risk from changes in foreign currency exchange rates that could impact our financial position, results of operations and cash flows. We manage our exposure to these market risks through our regular operating and financing activities and, when deemed appropriate, through the use of derivative financial instruments. We use derivative financial instruments as risk management tools and not for trading purposes. There were no derivative financial instruments outstanding at June 30, 2009 or 2008.

Critical Accounting Policies and Estimates Excerpt

1.19

FORTUNE BRANDS, INC. (DEC)

CRITICAL ACCOUNTING ESTIMATES AND POLICIES

Our significant accounting policies are described in Note 1 of Notes to Consolidated Financial Statements, Item 8 to this Form 10-K. The Consolidated Financial Statements are prepared in conformity with U.S. GAAP. Preparation of the financial statements requires us to make judgments, estimates and assumptions that affect the amounts of assets and liabilities in the financial statements and revenues and expenses during the reporting periods. We believe the following are the Company's critical accounting policies due to the more sig-

nificant, subjective and complex judgments and estimates used when preparing our consolidated financial statements. We regularly review our assumptions and estimates.

Allowances for Doubtful Accounts

Trade receivables are recorded at the stated amount, less allowances for discounts, doubtful accounts and returns. The allowances represent estimated uncollectible receivables associated with potential customer defaults on contractual obligations (usually due to customers' potential insolvency), or discounts related to early payment of accounts receivables by our customers. The allowances include amounts for certain customers where a risk of default has been specifically identified. In addition, the allowances include a provision for customer defaults on a general formula basis when it is determined the risk of some default is probable and estimable, but cannot yet be associated with specific customers. The assessment of the likelihood of customer defaults is based on various factors, including the length of time the receivables are past due, historical experience and existing economic conditions. In accordance with this policy, our allowance for discounts, doubtful accounts and returns for continuing operations was $72.0 million and $57.5 million as of December 31, 2009 and 2008, respectively.

Inventories

The first-in, first-out inventory method is our principal inventory method across all segments. In accordance with generally recognized trade practice, maturing spirits inventories are classified as current assets, although the majority of these inventories ordinarily will not be sold within one year due to the duration of aging processes. Inventory provisions are recorded to reduce inventory to the lower of cost or market value for obsolete or slow moving inventory based on assumptions about future demand and marketability of products, the impact of new product introductions, inventory turns, product spoilage and specific identification of items, such as product discontinuance or engineering/material changes.

Long-Lived Assets

In accordance with authoritative guidance on property, plant, and equipment (ASC 360), a long-lived asset (including amortizable identifiable intangible assets) or asset group is tested for recoverability whenever events or changes in circumstances indicate that its carrying amount may not be recoverable. When such events occur, the Company compares the sum of the undiscounted cash flows expected to result from the use and eventual disposition of the asset or asset group to the carrying amount of a long-lived asset or asset group. The cash flows are based on our best estimate of future cash flows derived from the most recent business projections. If this comparison indicates that there is an impairment, the amount of the impairment is calculated based on fair value. Fair value is estimated primarily using discounted expected future cash flows on a market participant basis.

Goodwill and Indefinite-Lived Intangible Assets

In accordance with authoritative guidance on goodwill and other intangibles assets (ASC 350), goodwill is tested for impairment at least annually, and written down when impaired. An interim impairment test is required if an event occurs or conditions change that would more likely than not reduce the fair value of the reporting unit below the carrying value.

We evaluate the recoverability of goodwill by estimating the future cash flows of the reporting units to which the goodwill relates, and then discount the future cash flows at a market-participant-derived weighted-average cost of capital. In determining the estimated future cash flows, we consider current and projected future levels of income based on management's plans for that business; business trends, prospects and market and economic conditions; and market-participant considerations. A reporting unit is an operating segment, or in the case of the Home & Security segment, one level below the operating segment. When the estimated fair value of a reporting unit is less than its carrying value, we measure and recognize the amount of the goodwill impairment loss, if any. Impairment losses, limited to the carrying value of goodwill, represent the excess of the carrying value of a reporting unit's goodwill over the implied fair value of that goodwill. The implied fair value of a reporting unit is estimated based on a hypothetical allocation of each reporting unit's fair value to all of its underlying assets and liabilities in accordance with the requirements of ASC 350.

ASC 350 requires that purchased intangible assets other than goodwill be amortized over their useful lives unless those lives are determined to be indefinite. Certain of our tradenames have been assigned an indefinite life as we currently anticipate that these tradenames will contribute cash flows to the Company indefinitely. Indefinite-lived intangible assets are not amortized, but are evaluated at each reporting period to determine whether the indefinite useful life is appropriate. We review indefinite-lived intangible assets for impairment annually, and whenever market or business events indicate there may be a potential impairment of that intangible. Impairment losses are recorded to the extent that the carrying value of the indefinite-lived intangible asset exceeds its fair value. We measure fair value using the standard relief-from-royalty approach which estimates the present value of royalty income that could hypothetically be earned by licensing the brand name to a third party over the remaining useful life.

The Company cannot predict the occurrence of certain events or changes in circumstances that might adversely affect the carrying value of goodwill and indefinite-lived intangible assets. Such events may include, but are not limited to, the impact of the economic environment; a material negative change in relationships with significant customers; or strategic decisions made in response to economic and competitive conditions.

Pension and Postretirement Benefit Plans

We provide a range of benefits to our employees and retired employees, including pension, postretirement, post-employment and health care benefits. We record amounts relating to these plans based on calculations specified by U.S. GAAP, which include various actuarial assumptions, including discount rates, assumed rates of return, compensation increases, turnover rates and health care cost trend rates. We review our actuarial assumptions on an annual basis and make modifications to the assumptions based on current economic conditions and trends. We use a market-related value method of plan assets to calculate pension costs, recognizing each year's asset gains or losses over a five-year period. Compensation increases reflect expected future compensation trends. The discount rate used to mea-

sure obligations is based on a spot-rate yield curve that matches projected future benefit payments with the appropriate interest rate applicable to the timing of the projected future benefit payments. The expected return on plan assets is determined based on the nature of the plans' investments and our expectations for long-term rates of return. The bond portfolio used for the selection of the interest rates is from the top quartile of bonds rated by nationally recognized statistical rating organizations, and includes only non-callable bonds and those that are deemed to be sufficiently marketable with a Moody's credit rating of Aa or higher. The weighted-average discount rate for pension and postretirement benefit liabilities as of December 31, 2009 and 2008 was 5.9% and 6.5%, respectively.

As required by U.S. GAAP, the effects of actuarial deviations from assumptions are generally accumulated and, if over a specified corridor, amortized over the average remaining service period of the employees. The weighted average remaining service period for the pension plans at December 31, 2009 was approximately 10.4 years. The cost or benefit of plan changes, such as increasing or decreasing benefits for prior employee service (prior service cost), is deferred and included in expense on a straight-line basis over the average remaining service period of the related employees. The total net actuarial losses for all pension and postretirement benefit plans were $429 million at December 31, 2009, a decrease of $18 million from December 31, 2008, primarily as a result of amortization of loss recognition in pension expense ($12 million) and recognition of curtailments and settlements ($15 million), partly offset by net actuarial losses in 2009 ($9 million). We believe that the assumptions utilized in recording our obligations under the Company's plans are reasonable based on our experience and on advice from our independent actuaries; however, differences in actual experience or changes in the assumptions may materially affect the Company's financial position or results of operations. For postretirement benefits, our health care trend rate assumption is based on historical cost increases and expectations for long-term increases. As of December 31, 2009, for postretirement medical and prescription drugs, our assumption was an assumed rate of increase of 7.5% in the next year, declining 50 basis points a year until reaching an ultimate assumed rate of increase of 5% per year. Our assumption as of December 31, 2008, for postretirement medical, was an assumed rate of increase of 6.75% in the next year, declining 75 basis points a year until reaching an ultimate assumed rate of increase of 5% per year, and, for postretirement prescription drugs, an assumed rate of increase of 9.75% in the next year, declining 75 basis points a year until reaching an ultimate assumed rate of increase of 5% per year.

Pension expenses were $48.9 million, $32.5 million, $41.8 million, respectively, for the years ended December 31, 2009, 2008 and 2007, including net curtailment and settlement losses of $17.6 million, $2.8 million, and zero for the years ended December 31, 2009, 2008 and 2007, respectively. Postretirement expenses were $7.9 million, $8.8 million and $9.3 million, respectively, for the years ended December 31, 2009, 2008 and 2007, including net curtailment gains of $0.1 million, $2.6 million, and $2.8 million for the years ended December 31, 2009, 2008 and 2007, respectively. A 25 basis point change in our discount rate assumption would lead to an increase or decrease in our pension expense and postretirement benefit expense of approximately $4.1 million and $0.2 million, respectively, for 2009. A 25 basis point change in the long-term rate of return on plan assets used in accounting for the Company's pension plans would have a $2.4 million impact on pension expense.

Income Taxes

In accordance with authoritative guidance on income taxes (ASC 740), we establish deferred tax liabilities or assets for temporary differences between financial and tax reporting bases and subsequently adjust them to reflect changes in tax rates expected to be in effect when the temporary differences reverse. The Company records a valuation allowance reducing deferred tax assets when it is more likely than not that such assets will not be realized.

We do not provide deferred income taxes on undistributed earnings of foreign subsidiaries that we expect to permanently reinvest or on foreign subsidiary earnings that will be remitted without incremental taxes.

We record liabilities for uncertain income tax positions based on a two step process. The first step is recognition, where we evaluate whether an individual tax position has a likelihood of greater than 50% of being sustained upon examination based on the technical merits of the position, including resolution of any related appeals or litigation processes. For tax positions that are currently estimated to have a less than 50% likelihood of being sustained, zero tax benefit is recorded. For tax positions that have met the recognition threshold in the first step, we perform the second step of measuring the benefit to be recorded. The actual benefits ultimately realized may differ from the Company's estimates. In future periods, changes in facts, circumstances, and new information may require the Company to change the recognition and measurement estimates with regard to individual tax positions. Changes in recognition and measurement estimates are recorded in results of operations and financial position in the period in which such changes occur. As of December 31, 2009, the Company has liabilities for unrecognized tax benefits pertaining to uncertain tax positions totaling $460.5 million. It is reasonably possible the unrecognized tax benefits may decrease in the range of $85 to $140 million in the next 12 months primarily as a result of the conclusion of U.S. federal, state and foreign income tax proceedings.

Customer Program Costs

Customer programs and incentives are a common practice in many of our businesses. These businesses incur customer program costs to obtain favorable product placement, to promote sell-through of that business's products and to maintain competitive pricing. Customer program costs and incentives, including rebates and promotion and volume allowances, are generally accounted for in either "net sales" or the category "advertising, selling, general and administrative expenses" at the time the program is initiated and/or the revenue is recognized. The costs recognized in "net sales" include, but are not limited to, general customer program generated expenses, cooperative advertising programs, volume allowances and promotional allowances. The costs typically recognized in "advertising, selling, general and administrative expenses" include point of sale materials and shared media. These costs are recorded at the latter of the time of sale or the implementation of the program based on management's best estimates. Estimates are based on historical and projected experience for each type of program or customer. Volume allowances are accrued based on management's estimates of customer volume achievement and other factors incorporated into customer agreements, such as new product purchases, store sell-through, merchandising support, levels of returns and customer training. Management periodically reviews accruals for these rebates and allowances, and adjusts accruals when circumstances indicate (typically as a result of a change in volume expectations).

SEGMENT INFORMATION

1.20 FASB *Accounting Standards Codification* (ASC) 280, *Segment Reporting*, requires an entity report information about a public business enterprise's operating segments. Operating segments are components of an enterprise about which separate financial information is available that is evaluated regularly by the chief operating decision maker in deciding how to allocate resources and in assessing performance.

1.21 FASB ASC 280, *Segment Reporting*, requires that a public business enterprise report a measure of segment profit or loss, certain specific revenue and expense items, and segment assets. It requires reconciliations of total segment revenues, total segment profit or loss, total segment assets, and other amounts disclosed for segments to corresponding amounts in the enterprise's general-purpose financial statements. It requires that all public business enterprises report information about the revenues derived from the enterprise's products or services (or groups of similar products and services), about the countries in which the enterprise earns revenues and holds assets, and about major customers regardless of whether that information is used in making operating decisions. However, this Statement does not require an enterprise to report information that is not prepared for internal use if reporting it would be impracticable. In addition to FASB ASC 280, FASB ASC 350, *Intangibles—Goodwill and Other*, requires that entities which report segment information shall provide information about the changes in the carrying amount of goodwill during the period for each reportable segment.

1.22 Table 1-3 shows the type of segment information most frequently presented as an integral part of the financial statements of the survey entities. Examples of segment information disclosures follow.

1.23

TABLE 1-3: SEGMENT INFORMATION

	Number of Entities			
	2009	2008	2007	2006
Industry segments				
Revenue	386	412	474	478
Operating income or loss	291	305	341	335
Identifiable assets	312	313	374	383
Depreciation expense	339	344	398	400
Capital expenditures	311	316	368	377
Goodwill	235	232	268	245
Geographic area				
Revenue	256	253	309	292
Operating income or loss	35	27	42	43
Identifiable assets	52	54	70	58
Depreciation expense	24	21	37	29
Capital expenditures	24	22	36	33
Goodwill	9	10	17	9
Export sales	20	19	27	28
Sales to major customers	99	117	142	144

2008–2009 based on 500 entities surveyed; 2006–2007 based on 600 entities surveyed.

1.24

CONVERGYS CORPORATION (DEC)

NOTES TO CONSOLIDATED FINANCIAL STATEMENTS
(Amounts in millions)

6. Goodwill and Other Intangible Assets

The Company tests goodwill for impairment annually as of October 1 and at other times if events have occurred or circumstances exist that indicate the carrying value of goodwill may no longer be recoverable. The impairment test for goodwill involves a two-step process. The first step compares the fair value of a reporting unit with its carrying amount, including the goodwill allocated to each reporting unit. If the carrying amount is in excess of the fair value, the second step requires the comparison of the implied fair value of the reporting unit goodwill with the carrying amount of the reporting unit goodwill. Any excess of the carrying value of the reporting unit goodwill over the implied fair value of the reporting unit goodwill will be recorded as an impairment loss. Fair value of the reporting units is determined using a combination of the market approach and the income approach. Under the market approach, fair value is based on actual stock price or transaction prices of comparable companies. Under the income approach, value is dependent on the present value of net cash flows to be derived from the ownership. Based on the results of its first-step impairment tests performed as of October 1, 2009, the Company had no goodwill impairment related to its five reporting units: Information Management International, Information Management North America, Customer Management, HR Management and Relationship Technology Management.

As more fully described in Note 7 of Notes to Consolidated Financial Statements, the impairment and implementation-related charges recorded at HR Management during 2009 and 2008 required a review of goodwill related to the HR Management segment both in 2009 and 2008. The reviews did not result in any goodwill impairment during 2009 and resulted in an impairment loss of $61.1 during 2008. The Company determined that the fair value of the HR Management segment was less than its carrying value in 2008 and, therefore, the second step of the test was required. This second step review resulted in a non-cash goodwill impairment charge of $61.1 recorded in the asset impairment caption in the accompanying Consolidated Statements of Operations. In determining the amount of the HR Management related goodwill impairment, the Company engaged a third-party appraisal firm to assist in valuing the significant intangible assets of the reporting unit. Key assumptions used by the Company in determining the fair value of the HR Management segment include revenue increases from existing contracts as services become operational and an estimate of future cash implementation costs and revenue. The approximate amount of the goodwill asset impairment charge that was deductible for tax purposes was $20. During the year ended December 31, 2008, the Company had no goodwill impairment related to any of its other reporting units. The Company believes it makes every reasonable effort to ensure that it accurately estimates the fair value of the reporting units. However, future changes in the assumptions used to make these estimates could result in impairment losses.

Below is a progression of goodwill for the Company's segments for 2009 and 2008:

	Customer Management	Information Management	HR Management	Total
Balance at January 1, 2008	$578.5	$187.8	$129.9	$ 896.2
Acquisitions	213.1	7.9	—	221.0
Impairment	—	—	(61.1)	(61.1)
Other	(15.2)	(6.3)	0.3	(21.2)
Balance at December 31, 2008	$776.4	$189.4	$ 69.1	$1,034.9
Acquisitions	(0.7)	3.1	—	2.4
Other	10.2	1.0	0.1	11.3
Balance at December 31, 2009	$785.9	$193.5	$ 69.2	$1,048.6

The goodwill additions to the Customer Management and Information Management segments for the years ended December 31, 2009 and 2008 resulted from the Intervoice acquisition and a few smaller Information Management acquisitions that are described in Note 5 of the Notes to Consolidated Financial Statements. The other changes to goodwill in 2009 and 2008 principally reflect foreign currency translation adjustments. Accumulated goodwill impairment charges at December 31, 2009 and 2008 were $61.1 and related entirely to HR Management.

The Company's other intangible assets, primarily acquired through business combinations, are evaluated periodically if events or circumstances indicate a possible inability to recover their carrying amounts. The evaluation of intangible assets during 2009 resulted in recording impairment charges of $6.8 related to certain acquired intangible assets. As of December 31, 2009 and 2008, the Company's other intangible assets consisted of the following:

	Gross Carrying Amount	Accumulated Amortization	Net
2009:			
Software (classified with Property, Plant & Equipment)	$ 92.2	$ (55.2)	$ 37.0
Trademarks	12.0	(5.3)	6.7
Customer relationships and other intangibles	164.0	(120.5)	43.5
Total	$268.2	$(181.0)	$ 87.2
2008:			
Software (classified with Property, Plant & Equipment)	$ 92.2	$ (46.3)	$ 45.9
Trademarks	12.0	(2.7)	9.3
Customer relationships and other intangibles	176.2	(116.7)	59.5
Total	$280.4	$(165.7)	$114.7

The intangible assets are being amortized using the following amortizable lives: two to eight years for software, four years for trademarks and five to twelve years for customer relationships and other. The remaining weighted average amortization period for intangible assets is 6.7 years.

Customer relationships, trademarks and other intangibles amortization expense was $11.7 for the year ended December 31, 2009 and the related estimated expense for the five subsequent fiscal years is as follows:

For the year ended 12/31/10	$10
For the year ended 12/31/11	$10
For the year ended 12/31/12	$ 9
For the year ended 12/31/13	$ 7
For the year ended 12/31/14	$ 3
Thereafter	$11

18. Industry Segment and Geographic Operations

Industry Segment Information

The Company has three segments, which are identified by service offerings. Customer Management provides agent-assisted services, self-service and technology solutions. Information Management provides business support system solutions for the global communications industry. HR Management provides global human resource business process outsourcing solutions. These segments are consistent with the Company's management of the business and reflect its internal financial reporting structure and operating focus.

The Company does not allocate activities below the operating income level to its reported segments. The Company's business segment information is as follows:

Revenues:	2009	2008	2007
Customer Management	$1,986.7	$1,954.8	$1,866.1
Information Management	434.3	571.5	723.0
HR Management	406.2	259.5	255.2
	$2,827.2	$2,785.8	$2,844.3
Depreciation:			
Customer Management	$ 66.9	$ 61.4	$ 55.9
Information Management	22.6	28.2	32.4
HR Management	8.6	9.3	8.7
Corporate and other[1]	20.8	20.1	18.4
	$ 118.9	$ 119.0	$ 115.4
Amortization:			
Customer Management	$ 7.3	$ 4.3	$ 2.7
Information Management	3.6	7.0	3.7
HR Management	0.8	2.2	2.6
	$ 11.7	$ 13.5	$ 9.0
Restructuring charges:			
Customer Management	$ 7.9	$ 14.0	$ —
Information Management	30.4	9.7	3.4
HR Management	3.7	10.5	—
Corporate and other	5.0	0.2	—
	$ 47.0	$ 34.4	$ 3.4
Asset impairments:			
Customer Management	$ —	$ —	$ 1.4
Information Management	3.1	—	1.3
HR Management	110.5	268.6	2.8
	$ 113.6	$ 268.6	$ 5.5

[1] Includes shared services-related capital expenditures and depreciation.

	2009	2008	2007
Operating income (loss):			
Customer Management	$ 133.9	$ 92.6	$176.7
Information Management	21.9	96.4	130.9
HR Management	(246.1)	(358.8)	(38.3)
Corporate[1]	(22.5)	(21.5)	(24.5)
	$(112.8)	$(191.3)	$244.8
Capital expenditures:			
Customer Management	$ 44.5	$ 49.7	$ 32.4
Information Management	10.8	17.9	18.4
HR Management	3.7	8.3	17.1
Corporate[1]	15.9	24.6	34.4
	$ 74.9	$ 100.5	$102.3

[1] Includes shared services-related capital expenditures and depreciation.

	2009	2008
Total assets:		
Customer Management	$1,503.1	$1,570.4
Information Management	464.6	516.7
HR Management	156.0	385.5
Corporate	489.9	368.8
	$2,613.6	$2,841.4

Geographic Operations

The following table presents certain geographic information regarding the Company's operations:

	2009	2008	2007
Revenues:			
North America	$2,361.2	$2,336.3	$2,449.8
Rest of world	466.0	449.5	394.5
	$2,827.2	$2,785.8	$2,844.3
Long-lived assets:			
North America	$1,490.8	$1,614.5	$1,465.5
Rest of world	161.7	240.5	230.2
	$1,652.5	$1,855.0	$1,695.7

Concentrations

The Customer Management and Information Management segments derive significant revenues from AT&T. Revenues from AT&T were 19.8%, 18.2% and 16.3% of the Company's consolidated revenues for 2009, 2008 and 2007, respectively. Related accounts receivable from AT&T totaled $85.8 and $93.1 at December 31, 2009 and 2008, respectively.

1.25

FORTUNE BRANDS, INC. (DEC)

NOTES TO CONSOLIDATED FINANCIAL STATEMENTS

3. Goodwill and Other Identifiable Intangible Assets

The change in the net carrying amount of goodwill by segment was as follows:

($ in millions)	Spirits	Home & Security	Golf	Total Goodwill
Balance at December 31, 2007				
Goodwill	$2,264.6	$1,920.1	$11.8	$4,196.5
Accumulated impairment losses	—	—	—	—
Total goodwill, net	$2,264.6	$1,920.1	$11.8	$4,196.5
2008 activity:				
Translation adjustments	(193.2)	(1.6)	—	(194.8)
Acquisition-related adjustments	26.8	(5.4)	—	21.4
Impairment charges	—	(451.3)	—	(451.3)
Balance at December 31, 2008				
Goodwill	$2,098.2	$1,913.1	$11.8	$4,023.1
Accumulated impairment losses	—	(451.3)	—	(451.3)
Total goodwill, net	$2,098.2	$1,461.8	$11.8	$3,571.8
2009 activity:				
Translation adjustments	44.3	6.9	—	35.2
Acquisition-related adjustments	(30.5)	(16.0)	—	(30.5)
Balance at December 31, 2009				
Goodwill	$2,112.0	$1,904.0	$11.8	$4,027.8
Accumulated impairment losses	—	(451.3)	—	(451.3)
Total goodwill, net	$2,112.0	$1,452.7	$11.8	$3,576.5

We also had indefinite-lived intangible assets, principally tradenames, of $2,623.1 million as of December 31, 2009 compared to $2,682.4 million as of December 31, 2008. The decrease of $59.3 million was primarily due to impairment charges related to certain tradenames in the Spirits business and the reclassification of a tradename from an indefinite-lived to amortizable intangible asset, partly offset by foreign currency translation adjustments. Refer to Note 2, "Asset Impairment Charges," for more information on the impairment charges in the Spirits business.

Amortizable identifiable intangible assets, principally tradenames and customer relationships, are subject to amortization over their estimated useful life, 5 to 30 years, based on the assessment of a number of factors that may impact useful life. These factors include historical and tradename performance with respect to consumer name recognition, geographic market presence, market share, plans for ongoing tradename support and promotion, financial results and other relevant factors. The gross carrying value and accumulated amortization of amortizable intangible assets were $932.1 million and $366.8 million, respectively, as of December 31, 2009, compared to $854.2 million and $325.2 million, respectively, as of December 31, 2008. The gross carrying value increase of $77.9 million was primarily due to changes in foreign currency translation adjustments and the reclassification of a tradename from an indefinite-lived to amortizable intangible asset.

The gross carrying value and accumulated amortization by class of intangible assets as of December 31, 2009 and 2008 were as follows:

(In millions)	2009			2008		
	Gross Carrying Amounts	Accumulated Amortization	Net Book Value	Gross Carrying Amounts	Accumulated Amortization	Net Book Value
Indefinite-lived intangible assets—tradenames	$2,695.1	$ (72.0)[a]	$2,623.1	$2,754.4	$ (72.0)[a]	$2,682.4
Amortizable intangible assets						
Tradenames	572.3	(179.8)	392.5	505.5	(161.2)	344.3
Customer and contractual relationships	274.0	(140.9)	133.1	262.9	(123.1)	139.8
Patents/proprietary technology	40.5	(31.0)	9.5	40.5	(29.0)	11.5
Licenses and other	45.3	(15.1)	30.2	45.3	(11.9)	33.4
Total	932.1	(366.8)	565.3	854.2	(325.2)	529.0
Total identifiable intangibles	$3,627.2	$(438.8)	$3,188.4	$3,608.6	$(397.2)	$3,211.4

[a] Accumulated amortization prior to the adoption of revised authoritative guidance on goodwill and other intangibles assets (ASC 350).

Intangible amortization was $33.7 million, $49.6 million and $47.6 million for the years ended December 31, 2009, 2008 and 2007, respectively. The Company expects to record intangible amortization of $34 million in 2010, trending down to $27 million by 2015.

The Company cannot predict the occurrence of certain events that might adversely affect the carrying value of goodwill and other intangible assets. Such events may include, but are not limited to, the impact of the economic environment; a material negative change in relationships with significant customers; or strategic decisions made in response to economic and competitive conditions.

19. Information on Business Segments

We report our operating segments (Spirits, Home & Security, and Golf) based on how we have organized our segments within the Company for making operating decisions and assessing performance based on the markets served. The Company's operating segments and types of products from which each segment derives revenues are described below.

Spirits includes products made, marketed or distributed by Beam Global Spirits & Wine, Inc. subsidiaries or affiliates.

Home & Security includes: kitchen and bathroom faucets and accessories manufactured, marketed or distributed by Moen; kitchen and bath cabinetry manufactured, marketed and distributed by MasterBrand Cabinets; residential entry door and patio door systems designed and manufactured by Therma-Tru; vinyl-framed windows manufactured, marketed and distributed by Simonton; locks, tool storage and organization products manufactured, marketed or distributed by Storage and Security.

Golf includes golf balls, golf clubs, golf shoes and gloves manufactured, marketed or distributed by Acushnet Company.

The Company's subsidiaries operate principally in the United States, Canada, Europe (primarily in Spain, the United Kingdom and France), Australia and Mexico.

(In millions)	2009	2008	2007
Net sales:			
Spirits	$ 2,469.6	$ 2,480.9	$ 2,606.8
Home & Security	3,006.8	3,759.1	4,550.9
Golf	1,218.3	1,368.9	1,405.4
Net sales	$ 6,694.7	$ 7,608.9	$ 8,563.1
Operating income (loss):			
Spirits	$ 484.7	$ 543.7	$ 766.7
Home & Security	87.0	(465.6)	503.0
Golf	25.0	125.3	165.5
Less: Corporate expenses[a]	(91.5)	(57.8)	(58.9)
Operating income	$ 505.2	$ 145.6	$ 1,376.3
Net sales by geographic region[b]:			
United States	$ 4,601.4	$ 5,312.2	$ 6,208.0
Canada	483.7	549.0	523.8
United Kingdom	239.2	435.6	504.7
Australia	276.8	258.4	280.5
Spain	178.9	156.5	189.5
Other countries	914.7	897.2	856.6
Net sales	$ 6,694.7	$ 7,608.9	$ 8,563.1
Total assets:			
Spirits	$ 7,482.7	$ 7,128.4	$ 7,855.6
Home & Security	3,747.9	3,924.1	5,057.5
Golf	813.2	895.0	840.3
Corporate[c]	326.8	144.4	203.5
Total assets	$12,370.6	$12,091.9	$13,956.9

[a] Corporate expenses include salaries, benefits and expenses related to Corporate office employees and functions that benefit all operating segments. Corporate expenses do not include expenses directly allocable to the reportable segments. Allocating these indirect expenses to operating segments would require an imprecise allocation methodology. There are no amounts that are the elimination or reversal of transactions between reportable segments.

[b] Based on country of destination.

[c] Corporate assets include cash, certain receivables related to taxes and insurance claims, and the cash surrender value on life insurance policies. Corporate assets do not include assets directly allocable to the reportable segments. Allocating these indirect assets to operating segments would require an imprecise allocation methodology.

(In millions)	2009	2008	2007
Property, plant and equipment, net:			
United States	$ 950.2	$1,064.3	$1,144.6
Spain	189.0	189.9	198.5
Mexico	79.4	83.0	92.9
Canada	61.8	56.4	71.6
United Kingdom	54.2	49.2	72.8
France	48.6	49.0	53.7
Other countries	84.7	62.1	64.1
Property, plant and equipment, net	$1,467.9	$1,553.9	$1,698.2
Depreciation expense:			
Spirits	$ 70.7	$ 68.4	$ 64.3
Home & Security	115.0	109.9	115.8
Golf	31.2	32.9	35.6
Corporate	1.4	2.0	1.7
Continuing operations	218.3	213.2	217.4
Discontinued operations	—	—	14.9
Depreciation expense	$ 218.3	$ 213.2	$ 232.3
Amortization of intangible assets:			
Spirits	$ 17.3	$ 16.4	$ 13.7
Home & Security	16.1	32.9	33.6
Golf	0.3	0.3	0.3
Continuing operations	33.7	49.6	47.6
Discontinued operations	—	—	0.5
Amortization of intangible assets	$ 33.7	$ 49.6	$ 48.1
Capital expenditures:			
Spirits	$ 77.9	$ 85.4	$ 111.3
Home & Security	43.2	57.0	75.1
Golf	36.3	33.6	63.0
Corporate	0.1	0.3	0.1
Continuing operations	157.5	176.3	249.5
Discontinued operations	—	—	17.6
Capital expenditures, gross	157.5	176.3	267.1
Less: proceeds from disposition of assets	(15.9)	(19.2)	(69.3)
Capital expenditures, net	$ 141.6	$ 157.0	$ 197.8

1.26

ROCK-TENN COMPANY (SEP)

NOTES TO CONSOLIDATED FINANCIAL STATEMENTS

Note 1 (In Part): Summary of Significant Accounting Policies

Goodwill and Long-Lived Assets

We review the recorded value of our goodwill annually at the beginning of the fourth quarter of each fiscal year, or more often if events or changes in circumstances indicate that the carrying amount may exceed fair value as set forth in ASC 350, *"Intangibles—Goodwill and Other."* We test goodwill for impairment at the reporting unit level, which is an operating segment or one level below an operating segment, which is referred to as a component. A component of an operating segment is a reporting unit if the component constitutes a business for which discrete financial information is available and segment management regularly reviews the operating results of that component. However, two or more components of an operating segment are aggregated and deemed a single reporting unit if the components have similar economic characteristics. The amount of goodwill acquired in a business combination that is assigned to one or more reporting units as of the acquisition date is the excess of the purchase price of the acquired businesses (or portion thereof) included in the reporting unit, over the fair value assigned to the individual assets acquired or liabilities assumed. Goodwill is assigned to the reporting unit(s) expected to benefit from the synergies of the combination even though other assets or liabilities of the acquired entity may not be assigned to that reporting unit. We determine recoverability by comparing the estimated fair value of the reporting unit to which the goodwill applies to the carrying value, including goodwill, of that reporting unit using a discounted cash flow model.

The goodwill impairment model is a two-step process. In step one, we utilize the present value of expected net cash flows to determine the estimated fair value of our reporting units. This present value model requires management to estimate future net cash flows, the timing of these cash flows, and a discount rate (based on a weighted average cost of capital), which represents the time value of money and the inherent risk and uncertainty of the future cash flows. Factors that management must estimate when performing this step in the process include, among other items, sales volume, prices, inflation, discount rates, exchange rates, tax rates and capital spending. The assumptions we use to estimate future cash flows are consistent with the assumptions that the reporting units use for internal planning purposes, updated to reflect current expectations. If we determine that the estimated fair value of the reporting unit exceeds its carrying amount, goodwill of the reporting unit is not impaired. If we determine that the carrying amount of the reporting unit exceeds its estimated fair value, we must complete step two of the impairment analysis. Step two involves determining the implied fair value of the reporting unit's goodwill and comparing it to the carrying amount of that goodwill. If the carrying amount of the reporting unit's goodwill exceeds the implied fair value of that goodwill, we recognize an impairment loss in an amount equal to that excess. We completed the annual test of the goodwill associated with each of our reporting units during fiscal 2009 and concluded the fair values were in excess of the carrying values of each of the report-

ing units. No events have occurred since the latest annual goodwill impairment assessment that would necessitate an interim goodwill impairment assessment.

We follow provisions included in ASC 360, *"Property, Plant and Equipment"* in determining whether the carrying value of any of our long-lived assets, including amortizing intangibles other than goodwill, is impaired. The ASC 360 test is a three-step test for assets that are "held and used" as that term is defined by ASC 360. First, we determine whether indicators of impairment are present. ASC 360 requires us to review long-lived assets for impairment only when events or changes in circumstances indicate that the carrying amount of the long-lived asset might not be recoverable. Accordingly, while we do routinely assess whether impairment indicators are present, we do not routinely perform tests of recoverability. Second, if we determine that indicators of impairment are present, we determine whether the estimated undiscounted cash flows for the potentially impaired assets are less than the carrying value. This requires management to estimate future net cash flows through operations over the remaining useful life of the asset and its ultimate disposition. The assumptions we use to estimate future cash flows are consistent with the assumptions we use for internal planning purposes, updated to reflect current expectations. Third, if such estimated undiscounted cash flows do not exceed the carrying value, we estimate the fair value of the asset and record an impairment charge if the carrying value is greater than the fair value of the asset. We estimate fair value using discounted cash flows, prices for similar assets, or other valuation techniques. We record assets classified as "held for sale" at the lower of their carrying value or estimated fair value less anticipated cost to sell.

Included in our long-lived assets are certain identifiable intangible assets. These intangible assets are amortized based on the estimated pattern in which the economic benefits are realized over their estimated useful lives ranging generally from 5 to 40 years and have a weighted average life of approximately 20.4 years.

Our judgments regarding the existence of impairment indicators are based on legal factors, market conditions and operational performance. Future events could cause us to conclude that impairment indicators exist and that assets associated with a particular operation are impaired. Evaluating impairment also requires us to estimate future operating results and cash flows, which also require judgment by management. Any resulting impairment loss could have a material adverse impact on our financial condition and results of operations.

Note 21. Segment Information

We report four business segments. The Consumer Packaging segment consists of facilities that manufacture coated paperboard products and convert paperboard into folding cartons. The Corrugated Packaging segment consists of facilities that manufacture containerboard and produce corrugated packaging and sheet stock. The Merchandising Displays segment consists of facilities that produce displays. The Specialty Paperboard Products segment consists of facilities that manufacture specialty paperboard and convert paperboard into interior packaging, convert specialty paperboard into laminated paperboard products, and facilities that collect recovered paper. The Specialty Paperboard Packaging segment consists of two operating segments that are

below the required quantitative thresholds; we have aggregated them into one segment which we disclose aggregated in our Specialty Paperboard Packaging segment.

Certain operations included in the segments are located in Canada, Mexico, Chile and Argentina. The table below reflects certain data of our foreign operations for each of the past three fiscal years (in millions, except percentages):

	2009	2008	2007
Foreign segment income	$25.8	$ 20.7	$12.3
Foreign long-lived assets	$97.3	$103.4	$88.2
Foreign operations as a percent of consolidated operations:			
Net sales to unaffiliated customers	8.5%	8.6%	8.4%
Segment income	5.5%	7.9%	5.1%
Identifiable assets	8.9%	8.2%	11.9%

We evaluate performance and allocate resources based, in part, on profit from operations before income taxes, interest and other items. The accounting policies of the reportable segments are the same as those described above in "Note 1. Description of Business and Summary of Significant Accounting Policies." We account for intersegment sales at prices that approximate market prices. For segment reporting purposes, we include our equity in income of unconsolidated entities, as well as our investments in unconsolidated entities, in the results of our business segments. Seven Hills is included in our Specialty Paperboard Products segment, QPSI and DSA are included in our Merchandising Displays segment, and Pohlig and Greenpine are included in the results of our Consumer Packaging segment.

Following is certain business segment information for each of the past three fiscal years (in millions):

	2009	2008	2007
Net sales (aggregate):			
Consumer Packaging	$1,503.1	$1,551.4	$1,459.6
Corrugated Packaging	752.9	607.5	236.7
Merchandising Displays	320.6	350.8	305.8
Specialty Paperboard Products	306.9	392.9	361.7
Total	$2,883.5	$2,902.6	$2,363.8
Less net sales (intersegment):			
Consumer Packaging	$ 25.1	$ 18.1	$ 15.0
Corrugated Packaging	37.3	31.1	22.7
Merchandising Displays	0.4	0.4	—
Specialty Paperboard Products	8.4	14.1	10.3
Total	$ 71.2	$ 63.7	$ 48.0
Net sales (unaffiliated customers):			
Consumer Packaging	$1,478.0	$1,533.3	$1,444.6
Corrugated Packaging	715.6	576.4	214.0
Merchandising Displays	320.2	350.4	305.8
Specialty Paperboard Products	298.5	378.8	351.4
Total	$2,812.3	$2,838.9	$2,315.8
Segment income:			
Consumer Packaging	$ 228.3	$ 119.8	$ 125.2
Corrugated Packaging	178.9	71.3	18.9
Merchandising Displays	31.9	41.9	38.8
Specialty Paperboard Products	26.5	30.3	28.8
Total	465.6	263.3	211.7
Restructuring and other costs, net	(13.4)	(15.6)	(4.7)
Non-allocated expenses	(33.6)	(29.3)	(24.1)
Interest expense	(96.7)	(86.7)	(49.8)
Loss on extinguishment of debt and related items	(4.4)	(1.9)	—
Interest income and other income (expense), net	—	1.6	(1.3)
Minority interest in consolidated subsidiaries	(3.6)	(5.3)	(4.8)
Income before income taxes	$ 313.9	$ 126.1	$ 127.0
Identifiable assets:			
Consumer Packaging	$1,286.2	$1,316.6	$1,362.2
Corrugated Packaging	1,183.3	1,313.5	89.3
Merchandising Displays	158.1	169.3	162.2
Specialty Paperboard Products	147.8	153.7	158.9
Assets held for sale	0.9	0.7	1.8
Corporate	108.1	59.3	26.3
Total	$2,884.4	$3,013.1	$1,800.7

	2009	2008	2007
Goodwill:			
Consumer Packaging	$296.1	$296.4	$299.1
Corrugated Packaging	392.8	383.7	18.5
Merchandising Displays	28.0	28.0	28.0
Specialty Paperboard Products	19.5	18.9	18.9
Total	$736.4	$727.0	$364.5
Depreciation and amortization:			
Consumer Packaging	$ 75.8	$ 79.3	$ 78.4
Corrugated Packaging	49.4	32.4	6.3
Merchandising Displays	6.1	6.4	6.6
Specialty Paperboard Products	8.6	8.9	9.3
Corporate	10.1	6.4	3.1
Total	$150.0	$133.4	$103.7
Capital expenditures:			
Consumer Packaging	$ 41.9	$ 46.8	$ 60.3
Corrugated Packaging	11.9	18.1	2.7
Merchandising Displays	4.0	6.3	1.2
Specialty Paperboard Products	8.4	6.6	4.7
Corporate	9.7	6.4	9.1
Total	$ 75.9	$ 84.2	$ 78.0
Investment in unconsolidated entities:			
Consumer Packaging	$ 0.9	$ 0.6	$ —
Merchandising Displays	10.4	11.4	11.1
Specialty Paperboard Products	12.5	17.4	17.8
Total	$ 23.8	$ 29.4	$ 28.9
Equity in income of unconsolidated entities:			
Consumer Packaging	$ 0.3	$ 0.1	$ —
Merchandising Displays	0.6	2.1	0.7
Specialty Paperboard Products	(0.8)	0.2	0.4
Total	$ 0.1	$ 2.4	$ 1.1

Identifiable assets as of September 30, 2008 reflect a reclassification adjustment to reduce Corrugated Packaging assets and increase Corporate assets by approximately $14.1 million. Depreciation and amortization for the year ended September 30, 2008 reflects an adjustment to reduce Corporate by approximately $1.9 million. Both of these reclassifications adjustments were recorded to conform to the current year presentation.

The changes in the carrying amount of goodwill for the fiscal years ended September 30, 2009, 2008 and 2007 are as follows (in millions):

	Consumer Packaging	Corrugated Packaging	Merchandising Displays	Specialty Paperboard Products	Total
Balance as of October 1, 2006	$290.9	$ 18.5	$28.7	$18.5	$356.6
Goodwill acquired	3.5	—	—	0.4	3.9
Translation and other adjustment	4.7	—	(0.7)	—	4.0
Balance as of September 30, 2007	$299.1	$ 18.5	$28.0	$18.9	$364.5
Goodwill acquired	0.1	365.4	—	—	365.5
Translation and other adjustment	(2.8)	(0.2)	—	—	(3.0)
Balance as of September 30, 2008	$296.4	$383.7	$28.0	$18.9	$727.0
Goodwill acquired	—	—	—	0.6	0.6
Purchase price allocation adjustments	—	9.4	—	—	9.4
Translation and other adjustment	(0.3)	(0.3)	—	—	(0.6)
Balance as of September 30, 2009	$296.1	$392.8	$28.0	$19.5	$736.4

1.27

TEXAS INDUSTRIES, INC. (DEC)

NOTES TO CONSOLIDATED FINANCIAL STATEMENTS

1. (In Part): Summary of Significant Accounting Policies

Goodwill and Goodwill Impairment

Management tests goodwill for impairment annually by reporting unit in the fourth quarter of our fiscal year using a two-step process. The first step of the impairment test identifies potential impairment by comparing the face value of a reporting unit to its carrying value including goodwill. In applying a fair-value-based test, estimates are made of the expected future cash flows to be derived from the reporting unit. Similar to the review for impairment of other long-lived assets, the resulting fair value determination is significantly impacted by estimates of future prices for our products, capital needs, economic trends and other factors. If the carrying value of the reporting unit exceeds its fair value the second step of the impairment test is performed to measure the amount of impairment loss, if any. The second step of the impairment test compares the implied fair value of the reporting unit goodwill with the carrying amount of that goodwill. If the carrying value of the reporting unit goodwill exceeds the implied fair value of the goodwill, an impairment loss is recognized in an amount equal to that excess. The implied fair value of goodwill is determined in the same manner as the amount of goodwill recognized in a business combination.

Goodwill resulting from the acquisition of Riverside Cement Company and identified with our California cement operations had a carrying value of $58.4 million at May 31, 2008. Based on an impairment test performed as of May 31, 2009 there was no implied fair value of the reporting unit goodwill, and therefore, an impairment charge of $58.4 million was recognized.

Goodwill resulting from the acquisition of ready-mix operations in Texas and Louisiana and identified with our consumer products operations has a carrying value of $1.7 million at both May 31, 2009 and 2008. Based on an impairment test performed as of March 31, 2009, the fair value of the reporting unit exceeds its carrying value, and therefore, no potential impairment was identified.

10. Business Segments

We have three business segments: cement, aggregates and consumer products. Our business segments are managed separately along product lines. Through the cement segment we produce and sell gray portland cement as our principal product, as well as specialty cements. Through the aggregates segment we produce and sell stone, sand and gravel as our principal products, as well as expanded shale and clay lightweight aggregates. Through the consumer products segment we produce and sell ready-mix concrete as our principal product, as well as packaged concrete mix, mortar, sand and related products. We account for intersegment sales at market prices. Segment operating profit consists of net sales less operating costs and expenses, including certain operating overhead and other income items not allocated to a specific segment. Corporate includes those administrative, financial, legal, human resources and real estate activities which are not allocated to operations and are excluded from segment operating profit. Identifiable assets by segment

are those assets that are used in each segment's operation. Corporate assets consist primarily of cash and cash equivalents, real estate and other financial assets not identified with a business segment. We currently report cement treated material operations and transportation overhead activities, both of which are not significant to operating profit, in our cement segment. Cement treated material operations were previously reported in our aggregate segment. Our transportation overhead activities were previously reported as a part of unallocated overhead and other income-net. Prior period information has been reclassified to conform to the current period presentation.

The following is a summary of operating results and certain other financial data for our business segments.

(In thousands)	2009	2008	2007
Net sales			
Cement			
Sales to external customers	$ 332,689	$ 424,199	$ 431,103
Intersegment sales	62,631	80,553	78,924
Aggregates			
Sales to external customers	200,623	239,494	233,233
Intersegment sales	36,868	45,836	35,621
Consumer products			
Sales to external customers	305,890	365,161	331,914
Intersegment sales	3,531	4,072	3,861
Eliminations	(103,030)	(130,461)	(118,406)
Total net sales	$ 839,202	$1,028,854	$ 996,250
Segment operating profit (loss)			
Cement	$ (13,263)	$ 103,751	$ 173,204
Aggregates	34,229	55,623	36,886
Consumer products	8,863	11,583	9,846
Unallocated overhead and other income—net	(11,720)	(11,065)	(12,164)
Total segment operating profit	18,109	159,892	207,772
Corporate			
Selling, general and administrative expense	(17,959)	(33,892)	(45,194)
Interest	(33,286)	(2,505)	(14,074)
Loss on debt retirements and spin-off charges	(907)	—	(48)
Other income	3,622	3,864	8,107
Income (loss) from continuing operations before income taxes	$ (30,421)	$ 127,359	$ 156,563

(In thousands)	2009	2008	2007
Identifiable assets			
Cement	$1,150,210	$1,044,981	$ 776,810
Aggregates	236,727	220,474	221,820
Consumer products	95,310	120,063	102,916
Corporate	90,297	146,016	173,824
Total assets	$1,572,544	$1,531,534	$1,275,370
Depreciation, depletion and amortization			
Cement	$ 37,821	$ 25,645	$ 23,234
Aggregates	21,919	21,166	16,093
Consumer products	7,434	7,998	6,493
Corporate	1,018	768	536
Total depreciation, depletion and amortization	$ 68,192	$ 55,577	$ 46,356
Capital expenditures			
Cement	$ 242,355	$ 267,118	$ 231,332
Aggregates	41,068	31,849	64,141
Consumer products	4,770	12,190	19,691
Corporate	351	1,368	2,494
Total capital expenditures	$ 288,544	$ 312,525	$ 317,658
Net sales by product			
Cement	$ 301,827	$ 388,136	$ 403,493
Stone, sand and gravel	99,206	127,399	124,491
Ready-mix concrete	247,766	310,170	277,725
Other products	113,006	118,347	111,691
Delivery fees	77,397	84,802	78,850
Total net sales	$ 839,202	$1,028,854	$ 996,250

All sales were made in the United States during the periods presented with no single customer representing more than 10 percent of sales. All of our identifiable assets are located in the United States.

Cement segment operating profit includes the recognition as of May 31, 2009 of a goodwill impairment charge of $58.4 million. In addition, operating profit in 2009 includes $2.8 million in lease bonus payments received upon the execution of oil and gas lease agreements on property we own in north Texas. Operating profit includes $1.7 million in 2009 and $3.9 million in 2008 from sales of emission credits associated with our California cement operations. Operating profit in 2007 includes $19.8 million representing distributions which we received pursuant to agreements that settled a 16-year dispute over the U.S. antidumping duty order on cement imports from Mexico.

Aggregates segment operating profit includes gains of $5.0 million in 2009 and $15.2 million in 2008 from sales of operating assets and real estate associated with our aggregate operations in north Texas and south Louisiana.

Cement capital expenditures, including capitalized interest, incurred in connection with the expansion of our Hunter, Texas cement plant were $222.1 million in 2009, $71.6 million in 2008 and $6.5 million in 2007. In addition, cement capital expenditures, including capitalized interest, incurred in connection with the expansion and modernization of our Oro Grande, California cement plant were $1.3 million in 2009, $176.0 million in 2008 and $208.4 million in 2007. Other capital expenditures incurred represent normal replacement and technological upgrades of existing equipment and acquisitions to sustain existing operations in each segment.

NATURAL BUSINESS YEAR

1.28 A natural business year is the period of 12 consecutive months which ends when the business activities of an entity have reached the lowest point in their annual cycle. In many instances, the natural business year of an entity ends December 31.

1.29 Table 1-4 summarizes, by the month in which a fiscal year ends, the fiscal year endings of the survey entities. For tabulation purposes, if a fiscal year ended in the first week of a month, the fiscal year was considered to have ended in the preceding month.

1.30 For 2009, 141 survey entities were on a 52–53 week fiscal year. During 2009, one survey entity changed the date of their fiscal year end. Examples of a fiscal year end change and fiscal year definitions follow.

1.31

TABLE 1-4: MONTH OF FISCAL YEAR END

	2009	2008	2007	2006
January	26	27	28	27
February	7	8	8	8
March	17	17	17	17
April	8	9	9	9
May	16	15	19	17
June	33	33	40	42
July	8	8	9	10
August	14	13	14	14
September	37	31	43	47
October	14	14	17	16
November	10	9	13	12
Subtotal	**190**	**184**	**217**	**219**
December	310	316	383	381
Total Entities	**500**	**500**	**600**	**600**

2008–2009 based on 500 entities surveyed; 2006–2007 based on 600 entities surveyed.

Change in Date of Fiscal Year End

1.32

ADC TELECOMMUNICATIONS, INC.

NOTES TO CONSOLIDATED FINANCIAL STATEMENTS

Note 1 (In Part): Summary of Significant Accounting Policies

Fiscal Year

On July 22, 2008, our Board of Directors approved a change in our fiscal year end from October 31st to September 30th commencing with our fiscal year 2009. This resulted in our fiscal year 2009 being shortened from 12 months to 11 months and ended on September 30th.

Definition of Fiscal Year

1.33

BELDEN INC.

NOTES TO CONSOLIDATED FINANCIAL STATEMENTS

Note 1 (In Part): Basis Presentation

Reporting Periods

Our fiscal year and fiscal fourth quarter both end on December 31. Typically, our fiscal first, second, and third quarter each have ended on the last Sunday falling on or before their respective calendar quarter-end. Beginning in 2010, our fiscal first quarter will end on the Sunday falling closest to 91 days after December 31. Our fiscal second and third quarter will each have 91 days. Our fiscal fourth quarter will end on December 31.

1.34

SNAP-ON INCORPORATED

NOTES TO CONSOLIDATED FINANCIAL STATEMENTS

Note 1 (In Part): Summary of Significant Accounting Policies

Fiscal Year Accounting Period

Snap-on's fiscal year ends on the Saturday nearest December 31. The 2009 fiscal year ended on January 2, 2010 ("2009"), and contained 52 weeks of operating results. The 2008 fiscal year ended on January 3, 2009 ("2008"), and contained 53 weeks of operating results, with the additional week occurring in the fourth quarter. The impact of the additional week of operations on full year 2008 net sales and operating earnings was not material. The 2007 fiscal year ended on December 29, 2007 ("2007") and contained 52 weeks of operating results.

COMPARATIVE FINANCIAL STATEMENTS

1.35   *Rule 14a-3* requires that annual reports to stockholders should include comparative balance sheets, and statements of income and of cash flows for each of the 3 most recent fiscal years. All of the survey entities are registered with the SEC and conformed to the aforementioned requirements of *Rule 14a-3*.

1.36   In their annual reports, the survey entities usually present an income statement as the first financial statement. For 2009, 276 survey entities presented an income statement first followed by a balance sheet; 184 survey entities presented a balance sheet first followed by an income statement; 14 survey entities presented an income statement first followed by a statement of cash flows; and 16 survey entities presented an income statement first combined with a statement of comprehensive income or followed by a separate statement of comprehensive income.

1.37   The financial statements, with rare exception, were presented on consecutive pages. Certain survey entities did not present their financial statements on consecutive pages but interspersed the Management's Discussion and Analysis of Financial Condition and Results of Operations among the financial statements by having comments discussing the content of a financial statement follow the presentation of a financial statement. Such interspersed material was not covered by an auditor's report and was not presented in lieu of notes. For 2009, one survey entity did not present their financial statements on consecutive pages.

ROUNDING OF AMOUNTS

1.38   Table 1-5 shows that most of the survey entities state financial statement amounts in either thousands or millions of dollars.

1.39

TABLE 1-5: ROUNDING OF AMOUNTS

	2009	2008	2007	2006
To nearest dollar	2	3	9	10
To nearest thousand dollars:				
Omitting 000	231	227	308	316
Presenting 000	1	1	2	3
To nearest million dollars	266	269	281	271
Total Entities	**500**	**500**	**600**	**600**

2008–2009 based on 500 entities surveyed; 2006–2007 based on 600 entities surveyed.

NOTES TO FINANCIAL STATEMENTS

1.40   SEC Regulations S-X, *Accounting Rules—Form and Content of Financial Statements*, and *S-K*, and Codification of Statements on Auditing Standards (AU) section 431, *Adequacy of Disclosure in Financial Statements*, state the need for adequate disclosure in financial statements. Normally the financial statements alone cannot present all information necessary for adequate disclosure without considering appended notes which disclose information of the sort listed below:
- Changes in accounting principles.
- Retroactive adjustments.
- Long-term lease agreements.
- Assets subject to lien.
- Preferred stock data.
- Pension and retirement plans.
- Restrictions on the availability of retained earnings for cash dividend purposes.
- Contingencies and commitments.

- Depreciation and depletion policies.
- Stock option or stock purchase plans.
- Consolidation policies.
- Computation of earnings per share.
- Subsequent events.
- Quarterly data.
- Segment information.
- Financial instruments.

1.41 Table 1-6 summarizes the manner in which financial statements refer to notes. Notes on specific topics are illustrated in this publication in the sections dealing with such topics.

1.42

TABLE 1-6: REFERENCING OF NOTES TO FINANCIAL STATEMENTS

	2009	2008	2007	2006
General reference only	448	445	517	512
General and direct references	51	53	82	87
No or direct reference only	1	2	1	1
Total Entities	**500**	**500**	**600**	**600**

2008–2009 based on 500 entities surveyed; 2006–2007 based on 600 entities surveyed.

DISCLOSURE OF ACCOUNTING POLICIES

1.43 FASB ASC 235, *Notes to Financial Statements* requires that the significant accounting policies of an entity be presented as an integral part of the financial statements of the entity. FASB ASC 235 sets forth guidelines as to the content and format of disclosures of accounting policies. FASB ASC 235 states that the preferable format is to present a Summary of Significant Accounting Policies preceding notes to financial statements or as the initial note. During 2009, 378 survey entities presented the Summary of Significant Accounting Policies as either the first footnote or as a separate presentation following the last financial statement and preceding the footnotes. Of the remainder, most survey entities presented the Summary of Significant Accounting Policies as the second footnote following a footnote which described the nature of operations.

1.44 Table 1-7 shows the nature of information frequently disclosed in summaries of accounting policies and the number of survey entities disclosing such information. Examples of summaries of accounting policies follow.

1.45

TABLE 1-7: DISCLOSURE OF ACCOUNTING POLICIES

	Number of Entities			
	2009	2008	2007	2006
Revenue recognition	485	486	587	590
Consolidation policy	477	481	561	570
Use of estimates	476	469	582	567
Property	475	453	570	572
Cash equivalents	474	475	551	546
Depreciation methods	456	469	513	514
Amortization of intangibles	456	451	548	540
Interperiod tax allocation	449	438	534	508
Impairment	436	415	517	546
Financial instruments	435	440	502	506
Inventory pricing	429	416	506	514
Stock-based compensation	414	408	493	507
Translation of foreign currency	383	376	445	428
Nature of operations	365	363	376	286
Earnings per share calculation	297	300	351	368
Accounts receivable	349	333	381	386
Advertising costs	244	250	293	288
Employee benefits	229	195	217	185
Research and development costs	185	172	228	224
Credit risk concentrations	181	190	213	211
Fiscal years	150	145	165	168
Environmental costs	129	131	145	144
Capitalization of interest	98	86	102	92

2008–2009 based on 500 entities surveyed; 2006–2007 based on 600 entities surveyed.

1.46

3M COMPANY (DEC)

NOTES TO CONSOLIDATED FINANCIAL STATEMENTS

Note 1. Significant Accounting Policies

Consolidation

3M is a diversified global manufacturer, technology innovator and marketer of a wide variety of products. All significant subsidiaries are consolidated. All significant intercompany transactions are eliminated. As used herein, the term "3M" or "Company" refers to 3M Company and subsidiaries unless the context indicates otherwise.

Foreign Currency Translation

Local currencies generally are considered the functional currencies outside the United States. Assets and liabilities for operations in local-currency environments are translated at year-end exchange rates. Income and expense items are translated at average rates of exchange prevailing during the year. Cumulative translation adjustments are recorded as a component of accumulated other comprehensive income (loss) in shareholders' equity.

The Company has a Venezuelan subsidiary with net sales and operating income representing less than one percent of 3M's related consolidated financial statement amounts for 2009. Regulations in Venezuela require the purchase and sale of foreign currency to be made at an official rate of exchange that is fixed from time to time by the Venezuelan government. Certain laws in the country, however, provide an exemption for the purchase and sale of certain securities and have resulted in an indirect "parallel" market through which companies may obtain foreign currency without having to purchase it from Venezuela's Commission for the Administration of Foreign Exchange (CADIVI). The average rate of exchange in the parallel market varies and is less favorable than the official rate. As of December 31, 2009, 3M began use of the parallel exchange rate for translation of the financial statements of its Venezuelan subsidiary. This change was based on a number of factors including 3M's ability to convert currency in the parallel market, the limited release of funds from CADIVI for the payment of dividends by the Venezuelan subsidiary, and conclusion that 3M will or could use the parallel market for repatriation of capital or dividends. This change resulted in a decrease in accumulated other comprehensive income (cumulative translation adjustment) of approximately $55 million with a corresponding decrease in the translated assets and liabilities of 3M's Venezuelan subsidiary at December 31, 2009. Additionally, 3M evaluates the highly inflationary status of Venezuela's economy by considering both the Consumer Price Index (which largely is associated with the cities of Caracas and Maracaibo) and the National Consumer Price Index (developed commencing in 2008 and covering the entire country of Venezuela). Under Accounting Standards Codification (ASC) 830, *Foreign Currency Matters*, the reporting currency of a foreign entity's parent is assumed to be that entity's functional currency when the economic environment of a foreign entity is highly inflationary. Generally, an economy is considered highly inflationary when its cumulative inflation is approximately 100 percent or more for the three years that precede the beginning of a reporting period. The blended cumulative inflation rate exceeded 100 percent in November 2009. Accordingly, the financial statements of the Venezuelan subsidiary will be remeasured as if its functional currency were that of its parent beginning January 1, 2010. This remeasurement will decrease net sales of the Venezuelan subsidiary by approximately two-thirds in 2010 in comparison to 2009 (based on exchange rates as of December 31, 2009), but will not otherwise have a material impact on operating income and 3M's consolidated results of operations.

Reclassifications

Certain amounts in the prior years' consolidated financial statements have been reclassified to conform to the current year presentation.

Use of Estimates

The preparation of financial statements in conformity with U.S. generally accepted accounting principles requires management to make estimates and assumptions that affect the reported amounts of assets and liabilities and the disclosure of contingent assets and liabilities at the date of the financial statements, and the reported amounts of revenues and expenses during the reporting period. Actual results could differ from these estimates.

Subsequent Events

3M has evaluated subsequent events through the date that the financial statements were issued, which was February 16, 2010, the date of 3M's Annual Report on 10-K for the period ended December 31, 2009.

Cash and Cash Equivalents

Cash and cash equivalents consist of cash and temporary investments with maturities of three months or less when purchased.

Investments

Investments primarily include equity and cost method investments and real estate not used in the business. Available-for-sale investments are recorded at fair value. Unrealized gains and losses relating to investments classified as available-for-sale are recorded as a component of accumulated other comprehensive income (loss) in shareholders' equity.

Other Assets

Other assets include deferred income taxes, product and other insurance receivables, the cash surrender value of life insurance policies, and other long-term assets. Investments in life insurance are reported at the amount that could be realized under contract at the balance sheet date, with any changes in cash surrender value or contract value during the period accounted for as an adjustment of premiums paid. Cash outflows and inflows associated with life insurance activity are included in "Purchases of marketable securities and investments" and "Proceeds from sale of marketable securities and investments," respectively.

Inventories

Inventories are stated at the lower of cost or market, with cost generally determined on a first-in, first-out basis.

Property, Plant and Equipment

Property, plant and equipment, including capitalized interest and internal engineering costs, are recorded at cost. Depreciation of property, plant and equipment generally is computed using the straight-line method based on the estimated useful lives of the assets. The estimated useful lives of buildings and improvements primarily range from 10 to 40 years, with the majority in the range of 20 to 40 years. The estimated useful lives of machinery and equipment primarily range from three to 15 years, with the majority in the range of five to 10 years. Fully depreciated assets are retained in property and accumulated depreciation accounts until disposal. Upon disposal, assets and related accumulated depreciation are removed from the accounts and the net amount, less proceeds from disposal, is charged or credited to operations. Property, plant and equipment amounts are reviewed for impairment whenever events or changes in circumstances indicate that the carrying amount of an asset (asset group) may not be recoverable. An impairment loss would be recognized when the carrying amount of an asset exceeds the estimated undiscounted future cash flows expected to result from the use of the asset and its eventual disposition. The amount of the impairment loss to be recorded is calculated by the excess of the asset's carrying value over its fair value. Fair value is generally determined using a discounted cash flow analysis.

Conditional Asset Retirement Obligations

A liability is initially recorded at fair value for an asset retirement obligation associated with the retirement of tangible long-lived assets in the period in which it is incurred if a reasonable estimate of fair value can be made. Conditional asset retirement obligations exist for certain long-term assets of the Company. The obligation is initially measured at fair value using expected present value techniques. Over time the liabilities are accreted for the change in their present value and the initial capitalized costs are depreciated over the remaining useful lives of the related assets. The asset retirement obligation liability was $64 million and $62 million, respectively, at December 31, 2009 and 2008.

Goodwill

Goodwill is the excess of cost of an acquired entity over the amounts assigned to assets acquired and liabilities assumed in a business combination. Goodwill is not amortized. Goodwill is tested for impairment annually, and is tested for impairment between annual tests if an event occurs or circumstances change that would indicate the carrying amount may be impaired. Impairment testing for goodwill is done at a reporting unit level, with all goodwill assigned to a reporting unit. Reporting units are one level below the business segment level, but can be combined when reporting units within the same segment have similar economic characteristics. An impairment loss generally would be recognized when the carrying amount of the reporting unit's net assets exceeds the estimated fair value of the reporting unit. The estimated fair value of a reporting unit is determined using earnings for the reporting unit multiplied by a price/earnings ratio for comparable industry groups, or by using a discounted cash flow analysis. The price/earnings ratio is adjusted, if necessary, to take into consideration the market value of the Company.

Intangible Assets

Intangible assets include patents, tradenames and other intangible assets acquired from an independent party. Intangible assets with an indefinite life, namely certain tradenames, are not amortized. Intangible assets with a definite life are amortized on a straight-line basis, with estimated useful lives ranging from one to 20 years. Indefinite-lived intangible assets are tested for impairment annually, and are tested for impairment between annual tests if an event occurs or circumstances change that would indicate that the carrying amount may be impaired. Intangible assets with a definite life are tested for impairment whenever events or circumstances indicate that the carrying amount of an asset (asset group) may not be recoverable. An impairment loss is recognized when the carrying amount of an asset exceeds the estimated undiscounted cash flows used in determining the fair value of the asset. The amount of the impairment loss to be recorded is calculated by the excess of the asset's carrying value over its fair value. Fair value is generally determined using a discounted cash flow analysis. Costs related to internally developed intangible assets, such as patents, are expensed as incurred, primarily in "Research, development and related expenses."

Revenue (Sales) Recognition

The Company sells a wide range of products to a diversified base of customers around the world and has no material concentration of credit risk. Revenue is recognized when the risks and rewards of ownership have substantively transferred to customers. This condition normally is met when the product has been delivered or upon performance of services. The Company records estimated reductions to revenue or records expense for customer and distributor incentives, primarily comprised of rebates and free goods, at the time of the initial sale. These sales incentives are accounted for in accordance with ASC 605, Revenue Recognition. The estimated reductions of revenue for rebates are based on the sales terms, historical experience, trend analysis and projected market conditions in the various markets served. Since the Company serves numerous markets, the rebate programs offered vary across businesses, but the most common incentive relates to amounts paid or credited to customers for achieving defined volume levels or growth objectives. Free goods are accounted for as an expense and recorded in cost of sales. Sales, use, value-added and other excise taxes are not recognized in revenue.

The majority of 3M's sales agreements are for standard products and services with customer acceptance occurring upon delivery of the product or performance of the service. 3M also enters into agreements that contain multiple elements (such as equipment, installation and service) or non-standard terms and conditions. For multiple-element arrangements, 3M recognizes revenue for delivered elements when it has stand-alone value to the customer, the fair values of undelivered elements are known, customer acceptance of the delivered elements has occurred, and there are only customary refund or return rights related to the delivered elements. In addition to the preceding conditions, equipment revenue is not recorded until the installation has been completed if equipment acceptance is dependent upon installation, or if installation is essential to the functionality of the equipment. Installation revenues are not recorded until installation has been completed. For prepaid service contracts, sales revenue is recognized on a straight-line basis over the term of the contract, unless historical evidence indicates the costs are incurred on other than a straight-line basis. License fee revenue is recognized as earned, and no revenue is recognized until the inception of the license term. On occasion, agreements will contain milestones, or 3M will recognize revenue based on proportional performance. For these agreements, and depending on the specifics, 3M may recognize revenue upon completion of a substantive milestone, or in proportion to costs incurred to date compared with the estimate of total costs to be incurred.

Accounts Receivable and Allowances

Trade accounts receivable are recorded at the invoiced amount and do not bear interest. The Company maintains allowances for bad debts, cash discounts, product returns and various other items. The allowance for doubtful accounts and product returns is based on the best estimate of the amount of probable credit losses in existing accounts receivable and anticipated sales returns. The Company determines the allowances based on historical write-off experience by industry and regional economic data and historical sales returns. The Company reviews the allowance for doubtful accounts monthly. The Company does not have any significant off-balance-sheet credit exposure related to its customers.

Advertising and Merchandising

These costs are charged to operations in the year incurred, and totaled $414 million in 2009, $468 million in 2008 and $469 million in 2007.

Research, Development and Related Expenses

These costs are charged to operations in the year incurred and are shown on a separate line of the Consolidated Statement of Income. Research, development and related expenses totaled $1.293 billion in 2009, $1.404 billion in 2008 and $1.368 billion in 2007. Research and development expenses, covering basic scientific research and the application of scientific advances in the development of new and improved products and their uses, totaled $838 million in 2009, $851 million in 2008 and $788 million in 2007. Related expenses primarily include technical support provided by 3M to customers who are using existing 3M products; internally developed patent costs, which include costs and fees incurred to prepare, file, secure and maintain patents; and amortization of acquired patents.

Internal-Use Software

The Company capitalizes direct costs of materials and services used in the development of internal-use software. Amounts capitalized are amortized on a straight-line basis over a period of three to seven years and are reported as a component of machinery and equipment within property, plant and equipment.

Environmental

Environmental expenditures relating to existing conditions caused by past operations that do not contribute to current or future revenues are expensed. Reserves for liabilities for anticipated remediation costs are recorded on an undiscounted basis when they are probable and reasonably estimable, generally no later than the completion of feasibility studies or the Company's commitment to a plan of action. Environmental expenditures for capital projects that contribute to current or future operations generally are capitalized and depreciated over their estimated useful lives.

Income Taxes

The provision for income taxes is determined using the asset and liability approach. Under this approach, deferred income taxes represent the expected future tax consequences of temporary differences between the carrying amounts and tax basis of assets and liabilities. The Company records a valuation allowance to reduce its deferred tax assets when uncertainty regarding their realizability exists. As of December 31, 2009, no significant valuation allowances were recorded. As of January 1, 2007, the Company adopted new standards related to accounting for uncertainty in income taxes. 3M follows this guidance to record uncertainties and judgments in the application of complex tax regulations in a multitude of jurisdictions (refer to Note 8 for additional information).

Earnings Per Share

The difference in the weighted average 3M shares outstanding for calculating basic and diluted earnings per share attributable to 3M common shareholders is the result of the dilution associated with the Company's stock-based compensation plans. Certain options outstanding under these stock-based compensation plans during the years 2009, 2008 and 2007 were not included in the computation of diluted earnings per share attributable to 3M common shareholders because they would not have had a dilutive effect (54.3 million average options for 2009, 41.0 million average options for 2008, and 21.6 million average options for 2007). As discussed in Note 10, the conditions for conversion related to the Company's Convertible Notes have never been met. If the conditions for conversion are met, 3M may choose to pay in cash and/or common stock; however, if this occurs, the Company has the intent and ability to settle this debt security in cash. Accordingly, there was no impact on diluted earnings per share attributable to 3M common shareholders. The computations for basic and diluted earnings per share for the years ended December 31 follow:

Earnings Per Share Computations

(Amounts in millions, except per share amounts)	2009	2008	2007
Numerator:			
Net income attributable to 3M	$3,193	$3,460	$4,096
Denominator:			
Denominator for weighted average 3M common shares outstanding—basic	700.5	699.2	718.3
Dilution associated with the Company's stock-based compensation plans	6.2	8.0	13.7
Denominator for weighted average 3M common shares outstanding—diluted	706.7	707.2	732.0
Earnings per share attributable to 3M common shareholders—basic	$ 4.56	$ 4.95	$ 5.70
Earnings per share attributable to 3M common shareholders—diluted	$ 4.52	$ 4.89	$ 5.60

Stock-Based Compensation

The Company recognizes compensation expense for both its General Employees' Stock Purchase Plan (GESPP) and the Long-Term Incentive Plan (LTIP). Under applicable accounting standards, the fair value of share-based compensation is determined at the grant date and the recognition of the related expense is recorded over the period in which the share-based compensation vests.

Comprehensive Income

Total comprehensive income and the components of accumulated other comprehensive income (loss) are presented in the Consolidated Statements of Changes in Equity and Comprehensive Income. Accumulated other comprehensive income (loss) is composed of foreign currency translation effects (including hedges of net investments in international companies), defined benefit pension and postretirement plan adjustments, unrealized gains and losses on available-for-sale debt and equity securities, and unrealized gains and losses on cash flow hedging instruments.

Derivatives and Hedging Activities

All derivative instruments within the scope of ASC 815, *Derivatives and Hedging*, are recorded on the balance sheet at fair value. The Company uses interest rate swaps, currency and commodity price swaps, and foreign currency forward and option contracts to manage risks generally associated with foreign exchange rate, interest rate and commodity market volatility. All hedging instruments that qualify for hedge accounting are designated and effective as hedges, in accordance with U.S. generally accepted accounting principles. If the underlying hedged transaction ceases to exist, all changes in fair value of the related derivatives that have not been settled are recognized in current earnings. Instruments that do not qualify for hedge accounting are marked to market with changes recognized in current earnings. The Company does not hold or issue derivative financial instruments for trading purposes and is not a party to leveraged derivatives. However, the Company does have contingently convertible debt that, if conditions for conversion are met, is convertible into shares of 3M common stock (refer to Note 10 in this document).

New Accounting Pronouncements

In June 2009, the Financial Accounting Standards Board (FASB) issued a standard that established the FASB Accounting Standards Codification™ (ASC) and amended the hierarchy of generally accepted accounting principles (GAAP) such that the ASC became the single source of authoritative non-governmental U.S. GAAP. The ASC did not change current U.S. GAAP, but was intended to simplify user access to all authoritative U.S. GAAP by providing all the authoritative literature related to a particular topic in one place. All previously existing accounting standard documents were superseded and all other accounting literature not included in the ASC is considered non-authoritative. New accounting standards issued subsequent to June 30, 2009 are communicated by the FASB through Accounting Standards Updates (ASUs). For 3M, the ASC was effective July 1, 2009. This standard did not have an impact on 3M's consolidated results of operations or financial condition. However, throughout the notes to the consolidated financial statements references that were previously made to various former authoritative U.S. GAAP pronouncements have been changed to coincide with the appropriate section of the ASC.

In June 2006, the FASB issued an accounting standard codified in ASC 740, *Income Taxes*, related to accounting for uncertainty in income taxes. This standard was adopted by 3M effective January 1, 2007. Refer to Note 8 for additional information concerning this standard.

In September 2006, the FASB issued an accounting standard codified in ASC 820, *Fair Value Measurements and Disclosures*. This standard established a single definition of fair value and a framework for measuring fair value, set out a fair value hierarchy to be used to classify the source of information used in fair value measurements, and required disclosures of assets and liabilities measured at fair value based on their level in the hierarchy. This standard applies under other accounting standards that require or permit fair value measurements. 3M adopted the standard as amended by

subsequent FASB standards beginning January 1, 2008 on a prospective basis. One of the amendments deferred the effective date for one year relative to nonfinancial assets and liabilities that are measured at fair value, but are recognized or disclosed at fair value on a nonrecurring basis. This deferral applied to such items as nonfinancial assets and liabilities initially measured at fair value in a business combination (but not measured at fair value in subsequent periods) or nonfinancial long-lived asset groups measured at fair value for an impairment assessment. These remaining aspects of the fair value measurement standard were adopted by the Company prospectively beginning January 1, 2009 and did not have a material impact on 3M's consolidated results of operations or financial condition. Refer to Note 13 for additional disclosures of assets and liabilities that are measured at fair value on a nonrecurring basis as a result of this adoption.

In February 2007, the FASB issued an accounting standard codified in ASC 825, *Financial Instruments*, that permits an entity to choose, at specified election dates, to measure eligible financial instruments and certain other items at fair value that were not currently required to be measured at fair value. An entity reports unrealized gains and losses on items for which the fair value option has been elected in earnings at each subsequent reporting date. Upfront costs and fees related to items for which the fair value option is elected are recognized in earnings as incurred and not deferred. This standard also established presentation and disclosure requirements designed to facilitate comparisons between entities that choose different measurement attributes for similar types of assets and liabilities. This standard was effective for financial statements issued for fiscal years beginning after November 15, 2007 (January 1, 2008 for 3M) and interim periods within those fiscal years. At the effective date, an entity could elect the fair value option for eligible items that existed at that date. The entity was required to report the effect of the first remeasurement to fair value as a cumulative-effect adjustment to the opening balance of retained earnings. The Company did not elect the fair value option for eligible items that existed as of January 1, 2008.

In June 2007, the FASB ratified a standard regarding the accounting for nonrefundable advance payments for goods or services to be used in future research and development activities that requires nonrefundable advance payments made by the Company for future R&D activities to be capitalized and recognized as an expense as the goods or services are received by the Company. This standard was effective for 3M with respect to new arrangements entered into beginning January 1, 2008 and did not have a material impact on 3M's consolidated results of operations or financial condition.

In December 2007, the FASB issued and, in April 2009, amended a new business combinations standard codified within ASC 805, which changed the accounting for business acquisitions. Accounting for business combinations under this standard requires the acquiring entity in a business combination to recognize all (and only) the assets acquired and liabilities assumed in the transaction and establishes the acquisition-date fair value as the measurement objective for all assets acquired and liabilities assumed in a business combination. Certain provisions of this standard impact the determination of acquisition-date fair value of consideration paid in a business combination (including contingent consideration); exclude transaction costs from acquisition accounting; and change accounting practices for acquisition-related restructuring costs, in-process research and development, indemnification assets, and tax benefits. For 3M, this standard was effective for business combinations and adjustments to an acquired entity's deferred tax asset and liability balances occurring after December 31, 2008. This standard had no immediate impact upon adoption by 3M, and was applied to the business combinations disclosed in Note 2 that were completed post-2008 and to applicable adjustments to acquired entity deferred tax items occurring after December 31, 2008. In December 2007, the FASB issued a new standard which established the accounting for and reporting of noncontrolling interests (NCIs) in partially owned consolidated subsidiaries and the loss of control of subsidiaries. Certain provisions of this standard indicate, among other things, that NCIs (previously referred to as minority interests) be treated as a separate component of equity, not as a liability (as was previously the case); that increases and decreases in the parent's ownership interest that leave control intact be treated as equity transactions, rather than as step acquisitions or gains or losses on purchases or sales; and that losses of a partially owned consolidated subsidiary be allocated to the NCI even when such allocation might result in a deficit balance. This standard also required changes to certain presentation and disclosure requirements. For 3M, the standard was effective beginning January 1, 2009. The provisions of the standard were applied to all NCIs prospectively, except for the presentation and disclosure requirements, which were applied retrospectively to all periods presented. As a result, upon adoption, 3M retroactively reclassified the "Minority interest in subsidiaries" balance previously included in the "Other liabilities" section of the consolidated balance sheet to a new component of equity with respect to NCIs in consolidated subsidiaries. The adoption also impacted certain captions previously used on the consolidated statement of income, largely identifying net income including NCI and net income attributable to 3M. Additional disclosures required by this standard are also included in Note 6. The adoption of this standard did not have a material impact on 3M's consolidated financial position or results of operations.

In December 2007, the FASB ratified a standard related to accounting for collaborative arrangements which discusses how parties to a collaborative arrangement (which does not establish a legal entity within such arrangement) should account for various activities. The standard indicates that costs incurred and revenues generated from transactions with third parties (i.e. parties outside of the collaborative arrangement) should be reported by the collaborators on the respective line items in their income statements pursuant to ASC 605-45, *Principle Agent Considerations*. Additionally, the guidance provides that income statement characterization of payments between the participants in a collaborative arrangement should be based upon existing authoritative standards; analogy to such standards if not within their scope; or a reasonable, rational, and consistently applied accounting policy election. This guidance was effective for 3M beginning January 1, 2009 and applied retrospectively to all periods presented for collaborative arrangements existing as of the date of adoption. The adoption of this standard did not have a material impact on 3M's consolidated results of operations or financial condition.

In March 2008, the FASB issued an accounting standard related to disclosures about derivative instruments and hedging activities, codified in ASC 815, which requires additional disclosures about an entity's strategies and objectives for using derivative instruments; the location and amounts of derivative instruments in an entity's financial statements; how derivative instruments and related hedged items are accounted for under ASC 815, and how derivative instruments and related hedged items affect its financial position, financial performance, and cash flows. Certain disclosures are also required with respect to derivative features that are credit-risk-related. The standard was effective for 3M beginning January 1, 2009 on a prospective basis. The additional disclosures required by this standard are included in Note 12.

In April 2008, the FASB issued an accounting standard which amended the list of factors an entity should consider in developing renewal or extension assumptions used in determining the useful life of recognized intangible assets under ASC 350, *Intangibles—Goodwill and Other*. This new standard applies to (1) intangible assets that are acquired individually or with a group of other assets and (2) intangible assets acquired in both business combinations and asset acquisitions. Under this standard, entities estimating the useful life of a recognized intangible asset must consider their historical experience in renewing or extending similar arrangements or, in the absence of historical experience, must consider assumptions that market participants would use about renewal or extension. For 3M, this standard required certain additional disclosures beginning January 1, 2009 (which are included in Notes 2 and 3) and application to useful life estimates prospectively for intangible assets acquired after December 31, 2008. The adoption of this standard did not have a material impact on 3M's consolidated results of operations or financial condition.

In May 2008, the FASB issued an accounting standard which addresses convertible debt securities that, upon conversion by the holder, may be settled by the issuer fully or partially in cash (rather than settled fully in shares) and specifies that issuers of such instruments should separately account for the liability and equity components in a manner that reflects the issuer's nonconvertible debt borrowing rate when related interest cost is recognized. This standard was effective for 3M beginning January 1, 2009 with retrospective application to all periods presented. This standard impacted the Company's "Convertible Notes" (refer to Note 10 to the Consolidated Financial Statements for more detail), and required that additional interest expense essentially equivalent to the portion of issuance proceeds be retroactively allocated to the instrument's equity component and be recognized over the period from the Convertible Notes' issuance on November 15, 2002 through November 15, 2005 (the first date holders of these Notes had the ability to put them back to 3M). 3M adopted this standard in January 2009. Its retrospective application had no impact on results of operations for periods following 2005, but on post-2005 consolidated balance sheets, it resulted in an increase of approximately $22 million in previously reported opening additional paid in capital and a corresponding decrease in previously reported opening retained earnings.

In early October 2008, the FASB issued an accounting standard codified in ASC 820, *Fair Value Measurements and Disclosures*, which illustrated key considerations in determining the fair value of a financial asset in an inactive market. This standard was effective for 3M beginning with the quarter ended September 30, 2008. Its additional guidance was incorporated in the measurements of fair value of applicable financial assets disclosed in Note 13 and did not have a material impact on 3M's consolidated results of operations or financial condition.

In November 2008, the FASB ratified a standard related to certain equity method investment accounting considerations. The standard indicates, among other things, that transaction costs for an investment should be included in the cost of the equity-method investment (and not expensed) and shares subsequently issued by the equity-method investee that reduce the investor's ownership percentage should be accounted for as if the investor had sold a proportionate share of its investment, with gains or losses recorded through earnings. For 3M, the standard was effective for transactions occurring after December 31, 2008. The adoption of this standard did not have a material impact on 3M's consolidated results of operations or financial condition.

In November 2008, the FASB ratified an accounting standard related to intangible assets acquired in a business combination or asset acquisition that an entity does not intend to use or intends to hold to prevent others from obtaining access (a defensive intangible asset). Under the standard a defensive intangible asset needs to be accounted for as a separate unit of accounting and would be assigned a useful life based on the period over which the asset diminishes in value. For 3M, the standard was effective for transactions occurring after December 31, 2008. The Company considered this standard in terms of intangible assets acquired in business combinations or asset acquisitions that closed after December 31, 2008.

In December 2008, the FASB issued an accounting standard regarding a company's disclosures about postretirement benefit plan assets. This standard requires additional disclosures about plan assets for sponsors of defined benefit pension and postretirement plans including expanded information regarding investment strategies, major categories of plan assets, and concentrations of risk within plan assets. Additionally, this standard requires disclosures similar to those required for fair value measurements and disclosures under ASC 820 with respect to the fair value of plan assets such as the inputs and valuation techniques used to measure fair value and information with respect to classification of plan assets in terms of the hierarchy of the source of information used to determine their value. For 3M, the disclosures under this standard are required beginning with the annual period ended December 31, 2009. The additional disclosures are included in Note 11.

In April 2009, the FASB issued an accounting standard which provides guidance on (1) estimating the fair value of an asset or liability when the volume and level of activity for the asset or liability have significantly declined and (2) identifying transactions that are not orderly. The standard also amended certain disclosure provisions for fair value measurements and disclosures in ASC 820 to require, among other things, disclosures in interim periods of the inputs and valuation techniques used to measure fair value as well as disclosure of the hierarchy of the source of underlying fair value information on a disaggregated basis by specific major category of investment. For 3M, this standard was effective prospectively beginning April 1, 2009. The adoption of this standard did not have a material impact on 3M's consolidated results of operations or financial condition.

In April 2009, the FASB issued an accounting standard which modifies the requirements for recognizing other-than-temporarily impaired debt securities and changes the existing impairment model for such securities. The standard also requires additional disclosures for both annual and interim periods with respect to both debt and equity securities. Under the standard, impairment of debt securities is considered other-than-temporary if an entity (1) intends to sell the security, (2) more likely than not will be required to sell the security before recovering its cost, or (3) does not expect to recover the security's entire amortized cost basis (even if the entity does not intend to sell). The standard further indicates that, depending on which of the above factor(s) causes the impairment to be considered other-than-temporary, (1) the entire shortfall of the security's fair value versus its amortized cost basis or (2) only the credit loss portion would be recognized in earnings while the remaining shortfall (if any) would be recorded in other comprehensive income. The standard requires entities to initially apply its provisions to previously other-than-temporarily impaired debt securities existing as of the date of initial adoption by making a cumulative-effect adjustment to the opening balance of retained earnings in the period of adoption. The cumulative-effect adjustment potentially reclassifies the noncredit portion of a previously other-than-temporarily impaired debt security held as of the date of initial adoption from retained earnings to accumulated other comprehensive income. For 3M, this standard was effective beginning April 1, 2009. The adoption of this standard did not have a material impact on 3M's consolidated results of operations or financial condition. Additional disclosures required by this standard are included in Note 9.

In April 2009, the FASB issued an accounting standard regarding interim disclosures about fair value of financial instruments. The standard essentially expands the disclosure about fair value of financial instruments that were previously required only annually to also be required for interim period reporting. In addition, the standard requires certain additional disclosures regarding the methods and significant assumptions used to estimate the fair value of financial instruments. This standard was effective for 3M beginning April 1, 2009 on a prospective basis. The additional disclosures required by this standard are included in Note 13.

In May 2009, the FASB issued a new accounting standard regarding subsequent events. This standard incorporates into authoritative accounting literature certain guidance that already existed within generally accepted auditing standards, with the requirements concerning recognition and disclosure of subsequent events remaining essentially unchanged. This guidance addresses events which occur after the balance sheet date but before the issuance of financial statements. Under the new standard, as under previous practice, an entity must record the effects of subsequent events that provide evidence about conditions that existed at the balance sheet date and must disclose but not record the effects of subsequent events which provide evidence about conditions that did not exist at the balance sheet date. This standard added an additional required disclosure relative to the date through which subsequent events have been evaluated and whether that is the date on which the financial statements were issued. For 3M, this standard was effective beginning April 1, 2009. The additional disclosures required by this standard are included in Note 1.

In June 2009, the FASB issued a new standard regarding the accounting for transfers of financial assets amending the existing guidance on transfers of financial assets to, among other things, eliminate the qualifying special-purpose entity concept, include a new unit of account definition that must be met for transfers of portions of financial assets to be eligible for sale accounting, clarify and change the derecognition criteria for a transfer to be accounted for as a sale, and require significant additional disclosure. For 3M, this standard is effective for new transfers of financial assets beginning January 1, 2010. Because 3M historically does not have significant transfers of financial assets, the adoption of this standard is not expected to have a material impact on 3M's consolidated results of operations or financial condition.

In June 2009, the FASB issued a new standard that revises the consolidation guidance for variable-interest entities. The modifications include the elimination of the exemption for qualifying special purpose entities, a new approach for determining who should consolidate a variable-interest entity, and changes to when it is necessary to reassess who should consolidate a variable-interest entity. For 3M, this standard is effective January 1, 2010. The Company does not expect the adoption of this standard to have a material impact on 3M's consolidated results of operations or financial condition.

In August 2009, the FASB issued ASU No. 2009-05, *Measuring Liabilities at Fair Value*, which provides additional guidance on how companies should measure liabilities at fair value under ASC 820. The ASU clarifies that the quoted price for an identical liability should be used. However, if such information is not available, a entity may use the quoted price of an identical liability when traded as an asset, quoted prices for similar liabilities or similar liabilities traded as assets, or another valuation technique (such as the market or income approach). The ASU also indicates that the fair value of a liability is not adjusted to reflect the impact of contractual restrictions that prevent its transfer and indicates circumstances in which quoted prices for an identical liability or quoted price for an identical liability traded as an asset may be considered level 1 fair value measurements (see Note 13 for a description of level 1 measurements). For 3M, this ASU was effective October 1, 2009. The adoption of this ASU did not have a material impact on 3M's consolidated results of operations or financial condition.

In September 2009, the FASB issued ASU No. 2009-12, *Investments in Certain Entities That Calculate Net Asset Value per Share (or Its Equivalent)*, that amends ASC 820 to provide guidance on measuring the fair value of certain alternative investments such as hedge funds, private equity funds and venture capital funds. The ASU indicates that, under certain circumstances, the fair value of such investments may be determined using net asset value (NAV) as a practical expedient, unless it is probable the investment will be sold at something other than NAV. In those situations, the practical expedient cannot be used and disclosure of the remaining actions necessary to complete the sale is required. The ASU also requires additional disclosures of the attributes of all investments within the scope of the new guidance, regardless of whether an entity used the practical expedient to measure the fair value of any of its investments. The disclosure provisions of this ASU are not applicable to an employer's disclosures about pension and other postretirement benefit plan assets. 3M does not have any significant direct investments within the scope of ASU No. 2009-12, but certain plan assets of the Company's benefit plans are valued based on NAV as indicated in Note 11. For 3M, this ASU was effective October 1, 2009. The adoption of this ASU did not have a material impact on 3M's consolidated results of operations or financial condition.

In October 2009, the FASB issued ASU No. 2009-13, *Multiple-Deliverable Revenue Arrangements—a consensus of the FASB Emerging Issues Task Force*, that provides amendments to the criteria for separating consideration in multiple-deliverable arrangements. As a result of these amendments, multiple-deliverable revenue arrangements will be separated in more circumstances than under existing U.S. GAAP. The ASU does this by establishing a selling price hierarchy for determining the selling price of a deliverable.

The selling price used for each deliverable will be based on vendor-specific objective evidence if available, third-party evidence if vendor-specific objective evidence is not available, or estimated selling price if neither vendor-specific objective evidence nor third-party evidence is available. A vendor will be required to determine its best estimate of selling price in a manner that is consistent with that used to determine the price to sell the deliverable on a standalone basis. This ASU also eliminates the residual method of allocation and will require that arrangement consideration be allocated at the inception of the arrangement to all deliverables using the relative selling price method, which allocates any discount in the overall arrangement proportionally to each deliverable based on its relative selling price. Expanded disclosures of qualitative and quantitative information regarding application of the multiple-deliverable revenue arrangement guidance are also required under the ASU. The ASU does not apply to arrangements for which industry specific allocation and measurement guidance exists, such as long-term construction contracts and software transactions. For 3M, ASU No. 2009-13 is effective beginning January 1, 2011. 3M may elect to adopt the provisions prospectively to new or materially modified arrangements beginning on the effective date or retrospectively for all periods presented. The Company is currently evaluating the impact of this standard on 3M's consolidated results of operations and financial condition.

In October 2009, the FASB issued ASU No. 2009-14, *Certain Revenue Arrangements That Include Software Elements—a consensus of the FASB Emerging Issues Task Force*, that reduces the types of transactions that fall within the current scope of software revenue recognition guidance. Existing software revenue recognition guidance requires that its provisions be applied to an entire arrangement when the sale of any products or services containing or utilizing software when the software is considered more than incidental to the product or service. As a result of the amendments included in ASU No. 2009-14, many tangible products and services that rely on software will be accounted for under the multiple-element arrangements revenue recognition guidance rather than under the software revenue recognition guidance. Under the ASU, the following components would be excluded from the scope of software revenue recognition guidance: the tangible element of the product, software products bundled with tangible products where the software components and non-software components function together to deliver the product's essential functionality, and undelivered components that relate to software that is essential to the tangible product's functionality. The ASU also provides guidance on how to allocate transaction consideration when an arrangement contains both deliverables within the scope of software revenue guidance (software deliverables) and deliverables not within the scope of that guidance (non-software deliverables). For 3M, ASU No. 2009-14 is effective beginning January 1, 2011. 3M may elect to adopt the provisions prospectively to new or materially modified arrangements beginning on the effective date or retrospectively for all periods presented. However, 3M must elect the same transition method for this guidance as that chosen for ASU No. 2009-13. The Company is currently evaluating the impact of this standard on 3M's consolidated results of operations and financial condition.

In January 2010, the FASB issued ASU No. 2010-6, *Improving Disclosures About Fair Value Measurements*, that amends existing disclosure requirements under ASC 820 by adding required disclosures about items transferring into and out of levels 1 and 2 in the fair value hierarchy; adding separate disclosures about purchase, sales, issuances, and settlements relative to level 3 measurements; and clarifying, among other things, the existing fair value disclosures about the level of disaggregation. For 3M this ASU is effective for the first quarter of 2010, except for the requirement to provide level 3 activity of purchases, sales, issuances, and settlements on a gross basis, which is effective beginning the first quarter of 2011. Since this standard impacts disclosure requirements only, its adoption will not have a material impact on 3M's consolidated results of operations or financial condition.

1.47

WHOLE FOODS MARKET, INC. (SEP)

NOTES TO CONSOLIDATED FINANCIAL STATEMENTS

2) Summary of Significant Accounting Policies

Definition of Fiscal Year

We report our results of operations on a 52- or 53-week fiscal year ending on the last Sunday in September. Fiscal years 2009 and 2008 were 52-week years and fiscal year 2007 was a 53-week year.

Principles of Consolidation

The accompanying consolidated financial statements have been prepared in accordance with U.S. generally accepted accounting principles. All significant majority-owned subsidiaries are consolidated on a line-by-line basis, and all significant intercompany accounts and transactions are eliminated upon consolidation.

Adoption of the FASB Accounting Standards Codification

In June 2009, the Financial Accounting Standards Board ("FASB") issued Accounting Standards Codification ("ASC") Update No. 2009-01 ("ASU No. 2009-01"), "Topic 105—Generally Accepted Accounting Principles," which amends the ASC for the issuance of Statement of Financial Accounting Standards No. 168 ("SFAS No. 168"), "The FASB Accounting Standards Codification and the Hierarchy of Generally Accepted Accounting Principles." ASU No. 2009-01 includes SFAS No. 168 in its entirety and establishes the ASC as the source of authoritative accounting principles recognized by FASB for all nongovernmental entities in the preparation of financial statements in accordance with GAAP. For SEC registrants, rules and interpretive releases of the SEC under federal securities laws are also considered authoritative sources of GAAP. The guidance is effective for financial statements issued for interim and annual periods ending after September 15, 2009. We adopted the FASB ASC for fiscal year ended September 27, 2009. The adoption had no impact on our financial statements. All references to authoritative guidance have been updated to cite relevant ASC Topics, as applicable.

Cash and Cash Equivalents

We consider all highly liquid investments with an original maturity of 90 days or less to be cash equivalents.

Restricted Cash

Restricted cash primarily relates to cash held as collateral to support a portion of our projected workers' compensation obligations.

Inventories

We value our inventories at the lower of cost or market. Cost was determined using the last-in, first-out ("LIFO") method for approximately 93.6% and 94.0% of inventories in fiscal years 2009 and 2008, respectively. Under the LIFO method, the cost assigned to items sold is based on the cost of the most recent items purchased. As a result, the costs of the first items purchased remain in inventory and are used to value ending inventory. The excess of estimated current costs over LIFO carrying value, or LIFO reserve, was approximately $27.1 million and $32.7 million at September 27, 2009 and September 28, 2008, respectively. Costs for remaining inventories are determined by the first-in, first-out ("FIFO") method.

Cost was determined using the retail method and the item cost method for inventories in fiscal years 2009 and 2008. Under the retail method, the valuation of inventories at cost and the resulting gross margins are determined by counting each item in inventory, then applying a cost-to-retail ratio for various groupings of similar items to the retail value of inventories. Inherent in the retail inventory method calculations are certain management judgments and estimates which could impact the ending inventory valuation at cost as well as the resulting gross margins. The item cost method involves counting each item in inventory, assigning costs to each of these items based on the actual purchase costs (net of vendor allowances) of each item and recording the actual cost of items sold. The item cost method of accounting enables management to more precisely manage inventory and purchasing levels when compared to the retail method of accounting. Our largest supplier, United Natural Foods, Inc., accounted for approximately 28%, 32%, and 24% of our total purchases in fiscal years 2009, 2008 and 2007, respectively.

Property and Equipment

Property and equipment is stated at cost, net of accumulated depreciation and amortization. We provide depreciation of equipment over the estimated useful lives (generally three to 15 years) using the straight-line method. We provide amortization of leasehold improvements and real estate assets under capital lease on the straight-line method over the shorter of the estimated useful lives of the improvements or the terms of the related leases. Terms of leases used in the determination of estimated useful lives may include renewal periods at the Company's option if exercise of the option is determined to be reasonably assured at the inception of the lease. We provide depreciation of buildings over the estimated useful lives (generally 20 to 30 years) using the straight-line method. Costs related to a projected site determined to be unsatisfactory and general site selection costs that cannot be identified with a specific store location are charged to operations currently. The Company recognizes a liability for the fair value of a conditional asset retirement obligation when the obligation is incurred. Repair and maintenance costs are expensed as incurred. Interest costs on significant projects constructed or developed for the Company's own use are capitalized as a separate component of the asset. Upon retirement or disposal of assets, the cost and related accumulated depreciation are removed from the balance sheet and any gain or loss is reflected in earnings.

Operating Leases

The Company leases stores, non-retail facilities and administrative offices under operating leases. Store lease agreements generally include rent holidays, rent escalation clauses and contingent rent provisions for percentage of sales in excess of specified levels. Most of our lease agreements include renewal periods at the Company's option. We recognize rent holiday periods and scheduled rent increases on a straight-line basis over the lease term beginning with the date the Company takes possession of the leased space for construction and other purposes. We record tenant improvement allowances and rent holidays as deferred rent liabilities and amortize the deferred rent over the terms of the lease to rent. We record rent liabilities for contingent percentage of sales lease provisions when we determine that it is probable that the specified levels will be reached as defined by the lease.

Goodwill

Goodwill consists of the excess of cost of acquired enterprises over the sum of the amounts assigned to identifiable assets acquired less liabilities assumed. Goodwill is reviewed for impairment annually at the beginning of the Company's fourth fiscal quarter, or more frequently if impairment indicators arise, on a reporting unit level. We allocate goodwill to one reporting unit for goodwill impairment testing. We compare our fair value, which is determined utilizing both a market value method and discounted projected future cash flows, to our carrying value for the purpose of identifying impairment. Our annual impairment review requires extensive use of accounting judgment and financial estimates.

Intangible Assets

Intangible assets include acquired leasehold rights, favorable lease assets, trade names, brand names, liquor licenses, license agreements, non-competition agreements and debt issuance costs. Indefinite-lived intangible assets are reviewed for impairment quarterly, or whenever events or changes in circumstances indicate the carrying amount of an intangible asset may not be recoverable. We amortize definite-lived intangible assets on a straight-line basis over the life of the related agreement. Currently the weighted average life of contract-based intangible assets and for marketing-related and other identifiable intangible assets is approximately 16 years and 2 years, respectively.

Impairment of Long-Lived Assets and Long-Lived Assets to Be Disposed of

We evaluate long-lived assets for impairment whenever events or changes in circumstances, such as unplanned negative cash flow or short lease life, indicate that the carrying amount of an asset may not be recoverable. Recoverability of assets to be held and used is measured by a comparison of the carrying amount of an asset to future undiscounted cash flows expected to be generated by the asset. If such assets are considered to be impaired, the impairment to be recognized is measured by the amount by which the carrying amount of the assets exceeds the fair value of the assets. Assets to be disposed of are reported at the lower of the carrying amount or fair value less costs to sell. When the Company impairs assets related to an operating location, a charge to write down the related assets is included in the "Direct store expenses" line item on the Consolidated Statements of Operations. When the Company commits to relocate, close, or dispose of a location, a charge to write down the related assets to their estimated recoverable value is included in the "Relocation, store closure and lease termination costs" line item on the Consolidated Statements of Operations.

Fair Value of Financial Instruments

The Company records its financial assets and liabilities at fair value, in accordance with the framework for measuring fair value in generally accepted accounting principles. This framework establishes a fair value hierarchy that prioritizes the inputs used to measure fair value:
- Level 1: Observable inputs that reflect unadjusted quoted prices for identical assets or liabilities traded in active markets.
- Level 2: Inputs other than quoted prices included within Level 1 that are observable for the asset or liability, either directly or indirectly.
- Level 3: Inputs that are generally unobservable. These inputs may be used with internally developed methodologies that result in management's best estimate of fair value.

The provisions of ASC 820, "Fair Value Measurements and Disclosures," are effective for the Company's nonfinancial assets and liabilities beginning in the first quarter of fiscal year ended September 26, 2010.

The Company holds money market fund investments that are classified as either cash equivalents or restricted cash that are measured at fair value on a recurring basis, based on quoted prices in active markets for identical assets. We had cash equivalent instruments and restricted cash investments totaling approximately $439.0 million and $70.4 million, respectively, at September 27, 2009. The carrying amount of the Company's interest rate swap agreement is measured at fair value on a recurring basis using a standard valuation model that incorporates inputs other than quoted prices that are observable. Declines in fair value below the Company's carrying value deemed to be other than temporary are charged against net earnings. Details on the fair value of the Company's interest rate swap agreement are included in Note 9 to the consolidated financial statements, "Derivatives."

The carrying amounts of trade and other accounts receivable, trade accounts payable, accrued payroll, bonuses and team member benefits, and other accrued expenses approximate fair value because of the short maturity of those instruments. Store closure reserves and estimated workers' compensation claims are recorded at net present value to approximate fair value. The carrying amount of our five-year term loan and revolving line of credit approximates fair value because each has a variable interest rate which reflects market changes to interest rates and contains variable risk premiums based on the Company's corporate ratings.

Derivative Instruments

The Company utilizes derivative financial instruments to hedge its exposure to changes in interest rates. All derivative financial instruments are recorded on the balance sheet at their respective fair value. The Company does not use financial instruments or derivatives for any trading or other speculative purposes. Hedge effectiveness is measured by comparing the change in fair value of the hedged item with the change in fair value of the derivative instrument. The effective portion of the gain or loss of the hedge is recorded on the Consolidated Balance Sheets under the caption "Accumulated other comprehensive income (loss)." Any ineffective portion of the hedge, as well as amounts not included in the assessment of effectiveness, is recorded on the Consolidated Statements of Operations under the caption "Interest expense."

Effective January 19, 2009 the Company adopted amendments to FASB guidance on ASC 815, "Derivatives and Hedging," that establishes, among other things, the disclosure requirements for derivative instruments and hedging activities. The guidance requires qualitative disclosures about objectives and strategies for using derivatives, quantitative disclosures about fair value amounts of gains and losses on derivative instruments, and disclosures about credit-risk-related contingent features in derivative agreements.

Insurance and Self-Insurance Reserves

The Company uses a combination of insurance and self-insurance plans to provide for the potential liabilities for workers' compensation, general liability, property insurance, director and officers' liability insurance, vehicle liability and employee health care benefits. Liabilities associated with the risks that are retained by the Company are estimated, in part, by considering historical claims experience, demographic factors, severity factors and other actuarial assumptions. The Company had insurance payables totaling approximately $86.9 million and $86.7 million at September 27, 2009 and September 28, 2008, respectively, included in the "Other current liabilities" line item on the Consolidated Balance Sheets.

Reserves for Closed Properties

The Company maintains reserves for retail stores and other properties that are no longer being utilized in current operations. The Company provides for closed property operating lease liabilities using a present value of the remaining noncancelable lease payments and lease termination fees after the closing date, net of estimated subtenant income. The closed property lease liabilities are expected to be paid over the remaining lease terms, which generally range from one to 16 years. The Company estimates subtenant income and future cash flows based on the Company's experience and knowledge of the area in which the closed property is located, the Company's previous efforts to dispose of similar assets and existing economic conditions. The reserves for closed properties include management's estimates for lease subsidies, lease terminations and future payments on exited real estate. Adjustments to closed property reserves primarily relate to changes in existing economic conditions, subtenant income or actual exit costs differing from original estimates. Adjustments are made for changes in estimates in the period in which the changes become known.

Capital lease properties that are closed are reduced to their estimated fair value. Reduction in the carrying values of property, equipment and leasehold improvements are recognized when expected net future cash flows are less than the assets' carrying value. The Company estimates net future cash flows based on its experience and knowledge of the area in which the closed property is located and, when necessary, utilizes local real estate brokers.

Revenue Recognition

We recognize revenue for sales of our products at the point of sale. Discounts provided to customers at the point of sale are recognized as a reduction in sales as the products are sold. Sales taxes are not included in revenue.

Cost of Goods Sold and Occupancy Costs

Cost of goods sold includes cost of inventory sold during the period, net of discounts and allowances, distribution and food preparation costs, and shipping and handling costs. The Company receives various rebates from third party vendors in the form of quantity discounts and payments under cooperative advertising agreements. Quantity discounts and cooperative advertising discounts in excess of identifiable advertising costs are recognized as a reduction of cost of goods sold when the related merchandise is sold. Occupancy costs include store rental costs, property taxes, utility costs, repair and maintenance, and property insurance.

Vendor Rebates and Allowances

The Company receives various rebates from third party vendors in the form of purchase or sales volume discounts and payments under cooperative advertising agreements. Purchase volume discounts are calculated based on actual purchase volumes. Volume discounts and cooperative advertising discounts in excess of identifiable advertising costs are recognized as a reduction of cost of goods sold when the related merchandise is sold.

Direct Store Expenses

Direct store expenses consist of store-level expenses such as salaries and benefits costs, supplies, depreciation, community marketing and other store-specific costs.

Advertising

Advertising and marketing expense for fiscal years 2009, 2008 and 2007 was approximately $32.9 million, $39.7 million, and $33.0 million, respectively. Advertising costs are charged to expense as incurred and are included in the "Direct store expenses" line item on the Consolidated Statements of Operations.

General and Administrative Expenses

General and administrative expenses consist of salaries and benefits costs, occupancy and other related costs associated with corporate and regional administrative support services.

Pre-Opening Expenses

Pre-opening expenses include rent expense incurred during construction of new stores and costs related to new store openings, including costs associated with hiring and training personnel, smallwares, supplies and other miscellaneous costs. Rent expense is generally incurred approximately thirteen months prior to a store's opening date. Other pre-opening expenses are incurred primarily in the 30 days prior to a new store opening. Pre-opening costs are expensed as incurred.

Relocation, Store Closure and Lease Termination Costs

Relocation costs consist of moving costs, estimated remaining net lease payments, accelerated depreciation costs, related asset impairment, and other costs associated with replaced facilities. Store closure costs consist of estimated remaining lease payments, accelerated depreciation costs, related asset impairment, and other costs associated with closed facilities. Lease termination costs consist of estimated remaining net lease payments for terminated leases and idle properties, and associated asset impairments.

Share-Based Payments

The Company maintains several share-based incentive plans. We grant options to purchase common stock under our Whole Foods Market 2009 Stock Incentive Plan, which was approved at our annual shareholders' meeting on March 16, 2009 and replaces the Whole Foods Market 2007 Stock Incentive Plan. All options outstanding are governed by the original terms and conditions of the grants. Options are granted at an option price equal to the market value of the stock at the grant date and are generally exercisable ratably over a four-year period beginning one year from grant date and have a five or seven year term. The grant date is established once the Company's Board of Directors approves the grant and all key terms have been determined. The exercise prices of our stock option grants are the closing price on the grant date. Stock option grant terms and conditions are communicated to team members within a relatively short period of time. Our Company generally approves one primary stock option grant annually, occurring during a trading window.

Our Company offers a team member stock purchase plan to all full-time team members with a minimum of 400 hours of service. Participating team members may purchase our common stock through payroll deductions. At our 2007 annual meeting, shareholders approved a new Team Member Stock Purchase Plan ("TMSPP") which became effective on April 1, 2007. The TMSPP replaces all previous stock purchase plans and provides for a 5% discount on the shares purchase date market value which meets the share-based payment, "Safe Harbor" provisions, and therefore is non-compensatory. As a result, no future compensation expense will be recognized for our employee stock purchase plan. Under the previous plans, participating team members could elect to purchase unrestricted shares at 100% of market value or restricted shares at 85% of market value on the purchase date.

The Company uses the Black-Scholes multiple option pricing model which requires extensive use of accounting judgment and financial estimates, including estimates of the expected term team members will retain their vested stock options before exercising them, the estimated volatility of the Company's common stock price over the expected term, and the number of options that will be forfeited prior to the completion of their vesting requirements. The related share-based payment expense is recognized on a straight-line basis over the vesting period. The tax savings resulting from tax deductions in excess of expense reflected in the Company's financial statements are reflected as a financing cash flow. Application of alternative assumptions could produce significantly different estimates of the fair value of share-based payment expense and consequently, the related amounts recognized in the Consolidated Statements of Operations.

Income Taxes

We recognize deferred income tax assets and liabilities by applying statutory tax rates in effect at the balance sheet date to differences between the book basis and the tax basis of assets and liabilities. Deferred tax assets and liabilities are measured using enacted tax rates expected to apply to taxable income in the years in which those temporary differences are expected to reverse. Deferred tax assets and liabilities are adjusted to reflect changes in tax laws or rates in the period that includes the enactment date. Significant accounting judgment is required in determining the provision for income taxes and related accruals, deferred tax assets and liabilities. The Company believes that its tax positions are consistent with applicable tax, but certain positions may be challenged by taxing authorities. In the ordinary course of business, there are transactions and calculations where the ultimate tax outcome is uncertain. In addition, we are subject to periodic audits and examinations by the Internal Revenue Service ("IRS") and other state and local taxing authorities. Although we believe that our estimates are reasonable, actual results could differ from these estimates.

In fiscal year 2008, the Company adopted amendments to ASC 740, "Income Taxes," which clarify the accounting for uncertainty in tax positions recognized in the financial statements. Under these provisions, the Company may recognize the tax benefit from an uncertain tax position only if it is more likely than not that the tax position will be sustained on examination by the taxing authorities based on the technical merits of the position. The tax benefits recognized in the financial statements from such a position should be measured based on the largest benefit that has a greater than 50% likelihood of being realized upon ultimate settlement. The related amendments also provide guidance on measurement, classification, interest and penalties associated with tax positions, and income tax disclosures. See Note 11 to the consolidated financial statements, "Income Taxes," for further discussion.

Treasury Stock

The Company maintains a stock repurchase program which expired subsequent to year end on November 8, 2009. Under this program, the Company may repurchase shares of the Company's common stock on the open market that are held in treasury at cost. The subsequent retirement of treasury stock is recorded as a reduction in retained earnings at cost. The Company's common stock has no par value.

Earnings Per Share

Basic earnings per share is calculated by dividing net income available to common shareholders by the weighted average number of common shares outstanding during the fiscal period. Net income available to common shareholders in fiscal year 2009 is calculated using the two-class method, which is an earnings allocation method for computing earnings per share when an entity's capital structure includes common stock and participating securities. The two-class method determines earnings per share based on dividends declared on common stock and participating securities (i.e., distributed earnings) and participation rights of participating securities in any undistributed earnings. The application of the two-class method is required since the Company's redeemable preferred shares contain a participation feature. See further discussion in Note 12 to the consolidated financial statements, "Redeemable Preferred Stock." Diluted earnings per share is based on the weighted average number of common shares outstanding plus, where applicable, the additional common shares that would have been outstanding as a result of the conversion of convertible debt, dilutive options, and redeemable preferred stock.

Comprehensive Income

Comprehensive income consists of net income; unrealized gains and losses on marketable securities; unrealized gains and losses on cash flow hedge instruments, including reclassification adjustments of unrealized losses to net income related to ongoing interest payments; and foreign currency translation adjustments, net of income taxes. Comprehensive income is reflected in the Consolidated Statements of Shareholders' Equity and Comprehensive Income. At September 27, 2009, accumulated other comprehensive income consisted of foreign currency translation adjustment losses of approximately $0.7 million and unrealized losses on cash flow hedge instruments of approximately $12.6 million. At September 28, 2008, accumulated other comprehensive income consisted of foreign currency translation adjustment gains of approximately $8.0 million and unrealized losses on cash flow hedge instruments of approximately $7.6 million.

Foreign Currency Translation

The Company's Canadian and United Kingdom operations use their local currency as their functional currency. Beginning in fiscal year 2009, foreign currency transaction gains and losses related to Canadian intercompany operations are charged to net income in the period incurred. The Company recognized foreign currency expense totaling approximately $0.9 million in fiscal year 2009. Intercompany transaction gains and losses associated with our United Kingdom operations are excluded from the determination of net income since these transactions are considered long-term investments in nature. Assets and liabilities are translated at exchange rates in effect at the balance sheet date. Income and expense accounts are translated at the average monthly exchange rates during the year. Resulting translation adjustments are recorded as a separate component of accumulated other comprehensive income.

Segment Information

The Company has one operating segment and a single reportable segment, natural and organic foods supermarkets. We currently have six stores in Canada and five stores in the United Kingdom. All of our remaining operations are domestic. The following is a summary of annual percentage sales and net long-lived assets by geographic area:

	2009	2008	2007
Sales:			
United States	97.2%	96.5%	97.3%
Canada and United Kingdom	2.8%	3.5%	2.7%
Total sales	100.0%	100.0%	100.0%
Long-lived assets, net:			
United States	96.5%	96.4%	95.1%
Canada and United Kingdom	3.5%	3.6%	4.9%
Total long-lived assets, net	100.0%	100.0%	100.0%

The following is a summary of annual percentage sales by product category:

	2009	2008	2007
Grocery	33.8%	33.2%	32.0%
Prepared foods	19.1%	19.3%	19.8%
Other perishables	47.1%	47.5%	48.3%
Total sales	100.0%	100.0%	100.0%

Figures may not sum due to rounding.

Use of Estimates

The preparation of financial statements in conformity with generally accepted accounting principles requires management to make estimates and assumptions that affect the reported amounts of assets and liabilities and disclosure of contingent assets and liabilities at the date of the financial statements and revenues and expenses during the period reported. Actual amounts could differ from those estimates.

Reclassifications

Where appropriate, we have reclassified prior years' financial statements to conform to current year presentation. Specifically we have reclassified the effect of the determination to retire treasury shares in fiscal year 2008 totaling approximately $200.0 million previously classified in "Common stock" to "Retained earnings" on the consolidated balance sheet as of September 28, 2008. The Company has determined that all or a portion of the excess of purchase price over par or stated value associated with the retirement of treasury shares is required to be charged to retained earnings in accordance with ASC 505-30, "Equity-Treasury Stock," and has elected to charge the entire excess to retained earnings. The Company's common stock has no par value. The Company has made a corresponding adjustment to its consolidated statements of shareholders' equity and comprehensive income to reflect the reclassification. There was no impact on previously reported statements of operations, earning per share amounts, statements of cash flows or total shareholders' equity as a result of this reclassification. Additionally, this reclassification does not impact compliance with any applicable debt covenants in the Company's credit agreements.

Recent Accounting Pronouncements

In December 2007, the FASB issued new guidance within ASC 805, "Business Combinations," which replaces previous guidance in this Topic and applies to all transactions or other events in which an entity obtains control of one or more businesses, including those sometimes referred to as "true mergers" or "mergers of equals" and combinations achieved without the transfer of consideration. The new provisions establish principles and requirements for how the acquirer recognizes and measures identifiable assets acquired, liabilities assumed, any noncontrolling interest and goodwill acquired, and also provide for disclosures to enable users of the financial statements to evaluate the nature and financial effects of the business combination. Additional amendments address the recognition and initial measurement, subsequent measurement, and disclosure of assets and liabilities arising from contingencies acquired as part of a business combination. The newly issued guidance is effective for fiscal years beginning after December 15, 2008 and is applied prospectively to business combinations completed on or after that date. The provisions are effective for the Company's fiscal year ending September 26, 2010. We will evaluate the impact, if any, that the adoption of these provisions could have on our consolidated financial statements.

In December 2007, the FASB issued amendments to ASC 810, "Consolidation." These provisions establish accounting and reporting standards for noncontrolling interests ("minority interests") in subsidiaries, and clarify that a noncontrolling interest in a subsidiary should be accounted for as a component of equity separate from the parent's equity. Additionally, these amendments serve to improve the consistency of guidance in ASC Topics 810 and 805. The amended guidance is effective for fiscal years, and interim periods within those fiscal years, beginning after December 15, 2008 and is applied prospectively, except for presentation and disclosure requirements, which will apply retrospectively. These provisions are effective for the Company's first quarter of fiscal year ending September 26, 2010. We are currently evaluating the impact, if any, that the adoption of these provisions will have on our consolidated financial statements.

In April 2008, the FASB issued amendments to ASC 350, "Intangibles—Goodwill and Other." These provisions amend the factors that should be considered in developing renewal or extension assumptions used to determine the useful life of a recognized intangible asset. The intent of the position is to improve the consistency between the determination of the useful life of a recognized intangible asset and the period of expected cash flows used to measure the fair value of the asset. The amended guidance is effective for fiscal years beginning after December 15, 2008. These provisions are effective for the Company's fiscal year ending September 26, 2010. We will evaluate the impact, if any, that the adoption of these provisions could have on our consolidated financial statements.

In May 2008, the FASB issued amendments to ASC 470, "Debt," which clarify that convertible debt instruments that may be settled in cash upon conversion (including partial cash settlement) were not addressed by previously existing guidance and specifies that such users should separately account for the liability and equity components in a manner that will reflect the entity's nonconvertible debt borrowing rate when interest cost is recognized in subsequent periods. The amended guidance is effective for fiscal years beginning after December 15, 2008, and interim periods within those fiscal years. These provisions are effective for the Company's first quarter of fiscal year ending September 26, 2010. We are currently evaluating the impact, if any, that the adoption of these provisions will have on our consolidated financial statements.

In August 2009, the FASB issued ASU No. 2009-04, "Accounting for Redeemable Equity Instruments—Amendment to Section 480-10-S99." The amended guidance represents technical changes to ASC 480, "Distinguishing Liabilities from Equity," to reflect SEC staff pronouncements on EITF Topic D-98, "Classification and Measurement of Redeemable Securities." The guidance provided in ASU No. 2009-04 is effective for the first reporting period, including interim periods, beginning after issuance. ASU No. 2009-04 is effective for the Company's first quarter of fiscal year ending September 26, 2010. We are currently evaluating the impact, if any, that the adoption of ASU No. 2009-04 will have on our consolidated financial statements.

In August 2009, the FASB issued ASU No. 2009-05, "Measuring Liabilities at Fair Value," which amends ASC 820, "Fair Value Measurements and Disclosures." ASU No. 2009-05 provides clarification for the valuation techniques available when valuing a liability when a quoted price for an identical liability is not available, and clarifies that no adjustment is necessary related to the existence of restrictions that prevent the transfer of the liability. The amendments in this update require the use of valuation techniques that use the quoted price of an identical liability when traded as an asset, or quoted prices for similar liabilities or similar liabilities when traded as assets. The guidance provided in ASU No. 2009-05 is effective for the first reporting period, including interim periods, beginning after issuance on August 26, 2009. ASU No. 2009-05 is effective for the Company's first quarter of fiscal year ending September 26, 2010. We are currently evaluating the impact, if any, that the adoption of ASU No. 2009-05 will have on our consolidated financial statements.

In September 2009, the FASB issued ASU No. 2009-08, "Earnings per Share—Amendments to Sections 260-10-S99." The amended guidance represents technical changes to ASC 260, "Earnings per Share," to reflect SEC staff pronouncements on EITF Topic D-53, "Computation of Earnings Per Share for a Period that Includes a Redemption or an Induced Conversion of a Portion of a Class of Preferred Stock," and EITF Topic D-42, "The Effect of the Calculation of Earnings per Share for the Redemption or Induced Conversion of Preferred Stock." The update consisted principally of formatting changes and removing out-of-date guidance. The provisions of ASU No. 2009-08 are effective for the first reporting period, including interim periods, beginning after issuance. ASU No. 2009-08 is effective for the Company's first quarter of fiscal year ending September 26, 2010. We are currently evaluating the impact, if any, that the adoption of ASU No. 2009-08 will have on our consolidated financial statements.

ACCOUNTING CHANGES

1.48 FASB ASC 250, *Accounting Changes and Error Corrections*, defines various types of accounting changes, including a change in accounting principle, and provided guidance on the manner of reporting each type.

1.49 FASB ASC 250 requires, unless impracticable or otherwise specified by applicable authoritative guidance, retrospective application to prior periods' financial statements of a change in accounting principle. Retrospective application is the application of a different accounting principle to prior accounting periods as if that principle had always been used. More specifically, retrospective application involves the following:

- The cumulative effect of the change on periods prior to those presented shall be reflected in the carrying amount of assets and liabilities as of the beginning of the first period presented.
- An offsetting adjustment, if any, shall be made to the opening balance of retained earnings (or other appropriate component of equity or net assets in the statement of financial position) for that period.
- Financial statements for each individual prior period presented shall be adjusted to reflect the period-specific effects of applying the new accounting principle.

1.50 FASB ASC 250 also requires that a change in depreciation, amortization, or depletion method be accounted for prospectively as a change in accounting estimate effected by a change in accounting principle. A change in accounting estimate is accounted for either in the period of change if the change affects that period only, or the period of change and future periods if the change affects both.

1.51 Table 1-8 lists the accounting changes disclosed by the survey entities. As indicated in Table 1-8, most of the accounting changes disclosed by the survey entities were changes made to conform to requirements stated in newly adopted authoritative pronouncements.

1.52 Examples of accounting change disclosures follow.

1.53

TABLE 1-8: ACCOUNTING CHANGES

	Number of Entities			
	2009	2008	2007	2006
Noncontrolling interests..............	96	N/C*	N/C*	N/C*
Fair value measurements............	51	175	2	—
Business combinations...............	46	N/C*	N/C*	N/C*
Defined benefit pension and postretirement plans.................	44	59	138	303
Financial instruments with debt and equity characteristics.........	20	N/C*	N/C*	N/C*
Derivatives and hedging activities..................................	18	5	—	—
Earnings per share	17	N/C*	N/C*	N/C*
Income tax uncertainties.............	5	161	369	1
Inventories.................................	4	4	3	8
Prior period financial statement misstatements	3	6	10	18
Consolidation of variable interest entities	3	—	—	—
Impairment or disposal of long-lived assets.....................	2	1	—	2
Asset retirement obligations........	2	—	—	29
Servicing of financial assets........	2	—	—	4
Stock based compensation.........	—	—	42	437
Other..	22	24	26	22

* N/C = Not compiled. Line item was not included in the table for the year shown.

2008–2009 based on 500 entities surveyed; 2006–2007 based on 600 entities surveyed.

Noncontrolling Interests

1.54

EMC CORPORATION (DEC)

NOTES TO CONSOLIDATED FINANCIAL STATEMENTS

A (In Part): Summary of Significant Accounting Policies

Principles of Consolidation

These consolidated financial statements include the accounts of EMC, its wholly-owned subsidiaries and VMware, a company that is majority-owned by EMC. All intercompany transactions have been eliminated.

As described in Note C, in August 2007, EMC and VMware completed transactions involving the sale of VMware common stock which reduced EMC's interest in VMware from 100% to approximately 84% and 81% as of December 31, 2008 and 2009, respectively. VMware's financial results have been consolidated with that of EMC for all periods presented as EMC is VMware's controlling stockholder. The portion of the results of operations of VMware allocable to its other owners is shown as net income attributable to the non-controlling interest in VMware, Inc. on EMC's consolidated income statements. Additionally, the cumulative portion of the results of operations of VMware allocable to its other owners, along with the interest in the net assets of VMware attributable to those other owners, is shown as non-controlling interest in VMware, Inc. on EMC's consolidated balance sheets.

B (In Part): Adoption of New Authoritative Guidance and Revised Financial Statements

Effective January 1, 2009, we adopted new authoritative guidance for non-controlling interests in Consolidated Financial Statements. The guidance requires that (a) the ownership interest in subsidiaries be clearly identified, labeled and presented in the consolidated statement of financial position within equity, but separate from the parent's equity, (b) the amount of consolidated net income attributable to the parent and to the non-controlling interest be clearly identified and presented on the face of the consolidated income statement, and (c) changes in a parent's ownership interest while the parent retains its controlling financial interest in its subsidiary be accounted for consistently within equity. A parent's ownership interest in a subsidiary changes if the parent purchases additional ownership interest in its subsidiary, the parent sells some of its ownership interest or the subsidiary issues additional ownership interests. Upon adoption of the guidance, previously reported financial statements were revised and we reclassified the previously reported Minority interest in VMware to a component of shareholders' equity as non-controlling interest in VMware, Inc. Previously reported Minority interest was renamed Net income attributable to the non-controlling interest in VMware, Inc. See Note C.

C. Non-controlling Interest in VMware, Inc.

In the third quarter of 2007, VMware completed an initial public offering ("IPO") of its Class A common stock. Prior to the IPO, EMC amended VMware's certificate of incorporation to authorize shares of Class A and Class B common stock. After a conversion of existing common stock into Class A and Class B common stock, EMC held 32.5 million shares of Class A common stock and 300.0 million shares of Class B common stock. The ownership rights of Class A and Class B common stock are the same, except with respect to voting, conversion, certain actions that require the consent of holders of Class B common stock and other protective provisions. Each share of Class B common stock has ten votes, while each share of Class A common stock has one vote for all matters to be voted on by stockholders. In the IPO, VMware sold 37.95 million shares of its Class A common stock at $29.00 per share, resulting in net proceeds of approximately $1,035.2 million. The gain of $551.1 million, net of taxes, of $330.7 million from this transaction was recorded as an increase to additional paid-in capital which reflects the amount of EMC's share of VMware's net assets (after non-controlling interest) in excess of EMC's carrying value prior to the IPO.

In October 2008, we purchased 500,000 shares of VMware's Class A common stock from Intel Capital Corporation for $13.3 million.

The non-controlling interests' share of equity in VMware is reflected as Non-controlling interest in VMware, Inc. in the accompanying consolidated balance sheets and was $510.6 million and $327.5 million as of December 31, 2009 and 2008, respectively. At December 31, 2009, EMC held approximately 98% of the combined voting power of VMware's outstanding common stock and approximately 81% of the economic interest in VMware.

The effects of changes in our ownership interest in VMware on our equity were as follows (table in thousands):

	2009	2008
Net income attributable to EMC Corporation	$1,088,077	$1,275,104
Transfers (to) from the non-controlling interest in VMware, Inc.:		
Increase in EMC Corporation's additional paid-in-capital for VMware's equity issuances	85,226	81,029
Decrease in EMC Corporation's additional paid-in-capital for VMware's other equity activity	(59,657)	(54,179)
Net transfers from non-controlling interest	25,569	26,850
Change from net income attributable to EMC Corporation and transfers from the non-controlling interest in VMware, Inc.	$1,113,646	$1,301,954

1.55

KIMBERLY-CLARK CORPORATION (DEC)

NOTES TO CONSOLIDATED FINANCIAL STATEMENTS

Note 1 (In Part): Accounting Policies

New Accounting Standards (In Part)
Also, effective January 1, 2009, as required:
- The Corporation adopted new FASB guidance with respect to the classification of noncontrolling interests (formerly minority interests) in its consolidated financial statements. See Note 11 for additional detail.
- The Corporation expanded disclosures about derivative instruments and hedging activities.
- Certain share-based payment awards entitled to non-forfeitable dividends or dividend equivalents were determined to be participating securities, which are included in the computation of basic and diluted earnings per share under the two-class method. Under the two-class method, earnings per share are computed by allocating net income between shares of common stock and participating securities.

Note 11 (In Part): Stockholders' Equity

Effective January 1, 2009, as required, the following changes were made with respect to the classification of noncontrolling interests (formerly minority owners' interest in subsidiaries). In addition, prior year amounts in the Consolidated Financial Statements have been recast to conform to the new requirements.
- Noncontrolling interests, which are not redeemable at the option of the noncontrolling interests, were reclassified from the mezzanine to equity, separate from the parent's stockholders' equity, in the Consolidated Balance Sheet. Common securities, redeemable at the option of the noncontrolling interest and carried at redemption values of approximately $41 million and $35

million as of December 31, 2009 and 2008, respectively, are classified in a line item combined with redeemable preferred securities of subsidiary in the Consolidated Balance Sheet.

- Consolidated net income was recast to include net income attributable to both the Corporation and noncontrolling interests.

Set forth below are reconciliations for each of the three years ending December 31, 2009 of the carrying amount of total stockholders' equity from the beginning of the period to the end of the period and an allocation of this equity to the stockholders of the Corporation and Noncontrolling Interests. In addition, because a portion of net income is allocable to redeemable securities of subsidiaries, which is classified outside of stockholders' equity, each of the reconciliations displays the amount of net income allocable to redeemable securities of subsidiaries.

(Millions of dollars)	Comprehensive Income	Stockholders' Equity Attributable to		Redeemable Securities of Subsidiaries
		The Corporation	Noncontrolling Interests	
Balance at December 31, 2006		$ 6,098	$404	$ 812
Comprehensive income:				
Net income	$1,951	1,823	85	43
Other comprehensive income, net of tax:				
Unrealized translation	377	365	12	—
Employee postretirement benefits	266	266	—	—
Other	10	10	—	—
Total comprehensive income	$2,604			
Stock-based awards		345	—	—
Income tax benefits on stock-based compensation		32	—	—
Shares repurchased		(2,811)	—	—
Recognition of stock-based compensation		63	—	—
Dividends declared		(933)	(30)	—
Additional investment in subsidiary and other		—	(5)	171
Return on noncontrolling interests		—	(3)	—
Adoption of uncertain tax positions accounting standard		(34)	—	—
Balance at December 31, 2007		$ 5,224	$463	$1,026
Comprehensive income:				
Net income	$1,829	1,690	82	57
Other comprehensive income, net of tax:				
Unrealized translation	(982)	(900)	(81)	(1)
Employee postretirement benefits	(689)	(687)	(2)	—
Other	(8)	(8)	—	—
Total comprehensive income	$ 150			
Stock-based awards		105	—	—
Income tax benefits on stock-based compensation		10	—	—
Shares repurchased		(636)	—	—
Recognition of stock-based compensation		47	—	—
Dividends declared		(966)	(51)	(1)
Additional investment in subsidiary and other		(1)	(25)	(2)
Return on redeemable preferred securities and noncontrolling interests		—	(3)	(47)
Balance at December 31, 2008		$ 3,878	$383	$1,032

(continued)

(Millions of dollars)	Comprehensive Income	Stockholders' Equity Attributable to		Redeemable Securities of Subsidiaries
		The Corporation	Noncontrolling Interests	
Balance at December 31, 2008		$3,878	$383	$1,032
Comprehensive income:				
Net income	$1,994	1,884	54	56
Other comprehensive income, net of tax:				
Unrealized translation	625	619	6	—
Employee postretirement benefits	(34)	(32)	(2)	—
Other	3	3	—	—
Total comprehensive income	$2,588			
Stock-based awards		150	—	—
Income tax benefits on stock-based compensation		7	—	—
Shares repurchased		(7)	—	—
Recognition of stock-based compensation		86	—	—
Dividends declared		(996)	(45)	(1)
Additional investment in subsidiary and other		(186)	(111)	18
Return on redeemable preferred securities and noncontrolling interests		—	(1)	(53)
Balance at December 31, 2009		$5,406	$ 284	$1,052

GAAP requires that the purchase of additional ownership in an already controlled subsidiary be treated as an equity transaction with no gain or loss recognized in consolidated net income or comprehensive income. GAAP also requires the presentation of the below schedule displaying the effect of a change in ownership interest between the Corporation and a noncontrolling interest.

(Millions of dollars)	
Net Income attributable to Kimberly-Clark Corporation	$1,884
Decrease in Kimberly-Clark Corporation's additional paid-in capital for purchase of remaining shares in its Andean subsidiary[a]	(133)
Change from net income attributable to Kimberly-Clark Corporation and transfers to noncontrolling interests	$1,751

[a] During the first quarter of 2009, the Corporation acquired the remaining approximate 31 percent interest in its Andean region subsidiary, Colombiana Kimberly Colpapel S.A., for $289 million. The acquisition was recorded as an equity transaction that reduced noncontrolling interests, AOCI and additional paid-in capital by approximately $278 million and increased investments in equity companies by approximately $11 million.

Fair Value Measurements

1.56

CHIQUITA BRANDS INTERNATIONAL, INC. (DEC)

NOTES TO CONSOLIDATED FINANCIAL STATEMENTS

Note 1 (In Part): Summary of Significant Accounting Policies

Goodwill, Trademarks and Intangible Assets

Impairment reviews are highly judgmental and involve the use of significant estimates and assumptions, which have a significant impact on whether there is potential impairment and the amount of any impairment charge recorded. Fair value assessments involve estimates of discounted cash flows that are dependent upon discount rates and long-term assumptions regarding future sales and margin trends, market conditions and cash flow, from which actual results may differ. Fair value measurements used in the impairment reviews of goodwill and intangible assets are Level 3 measurements, as described in Note 12. See further information about the company's policy for fair value measurements below under "Fair Value Measurements" and in Note 12.

Goodwill

Goodwill is reviewed for impairment each fourth quarter, or more frequently if circumstances indicate the possibility of impairment. Goodwill primarily relates to the company's salad operations, Fresh Express. The 2009 and 2007 reviews did not indicate impairment; however, as a result of the 2008 review, the company recorded a $375 million ($374 million after-tax) goodwill impairment charge in the fourth quarter of 2008. During the second half of 2008 and particularly in the fourth quarter, Fresh Express performed below prior periods and management expectations. Fresh Express' lower 2008 operating performance, along with slower growth expectations, negative category volume trends and a decline in market values resulting from weakness in the general economy as well as the financial markets, led to the 2008 goodwill impairment charge. These impairment indicators coincided with the company's annual impairment testing in the fourth quarter of 2008.

The first step of the impairment review compares the fair value of the reporting unit, Fresh Express, to the carrying value. Consistent with prior impairment reviews, the company estimated the fair value of the reporting unit using a combination of a market approach based on multiples of revenue and earnings before interest, taxes, depreciation and amortization ("EBITDA") from recent comparable transactions and an income approach based on expected future cash flows discounted at 9.4% in 2009 and 9.5% in 2008. The market approach and the income approach were weighted equally based on judgment of the comparability of the recent transactions and the risks inherent in estimating future cash flows in a difficult economic environment. Management considered recent economic and industry trends in estimating Fresh Express' expected future cash flows in the income approach. In 2009, the first step did not indicate potential impairment because the estimated fair value of Fresh Express was substantially greater than its carrying value; therefore, the second step was not required. In 2008, however, the first step indicated potential impairment, so the company performed the second step of the impairment review, which calculated the implied value of goodwill by subtracting the fair value of Fresh Express' assets and liabilities, including intangible assets, from the previously estimated fair value of Fresh Express as a whole. Impairment was measured as the difference between the implied value and the carrying value of goodwill.

Reasonably possible fluctuations in the discount rate, cash flows or market multiples in the 2009 analysis did not indicate impairment. In the 2008 impairment review, an increase in the discount rate of 0.5% would have increased the impairment charge by approximately $20 million and a 5.0% per year decrease in the expected future cash flows would have increased the impairment charge by $15 million.

Trademarks

Trademarks are indefinite-lived intangible assets that are not amortized and are also reviewed each fourth quarter or more frequently if circumstances indicate the possibility of impairment. The review compares the estimated fair values of the trademarks to the carrying values. The 2009, 2008 and 2007 reviews did not indicate impairment because the estimated fair values were greater than the carrying values. Consistent with prior reviews, the company estimated the fair values of the trademarks using the relief-from-royalty method. The relief-from-royalty method estimates the royalty expense that could be avoided in the operating business as a result of owning the respective trademarks. The royalty savings are measured by applying a royalty rate to projected sales, tax-effected and then converted to present value with a discount rate that considers the risk associated with owning the trademarks. In the 2009 review, the company assumed a 3.0% royalty rate, a 13.0% discount rate and a 38% tax rate for both Chiquita and Fresh Express trademarks. In the 2008 review, the company assumed a 3.0% royalty rate for Chiquita trademarks, a 1.0% royalty rate for Fresh Express trademarks, and a 12% discount rate and 38% tax rate for both Chiquita and Fresh Express trademarks. In 2009, the company changed the royalty rate assumed for the Fresh Express trademarks to more closely align it with market data for similar royalty agreements. The fair value estimate is most sensitive to the royalty rate but reasonably possible fluctuations in the royalty rates for both the Chiquita and Fresh Express trademarks also did not indicate impairment. The fair value estimate is less sensitive to the discount rate and reasonably possible changes to the discount rate would not indicate impairment for either trademark.

Other Intangible Assets

The company's intangible assets with a definite life consist of customer relationships and patented technology related to Fresh Express. These assets are amortized on a straight-line basis (which approximates the attrition method) over their estimated remaining lives. The weighted average remaining lives of the Fresh Express customer relationships and patented technology are 14 years and 12 years, respectively. As amortizable intangible assets, the company reviews the carrying value only when impairment indicators are present, by comparing (i) estimates of undiscounted future cash flows, before interest charges, included in the company's operating plans versus (ii) the carrying values of the related assets. Tests are performed over asset groups at the lowest level of identifiable cash flows. No impairment indicators existed in 2009. The goodwill impairment charge recorded in the fourth quarter of 2008 was an impairment indicator; however, no impairment resulted from testing these assets.

Fair Value Measurements

Effective January 1, 2008, the company adopted new accounting standards for fair value measurements of financial assets and financial liabilities. In February 2008, the effective date of these standards related to nonfinancial assets and nonfinancial liabilities was postponed until fiscal years beginning after November 15, 2008 and, accordingly, the company adopted these standards effective January 1, 2009. Fair value measurements of nonfinancial assets and nonfinancial liabilities are primarily used in goodwill and other intangible asset impairment reviews and in the valuation of assets held for sale.

The standards provide a framework for measuring fair value, which prioritizes the use of observable inputs in measuring fair value. Fair value is the price to hypothetically sell an asset or transfer a liability in an orderly manner in the principal market for that asset or liability. The standards address valuation techniques used to measure fair value including the market approach, the income approach and the cost approach. The market approach uses prices or relevant information generated by market transactions involving identical or comparable assets or liabilities. The income approach involves converting future cash flows to a single present value, with the fair value measurement based on current market expectations about those future cash flows. The cost approach is based on the amount that currently would be required to replace the service capacity of the asset.

See further information related to fair value measurements above under "Goodwill, Trademarks and Intangible Assets" and in Notes 12 and 14.

Note 12. Fair Value Measurements

Fair value is the price to hypothetically sell an asset or transfer a liability in an orderly manner in the principal market for that asset or liability. Accounting standards prioritize the use of observable inputs in measuring fair value. The level of a fair value measurement is determined entirely by the lowest level input that is significant to the measurement. The three levels are (from highest to lowest):

- Level 1—observable prices in active markets for identical assets and liabilities;
- Level 2—observable inputs other than quoted market prices in active markets for identical assets and liabilities, which include quoted prices for similar assets or liabilities in an active market and market-corroborated inputs; and
- Level 3—unobservable inputs.

At December 31, 2009, the company carried the following financial assets and liabilities at fair value:

| | | Fair Value Measurements Using | | |
(In thousands)	2009	Quoted Prices in Active Markets for Identical Assets (Level 1)	Significant Other Observable Inputs (Level 2)	Unobservable Inputs (Level 3)
Purchased euro put options	$ 6,527	$ —	$ 6,527	$—
Bunker fuel forward contracts	6,257	—	6,257	—
Available-for-sale investment	3,034	3,034	—	—
	$15,818	$3,034	$12,784	$—

At December 31, 2008, the company carried the following financial assets and liabilities at fair value:

| | | Fair Value Measurements Using | | |
(In thousands)	2008	Quoted Prices in Active Markets for Identical Assets (Level 1)	Significant Other Observable Inputs (Level 2)	Unobservable Inputs (Level 3)
Purchased euro put options	$ 47,239	$ —	$47,239	$ —
Bunker fuel forward contracts	(79,002)	—	—	(79,002)
30-day euro forward contracts	1,832	—	1,832	—
Available-for-sale investment	3,199	3,199	—	—
	$(26,732)	$3,199	$49,071	$(79,002)

The company values fuel hedging positions by applying an observable discount rate to the current forward prices of identical hedge positions. The company values currency hedging positions by utilizing observable or market-corroborated inputs such as exchange rates, volatility and forward yield curves. The company trades only with counterparties that meet certain liquidity and creditworthiness standards, and does not anticipate non-performance by any of these counterparties. The company does not require collateral from its counterparties, nor is it obliged to provide collateral when contracts are in a liability position. However, consideration of non-performance risk is required when valuing derivative instruments, and the company includes an adjustment for non-performance risk in the fair value measure of derivative instruments to reflect the full credit default spread ("CDS") applied to the net exposure by counterparty. When there is a net asset position, the company uses the counterparty's CDS, which is generally an observable input; when there is a net liability position, the company uses its own estimated CDS, which is an unobservable input. CDS is generally not a significant input in measuring fair value; however, at December 31, 2008 the company's own unobservable estimated CDS was significant to the fair value measurement of bunker fuel forward contracts, and accordingly, they were classified as Level 3 measurements. At December 31, 2009, the company's adjustment for non-performance risk was not significant for either the purchased euro put options or the bunker fuel forward contracts. At December 31, 2008, the company's adjustment for non-performance risk reduced the company's derivative assets for purchased euro put options by approximately $1 million, and reduced the derivative liabilities for bunker fuel forward contracts by approximately $8 million. CDS is not significant to the fair value measurement of 30-day euro forward contracts. See further discussion and tabular disclosure of hedging activity in Note 11.

The company has not elected to carry its debt at fair value. The carrying values of the company's debt represent amortized cost and are summarized below with estimated fair values:

	2009		2008	
(In thousands)	Carrying Value	Estimated Fair Value	Carrying Value	Estimated Fair Value
Financial instruments not carried at fair value:				
Parent company debt:				
7½% senior notes	$167,083	$168,000	$195,328	$133,000
8⅞% senior notes	179,185	182,000	188,445	126,000
4.25% convertible senior notes[1]	127,138	215,000	120,385	154,000
Subsidiary debt:				
Term loan (credit facility)	182,500	175,000	192,500	150,000
Other	163	100	653	600

[1] The principal amount of the Convertible Notes is $200 million. The carrying amount of the Convertible Notes is less than the principal amount due to the adoption of new accounting standards for Convertible Notes as described in Note 10.

The fair value of the parent company debt is based on quoted market prices (Level 1). The term loan may be traded on the secondary loan market, and the fair value of the term loan is based on either the last available trading price, if recent, or trading prices of comparable debt (Level 3). Level 3 fair value measurements described in Note 1 are used in the impairment reviews of goodwill and intangible assets. Fair value measurements of benefit plan assets included in net benefit plan liabilities are discussed in Note 14. The carrying amounts of cash and equivalents, accounts receivable and accounts payable approximate fair value.

Note 14 (In Part): Pension and Severance Benefits

Mutual funds, domestic common stock, corporate debt securities and mortgage-backed pass through securities held in the plans are publicly traded in active markets and are valued using the net asset value, or closing price of the investment at the measurement date. There have been no changes in the methodologies used at December 31, 2009 and 2008. The methods described above may produce a fair value calculation that may not be indicative of net realizable value or reflective of future fair values. Furthermore, while the company believes its valuation methods are appropriate and consistent with other market participants, the use of different methodologies or assumptions to determine the fair value of certain financial instruments could result in a different fair value measurement at the reporting date.

At December 31, 2009, the fair values of assets of the company's pension plans were as follows:

		Fair Value Measurements Using		
(In thousands)	2009	Quoted Prices in Active Markets for Identical Assets (Level 1)	Significant Other Observable Inputs (Level 2)	Unobservable Inputs (Level 3)
Domestic pension plans:				
Money market accounts	$ 236	$ 236	$ —	$—
Mutual funds:				
Domestic	6,606	6,606	—	—
International	2,023	2,023	—	—
Domestic large-cap common stock	4,929	4,929	—	—
Fixed income securities:				
Corporate bonds	2,352	—	2,352	—
Mortgage-backed pass-throughs	1,549	—	1,549	—
Other	678	—	678	—
Total assets of domestic pension plans	18,373	13,794	4,579	—
Foreign pension and severance plans:				
Cash and equivalents	3,508	3,508	—	—
Fixed income securities	1,481	—	1,481	—
Total assets of foreign pension and severance plans	4,989	3,508	1,481	—
Total assets of pension and severance plans	$23,362	$17,302	$6,060	$—

1.57

VARIAN MEDICAL SYSTEMS, INC. (SEP)

NOTES TO CONSOLIDATED FINANCIAL STATEMENTS

3. Fair Value

Effective September 27, 2008, the Company adopted the provisions of ASC 820, which defines fair value as the exchange price that would be received for an asset or paid to transfer a liability (an exit price) in the principal or most advantageous market for the asset or liability in an orderly transaction between market participants at the measurement date. ASC 820-10 establishes a three-level fair value hierarchy that prioritizes the inputs used to measure fair value. This hierarchy requires entities to maximize the use of observable inputs and minimize the use of unobservable inputs. The three levels of inputs used to measure fair value are as follows:

- Level 1—Quoted prices in active markets for identical assets or liabilities.
- Level 2—Observable inputs other than quoted prices included in Level 1, such as quoted prices for similar assets and liabilities in active markets; quoted prices for identical or similar assets and liabilities in markets that are not active; or other inputs that are observable or can be corroborated by observable market data.
- Level 3—Unobservable inputs that are supported by little or no market activity and that are significant to the fair value of the assets or liabilities.

The Company's financial assets and liabilities are valued using Level 1 and Level 2 inputs. Level 1 instrument valuations are obtained from quotes for transactions in active exchange markets involving identical assets. Level 2 instruments include valuations obtained from quoted prices for identical assets in markets that are not active. In addition, the Company has elected to use the income approach to value its derivative instruments using standard valuation techniques and Level 2 inputs, such as currency spot rates, forward points and credit default swap spreads. The Company's derivative instruments are short-term in nature, typically one month to twelve months in duration. As of October 2, 2009, the Company did not have any financial assets or liabilities without observable market values that would require a high level of judgment to determine fair value (Level 3 instruments).

The Company's adoption of the provisions of ASC 820-10 did not have a material impact on its consolidated financial statements. The Company has segregated all financial assets and liabilities that are measured at fair value on a recurring basis (at least annually) into the most appropriate level within the fair value hierarchy based on the inputs used to determine the fair value at the measurement date in the table below. The Company is not required to apply the provisions of ASC 820-10 for nonfinancial assets and liabilities until the first quarter of fiscal year 2010, except those that are recognized or disclosed at fair value in the financial statements on a recurring basis.

Effective September 27, 2008, the Company adopted the provisions of ASC 825-10-25, which provides entities the option to measure many financial instruments and certain other items at fair value. The Company has currently chosen not to elect the fair value option for any items that are not already required to be measured at fair value in accordance with GAAP.

Assets/Liabilities Measured at Fair Value on a Recurring Basis

The following tables present the Company's financial assets as of October 2, 2009 that are measured at fair value on a recurring basis. There were no financial liabilities that were measured at fair value as of October 2, 2009.

| | Fair Value Measurement Using | | | |
(In millions)	Quoted Prices in Active Markets for Identical Instruments (Level 1)	Significant Other Observable Inputs (Level 2)	Significant Unobservable Inputs (Level 3)	Total Balance
Type of instruments				
Assets:				
Money market funds	$85.0	$—	$—	$85.0
Total assets measured at fair value	$85.0	$—	$—	$85.0

| | Fair Value Measurement Using | | | |
(In millions)	Quoted Prices in Active Markets for Identical Instruments (Level 1)	Significant Other Observable Inputs (Level 2)	Significant Unobservable Inputs (Level 3)	Total Balance
Line item in condensed consolidated balance sheet				
Assets:				
Cash and cash equivalents	$84.0	$—	$—	$84.0
Other assets	1.0	—	—	1.0
Total assets measured at fair value	$85.0	$—	$—	$85.0

Business Combinations

1.58

ABBOTT LABORATORIES (DEC)

NOTES TO CONSOLIDATED FINANCIAL STATEMENTS

Note 11. Business Combinations, Technology Acquisitions and Related Transactions

On January 1, 2009, Abbott adopted the provisions of SFAS No. 141 (revised 2007), "Business Combinations," as codified in FASB ASC No. 805, "Business Combinations." Under ASC No. 805, acquired in-process research and development is accounted for as an indefinite-lived intangible asset until approval or discontinuation rather than as expense, acquisition costs in connection with an acquisition are expensed rather than added to the cost of an acquisition and the fair value of contingent consideration at the date of an acquisition is added to the cost of the acquisition.

In February 2009, Abbott acquired the outstanding shares of Advanced Medical Optics, Inc. (AMO) for approximately $1.4 billion in cash, net of cash held by AMO. Prior to the acquisition, Abbott held a small investment in AMO. Abbott acquired AMO to take advantage of increasing demand for vision care technologies due to population growth and demographic shifts and AMO's premier position in its field. Abbott acquired control of this business on February 25, 2009 and the financial results of the acquired operations are included in these financial statements beginning on that date. The acquisition was financed with long-term debt. The allocation of the fair value of the acquisition is shown in the table below:

(Dollars in billions)	
Goodwill, non-deductible	$ 1.7
Acquired intangible assets, non-deductible	0.9
Acquired in-process research and development, non-deductible	0.2
Acquired net tangible assets	0.4
Acquired debt	(1.5)
Deferred income taxes recorded at acquisition	(0.3)
Total allocation of fair value	$ 1.4

Acquired intangible assets consist of established customer relationships, developed technology and trade names and will be amortized over 2 to 30 years (average of 15 years). Acquired in-process research and development will be accounted for as an indefinite-lived intangible asset until regulatory approval or discontinuation. The net tangible assets acquired consist primarily of trade accounts receivable, inventory, property and equipment and other assets, net of assumed liabilities, primarily trade accounts payable, accrued compensation and other liabilities. Abbott incurred approximately $89 million of acquisition-related expenses in 2009 which are classified as Selling, general and administrative expense. In addition, subsequent to the acquisition, Abbott repaid substantially all of the acquired debt of AMO.

In October 2009, Abbott acquired 100 percent of Visiogen, Inc. for $400 million, in cash, providing Abbott with a next-generation accommodating intraocular lens (IOL) technology to address presbyopia for cataract patients. The preliminary allocation of the fair value of the acquisition resulted in non-deductible acquired in-process research and development

of approximately $195 million which will be accounted for as an indefinite-lived intangible asset until regulatory approval or discontinuation, non-deductible definite-lived intangible assets of approximately $33 million, goodwill of approximately $260 million and deferred income taxes of approximately $89 million. Acquired intangible assets consist of developed technology and will be amortized over 12 years. The allocation of the fair value of the acquisition will be finalized when the valuation is completed.

In October 2009, Abbott acquired Evalve, Inc. for $320 million, in cash, plus an additional payment of $90 million to be made upon completion of certain regulatory milestones. Abbott acquired Evalve to obtain a presence in the growing area of non-surgical treatment for structural heart disease. Including a previous investment in Evalve, Abbott has acquired 100 percent of the outstanding shares of Evalve. In connection with the acquisition, the carrying amount of this investment was revalued to fair value resulting in recording $28 million of income, which is reported as Other (income) expense, net. The preliminary allocation of the fair value of the acquisition resulted in non-deductible definite-lived intangible assets of approximately $145 million, non-deductible acquired in-process research and development of approximately $228 million which will be accounted for as an indefinite-lived intangible asset until regulatory approval or discontinuation, goodwill of approximately $158 million and deferred income taxes of approximately $136 million. Acquired intangible assets consist of developed technology and will be amortized over 12 years. The allocation of the fair value of the acquisition will be finalized when the valuation is completed.

In January 2009, Abbott acquired Ibis Biosciences, Inc. (Ibis) for $175 million, in cash, to expand Abbott's position in molecular diagnostics for infectious disease. Including a $40 million investment in Ibis in 2008, Abbott has acquired 100 percent of the outstanding shares of Ibis. A substantial portion of the fair value of the acquisition has been allocated to goodwill and amortizable intangible assets, and acquired in-process research and development that will be accounted for as an indefinite-lived intangible asset until regulatory approval or discontinuation. The investment in Ibis in 2008 resulted in a charge to acquired in-process research and development. In connection with the acquisition, the carrying amount of this investment was revalued to fair value resulting in recording $33 million of income, which is reported as Other (income) expense, net.

Had the above acquisitions taken place on January 1 of the previous year, consolidated net sales and income would not have been significantly different from reported amounts.

In December 2009, Abbott acquired the global rights to a novel biologic for the treatment of chronic pain for $170 million, in cash, resulting in a charge to acquired in-process research and development.

In September 2009, Abbott announced an agreement to acquire Solvay's pharmaceuticals business for EUR 4.5 billion (approximately $6.2 billion), in cash, plus additional payments of up to EUR 300 million if certain sales milestones are met. This acquisition will provide Abbott with a large and complementary portfolio of pharmaceutical products and a significant presence in key global emerging markets and will add approximately $500 million to Abbott's research and development spending. The transaction closed on February 15, 2010. Sales for the acquired business are forecast to be approximately $2.9 billion in 2010. The allocation of the fair value of the acquisition will be finalized when the valuation is completed.

1.59

BAXTER INTERNATIONAL INC. (DEC)

NOTES TO CONSOLIDATED FINANCIAL STATEMENTS

Note 1 (In Part): Summary of Significant Accounting Policies

Changes in Accounting Standards (In Part)

Business Combinations

On January 1, 2009, the company adopted a new accounting standard which changes the accounting for business combinations in a number of significant respects. The key changes include the expansion of transactions that qualify as business combinations, the capitalization of IPR&D as an indefinite-lived asset, the recognition of certain acquired contingent assets and liabilities at fair value, the expensing of acquisition costs, the expensing of costs associated with restructuring the acquired company, the recognition of contingent consideration at fair value on the acquisition date, the recognition of post-acquisition date changes in deferred tax asset valuation allowances and acquired income tax uncertainties as income tax expense or benefit, and the expansion of disclosure requirements. This standard was applicable for acquisitions made by the company on or after January 1, 2009, including the April 2009 consolidation of Sigma International General Medical Apparatus, LLC (SIGMA) and the August 2009 acquisition of certain assets of Edwards Lifesciences Corporation (Edwards CRRT) related to the hemofiltration business, also known as Continuous Renal Replacement Therapy (CRRT). Refer to Note 4 for further information regarding SIGMA and Edwards CRRT.

Note 4 (In Part): Acquisitions of and Investments in Businesses and Technologies

In 2009, 2008 and 2007, cash outflows related to the acquisitions of and investments in businesses and technologies totaled $156 million, $99 million and $112 million, respectively. The following are the more significant acquisitions and investments, including licensing agreements that require significant contingent milestone payments, entered into in 2009, 2008 and 2007.

2009

SIGMA

In April 2009, the company entered into an exclusive three-year distribution agreement with SIGMA covering the United States and international markets. The agreement, which enables Baxter to immediately provide SIGMA's SPECTRUM large volume infusion pumps to customers, as well as future products under development, complements Baxter's infusion systems portfolio and next generation technologies. The arrangement also included a 40% equity stake in SIGMA, and an option to purchase the remaining equity of SIGMA, exercisable at any time over a three-year term. The arrangement included a $100 million up-front payment and additional payments of up to $130 million for the exercise of the purchase option as well as for SIGMA's achievement of specified regulatory and commercial milestones.

Because Baxter's option to purchase the remaining equity of SIGMA limits the ability of the existing equity holders to participate significantly in SIGMA's profits and losses, and because the existing equity holders have the ability to make decisions about SIGMA's activities that have a significant effect on SIGMA's success, the company concluded that SIGMA is a VIE. Baxter is the primary beneficiary of the VIE due to its exposure to the majority of SIGMA's expected losses or expected residual returns and the relationship between Baxter and SIGMA created by the exclusive distribution agreement, and the significance of that agreement. Accordingly, the company consolidated the financial statements of SIGMA beginning in April 2009 (the acquisition date), with the fair value of the equity owned by the existing SIGMA equity holders reported as noncontrolling interests. The creditors of SIGMA do not have recourse to the general credit of Baxter.

The following table summarizes the preliminary allocation of fair value related to the arrangement at the acquisition date.

(In millions)	
Assets	
Goodwill	$ 87
IPR&D	24
Other intangible assets	94
Purchase option (other long-term assets)	111
Other assets	30
Liabilities	
Contingent payments	62
Other liabilities	25
Noncontrolling interests	159

The amount allocated to IPR&D is being accounted for as an indefinite-lived intangible asset until regulatory approval or discontinuation. The other intangible assets primarily relate to developed technology and are being amortized on a straight-line basis over an estimated average useful life of eight years. The fair value of the purchase option was estimated using the Black-Scholes model, and the fair value of the noncontrolling interests was estimated using a discounted cash flow model. The contingent payments of up to $70 million associated with SIGMA's achievement of specified regulatory and commercial milestones were recorded at their estimated fair value of $62 million. As of December 31, 2009, the estimated fair value of the contingent payments was $59 million, with the change in the estimated fair value since inception principally due to Baxter's payment of $5 million for the achievement of a commercial milestone in 2009. Other changes in the estimated fair value of the contingent payments are being recognized immediately in earnings. The results of operations and assets and liabilities of SIGMA are included in the Medication Delivery segment, and the goodwill is included in this reporting unit. The goodwill is deductible for tax purposes. The pro forma impact of the arrangement with SIGMA was not significant to the results of operations of the company.

Edwards CRRT

In August 2009, the company acquired Edwards CRRT. CRRT provides a method of continuous yet adjustable fluid removal that can gradually remove excess fluid and waste products that build up with the acute impairment of kidney function, and is usually administered in an intensive care setting in the hospital. The acquisition expands Baxter's existing CRRT business into new markets. The purchase price of $56 million was primarily allocated to other intangible assets and goodwill. The identified intangible assets of $28 million consisted of customer relationships and developed technology and are being amortized on a straight-line basis over an estimated average useful life of eight years. The goodwill of $28 million is deductible for tax purposes. Baxter will pay Edwards up to an additional $9 million in purchase price based on revenue objectives which are expected to be achieved over the next two years, and such contingent purchase price was recorded at its estimated fair value on the acquisition date. The results of operations and assets and liabilities of Edwards CRRT are included in the Renal segment, and the goodwill is included in this reporting unit. The pro forma impact of the Edwards CRRT acquisition was not significant to the results of operations of the company.

Defined Benefit Pension and Postretirement Plans

1.60

CLIFFS NATURAL RESOURCES INC. (DEC)

NOTES TO CONSOLIDATED FINANCIAL STATEMENTS

Note 1 (In Part): Business Summary and Significant Accounting Policies

Recent Accounting Pronouncements (In Part)

In December 2008, the FASB issued an update to ASC 715 regarding employers' disclosures about postretirement benefit plan assets. The amended guidance requires disclosure of additional information about investment allocation, fair values of major categories of assets, the development of fair value measurements, and concentrations of risk. The amendment is effective for fiscal years ending after December 15, 2009; however, earlier application is permitted. We adopted the amendment upon its effective date and have reported the required disclosures for our fiscal year ending December 31, 2009. Refer to NOTE 12—PENSIONS AND OTHER POSTRETIREMENT BENEFITS for further information.

Note 12 (In Part): Pensions and Other Postretirement Benefits

Plan Assets

The Company's financial objectives with respect to our pension and VEBA plan assets are to fully fund the actuarial accrued liability for each of the plans, to maximize investment returns within reasonable and prudent levels of risk, and to maintain sufficient liquidity to meet benefit obligations on a timely basis.

Our investment objective is to outperform the expected Return on Asset ("ROA") assumption used in the plans' actuarial reports over a full market cycle, which is considered a period during which the U.S. economy experiences the effects of both an upturn and a downturn in the level of economic activity. In general, these periods tend to last between three and five years. The expected ROA takes into account historical returns and estimated future long-term returns based on capital market assumptions applied to the asset allocation strategy.

The asset allocation strategy is determined through a detailed analysis of assets and liabilities by plan which defines the overall risk that is acceptable with regard to the expected level and variability of portfolio returns, surplus (assets compared to liabilities), contributions, and pension expense.

The asset allocation process involves simulating the effect of financial market performance for various asset allocation scenarios and factoring in the current funded status and likely future funded status levels by taking into account expected growth or decline in the contributions over time. The modeling is then adjusted by simulating unexpected changes in inflation and interest rates. The process also includes quantifying the effect of investment performance and simulated changes to future levels of contributions, determining the appropriate asset mix with the highest likelihood of meeting financial objectives, and regularly reviewing our asset allocation strategy.

The asset allocation strategy varies by plan. The following table reflects the actual asset allocations for pension and VEBA plan assets as of December 31, 2009 and 2008, as well as the 2010 weighted average target asset allocations as of December 31, 2009. Equity investments include securities in large-cap, mid-cap and small-cap companies located in the U.S. and worldwide. Fixed income investments primarily include corporate bonds and government debt securities. Alternative investments include hedge funds, private equity, structured credit and real estate.

	Pension Assets			VEBA Assets		
	Target Allocation	Percentage of Plan Assets at December 31		Target Allocation	Percentage of Plan Assets at December 31	
	2010	2009	2008	2010	2009	2008
Asset category						
Equity securities	37.0%	37.5%	35.8%	42.0%	46.4%	41.8%
Fixed income	30.0	29.9	32.8	35.0	38.3	36.6
Hedge funds	15.0	14.8	15.2	15.0	10.7	14.8
Private equity	9.0	6.6	7.4	8.0	4.4	6.6
Structured credit	5.0	8.1	3.5	—	—	—
Real estate	4.0	3.0	5.2	—	—	—
Cash	—	0.1	0.1	—	0.2	0.2
Total	100.0%	100.0%	100.0%	100.0%	100.0%	100.0%

Pension

The fair values of our pension plan assets at December 31, 2009 by asset category are as follows:

| | 2009 | | | |
	Quoted Prices in Active Markets for Identical Assets/Liabilities (Level 1)	Significant Other Observable Inputs (Level 2)	Significant Unobservable Inputs (Level 3)	Total
(In millions)				
Asset category				
Equity securities:				
U.S. large-cap	$ 88.1	$—	$ —	$ 88.1
U.S. small/mid-cap	35.1	—	—	35.1
International	57.8	—	—	57.8
Fixed income	144.8	—	—	144.8
Hedge funds	—	—	71.4	71.4
Private equity	13.6		18.2	31.8
Structured credit	—	—	39.1	39.1
Real estate	—	—	14.4	14.4
Cash	0.9	—	—	0.9
Total	$340.3	$—	$143.1	$483.4

Following is a description of the inputs and valuation methodologies used to measure the fair value of our plan assets.

Equity Securities

Equity securities classified as Level 1 investments include U.S. large, small and mid-cap investments and international equity. These investments are comprised of securities listed on an exchange, market or automated quotation system for which quotations are readily available. The valuation of these securities is determined using a market approach, and is based upon unadjusted quoted prices for identical assets in active markets.

Fixed Income

Fixed income securities classified as Level 1 investments include bonds and government debt securities. These investments are comprised of securities listed on an exchange, market or automated quotation system for which quotations are readily available. The valuation of these securities is determined using a market approach, and is based upon unadjusted quoted prices for identical assets in active markets.

Hedge Funds

Hedge funds are alternative investments comprised of direct or indirect investment in offshore hedge funds of funds with an investment objective to achieve an attractive risk-adjusted return with moderate volatility and moderate directional market exposure over a full market cycle. The valuation techniques used to measure fair value attempt to maximize the use of observable inputs and minimize the use of unobservable inputs. Considerable judgment is required to interpret the factors used to develop estimates of fair value. Valuations of the underlying investment funds are obtained and reviewed. The securities that are valued by the funds are interests in the investment funds and not the underlying holdings of such investment funds. Thus, the inputs used to value the investments in each of the underlying funds may differ from the inputs used to value the underlying holdings of such funds.

In determining the fair value of a security, the fund managers may consider any information that is deemed relevant, which may include one or more of the following factors regarding the portfolio security, if appropriate: type of security or asset; cost at the date of purchase; size of holding; last trade price; most recent valuation; fundamental analytical data relating to the investment in the security; nature and duration of any restriction on the disposition of the security; evaluation of the factors that influence the market in which the security is purchased or sold; financial statements of the issuer; discount from market value of unrestricted securities of the same class at the time of purchase; special reports prepared by analysts; information as to any transactions or offers with respect to the security; existence of merger proposals or tender offers affecting the security; price and extent of public trading in similar securities of the issuer or compatible companies and other relevant matters; changes in interest rates; observations from financial institutions; domestic or foreign government actions or pronouncements; other recent events; existence of shelf registration for restricted securities; existence of any undertaking to register the security; and other acceptable methods of valuing portfolio securities.

Hedge fund investments are valued monthly and recorded on a one-month lag. For alternative investment values reported on a lag, current market information is reviewed for any material changes in values at the reporting date. Share repurchases are available quarterly with notice of 65 business days.

Private Equity Funds

The private equity fund is an alternative investment that represents direct or indirect investments in partnerships, venture funds or a diversified pool of private investment vehicles (fund of funds).

Investment commitments are made in private equity funds of funds based on an asset allocation strategy, and capital calls are made over the life of the funds to fund the commitments. Until commitments are funded, the committed amount is reserved and invested in a selection of public equity mutual funds, including U.S. large, small and mid-cap investments and international equity, designed to approximate overall equity market returns. As of December 31, 2009, remaining commitments total $23.4 million, of which $16.5 million is reserved. Refer to the valuation methodologies for equity securities above for further information.

The valuation of investments in private equity funds of funds is initially performed by the underlying fund managers. In determining the fair value, the fund managers may consider any information that is deemed relevant, which may include: type of security or asset; cost at the date of purchase; size of holding; last trade price; most recent valuation; fundamental analytical data relating to the investment in the security; nature and duration of any restriction on the disposition of the security; evaluation of the factors that influence the market in which the security is purchased or sold; financial statements of the issuer; discount from market value of unrestricted securities of the same class at the time of purchase; special reports prepared by analysts; information as to any transactions or offers with respect to the security; existence of merger proposals or tender offers affecting the security; price and extent of public trading in similar securities of the issuer or compatible companies and other relevant matters; changes in interest rates; observations from financial institutions; domestic or foreign government actions or pronouncements; other recent events; existence of shelf registration for restricted securities; existence of any undertaking to register the security; and other acceptable methods of valuing portfolio securities.

The valuations are obtained from the underlying fund managers, and the valuation methodology and process is reviewed for consistent application and adherence to policies. Considerable judgment is required to interpret the factors used to develop estimates of fair value.

Private equity investments are valued quarterly and recorded on a one-quarter lag. For alternative investment values reported on a lag, current market information is reviewed for any material changes in values at the reporting date. Capital distributions for the funds do not occur on a regular frequency. Liquidation of these investments would require sale of the partnership interest.

Structured Credit

Structured credit investments are alternative investments comprised of collateralized debt obligations and other structured credit investments that are priced based on valuations provided by independent, third-party pricing agents, if available. Such values generally reflect the last reported sales price if the security is actively traded. The third-party pricing agents may also value structured credit investments at an evaluated bid price by employing methodologies that utilize actual market transactions, broker-supplied valuations, or other methodologies designed to identify the market value of such securities. Such methodologies generally consider such factors as security prices, yields, maturities, call features, ratings and developments relating to specific securities in arriving at valuations. Securities listed on a securities exchange, market or automated quotation system for which quotations are readily available are valued at the last quoted sale price on the primary exchange or market on which they are traded. Debt obligations with remaining maturities of 60 days or less may be valued at amortized cost, which approximates fair value.

Structured credit investments are valued monthly and recorded on a one-month lag. For alternative investment values reported on a lag, current market information is reviewed for any material changes in values at the reporting date. Redemption requests are considered quarterly subject to notice of 90 days; however, share repurchases are not permitted for a two-year lock-up period following each investment, which will expire in September 2010 for the plans' initial investments.

Real Estate

The real estate portfolio is an alternative investment comprised of three funds with strategic categories of real estate investments. All real estate holdings are externally appraised at least annually, and appraisals are conducted by reputable, independent appraisal firms that are members of the Appraisal Institute. All external appraisals are performed in accordance with the Uniform Standards of Professional Appraisal Practices. The property valuations and assumptions of each property are reviewed quarterly by the investment advisor and values are adjusted if there has been a significant change in circumstances relating to the property since the last external appraisal. The valuation methodology utilized in determining the fair value is consistent with the best practices prevailing within the real estate appraisal and real estate investment management industries, including the Real Estate Information Standards, and standards promulgated by the National Council of Real Estate Investment Fiduciaries, the National Association of Real Estate Investment Fiduciaries, and the National Association of Real Estate Managers. In addition, the investment advisor may cause additional appraisals to be performed. Two of the funds' fair values are updated monthly, and there is no lag in reported values. Redemption requests for these two funds are considered on a quarterly basis, subject to notice of 45 days.

Effective October 1, 2009, one of the real estate funds began an orderly wind-down over the next three to four years. The decision to wind down the fund was driven primarily by real estate market factors that adversely affected the availability of new investor capital. Third-party appraisals of this fund's assets will be eliminated; however, internal valuation updates for all assets and liabilities of the fund will be prepared quarterly. The fund's asset values are recorded on a one-quarter lag, and current market information is reviewed for any material changes in values at the reporting date. Distributions from sales of properties will be made on a pro-rata basis. Repurchase requests will not be honored during the wind-down period.

The following represents the effect of fair value measurements using significant unobservable inputs (Level 3) on changes in plan assets for the year ended December 31, 2009:

	2009				
(In millions)	Hedge Funds	Private Equity Funds	Structured Credit Fund	Real Estate	Total
Beginning balance—January 1, 2009	$69.3	$21.0	$15.9	$23.5	$129.7
Actual return on plan assets:					
Relating to assets still held at the reporting date	2.1	(5.6)	23.2	(9.5)	10.2
Relating to assets sold during the period	—	(0.5)	—	0.6	0.1
Purchases, sales and settlements	—	3.3	—	(0.2)	3.1
Transfers in (out) of Level 3	—	—	—	—	—
Ending balance—December 31, 2009	$71.4	$18.2	$39.1	$14.4	$143.1

The pension plan assets and asset allocation at December 31, 2008 were as follows:

($ in millions)	Assets at December 31, 2008	Percentage of Plan Assets at December 31, 2008
Asset category[1]		
Equity securities	$163.3	35.8%
Fixed income	149.6	32.8
Hedge funds	69.2	15.2
Private equity	33.9	7.4
Structured credit	15.8	3.5
Real estate	23.5	5.2
Cash	0.7	0.1
Total	$456.0	100.0%

[1] The 2008 presentation has been conformed in accordance with the asset categories presented for 2009.

The expected return on plan assets takes into account the weighted average of expected returns for each asset category. Expected returns are determined based on historical performance, adjusted for current trends. The expected return is net of investment expenses.

VEBA

Assets for other benefits include VEBA trusts pursuant to bargaining agreements that are available to fund retired employees' life insurance obligations and medical benefits. The fair values of our other benefit plan assets at December 31, 2009 by asset category are as follows:

	2009			
(In millions)	Quoted Prices in Active Markets for Identical Assets/Liabilities (Level 1)	Significant Other Observable Inputs (Level 2)	Significant Unobservable Inputs (Level 3)	Total
Asset category				
Equity securities:				
U.S. large-cap	$ 32.8	$—	$ —	$ 32.8
U.S. small/mid-cap	12.6	—	—	12.6
International	18.1	—	—	18.1
Fixed income	52.4	—	—	52.4
Hedge funds	—	—	14.6	14.6
Private equity	2.9	—	3.1	6.0
Cash	0.2	—	—	0.2
Total	$119.0	$—	$17.7	$136.7

Refer to the pension asset discussion above for further information regarding the inputs and valuation methodologies used to measure the fair value of each respective category of plan assets.

The following represents the effect of fair value measurements using significant unobservable inputs (Level 3) on changes in plan assets for the year ended December 31, 2009:

| (In millions) | 2009 | | |
	Hedge Funds	Private Equity Funds	Total
Beginning balance—January 1, 2009	$13.6	$ 3.0	$16.6
Actual return on plan assets:			
Relating to assets still held at the reporting date	0.5	(0.9)	(0.4)
Relating to assets sold during the period	—	—	—
Purchases, sales and settlements	0.5	1.0	1.5
Transfers in (out) of Level 3	—	—	—
Ending balance—December 31, 2009	$14.6	$ 3.1	$17.7

The other benefit plan assets and weighted average asset allocation at December 31, 2008 were as follows:

($ in millions)	Assets at December 31, 2008	Percentage of Plan Assets at December 31, 2008
Asset category[1]		
Equity securities	$38.3	41.8%
Fixed income	33.5	36.6
Hedge funds	13.6	14.8
Private equity	6.0	6.0
Cash	0.2	0.2
Total	$91.6	100.0%

[1] The 2008 presentation has been conformed in accordance with the asset categories presented for 2009.

The expected return on plan assets takes into account the weighted average of expected returns for each asset category. Expected returns are determined based on historical performance, adjusted for current trends. The expected return is net of investment expenses.

1.61

THE WASHINGTON POST COMPANY (DEC)

NOTES TO CONSOLIDATED FINANCIAL STATEMENTS

B (In Part): Summary of Significant Accounting Policies

Recently Adopted and Issued Accounting Pronouncements (In Part)

In December 2008, the FASB issued new guidance on an employer's disclosures about plan assets of a defined benefit pension or other postretirement plan. The additional disclosure requirements under this guidance include expanded disclosures about an entity's investment policies and strategies, the categories of plan assets, concentrations of credit risk and fair value measurements of plan assets. This new guidance is effective for fiscal years ending after December 15, 2009, and does not require comparative information for earlier periods presented. See Note L for additional disclosures following the implementation of this new guidance.

L (In Part): Pensions and Other Postretirement Plans

Defined Benefit Plan Assets

The Company's defined benefit pension obligations are funded by a portfolio made up of a relatively small number of stocks and high-quality fixed-income securities that are held by a third-party trustee. As of December 31, 2009 and December 31, 2008, the assets of the Company's pension plans were allocated as follows:

	Pension Plan Asset Allocations	
	2009	2008
U.S. equities	74%	73%
U.S. fixed income	18%	22%
International equities	8%	5%
Total	100%	100%

Essentially all of the assets are actively managed by two investment companies. The goal of the investment managers is to produce moderate long-term growth in the value of these assets, while protecting them against large decreases in value. Both of these managers may invest in a combination of equity and fixed-income securities and cash. The managers are not permitted to invest in securities of the Company or in alternative investments. The investment managers cannot invest more than 20% of the assets at the time of purchase in the stock of Berkshire Hathaway or more than 10% of the assets in the securities of any other single issuer, except for obligations of the U.S. Government, without receiving prior approval by the Plan administrator. As of December 31, 2009, up to 13% of the assets could be invested in international stocks, and no less than 9% of the assets could be invested in fixed-income securities. None of the assets is managed internally by the Company.

In determining the expected rate of return on plan assets, the Company considers the relative weighting of plan assets, the historical performance of total plan assets and individual asset classes and economic and other indicators of future performance. In addition, the Company may consult with and consider the input of financial and other professionals in developing appropriate return benchmarks.

The Company evaluated its defined benefit pension plans' asset portfolios for the existence of significant concentrations (defined as greater than 10% of plan assets) of credit risk as of January 3, 2010. Types of concentrations that were

evaluated include, but are not limited to, investment concentrations in a single entity, type of industry, foreign country and individual fund. Included in the assets are $274.3 million and $267.2 million of Berkshire Hathaway Class A and Class B common stock at December 31, 2009 and December 31, 2008, respectively. Approximately 41% of the Berkshire Hathaway common stock was subsequently sold in February 2010.

The following table presents the Company's pension plan assets using the fair value hierarchy as of January 3, 2010. The fair value hierarchy has three levels based on the reliability of the inputs used to determine fair value. Level 1 refers to fair values determined based on quoted prices in active markets for identical assets. Level 2 refers to fair values estimated using significant other observable inputs, and Level 3 includes fair values estimated using significant unobservable inputs.

(In thousands)	Level 1	Level 2	Level 3	Total
Cash equivalents and other short-term investments	$ 189,986	$42,419	$—	$ 232,405
Equity securities				
U.S. equities	1,061,957	—	—	1,061,957
International equities	115,153	—	—	115,153
Fixed-income securities				
Federal agency mortgage-backed securities	—	4,122	—	4,122
Corporate debt securities	—	17,270	—	17,270
Other fixed income	—	7,987	—	7,987
Total investments	$1,367,096	$71,798	$—	1,438,894
Cash				247
Receivables				1,675
Total				$1,440,816

Cash Equivalents and Other Short-Term Investments

These investments are primarily held in U.S Treasury securities and registered money market funds. These investments are valued using a market approach based on the quoted market prices of the security, or inputs that include quoted market prices for similar instruments, and are classified as either Level 1 or Level 2 in the valuation hierarchy.

U.S. Equities

These investments are held in common and preferred stock of U.S. and non-U.S. corporations traded on U.S. exchanges. Common and preferred shares are traded actively on exchanges, and price quotes for these shares are readily available. These investments are classified as Level 1 in the valuation hierarchy.

International Equities

These investments are held in common and preferred stock issued by non-U.S. corporations. Common and preferred shares are traded actively on exchanges, and price quotes for these shares are readily available. These investments are classified as Level 1 in the valuation hierarchy.

Federal Agency Mortgage-Backed Securities

These investments consist of fixed-income securities issued by Federal Agencies and are valued using a bid evaluation process, with bid data provided by independent pricing

sources. These investments are classified as Level 2 in the valuation hierarchy.

Corporate Debt Securities

These investments consist of fixed-income securities issued by U.S. corporations and are valued using a bid evaluation process, with bid data provided by independent pricing sources. These investments are classified as Level 2 in the valuation hierarchy.

Other Fixed Income

These investments consist of fixed-income securities issued in private placements and are valued using a bid evaluation process, with bid data provided by independent pricing sources. These investments are classified as Level 2 in the valuation hierarchy.

Financial Instruments With Debt and Equity Characteristics

1.62

INTEL CORPORATION (DEC)

NOTES TO CONSOLIDATED FINANCIAL STATEMENTS

Note 3 (In Part): Accounting Changes

2009

In the first quarter of 2009, we adopted new standards that changed the accounting for convertible debt instruments with cash settlement features. As of adoption, these new standards applied to our junior subordinated convertible debentures issued in 2005 (the 2005 debentures). Under the previous standards, our 2005 debentures were recognized entirely as a liability at historical value. In accordance with adopting these new standards, we retrospectively recognized both a liability and an equity component of the 2005 debentures at fair value. The liability component is recognized as the fair value of a similar instrument that does not have a conversion feature at issuance. The equity component, which is the value of the conversion feature at issuance, is recognized as the difference between the proceeds from the issuance of the 2005 debentures and the fair value of the liability component, after adjusting for the deferred tax impact. The 2005 debentures were issued at a coupon rate of 2.95%, which was below that of a similar instrument that did not have a conversion feature (6.45%). Therefore, the valuation of the debt component, using the income approach, resulted in a debt discount. The debt discount is reduced over the expected life of the debt, which is also the stated life of the debt. These new standards are also applicable in accounting for our convertible debt issued during 2009. See "Note 20: Borrowings" for further discussion.

As a result of applying these new standards retrospectively to all periods presented, we recognized the following incremental effects on individual line items on the consolidated balance sheets:

(In millions)	2008 Before Adoption	Adjustments	After Adoption
Property, plant and equipment, net	$17,544	$ 30	$17,574
Other long-term assets[1]	$ 6,092	$(273)	$ 5,819
Long-term debt	$ 1,886	$(701)	$ 1,185
Common stock and capital in excess of par value	$12,944	$ 458	$13,402

[1] Primarily related to the adjustment made to the net deferred tax asset.

The adoption of these new standards did not result in a change to our prior-period consolidated statements of operations, as the interest associated with our debt issuances is capitalized and added to the cost of qualified assets. The adoption of these new standards did not result in a significant change to depreciation expense or earnings per common share for 2009.

Note 20 (In Part): Borrowings

Long-Term Debt (In Part)

Our long-term debt as of December 26, 2009 and December 27, 2008 was as follows:

(In millions)	2009	2008[1]
2009 junior subordinated convertible debentures due 2039 at 3.25%	$1,030	$ —
2005 junior subordinated convertible debentures due 2035 at 2.95%	896	886
2005 Arizona bonds due 2035 at 4.375%	157	158
2007 Arizona bonds due 2037 at 5.3%	123	122
Other debt	—	21
	2,206	1,187
Less: current portion of long-term debt	(157)	(2)
Total long-term debt	$2,049	$1,185

[1] As adjusted due to changes to the accounting for convertible debt instruments. See "Note 3: Accounting Changes."

Convertible Debentures

In 2005, we issued $1.6 billion of junior subordinated convertible debentures (the 2005 debentures) due in 2035. In 2009, we issued $2.0 billion of junior subordinated convertible debentures (the 2009 debentures) due in 2039. Both the 2005 and 2009 debentures pay a fixed rate of interest semiannually. We capitalized all interest associated with these debentures during the periods presented.

	2005 Debentures	2009 Debentures
Coupon interest rate	2.95%	3.25%
Effective interest rate[1]	6.45%	7.20%
Maximum amount of contingent interest that will accrue per year[2]	0.40%	0.50%

[1] The effective rate is based on the rate for a similar instrument that does not have a conversion feature.

[2] Both the 2005 and 2009 debentures have a contingent interest component that will require us to pay interest based on certain thresholds and for certain events commencing on December 15, 2010 and August 1, 2019, for the 2005 and 2009 debentures, respectively, as outlined in the indentures governing the 2005 and 2009 debentures. The fair value of the related embedded derivative was $24 million and $15 million as of December 26, 2009 for the 2005 and 2009 debentures, respectively ($36 million as of December 27, 2008 for the 2005 debentures).

Both the 2005 and 2009 debentures are convertible, subject to certain conditions, into shares of our common stock. Holders can surrender the 2005 debentures for conversion at any time. Holders can surrender the 2009 debentures for conversion if the closing price of Intel common stock has been at least 130% of the conversion price then in effect for at least 20 trading days during the 30 trading-day period ending on the last trading day of the preceding fiscal quarter. We can settle any conversion or repurchase of the 2005 debentures in cash or stock at our option. However, we will settle any conversion or repurchase of the 2009 debentures in cash up to the face value, and any amount in excess of face value will be settled in cash or stock at our option. On or after December 15, 2012, we can redeem, for cash, all or part of the 2005 debentures for the principal amount, plus any accrued and unpaid interest, if the closing price of Intel common stock has been at least 130% of the conversion price then in effect for at least 20 trading days during any 30 consecutive trading-day period prior to the date on which we provide notice of redemption. On or after August 5, 2019, we can redeem, for cash, all or part of the 2009 debentures for the principal amount, plus any accrued and unpaid interest, if the closing price of Intel common stock has been at least 150% of the conversion price then in effect for at least 20 trading days during any 30 consecutive trading-day period prior to the date on which we provide notice of redemption. If certain events occur in the future, the indentures governing the 2005 and 2009 debentures provide that each holder of the debentures can, for a pre-defined period of time, require us to repurchase the holder's debentures for the principal amount plus any accrued and unpaid interest. Both the 2005 and 2009 debentures are subordinated in right of payment to our existing and future senior debt and to the other liabilities of our subsidiaries. We have concluded that both the 2005 and 2009 debentures are not conventional convertible debt instruments and that the embedded stock conversion options qualify as derivatives. In addition, we have concluded that the embedded conversion options would be classified in stockholders' equity if they were freestanding derivative instruments. As such, the embedded conversion options are not accounted for separately as derivatives.

(In millions, except per share amounts)	2005 Debentures		2009 Debentures
	2009	2008	2009
Outstanding principal	$1,600	$1,600	$2,000
Equity component carrying amount	$ 466	$ 466	$ 613
Unamortized discount[1]	$ 691	$ 701	$ 953
Net debt carrying amount	$ 896	$ 886	$1,030
Conversion rate (shares of common stock per $1,000 principal amount of debentures)[2]	32.12	31.72	44.09
Effective conversion price (per share of common stock)	$31.14	$31.53	$22.68

[1] The remaining amortization periods for the 2005 and 2009 debentures are approximately 26 and 30 years, respectively, as of December 26, 2009.

[2] The conversion rate adjusts for certain events outlined in the indentures governing the 2005 and 2009 debentures, such as quarterly dividend distributions in excess of $0.10 and $0.14 per share, for the 2005 and 2009 debentures, respectively, but does not adjust for accrued interest. In addition, the conversion rate will increase for a holder of either the 2005 or 2009 debentures who elects to convert the debentures in connection with certain share exchanges, mergers, or consolidations involving Intel, as described in the indentures governing the 2005 and 2009 debentures.

As of December 26, 2009, our aggregate debt maturities based on outstanding principal were as follows (in millions):

Year Payable	
2010	$ 157
2011	—
2012	—
2013	—
2014	—
2015 and thereafter	3,725
Total	$3,882

Substantially all of the difference between the total aggregate debt maturities above and the total carrying amount of our debt is due to the equity component of our convertible debentures.

Derivatives

1.63

HORMEL FOODS CORPORATION (OCT)

Note A (In Part): Summary of Significant Accounting Policies

Accounting Changes and Recent Accounting Pronouncements (In Part)

In March 2008, the FASB issued an update to ASC 815, *Derivatives and Hedging* (ASC 815). The update amends and expands the disclosure requirements previously required for derivative instruments and hedging activities. ASC 815 requires qualitative disclosures about objectives and strategies for using derivatives, quantitative disclosures about fair value amounts of gains and losses on derivative instruments, and disclosures about credit-risk-related contingent features in derivative agreements. The updated guidance was effective for financial statements issued for fiscal years and interim periods beginning after November 15, 2008. The Company adopted the updated provisions of ASC 815 in the second quarter of fiscal 2009, and the required disclosures are provided in Note J—Derivatives and Hedging. Adoption did not impact consolidated net earnings, cash flows, or financial position.

Note J. Derivatives and Hedging

The Company uses hedging programs to manage price risk associated with commodity purchases. These programs utilize futures contracts and swaps to manage the Company's exposure to price fluctuations in the commodities markets. The Company has determined its hedge programs to be highly effective in offsetting the changes in fair value or cash flows generated by the items hedged.

Cash Flow Hedges

The Company utilizes corn and soybean meal futures to offset the price fluctuation in the Company's future direct grain purchases, and has entered into various swaps to hedge the purchases of grain and natural gas at certain plant locations. The financial instruments are designated and accounted for as cash flow hedges, and the Company measures the effectiveness of the hedges on a regular basis. Effective gains or losses related to these cash flow hedges are reported in accumulated other comprehensive loss and reclassified into earnings, through cost of products sold, in the period or periods in which the hedged transactions affect earnings. Any gains or losses related to hedge ineffectiveness are recognized in the current period cost of products sold. The Company typically does not hedge its grain exposure beyond 24 months and its natural gas exposure beyond 36 months. As of October 25, 2009, the Company had the following outstanding commodity futures contracts and swaps that were entered into to hedge forecasted purchases:

Commodity	Volume
Corn	20.3 million bushels
Soybean meal	148,100 tons
Natural gas	4.6 million MMBTU's

As of October 25, 2009, the Company has included in accumulated other comprehensive loss, hedging losses of $19.2 million (before tax) relating to its positions. The Company expects to recognize the majority of these losses over the next 12 months.

Fair Value Hedges

The Company utilizes futures to minimize the price risk assumed when forward priced contracts are offered to the Company's commodity suppliers. The intent of the program is to make the forward priced commodities cost nearly the same as cash market purchases at the date of delivery. The futures contracts are designated and accounted for as fair value hedges, and the Company measures the effectiveness of the hedges on a regular basis. Changes in the fair value of the futures contracts, along with the gain or loss on the hedged purchase commitment, are marked-to-market through earnings and are recorded on the Consolidated Statement of Financial Position as a current asset and liability, respectively. Effective gains or losses related to these fair value hedges are recognized through cost of products sold in the period or periods in which the hedged transactions affect earnings. Any gains or losses related to hedge ineffectiveness are recognized in the current period cost of products sold. As of October 25, 2009, the Company had the following outstanding commodity futures contracts designated as fair value hedges:

Commodity	Volume
Corn	12.0 million bushels
Soybean meal	6,200 tons
Lean hogs	1.3 million cwt

Other Derivatives

During fiscal 2009, the Company has held certain futures contract positions as part of a merchandising program and to manage the Company's exposure to fluctuations in foreign currencies. The Company has not applied hedge accounting to these positions. All foreign exchange contracts were closed as of the end of the third quarter. As of October 25, 2009, the Company had the following outstanding commodity futures contracts related to its merchandising program:

Commodity	Volume
Pork bellies	14,800 cwt

Fair Values

The fair values of the Company's derivative instruments (in thousands) as of October 25, 2009, were as follows:

	2009	
	Location on Consolidated Statement of Financial Position	Fair Value[1]
Asset derivatives:		
Derivatives designated as hedges:		
Commodity contracts	Other current assets	$25,159
Derivatives not designated as hedges:		
Commodity contracts	Other current assets	(3,702)
Total asset derivatives		$21,457
Liability derivatives:		
Derivatives designated as hedges:		
Commodity contracts	Accounts payable	$17,563
Total liability derivatives		$17,563

[1] Amounts represent the gross fair value of derivative assets and liabilities. The Company nets its derivative assets and liabilities, including cash collateral, when a master netting arrangement exists between the Company and the counterparty to the derivative contract.

Derivative Gains and Losses

Gains or losses (before tax, in thousands) related to the Company's derivative instruments for the fiscal year ended October 25, 2009, were as follows:

Cash Flow Hedges	Gain/(Loss) Recognized in Accumulated Other Comprehensive Loss (AOCL) (Effective Portion)[1]	Location on Consolidated Statement of Operations	Gain/(Loss) Reclassified From AOCL into Earnings (Effective Portion)[1]	Gain/(Loss) Recognized in Earnings (Ineffective Portion)[2][4]
Commodity contracts	$(8,323)	Cost of products sold	$(55,053)	$2,082

Fair Value Hedges		Location on Consolidated Statement of Operations	Gain/(Loss) Recognized in Earnings (Effective Portion)[3]	Gain/(Loss) Recognized in Earnings (Ineffective Portion)[2][5]
Commodity contracts		Cost of products sold	$55,879	$(2,901)

Derivatives Not Designated as Hedges		Location on Consolidated Statement of Operations		Gain/(Loss) Recognized in Earnings
Commodity contracts		Cost of products sold		$ 414
Foreign exchange contracts		Interest and investment income (loss)		$(141)

[1] Amounts represent gains or losses in AOCL before tax.
[2] There were no gains or losses excluded from the assessment of hedge effectiveness during the fiscal year.
[3] Gains on commodity contracts designated as fair value hedges were offset by a corresponding loss on the underlying hedged purchase commitment.
[4] There were no gains or losses resulting from the discontinuance of cash flow hedges during the fiscal year.
[5] There were no gains or losses recognized as a result of a hedged firm commitment no longer qualifying as a fair value hedge during the fiscal year.

Earnings Per Share Calculation

1.64

RAYTHEON COMPANY (DEC)

NOTES TO CONSOLIDATED FINANCIAL STATEMENTS

Note 2 (In Part): Accounting Standards

In 2009, we adopted required new accounting standards related to the following:
- The accounting and disclosure of noncontrolling interests as discussed in Note 7;
- The disclosure of derivative instruments and hedging activities as discussed in Note 8;
- The accounting and disclosure of certain nonfinancial assets and liabilities not recognized or disclosed at fair value on a recurring basis, as discussed in Note 9;
- The earnings per share (EPS) impact of instruments granted in share-based payment transactions as discussed in Note 12;
- The disclosure of postretirement benefit plan assets as discussed in Note 14; and

- The accounting for business combinations, which we have applied prospectively to business combinations with acquisition dates after January 1, 2009.

Note 12 (In Part): Stockholders' Equity

Earnings Per Share (EPS)

We compute Basic EPS *attributable* to Raytheon Company common stockholders by dividing income from continuing operations attributable to Raytheon Company common stockholders, income from discontinued operations attributable to Raytheon Company common stockholders and net income attributable to Raytheon Company, by the weighted-average common shares outstanding, including participating securities outstanding as discussed below, during the period. Diluted EPS reflects the potential dilution beyond shares for basic EPS that could occur if securities or other contracts to issue common stock were exercised, converted into common stock or resulted in the issuance of common stock that would have shared in our earnings. We compute basic and diluted EPS using income from continuing operations attributable to Raytheon Company common stockholders, income from discontinued operations attributable to Raytheon Company common stockholders, net income attributable to Raytheon Company, and the actual weighted-average shares and participating securities outstanding rather than the numbers presented within our consolidated statements of operations, which are rounded to the nearest million. As a result, it may not be possible to recalculate EPS as presented in our consolidated statements of operations. Furthermore, it may not be possible to recalculate EPS attributable to Raytheon Company stockholders by adjusting EPS from continuing operations by EPS from discontinued operations.

In 2009, we adopted the required new accounting standard related to whether instruments granted in share-based payment transactions are participating securities. This accounting standard requires us to include all unvested stock awards which contain non-forfeitable rights to dividends or dividend equivalents, whether paid or unpaid, in the number of shares outstanding in our basic and diluted EPS calculations. As a result, we have included all of our outstanding unvested restricted stock and the LTPP awards that meet the retirement eligible criteria in our calculation of basic and diluted EPS for current and prior periods. Additionally, the accounting standard requires disclosure of EPS for common stock and unvested share-based payment awards, separately disclosing distributed and undistributed earnings. Distributed earnings represent common stock dividends and dividends earned on unvested share-based payment awards of retirement eligible employees. Undistributed earnings represent earnings that were available for distribution but were not distributed. Common stock and unvested share-based payment awards earn dividends equally as shown in the table below.

EPS from continuing operations attributable to Raytheon Company common stockholders and unvested share-based payment awards was as follows:

	2009	2008	2007
Basic EPS attributable to Raytheon Company common stockholders:			
Distributed earnings	$1.23	$1.11	$1.01
Undistributed earnings	3.73	2.90	2.85
Total	$4.96	$4.01	$3.86
Diluted EPS attributable to Raytheon Company common stockholders:			
Distributed earnings	$1.21	$1.09	$0.99
Undistributed earnings	3.68	2.84	2.79
Total	$4.89	$3.93	$3.78

EPS from discontinued operations attributable to Raytheon Company common stockholders and unvested share-based payment awards was as follows:

	2009	2008	2007
Basic EPS attributable to Raytheon Company common stockholders:			
Distributed earnings	$—	$ —	$ —
Undistributed earnings (loss)	—	(0.01)	2.02
Total	$—	$(0.01)	$2.02
Diluted EPS attributable to Raytheon Company common stockholders:			
Distributed earnings	$—	$ —	$ —
Undistributed earnings (loss)	—	(0.01)	1.97
Total	$—	$(0.01)	$1.97

EPS attributable to Raytheon Company common stockholders and unvested share-based payment awards was as follows:

	2009	2008	2007
Basic EPS attributable to Raytheon Company common stockholders:			
Distributed earnings	$1.23	$1.11	$1.01
Undistributed earnings	3.73	2.90	4.87
Total	$4.96	$4.01	$5.88
Diluted EPS attributable to Raytheon Company common stockholders:			
Distributed earnings	$1.21	$1.09	$0.99
Undistributed earnings	3.68	2.83	4.76
Total	$4.89	$3.92	$5.75

The amount of income from continuing operations attributable to participating securities was $29 million, $23 million and $22 million for 2009, 2008 and 2007, respectively. The amount of (loss) income from discontinued operations attributable to participating securities was a loss of less than $1 million for 2009 and 2008 and income of $11 million for 2007. The amount of net income attributable to participating securities was $29 million, $23 million and $33 million for 2009, 2008 and 2007, respectively.

The weighted-average shares outstanding for basic and diluted EPS were as follows:

(In millions)	2009	2008	2007
Shares for basic EPS (including 5.9, 5.7 and 5.6 participating securities for 2009, 2008 and 2007, respectively)	390.4	417.2	438.6
Dilutive effect of stock options and LTPP	3.1	5.1	5.7
Dilutive effect of warrants	2.2	4.2	4.1
Shares for diluted EPS	395.7	426.5	448.4

Stock options to purchase the following number of shares of common stock had exercise prices that were less than the average market price of our common stock during the applicable year and were included in our calculations of diluted EPS:

(In millions)	2009	2008	2007
Stock options	8.7	10.1	14.0

Stock options to purchase the following number of shares of common stock were not included in our calculations of diluted EPS, as the effect of including them would be anti-dilutive:

(In millions)	2009	2008	2007
Stock options	—	2.4	3.1

Our Board of Directors is authorized to issue up to 200 million shares of preferred stock, $0.01 par value per share, in multiple series with terms as determined by our Board of Directors. There were no shares of preferred stock outstanding at December 31, 2009 and December 31, 2008.

In June 2006, we issued 12.0 million warrants to purchase our common stock, of which 12.0 million were outstanding at

December 31, 2009, 2008 and 2007. These warrants, expiring in 2011, were issued with an exercise price of $37.50 per share and have been included in the calculation of diluted EPS.

Inventories

1.65

SILGAN HOLDINGS INC. (DEC)

NOTES TO CONSOLIDATED FINANCIAL STATEMENTS

Note 1 (In Part): Summary of Significant Accounting Policies

Change in Accounting Method

In the fourth quarter of 2009, we changed our method of valuing the inventory of the U.S. plastic container business from the last in, first out, or LIFO, method to the first in, first out, or FIFO, method. We believe the FIFO method of inventory valuation is preferable for our plastic container business because FIFO provides a better matching of revenues to expenses due to a lag in the pass through of changes in resin costs to customers and enhances the comparability of results to our peers. As a result of this change, all prior period amounts have been retrospectively adjusted as of the beginning of the earliest period presented. See Note 4 for further information.

Note 4. Inventories

The components of inventories at December 31 are as follows:

(Dollars in thousands)	2009	2008
Raw materials	$100,578	$110,480
Work-in-process	82,402	72,078
Finished goods	268,804	238,515
Other	14,334	14,057
	466,118	435,130
Adjustment to value domestic inventory at cost on the LIFO method	(78,904)	(57,412)
	$387,214	$377,718

Inventories include $68.6 million and $71.6 million recorded on the FIFO method at December 31, 2009 and 2008, respectively, and $65.1 million and $65.2 million recorded on the average cost method at December 31, 2009 and 2008, respectively.

Historically, the inventory value for our U.S. plastic container business was determined using the LIFO method of accounting. During the fourth quarter of 2009, we determined that the FIFO method of accounting was preferable for our plastic container business because FIFO provides a better matching of revenues to expenses due to a lag in the pass through of changes in resin costs to our customers and enhances the comparability of results to our peers. As a result, we changed the accounting method to value inventory of our U.S. plastic container business to the FIFO method. We have retrospectively adjusted all prior amounts as of the beginning of the earliest period presented. As a result of this retrospective adjustment, retained earnings at January 1, 2007 increased $3.1 million.

We have summarized the effects of this retrospective adjustment on our consolidated financial statements below (dollars in thousands, except per share amounts):

	2008		2007	
	As Reported	As Adjusted	As Reported	As Adjusted
Consolidated statements of income for the years ended December 31:				
Cost of goods sold	$2,683,466	$2,694,441	$2,509,336	$2,502,712
Provision for income taxes	72,922	68,582	70,422	73,042
Net income	131,627	124,992	122,779	126,783
Basic net income per share	$ 3.47	$ 3.30	$ 3.26	$ 3.37
Diluted net income per share	$ 3.44	$ 3.26	$ 3.22	$ 3.32
Consolidated balance sheets as of December 31:				
Inventories	$ 376,986	$ 377,718	$ 412,458	$ 424,165
Accrued liabilities	41,046	41,333	34,028	38,655
Retained earnings	497,732	498,177	392,108	399,188
Consolidated statements of cash flows for the years ended December 31:				
Change in inventories	$ 37,923	$ 48,898	$ 11,451	$ 4,827
Change in accrued liabilities	(3,458)	(7,798)	(10,079)	(7,459)

Had we not made this change in accounting method, cost of goods sold for the year ended December 31, 2009 would have been $2.3 million higher, provision for income taxes would have been $0.9 million lower and net income would have been $1.4 million lower than reported in our Consolidated Statements of Income. In addition, basic net income per share would have been $0.04 lower and diluted net income per share would have been $0.03 lower.

Revenue Recognition

1.66

HEWLETT-PACKARD COMPANY (OCT)

NOTES TO CONSOLIDATED FINANCIAL STATEMENTS

Note 1 (In Part): Summary of Significant Accounting Policies

Revenue Recognition

Net revenue is derived primarily from the sale of products and services. The following revenue recognition policies define the manner in which HP accounts for sales transactions.

HP recognizes revenue when persuasive evidence of a sales arrangement exists, delivery has occurred or services are rendered, the sales price or fee is fixed or determinable and collectibility is reasonably assured. Additionally, HP recognizes hardware revenue on sales to channel partners, including resellers, distributors or value-added solution providers at the time of sale and when the channel partners have economic substance apart from HP and HP has completed its obligations related to the sale.

In October 2009, the FASB issued Accounting Standards Update ("ASU") No. 2009-13, "Multiple-Deliverable Revenue Arrangements" ("ASU 2009-13"). The new standard changes the requirements for establishing separate units of accounting in a multiple element arrangement and requires the allocation of arrangement consideration to each deliverable to be based on the relative selling price. Concurrently to issuing ASU 2009-13, the FASB also issued ASU No. 2009-14, "Certain Revenue Arrangements That Include Software Elements" ("ASU 2009-14"). ASU 2009-14 excludes software that is contained on a tangible product from the scope of software revenue guidance if the software is essential to the tangible product's functionality.

HP early adopted these standards as of the beginning of fiscal 2009 for new and materially modified deals originating after November 1, 2008; therefore, the previously reported quarterly results have been restated to reflect the impact of adoption. As a result of the adoption, fiscal 2009 net revenues and net earnings were higher by $255 million and $55 million, respectively. The impact was due to the recognition of revenue previously deferred for certain deliverables bundled in multiple element arrangements where the arrangements also included services for which HP was unable to demonstrate fair value pursuant to the previous standards. The new standards allow for deliverables for which revenue was previously deferred to be separated and recognized as delivered, rather than over the longest service delivery period as a single unit with other elements in the arrangement. HP is not able to reasonably estimate the effect of adopting these standards on future financial periods as the impact will vary based on the nature and volume of new or materially modified deals in any given period.

For fiscal 2009 and future periods, pursuant to the guidance of ASU 2009-13, when a sales arrangement contains multiple elements, such as hardware and software products, licenses and/or services, HP allocates revenue to each element based on a selling price hierarchy. The selling price for a deliverable is based on its vendor specific objective evidence ("VSOE") if available, third party evidence ("TPE") if VSOE is not available, or estimated selling price ("ESP") if neither VSOE nor TPE is available. In multiple element arrangements where more-than-incidental software deliverables are included, revenue is allocated to each separate unit of accounting for each of the non-software deliverables and to the software deliverables as a group using the relative selling prices of each of the deliverables in the arrangement based on the aforementioned selling price hierarchy. If the arrangement contains more than one software deliverable, the arrangement consideration allocated to the software deliverables as a group is then allocated to each software deliverable using the guidance for recognizing software revenue, as amended.

HP limits the amount of revenue recognition for delivered elements to the amount that is not contingent on the future delivery of products or services, future performance obligations or subject to customer-specified return or refund privileges.

HP evaluates each deliverable in an arrangement to determine whether they represent separate units of accounting. A deliverable constitutes a separate unit of accounting when it has standalone value and there are no customer-negotiated refund or return rights for the delivered elements. If the arrangement includes a customer-negotiated refund or return right relative to the delivered item and the delivery and performance of the undelivered item is considered probable and substantially in HP's control, the delivered element constitutes a separate unit of accounting. In instances when the aforementioned criteria are not met, the deliverable is combined with the undelivered elements and the allocation of the arrangement consideration and revenue recognition is determined for the combined unit as a single unit. Allocation of the consideration is determined at arrangement inception on the basis of each unit's relative selling price.

HP establishes VSOE of selling price using the price charged for a deliverable when sold separately and, in rare instances, using the price established by management having the relevant authority. TPE of selling price is established by evaluating largely similar and interchangeable competitor products or services in standalone sales to similarly situated customers. The best estimate of selling price is established considering internal factors such as margin objectives, pricing practices and controls, customer segment pricing strategies and the product lifecycle. Consideration is also given to market conditions such as competitor pricing strategies and industry technology lifecycles.

For fiscal 2008 and fiscal 2007, pursuant to the previous guidance of revenue arrangements with multiple deliverables, for a sales arrangement with multiple elements, HP allocated revenue to each element based on its relative fair value, or for software, based on VSOE of fair value. In the absence of fair value for a delivered element, HP first allocated revenue to the fair value of the undelivered elements and the residual revenue to the delivered elements. Where the fair value for an undelivered element could not be determined, HP deferred revenue for the delivered elements until the undelivered elements were delivered or the fair value was determinable for the remaining undelivered elements. If the revenue for a delivered item was not recognized because it was not separable from the undelivered item, then HP also deferred the cost of the delivered item. HP limited the amount of revenue recognition for delivered elements to the amount that was not contingent on the future delivery of products or services, future performance obligations or subject to customer-specified return or refund privileges. For the purposes of income statement classification of products and services revenue, when HP could not determine fair value for all of the elements in an arrangement and the transaction was accounted for as a single unit of accounting, HP allocated revenue to products and services based on a rational and consistent methodology. This methodology utilized external and internal pricing inputs to derive HP's best estimate of fair value for the elements in the arrangement.

In instances when revenue is derived from sales of third-party vendor services, revenue is recorded at gross when HP is a principal to the transaction and net of costs when HP is acting as an agent between the customer and the vendor. Several factors are considered to determine whether HP is an agent or principal, most notably whether HP is the primary obligator to the customer, has established its own pricing, and has inventory and credit risks.

HP reports revenue net of any required taxes collected from customers and remitted to government authorities, with the collected taxes recorded as current liabilities until remitted to the relevant government authority.

Depreciation Method

1.67

VULCAN MATERIALS COMPANY (DEC)

NOTES TO CONSOLIDATED FINANCIAL STATEMENTS

Note 1 (In Part): Summary of Significant Accounting Policies

Depreciation, Depletion, Accretion and Amortization (In Part)
Depreciation is generally computed by the straight-line method at rates based on the estimated service lives of the various classes of assets, which include machinery and equipment (3 to 30 years), buildings (10 to 20 years) and land improvements (7 to 20 years).

Effective September 1, 2009, we changed our method of depreciation for our Newberry, Florida cement production facilities from straight-line to unit-of-production. We consider the change of depreciation method a change in accounting estimate effected by a change in accounting principle to be accounted for prospectively. The unit-of-production depreciation method is grounded on the assumption that depreciation of these assets is primarily a function of usage. The change to a unit-of-production method was based on information obtained by continued observation of the pattern of benefits derived from the cement plant assets and is preferable to a straight-line method as it results in depreciation that is more reflective of consumption of the assets. The effects of the partial year change in depreciation method increased 2009 earnings from continuing operations and net income by approximately $1,026,000, or $0.01 per basic and diluted

share when compared to the results using the straight-line method.

Estimated Useful Lives

1.68

KIMBALL INTERNATIONAL, INC. (JUN)

NOTES TO CONSOLIDATED FINANCIAL STATEMENTS

Note 1 (In Part): Summary of Significant Accounting Policies

Goodwill and Other Intangible Assets (In Part)
During fiscal year 2009, the Company performed an assessment of the useful lives of Enterprise Resource Planning (ERP) software. In evaluating useful lives, the Company considered how long assets would remain functionally efficient and effective, given levels of technology, competitive factors, and the economic environment as of fiscal year 2009. This assessment indicated that the assets will continue to be used for a longer period than previously anticipated. As a result, effective October 1, 2008, the Company revised the useful lives of ERP software from 7 years to 10 years. Changes in estimates are accounted for on a prospective basis, by amortizing assets' current carrying values over their revised remaining useful lives. The effect of this change in estimate, compared to the original amortization, for fiscal year 2009 was a pre-tax reduction in amortization expense of, in thousands, $1,402. The pre-tax (decrease) increase to amortization expense in future periods is expected to be, in thousands, ($1,227), ($299), $451, $911, and $664 in the five years ending June 30, 2014, and $902 thereafter.

Internal-use software is stated at cost less accumulated amortization and is amortized using the straight-line method. During the software application development stage, capitalized costs include external consulting costs, cost of software licenses, and internal payroll and payroll-related costs for employees who are directly associated with a software project. Upgrades and enhancements are capitalized if they result in added functionality which enable the software to perform tasks it was previously incapable of performing. Software maintenance, training, data conversion, and business process reengineering costs are expensed in the period in which they are incurred.

CONSOLIDATION POLICIES

1.69 FASB ASC 810, *Consolidation*, states in part:

1. The purpose of consolidated financial statements is to present, primarily for the benefit of the owners and creditors of the parent, the results of operations and the financial position of a parent and all its subsidiaries as if the consolidated group were a single economic entity. There is a presumption that consolidated financial statements are more meaningful than separate financial statements and that they are usually necessary for a fair presentation when one of the entities in the consolidated group directly or indirectly has a controlling financial interest in the other entities.

2. Consolidated financial statements shall disclose the consolidation policy that is being followed. In most cases, this can be made apparent by the headings or other information in the financial statements, but in other cases a footnote is required.

1.70 FASB ASC 810, *Consolidation*, requires the consolidation of subsidiaries having nonhomogenous operations. Consequently, with rare exception, the survey entities consolidate nonhomogenous operations. Table 1-9 shows the nature of nonhomogenous operations consolidated by the survey entities.

1.71 FASB ASC 810, *Consolidation*, clarifies the application of the general subsections of FASB ASC 810 to certain entities in which equity investors do not have the characteristics of a controlling financial interest or do not have sufficient equity at risk for the entity to finance its activities without additional subordinated financial support. FASB ASC 810 requires that consolidated financial statements include subsidiaries in which the reporting enterprise has a controlling financial interest, i.e., a majority voting interest. Application of the majority voting interest requirement to certain types of entities may not identify the party with a controlling financial interest because that interest may be achieved through other arrangements. Under FASB ASC 810, a reporting enterprise shall consolidate a variable interest entity if that reporting enterprise has a variable interest that will absorb a majority of the entity's expected losses, receive a majority of the entity's expected residual returns, or both. In determining whether it is a primary beneficiary of a variable interest entity, a reporting enterprise shall treat variable interests in that same entity held by the reporting enterprise's related parties as its own interest. FASB Accounting Standards Update (ASU) No. 2009-17, *Improvements to Financial Reporting by Enterprises Involved with Variable Interest Entities,* replaces the quantitative-based risks and rewards calculations for determining which reporting entity, if any, has a controlling financial interest in a variable interest entity with an approach focused on identifying which reporting entity has the power to direct the activities of a variable interest entity that most significantly impact the entity's economic performance and either has the obligation to absorb losses of the entity or the right to receive benefits from the entity. This approach that is expected to be primarily qualitative will be more effective for identifying which reporting entity has a controlling financial interest in a variable interest entity. FASB ASU No. 2009-17 also requires additional disclosures about a reporting entity's involvement in variable interest entities, which will enhance the information provided to users of financial statements. FASB ASU No. 2009-17 is effective for fiscal years beginning on or after November 15, 2009. Additionally, FASB ASU No. 2009-16, *Accounting for Transfers of Financial Assets,* eliminates from consolidation guidance the exception from consolidation of qualifying special purpose entities. FASB ASU No. 2009-16 is effective for fiscal years beginning on or after November 15, 2009.

1.72 FASB ASC 810, *Consolidation*, establishes accounting and reporting standards for the noncontrolling interest in a subsidiary and for the deconsolidation of a subsidiary. It clarifies that a noncontrolling interest in a subsidiary is an ownership interest in the consolidated entity that should be reported as equity in the consolidated financial statements. In addition, it changes the way the consolidated income statement is presented. The statement requires consolidated net income to be reported at amounts that include the amounts attributable to both the parent and the noncontrolling interest. It also requires disclosure, on the face of the consolidated statement of income, of the amounts of consolidated net income attributable to the parent and to the noncontrolling interest. Further, FASB ASC 810 requires that a change in a parent's ownership interest while the parent retains its controlling financial interest in its subsidiary shall be accounted for as equity transactions (investments by owners and distributions to owners acting in their capacity as owners). Therefore, no gain or loss shall be recognized in consolidated net income or comprehensive income. The carrying amount of the noncontrolling interest shall be adjusted to reflect the change in its ownership interest in the subsidiary. Any difference between the fair value of the consideration received or paid and the amount by which the noncontrolling interest is adjusted shall be recognized in equity attributable to the parent. When a change in a parent's ownership interest results in a deconsolidation of the subsidiary, the statement requires that a parent recognize a gain or loss in net income. If a parent retains a noncontrolling equity investment in the former subsidiary, that investment is measured at its fair value. The gain or loss on the deconsolidation of the subsidiary is measured using the fair value of the noncontrolling equity investment. Finally, FASB ASC 810 requires expanded disclosures in the consolidated financial statements that clearly identify and distinguish between the interests of the parent's owners and the interests of the noncontrolling owners of a subsidiary. Those expanded disclosures include a reconciliation of the beginning and ending balances of the equity attributable to the parent and the noncontrolling owners and a schedule showing the effects of changes in a parent's ownership interest in a subsidiary on the equity attributable to the parent.

1.73 Examples of consolidation practice disclosures follow.

1.74

TABLE 1-9: NONHOMOGENOUS OPERATIONS— CONSOLIDATED

| | Number of Entities | | | |
	2009	2008	2007	2006
Credit/Financing	36	31	53	66
Leasing	8	9	11	8
Insurance	6	7	10	15
Real estate	5	5	8	7

2008–2009 based on 500 entities surveyed; 2006–2007 based on 600 entities surveyed.

1.75

BRISTOL-MYERS SQUIBB COMPANY (DEC)

NOTES TO CONSOLIDATED FINANCIAL STATEMENTS

Note 1 (In Part): Accounting Policies

Basis of Consolidation

The consolidated financial statements, prepared in conformity with United States (U.S.) generally accepted accounting principles (GAAP), include the accounts of Bristol-Myers Squibb Company (which may be referred to as Bristol-Myers Squibb, BMS, or the Company) and all of its controlled majority-owned subsidiaries. All intercompany balances and transactions have been eliminated. Material subsequent events are evaluated and disclosed through the report issuance date, February 19, 2010.

Codevelopment, cocommercialization and license arrangements are entered into with other parties for various therapeutic areas, with terms including upfront licensing and contingent payments. These arrangements are assessed to determine whether the terms give economic or other control over the entity, which may require consolidation of the entity. Entities that are consolidated because they are controlled by means other than a majority voting interest are referred to as variable interest entities. Arrangements with material variable interest entities, including those associated with these codevelopment, cocommercialization and license arrangements, were determined not to exist.

Recently Issued Accounting Standards (In Part)

ASC 810-10-65-1, *Noncontrolling Interests in Consolidated Financial Statements—an amendment of ARB No. 51* (formerly SFAS No. 160, *Noncontrolling Interests in Consolidated Financial Statements—an amendment of ARB No. 51*) was adopted on January 1, 2009. As a result of adoption, the noncontrolling interest balance of $33 million, previously presented as $66 million of receivables and $33 million of noncurrent other liabilities, was presented as part of equity at December 31, 2008. Also, noncontrolling interest has been presented as a reconciling item in the consolidated statements of earnings, the consolidated statements of comprehensive income and retained earnings and the consolidated statements of cash flows.

Note 18 (In Part): Equity

The reconciliation of noncontrolling interest was as follows:

(Dollars in millions)	2009	2008	2007
Balance at January 1	$ (33)	$ (27)	$ 50
Mead Johnson IPO	(160)	—	—
Adjustments to the Mead Johnson net asset transfer	7	—	—
Mead Johnson split-off	105	—	—
Net earnings attributable to noncontrolling interest	1,808	1,468	1,132
Other comprehensive income attributable to noncontrolling interest	10	—	—
Distributions	(1,795)	(1,474)	(1,209)
Balance at December 31	$ (58)	$ (33)	$ (27)

Noncontrolling interest is primarily related to the partnerships with sanofi for the territory covering the Americas for net sales of PLAVIX. Net earnings attributable to noncontrolling interest are presented net of taxes of $589 million in 2009, $472 million in 2008 and $369 million in 2007, in the consolidated statements of earnings with a corresponding increase to the provision for income taxes. Distribution of the partnership profits to sanofi and sanofi's funding of ongoing partnership operations occur on a routine basis and are included within operating activities in the consolidated statements of cash flows. The above activity includes the pre-tax income and distributions related to these partnerships. Net earnings from noncontrolling interest included in discontinued operations was $69 million in 2009, and $7 million in 2008 and 2007.

1.76

THE DOW CHEMICAL COMPANY (DEC)

NOTES TO CONSOLIDATED FINANCIAL STATEMENTS

Note A (In Part): Summary of Significant Accounting Policies

Principles of Consolidation and Basis of Presentation

The accompanying consolidated financial statements of The Dow Chemical Company and its subsidiaries ("Dow" or the "Company") were prepared in accordance with accounting principles generally accepted in the United States of America ("U.S. GAAP") and include the assets, liabilities, revenues and expenses of all majority-owned subsidiaries over which the Company exercises control and, when applicable, entities for which the Company has a controlling financial interest or is the primary beneficiary. Intercompany transactions and balances are eliminated in consolidation. Investments in nonconsolidated affiliates (20-50 percent owned companies, joint ventures and partnerships) are accounted for using the equity method.

Note R (In Part): Variable Interest Entities

Consolidated Variable Interest Entities

The Company holds a variable interest in two joint ventures for which the Company is the primary beneficiary. One joint venture is in the early stages of constructing a manufacturing facility to produce propylene oxide in Thailand. The Company's variable interest in this joint venture relates to a cost-plus arrangement between the joint venture and the Company that involves a majority of the output and ensures a guaranteed return to the joint venture.

The other joint venture was acquired through the acquisition of Rohm and Haas on April 1, 2009. This joint venture manufactures products in Japan for the semiconductor industry. Each joint venture partner holds several equivalent variable interests, with the exception of a royalty agreement held exclusively between the joint venture and the Company. In addition, the entire output of the joint venture is sold to the Company for resale to third-party customers.

As the primary beneficiary of these two VIEs, the joint ventures' assets, liabilities and results of operations are included in the Company's consolidated financial statements. The other joint venture partners' interest in results of operations is reflected in "Net income attributable to noncontrolling interests" in the consolidated statements of income. The other joint venture partners' interest in the joint ventures' assets and liabilities is reflected in "Noncontrolling interests" in the consolidated balance sheet. The following table summarizes the carrying amount of the two joint ventures' assets and liabilities included in the Company's consolidated balance sheet, before intercompany eliminations, at December 31, 2009:

(In millions)	2009
Current assets	$102
Property	455
Other noncurrent assets	81
Total assets	$638
Current liabilities	$183
Long-term debt	125
Other noncurrent liabilities	43
Total liabilities	$351

In September 2001, Hobbes Capital S.A. ("Hobbes"), a former consolidated foreign subsidiary of the Company, issued $500 million of preferred securities in the form of equity certificates. The certificates provided a floating rate of return (which could be reinvested) based on LIBOR. Under the accounting guidance for consolidation, Hobbes was a VIE and the Company was the primary beneficiary. During the third quarter of 2008, the other partner of Hobbes redeemed its $674 million ownership in Hobbes. Prior to redemption, the equity certificates were classified as "Preferred Securities of Subsidiaries" and the reinvested preferred returns were included in "Noncontrolling interests" in the consolidated balance sheets. The preferred return was included in "Net income attributable to noncontrolling interests" in the consolidated statements of income.

1.77

SNAP-ON INCORPORATED (DEC)

NOTES TO CONSOLIDATED FINANCIAL STATEMENTS

Note 1 (In Part): Summary of Accounting Policies

Principles of Consolidation and Presentation

The Consolidated Financial Statements include the accounts of Snap-on Incorporated ("Snap-on" or "the company"), and its wholly-owned and majority-owned subsidiaries, including the accounts of Snap-on Credit LLC ("SOC"), the company's financial services operation in the United States. Prior to July 16, 2009, and since 2004, SOC was a consolidated financial services joint venture with CIT Group Inc. ("CIT"), as Snap-on was the primary beneficiary of the joint venture arrangement. On July 16, 2009, pursuant to the terms of the joint venture agreement, Snap-on terminated the joint venture agreement with CIT and subsequently purchased CIT's 50%-ownership interest in SOC for $8.1 million.

Investments in affiliates over which the company has a greater than 20% but less than 50% ownership interest are accounted for using the equity method of accounting. Investments in unconsolidated affiliates of $37.7 million at 2009

year end and $35.2 million at 2008 year end are included in "Other assets" on the accompanying Consolidated Balance Sheets. The Consolidated Financial Statements do not include the accounts of the company's independent franchisees. Snap-on's Consolidated Financial Statements are prepared in conformity with generally accepted accounting principles in the United States of America ("U.S. GAAP"). All significant intercompany accounts and transactions have been eliminated. The company has evaluated all subsequent events that occurred up to the time of the company's issuance of its financial statements on February 18, 2010.

Certain prior year amounts were reclassified on the Consolidated Financial Statements to reflect the company's adoption of accounting principles related to the presentation of noncontrolling interests in consolidated financial statements, which became effective for Snap-on at the beginning of its 2009 fiscal year. For all periods presented, noncontrolling interests in partially owned consolidated subsidiaries are classified in the Consolidated Balance Sheets as either a separate component of shareholders' equity or, for redeemable noncontrolling interests, as other long-term liabilities. The net earnings attributable to the controlling and noncontrolling interests are included on the face of the Consolidated Statements of Earnings. Distributions to noncontrolling interests are included in financing activities on the Consolidated Statements of Cash Flows for all years presented; previously, such distributions were included in net cash provided (used) by operating activities.

Certain prior year amounts were also reclassified on the Consolidated Financial Statements related to the company's Financial Services' operations. Following the July 16, 2009 acquisition of CIT's 50%-ownership interest in SOC, Snap-on began providing financing for the majority of new loans originated by SOC; previously, substantially all of the loans originated by SOC were sold to CIT. Depending on the type of loan, the new contracts originated by SOC, as well as the contracts originated by Snap-on's wholly owned international finance subsidiaries, are reflected as either contract or finance receivables on the Consolidated Balance Sheets. "Trade and other accounts receivable—net," and the current and long-term portions of net contract and finance receivables are also disclosed on the Consolidated Balance Sheets; previously, all current (payment terms of one year or less) accounts receivable were included in "Accounts receivable – net of allowances" and long-term (payment terms greater than one year) accounts receivable were included in "Other assets."

The Consolidated Statements of Cash Flows reflect the "Provision for losses on finance receivables" originated by (i) SOC after July 16, 2009, and (ii) Snap-on's wholly owned international finance subsidiaries, as part of "Net cash provided by operating activities." Beginning in the third quarter of 2009, following the acquisition of CIT's ownership interest in SOC, "Additions to finance receivables" and "Collections of finance receivables" are presented as part of "Net cash used by investing activities." For financial statement periods prior to October 3, 2009, the provision for losses on finance receivables and the net additions and collections of finance receivables, primarily related to the company's wholly owned international finance subsidiaries, are included in "(Increase) decrease in contract receivables" as part of "Net cash provided by operating activities;" prior period amounts were not restated as the amounts were not significant, individually or in the aggregate, to Snap-on's Consolidated Statements of Cash Flows.

Financial Services Revenue

Financial services revenue consists of installment contract revenue and finance loan receivable revenue and, prior to July 16, 2009, revenue from SOC's sales of originated loans to CIT; financial services revenue also includes service fee income received from CIT.

Snap-on generates financial services revenue from various financing programs that include (i) loans and vehicle leases to franchisees; (ii) loans to franchisees' customers; and (iii) loans to Snap-on's industrial and other customers for the purchase of tools, equipment and diagnostics products on an extended-term payment plan. These financing programs are offered through SOC and Snap-on's wholly owned international finance subsidiaries. Prior to the company's July 16, 2009 acquisition of CIT's 50%-ownership interest in SOC, financial services revenue in the United States was primarily generated from SOC's sales of originated contracts to CIT.

Financing revenue from originated loans retained by Snap-on's finance subsidiaries, including SOC, is recognized over the life of the contract, with interest computed on the average daily balances of the underlying contracts using the effective interest method. Financing revenue from sales of contracts to CIT was recognized on the date such contracts were sold. For contracts originated by SOC and subsequently sold to CIT, SOC continues to service the contracts for an estimated servicing fee and such revenue is recognized over the contractual term of the loan, with a portion of the servicing fee recognized at the time of sale since the contractual servicing fee provided SOC with more than adequate compensation for the level of services provided.

The decision to finance through Snap-on or another financing entity is solely at the election of the customer. When assessing customers for potential financing, Snap-on considers various factors regarding ability to pay including financial condition, collateral, debt-servicing ability, past payment experience and credit bureau information.

BUSINESS COMBINATIONS

1.78 FASB ASC 805, *Business Combinations*, requires that the acquisition method be used for all business combinations. FASB ASC 805 requires an acquirer to recognize the assets acquired, the liabilities assumed, and any noncontrolling interest in the acquiree at the acquisition date, measured at their fair values as of that date. This replaces the cost-allocation process, which required the cost of an acquisition to be allocated to the individual assets acquired and liabilities assumed based on their estimated fair values. Additionally, FASB ASC 805 requires costs incurred to affect the acquisition to be recognized separately from the acquisition rather than included in the cost allocated to the assets acquired and liabilities assumed. FASB ASC 805 also requires the acquirer in a step acquisition to recognize the identifiable assets and liabilities, as well as the noncontrolling interest in the acquiree, at the full amounts of their fair values. The guidance requires the acquirer to recognize goodwill as of the acquisition date, measured as a residual, which in most types of business combinations will result in measuring goodwill as the excess of the consideration transferred plus the fair value of any noncontrolling interest in the acquiree at the acquisition date over

the fair values of the identifiable net assets acquired. "Negative goodwill" resulting from a bargain purchase business combination in which the total acquisition-date fair value of the identifiable net assets acquired exceeds the fair value of the consideration transferred plus any noncontrolling interest in the acquiree, is to be recognized in earnings as a gain.

1.79 During 2009, 225 survey entities used the acquisition method to account for a business combination.

1.80 The nature of information commonly disclosed for business combinations is listed in Table 1-10. Examples of disclosures made by survey entities for business combinations accounted for by the acquisition method and for the formation of jointly owned entities follow.

1.81

TABLE 1-10: BUSINESS COMBINATION DISCLOSURES

	2009	2008	2007	2006
Method of payment:				
Cash only	147	194	261	251
Cash and stock	13	20	20	33
Stock only	8	5	8	9
Other—described	5	10	11	6
Intangible assets not subject to amortization	156	202	240	250
Intangible assets subject to amortization	114	176	211	200
Preliminary allocation of acquisition cost	81	118	162	159
Supplemental pro forma information	33	63	89	76
Contingent payments	26	42	48	48
Purchased research and development costs	25	25	37	39
Fair value of noncontrolling interest	4	N/C*	N/C*	N/C*
Bargain purchase gain (negative goodwill)	2	N/C*	N/C*	N/C*

* N/C = Not compiled. Line item was not included in the table for the year shown.

2008–2009 based on 500 entities surveyed; 2006–2007 based on 600 entities surveyed.

Acquisition Method

1.82

FIDELITY NATIONAL INFORMATION SERVICES, INC. (DEC)

NOTES TO CONSOLIDATED FINANCIAL STATEMENTS

3 (In Part): Summary of Significant Accounting Policies

u (In Part): Recent Accounting Pronouncements

In December 2007, the Financial Accounting Standards Board (FASB) issued new guidance requiring an acquirer in a business combination to recognize the assets acquired, the liabilities assumed, and any noncontrolling interest in the acquiree at their fair values at the acquisition date, with limited exceptions. The costs of the acquisition and any related restructuring costs are to be recognized separately. When the fair value of assets acquired exceeds the fair value of consideration transferred plus any noncontrolling interest in the acquiree, the excess will be recognized as a gain. All business combinations will be accounted for prospectively by applying the acquisition method, including combinations among mutual entities and combinations by contract alone. In April 2009, the FASB amended and clarified the initial recognition and measurement, subsequent measurement and accounting, and related disclosures arising from contingencies in a business combination. Assets and liabilities arising from contingencies in a business combination are to be recognized at their fair value on the acquisition date if fair value can be determined during the measurement period. If fair value cannot be determined, the existing guidance for contingencies and other authoritative literature should be followed. This new guidance is effective for periods beginning on or after December 15, 2008, and applies to business combinations occurring after the effective date. The Company has applied the provisions to the Metavante combination, and will apply the provisions prospectively for any future business combinations.

6 (In Part): Acquisitions and Dispositions

The results of operations and financial position of the entities acquired during the years ended December 31, 2009, 2008, and 2007 are included in the Consolidated Financial Statements from and after the date of acquisition. There were no significant acquisitions in 2008.

2009 Significant Acquisition

Metavante

On October 1, 2009, we completed the acquisition of Metavante (the "Metavante Acquisition"). Metavante expands the scale of FIS core processing and payment capabilities, adds trust and wealth management services and includes the NYCE Network, a leading national EFT network. In addition, Metavante adds significant scale to treasury and cash management offerings and provides an entry into the emerging markets of healthcare and government payments. Pursuant to the Agreement and Plan of Merger (the "Metavante Merger Agreement") dated as of March 31, 2009, Metavante became a wholly-owned subsidiary of FIS. Each issued and outstanding share of Metavante common stock, par value $0.01 per share, was converted into 1.35 shares of FIS common stock. In addition, outstanding Metavante stock options and other stock-based awards converted into comparable FIS stock options and other stock-based awards at the same conversion ratio.

The total purchase price was as follows (in millions):

Value of Metavante common stock	$4,066.4
Value of Metavante stock awards	121.4
Total purchase price	$4,187.8

We have recorded a preliminary allocation of the purchase price to Metavante tangible and identifiable intangible assets acquired and liabilities assumed based on their fair values as of October 1, 2009. Goodwill has been recorded based on

the amount by which the purchase price exceeds the fair value of the net assets acquired. The preliminary purchase price allocation is as follows (in millions):

Cash	$ 439.7
Trade and other receivables	237.9
Land, buildings, and equipment	119.8
Other assets	144.4
Computer software	287.7
Intangible assets	1,572.0
Goodwill	4,083.1
Liabilities assumed	(2,673.4)
Noncontrolling interest	(23.4)
Total purchase price	$ 4,187.8

The preliminary allocation of the purchase price to intangible assets, including computer software and customer relationships, is based on valuations performed to determine the fair value of such assets as of the merger date. The Company is still assessing the economic characteristics of certain software projects and customer relationships. The Company expects to substantially complete this assessment during the first quarter of 2010 and may adjust the amounts recorded as of December 31, 2009 to reflect any revised evaluations. Land and building valuations are based upon appraisals performed by certified property appraisers.

The following table summarizes the liabilities assumed in the Metavante Acquisition (in millions):

Long-term debt including current portion	$1,720.1
Deferred income taxes	544.4
Other liabilities	408.9
	$2,673.4

In connection with the Metavante Acquisition, we also acquired Metavante stock option plans and registered approximately 12.2 million options and 0.6 million restricted stock units in replacement of similar outstanding awards held by Metavante employees. The amounts attributable to vested options are included as an adjustment to the purchase price, and the amounts attributable to unvested options and restricted stock units will be expensed over the remaining vesting period based on a valuation as of the date of closing.

As of the acquisition date, WPM, L.P., a Delaware limited partnership affiliated with Warburg Pincus Private Equity IX, L.P. (collectively "Warburg Pincus") owned 25% of the outstanding shares of Metavante common stock, and was a party to a purchase right agreement with Metavante which granted Warburg Pincus the right to purchase additional shares of Metavante common stock under certain conditions in order to maintain its interest. The Company and Warburg Pincus entered into a replacement stock purchase right agreement effective upon consummation of the merger, granting Warburg Pincus the right to purchase comparable FIS shares in lieu of Metavante shares. The purchase right agreement relates to Metavante employee stock options that were outstanding as of the date of Warburg Pincus' initial investment in Metavante. The stock purchase right may be exercised quarterly for the difference between one-third of the number of said employee stock options exercised during the preceding quarter and the quotient of one-third of the aggregate exercise prices of such options exercised divided by the quoted closing price of a common share on the day immediately before exercise of the purchase right. As of October 1, 2009, approximately 7.0 million options remained outstanding that were subject to this purchase right, and approximately 0.5 million were exercised during the fourth quarter of 2009.

Pro Forma Results

Metavante's revenues of $404.1 million for the fourth quarter of 2009 are included in the Consolidated Statements of Earnings. Disclosure of the earnings of Metavante since the acquisition date is not practicable as it is not being operated as a standalone subsidiary.

Selected unaudited pro forma results of operations for the years ended December 31, 2009 and 2008, assuming the Metavante Acquisition had occurred as of January 1 of each respective year, are presented for comparative purposes below (in millions, except per share amounts):

	2009	2008
Total revenues	$4,983.1	$5,020.8
Net earnings from continuing operations attributable to FIS common stockholders	$ 155.1	$ 131.6
Pro forma earnings per share—basic from continuing operations attributable to FIS common stockholders	$ 0.41	$ 0.36
Pro forma earnings per share—diluted from continuing operations attributable to FIS common stockholders	$ 0.40	$ 0.35

Pro forma results include impairment charges of $136.9 million and Metavante merger and integration related costs of approximately $143.2 million, on a pre-tax basis. Excluding the impact of deferred revenue adjustments, total pro forma revenues would be $5,051.9 million and $5,092.0 million for 2009 and 2008, respectively.

1.83

PALL CORPORATION (JUL)

NOTES TO CONSOLIDATED FINANCIAL STATEMENTS (In thousands)

Note 2. Acquisitions

On September 2, 2008 (the "Closing Date"), the Company acquired 100% of the share capital and voting rights, on a fully diluted basis, of GeneSystems, SA ("GeneSystems"), a privately held French biotechnology company that has developed a patented approach to rapid microbiological detection equipment and disposables. On the Closing Date, the Company paid a cash purchase price of 25,000 Euros ($36,265 U.S. dollar equivalent at the foreign exchange rate on the Closing Date), subject to a post closing working capital adjustment. In the second quarter of fiscal year 2009, the Company paid the working capital adjustment of 289 Euros ($382 equivalent).

In the event that French regulations relating to the monitoring of possible contamination of hot water systems and/or water cooling towers by Legionella are amended by the second anniversary of the Closing Date, with effect within 12 months of such amendment, to either (i) make the use of Polymerase Chain Reaction technology mandatory for such monitoring in France or (ii) validate its use as the only or preferred method for such monitoring in France (the "Legionella Regulation"), a post closing payment equal to 11,500 Euros (less any indemnity related payments of up to 2,000 Euros) will also be paid. If the Legionella Regulation is published after the second anniversary of the Closing Date, but prior to the third anniversary of the Closing Date, and becomes effective within 12 months of publication, the sellers will be paid 5,000 Euros (less any indemnity related payments of up to 2,000 Euros). None of the aforementioned events that would require any post closing payments occurred through July 31, 2009. Accordingly, no liabilities for such payments have been recorded as of July 31, 2009.

The acquisition was accounted for using the purchase method of accounting in accordance with SFAS No. 141. SFAS No. 141 requires that the total cost of an acquisition be allocated to the tangible and intangible assets acquired and liabilities assumed based upon their respective fair values at the date of acquisition.

The following table summarizes the final allocation of the purchase price to the assets acquired and liabilities assumed at the date of the acquisition:

Purchase price	$36,647
Transaction costs	698
Total purchase price	37,345
Cash acquired	96
Total purchase price, net of cash acquired	37,249
Accounts receivable	909
Inventories	1,883
Other current assets	683
Property, plant and equipment	491
In-process research and development	1,743
Intangible assets	16,618
Total assets and in-process research and development acquired	22,327
Accounts payable and other current liabilities	2,260
Other non-current liabilities	4,785
Total liabilities assumed	7,045
Goodwill	$21,967

Based upon the valuation of in-process research and development, the Company recorded a charge to earnings of approximately $1,743, which has been included in Restructuring and other charges, net (see Note 3, Restructuring and Other Charges, Net) for the year ended July 31, 2009.

The amount of in-process research and development was determined by identifying research projects for which technological feasibility had not been established and for which no alternative future uses existed. As of the acquisition date, there was one project that met the above criteria. The project identified is targeted for the BioPharmaceuticals market. The value of the research project identified to be in-process was determined by estimating the future cash flows from the project once commercially feasible and discounting the net cash flows back to their present value. The key assumptions specifically underlying the valuation for purchased in-process research and development consist of an expected completion date for the in-process project, estimated costs to complete the project, revenue and expense projections, and discount rates based on the risks associated with the development life cycle of the in-process technology acquired. The weighted average discount rate used was approximately 40%. The project is expected to be completed by the end of calendar year 2010.

Based upon the markets GeneSystems serves, the goodwill was assigned to the Company's Life Sciences segment. The goodwill is not tax deductible. Pro forma financial information has not been provided as it would not be materially different from the financial information that was previously reported. The results of GeneSystems have been included in the results of operations of the Company since the date of acquisition.

Formation of Jointly Owned Entities

1.84

HASBRO, INC. (DEC)

NOTES TO CONSOLIDATED FINANCIAL STATEMENTS
(Thousands of dollars)

1 (In Part): Summary of Significant Accounting Policies

Equity Method Investments

For the Company's equity method investments, only the Company's investment in and amounts due to and from the equity method investments are included on the consolidated balance sheet and only the Company's share of the equity method investments' earnings (losses) is included on the consolidated statement of operations. Dividends, cash distributions, loans or other cash received from the equity method investments, additional cash investments, loan repayments or other cash paid to the investee are included in the consolidated statement of cash flows.

The Company reviews its investments in equity method investments for impairment on a periodic basis. If it has been determined that the equity investment is less than its related fair value and that this decline is other-than-temporary, the carrying value of the investment is adjusted downward to reflect these declines in value. The Company has one equity method investment that is material to the consolidated financial statements, its 50% interest in a joint venture with Discovery Communications, Inc. See note 5 for additional information.

5. Equity Method Investment

During 2009, the Company entered into an agreement to form a joint venture with Discovery Communications, Inc. ("Discovery") to create a television network in the United States dedicated to high-quality children's and family entertainment and educational programming. The transaction closed in May 2009 with the Company's purchase of a 50% interest in the joint venture, DHJV Company LLC ("DHJV"), which owns the DISCOVERY KIDS network in the United States. The Company purchased its 50% share in DHJV for a payment of $300,000 and certain future payments based on the value

of certain tax benefits expected to be received by the Company. The present value of the expected future payments at the acquisition date totaled approximately $67,900 and was recorded as a component of the Company's investment in the joint venture. The balance of the associated liability, including imputed interest, was $71,234 at December 27, 2009 and is included as a component of other liabilities in the accompanying balance sheet.

Voting control of the joint venture is shared 50/50 between the Company and Discovery. However, the Company believes that the joint venture qualifies as a variable interest entity pursuant to current accounting standards, and that it qualifies as the primary beneficiary, which would result in the Company consolidating the joint venture. In June 2009, the FASB revised the accounting guidance related to variable interest entity consolidation. The revised guidance is effective for the Company at the beginning of fiscal 2010. Under the revised guidance, the Company has determined that it does not meet the control requirements to consolidate the joint venture, and would be required to deconsolidate DHJV and utilize the equity method to account for its investment at the adoption date. The Company has elected to use the equity method in 2009 for financial statement presentation of the joint venture as it has determined that the difference between using consolidation and the equity method in 2009 is not material to the overall presentation of the financial statements. Additionally, there is no impact on net earnings or earnings per share. The Company's share in the earnings of the joint venture for the year ended December 27, 2009 totaled $3,856 of income and is included as a component of other (income) expense in the accompanying consolidated statements of operations.

The Company has entered into a license agreement with the joint venture that will require the payment of royalties by the Company to the joint venture based on a percentage of revenue derived from products related to television shows broadcast by the joint venture. The license agreement includes a minimum royalty guarantee of $125,000, payable in 5 annual installments of $25,000 per year, commencing in 2009, which can be earned out over approximately a 10-year period. During 2009, the Company paid the first annual installment of $25,000, which is included in other assets on the consolidated balance sheet at December 27, 2009. The Company and the joint venture are also parties to an agreement under which the Company will provide the joint venture with an exclusive first look in the U.S. to license certain types of programming developed by the Company based on its intellectual property. In the event the joint venture licenses the programming from the Company to air on the network, the joint venture is required to pay the Company a license fee.

The assets of the joint venture at inception consisted of goodwill and intangibles which were measured at fair value at inception. Intangible assets are primarily comprised of cable affiliate relationships, which are being amortized on a straight line basis over 30 years, and programming costs, which are being amortized primarily over 4 years on an accelerated basis. Hasbro's share of the assets underlying its investment at inception totaled $142,577 of goodwill, $211,850 of cable affiliate relationships, $12,400 of programming costs, and $1,100 of other intangibles. Amortization of the intangible assets is recorded in the results of the joint venture and, accordingly, the Company's share is included in its share of the joint venture earnings which is a component of other (income) expense. As of December 27, 2009, the Company's interest in the joint venture totaled $371,783 and is a component of other assets.

As of December 27, 2009, DHJV had current assets of $51,674, non-current assets of $696,842 and current liabilities of $27,209. Net income of the joint venture for the period from inception to December 27, 2009 was $7,711.

CONTINGENCIES

1.85 FASB ASC 450, *Contingencies*, defines a contingency as "an existing condition, situation or set of circumstances involving uncertainty as to possible gain or loss to an enterprise that will ultimately be resolved when one or more future events occur or fail to occur." FASB ASC 450-20, *Loss Contingencies*, sets forth standards of financial accounting and reporting for loss contingencies. FASB ASC 450-30, *Gain Contingencies*, states the accounting and reporting standards for gain contingencies. During 2009, 330 survey entities presented a caption for contingencies in the balance sheet. Table 1-11 lists the loss and gain contingencies disclosed in the annual reports of the survey entities.

1.86 Examples of contingency disclosures, except for tax carryforwards, follow. Examples of operating loss carryforwards are presented in Section 3.

1.87

TABLE 1-11: CONTINGENCIES

	Number of Entities			
	2009	2008	2007	2006
Loss Contingencies				
Litigation	379	404	489	476
Environmental	203	225	266	263
Possible tax assessments	145	166	185	117
Insurance	132	160	176	152
Government investigations	95	122	153	138
Other—described	63	66	45	70
Gain Contingencies				
Operating loss carryforward	429	423	499	496
Tax credits and other tax credit carryforwards	273	255	278	265
Capital loss carryforward	69	65	83	85
Alternative minimum tax carryforward	44	40	51	57
Plaintiff Litigation	42	55	40	40
Asset sale receivable	8	8	10	11
Investment credit carryforward	7	11	9	6
Potential tax refund	7	4	12	5
Charitable contribution carryforward	4	5	7	6
Other—described	6	3	6	5

2008–2009 based on 500 entities surveyed; 2006–2007 based on 600 entities surveyed.

LOSS CONTINGENCIES

Litigation

1.88

BJ SERVICES COMPANY (SEP)

NOTES TO CONSOLIDATED FINANCIAL STATEMENTS

11 (In Part): Commitments and Contingencies

Litigation

Through performance of our service operations, we are sometimes named as a defendant in litigation, usually relating to claims for personal injury or property damage (including claims for well or reservoir damage, and damage to pipelines or process facilities). We maintain insurance coverage against such claims to the extent deemed prudent by management. Further, through a series of acquisitions, we assumed responsibility for certain claims and proceedings made against the Western Company of North America, Nowsco Well Service Ltd., OSCA and other companies whose stock we acquired in connection with their businesses. Some, but not all, of such claims and proceedings will continue to be covered under insurance policies of our predecessors that were in place at the time of the acquisitions.

Although the outcome of the claims and proceedings against us cannot be predicted with certainty, management believes that there are no existing claims or proceedings that are likely to have a material adverse effect on our financial position, results of operations or cash flows.

Stockholder Lawsuits regarding Baker Hughes Merger

In connection with the pending Baker Hughes Merger, various lawsuits have been filed in the Court of Chancery of the State of Delaware (the "Delaware Lawsuits") on behalf of the public stockholders of the Company, naming the Company, current members of the Company's Board of Directors, and Baker Hughes as defendants. In the Delaware Lawsuits, the plaintiffs allege, among other things, that the Company's Board of Directors violated various fiduciary duties in approving the Merger Agreement and that the Company and/or Baker Hughes aided and abetted such alleged violations. Among other remedies, the plaintiffs seek to enjoin the Merger.

On September 25, 2009, the Delaware Chancery Court entered an order consolidating the Delaware Lawsuits into one class action, In re: BJ Services Company Shareholders Litigation, C.A. No. 4851-VCN. On October 6, 2009, the Delaware Chancery Court entered an order designating the law firm of Faruqi & Faruqi, LLP of New York, New York as lead counsel and Rosenthal, Monhait & Goddess, P.A. of Wilmington, Delaware as liaison counsel. On October 16, 2009, lead counsel for the plaintiffs filed an amended complaint in the Delaware Chancery Court which, among other things, adds Jeffrey E. Smith, the Company's Executive Vice President and Chief Financial Officer, as a defendant, contains new factual allegations about the merger negotiations, and alleges the preliminary joint proxy/prospectus filed on October 14, 2009, with the U.S. Securities and Exchange Commission (the "SEC") omits and misrepresents material information.

Various lawsuits have also been filed in the District Courts of Harris County, Texas (the "Texas Lawsuits"). The Texas

Lawsuits make substantially the same allegations as were initially asserted in the Delaware Lawsuits, and seek the same relief. On October 9, 2009, the Harris County Court consolidated the Texas Lawsuits into one class action, Garden City Employees' Retirement System, et al. v. BJ Services Company, et al., Cause No. 2009-57320, 80 th Judicial District of Harris County, Texas. On October 20, 2009, the Court of Appeals for the First District of Texas at Houston granted the defendants' emergency motion to stay the Texas Lawsuits pending its decision on the defendants' petition seeking a stay of the Texas Lawsuits pending adjudication of the Delaware Lawsuits, which were filed first.

The Company believes that the Delaware Lawsuits and the Texas Lawsuits are without merit, and it intends to vigorously defend itself against them. The outcome of this litigation is uncertain, however, and we cannot currently predict the manner and timing of the resolution of the suits, the likelihood of the issuance of an injunction preventing the consummation of the Merger, or an estimate of a range of possible losses or any minimum loss that could result in the event of an adverse verdict in these suits. These suits could prevent or delay the completion of the Merger and result in substantial costs to the Company and Baker Hughes. We have recorded an amount for estimated legal defense costs under our applicable insurance policies. However, there can be no assurance as to the ultimate outcome of these lawsuits or whether our applicable insurance policies will provide sufficient coverage for these claims.

Asbestos Litigation

In August 2004, certain predecessors of ours, along with numerous other defendants were named in four lawsuits filed in the Circuit Courts of Jones and Smith Counties in Mississippi. These four lawsuits included 118 individual plaintiffs alleging that they suffer various illnesses from exposure to asbestos and seeking damages. The lawsuits assert claims of unseaworthiness, negligence, and strict liability, all based upon the status of our predecessors as Jones Act employers. The plaintiffs were required to complete data sheets specifying the companies they were employed by and the asbestos-containing products to which they were allegedly exposed. Through this process, approximately 25 plaintiffs have identified us or our predecessors as their employer. Amended lawsuits were filed by four individuals against us and the remainder of the original claims (114) were dismissed. Of these four lawsuits, three failed to name us as an employer or manufacturer of asbestos-containing products so we were thereby dismissed. Subsequently an individual from one of these lawsuits brought his own action against us. As a result, we are currently named as a Jones Act employer in two of the Mississippi lawsuits. It is possible that as many as 21 other claimants who identified us or our predecessors as their employer could file suit against us, but they have not done so at this time. Only minimal medical information regarding the alleged asbestos-related disease suffered by the plaintiffs in the two lawsuits has been provided. Accordingly, we are unable to estimate our potential exposure to these lawsuits. We and our predecessors in the past maintained insurance which may be available to respond to these claims. In addition to the Jones Act cases, we have been named in a small number of additional asbestos cases. The allegations in these cases vary, but generally include claims that we provided some unspecified product or service which contained or utilized asbestos or that an employee was exposed to asbestos at one

of our facilities or customer job sites. Some of the allegations involve claims that we are the successor to the Byron Jackson Company. To date, we have been successful in obtaining dismissals of such successor cases without any payment in settlements or judgments, although some remain pending at the present time. We intend to defend ourselves vigorously in all of these cases based on the information available to us at this time. We do not expect the outcome of these lawsuits, individually or collectively, to have a material adverse effect on our financial position, results of operations or cash flows; however, there can be no assurance as to the ultimate outcome of these lawsuits or additional similar lawsuits, if any, that may be filed.

Halliburton—Python Litigation

On December 21, 2007, Halliburton Energy Services, Inc. re-filed a prior suit against us and another oilfield services company for patent infringement in connection with drillable bridge plug tools. These tools are used to isolate portions of a well for stimulation work, after which the plugs are milled out using coiled tubing or a workover rig. Halliburton claims that our tools (offered under the trade name "Python") and tools offered by the other company infringe various patents for a tool constructed of composite material. The lawsuit was filed in the United States District Court for the Northern District of Texas (Dallas). This lawsuit arises from litigation filed in 2003 by Halliburton regarding the patents at issue. The earlier case was dismissed without prejudice when Halliburton sought a re-examination of the patents by the United States Patent and Trademark Office on July 6, 2004. The parties have filed briefs with the Court arguing their positions on the construction of the coverage of Halliburton's patent. We expect that the Court will either issue a ruling or schedule a hearing on these issues within the next few months. We do not expect the outcome of this matter to have a material adverse effect on our financial position, results of operations or cash flows; however, there can be no assurance as to the ultimate outcome of this matter or future lawsuits, if any, that may be filed.

Halliburton—OptiFrac Litigation

In December 2008, Halliburton filed a lawsuit against us in the Eastern District of Texas (Marshall) and another lawsuit in Toronto, Canada against us and another oilfield services company for patent infringement. In both suits, Halliburton claims that our coiled tubing perforating system ("OptiFrac") infringes various patents for a coiled tubing fracturing system marketed by Halliburton. We are in the process of analyzing the methods, claims and causes of action alleged by Halliburton in the suits. We do not expect the outcome of these matters to have a material adverse effect on our financial position, results of operations or cash flows; however, there can be no assurance as to the ultimate outcome of these matters or future lawsuits, if any, that may be filed.

1.89

VERISIGN, INC. (DEC)

NOTES TO CONSOLIDATED FINANCIAL STATEMENTS

Note 15 (In Part): Commitments and Contingencies

Legal Proceedings

On July 6, 2006, a stockholder derivative complaint (Parnes v. Bidzos, et al., and VeriSign) was filed against VeriSign in the U.S. District Court for the Northern District of California, as a nominal defendant, and certain of its current and former directors and executive officers related to certain historical stock option grants. The complaint seeks unspecified damages on behalf of VeriSign, constructive trust and other equitable relief. Two other derivative actions were filed, one in the U.S. District Court for the Northern District of California (Port Authority v. Bidzos, et al., and VeriSign), and one in the Superior Court of the State of California, Santa Clara County (Port Authority v. Bidzos, et al., and VeriSign) on August 14, 2006. The state court derivative action is stayed pending resolution of the federal actions. The current directors and officers named in this state action are D. James Bidzos, William L. Chenevich, Roger H. Moore and Louis A. Simpson. The Company is named as a nominal defendant in these actions. The federal actions have been consolidated and plaintiffs filed a consolidated complaint on November 20, 2006 ("Federal Action"). The current directors and officers named in this consolidated Federal Action are D. James Bidzos, William L. Chenevich, Roger H. Moore, Louis A. Simpson and Timothy Tomlinson. Motions to dismiss the consolidated federal court complaint were heard on May 23, 2007. Those motions were granted on September 14, 2007. On November 16, 2007, a second amended shareholder derivative complaint was filed in the Federal Action wherein the Company was again named as a nominal defendant. By stipulation and Court order, defendants' obligation to respond to the second amended shareholder derivative complaint has been continued pending informal efforts by the parties to resolve the Federal Action. The parties have reached an agreement to resolve the option grant related matters. The Federal Action is subject to approval of the U.S. District Court for the Northern District of California. A motion for preliminary approval was filed on January 27, 2010 and the motion is scheduled to be heard on March 3, 2010. The parties have agreed that upon final approval of the settlement and dismissal of the Federal Action the parallel state court proceedings will be dismissed.

On May 15, 2007, a putative class action (Mykityshyn v. Bidzos, et al., and VeriSign) was filed in Superior Court for the State of California, Santa Clara County, naming the Company and certain current and former officers and directors, alleging false representations and disclosure failures regarding certain historical stock option grants. The plaintiff purports to represent all individuals who owned the Company's common stock between April 3, 2002, and August 9, 2006. The complaint seeks rescission of amendments to the 1998 and 2006 Option Plans and the cancellation of shares added to the 1998 Option Plan. The complaint also seeks to enjoin the Company from granting any stock options and from allowing the exercise of any currently outstanding options granted under the 1998 and 2006 Option Plans. The complaint seeks an unspecified amount of compensatory damages, costs and

attorneys fees. The identical case was filed in the Superior Court for the State of California, Santa Clara County under a separate name (Pace v. Bidzos, et al., and VeriSign) on June 19, 2007, and on October 3, 2007 (Mehdian v. Bidzos, et al.). On December 3, 2007, a consolidated complaint was filed in Superior Court for the State of California, Santa Clara County. The current directors and officers named in this consolidated class action are D. James Bidzos, William L. Chenevich, Roger H. Moore and Louis A. Simpson. VeriSign and the individual defendants dispute all of these claims. Defendants' collective pleading challenges to the putative consolidated class action complaint were granted with leave to amend in August 2008. By stipulation and Court order, plaintiff's obligation to file an amended consolidated class action complaint has been continued pending informal efforts by the parties to resolve the action. The parties have reached an agreement to resolve all of the option grant related matters. The Federal Action is subject to approval of the U.S. District Court for the Northern District of California. A motion for preliminary approval was filed on January 27, 2010 in that court and the motion is scheduled to be heard on March 3, 2010. The parties have agreed that upon final approval of the settlement and dismissal of the Federal Action the parallel state court proceedings will be dismissed.

On November 7, 2006, a judgment was entered against VeriSign by a trial court in Terni, Italy, in the matter of Penco v. VeriSign, Inc. in the amount of Euro 5.8 million plus fees arising from a lawsuit brought by a former consultant who claimed to be owed commissions. The Company was granted a stay on execution of the judgment and the Company filed an appeal. On July 9, 2008, the appellate court rejected all of plaintiff's claims. On or about April 2, 2009, plaintiff filed an appeal in the Supreme Court of Cassation, Rome, Italy. VeriSign filed a Writ of Reply on May 5, 2009.

On May 31, 2007, plaintiffs Karen Herbert, et al., on behalf of themselves and a nationwide class of consumers ("Herbert"), filed a complaint against VeriSign, m-Qube, Inc., and other defendants alleging that defendants collectively operate an illegal lottery under the laws of multiple states by allowing viewers of the NBC television show "Deal or No Deal" to incur premium text message charges in order to participate in an interactive television promotion called "Lucky Case Game." The lawsuit is pending in the U.S. District Court for the Central District of California, Western Division. On June 5, 2007, plaintiffs Cheryl Bentley, et al., on behalf of themselves and a nationwide class of consumers ("*Bentley*"), filed a complaint against VeriSign, m-Qube, Inc., and other defendants alleging that defendants collectively operate an illegal lottery under the laws of multiple states by allowing viewers of the NBC television show "The Apprentice" to incur premium text message charges in order to participate in an interactive television promotion called "Get Rich With Trump." The Bentley matter is currently stayed. A motion to dismiss the ruling in Herbert is on appeal in the U.S. Court of Appeals for the Ninth Circuit.

On September 12, 2008, Leon Stambler filed a declaratory judgment complaint against VeriSign in the U.S. District Court for the Eastern District of Texas. The complaint seeks an order permitting Stambler to proceed with patent infringement actions against VeriSign SSL certificate customers in actions in which VeriSign is not a party in view of Stambler's prior unsuccessful action in 2003 against VeriSign on the same patents in which a verdict was returned against Stambler and a judgment was entered thereon. VeriSign has received requests to indemnify certain SSL certificate customers in the patent infringement actions brought by Stambler. VeriSign and Stambler entered into a confidential settlement agreement on June 1, 2009. Certain indemnity requests from customers are still pending. The declaratory judgment complaint against VeriSign was dismissed on June 8, 2009.

On June 5, 2009, the U.S. Court of Appeals for the Ninth Circuit reversed and remanded a district court order dismissing a second amended complaint filed by plaintiff Coalition for ICANN Transparency, Inc. ("CFIT"). CFIT filed its initial complaint and an application for a temporary restraining order against VeriSign and Internet Corporation for Assigned Names and Numbers ("ICANN") in the U.S. District Court for the Northern District of California on November 28, 2005, asserting claims under Sections 1 and 2 of the Sherman Antitrust Act (the "Sherman Act"), the Cartwright Act, and Cal. Bus. & Prof. Code § 17200. The district court denied CFIT's application for a temporary restraining order on November 30, 2005. Shortly after the action was initiated and CFIT's application was denied, the district court granted defendants' Motion for Judgment on the Pleadings on February 28, 2006, with leave to amend. CFIT filed a First Amended Complaint on March 14, 2006. The Court granted defendants' Motion to Dismiss the First Amended Complaint, with leave to amend, on December 8, 2006. CFIT filed a Second Amended Complaint on December 28, 2006; ICANN was not included as a defendant in the Second Amended Complaint. The Second Amended Complaint, which VeriSign has not yet answered, asserted claims, among others, under Sections 1 and 2 of the Sherman Act against VeriSign, challenging in part VeriSign's conduct in entering into, and the pricing, renewal and certain other terms of, the .com and .net registry agreements with ICANN. The same renewal and pricing terms in the .com registry agreement are incorporated by reference in the Cooperative Agreement between VeriSign and the U.S. Department of Commerce, which approved the .com Registry Agreement as in the public interest. The Court granted VeriSign's Motion to Dismiss the Second Amended Complaint on May 14, 2007, without leave to amend, and entered judgment for VeriSign. CFIT filed a Notice of Appeal to the U.S. Court of Appeals for the Ninth Circuit on June 13, 2007. After briefing, the appeal was argued on December 8, 2008. The Ninth Circuit filed its Opinion reversing and remanding the dismissal of the Second Amended Complaint on June 5, 2009. VeriSign filed a motion for rehearing in the Ninth Circuit on July 2, 2009.

VeriSign is involved in various other investigations, claims and lawsuits arising in the normal conduct of its business, none of which, in its opinion will have a material effect on its business. The Company cannot assure you that it will prevail in any litigation. Regardless of the outcome, any litigation may require the Company to incur significant litigation expense and may result in significant diversion of management attention.

Environmental Matters

1.90

CRANE CO. (DEC)

NOTES TO CONSOLIDATED FINANCIAL STATEMENTS

Note 11 (In Part): Commitments and Contingencies

Other Contingencies

For environmental matters, the Company records a liability for estimated remediation costs when it is probable that the Company will be responsible for such costs and they can be reasonably estimated. Generally, third party specialists assist in the estimation of remediation costs. The environmental remediation liability at December 31, 2009 is substantially all for the former manufacturing site in Goodyear, Arizona (the "Goodyear Site") discussed below.

Estimates of the Company's environmental liabilities at the Goodyear Site are based on currently available facts, present laws and regulations and current technology available for remediation, and are recorded on an undiscounted basis. These estimates consider the Company's prior experience in the Goodyear Site investigation and remediation, as well as available data from, and in consultation with, the Company's environmental specialists. Estimates at the Goodyear Site are subject to significant uncertainties caused primarily by the dynamic nature of the Goodyear Site conditions, the range of remediation alternatives available, together with the corresponding estimates of cleanup methodology and costs, as well as ongoing, required regulatory approvals, primarily from the EPA. Accordingly, it is likely that adjustments to the Company's liability estimate will be necessary as further information and circumstances regarding the Goodyear Site characterization develop. While actual remediation cost therefore may be more than amounts accrued, the Company believes it has established adequate reserves for all probable and reasonably estimable costs.

The Goodyear Site was operated by UniDynamics/Phoenix, Inc. ("UPI"), which became an indirect subsidiary of the Company in 1985 when the Company acquired UPI's parent company, UniDynamics Corporation. UPI manufactured explosive and pyrotechnic compounds, including components for critical military programs, for the U.S. government at the Goodyear Site from 1962 to 1993, under contracts with the Department of Defense and other government agencies and certain of their prime contractors. No manufacturing operations have been conducted at the Goodyear Site since 1994. The Goodyear Site was placed on the National Priorities List in 1983, and is now part of the Phoenix-Goodyear Airport North Superfund Goodyear Site. In 1990, the EPA issued administrative orders requiring UPI to design and carry out certain remedial actions, which UPI has done. Groundwater extraction and treatment systems have been in operation at the Goodyear Site since 1994. A soil vapor extraction system was in operation from 1994 to 1998, was restarted in 2004, and is currently in operation. On July 26, 2006, the Company entered into a consent decree with the EPA with respect to the Goodyear Site providing for, among other things, a work plan for further investigation and remediation activities at the Goodyear Site. The Company recorded a liability in 2004 for estimated costs through 2014 after reaching substantial agreement on the scope of work with the EPA. At the end of September 2007, the liability totaled $15.4 million. During the fourth quarter of 2007, the Company and its technical advisors determined that changing groundwater flow rates and contaminant plume direction at the Goodyear Site required additional extraction systems as well as modifications and upgrades of the existing systems. In consultation with its technical advisors, the Company prepared a forecast of the expenditures required for these new and upgraded systems as well as the costs of operation over the forecast period through 2014. Taking these additional costs into consideration, the Company estimated its liability for the costs of such activities through 2014 to be $41.5 million as of December 31, 2007. During the fourth quarter of 2008, based on further consultation with our advisors and the EPA and in response to groundwater monitoring results that reflected a continuing migration in contaminant plume direction during the year, the Company revised its forecast of remedial activities to increase the level of extraction systems and the number of monitoring wells in and around the Goodyear Site, among other things. As of December 31, 2008, the revised liability estimate was $65.2 million which resulted in an additional charge of $24.3 million during the fourth quarter of 2008. The total estimated gross liability was $53.8 million as of December 31, 2009, as described below; a portion is reimbursable by the U.S. Government. The current portion was approximately $12.8 million and represents the Company's best estimate, in consultation with its technical advisors, of total remediation costs expected to be paid during the twelve-month period.

It is not possible at this point to reasonably estimate the amount of any obligation in excess of the Company's current accruals through the 2014 forecast period because of the aforementioned uncertainties, in particular, the continued significant changes in the Goodyear Site conditions experienced in recent years.

On July 31, 2006, the Company entered into a consent decree with the U.S. Department of Justice on behalf of the Department of Defense and the Department of Energy pursuant to which, among other things, the U.S. Government reimburses the Company for 21 percent of qualifying costs of investigation and remediation activities at the Goodyear Site. As of December 31, 2009 the Company has recorded a receivable of $11.3 million for the expected reimbursements from the U.S. Government in respect of the aggregate liability as at that date. In the first quarter of 2009, the Company issued a $35 million letter of credit to support requirements of the consent decree for the Goodyear Site.

The Company has been identified as a potentially responsible party ("PRP") with respect to environmental contamination at the Crab Orchard National Wildlife Refuge Superfund Site (the "Crab Orchard Site"). The Crab Orchard Site is located about five miles west of Marion, Illinois, and consists of approximately 55,000 acres. Beginning in 1941, the United States used the Crab Orchard Site for the production of ordnance and other related products for use in World War II. In 1947, the Crab Orchard Site was transferred to the United States Fish and Wildlife Service, and about 30,000 acres of the Crab Orchard Site were leased to a variety of industrial tenants whose activities (which continue to this day) included manufacturing ordnance and explosives. A predecessor to the Company formerly leased portions of the Crab Orchard Site, and conducted manufacturing operations at the Crab Orchard Site from 1952 until 1964. General Dynamics Ordnance and Tactical Systems, Inc. ("GD-OTS") is in the process of conducting the remedial investigation and feasibility study at the Crab Orchard Site, pursuant to an Administrative

Order on Consent between GD-OTS and the U.S. Fish and Wildlife Service, the U.S. Environmental Protection Agency ("EPA") and the Illinois Environmental Protection Agency. The Company is not a party to that agreement, and has not been asked by any agency of the United States Government to participate in any activity relative to the Crab Orchard Site. The Company is informed that GD-OTS completed a Phase I remedial investigation in 2008, that GD-OTS is performing a Phase II remedial investigation scheduled for completion in 2010, and that the feasibility study is projected to be complete in mid to late 2012. GD-OTS has asked the Company to participate in a voluntary cost allocation exercise, but the Company, along with a number of other PRPs that were contacted, declined citing the absence of certain necessary parties as well as an undeveloped environmental record. The Company does not believe that it is likely that any discussion about the allocable share of the various PRPs, including the U.S. Government, will take place before the end of 2010. Although a loss is probable, it is not possible at this time to reasonably estimate the amount of any obligation for remediation of the Crab Orchard Site because the extent of the environmental impact, allocation among PRPs, remediation alternatives, and concurrence of regulatory authorities have not yet advanced to the stage where a reasonable estimate can be made. The Company has notified its insurers of this potential liability and will seek coverage under its insurance policies.

1.91

THOMAS & BETTS CORPORATION (DEC)

NOTES TO CONSOLIDATED FINANCIAL STATEMENTS

19 (In Part): Contingencies

Environmental Matters

Under the requirements of the Comprehensive Environmental Response Compensation and Liability Act of 1980, as amended, (the "Superfund Act") and certain other laws, the Corporation is potentially liable for the cost of clean-up at various contaminated sites identified by the United States Environmental Protection Agency and other agencies. The Corporation has been notified that it is named a potentially responsible party ("PRP") at various sites for study and clean-up costs. In some cases there are several named PRPs and in others there are hundreds. The Corporation generally participates in the investigation or clean-up of potentially contaminated sites through cost-sharing agreements with terms which vary from site to site. Costs are typically allocated based upon the volume and nature of the materials sent to the site. However, under the Superfund Act and certain other laws, as a PRP, the Corporation can be held jointly and severally liable for all environmental costs associated with the site.

In conjunction with the acquisition of Lamson & Sessions Co., Joslyn Hi-Voltage, Power Solutions, Drilling Technical Supply SA, The Homac Manufacturing Company and Boreal Braidings Inc., the Corporation assumed responsibility for environmental matters for those entities. Related to the acquisition of Lamson & Sessions Co., the Corporation assumed responsibility for environmental liabilities involving a site in Ohio.

When the Corporation becomes aware of a potential liability at a particular site, it conducts studies to estimate the amount of the liability. If determinable, the Corporation accrues what it considers to be the most accurate estimate of its liability at that site, taking into account the other participants involved in the site and their ability to pay. The Corporation has acquired facilities subject to environmental liability where, in one case, the seller has committed to indemnify the Corporation for those liabilities, and, in another, subject to an asset purchase agreement, the seller assumed responsibility for paying its proportionate share of the environmental clean-up costs.

The Corporation's accrual for probable environmental costs was approximately $11 million and $14 million as of December 31, 2009 and 2008, respectively. The Corporation is not able to predict the extent of its ultimate liability with respect to all of its pending or future environmental matters, and liabilities arising from potential environmental obligations that have not been reserved at this time may be material to the operating results of any single quarter or year in the future. The operation of manufacturing plants involves a high level of susceptibility in these areas, and there is no assurance that the Corporation will not incur material environmental or occupational health and safety liabilities in the future. Moreover, expectations of remediation expenses could be affected by, and potentially significant expenditures could be required to comply with, environmental regulations and health and safety laws that may be adopted or imposed in the future. Future remediation technology advances could adversely impact expectations of remediation expenses.

Possible Tax Assessments

1.92

AIR PRODUCTS AND CHEMICALS, INC. (SEP)

NOTES TO CONSOLIDATED FINANCIAL STATEMENTS

20 (In Part): Income Taxes

The Company is currently under examination in a number of tax jurisdictions, some of which may be resolved in the next twelve months. As a result, it is reasonably possible that a change in the unrecognized tax benefits may occur during the next twelve months. However, quantification of an estimated range cannot be made at this time. A reconciliation

of the beginning and ending amount of the unrecognized tax benefits is as follows:

	2009	2008
Unrecognized tax benefits		
Balance, beginning of year	$184.1	$116.5
Additions for tax positions of the current year	25.6	58.3
Additions for tax positions of prior years	39.0	20.1
Reductions for tax positions of prior years	(45.2)	(5.2)
Settlements	(5.4)	(4.6)
Statute of limitations expiration	(5.4)	(3.4)
Foreign currency translation	2.2	2.4
Balance, end of year	$194.9	$184.1

The Company remains subject to examination in the following major tax jurisdictions for the years indicated below.

	Open Tax Fiscal Years
Major tax jurisdiction	
North America	
United States	2007–2009
Canada	2006–2009
Europe	
United Kingdom	2006–2009
Germany	2006–2009
Netherlands	2005–2009
Poland	2003–2009
Spain	2005–2009
Asia	
Taiwan	2004–2009
Korea	2004–2009

1.93

GOODRICH CORPORATION (DEC)

NOTES TO CONSOLIDATED FINANCIAL STATEMENTS

Note 15 (In Part): Income Taxes

The Company or one of its subsidiaries files income tax returns in the U.S. federal jurisdiction, various U.S. state jurisdictions and foreign jurisdictions. The Company is no longer subject to U.S. federal examination for years before 2006 and with few exceptions, state and local examinations for years before 2000 and non-U.S. income tax examinations for years before 2002. In late 2009, the U.S. Internal Revenue Service (IRS) began examination of the tax years 2007 and 2008. For a discussion of uncertainties related to tax matters see Note 17, "Contingencies."

Note 17 (In Part): Contingencies

Tax

The Company is continuously undergoing examination by the IRS as well as various state and foreign jurisdictions. The IRS and other taxing authorities routinely challenge certain deductions and credits reported by the Company on its income tax returns. See Note 15 "Income Taxes," for additional detail.

Tax Years 2005 and 2006

During 2009, the IRS issued a Revenue Agent's Report for the tax years 2005 and 2006. In July 2009, the Company submitted a protest to the Appeals Division of the IRS with respect to certain unresolved issues which involve the proper timing of deductions. Although it is reasonably possible that these matters could be resolved during the next 12 months, the timing or ultimate outcome is uncertain.

Tax Years 2000 to 2004

During 2007, the IRS and the Company reached agreement on substantially all of the issues raised with respect to the examination of taxable years 2000 to 2004. The Company submitted a protest to the Appeals Division of the IRS with respect to the remaining unresolved issues which involve the proper timing of certain deductions. The Company and the IRS were unable to reach agreement on the remaining issues and in December 2009, the Company filed a petition to the U.S. Tax Court. The Company believes the amount of the estimated tax liability if the IRS were to prevail is fully reserved. The Company cannot predict the timing or ultimate outcome of a final resolution of the remaining unresolved issues.

Tax Years Prior to 2000

The previous examination cycle included the consolidated income tax groups for the audit periods identified below:

Coltec Industries Inc. and Subsidiaries	December, 1997–July, 1999 (through date of acquisition)
Goodrich Corporation and Subsidiaries	1998–1999 (including Rohr, Inc. (Rohr) and Coltec)

The IRS and the Company previously reached final settlement on all but one of the issues raised in this examination cycle. The Company received statutory notices of deficiency dated June 14, 2007 related to the remaining unresolved issue which involves the proper timing of certain deductions. The Company filed a petition with the U.S. Tax Court in September 2007 to contest the notices of deficiency. The Company believes the amount of the estimated tax liability if the IRS were to prevail is fully reserved. Although it is reasonably possible that this matter could be resolved during the next 12 months, the timing or ultimate outcome is uncertain.

Rohr was examined by the State of California for the tax years ended July 31, 1985, 1986 and 1987. The State of California disallowed certain expenses incurred by one of Rohr's subsidiaries in connection with the lease of certain tangible property. California's Franchise Tax Board held that the deductions associated with the leased equipment were non-business deductions. The additional tax associated with the Franchise Tax Board's position is $4.5 million. The amount of accrued interest associated with the additional tax is approximately $29 million at December 31, 2009. In addition, the State of California enacted an amnesty provision that imposes nondeductible penalty interest equal to 50% of the unpaid interest amounts relating to taxable years ended before 2003. The penalty interest is approximately $14.5 million at December 31, 2009. The tax and interest amounts continue to be contested by Rohr. No payment has been made for the $29 million of interest or $14.5 million of penalty interest. In April 2009, the Superior Court of California issued a ruling granting the Company's motion for summary judg-

ment. In August 2009 the State of California appealed the ruling. Once the State's appeals have been exhausted and if the Superior Court's decision is not overturned, the Company will be entitled to a refund of the $4.5 million of tax, together with interest from the date of payment.

Following settlement of the U.S. Tax Court for Rohr's tax years 1986 to 1997, California audited the Company's amended tax returns and issued an assessment based on numerous issues including proper timing of deductions and allowance of tax credits. The Company submitted a protest of the assessment to the California Franchise Tax Board in November 2008. The Company believes that it is adequately reserved for this contingency. Although it is reasonably possible that this matter could be resolved during the next 12 months, the timing or ultimate outcome is uncertain.

Insurance Coverage/Self-Insurance

1.94

ROCK-TENN COMPANY (SEP)

NOTES TO CONSOLIDATED FINANCIAL STATEMENTS

Note 20 (In Part): Commitments and Contingencies

Insurance Placed With Kemper

During fiscal 1985 through 2002, Kemper Insurance Companies/Lumbermens Mutual provided us with workers' compensation insurance, auto liability insurance and general liability insurance. Kemper has made public statements that they are uncertain that they will be able to pay all of their claims liabilities in the future. At present, based on public comments made by Kemper, we believe it is reasonably possible they will not be able to pay some or all of the future liabilities associated with our open and reopened claims. However, we cannot reasonably estimate the amount that Kemper may be unable to pay. Additionally, we cannot reasonably estimate the impact of state guarantee funds and any facultative and treaty reinsurance that may be available to pay such liabilities. If Kemper is ultimately unable to pay such liabilities, we believe the range of our liability is between approximately $0 and $2 million, and we are unable to estimate the liability more specifically because of the factors described above.

Governmental Investigations

1.95

BOSTON SCIENTIFIC CORPORATION (DEC)

NOTES TO CONSOLIDATED FINANCIAL STATEMENTS

Note L (In Part): Commitments and Contingencies

Governmental Proceedings—BSC

In December 2007, we were informed by the DOJ that it was conducting an investigation of allegations that we and other suppliers improperly promoted biliary stents for off-label uses. The allegations were brought as part of a *qui tam* complaint that remained under confidential seal. On December 11, 2009, the Federal government filed a notice of non-intervention with the U.S. District Court for the Northern District of Texas and, subsequently, on January 11, 2010, the *qui tam* complaint was unsealed by the Court. On June 26, 2008, the Department of Justice issued a subpoena to us under the Health Insurance Portability & Accountability Act of 1996 requiring the production of documents to the U.S. Attorney's Office in the District of Massachusetts. We are cooperating with the investigation.

On June 27, 2008, the Republic of Iraq filed a complaint against our wholly-owned subsidiary, BSSA France, and ninety-two other defendants in the U.S. District Court of the Southern District of New York. The complaint alleges that the defendants acted improperly in connection with the sale of products under the United Nations Oil for Food Program. The complaint alleges Racketeer Influenced and Corrupt Organizations Act (RICO) violations, conspiracy to commit fraud and the making of false statements and improper payments, and seeks monetary and punitive damages. We intend to vigorously defend against its allegations. On May 6, 2009, BSSA France was served the complaint. On July 31, 2009, the plaintiff filed an amended complaint. On January 15, 2010, defendant's filed a motion to dismiss the amended complaint.

On July 14, 2008, we received a subpoena from the State of New Hampshire, Office of the Attorney General requesting information in connection with our refusal to sell medical devices or equipment intended to be used in the administration of spinal cord stimulation trials to practitioners other than practicing medical doctors. We have responded to the Attorney General's request.

Governmental Proceedings—Guidant

On November 2, 2005, the Attorney General of the State of New York filed a civil complaint against Guidant pursuant to the New York's Consumer Protection Law. In the complaint, the Attorney General alleges that Guidant concealed from physicians and patients a design flaw in its VENTAK PRIZM® 2 1861 defibrillator from approximately February of 2002 until May 23, 2005. The complaint further alleges that due to Guidant's concealment of this information, Guidant has engaged in repeated and persistent fraudulent conduct in violation of the law. The Attorney General is seeking permanent injunctive relief, restitution for patients in whom a VENTAK PRIZM® 2 1861 defibrillator manufactured before April 2002 was implanted, disgorgement of profits, and all other proper relief. This case is currently pending in the MDL in the U.S. District Court for the District of Minnesota.

In October 2005, Guidant received an administrative subpoena from the DOJ U.S. Attorney's office in Boston, issued under the Health Insurance Portability & Accountability Act of 1996. The subpoena requests documents concerning certain marketing practices for pacemakers, implantable cardioverter defibrillators, leads and related products arising prior to our acquisition of Guidant in 2006. In December 2009, Guidant settled this matter for $22 million and agreed to enter into a Corporate Integrity Agreement.

In October 2005, Guidant received an administrative subpoena from the DOJ U.S. Attorney's office in Minneapolis, issued under the Health Insurance Portability & Accountability Act of 1996. The subpoena requests documents relating to alleged violations of the Food, Drug, and Cosmetic Act occurring prior to our acquisition of Guidant involving

Guidant's VENTAK PRIZM® 2 and CONTAK RENEWAL® and CONTAK RENEWAL 2 devices. Guidant is cooperating with the request, including producing a significant volume of documents and providing witnesses for grand jury proceedings. On November 3, 2009, Guidant and the DOJ reached an agreement in principle to resolve the matters raised in the Minneapolis subpoena. Under the terms of the agreement, Guidant will plead to two misdemeanor charges related to failure to include information in reports to the FDA and Boston Scientific will pay approximately $296 million in fines and forfeitures on behalf of Guidant. We recorded a charge of $294 million in the third quarter of 2009 as a result of the agreement in principle, which represents the $296 million charge associated with the agreement, net of a $2 million reversal of a related accrual. On February 24, 2010, Guidant entered into a plea agreement and sentencing stipulations with the U.S. Attorney for the District of Minnesota and the Office of Consumer Litigation of the DOJ documenting the agreement in principle. We expect to satisfy the obligation during the second quarter of 2010. The DOJ is also investigating whether there were civil violations under the False Claims Act related to these products.

In January 2006, Guidant was served with a civil False Claims Act *qui tam* lawsuit filed in the U.S. District Court for the Middle District of Tennessee in September 2003 by Robert Fry, a former employee alleged to have worked for Guidant from 1981 to 1997. The lawsuit claims that Guidant violated federal law and the laws of the States of Tennessee, Florida and California, by allegedly concealing limited warranty and other credits for upgraded or replacement medical devices, thereby allegedly causing hospitals to file reimbursement claims with federal and state healthcare programs for amounts that did not reflect the providers' true costs for the devices. On October 16, 2006, the United States filed a motion to intervene in this action, which was approved by the Court on November 2, 2006. Fact discovery has been ongoing and mediation is scheduled for late Q1 2010.

On July 1, 2008, Guidant Sales Corporation received a subpoena from the Maryland office of the U.S. Department of Health and Human Services, Office of Inspector General. This subpoena seeks information concerning payments to physicians, primarily related to the training of sales representatives. We are cooperating with this request.

On October 17, 2008, we received a subpoena from the U.S. Department of Health and Human Services, Office of the Inspector General, requesting information related to the alleged use of a skin adhesive in certain of our CRM products. We are cooperating with the request.

On October 24, 2008, we received a letter from the DOJ informing us of an investigation relating to alleged off-label promotion of surgical cardiac ablation system devices to treat atrial fibrillation. We have divested the surgical cardiac ablation business and the devices at issue are no longer sold by us. We are cooperating with the government's investigation. On July 13, 2009, we became aware that a judge in Texas partially unsealed a *qui tam* whistleblower complaint which is the basis for the DOJ investigation. In August 2009, the government, which has the right to intervene and take over the conduct of the *qui tam* case, filed a notice indicating that it has elected not to intervene in this matter at this time.

Following the unsealing of the whistleblower complaint, we received in August 2009 shareholder letters demanding that our Board of Directors take action against certain directors and executive officers as a result of the alleged off-label promotion of surgical cardiac ablation system devices to treat atrial fibrillation. The matter was referred to a special committee of the Board to investigate and then to make a recommendation to the full Board.

On November 7, 2008, Guidant/Boston Scientific received a request from the U.S. Department of Defense (DOD), Defense Criminal Investigative Service and the Department of the Army, Criminal Investigation Command seeking information concerning sales and marketing interactions with physicians at Madigan Army Medical Center in Tacoma, Washington. Since that date, we have been cooperating with the DOD and the DOJ to review CRM's financial interactions with military personnel.

On September 25, 2009, we received a subpoena from the U.S. Department of Health and Human Services, Office of Inspector General, requesting certain information relating to contributions made by us to charities with ties to physicians or their families. We are currently working with the government to understand the scope of the subpoena.

Multi-Employer Plan Contributions

1.96

SARA LEE CORPORATION (JUN)

NOTES TO CONSOLIDATED FINANCIAL STATEMENTS

Note 16 (In Part): Contingencies and Commitments

Multi-Employer Pension Plans

The corporation participates in various multi-employer pension plans that provide retirement benefits to certain employees covered by collective bargaining agreements (MEPP). MEPPs are managed by trustee boards comprised of participating employer and labor union representatives, and participating employers are jointly responsible for any plan underfunding. The corporation's MEPP contributions are established by the applicable collective bargaining agreements; however, our required contributions may increase based on the funded status of the plan and the provisions of the Pension Protection Act, which requires substantially underfunded MEPPs to implement rehabilitation plans to improve funded status. Factors that could impact funded status of a MEPP include investment performance, changes in the participant demographics, financial stability of contributing employers and changes in actuarial assumptions. In addition to regular scheduled contributions, the corporation could be obligated to make additional contributions (known as a complete or partial withdrawal liability) if a MEPP has unfunded vested benefits. These complete or partial withdrawal liabilities would be triggered if the corporation ceases to make contributions to that MEPP, either completely or with respect to only one or more collective bargaining units. The withdrawal liability would equal the corporation's proportionate share of the unfunded vested benefits, based on the year in which the withdrawal liability is triggered. The corporation believes that certain of the MEPPs in which we participate have unfunded vested benefits. Due to uncertainty regarding future factors that could trigger withdrawal liability, such as the corporation's decision to close a plant or the dissolution of a collective bargaining unit, we are unable to determine the amount and timing of the corporation's future withdrawal liability, if any, or whether the corporation's participation in these MEPPs could have any material adverse impact on its financial condition, results of operations or liquidity. The corporation's regular scheduled contributions to MEPPs totaled $49 in 2009, $48 in 2008 and $47 in 2007. The corporation has incurred withdrawal liabilities of approximately $31 in 2009, and immaterial amounts in 2008 and 2007.

GAIN CONTINGENCIES

Plaintiff Litigation

1.97

ELI LILLY AND COMPANY (DEC)

NOTES TO CONSOLIDATED FINANCIAL STATEMENTS

Note 14 (In Part): Contingencies

Patent Litigation

We are engaged in the following patent litigation matters brought pursuant to procedures set out in the Hatch-Waxman Act (the Drug Price Competition and Patent Term Restoration Act of 1984):

- Cymbalta: Sixteen generic drug manufacturers have submitted Abbreviated New Drug Applications (ANDAs) seeking permission to market generic versions of Cymbalta prior to the expiration of our relevant U.S. patents (the earliest of which expires in 2013). Of these challengers, all allege non-infringement of the patent claims directed to the commercial formulation, and nine allege invalidity of the patent claims directed to the active ingredient duloxetine. Of the nine challengers to the compound patent claims, one further alleges invalidity of the claims directed to the use of Cymbalta for treating fibromyalgia, and one alleges the patent having claims directed to the active ingredient is unenforceable. In November 2008 we filed lawsuits in U.S. District Court for the Southern District of Indiana against Actavis Elizabeth LLC; Aurobindo Pharma Ltd.; Cobalt Laboratories, Inc.; Impax Laboratories, Inc.; Lupin Limited; Sandoz Inc.; and Wockhardt Limited, seeking rulings that the patents are valid, infringed, and enforceable. We filed similar lawsuits in the same court against Sun Pharma Global, Inc. in December 2008 and against Anchen Pharmaceuticals, Inc. in August 2009. The cases have been consolidated and actions against all but Wockhardt Limited have been stayed pursuant to stipulations by the defendants to be bound by the outcome of the litigation through appeal.
- Gemzar: Mayne Pharma (USA) Inc., now Hospira, Inc. (Hospira); Fresenius Kabi Oncology Plc (Fresenius); Sicor Pharmaceuticals, Inc., now Teva Parenteral Medicines, Inc. (Teva); and Sun Pharmaceutical Industries Inc. (Sun) each submitted an ANDA seeking permission to market generic versions of Gemzar prior to the expiration of our relevant U.S. patents (compound patent expiring in 2010 and method-of-use patent expiring in 2013), and alleging that these patents are

invalid. Sandoz Inc. (Sandoz) and APP Pharmaceuticals, LLC (APP) have similarly challenged our method-of-use patent. We filed lawsuits in the U.S. District Court for the Southern District of Indiana against Teva (February 2006), Hospira (October 2006 and January 2008), Sandoz (October 2009), APP (December 2009), and Fresenius (February 2010), seeking rulings that our patents are valid and are being infringed. Sandoz withdrew its ANDA and the suit against it was dismissed in February 2010. The trial against Teva was held in September 2009 and we are waiting for a ruling. Teva's ANDAs have been approved by the FDA; however, Teva must provide 90 days notice prior to marketing generic Gemzar to allow time for us to seek a preliminary injunction. Both suits against Hospira have been administratively closed, and the parties have agreed to be bound by the results of the Teva suit. In November 2007, Sun filed a declaratory judgment action in the United States District Court for the Eastern District of Michigan, seeking rulings that our method-of-use and compound patents are invalid or unenforceable, or would not be infringed by the sale of Sun's generic product. In August 2009, the District Court granted a motion by Sun for partial summary judgment, invalidating our method-of-use patent. We have appealed this decision. This ruling has no bearing on the compound patent. The trial originally scheduled for December 2009 has been postponed while the court considers Sun's second summary judgment motion, related to the validity of our compound patent. Sun and APP have received tentative approval for their products from the FDA, but are prohibited from entering the market by 30-month stays, which expire in June 2010 for Sun and May 2012 for APP.

- Alimta: Teva Parenteral Medicines, Inc. (Teva), APP, and Barr Laboratories, Inc. (Barr) each submitted ANDAs seeking approval to market generic versions of Alimta prior to the expiration of the relevant U.S. patent (licensed from the Trustees of Princeton University and expiring in 2016), and alleging the patent is invalid. We, along with Princeton, filed lawsuits in the U.S. District Court for the District of Delaware against Teva, APP, and Barr seeking rulings that the compound patent is valid and infringed. Trial is scheduled for November 2010 against Teva and APP.

- Evista: In 2006, Teva Pharmaceuticals USA, Inc. (Teva) submitted an ANDA seeking permission to market a generic version of Evista prior to the expiration of our relevant U.S. patents (expiring in 2012-2017) and alleging that these patents are invalid, not enforceable, or not infringed. In June 2006, we filed a lawsuit against Teva in the U.S. District Court for the Southern District of Indiana, seeking a ruling that these patents are valid, enforceable, and being infringed by Teva. The trial against Teva was completed in March 2009. In September 2009, the court upheld our method-of-use patents (the last expires in 2014). Teva has appealed that ruling. In addition, the court held that our particle-size patent (expiring 2017) is invalid. We have appealed that ruling.

- Strattera: Actavis Elizabeth LLC (Actavis), Apotex Inc. (Apotex), Aurobindo Pharma Ltd. (Aurobindo), Mylan Pharmaceuticals Inc. (Mylan), Sandoz Inc. (Sandoz), Sun Pharmaceutical Industries Limited (Sun), and Teva Pharmaceuticals USA, Inc. (Teva) each submitted an ANDA seeking permission to market generic versions

of Strattera prior to the expiration of our relevant U.S. patent (expiring in 2017), and alleging that this patent is invalid. In 2007, we brought a lawsuit against Actavis, Apotex, Aurobindo, Mylan, Sandoz, Sun, and Teva in the United States District Court for the District of New Jersey. The court has ruled on all pending summary judgment motions, and granted our infringement motion. The remaining invalidity defenses will be decided at trial, which could take place as early as the third quarter of 2010. Several companies have received tentative approval to market generic atomoxetine, but are prohibited from entering the market by a 30-month stay which expires in November 2010.

We believe each of these Hatch-Waxman challenges is without merit and expect to prevail in this litigation. However, it is not possible to determine the outcome of this litigation, and accordingly, we can provide no assurance that we will prevail. An unfavorable outcome in any of these cases could have a material adverse impact on our future consolidated results of operations, liquidity, and financial position.

1.98

TUTOR PERINI CORPORATION (DEC)

NOTES TO CONSOLIDATED FINANCIAL STATEMENTS

9 (In Part): Contingencies and Commitments

The Company and certain of its subsidiaries are involved in litigation and are contingently liable for commitments and performance guarantees arising in the ordinary course of business. The Company and certain of its clients have made claims arising from the performance under its contracts. The Company recognizes certain significant claims for recovery of incurred cost when it is probable that the claim will result in additional contract revenue and when the amount of the claim can be reliably estimated. As of December 31, 2009, several matters were in the litigation and dispute resolution process. The following discussion provides a background and current status of these matters.

Tutor-Saliba-Perini Joint Venture vs. Los Angeles MTA Matter

During 1995, a joint venture, Tutor-Saliba-Perini, ("Joint Venture"), in which the Company and Tutor-Saliba were partners, filed a complaint in the Superior Court of the State of California for the County of Los Angeles against the Los Angeles County Metropolitan Transportation Authority ("LAMTA"), seeking to recover costs for extra work required by LAMTA in connection with the construction of certain tunnel and station projects. In 1999, LAMTA countered with civil claims under the California False Claims Act ("CFCA") against the Joint Venture, Tutor-Saliba and the Company jointly and severally (together, "TSP"). In September, 2008, Tutor-Saliba merged with the Company.

Claims concerning the construction of LAMTA projects were tried in 2001. During the trial, based on the Joint Venture's alleged failure to comply with the court's discovery orders, the judge issued terminating sanctions that resulted in a substantial judgment against TSP.

TSP appealed and, in January 2005, the State of California Court of Appeal reversed the trial court's entire judgment and found that the trial court judge had abused his discretion, had violated TSP's due process rights, and had imposed impermissibly overbroad terminating sanctions. The Court of Appeal also directed the trial court to dismiss LAMTA's claims that TSP had violated the Unfair Competition Law ("UCL") because LAMTA lacked standing to bring such a claim, and remanded the Joint Venture's claims against LAMTA for extra work required by LAMTA and LAMTA's counterclaim under the CFCA against TSP to the trial court for further proceedings, including a new trial.

In 2006, upon remand, the trial court allowed LAMTA to amend its cross-complaint to add the District Attorney as a party in order to have a plaintiff with standing to assert a UCL claim, and allowed a UCL claim to be added. The court also ordered that individual issues of the case be tried separately.

In December 2006, in the trial of the first issue, which arose out of a 1994 change order involving a Disadvantaged Business Enterprise ("DBE") subcontractor pass-through claim, the jury found that the Joint Venture had submitted two false claims for payment and had breached its contract with LAMTA and awarded LAMTA $111,651 in direct damages. The court has awarded penalties of $10,000 for each of the two claims and will treble the damages awarded by the Jury. A final judgment with respect to these claims will not be entered until the entire case has been resolved and is subject to appeal. In addition, the court will determine whether there were any violations of the UCL, but has deferred its decision on those claims until the case is completed. Each such violation may bear a penalty of up to $2,500.

In February 2007, the court granted a Joint Venture motion and precluded LAMTA in future proceedings from presenting its claims that the Joint Venture breached its contract and violated the CFCA by allegedly "frontloading" the so-called "B Series" contracts. The court ordered further briefing on LAMTA's UCL claim on this issue.

In March 2009, the court ruled that LAMTA could not proceed with its breach of contract claims unless it can prove the contracts are constitutional under a "strict scrutiny" standard. LAMTA has informed the court it will drop the contract claims. The court also ruled that LAMTA may proceed with a trial on its DBE false claims.

In a series of hearings commencing on November 23, 2009, the court ruled on a number of TSP's and LAMTA's Motions in limine. Subsequently, LAMTA has agreed to concede to TSP's entitlement to be paid on five of TSP's claims and to the amount requested by TSP with respect to four of the five. LAMTA will contest the amount of the fifth claim. LAMTA also abandoned its alleged false claim related to delay.

Trial is expected to start in March 2010.

The ultimate financial impact of the lawsuit is not yet determinable. Therefore, no provision for loss, if any, has been recorded in the financial statements.

Perini/Kiewit/Cashman Joint Venture-Central Artery/Tunnel Project Matter

Perini/Kiewit/Cashman Joint Venture ("PKC") a joint venture in which the Company holds a 56% interest and is the managing partner, is currently pursuing a series of claims, instituted at different times over the course of the past ten years, for additional contract time and/or compensation against the Massachusetts Highway Department ("MHD") for work per-

formed by PKC on a portion of the Central Artery/Tunnel project in Boston, Massachusetts. During construction, MHD ordered PKC to perform changes to the work and issued related direct cost changes with an estimated value, excluding time delay and inefficiency costs, in excess of $100 million. In addition, PKC encountered a number of unforeseen conditions during construction that greatly increased PKC's cost of performance. MHD has asserted counterclaims for liquidated damages.

Certain of PKC's claims have been presented to a Disputes Review Board, or DRB, which consists of three construction experts chosen by the parties. To date, the various DRB panels have issued eight awards and several interim decisions on PKC's claims. The second panel (the "Second DRB") ruled on a binding basis that PKC is entitled to five compensation awards, less credits, totaling $57.2 million for delays, impacts and inefficiencies caused by MHD to certain of PKC's work. The first three such awards, totaling $34.5 million, have been confirmed by the Superior Court and were not appealed. The other two awards, totaling $22.7 million, were confirmed by the Superior Court in January 2009 and have been appealed by MHD. The January 2009 Superior Court decision also held that PKC was entitled to post-award, pre-judgment interest on those two awards, albeit at a lower rate than awarded by the Second DRB.

The third panel (the "Third DRB") made three awards. The first is an award to PKC in the amount of $50.7 million for further delays, impacts and inefficiencies. Of that total award, $41.1 million was issued as a binding arbitration award, and the remaining $9.6 million was issued as a non-binding recommendation. The second award is in the amount of $5.8 million for delay damages. Of that amount, $3.3 million was issued as a binding arbitration award, and $2.5 million was issued as a non-binding recommendation. MHD has appealed both of these awards. The third award is a binding arbitration award, denying PKC's $3.7 million claim for further compensable delays. That award was not appealed by PKC.

The Third DRB also issued three interim decisions. The first interim decision held that PKC's claim for delays, on which it later issued an award, is not barred or limited by the 10% markups for overhead and profit on change orders.

The second interim decision held that the date of the project's substantial completion, for purposes of calculating any liquidated damages, is August 23, 2003. The third interim decision was issued in which the Third DRB decided which portions of PKC's claims are subject to binding arbitration. MHD has appealed that decision.

It is PKC's position that the remaining claims to be decided by the DRB on a binding basis have an anticipated value of approximately $28 million, plus interest. PKC also claims it is due interest on the amounts awarded by the Third DRB. MHD disputes that the remaining claims before the DRB may be decided on a binding basis, and further disputes that any interest is due. Hearings before the DRB occurred throughout 2009 and are scheduled to continue during 2010.

Management has made an estimate of the total anticipated cost recovery on this project and it is included in revenue recorded to date. To the extent new facts become known or the final cost recovery included in the claim settlement varies from the estimate, the impact of the change will be reflected in the financial statements at that time.

Contingent Receivables

1.99

ANALOG DEVICES, INC. (OCT)

NOTES TO CONSOLIDATED FINANCIAL STATEMENTS

u (In Part): Discontinued Operations

In November 2007, the Company entered into a purchase and sale agreement with certain subsidiaries of ON Semiconductor Corporation to sell the Company's CPU voltage regulation and PC thermal monitoring business which consists of core voltage regulator products for the central processing unit in computing and gaming applications and temperature sensors and fan-speed controllers for managing the temperature of the central processing unit. During the first quarter of fiscal 2008, the Company completed the sale of this business for net cash proceeds of $138 million, which was net of other cash payments of approximately $1.4 million. The Company made final additional cash payments of approximately $2.2 million in the second quarter of fiscal 2008. In connection with the purchase and sale agreement, $7.5 million was placed into escrow and was excluded from the gain calculations. The Company recorded a pre-tax gain in the first quarter of fiscal 2008 of $78 million, or $43 million net of tax, which was recorded as a gain on sale of discontinued operations. During the third quarter of fiscal 2008, additional proceeds were released from escrow and an additional pre-tax gain of $6.6 million, or $3.8 million net of tax, was recorded as a gain on sale of discontinued operations. Additionally, at the time of the sale, the Company entered into a one-year manufacturing supply agreement with a subsidiary of ON Semiconductor Corporation for an additional $37 million. The Company has allocated the proceeds from this arrangement based on the fair value of the two elements of this transaction: 1) the sale of a business and 2) the obligation to manufacture product for a one-year period. As a result, $85 million was recorded as a liability related to the manufacturing supply agreement, all of which has been utilized. The liability was included in current liabilities of discontinued operations on the Company's consolidated balance sheet. The Company recorded the revenue associated with this manufacturing supply agreement in discontinued operations. As a result, the Company classified inventory for this arrangement as a current asset of discontinued operations. The Company may receive additional proceeds of up to $1 million, currently held in escrow, upon the resolution of certain contingent items, which would be recorded as additional gain from the sale of discontinued operations.

In September 2007, the Company entered into a definitive agreement to sell its Baseband Chipset Business to MediaTek Inc. The decision to sell the Baseband Chipset Business was due to the Company's decision to focus its resources in areas where its signal processing expertise can provide unique capabilities and earn superior returns. On January 11, 2008, the Company completed the sale of its Baseband Chipset Business for net cash proceeds of $269 million. The cash proceeds received were net of a refundable withholding tax of $62 million and other cash payments of approximately $9 million. The Company made additional cash payments of $7.8 million during fiscal 2008, primarily related to transaction fees and retention payments to employees that transferred to MediaTek Inc. The Company made additional cash payments of $1.7 million during fiscal 2009 related to retention payments for employees who transferred to MediaTek Inc and for the reimbursement of intellectual property license fees incurred by MediaTek Inc. The Company recorded a pre-tax gain in fiscal 2008 of $278 million, or $202 million net of tax, which is recorded as a gain on sale of discontinued operations. The Company may receive additional proceeds of up to $10 million, currently held in escrow, upon the resolution of certain contingent items, which would be recorded as additional gain from the sale of discontinued operations.

RISKS AND UNCERTAINTIES

1.100 FASB ASC 275, *Risks and Uncertainties*, requires reporting entities to disclose information about the nature of their operations, the use of estimates in preparing financial statements, certain significant estimates, and vulnerabilities due to certain concentrations.

1.101 Examples of disclosures made by the survey entities to conform to the requirements of FASB ASC 275, *Risks and Uncertainties*, follow.

Nature of Operations

1.102

CATERPILLAR INC. (DEC)

NOTES TO CONSOLIDATED FINANCIAL STATEMENTS

1 (In Part): Operations and Summary of Significant Accounting Policies

A. Nature of Operations

We operate in three principal lines of business:

Machinery

A principal line of business which includes the design, manufacture, marketing and sales of construction, mining and forestry machinery—track and wheel tractors, track and wheel loaders, pipelayers, motor graders, wheel tractor-scrapers, track and wheel excavators, backhoe loaders, log skidders, log loaders, off-highway trucks, articulated trucks, paving products, skid steer loaders, underground mining equipment, tunnel boring equipment and related parts. Also includes logistics services for other companies and the design, manufacture, remanufacture, maintenance and services of rail-related products.

Engines

A principal line of business including the design, manufacture, marketing and sales of engines for Caterpillar machinery, electric power generation systems, locomotives, marine, petroleum, construction, industrial, agricultural and other applications, and related parts. Also includes remanufacturing of Caterpillar engines and a variety of Caterpillar machine and engine components and remanufacturing services for other companies. Reciprocating engines meet power needs ranging from 10 to 21,800 horsepower (8 to over 16,000 kilowatts). Turbines range from 1,600 to 30,000 horsepower (1,200 to 22,000 kilowatts).

Financial Products

A principal line of business consisting primarily of Caterpillar Financial Services Corporation (Cat Financial), Caterpillar Insurance Holdings, Inc. (Cat Insurance) and their respective subsidiaries. Cat Financial provides a wide range of financing alternatives to customers and dealers for Caterpillar machinery and engines, Solar gas turbines as well as other equipment and marine vessels. Cat Financial also extends loans to customers and dealers. Cat Insurance provides various forms of insurance to customers and dealers to help support the purchase and lease of our equipment.

1.103

LOUISIANA-PACIFIC CORPORATION (DEC)

NOTES TO FINANCIAL STATEMENTS

1 (In Part): Summary of Significant Accounting Policies

Nature of Operations

Louisiana-Pacific Corporation and its subsidiaries (collectively LP or the Company) are principally engaged in the manufacture of building products. In addition to its U.S. operations, the Company also maintains manufacturing facilities in Canada, Chile and Brazil through foreign subsidiaries and joint ventures. The principal customers for the Company's building products are retail home centers, manufactured housing producers, distributors and wholesalers in North America and South America, with minor sales to Asia and Europe.

1.104

TEXAS INSTRUMENTS INCORPORATED (DEC)

NOTES TO FINANCIAL STATEMENTS

1 (In Part): Description of Business and Significant Accounting Policies and Practices

Business

At Texas Instruments (TI), we design and make semiconductors that we sell to electronics designers and manufacturers all over the world. We have three reportable segments, which are established along major product categories as follows:

- Analog—consists of high-performance analog (includes data converters, amplifiers and interface products), high-volume analog & logic and power management,

- Embedded Processing—consists of digital signal processors (DSPs) and microcontrollers used in catalog, communications infrastructure and automotive applications, and
- Wireless—consists of DSPs and analog used in basebands for handsets, OMAP™ applications processors and connectivity products for wireless applications.

In addition, we report the results of our remaining business activities in Other. Other includes DLP® products, calculators, reduced-instruction set computing (RISC) microprocessors, application-specific integrated circuits (ASIC) products and royalties received for our patented technology that we license to other electronics companies. See Note 14 for additional information on our business segments.

Use of Estimates

1.105

GENERAL MILLS, INC. (MAY)

NOTES TO CONSOLIDATED FINANCIAL STATEMENTS

Note 2 (In Part): Summary of Significant Accounting Policies

Use of Estimates

Preparing our Consolidated Financial Statements in conformity with accounting principles generally accepted in the United States requires us to make estimates and assumptions that affect reported amounts of assets and liabilities, disclosures of contingent assets and liabilities at the date of the financial statements, and the reported amounts of revenues and expenses during the reporting period. These estimates include our accounting for promotional expenditures, valuation of long-lived assets, intangible assets, stock-based compensation, income taxes, and defined benefit pension, post-retirement and post-employment benefits. Actual results could differ from our estimates.

1.106

JOHNSON & JOHNSON (DEC)

NOTES TO CONSOLIDATED FINANCIAL STATEMENTS

1 (In Part): Summary of Significant Accounting Policies

Use of Estimates

The preparation of consolidated financial statements in conformity with accounting principles generally accepted in the U.S. requires management to make estimates and assumptions that affect the amounts reported. Estimates are used when accounting for sales discounts, rebates, allowances and incentives, product liabilities, income taxes, depreciation, amortization, employee benefits, contingencies and intangible asset and liability valuations. For instance, in determining annual pension and post-employment benefit costs, the Company estimates the rate of return on plan assets, and the cost of future health care benefits. Actual results may or may not differ from those estimates.

Significant Estimates

1.107

ASHLAND INC. (SEP)

NOTES TO CONSOLIDATED FINANCIAL STATEMENTS

Note A (In Part): Significant Accounting Policies

Use of Estimates, Risks and Uncertainties

The preparation of Ashland's Consolidated Financial Statements in conformity with U.S. GAAP requires management to make estimates and assumptions that affect the reported amounts of assets, liabilities, revenues and expenses, and the disclosures of contingent assets and liabilities. Significant items that are subject to such estimates and assumptions include, but are not limited to, long-lived assets (including goodwill and other intangible assets), employee benefit obligations, income taxes, other liabilities and associated receivables for asbestos litigation and environmental remediation. Although management bases its estimates on historical experience and various other assumptions that are believed to be reasonable under the circumstances, actual results could differ significantly from the estimates under different assumptions or conditions.

Ashland has evaluated the period from September 30, 2009, the date of the financial statements, through November 23, 2009, the date of the issuance and filing of the financial statements, and determined that no material subsequent event has occurred that would affect the information presented within these financial statements, nor require additional disclosure, except for the $100 million Ashland Common Stock contribution made to the U.S. pension plan in November 2009.

Ashland's results are affected by domestic and international economic, political, legislative, regulatory and legal actions. Economic conditions, such as recessionary trends, inflation, interest and monetary exchange rates, government fiscal policies, and changes in the prices of hydrocarbon-based products and other raw materials, can have a significant effect on operations. While Ashland maintains reserves for anticipated liabilities and carries various levels of insurance, Ashland could be affected by civil, criminal, regulatory or administrative actions, claims or proceedings relating to asbestos, environmental remediation or other matters.

Goodwill and Other Indefinite-Lived Intangibles

In accordance with U.S. GAAP for goodwill and other indefinite-lived intangibles, Ashland tests these assets for impairment annually as of July 1 and whenever events or circumstances made it more likely than not that an impairment may have occurred. Ashland reviews goodwill for impairment based on its identified reporting units, which are defined as reportable segments or groupings of businesses one level below the reportable segment level. Ashland tests goodwill for impairment by comparing the carrying value to the estimated fair value of its reporting units, determined using ex-

ternally quoted prices (if available) or a discounted cash flow model and, when deemed necessary, a market approach. Ashland tests its indefinite-lived intangible assets, principally trademarks and trade names, using a "relief-from-royalty" valuation method compared to the carrying value. Significant assumptions inherent in the valuation methodologies for goodwill and other intangibles are employed and include, but are not limited to, such estimates as projected business results, growth rates, Ashland's weighted-average cost of capital, royalty and discount rates.

Income Taxes

Ashland is subject to income taxes in the United States and numerous foreign jurisdictions. Significant judgment in the forecasting of taxable income using historical and projected future operating results is required in determining Ashland's provision for income taxes and the related assets and liabilities. The provision for income taxes includes income taxes paid, currently payable or receivable, and those deferred. Under U.S. GAAP, deferred tax assets and liabilities are determined based on differences between financial reporting and tax basis of assets and liabilities, and are measured using enacted tax rates and laws that are expected to be in effect when the differences reverse. Deferred tax assets are also recognized for the estimated future effects of tax loss carryforwards. The effect on deferred taxes of changes in tax rates is recognized in the period in which the enactment date changes. Valuation allowances are established when necessary on a jurisdictional basis to reduce deferred tax assets to the amounts expected to be realized. In the event that the actual outcome of future tax consequences differs from Ashland's estimates and assumptions due to changes or future events such as tax legislation, geographic mix of earnings, completion of tax audits or earnings repatriation plans, the resulting change to the provision for income taxes could have a material effect on the Consolidated Statement of Income and Consolidated Balance Sheet.

Asbestos-Related Litigation

Ashland is subject to liabilities from claims alleging personal injury caused by exposure to asbestos. Such claims result from indemnification obligations undertaken in 1990 in connection with the sale of Riley Stoker Corporation (Riley) and the acquisition of Hercules in November 2008. Although Riley, a former subsidiary, was neither a producer nor a manufacturer of asbestos, its industrial boilers contained some asbestos-containing components provided by other companies. Hercules, a wholly owned subsidiary of Ashland, has liabilities from claims alleging personal injury caused by exposure to asbestos. Such claims typically arise from alleged exposure to asbestos fibers from resin encapsulated pipe and tank products sold by one of Hercules' former subsidiaries to a limited industrial market.

Ashland retained Hamilton, Rabinovitz & Associates, Inc. (HR&A) to assist in developing and annually updating independent reserve estimates for future asbestos claims and related costs given various assumptions. The methodology used by HR&A to project future asbestos costs is based largely on Ashland's recent experience, including claim-filing and settlement rates, disease mix, enacted legislation, open claims, and litigation defense. Ashland's claim experience is compared to the results of previously conducted epidemiological studies estimating the number of people likely to develop asbestos-related diseases. Those studies were undertaken in connection with national analyses of the population expected to have been exposed to asbestos. Using that information, HR&A estimates a range of the number of future claims that may be filed, as well as the related costs that may be incurred in resolving those claims. From the range of estimates, Ashland records the amount it believes to be the best estimate of future payments for litigation defense and claim settlement costs.

Environmental Remediation

Accruals for environmental remediation are recognized when it is probable a liability has been incurred and the amount of that liability can be reasonably estimated. Such costs are charged to expense if they relate to the remediation of conditions caused by past operations or are not expected to mitigate or prevent contamination from future operations. Liabilities are recorded at estimated cost values based on experience, assessments and current technology, without regard to any third-party recoveries and are regularly adjusted as environmental assessments and remediation efforts continue.

1.108

TIME WARNER INC. (DEC)

NOTES TO CONSOLIDATED FINANCIAL STATEMENTS

1 (In Part): Summary of Significant Accounting Policies

Sales Returns, Pricing Rebates and Uncollectible Accounts
Management's estimate of product sales that will be returned and the amount of receivables that will ultimately be collected is an area of judgment affecting reported revenues and net income. In estimating product sales that will be returned, management analyzes vendor sell-off of product, historical return trends, current economic conditions, and changes in customer demand. Based on this information, management reserves a percentage of any product sales that provide the customer with the right of return. The provision for such sales returns is reflected as a reduction in the revenues from the related sale. The Company's products subject to return include home video product at the Filmed Entertainment and Networks segments and magazines and direct sales merchandise at the Publishing segment. In estimating the reserve for pricing rebates, management considers the terms of the Company's agreements with its customers that contain purchasing targets which, if met, would entitle the customer to a rebate. In those instances, management evaluates the customer's actual and forecasted purchases to determine the appropriate reserve. At December 31, 2009, total reserves for returns (which also reflects reserves for certain pricing allowances provided to customers) were $1.493 billion at the Filmed Entertainment and Networks segments primarily related to film products (e.g., DVD sales) and $387 million at the Publishing segment for magazines and direct sales merchandise.

Similarly, management evaluates accounts receivable to determine if they will ultimately be fully collected. In performing this evaluation, significant judgments and estimates are involved, including management's views on trends in the overall receivable agings at the different divisions, and for larger accounts, analyses of specific risks on a customer specific basis. Using this information, management reserves an amount that is expected to be uncollectible. At December 31, 2009 and 2008, total reserves for uncollectible accounts were approximately $373 million and $438 million, respectively. Bad debt expense recognized during the years ended December 31, 2009, 2008 and 2007 totaled $87 million, $122 million and $70 million, respectively.

Based on management's analyses of sales returns and allowances and uncollectible accounts, the Company had total reserves of $2.253 billion and $2.229 billion at December 31, 2009 and 2008, respectively. Total gross accounts receivable were $7.364 billion and $7.400 billion at December 31, 2009 and 2008, respectively. As of December 31, 2009, no single counterparty comprised greater than 5% of the Company's total receivables balance. In general, the Company does not require collateral with respect to its trade receivable arrangements. The Company performs ongoing credit evaluations of its customers and adjusts credit limits based on payment histories, current credit ratings and other factors.

Vulnerability Due to Certain Concentrations

1.109

AMERICAN GREETINGS CORPORATION (FEB)

NOTES TO CONSOLIDATED FINANCIAL STATEMENTS

Note 1 (In Part): Significant Accounting Policies

Concentration of Credit Risks
The Corporation sells primarily to customers in the retail trade, including those in the mass merchandise, drug store, supermarket and other channels of distribution. These customers are located throughout the United States, Canada, the United Kingdom, Australia, New Zealand and Mexico. Net sales from continuing operations to the Corporation's five largest customers accounted for approximately 36%, 37% and 36% of total revenue in 2009, 2008 and 2007, respectively. Net sales to Wal-Mart Stores, Inc. and its subsidiaries accounted for approximately 15%, 16% and 16% of total revenue from continuing operations in 2009, 2008 and 2007, respectively.

The Corporation conducts business based on periodic evaluations of its customers' financial condition and generally does not require collateral to secure their obligation to the Corporation. While the competitiveness of the retail industry presents an inherent uncertainty, the Corporation does not believe a significant risk of loss exists from a concentration of credit.

1.110

HEWLETT-PACKARD COMPANY (OCT)

NOTES TO CONSOLIDATED FINANCIAL STATEMENTS

Note 1 (In Part): Summary of Significant Accounting Policies

Concentrations of Credit Risk

Financial instruments that potentially subject HP to significant concentrations of credit risk consist principally of cash and cash equivalents, investments, accounts receivable from trade customers and from contract manufacturers, financing receivables and derivatives.

HP maintains cash and cash equivalents, short and long-term investments, derivatives and certain other financial instruments with various financial institutions. These financial institutions are located in many different geographical regions and HP's policy is designed to limit exposure with any one institution. As part of its cash and risk management processes, HP performs periodic evaluations of the relative credit standing of the financial institutions. HP has not sustained material credit losses from instruments held at financial institutions. HP utilizes forward contracts and other derivative contracts to protect against the effects of foreign currency fluctuations. Such contracts involve the risk of nonperformance by the counterparty, which could result in a material loss.

HP sells a significant portion of its products through third-party distributors and resellers and, as a result, maintains individually significant receivable balances with these parties. If the financial condition or operations of these distributors and resellers deteriorate substantially, HP's operating results could be adversely affected. The ten largest distributor and reseller receivable balances collectively, which were concentrated primarily in North America and Europe, represented approximately 22% of gross accounts receivable at October 31, 2009 and 18% at October 31, 2008. No single customer accounts for more than 10% of accounts receivable. Credit risk with respect to other accounts receivable and financing receivables is generally diversified due to the large number of entities comprising HP's customer base and their dispersion across many different industries and geographical regions. HP performs ongoing credit evaluations of the financial condition of its third-party distributors, resellers and other customers and requires collateral, such as letters of credit and bank guarantees, in certain circumstances. To ensure a receivable balance is not overstated due to uncollectibility, an allowance for doubtful accounts is maintained as required under U.S. GAAP. The past due or delinquency status of a receivable is based on the contractual payment terms of the receivable. The need to write off a receivable balance depends on the age, size and a determination of collectability of the receivable. HP generally has experienced longer accounts receivable collection cycles in its emerging markets, in particular Asia Pacific and Latin America, compared to its United States and European markets. In the event that accounts receivable collection cycles in emerging markets significantly deteriorate or one or more of HP's larger resellers or enterprise customers fail, HP's operating results could be adversely affected.

Other Concentration

HP obtains a significant number of components from single source suppliers due to technology, availability, price, quality or other considerations. The loss of a single source supplier, the deterioration of its relationship with a single source supplier, or any unilateral modification to the contractual terms under which HP is supplied components by a single source supplier could adversely affect HP's revenue and gross margins.

1.111

ROCKWELL COLLINS, INC. (SEP)

NOTES TO CONSOLIDATED FINANCIAL STATEMENTS

2 (In Part): Significant Accounting Policies

Concentration of Risks

The Company's products and services are concentrated within the aerospace and defense industries with customers consisting primarily of military and commercial aircraft manufacturers, commercial airlines, and the U.S. and non-U.S. governments. As a result of this industry focus, the Company's current and future financial performance is largely dependent upon the overall economic conditions within these industries. In particular, the commercial aerospace market has been historically cyclical and subject to downturns during periods of weak economic conditions, which could be prompted by or exacerbated by political or other domestic or international events. The defense market may be affected by changes in budget appropriations, procurement policies, political developments both domestically and abroad, and other factors. While management believes the Company's product offerings are well positioned to meet the needs of its customer base, any material deterioration in the economic and environmental factors that impact the aerospace and defense industries could have a material adverse effect on the Company's results of operations, financial position or cash flows.

In addition to the overall business risks associated with the Company's concentration within the aerospace and defense industries, the Company is also exposed to a concentration of collection risk on credit extended to commercial airlines and business jet aircraft manufacturers. At September 30, 2009, accounts receivable due from U.S. and international commercial airlines were approximately $18 million and $63 million, respectively. At September 30, 2009, accounts receivable due from business jet aircraft manufacturers were approximately $82 million. The Company performs ongoing credit evaluations on the financial condition of all of its customers and maintains allowances for uncollectible accounts receivable based on expected collectability. Although management believes its allowances are adequate, the Company is not able to predict with certainty the changes in the financial stability of its customers. Any material change in the financial status of any one or group of customers could have a material adverse effect on the Company's results of operations, financial position or cash flows.

As of September 30, 2009, approximately 11 percent of the Company's employees were represented by collective bargaining agreements, which are generally set to expire between September 2010 and May 2013. Collective bargaining agreements representing approximately 1 percent of the Company's employees expire within one year.

1.112

VISHAY INTERTECHNOLOGY, INC. (DEC)

NOTES TO CONSOLIDATED FINANCIAL STATEMENTS

Note 14. Current Vulnerability Due to Certain Concentrations

Market Concentrations

While no single customer comprises greater than 10% of net revenues, a material portion of the Company's revenues are derived from the worldwide communications and computer markets. These markets have historically experienced wide variations in demand for end products. If demand for these end products should decrease, the producers thereof could reduce their purchases of the Company's products, which could have a material adverse effect on the Company's results of operations and financial position.

Credit Risk Concentrations

Financial instruments with potential credit risk consist principally of cash and cash equivalents, accounts receivable, and notes receivable. The Company maintains cash and cash equivalents with various major financial institutions. Concentrations of credit risk with respect to receivables are generally limited due to the Company's large number of customers and their dispersion across many countries and industries. At December 31, 2009 and 2008, the Company had no significant concentrations of credit risk.

Sources of Supplies

Many of the Company's products require the use of raw materials that are produced in only a limited number of regions around the world or are available from only a limited number of suppliers. The Company's consolidated results of operations may be materially and adversely affected if the Company has difficulty obtaining these raw materials, the quality of available raw materials deteriorates or there are significant price increases for these raw materials. For periods in which the prices of these raw materials are rising, the Company may be unable to pass on the increased cost to the Company's customers, which would result in decreased margins for the products in which they are used. For periods in which the prices are declining, the Company may be required to write down its inventory carrying cost of these raw materials which, depending on the extent of the difference between market price and its carrying cost, could have a material adverse effect on the Company's net earnings.

From time to time, there have been short-term market shortages of raw materials utilized by the Company. While these shortages have not historically adversely affected the Company's ability to increase production of products containing these raw materials, they have historically resulted in higher raw material costs for the Company. The Company cannot assure that any of these market shortages in the future would not adversely affect the Company's ability to increase production, particularly during periods of growing demand for the Company's products.

Tantalum

Vishay is a major consumer of the world's annual production of tantalum. Tantalum, a metal purchased in powder or wire form, is the principal material used in the manufacture of tantalum capacitors. There are few suppliers that process tantalum ore into capacitor grade tantalum powder.

The Company was obligated under two contracts entered into in 2000 with Cabot Corporation to make purchases of tantalum through 2006. The Company's purchase commitments were entered into at a time when market demand for tantalum capacitors was high and tantalum powder was in short supply. Since that time, the price of tantalum has decreased significantly, and accordingly, the Company wrote down the carrying value of its tantalum inventory on-hand and recognized losses on purchase commitments. As of December 31, 2006, the Company has fulfilled all obligations under the Cabot contracts and is no longer required to purchase tantalum from Cabot at prices fixed by the contracts.

Our minimum tantalum purchase commitments under the contracts with Cabot exceeded our production requirements for tantalum capacitors over the term of the contract. Tantalum powder and wire have an indefinite shelf life; therefore, we believe that we will eventually use all of the material in our inventory. At December 31, 2009 and 2008, the Company had tantalum with a book value of $32,578,000 and $46,750,000, respectively. Of these amounts, the Company classified $13,032,000 and $19,700,000, respectively, as other assets, representing the value of quantities which are not expected to be used within one year.

Geographic Concentration

We have operations outside the United States, and approximately 75% of our revenues during 2009 were derived from sales to customers outside the United States. Some of our products are produced in countries which are subject to risks of political, economic, and military instability. This instability could result in wars, riots, nationalization of industry, currency fluctuations, and labor unrest. These conditions could have an adverse impact on our ability to operate in these regions and, depending on the extent and severity of these conditions, could materially and adversely affect our overall financial condition and operating results.

Our business has been in operation in Israel for 39 years. We have never experienced any material interruption in our operations attributable to these factors, in spite of several Middle East crises, including wars. However, we might be adversely affected if events were to occur in the Middle East that interfered with our operations in Israel.

COMMITMENTS

1.113 FASB ASC 440, *Commitments*, requires the disclosure of commitments such as those for capital expenditures or an obligation to restrict dividends. Table 1-12 lists the various commitments disclosed in the annual reports of the survey entities.

1.114 Examples of commitment disclosures follow.

1.115

TABLE 1-12: COMMITMENTS

	Number of Entities			
	2009	2008	2007	2006
Debt covenant restrictions......	348	328	390	401
Purchase agreements............	248	220	254	250
Capital expenditures.............	72	77	87	80
Financing/support agreements........................	47	45	50	41
Sales agreements.................	41	40	50	48
Additional payments related to acquisitions.....................	38	46	61	50
Employment contracts...........	35	35	41	45
Licensing agreements............	26	34	36	45
Other—described.................	44	27	33	31

2008–2009 based on 500 entities surveyed; 2006–2007 based on 600 entities surveyed.

Debt Covenant Restrictions

1.116

DEAN FOODS COMPANY (DEC)

NOTES TO CONSOLIDATED FINANCIAL STATEMENTS

Note 9 (In Part): Debt

Under the senior secured credit facility, we are required to comply with certain financial covenants, including, but not limited to, maximum leverage and minimum interest coverage ratio. As of December 31, 2009, we were in compliance with all covenants contained in their agreement. Our Leverage Ratio at December 31, 2009 was 4.16 times consolidated funded indebtedness to consolidated EBITDA for the prior four consecutive quarters, each as defined under and calculated in accordance with the terms of our senior secured credit facility and our receivables-backed facility. The maximum permitted Leverage Ratio as of December 31, 2009 is 5.00 times declining to a final step down to 4.50 times as of December 31, 2010.

Our credit agreement permits us to complete acquisitions that meet all of the following conditions without obtaining prior approval: (1) the acquired company is involved in the manufacture, processing and distribution of food or packaging products or any other line of business in which we are currently engaged, (2) the net cash purchase price for any single acquisition is not greater than $500 million, (3) we acquire at least 51% of the acquired entity, (4) the transaction is approved by the board of directors or shareholders, as appropriate, of the target and (5) after giving effect to such acquisition on a pro forma basis, we would have been in compliance with all financial covenants. All other acquisitions must be approved in advance by the required lenders.

The senior secured credit facility contains limitations on liens, investments and the incurrence of additional indebtedness, prohibits certain dispositions of property and conditionally restricts certain payments, including dividends. There are no restrictions on these certain payments, including dividends, when our Leverage Ratio is below 5.00 times. The senior secured credit facility is secured by liens on substantially all of our domestic assets including the assets of our subsidiaries, but excluding the capital stock of subsidiaries of the former Dean Foods Company ("Legacy Dean"), and the real property owned by Legacy Dean and its subsidiaries.

The credit agreement contains standard default triggers, including without limitation: failure to maintain compliance with the financial and other covenants contained in the credit agreement, default on certain of our other debt, a change in control and certain other material adverse changes in our business. The credit agreement does not contain any requirements to maintain specific credit rating levels.

Interest on the outstanding balances under the senior secured credit facility is payable, at our election, at the Alternative Base Rate (as defined in our credit agreement) plus a margin depending on our Leverage Ratio (as defined in our credit agreement) or LIBOR plus a margin depending on our Leverage Ratio. The Applicable Base Rate margin under our revolving credit and term loan A varies from zero to 75 basis points, while the Applicable LIBOR Rate margin varies from 62.5 to 175 basis points. The Applicable Base Rate margin under our term loan B varies from 37.5 to 75 basis points, while the Applicable LIBOR Rate margin varies from 137.5 to 175 basis points.

In consideration for the revolving commitment, we are required to pay a quarterly commitment fee on unused amounts of the senior secured revolving credit facility that ranges from 12.5 to 37.5 basis points, depending on our Leverage Ratio.

1.117

THE L.S. STARRETT COMPANY (JUN)

NOTES TO CONSOLIDATED FINANCIAL STATEMENTS

Note 11 (In Part): Debt

The obligations under the New Credit Facility are unsecured. However, in the event of certain triggering events, the obligations under the New Credit Facility will become secured by the assets of the Company and the Subsidiaries.

Availability under the New Credit Facility is subject to a borrowing base comprised of accounts receivable and inventory. The Company believes that the borrowing base will consistently produce availability under the New Credit Facility in excess of $23 million. In addition, the Company anticipates that it will not need to fully utilize the amounts available to the Company and the Subsidiaries under the New Credit Facility. As of September 8, 2009, the Company had borrowings of $3.3 million under this facility. A .25% commitment fee is charged on the unused portion of the line of credit.

The New Credit Facility contains financial covenants with respect to leverage, tangible net worth, and interest coverage, and also contains customary affirmative and negative covenants, including limitations on indebtedness, liens, acquisitions, asset dispositions, and fundamental corporate changes, and certain customary events of default. Upon the occurrence and continuation of an event of default, the lender may terminate the revolving credit commitment and require immediate payment of the entire unpaid principal amount of the New Credit Facility, accrued interest and all other obligations. As of June 30, 2009, the Company was in compliance with all covenants required to be tested at that time.

1.118

POTLATCH CORPORATION (DEC)

NOTES TO CONSOLIDATED FINANCIAL STATEMENTS

Note 8 (In Part): Debt and Note Receivable

The bank credit facility is secured by a pledge of the capital stock of our subsidiaries and by 659,600 acres of our timberlands in Idaho to satisfy the minimum collateral coverage ratio, as described below. This pledge is on an equal rights of payment and level of seniority basis with the $22.5 million principal amount of 6.95% debentures due 2015 and the $48.8 million principal amount of medium-term notes due 2011 through 2022.

The agreement governing our bank credit facility contains certain covenants that limit our ability and that of our subsidiaries to create liens, merge or consolidate, dispose of assets, incur indebtedness and guarantees, repurchase or redeem capital stock and indebtedness, make certain investments or acquisitions, enter into certain transactions with affiliates or change the nature of our business. The credit facility also contains financial maintenance covenants establishing a minimum interest coverage ratio, a minimum collateral coverage ratio and a maximum funded indebtedness to capitalization ratio. We will be permitted to pay distributions to our stockholders under the terms of the credit facility so long as we remain in pro forma compliance with the financial maintenance covenants.

The table below sets forth the most restrictive covenants in the credit facility and our status with respect to these covenants as of December 31, 2009:

	Covenant Requirement	Actual Ratio at December 31, 2009
Minimum interest coverage ratio	2.50 to 1.00	5.98 to 1.00
Minimum collateral coverage ratio	2.25 to 1.00	3.87 to 1.00
Maximum funded indebtedness to capitalization ratio	60.0%	51.4%

Events of default under the credit facility include, but are not limited to, payment defaults, covenant defaults, breaches of representations and warranties, cross defaults to certain other material agreements and indebtedness, bankruptcy and other insolvency events, material adverse judgments, actual or asserted invalidity of security interests or loan documentation, and certain change of control events.

We and several of our subsidiaries are parties to the credit agreement and eligible to borrow thereunder, subject to the specified borrowing limits and continued compliance with debt covenants. Any borrowings by one of these entities under the credit facility reduces the credit available for all the entities. As a result, borrowings by Potlatch TRS under the

credit facility will, until repaid, reduce the amount of borrowings otherwise available to us for purposes such as the funding of quarterly distributions.

Purchase Agreements

1.119

PRAXAIR, INC. (DEC)

NOTES TO CONSOLIDATED FINANCIAL STATEMENTS

Note 17 (In Part): Commitments and Contingencies

The following table sets forth Praxair's material commitments and contractual obligations as of December 31, 2009, excluding leases, tax liabilities for uncertain tax positions, other post retirement and pension obligations which are summarized elsewhere in the financial statements:

(Millions of dollars)	Unconditional Purchase Obligations	Construction Commitments	Guarantees and Other
Expiring through December 31,			
2010	$ 483	746	$177
2011	335	207	—
2012	283	14	—
2013	269	—	—
2014	299	—	—
Thereafter	1,795	—	19
	$3,464	967	$196

Unconditional purchase obligations of $3,464 million represent contractual commitments under various long- and short-term, take-or-pay arrangements with suppliers and are not included on Praxair's balance sheet. These obligations are primarily minimum purchase commitments for helium, electricity, natural gas and feedstock used to produce atmospheric and process gases. During 2009, payments under these contracts totaled $1,020 million, including $581 million for electricity and $195 million for natural gas. A significant portion of these obligations is passed on to customers through similar take-or-pay contractual arrangements. Purchase obligations which are not passed along to customers do not represent a significant risk to Praxair.

1.120

THERMO FISHER SCIENTIFIC INC. (DEC)

NOTES TO CONSOLIDATED FINANCIAL STATEMENTS

Note 10 (In Part): Commitments and Contingencies

Purchase Obligations

The company has entered into unconditional purchase obligations, in the ordinary course of business, that include agreements to purchase goods or services that are enforceable and legally binding and that specify all significant terms including: fixed or minimum quantities to be purchased; fixed, minimum or variable price provisions; and the approximate timing of the transaction. Purchase obligations exclude agreements that are cancelable at any time without penalty. The aggregate amount of the company's unconditional purchase obligations totaled $172.2 million at December 31, 2009 and the majority of these obligations are expected to be settled during 2010.

Capital Expenditures

1.121

CLIFFS NATURAL RESOURCES INC. (DEC)

NOTES TO CONSOLIDATED FINANCIAL STATEMENTS

Note 18 (In Part): Commitments and Contingencies

We have total contractual obligations and binding commitments of approximately $2.7 billion as of December 31, 2009 compared with $2.5 billion as of December 31, 2008, primarily related to purchase commitments, principal and interest payments on long-term debt, lease obligations, pension and OPEB funding minimums, and mine closure obligations. Such future commitments total $661.0 million in 2010, $314.9 million in 2011, $429.7 million in 2012, $470.0 million in 2013, $183.4 million in 2014 and $597.4 million thereafter.

Purchase Commitments

In 2008, we incurred a capital commitment for the purchase of a new longwall plow system for our Pinnacle mine in West Virginia. The system, which requires a capital investment of approximately $83 million, will replace the current longwall plow system in an effort to reduce maintenance costs and increase production at the mine. As of December 31, 2009, capital expenditures related to this purchase were approximately $29 million. Remaining expenditures of approximately $40 million and $14 million are scheduled to be made in 2010 and 2011, respectively, based upon revised payment and delivery terms negotiated with the supplier.

Financing/Support Agreement

1.122

THE BOEING COMPANY (DEC)

NOTES TO CONSOLIDATED FINANCIAL STATEMENTS

Note 11 (In Part): Liabilities, Commitments and Contingencies

Financing Commitments

Financing commitments totaled $10,409 and $10,145 as of December 31, 2009 and 2008. We anticipate that a significant portion of these commitments will not be exercised by the customers as we continue to work with third party financiers to provide alternative financing to customers. However, there can be no assurances that we will not be required to fund greater amounts than historically required.

In connection with the formation of ULA, we and Lockheed Martin Corporation (Lockheed) each agreed to extend a line of credit to ULA of up to $200 to support its working capital requirements during the five-year period following December 1, 2006. ULA did not request any funds under the line of credit as of December 31, 2009. We and Lockheed have also each committed to provide ULA with up to $122 of additional capital contributions in the event ULA does not have sufficient funds to make a required payment to us under an inventory supply agreement. See Note 7.

We have entered into standby letters of credit agreements and surety bonds with financial institutions primarily relating to the guarantee of future performance on certain contracts. Contingent liabilities on outstanding letters of credit agreements and surety bonds aggregated approximately $7,052 and $5,763 as of December 31, 2009 and 2008.

Agreement to Sell

1.123

SEABOARD CORPORATION (DEC)

NOTES TO CONSOLIDATED FINANCIAL STATEMENTS

Note 13 (In Part): Segment Information

On March 2, 2009, an agreement became effective under which Seaboard will sell its two power barges in the Dominican Republic for $70,000,000, which will use such barges for private use. The agreement calls for the sale to occur on or around January 1, 2011. During March 2009, $15,000,000 was paid to Seaboard (recorded as long-term deferred revenue) and the $55,000,000 balance of the purchase price was paid into escrow and will be paid to Seaboard at the closing of the sale. The net book value of the two barges was $20,090,000 as of December 31, 2009 and is classified as held for sale in non-current other assets. Accordingly, Seaboard will cease depreciation on January 1, 2010 for these two barges but continue to operate these two barges until a few weeks prior to the closing date of the sale. Seaboard will be responsible for the wind down and decommissioning costs of the barges. Completion of the sale is dependent upon several issues, including meeting certain baseline performance and emission tests. Failure to satisfy or cure any deficiencies could result in the agreement being terminated and the sale abandoned. Seaboard could be responsible to pay liquidated damages of up to approximately $15,000,000 should it fail to perform its obligations under the agreement, after expiration of applicable cure and grace periods. Seaboard will retain all other physical properties of this business and is considering options to continue its power business in the Dominican Republic after the sale of these assets is completed.

Additional Payments Related to Acquisitions

1.124

ABM INDUSTRIES INCORPORATED (OCT)

NOTES TO CONSOLIDATED FINANCIAL STATEMENTS

Note 3 (In Part): Acquisitions

On April 2, 2007, the Company acquired substantially all of the operating assets of HealthCare Parking Systems of America, Inc., a provider of healthcare-related parking services based in Tampa, Florida, for $7.1 million in cash, plus additional consideration based on the financial performance of the acquired business over the three years following the acquisition. Additional consideration paid in the years ended October 31, 2009 and 2008 were $4.0 million and $1.7 million, respectively, which were allocated to goodwill. If certain growth thresholds are achieved, additional payments will be required in years four and five. HealthCare Parking Systems of America, Inc. was a provider of premium parking management services exclusively to hospitals, health centers, and medical office buildings across the United States. Of the total initial payment, $5.2 million was allocated to customer relationship intangible assets (amortized over a useful life of 14 years under the sum-of-the-year-digits method), $0.8 million to trademarks intangible assets (amortized over a useful life of 10 years under the straight-line method), $1.0 million to goodwill, and $0.1 million to other assets.

Employment Contracts

1.125

ARDEN GROUP, INC. (DEC)

NOTES TO CONSOLIDATED STATEMENTS

11 (In Part): Retirement Plans

An employment agreement with a key executive officer provides for annual post-employment compensation equal to 25% of his average base salary and bonus earned in the last three fiscal years prior to the cessation of his employment with the Company. The officer is entitled to monthly payments during his lifetime beginning with the termination of his employment for any reason other than his breach of the employment agreement or termination for cause. The Company has accrued its obligation under the terms of the employment agreement. The Company decreased the accrual during 2009, 2008 and 2007 and recognized income of approximately $249,000, $45,000 and $44,000, respectively. The decrease in the accrual is primarily due to a change in estimate based on the refining of the assumptions and underlying data, including the estimated payout term. This accrual is recorded under other liabilities on the Consolidated Balance Sheets and totaled approximately $1,873,000 as of January 2, 2010.

16 (In Part): Commitments and Contingent Liabilities

The Company has an employment agreement with a key executive officer and shareholder which currently expires on January 1, 2012. In addition to a base salary, the agreement provides for a bonus based on pre-tax earnings. No maximum compensation limit exists. Total salary and bonus expensed in 2009, 2008 and 2007 was approximately $1,709,000, $2,154,000 and $2,385,000, respectively. The unpaid bonus at year end is recorded under other current liabilities on the Consolidated Balance Sheets. For fiscal 2009, this key executive voluntarily reduced the bonus to which he was contractually entitled to 70% of his prior year bonus. The officer is also entitled to monthly payments during his lifetime beginning with the termination of his employment for any reason other than his breach of the employment agreement or termination for cause. The Company has accrued its obligation under the terms of the employment agreement as discussed in Note 11.

Licensing Agreement

1.126

POLO RALPH LAUREN CORPORATION (MAR)

NOTES TO CONSOLIDATED FINANCIAL STATEMENTS

Note 23 (In Part): Additional Financial Information

Licensing-Related Transactions

Eyewear Licensing Agreement

In February 2006, the Company announced that it had entered into a ten-year exclusive licensing agreement with Luxottica Group, S.p.A. and affiliates for the design, production, sale and distribution of prescription frames and sunglasses under the *Polo Ralph Lauren* brand (the "Eyewear Licensing Agreement").

The Eyewear Licensing Agreement took effect on January 1, 2007 after the Company's pre-existing licensing agreement with another licensee expired. In early January, the Company received a prepayment of approximately $180 million, net of certain tax withholdings, in consideration of the annual minimum royalty and design-services fees to be earned over the life of the contract. The prepayment is non-refundable, except with respect to certain breaches of the agreement by the Company, in which case only the unearned portion of the prepayment as determined based on the specific terms of the agreement would be required to be repaid. The prepayment was recorded by the Company as deferred income and is being recognized in earnings as earned in accordance with the terms of the agreement based upon the higher of (a) contractually guaranteed minimum royalty levels or (b) estimates of sales and royalty data received from the licensee.

Underwear Licensing Agreement

The Company licensed the right to manufacture and sell Chaps-branded underwear under a long-term license agreement, which was scheduled to expire in December 2009. During Fiscal 2007, the Company and the licensee agreed to terminate the licensing and related design-services agreements. In connection with this agreement, the Company received a portion of the minimum royalty and design-service fees due to it under the underlying agreements on an accelerated basis. The approximate $8 million of proceeds received by the Company has been recognized as licensing revenue in the consolidated financial statements for Fiscal 2007.

FINANCIAL INSTRUMENTS

1.127 There are several sections of the FASB Accounting Standards Codification that deal with financial instruments. FASB ASC 825, *Financial Instruments*, requires reporting entities to disclose the fair value of financial instruments, and FASB ASC 815, *Derivatives and Hedging*, includes the disclosure requirements of credit risk concentrations. FASB ASC 815 establishes accounting and reporting standards for derivative instruments, including certain derivative instruments embedded in other contracts (collectively referred to as derivatives), and for hedging activities. FASB ASC 815 requires that an entity recognize all derivatives as either assets or liabilities in the statement of financial position and measure those instruments at fair value. FASB ASC 480, *Distinguishing Liabilities from Equity*, requires that an issuer classify certain financial instruments with characteristics of both liabilities and equity as liabilities. In addition, FASB ASC 815 simplifies the accounting for certain hybrid financial instruments by permitting fair value remeasurement of any hybrid financial instrument that contains an embedded derivative that would require bifurcation, including beneficial interests in securitized financial assets.

1.128 More recently, FASB ASC 815, *Derivatives and Hedging*, amended and expanded the disclosure requirements to enable users of financial statements to understand (a) how and why an entity uses derivative instruments, (b) how derivative instruments and related hedged items are accounted for under this statement and related interpretations, (c) how derivative instruments and related hedged items affect an entity's financial position, financial performance, and cash flows. To meet those objectives, FASB ASC 815 requires qualitative disclosures about objectives and strategies for using derivatives, qualitative disclosures about fair value amounts of gains and losses on derivative instruments, and disclosures about credit-risk-related contingent features in derivative agreements. Information about those instruments shall be disclosed in the context of each instrument's primary underlying risk exposure: for example, interest rate risk, credit risk, foreign currency exchange rate risk, commodity price risk or equity price risk. Further, those instruments shall be distinguished between those used for risk management purposes and those used for other purposes. FASB ASC 815 requires disclosure of the location and fair value amounts of derivative instruments reported in the statement of financial position. The fair value of those instruments shall be presented on a gross basis. Fair value amounts shall be presented as separate asset and liability values segregated between derivatives that are designated and qualifying as hedging instruments and those that are not. The disclosure shall identify the line item(s) in the statement of financial position in which the fair value amounts for these categories of derivative instruments are included. Also, the statement requires disclosure of the location and amount of the gains and losses on derivative instruments and related hedged items in the statement of financial performance or when applicable, in other comprehensive income. These gain and loss disclosures shall be presented separately by type of derivative contract. These quantitative disclosures are generally required to be presented in tabular format. Additionally, FASB ASC 815 requires disclosure of the nature and fair value amounts of derivative instruments that contain credit-risk-related features.

1.129 FASB ASC 820, *Fair Value Measurements and Disclosures*, defines fair value, establishes a framework for measuring fair value, and requires certain disclosures about fair value measurements. FASB ASC 820 clarifies the definition of fair value as an exit price, i.e., a price that would be received to sell, as opposed to acquire, an asset or transfer a liability. FASB ASC 820 emphasizes that fair value is a market-based measurement. It establishes a fair value hierarchy that distinguishes between assumptions developed based on market data obtained from independent external sources and the reporting entity's own assumptions. Further, FASB ASC 820 specifies that fair value measurement should consider adjustment for risk, such as the risk inherent in a valuation technique or its inputs. For assets and liabilities measured at fair value, whether on a recurring or a nonrecurring basis, FASB ASC 820 specifies the required disclosures concerning the inputs used to measure fair value. Since there has been an expressed concern about the potential difficulty associated with measuring the fair value of some liabilities, FASB Accounting Standards Update (ASU) No. 2009-05, *Measuring Liabilities at Fair Value*, provides clarification of the techniques used to measure fair value of a liability. FASB ASU No. 2009-05 is effective for the first reporting period beginning after issuance of the update, August 2009. Additionally, FASB Accounting Standards Update (ASU) No. 2010-06, *Improving Disclosures about Fair Value Measurements*, requires more robust disclosures about different classes of assets and liabilities measured at fair value, the valuation techniques and inputs used, the activity in Level 3 fair value measurements, and the transfers between Levels 1, 2, and 3. FASB ASU No. 2010-06 is effective for fiscal years beginning after December 15, 2009, except for the disclosures about certain Level 3 activity. Those disclosures are effective for fiscal years beginning after December 15, 2010.

1.130 FASB ASC 825, *Financial Instruments*, permits entities to choose to measure many financial instruments and certain other items at fair value that are not currently required to be measured at fair value. Further, under FASB ASC 825 a business entity shall report unrealized gains and losses on eligible items for which the fair value option has been elected in earnings at each subsequent reporting date. The irrevocable election of the fair value option is made on an instrument by instrument basis, and applied to the entire instrument, not just a portion of it. FASB ASC 825 also establishes presentation and disclosure requirements designed to facilitate comparison between entities that choose different measurement attributes for similar types of assets and liabilities.

1.131 Table 1-13 lists the frequencies of the various types of financial instruments of the survey entities. 218 survey entities entered into interest rate swaps. 297 survey entities entered into forward foreign currency contracts, options, or foreign exchange contracts. Swaps, futures, forward contracts, collars, and options were common types of commodity contracts reported by the survey entities. 126 survey entities entered into these types of contracts. The most frequent bases used by the survey entities to estimate fair value were market based approaches utilizing observable market-corroborated (level 2) inputs.

1.132 Examples of fair value disclosure for financial instruments and of disclosures for concentration of credit risk follow.

1.133

TABLE 1-13: FINANCIAL INSTRUMENTS

| | Number of Entities | | | |
	2009	2008	2007	2006
Foreign currency contracts	294	298	323	330
Interest rate contracts	235	239	289	297
Commodity contracts	124	126	128	128
Guarantees/ indemnifications:				
Debt	172	188	237	238
Contract performance	95	107	121	94
Lease payments	90	70	124	102
Product/service related	61	55	47	49
Environmental	60	60	58	61
Employee related	53	47	52	49
Tax	51	41	39	39
Intellectual property related	41	45	46	39
Other	47	37	37	56
Letters of credit	314	286	370	353
Sale of receivables with recourse	11	20	30	26

2008–2009 based on 500 entities surveyed; 2006–2007 based on 600 entities surveyed.

DERIVATIVE FINANCIAL INSTRUMENTS

1.134

ANADARKO PETROLEUM CORPORATION (DEC)

NOTES TO CONSOLIDATED FINANCIAL STATEMENTS

1 (In Part): Summary of Significant Accounting Policies

Fair Value (In Part)

Fair value is defined as the price that would be received to sell an asset or price paid to transfer a liability in an orderly transaction between market participants at the measurement date. The standard characterizes inputs used in determining fair value according to a hierarchy that prioritizes those inputs based upon the degree to which they are observable. The three levels of the fair-value-measurement hierarchy are as follows:

- Level 1—inputs represent quoted prices in active markets for identical assets or liabilities (for example, exchange-traded commodity derivatives).
- Level 2—inputs other than quoted prices included within Level 1 that are observable for the asset or liability, either directly or indirectly (for example, quoted market prices for similar assets or liabilities in active markets or quoted market prices for identical assets or liabilities in markets not considered to be active, inputs other than quoted prices that are observable for the asset or liability, or market-corroborated inputs).
- Level 3—inputs that are not observable from objective sources, such as the Company's internally developed assumptions used in pricing an asset or liability (for example, an estimate of future cash flows used in the Company's internally developed present value of future cash flows model that underlies the fair-value measurement).

In determining fair value, the Company utilizes observable market data when available, or models that incorporate observable market data. In addition to market information, the Company incorporates transaction-specific details that, in management's judgment, market participants would take into account in measuring fair value.

In arriving at fair-value estimates, the Company utilizes the most observable inputs available for the valuation technique employed. If a fair-value measurement reflects inputs at multiple levels within the hierarchy, the fair-value measurement is characterized based upon the lowest level of input that is significant to the fair-value measurement. For Anadarko, recurring fair-value measurements are performed for interest-rate derivatives, commodity derivatives, investments in trading securities and pension assets.

Derivative Instruments

Anadarko utilizes derivative instruments in its marketing and trading activities and to manage price risk attributable to the Company's forecasted sales of oil, natural-gas and NGLs production. Anadarko also periodically utilizes derivatives to manage its exposure associated with natural-gas processing, interest rates and foreign currency exchange rates. All derivatives that do not satisfy the normal purchases and sales exception criteria are carried on the balance sheet at fair value and are included in other current assets, other assets, accrued expenses or other long-term liabilities, depending on the derivative position and the expected timing of settlement. To the extent a legal right of offset with a counterparty exists, the Company reports derivative assets and liabilities on a net basis. Anadarko has exposure to credit risk to the extent the derivative-instrument counterparty is unable to satisfy its settlement commitment. The Company actively monitors the creditworthiness of each counterparty and assesses the impact, if any, on its derivative positions.

Through the end of 2006, Anadarko applied hedge accounting to certain commodity and interest-rate derivatives whereby gains and losses on these instruments were recognized in earnings in the same period in which the specifically identified hedged transactions affected earnings. Effective January 1, 2007, Anadarko discontinued its application of hedge accounting to all derivatives. As a result of this change, both realized and unrealized gains and losses on derivative instruments are recognized on a current basis. Net derivative losses attributable to derivatives previously subject to hedge accounting reside in accumulated other comprehensive income as of December 31, 2009 and will be reclassified to earnings in future periods as the economic transactions to which the derivatives relate affect earnings. See Note 8.

Changes in Accounting Principles (In Part)

The Company adopted a new fair-value-measurement standard as of January 1, 2008. The standard defines fair value, establishes a framework for measuring fair value under existing accounting pronouncements that require fair-value measurements and expands fair-value-measurement disclosures. The Company elected to implement the standard with the one-year deferral permitted for nonfinancial assets and nonfinancial liabilities, except those nonfinancial items recognized or disclosed at fair value on a recurring basis (at least annually). The deferral period ended on January 1, 2009. Accordingly, the Company now applies the fair-value framework to nonfinancial assets and nonfinancial liabilities initially measured at fair value, such as assets and liabilities acquired in a business combination, impaired long-lived assets (asset groups), intangible assets and goodwill, and initial recognition of asset retirement obligations and exit or disposal costs. Also, during the fourth quarter of 2009, Anadarko adopted a standard that requires expanded fair-value-measurement disclosures related to pensions.

The Company adopted a new standard for its derivative instruments and hedging activities, effective January 1, 2009. The standard does not change the Company's accounting for derivatives, but requires enhanced disclosures regarding the Company's methodology and purpose for entering into derivative instruments, accounting for derivative instruments and related hedged items (if any), and the impact of derivative instruments on the Company's consolidated financial position, results of operations and cash flows. See Note 8.

8. Derivative Instruments

Objective and Strategy

The Company is exposed to commodity price and interest-rate risk, and management considers it prudent to periodically reduce the Company's exposure to cash flow variability resulting from commodity price changes and interest-rate fluctuations. Accordingly, the Company enters into certain derivative instruments in order to manage its exposure to these risks.

Futures, swaps and options are used to manage the Company's cash flow exposure to commodity price risk inherent in the Company's oil and gas production and gas-processing operations (Oil and Gas Production/Processing Derivative Activities). Futures contracts and commodity swap agreements are used to fix the price of expected future oil and gas sales at major industry trading locations, such as Henry Hub, Louisiana for gas and Cushing, Oklahoma for oil. Basis swaps are used to fix or float the price differential between the product price at one market location versus another. Options are used to establish a floor and a ceiling price (collar) for expected future oil and gas sales. Derivative instruments are also used to manage commodity price risk inherent in customer pricing requirements and to fix margins on the future sale of natural gas and NGLs from the Company's leased storage facilities (Marketing and Trading Derivative Activities).

The Company may also enter into physical-delivery sales contracts to manage cash flow variability. These contracts call for the receipt or delivery of physical product at a specified location and price, which may be fixed or market-based.

Interest-rate swaps are used to fix or float interest rates on existing or anticipated indebtedness. The purpose of these instruments is to mitigate the Company's existing or anticipated exposure to unfavorable interest-rate changes.

The Company does not apply hedge accounting to any of its derivative instruments. The application of hedge accounting was discontinued by the Company for periods beginning on or after January 1, 2007. As a result, both realized and unrealized gains and losses associated with derivative instruments are recognized in earnings. Net derivative losses attributable to derivatives previously subject to hedge accounting reside in accumulated other comprehensive income (loss) and are reclassified to earnings in future periods as the economic transactions to which the derivatives relate are recorded in earnings.

The accumulated other comprehensive loss balances related to commodity derivatives at December 31, 2009 and December 31, 2008, were $10 million ($7 million after tax) and $22 million ($14 million after tax), respectively. The accumulated other comprehensive loss balances related to interest-rate derivatives at December 31, 2009 and December 31, 2008, were $141 million ($89 million after tax) and $163 million ($104 million after tax), respectively.

Oil and Gas Production/Processing Derivative Activities

Below is a summary of the Company's derivative instruments related to its oil and gas production as of December 31, 2009. The natural-gas prices listed below are New York Mercantile Exchange (NYMEX) Henry Hub prices. The crude-oil prices listed below reflect a combination of NYMEX Cushing and London Brent Dated prices.

	2010	2011	2012
Natural gas			
Three-way collars (thousand MMBtu/d)	1,630	480	500
Average price per MMBtu			
Ceiling sold price (call)	$8.23	$8.29	$9.03
Floor purchased price (put)	$5.59	$6.50	$6.50
Floor sold price (put)	$4.22	$5.00	$5.00
Fixed-price contracts (thousand MMBtu/d)	90	90	—
Average price per MMBtu	$6.10	$6.17	$—
Basis swaps (thousand MMBtu/d)	620	45	—
Price per MMBtu	$(0.98)	$(1.74)	$—

MMBtu—million British thermal units.
MMBtu/d—million British thermal units per day.

	2010	2011	2012
Crude oil			
Three-way collars (MBbls/d)	129	3	2
Average price per barrel			
Ceiling sold price (call)	$90.73	$86.00	$92.50
Floor purchased price (put)	$64.34	$50.00	$50.00
Floor sold price (put)	$49.34	$35.00	$35.00

MBbls/d—thousand barrels per day.

A three-way collar is a combination of three options: a sold call, a purchased put and a sold put. The sold call establishes the maximum price that the Company will receive for the contracted commodity volumes. The purchased put establishes the minimum price that the Company will receive for the contracted volumes unless the market price for the commodity falls below the sold put strike price, at which point the minimum price equals the reference price (*i.e.*, NYMEX) plus the excess of the purchased put strike price over the sold put strike price.

Marketing and Trading Derivative Activities

In addition to the positions in the above tables, the Company also engages in marketing and trading activities, which include physical product sales and derivative transactions entered into to reduce commodity price risk associated with certain physical product sales. At December 31, 2009 and December 31, 2008, the Company had outstanding physical transactions for 46 billion cubic feet (Bcf) and 51 Bcf, respectively, offset by derivative transactions for 17 Bcf and 34 Bcf, respectively, for net positions of 29 Bcf and 17 Bcf, respectively.

Interest-Rate Derivatives

As discussed in Note 10, during 2009, Anadarko issued fixed-rate senior notes in the aggregate principal amount of $2.0 billion. In advance of certain of these debt issuances, Anadarko entered into derivative financial instruments, effectively hedging the U.S. Treasury portion of the coupon rate on a portion of this debt. These derivative instruments were settled concurrently with the associated debt issuances, resulting in a realized loss of $16 million for the year ended December 31, 2009, reflected in (gains) losses on other derivatives, net.

As of December 31, 2009, the Company had scheduled debt maturities of approximately $3.5 billion in 2011 and 2012. In anticipation of refinancing a portion of these maturing debt obligations, in December 2008 and January 2009 Anadarko entered into interest-rate swap agreements to hedge a portion of the fixed interest rate it would pay on an aggregate notional principal amount of $3.0 billion, over a reference term of either 10 years or 30 years, beginning in 2011 and 2012. The swap instruments include a provision that requires both the termination of the swaps and cash settlement in full at the start of the reference period. A summary of the swaps detailing the outstanding notional principal amounts and the associated reference periods is shown in the table below.

Increases in the reference U.S. Treasury rates since contract inception have increased the value of this swap portfolio to Anadarko, the fixed-rate payor. During the second quarter of 2009, the Company revised the contractual terms of this swap portfolio to increase the weighted-average interest rate it is required to pay from approximately 3.25% to approximately 4.80%, and realized $552 million in cash. This realized gain was recorded to (gains) losses on other derivatives, net, as were unrealized gains of $57 million, for the year ended December 31, 2009, which were attributable to further fair-value changes of the Company's swap portfolio.

The Company's interest-rate derivative positions outstanding as of December 31, 2009, are as follows:

(Millions)	Reference Period		Weighted-Average Interest Rate
	Start	End	
Notional principal amount:			
$750	October 2011	October 2021	4.72%
$1,250	October 2011	October 2041	4.83%
$250	October 2012	October 2022	4.91%
$750	October 2012	October 2042	4.80%

Effect of Derivative Instruments—Balance Sheet

The fair value of all oil and gas and interest-rate derivative instruments not designated as hedging instruments (including physical-delivery sales contracts) is included in the table below.

(Millions)	Balance Sheet Classification	Gross Asset Derivatives		Gross Liability Derivatives	
		2009	2008	2009	2008
Derivatives					
Commodity	Other current assets	$140	$709	$ (63)	$(134)
	Other assets	82	156	(6)	(24)
	Accrued expenses	195	—	(417)	(14)
	Other liabilities	25	1	(52)	(28)
Total commodity derivatives		442	866	(538)	(200)
Interest rate	Other assets	53	3	—	—
	Accrued expenses	—	—	—	(10)
	Other liabilities	—	—	(3)	—
Total derivatives		$495	$869	$(541)	$(210)

Effect of Derivative Instruments—Statement of Income

The unrealized and realized gain or loss amounts and classification related to derivative instruments not designated as hedging instruments are as follows:

(Millions)	Classification of (Gain) Loss Recognized	Amount of (Gain) Loss Recognized		
		2009	2008	2007
Derivatives				
Commodity	Gathering, processing and marketing sales*	$ 37	$ (4)	$ 80
	(Gains) losses on commodity derivatives, net	408	(561)	524
Interest rate	(Gains) losses on other derivatives, net	(582)	10	9
Total derivative (gain) loss		$(137)	$(555)	$ 613

* Represents the effect of marketing and trading derivative activities.

The unrealized gain or loss amounts and classification related to derivative instruments included in the table above not designated as hedging instruments are as follows:

(Millions)	Classification of Unrealized (Gain) Loss Recognized	Amount of Unrealized (Gain) Loss Recognized		
		2009	2008	2007
Derivatives				
Commodity	Gathering, processing and marketing sales	$ 39	$ (29)	$ 52
	(Gains) losses on commodity derivatives, net	735	(900)	1,048
Interest rate	(Gains) losses on other derivatives, net	(57)	10	9
Total derivative unrealized (gain) loss		$ 717	$(919)	$1,109

Credit-Risk Considerations

The financial integrity of exchange-traded contracts are assured by NYMEX or the Intercontinental Exchange through their systems of financial safeguards and transaction guarantees and are subject to nominal credit risk. Over-the-counter traded swaps, options and futures contracts expose the Company to counterparty credit risk. The Company monitors the creditworthiness of each of its counterparties, establishes credit limits according to the Company's credit policies and guidelines, and assesses the impact, if any, of counterparties' creditworthiness on fair value. The Company has the ability to require cash collateral or letters of credit to mitigate credit-risk exposure. The Company also routinely exercises its contractual right to net realized gains against realized losses when settling with its counterparties.

The Company's net asset derivatives recorded at fair value on the balance sheet include amounts attributable to agreements entered into with financial institutions. Approximately $442 million of the Company's $495 million gross derivative asset balance at December 31, 2009 was attributable to open positions with financial institutions. The Company has netting and setoff agreements with each of these counterparties, which permit the net settlement of these gross derivative assets against gross derivative liabilities with this same group of counterparties. As of December 31, 2009, $321 million of the Company's $541 million gross derivative liability balance is permitted to offset the gross derivative asset balance. The table below includes the financial impact of our netting arrangements on the fair value of the Company's outstanding derivative positions.

Certain of the Company's derivative instruments contain provisions requiring either full or partial collateralization of the Company's obligations, or the immediate settlement of all such obligations in the event of a downgrade in the Company's credit rating to a level below investment grade from major credit rating agencies. The aggregate fair value of all derivative instruments with credit-risk-related contingent features for which a net liability position existed on December 31, 2009 was $146 million. This amount represents the amount that the Company would have to either collateralize or cash settle in the event the Company's credit rating was downgraded to a level below investment grade and the credit-risk-related features of such instruments were exercised.

Fair Value

The fair value of commodity-futures contracts are based on inputs that are quoted prices in active markets for identical assets or liabilities, resulting in Level 1 categorization of such measurements. The valuation of physical-delivery purchase and sale agreements, over-the-counter financial swaps and three-way collars are based on similar transactions observable in active markets or industry-standard models that primarily rely on market-observable inputs. Substantially all of the assumptions for industry-standard models are observable in active markets throughout the full term of the instrument. Therefore, the Company categorizes these measurements as Level 2.

The following tables set forth, by level within the fair-value hierarchy, the fair value of the Company's financial assets and liabilities.

(Millions)	Level 1	Level 2	Level 3	Netting and Collateral[1]	Total
December 31, 2009					
Assets:					
Commodity derivatives	$ 4	$ 438	$—	$(289)	$ 153
Interest-rate derivatives	—	53	—	—	53
Total	$ 4	$ 491	$—	(289)	$ 206
Liabilities:					
Commodity derivatives	$(6)	$(532)	$—	333	$(205)
Interest-rate derivatives	—	$ (3)	—	—	(3)
Total	$(6)	$(535)	$—	$ 333	$(208)

[1] Represents the impact of netting assets, liabilities and collateral with counterparties with which the right of setoff exists. Cash collateral held by counterparties from Anadarko was $105 million at December 31, 2009. Anadarko held no cash collateral from counterparties at December 31, 2009.

(Millions)	Level 1	Level 2	Level 3	Netting and Collateral[1]	Total
December 31, 2008					
Assets:					
Commodity derivatives	$ 34	$ 832	$—	$(161)	$705
Interest-rate derivatives	—	3	—	—	3
Total	$ 34	$ 835	$—	$(161)	$708
Liabilities:					
Commodity derivatives	$(13)	$(187)	$—	$ 158	$(42)
Interest-rate derivatives	—	(10)	—	—	(10)
Total	$(13)	$(197)	$—	$ 158	$(52)

[1] Represents the impact of netting assets, liabilities and collateral with counterparties with which the right of setoff exists. Cash collateral held by counterparties was $10 million at December 31, 2008. Cash collateral held by Anadarko from counterparties was $3 million at December 31, 2008.

1.135

CAMPBELL SOUP COMPANY (JUL)

NOTES TO CONSOLIDATED FINANCIAL STATEMENTS (Currency in millions)

1 (In Part): Summary of Significant Accounting Policies

Derivative Financial Instruments

The company uses derivative financial instruments primarily for purposes of hedging exposures to fluctuations in foreign currency exchange rates, interest rates, commodities and equity-linked employee benefit obligations. These derivative contracts are entered into for periods consistent with the related underlying exposures and do not constitute positions independent of those exposures. The company does not enter into derivative contracts for speculative purposes and does not use leveraged instruments. The company's derivative programs include strategies that both qualify and do not qualify for hedge accounting treatment under SFAS No. 133 "Accounting for Derivative Instruments and Hedging Activities," as amended.

All derivatives are recognized on the balance sheet at fair value. On the date the derivative contract is entered into, the company designates the derivative as a hedge of the fair value of a recognized asset or liability or a firm commitment (fair-value hedge), a hedge of a forecasted transaction or of the variability of cash flows to be received or paid related to a recognized asset or liability (cash-flow hedge), or a hedge of a net investment in a foreign operation. Some derivatives may also be considered natural hedging instruments (changes in fair value act as economic offsets to changes in fair value of the underlying hedged item) and are not designated for hedge accounting under SFAS No. 133.

Changes in the fair value of a fair-value hedge, along with the gain or loss on the underlying hedged asset or liability (including losses or gains on firm commitments), are recorded in current-period earnings. The effective portion of gains and losses on cash-flow hedges are recorded in other comprehensive income (loss), until earnings are affected by the variability of cash flows. If a derivative is used as a hedge of a net investment in a foreign operation, its changes in fair value, to the extent effective as a hedge, are recorded in other comprehensive income (loss). Any ineffective portion of designated hedges is recognized in current-period earnings. Changes in the fair value of derivatives that are not designated for hedge accounting are recognized in current-period earnings.

Cash flows from derivative contracts are included in Net cash provided by operating activities.

2 (In Part): Recent Accounting Pronouncements

Recently Adopted Accounting Pronouncements (In Part)

In September 2006, the FASB issued SFAS No. 157 "Fair Value Measurements," which provides guidance for using fair value to measure assets and liabilities. SFAS No. 157 establishes a definition of fair value, provides a framework for measuring fair value and expands the disclosure requirements about fair value measurements. This statement does not require any new fair value measurements but rather applies to all other accounting pronouncements that require or permit fair value measurements. In February 2008, FASB Staff Position (FSP) No. FAS 157-2 was issued, which delayed by a year the effective date for certain nonfinancial assets and liabilities. The company adopted SFAS No. 157 for financial assets and liabilities in the first quarter of fiscal 2009. See Note 13 for additional information.

● ● ● ● ● ●

In March 2008, the FASB issued SFAS No. 161 "Disclosures about Derivative Instruments and Hedging Activities—an amendment of FASB Statement No. 133," which enhances the disclosure requirements for derivative instruments and hedging activities. Entities are required to provide enhanced disclosures about (a) the location and amounts of derivative instruments in an entity's financial statements, (b) how derivative instruments and related hedged items are accounted for under Statement 133 and its related interpretations, and (c) how derivative instruments and related hedged items affect an entity's financial position, financial performance, and cash flows. The guidance in SFAS No. 161 is effective for financial statements issued for fiscal years and interim periods beginning after November 15, 2008, with early application encouraged. This Statement encouraged, but did not require, comparative disclosures for earlier periods at initial adoption. The company adopted SFAS No. 161 in the third quarter of fiscal 2009. See Note 12 for additional information.

12. Financial Instruments

The carrying value of cash and cash equivalents, accounts receivable, accounts payable and short-term debt approximate fair value. The fair value of long-term debt as indicated in Note 11 is based on quoted market prices or pricing models using current market rates.

The principal market risks to which the company is exposed are changes in foreign currency exchange rates, interest rates, and commodity prices. In addition, the company is exposed to equity price changes related to certain deferred compensation obligations. In order to manage these exposures, the company follows established risk management policies and procedures, including the use of derivative contracts such as swaps, forwards and commodity futures and option contracts. These derivative contracts are entered into for periods consistent with the related underlying exposures and do not constitute positions independent of those exposures. The company does not enter into derivative contracts for speculative purposes and does not use leveraged instruments. The company's derivative programs include strategies that both qualify and do not qualify for hedge accounting treatment under SFAS No. 133, "Accounting for Derivative Instruments and Hedging Activities."

The company is exposed to the risk that counterparties to derivative contracts will fail to meet their contractual obligations. The company minimizes the counterparty credit risk on these transactions by dealing only with leading, creditworthy financial institutions having long-term credit ratings of "A" or better and, therefore, does not anticipate nonperformance. In addition, the contracts are distributed among several financial institutions, thus minimizing credit risk concentration. The company does not have credit-risk-related contingent features in its derivative instruments as of August 2, 2009.

Foreign Currency Exchange Risk

The company is exposed to foreign currency exchange risk related to its international operations, including non-functional currency intercompany debt and net investments in subsidiaries. The company is also exposed to foreign exchange risk as a result of transactions in currencies other than the functional currency of certain subsidiaries. The company utilizes foreign exchange forward purchase and sale contracts as well as cross-currency swaps to hedge these exposures. The contracts are either designated as cash-flow hedging instruments or are undesignated. The company typically hedges portions of its forecasted foreign currency transaction exposure with foreign exchange forward contracts for up to eighteen months. To hedge currency exposures related to intercompany debt, cross-currency swap contracts are entered into for periods consistent with the underlying debt. As of August 2, 2009, cross-currency swap contracts mature in 2010 through 2014. Principal currencies hedged include the Australian dollar, Canadian dollar, euro, Swedish krona, New Zealand dollar, British pound and Japanese yen. The notional amount of foreign exchange forward and cross-currency swap contracts accounted for as cash-flow hedges was $322 and $307 at August 2, 2009 and August 3, 2008, respectively. The effective portion of the changes in fair value on these instruments is recorded in other comprehensive income (loss) and is reclassified into the Statements of Earnings on the same line item and same period in which the underlying hedge transaction affects earnings. The notional amount of foreign exchange forward and cross-currency swap contracts that are not designated as accounting hedges was $802 and $582 at August 2, 2009 and August 3, 2008, respectively.

Interest Rate Risk

The company manages its exposure to changes in interest rates by optimizing the use of variable-rate and fixed-rate debt and by utilizing interest rate swaps in order to maintain its variable-to-total debt ratio within targeted guidelines. Receive fixed rate/pay variable rate interest rate swaps are accounted for as fair-value hedges. The notional amount of outstanding fair-value interest rate swaps at August 2, 2009 and August 3, 2008, totaled $500 and $675, respectively.

In June 2008, the company entered into two forward starting interest rate swap contracts accounted for as cash-flow hedges with a combined notional value of $200 to hedge an anticipated debt offering in fiscal 2009. These swaps were settled as of November 2, 2008, at a loss of $13, which was recorded in other comprehensive income (loss). In January 2009, the company issued $300 ten-year 4.50% notes. The loss on the swap contracts will be amortized over the life of the debt as additional interest expense.

Commodity Price Risk

The company principally uses a combination of purchase orders and various short- and long-term supply arrangements in connection with the purchase of raw materials, including certain commodities and agricultural products. The company also enters into commodity futures and options contracts to reduce the volatility of price fluctuations of natural gas, diesel fuel, wheat, soybean oil, cocoa, aluminum and corn which impact the cost of raw materials. Commodity futures and option contracts are typically accounted for as cash-flow hedges or are not designated as accounting hedges. Commodity futures and option contracts are typically entered into to hedge a portion of commodity requirements for periods up to 18 months. The notional amount of commodity contracts accounted for as cash-flow hedges was $7 and $66 at August 2, 2009 and August 3, 2008, respectively. The notional amount of commodity contracts that are not designated as

accounting hedges was $44 and $80 at August 2, 2009 and August 3, 2008, respectively. As of August 2, 2009, the contracts mature within 12 months.

Equity Price Risk

The company hedges a portion of exposures relating to certain deferred compensation obligations linked to the total return of the Standard & Poor's 500 Index, the total return of the company's capital stock and the total return of the Puritan Fund. Under these contracts, the company pays variable interest rates and receives from the counterparty either the total return of the Standard & Poor's 500 Index, the total return of the Puritan Fund, or the total return on company capital stock. These instruments are not designated as hedges for accounting purposes. The contracts are typically entered into for periods not exceeding 12 months. The notional amount of the company's deferred compensation hedges as of August 3, 2009 and August 3, 2008 were $48 and $56, respectively.

The following table summarizes the fair value of derivative instruments recorded in the Consolidated Balance Sheets as of August 2, 2009 and August 3, 2008:

	Balance Sheet Classification	2009	2008
Asset derivatives			
Derivatives designated as hedges:			
Foreign exchange forward contracts	Other current assets	$ 1	$ 2
Cross-currency swap contracts	Other current assets	3	—
Commodity contracts	Other current assets	—	6
Interest rate swaps	Other current assets	—	2
Interest rate swaps	Other assets	38	13
Total derivatives designated as hedges		$42	$ 23
Derivatives not designated as hedges:			
Foreign exchange forward contracts	Other current assets	$ 3	$1
Commodity contracts	Other current assets	6	1
Cross-currency swap contracts	Other current assets	—	1
Cross-currency swap contracts	Other assets	7	—
Deferred compensation contracts	Other current assets	4	1
Total derivatives not designated as hedges		$20	$ 4
Total asset derivatives		$62	$ 27
Liability derivatives			
Derivatives designated as hedges:			
Foreign exchange forward contracts	Accrued liabilities	$ 3	$ 1
Commodity contracts	Accrued liabilities	—	2
Cross-currency swap contracts	Accrued liabilities	1	22
Cross-currency swap contracts	Other liabilities	31	47
Total derivatives designated as hedges		$35	$ 72
Derivatives not designated as hedges:			
Foreign exchange forward contracts	Accrued liabilities	$11	$ 1
Commodity contracts	Accrued liabilities	6	8
Cross-currency swap contracts	Accrued liabilities	5	14
Cross-currency swap contracts	Other liabilities	8	35
Total derivatives not designated as hedges		$30	$ 58
Total liability derivatives		$65	$130

The derivative assets and liabilities are presented on a gross basis in the table. In accordance with FIN 39, "Offsetting Amounts Related to Certain Contracts," as amended, certain derivative asset and liability balances, including cash collat-

eral, are offset in the balance sheet when a legally enforceable right of offset exists.

The following table shows the effect of the company's derivative instruments designated as cash-flow hedges for the years ended August 2, 2009 and August 3, 2008 on other comprehensive income (loss) (OCI) and the Consolidated Statements of Earnings:

Derivatives Designated as Cash-Flow Hedges

	Location in Earnings	Total Cash-Flow Hedge OCI Activity	
		2009	2008
OCI derivative gain/(loss) at beginning of year		$ 8	$(8)
Effective portion of changes in fair value recognized in OCI:			
Foreign exchange forward contracts		(6)	(4)
Cross-currency swap contracts		(6)	6
Forward starting interest rate swaps		(15)	1
Commodity contracts		(11)	5
Amount of (gain) or loss reclassified from OCI to earnings:			
Foreign exchange forward contracts	Other expenses/income	(2)	2
Foreign exchange forward contracts	Cost of products sold	(5)	5
Cross-currency swap contracts	Other expenses/income	—	—
Forward starting interest rate swaps	Interest expense	1	1
Commodity contracts	Cost of products sold	5	—
OCI derivative gain/(loss) at end of year		$(31)	$ 8

The amount expected to be reclassified from other comprehensive income into earnings in 2010 is $20. The ineffective portion and amount excluded from effectiveness testing were not material.

The following table shows the effect of the company's derivative instruments designated as fair-value hedges on the Consolidated Statements of Earnings:

Derivatives Designated as Fair-Value Hedges	Location of Gain or (Loss) Recognized in Earnings	Amount of Gain or (Loss) Recognized in Earnings on Derivatives		Amount of Gain or (Loss) Recognized in Earnings on Hedged Item	
		2009	2008	2009	2008
Interest rate swaps	Interest expense	$24	$33	$(24)	$(33)

The following table shows the effects of the company's derivative instruments not designated as hedges in the Consolidated Statements of Earnings:

Derivatives Not Designated as Hedges	Location of Gain or (Loss) Recognized in Earnings	Amount of Gain or (Loss) Recognized in Earnings on Derivatives	
		2009	2008
Foreign exchange forward contracts	Other expenses/income	$ 7	$ 1
Foreign exchange forward contracts	Cost of products sold	1	—
Cross-currency swap contracts	Other expenses/income	44	(76)
Commodity contracts	Cost of products sold	(24)	(17)
Deferred compensation contracts	Administrative expenses	(8)	(6)
Total		$20	$(98)

13. Fair Value Measurements

In the first quarter of fiscal 2009, the company adopted the provisions of SFAS No. 157 "Fair Value Measurements" for financial assets and liabilities, as described in Note 2. The provisions have been applied prospectively beginning August 4, 2008. Under SFAS No. 157, the company is required to categorize financial assets and liabilities based on the following fair value hierarchy:

- Level 1: Observable inputs that reflect quoted prices (unadjusted) for identical assets or liabilities in active markets.

- Level 2: Inputs other than quoted prices included in Level 1 that are observable for the asset or liability through corroboration with observable market data.
- Level 3: Unobservable inputs that reflect the reporting entity's own assumptions.

The following table presents the company's financial assets and liabilities that are measured at fair value on a recurring basis at August 2, 2009 consistent with the fair value hierarchy of SFAS No. 157:

| | Fair Value 2009 | Fair Value Measurements 2009 Using Fair Value Hierarchy | | |
		Level 1	Level 2	Level 3
Assets				
Interest rate swaps[1]	$ 38	$ —	$ 38	$—
Foreign exchange forward contracts[2]	4	—	4	—
Cross-currency swap contracts[3]	10	—	10	—
Deferred compensation derivatives[4]	4	—	4	—
Commodity derivatives[5]	6	6	—	—
Total assets at fair value	$ 62	$ 6	$ 56	$—
Liabilities				
Commodity derivatives[5]	$ 6	$ 6	$ —	$—
Foreign exchange forward contracts[2]	14	—	14	—
Cross-currency swap contracts[3]	45	—	45	—
Deferred compensation obligation[6]	142	80	62	—
Total liabilities at fair value	$207	$86	$121	$—

[1] Based on LIBOR swap rates.
[2] Based on observable market transactions of spot currency rates and forward rates.
[3] Based on observable local benchmarks for currency and interest rates.
[4] Based on LIBOR and equity index swap rates.
[5] Based on quoted futures exchanges.
[6] Based on the fair value of the participants' investments.

1.136

COOPER TIRE & RUBBER COMPANY (DEC)

NOTES TO CONSOLIDATED FINANCIAL STATEMENTS
(Dollar amounts in thousands)

Note 1 (In Part): Significant Accounting Policies

Derivative Financial Instruments

Derivative financial instruments are utilized by the Company to reduce foreign currency exchange risks. The Company has established policies and procedures for risk assessment and the approval, reporting and monitoring of derivative financial instrument activities. The Company does not enter into financial instruments for trading or speculative purposes.

The Company uses foreign currency forward contracts as hedges of the fair value of certain non-U.S. dollar denominated asset and liability positions, primarily accounts receivable. Gains and losses resulting from the impact of currency exchange rate movements on these forward contracts are recognized in the accompanying consolidated statements of income in the period in which the exchange rates change and offset the foreign currency gains and losses on the underlying exposure being hedged.

Foreign currency forward contracts are also used to hedge variable cash flows associated with forecasted sales and purchases denominated in currencies that are not the functional currency of certain entities. The forward contracts have maturities of less than twelve months pursuant to the Company's policies and hedging practices. These forward contracts meet the criteria for and have been designated as cash flow hedges. Accordingly, the effective portion of the change in fair value of unrealized gains and losses on such forward contracts are recorded as a separate component of stockholders' equity in the accompanying consolidated balance sheets and reclassified into earnings as the hedged transaction affects earnings.

The Company assesses hedge effectiveness quarterly. In doing so, the Company monitors the actual and forecasted foreign currency sales and purchases versus the amounts hedged to identify any hedge ineffectiveness. The Company also performs regression analysis comparing the change in value of the hedging contracts versus the underlying foreign currency sales and purchases, which confirms a high correlation and hedge effectiveness. Any hedge ineffectiveness is recorded as an adjustment in the accompanying consolidated financial statements of operations in the period in which the ineffectiveness occurs. For periods presented, an immaterial amount of ineffectiveness has been identified and recorded.

Accounting Pronouncements (In Part)

Disclosures About Derivative Instruments and Hedging Activities

In March 2008, the FASB issued accounting guidance on disclosures about derivative instruments and hedging activities. This guidance expands disclosures for derivative instruments by requiring entities to disclose the fair value of derivative instruments and their gains or losses in tabular format. It also requires disclosure of information about credit risk-related contingent features in derivative agreements, counterparty credit risk, and strategies and objectives for using derivative instruments. The Company adopted this new guidance on January 1, 2009. The adoption of this guidance did not have a material impact on the Company's consolidated financial statements. See Note 9—Fair Value of Financial Instruments for additional information.

Note 9. Fair Value of Financial Instruments

Derivative financial instruments are utilized by the Company to reduce foreign currency exchange risks. The Company has established policies and procedures for risk assessment and the approval, reporting and monitoring of derivative financial instrument activities. The Company does not enter into financial instruments for training or speculative purposes. The derivative financial instruments include fair value and cash flow hedges of foreign currency exposures. Exchange rate fluctuations on the foreign currency-denominated intercompany loans and obligations are offset by the change in values of the fair value foreign currency hedges. The Company presently hedges exposures in the Euro, Canadian dollar, British pound sterling, Swiss franc, Swedish krona, Mexican peso and Chinese yuan generally for transactions expected to occur within the next 12 months. The notional amount of these foreign currency derivative instruments at December 31, 2008 and 2009 was $178,100 and $207,600, respectively.

The counterparties to each of these agreements are major commercial banks. Management believes that the probability of losses related to credit risk on investments classified as cash and cash equivalents is unlikely.

The Company uses foreign currency forward contracts as hedges of the fair value of certain non-U.S. dollar denominated asset and liability positions, primarily accounts receivable and debt. Gains and losses resulting from the impact of currency exchange rate movements on these forward contracts are recognized in the accompanying consolidated statements of income in the period in which the exchange rates change and offset the foreign currency gains and losses on the underlying exposure being hedged.

Foreign currency forward contracts are also used to hedge variable cash flows associated with forecasted sales and purchases denominated in currencies that are not the functional currency of certain entities. The forward contracts have maturities of less than twelve months pursuant to the Company's policies and hedging practices. These forward contracts meet the criteria for and have been designated as cash flow hedges. Accordingly, the effective portion of the change in fair value of such forward contracts (approximately $3,272 and $(2,136) as of December 31, 2008 and 2009, respectively) are recorded as a separate component of stockholders' equity in the accompanying consolidated balance sheets and reclassified into earnings as the hedged transaction affects earnings.

The Company assesses hedge ineffectiveness quarterly using the hypothetical derivative methodology. In doing so, the Company monitors the actual and forecasted foreign currency sales and purchases versus the amounts hedged to identify any hedge ineffectiveness. Any hedge ineffectiveness is recorded as an adjustment in the accompanying consolidated financial statements of operations in the period in which the ineffectiveness occurs. The Company also performs regression analysis comparing the change in value of the hedging contracts versus the underlying foreign currency sales and purchases, which confirms a high correlation and hedge effectiveness.

The following table presents the location and amounts of derivative instrument fair values in the Statement of Financial Position:

	2008	2009
(Assets)/liabilities		
Derivatives designated as hedging instruments	Accrued liabilities $(1,058)	Accrued liabilities $2,158
Derivatives not designated as hedging instruments	Accrued liabilities $ (194)	Accrued liabilities $ (78)

The following table presents the location and amount of gains and losses on derivative instruments in the Consolidated Statement of Operations:

	Amount of Gain (Loss) Recognized in Other Comprehensive Income on Derivative (Effective Portion)	Amount of Gain (Loss) Reclassified From Cumulative Other Comprehensive Loss into Net Sales (Effective Portion)	Amount of Gain (Loss) Recognized in Other—Net on Derivative (Ineffective Portion)
Derivatives Designated as Cash Flow Hedges	2009	2009	2009
Foreign exchange contracts	$(7,208)	$(4,198)	$(458)

Derivatives Not Designated as Hedging Instruments	Location of Gain (Loss) Recognized in Income on Derivatives	Amount of Gain (Loss) Recognized in Income on Derivatives 2009
Foreign exchange contracts	Other—net	$ 142
Interest swap contracts	Interest expense	1,855
		$1,997

For effective designated foreign exchange hedges, the Company reclassifies the gain (loss) from Other Comprehensive Income into Net Sales and the ineffective portion is recorded directly into Other—net.

The Company has categorized its financial instruments, based on the priority of the inputs to the valuation technique, into the three-level fair value hierarchy. The fair value hierarchy gives the highest priority to quoted prices in active markets for identical assets or liabilities (Level 1) and the lowest priority to unobservable inputs (Level 3). If the inputs used to measure the financial instruments fall within the different levels of the hierarchy, the categorization is based on the lowest level input that is significant to the fair value measurement of the instrument.

Financial assets and liabilities recorded on the Consolidated Balance Sheet are categorized based on the inputs to the valuation techniques as follows:

- Level 1. Financial assets and liabilities whose values are based on unadjusted quoted prices for identical assets or liabilities in an active market that the Company has the ability to access.
- Level 2. Financial assets and liabilities whose values are based on quoted prices in markets that are not active or model inputs that are observable either directly or indirectly for substantially the full term of the asset or liability. Level 2 inputs include the following.
  a. Quoted prices for similar assets or liabilities in active markets;
  b. Quoted prices for identical or similar assets or liabilities in non-active markets;
  c. Pricing models whose inputs are observable for substantially the full term of the asset or liability; and
  d. Pricing models whose inputs are derived principally from or corroborated by observable market data through correlation or other means for substantially the full term of the asset or liability.
- Level 3. Financial assets and liabilities whose values are based on prices or valuation techniques that require inputs that are both unobservable and significant to the overall fair value measurement. These inputs reflect management's own assumptions about the assumptions a market participant would use in pricing the asset or liability.

The Company defines the fair value of foreign exchange contracts as the amount of the difference between the contracted and current market value at the end of the period. The Company estimates the current market value of foreign exchange contracts by obtaining month-end market quotes of foreign exchange rates and forward rates for contracts with similar terms.

The following table presents the Company's fair value hierarchy for those assets and liabilities measured at fair value on a recurring basis as of December 31, 2008 and 2009:

Foreign Exchange Contracts	Total Derivative (Assets) Liabilities	Quoted Prices in Active Markets for Identical Assets Level (1)	Significant Other Observable Inputs Level (2)	Significant Unobservable Inputs Level (3)
2009	$(2,080)		$(2,080)	
2008	$(1,252)		$(1,252)	

OFF-BALANCE-SHEET FINANCIAL INSTRUMENTS

Financial Guarantees/Indemnifications

1.137

THE BOEING COMPANY (DEC)

NOTES TO CONSOLIDATED FINANCIAL STATEMENTS (Dollars in millions)

Note 1 (In Part): Summary of Significant Accounting Policies

Guarantees

We record a liability in Other accrued liabilities for the fair value of guarantees that are issued or modified after December 31, 2002. For a residual value guarantee where we received a cash premium, the liability is equal to the cash premium received at the guarantee's inception. For credit and performance guarantees, the liability is equal to the present value of the expected loss. We determine the expected loss by multiplying the creditor's default rate by the guarantee amount reduced by the expected recovery, if applicable, for each future period the credit or performance guarantee will be outstanding. If at inception of a guarantee, we determine there is a probable related contingent loss, we will recognize a liability for the greater of (a) the fair value of the guarantee as described above or (b) the probable contingent loss amount.

Note 11 (In Part): Liabilities, Commitments and Contingencies

Financing Commitments (In Part)

We have entered into standby letters of credit agreements and surety bonds with financial institutions primarily relating to the guarantee of future performance on certain contracts. Contingent liabilities on outstanding letters of credit agreements and surety bonds aggregated approximately $7,052 and $5,763 as of December 31, 2009 and 2008.

Note 12 (In Part): Arrangements With Off-Balance Sheet Risk

We enter into arrangements with off-balance sheet risk in the normal course of business, primarily in the form of guarantees.

Third-Party Guarantees

The following tables provide quantitative data regarding our third-party guarantees. The maximum potential payments represent a "worst-case scenario," and do not necessarily reflect our expected results. Estimated proceeds from collateral and recourse represent the anticipated values of assets we could liquidate or receive from other parties to offset our payments under guarantees.

	Maximum Potential Payments	Estimated Proceeds From Collateral/ Recourse	Carrying Amount of Liabilities*
As of December 31, 2009			
Contingent repurchase commitments	$3,958	$3,940	$ 7
Indemnifications to ULA	682		23
Other credit guarantees	119	109	2
Residual value guarantees	51	44	10
As of December 31, 2008			
Contingent repurchase commitments	$4,024	$4,014	$ 7
Indemnifications to ULA	1,184		7
Credit guarantees related to the Sea Launch venture	451	271	180
Other credit guarantees	158	145	11
Residual value guarantees	51	47	10

* Amounts included in Other accrued liabilities.

Indemnifications to ULA

We agreed to indemnify ULA against losses in the event that costs associated with $1,360 of Delta launch program inventories included in contributed assets and $1,860 of Delta program inventories subject to an inventory supply agreement are not recoverable and allowable from existing and future orders. The term of the inventory indemnification extends to December 31, 2020. Since inception, ULA has consumed $1,111 of inventories that were contributed by us and has made advances of $120 to us under the inventory supply agreement. The table above includes indemnifications to ULA for contributed Delta launch program inventory of $277 and $813, plus $348 related to the pricing of certain contracts and $57 and $23 related to miscellaneous Delta contracts at December 31, 2009 and 2008.

We agreed to indemnify ULA against potential losses that ULA may incur in the event ULA is unable to obtain certain additional contract pricing from the USAF for four satellite missions. We believe ULA is entitled to additional contract pricing. In December 2008, ULA submitted a claim to the USAF to re-price the contract value for two of the four satellite missions covered by the indemnification. In March 2009, the USAF issued a denial of that claim and in June 2009, ULA filed an appeal. During 2009, the USAF exercised its option for a third satellite mission. ULA intends to submit a claim to the USAF in 2010 to re-price the contract value of the third mission. If ULA is unsuccessful obtaining additional pricing, we may be responsible for a portion of the shortfall and may record up to $382 in pre-tax losses associated with the four missions.

Other Credit Guarantees

We have issued credit guarantees, principally to facilitate the sale and/or financing of commercial aircraft. Under these arrangements, we are obligated to make payments to a guaranteed party in the event that lease or loan payments are not made by the original lessee or debtor or certain specified services are not performed. A substantial portion of these guarantees has been extended on behalf of original lessees or debtors with less than investment-grade credit. Our commercial aircraft credit-related guarantees are collateralized by the underlying commercial aircraft and certain other assets. Current outstanding credit guarantees expire within the next 11 years.

Residual Value Guarantees

We have issued various residual value guarantees principally to facilitate the sale and financing of certain commercial aircraft. Under these guarantees, we are obligated to make payments to the guaranteed party if the related aircraft or equipment fair values fall below a specified amount at a future time. These obligations are collateralized principally by commercial aircraft and expire within the next 9 years.

1.138

E. I. DU PONT DE NEMOURS AND COMPANY (DEC)

NOTES TO CONSOLIDATED FINANCIAL STATEMENTS
(Dollars in millions)

20 (In Part): Commitments and Contingent Liabilities

Guarantees (In Part)

Indemnifications

In connection with acquisitions and divestitures, the company has indemnified respective parties against certain liabilities that may arise in connection with these transactions and business activities prior to the completion of the transaction. The term of these indemnifications, which typically pertain to environmental, tax and product liabilities, is generally indefinite. In addition, the company indemnifies its duly elected or appointed directors and officers to the fullest extent permitted by Delaware law, against liabilities incurred as a result of their activities for the company, such as adverse judgments relating to litigation matters. If the indemnified party were to incur a liability or have a liability increase as a result of a successful claim, pursuant to the terms of the indemnification, the company would be required to reimburse the indemnified party. The maximum amount of potential future payments is generally unlimited. The carrying amount recorded for all indemnifications as of December 31, 2009 and December 31, 2008 was $100 and $110, respectively. Although it is reasonably possible that future payments may exceed amounts accrued, due to the nature of indemnified items, it is not possible to make a reasonable estimate of the maximum potential loss or range of loss. No assets are held as collateral and no specific recourse provisions exist.

In connection with the 2004 sale of the majority of the net assets of Textiles and Interiors, the company indemnified the purchasers, subsidiaries of Koch Industries, Inc. (INVISTA), against certain liabilities primarily related to taxes, legal and environmental matters and other representations and warranties under the Purchase and Sale Agreement. The estimated fair value of the indemnity obligations under the Purchase and Sale Agreement was $70 and was included in the indemnifications balance of $100 at December 31, 2009. Under the Purchase and Sale Agreement, the company's total indemnification obligation for the majority of the representations and warranties cannot exceed $1,400. The other indemnities are not subject to this limit. In March 2008, INVISTA filed suit in the Southern District of New York alleging that certain representations and warranties in the Purchase and Sale Agreement were breached and, therefore, that DuPont is obligated to indemnify it. DuPont disagrees with the extent and value of INVISTA's claims. DuPont has not changed its estimate of its total indemnification obligation under the Purchase and Sale Agreement as a result of the lawsuit.

Obligations for Equity Affiliates & Others

The company has directly guaranteed various debt obligations under agreements with third parties related to equity affiliates, customers, suppliers and other affiliated and unaffiliated companies. At December 31, 2009, the company had directly guaranteed $684 of such obligations, and $119 relating to guarantees of historical obligations for divested subsidiaries. This represents the maximum potential amount of future (undiscounted) payments that the company could be required to make under the guarantees. The company would be required to perform on these guarantees in the event of default by the guaranteed party.

The company assesses the payment/performance risk by assigning default rates based on the duration of the guarantees. These default rates are assigned based on the external credit rating of the counterparty or through internal credit analysis and historical default history for counterparties that do not have published credit ratings. For counterparties without an external rating or available credit history, a cumulative average default rate is used.

At December 31, 2009 and December 31, 2008, a liability of $146 and $121, respectively, was recorded for these obligations, representing the amount of payment/performance risk for which the company deems probable. This liability is principally related to obligations of the company's polyester films joint venture, which are guaranteed by the company.

In certain cases, the company has recourse to assets held as collateral, as well as personal guarantees from customers and suppliers. Assuming liquidation, these assets are estimated to cover approximately 32 percent of the $358 of guaranteed obligations of customers and suppliers. Set forth below are the company's guaranteed obligations at December 31, 2009:

	Short-Term	Long-Term	Total
Obligations for customers, suppliers and other affiliated and unaffiliated companies[1,2]:			
Bank borrowings (terms up to 6 years)	$505	$134	$639
Leases on equipment and facilities (terms up to 3 years)	12	1	13
Obligations for equity affiliates[2]:			
Bank borrowings (terms up to 3 years)	7	22	29
Leases on equipment and facilities (terms up to 1 year)	3	—	3
Total obligations for customers, suppliers, affiliated and other unaffiliated companies, and equity affiliates	527	157	684
Obligations for divested subsidiaries[3]:			
Conoco (terms up to 17 years)	—	16	16
Consolidation Coal Sales Company (terms up to 2 years)	31	72	103
Total obligations for divested subsidiaries	31	88	119
	$558	$245	$803

[1] Existing guarantees for customers, suppliers, and other unaffiliated companies arose as part of contractual agreements.

[2] Existing guarantees for equity affiliates and other affiliated companies arose for liquidity needs in normal operations.

[3] The company has guaranteed certain obligations and liabilities related to divested subsidiaries Conoco and Consolidation Coal Sales Company. Conoco and Consolidation Coal Sales Company have indemnified the company for any liabilities the company may incur pursuant to these guarantees.

1.139

NETAPP, INC. (APR)

NOTES TO CONSOLIDATED FINANCIAL STATEMENTS
(Dollar and share amounts in thousands)

14 (In Part): Commitments and Contingencies

Guarantees

As of April 24, 2009, our financial guarantees consisted of standby letters of credit outstanding, bank guarantees, foreign rent guarantees, service performance guarantees, customs and duties guarantees, VAT requirements, workers' compensation plans and surety bonds, which were primarily related to self insurance. The maximum amount of potential future payments under these arrangements was $12,104 as of April 24, 2009, of which $1,001 and $5,182 were collateralized as short-term and long-term restricted cash and investments, respectively, on our balance sheet. The maximum amount of potential future payments under these arrangements was $253,350 as of April 25, 2008, of which $2,953 and $247,234 were collateralized by short-term and long-term restricted cash, respectively, on our consolidated balance sheets.

Recourse and Nonrecourse Leases

We have both recourse and nonrecourse lease financing arrangements with third-party leasing companies through preexisting relationships with customers. Under the terms of recourse leases, which are generally three years or less, we remain liable for the aggregate unpaid remaining lease payments to the third-party leasing company in the event that any customers default. These arrangements are generally collateralized by a security interest in the underlying assets. For these recourse arrangements, revenues on the sale of our product to the leasing company are deferred and recognized into income as payments to the leasing company are received. As of April 24, 2009, and April 25, 2008, the maximum recourse exposure under such leases totaled approximately $25,682 and $24,842, respectively. Under the terms of the nonrecourse leases, we do not have any continuing obligations or liabilities. To date, we have not experienced material losses under our lease financing programs.

Indemnification Agreements

We enter into standard indemnification agreements in the ordinary course of business. Pursuant to these agreements, we agree to defend and indemnify the other party—primarily our customers or business partners or subcontractors—for damages and reasonable costs incurred in any suit or claim brought against them alleging that our products sold to them infringe any U.S. patent, copyright, trade secret, or similar right. If a product becomes the subject of an infringement claim, we may, at our option: (i) replace the product with another noninfringing product that provides substantially similar performance; (ii) modify the infringing product so that it no longer infringes but remains functionally equivalent; (iii) obtain the right for the customer to continue using the product at our expense and for the reseller to continue selling the product; (iv) take back the infringing product and refund to customer the purchase price paid less depreciation amortized on a straight-line basis. We have not been required to make material payments pursuant to these provisions historically. We have not recorded any liability at April 24, 2009, and April 25, 2008, respectively, related to these guarantees since the maximum amount of potential future payments under such guarantees, indemnities and warranties is not determinable, other than as described above.

Letters of Credit

1.140

TARGET CORPORATION (JAN)

NOTES TO CONSOLIDATED FINANCIAL STATEMENTS

18 (In Part): Commitments and Contingencies

Trade letters of credit totaled $1,359 million and $1,861 million at January 31, 2009 and February 2, 2008, respectively, a portion of which are reflected in accounts payable. Standby letters of credit, relating primarily to retained risk on our insurance claims, totaled $64 million and $69 million at January 31, 2009 and February 2, 2008, respectively.

Sale of Receivables With Recourse

1.141

MONSANTO COMPANY (AUG)

NOTES TO CONSOLIDATED FINANCIAL STATEMENTS

Note 7 (In Part): Customer Financing Programs

In August 2009, Monsanto entered into an agreement in the United States to sell customer receivables up to a maximum of $500 million annually and to service such accounts. The program will terminate in August 2012. These receivables qualify for sales treatment under SFAS 140 and accordingly, the proceeds are included in net cash provided by operating activities in the Statements of Consolidated Cash Flows. The gross amount of receivables sold totaled $319 million for fiscal year 2009. The agreement includes recourse provisions and thus a liability was established at the time of sale which approximates fair value based upon the company's historical collection experience with such receivables and a current assessment of credit exposure. The recourse liability recorded by Monsanto was $2 million as of Aug. 31, 2009. The maximum potential amount of future payments under the recourse provisions of the agreement was $18 million as of Aug. 31, 2009. The outstanding balance of the receivables sold was $319 million as of Aug. 31, 2009. There were no delinquent accounts as of Aug. 31, 2009.

Monsanto sells accounts receivable, both with and without recourse, outside of the United States. These sales qualify for sales treatment under SFAS 140 and accordingly, the proceeds are included in net cash provided by operating activities in the Statements of Consolidated Cash Flows. The gross amounts of receivables sold totaled $72 million, $48 million and $46 million for fiscal years 2009, 2008 and 2007, respectively. The liability for the guarantees for sales with recourse is recorded at an amount that approximates fair value and is based on the company's historical collection experience for the customers associated with the sale of the receivables and a current assessment of credit exposure. The liability recorded by Monsanto was less than $1 million as of Aug. 31, 2009, and Aug. 31, 2008. The maximum potential amount of future payments under the recourse provisions of the agreements was $51 million as of Aug. 31, 2009. The outstanding balance of the receivables sold was $57 million and $33 million as of Aug. 31, 2009, and Aug. 31, 2008, respectively. There were no delinquent loans as of Aug. 31, 2009, or Aug. 31, 2008.

DISCLOSURES OF FAIR VALUE

1.142

CLIFFS NATURAL RESOURCES INC. (DEC)

NOTES TO CONSOLIDATED FINANCIAL STATEMENTS

Note 1 (In Part): Business Summary and Significant Accounting Policies

Accounting Policies (In Part)

Fair Value Measurements (In Part):

Valuation Hierarchy
ASC 820 establishes a three-level valuation hierarchy for classification of fair value measurements. The valuation hierarchy is based upon the transparency of inputs to the valuation of an asset or liability as of the measurement date. Inputs refer broadly to the assumptions that market participants would use in pricing an asset or liability. Inputs may be observable or unobservable. Observable inputs are inputs that reflect the assumptions market participants would use in pricing the asset or liability developed based on market data obtained from independent sources. Unobservable inputs are inputs that reflect our own assumptions about the assumptions market participants would use in pricing the asset or liability developed based on the best information available in the circumstances. The three-tier hierarchy of inputs is summarized below:
* Level 1—Valuation is based upon quoted prices (unadjusted) for identical assets or liabilities in active markets.
* Level 2—Valuation is based upon quoted prices for similar assets and liabilities in active markets, or other inputs that are observable for the asset or liability, either directly or indirectly, for substantially the full term of the financial instrument.
* Level 3—Valuation is based upon other unobservable inputs that are significant to the fair value measurement.
The classification of assets and liabilities within the valuation hierarchy is based upon the lowest level of input that is significant to the fair value measurement in its entirety. Valuation

methodologies used for assets and liabilities measured at fair value are as follows.

Cash Equivalents

Where quoted prices are available in an active market, cash equivalents are classified within Level 1 of the valuation hierarchy. Cash equivalents classified in Level 1 at December 31, 2009 and 2008 include money market funds. The valuation of these instruments is determined using a market approach and is based upon unadjusted quoted prices for identical assets in active markets. If quoted market prices are not available, then fair values are estimated by using pricing models, quoted prices of securities with similar characteristics, or discounted cash flows. In these instances, the valuation is based upon quoted prices for similar assets and liabilities in active markets, or other inputs that are observable for substantially the full term of the financial instrument, and the related financial instrument is therefore classified within Level 2 of the valuation hierarchy. Level 2 securities include short-term investments for which the value of each investment is a function of the purchase price, purchase yield, and maturity date.

Marketable Securities

Where quoted prices are available in an active market, marketable securities are classified within Level 1 of the valuation hierarchy. Marketable securities classified in Level 1 at December 31, 2009 and 2008 include available-for-sale securities. The valuation of these instruments is determined using a market approach and is based upon unadjusted quoted prices for identical assets in active markets.

Derivative Financial Instruments

Derivative financial instruments valued using financial models that use as their basis readily observable market parameters are classified within Level 2 of the valuation hierarchy. Such derivative financial instruments include substantially all of our foreign currency exchange contracts and interest rate swap agreements. Derivative financial instruments that are valued based upon models with significant unobservable market parameters, and that are normally traded less actively, are classified within Level 3 of the valuation hierarchy.

Recent Accounting Pronouncements (In Part)

In April 2009, the FASB issued an update to ASC 825, which requires disclosures about fair value of financial instruments for interim reporting periods of publicly traded companies as well as in annual financial statements, including significant assumptions used to estimate the fair value of financial instruments and changes in methods and significant assumptions, if any, during the period. The new guidance is effective for interim reporting periods ending after June 15, 2009, with early adoption permitted for periods ending after March 15, 2009. We adopted this amendment upon its effective date beginning with the interim period ending June 30, 2009.

Note 8 (In Part): Fair Value of Financial Instruments

The following represents the assets and liabilities of the Company measured at fair value at December 31, 2009 and 2008:

| (In millions) | 2009 | | | |
	Quoted Prices in Active Markets for Identical Assets/Liabilities (Level 1)	Significant Other Observable Inputs (Level 2)	Significant Unobservable Inputs (Level 3)	Total
Assets:				
Cash equivalents	$376.0	$—	$ —	$376.0
Derivative assets	—	—	63.2	63.2
Marketable securities	81.0	—	—	81.0
Foreign exchange contracts	—	4.2	—	4.2
Total	$457.0	$4.2	$63.2	$524.4

We had no financial instruments measured at fair value that were in a liability position at December 31, 2009.

| (In millions) | 2008 | | | |
	Quoted Prices in Active Markets for Identical Assets/Liabilities (Level 1)	Significant Other Observable Inputs (Level 2)	Significant Unobservable Inputs (Level 3)	Total
Assets:				
Cash equivalents	$40.4	$ —	$ —	$ 40.4
Derivative assets	—	—	76.6	76.6
Marketable securities	10.9	0.3	—	11.2
Foreign exchange contracts	—	0.9	—	0.9
Total	$51.3	$ 1.2	$ 76.6	$129.1
Liabilities:				
Interest rate swap	$ —	$ 2.6	$ —	$ 2.6
Foreign exchange contracts	—	111.8	—	111.8
Derivative liabilities	—	—	114.2	114.2
Total	$ —	$114.4	$114.2	$228.6

Financial assets classified in Level 1 at December 31, 2009 and 2008 include money market funds and available-for-sale marketable securities. The valuation of these instruments is determined using a market approach, taking into account current interest rates, creditworthiness, and liquidity risks in relation to current market conditions, and is based upon unadjusted quoted prices for identical assets in active markets.

The valuation of financial assets and liabilities classified in Level 2 is determined using a market approach based upon quoted prices for similar assets and liabilities in active markets, or other inputs that are observable for substantially the full term of the financial instrument. Level 2 securities primarily include derivative financial instruments valued using financial models that use as their basis readily observable market parameters. At December 31, 2009 and 2008, such derivative financial instruments include substantially all of our foreign exchange hedge contracts. As of December 31, 2008, such derivative instruments also included our interest rate swap agreement, which terminated in October 2009. The fair value of the interest rate swap and foreign exchange hedge contracts is based on a forward LIBOR curve and forward market prices, respectively, and represents the estimated amount we would receive or pay to terminate these agreements at the reporting date, taking into account current interest rates, creditworthiness, nonperformance risk, and liquidity risks associated with current market conditions.

The derivative financial asset classified within Level 3 is an embedded derivative instrument included in certain supply agreements with one of our customers. The agreements include provisions for supplemental revenue or refunds based on the customer's annual steel pricing at the time the product is consumed in the customer's blast furnaces. We account for this provision as a derivative instrument at the time of sale and record this provision at fair value, based on an income approach when the product is consumed and the amounts are settled, as an adjustment to revenue. The fair value of the instrument is determined using an income approach based on an estimate of the annual realized price of hot rolled steel at the steelmaker's facilities, and takes into consideration current market conditions and nonperformance risk.

The derivative liabilities classified within Level 3 at December 31, 2008 were comprised of two instruments. One of the instruments was a derivative included in the purchase agreement for the acquisition of the remaining 30 percent interest in United Taconite in 2008. The agreement contained a penalty provision in the event the 1.2 million tons of pellets included as part of the purchase consideration were not delivered by December 31, 2009. The penalty provision, which was not a fixed amount or a fixed amount per unit, was a net settlement feature in this arrangement, and therefore required the obligation to be accounted for as a derivative instrument, which was based on the future Eastern Canadian pellet price.

The instrument was marked to fair value each reporting period until the pellets were delivered and the amounts were settled. A derivative liability of $106.5 million, representing the fair value of the pellets that had not yet been delivered, was recorded as current *Derivative liabilities* on the Statement of Consolidated Financial Position as of December 31, 2008. As of December 31, 2009 the entire 1.2 million tons of pellets have been delivered, thereby resulting in settlement of the derivative liability.

The Level 3 derivative liabilities at December 31, 2008 also consisted of freestanding derivatives related to certain supply agreements primarily with our Asia Pacific customers that provided for discounts on December 2008 shipments based on the ultimate settlement of the 2009 international benchmark pricing provisions. The discount provisions were characterized as freestanding derivatives and were required to be accounted for separately once the iron ore was shipped. The derivative instrument, which was settled and billed once the annual international benchmark price was settled, was marked to fair value as a revenue adjustment each reporting period based upon the estimated forward settlement until the

benchmark was actually settled. The fair value of the instrument was determined based on the forward price expectation of the 2009 annual international benchmark price and took into account current market conditions and other risks, including nonperformance risk. As of December 31, 2008, the 2009 international benchmark prices had not yet settled. Therefore, we had recorded approximately $7.7 million as current *Derivative liabilities* on the Statement of Consolidated Financial Position at December 31, 2008. The derivative instrument was settled in the fourth quarter of 2009 upon settlement of the pricing provisions with each of our customers, and is therefore not reflected on the Statement of Consolidated Financial Position at December 31, 2009.

Substantially all of the financial assets and liabilities are carried at fair value or contracted amounts that approximate fair value. We had no financial assets and liabilities measured at fair value on a non-recurring basis at December 31, 2009 and 2008.

The following represents a reconciliation of the changes in fair value of financial instruments measured at fair value on a recurring basis using significant unobservable inputs (Level 3) for the years ended December 31, 2009 and 2008.

	Derivative Assets		Derivative Liabilities	
(In millions)	2009	2008	2009	2008
Beginning balance—January 1	$ 76.6	$ 53.8	$(114.2)	$ —
Total gains (losses)				
Included in earnings	22.2	386.0	78.3	50.6
Included in other comprehensive income	—	—	—	—
Settlements	(35.6)	(363.2)	35.9	24.2
Transfers in to Level 3	—	—	—	(189.0)
Ending balance—December 31	$ 63.2	$ 76.6	$ —	$(114.2)
Total gains (losses) for the period included in earnings attributable to the change in unrealized gains or losses on assets and liabilities still held at the reporting date	$ 22.2	$ 225.5	$ —	$ 50.6

Gains and losses included in earnings are reported in *Product revenue* on the Statements of Consolidated Operations for the years ended December 31, 2009 and 2008.

1.143

KELLOGG COMPANY (DEC)

NOTES TO CONSOLIDATED FINANCIAL STATEMENTS

Note 11(In Part): Fair Value Measurements

The Company has categorized its financial assets and liabilities into a three-level fair value hierarchy, based on the nature of the inputs used in determining fair value. The hierarchy gives the highest priority to quoted prices in active markets for identical assets or liabilities (level 1) and the lowest priority to unobservable inputs (level 3). Following is a description of each category in the fair value hierarchy and the financial assets and liabilities of the Company that are included in each category at January 2, 2010 and January 3, 2009.

- *Level 1*—Financial assets and liabilities whose values are based on unadjusted quoted prices for identical

assets or liabilities in an active market. For the Company, level 1 financial assets and liabilities consist primarily of commodity derivative contracts.
- *Level 2*—Financial assets and liabilities whose values are based on quoted prices in markets that are not active or model inputs that are observable either directly or indirectly for substantially the full term of the asset or liability. For the Company, level 2 financial assets and liabilities consist of interest rate swaps and over-the-counter commodity and currency contracts.
  The Company's calculation of the fair value of interest rate swaps is derived from a discounted cash flow analysis based on the terms of the contract and the interest rate curve. Commodity derivatives are valued using an income approach based on the commodity index prices less the contract rate multiplied by the notional amount. Foreign currency contracts are valued using an income approach based on forward rates less the contract rate multiplied by the notional amount.

- *Level 3*—Financial assets and liabilities whose values are based on prices or valuation techniques that require inputs that are both unobservable and significant to the overall fair value measurement. These inputs reflect management's own assumptions about the assumptions a market participant would use in pricing the asset or liability. The Company did not have any level 3 financial assets or liabilities as of January 2, 2010, or January 3, 2009.

The following table presents the Company's fair value hierarchy for those assets and liabilities measured at fair value on a recurring basis as of January 2, 2010 and January 3, 2009:

	Level 1		Level 2		Total	
(Millions)	2009	2008	2009	2008	2009	2008
Assets:						
Derivatives (recorded in other current assets)	$ 4	$ 9	$ 7	$ 34	$ 11	$ 43
Derivatives (recorded in other assets)	—	—	44	43	44	43
Total assets	$ 4	$ 9	$ 51	$ 77	$ 55	$ 86
Liabilities:						
Derivatives (recorded in other current liabilities)	$—	$—	$(37)	$(17)	$(37)	$(17)
Derivatives (recorded in other liabilities)	—	—	(15)	(4)	(15)	(4)
Total liabilities	$—	$—	$(52)	$(21)	$(52)	$(21)

Financial Instruments

The carrying values of the Company's short-term items, including cash, cash equivalents, accounts receivable, accounts payable and notes payable approximate fair value. The fair value of the Company's long-term debt is calculated based on broker quotes and was approximately $5.2 billion at January 2, 2010, as compared to the carrying value of $4.8 billion.

Note 12. Derivative Instruments and Hedging Activities

The Company adopted a new accounting standard regarding disclosures about derivative instruments and hedging activities as of the beginning of its 2009 fiscal year.

The Company is exposed to certain market risks such as changes in interest rates, foreign currency exchange rates, and commodity prices, which exist as a part of its ongoing business operations. Management uses derivative financial and commodity instruments, including futures, options, and swaps, where appropriate, to manage these risks. Instruments used as hedges must be effective at reducing the risk associated with the exposure being hedged and must be designated as a hedge at the inception of the contract.

The Company designates derivatives as cash flow hedges, fair value hedges, net investment hedges, or other contracts used to reduce volatility in the translation of foreign currency earnings to U.S. dollars. The fair value of derivative instruments is recorded in other current assets, other assets, other current liabilities or other liabilities. Gains and losses representing either hedge ineffectiveness, hedge components excluded from the assessment of effectiveness, or hedges of translational exposure are recorded in the Consolidated Statement of Income in other income (expense), net. Within the Consolidated Statement of Cash Flows, settlements of cash flow and fair value hedges are classified as an operating activity; settlements of all other derivatives are classified as a financing activity. As a matter of policy, the Company does not engage in trading or speculative hedging transactions.

Cash Flow Hedges

Qualifying derivatives are accounted for as cash flow hedges when the hedged item is a forecasted transaction. Gains and losses on these instruments are recorded in other comprehensive income until the underlying transaction is recorded in earnings. When the hedged item is realized, gains or losses are reclassified from accumulated other comprehensive income (loss) (AOCI) to the Consolidated Statement of Income on the same line item as the underlying transaction.

The cumulative net loss attributable to cash flow hedges recorded in AOCI at January 2, 2010, was $30 million, related to forward interest rate contracts settled during 2001, 2003 and 2009 in conjunction with fixed rate long-term debt issuances, 10-year natural gas price swaps entered into in 2006, commodity price cash flow hedges and net losses on foreign currency cash flow hedges. The interest rate contract losses will be reclassified into interest expense over the next 22 years. The natural gas swap losses will be reclassified to COGS over the next 7 years. Losses related to foreign currency and commodity price cash flow hedges will be reclassified into earnings during the next 18 months.

Fair Value Hedges

Qualifying derivatives are accounted for as fair value hedges when the hedged item is a recognized asset, liability, or firm commitment. Gains and losses on these instruments are recorded in earnings, offsetting gains and losses on the hedged item.

Net Investment Hedges

Qualifying derivative and nonderivative financial instruments are accounted for as net investment hedges when the hedged item is a nonfunctional currency investment in a subsidiary. Gains and losses on these instruments are included in foreign currency translation adjustments in AOCI.

Other Contracts

The Company also periodically enters into foreign currency forward contracts and options to reduce volatility in the translation of foreign currency earnings to U.S. dollars. Gains and losses on these instruments are recorded in other income (expense), net, generally reducing the exposure to translation volatility during a full-year period.

Foreign Currency Exchange Risk

The Company is exposed to fluctuations in foreign currency cash flows related primarily to third-party purchases, intercompany transactions and nonfunctional currency denominated third-party debt. The Company is also exposed to fluctuations in the value of foreign currency investments in subsidiaries and cash flows related to repatriation of these investments. Additionally, the Company is exposed to volatility in the translation of foreign currency denominated earnings to U.S. dollars. Management assesses foreign currency risk based on transactional cash flows and translational volatility and enters into forward contracts, options, and currency swaps to reduce fluctuations in net long or short currency positions. Forward contracts and options are generally less than 18 months duration. Currency swap agreements are established in conjunction with the term of underlying debt issues.

For foreign currency cash flow and fair value hedges, the assessment of effectiveness is generally based on changes in spot rates. Changes in time value are reported in other income (expense), net.

The total notional amount of foreign currency derivative instruments was $1,588 million and $924 million at January 2, 2010 and January 3, 2009, respectively.

Interest Rate Risk

The Company is exposed to interest rate volatility with regard to future issuances of fixed rate debt. The Company periodically uses interest rate swaps, including forward-starting swaps, to reduce interest rate volatility and funding costs associated with certain debt issues, and to achieve a desired proportion of variable versus fixed rate debt, based on current and projected market conditions.

Fixed-to-variable interest rate swaps are accounted for as fair value hedges and the assessment of effectiveness is based on changes in the fair value of the underlying debt, using incremental borrowing rates currently available on loans with similar terms and maturities.

The total notional amount of interest rate derivative instruments was $1,900 million and $750 million at January 2, 2010 and January 3, 2009, respectively.

Price Risk

The Company is exposed to price fluctuations primarily as a result of anticipated purchases of raw and packaging materials, fuel, and energy. The Company has historically used the combination of long-term contracts with suppliers, and exchange-traded futures and option contracts to reduce price fluctuations in a desired percentage of forecasted raw material purchases over a duration of generally less than 18 months. During 2006, the Company entered into two separate 10-year over-the-counter commodity swap transactions to reduce fluctuations in the price of natural gas used principally in its manufacturing processes. The notional amount of the swaps totaled $146 million as of January 2, 2010 and $167 million as of January 3, 2009.

Commodity contracts are accounted for as cash flow hedges. The assessment of effectiveness for exchange-traded instruments is based on changes in futures prices. The assessment of effectiveness for over-the-counter transactions is based on changes in designated indexes.

The total notional amount of commodity derivative instruments, including the natural gas swaps was $213 million and $267 million at January 2, 2010 and January 3, 2009, respectively.

Credit-Risk-Related Contingent Features

Certain of the Company's derivative instruments contain provisions requiring the Company to post collateral on those derivative instruments that are in a liability position if the Company's credit rating falls below BB+ (S&P), or Baa1 (Moody's). The fair value of all derivative instruments with credit-risk-related contingent features in a liability position on January 2, 2010 was $18 million. If the credit-risk-related contingent features were triggered as of January 2, 2010, the Company would be required to post collateral of $18 million. In addition, certain derivative instruments contain provisions that would be triggered in the event the Company defaults on its debt agreements. There were no collateral posting requirements as of January 2, 2010 triggered by credit-risk-related contingent features.

Fair values of derivative instruments in the Consolidated Balance Sheet designated as hedging instruments as of January 2, 2010 were as follows:

(Millions)	Asset Derivatives		Liability Derivatives	
	Balance Sheet Location	Fair Value	Balance Sheet Location	Fair Value
Foreign currency exchange contracts	Other current assets	$ 7	Other current liabilities	$(31)
Interest rate contracts	Other assets	44	Other liabilities	(1)
Commodity contracts	Other current assets	4	Other current liabilities	(6)
Commodity contracts	Other assets	—	Other liabilities	(14)
Total		$55		$(52)

The effect of derivative instruments on the Consolidated Statement of Income for the year ended January 2, 2010 was as follows:

(Millions)	Gain (Loss) Recognized in AOCI	Location of Gain (Loss) Reclassified From AOCI	Gain (Loss) Reclassified From AOCI into Income	Location of Gain (Loss) Recognized in Income	Gain (Loss) Recognized in Income
Derivatives in fair value hedging relationships					
Foreign currency exchange contracts				Other income (expense), net	$(46)
Interest rate contracts				Interest expense	28
Total					$(18)
Derivatives in cash flow hedging relationships					
Foreign currency exchange contracts	$(23)	Cost of goods sold	$19	Other income (expense), net[a]	$ (8)
Foreign currency exchange contracts	3	Selling, general and administrative expense	(3)	Other income (expense), net[a]	—
Interest rate contracts	—	Interest expense	(8)	N/A	—
Commodity contracts	14	Cost of goods sold	(5)	Other income (expense), net[a]	(2)
Total	$ (6)		$ 3		$(10)
Derivatives not designated as hedging instruments (millions)					
Foreign currency exchange contracts				Other income (expense), net	$ 1

[a] Includes the ineffective portion and amount excluded from effectiveness testing.

Refer to Note 11 for disclosures regarding the fair value of the Company's derivatives.

CONCENTRATIONS OF CREDIT RISK

1.144

ANALOG DEVICES, INC. (OCT)

NOTES TO CONSOLIDATED FINANCIAL STATEMENTS

Note 2 (In Part): Summary of Significant Accounting Policies

i. (In Part): Derivative Instruments and Hedging Agreements

The market risk associated with the Company's derivative instruments results from currency exchange rate or interest rate movements that are expected to offset the market risk of the underlying transactions, assets and liabilities being hedged. The counterparties to the agreements relating to the Company's derivative instruments consist of a number of major international financial institutions with high credit ratings. The Company does not believe that there is significant risk of nonperformance by these counterparties because the Company continually monitors the credit ratings of such counterparties. Furthermore, none of the Company's derivative transactions are subject to collateral or other security arrangements and none contain provisions that are dependent on the Company's credit ratings from any credit rating agency. While the contract or notional amounts of derivative financial instruments provide one measure of the volume of these transactions, they do not represent the amount of the Company's exposure to credit risk. The amounts potentially subject to credit risk (arising from the possible inability of counterparties to meet the terms of their contracts) are generally limited to the amounts, if any, by which the counterparties' obligations under the contracts exceed the obligations of the Company to the counterparties. As a result of the above considerations, the Company does not consider the risk of counterparty default to be significant.

1.145

C. R. BARD, INC. (DEC)

NOTES TO CONSOLIDATED FINANCIAL STATEMENTS

6 (In Part): Financial Instruments

Concentration Risks

The company is potentially subject to financial instrument concentration of credit risk through its cash equivalents and trade accounts receivable. The company performs periodic evaluations of the relative credit standing of these financial institutions and limits the amount of credit exposure with any one institution. Concentrations of risk with respect to trade accounts receivable are limited due to the large number of customers and their dispersion across many geographic areas. However, a significant amount of trade accounts receivable is with the national healthcare systems of several countries, including Greece. The company is currently experiencing delays in the collection of accounts receivable associated with the national healthcare system in Greece, which amounted to $36.7 million of net receivables as of December 31, 2009. Although the company does not currently foresee

a credit risk associated with any of these receivables, including Greece, payment is dependent upon the financial stability and creditworthiness of those countries' national economies. Sales to distributors, which supply the company's products to many end users, accounted for approximately 33% of the company's net sales in 2009, and the five largest distributors combined, including the company's Medicon joint venture, accounted for approximately 65% of distributors' sales. One large distributor accounted for approximately 10%, 10% and 9% of the company's net sales in 2009, 2008 and 2007, respectively, and represented gross receivables of approximately $36.0 million and $38.6 million as of December 31, 2009 and 2008, respectively.

1.146

KIMBALL INTERNATIONAL, INC. (JUN)

NOTES TO CONSOLIDATED FINANCIAL STATEMENTS

Note 1 (In Part): Summary of Significant Accounting Policies

Concentration of Credit Risk (In Part)

The Company has business and credit risks concentrated in the medical, automotive, and furniture industries. Two customers, Bayer AG and TRW Automotive, Inc., represented 19% and 11%, respectively, of consolidated accounts receivable at June 30, 2009. Bayer AG and Siemens AG, represented 16% and 15%, respectively, of consolidated accounts receivable at June 30, 2008. The Company currently does not foresee a credit risk associated with these receivables. The Company also has an agreement with a contract customer and a note receivable related to the sale of an Indiana facility. At June 30, 2009, $4.7 million was outstanding. The Company recorded a provision for potential credit losses.

SUBSEQUENT EVENTS

1.147   Events or transactions which occur subsequent to the balance sheet date but prior to the issuance of the financial statements and which have a material effect on the financial statements should be either recorded or disclosed in the financial statements. AU section 560, *Subsequent Events*, sets forth criteria for the proper treatment of subsequent events. FASB ASC 855, *Subsequent Events*, introduces the concept of financial statements being available to be issued. Financial statements are considered available to be issued when they are complete in a form and format that complies with GAAP and all approvals necessary for issuance have been obtained, for example, from management, the board of directors, and/or significant shareholders. An entity that is a Securities and Exchange Commission (SEC) filer shall evaluate subsequent events through the date that the financial statements are issued. All other entities shall evaluate subsequent events through the date that the financial statements are available to be issued. Further, FASB ASC 855 requires of an entity that is not an SEC filer the disclosure of the date through which that entity has evaluated subsequent events and whether that date represents the date the financial statements were issued or were available to be issued. Table 1-14 lists the subsequent events disclosed in the financial statements of the survey entities.

1.148 Examples of subsequent event disclosures follow.

1.149

TABLE 1-14: SUBSEQUENT EVENTS

	Number of Entities			
	2009	2008	2007	2006
Debt incurred, reduced or refinanced...........................	56	73	77	63
Business combinations pending or affected.............	44	46	80	94
Litigation.....................................	37	52	37	42
Discontinued operations or asset disposals..................	33	24	52	60
Employee benefits................	17	26	13	12
Capital stock issued or purchased...........................	17	17	42	27
Restructuring/bankruptcy.......	16	26	15	28
Stock splits or dividends........	4	6	6	18
Other—described..................	51	59	50	63

2008–2009 based on 500 entities surveyed; 2006–2007 based on 600 entities surveyed.

Debt Incurred, Reduced, or Refinanced

1.150

GENCORP INC. (NOV)

NOTES TO CONSOLIDATED FINANCIAL STATEMENTS

15. Subsequent Events

In December 2009, the Company issued $200.0 million in aggregate principal amount of 4.0625% Convertible Subordinated Debentures ("$4^1/_{16}$% Debentures") in a private placement to qualified institutional buyers pursuant to Rule 144A under the Securities Act of 1933. The $4^1/_{16}$% Debentures mature on December 31, 2039. Interest on the $4^1/_{16}$% Debentures accrues at 4.0625% per annum and is payable semiannually in arrears on June 30 and December 31 of each year, beginning June 30, 2010 (or if any such day is not a business day, payable on the following business day), and the Company may elect to pay interest in cash or, generally on any interest payment that is at least one year after the original issuance date of the $4^1/_{16}$% Debentures, in shares of the Company's common stock or a combination of cash and shares of the Company's common stock, at the Company's option. The valuation methodology the Company will use in determining the value of any shares to be so delivered is discussed in the indenture governing the $4^1/_{16}$% Debentures.

The $4^1/_{16}$% Debentures are general unsecured obligations and rank equal in right of payment to all of the Company's other existing and future unsecured subordinated indebtedness, including the 4% Notes and $2^1/_4$% Debentures. The $4^1/_{16}$% Debentures rank junior in right of payment to all of the Company's existing and future senior indebtedness, including all of its obligations under its Senior Credit Facility and all of its existing and future senior subordinated indebtedness, including the Company's outstanding $9^1/_2$% Notes. In addition, the $4^1/_{16}$% Debentures are effectively subordinated to any of the Company's collateralized debt and to any and all debt and liabilities, including trade debt of its subsidiaries.

Each holder of the $4^1/_{16}$% Debentures may convert their $4^1/_{16}$% Debentures into shares of the Company's common stock at a conversion rate of 111.0926 shares per $1,000 principal amount, representing a conversion price of approximately $9.00 per share, subject to adjustment. In addition, if the holders elect to convert their $4^1/_{16}$% Debentures in connection with the occurrence of certain fundamental changes, the holders will be entitled to receive additional shares of common stock upon conversion in some circumstances. Upon any conversion of the $4^1/_{16}$% Debentures, subject to certain exceptions, the holders will not receive any cash payment representing accrued and unpaid interest.

The Company may at any time redeem any $4^1/_{16}$% Debentures for cash (except as described below with respect to any make-whole premium that may be payable) if the last reported sale price of the Company's common stock has been at least 150% of the conversion price then in effect for at least twenty (20) trading days during any thirty (30) consecutive trading day period ending within five (5) trading days prior to the date on which the Company provides the notice of redemption.

The Company may redeem the $4^1/_{16}$% Debentures either in whole or in part at a redemption price equal to (i) 100% of the principal amount of the $4^1/_{16}$% Debentures to be redeemed, plus (ii) accrued and unpaid interest, if any, up to, but excluding, the redemption date, plus (iii) if the Company redeems the $4^1/_{16}$% Debentures prior to December 31, 2014, a "make-whole premium" equal to the present value of the remaining scheduled payments of interest that would have been made on the $4^1/_{16}$% Debentures to be redeemed had such $4^1/_{16}$% Debentures remained outstanding from the redemption date to December 31, 2014. Any make-whole premium is payable in cash, shares of the Company's common stock or a combination of cash and shares, at the Company's option, subject to certain conditions.

Each holder may require the Company to repurchase all or part of their $4^1/_{16}$% Debentures on December 31, 2014, 2019, 2024, 2029 and 2034 (each, an "optional repurchase date") at an optional repurchase price equal to (1) 100% of their principal amount plus (2) accrued and unpaid interest, if any, up to, but excluding, the date of repurchase. The Company may elect to pay the optional repurchase price in cash, shares of the Company's common stock, or a combination of cash and shares of the Company's common stock, at the Company's option, subject to certain conditions.

If a fundamental change, as described in the indenture governing the $4^1/_{16}$% Debentures, occurs prior to maturity, each holder will have the right to require the Company to purchase all or part of their $4^1/_{16}$% Debentures for cash at a repurchase price equal to 100% of their principal amount, plus accrued and unpaid interest, if any, up to, but excluding, the repurchase date.

If the Company delivers shares of its common stock as all or part of any interest payment, any make-whole premium or any optional repurchase price, such shares will be valued at the product of (x) the price per share of the Company's common stock determined during: (i) in the case of any interest payment, the twenty (20) consecutive trading days ending on the second trading day immediately preceding the record date for such interest payment; (ii) in the case of any make-whole premium payable as part of the redemption price, the twenty (20) consecutive trading days ending on the second trading day immediately preceding the redemption date; and (iii) in the case of any optional repurchase price, the forty (40) consecutive trading days ending on the second trading day immediately preceding the optional repurchase date; (in each case, the "averaging period" with respect to such date) using the sum of the daily price fractions (where "daily price fraction" means, for each trading day during the relevant averaging period, 5% in the case of any interest payment or any make-whole premium or 2.5% in the case of any optional repurchase, multiplied by the daily VWAP (VWAP as defined by the indenture), per share of the Company's common stock for such day), multiplied by (y) 97.5%. The Company will notify holders at least five (5) business days prior to the start of the relevant averaging period of the extent to which the Company will pay any portion of the related payment using shares of common stock.

Issuance of the $4^1/_{16}$% Debentures generated net proceeds of $195.0 million, which were used to repurchase $124.7 million of the 4% Notes and will be used to redeem a portion of the $9^1/_2$% Notes; pay accrued interest on the 4% Notes and $9^1/_2$% Notes; and pay other debt issuance costs.

1.151

THE MCCLATCHY COMPANY (DEC)

NOTES TO CONSOLIDATED FINANCIAL STATEMENTS

Note 6 (In Part): Long Term Debt

Debt Refinancing

On January 26, 2010, the Company entered into an amendment to the original credit agreement that became effective on February 11, 2010, immediately prior to the closing of an offering of $875 million of senior secured public notes. The original credit agreement was amended and restated in its entirety (the "Amended and Restated Credit Agreement" or "Credit Agreement"). The Amended and Restated Credit Agreement provides for a $262.0 million term loan and a $249.3 million revolving credit facility, including a $100 million letter of credit sub-facility, and extended the term of certain of the credit commitments to July 1, 2013. In connection with the Amended and Restated Credit Agreement, certain of the lenders did not extend the maturity of their commitments from the original maturity date of June 27, 2011. Non-extended term loans equaling $72.3 million will mature on June 27, 2011 as will revolving loan commitments equal to $42.2 million. The remaining term loans and revolving loan commitments under the Amended and Restated Credit Agreement will mature on July 1, 2013.

In connection with the Credit Agreement, the Company issued new 11.5% senior secured notes due February 15, 2017, totaling $875 million. The notes are secured by a first-priority lien on certain of McClatchy's and the subsidiary guar-

antors' assets, and will rank pari passu with liens granted under McClatchy's Credit Agreement. The assets securing the debt are unchanged from the original credit agreement and include intangible assets, inventory, receivables and certain other assets. In addition, the Company completed tender offers for its 7.125% notes due in 2011 and 15.75% senior notes due 2014, paying $187.3 million in cash for $171.9 million of principal 2011 and 2014 notes.

Debt under the Credit Agreement incurs interest at the London Interbank Offered Rate (LIBOR) plus a spread ranging from 425 basis points to 575 basis points or at a base rate plus a spread ranging from 325 basis points to 475 basis points, in each case, based upon the consolidated total leverage ratio (as defined in the Credit Agreement) and sets a floor on LIBOR for the purposes of interest payments under the Credit Agreement of no less than 300 basis points. A commitment fee for the unused revolving credit is priced at 50 basis points to 75 basis points, based upon the Company's consolidated total leverage ratio (as defined in the Credit Agreement). The Company currently pays interest on borrowings under the Credit Agreement at a rate of 500 basis points over the 300 basis point LIBOR floor and pays 62.5 basis points for commitment fees.

The Credit Agreement contains quarterly financial covenants including requirements that the Company maintain a minimum consolidated interest coverage ratio (as defined in the Credit Agreement) of 1.50 to 1.00 from the quarter ending in March 2010 through the quarter ending in September 2011; increasing it to 1.60 to 1.00 from the quarter ending in December 2011 through the quarter ending in September 2012; and further increasing to 1.70 to 1.00 thereafter. The Company is required to maintain a maximum consolidated leverage ratio (as defined in the Credit Agreement) of 6.75 to 1.00 from the quarter ending in March 2010 through the quarter ending December 2010; declining to 6.50 to 1.00 from the quarter ending in March 2011 through the quarter ending in December 2011; to 6.25 to 1.00 from the quarter ending in March 2012 through the quarter ending in December 2012 and declining to 6.00 to 1.00 thereafter. Because of the significance of the Company's outstanding debt, remaining in compliance with debt covenants is critical to the Company's operations. If revenue declines continue beyond those currently anticipated, the Company expects to continue to restructure operations and reduce debt to maintain compliance with its covenants.

The Credit Agreement includes requirements for mandatory prepayments of bank debt from certain sources of cash; limitations on cash dividends allowed to be paid at certain leverage levels; and other covenants including limitations on additional debt and the ability to retire public bonds early, amongst other changes.

Business Combinations

1.152

BAKER HUGHES INCORPORATED (DEC)

NOTES TO CONSOLIDATED FINANCIAL STATEMENTS

Note 2. Pending Merger With BJ Services

On August 30, 2009, the Company and its subsidiary and BJ Services Company ("BJ Services") entered into a merger agreement (the "Merger Agreement") pursuant to which the Company will acquire 100% of the outstanding common stock of BJ Services in exchange for newly issued shares of the Company's common stock and cash. BJ Services is a leading provider of pressure pumping and oilfield services. The Merger Agreement and the merger have been approved by the Board of Directors of both the Company and BJ Services. Consummation of the merger is subject to the approval of the stockholders of the Company and BJ Services' stockholders at special meetings scheduled on March 19, 2010 subject to adjournment or postponement, regulatory approvals, and the satisfaction or waiver of various other conditions as more fully described in the Merger Agreement.

Subject to receipt of all required approvals, it is anticipated that closing of the merger will occur in March of 2010. Under the terms of the Merger Agreement, each share of BJ Services common stock will be converted into the right to receive 0.40035 shares of the Company's common stock and $2.69 in cash. Baker Hughes has estimated the total consideration expected to be issued and paid in the merger to be approximately $6.4 billion, consisting of approximately $0.8 billion to be paid in cash and approximately $5.6 billion to be paid through the issuance of approximately 118 million shares of Baker Hughes common stock valued at the February 11, 2010 closing share price of $46.68 per share. The value of the merger consideration will fluctuate based upon changes in the price of shares of Baker Hughes common stock and the number of BJ Services common shares and options outstanding at the closing date.

1.153

TERRA INDUSTRIES INC. (DEC)

NOTES TO CONSOLIDATED FINANCIAL STATEMENTS

27. Subsequent Events

On February 12, 2010, Terra entered into an Agreement and Plan of Merger (the "Yara Merger Agreement") with Yara International ASA ("Yara") and Yukon Merger Sub, Inc. ("Merger Sub"), an indirect, wholly owned subsidiary of Yara. If the transactions contemplated by the Yara Merger Agreement are consummated, Merger Sub will merge with and into Terra (the "Yara Merger"), with the result that Terra will become an indirect, wholly owned subsidiary of Yara.

Upon consummation of the Yara Merger, each outstanding share of Terra common stock will be converted into the right to receive $41.10 in cash, without interest and less any

taxes required to be withheld. The purchase price is subject to increase as provided in the Yara Merger Agreement if Yara does not hold its stockholders meeting to obtain the Yara Stockholder Approval (as defined below) within 90 days from the date of execution of the Yara Merger Agreement.

The consummation of the Yara Merger is subject to certain conditions, including, among others, (i) the approval by Terra's stockholders (the "Terra Stockholder Approval") of the Yara Merger, (ii) the approval by Yara's stockholders (the "Yara Stockholder Approval") of the issuance of Yara common stock to finance a portion of the Yara Merger consideration, (iii) the receipt of regulatory approvals (or the expiration of applicable waiting periods) in the United States, Canada and the European Union, (iv) the absence of legal restraints preventing consummation of the Yara Merger, (v) the absence of pending lawsuits by any governmental entity seeking to prevent consummation of the Yara Merger that would reasonably be expected to result in certain material adverse effects on Terra and (vi) the absence since January 1, 2009 of any change or event that, individually or in the aggregate, has resulted in or would reasonably be expected to result in a material adverse effect on Terra. The Yara Merger is not subject to any financing condition.

The Yara Merger Agreement contains certain termination rights and provides that (i) upon the termination of the Yara Merger Agreement under specified circumstances, including, among others, by Terra to accept a superior proposal or by Yara upon a change in the recommendation of Terra's board of directors, Terra will owe Yara a cash termination fee of $123 million and (ii) upon the termination of the Yara Merger Agreement due to Yara's failure to obtain the Yara Stockholder Approval, Yara will owe Terra a cash termination fee of $123 million.

Litigation

1.154

VALASSIS COMMUNICATIONS, INC. (DEC)

NOTES TO THE CONSOLIDATED FINANCIAL STATEMENTS

15) Subsequent Events

On January 30, 2010, Valassis announced that it had reached an agreement to settle its outstanding lawsuits against News America Incorporated, a/k/a News America Marketing Group, News America Marketing, FSI, Inc. a/k/a News America Marketing FSI, LLC and News America Marketing In-Store Services, Inc. a/k/a News America Marketing In-Store Services, LLC (collectively "News"). The operative complaint alleged violation of the Sherman Act, various state competitive statutes and the commission of torts by News in connection with the marketing and sale of FSI space and in-store promotion and advertising services.

On February 4, 2010, Valassis and News executed a settlement agreement and release (the "Settlement Agreement"), and pursuant to the terms of the Settlement Agreement, News paid Valassis $500.0 million, which will be recorded in our financial statements in the first quarter of 2010. News America, Inc. also entered into a 10-year shared mail distribution agreement with Valassis Direct Mail, Inc., a Valassis subsidiary, which provides for the sale by Valassis of certain shared mail services to News on specified terms.

In connection with the settlement, the parties are working with the Court, under the Honorable Arthur J. Tarnow, on a set of procedures to handle future disputes among the parties with respect to conduct at issue in the litigation. The precise timing and form of the relief rests with the Court.

The settlement resolves all outstanding claims between Valassis and News as of February 4, 2010. As a result, the parties agreed to dismiss all outstanding litigation between them and release all existing and potential claims against each other that were or could have been asserted in the litigation as of the date of the Settlement Agreement.

1.155

VALERO ENERGY CORPORATION (DEC)

NOTES TO CONSOLIDATED FINANCIAL STATEMENTS

25. Litigation Matters

MTBE Litigation

As of February 26, 2010, we were named as a defendant in 34 active cases alleging liability related to MTBE contamination in groundwater. The plaintiffs are generally water providers, governmental authorities, and private water companies alleging that refiners and marketers of MTBE and gasoline containing MTBE are liable for manufacturing or distributing a defective product. We have been named in these lawsuits together with many other refining industry companies. We are being sued primarily as a refiner and marketer of MTBE and gasoline containing MTBE. We do not own or operate gasoline station facilities in most of the geographic locations in which damage is alleged to have occurred. The lawsuits generally seek individual, unquantified compensatory and punitive damages, injunctive relief, and attorneys' fees. Many of the cases are pending in federal court and are consolidated for pre-trial proceedings in the U.S. District Court for the Southern District of New York (Multi-District Litigation Docket No. 1358, *In re: Methyl-Tertiary Butyl Ether Products Liability Litigation*). Sixteen cases are pending in state court. Discovery is open in all cases. We believe that we have strong defenses to all claims and are vigorously defending the lawsuits.

We have recorded a loss contingency liability with respect to our MTBE litigation portfolio. However, due to the inherent uncertainty of litigation, we believe that it is reasonably possible that we may suffer a loss with respect to one or more of the lawsuits in excess of the amount accrued. We believe that such an outcome in any one of these lawsuits would not have a material adverse effect on our results of operations or financial position. An estimate of the possible loss or range of loss from an adverse result in all or substantially all of these cases cannot reasonably be made.

Retail Fuel Temperature Litigation

As of February 26, 2010, we were named in 21 consumer class action lawsuits relating to fuel temperature. We have been named in these lawsuits together with several other

defendants in the retail and wholesale petroleum marketing business. The complaints, filed in federal courts in several states, allege that because fuel volume increases with fuel temperature, the defendants have violated state consumer protection laws by failing to adjust the volume or price of fuel when the fuel temperature exceeded 60 degrees Fahrenheit. The complaints seek to certify classes of retail consumers who purchased fuel in various locations. The complaints seek an order compelling the installation of temperature correction devices as well as monetary relief. The federal lawsuits are consolidated into a multi-district litigation case in the U.S. District Court for the District of Kansas (Multi-District Litigation Docket No. 1840, *In re: Motor Fuel Temperature Sales Practices Litigation*). Discovery has commenced. The court has indicated that it will rule on the Kansas-based class certification motion only (possibly in the spring of 2010), and then make a decision on how to further proceed with the rest of the docket. We believe that we have several strong defenses to these lawsuits and intend to contest them. We have not recorded a loss contingency liability with respect to this matter, but due to the inherent uncertainty of litigation, we believe that it is reasonably possible that we may suffer a loss with respect to one or more of the lawsuits. An estimate of the possible loss or range of loss from an adverse result in all or substantially all of these cases cannot reasonably be made.

Asset Disposals

1.156

EMC CORPORATION (DEC)

NOTES TO CONSOLIDATED FINANCIAL STATEMENTS

U (In Part): Subsequent Events

On February 25, 2010, EMC entered into a definitive agreement with VMware to transfer key management technologies to VMware, including solutions aimed at delivering configuration compliance for virtualized environments. The acquisition by VMware will further enhance its mission of driving complexity out of the data center, desktop, application development and core IT services, while delivering a fundamentally new and more efficient approach to IT. VMware will pay EMC up to $200 million. The transaction is expected to close during the second quarter of 2010.

Employee Benefits

1.157

ILLINOIS TOOL WORKS INC. (DEC)

NOTES TO CONSOLIDATED FINANCIAL STATEMENTS

Stock-Based Compensation (In Part)

As of February 12, 2010, the Compensation Committee of the Board of Directors approved an annual equity award consisting of stock options, restricted stock units ("RSUs") and performance restricted stock units ("PRSUs"). The form of RSU provides for full "cliff" vesting three years from the date of grant. The form of PRSU provides for full "cliff" vesting after three years if the Compensation Committee certifies that the performance goals set with respect to the PRSU are met. Upon vesting, the holder will receive one share of common stock of the Company for each vested RSU or PRSU. Stock options were granted on 2,287,974 shares at an exercise price of $43.64 per share. Additionally, 711,813 RSUs and PRSUs were issued at the grant date share price of $43.64. The Company uses a binomial option pricing model to estimate the fair value of the stock options granted. The following summarizes the assumptions used in the models:

	2010	2009	2008
Risk-free interest rate	0.4–3.9%	0.6–3.3%	1.9–3.9%
Weighted-average volatility	25.0%	33.0%	27.0%
Dividend yield	2.78%	2.34%	1.96%
Expected years until exercise	7.5–7.8	7.3–7.7	7.3–7.9

Capital Stock Issued or Repurchased

1.158

JUNIPER NETWORKS, INC. (DEC)

NOTES TO CONSOLIDATED FINANCIAL STATEMENTS

Note 16. Subsequent Event

Stock Repurchases

Subsequent to December 31, 2009, through the filing of this report, the Company repurchased 2.1 million shares of its common stock, for $55.3 million at an average purchase price of $26.28 per share, under its 2008 Stock Repurchase Program. As of the filing of this Annual Report on Form 10-K, the Company's 2008 Stock Repurchase Programs had remaining authorized funds of $263.3 million. Purchases under this program are subject to a review of the circumstances in place at the time. Acquisitions under the Company's share repurchase program may be made from time to time as permitted by securities laws and other legal requirements. This program may be discontinued at any time.

In February 2010, the Company's Board approved a new stock repurchase program which authorized the Company to repurchase up to $1.0 billion of its common stock. This new authorization is in addition to the Company's 2008 Stock Repurchase Program. Share repurchases under the Company's stock repurchase programs will be subject to a review of the circumstances in place at the time and will be made from time to time in private transactions or open market purchases as permitted by securities laws and other legal requirements. These programs may be discontinued at any time.

Restructuring/Bankruptcy

1.159

BOSTON SCIENTIFIC CORPORATION (DEC)

NOTES TO CONSOLIDATED FINANCIAL STATEMENTS

Note H (In Part): Restructuring-Related Activities

On an on-going basis, we monitor the dynamics of the economy, the healthcare industry, and the markets in which we compete; and we continue to assess opportunities for improved operational effectiveness and efficiency, and better alignment of expenses with revenues, while preserving our ability to make the investments in quality, research and development projects, capital and our people that are essential to our long-term success. As a result of these assessments, we have undertaken various restructuring initiatives to focus our business, diversify and reprioritize our product portfolio and redirect research and development and other spending toward higher payoff products in order to enhance our growth potential. These initiatives are described below.

Further, on February 6, 2010, our Board of Directors approved, and we committed to, a series of management changes and restructuring initiatives (the 2010 Restructuring plan) designed to strengthen and position us for long-term success. Key activities under the plan include the integration of our Cardiovascular and CRM businesses, as well as the restructuring of certain other businesses and corporate functions; the centralization of our R&D organization; the realignment of our international structure, and the reprioritization and diversification of our product portfolio, in order to drive innovation, accelerate profitable growth and increase both accountability and shareholder value. Activities under the 2010 Restructuring plan will be initiated in early 2010 and are expected to be substantially completed by the end of 2011. We estimate that the 2010 Restructuring plan will result in total pre-tax charges of approximately $180 million to $200 million, and that approximately $170 million to $190 million of these charges will result in future cash outlays. We expect the execution of the plan will result in the elimination of approximately 1,000 to 1,300 positions by the end of 2011. The following provides a summary of our expected total costs associated with the plan by major type of cost:

Type of Cost	Total Expected Amounts
Restructuring charges:	
Termination benefits	$115 million to $125 million
Asset write-offs	$5 million
Other[1]	$35 million to $40 million
Restructuring-related expenses:	
Other[2]	$25 million to $30 million
	$180 million to $200 million

[1] Includes primarily consulting fees and costs associated with contractual cancellations.

[2] Comprised of other costs directly related to restructuring plan, including accelerated depreciation and infrastructure-related costs.

Stock Purchase Rights

1.160

THE J. M. SMUCKER COMPANY (APR)

NOTES TO CONSOLIDATED FINANCIAL STATEMENTS

Note Q (In Part): Common Shares

Shareholders' Rights Plan

Pursuant to a shareholders' rights plan adopted by the Company's Board of Directors on May 20, 2009, one share purchase right is associated with each of the Company's outstanding common shares.

Under the plan, the rights will initially trade together with the Company's common shares and will not be exercisable. In the absence of further action by the directors, the rights generally will become exercisable and allow the holder to acquire the Company's common shares at a discounted price if a person or group acquires 10 percent or more of the outstanding common shares. Rights held by persons who exceed the applicable thresholds will be void. Shares held by members of the Smucker family are not subject to the thresholds. If exercisable, each right entitles the shareholder to buy one common share at a discounted price. Under certain circumstances, the rights will entitle the holder to buy shares in an acquiring entity at a discounted price.

The plan also includes an exchange option. In general, if the rights become exercisable, the directors may, at their option, effect an exchange of part or all of the rights, other than rights that have become void, for common shares. Under this option, the Company would issue one common share for each right, in each case subject to adjustment in certain circumstances.

The Company's directors may, at their option, redeem all rights for $0.001 per right, generally at any time prior to the rights becoming exercisable. The rights will expire June 3, 2019, unless earlier redeemed, exchanged, or amended by the directors.

Tax Assessment

1.161

SYSCO CORPORATION (JUN)

NOTES TO CONSOLIDATED FINANCIAL STATEMENTS

22. Subsequent Events

Sysco's affiliate, Baugh Supply Chain Cooperative (BSCC), is a cooperative taxed under subchapter T of the United States Internal Revenue Code the operation of which has resulted in a deferral of tax payments. The IRS, in connection with its audits of the company's 2003 through 2006 federal income tax returns proposed adjustments that would have accelerated amounts that the company had previously deferred and would have resulted in the payment of interest on those deferred amounts. Sysco reached a settlement with the IRS on August 21, 2009 to cease paying U.S. federal taxes related to BSCC on a deferred basis, pay the amounts currently recorded within deferred taxes related to BSCC over a three year period and make a one-time payment of $41,000,000, of which approximately $39,000,000 is non-deductible. The settlement addresses the BSCC deferred tax issue as it relates to the IRS audit of the company's 2003 through 2006 federal income tax returns, and settles the matter for all subsequent periods, including the 2007 and 2008 federal income tax returns already under audit. As a result of the settlement, the company will pay the amounts owed in the following schedule:

Amounts paid annually:	
Fiscal 2010	$528,000,000
Fiscal 2011	212,000,000
Fiscal 2012	212,000,000

Of the amounts to be paid in fiscal 2010 included in the table above, $316,000,000 will be paid in the first quarter of fiscal 2010 and the remaining payments will be paid in quarterly installments beginning in the second quarter of fiscal 2010. Amounts to be paid in fiscal 2011 and 2012 will be paid with Sysco's quarterly tax payments. The company believes it has access to sufficient cash on hand, cash flow from operations and current access to capital to make payments on all of the amounts noted above. As of June 27, 2009, Sysco has recorded deferred income tax liabilities of $750,755,000, net of federal benefit, and $429,189,000 within accrued income taxes related to the BSCC supply chain distributions. The company had previously accrued interest during the period of appeals and as a result of the settlement with the IRS, Sysco will record an income tax benefit of approximately $30,000,000 in the first quarter of fiscal 2010.

Devaluation of Monetary Assets

1.162

XEROX CORPORATION (DEC)

NOTES TO CONSOLIDATED FINANCIAL STATEMENTS

Note 1 (In Part): Summary of Significant Accounting Policies

Summary of Accounting Policies (In Part)

Foreign Currency Translation and Re-Measurement (In Part)
We have operations in Venezuela where the U.S. Dollar is the functional currency. At December 31, 2009 our Venezuelan operations had approximately 90 million in net Bolivar-denominated monetary assets that were re-measured to U.S. Dollars at the official exchange rate of 2.15 Bolivars to the Dollar. In January 2010, Venezuela announced a devaluation of the Bolivar to an official rate of 4.30 Bolivars to the Dollar for our products. As a result of this devaluation, we expect to record a loss of approximately $21 in the first quarter of 2010 for the re-measurement of our net Bolivar-denominated monetary assets.

RELATED PARTY TRANSACTIONS

1.163 FASB ASC 850, *Related Party Disclosures*, specifies the nature of information which should be disclosed in financial statements about related party transactions. In 2009, 200 survey entities disclosed related party transactions. Examples of related party disclosures follow.

Sale of Receivables to Subsidiary

1.164

DEERE & COMPANY (OCT)

NOTES TO CONSOLIDATED FINANCIAL STATEMENTS

2 (In Part): Summary of Significant Accounting Policies

Securitization of Receivables

Certain financing receivables are periodically transferred to special purpose entities (SPEs) in securitization transactions (see Note 13). These securitizations qualify as collateral for secured borrowings and no gains or losses are recognized at the time of securitization. The receivables remain on the balance sheet and are classified as "Restricted financing receivables—net." The company recognizes finance income over the lives of these receivables using the interest method.

13. Securitization of Financing Receivables

The company, as a part of its overall funding strategy, periodically transfers certain financing receivables (retail notes) into variable interest entities (VIEs) that are special purpose entities (SPEs) as part of its asset-backed securities programs (securitizations). The structure of these transactions is such that the transfer of the retail notes did not meet the criteria of sales of receivables, and is, therefore, accounted for as a secured borrowing. SPEs utilized in securitizations of retail notes differ from other entities included in the company's consolidated statements because the assets they hold are legally isolated. For bankruptcy analysis purposes, the company has sold the receivables to the SPEs in a true sale and the SPEs are separate legal entities. Use of the assets held by the SPEs is restricted by terms of the documents governing the securitization transaction.

In securitizations of retail notes related to secured borrowings, the retail notes are transferred to certain SPEs which in turn issue debt to investors. The resulting secured borrowings are included in short-term borrowings on the balance sheet. The securitized retail notes are recorded as "Restricted financing receivables—net" on the balance sheet. The total restricted assets on the balance sheet related to these securitizations include the restricted financing receivables less an allowance for credit losses, and other assets primarily representing restricted cash. The SPEs supporting the secured borrowings to which the retail notes are transferred are consolidated unless the company is not the primary beneficiary. No additional support to these SPEs beyond what was previously contractually required has been provided during fiscal year 2009.

In certain securitizations, the company is the primary beneficiary of the SPEs and, as such, consolidates the entities. The restricted assets (retail notes, allowance for credit losses and other assets) of the consolidated SPEs totaled $2,157 million and $1,303 million at October 31, 2009 and 2008, respectively. The liabilities (short-term borrowings and accrued interest) of these SPEs totaled $2,133 million and $1,287 million at October 31, 2009 and 2008, respectively. The credit holders of these SPEs do not have legal recourse to the company's general credit.

In other securitizations, the company transfers retail notes into bank-sponsored, multi-seller, commercial paper conduits, which are SPEs that are not consolidated. The company is not considered to be the primary beneficiary of these conduits, because the company's variable interests in the conduits will not absorb a majority of the conduits' expected losses, residual returns, or both. This is primarily due to these interests representing significantly less than a majority of the conduits' total assets and liabilities. These conduits provide a funding source to the company (as well as other transferors into the conduit) as they fund the retail notes through the issuance of commercial paper. The company's carrying values and variable interest related to these conduits were restricted assets (retail notes, allowance for credit losses and other assets) of $1,059 million and $398 million at October 31, 2009 and 2008, respectively. The liabilities (short-term borrowings and accrued interest) related to these conduits were $1,004 million and $398 million at October 31, 2009 and 2008, respectively.

The company's carrying amount of the liabilities to the unconsolidated conduits, compared to the maximum exposure to loss related to these conduits, which would only be incurred in the event of a complete loss on the restricted assets, was as follows at October 31 in millions of dollars:

	2009
Carrying value of liabilities	$1,004
Maximum exposure to loss	1,059

The assets of unconsolidated conduits related to securitizations in which the company's variable interests were considered significant were approximately $35 billion at October 31, 2009.

The components of consolidated restricted assets related to secured borrowings in securitization transactions at October 31 were as follows in millions of dollars:

	2009	2008
Restricted financing receivables (retail notes)	$3,133	$1,656
Allowance for credit losses	(25)	(11)
Other assets	108	56
Total restricted securitized assets	$3,216	$1,701

The components of consolidated secured borrowings and other liabilities related to securitizations at October 31 were as follows in millions of dollars:

	2009	2008
Short-term borrowings	$3,132	$1,682
Accrued interest on borrowings	5	3
Total liabilities related to restricted securitized assets	$3,137	$1,685

The secured borrowings related to these restricted securitized retail notes are obligations that are payable as the retail notes are liquidated. Repayment of the secured borrowings depends primarily on cash flows generated by the restricted assets. Due to the company's short-term credit rating, cash collections from these restricted assets are not required to be placed into a segregated collection account until immediately prior to the time payment is required to the secured creditors. At October 31, 2009, the maximum remaining term of all restricted receivables was approximately five years.

Transaction Between Reporting Entity and Investee

1.165

TOLL BROTHERS, INC. (OCT)

NOTES TO CONSOLIDATED FINANCIAL STATEMENTS

16 (In Part): Related Party Transactions

The Company formed the Trust in 1998 to take advantage of commercial real estate opportunities. The Trust is effectively owned one-third by the Company; one-third by Robert I. Toll, Bruce E. Toll (and members of his family), Zvi Barzilay (and members of his family), Joel H. Rassman, Douglas C. Yearley, Jr. and other members of the Company's current and former senior management; and one-third by an affiliate of PASERS (collectively, the "Shareholders"). At October 31, 2009, the Company's investment in the Trust was $0.9 million. The Company provides development, finance and management services to the Trust and recognized fees under the terms of various agreements in the amounts of $2.1 million, $2.2 million and $5.9 million in the fiscal years ended October 31, 2009, 2008 and 2007, respectively. The Company believes that the transactions between itself and the Trust were on terms no less favorable than it would have agreed to with unrelated parties.

Transaction Between Reporting Entity and Major Stockholder

1.166

THE MOSAIC COMPANY (MAY)

NOTES TO CONSOLIDATED FINANCIAL STATEMENTS

22. Related Party Transactions

Cargill is considered a related party due to its ownership interest in us. At May 31, 2009, Cargill and certain of its subsidiaries owned approximately 64.3% of our outstanding common stock. At May 31, 2005, Cargill owned all of our Class B Common stock, which was automatically converted to common stock on July 1, 2006. We have entered into transactions and agreements with Cargill and its non-consolidated subsidiaries (affiliates), from time to time, and we expect to enter into additional transactions and agreements with Cargill and its affiliates in the future. Certain agreements and transactions between Cargill and its affiliates and us are described below.

Approval of Transactions With Cargill

Pursuant to an Investor Rights Agreement between us and Cargill that expired in October 2008, we had established special approval requirements for commercial and other transactions, arrangements or agreements between Cargill and us. These provisions required the approval of the transactions, arrangements or agreements by a majority of our directors who were former directors of IMC, or their successors, who were deemed "non-associated," or independent, unless approval authority for the transactions, arrangements or agreements was delegated to an internal management committee as described below. These independent former IMC directors comprised the Special Transactions Committee of our Board. The Special Transactions Committee's charter provided for it to oversee transactions involving Cargill with the objective that they be fair and reasonable to us. Further, pursuant to its charter, the Special Transactions Committee had a policy under which the Special Transactions Committee delegated approval authority for certain transactions with Cargill to an internal management committee. The internal management committee was required to report its activities to the Special Transactions Committee on a periodic basis.

On December 11, 2008, our Board, on the recommendation of the Special Transactions Committee and our Corporate Governance and Nominating Committee, replaced the special approval requirements for transactions, arrangements or agreements between Cargill and us that had been established under the expired Investor Rights Agreement with new special approval requirements under which responsibility for approval of these transactions has been transferred to a subcommittee of the Corporate Governance and Nominating Committee comprised solely of independent directors in accordance with procedures it establishes. The subcommittee has delegated approval authority for certain transactions with Cargill to the internal management committee in accordance with our Related Person Transactions Approval Policy. The internal management committee is required to report its activities to the subcommittee of the Corporate Governance and Nominating Committee on a periodic basis.

During fiscal 2009, we engaged in various transactions, arrangements or agreements with Cargill which are described below. The Special Transactions Committee, the subcommittee of the Corporate Governance and Nominating Committee or the internal management committee have either approved or ratified these transactions, arrangements or agreements in accordance with either the charter and policies of the Special Transactions Committee or our Related Person Transactions Approval Policy.

We negotiated each of the following transactions, arrangements and agreements with Cargill on the basis of what we believe to be competitive market practices.

Master Transition Services Agreement and Amendment; Master Services Agreement

In connection with the combination between IMC and the fertilizer businesses of Cargill, we and Cargill entered into a master transition services agreement. Pursuant to the master transition services agreement, Cargill agreed to provide us with various transition-related services pursuant to individual work orders negotiated with us. We have entered into individual work orders for services in various countries, including Argentina, Australia, Brazil, Canada, Chile, China, Hong Kong, India, Mexico, Thailand, and the United States. Each of these work orders has been approved by the Special Transactions Committee or our internal management committee. Generally speaking, each work order is related to services provided by Cargill for its fertilizer businesses prior to the combination which were continued for our benefit post-combination. Services provided by Cargill include, but are not limited to, accounting, accounts payable and receivable processing, certain financial reporting, financial service center, graphics, human resources, information technology, insurance, legal, license and tonnage reporting, mail services, maintenance, marketing, office services, procurement, public relations, records, strategy and business development, tax, travel services and expense reporting, treasury, and other administrative and functional related services. The services performed may be modified by our mutual agreement with Cargill. The initial master transition services agreement with Cargill expired in October 2005 and was renewed through October 2006. In October 2006 Cargill agreed to continue to provide certain services to us and the parties entered into a master services agreement on terms similar to the master transition services agreement. We have renewed several work orders under which Cargill had been performing services on a transitional basis. Each of these work orders has been approved by the Special Transactions Committee or by our internal management committee.

Fertilizer Supply Agreement (U.S.)

We sell fertilizer products to Cargill's AgHorizons business unit which it resells through its retail fertilizer stores in the U.S. Under a fertilizer supply agreement, we sell nitrogen, phosphate and potash products at prices set forth in price lists that we issue from time to time to our customers. In addition, we may sell to Cargill certain products produced by third parties. We have also agreed to make available to Cargill AgHorizons, on regular commercial terms, new fertilizer products and agronomic services that are developed. Cargill AgHorizons is not obligated to purchase any minimum volume of fertilizer products and we are under no obligation to supply such products unless the parties agree to specific volumes and prices on a transaction-by-transaction basis. Our supply agreement is in effect until terminated by either party on three months written notice.

Fertilizer Supply Agreement (Canada)

We sell fertilizer products produced to a Canadian subsidiary of Cargill. Cargill purchases the substantial majority of its Canadian fertilizer requirements from us for its retail fertilizer stores in Western Canada. The agreement provides that we will sell nitrogen, phosphate and potash products at prices set forth in price lists we issue from time to time to our customers. In addition, we may sell Cargill certain products produced by third parties for a per tonne sourcing fee. In exchange for Cargill's commitment to purchase the substantial majority of its fertilizer needs from us and because it is one of our largest customers in Canada, we have also agreed to make new fertilizer products and agronomic services, to the extent marketed by us, available to Cargill on regular commercial terms. In addition, because of the volume of purchases by Cargill, we have agreed to pay a per tonne rebate at the end of each contract year if annual purchase volumes exceed certain thresholds. This agreement is in effect until June 30, 2010.

Phosphate Supply Agreement

We have a supply agreement with Cargill's subsidiary in Argentina for phosphate-based fertilizers. Cargill has no obligation to purchase any minimum quantities of fertilizer products from us and we have no obligation to supply any minimum quantities of products to Cargill. This agreement has been renewed through May 31, 2009.

Spot Fertilizer Sales

From time to time, we make spot fertilizer sales to Cargill's subsidiaries in Paraguay and Bolivia. We are under no obligation to sell fertilizer to Cargill under this relationship. This agreement is in effect until December 22, 2009.

Feed Supply Agreements and Renewals

We have various agreements relating to the supply of feed grade phosphate, potash and urea products to Cargill's animal nutrition, grain and oilseeds, and poultry businesses. The sales are generally on a spot basis in Brazil, Canada, Indonesia, Malaysia, Mexico, Philippines, Taiwan, Thailand, United States, Vietnam, Bolivia, and Venezuela. Cargill has no obligation to purchase any minimum of feed grade products from us and we have no obligation to supply any minimum amount of feed grade products to Cargill. These supply agreements are in effect until May 31, 2010.

Ocean Transportation Agreement

We have a non-exclusive agreement with Cargill's Ocean Transportation Division to perform various freight related services for us. Freight services include, but are not limited to: (i) vessel and owner screening, (ii) freight rate quotes in specified routes and at specified times, (iii) advice on market opportunities and freight strategies for the shipment of our fertilizer products to international locations, and (iv) the execution of various operational tasks associated with the international shipment of our products. We pay a fee (1) in the case of voyage charters, an address commission calculated as a percentage of the voyage freight value, (2) in the case of time charters, an address commission calculated as a percentage of the time-charter hire, and (3) in the case of forward freight agreements, a commission calculated as a percentage of the forward freight agreement notional value. Our agreement provides that the parties may renegotiate fees during its term, and the agreement is in effect until either party terminates it by providing 60 days prior written notice to the other party.

Services Agreements for Logistics and General Services

Our Argentine subsidiary has entered into services agreements with Cargill's Argentine subsidiary, which originates fertilizer and sells crop nutrients to farmers from its country stations in Argentina. Under the terms of the services agreement, we supply services related to fertilizer origination, administration, storage and dispatch. This agreement is in effect until May 31, 2009, unless terminated earlier by the parties and will automatically renew for an additional two-year term unless terminated by either party at least 90 days prior to the expiration of the original term. We have also agreed to make available to Cargill 50,000 tonnes of storage space per month as well as to a daily dispatch of 30 trucks for fertilizer shipments.

Barter Agreements

We have a barter relationship with Cargill's grain and oilseed business in Brazil. Cargill's Brazilian subsidiary, Mosaic and Brazilian farmers may, from time to time, enter into commercial arrangements pursuant to which farmers agree to forward delivery grain contracts with Cargill, and in turn, use cash generated from the transactions to purchase fertilizer from us. Similarly, in Argentina, we enter into agreements with farmers who purchase fertilizer products from us and agree to sell their grain to us upon harvest. Upon receipt of the grain, we have agreements to sell it to Cargill's grain and oilseed business in Argentina. The number of barter transactions with Cargill's subsidiaries varies from year to year. The Brazil agreement remains in effect until either party terminates it by providing 90 days prior written notice to the other party. In Argentina, the agreement is in effect until May 31, 2010.

Offer of Single Superphosphate

We have a supply agreement with Cargill's subsidiary in Argentina for single superphosphate. Cargill has no obligation to purchase any minimum quantities of fertilizer products from us and we have no obligation to supply any minimum quantities of products to Cargill. This agreement has been renewed through May 31, 2009.

Fertilizer Supply Agreement

On July 18, 2008, Phosphate Chemicals Export Association, Inc. ("PhosChem"), a consolidated subsidiary of ours, and of which one of our subsidiaries is a member, and Cargill S.A.C.I. entered into a supply agreement for sales of fertilizer products to Cargill in Argentina.

Miscellaneous Co-Location Agreements

We have various office sharing and sublease arrangements with Cargill in various geographic locations, including with respect to certain offices in Argentina, China, Brazil and the United States.

Miscellaneous

There are various other agreements between us and Cargill which we believe are not significant to us.

Summary

As of May 31, 2009 and 2008, the net amount due (to) from Cargill related to the above transactions amounted to ($3.1) million and $12.5 million, respectively.

Cargill made net equity (distributions) contributions of $(0.6) million, $4.6 million and $2.3 million to us during fiscal 2009, 2008 and 2007, respectively.

In summary, the Consolidated Statements of Earnings included the following transactions with Cargill:

(In millions)	2009	2008	2007
Transactions with Cargill included in net sales	$286.3	$299.1	$180.5
Transactions with Cargill included in cost of goods sold	173.1	228.0	71.8
Transactions with Cargill included in selling, general and administrative expenses	11.6	16.1	11.4
Interest (income) expense (received from) paid to Cargill	(0.8)	0.2	(0.6)

We have also entered into transactions and agreements with certain of our non-consolidated companies. As of May 31, 2009 and 2008, the net amount due from our non-consolidated companies totaled $220.0 million and $191.4 million, respectively.

The Consolidated Statements of Earnings included the following transactions with our non-consolidated companies:

(In millions)	2009	2008	2007
Transactions with non-consolidated companies included in net sales	$1,315.9	$871.0	$455.7
Transactions with non-consolidated companies included in cost of goods sold	384.8	327.8	211.7

Transaction Between Reporting Entity and Officer/Director

1.167

NEWS CORPORATION (JUN)

NOTES TO CONSOLIDATED FINANCIAL STATEMENTS

Note 15 (In Part): Related Parties

Director Transactions

The Company has engaged Mrs. Wendi Murdoch, the wife of Mr. K.R. Murdoch, the Company's Chairman and Chief Executive Officer, to provide strategic advice for the development of the MySpace business in China. The fees paid to Mrs. Murdoch pursuant to this arrangement are $100,000 per annum and Mrs. Murdoch received $100,000 in both the fiscal year ended June 30, 2009 and 2008 and $83,333 in the fiscal year ended June 30, 2007. Mrs. Murdoch is a Director of MySpace China Holdings Limited ("MySpace China"), a joint venture in which the Company owns a 51.7% interest on a fully diluted basis, which licenses the technology and brand to the local company in China that operates the MySpace China website. Similar to other Directors of MySpace China, Mrs. Murdoch received options over 2.5% of the fully diluted shares of MySpace China that will vest over four years under the MySpace China option plan.

Freud Communications, which is controlled by Matthew Freud, Mr. K.R. Murdoch's son-in-law, provided external support to the press and publicity activities of the Company during fiscal years 2009, 2008 and 2007. The fees paid by the Company to Freud Communications were approximately $473,000, $669,000 and $500,000 in fiscal 2009, 2008, and 2007, respectively. At June 30, 2009, there were no outstanding amounts due to or from Freud Communications.

The Shine Group ("Shine"), a television production and distribution company, is controlled by Ms. Elisabeth Murdoch, the daughter of Mr. K.R. Murdoch. Through the normal course of business, certain subsidiaries of the Company have entered into various production and distribution arrangements with Shine. Pursuant to these arrangements, the Company paid Shine an aggregate of approximately $453,000 and $300,000 in the fiscal years ended June 30, 2008 and 2007, respectively. No amounts were paid to Shine in fiscal year 2009.

Mr. Mark Hurd, a Director of the Company, is also the Chairman and Chief Executive Officer of Hewlett-Packard Company ("HP"). Through the normal course of business, HP sells certain equipment and provides services to the Company and its subsidiaries pursuant to a worldwide agreement entered into by the Company and HP in August 2007. Pursuant to this agreement, the Company paid HP approximately $47 million and $68 million in the fiscal years ended June 30, 2009 and 2008, respectively.

Dr. Roderick R. Paige was a Director of the Company until February 2008. Upon his resignation from the Board, the Company and Dr. Paige entered into a consultancy arrangement pursuant to which Dr. Paige advised the Company on certain educational matters. The consultancy arrangement was terminated in March 2009. The fees paid by the Company to Dr. Paige pursuant to this arrangement were $240,000 per annum and Dr. Paige received $90,668 in the fiscal year ended June 30, 2008. Other than fees related to his Directorship, no amounts were paid to Dr. Paige in fiscal 2007.

Mr. Stanley Shuman, Director Emeritus, and Mr. Kenneth Siskind, son of Mr. Arthur M. Siskind, who is a Director and senior advisor to the Chairman, are Managing Directors of Allen & Company LLC, a U.S. based investment bank, which provided investment advisory services to the Company. Total fees paid to Allen & Company LLC were $17.5 million and $7.5 million in fiscal 2009 and 2008, respectively. No fees were paid to Allen & Company LLC during fiscal 2007.

Transaction Between Reporting Entity and Variable Interest Entity

1.168

KIMBERLY-CLARK CORPORATION (DEC)

NOTES TO CONSOLIDATED FINANCIAL STATEMENTS

Note 2. Monetization Financing Entities

Prior to November 2009, the Corporation had minority voting interests in two financing entities ("Entity 1" and "Entity 2," collectively the "Financing Entities") used to monetize long-term notes (the "Notes") received from the sale of certain nonstrategic timberlands and related assets to nonaffiliated buyers. The Notes have an aggregate face value of $617 million and are backed by irrevocable standby letters of credit issued by money center banks. The Notes and certain other assets were transferred to the Financing Entities in 1999 and 2000. A nonaffiliated financial institution (the "Third Party") made substantive capital investments in each of the Financing Entities and had majority voting control over each of them. The Third Party also made monetization loans aggregating $617 million to the Corporation, which were assumed by the Financing Entities at the time they acquired the Notes. These monetization loans are secured by the Notes. The Corporation also contributed to the Financing Entities intercompany notes receivable aggregating $662 million and intercompany preferred stock of $50 million, which serve as secondary collateral for the monetization loans.

In 2003, the Third Party was determined to be the primary beneficiary of the Financing Entities as a result of the interest rate variability allocated to it. On June 30, 2008, the maturity dates of the lending arrangements with the Third Party were extended. In connection with the extensions, the primary beneficiary determination was reconsidered and, after excluding the interest rate variability as required by an accounting standard change, the Corporation became the primary beneficiary and began consolidating the Financing Entities. The assets and liabilities of the Financing Entities were recorded at fair value as of June 30, 2008. Because the fair value of the monetization loans exceeded the fair value of the Notes, the Corporation recorded an after-tax extraordinary charge of $8 million on its Consolidated Income Statement for the period ended June 30, 2008. Prior period financial statements have not been adjusted to reflect the consolidation of the Financing Entities. The maturity dates of the two loans were extended in June 2009. These extensions had no effect on the primary beneficiary determination.

In November 2009, the Corporation acquired the Third Party's equity voting interest in Entity 2 and acquired the Third Party's Entity 2 monetization loan rights for approximately $235 million. As a result, Entity 2 became a wholly-owned subsidiary of the Corporation. In addition, the maturity date of the Entity 1 monetization loan was extended. This extension had no effect on the primary beneficiary determination.

The following summarizes the terms of the Notes and the Entity 1 loan as of December 31, 2009 (millions of dollars):

Description	Face Value	Carrying Amount	Fair Value	Maturity	Interest Rate[1][2]
Note 1	$397	$392	$375	09/30/2014	LIBOR minus 15 bps
Loan	397	397	398	01/31/2011	LIBOR plus 127 bps
Note 2	220	215	216	07/07/2011	LIBOR minus 12.5 bps

[1] Payable quarterly.
[2] 3-month LIBOR.

The Notes and the loan are not traded in active markets. Accordingly, their fair values were calculated using a floating rate pricing model that compared the stated spread to the fair value spread to determine the price at which each of the financial instruments should trade. The model used the following inputs to calculate fair values: face value, current LIBOR rate, fair value credit spread, stated spread, maturity date and interest payment dates.

The difference between the carrying amount of the Notes and their fair value represents an unrealized loss position for which an other-than-temporary impairment has not been recognized in earnings because the Corporation does not have the intent to sell, and has both the intent and ability to hold, the Notes for a period of time sufficient to allow for an anticipated recovery of fair value to the carrying amount of the Notes.

Interest income on the Notes of $8 million and $14 million and interest expense on the monetization loans of $14 million and $15 million have been reported on the Corporation's 2009 and 2008 Consolidated Income Statement, respectively.

1.169

WASTE MANAGEMENT, INC. (DEC)

NOTES TO CONSOLIDATED FINANCIAL STATEMENTS

20 (In Part): Variable Interest Entities

Following is a description of our financial interests in variable interest entities that we consider significant, including (i) those for which we have determined that we are the primary beneficiary of the entity and, therefore, have consolidated the entity into our financial statements; and (ii) those that represent a significant interest in an unconsolidated entity. As disclosed in Note 24, we are in the process of assessing revised guidance from the FASB related to variable interest entities that is effective for the Company January 1, 2010.

Consolidated Variable Interest Entities

Waste-to-Energy LLCs

On June 30, 2000, two limited liability companies were established to purchase interests in existing leveraged lease financings at three waste-to-energy facilities that we lease, operate and maintain. We own a 0.5% interest in one of the LLCs ("LLC I") and a 0.25% interest in the second LLC ("LLC II"). John Hancock Life Insurance Company owns 99.5% of LLC I and 99.75% of LLC II is owned by LLC I and the CIT Group. In 2000, Hancock and CIT made an initial investment of $167 million in the LLCs, which was used to purchase the three waste-to-energy facilities and assume the seller's indebtedness. Under the LLC agreements, the LLCs shall be dissolved upon the occurrence of any of the following events: (i) a written decision of all members of the LLCs; (ii) December 31, 2063; (iii) a court's dissolution of the LLCs; or (iv) the LLCs ceasing to own any interest in the waste-to-energy facilities.

Income, losses and cash flows of the LLCs are allocated to the members based on their initial capital account balances until Hancock and CIT achieve targeted returns; thereafter, we will receive 80% of the earnings of each of the LLCs and Hancock and CIT will be allocated the remaining 20% based on their respective equity interests. All capital allocations made through December 31, 2009 have been based on initial capital account balances as the target returns have not yet been achieved.

Our obligations associated with our interests in the LLCs are primarily related to the lease of the facilities. In addition to our minimum lease payment obligations, we are required to make cash payments to the LLCs for differences between fair market rents and our minimum lease payments. These payments are subject to adjustment based on factors that include the fair market value of rents for the facilities and lease payments made through the re-measurement dates. In addition, we may be required under certain circumstances to make capital contributions to the LLCs based on differences between the fair market value of the facilities and defined termination values as provided for by the underlying lease agreements, although we believe the likelihood of the occurrence of these circumstances is remote.

We determined that we are the primary beneficiary of the LLCs because our interest in the entities is subject to variability based on changes in the fair market value of the leased facilities, while Hancock's and CIT's interests are structured to provide targeted returns based on their respective initial investments. As of December 31, 2009, our Consolidated Balance Sheet includes $331 million of net property and equipment associated with the LLCs' waste-to-energy facilities and $234 million in noncontrolling interests associated with Hancock's and CIT's interests in the LLCs. During the years ended December 31, 2009, 2008 and 2007, we recognized noncontrolling interest expense of $50 million, $41 million and $35 million, respectively, for Hancock's and CIT's interests in the LLCs' earnings, which are largely eliminated in WMI's consolidation.

Trusts for Closure, Post-Closure or Environmental Remediation Obligations

We have determined that we are the primary beneficiary of trust funds that were created to settle certain of our closure, post-closure or environmental remediation obligations. Although we are not always the sole beneficiary of these trust funds, we have determined that we are the primary beneficiary because we retain a majority of the risks and re-wards associated with changes in the fair value of the assets held in trust. As the trust funds are expected to continue to meet the statutory requirements for which they were estab-lished, we do not believe that there is any material exposure to loss associated with the trusts. The consolidation of these variable interest entities has not materially affected our finan-cial position or results of operations.

24 (In Part): New Accounting Pronouncements

Consolidation of Variable Interest Entities

In June 2009, the FASB issued revised authoritative guidance associated with the consolidation of variable interest enti-ties. This revised guidance replaces the current quantitative-based assessment for determining which enterprise has a controlling interest in a variable interest entity with an ap-proach that is now primarily qualitative. This qualitative ap-proach focuses on identifying the enterprise that has (i) the power to direct the activities of the variable interest entity that can most significantly impact the entity's performance; and (ii) the obligation to absorb losses and the right to receive benefits from the entity that could potentially be significant to the variable interest entity. This revised guidance also re-quires an ongoing assessment of whether an enterprise is the primary beneficiary of a variable interest entity rather than a reassessment only upon the occurrence of specific events. The new FASB-issued authoritative guidance associated with the consolidation of variable interest entities is effective for the Company January 1, 2010. The change in accounting may either be applied by recognizing a cumulative-effect ad-justment to retained earnings on the date of adoption or by retrospectively restating one or more years and recognizing a cumulative-effect adjustment to retained earnings as of the beginning of the earliest year restated. We are currently in the process of assessing the provisions of this revised guidance and have not determined whether the adoption will have a material impact on our consolidated financial statements.

Consolidated Tax Return

1.170

AK STEEL HOLDING CORPORATION (DEC)

NOTES TO CONSOLIDATED FINANCIAL STATEMENTS

Note 4 (In Part): Income Taxes

The Company and its subsidiaries file a consolidated federal income tax return. This return includes all domestic com-panies 80% or more owned by the Company and the pro-portionate share of the Company's interest in partnership investments. State tax returns are filed on a consolidated, combined or separate basis depending on the applicable laws relating to the Company and its domestic subsidiaries.

Tax Sharing Agreement

1.171

THE WESTERN UNION COMPANY (DEC)

NOTES TO CONSOLIDATED FINANCIAL STATEMENTS

10 (In Part): Taxes

Tax Allocation Agreement With First Data

The Company and First Data each are liable for taxes im-posed on their respective businesses both prior to and after the Spin-off. If such taxes have not been appropriately ap-portioned between First Data and the Company, subsequent adjustments may occur that may impact the Company's fi-nancial position or results of operations.

Also under the tax allocation agreement, with respect to taxes and other liabilities that result from a final determination that is inconsistent with the anticipated tax consequences of the Spin-off (as set forth in the private letter ruling and relevant tax opinion), ("Spin-off Related Taxes"), the Com-pany will be liable to First Data for any such Spin-off Related Taxes attributable solely to actions taken by or with respect to the Company. In addition, the Company will also be li-able for 50% of any Spin-off Related Taxes (i) that would not have been imposed but for the existence of both an action by the Company and an action by First Data or (ii) where the Company and First Data each take actions that, standing alone, would have resulted in the imposition of such Spin-off Related Taxes. The Company may be similarly liable if it breaches certain representations or covenants set forth in the tax allocation agreement. If the Company is required to indemnify First Data for taxes incurred as a result of the Spin-off being taxable to First Data, it likely would have a material adverse effect on the Company's business, finan-cial position and results of operations. First Data generally will be liable for all Spin-off Related Taxes, other than those described above.

INFLATION ACCOUNTING

1.172 FASB ASC 255, *Changing Prices*, states that entities previously required to disclose current cost information are no longer required to disclose such information.

1.173 Many of the survey entities include comments about inflation in Management's Discussion and Analysis of Fi-nancial Condition and Results of Operations. An example follows.

1.174

SPAN-AMERICA MEDICAL SYSTEMS, INC. (SEP)

IMPACT OF INFLATION AND COST OF RAW MATERIALS

Based on current conditions in the markets for our primary raw materials, we expect inflation to be a moderate factor for our operations in fiscal 2010. We experienced increases in the cost of polyurethane foam, our primary raw material, during the first quarter of 2009, followed by cost decreases on selected raw materials later in fiscal 2009. We have been able to offset previous raw material cost increases through a combination of sales price increases, efficiency improvements and other expense reduction efforts. However, we can give no assurance that we will be able to offset future cost increases, which could negatively affect our profitability.

The cost of polyurethane foam is indirectly influenced by oil prices. However, other market factors also affect foam prices, including supply availability of component chemicals, demand for related products from domestic and international manufacturers, competition among domestic suppliers, our purchase volumes and regulatory requirements. Consequently, it is difficult for us to accurately predict the impact that inflation might have on our operations.

FASB REFERENCES IN POST-CODIFICATION FINANCIAL STATEMENTS

1.175   In June 2009, the Financial Accounting Standards Board (FASB) issued the last FASB statement referenced in that form: FASB Statement No. 168, *The FASB Accounting Standards Codification*™ *and the Hierarchy of Generally Accepted Accounting Principles—a replacement of FASB Statement No. 162.* This standard establishes FASB *Accounting Standards Codification*™ (ASC) as the source of authoritative U.S. accounting and reporting standards for nongovernmental companies, in addition to guidance issued by the Securities and Exchange Commission (SEC), and is effective for financial statements issued for interim and annual periods ending after September 15, 2009. In the ASC Notice to Constituents, FASB suggests the use of plain English references going forward in financial statements and related footnote disclosures.

1.176   FASB provides the following example of plain English references in the Notice to Constituents when referring to the requirements of FASB ASC 815, *Derivatives and Hedging*: "as required by the Derivatives and Hedging Topic of the FASB Accounting Standards Codification."

1.177   Table 1-15 shows the referencing techniques used by the 500 survey entities. As indicated in the table, the four types of referencing used were:
- Plain English referencing only, with no specific references to FASB ASC (including entities whose only reference to a specific FASB ASC is in the "recently issued accounting standards" section of the notes).
- FASB ASC referencing, at either the topic, subtopic, section, or even paragraph level.
- Dual referencing, where entities used both the legacy FASB references (for example, SFAS No. 157) in addition to the new FASB ASC references.
- Legacy FASB referencing only.

For survey entities with fiscal years ending on or before September 15, 2009, this measure of referencing techniques is not applicable.

1.178   Examples of FASB referencing in financial statements follow.

1.179

TABLE 1-15: USE OF FASB REFERENCES IN FINANCIAL STATEMENTS

	Number of Entities			
	2009	2008	2007	2006
Plain English referencing only	236	—	—	—
FASB ASC referencing	98	—	—	—
Dual referencing	35	—	—	—
Legacy FASB referencing only	2	—	—	—
Pre-codification financial statements	129	500	600	600
Total Entities	**500**	**500**	**600**	**600**

2008–2009 based on 500 entities surveyed; 2006–2007 based on 600 entities surveyed.

Plain English Referencing

1.180

AMPHENOL CORPORATION (DEC)

NOTES TO CONSOLIDATED FINANCIAL STATEMENTS

Note 3 (In Part): Fair Value Measurements

Effective January 1, 2008, the Company adopted standards set forth in the Fair Value Measurements and Disclosures Topic of the ASC, which includes a new framework for measuring fair value of financial and non-financial instruments and expands related disclosures. The Company does not have any non-financial instruments accounted for at fair value on a recurring basis. Broadly, the framework within the Fair Value Measurements and Disclosures Topic requires fair value to be determined based on the exchange price that would be received for an asset or paid to transfer a liability (an exit price) in the principal or most advantageous market for the asset or liability in an orderly transaction between market participants. These standards establish market or observable inputs as the preferred source of values. Assumptions based on hypothetical transactions are used in the absence of market inputs.

Note 4 (In Part): Derivative Instruments

Effective January 1, 2009, the Company adopted standards set forth in the Derivatives and Hedging Topic of the ASC, which require disclosure of: (1) how and why an entity uses derivative instruments; (2) how derivative instruments and related hedged items are accounted for in accordance with the Derivatives and Hedging Topic; and (3) how derivative instruments and related hedged items affect an entity's financial position, financial performance, and cash flows.

Note 10 (In Part): Business Combinations

Effective January 1, 2009, the Company adopted amended standards set forth in the Business Combinations Topic of the ASC. Such standards are applicable to the Company for acquisitions completed on or after January 1, 2009 and establish principles and requirements for how the acquirer: (1) recognizes and measures in its financial statements the identifiable assets acquired, the liabilities assumed, and any noncontrolling interest in the acquiree; (2) recognizes and measures the goodwill acquired in the business combination; and (3) determines what information to disclose in the financial statements. The principles in the Business Combinations Topic that are most applicable to the Company are: (1) companies are required to expense transaction costs as incurred; (2) any subsequent adjustments to a recorded performance-based liability after its recognition are adjusted through income as opposed to goodwill; and (3) any noncontrolling interests are recorded at fair value.

1.181

C. R. BARD, INC. (DEC)

NOTES TO CONSOLIDATED FINANCIAL STATEMENTS

2 (In Part): Acquisitions and Divestitures

Acquisitions (In Part)

On January 1, 2009, the company adopted new FASB guidance on accounting for business combinations. This guidance requires an acquirer to measure the identifiable assets acquired and liabilities assumed at their fair value on the acquisition date, with goodwill being the excess value of consideration paid over the fair value of the net identifiable assets acquired. This guidance also requires that purchased R&D be capitalized and recorded as an intangible asset at the acquisition date, that contingent consideration be recorded at fair value at the acquisition date and that transaction costs be expensed.

4 (In Part): Income Taxes

Effective January 1, 2007, the company adopted FASB authoritative guidance on the accounting for uncertainty in income taxes. This guidance states that a tax benefit from an uncertain tax position may be recognized only if it is more likely than not that the position is sustainable based on its technical merits. The tax benefit of a qualifying position is the largest amount of tax benefit that is greater than 50% likely of being realized upon settlement with a taxing authority having full knowledge of all relevant information. A tax benefit from an uncertain position was previously recognized if it was probable of being sustained. The company increased its January 1, 2007 retained earnings by $5.3 million as a result of the adoption of this guidance.

5 (In Part): Earnings Per Common Share

On January 1, 2009, the company adopted new FASB guidance on determining whether awards granted in share-based payment transactions are participating securities prior to vesting and therefore need to be included in the earnings allocation in computing earnings per share ("EPS") using the two-class method. This guidance requires nonvested share-based payment awards that have non-forfeitable rights to dividend or dividend equivalents to be treated as a separate class of securities in calculating EPS. Participating securities include nonvested restricted stock, nonvested shares or units under the management stock purchase program, and certain other nonvested stock-based awards. This guidance was applied retrospectively and therefore prior period information was adjusted.

ASC Referencing Only

1.182

CRANE CO. (DEC)

NOTES TO CONSOLIDATED FINANCIAL STATEMENTS

Note 9. Fair Value of Financial Instruments

The Company adopted the provisions under ASC Topic 820, "Fair Value Measurements and Disclosures" ("ASC 820") as of January 1, 2008, with the exception of the application to non-recurring nonfinancial assets and nonfinancial liabilities, which was delayed and therefore adopted as of January 1, 2009. The provisions under ASC 820 define fair value, establish a framework for measuring fair value and generally accepted accounting principles and expand disclosures about fair value measurements.

Fair value is defined in ASC 820 as the price that would be received to sell an asset or paid to transfer a liability in an orderly transaction between market participants at the measurement date. Fair value measurements are to be considered from the perspective of a market participant that holds the asset or owes the liability. The provisions under ASC 820 also establish a fair value hierarchy which requires an entity to maximize the use of observable inputs and minimize the use of unobservable inputs when measuring fair value.

ASC 820 describes three levels of inputs that may be used to measure fair value:

- Level 1—Quoted prices in active markets for identical or similar assets and liabilities.
- Level 2—Quoted prices for identical or similar assets and liabilities in markets that are not active or observable inputs other than quoted prices in active markets for identical or similar assets and liabilities.

- Level 3—Unobservable inputs that are supported by little or no market activity and that are significant to the fair value of the assets or liabilities.

● ● ● ● ● ●

The Company adopted the provisions under ASC Topic 825, "Financial Instruments" as of January 1, 2008. These provisions provide companies with an option to report selected financial assets and liabilities at fair value. The Company did not elect the fair value option for any of such eligible financial assets or financial liabilities as of the adoption date.

Note 10 (In Part): Derivative Instruments and Hedging Activities

In March 2009, the Company adopted the provisions under ASC Topic 815, "Derivatives and Hedging" ("ASC 815") as it relates to disclosures about derivative instruments and hedging activities. The provisions under ASC 815 are intended to improve transparency in financial reporting by requiring enhanced disclosures of an entity's derivative instruments and hedging activities and their effects on the entity's financial position, financial performance, and cash flows.

Dual Referencing

1.183

GREIF, INC. (OCT)

NOTES TO CONSOLIDATED FINANCIAL STATEMENTS

Note 1 (In Part): Summary of Significant Accounting Policies

Net Assets Held for Sale

Net assets held for sale represent land, buildings and land improvements for locations that have met the criteria of "held for sale" accounting, as specified by Statement of Financial Accounting Standards ("SFAS") No. 144, "Accounting for Impairment or Disposal of Long-Lived Assets" (codified under ASC 360 "Property, Plant, and Equipment"). As of October 31, 2009, there were fourteen locations held for sale (twelve in the Industrial Packaging segment and two in the Paper Packaging segment). In 2009, the Company recorded net sales of $5.5 million and net loss before taxes of $3.9 million associated with these properties, primarily related to the Industrial Packaging segment. For 2008, the Company recorded net sales of $15.4 million and net loss before taxes of $8.2 million, primarily related to the Industrial Packaging segment. The effect of suspending depreciation on the facilities held for sale is immaterial to the results of operations. The properties classified within net assets held for sale have been listed for sale and it is the Company's intention to complete these sales within the upcoming year.

Goodwill and Other Intangibles (In Part)

Goodwill is the excess of the purchase price of an acquired entity over the amounts assigned to assets and liabilities assumed in the business combination. The Company accounts for purchased goodwill and other intangible assets in accordance with SFAS No. 142, "Goodwill and Other Intangible Assets" (codified under ASC 350 "Intangibles—Goodwill and Other"). Under SFAS 142, purchased goodwill and intangible assets with indefinite lives are not amortized, but instead are tested for impairment at least annually. Intangible assets with finite lives, primarily customer relationships, patents and trademarks, continue to be amortized over their useful lives. The Company tests for impairment during the fourth quarter of each fiscal year, or more frequently if certain indicators are present or changes in circumstances suggest that impairment may exist.

Internal Use Software

Internal use software is accounted for under Statement of Position 98-1 "Accounting for the Costs of Computer Software Developed or Obtained for Internal Use" (codified under ASC 985 "Software"). Internal use software is software that is acquired, internally developed or modified solely to meet the Company's needs and for which, during the software's development or modification, a plan does not exist to market the software externally. Costs incurred to develop the software during the application development stage and for upgrades and enhancements that provide additional functionality are capitalized and then amortized over a three- to ten-year period.

Note 8 (In Part): Financial Instruments and Fair Value Measurements

The Company uses derivatives from time to time to partially mitigate the effect of exposure to interest rate movements, exposure to currency fluctuations, and energy cost fluctuations. Under SFAS No. 133 (*codified under ASC 815 "Derivatives and Hedging"*), all derivatives are to be recognized as assets or liabilities in the balance sheet and measured at fair value. Changes in the fair value of derivatives are recognized in either net income or in other comprehensive income, depending on the designated purpose of the derivative.

SFAS No. 157 (codified under ASC 820—"Fair Value Measurements and Disclosures") established a three-tier fair value hierarchy, which prioritizes the inputs used in measuring fair value. These tiers include: Level 1, defined as observable inputs such as quoted prices in active markets; Level 2, defined as inputs other than quoted prices in active markets that are either directly or indirectly observable; and Level 3, defined as unobservable inputs in which little or no market data exists, therefore requiring an entity to develop its own assumptions. As of October 31, 2009, the Company held certain derivative asset and liability positions that lack level 1 inputs and are thus required to be measured at fair value on a Level 2 basis. The majority of the Company's derivative instruments related to receive floating-rate, pay fixed-rate interest rate swaps and receive fixed-rate, pay fixed-rate cross-currency interest rate swaps.

Note 11 (In Part): Income Taxes

On November 1, 2007, the Company adopted FIN 48, "Accounting for Uncertainty in Income Taxes," FIN 48 is an interpretation of SFAS No. 109, "Accounting for Income Taxes," and clarifies the accounting for uncertainty in income tax positions (codified under ASC 740 "Income Taxes"). FIN 48 prescribes a recognition threshold and measurement process for recording in the financial statements uncertain tax positions taken or expected to be taken in a tax return. Additionally,

FIN 48 provides guidance regarding uncertain tax positions relating to de-recognition, classification, interest and penalties, accounting in interim periods, disclosure and transition.

Note 12 (In Part): Retirement Plans

In September 2006, the guidance was updated within SFAS No. 158, "Employers' Accounting for Defined Benefit Pension and Other Postretirement Plans (codified under ASC 715 "Compensation—Retirement Benefits"). Under SFAS No. 158, employers recognize the funded status of their defined benefit pension and other postretirement plans on the consolidated balance sheet and record as a component of other comprehensive income, net of tax, the gains or losses and prior service costs or credits that have not been recognized as components of the net periodic benefit cost. The Company adopted the recognition and related disclosure provisions of this standard, prospectively, on October 31, 2007. Under SFAS No. 158, companies must change the plan measurement date to the end of the employer's fiscal year.

Section 2: Balance Sheet

BALANCE SHEET TITLE

2.01 Table 2-1 summarizes the titles used to describe the statement of assets, liabilities and stockholders' equity.

2.02

TABLE 2-1: BALANCE SHEET TITLE

	2009	2008	2007	2006
Balance Sheet......................................	476	478	577	578
Statement of Financial Position...........	24	22	23	21
Statement of Financial Condition.........	—	—	—	1
Total Entities.....................................	**500**	**500**	**600**	**600**

2008–2009 based on 500 entities surveyed; 2006–2007 based on 600 entities surveyed.

BALANCE SHEET FORMAT

2.03 Table 2-2 summarizes the different balance sheet formats used by the survey entities. Balance sheet formats include the account form, the report form, and the financial position form. The account form shows total assets on the left-hand side equal to the sum of liabilities and stockholders' equity on the right-hand side. The report form shows a downward sequence of either total assets minus total liabilities equal to stockholders' equity or total assets equal to total liabilities plus stockholders' equity. The financial position form, a variation of the report form, shows noncurrent assets added to and noncurrent liabilities deducted from working capital to arrive at a balance equal to stockholders' equity.

2.04 FASB ASC 810, *Consolidation*, requires that entities consolidate subsidiaries having nonhomogenous operations. This requirement resulted in certain survey entities presenting an unclassified balance sheet (15 entities in 2009) or a balance sheet classified as to industrial operations but showing assets and liabilities of nonhomogenous operations as segregated amounts (three entities in 2009).

2.05 Occasionally, the survey entities disclose reclassifications of balance sheet amounts. Examples of a reclassification follow.

2.06

TABLE 2-2: BALANCE SHEET FORMAT

	2009	2008	2007	2006
Report form...........................	437	438	523	524
Account form.........................	63	62	74	76
Financial position form.........................	—	—	—	—
Total Entities.....................................	**500**	**500**	**600**	**600**

2008–2009 based on 500 entities surveyed; 2006–2007 based on 600 entities surveyed.

Reclassifications

2.07

HARRIS CORPORATION (JUN)

NOTES TO CONSOLIDATED FINANCIAL STATEMENTS

Note 1 (In Part): Significant Accounting Policies

Reclassifications
Certain prior-year amounts have been reclassified in our Consolidated Financial Statements to conform with current-year classifications. These reclassifications include:

- Reclassifying $5.8 million and $63.1 million of investments associated with our non-qualified deferred compensation plans from the "Compensation and benefits" line item to the "Other current assets" and "Other noncurrent assets" line items, respectively, in our Consolidated Balance Sheet;
- Reclassifying $58.6 million of obligations to pay benefits under our non-qualified deferred compensation plans from the "Compensation and benefits" line item to the "Other long-term liabilities" line item in our Consolidated Balance Sheet; and
- Reclassifying $14.1 million of advance payments on extended warranty contracts from the "Advanced payments and unearned income" line item to the "Other long-term liabilities" line item in our Consolidated Balance Sheet.

2.08

LEGGETT & PLATT, INCORPORATED (DEC)

NOTES TO CONSOLIDATED FINANCIAL STATEMENTS

A (In Part): Summary of Significant Accounting Policies

Reclassifications

Certain reclassifications have been made to the prior years' consolidated financial statements to conform to the 2009 presentation:

- In the Consolidated Balance Sheets—noncontrolling interests have been reclassified from "Other long-term liabilities" to "Noncontrolling interest" within "Equity."
- In the Consolidated Statements of Operations— noncontrolling interests have been reclassified from "Other expense (income), net" to "(Earnings) attributable to noncontrolling interest, net of tax."
- In the Consolidated Statements of Cash Flows— noncontrolling interests have been reclassified between "Net earnings" and "Other adjustments to reconcile net earnings to net cash provided by operating activities" and to reflect separate presentation of "Provision for losses on accounts and notes receivables."
- In the Consolidated Statements of Changes in Equity— balance sheet activity as well as comprehensive income information has been added for noncontrolling interest.
- In Notes to Consolidated Financial Statements— Segment Information, EBIT for Commercial Fixturing & Components and Specialized Products has been retrospectively adjusted to include noncontrolling interest.
- In Notes to Consolidated Financial Statements— Segment Information, long-lived assets by geographic location have been retrospectively adjusted to include only tangible long-lived assets.

CASH AND CASH EQUIVALENTS

2.09   Cash is commonly considered to consist of currency and demand deposits. FASB ASC 230, *Statement of Cash Flows*, defines cash equivalents as "short-term, highly liquid investments" that are both readily convertible into known amounts of cash and so near their maturity that they present insignificant risk of changes in value because of changes in interest rates. Generally, only investments with original maturities of three months or less qualify under that definition. 376 survey entities stated explicitly that the carrying amount of cash and cash equivalents approximated fair value.

2.10   Table 2-3 lists the balance sheet captions used by the survey entities to describe cash and cash equivalents. As indicated in Table 2-3, the most frequently used caption is cash and cash equivalents. Examples of cash and cash equivalents presentations and disclosures follow.

2.11

TABLE 2-3: CASH AND CASH EQUIVALENTS— BALANCE SHEET CAPTIONS

	2009	2008	2007	2006
Cash	12	12	20	19
Cash and cash equivalents	444	446	538	536
Cash and equivalents	31	33	31	33
Cash includes certificates of deposit or time deposits	3	1	2	1
Cash combined with marketable securities	10	8	9	11
No amount for cash	—	—	—	—
Total Entities	**500**	**500**	**600**	**600**

2008–2009 based on 500 entities surveyed; 2006–2007 based on 600 entities surveyed.

2.12

FREEPORT-MCMORAN COPPER & GOLD INC. (DEC)

NOTES TO CONSOLIDATED FINANCIAL STATEMENTS

Note 1 (In Part): Summary of Significant Accounting Policies

Cash Equivalents

Highly liquid investments purchased with maturities of three months or less are considered cash equivalents.

Note 17 (In Part): Fair Value Measurement

A summary of FCX's financial assets and liabilities measured at fair value on a recurring basis follows:

	Fair Value at December 31, 2009			
(In millions)	Total	Level 1	Level 2	Level 3
Cash equivalents	$2,610	$2,610	$—	$—
Trust assets (current and long-term)	146	146	—	—
Available-for-sale securities (current and long-term)	74	74	—	—
Embedded derivatives in provisional sales/purchases contracts, net	165	165	—	—
Other derivative financial instruments, net	14	14	—	—
	$3,009	$3,009	$—	$—

Valuation Techniques (In Part)

Cash Equivalents

The fair value of FCX's cash equivalents are classified within Level 1 of the fair value hierarchy because they are valued using quoted market prices in active markets. FCX's cash equivalents are primarily money market securities, time deposits and U.S. treasury securities.

A summary of the carrying amount and fair value of FCX's financial instruments at December 31, 2009 and 2008 follows:

	2009		2008	
(In millions)	Carrying Amount	Fair Value	Carrying Amount	Fair Value
Cash and cash equivalents[a]	$ 2,656	$ 2,656	$ 872	$ 872
Accounts receivable	1,803	1,803	1,212	1,212
Trust assets (current and long-term)	146	146	260	260
Available-for-sale securities (current and long-term)	74	74	84	84
Derivative assets	14	14	—	—
Accounts payable and accrued liabilities	(1,837)	(1,837)	(2,644)	(2,644)
Rio Tinto share of joint venture cash flows	(161)	(161)	—	—
Dividends payable	(99)	(99)	(44)	(44)
Debt (including amounts due within one year)	(6,346)	(6,735)	(7,351)	(5,889)

[a] Recorded at fair value. Quoted market prices are used to determine fair value.

2.13

SILGAN HOLDINGS INC. (DEC)

NOTES TO CONSOLIDATED FINANCIAL STATEMENTS

Note 1 (In Part): Summary of Significant Accounting Policies

Cash and Cash Equivalents

Cash equivalents represent short-term, highly liquid investments which are readily convertible to cash and have maturities of three months or less at the time of purchase. As a result of our cash management system, checks issued for payment may create negative book balances.

Checks outstanding in excess of related book balances totaling $104.8 million at December 31, 2009 and $63.9 million at December 31, 2008 are included in trade accounts payable in our Consolidated Balance Sheets. Changes in outstanding checks are included in financing activities in our Consolidated Statements of Cash Flows to treat them as, in substance, cash advances.

Note 8 (In Part): Financial Instruments

The financial instruments recorded in our Consolidated Balance Sheets include cash and cash equivalents, trade accounts receivable, trade accounts payable, debt obligations and swap agreements. Due to their short-term maturity, the carrying amounts of trade accounts receivable and trade accounts payable approximate their fair market values. The following table summarizes the carrying amounts and estimated fair values of our other financial instruments at December 31:

	2009		2008	
(Dollars in thousands)	Carrying Amount	Fair Value	Carrying Amount	Fair Value
Assets:				
Cash and cash equivalents	$305,754	$305,754	$163,006	$163,006
Natural gas swap agreements	355	355	—	—
Liabilities:				
Bank debt	355,766	355,766	684,913	684,913
7 $\frac{1}{4}$% notes	243,648	257,500	—	—
6 $\frac{3}{4}$% notes	200,000	201,500	200,000	172,000
Interest rate swap agreements	13,946	13,946	12,120	12,120
Natural gas swap agreements	—	—	158	158

Fair Value Measurement

Financial Instruments Measured at Fair Value

GAAP defines fair value as the price that would be received to sell an asset or paid to transfer a liability in an orderly transaction between market participants at the measurement date (exit price). GAAP classifies the inputs used to measure fair value into a hierarchy consisting of three levels. Level 1 inputs represent unadjusted quoted prices in active markets for identical assets or liabilities. Level 2 inputs represent unadjusted quoted prices in active markets for similar assets or liabilities, or unadjusted quoted prices for identical or similar assets or liabilities in markets that are not active, or inputs other than quoted prices that are observable for the asset or liability. Level 3 inputs represent unobservable inputs for the asset or liability. Financial assets and liabilities are classified in their entirety based on the lowest level of input that is significant to the fair value measurement.

The financial assets and liabilities that are measured on a recurring basis at December 31, 2009 and 2008 consist of our cash and cash equivalents, interest rate swap agreements and natural gas swap agreements. We measured the fair value of cash and cash equivalents using Level 1 inputs. We measured the fair value of the swap agreements using the income approach. The fair value of these agreements reflects the estimated amounts that we would pay or receive based on the present value of the expected cash flows derived from market rates and prices. As such, these derivative instruments are classified within Level 2.

MARKETABLE SECURITIES

2.14   FASB ASC 320, *Investments—Debt and Equity Securities*, provides guidance on accounting for and reporting investments in equity securities that have readily determinable fair value and all investments in debt securities. FASB ASC 320 also states the disclosure requirements for such investments.

2.15   By definition, investments in debt and equity securities are financial instruments. FASB ASC 825, *Financial Instruments*, requires disclosure of the fair value of those investments for which it is practicable to estimate that value, the methods and assumptions used in estimating the fair value of marketable securities, and a description of any changes in the methods and assumptions during the period.

2.16   FASB ASC 320 requires that certain debt and equity securities be classified into one of three categories: held-to-maturity, available-for-sale, or trading securities. Investments in debt securities that the enterprise has the positive intent and ability to hold to maturity are classified as held-to-maturity and reported at amortized cost in the statement of financial position. Securities that are bought and held principally for the purpose of selling them in the near term (thus held for only a short period of time) are classified as trading securities and reported at fair value. Trading generally reflects active and frequent buying and selling, and trading securities are generally used to generate profit on short-term differences in price. Investments not classified as either held-to-maturity or trading securities are classified as available-for-sale securities and reported at fair value. 122 survey entities identified their marketable securities as available-for-sale.

2.17   FASB ASC 820, *Fair Value Measurements and Disclosures*, defines fair value, establishes a framework for measuring fair value, and requires certain disclosures about fair value measurements. FASB ASC 820 clarifies the definition of fair value as an exit price, i.e., a price that would be received to sell, as opposed to acquire, an asset or transfer a liability. FASB ASC 820 emphasizes that fair value is a market-based

measurement. It establishes a fair value hierarchy that distinguishes between assumptions developed based on market data obtained from independent external sources and the reporting entity's own assumptions. Further, FASB ASC 820 specifies that fair value measurement should consider adjustment for risk, such as the risk inherent in a valuation technique or its inputs. For assets measured at fair value, whether on a recurring or a nonrecurring basis, FASB ASC 820 specifies the required disclosures concerning the inputs used to measure fair value. FASB Accounting Standards Update (ASU) No. 2010-06, *Improving Disclosures about Fair Value Measurements*, requires more robust disclosures about different classes of assets and liabilities measured at fair value, the valuation techniques and inputs used, the activity in Level 3 fair value measurements, and the transfers between Levels 1, 2, and 3. FASB ASU No. 2010-06 is effective for fiscal years beginning after December 15, 2009, except for the disclosures about certain Level 3 activity. Those disclosures are effective for fiscal years beginning after December 15, 2010. During 2009, 211 survey companies made 385 disclosures of fair value related to marketable securities. 141 of those disclosures were based on the quoted price of the identical item in an active market (level 1 input). 93 of those disclosures were primarily based on other market-corroborated (level 2) inputs. 32 disclosures estimated fair value using nonmarket-corroborated (level 3) inputs. 51 disclosures presented carrying amounts which approximated fair value of marketable securities. In addition, there were 61 disclosures in which carrying value was compared to fair value in an exposition or a table.

2.18   FASB ASC 825, *Financial Instruments*, permits entities to choose to measure many financial instruments and certain other items at fair value that are not currently required to be measured at fair value. Further, under FASB ASC 825 a business entity shall report unrealized gains and losses on eligible items for which the fair value option has been elected in earnings at each subsequent reporting date. The irrevocable election of the fair value option is made on an instrument by instrument basis, and applied to the entire instrument, not just a portion of it. FASB ASC 825 also establishes presentation and disclosure requirements designed to facilitate comparison between entities that choose different measurement attributes for similar types of assets and liabilities.

2.19   FASB ASC 320, *Investments—Debt and Equity Securities*, should be used to determine when certain investments are considered impaired, whether that impairment is other than temporary, and the measurement and recognition of an impairment loss. FASB ASC 320 also provides guidance on accounting considerations subsequent to the recognition of an other-than-temporary impairment and requires certain disclosures about unrealized losses that have not been recognized as other-than-temporary impairments.

2.20 Table 2-4 lists the balance sheet carrying bases for investments in debt and equity securities presented as current assets. Examples of presentations and disclosures for such investments follow.

2.21

TABLE 2-4: MARKETABLE SECURITIES—CARRYING BASES*

	Number of Entities			
	2009	2008	2007	2006
Market/fair value	148	151	209	211
Cost	26	23	35	39

* Appearing in either the balance sheet and/or the notes to financial statements.

2008–2009 based on 500 entities surveyed; 2006–2007 based on 600 entities surveyed.

Available-for-Sale Securities

2.22

COSTCO WHOLESALE CORPORATION (AUG)

(In millions)	2009	2008
Current assets		
Cash and cash equivalents	$ 3,157	$2,619
Short-term investments	570	656
Receivables, net	834	748
Merchandise inventories	5,405	5,039
Deferred income taxes and other current assets	371	400
Total current assets	$10,337	$9,462

NOTES TO CONSOLIDATED FINANCIAL STATEMENTS (In millions)

Note 1 (In Part): Summary of Significant Accounting Policies

Short-Term Investments

In general, short-term investments have a maturity of three months to five years at the date of purchase. Investments with maturities beyond five years may be classified as short-term based on their highly liquid nature and because such marketable securities represent the investment of cash that is available for current operations. Short-term investments classified as available-for-sale are recorded at fair value as described in Notes 2 and 3, using the specific identification method with the unrealized gains and losses reflected in accumulated other comprehensive income until realized. Realized gains and losses from the sale of available-for-sale securities, if any, are determined on a specific identification basis.

Note 2. Investments

The major categories of the Company's investments are as follows:

Money Market Mutual Funds

The Company invests in money funds that seek to maintain a net asset value of a $1.00, while limiting overall exposure to credit, market, and liquidity risks.

U.S. Government and Agency Securities

These U.S. government secured debt instruments are publically traded and valued. Losses in this category are primarily due to market liquidity and interest rate reductions.

Corporate Notes and Bonds

The Company evaluates its corporate debt securities based on a variety of factors including, but not limited to, the credit rating of the issuer. The vast majority of the Company's corporate debt securities are rated investment grade by the major rating agencies.

Asset and Mortgage-Backed Securities

The vast majority of the Company's asset and mortgage-backed securities have investment grade credit ratings from the major rating agencies. These investments are collateralized by residential sub-prime credit, credit card receivables, commercial real estate, foreign mortgage receivables, and lease receivables. Estimates of fair value are based upon a variety of factors including, but not limited to, credit rating of the issuer, internal credit risk, interest rate variation, prepayment assumptions, and the potential for default.

Certificates of Deposit

Certificates of deposit are short-term interest-bearing debt instruments issued by various financial institutions with which the Company has an established banking relationship. Those certificates of deposit issued by U.S. financial institutions are insured by the Federal Deposit Insurance Corporation.

The Company's investments at August 30, 2009 and August 31, 2008, were as follows:

| | Cost Basis | Unrealized Gains | Unrealized Losses | Recorded Basis | Balance Sheet Classification | |
					Short-Term Investments	Other Assets
2009:						
Available-for-sale:						
Money market mutual funds	$ 13	$—	$—	$ 13	$ 13	$—
U.S. government and agency securities	400	3	—	403	403	—
Corporate notes and bonds	49	1	(1)	49	49	—
Asset and mortgage-backed securities	48	1	—	49	46	3
Total available-for-sale	510	5	(1)	514	511	3
Held-to-maturity:						
Certificates of deposit	59	—	—	59	59	—
Total investments	$569	$ 5	$(1)	$573	$570	$ 3
2008:						
Available-for-sale:						
Money market mutual funds	$ 16	$—	$—	$ 16	$ 16	$—
U.S. government and agency securities	355	2	(1)	356	356	—
Corporate notes and bonds	115	1	(1)	115	99	16
Asset and mortgage-backed securities	113	—	(2)	111	84	27
Total available-for-sale	599	3	(4)	598	555	43
Held-to-maturity:						
Certificates of deposit	1	—	—	1	1	—
Enhanced money funds	125	—	—	125	100	25
Total held-to-maturity	126	—	—	126	101	25
Total investments	$725	$ 3	$(4)	$724	$656	$68

For available-for-sale securities, proceeds from sales were $183, $165, and $496 in 2009, 2008, and 2007, respectively. Gross realized gains from sales were $5, $2, and $1 in 2009, 2008 and 2007, respectively, and gross realized losses from sales were $2 and $1 in 2009 and 2007, respectively. In 2008, gross realized losses from sales were not significant.

The following tables present the length of time available-for-sale securities were in continuous unrealized loss positions, but were not deemed to be other-than-temporarily impaired:

| | Less Than 12 Months | | Greater Than or Equal to 12 Months | |
	Gross Unrealized Holding Losses	Fair Value	Gross Unrealized Holding Losses	Fair Value
2009				
U.S. government and agency	$—	$ —	$—	$—
Corporate notes and bonds	—	—	(1)	8
Asset and mortgage-backed securities	—	—	—	—
	$—	$ —	$(1)	$ 8
2008				
U.S. government and agency	$(1)	$187	$—	$—
Corporate notes and bonds	(1)	61	—	—
Asset and mortgage-backed securities	(2)	58	—	—
	$(4)	$306	$—	$—

Gross unrealized holding losses of $1, at August 30, 2009, for investments held greater than or equal to twelve months pertained to the Company's holdings in corporate notes and bonds. The unrealized loss on these securities largely reflects changes in interest rates and higher spreads driven by the challenging conditions in the credit markets. The $1 of gross unrealized losses is attributable to the Company's holdings in eight individual securities from five issuers.

ATT-SEC 2.22

As the Company presently does not intend to sell its debt securities and believes that it is not more-likely-than-not that it will be required to sell the securities that are in an unrealized loss position before recovery of their amortized cost, the Company does not consider these securities to be other-than-temporarily impaired.

In 2008, one of the Company's enhanced money fund investments, Columbia Strategic Cash Portfolio Fund (Columbia), ceased accepting cash redemption requests and changed to a floating net asset value. In light of the restricted liquidity, the Company elected to receive a pro-rata allocation of the underlying securities in a separately managed account. The Company assessed the fair value of these securities through market quotations and review of current investment ratings, as available, coupled with an evaluation of the liquidation value of each investment and its current performance in meeting scheduled payments of principal and interest. During 2009 and 2008, the Company recognized $12 and $5, respectively, of other-than-temporary impairment losses related to these securities. The losses are included in interest income and other in the accompanying consolidated statements of income. At August 30, 2009 and August 31, 2008, the balance of the Columbia fund was $27 and $104, respectively, on the consolidated balance sheets.

In 2008, two other enhanced money fund investments, BlackRock Cash Strategies, LLC (BlackRock) and Merrill Lynch Capital Reserve Fund, LLC (Merrill Lynch), ceased accepting redemption requests and commenced liquidation. As of August 31, 2008, the balance of the BlackRock and Merrill Lynch funds was $82 and $43, respectively, on the consolidated balance sheets. During 2009, these funds were liquidated and the Company received the remaining balances of its investment.

During 2008, the Company reclassified $371 of these three funds from cash and cash equivalents to short-term investments and other assets. At August 30, 2009, $24 remained in short-term investments and $3 remained in other assets on the consolidated balance sheets, reflecting the timing of the expected distributions. At August 31, 2008, $161 was in short-term investments and $68 in other assets on the consolidated balance sheets.

The markets relating to these investments remain uncertain, and there may be further declines in the value of these investments that may cause additional losses in future periods.

The maturities of available-for-sale and held-to-maturity securities at August 30, 2009 are as follows:

	Available-for-Sale		Held-to-Maturity	
	Cost Basis	Fair Value	Cost Basis	Fair Value
Due in one year or less	$324	$325	$59	$59
Due after one year through five years	178	181	—	—
Due after five years	8	8	—	—
	$510	$514	$59	$59

2.23

GOOGLE INC. (DEC)

(In thousands)	2008	2009
Current assets:		
Cash and cash equivalents	$ 8,656,672	$10,197,588
Marketable securities	7,189,099	14,287,187
Accounts receivable, net of allowance of $80,086 and $78,884	2,642,192	3,178,471
Deferred income taxes, net	286,105	644,406
Income taxes receivable, net	—	23,244
Prepaid revenue share, expenses and other assets	1,404,114	836,062
Total current assets	$20,178,182	$29,166,958

NOTES TO CONSOLIDATED FINANCIAL STATEMENTS

Note 1 (In Part): Summary of Significant Accounting Policies

Cash and Cash Equivalents and Marketable Securities

We invest our excess cash primarily in highly liquid debt instruments of the U.S. government and its agencies, municipalities in the U.S., debt instruments issued by foreign government, time deposits, money market mutual funds, mortgage-backed securities, and corporate securities. We classify all highly liquid investments with stated maturities of three months or less from date of purchase as cash equivalents and all highly liquid investments with stated maturities of greater than three months as marketable securities.

We determine the appropriate classification of our investments in marketable securities at the time of purchase and reevaluate such designation at each balance sheet date. We have classified and accounted for our marketable securities as available-for-sale. We may or may not hold securities with stated maturities greater than 12 months until maturity. After consideration of our risk versus reward objectives, as well as our liquidity requirements, we may sell these securities prior to their stated maturities. As we view these securities as available to support current operations, we classify securities with maturities beyond 12 months as current assets under the caption marketable securities in the accompanying Consolidated Balance Sheets. We carry these securities at fair value, and report the unrealized gains and losses, net of taxes, as a component of stockholders' equity, except for unrealized losses determined to be other than temporary which we record as interest income and other, net. We determine any realized gains or losses on the sale of marketable securities on a specific identification method, and we record such gains and losses as a component of interest income and other, net.

Note 3 (In Part): Cash and Investments

Cash, cash equivalents, and marketable securities consist of the following (in thousands):

	2008	2009
Cash and cash equivalents:		
Cash	$ 3,330,658	$ 4,302,578
Cash equivalents:		
Municipal securities	14,250	—
Time deposits	3,015,557	3,739,875
Money market mutual funds	2,296,207	2,153,175
U.S. government agencies	—	1,960
Total cash and cash equivalents	8,656,672	10,197,588
Marketable securities:		
Time deposits	—	1,250,000
U.S. government agencies	3,342,406	3,703,868
U.S. government notes	—	2,491,709
Foreign government bonds	—	36,643
Municipal securities	2,721,603	2,129,774
Money market mutual funds	73,034	27,899
Corporate debt securities	907,056	2,822,111
Agency residential mortgage-backed securities	—	1,578,644
Commercial mortgage-backed securities	—	47,716
Marketable equity security	145,000	198,823
Total marketable securities	7,189,099	14,287,187
Total cash, cash equivalents and marketable securities	$15,845,771	$24,484,775

The following tables summarize unrealized gains and losses related to our investments in marketable securities designated as available-for-sale (in thousands):

	Adjusted Cost	Gross Unrealized Gains	Gross Unrealized Losses	Fair Value
2008				
U.S. government agencies	$3,324,750	$17,747	$ (91)	$3,342,406
Municipal securities	2,690,270	34,685	(3,352)	2,721,603
Money market mutual funds	73,034	—	—	73,034
Corporate debt securities	903,963	3,265	(172)	907,056
Marketable equity security	145,000	—	—	145,000
Total	$7,137,017	$55,697	$(3,615)	$7,189,099

	Adjusted Cost	Gross Unrealized Gains	Gross Unrealized Losses	Fair Value
2009				
Time deposits	$ 1,250,000	$ —	$ —	$ 1,250,000
U.S. government agencies	3,700,476	5,396	(2,004)	3,703,868
U.S. government notes	2,519,780	—	(28,071)	2,491,709
Foreign government bonds	36,662	—	(19)	36,643
Municipal securities	2,100,241	29,626	(93)	2,129,774
Money market mutual funds	27,899	—	—	27,899
Corporate debt securities	2,826,461	12,910	(17,260)	2,822,111
Agency residential mortgage-backed securities	1,584,537	5,511	(11,404)	1,578,644
Commercial mortgage-backed securities	47,141	575	—	47,716
Marketable equity security	145,000	53,823	—	198,823
Total	$14,238,197	$107,841	$(58,851)	$14,287,187

Gross unrealized gains and losses on cash equivalents were not material at December 31, 2008 and December 31, 2009.

Our corporate debt securities are primarily guaranteed by the full faith and credit of the U.S. government under the Federal Deposit Insurance Corporation's Temporary Liquidity Guarantee Program (TLGP) or the sovereign guarantee of foreign governments under similar programs to the TLGP.

Our agency residential mortgage-backed securities are specified pools of mortgage pass-through securities that are guaranteed by government-sponsored enterprises. Our commercial mortgage-backed securities are fully defeased securities with underlying collateral loans replaced by U.S. Treasury notes.

Our marketable equity security consists of our investment in Clearwire.

We recognized gross realized gains of $105.8 million and $118.3 million for the years ended December 31, 2008 and 2009. Gross realized losses were not material in all periods presented. We determine realized gains or losses on the sale of marketable securities on a specific identification method, and we reflect such gains and losses as a component of interest income and other, net, in our accompanying Consolidated Statements of Income.

The following table summarizes the estimated fair value of our investments in marketable securities, excluding the marketable equity security, designated as available-for-sale and classified by the contractual maturity date of the security (in thousands):

	2009
Due in 1 year	$ 1,400,583
Due in 1 year through 5 years	8,442,820
Due in 5 years through 10 years	1,557,923
Due after 10 years	2,687,038
Total	$14,088,364

The following tables present gross unrealized losses and fair values for those investments that were in an unrealized loss position as of December 31, 2008 and 2009, aggregated by investment category and the length of time that individual securities have been in a continuous loss position (in thousands):

	Less Than 12 Months	
Security Description	Fair Value	Unrealized Loss
2008		
U.S. government agencies	$183,054	$ (91)
Municipal securities	274,042	(3,352)
Corporate debt securities	199,828	(172)
Total	$656,924	$(3,615)

	Less Than 12 Months	
Security Description	Fair Value	Unrealized Loss
2009		
U.S. government agencies	$1,273,165	$ (2,004)
U.S. government notes	2,491,709	(28,071)
Foreign government bonds	36,643	(19)
Municipal securities	60,212	(93)
Corporate debt securities	1,174,769	(17,260)
Agency mortgage-backed securities	1,040,486	(11,404)
Total	$6,076,984	$(58,851)

As of December 31, 2008 and 2009, we did not have any investments in marketable securities that were in an unrealized loss position for 12 months or greater.

Held-to-Maturity Securities

2.24

3COM CORPORATION (MAY)

(In thousands)	2009	2008
Current assets:		
Cash and equivalents	$545,818	$503,644
Short-term investments	98,357	—
Notes receivable	40,590	65,116
Accounts receivable, less allowance for doubtful accounts of $9,645 and $12,253, respectively	112,771	116,281
Inventories	90,395	90,831
Other current assets	56,982	34,033
Total current assets	$944,913	$809,905

NOTES TO CONSOLIDATED FINANCIAL STATEMENTS

Note 2 (In Part): Significant Accounting Policies

Short-Term Investments

Short-term investments are invested in Chinese government bonds and central bank bills, with maturity periods from three months to one year. These investments were classified as held-to-maturity. As of March 31, 2009, held-to-maturity securities have amortized costs of $98.4 million which approximates fair value according to prevailing market prices.

2.25

CLIFFS NATURAL RESOURCES INC. (DEC)

(In millions)	2009	2008
Current assets		
Cash and cash equivalents	$ 502.7	$179.0
Accounts receivable	103.5	68.5
Inventories	272.5	265.4
Supplies and other inventories	102.7	101.2
Deferred and refundable taxes	61.4	54.8
Derivative assets	51.5	76.9
Other current assets	66.9	115.9
Total current assets	$1,161.2	$861.7

NOTES TO CONSOLIDATED FINANCIAL STATEMENTS

Note 1 (In Part): Significant Accounting Policies

Marketable Securities

Our marketable securities consist of debt and equity instruments and are classified as either held-to-maturity or available-for-sale. Securities investments that we have the intent and ability to hold to maturity are classified as held-to-maturity and recorded at amortized cost. Investments in marketable equity securities that are being held for an indefinite period are classified as available-for-sale. We determine the appropriate classification of debt and equity securities at the time of purchase and re-evaluate such designation as of each balance sheet date. In addition, we review our investments on an ongoing basis for indications of possible impairment. Once identified, the determination of whether the impairment is temporary or other-than-temporary requires significant judgment. The primary factors that we consider in classifying the impairment include the extent and time the fair value of each investment has been below cost, and the existence of a credit loss in relation to our debt securities. If a decline in fair value is judged other than temporary, the basis of the individual security is written down to fair value as a new cost basis, and the amount of the write-down is included as a realized loss. For our held-to-maturity debt securities, if the fair value is less than cost, and we do not expect to recover the entire amortized cost basis of the security, the other-than-temporary impairment is separated into the amount representing the credit loss, which is recognized in earnings, and the amount representing all other factors, which is recognized in other comprehensive income. Refer to Note 4—Marketable Securities for additional information.

Note 4 (In Part): Marketable Securities

At December 31, 2009 and 2008, we had $99.3 million and $30.2 million, respectively, of marketable securities as follows:

(In millions)	2009	2008
Held to maturity—current	$11.2	$ 4.8
Held to maturity—non-current	7.1	14.2
	18.3	19.0
Available for sale—non-current	81.0	11.2
Total	$99.3	$30.2

Marketable securities classified as held-to-maturity are measured and stated at amortized cost. The amortized cost, gross unrealized gains and losses and fair value of investment securities held-to-maturity at December 31, 2009 and 2008 are summarized as follows:

(In millions)	Amortized Cost	Gross Unrealized Gains	Gross Unrealized Losses	Fair Value
2009				
Asset backed securities	$ 2.7	$—	$(1.2)	$ 1.5
Floating rate notes	15.6	—	(0.2)	15.4
Total	$18.3	$—	$(1.4)	$16.9
2008				
Asset backed securities	$ 2.1	$—	$(0.6)	$ 1.5
Floating rate notes	16.9	—	(1.1)	15.8
Total	$19.0	$—	$(1.7)	$17.3

Investment securities held-to-maturity at December 31, 2009 and 2008 have contractual maturities as follows:

(In millions)	2009	2008
Asset backed securities:		
Within 1 year	$ —	$ —
1 to 5 years	2.7	2.1
	$ 2.7	$ 2.1
Floating rate notes:		
Within 1 year	$11.2	$ 4.8
1 to 5 years	4.4	12.1
	$15.6	$16.9

The following table shows our gross unrealized losses and fair value of securities classified as held-to-maturity, aggregated by investment category and length of time that individual securities have been in a continuous unrealized loss position, at December 31, 2009 and 2008:

	Less Than 12 Months			
	2009		2008	
(In millions)	Unrealized Losses	Fair Value	Unrealized Losses	Fair Value
Asset backed securities	$—	$—	$ —	$ —
Floating rate notes	—	—	(0.1)	1.7
	$—	$—	$(0.1)	$1.7

	12 Months or Longer			
	2009		2008	
(In millions)	Unrealized Losses	Fair Value	Unrealized Losses	Fair Value
Asset backed securities	$(1.2)	$ 1.5	$(0.6)	$ 1.5
Floating rate notes	(0.2)	13.2	(1.0)	14.1
	$(1.4)	$14.7	$(1.6)	$15.6

We believe that the unrealized losses on the held-to-maturity portfolio at December 31, 2009 are temporary and are related to market interest rate fluctuations and not to deterioration in the creditworthiness of the issuers. We expect to recover the entire amortized cost basis of the held-to-maturity debt securities, and we intend to hold these investments until maturity.

Trading Securities

2.26

STARBUCKS CORPORATION (SEP)

(In millions)	2009	2008
Current assets:		
Cash and cash equivalents	$ 599.8	$ 269.8
Short-term investments—available-for-sale securities	21.5	3.0
Short-term investments—trading securities	44.8	49.5
Accounts receivable, net	271.0	329.5
Inventories	664.9	692.8
Prepaid expenses and other current assets	147.2	169.2
Deferred income taxes, net	286.6	234.2
Total current assets	$2,035.8	$1,748.0

NOTES TO CONSOLIDATED FINANCIAL STATEMENTS

Note 1 (In Part): Summary of Significant Accounting Policies

Short-Term and Long-Term Investments

The Company's short-term and long-term investments consist primarily of investment grade debt securities, equity mutual funds, and equity exchange-traded funds, all of which are classified as available-for-sale or trading. As of September 27, 2009, a substantial portion of the Company's available-for-sale investments consisted of auction rate securities, as described in more detail in Note 3. Trading securities are recorded at fair value with unrealized holding gains and losses included in net earnings. Available-for-sale securities are recorded at fair value, and unrealized holding gains and losses are recorded, net of tax, as a component of accumulated other comprehensive income. Available-for-sale securities with remaining maturities of less than one year and those identified by management at time of purchase for funding operations in less than one year are classified as short term, and all other available-for-sale securities are classified as long term. Unrealized losses are charged against net earnings when a decline in fair value is determined to be other than temporary. Management reviews several factors to determine whether a loss is other than temporary, such as the length and extent of the fair value decline, the financial condition and near term prospects of the issuer, and for equity investments, the Company's intent and ability to hold the security for a period of time sufficient to allow for any anticipated recovery in fair value. For debt securities, management also evaluates whether the Company has the intent to sell or will likely be required to sell before its anticipated recovery. Realized gains and losses are accounted for on the specific identification method. Purchases and sales are recorded on a trade date basis.

Note 3 (In Part): Investments

Trading Securities

Trading securities are comprised of marketable equity mutual funds and equity exchange-traded funds that approximate a portion of the Company's liability under the Management Deferred Compensation Plan ("MDCP"), a defined contribution plan. The corresponding deferred compensation liability of $68.3 million and $68.0 million in fiscal 2009 and 2008, respectively, is included in Accrued compensation and related costs on the consolidated balance sheets. The changes in net unrealized holding gains/losses in the trading portfolio included in earnings for the years ended September 27, 2009 and September 28, 2008 were a net loss of $4.9 million and $14.5 million, respectively.

Note 5 (In Part): Fair Value Measurements

The Company adopted the new fair value accounting guidance related to financial assets and liabilities effective September 29, 2008, and will adopt the new fair value accounting guidance for nonfinancial assets and liabilities in the first fiscal quarter of 2010. The new fair value accounting guidance allows for this two-step adoption approach. The Company continues to evaluate the potential impact of the adoption of fair value measurements related to its property, plant and equipment, goodwill and other intangible assets.

The guidance defines fair value, establishes a framework for measuring fair value under GAAP and expands disclosures about fair value measurements. It also establishes a fair value hierarchy that prioritizes the inputs used to measure fair value:

- Level 1—Observable inputs that reflect unadjusted quoted prices for identical assets or liabilities traded in active markets.
- Level 2—Inputs other than quoted prices included within Level 1 that are observable for the asset or liability, either directly or indirectly.
- Level 3—Inputs that are generally unobservable. These inputs may be used with internally developed methodologies that result in management's best estimate of fair value.

Financial Assets and Liabilities Measured at Fair Value on a Recurring Basis

(In millions)	2009	Level 1	Level 2	Level 3
Assets:				
Trading securities	$ 44.8	$44.8	$ —	$ —
Available-for-sale securities	92.7	19.0	18.0	55.7
Derivatives	13.2	—	13.2	—
Total	$150.7	$63.8	$31.2	$55.7
Liabilities:				
Derivatives	$ 33.2	$ —	$33.2	$ —

Trading securities include equity mutual funds and exchange-traded funds. For these securities, the Company uses quoted prices in active markets for identical assets to determine their fair value, thus they are considered to be Level 1 instruments.

Note 4. Trading Assets

Trading assets outstanding at fiscal year-ends were as follows:

(In millions)	2008 Net Unrealized Gains (Losses)	Fair Value	2007 Net Unrealized Gains (Losses)	Fair Value
Marketable debt instruments	$ (96)	$2,863	$ 51	$2,074
Equity securities offsetting deferred compensation	(41)	299	163	492
Total trading assets	$(137)	$3,162	$214	$2,566

Net losses on marketable debt instruments that we classified as trading assets held at the reporting date were $132 million in 2008 (gains of $19 million in 2007 and $31 million in 2006). Our net losses in 2008 on marketable debt instruments that we classified as trading assets held at the reporting date included $87 million of losses related to asset-backed securities. Net losses on the related derivatives were $5 million in 2008 (losses of $37 million in 2007 and $22 million in 2006). We maintain certain equity securities within our trading assets portfolio to generate returns that seek to offset changes in liabilities related to the equity market risk of certain deferred compensation arrangements. These deferred compensation liabilities were $332 million in 2008 ($483 million in 2007) and are included in other accrued liabilities. Net losses on equity securities offsetting deferred compensation arrangements still held at the reporting date were $209 million in 2008 (gains of $28 million in 2007 and $45 million in 2006).

CURRENT RECEIVABLES

2.27 Under FASB ASC 825, *Financial Instruments*, fair value disclosure is not required for trade receivables when the carrying amount of the trade receivable approximates its fair value. 296 survey entities made 327 fair value disclosures. 279 disclosures presented carrying amounts which approximated fair value of trade receivables.

2.28 FASB ASC 310, *Receivables*, requires that loans or trade receivables may be presented on the balance sheet as aggregate amounts. However, such receivables held for sale should be a separate balance-sheet category. Major categories of loans or trade receivables should be presented separately either in the balance sheet or in the notes to the financial statements. The allowance for credit losses, the allowance for doubtful accounts, and, as applicable, any unearned income, any unamortized premium and discounts, and any net unamortized deferred fees and costs, should be disclosed in the financial statements.

2.29 Table 2-5 summarizes both the descriptive titles used in the balance sheet to describe trade receivables, and the types of receivables, other than trade receivables, which the survey entities most frequently presented as current assets. Examples of presentations and disclosures for current receivables follow.

2.30

TABLE 2-5: CURRENT RECEIVABLES*

	2009	2008	2007	2006
Trade Receivable Captions:				
Accounts receivable	230	234	301	303
Receivables	108	103	126	126
Trade accounts receivable	104	95	99	106
Accounts and notes receivable	38	45	51	49
No caption for current receivables	20	23	23	16
Total Entities	500	500	600	600
Receivables Other Than Trade Receivables:	Number of Entities			
Tax refund claims	105	75	67	63
Investees/affiliates	38	43	47	47
Contracts	38	31	36	42
Finance	29	25	28	28
Retained interest in sold receivables	22	21	26	16
Insurance claims	15	17	23	27
Vendors/suppliers	15	14	10	11
Asset disposals	4	6	9	4
Employees	2	2	2	4

* Appearing in either the balance sheet and/or the notes to financial statements.

2008–2009 based on 500 entities surveyed; 2006–2007 based on 600 entities surveyed.

RECEIVABLES OTHER THAN TRADE RECEIVABLES

Tax Refund Claims

2.31

TENET HEALTHCARE CORPORATION (DEC)

(Dollars in millions)	2009	2008
Current assets:		
Cash and cash equivalents	$ 690	$ 507
Investments in Reserve Yield Plus Fund	2	14
Investments in marketable securities	11	2
Accounts receivable, less allowance for doubtful accounts ($369 at December 31, 2009 and $396 at December 31, 2008)	1,158	1,337
Inventories of supplies, at cost	153	161
Income tax receivable	35	6
Deferred income taxes	108	82
Assets held for sale	29	310
Other current assets	286	290
Total current assets	$2,472	$2,709

NOTES TO CONSOLIDATED FINANCIAL STATEMENTS

Note 1 (In Part): Significant Accounting Policies

Income Taxes (In Part)

While we believe we have adequately provided for our income tax receivables or liabilities and our deferred tax assets or liabilities in accordance with FASB income tax guidance, adverse determinations by taxing authorities or changes in tax laws and regulations could have a material adverse effect on our consolidated financial condition, results of operations or cash flows.

Receivables From Affiliates

2.32

ARCHER DANIELS MIDLAND COMPANY (JUN)

(In millions)	2009	2008
Current assets		
Cash and cash equivalents	$ 1,055	$ 810
Short-term marketable securities	500	455
Segregated cash and investments	2,430	2,035
Receivables	7,311	11,483
Inventories	7,782	10,160
Other assets	330	512
Total current assets	$19,408	$25,455

NOTES TO CONSOLIDATED FINANCIAL STATEMENTS

Note 1 (In Part): Summary of Significant Accounting Policies

Receivables (In Part)

The Company records trade accounts receivable at net realizable value. This value includes an appropriate allowance for estimated uncollectible accounts, $103 million and $89 million at June 30, 2009 and 2008, respectively, to reflect any loss anticipated on the trade accounts receivable balances. The Company calculates this allowance based on its history of write-offs, level of past-due accounts, and its relationships with, and the economic status of, its customers.

Credit risk on trade receivables is minimized as a result of the large and diversified nature of the Company's worldwide customer base. The Company controls its exposure to counter party credit risk through credit analysis and approvals, credit limits, and monitoring procedures. Collateral is generally not required for the Company's trade receivables. Trade accounts receivable due from unconsolidated affiliates as of June 30, 2009 and 2008 was $301 million and $199 million, respectively.

Contracts

2.33

ALLIANT TECHSYSTEMS INC. (MAR)

(Amounts in thousands)	2009	2008
Current assets:		
Cash and cash equivalents	$ 336,700	$ 119,773
Net receivables	899,543	798,468
Net inventories	238,600	205,825
Income tax receivable	34,835	—
Deferred income tax assets	30,751	88,282
Other current assets	39,843	35,568
Total current assets	$1,580,272	$1,247,916

NOTES TO CONSOLIDATED FINANCIAL STATEMENTS

5 (In Part): Receivables

Receivables, including amounts due under long-term contracts (contract receivables), are summarized as follows:

(Amounts in thousands)	2009	2008
Billed receivables		
U.S. Government contracts	$203,534	$200,871
Commercial and other	145,905	155,061
Unbilled receivables		
U.S. Government contracts	485,511	426,062
Commercial and other	76,042	25,083
Less allowance for doubtful accounts	(11,449)	(8,609)
Net receivables	$899,543	$798,468

Receivable balances are shown net of customer progress payments received of $320,826 as of March 31, 2009 and $316,022 as of March 31, 2008.

Unbilled receivables represent the balance of recoverable costs and accrued profit, comprised principally of revenue recognized on contracts for which billings have not been presented to the customer because the amounts were earned but not contractually billable as of the balance sheet date. These amounts include expected additional billable general overhead costs and fees on flexibly priced contracts awaiting final rate negotiations, and are expected to be billable and collectible within one year.

Finance Receivables

2.34

SNAP-ON INCORPORATED (DEC)

(Amounts in millions)	2009	2008
Current assets		
Cash and cash equivalents	$ 699.4	$ 115.8
Trade and other accounts receivable—net	414.4	462.2
Contract receivables—net	32.9	22.8
Finance receivables—net	122.3	37.1
Inventories—net	274.7	359.2
Deferred income tax assets	69.5	64.1
Prepaid expenses and other assets	62.9	79.5
Total current assets	$1,676.1	$1,140.7

NOTES TO CONSOLIDATED FINANCIAL STATEMENTS

Note 3 (In Part): Accounts Receivable

Snap-on's accounts receivable consist of (i) trade and other accounts receivable; (ii) contract receivables; and (iii) finance receivables. Trade and other accounts receivable primarily arise from the sale of tools, diagnostics and equipment to a broad range of industrial and commercial customers and to Snap-on's independent franchise van channel on a non-extended-term basis with payment terms generally ranging from 30 to 120 days. Contract receivables, with payment terms of up to 10 years, are comprised of extended-term installment loans to a broad base of industrial and other customers worldwide, including shop owners, both independents and national chains, for their purchase of tools, diagnostics and equipment. Contract receivables also include extended-term installment loans to franchisees to meet a number of financing needs including van and truck leases, working capital loans, and loans to enable new franchisees to fund the purchase of the franchise. Finance receivables are comprised of extended-term installment loans to technicians (i.e. franchisees' customers) to enable them to purchase tools, diagnostics and equipment on an extended-term payment plan, generally with average payment terms of 32 months. Contract and finance receivables are generally secured by the underlying tools, diagnostics or equipment financed and, for installment loans to franchisees, other franchisee assets.

The components of Snap-on's current accounts receivable at 2009 and 2008 year end are as follows:

(Amounts in millions)	2009	2008
Trade and other accounts receivable	$440.8	$486.5
Contract receivables, net of unearned finance charges of $4.0 million and $2.6 million	34.5	22.8
Finance receivables, net of unearned finance charges of $6.8 million and $5.7 million	126.2	39.1
Total	601.5	548.4
Allowances for doubtful accounts:		
Trade and other accounts receivable	(26.4)	(24.3)
Contract receivables	(1.6)	—
Finance receivables	(3.9)	(2.0)
Total	(31.9)	(26.3)
Total current accounts receivable—net	$569.6	$522.1
Trade and other accounts receivable—net	$414.4	$462.2
Contract receivables—net	32.9	22.8
Finance receivables—net	122.3	37.1
Total current accounts receivable—net	$569.6	$522.1

The components of Snap-on's contract and finance receivables with payment terms beyond one year at 2009 and 2008 year end are as follows:

(Amounts in millions)	2009	2008
Contract receivables, net of unearned finance charges of $5.9 million and $6.5 million	$ 73.2	$38.0
Finance receivables, net of unearned finance charges of $8.0 million and $6.9 million	184.1	29.3
Total	257.3	67.3
Allowances for doubtful accounts:		
Contract receivables	(2.5)	—
Finance receivables	(6.2)	—
Total	(8.7)	—
Total long-term accounts receivable—net	$248.6	$67.3
Contract receivables—net	$70.7	$38.0
Finance receivables—net	177.9	29.3
Total long-term accounts receivable—net	$248.6	$67.3

Long-term contract and finance receivables installments, net of unearned finance charges, as of 2009 year end are scheduled as follows:

	2009	
(Amounts in millions)	Contract Receivables	Finance Receivables
Due in months:		
13–24	$22.3	$ 84.8
25–36	16.5	63.9
37–48	11.5	23.8
49–60	8.2	11.4
Thereafter	14.7	0.2
Total	$73.2	$184.1

Retained Interest in Sold Receivables

2.35

POLYONE CORPORATION (DEC)

(In millions)	2009	2008
Current assets		
Cash and cash equivalents	$222.7	$ 44.3
Accounts receivable (less allowance of $5.9 in 2009 and $6.7 in 2008)	274.4	262.1
Inventories	159.6	197.8
Deferred income tax assets	—	1.0
Other current assets	38.0	19.9
Total current assets	$694.7	$525.1

NOTES TO FINANCIAL STATEMENTS

Note 7 (In Part): Accounts Receivable

Accounts receivable as of December 31 consist of the following:

(In millions)	2009	2008
Trade accounts receivable	$129.2	$141.6
Retained interest in securitized accounts receivable	151.1	127.2
Allowance for doubtful accounts	(5.9)	(6.7)
	$274.4	$262.1

Sale of Accounts Receivable

Under the terms of our receivables sale facility, we sell accounts receivable to PolyOne Funding Corporation (PFC) and PolyOne Funding Canada Corporation (PFCC), both wholly-owned, bankruptcy-remote subsidiaries. PFC and PFCC, in turn, may sell an undivided interest in up to $175.0 million and $25.0 million of these accounts receivable, respectively, to certain investors. The receivables sale facility was amended in June 2007 to extend the maturity of the facility to June 2012 and to, among other things, modify certain financial covenants and reduce the cost of utilizing the facility.

As of December 31, 2009 and 2008, accounts receivable totaling $151.1 million and $141.4 million, respectively, were sold by us to PFC and PFCC. The maximum proceeds that PFC and PFCC may receive under the facility is limited to the lesser of $200.0 million or 85% of the eligible domestic and Canadian accounts receivable sold. As of December 31, 2009, neither PFC nor PFCC had sold any of their undivided interests in accounts receivable. As of December 31, 2008, PFC and PFCC had sold $14.2 million of their undivided interests in accounts receivable.

We retain an interest in the difference between the amount of trade receivables sold by us to PFC and PFCC and the undivided interest sold by PFC and PFCC as of December 31, 2009 and 2008. As a result, the interest retained by us is $151.1 million and $127.2 million and is included in accounts receivable on the accompanying consolidated balance sheets as of December 31, 2009 and 2008, respectively.

The receivables sale facility also makes up to $40.0 million available for the issuance of standby letters of credit as a sub-limit within the $200.0 million limit under the facility, of which $12.8 million was used at December 31, 2009.

The level of availability under the receivables sale facility is based on the prior month's total accounts receivable sold to PFC and PFCC, as reduced by outstanding letters of credit. Additionally, availability is dependent upon compliance with a fixed charge coverage ratio covenant related primarily to operating performance that is set forth in the related agreements. As of December 31, 2009, we were in compliance with these covenants. As of December 31, 2009, $112.8 million was available for sale.

We also service the underlying accounts receivable and receive a service fee of 1% per annum on the average daily amount of the outstanding interests in our receivables. The net discount and other costs of the receivables sale facility are included in *Other expense, net* in the accompanying consolidated statements of operations.

Insurance Claims

2.36

CRANE CO. (DEC)

(In thousands)	2009	2008
Current assets:		
Cash and cash equivalents	$ 372,714	$ 231,840
Current insurance receivable—asbestos	35,300	41,300
Accounts receivable, net	282,463	334,263
Inventories, net	284,552	349,926
Current deferred tax assets	58,856	50,457
Other current assets	12,461	13,454
Total current assets	1,046,346	1,021,240
Property, plant and equipment, net	285,224	290,814
Insurance receivable—asbestos	213,004	260,660
Long-term deferred tax assets	204,386	233,165
Other assets	83,229	80,676
Intangible assets, net	118,731	106,701
Goodwill	761,978	781,232
Total assets	$2,712,898	$2,774,488

NOTES TO CONSOLIDATED FINANCIAL STATEMENTS

Note 11 (In Part): Commitments and Contingencies

Asbestos Liability (In Part)

Insurance Coverage and Receivables

Prior to 2005, a significant portion of the Company's settlement and defense costs were paid by its primary insurers. With the exhaustion of that primary coverage, the Company began negotiations with its excess insurers to reimburse the Company for a portion of its settlement and defense costs as incurred. To date, the Company has entered into agreements providing for such reimbursements, known as "coverage-in-place," with ten of its excess insurer groups. Under such coverage-in-place agreements, an insurer's policies remain in force and the insurer undertakes to provide coverage for the Company's present and future asbestos claims on specified terms and conditions that address, among other things, the share of asbestos claims costs to be paid by the insurer, payment terms, claims handling procedures and the expiration of the insurer's obligations. The most recent such agreement became effective April 21, 2009, between the Company and Employers Mutual Casualty Company, by and through its managing general agent and attorney-in-fact Mutual Marine Office, Inc. On March 3, 2008, the Company reached agreement with certain London Market Insurance Companies, North River Insurance Company and TIG Insurance Company, confirming the aggregate amount of available coverage under certain London policies and setting forth a schedule for future reimbursement payments to the Company based on aggregate indemnity and defense payments made. In addition, with four of its excess insurer groups, the Company entered into policy buyout agreements, settling all asbestos and other coverage obligations for an agreed sum, totaling $61.3 million in aggregate. The most recent of these buyouts was reached in October 2008 with Highlands Insurance Company, which currently is in receivership in the State of Texas. The settlement agreement with Highlands was formally approved by the Texas receivership court on December 8, 2008, and Highlands paid the full settlement amount, $14.5 million, to the Company on January 12, 2009. Reimbursements from insurers for past and ongoing settlement and defense costs allocable to their policies have been made as coverage-in-place and other agreements are reached with such insurers. All of these agreements include provisions for mutual releases, indemnification of the insurer and, for coverage-in-place, claims handling procedures. The Company is in discussions with or expects to enter into additional coverage-in-place or other agreements with other of its solvent excess insurers not currently subject to a settlement agreement whose policies are expected to respond to the aggregate costs included in the updated liability estimate. If it is not successful in concluding such coverage-in-place or other agreements with such insurers, then the Company anticipates that it would pursue litigation to enforce its rights under such insurers' policies. There are no pending legal proceedings between the Company and any insurer contesting the Company's asbestos claims under its insurance policies.

In conjunction with developing the aggregate liability estimate referenced above, the Company also developed an estimate of probable insurance recoveries for its asbestos liabilities. In developing this estimate, the Company considered its coverage-in-place and other settlement agreements described above, as well as a number of additional factors. These additional factors include the financial viability of the insurance companies, the method by which losses will be allocated to the various insurance policies and the years covered by those policies, how settlement and defense costs will be covered by the insurance policies and interpretation of the effect on coverage of various policy terms and limits and their interrelationships. In addition, the timing and amount of reimbursements will vary because the Company's insurance coverage for asbestos claims involves multiple insurers, with different policy terms and certain gaps in coverage. In addition to consulting with legal counsel on these insurance matters, the Company retained insurance consultants to assist management in the estimation of probable insurance recoveries based upon the aggregate liability estimate described above and assuming the continued viability of all solvent insurance carriers. Based upon the analysis of policy terms and other factors noted above by the Company's legal counsel, and incorporating risk mitigation judgments by the Company where policy terms or other factors were not certain, the Company's insurance consultants compiled a model indicating how the Company's historical insurance policies would respond to varying levels of asbestos settle-

ment and defense costs and the allocation of such costs between such insurers and the Company. Using the estimated liability as of September 30, 2007 (for claims filed through 2017), the insurance consultant's model forecasted that approximately 33% of the liability would be reimbursed by the Company's insurers. An asset of $351 million was recorded as of September 30, 2007 representing the probable insurance reimbursement for such claims. The asset is reduced as reimbursements and other payments from insurers are received. The asset was $248 million as of December 31, 2009.

The Company reviews the aforementioned estimated reimbursement rate with its insurance consultants on a periodic basis in order to confirm its overall consistency with the Company's established reserves. Since September 2007, there have been no developments that have caused the Company to change the estimated 33% rate, although actual insurance reimbursements vary from period to period for the reasons cited above. While there are overall limits on the aggregate amount of insurance available to the Company with respect to asbestos claims, those overall limits were not reached by the total estimated liability currently recorded by the Company, and such overall limits did not influence the Company in its determination of the asset amount to record. The proportion of the asbestos liability that is allocated to certain insurance coverage years, however, exceeds the limits of available insurance in those years. The Company allocates to itself the amount of the asbestos liability (for claims filed through 2017) that is in excess of available insurance coverage allocated to such years.

Uncertainties

Estimation of the Company's ultimate exposure for asbestos-related claims is subject to significant uncertainties, as there are multiple variables that can affect the timing, severity and quantity of claims. The Company cautions that its estimated liability is based on assumptions with respect to future claims, settlement and defense costs based on recent experience during the last few years that may not prove reliable as predictors. A significant upward or downward trend in the number of claims filed, depending on the nature of the alleged injury, the jurisdiction where filed and the quality of the product identification, or a significant upward or downward trend in the costs of defending claims, could change the estimated liability, as would substantial adverse verdicts at trial. A legislative solution or a revised structured settlement transaction could also change the estimated liability.

The same factors that affect developing estimates of probable settlement and defense costs for asbestos-related liabilities also affect estimates of the probable insurance payments, as do a number of additional factors. These additional factors include the financial viability of the insurance companies, the method by which losses will be allocated to the various insurance policies and the years covered by those policies, how settlement and defense costs will be covered by the insurance policies and interpretation of the effect on coverage of various policy terms and limits and their interrelationships. In addition, due to the uncertainties inherent in litigation matters, no assurances can be given regarding the outcome of any litigation, if necessary, to enforce the Company's rights under its insurance policies.

Many uncertainties exist surrounding asbestos litigation, and the Company will continue to evaluate its estimated asbestos-related liability and corresponding estimated insurance reimbursement as well as the underlying assumptions and process used to derive these amounts. These uncertainties may result in the Company incurring future charges or increases to income to adjust the carrying value of recorded liabilities and assets, particularly if the number of claims and settlement and defense costs change significantly or if legislation or another alternative solution is implemented; however, the Company is currently unable to estimate such future changes and, accordingly, while it is probable that the Company will incur additional charges for asbestos liabilities and defense costs in excess of the amounts currently provided, the Company does not believe that any such amount can be reasonably determined. Although the resolution of these claims may take many years, the effect on the results of operations, financial position and cash flow in any given period from a revision to these estimates could be material.

Vendors/Suppliers

2.37

APPLE INC. (SEP)

(In millions)	2009	2008
Current assets:		
Cash and cash equivalents	$ 5,263	$11,875
Short-term marketable securities	18,201	10,236
Accounts receivable, less allowances of $52 and $47, respectively	3,361	2,422
Inventories	455	509
Deferred tax assets	2,101	1,447
Other current assets	6,884	5,822
Total current assets	$36,265	$32,311

NOTES TO CONSOLIDATED FINANCIAL STATEMENTS

Note 2 (In Part): Financial Instruments

Accounts Receivable (In Part)

Vendor Non-Trade Receivables

The Company has non-trade receivables from certain of its manufacturing vendors resulting from the sale of raw material components to these manufacturing vendors who manufacture sub-assemblies or assemble final products for the Company. The Company purchases these raw material components directly from suppliers. These non-trade receivables, which are included in the Consolidated Balance Sheets in other current assets, totaled $1.7 billion and $2.3 billion as of September 26, 2009 and September 27, 2008, respectively. Vendor non-trade receivables from two of the Company's vendors accounted for 40% and 36%, respectively, of non-trade receivables as of September 26, 2009 and two of the Company's vendors accounted for 47% and 38%, respectively, of non-trade receivables as of September 27, 2008. The Company does not reflect the sale of these components in net sales and does not recognize any profits on these sales

until the related products are sold by the Company, at which time any profit is recognized as a reduction of cost of sales.

Sale of Assets

2.38

ARVINMERITOR, INC. (SEP)

(In millions)	2009	2008
Current assets:		
Cash and cash equivalents	$ 95	$ 497
Receivables, trade and other, net	694	1,114
Inventories	374	623
Other current assets	97	218
Assets of discontinued operations	56	—
Total current assets	$1,316	$2,452

NOTES TO CONSOLIDATED FINANCIAL STATEMENTS

3 (In Part): Discontinued Operations

Gabriel Ride Control Products North America

The company's Gabriel Ride Control Products North America (Gabriel Ride Control) business supplied motion control products, shock absorbers, struts, ministruts and corner modules, as well as other automotive parts to the passenger car, light truck and sport utility vehicle aftermarket industries. During fiscal year 2009, the company completed the sale of Gabriel Ride Control to Ride Control, LLC, a wholly owned subsidiary of OpenGate Capital, a private equity firm. The company recognized a pre-tax loss on sale of approximately $42 million ($42 million after-tax).

In the first quarter of fiscal year 2009, the company recognized a $19 million ($14 million after-tax) non-cash impairment charge associated with the long-lived assets of this business (see Note 5). Charges associated with the sale of Gabriel Ride Control are included in the results of discontinued operations in the consolidated statement of operations.

In connection with the sale, the company provided funding of $9 million to Ride Control, LLC. The terms of the sale agreement requires a purchase price adjustment based upon closing working capital. Settlement of the working capital purchase price adjustment is subject to negotiations and is expected to occur in the first quarter of fiscal year 2010. Included in receivables, trade and other, net, in the consolidated balance sheet is $7 million based upon management's best estimate of this adjustment. The agreement also contains arrangements for royalties and other items which are not expected to materially impact the company in the future.

RECEIVABLES SOLD OR COLLATERALIZED

2.39 Table 2-6 shows that 2009 annual reports of 123 survey entities disclosed either the sale of receivables or the pledging of receivables as collateral. Of those 123 survey entities, eight disclosed a factoring agreement and 58 disclosed that the receivables were transferred to a special-purpose entity.

2.40   FASB ASC 860, *Transfers and Servicing*, establishes criteria for determining whether a transfer of financial assets in exchange for cash or other consideration should be accounted for as a sale or as a pledge of collateral in a secured borrowing. FASB ASC 860 establishes the criteria for accounting for securitizations and other transfers of financial assets and collateral, and requires certain disclosures.

2.41   FASB ASC 860 requires that all separately recognized servicing assets and liabilities be initially measured at fair value. Further, FASB ASC 860 permits, but does not require, the subsequent measurement of servicing assets and liabilities at fair value. Moreover, FASB ASC 860 requires additional disclosures and separate balance sheet presentation of the carrying amounts of servicing assets and liabilities that are subsequently measured at fair value.

2.42   FASB Accounting Standards Update (ASU) No. 2009-16, *Accounting for Transfers of Financial Assets*, eliminates the exceptions for qualifying special-purpose entities from the consolidation guidance. In addition, the amendments require enhanced disclosures about the risks that a transferor continues to be exposed to because of its continuing involvement in transferred financial assets. Further, ASU No. 2009-16 provides clarifications of the requirements for isolation and limitations on portions of financial assets that are eligible for sale accounting. ASU No. 2009-16 is effective for fiscal years beginning after November 15, 2009.

2.43   Examples of disclosures made in the reports of the survey entities having sold or collateralized receivables follow.

2.44

TABLE 2-6: RECEIVABLES SOLD OR COLLATERALIZED

	2009	2008	2007	2006
Receivables sold				
With recourse.................................	2	13	23	22
With limited recourse......................	9	7	7	4
Without recourse.............................	45	39	37	43
Recourse not discussed.................	46	51	49	47
	102	110	116	116
Receivables used as collateral...........	21	13	11	11
	123	123	127	127
No reference to receivables sold or				
collateralized.....................................	377	377	473	473
Total Entities.....................................	**500**	**500**	**600**	**600**

2008–2009 based on 500 entities surveyed; 2006–2007 based on 600 entities surveyed.

Receivables Sold With Recourse

2.45

MONSANTO COMPANY (AUG)

(Dollars in millions)	2009	2008
Current assets:		
Cash and cash equivalents	$1,956	$1,613
Trade receivables, net	1,556	2,067
Miscellaneous receivables	654	742
Deferred tax assets	662	338
Inventory, net	2,934	2,453
Assets of discontinued operations	—	153
Other current assets	121	243
Total current assets	$7,883	$7,609

NOTES TO CONSOLIDATED FINANCIAL STATEMENTS

Note 7 (In Part): Customer Financing Programs

Monsanto has agreements with lenders to establish programs that provide financing of up to $300 million for selected customers in Brazil. These agreements qualify for sales treatment under SFAS 140. Proceeds from the transfer of receivables are included in net cash provided by operating activities in the Statements of Consolidated Cash Flows. Proceeds from the transfer of receivables through these programs totaled $197 million, $239 million and $139 million for fiscal years 2009, 2008 and 2007, respectively. Monsanto provides a guarantee of the loans in the event of customer default. The term of the guarantee is equivalent to the term of the bank loans. The liability for the guarantees is recorded at an amount that approximates fair value and is based on the company's historical collection experience with customers that participate in the program and a current assessment of credit exposure. The guarantee liability recorded by Monsanto was $6 million and $10 million as of Aug. 31, 2009, and Aug. 31, 2008, respectively. If performance is required under the guarantee, Monsanto may retain amounts that are subsequently collected from customers. The maximum potential amount of future payments under the guarantee was $160 million as of Aug. 31, 2009. The loan balance outstanding for these programs was $160 million and $187 million as of Aug. 31, 2009, and Aug. 31, 2008, respectively. As of Aug. 31, 2009, $2 million of loans sold through these financing programs were delinquent, and no loans were delinquent as of Aug. 31, 2008.

Monsanto also has similar agreements with banks that provide financing to its customers in Brazil through credit programs that are subsidized by the Brazilian government. In addition, Monsanto has similar financing programs in Europe and Argentina. Proceeds from the transfer of receivables are included in net cash provided by operating activities in the Statements of Consolidated Cash Flows and totaled $91 million, $146 million and $115 million for fiscal years 2009, 2008 and 2007, respectively. Under most of these programs, Monsanto provides a guarantee of the loans in the event of customer default. The terms of the guarantees are equivalent to the terms of the bank loans. The liability for the guarantees is recorded at an amount that approximates fair value and is based on the company's historical collection experience with customers that participate in the program and a current assessment of credit exposure. The guarantee liability recorded by Monsanto was $5 million and $11 million as of Aug. 31, 2009, and Aug. 31, 2008, respectively. If performance is required under the guarantee, Monsanto may retain amounts that are subsequently collected from customers. The maximum potential amount of future payments under the guarantees was $44 million as of Aug. 31, 2009. The loan balance outstanding for these programs was $48 million and $92 million as of Aug. 31, 2009, and Aug. 31, 2008, respectively. There were no delinquent loans as of Aug. 31, 2009, or Aug. 31, 2008.

In August 2009, Monsanto entered into an agreement in the United States to sell customer receivables up to a maximum of $500 million annually and to service such accounts. The program will terminate in August 2012. These receivables qualify for sales treatment under SFAS 140 and accordingly, the proceeds are included in net cash provided by operating activities in the Statements of Consolidated Cash Flows. The gross amount of receivables sold totaled $319 million for fiscal year 2009. The agreement includes recourse provisions and thus a liability was established at the time of sale which approximates fair value based upon the company's historical collection experience with such receivables and a current assessment of credit exposure. The recourse liability recorded by Monsanto was $2 million as of Aug. 31, 2009. The maximum potential amount of future payments under the recourse provisions of the agreement was $18 million as of Aug. 31, 2009. The outstanding balance of the receivables sold was $319 million as of Aug. 31, 2009. There were no delinquent accounts as of Aug. 31, 2009.

Monsanto sells accounts receivable, both with and without recourse, outside of the United States. These sales qualify for sales treatment under SFAS 140 and accordingly, the proceeds are included in net cash provided by operating activities in the Statements of Consolidated Cash Flows. The gross amounts of receivables sold totaled $72 million, $48 million and $46 million for fiscal years 2009, 2008 and 2007, respectively. The liability for the guarantees for sales with recourse is recorded at an amount that approximates fair value and is based on the company's historical collection experience for the customers associated with the sale of the receivables and a current assessment of credit exposure. The liability recorded by Monsanto was less than $1 million as of Aug. 31, 2009, and Aug. 31, 2008. The maximum potential amount of future payments under the recourse provisions of the agreements was $51 million as of Aug. 31, 2009. The outstanding balance of the receivables sold was $57 million and $33 million as of Aug. 31, 2009, and Aug. 31, 2008, respectively. There were no delinquent loans as of Aug. 31, 2009, or Aug. 31, 2008.

Receivables Sold With Limited Recourse

2.46

LEXMARK INTERNATIONAL, INC. (DEC)

(In millions)	2009	2008
Current assets:		
Cash and cash equivalents	$ 459.3	$ 279.2
Marketable securities	673.2	694.1
Trade receivables, net of allowances of $33.7 and $36.1 in 2009 and 2008, respectively	424.9	427.3
Inventories	357.3	438.3
Prepaid expenses and other current assets	226.0	223.8
Total current assets	$2,140.7	$2,062.7

NOTES TO CONSOLIDATED FINANCIAL STATEMENTS
(Tabular dollars in millions)

7 (In Part): Trade Receivables

The Company's trade receivables are reported in the Consolidated Statements of Financial Position net of allowances for doubtful accounts and product returns. *Trade receivables* consisted of the following at December 31:

	2009	2008
Gross trade receivables	$458.6	$463.4
Allowances	(33.7)	(36.1)
Trade receivables, net	$424.9	$427.3

In the U.S., the Company transfers a majority of its receivables to its wholly-owned subsidiary, Lexmark Receivables Corporation ("LRC"), which then may transfer the receivables on a limited recourse basis to an unrelated third party. The financial results of LRC are included in the Company's consolidated financial results since it is a wholly owned subsidiary. LRC is a separate legal entity with its own separate creditors who, in a liquidation of LRC, would be entitled to be satisfied out of LRC's assets prior to any value in LRC becoming available for equity claims of the Company. The Company accounts for transfers of receivables from LRC to the unrelated third party as a secured borrowing with the pledge of its receivables as collateral since LRC can repurchase receivables previously transferred to the unrelated third party. The maximum capital available under the facility is $100 million. In October 2009, the agreement was amended to extend the term of the facility to October 1, 2010.

This facility contains customary affirmative and negative covenants as well as specific provisions related to the quality of the accounts receivables transferred. As collections reduce previously transferred receivables, the Company may replenish these with new receivables. Lexmark bears a limited risk of bad debt losses on the trade receivables transferred, since the Company over-collateralizes the receivables transferred with additional eligible receivables. Lexmark addresses this risk of loss in its allowance for doubtful accounts. Receivables transferred to the unrelated third-party may not include amounts over 90 days past due or concentrations over certain limits with any one customer. The facility also contains customary cash control triggering events which, if triggered, could adversely affect the Company's liquidity and/or its ability to obtain secured borrowings. A downgrade in the Company's credit rating would reduce the amount of secured borrowings available under the facility.

At the end of years 2009 and 2008, there were no secured borrowings under the facility. Expenses incurred under this program totaled $0.4 million, $0.3 million and $0.6 million in 2009, 2008 and 2007 respectively. The expenses are primarily included in *Other (income) expense, net* on the Consolidated Statements of Earnings in 2009 and 2007. In 2008, the expenses are included in *Interest (income) expense, net* on the Consolidated Statements of Earnings.

Receivables Sold Without Recourse

2.47

COMMERCIAL METALS COMPANY (AUG)

(In thousands)	2009	2008
Current assets:		
Cash and cash equivalents	$ 405,603	$ 219,026
Accounts receivable (less allowance for collection losses of $42,134 and $17,652)	731,282	1,369,453
Inventories	678,541	1,400,332
Other	182,126	228,632
Total current assets	$1,997,552	$3,217,443

NOTES TO CONSOLIDATED FINANCIAL STATEMENTS

Note 3. Sales of Accounts Receivable

The Company has an accounts receivable securitization program which it utilizes as a cost-effective, short-term financing alternative. Under this program, the Company and several of its subsidiaries periodically sell certain eligible trade accounts receivable to the Company's wholly-owned consolidated special purpose subsidiary ("CMCRV"). CMCRV is structured to be a bankruptcy-remote entity and was formed for the sole purpose of buying and selling receivables generated by the Company. The Company, irrevocably and without recourse, transfers all applicable trade accounts receivable to CMCRV. CMCRV, in turn, sells an undivided percentage ownership interest in the pool of receivables to affiliates of two third party financial institutions. On June 12, 2009, the agreement with the financial institution affiliates was amended and extended to December 18, 2009. The amended agreement reduced the total facility from $200 million to $100 million. The Company intends to amend and extend the facility in fiscal year 2010.

The Company accounts for its transfers of receivables to CMCRV together with CMCRV's sales of undivided interests in these receivables to the financial institutions as sales in accordance with SFAS No. 140, *Accounting for Transfers and Servicing of Financial Assets and Extinguishments of Liabilities*. Additionally, during the second quarter of 2009, the Company adopted FSP No. 140-4 and FIN 46(R)-8, *Disclosures by Public Entities (Enterprises) about Transfers of Financial Assets and Interests in Variable Interest Entities*, to provide additional disclosures about transfers of financial assets and involvement with variable interest entities. At the

time an undivided interest in the pool of receivables is sold, the amount is removed from the consolidated balance sheet and the proceeds from the sale are reflected as cash provided by operating activities.

At August 31, 2009 and 2008, accounts receivable of $141 million and $420 million, respectively, had been sold to CMCRV. The Company's undivided interest in these receivables (representing the Company's retained interest) was 100% at August 31, 2009 and 2008. The sale of receivables to institutional buyers provides the Company with added financial flexibility, if needed, to fund the Company's ongoing operations. The average monthly amounts of undivided interests owned by the financial institutional buyers were $20.8 million, $8.3 million and $6.2 million for the years ended August 31, 2009, 2008 and 2007, respectively. The carrying amount of the Company's retained interest in the receivables approximated fair value due to the short-term nature of the collection period. No other material assumptions are made in determining the fair value of the retained interest. This retained interest is subordinate to, and provides credit enhancement for, the financial institution buyers' ownership interest in CMCRV's receivables, and is available to the financial institution buyers to pay any fees or expenses due to them and to absorb all credit losses incurred on any of the receivables. The Company is responsible for servicing the entire pool of receivables; however, no servicing asset or liability is recorded as these receivables are collected in the normal course of business and the collection of receivables related to any sales to third party institutional buyers are normally short term in nature. This U.S. securitization program contains certain cross-default provisions whereby a termination event could occur if the Company defaulted under one of its credit arrangements.

In addition to the securitization program described above, the Company's international subsidiaries in Australia, Europe, Poland and a domestic subsidiary periodically sell accounts receivable without recourse. These arrangements constitute true sales and, once the accounts are sold, are no longer available to satisfy the Company's creditors in the event of bankruptcy. Uncollected accounts receivable sold under these international arrangements and removed from the consolidated balance sheets were $93.7 million and $222.9 million at August 31, 2009 and 2008, respectively. The average monthly amounts of international accounts receivable sold were $110.8 million, $206.8 million and $99.0 million for the years ended August 31, 2009, 2008 and 2007, respectively. The Company's Australian subsidiary entered into an agreement with a financial institution to periodically sell certain trade accounts receivable up to a maximum of AUD 126 million ($107 million). This Australian program contains financial covenants whereby our subsidiary must meet certain coverage and tangible net worth levels, as defined. At August 31, 2009, our Australian subsidiary was not in compliance with these covenants. As a result, the financial institution could terminate the accounts receivable program. On October 15, 2009, Commercial Metals Company provided a guarantee of our subsidiary's performance resulting in the financial covenants at August 31, 2009 being waived. The guarantee will cease to be effective when the subsidiary is in compliance with the financial covenants for two consecutive quarters.

During 2009, proceeds from the sale of receivables were $966.5 million and cash payments to the owners of receivables were $1,095.7 million. Discounts on domestic and international sales of accounts receivable were $4.9 million,

$11.1 million and $5.6 million for the years ended August 31, 2009, 2008 and 2007, respectively. These losses primarily represented the costs of funds and were included in selling, general and administrative expenses.

2.48

XEROX CORPORATION (DEC)

(In millions)	2009	2008
Cash and cash equivalents	$3,799	$1,229
Accounts receivable, net	1,702	2,184
Billed portion of finance receivables, net	226	254
Finance receivables, net	2,396	2,461
Inventories	900	1,232
Other current assets	708	790
Total current assets	$9,731	$8,150

NOTES TO CONSOLIDATED FINANCIAL STATEMENTS
(Dollars in millions)

Note 4 (In Part): Receivables, Net

Accounts Receivable Sales Arrangements
We have facilities in the U.S., Canada and several countries in Europe that enable us to sell, on an on-going basis, certain accounts receivable without recourse to third-parties. The accounts receivables sold are generally short-term trade receivables with a payment due date of less than 60 days. In some of the agreements we continue to service the sold receivables and hold beneficial interests. When applicable, a servicing liability is recorded for the estimated fair value of the servicing. Beneficial interests are included in the caption "Other current assets" in the accompanying Consolidated Balance Sheets and are recorded at estimated fair value. The amounts associated with the servicing liability and beneficial interests were not material at December 31, 2009 and 2008, respectively. Accounts receivables sales for the three years ended December 31, 2009 were as follows:

	2009	2008	2007
Accounts receivables sales	$1,566	$717	$326
Fees associated with sales	13	4	2
Estimated impact of sales on operating cash flows	309	51	147

Receivables Used as Collateral

2.49

SUPERVALU INC. (FEB)

NOTES TO CONSOLIDATED FINANCIAL STATEMENTS

Note 7 (In Part): Long-Term Debt

The Company's long-term debt and capital lease obligations consisted of the following:

(In millions)	2009	2008
1.32% to 3.25% revolving credit facility and variable rate notes due June 2011–June 2012	$1,920	$1,933
7.50% notes due February 2011	700	700
7.45% debentures due August 2029	650	650
6.10% to 7.15% medium term notes due July 2009–June 2028	512	622
7.50% notes due November 2014	500	500
8.00% debentures due May 2031	400	400
7.875% notes due August 2009	350	350
6.95% notes due August 2009	350	350
7.50% notes due May 2012	300	300
8.35% notes due May 2010	275	275
8.00% debentures due June 2026	272	272
8.70% debentures due May 2030	225	225
7.75% debentures due June 2026	200	200
7.25% notes due May 2013	200	200
7.50% debentures due May 2037	191	200
7.90% debentures due May 2017	96	96
Accounts receivable securitization facility, currently 1.21%	120	272
Other	97	112
Net discount on acquired debt, using an effective interest rate of 5.44% to 8.97%	(208)	(206)
Capital lease obligations	1,334	1,382
Total debt and capital lease obligations	8,484	8,833
Less current maturities of long-term debt and capital lease obligations	(516)	(331)
Long-term debt and capital lease obligations	$7,968	$8,502

In May 2008, the Company amended and extended its 364-day accounts receivable securitization program. The Company can continue to borrow up to $300 on a revolving basis, with borrowings secured by eligible accounts receivable, which remain under the Company's control. Facility fees under this program range from 0.225 percent to 2.00 percent, based on the Company's credit ratings. The facility fee in effect on February 28, 2009, based on the Company's current credit ratings, is 0.25 percent. As of February 28, 2009, there were $353 of accounts receivable pledged as collateral, classified in Receivables in the Consolidated Balance Sheet. Due to the Company's intent to renew the facility or refinance it with the Revolving Credit Facility, the facility is classified in Long-term debt in the Consolidated Balance Sheets.

ALLOWANCE FOR DOUBTFUL ACCOUNTS

2.50 Table 2-7 summarizes the captions used by the survey entities to describe an allowance for doubtful accounts. FASB ASC 310, *Receivables*, states that such allowances should be deducted from the related receivables and appropriately disclosed.

2.51

TABLE 2-7: DOUBTFUL ACCOUNT CAPTIONS*

	2009	2008	2007	2006
Allowance for doubtful accounts..........	287	272	340	333
Allowance...	107	112	126	132
Allowance for uncollectible accounts...	16	15	20	26
Reserve..	13	12	13	12
Allowance for losses.............................	7	11	12	13
Reserve for doubtful accounts.............	5	7	7	5
Other caption titles...............................	1	1	6	10
	436	430	524	531
Receivables shown net.........................	23	23	27	26
No reference to doubtful accounts.......	41	47	49	43
Total Entities.....................................	**500**	**500**	**600**	**600**

* Appearing in either the balance sheet and/or the notes to financial statements.
2008–2009 based on 500 entities surveyed; 2006–2007 based on 600 entities surveyed.

INVENTORIES

2.52 FASB ASC 330, *Inventory*, states that the "primary basis of accounting for inventories is cost . . ." but "a departure from the cost basis of pricing the inventory is required when the utility of the goods is no longer as great as their cost." Approximately 81% of the survey entities use lower of cost or market, an acceptable basis for pricing inventories when circumstances require a departure from cost, to price all or a portion of their inventories.

2.53 Table 2-8 shows the captions frequently used to identify the nature of inventory items owned by the survey entities. 98 survey entities either had no inventory items or did not disclose details as to the nature of inventory items.

2.54 Table 2-9 summarizes the methods used by the survey entities to determine inventory costs and indicates the portion of inventory cost determined by LIFO. As indicated in Table 2-9, it is not uncommon for an entity to use more than one method in determining the total cost of inventory. Methods of inventory cost determination classified as Other in Table 2-9 include specific identification and accumulated costs for contracts in process.

2.55 A number of survey entities made supplemental disclosures concerning inventories, including information about items such as valuation accounts, obsolescence, and the effects of using LIFO. 50 survey entities disclosed that certain LIFO inventory layers were reduced which increased net income due to the matching of older, lower historical costs with current sales dollars. Eighteen survey entities disclosed the effect of income from using LIFO rather than FIFO or average cost to determine inventory cost.

2.56 Valuation accounts are used to adjust an inventory cost. 184 survey entities disclosed that they have inventory valuation accounts. 135 entities disclosed that a valuation account was used to reduce inventories to a LIFO basis. 64 survey entities disclosed that a valuation account was used for inventory obsolescence.

2.57 Table 2-10 shows, by industry classification, the number of entities using LIFO and the percentage relationship of those entities using LIFO to the total number of entities in a particular industry classification in the current year.

2.58 Each year, entities are selected from the latest Fortune 1000 listing to replace those entities that were deleted from the survey (see the *Appendix of 500 Entities* for a comprehensive listing of the 500 entities as well as those that were added and removed in this edition). Generally, entities are deleted from the survey when they have either been acquired, become privately held (and are, therefore, no longer registered with the SEC), failed to timely issue a report, or ceased operations. The decrease in the number of survey entities using LIFO was caused in part by the fact that more entities deleted from the survey used LIFO than those entities selected as replacements. Four survey entities changed from the LIFO method to another method of determining inventory cost.

2.59 Examples of presentations and disclosures for inventories follow.

2.60

TABLE 2-8: INVENTORY CAPTIONS*

	Number of Entities			
	2009	2008	2007	2006
Finished goods	280	273	337	345
Finished goods and work in process	23	21	27	29
Work in process	211	214	270	270
Work in process and raw materials	33	31	39	37
Raw materials	156	149	208	206
Raw materials and supplies/parts	89	91	92	100
Supplies and/or materials	78	77	100	97

* Appearing in either the balance sheet and/or the notes to financial statements.

2008–2009 based on 500 entities surveyed; 2006–2007 based on 600 entities surveyed.

2.61

TABLE 2-9: INVENTORY COST DETERMINATION

	Number of Entities			
	2009	2008	2007	2006
Methods				
First-in first-out (FIFO)	325	323	391	385
Last-in first-out (LIFO)	176	179	213	228
Average cost	147	146	155	159
Other	18	17	24	30
Use of LIFO				
All inventories	4	7	14	11
50% or more of inventories	82	86	91	109
Less than 50% of inventories	78	72	88	88
Not determinable	12	14	20	20
Entities Using LIFO	**176**	**179**	**213**	**228**

2008–2009 based on 500 entities surveyed; 2006–2007 based on 600 entities surveyed.

2.62

TABLE 2-10: INDUSTRY CLASSIFICATION OF ENTITIES USING LIFO

	2009		2008	
	No.	%[1]	No.	%[1]
Advertising, marketing	—	—	—	—
Aerospace	5	36	5	36
Apparel	3	25	2	20
Beverages	2	25	2	25
Building materials, glass	5	56	5	63
Chemicals	16	64	17	68
Computer peripherals	—	—	—	—
Computer software	—	—	—	—
Computers, office equipment	1	11	1	13
Diversified outsourcing services	—	—	—	—
Electronics, electrical equipment	8	29	8	29
Engineering, construction	1	11	1	11
Entertainment	—	—	—	—
Food	7	32	6	29
Food and drug stores	12	92	13	93
Food services	—	—	—	—
Forest and paper products	8	73	7	70
Furniture	7	78	7	78
General merchandisers	7	64	7	64
Health care	1	17	1	9
Homebuilders	—	—	—	—
Hotels, casinos, resorts	—	—	—	—
Household and personal products	5	62	4	50
Industrial and farm equipment	18	69	18	69
Information technology services	—	—	—	—
Mail, package and freight delivery	—	—	—	—
Medical products and equipment	4	36	4	40
Metal products	5	62	6	67
Metals	9	75	9	75
Mining, crude-oil production	2	17	2	17
Miscellaneous	—	—	—	—
Motor vehicles and parts	5	38	7	47
Network communications	—	—	—	—
Packaging, containers	4	50	5	63
Petroleum refining	10	83	10	83
Pharmaceuticals	2	25	3	30
Publishing, printing	6	50	7	58
Rubber and plastic products	2	50	2	50
Scientific, photographic, and control equipment	4	27	3	23
Semiconductors	—	—	—	—
Soaps, cosmetics	2	33	2	40
Specialty retailers	4	21	4	20
Telecommunications	—	—	—	—
Temporary help	—	—	—	—
Textiles	—	—	—	—
Tobacco	2	50	2	50
Toys, sporting goods	—	—	—	—
Transportation equipment	2	50	2	50
Trucking, truck leasing	—	—	—	—
Waste management	—	—	—	—
Wholesalers	7	58	7	58
Total Entities	**176**	**35**	**179**	**36**

[1] This represents the percentage of survey entities that use LIFO in a particular industry classification. For example, 2009 data shows that 5 entities in the Aerospace industry use LIFO. Those 5 entities represent 36% of the total number of Aerospace entities surveyed.

First-In First-Out

2.63

AVON PRODUCTS, INC. (DEC)

(In millions)	2009	2008
Current assets		
Cash, including cash equivalents of $670.5 and $704.8	$1,311.6	$1,104.7
Accounts receivable (less allowances of $165.5 and $127.9)	779.7	687.8
Inventories	1,067.5	1,007.9
Prepaid expenses and other	1,030.5	756.5
Total current assets	$4,189.3	$3,556.9

NOTES TO FINANCIAL STATEMENTS
(Dollars in millions)

Note 1 (In Part): Summary of Significant Accounting Policies

Inventories

Inventories are stated at the lower of cost or market. Cost is determined using the first-in, first-out ("FIFO") method. We classify inventory into various categories based upon their stage in the product life cycle, future marketing sales plans and disposition process. We assign a degree of obsolescence risk to products based on this classification to determine the level of obsolescence provision.

Note 3. Inventories

Inventories at December 31 consisted of the following:

	2009	2008
Raw materials	$ 335.9	$ 292.7
Finished goods	731.6	715.2
Total	$1,067.5	$1,007.9

2.64

FORTUNE BRANDS, INC. (DEC)

(In millions)	2009	2008
Current assets		
Cash and cash equivalents	$ 417.2	$ 163.3
Accounts receivable from customers less allowances for discounts, doubtful accounts and returns	906.7	856.4
Accounts receivable from related parties	42.3	62.1
Inventories		
Maturing spirits	1,243.0	1,128.1
Other raw materials, supplies and work in process	322.7	366.7
Finished products	450.9	480.6
Total inventories	2,016.6	1,975.4
Other current assets	488.9	410.9
Total current assets	$3,871.7	$3,468.1

NOTES TO CONSOLIDATED FINANCIAL STATEMENTS

1 (In Part): Significant Accounting Policies

Inventories

The first-in, first-out (FIFO) inventory method is our principal inventory method across all segments. In accordance with generally recognized trade practice, maturing spirits inventories are classified as current assets, although the majority of these inventories ordinarily will not be sold within one year, due to the duration of aging processes. Inventory provisions are recorded to reduce inventory to the lower of cost or market value for obsolete or slow moving inventory based on assumptions about future demand and marketability of products, the impact of new product introductions, inventory turns, product spoilage and specific identification of items, such as product discontinuance or engineering/material changes.

In our Home & Security segment, we use the last-in, first-out (LIFO) inventory method in those product groups in which metals inventories comprise a significant portion of our inventories. LIFO inventories at December 31, 2009 and 2008 were $153.6 million (with a current cost of $176.9 million) and $165.8 million (with a current cost of $184.3 million), respectively.

Last-In First-Out

2.65

KIMBERLY-CLARK CORPORATION (DEC)

(Millions of dollars)	2009	2008
Current assets		
Cash and cash equivalents	$ 798	$ 364
Accounts receivable, net	2,566	2,492
Inventories	2,033	2,493
Deferred income taxes	136	131
Time deposits	189	141
Other current assets	142	192
Total current assets	$5,864	$5,813

NOTES TO CONSOLIDATED FINANCIAL STATEMENTS

Note 1 (In Part): Accounting Policies

Inventories and Distribution Costs

For financial reporting purposes, most U.S. inventories are valued at the lower of cost, using the Last-In, First-Out (LIFO) method, or market. The balance of the U.S. inventories and inventories of consolidated operations outside the U.S. are valued at the lower of cost, using either the First-In, First-Out (FIFO) or weighted-average cost methods, or market. Distribution costs are classified as cost of products sold.

Note 21 (In Part): Supplemental Data

(Millions of dollars)	2009			2008		
	LIFO	Non-LIFO	Total	LIFO	Non-LIFO	Total
Summary of inventories						
Inventories by major class:						
At the lower of cost determined on the FIFO or weighted-average cost methods or market:						
Raw materials	$ 137	$ 282	$ 419	$ 150	$ 367	$ 517
Work in process	177	111	288	246	133	379
Finished goods	573	685	1,258	758	832	1,590
Supplies and other	—	277	277	—	262	262
	887	1,355	2,242	1,154	1,594	2,748
Excess of FIFO or weighted-average cost over LIFO cost	(209)	—	(209)	(255)	—	(255)
Total	$ 678	$1,355	$2,033	$ 899	$1,594	$2,493

2.66

SUPERVALU INC. (FEB)

(In millions)	2009	2008
Current assets		
Cash and cash equivalents	$ 240	$ 243
Receivables, less allowance for losses of $13 in 2009 and $14 in 2008	874	951
Inventories	2,709	2,776
Other current assets	282	177
Total current assets	$4,105	$4,147

NOTES TO CONSOLIDATED FINANCIAL STATEMENTS
(Dollars in millions)

Note 1 (In Part): Summary of Significant Accounting Policies

Inventories

Inventories are valued at the lower of cost or market. Substantially all of the Company's inventory consists of finished goods.

Approximately 81 percent and 82 percent of the Company's inventories were valued using the last-in, first-out ("LIFO") method for fiscal 2009 and 2008, respectively. The Company uses a combination of the retail inventory method ("RIM") and replacement cost method to determine the current cost of its inventory before any LIFO reserve is applied. Under RIM, the current cost of inventories and the gross margins are calculated by applying a cost-to-retail ratio to the current retail value of inventories. Under the replacement cost method, the most current unit purchase cost is used to calculate the current cost of inventories. The first-in, first-out method ("FIFO") is primarily used to determine cost for some of the remaining highly perishable inventories. If the FIFO method had been used to determine cost of inventories for which the LIFO method is used, the Company's inventories would have been higher by approximately $258 and $180 as of February 28, 2009 and February 23, 2008, respectively. In addition, the LIFO reserve was reduced by $28 as a result of the finalization of the fair value of inventory for the Acquired Operations during the first quarter of fiscal 2008.

During fiscal 2009, 2008 and 2007, inventory quantities in certain LIFO layers were reduced. These reductions resulted in a liquidation of LIFO inventory quantities carried at lower costs prevailing in prior years as compared with the cost of fiscal 2009, 2008 and 2007 purchases. As a result, Cost of sales decreased by $10, $5 and $6 in fiscal 2009, 2008 and 2007, respectively.

The Company evaluates inventory shortages throughout each fiscal year based on actual physical counts in its facilities. Allowances for inventory shortages are recorded based on the results of these counts to provide for estimated shortages as of the end of each fiscal year.

2.67

VULCAN MATERIALS COMPANY (DEC)

(Amounts in thousands)	2009	2008
Current assets		
Cash and cash equivalents	$ 22,265	$ 10,194
Medium-term investments	4,111	36,734
Accounts and notes receivable		
Customers, less allowance for doubtful accounts 2009—$8,722; 2008—$8,711	254,753	326,204
Other	13,271	30,773
Inventories	325,033	364,311
Deferred income taxes	57,967	71,205
Prepaid expenses	50,817	54,469
Assets held for sale	15,072	0
Total current assets	$743,289	$893,890

NOTES TO CONSOLIDATED FINANCIAL STATEMENTS

Note 1 (In Part): Summary of Significant Accounting Policies

Inventories

Inventories and supplies are stated at the lower of cost or market. We use the last-in, first-out (LIFO) method of valuation for most of our inventories because it results in a better matching of costs with revenues. Such costs include fuel, parts and supplies, raw materials, direct labor and production overhead. An actual valuation of inventory under the LIFO method can be made only at the end of each year based on the inventory levels and costs at that time. Accordingly, interim LIFO calculations are based on our estimates of expected year-end inventory levels and costs and are subject to the final year-end LIFO inventory valuation. Substantially all operating supplies inventory is carried at average cost. For additional information regarding our inventories, see Note 3.

Note 3. Inventories

Inventories at December 31 are as follows (in thousands of dollars):

	2009	2008
Finished products	$261,752	$295,525
Raw materials	21,807	28,568
Products in process	3,907	4,475
Operating supplies and other	37,567	35,743
Total inventories	$325,033	$364,311

In addition to the inventory balances presented above, as of December 31, 2009, we have $21,091,000 of inventory classified as long-term assets (Other assets) as we do not expect to sell the inventory within one year. Inventories valued under the LIFO method total $252,494,000 at December 31, 2009 and $269,598,000 at December 31, 2008. During 2009, 2008 and 2007, inventory reductions resulted in liquidations of LIFO inventory layers carried at lower costs prevailing in prior years as compared to the cost of current-year purchases. The effect of the LIFO liquidation on 2009 results was to decrease cost of goods sold by $3,839,000; increase earnings from continuing operations by $2,273,000; and increase net earnings by $2,273,000. The effect of the LIFO liquidation on 2008 results was to decrease cost of goods sold by $2,654,000; increase earnings from continuing operations by $1,605,000; and increase net earnings by $1,605,000. The effect of the LIFO liquidation on 2007 results was to decrease cost of goods sold by $85,000; increase earnings from continuing operations by $52,000; and increase net earnings by $52,000.

Estimated current cost exceeded LIFO cost at December 31, 2009 and 2008 by $129,424,000 and $125,997,000, respectively. We use the LIFO method of valuation for most of our inventories as it results in a better matching of costs with revenues. We provide supplemental income disclosures to facilitate comparisons with companies not on LIFO. The supplemental income calculation is derived by tax-effecting the change in the LIFO reserve for the periods presented. If all inventories valued at LIFO cost had been valued under the methods (substantially average cost) used prior to the adoption of the LIFO method, the approximate effect on net earnings would have been an increase of $2,043,000 in 2009, an increase of $26,192,000 in 2008 and an increase of $15,518,000 in 2007.

Average Cost

2.68

SCHNITZER STEEL INDUSTRIES, INC. (AUG)

(In thousands)	2009	2008
Current assets		
Cash and cash equivalents	$ 41,026	$ 15,039
Accounts receivable, net of allowance of $7,509 in 2009 and $3,049 in 2008	117,666	314,993
Inventories, net	184,455	429,061
Deferred income taxes	10,027	7,808
Refundable income taxes	46,972	825
Prepaid expenses and other current assets	10,868	11,800
Total current assets	$411,014	$779,526

NOTES TO CONSOLIDATED FINANCIAL STATEMENTS

Note 2 (In Part): Summary of Significant Accounting Policies

Inventories, Net

The Company's inventories primarily consist of ferrous and nonferrous unprocessed metal, ferrous processed metal, nonferrous recovered joint product, used and salvaged vehicles and semi-finished (billets) and finished steel products consisting of rebar, coiled rebar, merchant bar and wire rod. Inventories are stated at the lower of cost or market. MRB determines the cost of ferrous and nonferrous inventories principally using the average cost method and capitalizes substantially all direct costs and yard costs into inventory. MRB allocates material and production costs to joint products using the gross margin method. APB determines the cost for used and salvaged vehicle inventory based on the average price the Company pays for a vehicle. The self-service business capitalizes only the vehicle cost into inventory, while the full-service business capitalizes the vehicle cost, dismantling and, where applicable, storage and towing fees into inventory. SMB determines the cost of its finished steel product inventory based on weighted average costs and capitalizes all direct and indirect costs of manufacturing into inventory. Indirect costs of manufacturing include general plant costs, maintenance, human resources and yard costs. The Company evaluates whether its inventory is properly valued at the lower of cost or market on a quarterly basis. The Company considers estimated future selling prices when determining the estimated net realizable value for its inventory. However, as MRB generally sells its export recycled ferrous metal under contracts that provide for shipment within 30 to 90 days after the price is agreed, it utilizes the selling prices under committed contracts and sales orders for determining the estimated market price of quantities on hand that will be shipped under these contracts and orders.

The Company performs periodic physical inventories to verify the quantity of inventory on hand. Due to variations in product density, holding period and production processes utilized to manufacture the product, physical inventories will not necessarily detect all variances. To mitigate this risk, the Company adjusts its ferrous physical inventories when the volume of a commodity is low and a physical inventory count can more accurately predict the remaining volume.

Note 4. Inventories, Net

Inventories consisted of the following at August 31 (in thousands):

	2009	2008
Processed and unprocessed scrap metal	$ 77,607	$279,019
Semi-finished goods (billets)	9,600	17,328
Finished goods	66,936	101,844
Supplies	31,581	31,995
Inventory reserve	(1,269)	(1,125)
Inventories, net	$184,455	$429,061

The Company makes certain assumptions regarding future demand and net realizable value in order to assess that inventory is properly recorded at the lower of cost or market. The assumptions are based on both historical experience and current information.

Due to reduced production levels during fiscal 2009, the Company recognized $19 million of expense during fiscal 2009 for production costs that could not be capitalized in inventory.

Production Cost

2.69

THE BOEING COMPANY (DEC)

(Dollars in millions)	2009	2008
Current assets		
Cash and cash equivalents	$ 9,215	$ 3,268
Short-term investments	2,008	11
Accounts receivable, net	5,785	5,602
Current portion of customer financing, net	368	425
Deferred income taxes	966	1,046
Inventories, net of advances and progress billings	16,933	15,612
Total current assets	$35,275	$25,964

NOTES TO CONSOLIDATED FINANCIAL STATEMENTS (Dollars in millions)

Note 1 (In Part): Summary of Significant Accounting Policies

Inventories

Inventoried costs on commercial aircraft programs and long-term contracts include direct engineering, production and tooling costs, and applicable overhead, which includes fringe benefits, production related indirect and plant management salaries and plant services, not in excess of estimated net realizable value. To the extent a material amount of such costs are related to an abnormal event or are fixed costs not appropriately attributable to our programs or contracts, they are expensed in the current period rather than inventoried. Inventoried costs include amounts relating to programs and contracts with long-term production cycles, a portion of which is not expected to be realized within one year. Included in inventory for federal government contracts is an allocation of allowable costs related to manufacturing process reengineering.

Because of the higher unit production costs experienced at the beginning of a new or derivative commercial airplane program, the actual costs incurred for production of the early units in the program may exceed the amount reported as cost of sales for those units. In addition, the use of a total program gross profit rate to delivered units may result in costs assigned to delivered units in a reporting period being less than the actual cost of those units. The excess actual costs incurred over the amount reported as cost of sales is disclosed as deferred production costs, which are included in inventory along with unamortized tooling costs.

The determination of net realizable value of long-term contract costs is based upon quarterly reviews that determine an estimate of costs to be incurred to complete all contract requirements. When actual contract costs and the estimate to complete exceed total estimated contract revenues, a loss provision is recorded. The determination of net realizable value of commercial aircraft program costs is based upon quarterly program reviews that determine an estimate of revenue and cost to be incurred to complete the program accounting quantity. When estimated costs to complete exceed estimated program revenues to go, a program loss provision is recorded in the current period for the estimated loss on all undelivered units in the accounting quantity.

Used aircraft purchased by the Commercial Airplanes segment and general stock materials are stated at cost not in excess of net realizable value. See 'Aircraft valuation' within this Note for our valuation of used aircraft. Spare parts inventory is stated at lower of average unit cost or market. We review our commercial spare parts and general stock materials quarterly to identify impaired inventory, including excess or obsolete inventory, based on historical sales trends, expected production usage, and the size and age of the aircraft fleet using the part. Impaired inventories are charged to Cost of products in the period the impairment occurs.

Included in inventory for commercial aircraft programs are amounts paid or credited in cash, or other consideration to certain airline customers, that are referred to as early issue sales consideration. Early issue sales consideration is recognized as a reduction to revenue when the delivery of the aircraft under contract occurs. In the unlikely situation that an airline customer was not able to perform and take delivery of the contracted aircraft, we believe that we would have the ability to recover amounts paid through retaining amounts secured by advances received on aircraft to be delivered. However, to the extent early issue sales consideration exceeds advances and is not considered to be recoverable, it would be recognized as a current period expense.

We net advances and progress billings on long-term contracts against inventory in the Consolidated Statements of Financial Position. Advances and progress billings in excess of related inventory are reported in Advances and billings in excess of related costs.

Note 7. Inventories

Inventories at December 31 consisted of the following:

	2009	2008
Long-term contracts in progress	$ 14,673	$ 14,051
Commercial aircraft programs	18,568	19,309
Commercial spare parts, used aircraft, general stock materials and other	5,004	4,340
	38,245	37,700
Less advances and progress billings	(21,312)	(22,088)
	$ 16,933	$ 15,612

Long-Term Contracts in Progress

Delta launch program inventories that will be sold at cost to United Launch Alliance (ULA) under an inventory supply agreement that terminates on March 31, 2021 are included in long-term contracts in progress inventories. At December 31, 2009, and 2008, the inventory balance was $1,685 (net of $120 of advances received under the inventory supply agreement) and $1,822, of which $1,070 relates to yet unsold launches at December 31, 2009. ULA is continuing to assess the future of the Delta II program. In the event ULA is unable to sell additional Delta II inventory, earnings could be reduced by up to $62.

Commercial Aircraft Programs

Inventory includes deferred production costs which represent commercial aircraft programs production costs incurred on in-process and delivered units in excess of the estimated average cost of such units. As of December 31, 2009 and 2008, the balance of deferred production costs and unamortized tooling related to commercial aircraft programs in production, except the 777 and 787 programs, was insignificant relative to the programs' balance-to-go estimates. As of December 31, 2009 and 2008, all significant excess deferred production costs or unamortized tooling costs are recoverable from existing firm orders for the 777 program.

For the 777 program, inventory included $510 and $1,223 for deferred production cost, and $211 and $255 of unamortized tooling at December 31, 2009 and 2008.

For the 787 program, inventory included $3,885 and $3,021 of work in process (including deferred production costs), $2,187 and $2,548 of supplier advances, and $1,231 and $755 of tooling and other non-recurring costs at December 31, 2009 and 2008. In August 2009, we concluded that the first three flight-test airplanes for the 787 program will not be sold as previously anticipated due to the inordinate amount of rework and unique and extensive modifications made to those aircraft. Therefore, $2,481 in costs previously recorded for the first three flight-test airplanes were reclassified from program inventory to research and development expense during the third quarter of 2009. Additionally, production costs incurred from August to December 2009 of $212 related to these flight-test airplanes were also included in research and development expense.

Commercial aircraft program inventory included amounts credited in cash or other consideration (early issue sales consideration), to airline customers totaling $1,577 and $1,271 at December 31, 2009 and 2008.

Commercial Spare Parts, Used Aircraft, General Stock Materials and Other

As a normal course of our Commercial Airplanes segment production process, our inventory may include a small quantity of airplanes that are completed but unsold. As of December 31, 2009 and 2008, the value of completed but unsold aircraft in inventory was insignificant. Inventory balances included $235 subject to claims or other uncertainties relating to the A-12 program at December 31, 2009 and 2008.

PREPAID EXPENSES

2.70   Table 2-11 summarizes the number of survey entities disclosing, either on the balance sheet or in the notes to financial statements, an amount for prepaid expenses. Rarely is the nature of prepaid expenses disclosed. Examples of items identified as prepaid expenses follow.

2.71

TABLE 2-11: PREPAID EXPENSES*

	Number of Entities			
	2009	2008	2007	2006
Prepaid expenses	73	71	86	94
Prepaid expenses and other current assets	207	206	240	236
Prepaid expenses and deferred taxes	2	3	7	8
Prepaid expenses and advances	5	5	6	7
Prepaid expenses and other receivables	3	2	2	2
Employee benefits	7	5	4	9
Advertising costs	15	14	27	20
Other captions indicating prepaid expenses	18	9	18	12

* Appearing in either the balance sheet and/or the notes to financial statements.

2008–2009 based on 500 entities surveyed; 2006–2007 based on 600 entities surveyed.

2.72

NEWMARKET CORPORATION (DEC)

(In thousands)	2009	2008
Current assets		
Cash and cash equivalents	$151,831	$ 21,761
Short-term investments	300	—
Trade and other accounts receivable, net	214,887	203,551
Inventories	192,903	201,072
Deferred income taxes	4,118	14,090
Prepaid expenses and other current assets	39,100	5,704
Total current assets	$603,139	$446,178

NOTES TO CONSOLIDATED FINANCIAL STATEMENTS

8. Prepaid Expenses and Other Current Assets

(In thousands)	2009	2008
Income taxes on intercompany profit	$30,141	$ —
Dividend funding	4,992	2,646
Insurance	2,537	1,996
Other	1,430	1,062
	$39,100	$5,704

2.73

STARBUCKS CORPORATION (SEP)

(In millions)	2009	2008
Current assets		
Cash and cash equivalents	$ 599.8	$ 269.8
Short-term investments—available-for-sale securities	21.5	3.0
Short-term investments—trading securities	44.8	49.5
Accounts receivable, net	271.0	329.5
Inventories	664.9	692.8
Prepaid expenses and other current assets	147.2	169.2
Deferred income taxes, net	286.6	234.2
Total current assets	$2,035.8	$1,748.0

NOTES TO CONSOLIDATED FINANCIAL STATEMENTS

Note 1 (In Part): Summary of Significant Accounting Policies

Advertising

The Company expenses most advertising costs as they are incurred, except for certain production costs that are expensed the first time the advertising campaign takes place and direct-response advertising, which is capitalized and amortized over its expected period of future benefits.

Advertising expenses, recorded in Store operating expenses, Other operating expenses and General and administrative expenses on the consolidated statements of earnings, totaled $126.3 million, $129.0 million and $103.5 million in fiscal 2009, 2008 and 2007, respectively. As of September 27, 2009 and September 28, 2008, $7.2 million and $8.8 million, respectively, of capitalized advertising costs were recorded in Prepaid expenses and other current assets, and Other assets on the consolidated balance sheets.

OTHER CURRENT ASSETS

2.74 Table 2-12 summarizes the nature of accounts (other than cash, marketable securities, inventories, and prepaid expenses) appearing in the current asset section of the balance sheets of the survey entities. Examples of such other current asset captions follow.

2.75

TABLE 2-12: OTHER CURRENT ASSET CAPTIONS*

	Number of Entities			
Nature of Asset	2009	2008	2007	2006
Deferred & prepaid income taxes	381	371	450	434
Derivatives	232	55	50	56
Property held for sale	79	80	120	120
Unbilled costs	15	13	24	21
Advances or deposits	8	22	23	18
Other—identified	33	48	41	37

* Appearing in either the balance sheet and/or the notes to financial statements.
2008–2009 based on 500 entities surveyed; 2006–2007 based on 600 entities surveyed.

Deferred Taxes

2.76

ADMINISTAFF, INC. (DEC)

(In thousands)	2009	2008
Current assets:		
Cash and cash equivalents	$227,085	$252,190
Restricted cash	36,436	36,466
Marketable securities	6,037	225
Accounts receivable, net:		
Trade	2,899	4,908
Unbilled	106,601	116,173
Other	13,092	4,012
Prepaid insurance	14,484	28,911
Other current assets	6,317	6,735
Income taxes receivable	2,692	—
Deferred income taxes	2,578	—
Total current assets	$418,221	$449,620

NOTES TO CONSOLIDATED FINANCIAL STATEMENTS

5 (In Part): Income Taxes

Deferred taxes reflect the net tax effects of temporary differences between the carrying amounts of assets and liabilities used for financial reporting purposes and the amounts used for income tax purposes. Significant components of the net deferred tax assets and net deferred tax liabilities as reflected on the Consolidated Balance Sheets are as follows:

(In thousands)	2009	2008
Deferred tax liabilities:		
Prepaid assets	$ (6,021)	$(10,968)
Depreciation	(7,842)	(8,160)
Software development costs	(1,270)	(706)
Other	(406)	(142)
Total deferred tax liabilities	(15,539)	(19,976)
Deferred tax assets:		
Workers' compensation accruals	2,648	2,778
Long-term capital loss carry-forward	184	184
State unemployment tax accruals	—	164
Accrued rent	1,343	1,340
Stock-based compensation	2,931	2,807
Uncollectible accounts receivable	493	366
Total deferred tax assets	7,599	7,639
Valuation allowance	(184)	(184)
Total net deferred tax assets	7,415	7,455
Net deferred tax liabilities	$ (8,124)	$(12,521)
Net current deferred tax assets (liabilities)	$ 2,578	$ (1,956)
Net noncurrent deferred tax liabilities	(10,702)	(10,565)
	$ (8,124)	$(12,521)

•   •   •   •   •   •   •

The Company has capital loss carryforwards totaling approximately $500,000 that will expire during 2012, but can only be used to offset future capital gains. The Company has a valuation allowance of $500,000 against these related deferred tax assets as it is uncertain that the Company will be able to utilize the capital loss carryforwards prior to their expiration. In addition, the Company has incurred net operating losses at the subsidiary level for state income tax purposes totaling $3.5 million ($262,000 tax effected) that expire from 2010 to 2028.

2.77

HNI CORPORATION (DEC)

(Amounts in thousands of dollars)	2009	2008	2007
Current assets			
Cash and cash equivalents	$ 87,374	$ 39,538	$ 33,881
Short-term investments	5,994	9,750	9,900
Receivables, net	163,732	238,327	288,777
Inventories	65,144	84,290	108,541
Deferred income taxes	20,299	16,313	17,828
Prepaid expenses and other current assets	17,728	29,623	30,145
Total current assets	$360,271	$417,841	$489,072

Summary of Significant Accounting Policies (In Part)

Income Taxes

The Corporation uses an asset and liability approach that requires the recognition of deferred tax assets and liabilities for the expected future tax consequences of events that have been recognized in the Corporation's financial statements or tax returns. Deferred income taxes are provided to reflect the differences between the tax bases of assets and liabilities and their reported amounts in the financial statements. The Corporation provides for taxes that may be payable if undistributed earnings of overseas subsidiaries were to be remitted to the United States, except for those earnings it considers to be permanently reinvested. There were approximately $12.4 million of accumulated earnings considered to be permanently reinvested as of January 2, 2010. See the Income Tax footnote for further information.

Income Taxes (In Part)

The Corporation recorded additional deferred tax assets in 2008 for the tax basis in the stock of a subsidiary in excess of the net tax basis of the subsidiary's assets and liabilities. As a result of managements change in intent of potential disposition of this subsidiary the deferred tax assets and related valuation allowance were reduced.

Deferred income taxes reflect the net tax effects of temporary differences between the carrying amounts of assets and liabilities for financial reporting purposes and the amounts used for income tax purposes.

Significant components of the Corporation's deferred tax liabilities and assets are as follows:

(In thousands)	2009	2008	2007
Net long-term deferred tax liabilities:			
Tax over book depreciation	$ 1,334	$ (1,028)	$ 1,614
Compensation	3,221	3,175	4,624
Goodwill	(40,314)	(42,802)	(38,559)
Basis in subsidiary	—	5,314	—
Valuation allowance	—	(1,981)	—
Other—net	11,532	12,051	5,649
Total net long-term deferred tax liabilities	(24,227)	(25,271)	(26,672)
Net current deferred tax assets:			
Allowance for doubtful accounts	2,337	2,601	3,491
Vacation accrual	4,029	3,646	5,302
Inventory differences	3,845	3,878	2,572
Deferred income	(2,798)	(3,836)	(4,484)
Warranty accruals	4,742	5,177	4,234
Valuation allowance	—	(1,092)	—
Other—net	8,144	5,939	6,713
Total net current deferred tax assets	20,299	16,313	17,828
Net deferred tax (liabilities) assets	$ (3,928)	$ (8,958)	$ (8,844)

Derivatives

2.78

ALLIANCE ONE INTERNATIONAL, INC. (MAR)

(In thousands)	2009	2008
Current assets		
Cash and cash equivalents	$ 87,665	$ 112,214
Trade and other receivables, net	175,705	180,997
Accounts receivable, related parties	29,765	—
Inventories:		
Tobacco	627,496	649,555
Other	59,693	39,267
Advances on purchases of tobacco, net	137,824	112,989
Recoverable income taxes	3,995	12,841
Current deferred taxes	24,837	20,836
Prepaid expenses	47,800	50,668
Assets held for sale	4,411	4,885
Current derivative asset	23,469	—
Other current assets	9,603	7,382
Assets of discontinued operations	—	236
Total current assets	$1,232,263	$1,191,870

NOTES TO CONSOLIDATED FINANCIAL STATEMENTS
(In thousands)

Note A (In Part): Significant Accounting Policies

Derivative Financial Instruments

The Company uses forward or option currency contracts to protect against volatility associated with certain non-U.S. dollar denominated forecasted transactions. The Company does not currently deem underlying criteria to be perfectly matched and therefore does not believe the currency contracts qualify for hedge accounting as defined by SFAS No. 133. As a result, the Company has recorded a loss of $3,702 and income of $834 and $12,914 in its cost of goods and services sold for the years ended March 31, 2009, 2008 and 2007, respectively. The Company has also recorded expense of $879 and $94 in its selling, administrative and general expenses for the years ended March 31, 2009 and 2008, respectively. In fiscal year 2007 the Company also utilized interest rate swaps to convert a portion of its debt from floating rate to fixed rate to reduce interest rate volatility. These instruments did not qualify for hedge accounting under SFAS No. 133 and resulted in non-cash income of $290 for March 31, 2007. See Note F "Derivative and Other Financial Instruments" to the "Notes to Consolidated Financial Statements" for further information.

Note F (In Part): Derivative and Other Financial Instruments

On January 1, 2009, the Company adopted SFAS No. 161, *Disclosures about Derivative Instruments and Hedging Activities—An Amendment of FASB Statement No. 133* (SFAS No. 133). The standard supplements the required disclosures provided under SFAS No. 133, as amended, with additional qualitative and quantitative information.

Fair Value of Derivative Financial Instruments

In accordance with SFAS No. 133, the Company recognizes all derivative financial instruments, such as interest rate swap contracts and foreign exchange contracts at fair value.

Changes in the fair value of derivative financial instruments are either recognized periodically in income or in shareholders' equity as a component of other comprehensive income depending on whether the derivative financial instrument qualifies for hedge accounting, and if so, whether it qualifies as a fair value hedge or a cash flow hedge. Changes in fair values of derivatives accounted for as fair value hedges are recorded in income along with the portions of the changes in the fair values of the hedged items that relate to the hedged risk(s). Changes in fair values of derivatives accounted for as cash flow hedges, to the extent they are effective as hedges, are recorded in other comprehensive income net of deferred taxes. Changes in fair values of derivatives not qualifying as hedges are reported in income. During the years ended March 31, 2009 and 2008, there were no qualified cash flow or fair value hedges. Estimates of fair value were determined in accordance with SFAS No. 107, as amended by SFAS No. 157. See Note R "Fair Value Measurements" to the "Notes to Consolidated Financial Statements" for further information of fair value methodology. The following table summarizes the fair value of the Company's derivatives by type at March 31, 2009.

Fair Values of Derivative Instruments

	Assets		Liabilities	
	Balance Sheet Account	Fair Value	Balance Sheet Account	Fair Value
Derivatives not designated as hedging instruments under FAS 133:				
Foreign currency contracts	Current derivative asset	$23,469	Current derivative liability	$25,670

Credit Risk

Financial instruments, including derivatives, expose the Company to credit loss in the event of non-performance by counterparties. The Company manages its exposure to counterparty credit risk through specific minimum credit standards, diversification of counterparties, and procedures to monitor concentrations of credit risk. If a counterparty fails to meet the terms of an arrangement, the Company's exposure is limited to the net amount that would have been received, if any, over the arrangement's remaining life. The Company does not anticipate non-performance by the counterparties and no material loss would be expected from non-performance by any one of such counterparties.

Note R (In Part): Fair Value Measurements

The Company adopted SFAS No. 157, *Fair Value Measurements* as of April 1, 2008 for all recurring financial assets and liabilities. It utilized the deferral provision of FSP No. FAS 157-2 for all non-recurring non-financial assets and liabilities within its scope. SFAS No. 157 defines fair value as the exchange price that would be received for an asset or paid to transfer a liability (an exit price) in the principal or most advantageous market for the asset or liability in an orderly transaction between market participants. SFAS No. 157 also specifies a fair value hierarchy based upon the observability of inputs used in valuation techniques. Observable inputs (highest level) reflect market data obtained from independent sources, while unobservable inputs (lowest level) reflect internally developed market assumptions. In accordance with SFAS No. 157, fair value measurements are classified under the following hierarchy:

- Level 1—Quoted prices for identical instruments in active markets. Active markets are those in which transactions for the asset or liability occur in sufficient frequency and volume to provide pricing information on an ongoing basis.
- Level 2—Quoted prices for similar instruments in active markets; quoted prices for identical or similar instruments in markets that are not active; and model-derived valuations in which all significant inputs or significant value-drivers are observable in active markets.
- Level 3—Model-derived valuations in which one or more significant inputs or significant value-drivers are unobservable.

When available, the Company uses quoted market prices to determine fair value, and it classifies such measurements within Level 1. In some cases where market prices are not available, it makes use of observable market based inputs to calculate fair value, in which case the measurements are classified within Level 2. If quoted or observable market prices are not available, fair value is based upon internally developed models that use, where possible, current market-based parameters such as interest rates, yield curves, currency rates, etc. These measurements are classified within Level 3.

Fair value measurements are classified according to the lowest level input or value-driver that is significant to the valuation. A measurement may therefore be classified within Level 3 even though there may be significant inputs that are readily observable.

Derivative Financial Instruments

The fair value of foreign currency and interest rate swap contracts are based on third-party market maker valuation models that discount cash flows resulting from the differential between the contract rate and the market-based forward rate or curve capturing volatility and establishing intrinsic and carrying values. The amounts include fair value adjustments related to the Company's own credit risk and counterparty credit risk.

•   •   •   •   •   •

Assets measured at fair value included in the Consolidated Balance Sheet as of March 31, 2009 are summarized below:

	2009			
	Level 1	Level 2	Level 3	Total Assets/ Liabilities, at Fair Value
Assets				
Derivative financial instruments	$—	$23,469	$ —	$23,469
Securitized retained interests	—	—	26,833	26,833
Total assets	$—	$23,469	$26,833	$50,302
Liabilities				
Derivative financial instruments	$—	$25,670	$ —	$25,670

2.79

FLOWERS FOODS, INC. (DEC)

(Amounts in thousands)	2009	2008
Current assets:		
Cash and cash equivalents	$ 18,948	$ 19,964
Accounts and notes receivable, net	178,708	178,077
Inventories, net:		
Raw materials	20,952	18,032
Packaging materials	12,065	12,162
Finished goods	27,979	23,984
	60,996	54,178
Spare parts and supplies	35,437	32,541
Deferred income taxes	20,714	38,745
Other	24,152	28,738
Total current assets	$338,955	$352,243

NOTES TO CONSOLIDATED FINANCIAL STATEMENTS

Note 2 (In Part): Summary of Significant Accounting Policies

Derivative Financial Instruments

The company enters into commodity derivatives, designated as cash flow hedges of existing or future exposure to changes in commodity prices. The company's primary raw materials are flour, sweeteners and shortening, along with pulp, paper, and petroleum-based packaging products. The company uses natural gas and propane as fuel for firing ovens. The company also periodically enters into interest rate derivatives to hedge exposure to changes in interest rates. See Note 10, *Derivative Financial Instruments*, for further details.

Note 10 (In Part): Derivative Financial Instruments

In the first fiscal quarter of fiscal 2008, the company began measuring the fair value of its derivative portfolio using the fair value as the price that would be received to sell an asset or paid to transfer a liability in the principal market for that asset or liability. These measurements are classified into a hierarchy by the inputs used to perform the fair value calculation as follows:

- Level 1—Fair value based on unadjusted quoted prices for identical assets or liabilities in active markets
- Level 2—Modeled fair value with model inputs that are all observable market values
- Level 3—Modeled fair value with at least one model input that is not an observable market value

This change in measurement technique had no material impact on the reported value of our derivative portfolio.

Commodity Price Risk

The company enters into commodity derivatives, designated as cash-flow hedges of existing or future exposure to changes in commodity prices. The company's primary raw materials are flour, sweeteners and shortening, along with pulp, paper and petroleum-based packaging products. Natural gas, which is used as oven fuel, is also an important commodity input to production.

As of January 2, 2010, the company's commodity hedge portfolio contained derivatives with a fair value of $(3.7) million, which is recorded in the following accounts with fair values measured as indicated (amounts in millions):

	Level 1	Level 2	Level 3	Total
Assets:				
Other current	$ 2.5	$ —	$—	$ 2.5
Other long-term	—	—	—	—
Total	2.5	—	—	2.5
Liabilities:				
Other current	(4.2)	(1.9)	—	(6.1)
Other long-term	—	(0.1)	—	(0.1)
Total	(4.2)	(2.0)	—	(6.2)
Net fair value	$(1.7)	$(2.0)	$—	$(3.7)

The positions held in the portfolio are used to hedge economic exposure to changes in various raw material and production input prices and effectively fix the price, or limit increases in prices, for a period of time extending into fiscal 2011. These instruments are designated as cash-flow hedges. The effective portion of changes in fair value for these derivatives is recorded each period in other comprehensive income (loss), and any ineffective portion of the change in fair value is recorded to current period earnings in selling, marketing and administrative expenses. The company held no commodity derivatives at January 2, 2010 that did not qualify for hedge accounting. During fiscal years 2009, 2008 and 2007 there was no income or expense recorded due to ineffectiveness in current earnings due to changes in fair value of these instruments.

As of January 2, 2010, the balance in accumulated other comprehensive income related to commodity derivative transactions was $7.7 million. Of this total, approximately $2.2 million and $0.1 million were related to instruments expiring in 2010 and 2011, respectively, and $5.4 million was related to deferred gains on cash flow hedge positions.

The company routinely transfers amounts from other comprehensive income ("OCI") to earnings as transactions for which cash flow hedges were held occur. Significant situations which do not routinely occur that could cause transfers from OCI to earnings are as follows: (i) an event that causes a hedge to be suddenly ineffective and significant enough that hedge accounting must be discontinued and (ii) cancellation of a forecasted transaction for which a derivative was held as a hedge or a significant and material reduction in volume used of a hedged ingredient such that the company is over-hedged and must discontinue hedge accounting. During the 53 weeks ended January 3, 2009, $0.6 million was recorded to income for net gains obtained from exiting derivative positions acquired with ButterKrust and Holsum that did not qualify for hedge accounting treatment. During fiscal 2009, $0.4 million was recorded to expense for net losses from discontinuing hedge accounting and exiting of a position in the commodity hedge portfolio.

Interest Rate Risk

The company entered interest rate swaps with initial notional amounts of $85.0 million, and $65.0 million, respectively, to fix the interest rate on the $150.0 million term loan entered into on August 1, 2008 to fund the acquisitions of ButterKrust and Holsum. The notional amounts are adjusted to match the scheduled quarterly principal payments on the $150 million term loan so that the remaining outstanding term loan balance at any reporting date is fully covered by the swap arrangements through the August 2013 maturity of the term loan. In addition, on October 27, 2008, the company entered an interest rate swap with a notional amount of $50.0 million to fix the interest rate through September 30, 2009 on $50.0 million of borrowings outstanding under the company's unsecured credit facility.

The interest rate swap agreements result in the company paying or receiving the difference between the fixed and floating rates at specified intervals calculated based on the notional amount. The interest rate differential to be paid or received is recorded as interest expense. These swap transactions are designated as cash-flow hedges. Accordingly, the effective portion of changes in the fair value of the swaps is recorded each period in other comprehensive income. Any ineffective portions of changes in fair value are recorded to current period earnings in selling, marketing and administrative expenses.

As of January 2, 2010, the fair value of the interest rate swaps was $(6.7) million, which is recorded in the following accounts with fair values measured as indicated (amounts in millions):

	Level 1	Level 2	Level 3	Total
Liabilities:				
Other current	$—	$(4.3)	$—	$(4.3)
Other long-term	—	(2.4)	—	(2.4)
Total	—	(6.7)	—	(6.7)
Net fair value	$—	$(6.7)	$—	$(6.7)

●   ●   ●   ●   ●   ●

The company had the following derivative instruments recorded on the consolidated balance sheet, all of which are utilized for the risk management purposes detailed above (amounts in thousands):

| | Derivative Assets | | | | Derivative Liabilities | | | |
| | 2009 | | 2008 | | 2009 | | 2008 | |
Derivatives Designated as Hedging Instruments	Balance Sheet Location	Fair Value	Balance Sheet Location	Fair Value	Balance Sheet Location	Fair Value	Balance Sheet Location	Fair Value
Interest rate contracts	—	$ —	—	$ —	Other current liabilities	$ 4,271	Other current liabilities	$ 4,311
Interest rate contracts	—	—	—	—	Other long term liabilities	2,459	Other long term liabilities	5,137
Commodity contracts	Other current assets	2,501	Other current assets	—	Other current liabilities	6,143	Other current liabilities	20,668
Commodity contracts	Other long term assets	—	Other long term assets	249	Other long term liabilities	78	Other long term liabilities	618
Total		$2,501		$249		$12,951		$30,734

As of January 2, 2010, the company had entered into the following financial contracts to hedge commodity and interest rate risk:

(Millions)	Notional Amount
Derivatives in cash flow hedging relationships	
Interest rate contracts	$131.3
Wheat contracts	66.0
Soybean oil contracts	14.1
Natural gas contracts	10.5
Total	$221.9

The company's derivative instruments contained no credit-risk-related contingent features at January 2, 2010. As of January 2, 2010 and January 3, 2009, the company had $7.0 million and $16.5 million, respectively, recorded in other current assets, and $0.8 million and $0.0 million, respectively, recorded in other accrued liabilities representing cash collateral for hedged positions.

Note 11. Other Current Assets

Other current assets consist of:

(Amounts in thousands)	2009	2008
Prepaid assets	$ 9,022	$ 8,306
Collateral for derivative positions	7,023	16,533
Derivative instruments	2,501	—
Federal income tax receivable	3,616	—
Other	1,990	3,899
Total	$24,152	$28,738

Property Held for Sale

2.80

AUTOMATIC DATA PROCESSING, INC. (JUN)

(In millions)	2009	2008
Current assets:		
Cash and cash equivalents	$ 2,265.3	$ 917.5
Short-term marketable securities	30.8	666.3
Accounts receivable, net	1,055.4	1,034.6
Other current assets	921.1	771.6
Assets held for sale	12.1	—
Total current assets before funds held for clients	4,284.7	3,390.0
Funds held for clients	16,419.2	15,418.9
Total current assets	$20,703.9	$18,808.9

NOTES TO CONSOLIDATED FINANCIAL STATEMENTS

Note 9. Assets Held for Sale

During fiscal 2009, the Company reclassified assets related to three buildings as assets held for sale on the Consolidated Balance Sheets. Such assets were previously reported in property, plant and equipment, net on the Consolidated Balance Sheets. At June 30, 2009, the Company had $12.1 million classified as assets held for sale on the Consolidated Balance Sheets.

In fiscal 2009, the Company sold a building and realized a gain of $2.2 million in other income, net, on the Statements of Consolidated Earnings. In July 2009, the Company sold a building and expects to realize a gain of $1.5 million during the three months ended September 30, 2009. The Company currently expects to complete the sale of the remaining building during fiscal 2010.

Unbilled Costs

2.81

EMCOR GROUP, INC. (DEC)

(In thousands)	2009	2008
Current assets:		
Cash and cash equivalents	$ 726,975	$ 405,869
Accounts receivable, less allowance for doubtful accounts of $36,188 and $34,832, respectively	1,057,171	1,390,973
Costs and estimated earnings in excess of billings on uncompleted contracts	90,049	105,441
Inventories	34,468	54,601
Prepaid expenses and other	68,702	56,691
Total current assets	$1,977,365	$2,013,575

NOTES TO CONSOLIDATED FINANCIAL STATEMENTS

Note B (In Part): Summary of Significant Accounting Policies

Revenue Recognition

Revenues from long-term construction contracts are recognized on the percentage-of-completion method in accordance with ASC Topic 605–35, "Revenue Recognition—Construction-Type and Production-Type Contracts." Percentage-of-completion is measured principally by the percentage of costs incurred to date for each contract to the estimated total costs for such contract at completion. Certain of our electrical contracting business units measure percentage-of-completion by the percentage of labor costs incurred to date for each contract to the estimated total labor costs for such contract. Revenues from the performance of facilities services for maintenance, repair and retrofit work are recognized consistent with the performance of services, which are generally on a pro-rata basis over the life of the contractual arrangement. Expenses related to all services arrangements are recognized as incurred. Revenues related to the engineering, manufacturing and repairing of shell and tube heat exchangers are recognized when the product is shipped and all other revenue recognition criteria have been met. Costs related to this work are included in inventory until the product is shipped. These costs include all direct material, labor and subcontracting costs and indirect costs related to performance such as supplies, tools and repairs. Provisions for estimated losses on uncompleted contracts are made in the period in which such losses are determined. In the case of customer change orders for uncompleted long-term construction contracts, estimated recoveries are included for work performed in forecasting ultimate profitability on certain contracts. Due to uncertainties inherent in the estimation process, it is possible that completion costs, including those arising from contract penalty provisions and final contract settlements, will be revised in the near-term. Such revisions to costs and income are recognized in the period in which the revisions are determined.

Costs and Estimated Earnings on Uncompleted Contracts

Costs and estimated earnings in excess of billings on uncompleted contracts arise in the consolidated balance sheets when revenues have been recognized but the amounts cannot be billed under the terms of the contracts. Such amounts are recoverable from customers upon various measures of performance, including achievement of certain milestones, completion of specified units, or completion of a contract. Also included in costs and estimated earnings on uncompleted contracts are amounts we seek or will seek to collect from customers or others for errors or changes in contract specifications or design, contract change orders in dispute or unapproved as to both scope and price or other customer-related causes of unanticipated additional contract costs (claims and unapproved change orders). Such amounts are recorded at estimated net realizable value when realization is probable and can be reasonably estimated. No profit is recognized on construction costs incurred in connection with claim amounts. Claims and unapproved change orders made by us involve negotiation and, in certain cases, litigation. In the event litigation costs are incurred by us in connection with claims or unapproved change orders, such litigation costs are expensed as incurred, although we may seek to recover these costs. We believe that we have established legal bases for pursuing recovery of our recorded unapproved change orders and claims, and it is management's intention to pursue and litigate such claims, if necessary, until a decision or settlement is reached. Unapproved change orders and claims also involve the use of estimates, and it is reasonably possible that revisions to the estimated recoverable amounts of recorded claims and unapproved change orders may be made in the near term. If we do not successfully resolve these matters, a net expense (recorded as a reduction in revenues) may be required, in addition to amounts that may have been previously provided for. We record the profit associated with the settlement of claims upon receipt of final payment. Claims against us are recognized when a loss is considered probable and amounts are reasonably determinable.

Costs and estimated earnings on uncompleted contracts and related amounts billed as of December 31, 2009 and 2008 were as follows (in thousands):

	2009	2008
Costs incurred on uncompleted contracts	$8,156,428	$ 8,990,785
Estimated earnings, thereon	795,407	751,041
	8,951,835	9,741,826
Less: billings to date	9,388,027	10,238,219
	$ (436,192)	$ (496,393)

Such amounts were included in the accompanying Consolidated Balance Sheets at December 31, 2009 and 2008 under the following captions (in thousands):

	2009	2008
Costs and estimated earnings in excess of billings on uncompleted contracts	$ 90,049	$ 105,441
Billings in excess of costs and estimated earnings on uncompleted contracts	(526,241)	(601,834)
	$(436,192)	$(496,393)

As of December 31, 2009 and 2008, costs and estimated earnings in excess of billings on uncompleted contracts included unbilled revenues for unapproved change orders of approximately $11.2 million and $12.2 million, respectively, and claims of approximately $4.9 million and $5.8 million, respectively. In addition, accounts receivable as of December 31, 2009 and 2008 included claims of approximately $2.5 million and $1.7 million, respectively, plus contractually billed amounts related to such contracts of $29.6 million and $45.0 million, respectively. Generally, contractually billed amounts will not be paid by the customer to us until final resolution of related claims.

Classification of Contract Amounts

In accordance with industry practice, we classify as current all assets and liabilities related to the performance of long-term contracts. The contracting cycle for certain long-term contracts may extend beyond one year, and, accordingly, collection or payment of amounts related to these contracts may extend beyond one year. Accounts receivable at December 31, 2009 and 2008 included $221.0 million and $275.0 million, respectively, of retainage billed under terms of these contracts. We estimate that approximately 75% of retainage recorded at December 31, 2009 will be collected during 2010. Accounts payable at December 31, 2009 and 2008 included $38.6 million and $45.5 million, respectively, of retainage withheld under terms of the contracts. We estimate that approximately 69% of retainage withheld at December 31, 2009 will be paid during 2010. Specific accounts receivable are evaluated when we believe a customer may not be able to meet its financial obligations due to deterioration of its financial condition or its credit ratings. The allowance for doubtful accounts requirements are based on the best facts available and are reevaluated and adjusted on a regular basis and as additional information is received.

PROPERTY, PLANT, AND EQUIPMENT

2.82 Property, Plant, and Equipment are the long-lived, physical assets of the firm acquired for use in the firm's normal business operations and not intended for resale by the firm. These assets are usually valued at historical cost. FASB ASC 835, *Interest*, establishes standards of financial accounting and reporting for capitalizing interest cost as part of the historical cost of acquiring certain assets such as plant assets that an entity constructs for its own use. In 2009, 122 survey entities disclosed that interest costs were capitalized during the period.

2.83 FASB ASC 350-40, *Internal-Use Software*, provides guidance on accounting for the costs of internal-use computer software other than software used in research and development activities. Under FASB ASC 350-40, certain computer software costs should be capitalized and amortized over their estimated useful lives. Accounting for computer software costs is also addressed by FASB ASC 985-20, *Costs of Software to be Sold, Leased or Marketed*. Under FASB ASC 985-20, certain computer software production costs incurred subsequent to establishing technological feasibility should be capitalized and amortized on a product-by-product basis. Presentations of capitalized computer soft-

ware costs by survey entities vary. Examples of capitalized software cost disclosures are included here and in the Other Noncurrent Asset section.

2.84 FASB ASC 360, *Property, Plant, and Equipment*, states:

> Because of the significant effects on financial position and results of operations of the depreciation method or methods used, the following disclosures should be made in the financial statements or in notes thereto:
> a. Depreciation expense for the period,
> b. Balance of major classes of depreciable assets, by nature or function, at the balance sheet date,
> c. Accumulated depreciation, either by major classes of depreciable assets or in total, at the balance sheet date, and
> d. A general description of the method or methods used in computing depreciation with respect to major classes of depreciable assets.

2.85 FASB ASC 250, *Accounting Changes and Error Corrections*, defines various types of accounting changes, including a change in depreciation, amortization or depletion method, and provides guidance on the manner of reporting each type. FASB ASC 250 specifies the requirements for the accounting for and reporting of a change in accounting principle. FASB ASC 250 also requires that a change in depreciation, amortization, or depletion method be accounted for prospectively as a change in accounting estimate effected by a change in accounting principle. A change in accounting estimate is accounted for either in the period of change if the change affects that period only, or the period of change and future periods if the change affects both.

2.86 Tables 2-13 and 2-14 show the assets classified as Property, Plant, and Equipment by the survey entities. Table 2-15 summarizes the descriptive captions used to describe the accumulated allowance for depreciation.

2.87 Examples of Property, Plant, and Equipment disclosures follow.

2.88

TABLE 2-13: LAND CAPTIONS*

	2009	2008	2007	2006
Land..	282	289	343	325
Land and improvements..........	111	104	131	140
Land and buildings...................	47	50	57	60
Land combined with other identified assets...................	7	6	9	7
No caption with term land........	42	39	45	42
	489	488	585	574
Lines of business classification	11	12	15	26
Total Entities.........................	**500**	**500**	**600**	**600**

* Appearing in either the balance sheet and/or the notes to financial statements.

2008–2009 based on 500 entities surveyed; 2006–2007 based on 600 entities surveyed.

2.89

TABLE 2-14: DEPRECIABLE ASSET CAPTIONS*

Buildings	2009	2008	2007	2006
Buildings	137	144	183	183
Buildings and improvement	235	235	271	275
Building and land or equipment	63	70	76	78
Buildings combined with other identified assets	11	5	7	11
No caption with term buildings	41	37	50	42
	487	491	587	589
Line of business classification	13	9	13	11
Total Entities	**500**	**500**	**600**	**600**

Other Depreciable Asset Captions	Number of Entities			
Machinery and/or equipment	308	304	378	377
Machinery and/or equipment combined with other assets	115	104	126	130
Construction in progress	262	250	301	289
Leasehold improvements	112	103	132	129
Furniture and fixtures	82	89	126	106
Automobiles and other specific type equipment	73	75	104	99
Software	74	75	85	67
Lease assets	68	66	64	62
Computer equipment	59	64	61	69
Assets leased to others	12	14	18	25

* Appearing in either the balance sheet and/or the notes to financial statements.

2008–2009 based on 500 entities surveyed; 2006–2007 based on 600 entities surveyed.

2.90

TABLE 2-15: ACCUMULATED DEPRECIATION*

	2009	2008	2007	2006
Accumulated depreciation	279	283	346	357
Accumulated depreciation and amortization	158	156	191	184
Accumulated depreciation, amortization and depletion	15	16	18	14
Accumulated depreciation and depletion	5	4	3	5
Allowance for depreciation	11	14	14	15
Allowance for depreciation and amortization	3	4	4	5
Other captions	29	23	24	20
Total Entities	**500**	**500**	**600**	**600**

* Appearing in either the balance sheet and/or the notes to financial statements.

2008–2009 based on 500 entities surveyed; 2006–2007 based on 600 entities surveyed.

2.91

IRON MOUNTAIN INCORPORATED (DEC)

(In thousands)	2008	2009
Total current assets	$ 976,392	$ 1,211,425
Property, plant and equipment:		
Property, plant and equipment	3,750,515	4,184,631
Less—accumulated depreciation	(1,363,761)	(1,616,431)
Net property, plant and equipment	2,386,754	2,568,200
Other assets, net:		
Goodwill	2,452,304	2,534,713
Customer relationships and acquisition costs	443,729	438,812
Deferred financing costs	33,186	35,206
Other	64,489	58,478
Total other assets, net	2,993,708	3,067,209
Total assets	$ 6,356,854	$ 6,846,834

NOTES TO CONSOLIDATED FINANCIAL STATEMENTS
(In thousands)

2 (In Part): Summary of Significant Accounting Policies

f. Property, Plant and Equipment

Property, plant and equipment are stated at cost and depreciated using the straight-line method with the following useful lives:

Building and building improvements	5 to 50 years
Leasehold improvements	8 to 10 years or the life of the lease, whichever is shorter
Racking	3 to 20 years
Warehouse equipment	3 to 10 years
Vehicles	2 to 10 years
Furniture and fixtures	2 to 10 years
Computer hardware and software	3 to 5 years

Property, plant and equipment (including capital leases in the respective category), at cost, consist of the following:

	2008	2009
Land, buildings and building improvements	$1,091,340	$1,202,406
Leasehold improvements	346,837	429,331
Racking	1,198,015	1,318,501
Warehouse equipment/vehicles	275,866	343,591
Furniture and fixtures	72,678	78,265
Computer hardware and software	620,922	663,739
Construction in progress	144,857	148,798
	$3,750,515	$4,184,631

Minor maintenance costs are expensed as incurred. Major improvements which extend the life, increase the capacity or improve the safety or the efficiency of property owned are capitalized. Major improvements to leased buildings are capitalized as leasehold improvements and depreciated.

We develop various software applications for internal use. Payroll and related costs for employees who are directly associated with, and who devote time to, the development of internal use computer software projects (to the extent of the time spent directly on the project) are capitalized. Capitalization begins when the design stage of the application has been completed and it is probable that the project will be completed and used to perform the function intended. Capitalized software costs are depreciated over the estimated useful life of the software beginning when the software is placed in service. During the years ended December 31, 2007, 2008 and 2009, we wrote-off $1,263, $610 and $600, respectively, of previously deferred software costs (primarily in Corporate), primarily internal labor costs, associated with internal use software development projects that were discontinued after implementation, which resulted in a loss on disposal/writedown of property, plant and equipment, net in the accompanying consolidated statement of operations.

Entities are required to record the fair value of a liability for an asset retirement obligation in the period in which it is incurred. Asset retirement obligations represent the costs to repair, replace or remove tangible long-lived assets required by law, regulatory rule or contractual agreement. When the liability is initially recorded, the entity capitalizes the cost by increasing the carrying amount of the related long-lived asset, which is then depreciated over the useful life of the related asset. The liability is increased over time through income such that the liability will equate to the future cost to retire the long-lived asset at the expected retirement date. Upon settlement of the liability, an entity either settles the obligation for its recorded amount or realizes a gain or loss upon settlement. Our obligations are primarily the result of requirements under our facility lease agreements which generally have "return to original condition" clauses which would require us to remove or restore items such as shred pits, vaults, demising walls and office build-outs, among others. The significant assumptions used in estimating our aggregate asset retirement obligation are the timing of removals, estimated cost and associated expected inflation rates that are consistent with historical rates and credit-adjusted risk-free rates that approximate our incremental borrowing rate.

A reconciliation of liabilities for asset retirement obligations (included in other long-term liabilities) is as follows:

	2008	2009
Asset retirement obligations, beginning of the year	$7,775	$ 9,096
Liabilities incurred	797	882
Liabilities settled	(486)	(312)
Accretion expense	1,010	1,233
Asset retirement obligations, end of the year	$9,096	$10,899

2.92

NORDSTROM, INC. (JAN)

(In millions)	2009	2008
Total current assets	$3,217	$3,361
Land, buildings and equipment, net	2,221	1,983
Goodwill	53	53
Other assets	170	203
Total assets	$5,661	$5,600

NOTES TO CONSOLIDATED FINANCIAL STATEMENTS
(Dollar amounts in millions)

Note 1 (In Part): Summary of Significant Accounting Policies

Land, Buildings and Equipment
Depreciation is computed using the straight-line method. Estimated useful lives by major asset category are as follows:

Asset	Life (In years)
Buildings and improvements	5–40
Store fixtures and equipment	3–15
Leasehold improvements	Shorter of initial lease term or asset life
Software	3–7

Impairment of Long-Lived Assets

In accordance with Statement of Financial Accounting Standards No. 144, Accounting for the Impairment or Disposal of Long-lived Assets, when facts and circumstances indicate that the carrying values of long-lived assets may be impaired, we perform an evaluation of recoverability by comparing the carrying values of the net assets to projected undiscounted future cash flows in addition to other quantitative and qualitative analyses. Upon indication that the carrying values of long-lived assets may not be recoverable, we recognize an impairment loss. We estimate the fair value of the assets using the discounted future cash flows of the assets. Property, plant and equipment assets are grouped at the lowest level for which there are identifiable cash flows when assessing impairment. Cash flows for our retail store assets are identified at the individual store level.

Note 3. Land, Buildings and Equipment

Land, buildings and equipment consist of the following:

	2009	2008
Land and land improvements	$ 67	$ 65
Buildings and building improvements	847	842
Leasehold improvements	1,631	1,313
Store fixtures and equipment	2,214	1,995
Software	347	303
Construction in progress	222	391
	5,328	4,909
Less: accumulated depreciation and amortization	(3,107)	(2,926)
Land, buildings and equipment, net	$ 2,221	$ 1,983

The total cost of buildings and equipment held under capital lease obligations was $28 at the end of both 2008 and 2007, with related accumulated amortization of $21 in 2008 and $20 in 2007. The amortization of capitalized leased buildings and equipment of $1 in both 2008 and 2007 was recorded in depreciation expense.

2.93

UNITED STATIONERS INC. (DEC)

(Dollars in thousands)	2009	2008
Total current assets	$1,283,752	$1,335,245
Property, plant and equipment, at cost:		
Land	12,259	12,259
Buildings	58,768	58,768
Fixtures and equipment	272,401	268,368
Leasehold improvements	22,994	20,786
Capitalized software costs	55,912	50,971
Total property, plant and equipment	422,334	411,152
Less—accumulated depreciation and amortization	287,302	258,138
Net property, plant and equipment	135,032	153,014
Intangible assets, net	62,932	67,982
Goodwill	314,429	314,441
Other	12,371	10,834
Total assets	$1,808,516	$1,881,516

NOTES TO CONSOLIDATED FINANCIAL STATEMENTS

2 (In Part): Summary of Significant Accounting Policies

Property, Plant and Equipment

Property, plant and equipment is recorded at cost. Depreciation and amortization are determined by using the straight-line method over the estimated useful lives of the assets. The estimated useful life assigned to fixtures and equipment is from two to 10 years; the estimated useful life assigned to buildings does not exceed 40 years; leasehold improvements are amortized over the lesser of their useful lives or the term of the applicable lease. Repair and maintenance costs are charged to expense as incurred.

On July 11, 2008, the Company completed the sale of its distribution center located in Jacksonville, FL for approximately $3.5 million. The net book value of this building and related assets was $1.8 million as of the closing date. In addition, the Company closed on the sale of its distribution center in Tampa, FL on August 8, 2008, with a sales price of approximately $4.8 million compared with a net book value of $1.5 million. As of December 31, 2007, the Company had one building and associated assets, related to its former corporate headquarters, with total net book value of $5.4 million classified as "assets held for sale" within "Other assets" on the Consolidated Balance Sheets. On May 7, 2008, the Company completed the sale of this building for approximately $9.8 million. During 2007, the Company recognized an impairment loss of $0.6 million on certain Information Technology (IT) hardware "held for sale."

Software Capitalization

The Company capitalizes internal use software development costs in accordance with accounting guidance on accounting for costs of computer software developed or obtained for internal use. Amortization is recorded on a straight-line basis over the estimated useful life of the software, generally not to exceed ten years. Capitalized software is included in

"Property, plant and equipment, at cost" on the Consolidated Balance Sheet. The total costs are as follows (in thousands):

	2009	2008
Capitalized software development costs	$ 56,183	$ 57,706
Write-off of capitalized software development costs	(271)	(6,735)
Accumulated amortization	(40,375)	(36,498)
Net capitalized software development costs	$ 15,537	$ 14,473

Capitalized software development costs related to the Company's Reseller Technology Solution (RTS) investment were being amortized over five years, with $1.6 million amortized for the year ending December 31, 2008. During 2008, the Company wrote off the remaining $6.7 million of capitalized software development costs related to the RTS investment. The charge reflected delays in bringing this solution to market and the acceleration of development of other such software solutions. As a result of these changing developments, the Company's undiscounted forecasted cash flows and fair value analysis associated with this investment declined such that a write-off of the remaining asset-value was required. This pre-tax write-off is reflected in "Warehousing, marketing and administrative expenses" on the Consolidated Statement of Income for 2008.

INVESTMENTS

2.94 FASB ASC 323, *Investments—Equity Method and Joint Ventures*, stipulates that the equity method should be used to account for investments in corporate joint ventures and certain other entities when an investor has "the ability to exercise significant influence over operating and financial policies of an investee even though the investor holds 50% or less of the voting stock." FASB ASC 323 considers an investor to have the ability to exercise significant influence when it owns 20% or more of the voting stock of an investee. FASB ASC 323 specifies the criteria for applying the equity method of accounting to 50% or less owned entities, and lists circumstances under which, despite 20% ownership, an investor may not be able to exercise significant influence.

2.95 In addition to investments accounted for by the equity method, many survey entities disclosed investments in equity and debt securities subject to the requirements of FASB ASC 320, *Investments—Debt and Equity Securities*. FASB ASC 320 provides guidance on accounting for and reporting investments in equity securities that have readily determinable fair value and all investments in debt securities. FASB ASC 320 states the disclosure requirements for such investments. FASB ASC 320 does not apply to investments accounted for by the equity method.

2.96 For investments subject to FASB ASC 320 requirements, FASB ASC 820, *Fair Value Measurements and Disclosures*, requires disclosure of both the fair value and the bases for estimating the fair value of investments unless it is not practicable to estimate that value.

2.97 FASB ASC 820, *Fair Value Measurements and Disclosures*, defines fair value, establishes a framework for measuring fair value, and requires certain disclosures about fair value measurements. FASB ASC 820 clarifies the definition of fair value as an exit price, i.e., a price that would be received to sell, as opposed to acquire, an asset or transfer a liability. FASB ASC 820 emphasizes that fair value is a market-based measurement. It establishes a fair value hierarchy that distinguishes between assumptions developed based on market data obtained from independent external sources and the reporting entity's own assumptions. Further, FASB ASC 820 specifies that fair value measurement should consider adjustment for risk, such as the risk inherent in a valuation technique or its inputs. For assets measured at fair value, whether on a recurring or a nonrecurring basis, FASB ASC 820 specifies the required disclosures concerning the inputs used to measure fair value. FASB Accounting Standards Update (ASU) No. 2010-06, *Improving Disclosures about Fair Value Measurements*, requires more robust disclosures about different classes of assets and liabilities measured at fair value, the valuation techniques and inputs used, the activity in Level 3 fair value measurements, and the transfers between Levels 1, 2, and 3. FASB ASU No. 2010-06 is effective for fiscal years beginning after December 15, 2009, except for the disclosures about certain Level 3 activity. Those disclosures are effective for fiscal years beginning after December 15, 2010. During 2009, 214 survey companies made 389 disclosures of fair value related to investments. 145 of those disclosures were based on the quoted price of the identical item in an active market (level 1 input). 87 of those disclosures were primarily based on other market-corroborated (level 2) inputs. 61 disclosures estimated fair value using nonmarket-corroborated (level 3) inputs. 27 disclosures presented carrying amounts which approximated fair value of investments. In addition, there were 63 disclosures in which carrying value was compared to fair value in an exposition or a table.

2.98 FASB ASC 825, *Financial Instruments*, permits entities to choose to measure many financial instruments and certain other items at fair value that are not currently required to be measured at fair value. Further, under FASB ASC 825, a business entity shall report unrealized gains and losses on eligible items for which the fair value option has been elected in earnings at each subsequent reporting date. The irrevocable election of the fair value option is made on an instrument by instrument basis, and applied to the entire instrument, not just a portion of it. FASB ASC 825 also establishes presentation and disclosure requirements designed to facilitate comparison between entities that choose different measurement attributes for similar types of assets and liabilities.

2.99 FASB ASC 320, *Investments—Debt and Equity Securities*, should be used to determine when certain investments are considered impaired, whether that impairment is other than temporary, and the measurement and recognition of an impairment loss. FASB ASC 320 also provides guidance on accounting considerations subsequent to the recognition of an other-than-temporary impairment and requires certain disclosures about unrealized losses that have not been recognized as other-than-temporary impairments.

2.100 Table 2-16 lists the balance sheet carrying bases for investments presented as noncurrent assets.

2.101 Table 2-17 lists descriptions of investments presented as non-current investments. Examples of presentations and disclosures for such investments follow.

2.102

TABLE 2-16: NONCURRENT INVESTMENTS— CARRYING BASES*

	Number of Entities			
	2009	2008	2007	2006
Equity..........................	237	262	302	300
Fair value...................	131	120	133	124
Cost...........................	88	100	109	123
Lower of cost or market..........	2	3	4	5

* Appearing in either the balance sheet and/or the notes to financial statements.

2008–2009 based on 500 entities surveyed; 2006–2007 based on 600 entities surveyed.

2.103

TABLE 2-17: NONCURRENT INVESTMENTS— DESCRIPTION*

	Number of Entities			
	2009	2008	2007	2006
Common stock..........................	175	195	246	232
Marketable equity securities....	112	99	116	111
Joint ventures.........................	80	84	111	84
Debt..	43	49	41	42
Leases....................................	8	7	11	7
Real estate..............................	7	3	5	5
Preferred stock........................	5	2	10	11
Other.......................................	11	18	31	24
No details................................	15	14	10	8

* Appearing in either the balance sheet and/or the notes to financial statements.

2008–2009 based on 500 entities surveyed; 2006–2007 based on 600 entities surveyed.

Equity Method

2.104

AT&T INC. (DEC)

Consolidated Balance Sheets

(Dollars in millions)	2009	2008
Total current assets	$ 24,334	$ 22,556
Property, plant and equipment—net	100,093	99,088
Goodwill	73,259	71,829
Licenses	48,759	47,306
Customer lists and relationships—net	7,420	10,582
Other intangible assets—net	5,644	5,824
Investments in equity affiliates	2,921	2,332
Other assets	6,322	5,728
Total assets	$268,752	$265,245

Consolidated Statements of Operations

(Dollars in millions)	2009	2008	2007
Operating revenues			
Wireless service	$ 48,563	$ 44,249	$ 38,568
Voice	32,314	37,321	40,798
Data	25,454	24,373	23,206
Directory	4,724	5,416	4,806
Other	11,963	12,669	11,550
Total operating revenues	123,018	124,028	118,928
Operating expenses			
Cost of services and sales (exclusive of depreciation and amortization shown separately below)	50,405	49,556	46,801
Selling, general and administrative	31,407	31,526	30,146
Depreciation and amortization	19,714	19,883	21,577
Total operating expenses	101,526	100,965	98,524
Operating income	21,492	23,063	20,404
Other income (expense)			
Interest expense	(3,379)	(3,390)	(3,507)
Equity in net income of affiliates	734	819	692
Other income (expense)—net	152	(328)	810
Total other income (expense)	(2,493)	(2,899)	(2,005)
Income before income taxes	18,999	20,164	18,399
Income taxes	6,156	7,036	6,252
Net income	12,843	13,128	12,147
Less: net income attributable to noncontrolling interest	(308)	(261)	(196)
Net income attributable to AT&T	$ 12,535	$ 12,867	$ 11,951

NOTES TO CONSOLIDATED FINANCIAL STATEMENTS

1 (In Part): Summary of Significant Accounting Policies

Basis of Presentation (In Part)

All significant intercompany transactions are eliminated in the consolidation process. Investments in partnerships and less-than-majority-owned subsidiaries where we have significant influence are accounted for under the equity method. Earnings from certain foreign equity investments accounted for using the equity method are included for periods ended within up to one month of our year-end (see Note 7).

Recent Accounting Standards (In Part)

Equity Method Investments Accounting

In November 2008, the Emerging Issues Task Force (EITF) reached a consensus on new clarification guidance regarding the application of the equity method. It states equity method investments should be recognized using a cost accumulation model. It also requires that equity method investments as a whole be assessed for other-than-temporary impairment in accordance with existing GAAP for equity method investments. The new guidance was effective, on a prospective basis, for initial or additional equity method investments transactions and subsequent impairments recognized in interim and annual periods that began on or after December 15, 2008 (i.e., as of January 1, 2009, for us). The new guid-ance did not have a material impact on our financial position or results of operations.

Note 7. Equity Method Investments

Investments in partnerships, joint ventures and less-than-majority-owned subsidiaries in which we have significant influence are accounted for under the equity method.

Our investments in equity affiliates include primarily international investments. As of December 31, 2009, our investments in equity affiliates included a 9.8% interest in Téléfonos de México, S.A. de C.V. (Telmex), Mexico's national telecommunications company, and an 8.8% interest in América Móvil S.A. de C.V. (América Móvil), primarily a wireless provider in Mexico with telecommunications investments in the United States and Latin America. In 2007, Telmex's Board of Directors and shareholders approved a strategic initiative to split off its Latin American businesses and its Mexican yellow pages business to a new holding company, Telmex Internacional, S.A.B. de C.V. (Telmex Internacional). Our investment in Telmex Internacional is 9.9%. We are a member of a consortium that holds all of the class AA shares of Telmex stock, representing voting control of the company. Another member of the consortium, Carso Global Telecom, S.A. de C.V. (CGT), has the right to appoint a majority of the directors of Telmex. We also are a member of a consortium that holds all of the class AA shares of América Móvil stock, representing voting control of the company. Another member of the consortium has the right to appoint a majority of the directors of América Móvil. On January 13, 2010, América Móvil announced that its Board of Directors had authorized it to submit an offer for 100% of the equity of CGT, a holding company that owns 59.4% of Telmex and 60.7% of Telmex Internacional, in exchange for América Móvil shares; and an offer for Telmex Internacional shares not owned by CGT, to be purchased for cash or to be exchanged for América Móvil shares, at the election of the shareholders.

The following table is a reconciliation of our investments in equity affiliates as presented on our consolidated balance sheets:

(Dollars in millions)	2009	2008
Beginning of year	$2,332	$2,270
Additional investments	44	—
Equity in net income of affiliates	734	819
Dividends received	(317)	(164)
Currency translation adjustments	125	(574)
Other adjustments	3	(19)
End of year	$2,921	$2,332

Undistributed earnings from equity affiliates were $3,408 and $2,989 at December 31, 2009 and 2008. The currency translation adjustment for 2009 and 2008 reflects the effect of exchange rate fluctuations on our investments in Telmex, Telmex Internacional and América Móvil.

The fair value of our investment in Telmex, based on the equivalent value of Telmex L shares at December 31, 2009, was $1,492. The fair value of our investment in América Móvil, based on the equivalent value of América Móvil L shares at December 31, 2009, was $6,741. The fair value of our investment in Telmex Internacional, based on the equivalent value of Telmex Internacional L shares at December 31, 2009, was $1,597.

2.105

TERRA INDUSTRIES INC. (DEC)

Consolidated Statements of Financial Position

(In thousands)	2009	2008
Total current assets	$ 826,302	$1,392,464
Property, plant and equipment, net	456,702	403,313
Equity method investments	258,860	270,915
Deferred plant turnaround costs, net	25,011	23,467
Other assets	32,868	22,858
Total assets	$1,599,743	$2,113,017

Consolidated Statements of Operations

(In thousands)	2009	2008	2007
Product revenues	$1,576,528	$2,880,255	$2,335,874
Other income	4,904	11,224	7,055
Total revenue	1,581,432	2,891,479	2,342,929
Cost and expenses			
Cost of sales	1,195,176	2,028,252	1,815,421
Selling, general and administrative expenses	67,137	70,736	91,971
Other operating expenses	18,000	—	—
Equity in earnings of North American affiliates	(17,702)	(56,237)	(16,209)
	1,262,611	2,042,751	1,891,183
Income from operations	318,821	848,728	451,746
Interest income	4,136	23,370	17,262
Interest expense	(31,860)	(27,369)	(29,100)
Loss on early retirement of debt	(53,476)	—	(38,836)
Income before income taxes, noncontrolling interest and equity earnings (loss) of GrowHow UK Limited	237,621	844,729	401,072
Income tax provision	(74,299)	(239,851)	(127,316)
Equity earnings (loss) of GrowHow UK Limited	14,177	95,578	(2,718)
Income from continuing operations, net of tax	177,499	700,456	271,038
Income (loss) from discontinued operations, net of tax	1,118	8,269	(18,861)
Net income	178,617	708,725	252,177
Less: net income attributable to the noncontrolling interest	25,984	67,684	50,281
Net income attributable to Terra Industries, Inc.	$ 152,633	$ 641,041	$ 201,896

NOTES TO CONSOLIDATED FINANCIAL STATEMENTS

1 (In Part): Summary of Significant Accounting Policies

Equity Investments

Equity investments are carried at original cost adjusted for the proportionate share of the investees' income, losses and distributions. We have a basis difference between carrying value and the affiliates' book value primarily due to the step-up in basis for fixed asset values, which is being depreciated over a period of 12 to 15 years. We assess the carrying value of our equity investments when an indicator of a loss in value is present and record a loss in value of the investment when the assessment indicates that an other-than-temporary decline in the investment exists.

We classify our equity in earnings of unconsolidated affiliates for our North America and Trinidad equity investments as a component of income from operations because these investments provide additional nitrogen capacity and are integrated with our supply chain and sales activities in our nitrogen segment. We classify our equity earnings of unconsolidated affiliates for our U.K. equity investment as a component of net income, but not income from operations, because this investment does not provide additional nitrogen capacity nor is it integrated with any sales, supply chain or administrative activities.

8. Equity Investments

North America

Our investments in North American companies that are accounted for on the equity method of accounting consist of the following: (1) 50 percent ownership interest in Point Lisas Nitrogen Limited (PLNL), which operates an ammonia production plant in Trinidad, (2) 50 percent interest in an ammonia storage joint venture located in Houston, Texas and (3) 50 percent interest in a joint venture in Oklahoma CO 2, located in Verdigris, Oklahoma, which produces CO 2 at our Verdigris nitrogen plant. These investments were $113.9 million and $131.6 million at December 31, 2009 and 2008, respectively. We include the net earnings of these investments as equity in earnings of North American affiliates as an element of income from operations because the investees' operations provide additional capacity to our operations.

The combined results of operations and financial position of our North American equity method investments are summarized below:

(In thousands)	2009	2008	2007
Condensed income statement information:			
Net sales	$168,234	$380,540	$151,723
Net income	48,554	123,019	38,411
Terra's equity in earnings of North American affiliates	17,702	56,237	16,209

(In thousands)	2009	2008
Condensed balance sheet information:		
Current assets	$ 52,701	$ 50,582
Long-lived assets	156,825	173,631
Total assets	$209,526	$224,213
Current liabilities	$ 23,041	$ 20,212
Long-term liabilities	19,083	19,380
Equity	167,402	184,621
Total liabilities and equity	$209,526	$224,213

The carrying value of these investments at December 31, 2009 was $30.2 million more than our share of the affiliates' book value. The excess is attributable primarily to the step-up in basis for fixed asset values, which is being depreciated over a period of approximately 15 years. Our equity in earnings of unconsolidated subsidiaries is different than our ownership interest in income reported by the unconsolidated subsidiaries due to deferred profits on intergroup transactions and amortization of basis differences.

We have transactions in the normal course of business with PLNL, whereby we are obliged to purchase 50 percent of the ammonia produced by PLNL at current market prices. During the year ended December 31, 2009, we purchased approximately $79.1 million of ammonia from PLNL. During the year ended December 31, 2008, we purchased approximately $182.4 million of ammonia from PLNL.

The total cash distributions from our North American equity method investments were $35.8 million, $72.8 million, and $29.5 million at December 31, 2009, 2008 and 2007, respectively.

United Kingdom

On September 14, 2007, we completed the formation of GrowHow UK Limited (GrowHow), a joint venture between Terra and Kemira GrowHow Oyj (Kemira). Pursuant to the joint venture agreement, we contributed our United Kingdom subsidiary Terra Nitrogen (UK) Limited to the joint venture for a 50 percent interest. Subsequent to the formation, we have accounted for our investment in GrowHow as a non-operating equity method investment. We do not include the net earnings of this investment as an element of income from operations since the investees' operations do not provide additional capacity to us, nor are its operations integrated with

our supply chain in North America. The GrowHow joint venture includes the Kemira site at Ince and our former Teeside and Severnside sites.

In conjunction with the formation of GrowHow, we commenced the closure of our Severnside, U.K. facility. Pursuant to the agreement with Kemira, we are responsible for the remediation costs required to prepare the Severnside site for disposal. During 2009, Severnside underwent remediation and we incurred $8.7 million in relation to the remediation costs. We estimate a remaining $2-3 million in remediation cost to be incurred in 2010. Upon the disposition of Severnside, Terra is entitled to receive the net sales proceeds. We anticipate the proceeds related to the sale of the Severnside land will exceed the total cost of reclamation of the site.

The Joint Venture Contribution Agreement specifies that we are entitled to receive balancing consideration payments up to £60 million based on GrowHow's operating results for fiscal 2008 to 2010. Pursuant to agreements with Kemira, we received minimum balancing consideration and other payments totaling £13.7 million ($21.2 million) and £38.0 million ($61.3 million) during the year ended December 31, 2009 and 2008, respectively. We also received $27.4 million from GrowHow during 2008 for the refund of working capital contributions in excess of amounts specified in the Joint Venture Contribution Agreement. The carrying value of this equity method investment was $144.9 million and $139.3 million at December 31, 2009 and 2008, respectively.

The financial position of our equity method investment in GrowHow at December 31, 2009 and 2008 and the results of operations for the year ended December 31, 2009, 2008 and 2007 are summarized below.

(In thousands)	2009	2008	2007
Condensed income statement information:			
Net sales	$494,202	$1,111,272	$233,103
Net income	38,691	191,781	4,253
Terra's equity in earnings (losses) of GrowHow	14,177	95,578	(2,718)

(In thousands)	2009	2008
Condensed balance sheet information:		
Current assets	$206,225	$212,992
Long-lived assets	288,101	239,589
Total assets	$494,326	$452,581
Current liabilities	$ 82,877	$ 86,471
Long-term liabilities	186,257	132,754
Equity	225,192	233,356
Total liabilities and equity	$494,326	$452,581

The carrying value of these investments at December 31, 2009 and 2008, was $32.3 million and $22.7 million, respectively, more than our share of GrowHow's book value. The excess is attributable to basis differences for fixed asset values, which is being depreciated over a period of 12 years, and the balancing consideration payment from GrowHow as previously discussed. Our equity in earnings of GrowHow is different than our ownership interest in GrowHow's net income due to the amortization of basis differences.

Fair Value

2.106

BRISTOL-MYERS SQUIBB COMPANY (DEC)

(In millions)	2009	2008
Total current assets	$13,958	$14,697
Property, plant and equipment	5,055	5,405
Goodwill	5,218	4,827
Other intangible assets	2,865	1,151
Deferred income taxes	1,636	2,137
Marketable securities	1,369	188
Other assets	907	1,081
Total assets	$31,008	$29,486

NOTES TO CONSOLIDATED FINANCIAL STATEMENTS

Note 1 (In Part): Accounting Policies

Marketable Securities and Investments in Other Companies

All marketable securities were classified as "available for sale" on the date of purchase. As such, all investments in marketable securities were reported at fair value at December 31, 2009 and 2008. Fair value is determined based on observable market quotes or valuation models using assessments of counterparty credit worthiness, credit default risk or underlying security and overall capital market liquidity. Declines in fair value considered other than temporary are charged to earnings and those considered temporary are reported as a component of accumulated other comprehensive income (OCI) in shareholders' equity. Declines in fair value determined to be credit related are charged to earnings.

An average cost method is used in determining realized gains and losses on the sale of "available for sale" securities which are included in other (income)/expense.

Investments in 50% or less owned companies for which the ability to exercise significant influence is maintained are accounted for using the equity method of accounting. The share of net income or losses of equity investments is included in equity in net income of affiliates in the consolidated statements of earnings. Equity investments are reviewed for impairment by assessing if the decline in market value of the investment below the carrying value is other than temporary. In making this determination, factors are evaluated in determining whether a loss in value should be recognized. This includes consideration of the intent and ability to hold investments, the market price and market price fluctuations of the investment's publicly traded shares, and inability of the investee to sustain an earnings capacity, justifying the carrying amount of the investment. Impairment losses are recognized in other expense when a decline in market value is deemed to be other than temporary.

Note 11. Fair Value Measurement

The fair value of financial assets and liabilities are classified in one of the following categories:
- Level 1—Quoted prices (unadjusted) in active markets that are accessible at the measurement date for identical assets or liabilities. The fair value hierarchy gives the highest priority to Level 1 inputs.
- Level 2—Observable prices that are based on inputs not quoted on active markets, but corroborated by market data.
- Level 3—Unobservable inputs are used when little or no market data is available. The fair value hierarchy gives the lowest priority to Level 3 inputs.

	2009				2008			
(Dollars in millions)	Level 1	Level 2	Level 3	Total	Level 1	Level 2	Level 3	Total
Available for sale:								
U.S. government agency securities	$225	$ —	$ —	$ 225	$180	$ —	$ —	$ 180
Equity securities	11	—	—	11	21	—	—	21
Prime money market funds	—	5,807	—	5,807	—	—	—	—
Corporate debt securities	—	837	—	837	—	—	—	—
Commercial paper	—	518	—	518	—	—	—	—
FDIC insured debt securities	—	252	—	252	—	—	—	—
U.S. treasury money market funds	—	218	—	218	—	7,049	—	7,049
U.S. government agency money market funds	—	24	—	24	—	—	—	—
Floating rate securities (FRS)	—	—	91	91	—	—	203	203
Auction rate securities	—	—	88	88	—	—	94	94
Total available for sale assets	236	7,656	179	8,071	201	7,049	297	7,547
Derivatives:								
Interest rate swap derivatives	—	165	—	165	—	647	—	647
Foreign currency forward derivatives	—	21	—	21	—	90	—	90
Total derivative assets	—	186	—	186	—	737	—	737
Total assets at fair value	$236	$7,842	$179	$8,257	$201	$7,786	$297	$8,284
Derivatives:								
Foreign currency forward derivatives	$ —	$ 31	$ —	$ 31	$ —	$ 45	$ —	$ 45
Interest rate swap derivatives	—	5	—	5	—	—	—	—
Natural gas contracts	—	1	—	1	—	7	—	7
Total derivative liabilities	—	37	—	37	—	52	—	52
Total liabilities at fair value	$ —	$ 37	$ —	$ 37	$ —	$ 52	$ —	$ 52

A majority of the ARS were rated 'A' by Standard and Poor's, and primarily represent interests in insurance securitizations. Valuation models are utilized that rely exclusively on Level 3 inputs due to the lack of observable market quotes for the ARS portfolio. These inputs are based on expected cash flow streams and collateral values including assessments of counterparty credit quality, default risk underlying the security, discount rates and overall capital market liquidity. The fair value of ARS was determined using internally developed valuations that were based in part on indicative bids received on the underlying assets of the securities and other evidence of fair value. These investments are expected to be sold before recovery of their amortized cost basis and any further decline in fair value will be considered other-than-temporary.

FRS are long-term debt securities with coupons that reset periodically against a benchmark interest rate. During 2009, $141 million of principal at par for FRS was received. There were no known reported defaults of the FRS. The underlying assets of the FRS primarily consist of consumer loans, auto loans, collateralized loan obligations, monoline securities, asset-backed securities and corporate bonds and loans. Due to the current lack of an active market for FRS and the general lack of transparency into their underlying assets, other qualitative analysis are relied upon to value FRS including discussion with brokers and fund managers, default risk underlying the security and overall capital market liquidity (Level 3 inputs). Declines in fair value are reported as a temporary loss in other comprehensive income because there are no intentions to sell these investments nor is it more likely than not that these investments will be required to be sold before recovery of their amortized cost basis.

For financial assets and liabilities that utilize Level 1 and Level 2 inputs, both direct and indirect observable price quotes are utilized, including LIBOR and EURIBOR yield curves, foreign exchange forward prices, NYMEX futures pricing and common stock price quotes. Below is a summary of valuation techniques for Level 1 and Level 2 financial assets and liabilities:

- U.S. Government Agency Securities and U.S. Government Agency Money Market Funds—valued at the quoted market price from observable pricing sources at the reporting date.
- Equity Securities—valued using quoted stock prices from New York Stock Exchange or National Association of Securities Dealers Automated Quotation System at the reporting date.
- Prime Money Market Funds—net asset value of $1 per share.
- Corporate Debt Securities and Commercial Paper—valued at the quoted market price from observable pricing sources at the reporting date.
- FDIC Insured Debt Securities—valued at the quoted market price from observable pricing sources at the reporting date.

- U.S. Treasury Money Market Funds—valued at the quoted market price from observable pricing sources at the reporting date.
- Foreign currency forward derivative assets and liabilities—valued using quoted forward foreign exchange prices at the reporting date. Counterparties to these contracts are highly-rated financial institutions, none of which experienced any significant downgrades during 2009. Valuations may fluctuate considerably from period-to-period due to volatility in the underlying foreign currencies. Short-term maturities of the foreign currency forward derivatives are 17 months or less, therefore, counterparty credit risk is not significant.
- Interest rate swap derivative assets and liabilities—valued using LIBOR and EURIBOR yield curves, less credit valuation adjustments, at the reporting date. Counterparties to these contracts are highly-rated financial institutions, none of which experienced any significant downgrades during 2009. Valuations may fluctuate considerably from period-to-period due to volatility in underlying interest rates, driven by market conditions and the duration of the swap. In addition, credit valuation adjustment volatility may have a significant impact on the valuation of interest rate swaps due to changes in counterparty credit ratings and credit default swap spreads.

Note 12. Cash, Cash Equivalents and Marketable Securities

Cash and cash equivalents were $7,683 million at December 31, 2009 and $7,976 million at December 31, 2008 and consisted of prime money market funds, government agency securities and treasury securities. Cash equivalents primarily consist of highly liquid investments with original maturities of three months or less at the time of purchase and are recognized at cost, which approximates fair value.

The following table summarizes current and non-current marketable securities, accounted for as "available for sale" debt securities and equity securities:

(Dollars in millions)	2009				2008			
	Cost	Fair Value	Carrying Value	Unrealized (Loss)/Gain in Accumulated OCI	Cost	Fair Value	Carrying Value	Unrealized (Loss)/Gain in Accumulated OCI
Current marketable securities:								
Certificates of deposit	$ 501	$ 501	$ 501	$ —	$ —	$ —	$ —	$ —
Commercial paper	205	205	205	—	—	—	—	—
U.S. government agency securities	125	125	125	—	—	—	—	—
U.S. treasury bills	—	—	—	—	179	180	180	1
Floating rate securities	—	—	—	—	115	109	109	(6)
Total current	$ 831	$ 831	$ 831	$ —	$294	$289	$289	$ (5)
Non-current marketable securities:								
Corporate debt securities	$ 836	$ 837	$ 837	$ 3	$ —	$ —	$ —	$ —
FDIC insured debt securities	252	252	252	—	—	—	—	—
U.S. government agency securities	100	100	100	—	—	—	—	—
Auction rate securities	114	88	88	8	169	94	94	—
Floating rate securities[1]	113	91	91	(22)	139	94	94	(45)
Other	1	1	1	—	—	—	—	—
Total non-current	$1,416	$1,369	$1,369	$(11)	$308	$188	$188	$(45)
Other assets:								
Equity securities	$ 11	$ 11	$ 11	$ —	$ 31	$ 21	$ 21	$(10)

[1] All FRS have been in an unrealized loss position for 12 months or more at December 31, 2009.

The following table summarizes the activity for financial assets utilizing Level 3 fair value measurements:

(Dollars in millions)	2009				2008			
	Current FRS	Non-Current		Total	Current FRS	Non-Current		Total
		FRS	ARS			FRS	ARS	
Fair value at January 1	$ 109	$ 94	$ 94	$ 297	$ 337	$ —	$ 419	$ 756
Sales and settlements	(115)	(26)	(14)	(155)	(106)	(2)	(118)	(226)
Transfers between current and non-current	—	—	—	—	(104)	104	—	—
Realized losses	—	—	—	—	—	—	(324)	(324)
Unrealized gains/(losses)	6	23	8	37	(18)	(8)	117	91
Fair value at December 31	$ —	$ 91	$ 88	$ 179	$ 109	$ 94	$ 94	$ 297

The contractual maturities of "available for sale" debt securities at December 31, 2009 were as follows:

(Dollars in millions)	Within 1 Year	1 to 5 Years	5 to 10 Years	Over 10 Years	Total
Available for sale:					
Certificates of deposit	$501	$ —	$—	$—	$ 501
Commercial paper	205	—	—	—	205
U.S. government agency securities	125	100	—	—	225
Corporate debt securities	—	837	—	—	837
FDIC insured debt securities	—	252	—	—	252
Floating rate securities	—	91	—	—	91
Auction rate securities	—	—	—	88	88
Other	—	1	—	—	1
Total available for sale	$831	$1,281	$—	$88	$2,200

2.107

LOWE'S COMPANIES, INC. (JAN)

(In millions)	2009	2008
Total current assets	$ 9,251	$ 8,686
Property, less accumulated depreciation	22,722	21,361
Long-term investments (Notes 1, 2 and 3)	253	509
Other assets	460	313
Total assets	$32,686	$30,869

NOTES TO CONSOLIDATED FINANCIAL STATEMENTS

Note 1 (In Part): Summary of Significant Accounting Policies

Investments

The Company has a cash management program which provides for the investment of cash balances not expected to be used in current operations in financial instruments that have maturities of up to 10 years. Variable-rate demand notes, which have stated maturity dates in excess of 10 years, meet this maturity requirement of the cash management program because the maturity date of these investments is determined based on the interest rate reset date or par value put date for the purpose of applying this criteria.

Investments, exclusive of cash equivalents, with a stated maturity date of one year or less from the balance sheet date or that are expected to be used in current operations, are classified as short-term investments. The Company's trading securities are also classified as short-term investments. All other investments are classified as long-term. As of January 30, 2009, investments consisted primarily of money market funds, certificates of deposit, municipal obligations and mutual funds. Restricted balances pledged as collateral for letters of credit for the Company's extended warranty program and for a portion of the Company's casualty insurance and Installed Sales program liabilities are also classified as investments.

The Company maintains investment securities in conjunction with certain employee benefit plans that are classified as trading securities. These securities are carried at fair market value with unrealized gains and losses included in SG&A expense. All other investment securities are classified as available-for-sale and are carried at fair market value with unrealized gains and losses included in accumulated other comprehensive (loss) income in shareholders' equity.

Note 2. Fair Value Measurements and Financial Instruments

Statement of Financial Accounting Standards (SFAS) No. 157, "Fair Value Measurements," provides a single definition of fair value, together with a framework for measuring it, and requires additional disclosure about the use of fair value to measure assets and liabilities. FASB Staff Position (FSP) FAS 157-2, "Effective Date of FASB Statement No. 157" delayed the effective date for one year for all nonrecurring fair value measurements of nonfinancial assets and liabilities. As a result, the Company's adoption of SFAS No. 157, effective February 2, 2008, is currently limited to financial assets and liabilities measured at fair value and other nonfinancial assets and liabilities measured at fair value on a recurring basis. The Company elected a partial deferral under the provisions of FSP FAS 157-2 related to the measurement of fair value used when evaluating long-lived assets for impairment and liabilities for exit or disposal activities.

SFAS No. 157 defines fair value as the price that would be received to sell an asset or paid to transfer a liability in an orderly transaction between market participants at the measurement date. SFAS No. 157 establishes a three-level hierarchy, which encourages an entity to maximize the use of observable inputs and minimize the use of unobservable inputs when measuring fair value. The three levels of the hierarchy are defined as follows:

- Level 1—inputs to the valuation techniques that are quoted prices in active markets for identical assets or liabilities
- Level 2—inputs to the valuation techniques that are other than quoted prices but are observable for the assets or liabilities, either directly or indirectly
- Level 3—inputs to the valuation techniques that are unobservable for the assets or liabilities

The effect of partially adopting this standard did not result in changes to the valuation techniques the Company had previously used to measure the fair value of its financial assets and liabilities. Therefore, the primary impact to the Company upon partial adoption of SFAS No. 157 was expanded fair value measurement disclosure.

The following table presents the Company's financial assets measured at fair value on a recurring basis as of January 30, 2009, classified by SFAS No. 157 fair value hierarchy:

		Fair Value Measurements at Reporting Date Using		
		Quoted Prices in Active Markets for Identical Assets	Significant Other Observable Inputs	Significant Unobservable Inputs
(In millions)	2009	(Level 1)	(Level 2)	(Level 3)
Short-term investments:				
Available-for-sale securities	$385	$ 81	$304	$—
Trading securities	31	31	—	—
Long-term investments:				
Available-for-sale securities	253	—	253	—
Total investments	$669	$112	$557	$—

When available, quoted prices are used to determine fair value. When quoted prices in active markets are available, investments are classified within Level 1 of the fair value hierarchy. The Company's Level 1 investments primarily consist of investments in money market and mutual funds. When quoted prices in active markets are not available, fair values are determined using pricing models and the inputs to those pricing models are based on observable market inputs in active markets. The inputs to the pricing models are typically benchmark yields, reported trades, broker-dealer quotes, issuer spreads and benchmark securities, among others. The Company's Level 2 investments primarily consist of investments in municipal obligations.

The Company's other financial instruments not measured at fair value on a recurring basis include cash and cash equivalents, accounts receivable, short-term borrowings, accounts payable, accrued liabilities, and long-term debt and are reflected in the financial statements at cost. With the exception of long-term debt, cost approximates fair value for these items due to their short-term nature. Estimated fair values for long-term debt have been determined using available market information. For debt issues that are not quoted on an exchange, interest rates that are currently available to the Company for issuance of debt with similar terms and remaining maturities are used to estimate fair value.

Carrying amounts and the related estimated fair value of the Company's long-term debt, excluding capital leases and other, is as follows:

| | 2009 | | 2008 | |
| | Carrying Amount | Fair Value | Carrying Amount | Fair Value |
(In millions)				
Liabilities:				
Long-term debt (excluding capital leases and other)	$4,726	$4,653	$5,245	$5,406

Note 3. Investments

The amortized costs, gross unrealized holding gains and losses, and fair values of the Company's investment securities classified as available-for-sale at January 30, 2009, and February 1, 2008, are as follows:

| | 2009 | | | |
(In millions)	Amortized Cost	Gross Unrealized Gains	Gross Unrealized Losses	Fair Value
Municipal obligations	$301	$3	$—	$304
Money market funds	79	—	—	79
Certificates of deposit	2	—	—	2
Classified as short-term	382	3	—	385
Municipal obligations	248	5	—	253
Classified as long-term	248	5	—	253
Total	$630	$8	$—	$638

| | 2008 | | | |
(In millions)	Amortized Cost	Gross Unrealized Gains	Gross Unrealized Losses	Fair Value
Municipal obligations	$117	$1	$—	$118
Money market funds	128	—	—	128
Certificates of deposit	3	—	—	3
Classified as short-term	248	1	—	249
Municipal obligations	462	5	—	467
Mutual funds	42	1	(1)	42
Classified as long-term	504	6	(1)	509
Total	$752	$7	$(1)	$758

The proceeds from sales of available-for-sale securities were $1.0 billion, $1.2 billion and $412 million for 2008, 2007 and 2006, respectively. Gross realized gains and losses on the sale of available-for-sale securities were not significant for any of the periods presented. The municipal obligations classified as long-term at January 30, 2009, will mature in one to 32 years, based on stated maturity dates.

The Company adopted SFAS No. 159, "The Fair Value Option for Financial Assets and Financial Liabilities, Including an Amendment of FASB Statement No. 115," effective February 2, 2008. SFAS No. 159 provides entities with an option to measure many financial instruments and certain other items at fair value, including available-for-sale securities previously accounted for under SFAS No. 115, "Accounting for Certain Investments in Debt and Equity Securities." Under SFAS No. 159, unrealized gains and losses on items for which the fair value option has been elected are reported in earnings at each reporting period. Upon adoption of SFAS No. 159, the Company elected the fair value option for certain pre-existing investments, which had a carrying value of $42 million and were included in long-term investments in the consolidated balance sheet at February 2, 2008. These investments are now reported as trading securities under SFAS No. 115. Trading securities are included in short-term investments and were $31 million at January 30, 2009. For the year ended January 30, 2009, unrealized losses on those trading securities totaled $14 million and were included in SG&A expense. Cash flows from purchases, sales and maturities of trading securities continue to be included in cash flows from investing activities in the consolidated statements of cash flows because the nature and purpose for which the securities were acquired has not changed as a result of the SFAS No. 159 election. The adoption of SFAS No. 159 did not have a material impact on the Company's consolidated financial statements.

Short-term and long-term investments include restricted balances pledged as collateral for letters of credit for the Company's extended warranty program and for a portion of the Company's casualty insurance and Installed Sales program liabilities. Restricted balances included in short-term investments were $214 million at January 30, 2009 and $167 million at February 1, 2008. Restricted balances included in long-term investments were $143 million at January 30, 2009 and $172 million at February 1, 2008.

Cost

2.108

UTSTARCOM, INC. (DEC)

(Dollars in thousands)	2009	2008
Total current assets	$587,761	$ 932,592
Property, plant and equipment, net	130,612	175,287
Long-term investments	8,402	17,691
Long-term deferred costs	184,978	149,258
Long-term deferred tax assets	4,822	13,464
Other long-term assets	12,536	22,514
Total assets	$929,111	$1,310,806

NOTES TO CONSOLIDATED FINANCIAL STATEMENTS

Note 2 (In Part): Summary of Significant Accounting Policies

Investments

The Company's investments consist principally of bank notes and equity securities of publicly traded and privately held companies. The Company's investments in publicly traded equity securities are accounted for under ASC 320, "Investment, Debt and Equity Securities" and are classified as available-for-sale. These investments are recorded at fair value with the unrealized gains and losses included as a separate component of accumulated other comprehensive income, net of tax. During 2009, the Company sold its remaining investment in publicly traded equity securities. The investments in equity securities of privately held companies in which the Company holds less than 20% voting interest and on which the Company does not have the ability to exercise significant influence are accounted for under ASC 325, "Investments-Other" using the cost method. Under the cost method, these investments are carried at the lower of cost or fair market value.

The Company recognizes an impairment charge when a decline in the fair value of its investments below the cost basis is judged to be other-than-temporary. In making this determination, the Company reviews several factors to determine whether the losses are other-than-temporary, including but not limited to: (i) the length of time the investment was in an unrealized loss position, (ii) the extent to which fair value was less than cost, (iii) the financial condition and near term prospects of the issuer and (iv) the Company's intent and ability to hold the investment for a period of time sufficient to allow for any anticipated recovery in fair value.

Joint Ventures

Investments in unconsolidated joint ventures or affiliates ("joint ventures") over which the Company has significant influence are accounted for under the equity method of accounting, whereby the investment is carried at the cost of acquisition, plus the Company's equity in undistributed earnings or losses since acquisition. Investments in joint ventures over which the Company does not have the ability to exert significant influence over the investees' operating and financing activities are accounted for under the cost method of accounting. The Company's investment in TAMCO, a steel mini-mill in California, is accounted for under the equity method. Investments in Ameron Saudi Arabia, Ltd. and Bondstrand, Ltd. are accounted for under the cost method due to

Management's current assessment of the Company's influence over these joint ventures.

Note 4 (In Part): Cash, Cash Equivalents and Investments

At December 31, 2008, MRV Communications ("MRV") was the only available-for-sale security investment recorded at fair value. Any unrealized holding gains or losses are reported as a component of other comprehensive income, net of related income tax effects. Realized gains and losses are reported in earnings. Accumulated other comprehensive income included approximately $3.3 million of unrealized holding loss at December 31, 2008 related to the Company's investment in MRV. During the fourth quarter of 2009, the Company disposed all of its holdings in MRV (see below for additional discussion). As a result, there were no available-for-sale securities subject to fair value accounting at December 31, 2009. All long-term investments at December 31, 2009 are in privately-held companies and are accounted for under the cost method.

The following table shows the break-down of the Company's total investments at December 31, 2009 and December 31, 2008:

(In thousands)	2009	2008
TET	$ —	$ 4,800
Cortina	3,348	3,348
MRV	—	1,170
GCT SemiConductor, Inc.	3,000	3,000
Xalted Networks	1,583	3,302
PCD LLC	—	1,600
Other	471	471
Total equity securities	$8,402	$17,691

TET

In October 2008, the Company invested $4.8 million into Turnstone Environment Technologies LLC ("TET"), in exchange for approximately 22% of voting interest. The Company is not obligated to make further capital contributions. TET's mission is to secure the exclusive licensing rights to technologically-proven environmentally friendly, renewable energy technologies for distribution to various emerging markets, with an initial focus on India. TET is considered as a variable interest entity where the Company is the primary beneficiary and does not hold a majority voting interest. The assets, liabilities and operating results of TET were determined to be immaterial as of December 31, 2008 and, therefore, were not consolidated. Beginning January 1, 2009, the financial statements of TET were included in the consolidated financial statement of the Company (see Note 18).

Cortina

In September 2004, the Company invested $2.0 million in Series A preferred stock of ImmenStar, Inc. ("ImmenStar"). ImmenStar was a development stage company that designed a chip that was used in the Company's product. This investment was accounted for under the cost method. In February 2007, ImmenStar was acquired by Cortina Systems, Inc. ("Cortina"). In exchange for the Company's investment in ImmenStar, the Company received 3.6 million shares of Series D Preferred Stock of Cortina at $0.837 per share, $1.8 million cash in March 2007 and received an additional 0.4 million shares of Series D Preferred Stock at $0.837 per share and $0.2 million cash from escrow during 2008. As a result of the acquisition, the Company recorded a gain on investment of $2.8 million, in other income, net in 2007 and $0.5 million in 2008. The Company owns approximately 1% interest of Cortina at both December 31, 2009 and 2008 and accounts for the investment in Cortina using the cost method.

MRV

On July 1, 2007, Fiberxon, an investment in which the Company had a 7% ownership interest, completed a merger with MRV, which was a publicly-traded company in an active market. In exchange for the Company's interest in Fiberxon, the Company was entitled to receive $1.5 million in cash, 1,519,365 shares of MRV common stock valued at approximately $4.5 million and deferred consideration of approximately $2.7 million. The deferred consideration becomes payable upon the completion of certain milestones and may be reduced by legitimate claims of MRV for certain matters related to the merger. In the third quarter of 2007, the Company was paid the cash consideration of $1.5 million, received 1,519,365 shares of MRV common stock and recognized a gain on investment of $2.9 million.

During the second quarter of 2009, the trading of MRV common stock on the NASDAQ Global Market was suspended as a result of MRV's failure to file its delinquent periodic reports with the SEC after numerous extensions granted by the staff of the Nasdaq Stock Market, Inc. As a result of the delisting from the NASDAQ Global Market, management re-evaluated the carrying value of this investment, including reviewing MRV's cash position, recent financing activities, financing needs, earnings/revenue outlook, operational performance, and competition. Based on this review and consideration of the duration and extent of the decline in MRV fair value, the Company determined that the decline in MRV fair value was other-than-temporary and recorded a $3.8 million impairment charge for this investment in other income, net in the second quarter of 2009. The $3.8 million impairment charge included recognition of previously unrealized loss of approximately $3.3 million at December 31, 2008. During the fourth quarter of 2009, the Company sold its entire equity position of 1,519,365 MRV shares for approximately $1.0 million in cash proceeds and recognized a gain of $0.4 million in other income, net.

In December 2009, the Company, together with other Fiberxon shareholders, agreed to a settlement with MRV related to the deferred consideration. The Company's proportionate share of the settlement proceeds is expected to be less than $0.5 million, to be paid in several installments during fiscal 2010. The Company will record this contingent gain upon receipt of the settlement proceeds.

GCT Semiconductor

In October 2004, the Company invested $3.0 million in GCT Semiconductor, Inc. This investment represents approximately a 2% interest in GCT Semiconductor, Inc., which designs, develops and markets integrated circuit products for the wireless communications industry. This investment is accounted for under the cost method.

Xalted Networks

In May 2005 and August 2005, the Company invested $2.0 million and $1.0 million, respectively, in Xalted Networks ("Xalted"). In March 2006, the Company invested an additional $0.3 million in Xalted. Xalted is a development stage company providing telecommunication operator customers with a comprehensive set of network systems, software solutions and service offerings. The Company had less than a 10% ownership interest at December 31, 2009 and 2008, on a fully diluted basis, in Xalted and accounts for the investment using the cost method. During the third quarter of 2009, management re-evaluated the carrying value of this investment, including reviewing Xalted's cash position, recent financing activities, financing needs, earnings/revenue outlook, operational performance, and competition. Based on this review, the Company determined that the decline in Xalted's fair value was other-than-temporary and recorded a $1.7 million impairment charge for this investment in other income (expense) in the third quarter of 2009.

PCD LLC

In connection with the divestiture of PCD, the Company invested $1.6 million in equity units representing approximately a 2.6% ownership interest of PCD LLC. Under the Settlement Agreement dated June 30, 2009, the Company granted PCD LLC an option to repurchase the Company's current equity position in PCD LLC within 90 days of the date of the Settlement Agreement at its original investment cost of $1.6 million. In the third quarter of 2009, PCD LLC elected to exercise the call option to repurchase all 2,199,214 Class A Units owned by the Company. The Company received cash of $1.6 million in September 2009 and transferred all its equity holdings in Class A Units to PCD LLC. No gain or loss was recorded on this transfer as the carrying value of the equity holdings was equal to the proceeds received.

NONCURRENT RECEIVABLES

2.109   FASB ASC 210, *Balance Sheet*, states that the concept of current assets excludes "receivables arising from unusual transactions (such as the sale of capital assets, or loans or advances to affiliates, officers, or employees) which are not expected to be collected within twelve months."

2.110   FASB ASC 825, *Financial Instruments*, defines noncurrent receivables as financial instruments. FASB ASC 820, *Fair Value Measurements and Disclosures*, requires disclosure of both the fair value and the bases for estimating the fair value of noncurrent receivables unless it is not practicable to estimate that value.

2.111   FASB ASC 820, *Fair Value Measurements and Disclosures*, defines fair value, establishes a framework for measuring fair value, and requires certain disclosures about fair value measurements. FASB ASC 820 clarifies the definition of fair value as an exit price, i.e., a price that would be received to sell, as opposed to acquire, an asset or transfer a liability. FASB ASC 820 emphasizes that fair value is a market-based measurement. It establishes a fair value hierarchy that distinguishes between assumptions developed based on market data obtained from independent external sources and the reporting entity's own assumptions. Further, FASB ASC 820 specifies that fair value measurement should consider adjustment for risk, such as the risk inherent in a valuation technique or its inputs. For assets measured at fair value, whether on a recurring or a nonrecurring basis, FASB ASC 820 specifies the required disclosures concerning the inputs used to measure fair value. FASB Accounting Standards Update (ASU) No. 2010-06, *Improving Disclosures about Fair Value Measurements*, requires more robust disclosures about different classes of assets and liabilities measured at fair value, the valuation techniques and inputs used, the activity in Level 3 fair value measurements, and the transfers between Levels 1, 2, and 3. FASB ASU No. 2010-06 is effective for fiscal years beginning after December 15, 2009, except for the disclosures about certain Level 3 activity. Those disclosures are effective for fiscal years beginning after December 15, 2010. During 2009, 65 survey companies made 104 disclosures of fair value related to noncurrent receivables. Five of those disclosures were based on the quoted price of the identical item in an active market (level 1 input). 23 of those disclosures were primarily based on other market-corroborated (level 2) inputs. 11 disclosures estimated fair value using nonmarket-corroborated (level 3) inputs. 34 disclosures presented carrying amounts which approximated fair value of noncurrent receivables. In addition, there were 27 disclosures in which carrying value was compared to fair value in an exposition or a table.

2.112 FASB ASC 825, *Financial Instruments*, permits entities to choose to measure many financial instruments and certain other items at fair value that are not currently required to be measured at fair value. Further, under FASB ASC 825 a business entity shall report unrealized gains and losses on eligible items for which the fair value option has been elected in earnings at each subsequent reporting date. The irrevocable election of the fair value option is made on an instrument by instrument basis, and applied to the entire instrument, not just a portion of it. FASB ASC 825 also establishes presentation and disclosure requirements designed to facilitate comparison between entities that choose different measurement attributes for similar types of assets and liabilities.

2.113 FASB ASC 860, *Transfers and Servicing*, establishes criteria for determining whether a transfer of financial assets in exchange for cash or other consideration should be accounted for as a sale or as a pledge of collateral in a secured borrowing. This topic and the related examples are covered under the "Receivables Sold or Collateralized" part of this section.

2.114 Table 2-18 summarizes the balance sheet captions used to describe noncurrent receivables. Examples of noncurrent receivable presentations and disclosures follow.

2.115

TABLE 2-18: NONCURRENT RECEIVABLES*

Caption Title	2009	2008	2007	2006
Finance receivable	30	22	29	35
Long-term receivables	24	29	23	22
Notes receivable	24	23	30	29
Receivables from related party	14	11	9	8
Taxes receivable	12	14	5	2
Insurance receivable	11	14	21	25
Other	31	25	35	43
Receivables combined with other investments, deposits, etc.	6	2	1	2
Total Presentations	**152**	**140**	**153**	**166**
	Number of Entities			
Presenting noncurrent receivables	128	119	131	148
Not presenting noncurrent receivables	372	381	469	452
Total Entities	**500**	**500**	**600**	**600**

* Appearing in either the balance sheet and/or the notes to financial statements.

2008–2009 based on 500 entities surveyed; 2006–2007 based on 600 entities surveyed.

2.116

3M COMPANY (DEC)

(Dollars in millions)	2009	2008
Total current assets	$ 10,795	$ 9,598
Marketable securities—non-current	825	352
Investments	103	111
Property, plant and equipment	19,440	18,812
Less: accumulated depreciation	(12,440)	(11,926)
Property, plant and equipment—net	7,000	6,886
Goodwill	5,832	5,753
Intangible assets—net	1,342	1,398
Prepaid pension benefits	78	36
Other assets	1,275	1,659
Total assets	$ 27,250	$ 25,793

NOTES TO CONSOLIDATED FINANCIAL STATEMENTS

Note 5 (In Part): Supplemental Balance Sheet Information

(Millions)	2009	2008
Other assets		
Deferred income taxes	$ 625	$1,053
Product and other insurance receivables	171	206
Cash surrender value of life insurance policies	202	175
Other	277	225
Total other assets	$1,275	$1,659

Note 14 (In Part): Commitments and Contingencies

Accrued Liabilities and Insurance Receivables Related to Legal Proceedings

The Company complies with the requirements of ASC 450, *Contingencies,* and related guidance, and records liabilities for legal proceedings in those instances where it can reasonably estimate the amount of the loss and where liability is probable. Where the reasonable estimate of the probable loss is a range, the Company records the most likely estimate of the loss, or the low end of the range if there is no one best estimate. The Company either discloses the amount of a possible loss or range of loss in excess of established reserves if estimable, or states that such an estimate cannot be made. For those insured matters where the Company has taken a reserve, the Company also records receivables for the amount of insurance that it expects to recover under the Company's insurance program. For those insured matters where the Company has not taken a reserve because the liability is not probable or the amount of the liability is not estimable, or both, but where the Company has incurred an expense in defending itself, the Company records receivables for the amount of insurance that it expects to recover for the expense incurred. The Company discloses significant legal proceedings even where liability is not probable or the amount of the liability is not estimable, or both, if the Company believes there is at least a reasonable possibility that a loss may be incurred.

Because litigation is subject to inherent uncertainties, and unfavorable rulings or developments could occur, there can be no certainty that the Company may not ultimately incur charges in excess of presently recorded liabilities. A future adverse ruling, settlement, or unfavorable development could result in future charges that could have a material adverse effect on the Company's results of operations or cash flows in the period in which they are recorded. The Company currently believes that such future charges, if any, would not have a material adverse effect on the consolidated financial position of the Company, taking into account its significant available insurance coverage. Based on experience and developments, the Company periodically reexamines its estimates of probable liabilities and associated expenses and receivables, and whether it is able to estimate a liability previously determined to be not estimable and/or not probable. Where appropriate, the Company makes additions to or adjustments of its estimated liabilities. As a result, the current estimates of the potential impact on the Company's consolidated financial position, results of operations and cash flows for the legal proceedings and claims pending against the Company could change in the future.

The Company estimates insurance receivables based on an analysis of its numerous policies, including their exclusions, pertinent case law interpreting comparable policies, its experience with similar claims, and assessment of the nature of the claim, and records an amount it has concluded is likely to be recovered.

The following table shows the major categories of on-going litigation, environmental remediation and other environmental liabilities for which the Company has been able to estimate its probable liability and for which the Company has taken reserves and the related insurance receivables:

(Millions)	2009	2008	2007
Respirator mask/asbestos liabilities (includes Aearo in December 31, 2009 and 2008 balances)	$138	$140	$121
Respirator mask/asbestos insurance receivables	143	193	332
Environmental remediation liabilities	31	31	37
Environmental remediation insurance receivables	15	15	15
Other environmental liabilities	117	137	147

For those significant pending legal proceedings that do not appear in the table and that are not the subject of pending settlement agreements, the Company has determined that liability is not probable or the amount of the liability is not estimable, or both, and the Company is unable to estimate the possible loss or range of loss at this time. The Company does not believe that there is any single best estimate of the respirator/mask/asbestos liability, the environmental remediation or the other environmental liabilities shown above, nor that it can reliably estimate the amount or range of amounts by which those liabilities may exceed the reserves the Company has established.

Respirator Mask/Asbestos Liabilities and Insurance Receivables

The Company estimates its respirator mask/asbestos liabilities, including the cost to resolve the claim and defense costs, by examining: (i) the Company's experience in resolving claims, (ii) apparent trends, (iii) the apparent quality of claims (*e.g.,* whether the claim has been asserted on behalf of asymptomatic claimants), (iv) changes in the nature and mix of claims (*e.g.,* the proportion of claims asserting usage of the Company's mask or respirator products and alleging exposure to each of asbestos, silica, coal or other occupational dusts, and claims pleading use of asbestos-containing products allegedly manufactured by the Company), (v) the number of current claims and a projection of the number of future asbestos and other claims that may be filed against the Company, (vi) the cost to resolve recently settled claims, and (vii) an estimate of the cost to resolve and defend against current and future claims. Because of the inherent difficulty in projecting the number of claims that have not yet been asserted, particularly with respect to the Company's respiratory products that themselves did not contain any harmful materials (which makes the various published studies that purport to project future asbestos claims substantially removed from the Company's principal experience and which themselves vary widely), the Company does not believe that there is any single best estimate of this liability, nor that it can reliably estimate the amount or range of amounts by which the liability may exceed the reserve the Company has established. No liability has been recorded regarding the pending action brought by the West Virginia Attorney General previously described.

Developments may occur that could affect the Company's estimate of its liabilities. These developments include, but are not limited to, significant changes in (i) the number of future claims, (ii) the average cost of resolving claims, (iii) the legal costs of defending these claims and in maintaining trial readiness, (iv) changes in the mix and nature of claims received, (v) trial and appellate outcomes, (vi) changes in the law and procedure applicable to these claims, and (vii) the financial viability of other co-defendants and insurers.

As a result of the costs of aggressively defending itself and the greater cost of resolving claims of persons with malignant conditions, the Company increased its reserves in 2009 for respirator mask/asbestos liabilities by $33 million. As of December 31, 2009, the Company had reserves for respirator mask/asbestos liabilities of $104 million (excluding Aearo reserves).

As of December 31, 2009, the Company's receivable for insurance recoveries related to the respirator mask/asbestos litigation was $143 million. The Company increased its receivables for insurance recoveries by $7 million in 2009 related to this litigation. As a result of settlements reached with its insurers, the Company was paid approximately $57 million in 2009 and has an agreement in principle to receive an additional $28 million in connection with the respirator mask/asbestos litigation.

Various factors could affect the timing and amount of recovery of this receivable, including (i) delays in or avoidance of payment by insurers; (ii) the extent to which insurers may become insolvent in the future, and (iii) the outcome of negotiations with insurers and legal proceedings with respect to respirator mask/asbestos liability insurance coverage. The difference between the accrued liability and insurance receivable represents in part the time delay between payment of claims on the one hand and receipt of insurance reimbursements on the other hand. Because of the lag time between settlement and payment of a claim, no meaningful conclusions may be drawn from quarterly or annual changes in the amount of receivables for expected insurance recoveries or changes in the number of claimants.

On January 5, 2007 the Company was served with a declaratory judgment action filed on behalf of two of its insurers (Continental Casualty and Continental Insurance Co.—both part of the Continental Casualty Group) disclaiming coverage for respirator mask/asbestos claims. These insurers represent approximately $14 million of the $143 million insurance recovery receivable referenced in the above table. The action seeks declaratory judgment regarding the allocation of covered costs among the policies issued by the various insurers. It was filed in Hennepin County, Minnesota and named, in addition to the Company, over 60 of the Company's insurers. This action is similar in nature to an action filed in 1994 with respect to breast implant coverage, which ultimately resulted in the Minnesota Supreme Court's ruling of 2003 that was largely in the Company's favor. At the Company's request, the case was transferred to Ramsey County, over the objections of the insurers. The Minnesota Supreme Court heard oral argument of the insurers' appeal of that decision in March 2008 and ruled in May 2008 that the proper venue of that case is Ramsey County. The case has been assigned to a judge in Ramsey County District Court. The plaintiff insurers have served an amended complaint that names

some additional insurers and deletes others. Several of the insurer defendants named in the amended complaint have been dismissed because of settlements they have reached with 3M regarding the matters at issue in the lawsuit. The case remains in its early stages with a trial scheduled to begin in June, 2012.

*Environmental and Other Liabilities
and Insurance Receivables*

As of December 31, 2009, the Company had recorded liabilities of $31 million for estimated environmental remediation costs based upon an evaluation of currently available facts with respect to each individual site and also recorded related insurance receivables of $15 million. The Company records liabilities for remediation costs on an undiscounted basis when they are probable and reasonably estimable, generally no later than the completion of feasibility studies or the Company's commitment to a plan of action. Liabilities for estimated costs of environmental remediation, depending on the site, are based primarily upon internal or third-party environmental studies, and estimates as to the number, participation level and financial viability of any other potentially responsible parties, the extent of the contamination and the nature of required remedial actions. The Company adjusts recorded liabilities as further information develops or circumstances change. The Company expects that it will pay the amounts recorded over the periods of remediation for the applicable sites, currently ranging up to 30 years.

As of December 31, 2009, the Company had recorded liabilities of $117 million for estimated other environmental liabilities based upon an evaluation of currently available facts for addressing trace amounts of perfluorinated compounds in drinking water sources in the City of Oakdale and Lake Elmo, Minnesota, as well as presence in the soil and groundwater at the Company's manufacturing facilities in Decatur, Alabama, and Cottage Grove, Minnesota, and at two former disposal sites in Minnesota. The Company expects that most of the spending will occur over the next seven years.

It is difficult to estimate the cost of environmental compliance and remediation given the uncertainties regarding the interpretation and enforcement of applicable environmental laws and regulations, the extent of environmental contamination and the existence of alternate cleanup methods. Developments may occur that could affect the Company's current assessment, including, but not limited to: (i) changes in the information available regarding the environmental impact of the Company's operations and products; (ii) changes in environmental regulations, changes in permissible levels of specific compounds in drinking water sources, or changes in enforcement theories and policies, including efforts to recover natural resource damages; (iii) new and evolving analytical and remediation techniques; (iv) success in allocating liability to other potentially responsible parties; and (v) the financial viability of other potentially responsible parties and third-party indemnitors.

2.117

RYDER SYSTEM, INC. (DEC)

(Dollars in thousands)	2009	2008
Total current assets	$ 880,373	$ 957,581
Revenue earning equipment, net of accumulated depreciation of $3,013,179 and $2,749,654, respectively	4,178,659	4,565,224
Operating property and equipment, net of accumulated depreciation of $855,657 and $842,427, respectively	543,910	546,816
Goodwill	216,444	198,253
Intangible assets	39,120	36,705
Direct financing leases and other assets	401,324	384,929
Total assets	$6,259,830	$6,689,508

NOTES TO CONSOLIDATED FINANCIAL STATEMENTS

12. Direct Financing Leases and Other Assets

(In thousands)	2009	2008
Direct financing leases, net	$285,273	$285,506
Investments held in Rabbi Trusts	19,686	16,950
Insurance receivables	13,300	10,401
Debt issuance costs	17,009	11,731
Prepaid pension asset	10,588	5,270
Contract incentives	21,776	21,896
Swap agreement	12,101	18,391
Other	21,591	14,784
Total	$401,324	$384,929

15 (In Part): Leases

Leases as Lessor

We lease revenue earning equipment to customers for periods generally ranging from three to seven years for trucks and tractors and up to ten years for trailers. From time to time, we may also lease facilities to third parties. The majority of our leases are classified as operating leases. However, some of our revenue earning equipment leases are classified as direct financing leases and, to a lesser extent, sales-type leases. The net investment in direct financing and sales-type leases consisted of:

(In thousands)	2009	2008
Total minimum lease payments receivable	$ 582,532	$ 602,577
Less: executory costs	(189,057)	(204,601)
Minimum lease payments receivable	393,475	397,976
Less: allowance for uncollectibles	(813)	(4,724)
Net minimum lease payments receivable	392,662	393,252
Unguaranteed residuals	59,049	58,989
Less: unearned income	(98,142)	(97,215)
Net investment in direct financing and sales-type leases	353,569	355,026
Current portion	(68,296)	(69,520)
Non-current portion	$ 285,273	$ 285,506

2.118

VARIAN MEDICAL SYSTEMS, INC. (SEP)

(In thousands)	2009	2008
Total current assets	$1,672,451	$1,394,401
Property, plant and equipment, net	264,060	218,183
Goodwill	210,346	209,146
Other assets	161,391	150,694
Long-term assets of discontinued operations	—	3,088
Total assets	$2,308,248	$1,975,512

NOTES TO CONSOLIDATED FINANCIAL STATEMENTS

5 (In Part): Related Party Transactions

In fiscal years 1999 and 2000, VMS invested a total of $5 million in a three member consortium for a 20% ownership interest in dpiX Holding LLC ("dpiX Holding"), which in turn invested $25 million for an 80.1% ownership interest in dpiX LLC ("dpiX"), a supplier of amorphous silicon based thin-film transistor arrays ("flat panels") for the Company's X-ray Products' digital image detectors and for its Oncology Systems' On-Board Imager®, or OBI, and PortalVision™ imaging products. VMS had the right to appoint one manager of the five person board of managers. In accordance with the dpiX Holding agreement, net losses were to be allocated to the three members, in succession, until their capital accounts equaled zero, then to the three members in accordance with their ownership interests. The dpiX Holding agreement also provided that net profits were to be allocated to the three members, in succession, until their capital accounts equaled the net losses previously allocated, then to the three members in accordance with their ownership interests.

•   •   •   •   •   •

In December 2004, VMS agreed to loan $2 million to dpiX in four separate installments, with the loan bearing interest at prime plus 1% per annum. The principal balance was due and payable to VMS in twelve equal quarterly installments that began in October 2006; interest was payable in full according to a quarterly schedule, which began in April 2005; and the entire principal balance, together with accrued and unpaid interest thereon and all other related amounts payable thereunder, was due and payable on July 10, 2009. The note receivable of $0.7 million from dpiX at September 26, 2008 was included in "Prepaid expense and other current assets" in the Consolidated Balance Sheets, and has been paid as of October 2, 2009.

In February 2008, VMS agreed to loan an additional $1.6 million to dpiX, with the loan bearing interest at prime plus 1% per annum. The principal balance is due and payable to VMS in twelve equal quarterly installments beginning in January 2010; interest is payable in full according to a quarterly schedule which began in April 2008; and the entire principal balance, together with accrued and unpaid interest thereon and all other related amounts payable thereunder, is due and payable on October 10, 2012. The additional note receivable from dpiX was $1.6 million at both October 2, 2009 and September 26, 2008. The current portion of the note receivable was included in "Prepaid expense and other current assets" and the long-term portion was included in "Other Assets" in the Consolidated Balance Sheets.

In February 2009, VMS agreed to loan a further $14 million to dpiX in four separate installments over a period through December 2009. The loan bears interest at prime plus 1% per annum. The principal balance is due and payable to VMS in four installments beginning in December 2011; interest is payable in full according to a quarterly schedule which began in April 2009; and the entire principal balance, together with accrued and unpaid interest thereon and all other related amounts payable thereunder, is due and payable on September 10, 2012. As of October 2, 2009, VMS had loaned $6.8 million to dpiX under this loan agreement, which was included in "Other assets" in the Consolidated Balance Sheet.

In March 2006, VMS and the other member of dpiX Holding agreed to invest an aggregate $92 million in dpiX Holding, with each member's contribution based on its percentage ownership interest in dpiX Holding, for dpiX to acquire and construct a manufacturing facility in Colorado to increase its production capacity. As of October 2, 2009 and September 26, 2008, VMS's contribution of $36.8 million to dpiX Holding for the Colorado manufacturing facility was included in "Other assets" in the Consolidated Balance Sheets as of October 2, 2009 and September 26, 2008.

INTANGIBLE ASSETS

2.119 FASB ASC 350, *Intangibles—Goodwill and Other*, specifies that goodwill and intangible assets that have indefinite useful lives will not be subject to amortization, but rather will be tested at least annually for impairment. In addition, FASB ASC 350 provides specific guidance on how to determine and measure goodwill impairment. Intangible assets that have finite useful lives will be amortized over their useful lives. FASB ASC 350 requires additional disclosures including information about carrying amounts of goodwill and other intangible assets, and estimates as to future intangible asset amortization expense. Also, FASB ASC 350 provides guidance on the impairment testing of acquired research and development intangible assets and assets that the acquirer intends not to use.

2.120 Table 2-19 lists those intangible assets, amortized or not, which are most frequently disclosed by the survey entities. Table 2-20 summarizes the amortization periods used by the survey entities to amortize intangible assets that have finite useful lives.

2.121 Examples of intangible asset presentations and disclosures follow.

2.122

TABLE 2-19: INTANGIBLE ASSETS*

	Number of Entities			
	2009	2008	2007	2006
Goodwill recognized in a business combination..	434	444	542	542
Trademarks, brand names, copyrights	307	295	330	296
Customer lists/relationships.................	277	272	320	290
Technology...	148	138	162	142
Patents, patent rights..........................	128	139	161	153
Noncompete covenants......................	97	93	112	103
Licenses, franchises, memberships....	96	96	114	111
Contracts, agreements........................	93	92	104	89
Research and development acquired in a business combination...............	12	N/C**	N/C**	N/C**
Other—described..................................	62	62	65	77

* Appearing in either the balance sheet and/or the notes to financial statements.

** N/C = Not Compiled. Line item was not included in the table for the year shown.

2008–2009 based on 500 entities surveyed; 2006–2007 based on 600 entities surveyed.

2.123

TABLE 2-20: AMORTIZATION PERIOD—2009

Intangible Asset	Number of Entities					
	Exceeding 40 Years	31–40 Years	21–30 Years	11–20 Years	10 Years or Less	Estimated or Legal Life
Trademarks, brand names, copyrights......	—	6	15	69	70	35
Customer lists/relationships......................	—	—	11	109	110	46
Technology...	—	1	2	52	63	30
Patents, patent rights...............................	—	1	5	57	35	30
Noncompete covenants............................	—	—	1	16	59	21
Licenses, franchises, memberships..........	—	2	4	19	24	22
Contracts, agreements..............................	1	1	5	30	34	22
Research and development acquired in a business combination.............................	—	—	—	—	2	2

Goodwill

2.124

BALL CORPORATION (DEC)

($ in millions)	2009	2008
Total current assets	$1,923.3	$2,165.3
Property, plant and equipment, net	1,949.0	1,866.9
Goodwill (Notes 3 and 12)	2,114.8	1,825.5
Noncurrent derivative contracts	80.6	139.0
Intangibles and other assets, net	420.6	372.0
Total assets	$6,488.3	$6,368.7

NOTES TO CONSOLIDATED FINANCIAL STATEMENTS

1 (In Part): Critical and Significant Accounting Policies

Recoverability of Goodwill and Intangible Assets

On an annual basis and at interim periods when circumstances require, the company tests the recoverability of its goodwill and indefinite-lived intangible assets. The company's indefinite-lived intangible assets are not significant to the consolidated financial statements. The goodwill testing utilizes a two-step impairment analysis, whereby the company compares the carrying value of each identified reporting unit to its fair value. If the carrying value of the reporting unit is greater than its fair value, the second step is performed, where the implied fair value of goodwill is compared to its carrying value. The company recognizes an impairment charge for the amount by which the carrying amount of goodwill exceeds its fair value. The fair values of the reporting units are estimated using the net present value of discounted cash flows, excluding any financing costs or dividends, generated by each reporting unit. The company's discounted cash flows are based upon reasonable and appropriate assumptions, which are weighted for their likely probability of occurrence, about the underlying business activities of the company's reporting units.

3 (In Part): Acquisitions

Anheuser-Busch InBev n.a./s.a.

On October 1, 2009, the company acquired three of Anheuser-Busch InBev n.v./s.a.'s (AB InBev) beverage can manufacturing plants and one of its beverage can end manufacturing plants, all of which are located in the U.S., for $574.7 million in cash. The additional plants will enhance Ball's ability to better serve its customers. The facilities acquired employ approximately 635 people.

• • • • • •

Management's fair market valuation of acquired assets and liabilities has been completed and is summarized in the table below:

($ in millions)	
Inventories	$ 63.3
Property, plant and equipment	191.5
Goodwill	279.3
Other intangible assets	42.5
Current liabilities	(1.9)
Net assets acquired	$574.7

12. Goodwill

($ in millions)	Metal Beverage Packaging, Americas & Asia	Metal Beverage Packaging, Europe	Metal Food & Household Products Packaging, Americas	Plastic Packaging, Americas	Total
Balance at December 31, 2007	$279.4	$1,115.3	$354.3	$114.1	$1,863.1
Transfers of Ball's PRC operations	30.6	(30.6)	—	—	—
Effects of foreign currency exchange rates and other	—	(36.4)	(0.7)	(0.5)	(37.6)
Balance at December 31, 2008	310.0	1,048.3	353.6	113.6	1,825.5
Acquisition of AB InBev plants	279.3	—	—	—	279.3
Sale of plastics pail business	—	—	—	(7.5)	(7.5)
Effects of foreign currency exchange rates and other	(0.5)	17.6	—	0.4	17.5
Balance at December 31, 2009	$588.8	$1,065.9	$353.6	$106.5	$2,114.8

There has been no impairment on the company's goodwill since January 1, 2002.

Since January 1, 2002, the company has tested the recoverability of goodwill annually during the first quarter of each year. The testing was completed at the appropriate time, and no impairments resulted from this review. During the fourth quarter of 2009, Ball adopted a new accounting policy whereby our annual impairment test of goodwill is performed in the fourth quarter instead of the first quarter. The change in the company's annual goodwill impairment testing date was made to coincide with the timing of the annual strategic planning process. As a result of the change, Ball performed the annual impairment tests again in the fourth quarter. No impairments resulted from the fourth quarter test.

2.125

V.F. CORPORATION (DEC)

(In thousands)	2009	2008
Total current assets	$2,629,356	$2,653,010
Property, plant and equipment	614,178	642,727
Intangible assets	1,535,121	1,366,222
Goodwill	1,367,680	1,313,798
Other assets	324,322	458,111
Total assets	$6,470,657	$6,433,868

NOTES TO CONSOLIDATED FINANCIAL STATEMENTS

Note A (In Part): Significant Accounting Policies

VF's policy is to review property and intangible assets with identified useful lives for possible impairment whenever events or changes in circumstances indicate that the carrying amount of an asset or asset group may not be recoverable. If forecasted undiscounted cash flows to be generated by

the asset are not expected to be adequate to recover the asset's carrying value, an impairment charge is recorded for the excess of the asset's carrying value over its estimated fair value.

VF's policy is to evaluate indefinite-lived intangible assets and goodwill for possible impairment at least annually or whenever events or changes in circumstances indicate that the carrying amount of such assets may not be recoverable. An intangible asset with an indefinite life (a major trademark) is evaluated for possible impairment by comparing the fair value of the asset with its carrying value. Fair value is estimated as the discounted value of future revenues arising from a trademark using a royalty rate that an independent party would pay for use of that trademark. An impairment charge is recorded if the trademark's carrying value exceeds its estimated fair value. Goodwill is evaluated for possible impairment by comparing the fair value of a business unit with its carrying value, including the goodwill assigned to that business unit. Fair value of a business unit is estimated using a combination of income-based and market-based valuation methodologies. Under the income approach, forecasted cash flows of a business unit are discounted to a present value using a discount rate commensurate with the risks of those cash flows. Under the market approach, the fair value of a business unit is estimated based on the revenues and earnings multiples of a group of comparable public companies and from recent transactions involving comparable companies. An impairment charge is recorded if the carrying value of the goodwill exceeds its implied fair value. See Notes H and U for information related to impairment charges recorded in 2009 for indefinite-lived trademark intangible assets and goodwill.

Note H. Goodwill

Activity is summarized by business segment as follows:

(In thousands)	Outdoor & Action Sports	Jeanswear	Imagewear	Sportswear	Contemporary Brands
Balance, December 2006	$531,884	$225,202	$56,246	$217,593	
Change in accounting policy	(1,014)	—	—	(1,809)	
2007 acquisitions	12,785	—	—	—	$209,215
Additional purchase cost	—	50	—	—	—
Adjustments to purchase price allocation	(6,240)	(5,027)	—	(17)	—
Currency translation	27,452	11,843	—	—	—
Balance, December 2007	564,867	232,068	56,246	215,767	209,215
2008 acquisition	—	15,678	—	—	—
Contingent consideration	5,309	—	457	—	—
Adjustments to purchase price allocation	(426)	—	—	—	41,215*
Currency translation	(15,040)	(11,928)	—	—	370
Balance, December 2008	554,710	235,818	56,703	215,767	250,800
2009 acquisition	—	—	—	—	142,361
Impairment charges	(31,142)	—	—	(58,453)	(12,256)
Contingent consideration	3,818	—	—	—	—
Adjustments to purchase price allocation	—	—	—	—	(3,454)
Currency translation	8,149	3,112	—	—	1,747
Balance, December 2009	$535,535	$238,930	$56,703	$157,314	$379,198

* Represents reclassification from indefinite-lived Intangible Assets upon finalization of purchase price allocation.

VF completed its annual impairment testing for goodwill and indefinite-lived intangible assets in the fourth quarter of 2009. Based on (i) assessment of current and expected future economic conditions, (ii) trends, strategies and forecasted cash flows at each business unit and (iii) assumptions similar to those that market participants would make in valuing VF's business units, VF management determined that the carrying values of goodwill and trademark intangible assets at its Reef ®, Nautica® and lucy® business units exceeded their fair value. Accordingly, VF recorded noncash impairment charges totaling $122.0 million in the Consolidated Statement of Income. These impairment charges consisted of $31.1 million, $58.5 million and $12.3 million to reduce goodwill at its Reef ®, Nautica® and lucy® business units to their respective implied fair values and $5.6 million and $14.5 million to reduce the Reef ® and lucy® trademark assets to their respective fair values. The Reef ® business unit is a component of the Outdoor & Action Sports Coalition, the Nautica® business unit is a component of the Sportswear Coalition, and the lucy® business unit is a component of the Contemporary Brands Coalition.

Note U (In Part): Fair Value Measurements

Nonrecurring Fair Value Measurements

Goodwill and indefinite-lived intangible assets are tested for possible impairment as of the beginning of the fourth quarter of each year. During 2009, management concluded that the carrying values of goodwill at its Reef ®, Nautica® and lucy® business units exceeded their respective fair values and, accordingly, recorded impairment charges totaling $101.9 million to write down the goodwill to their respective implied fair values (Note H). Management also concluded that the carrying values of its Reef ® and lucy® trademark intangible assets exceeded their respective fair values and, accordingly, recorded impairment charges totaling $20.1 million to write down the assets to their respective fair values. Impairment charges included in the 2009 Consolidated Statement of Income are summarized as follows:

| (In thousands) | Business Unit | | | |
	Reef ®	Nautica®	lucy ®	Total
Goodwill	$31,142	$58,453	$12,256	$101,851
Trademarks	5,600	—	14,502	20,102
Total	$36,742	$58,453	$26,758	$121,953

These nonrecurring fair value measurements were developed using significant unobservable inputs (Level 3). For goodwill, the primary valuation technique used was an income methodology based on management's estimates of forecasted cash flows for each business unit, with those cash flows discounted to present value using rates commensurate with the risks of those cash flows. In addition, management used a market-based valuation method involving analysis of market multiples of revenues and earnings before interest, taxes, depreciation and amortization ("EBITDA") for (i) a group of comparable public companies and (ii) recent transactions, if any, involving comparable companies. For trademark intangible assets, management used the income-based relief-from-royalty valuation method in which fair value is the discounted value of forecasted royalty revenues arising from a trademark using a royalty rate that an independent party would pay for use of that trademark. Assumptions used by management were similar to those that would be used by market participants performing valuations of these business units.

Management's assumptions were based on analysis of current and expected future economic conditions and the updated strategic plan for each business unit. On a macro level, management's assumptions included continuation of the current difficult economic environment with only a gradual recovery over the next 2-3 years. Information regarding the fair value assessments of the Reef ®, Nautica® and lucy® business units is provided below:

Reef ®

The Reef ® business unit has not met the revenue and earnings growth forecasted at its acquisition in 2005. Although its core sandals revenues have grown in both the United States and international markets, the expansion of Reef ® apparel lines has not been as successful. Factors that led to management's current expectation of reduced revenue and earnings growth included (i) current economic conditions and expectation of a slow economic recovery and continued low consumer spending for the next several years and (ii) a revised business strategy, led by a new management team installed in 2009, to focus on the brand's core sandals business and to reduce the brand's apparel lines, in part by licensing rights to certain product categories to independent parties. After the charges in the table above, there was $48.3 million of goodwill and $74.4 million of indefinite-lived trademark intangible assets remaining at the end of December 2009.

Nautica®

The department store channel of distribution in the United States has undergone consolidation over the last several years, resulting in the closing of a number of stores. Recessionary conditions since 2008 have negatively impacted retail sales in the department store channel, including sales of Nautica® brand products, and have also impacted sales at Nautica® retail outlet stores. Accordingly, in connection with our strategic planning process, management has reassessed the financial expectations of this business. Factors that led to management's current expectation of reduced revenue and earnings growth included (i) current economic conditions and expectation of a slow economic recovery and continued low consumer spending for the next several years and (ii) continued challenging conditions in the department store channel. After the impairment charge, there was $153.7 million of goodwill remaining at the end of December 2009.

lucy®

The lucy® business unit was acquired in August 2007, shortly before the start of the current recession. Management's intent at the acquisition date was to refine the product offerings and store design and then to aggressively open new stores for several years. Because we have not made as much progress as planned, along with recessionary conditions in the United States, the number of stores has not been expanded, and the business has not been profitable. In late 2009 responsibility for the lucy® business was transferred from the Contemporary Brands Coalition to the Outdoor & Action Sports Coalition where the lucy® business unit will benefit from the technical product expertise, design staff and retail competencies of The North Face®. Further, several underperforming stores will be closed in 2010. These factors, and particularly management's expectation of a slow economic recovery, have led to a reduced revenue forecast. After the charges in the table above, there was $39.3 million of goodwill and $40.3 million of indefinite-lived trademark intangible assets remaining at the end of December 2009.

Trademarks

2.126

ASHLAND INC. (SEP)

(In millions)	2009	2008
Total current assets	$ 2,473	$ 3,026
Noncurrent assets		
Auction rate securities	170	243
Goodwill	2,220	283
Intangibles—Note H	1,204	109
Asbestos insurance receivable (noncurrent portion)	510	428
Deferred income taxes	161	153
Other noncurrent assets	596	388
Noncurrent assets held for sale	17	46
	$ 4,878	$ 1,650
Property, plant and equipment		
Cost		
Land	258	82
Buildings	723	552
Machinery and equipment	2,317	1,497
Construction in progress	195	140
	3,493	2,271
Accumulated depreciation and amortization	(1,397)	(1,176)
	2,096	1,095
Total assets	$ 9,447	$ 5,771

NOTES TO CONSOLIDATED FINANCIAL STATEMENTS

Note A (In Part): Significant Accounting Policies

Goodwill and Other Indefinite-Lived Intangibles

In accordance with U.S. GAAP for goodwill and other indefinite-lived intangibles, Ashland tests these assets for impairment annually as of July 1 and whenever events or circumstances made it more likely than not that an impairment may have occurred. Ashland reviews goodwill for impairment based on its identified reporting units, which are defined as reportable segments or groupings of businesses one level below the reportable segment level. Ashland tests goodwill for impairment by comparing the carrying value to the estimated fair value of its reporting units, determined using externally quoted prices (if available) or a discounted cash flow model and, when deemed necessary, a market approach. Ashland tests its indefinite-lived intangible assets, principally trademarks and trade names, using a "relief-from-royalty" valuation method compared to the carrying value. Significant assumptions inherent in the valuation methodologies for goodwill and other intangibles are employed and include, but are not limited to, such estimates as projected business results, growth rates, Ashland's weighted-average cost of capital, royalty and discount rates. For further information on goodwill and other intangible assets, see Note H.

Note H (In Part): Goodwill and Other Intangibles

Intangible assets principally consist of trademarks and trade names, intellectual property, customer lists and sale contracts. Intangibles are amortized on a straight-line basis over their estimated useful lives. The cost of trademarks and trade names is amortized principally over 15 to 25 years, intellectual property over 5 to 20 years, customer relationships over 3 to 24 years and other intangibles over 2 to 50 years. As part of recording the Hercules acquisition during 2009, Ashland recorded $1,116 million in intangible assets of which $255 million were related to indefinite-lived assets. Ashland reviews intangible assets for possible impairment whenever events or changes in circumstances indicate that carrying amounts may not be recoverable. In conjunction with the July 1 annual assessment of indefinite-lived intangible assets, Ashland's model did not indicate any impairment. Intangible assets were comprised of the following as of September 30, 2009 and 2008.

	2009			2008		
(In millions)	Gross Carrying Amount	Accumulated Amortization	Net Carrying Amount	Gross Carrying Amount	Accumulated Amortization	Net Carrying Amount
Trademarks and trade names	$ 353	$ (24)	$ 329	$ 67	$(22)	$ 45
Intellectual property	331	(41)	290	54	(21)	33
Customer relationships	586	(40)	546	13	(3)	10
Other intangibles	63	(24)	39	38	(17)	21
Total intangible assets	$1,333	$(129)	$1,204	$172	$(63)	$109

Amortization expense recognized on intangible assets was $68 million for 2009, $11 million for 2008 and $11 million for 2007, and is primarily included in the selling, general and administrative expense caption of the Statements of Consolidated Income. As of September 30, 2009, all of Ashland's intangible assets that had a carrying value were being amortized except for certain trademarks and trade names that

currently have been determined to have indefinite lives. These assets had a balance of $290 million and $35 million as of September 30, 2009 and 2008, respectively. In accordance with U.S. GAAP, Ashland annually reviews these assets to determine whether events and circumstances continue to support the indefinite useful life designation. Estimated amortization expense for future periods is $66 million in 2010, $64 million in 2011, $63 million in 2012, $62 million in 2013 and $60 million in 2014.

2.127

THE ESTÉE LAUDER COMPANIES INC. (JUN)

(In millions)	2009	2008
Total current assets	$2,912.5	$2,787.2
Property, plant and equipment, net	1,026.7	1,043.1
Other assets		
Investments, at cost or market value	12.7	24.1
Goodwill	759.9	708.9
Other intangible assets, net	150.1	191.9
Other assets	314.7	256.0
Total other assets	1,237.4	1,180.9
Total assets	$5,176.6	$5,011.2

NOTES TO CONSOLIDATED FINANCIAL STATEMENTS

Note 2 (In Part): Summary of Significant Accounting Policies

Goodwill and Other Indefinite-Lived Intangible Assets

Goodwill is calculated as the excess of the cost of purchased businesses over the fair value of their underlying net assets. Other indefinite-lived intangible assets principally consist of trademarks. Goodwill and other indefinite-lived intangible assets are not amortized.

The Company assesses goodwill and other indefinite-lived intangibles at least annually for impairment as of the beginning of the fiscal fourth quarter, or more frequently if certain events or circumstances warrant. The Company tests goodwill for impairment at the reporting unit level, which is one level below the Company's operating segments. The Company identifies its reporting units by assessing whether the components of its operating segments constitute businesses for which discrete financial information is available and man-

agement of each reporting unit regularly reviews the operating results of those components. Impairment testing is performed in two steps: (i) the Company determines impairment by comparing the fair value of a reporting unit with its carrying value, and (ii) if there is an impairment, the Company measures the amount of impairment loss by comparing the implied fair value of goodwill with the carrying amount of that goodwill. The impairment test for indefinite-lived intangible assets encompasses calculating a fair value of an indefinite-lived intangible asset and comparing the fair value to its carrying value. If the carrying value exceeds the fair value, impairment is recorded.

•   •   •   •   •   •

To determine fair value of other indefinite-lived intangible assets, the Company uses an income approach, the relief-from-royalty method. This method assumes that, in lieu of ownership, a third party would be willing to pay a royalty in order to obtain the rights to use the comparable asset. Other indefinite-lived intangible assets' fair values require significant judgments in determining both the assets' estimated cash flows as well as the appropriate discount and royalty rates applied to those cash flows to determine fair value. Changes in such estimates or the application of alternative assumptions could produce significantly different results.

Note 5 (In Part): Goodwill and Other Intangible Assets

Other Intangible Assets (In Part)

Other intangible assets include trademarks and patents, as well as license agreements and other intangible assets resulting from or related to businesses and assets purchased by the Company. Indefinite-lived intangible assets (e.g., trademarks) are not subject to amortization and are assessed at least annually for impairment during the fiscal fourth quarter, or more frequently if certain events or circumstances warrant. Other intangible assets (e.g., non-compete agreements, customer lists) are amortized on a straight-line basis over their expected period of benefit, approximately 5 years to 14 years. Intangible assets related to license agreements are amortized on a straight-line basis over their useful lives based on the term of the respective agreement, currently approximately 10 years.

Other intangible assets consist of the following:

	2009			2008		
(In millions)	Gross Carrying Value	Accumulated Amortization	Total Net Book Value	Gross Carrying Value	Accumulated Amortization	Total Net Book Value
Amortizable intangible assets:						
Customer lists and other	$199.2	$115.9	$ 83.3	$184.5	$102.8	$ 81.7
License agreements	43.2	43.0	0.2	43.2	28.1	15.1
	242.4	158.9	83.5	227.7	130.9	96.8
Non-amortizable intangible assets:						
Trademarks and other	73.4	6.8	66.6	99.7	4.6	95.1
Total intangible assets	$315.8	$165.7	$150.1	$327.4	$135.5	$191.9

The aggregate amortization expense related to amortizable intangible assets for the years ended June 30, 2009, 2008 and 2007 was $11.5 million, $14.0 million and $6.3 million, respectively. The estimated aggregate amortization expense for each of the next five fiscal years is as follows:

| (In millions) | Estimated Expense in Fiscal | | | | |
	2010	2011	2012	2013	2014
Aggregate amortization expense	$9.5	$9.3	$8.9	$8.5	$6.2

As previously discussed, the Company performed an interim impairment test as of March 31, 2009 for trademarks related to the Darphin reporting unit. The Company concluded that the carrying value of the Darphin trademark exceeded its estimated fair value and, as a result, recognized an impairment charge of $12.3 million at the exchange rate in effect at that time. This charge was reflected in the skin care product category and in the Europe, the Middle East & Africa region. In

addition, during the third quarter of fiscal 2009, the Company identified a license agreement intangible asset which was tested for impairment based upon a history of operating losses in excess of projections and revisions in internal forecasts. The Company determined that the intangible asset was impaired and therefore recorded an asset impairment charge of $2.3 million in the fragrance product category and in the Americas region.

• • • • • •

The Company completed its annual impairment test of indefinite-lived intangible assets during the fourth quarter of fiscal 2009. Due to the current economic environment and revised expectations regarding future net sales generated from the use of Ojon and Bumble and bumble trademarks, the Company determined that their carrying values exceeded the estimated fair value, by approximately $9.8 million, predominantly in the hair care product category and in the Americas region. Additionally, during the fourth quarter of fiscal 2009, the Company wrote-off approximately $1.2 million of trademarks, primarily in the makeup and skin care product categories and in the Americas region, which are no longer expected to generate operating cash flows.

Customer Lists/Relationships

2.128

IRON MOUNTAIN INCORPORATED (DEC)

(In thousands)	2008	2009
Total current assets	$ 976,392	$ 1,211,425
Property, plant and equipment		
Property, plant and equipment	3,750,515	4,184,631
Less—accumulated depreciation	(1,363,761)	(1,616,431)
Net property, plant and equipment	2,386,754	2,568,200
Other assets, net:		
Goodwill	2,452,304	2,534,713
Customer relationships and acquisition costs	443,729	438,812
Deferred financing costs	33,186	35,206
Other	64,489	58,478
Total other assets, net	2,993,708	3,067,209
Total assets	$ 6,356,854	$ 6,846,834

NOTES TO CONSOLIDATED FINANCIAL STATEMENTS (In thousands)

2 (In Part): Summary of Significant Accounting Policies

g (In Part): Goodwill and Other Intangible Assets
Goodwill and intangible assets with indefinite lives are not amortized but are reviewed annually for impairment or more frequently if impairment indicators arise. We currently have no intangible assets that have indefinite lives and which are not amortized, other than goodwill. Separable intangible assets that are not deemed to have indefinite lives are amortized over their useful lives. We periodically assess whether events or circumstances warrant a change in the life over which our intangible assets are amortized.

h (In Part): Long-Lived Assets

We review long-lived assets and all amortizable intangible assets for impairment whenever events or changes in circumstances indicate the carrying amount of such assets may not be recoverable. Recoverability of these assets is determined by comparing the forecasted undiscounted net cash flows of the operation to which the assets relate to their carrying amount. The operations are generally distinguished by the business segment and geographic region in which they operate. If the operation is determined to be unable to recover the carrying amount of its assets, then intangible assets are written down first, followed by the other long-lived assets of the operation, to fair value. Fair value is determined based on discounted cash flows or appraised values, depending upon the nature of the assets.

i. Customer Relationships and Acquisition Costs and Other Intangible Assets

Costs related to the acquisition of large volume accounts, net of revenues received for the initial transfer of the records, are capitalized. Initial costs incurred to transport the boxes to one of our facilities, which includes labor and transportation charges, are amortized over periods ranging from one to 30 years (weighted average of 25 years at December 31, 2009), and are included in depreciation and amortization in the accompanying consolidated statements of operations. Payments to a customer's current records management vendor or direct payments to a customer are amortized over periods ranging from one to 10 years (weighted average of 4 years at December 31, 2009) to the storage and service revenue line items in the accompanying consolidated statements of operations. If the customer terminates its relationship with us, the unamortized cost is charged to expense or revenue. However, in the event of such termination, we generally collect, and record as income, permanent removal fees that generally equal or exceed the amount of the unamortized costs. Customer relationship intangible assets acquired through business combinations, which represents the majority of the balance, are amortized over periods ranging from six to 30 years (weighted average of 22 years at December 31, 2009). Amounts allocated in purchase accounting to customer relationship intangible assets are calculated based upon estimates of their fair value. Other intangible assets, including noncompetition agreements, acquired core technology and trademarks, are capitalized and amortized over periods ranging from two to 25 years (weighted average of 9 years at December 31, 2009).

The gross carrying amount and accumulated amortization are as follows:

	2008	2009
Gross carrying amount		
Customer relationship and acquisition costs	$541,300	$574,223
Other intangible assets (included in other assets, net)	55,682	56,738
Accumulated amortization		
Customer relationship and acquisition costs	97,571	135,411
Other intangible assets (included in other assets, net)	20,815	29,208

The amortization expense for the years ended December 31, 2007, 2008 and 2009 are as follows:

	2007	2008	2009
Customer relationship and acquisition costs:			
Amortization expense included in depreciation and amortization	$22,110	$28,366	$27,202
Amortization expense charged to revenues	4,864	6,528	8,096
Other intangible assets:			
Amortization expense included in depreciation and amortization	4,526	7,753	8,299

Estimated amortization expense for existing intangible assets (excluding deferred financing costs, which are amortized through interest expense, of $5,156, $5,156, $4,596, $4,409

and $3,577 for 2010, 2011, 2012, 2013 and 2014, respectively) for the next five succeeding fiscal years is as follows:

Estimated Amortization		
	Included in Depreciation and Amortization	Charged to Revenues
2010	$29,915	$4,317
2011	27,976	3,274
2012	26,894	1,852
2013	26,009	951
2014	25,102	458

Technology

2.129

COVANCE INC. (DEC)

(Dollars in thousands)	2009	2008
Total current assets	$ 877,672	$ 737,690
Property and equipment, net	921,995	860,957
Goodwill, net	127,653	105,486
Other assets	47,624	48,955
Total assets	$1,974,944	$1,753,088

NOTES TO CONSOLIDATED FINANCIAL STATEMENTS (Dollars in thousands)

2 (In Part): Summary of Significant Accounting Policies

Goodwill and Other Intangible Assets and Impairment (In Part)

Intangible assets with finite lives are amortized on a straight-line basis over their estimated useful lives, which range in term from one to ten years. The Company periodically evaluates the reasonableness of the estimated useful lives of these intangible assets. See Note 4.

4 (In Part): Goodwill and Amortizable Intangible Assets

The following table summarizes the Company's acquired amortizable intangible assets, which are reflected in other assets on the consolidated balance sheet, as of December 31, 2009 and 2008:

	2009	2008
Intangible assets at cost:		
Customer lists (10 year weighted average useful life)	$ 5,753	$ 4,510
Technology (5 year weighted average useful life)	2,340	2,340
Other—patient list, backlog and non-compete agreements (weighted average useful lives ranging from 1 to 4 years)	1,419	820
	9,512	7,670
Less: accumulated amortization	(4,039)	(3,016)
Net carrying value	$ 5,473	$ 4,654

Amortization expense for the years ended December 31, 2009, 2008 and 2007 was $1.0 million, $1.0 million and $1.2

million, respectively. Amortization expense expected to be recorded for each of the next five years is as follows:

Year Ending December 31	
2010	$1,194
2011	918
2012	627
2013	590
2014	590

Patents

2.130

NETAPP, INC. (APR)

(In thousands)	2009	2008
Total current assets	$3,438,784	$2,067,433
Property and equipment, net	807,923	693,792
Goodwill	680,986	680,054
Intangible assets, net	45,744	90,075
Long-term investments and restricted cash	127,317	331,105
Long-term deferred income taxes and other assets	372,065	208,529
Total assets	$5,472,819	$4,070,988

NOTES TO CONSOLIDATED FINANCIAL STATEMENTS
(Dollar and share amounts in thousands)

Note 2 (In Part): Significant Accounting Policies

Goodwill and Purchased Intangible Assets (In Part)

Goodwill is recorded when the consideration paid for an acquisition exceeds the fair value of net tangible and intangible assets acquired. Acquisition-related intangible assets are amortized on a straight-line basis over their economic lives of five years for patents, four to five years for existing technology, 18 months to eight years for customer relationships and two to seven years for trademarks and tradenames as we believe this method would most closely reflect the pattern in which the economic benefits of the assets will be consumed.

Note 12 (In Part): Goodwill and Purchased Intangible Assets

The change in the net carrying amount of intangibles for the periods ended April 24, 2009 and April 25, 2008 is as follows:

	2009	2008
Beginning balance	$ 90,075	$ 83,009
Recognized in connection with acquisitions	—	36,000
Amortization	(29,414)	(28,934)
Impairment charges	(14,917)	—
Ending balance	$ 45,744	$ 90,075

Intangible assets balances are summarized as follows:

		2009			2008		
	Amortization Period (Years)	Gross Assets	Accumulated Amortization	Net Assets	Gross Assets	Accumulated Amortization	Net Assets
Identified intangible assets:							
Patents	5	$ 10,040	$ (9,891)	$ 149	$ 10,040	$ (9,411)	$ 629
Existing technology	4–5	107,860	(71,210)	36,650	126,660	(56,095)	70,565
Trademarks/tradenames	2–7	6,600	(3,419)	3,181	6,600	(2,328)	4,272
Customer contracts/relationships	1.5–8	12,500	(6,736)	5,764	20,800	(6,191)	14,609
Total identified intangible assets, net		$137,000	$(91,256)	$45,744	$164,100	$(74,025)	$90,075

Amortization expense for identified intangibles is summarized below:

	2009	2008	2007
Patents	$ 479	$ 1,982	$ 1,982
Existing technology	24,515	22,582	17,581
Other identified intangibles	4,420	4,370	3,879
	$29,414	$28,934	$23,442

Our acquired patents are intended to enhance our technology base to build next-generation network-attached storage, storage area network, and fabric-attached storage systems for the benefit of our enterprise customers. The costs of such patents for use in research and development activities that have alternative future uses have been capitalized and amortized over an estimated useful life of five years as research and development expenses.

•   •   •   •   •   •

Based on the identified intangible assets recorded at April 24, 2009, the future amortization expense of identified intangibles for the next five fiscal years is as follows:

Fiscal Year Ending April	Amount
2010	$20,636
2011	11,701
2012	7,150
2013	4,963
2014	554
Thereafter	740
Total	$45,744

Covenants Not to Compete

2.131

JOY GLOBAL INC. (OCT)

(In thousands)	2009	2008
Total current assets	$1,950,027	$1,738,129
Property, plant and equipment:		
Land and improvements	24,971	23,395
Buildings	119,654	94,220
Machinery and equipment	455,894	385,656
	600,519	503,271
Accumulated depreciation	(253,461)	(214,270)
Total property, plant and equipment	347,058	289,001
Other assets:		
Other intangible assets, net	187,037	195,033
Goodwill	127,732	124,994
Deferred income taxes	332,474	255,313
Other non-current assets	63,951	41,843
Total other assets	711,194	617,183
Total assets	$3,008,279	$2,644,313

NOTES TO CONSOLIDATED FINANCIAL STATEMENTS

2 (In Part): Significant Accounting Policies

Goodwill and Intangible Assets (In Part):

Intangible assets include drawings, patents, trademarks, technology, customer relationships and other specifically identifiable assets. Indefinite-lived intangible assets are not being amortized. Assets not subject to amortization are evaluated for impairment annually or more frequently if events or changes occur that suggest impairment in carrying value. Finite-lived intangible assets are amortized to reflect the pattern of economic benefits consumed, which is principally the straight-line method. Intangible assets that are subject to amortization are evaluated for potential impairment whenever events or circumstances indicate that the carrying amount may not be recoverable.

3. Goodwill and Intangible Assets

The gross carrying amount and accumulated amortization of our intangible assets other than goodwill as of October 30, 2009 and October 31, 2008, were as follows:

		2009		2008	
(In thousands)	Weighted Average Amortization Period	Gross Carrying Amount	Accumulated Amortization	Gross Carrying Amount	Accumulated Amortization
Finite lived other intangible assets:					
Engineering drawings	6 years	$ 2,900	$ (1,571)	$ 2,900	$ (1,088)
Customer relationships	20 years	105,200	(12,754)	105,200	(7,127)
Backlog	1 year	16,389	(16,132)	15,089	(15,007)
Non-compete agreements	5 years	5,800	(3,419)	5,800	(2,435)
Patents	17 years	21,123	(6,851)	21,118	(5,853)
Unpatented technology	31 years	1,235	(283)	1,236	(200)
Subtotal	17 years	152,647	(41,010)	151,343	(31,710)
Indefinite lived other intangible assets:					
Trademarks		75,400	—	75,400	—
Total other intangible assets		$228,047	$(41,010)	$226,743	$(31,710)

•   •   •   •   •   •

Amortization expense for finite-lived intangible assets was $9.3 million, $16.2 million and $8.9 million, for fiscal 2009, 2008, and 2007, respectively.

Estimated future annual amortization expense is as follows:

(In thousands)	
For the fiscal year ending:	
2010	$8,347
2011	8,015
2012	7,218
2013	6,489
2014	6,386

Licenses and Franchises

2.132

THE DOW CHEMICAL COMPANY (DEC)

(In millions)	2009	2008
Total current assets	$19,560	$16,060
Investments		
Investment in nonconsolidated affiliates	3,224	3,204
Other investments (investments carried at fair value—2009: $2,136; 2008: $1,853)	2,561	2,245
Noncurrent receivables	210	276
Total investments	5,995	5,725
Property		
Property	53,567	48,391
Less accumulated depreciation	35,426	34,097
Net property	18,141	14,294
Other assets		
Goodwill	13,114	3,394
Other intangible assets (net of accumulated amortization—2009: $1,302; 2008: $825)	5,966	829
Deferred income tax assets—noncurrent	2,039	3,900
Asbestos-related insurance receivables—noncurrent	330	658
Deferred charges and other assets	792	614
Total other assets	22,241	9,395
Total assets	$65,937	$45,474

NOTES TO CONSOLIDATED FINANCIAL STATEMENTS

Note A (In Part): Summary of Significant Accounting Policies

Goodwill and Other Intangible Assets (In Part)

Finite-lived intangible assets such as purchased customer lists, licenses, intellectual property, patents, trademarks and software, are amortized over their estimated useful lives, generally on a straight-line basis for periods ranging from three to twenty years. Finite-lived intangible assets are reviewed for impairment or obsolescence annually, or more frequently if events or changes in circumstances indicate that the carrying amount of an intangible asset may not be recoverable. If impaired, intangible assets are written down to fair value based on discounted cash flows.

Note I (In Part): Goodwill and Other Intangible Assets

Other Intangible Assets

The following table provides information regarding the Company's other intangible assets:

(In millions)	2009			2008		
	Gross Carrying Amount	Accumulated Amortization	Net	Gross Carrying Amount	Accumulated Amortization	Net
Other intangible assets						
Intangible assets with finite lives:						
Licenses and intellectual property	$1,729	$ (320)	$1,409	$ 316	$(192)	$124
Patents	140	(107)	33	139	(100)	39
Software	875	(439)	436	700	(363)	337
Trademarks	694	(110)	584	169	(61)	108
Customer related	3,613	(261)	3,352	210	(66)	144
Other	142	(65)	77	120	(43)	77
Total other intangible assets, finite lives	$7,193	$(1,302)	$5,891	$1,654	$(825)	$829
IPR&D, indefinite lives	75	—	75	—	—	—
Total other intangible assets	$7,268	$(1,302)	$5,966	$1,654	$(825)	$829

Intangible assets acquired with the April 1, 2009 acquisition of Rohm and Haas amounted to $5,305 million including net adjustments made since the acquisition that increased the fair value of these assets $830 million. These adjustments are reflected in the values presented in the tables above and below:

(In millions)	Gross Carrying Amount	Weighted-Average Amortization Period
Rohm and Haas intangible assets		
Intangible assets with finite lives:		
Licenses and intellectual property	$1,410	10 years
Software	73	3 years
Trademarks	513	10 years
Customer related	3,235	16 years
Total intangible assets, finite lives	$5,231	14 years
IPR&D, indefinite lives	74	—
Total intangible assets	$5,305	

During 2009, the Company acquired software for $201 million, including $73 million of software acquired from Rohm and Haas. The weighted-average amortization period for the acquired software is four years.

The following table provides information regarding amortization expense:

(In millions)	2009	2008	2007
Amortization expense			
Other intangible assets, excluding software	$399	$92	$72
Software, included in "cost of sales"	$ 76	$48	$47

Total estimated amortization expense for the next five fiscal years is as follows:

(In millions)	Estimated Amortization Expense for Next Five Years
2010	$575
2011	$566
2012	$548
2013	$527
2014	$504

Contracts

2.133

ANADARKO PETROLEUM CORPORATION (DEC)

(Millions)	2009	2008
Total current assets	$ 6,083	$ 5,095
Properties and equipment		
Cost	50,344	47,073
Less accumulated depreciation, depletion and amortization	13,140	10,026
Net properties and equipment	37,204	37,047
Other assets	1,514	1,368
Goodwill and other intangible assets	5,322	5,413
Total assets	$50,123	$48,923

NOTES TO CONSOLIDATED FINANCIAL STATEMENTS

1 (In Part): Summary of Significant Accounting Policies

Goodwill and Other Intangible Assets (In Part)

Other intangible assets represent contractual rights obtained in connection with a business combination that had favorable contractual terms relative to market as of the acquisition date. Other intangible assets are amortized over their estimated useful lives and are reviewed for impairment whenever impairment indicators are present. See Note 7.

7 (In Part): Goodwill and Other Intangible Assets

Intangible assets subject to amortization at December 31, 2009 and 2008 are as follows:

(Millions)	Gross Carrying Amount	Accumulated Amortization	Net Carrying Amount
Balance at December 31, 2009			
Drilling contracts	$155	$(155)	$ —
Transportation contracts	171	(163)	8
Offshore platform leases	60	(28)	32
	$386	$(346)	$ 40
Balance at December 31, 2008			
Drilling contracts	$155	$(153)	$ 2
Transportation contracts	171	(76)	95
Offshore platform leases	60	(26)	34
	$386	$(255)	$131

Costs associated with acquired drilling contract intangibles were initially capitalized as intangible assets. Amortization of these costs is recorded to oil and gas properties as exploratory and development drilling costs and ultimately expensed through depletion. In 2009, 2008 and 2007, $2 million, $35 million and $81 million, respectively, of drilling contract intangible value was amortized and recorded to oil and gas properties. Drilling contract intangibles relate to the Company's oil and gas exploration and production operating segment.

The Company recognized impairments of $74 million, $12 million and zero for 2009, 2008 and 2007, respectively, related to certain transportation contracts included in intangible assets due to changes in price differentials at specific locations. These assets were impaired to fair value, determined using a discounted cash flow approach, which incorporates market-based inputs that represent a Level 2 fair-value measurement. Amortization expense for the transportation contracts was $13 million, $26 million and $28 million for 2009, 2008 and 2007, respectively. The transportation contract impairments and amortization relate to the marketing operating segment.

Costs associated with offshore platform leases were capitalized as intangible assets. Amortization expense for the offshore platform lease intangibles was $2 million, $7 million and $19 million for 2009, 2008 and 2007, respectively. Offshore platform lease intangibles relate to the Company's oil and gas exploration and production operating segment.

The estimated aggregate amortization expense for all intangible assets for the next five years is $3 million, $5 million, $6 million, $1 million, and $1 million, respectively.

Research and Development Acquired in a Business Combination

2.134

AMGEN INC. (DEC)

(In millions)	2009	2008
Total current assets	$18,932	$15,221
Property, plant and equipment, net	5,738	5,879
Intangible assets, net	2,567	2,988
Goodwill	11,335	11,339
Other assets	1,057	1,000
Total assets	$39,629	$36,427

NOTES TO CONSOLIDATED FINANCIAL STATEMENTS

1 (In Part): Summary of Significant Accounting Policies

Acquired In-Process Research and Development

For business combinations that occurred prior to January 1, 2009, under the then existing accounting rules the estimated fair value of acquired in-process R&D ("IPR&D") projects, which had not reached technological feasibility at the date of acquisition and which did not have an alternative future use, were immediately expensed. In 2007, we wrote-off $270 million and $320 million of acquired IPR&D related to the Ilypsa, Inc. ("Ilypsa") and Alantos Pharmaceuticals Holding, Inc. ("Alantos") acquisitions, respectively. Acquired IPR&D for acquisitions prior to January 1, 2009 is considered part of total R&D expense.

For business combinations that occur on or after January 1, 2009, under current GAAP the estimated fair values of acquired IPR&D projects which have not reached technological feasibility at the date of acquisition are capitalized and subsequently tested for impairment through completion of the development process, at which point the capitalized amounts are amortized over their estimated useful life. If a project is abandoned rather than completed, all capitalized amounts are written-off immediately.

Intangible Assets and Goodwill (In Part)

Intangible assets other than goodwill are recorded at cost, net of accumulated amortization. Amortization of intangible assets is provided over their estimated useful lives on a straight-line basis. We review our intangible assets for impairment whenever events or changes in circumstances indicate that the carrying amount of an asset may not be recoverable. See Note 14, "Intangible Assets."

14. Intangible Assets

Amortization of intangible assets other than goodwill is provided over their estimated useful lives ranging from 5 to 15 years on a straight-line basis (weighted average remaining amortization period of 7 years at December 31, 2009). Intangible assets other than goodwill consisted of the following (in millions):

	Weighted Average Amortization Period	2009	2008
Intangible assets subject to amortization			
Acquired product technology rights:			
Developed product technology	15 years	$ 2,872	$ 2,872
Core technology	15 years	1,348	1,348
Trade name	15 years	190	190
Acquired R&D technology rights	5 years	350	350
Other intangible assets	10 years	541	537
		5,301	5,297
Less accumulated amortization		(2,734)	(2,309)
		$ 2,567	$ 2,988

Acquired product technology rights relate to the identifiable intangible assets acquired in connection with the 2002 Immunex acquisition and the amortization is included in "Amortization of certain acquired intangible assets" in the Consolidated Statements of Income. Intangible assets also include acquired R&D technology rights consisting of technology used in R&D with alternative future uses and the amortization is included in "Research and development" expense in the Consolidated Statements of Income. Acquired R&D technology rights principally include certain technology acquired in the Abgenix, Inc. ("Abgenix") acquisition in 2006. The amortization of other intangible assets is principally included in "Cost of sales" and "Selling, general and administrative" expense in the Consolidated Statements of Income. During the years ended December 31, 2009, 2008 and 2007, we recognized amortization charges associated with our intangible assets of $425 million, $425 million and $416 million, respectively. The total estimated amortization for each of the next five years for our intangible assets is $418 million, $366 million, $338 million, $338 million and $321 million in 2010, 2011, 2012, 2013 and 2014, respectively.

OTHER NONCURRENT ASSETS

2.135 Table 2-21 summarizes the nature of assets (other than property, investments, noncurrent receivables, and intangible assets) classified as noncurrent assets on the balance sheet of the survey entities. Examples of other noncurrent asset presentations and disclosures, except assets leased to others, follow. Examples of assets leased to others are presented under "Lessor Leases" in the "Long-Term Leases" section.

2.136

TABLE 2-21: OTHER NONCURRENT ASSETS*

	Number of Entities			
	2009	2008	2007	2006
Deferred income taxes	277	261	287	261
Pension asset	160	169	235	200
Derivatives	150	47	50	46
Segregated cash or securities	103	100	105	82
Software	87	98	116	117
Debt issue costs	68	79	110	104
Property held for sale	43	45	57	68
Cash surrender value of life insurance	42	32	39	43
Assets of nonhomogeneous operations	9	10	10	8
Contracts	8	10	21	16
Estimated insurance recoveries	5	6	9	12
Assets leased to others	5	4	11	13
Other identified noncurrent assets	58	62	68	60

* Appearing in either the balance sheet and/or the notes to financial statements.

2008–2009 based on 500 entities surveyed; 2006–2007 based on 600 entities surveyed.

Deferred Income Taxes

2.137

AVIS BUDGET GROUP, INC. (DEC)

(In millions)	2009	2008
Total current assets	$ 1,730	$ 1,073
Property and equipment, net	442	485
Deferred income taxes	597	503
Goodwill	76	75
Other intangibles, net	478	467
Other non-current assets	248	889
Total assets exclusive of assets under vehicle programs	3,571	3,492
Assets under vehicle programs:		
Program cash	157	12
Vehicles, net	5,967	7,164
Receivables from vehicle manufacturers and other	170	533
Investment in Avis Budget Rental Car Funding (AESOP) LLC—related party	228	117
	6,522	7,826
Total assets	$10,093	$11,318

NOTES TO CONSOLIDATED FINANCIAL STATEMENTS (Dollar amounts are in millions)

Note 2 (In Part): Summary of Significant Accounting Policies

Taxes (In Part)

The Company accounts for income taxes under the asset and liability method, which requires the recognition of deferred tax assets and liabilities for the expected future tax consequences of events that have been included in the financial statements. Under this method, deferred tax assets and liabilities are determined based on the differences between the financial statement and tax basis of assets and liabilities using enacted tax rates in effect for the year in which the differences are expected to reverse. The effect of a change in tax rates on deferred tax assets and liabilities is recognized in income in the period that includes the enactment date.

The Company records net deferred tax assets to the extent it believes that it is more likely than not that these assets will be realized. In making such determination, the Company considers all available positive and negative evidence, including scheduled reversals of deferred tax liabilities, projected future taxable income, tax planning strategies and recent results of operations. In the event the Company were to determine that it would be able to realize the deferred income tax assets in the future in excess of their net recorded amount, the Company would adjust the valuation allowance, which would reduce the provision for income taxes.

10 (In Part): Income Taxes

Current and non-current deferred income tax assets and liabilities are comprised of the following:

	2009	2008
Current deferred income tax assets:		
Accrued liabilities and deferred income	$ 165	$ 115
Provision for doubtful accounts	4	6
Acquisition and integration-related liabilities	—	2
Unrealized hedge loss	—	9
Convertible note hedge	8	—
Valuation allowance[a]	(25)	(20)
Current deferred income tax assets	152	112
Current deferred income tax liabilities:		
Prepaid expenses	38	37
Unrealized hedge gain	7	—
Current deferred income tax liabilities	45	37
Current net deferred income tax asset	$ 107	$ 75
Non-current deferred income tax assets:		
Net tax loss carryforwards	$ 351	$ 287
Accrued liabilities and deferred income	130	134
Tax credit carryforward	50	48
Acquisition and integration-related liabilities	23	24
Unrealized hedge loss	15	12
Depreciation and amortization	117	129
Convertible note hedge	28	—
Other	24	6
Valuation allowance[a]	(141)	(137)
Non-current deferred income tax assets	$ 597	$ 503

[a] The valuation allowance of $166 million at December 31, 2009, relates to tax loss carryforwards, foreign tax credits and certain state deferred tax assets of $123 million, $32 million and $11 million, respectively. The valuation allowance will be reduced when and if the Company determines it is more likely than not that the related deferred income tax assets will be realized.

● ● ● ● ● ●

As of December 31, 2009, the Company had federal net operating loss carryforwards of approximately $523 million (net of valuation allowances), most of which expire in 2027, 2028

and 2029. Currently the Company does not record valuation allowances on the majority of its tax loss carryforwards as there are adequate deferred tax liabilities that could be realized within the carryforward period. No provision has been made for U.S. federal deferred income taxes on approximately $429 million of accumulated and undistributed earnings of foreign subsidiaries at December 31, 2009, since it is the present intention of management to reinvest the undistributed earnings indefinitely in those foreign operations. The determination of the amount of unrecognized U.S. federal deferred income tax liability for unremitted earnings is not practicable.

2.138

W.W. GRAINGER, INC. (DEC)

(In thousands of dollars)	2009	2008	2007
Total current assets	$2,131,515	$2,144,109	$1,800,817
Property, buildings and equipment			
Land	237,867	192,916	178,321
Buildings, structures and improvements	1,078,439	1,048,440	977,837
Furniture, fixtures, machinery and equipment	950,187	890,507	848,118
	2,266,493	2,131,863	2,004,276
Less accumulated depreciation and amortization	1,313,222	1,201,552	1,125,931
Property, buildings and equipment—net	953,271	930,311	878,345
Deferred income taxes	79,472	97,442	54,658
Investments in unconsolidated entities	3,508	20,830	14,759
Goodwill	351,182	213,159	233,028
Other assets and intangibles—net	207,384	109,566	112,421
Total assets	$3,726,332	$3,515,417	$3,094,028

NOTES TO CONSOLIDATED FINANCIAL STATEMENTS

Note 2 (In Part): Summary of Significant Accounting Policies

Income Taxes

Income taxes are recognized during the year in which transactions enter into the determination of financial statement income, with deferred taxes being provided for temporary differences between financial and tax reporting.

Note 16 (In Part): Income Taxes

The Company recognizes deferred tax assets and liabilities for the expected future tax consequences of events that have been included in the financial statements or tax returns. Under this method, deferred tax assets and liabilities are determined based on the differences between the financial reporting and tax bases of assets and liabilities, using enacted tax rates in effect for the year in which the differences are expected to reverse.

•   •   •   •   •   •

The income tax effects of temporary differences that gave rise to the net deferred tax asset were (in thousands of dollars):

	2009	2008	2007
Deferred tax assets:			
Inventory	$ 11,554	$ 22,674	$ 19,577
Accrued expenses	29,262	29,966	30,295
Accrued employment-related benefits	163,333	144,125	111,147
Foreign operating loss carryforwards	12,547	10,833	10,239
Property, buildings and equipment	—	921	3,189
Other	13,947	11,352	8,064
Deferred tax assets	230,643	219,871	182,511
Less valuation allowance	(20,810)	(15,977)	(13,551)
Deferred tax assets, net of valuation allowance	$ 209,833	$203,894	$168,960
Deferred tax liabilities:			
Purchased tax benefits	$ (5,178)	$ (5,812)	$ (6,779)
Property, buildings and equipment	(7,318)	—	—
Intangibles	(67,821)	(17,083)	(16,884)
Software	(8,835)	(12,774)	(9,710)
Prepaids	(22,889)	(21,893)	(16,625)
Foreign currency gain	(10,020)	(2,206)	(13,661)
Deferred tax liabilities	(122,061)	(59,768)	(63,659)
Net deferred tax asset	$ 87,772	$144,126	$105,301
The net deferred tax asset is classified as follows:			
Current assets	$ 42,023	$ 52,556	$ 56,663
Noncurrent assets	79,472	97,442	54,658
Noncurrent liabilities (foreign)	(33,723)	(5,872)	(6,020)
Net deferred tax asset	$ 87,772	$144,126	$105,301

At December 31, 2009, the Company had $44.8 million of operating loss carryforwards related primarily to foreign operations, some of which begin to expire in 2010. The valuation allowance represents a provision for uncertainty as to the realization of the tax benefits of these carryforwards. In addition, the Company recorded a valuation allowance to reflect the estimated amount of deferred tax assets that may not be realized.

The changes in the valuation allowance were as follows (in thousands of dollars):

	2009	2008	2007
Beginning balance	$15,977	$13,551	$13,461
Increase related to foreign net operating loss carryforwards	4,833	86	1,329
Increase (decrease) related to capital losses and other	—	2,340	(1,239)
Ending balance	$20,810	$15,977	$13,551

Pension Asset

2.139

LEGGETT & PLATT, INCORPORATED (DEC)

(Amounts in millions)	2009	2008
Total current assets	$1,213.6	$1,306.8
Property, plant and equipment—at cost		
Machinery and equipment	1,127.7	1,103.4
Buildings and other	612.8	592.7
Land	49.6	44.7
Total property, plant and equipment	1,790.1	1,740.8
Less accumulated depreciation	1,121.5	1,059.4
Net property, plant and equipment	668.6	681.4
Other assets		
Goodwill	928.2	875.6
Other intangibles, less accumulated amortization of $98.2 and $76.9 at December 31, 2009 and 2008, respectively	171.1	197.4
Sundry	52.5	70.5
Non-current assets held for sale	27.2	30.2
Total other assets	1,179.0	1,173.7
Total assets	$3,061.2	$3,161.9

NOTES TO CONSOLIDATED FINANCIAL STATEMENTS
(Dollar amounts in millions)

I (In Part): Supplemental Balance Sheet Information

Sundry assets, accrued expenses, other current liabilities and other long-term liabilities at December 31 consisted of the following:

	2009	2008
Sundry assets		
Pension plan assets	$ 3.1	$ .5
Notes receivable, net of allowance of $1.3 and $10.3 at December 31, 2009 and 2008, respectively	18.2	45.9
Deferred tax assets	14.2	10.6
Other	17.0	13.5
	$52.5	$70.5

M (In Part): Employee Benefit Plans

The accompanying balance sheets reflect an asset or liability for the funded status of our domestic and foreign defined benefit pension plans. On January 1, 2008, we adopted new guidance that required the funded status of our plans to be measured as of year end beginning with the December 31, 2008 balance sheet. We previously used September 30 as the measurement date for our most significant plans. We chose to perform a measurement that covered the 15-month period of October 1, 2007 through December 31, 2008. Upon implementation, a proportionate allocation was made to cover the net benefit income for the transition period and we recorded a $.5 (net of tax) increase to beginning retained earnings on January 1, 2008.

A summary of our pension obligations and funded status as of December 31, 2009, 2008 and 2007 and changes during the years then ended, is as follows:

	2009	2008	2007
Change in benefit obligation			
Benefit obligation, beginning of period	$226.7	$239.4	$241.6
Service cost	2.3	2.2	4.4
Interest cost	13.5	13.1	13.3
Plan participants' contributions	.6	.8	2.2
Actuarial losses (gains)	7.2	3.7	(6.6)
Benefits paid	(18.4)	(19.0)	(15.7)
Foreign currency exchange rate changes	2.6	(9.1)	2.6
(Divestitures) acquisitions	—	(4.4)	10.1
Plan amendments and curtailments	—	—	(12.5)
Benefit obligation, end of period	234.5	226.7	239.4
Change in plan assets			
Fair value of plan assets, beginning of period	197.6	263.0	226.8
Actual return (loss) on plan assets	13.1	(35.7)	34.4
Employer contributions	2.9	1.3	2.6
Plan participants' contributions	.6	.8	2.2
Benefits paid	(18.4)	(19.0)	(15.7)
(Divestitures) acquisitions	—	(4.6)	10.1
Foreign currency exchange rate changes	1.6	(8.2)	2.6
Fair value of plan assets, end of period	197.4	197.6	263.0
Plan assets (under) over benefit obligations	$ (37.1)	$ (29.1)	$ 23.6
Funded status recognized in the consolidated balance sheets			
Other assets—sundry	$ 3.1	$ .5	$ 35.2
Other current liabilities	(.6)	(.5)	(.6)
Other long-term liabilities	(39.6)	(29.1)	(11.0)
Total net funded status	$ (37.1)	$ (29.1)	$ 23.6

Those plans that have benefit obligations in excess of plan assets at December 31 are recapped below:

	2009	2008	2007
Aggregated plans with accumulated benefit obligations in excess of plan assets:			
Projected benefit obligation	$197.7	$191.6	$35.7
Accumulated benefit obligation	195.9	189.4	34.9
Fair value of plan assets	160.8	162.3	25.2
Aggregated plans with projected benefit obligations in excess of plan assets:			
Projected benefit obligation	197.7	194.2	71.2
Fair value of plan assets	160.8	164.4	59.5

The accumulated benefit obligation for all defined benefit pension plans was $230.8, $222.2 and $234.6 at December 31, 2009, 2008 and 2007, respectively.

Included in the above plans is a subsidiary's unfunded supplemental executive retirement plan. The subsidiary owns insurance policies with cash surrender values of $2.4, $2.3 and $2.2 at December 31, 2009, 2008 and 2007, respectively, for the participants in this non-qualified plan. These insurance policies are not included in the plan's assets.

•   •   •   •   •   •

Pension Plan Assets

In December 2008, the FASB issued guidance for additional disclosure surrounding plan assets of defined benefit pension plans effective for the December 31, 2009 financial statements. The fair value of our major categories of pension plan assets is disclosed below using a three level valuation hierarchy that prioritizes the inputs to valuation techniques used to measure fair value into the following categories:
- Level 1—Quoted prices for identical assets or liabilities in active markets.
- Level 2—Other significant inputs observable either directly or indirectly (including quoted prices for similar securities, interest rates, yield curves, credit risk, etc.).
- Level 3—Unobservable inputs that are not corroborated by market data.

Presented below are our major categories of investments at December 31, 2009:

	Level 1	Level 2	Level 3	Total
Mutual and pooled funds				
Fixed income	$ 90.9	$—	$—	$ 90.9
Equities	59.4	—	—	59.4
Common stock	31.0	—	—	31.0
Money market funds, cash and other	15.9	.2	—	16.1
Total investments at fair value	$197.2	$.2	$—	$197.4

Plan assets are invested in diversified portfolios of equity, debt and government securities. The aggregate allocation of these investments is as follows:

	2009	2008	2007
Asset category			
Equity securities	46%	43%	75%
Debt securities	46	54	17
Other, including cash	8	3	8
Total	100%	100%	100%

Our investment policy and strategies are established with a long-term view in mind. We strive for a sufficiently diversified asset mix to minimize the risk of a material loss to the portfolio value due to the devaluation of any single investment. In determining the appropriate asset mix, our financial strength and ability to fund potential shortfalls that might result from poor investment performance are considered. Approximately 60% of our significant plans (the "frozen" plans) are employing a Liability Driven Investment strategy and have a target allocation of 75% bonds and 25% equities. The remaining significant plans (the "active" plans) have a target allocation of 75% equities and 25% bonds, as historical equity returns have tended to exceed bond returns over the long term.

Assets of our domestic plans represent the majority of plan assets and are allocated to seven different investments: five mutual funds and two separate accounts.

The mutual funds, all passively managed low-cost index funds, include:

- Total Stock Market Index: Large, mid-, and small-cap equity diversified across growth and value styles; using index sampling.
- Developed Markets Index: International large-cap equity; developed markets in Europe and the Pacific region; full-replication approach.
- Total Bond Market Index: Broadly diversified exposure to investment-grade U.S. bond market; using index sampling.
- Long-term Bond Index: Diversified exposure to the long-term, investment-grade U.S. bond market; index sampling.
- Extended Duration Treasury Index: Diversified exposure to the long-term Treasury STRIPS market; using index sampling.

The separate accounts are invested as follows:

- Small cap U.S. equities: Portfolio of small capitalization U.S. stocks benchmarked to the Russell 2000 Value Index.
- U.S. equities: Broad portfolio of U.S. stocks benchmarked to the Russell 1000 Index.

2.140

MEADWESTVACO CORPORATION (DEC)

(In millions)	2009	2008
Current assets	$2,530	$2,161
Property, plant, equipment and forest lands, net	3,442	3,518
Prepaid pension asset	938	634
Goodwill	818	805
Other assets	1,293	1,337
Total assets	$9,021	$8,455

NOTES TO CONSOLIDATED FINANCIAL STATEMENTS

A (In Part): Fair Value Measurements

The following information is presented for assets and liabilities that are recorded in the consolidated balance sheet at fair value at December 31, 2009, measured on a recurring and non-recurring basis:

(In millions)	2009	Level 1[1]	Level 2[2]	Level 3[3]
Recurring fair value measurements:				
Derivatives-assets	$ 1	$ —	$ 1	$ —
Derivatives-liabilities	(23)	—	(23)	—
Cash equivalents	670	670	—	—
Pension plan assets:				
Asset backed securities	$ 20	$ —	$ 19	$ 1
Equity investments	751	707	43	1
Preferred stock	2	2	—	—
Government securities	702	—	702	—
Corporate debt investments	548	—	536	12
Partnerships and joint ventures	104	—	—	104
Real estate	45	—	—	45
Common collective trust	1,125	—	1,125	—
Registered investment companies	55	—	55	—
103-12 investment entities	114	—	114	—
Other pension (payables) receivables	(4)	(32)	7	21
Total pension plan assets	$3,462	$677	$2,601	$184
Non-recurring fair value measurements:				
Long-lived assets held and used	$ 1	$ —	$ —	$ 1
Long-lived assets held for sale	8	—	—	8

[1] Quoted prices in active markets for identical assets.
[2] Quoted prices for similar assets and liabilities in active markets.
[3] Significant unobservable inputs.

The following information is presented for those assets measured at fair value on a recurring basis using significant unobservable inputs (Level 3) at December 31, 2009:

(In millions)	Asset Backed Securities	Equity Investments	Government Securities	Corporate Debt Investments	Partnerships and Joint Ventures	Real Estate	Other Pension Receivables and Payables	Total
December 31, 2008	$ 1	$—	$40	$ 49	$133	$ 61	$ 282	$ 566
Purchases	1	2	—	4	19	6	4	36
Sales	(1)	(1)	(11)	(27)	(37)	(1)	(209)	(287)
Realized gains (losses)	—	—	(1)	(3)	(10)	—	208	194
Unrealized gains (losses)	—	—	2	4	(1)	(21)	(264)	(280)
Transfers in (out) of Level 3	—	—	(30)	(15)	—	—	—	(45)
December 31, 2009	$ 1	$ 1	$—	$ 12	$104	$ 45	$ 21	$ 184

The fair values of the pension plan assets were determined using a market approach based on quoted prices in active markets for identical or similar assets or where there were no observable market inputs an income approach based on estimated investment returns and cash flows.

L (In Part): Employee Retirement, Postretirement and Postemployment Benefits

Retirement Plans

MeadWestvaco provides retirement benefits for substantially all U.S. and certain non-U.S. employees under several noncontributory trusteed plans and also provides benefits to employees whose retirement benefits exceed maximum amounts permitted by current tax law under unfunded benefit plans. U.S. benefits are based on either a final average pay formula or a cash balance formula for the salaried plans and a unit-benefit formula for the bargained hourly plan. Contributions are made to the U.S. funded plans in accordance with ERISA requirements.

In August 2006, the President signed into law the Pension Protection Act of 2006 ("PPA"). The PPA established new minimum funding rules for defined benefit pension plans beginning in 2008. The company does not anticipate any required funding to the U.S. qualified retirement plans as a result of this legislation in the foreseeable future due to the overfunded status of the plans.

In October 2006, the Board of Directors approved the creation of a cash balance formula within the Company's existing retirement plans for salaried and non-bargained hourly employees. The formula provides cash balance credits at the rate of 4%-8% of eligible earnings, depending upon age and years of service points, with interest credited annually at the 30-year Treasury rate. Effective January 1, 2007, all newly hired U.S. employees began accruing benefits under this formula. Effective January 1, 2008, all U.S. employees age 40 and over at that time were provided the opportunity to make a one-time choice between the existing final average pay and cash balance formulas and all U.S. employees less than age 40 at that time began accruing cash balance credits under this formula.

•   •   •   •   •   •

The following table also sets forth the funded status of the plans and amounts recognized in the consolidated balance sheets at December 31, 2009 and 2008, based on a measurement date of December 31 for each period.

Obligations, Assets and Funded Status

(In millions)	Qualified U.S. Retirement Plans		Nonqualified U.S. and Non-U.S. Retirement Plans		Postretirement Benefits	
	2009	2008	2009	2008	2009	2008
Change in benefit obligation:						
Benefit obligation at beginning of year	$2,404	$2,324	$ 180	$ 188	$ 116	$ 124
Service cost	42	40	4	4	3	3
Interest cost	144	142	11	10	7	7
Actuarial loss (gain)	107	56	14	6	3	(3)
Plan amendments	(37)	2	(3)	—	(6)	—
Foreign currency exchange rate changes	—	—	7	(18)	1	—
Employee contributions	—	—	—	—	7	14
Termination benefit costs	25	9	—	—	—	—
Curtailments	1	(2)	1	—	—	—
Benefits paid (including termination benefits)	(226)	(167)	(18)	(10)	(24)	(29)
Benefit obligation at end of year	$2,460	$2,404	$ 196	$ 180	$ 107	$ 116
Change in plan assets:						
Fair value of plan assets at beginning of year	$3,038	$3,538	$ 49	$ 69	$ —	$ —
Actual return on plan assets	586	(333)	7	(6)	—	—
Company contributions	—	—	20	12	17	15
Foreign currency exchange rate changes	—	—	6	(16)	—	—
Employee contributions	—	—	—	—	7	14
Benefits paid (including termination benefits)	(226)	(167)	(18)	(10)	(24)	(29)
Fair value of plan assets at end of year	$3,398	$3,038	$ 64	$ 49	$ —	$ —
Over (under) funded status at end of year	$ 938	$ 634	$(132)	$(131)	$(107)	$(116)
Amounts recognized in the balance sheet consist of:						
Noncurrent assets—prepaid pension asset	$ 938	$ 634	$ —	$ —	$ —	$ —
Current liabilities	—	—	(10)	(6)	(14)	(14)
Noncurrent liabilities	—	—	(122)	(125)	(93)	(102)
Total net pension asset (liability)	$ 938	$ 634	$(132)	$(131)	$(107)	$(116)
Amounts recognized in accumulated other comprehensive income (loss) (pre-tax) consist of:						
Net actuarial loss (gain)	$ 302	$ 516	$ 42	$ 34	$ (19)	$ (18)
Prior service cost (benefit)	4	36	(4)	(2)	(35)	(31)
Total loss (gain) recognized in accumulated other comprehensive income (loss)	$ 306	$ 552	$ 38	$ 32	$ (54)	$ (49)

The accumulated benefit obligation for all defined benefit plans was $2.58 billion and $2.49 billion at December 31, 2009 and 2008, respectively.

Information for pension plans with an accumulated benefit obligation in excess of plan assets as of December 31:

(In millions)	2009	2008
Projected benefit obligation	$155	$148
Accumulated benefit obligation	142	130
Fair value of plan assets	20	16

Assumptions

The weighted average assumptions used to determine the company's benefit obligations at December 31:

	2009	2008
Retirement benefits:		
Discount rate	5.74%	6.25%
Rate of compensation increase	3.98%	3.98%
Postretirement benefits:		
Discount rate	5.75%	6.26%
Healthcare cost increase	7.76%	7.99%
Prescription drug cost increase	8.99%	9.47%

●　　●　　●　　●　　●　　●

MeadWestvaco's approach to developing capital market assumptions combines an analysis of historical performance, the drivers of investment performance by asset class and current economic fundamentals. For returns, the company utilizes a building block approach starting with an inflation expectation and adds an expected real return to arrive at a long-term nominal expected return for each asset class. Long-term expected real returns are derived in the context of future expectations for the U.S. Treasury real yield curve. The company derives return assumptions for all other equity and fixed income asset classes by starting with either the U.S. Equity or U.S. Fixed Income return assumption and adding a risk premium, which reflects any additional risk inherent in the asset class.

The company determined the discount rates for 2009, 2008, and 2007 by referencing the Citigroup Pension Discount Curve. The company believes that using a yield curve approach more accurately reflects changes in the present value of liabilities over time since each cash flow is discounted at the rate at which it could effectively be settled.

Retirement Plan Assets

The MeadWestvaco U.S. retirement plan asset allocation at December 31, 2009 and 2008, long-term target allocation, and expected long-term rate of return by asset category are as follows:

	Target Allocation	Percentage of Plan Assets at December 31		Weighted Average Expected Long-Term Rate of Return
		2009	2008	2009
Asset category:				
Equity securities	40%	47%	38%	10.1%
Debt securities	50%	48%	56%	6.3%
Real estate and private equity	10%	5%	6%	12.5%
Total	100%	100%	100%	

The MeadWestvaco Master Retirement Trust maintains a well-diversified investment program through both the long-term allocation of trust fund assets among asset classes and the selection of investment managers whose various styles are fundamentally complementary to one another and serve to achieve satisfactory rates of return. Target asset allocation among asset classes is set through periodic asset/liability studies that emphasize protecting the funded status of the plan.

Portfolio risk and return is evaluated based on capital market assumptions for asset class long-term rates of return, volatility, and correlations. Target allocation to asset classes is set so that target expected asset returns modestly outperform expected liability growth while expected portfolio risk is low enough to make it unlikely that the funded status of the plan will drop below 100%. Active management of assets is used in asset classes and strategies where there is the potential to add value over a benchmark. The equity class of securities is expected to provide the long-term growth necessary to cover the growth of the plans' obligations.

Equity market risk is the most concentrated type of risk in the trust which has significant investments in common stock and in collective trusts with equity exposure. This risk is mitigated by maintaining diversification in geography and mar-ket capitalization. Investment manager guidelines limit the amount that can be invested in any one security. Approximately 13% of the trust's equity portfolio is hedged against equity market risk. The policy also allows allocation of funds to other asset classes that serve to enhance long-term, risk-adjusted return expectations.

Liquidity risk is present in the trust's investments in partnerships/joint ventures, real estate, registered investment companies, and 103-12 investment entities. The policy limits target allocations to these asset classes to 10%.

Concentrated interest rate risk, credit spread risk, and inflation risk are present in the trust's investments in government securities, corporate debt instruments, and common collective trusts. These investment risks are meant to offset the risks in the plan liabilities. Long-duration fixed income securities and interest rate swaps are used to better match the interest rate sensitivity of plan assets and liabilities. The portfolio's interest rate risk is hedged at approximately 75% of the value of the plans' accumulated benefit obligation. The tabular percentages above exclude the market value of the interest rate hedge used in rebalancing the asset allocation targets. Treasury inflation protected securities are used to better match inflation risk of plan assets and liabilities. Corporate debt instruments mitigate the credit risk in the discount rate used to value the plan liabilities. Investment risk is measured and monitored on an ongoing basis through annual liability measurements, periodic asset/liability studies and quarterly investment portfolio reviews. A portion of the overall fund will remain in short-term fixed income investments in order to meet the ongoing operating cash requirements of the plans.

Derivatives

2.141

BALL CORPORATION (DEC)

($ in millions)	2009	2008
Total current assets	$1,923.3	$2,165.3
Property, plant and equipment, net	1,949.0	1,866.9
Goodwill	2,114.8	1,825.5
Noncurrent derivative contracts (Note 21)	80.6	139.0
Intangibles and other assets, net	420.6	372.0
Total assets	$6,488.3	$6,368.7

NOTES TO CONSOLIDATED FINANCIAL STATEMENTS

1 (In Part): Critical and Significant Accounting Policies

Critical Accounting Policies (In Part)

Derivative Financial Instruments

The company uses derivative financial instruments for the purpose of hedging exposures to fluctuations in interest rates, foreign currency exchange rates, raw materials purchasing, inflation rates and common share repurchases. The company's derivative instruments are recorded in the consolidated balance sheets at fair value. For a derivative designated as a cash flow hedge, the effective portion of the derivative's gain or loss is initially reported as a component of accumulated other comprehensive earnings and subsequently reclassified into earnings when the forecasted transaction affects earnings. The ineffective portion of the gain or loss associated with all hedges is reported in earnings immediately. Derivatives that do not qualify for hedge accounting are marked to market with gains and losses also reported immediately in earnings. In the statements of cash flows, derivative activities are classified based on the items being hedged. The accounting for our cash collateral calls related to our derivative activities are classified as investing activities as discussed in Note 9.

Realized gains and losses from hedges are classified in the consolidated statements of earnings consistent with the accounting treatment of the items being hedged. Upon the early dedesignation of an effective derivative contract, the gains or losses are deferred in accumulated other comprehensive earnings until the originally hedged item affects earnings. Any gains or losses incurred after the dedesignation date are reported in earnings immediately.

21 (In Part): Financial Instruments and Risk Management

Policies and Procedures

In the ordinary course of business, Ball employs established risk management policies and procedures, which seek to reduce Ball's exposure to fluctuations in commodity prices, interest rates, foreign currencies and prices of the company's common stock in regard to common share repurchases, although there can be no assurance that these policies and procedures will be successful. Although the instruments utilized involve varying degrees of credit, market and interest risk, the counterparties to the agreements are expected to perform fully under the terms of the agreements. The company monitors counterparty credit risk, including lenders, on a regular basis, but Ball cannot be certain that all risks will be discerned or that its risk management policies and procedures will always be effective.

Commodity Price Risk

Ball's metal beverage container operations in North America, Europe and Asia manage commodity price risk in connection with market price fluctuations of aluminum ingot through two different methods. First, the company enters into container sales contracts that include aluminum ingot-based pricing terms that generally reflect price fluctuations under our commercial supply contracts for aluminum sheet purchases. The terms include fixed, floating or pass-through aluminum ingot component pricing. This matched pricing affects most of Ball's North American metal beverage packaging net sales. Second, Ball uses certain derivative instruments such as option and forward contracts as cash flow hedges of commodity price risk where there is not a pass-through arrangement in the sales contract to match underlying purchase volumes and pricing with sales volumes and pricing.

Most of the plastic packaging, Americas, sales contracts include provisions to fully pass through resin cost changes. As a result, Ball has minimal exposure related to changes in the cost of plastic resin. Most metal food and household products packaging, Americas, sales contracts either include provisions permitting Ball to pass through some or all steel cost changes incurred, or they incorporate annually negotiated steel costs. In 2009 and 2008, Ball was able to pass through to customers the majority of steel cost increases. Ball anticipates at this time that it will be able to pass through the majority of the steel price increases that occur over the next 12 months.

The company had aluminum contracts limiting its aluminum exposure with notional amounts of approximately $1.1 billion and $1.4 billion at December 31, 2009 and 2008, respectively. The aluminum contracts include derivative instruments that are undesignated and receive mark-to-market accounting, as well as cash flow hedges that offset sales contracts of various terms and lengths. Cash flow hedges relate to forecasted transactions that expire within the next four years. Included in shareholders' equity at December 31, 2009, within accumulated other comprehensive earnings is a net after-tax gain of $27.2 million associated with these contracts. However, a net loss of $2.9 million is expected to be recognized in the consolidated statement of earnings during the next 12 months, which will be passed through to customers by higher revenue from sales contracts resulting in no earnings impact to Ball.

During the fourth quarter of 2008, Ball recorded a pre-tax charge of $11.5 million for mark-to-market losses related to aluminum derivative instruments, which were no longer deemed highly effective for hedge accounting purposes. These losses were largely recovered in 2009 through customer contracts.

Interest Rate Risk

Ball's objective in managing exposure to interest rate changes is to minimize the impact of interest rate changes on earnings and cash flows and to lower our overall borrowing costs. To achieve these objectives, Ball uses a variety of interest rate swaps, collars and options to manage our mix of floating and fixed-rate debt. Interest rate instruments held by the company at December 31, 2009, included pay-fixed interest rate swaps and interest rate collars. Pay-fixed swaps effectively convert variable rate obligations to fixed rate instruments. Collars create an upper and lower threshold within which interest rates will fluctuate.

At December 31, 2009, the company had outstanding interest rate swap agreements in Europe with notional amounts of €135 million ($193.5 million) paying fixed rates expiring within the next three years. An approximate $5.2 million net after-tax loss associated with these contracts is included in accumulated other comprehensive earnings at December 31, 2009, of which $4.6 million is expected to be recognized in the consolidated statement of earnings during the next 12 months. At December 31, 2009, the company had outstanding interest rate collars in the U.S. totaling $50 million that expired at the end of January 2010. Ball additionally has $100 million of forward rate agreements expiring in February 2010. The value of these contracts in accumulated other comprehensive earnings at December 31, 2009, was insignificant. Approximately $2.1 million of net gain related to the termination or dedesignation of hedges is included in accumulated other comprehensive earnings at December 31, 2009. The amount recognized in 2009 earnings related to the dedesignation of hedges was insignificant.

Ball also uses inflation option contracts in Europe to limit the impacts from spikes in inflation against certain multi-year contracts. At December 31, 2009, the company had inflation options in Europe with notional amounts of €115 million ($164.8 million). These options are undesignated for hedge accounting purposes and receive mark-to-market accounting. The fair value at December 31, 2009, was €1 million and the option contracts expire within the next three years.

The fair value of derivatives generally reflects the estimated amounts that we would pay or receive upon termination of the contracts at December 31, taking into account any unrealized gains and losses on open contracts. The unrealized pretax loss on interest rate derivative contracts was $7.3 million and $10.6 million at December 31, 2009 and 2008, respectively.

Foreign Currency Exchange Rate Risk

Ball's objective in managing exposure to foreign currency fluctuations is to protect foreign cash flows and earnings from changes associated with foreign currency exchange rate changes through the use of various derivative contracts. In addition, at times Ball manages foreign earnings translation volatility through the use of foreign currency option strategies, and the change in the fair value of those options is recorded in the company's net earnings. Ball's foreign currency translation risk results from the European euro, British pound, Canadian dollar, Polish zloty, Chinese renminbi, Hong Kong dollar, Brazilian real, Argentine peso and Serbian dinar. Ball faces currency exposures in our global operations as a result of purchasing raw materials in U.S. dollars and, to a lesser extent, in other currencies. Sales contracts are negotiated with customers to reflect cost changes and, where there is not a foreign exchange pass-through arrangement, the company uses forward and option contracts to manage foreign currency exposures. Such contracts outstanding at December 31, 2009, expire within 12 months, and the amounts included in accumulated other comprehensive earnings related to these contracts were not significant.

Fair Value Measurements

Ball has classified all applicable financial derivative assets and liabilities as Level 2 within the fair value hierarchy as of December 31, 2009 and 2008, and presented those values in the table below. The company's assessment of the significance of a particular input to the fair value measurement requires judgment and may affect the valuation of fair value assets and liabilities and their placement within the fair value hierarchy levels. The fair value of debt is discussed in Note 15 to the consolidated financial statements.

The company uses closing spot and forward market prices as published by the London Metal Exchange, the New York Mercantile Exchange, Reuters and Bloomberg to determine the fair value of its aluminum, currency, energy, inflation and interest rate spot and forward contracts. Option contracts are valued using a Black-Scholes model with observable market inputs for aluminum, currency and interest rates. We do not obtain multiple quotes to determine the value for our financial instruments, as we value each of our financial instruments either internally using a single valuation technique or from a reliable observable market source. The company also does not adjust the value of its financial instruments except in determining the fair value of a trade that settles in the future by discounting the value to its present value using 12-month LIBOR as the discount factor. Ball performs validations of our internally derived fair values reported for our financial instruments on a quarterly basis utilizing counterparty valuation statements. The company additionally evaluates counterparty creditworthiness and, as of December 31, 2009, has not identified any circumstances requiring that the reported values of our financial instruments be adjusted.

At December 31, 2009, the company's investment in shares of DigitalGlobe (as discussed in Note 4) was measured using Level 1 inputs, and net receivables totaling $11.2 million related to the European scrap metal program were classified as Level 2 within the fair value hierarchy.

Fair Value of Derivative Instruments as of December 31, 2009

($ in millions)	Derivatives Designated as Hedging Instruments	Derivatives Not Designated as Hedging Instruments	Total
Assets:			
Commodity contracts	$36.2	$51.7	$ 87.9
Foreign currency contracts	0.1	12.1	12.2
Total current derivative contracts	$36.3	$63.8	$100.1
Noncurrent commodity contracts	$40.1	$39.1	$ 79.2
Other contracts	—	1.4	1.4
Total noncurrent derivative contracts	$40.1	$40.5	$ 80.6
Liabilities:			
Commodity contracts	$27.5	$51.9	$ 79.4
Foreign currency contracts	0.6	3.2	3.8
Total current derivative contracts	$28.1	$55.1	$ 83.2
Noncurrent commodity contracts	$ 1.9	$38.9	$ 40.8
Interest rate contracts	7.2	—	7.2
Total noncurrent derivative contracts	$ 9.1	$38.9	$ 48.0

Segregated Funds

2.142

JUNIPER NETWORKS, INC. (DEC)

(In thousands)	2009	2008
Total current assets	$7,590,263	$7,590,263
Property and equipment, net	455,651	436,433
Long-term investments	483,505	101,415
Restricted cash	53,732	43,442
Purchased intangible assets, net	13,834	28,861
Goodwill	3,658,602	3,658,602
Long-term deferred tax assets, net	10,555	71,079
Other long-term assets	35,425	31,303
Total assets	$7,590,263	$7,187,341

NOTES TO CONSOLIDATED FINANCIAL STATEMENTS

Note 3 (In Part): Cash, Cash Equivalents, and Investments

Restricted Cash

Restricted cash as of December 31, 2009, consisted of escrow accounts required by certain acquisitions completed in 2005, the D&O indemnification trust, and the India Gratuity Trust. The India Gratuity Trust was established in 2008 to cover statutory severance obligations in the event of termination of its India employees who have provided five or more years of continuous service. The D&O trust was established to secure the Company's indemnification obligations to certain directors, officers, and other specified employees, arising from their activities as such, in the event that the Company does not provide or is financially incapable of providing indemnification. In 2009, the Company distributed $1.0 million of its restricted cash in connection with the escrow fund associated with the acquisition of Funk Software. The Company also increased its restricted cash by an aggregate of $11.3 million to fund both its India Gratuity and D&O Trusts due to overall growth of the Company. In 2008, the Company made no distributions from restricted cash and increased its restricted cash by an aggregate of $8.1 million to fund both the India Gratuity and D&O Trusts due to overall growth of the Company.

The following table summarizes the Company's restricted cash as reported in the consolidated balance sheets (in millions):

	2009	2008
Restricted cash:		
Demand deposits	$ 3.8	$ 0.8
Time deposits	—	—
Total restricted cash	3.8	0.8
Restricted investments:		
U.S. government securities	19.8	1.6
Government-sponsored enterprise obligations	—	20.0
Corporate debt securities	—	6.0
Money market funds	30.1	15.0
Total restricted investments	49.9	42.6
Total restricted cash and investments	$53.7	$43.4

As of December 31, 2009, and 2008, the unrealized gain and losses related to restricted investments were immaterial.

Note 4 (In Part): Fair Value Measurements

Fair Value Hierarchy

The Company determines the fair values of its financial instruments based on the fair value hierarchy, which requires an entity to maximize the use of observable inputs and minimize the use of unobservable inputs when measuring fair value. Fair value is defined as the price that would be received to sell an asset or paid to transfer a liability in an orderly transaction between market participants at the measurement date. The fair value assumes that the transaction to sell the asset or transfer the liability occurs in the principal or most advantageous market for the asset or liability and establishes that the fair value of an asset or liability shall be determined based on the assumptions that market participants would use in pricing the asset or liability. The classification of a financial asset or liability within the hierarchy is based upon the lowest level input that is significant to the fair value measurement. The fair value hierarchy prioritizes the inputs into three levels that may be used to measure fair value:

- Level 1—Inputs are unadjusted quoted prices in active markets for identical assets or liabilities.
- Level 2—Inputs are quoted prices for similar assets and liabilities in active markets or inputs that are observable for the asset or liability, either directly or indirectly through market corroboration, for substantially the full term of the financial instrument.
- Level 3—Inputs are unobservable inputs based on the Company's assumptions.

Assets and Liabilities Measured at Fair Value on a Recurring Basis

The following tables provide a summary of the assets and liabilities measured at fair value on a recurring basis (in millions):

	Fair Value Measurements at December 31, 2009, Using			
	Quoted Prices in Active Markets for Identical Assets (Level 1)	Significant Other Observable Remaining Inputs (Level 2)	Significant Other Unobservable Remaining Inputs (Level 3)	Total
Assets measured at fair value:				
U.S. government securities[1]	$ 72.6	$192.3	$—	$ 264.9
Government-sponsored enterprise obligations	193.3	19.0	—	212.3
Foreign government debt securities	26.3	70.3	—	96.6
Corporate debt securities	—	489.9	—	489.9
Commercial paper	—	17.0	—	17.0
Money market funds[2]	1,062.7	—	—	1,062.7
Publicly-traded securities	10.1	—	—	10.1
Total assets	1,365.0	788.5	—	2,153.5
Liabilities measured at fair value:				
Derivative liability	—	(1.3)	—	(1.3)
Total liabilities	—	(1.3)	—	(1.3)
Total	$1,365.0	$787.2	$—	$2,152.2

[1] Balance includes $19.8 million of restricted investments measured at fair market value, related to the Company's Directors and Officers ("D&O") indemnification trust. For additional information regarding the D&O trust, see Note 3, *Cash, Cash Equivalents, and Investments,* under the heading "Restricted Cash." Restricted investments are included in the restricted cash balance in the consolidated balance sheet.
[2] Balance includes $30.1 million of restricted investments measured at fair market value, related to the Company's D&O trust.

	Fair Value Measurements at December 31, 2008, Using			
	Quoted Prices in Active Markets for Identical Assets (Level 1)	Significant Other Observable Remaining Inputs (Level 2)	Significant Other Unobservable Remaining Inputs (Level 3)	Total
Assets measured at fair value:				
U.S. government securities[1]	$ 26.3	$203.8	$—	$ 230.1
Government-sponsored enterprise obligations[2]	71.9	114.8	—	186.7
Corporate debt securities[3]	—	116.3	—	116.3
Commercial paper	—	90.4	—	90.4
Money market funds[4]	1,296.1	—	—	1,296.1
Publicly-traded securities	5.4	—	—	5.4
Derivative asset	—	2.6	—	2.6
Total	$1,399.7	$527.9	$—	$1,927.6

[1] Balance includes $1.6 million of restricted investments measured at fair market value, related to an acquisition completed in 2005.
[2] Balance includes $20.0 million of restricted investments measured at fair market value, related to the Company's D&O trust.
[3] Balance includes $6.0 million of restricted investments measured at fair market value, related to the Company's D&O trust.
[4] Balance includes $15.0 million of restricted investments measured at fair market value, related to the Company's D&O trust.

Assets and liabilities measured at fair value on a recurring basis are presented on the Company's consolidated balance sheets as follows (in millions):

	Fair Value Measurements at December 31, 2009, Using			
	Quoted Prices in Active Markets for Identical Assets (Level 1)	Significant Other Observable Remaining Inputs (Level 2)	Significant Other Unobservable Remaining Inputs (Level 3)	Total
Reported as:				
Cash equivalents	$1,032.6	$ 17.0	$—	$1,049.6
Short-term investments	101.3	469.2	—	570.5
Long-term investments	181.2	302.3	—	483.5
Restricted cash	49.9	—	—	49.9
Other accrued liabilities	—	(1.3)	—	(1.3)
Total	$1,365.0	$787.2	$—	$2,152.2

	Fair Value Measurements at December 31, 2008, Using			
	Quoted Prices in Active Markets for Identical Assets (Level 1)	Significant Other Observable Remaining Inputs (Level 2)	Significant Other Unobservable Remaining Inputs (Level 3)	Total
Reported as:				
Cash equivalents	$1,281.1	$327.0	$—	$1,608.1
Short-term investments	57.1	115.8	—	172.9
Long-term investments	46.5	54.9	—	101.4
Restricted cash	15.0	27.6	—	42.6
Other assets	—	2.6	—	2.6
Total	$1,399.7	$527.9	$—	$1,927.6

Software Development Costs

2.143

BMC SOFTWARE, INC. (MAR)

(In millions)	2009	2008
Total current assets	$1,560.5	$1,802.6
Property and equipment, net	103.0	99.8
Software development costs	122.6	113.4
Long-term investments	72.3	124.7
Long-term trade finance receivables, net	92.1	56.4
Intangible assets, net	189.9	46.8
Goodwill	1,288.7	756.5
Other long-term assets	268.4	345.3
Total assets	$3,697.5	$3,345.5

NOTES TO CONSOLIDATED FINANCIAL STATEMENTS

1 (In Part): Summary of Significant Accounting Policies

Long-Lived Assets (In Part)

Software Development Costs

Costs of software developed internally for licensing to third-parties are expensed until the technological feasibility of the software product has been established. Thereafter, software development costs are capitalized through the general release of the software products and subsequently reported at the lower of unamortized cost or net realizable value. Capitalized software development costs are amortized on a straight-line basis over the products' respective estimated economic lives, which are typically three years. The amortization of capitalized software development costs, including amounts accelerated for products that were not expected to generate sufficient future revenue to realize their carrying values, is included in cost of license revenue in the consolidated statements of operations. During fiscal 2009, 2008 and 2007, amounts capitalized were $72.5 million, $71.8 million and $55.4 million, respectively, amounts amortized were $62.9 million, $64.5 million and $64.2 million, respectively, and the change in foreign exchange rates impacted capitalized software development costs by $(0.4) million, $2.0 million and $2.1 million, respectively. Amounts capitalized during fiscal 2009 included $1.7 million of capitalized interest.

2.144

CENTURYTEL, INC. (DEC)

(Dollars in thousands)	2009	2008
Total current assets	$ 1,123,591	$ 555,407
Net property, plant and equipment	9,097,139	2,895,892
Goodwill and other assets		
Goodwill	10,251,758	4,015,674
Other intangible assets		
Customer list	1,130,817	146,283
Other	315,601	42,750
Other assets	643,823	598,189
Total goodwill and other assets	12,341,999	4,802,896
Total assets	$22,562,729	$8,254,195

NOTES TO CONSOLIDATED FINANCIAL STATEMENTS

3 (In Part): Goodwill and Other Assets

Goodwill and other assets at December 31, 2009 and 2008 were composed of the following:

(Dollars in thousands)	2009	2008
Goodwill	$10,251,758	$4,015,674
Intangible assets subject to amortization		
Customer list, less accumulated amortization of $148,491 and $35,026	1,130,817	146,283
Other, less accumulated amortization of $22,466	47,101	42,750
Intangible assets not subject to amortization	268,500	—
Billing system development costs, less accumulated amortization of $61,672 and $49,979	174,872	181,210
Investment in 700 MHz wireless spectrum licenses	149,425	148,964
Cash surrender value of life insurance contracts	100,945	96,606
Deferred costs associated with installation activities	91,865	77,202
Investment in unconsolidated cellular partnership	32,679	33,662
Other	94,037	60,545
	$12,341,999	$4,802,896

We accounted for the costs to develop an integrated billing and customer care system in accordance with Statement of Position 98-1, "Accounting for the Costs of Computer Software Developed or Obtained for Internal Use." Aggregate capitalized costs (before accumulated amortization) totaled $236.5 million and are being amortized over a twenty-year period.

Debt Issue Costs

2.145

NEWMARKET CORPORATION (DEC)

(In thousands)	2009	2008
Total current assets	$ 603,139	$446,178
Property, plant, and equipment, at cost	934,382	848,011
Less accumulated depreciation and amortization	631,967	606,275
Net property, plant, and equipment	302,415	241,736
Prepaid pension cost	2,430	159
Deferred income taxes	34,670	37,744
Other assets and deferred charges	37,475	31,566
Intangibles, net of amortization and goodwill	45,063	54,069
Total assets	$1,025,192	$811,452

*NOTES TO CONSOLIDATED FINANCIAL STATEMENTS
(Tabular amounts in thousands)*

10 (In Part): Other Assets and Deferred Charges

	2009	2008
Interest rate swap deposits	$15,283	$ —
Foundry Park I deferred leasing costs	5,528	3,858
Deferred financing costs, net of amortization	3,946	4,728
Interest rate lock agreement deposits	—	10,500
Other	12,718	12,480
	$37,475	$31,566

The accumulated amortization on the deferred financing fees relating to our 7.125% senior notes and senior credit facility was $6 million at December 31, 2009 and $5 million at December 31, 2008. We incurred $500 thousand of additional deferred financing fees in 2009 related to the senior credit facility. See Note 13 in the Notes to Consolidated Financial Statements for further information on our long-term debt.

13 (In Part): Long-Term Debt

Senior Credit Facility (In Part)

On December 21, 2006, we entered into a Second Amended and Restated Credit Agreement. This credit agreement amended and restated the credit agreement that we entered into on June 18, 2004. We incurred additional financing costs of approximately $600 thousand, which resulted in the total unamortized deferred financing costs of approximately $3 million related to the senior credit facility. These costs are being amortized over five years.

Beginning in late 2008, we entered into several additional agreements related to the Second Amended and Restated Credit Agreement. These additional agreements were as follows:

- On December 22, 2008, we entered into a Supplement Agreement to the Second Amended and Restated Credit Agreement to increase the commitment level by $7 million.
- On January 5, 2009, we entered into another Supplement Agreement to increase the commitment level by an additional $5 million.
- On March 24, 2009, we entered into a Second Amendment to the Second Amended and Restated Revolving Credit Agreement (Second Amendment). The Second Amendment increased the commitment level by an additional $5 million, increased the letter of credit commitment level from $50 million to $75 million, increased the interest rate paid for borrowings, and amended certain defined terms and covenant calculations.
- Also, on March 24, 2009, we entered into a Supplement Agreement to the Second Amended and Restated Revolving Credit Agreement to increase the commitment level of the revolving credit facility by $2.25 million.
- On April 20, 2009, we entered into an agreement to add an additional lender under the revolving credit facility and increase the commitment level by $10 million.
- Subsequently, on June 30, 2009, that lender increased its commitment level by another $10 million.
- On December 7, 2009, we entered into an agreement to add an additional lender under the revolving credit facility and increase the commitment level by $10.75 million.
- On December 30, 2009, we entered into a Third Amendment to the Second Amended and Restated Revolving Credit Agreement (Third Amendment). The Third Amendment amends the definition of Subsidiary; allows liens on cash in an amount not to exceed $20 million specifically related to the Foundry Park rate lock transactions; allows investments in Real Estate Subsidiaries (as defined in the Second Amended and Restated Credit Agreement) not to exceed $55 million; and provides that transactions with the Charitable Foundation (as defined in the Third Amendment) will not be considered transactions with an Affiliate (as defined in the Second Amended and Restated Credit Agreement).

We paid financing costs in 2009 and late 2008 of approximately $700 thousand related to these agreements, and we are amortizing these deferred financing costs over the remaining term of the credit agreement.

Property Held for Sale

2.146

DANA HOLDING CORPORATION (DEC)

(In millions)	2009	2008
Total current assets	$2,582	$2,747
Goodwill	111	108
Intangibles	438	515
Investments and other assets	233	200
Investments in affiliates	112	119
Property, plant and equipment, net	1,484	1,636
Non-current assets held for sale	104	282
Total assets	$5,064	$5,607

NOTES TO CONSOLIDATED FINANCIAL STATEMENTS
(In millions)

Note 2 (In Part): Divestitures and Acquisitions

Structural Products Business

In December 2009, we entered into an agreement with Metalsa S.A. de C.V. (Metalsa) to sell substantially all of our Structural Products business to Metalsa. We had previously evaluated a number of strategic options in our non-driveline light vehicle businesses and had concluded that this product line was not strategic to our core driveline business. Dana will retain a facility of this business in Longview, Texas and will continue to produce products for a large customer at this facility. Accordingly, we have not reported the Structures segment as discontinued operations. The parties expect to complete the sale of all but the Venezuelan operations in March 2010, with Venezuela being completed as soon as the necessary governmental approvals are obtained.

As a result of this agreement we recorded $150 as an impairment of the intangible and long-lived assets in December 2009 and we recorded strategic transaction expenses of $11 associated with the sale in other income, net. The impairment loss was based on expected proceeds of $150 less projected working capital adjustments. Under the terms of our amended Term Facility, we will be required to utilize the proceeds of the sale to pay down our Term Facility debt.

The assets to be sold in this transaction are reported as assets held for sale in our consolidated balance sheet and consist of the following:

	2009	2008
Assets		
Accounts receivable	$ 62	$ 69
Inventories	34	46
Other current assets	3	6
Current assets held for sale	$ 99	$121
Intangibles	16	54
Investments and other assets	6	7
Investments in affiliates	17	16
Property, plant and equipment, net	65	205
Non-current assets held for sale	$104	$282
Liabilities		
Accounts payable	$ 54	$ 65
Accrued payroll	7	8
Other accrued liabilities	18	16
Current liabilities held for sale	$ 79	$ 89

Cash Value of Life Insurance

2.147

STEELCASE INC. (FEB)

(In millions)	2009	2008
Total current assets	$ 751.4	$ 934.7
Property, plant and equipment, net of accumulated depreciation of $1,280.3 and $1,290.1	433.3	478.4
Company-owned life insurance	171.6	210.6
Deferred income taxes	108.9	125.9
Goodwill	181.1	252.1
Other intangible assets, net of accumulated amortization of $50.2 and $64.7	29.6	48.9
Other assets	74.1	73.8
Total assets	$1,750.0	$2,124.4

NOTES TO CONSOLIDATED FINANCIAL STATEMENTS
(Dollars in millions)

7. Company-Owned Life Insurance

Investments in company-owned life insurance policies ("COLI") were made with the intention of utilizing them as a long-term funding source for post-retirement medical benefits, deferred compensation and supplemental retirement plan obligations, which as of February 27, 2009 aggregated $165.5, with a related deferred tax asset of $63.4. However, they do not represent a committed funding source for these obligations. They are subject to claims from creditors, and we can designate them to another purpose at any time. The policies are recorded at their net cash surrender values, as reported by the four issuing insurance companies, whose Standard & Poor's financial strength ratings range from AA- to AAA. The net cash surrender values totaled $171.6 as of February 27, 2009 and $210.6 as of February 29, 2008.

A summary of investments in COLI as of February 27, 2009 and February 29, 2008 is as follows:

Type	Ability to Choose Investments	Net Return	Target Asset Allocation	2009	2008
Whole life insurance policies	No ability	A set dividend rate periodically adjusted by insurance companies	Not applicable	$103.9	$100.8
Variable life insurance policies	Can allocate across a set of choices provided by the insurance companies	Fluctuates depending on changes in market interest rates and equity values	25% fixed income 75% equity	67.7	109.8
				$171.6	$210.6

During 2009, our cash surrender value of COLI declined ($39.0), of which ($42.1) related to significant declines in equity investments within our variable life insurance policies. The net returns in cash surrender value, normal insurance expenses and any death benefit gains are generally allocated 60% to *Cost of sales* and 40% to *Operating expenses* on the Consolidated Statements of Operations. This allocation is consistent with the costs associated with the long-term employee benefit obligations that COLI is intended to fund. The net effect of these items resulted in a non-tax deductible loss of ($36.6) in 2009, and non-taxable income in 2008 and 2007 of approximately $4.1 and $15.9, respectively.

Contracts

2.148

FIDELITY NATIONAL INFORMATION SERVICES, INC. (DEC)

(In millions)	2009	2008
Total current assets	$ 1,666.1	$1,166.2
Property and equipment, net	375.9	272.6
Goodwill	8,232.9	4,194.0
Intangible assets, net	2,396.8	924.3
Computer software, net	932.7	617.0
Deferred contract costs	261.4	241.2
Long term note receivable from FNF	—	5.5
Other noncurrent assets	131.8	79.6
Total assets	$13,997.6	$7,500.4

NOTES TO CONSOLIDATED FINANCIAL STATEMENTS

3 (In Part): Summary of Significant Accounting Policies

k. Deferred Contract Costs

Costs of software sales and outsourced data processing and application management arrangements, including costs incurred for bid and proposal activities, are generally expensed as incurred. However, certain costs incurred upon initiation of a contract are deferred and expensed over the contract life. These costs represent incremental external costs or certain specific internal costs that are directly related to the contract acquisition or transition activities and are primarily associated with installation of systems/processes and data conversion.

In the event indications exist that a particular deferred contract cost balance may be impaired, undiscounted estimated cash flows of the contract are projected over its remaining term and compared to the unamortized deferred contract cost balance. If the projected cash flows are not adequate to recover the unamortized cost balance, the balance would be adjusted to equal the contract's net realizable value, including any termination fees provided for under the contract, in the period such a determination is made.

12. Deferred Contract Costs

A summary of deferred contract costs as of December 31, 2009 and 2008 was as follows (in millions):

	2009	2008
Installations and conversions in progress	$ 31.8	$ 22.5
Installations and conversions completed, net	193.5	181.0
Other, net	36.1	37.7
Total deferred contract costs	$261.4	$241.2

Amortization of deferred contract costs was $49.4 million, $39.8 million and $34.8 million for the years ended December 31, 2009, 2008 and 2007 respectively. Included in discontinued operations in the Consolidated Statements of Earnings was amortization expense on deferred contract costs of $1.1 million and $2.0 million for the years ended December 31, 2008 and 2007, respectively.

Turnaround Costs

2.149

TERRA INDUSTRIES INC. (DEC)

(In thousands)	2009	2008
Total current assets	$ 826,302	$1,392,464
Property, plant and equipment, net	456,702	403,313
Equity method investments	258,860	270,915
Deferred plant turnaround costs, net	25,011	23,467
Other assets	32,868	22,858
Total assets	$1,599,743	$2,113,017

NOTES TO CONSOLIDATED FINANCIAL STATEMENTS

1 (In Part): Summary of Significant Accounting Policies

Plant Turnaround Costs

Plant turnarounds are periodically performed to extend the useful life, increase output and/or efficiency and ensure the long-term reliability and safety of integrated plant machinery at our continuous process production facilities. The nature of a turnaround is such that it occurs on less than an annual basis and requires a multi-week shutdown of plant operations. Specific procedures performed during the turnaround include the disassembly, inspection and replacement or overhaul of plant machinery (boilers, pressure vessels, piping, heat exchangers, etc.) and rotating equipment (compressors, pumps, turbines, etc.), equipment recalibration and internal equipment efficiency assessments.

Preceding a turnaround, plants experience decreased efficiency in resource conversion to finished products. Replacement or overhaul of equipment and items such as compressors, turbines, pumps, motors, valves, piping and other parts that have an estimated useful life of at least two years, the internal assessment of production equipment, replacement of aged catalysts, and new installation/recalibration of measurement and control devices result in increased production output and/or improved plant efficiency after the turnaround. Turnaround activities are betterments that meet at least one of the following criteria: 1) extend the equipment useful life, or 2) increase the output and/or efficiency of the equipment. As a result, we follow the deferral method of accounting for these turnaround costs and thus they are capitalized and amortized over the period benefited, which is generally the

two-year period until the next turnaround. Turnaround activities may extend the useful life of the assets since the overhaul of heat exchangers, pressure vessels, compressors, turbines, pumps, motors, etc. allow the continued use beyond the original design. If criteria for betterment or useful life extension are not met, we expense the turnaround expenditures as repair and maintenance activities in the period performed.

In addition, state and certain other regulatory agencies require a scheduled biennial safety inspection of plant components, such as steam boilers and registered pressure vessels and piping, which can only be performed during the period of shut down. A full shutdown and dismantling of components of the plant is generally mandatory to facilitate the inspection and certification. We defer costs associated with regulatory safety inspection mandates that are incurred during the turnaround. These costs are amortized over the period benefited, which is generally the two-year period until the next turnaround.

During a turnaround event, there will also be routine repairs and maintenance activities performed for normal operating purposes. The routine repairs and maintenance costs are expensed as incurred. We do not classify routine repair and maintenance activities as part of the turnaround cost capitalization since they are not considered asset betterments.

The installation of major equipment items can occur at any time, but frequently occurs during scheduled plant outages, such as a turnaround. During a plant turnaround, expenditures for replacing major equipment items are capitalized as separate fixed assets.

We classify capitalized turnaround costs as an investing activity under the caption "Capital expenditures and plant turnaround expenditures" in the Statement of Cash Flows, since this cash outflow relates to expenditures related to productive assets. Repair, maintenance costs, and gas costs are expensed as incurred and are included in the operating cash flow.

There are three acceptable methods of accounting for turnaround costs: 1) direct expensing method, 2) built-in overhaul method and 3) deferral method. We utilize the deferral method and recognize turnaround expense over the period benefited since these expenditures are asset betterments. If the direct expense method was utilized, all turnaround expenditures would be recognized in the statement of operations as a period cost when incurred and reflected in cash flows from operating activities in the statement of cash flows.

10. Turnaround Costs

The following represents a summary of the deferred plant turnaround costs for the years ended December 31, 2009 and 2008:

(In thousands)	Beginning Balance	Turnaround Costs Capitalized	Turnaround Amortization	Currency Translation Adjustments	Ending Balance
Year ended:					
December 31, 2009	$23,467	$25,427	$(24,267)	$ 384	$25,011
December 31, 2008	42,190	10,125	(27,017)	(1,831)	23,467

CURRENT LIABILITIES

2.150   FASB ASC 210, *Balance Sheet*, discusses the nature of current liabilities. Examples of the various types of current liabilities follow.

SHORT-TERM DEBT

2.151   Table 2-22 lists the captions used by the survey entities to describe short-term notes payable, loans payable and commercial paper. By definition, such short-term obligations are financial instruments.

2.152   FASB ASC 825, *Financial Instruments*, requires disclosure of both the fair value and the bases for estimating the fair value of short-term notes payable, loans payable, and commercial paper unless it is not practicable to estimate that value.

2.153   FASB ASC 820, *Fair Value Measurements and Disclosures*, defines fair value, establishes a framework for measuring fair value, and requires certain disclosures about fair value measurements. FASB ASC 820 clarifies the definition of fair value as an exit price, i.e., a price that would be received to sell, as opposed to acquire, an asset or transfer a liability. FASB ASC 820 emphasizes that fair value is a market-based measurement. It establishes a fair value hierarchy that distinguishes between assumptions developed based on market data obtained from independent external sources and the reporting entity's own assumptions. Further, FASB ASC 820 specifies that fair value measurement should consider adjustment for risk, such as the risk inherent in a valuation technique or its inputs. For assets measured at fair value, whether on a recurring or a nonrecurring basis, FASB ASC 820 specifies the required disclosures concerning the inputs used to measure fair value. FASB Accounting Standards Update (ASU) No. 2010-06, *Improving Disclosures about Fair Value Measurements*, requires more robust disclosures about different classes of assets and liabilities measured at fair value, the valuation techniques and inputs used, the activity in Level 3 fair value measurements, and the transfers between Levels 1, 2, and 3. FASB ASU No. 2010-06 is effective for fiscal years beginning after December 15, 2009, except for the disclosures about certain Level 3 activity. Those disclosures are effective for fiscal years beginning after December 15, 2010. During 2009, 193 survey companies made 258 disclosures of fair value related to short-term debt. 28 of those disclosures were based on the quoted price of the identical item in an active market (level 1 input). 40 of those disclosures were primarily based on other market-corroborated (level 2) inputs. 3 disclosures estimated fair value using nonmarket-corroborated (level 3) inputs. 137 disclosures presented carrying amounts which approximated fair value of short-term debt. In addition, there were 49 disclosures in which carrying value was compared to fair value in an exposition or a table.

2.154   FASB ASC 825, *Financial Instruments*, permits entities to choose to measure many financial instruments and certain other items at fair value that are not currently required to be measured at fair value. Further, under FASB ASC 825 a business entity shall report unrealized gains and losses on eligible items for which the fair value option has been elected in earnings at each subsequent reporting date. The irrevocable election of the fair value option is made on an instrument by instrument basis, and applied to the entire instrument, not just a portion of it. FASB ASC 825 also establishes presentation and disclosure requirements designed to facilitate comparison between entities that choose different measurement attributes for similar types of assets and liabilities.

2.155   Examples of short-term debt presentations and disclosures follow.

2.156

TABLE 2-22: SHORT-TERM DEBT*

Description	2009	2008	2007	2006
Notes or loans				
Payee indicated	22	19	29	22
Payee not indicated	61	60	78	77
Short-term debt or borrowings	113	138	135	133
Commercial paper	39	43	54	45
Credit agreements	39	43	40	38
Other	14	19	26	24
Total Presentations	**288**	**322**	**362**	**339**
	Number of Entities			
Showing short-term debt	243	263	297	293
Not showing short-term debt	257	237	303	307
Total Entities	**500**	**500**	**600**	**600**

* Appearing in either the balance sheet and/or the notes to financial statements.

2008–2009 based on 500 entities surveyed; 2006–2007 based on 600 entities surveyed.

2.157

BEST BUY CO., INC. (FEB)

($ in millions)	2009	2008
Current liabilities		
Accounts payable	$4,997	$4,297
Unredeemed gift card liabilities	479	531
Accrued compensation and related expenses	459	373
Accrued liabilities	1,382	975
Accrued income taxes	281	404
Short-term debt	783	156
Current portion of long-term debt	54	33
Total current liabilities	$8,435	$6,769
Long-term liabilities	$1,109	$ 838
Long-term debt	1,126	627
Minority interests	513	40

NOTES TO CONSOLIDATED FINANCIAL STATEMENTS
($ in millions)

Note 6 (In Part): Debt

Short-Term Debt

Short-term debt consisted of the following:

	2009		2008	
	Principal Balance	Interest Rate	Principal Balance	Interest Rate
JPMorgan credit facility	$162	0.7% to 1.5%	$120	3.6%
ARS revolving credit line	—		—	
Europe revolving credit facility	584	1.2% to 3.9%	—	
Canada revolving demand facility	2	4.0%	—	
China revolving demand facilities	35	4.6% to 5.0%	36	6.5% to 8.0%
Total short-term debt	$783		$156	

Fiscal Year	2009	2008
Maximum month-end outstanding during the year	$2,712	$1,955
Average amount outstanding during the year	$1,167	$ 655
Weighted-average interest rate	3.2%	4.5%

JPMorgan Credit Facility

In September 2007, we entered into a $2,500 five-year unsecured revolving credit agreement ("Credit Agreement"), as amended, with JPMorgan Chase Bank, N.A. ("JPMorgan"), as administrative agent, and a syndication of banks (collectively, "Lenders"). The Credit Agreement permits borrowings up to $2,500, which may be increased up to $3,000 at our option upon the consent of JPMorgan and each of the Lenders providing an incremental credit commitment. The Credit Agreement includes a $300 letter of credit sub-limit and a $200 foreign currency sub-limit. The Credit Agreement expires in September 2012.

Interest rates under the Credit Agreement are variable and are determined at our option at: (i) the greater of the federal funds rate plus 0.5% or JPMorgan's prime rate, or (ii) the London Interbank Offered Rate ("LIBOR") plus an applicable LIBOR margin. A facility fee is assessed on the commitment amount. Both the LIBOR margin and the facility fee are based upon our then current senior unsecured debt rating. The LIBOR margin ranges from 0.32% to 0.60%, and the facility fee ranges from 0.08% to 0.15%.

The Credit Agreement is guaranteed by certain of our subsidiaries and contains customary affirmative and negative covenants. Among other things, these covenants restrict or prohibit our ability to incur certain types or amounts of indebtedness, incur liens on certain assets, make material changes to our corporate structure or the nature of our business, dispose of material assets, allow non-material subsidiaries to make guarantees, engage in a change in control transaction, or engage in certain transactions with our affiliates. The Credit Agreement also contains covenants that require us to maintain a maximum quarterly cash flow leverage ratio and a minimum quarterly interest coverage ratio. We were in compliance with all such covenants at February 28, 2009.

On September 15, 2008, Lehman Brothers Holdings Inc. ("Lehman") filed a petition under Chapter 11 of the U.S. Bankruptcy Code. A subsidiary of Lehman, Lehman Commercial Paper Inc. ("Lehman CPI"), is one of the lenders under the Credit Agreement and represents a commitment of $180. Since September 2008, Lehman CPI has declined requests for funding under our Credit Agreement and no other lender has assumed Lehman CPI's obligation to fund. As a result, our borrowing base of $2,500 has been effectively reduced by $180.

At February 28, 2009, $162 was outstanding and $2,095 was available under the Credit Agreement, which excludes Lehman CPI's $180 commitment. Amounts outstanding under letters of credit may reduce amounts available under the Credit Agreement.

ARS Revolving Credit Line

We entered into an agreement with UBS Bank ("UBS Credit Agreement") for a $89 revolving credit line that is secured by the $89 par value of our UBS-brokered ARS. Interest rates under the UBS Credit Agreement are variable based on the weighted-average rate of interest we earn on our UBS-brokered ARS. The UBS Credit Agreement will terminate at the time UBS buys back our UBS-brokered ARS pursuant to the settlement agreement which will be no later than July 2, 2012. If we sell any of the UBS-brokered ARS at par during the term of the UBS Credit Agreement, the amount available to us will be reduced accordingly.

Europe Revolving Credit Facility

We have a $699 (or £475 million) revolving credit facility available to Best Buy Europe with CPW as the lender, of which $115 (or £78 million) was available for borrowing at February 28, 2009. Best Buy Co., Inc. is named as the guarantor in the credit agreement for the facility, up to 50% of the amount outstanding. The facility terminates in March 2013. Borrowings bear interest at LIBOR plus 0.75%. The credit agreement contains one financial covenant, requiring Best Buy Europe to maintain a minimum net debt to EBITDA ratio computed semi-annually beginning March 31, 2009.

Canada Revolving Demand Facility

We have a $39 revolving demand facility available to our Canada operations, of which $37 was available for borrowing at February 28, 2009. There is no set expiration date for the facility. All borrowings under the facility are made available at the sole discretion of the lender and are payable on demand. Borrowings under the facility bear interest at rates specified in the credit agreement for the facility. Borrowings are secured by a guarantee of Best Buy Co., Inc.

China Revolving Demand Facilities

We have $141 in revolving demand facilities available to our China operations, of which $106 was available to us at February 28, 2009. The facilities are renewed annually with the respective banks. All borrowings under these facilities bear interest at rates specified in the credit agreements, are made available at the sole discretion of the respective lenders and are payable on demand. Certain borrowings are secured by a guarantee of Best Buy Co., Inc.

Long-Term Debt (In Part)

Other (In Part)

The fair value of debt approximated $1,904 and $853 at February 28, 2009, and March 1, 2008, respectively, based on the ask prices quoted from external sources, compared with carrying values of $1,963 and $816, respectively.

2.158

THE CLOROX COMPANY (JUN)

(Dollars in millions)	2009	2008
Current liabilities		
Notes and loans payable	$ 421	$ 755
Current maturities of long-term debt	577	—
Accounts payable	381	418
Accrued liabilities	472	440
Income taxes payable	86	52
Total current liabilities	$1,937	$1,665

NOTES TO CONSOLIDATED FINANCIAL STATEMENTS

Note 11 (In Part): Debt

Notes and loans payable, which mature in less than one year, included the following at June 30:

(Dollars in millions)	2009	2008
Commercial paper	$419	$748
Foreign borrowings	2	7
Total	$421	$755

The weighted average interest rate on notes and loans payable was 0.59% and 2.95% at June 30, 2009 and 2008, respectively. During the fiscal years ended June 30, 2009, 2008 and 2007, the weighted average interest rates on notes and loans payable was 2.85%, 4.45%, and 5.72%, respectively. The carrying value of notes and loans payable at June 30, 2009 and 2008, approximated the fair value of such debt.

Note 12 (In Part): Financial Instruments and Fair Value Measurements

The Company adopted the required portions of SFAS No. 157 on July 1, 2008. SFAS No. 157 applies to all assets and liabilities that are being measured and reported at fair value. SFAS No. 157 defines fair value as the price that would be received to sell an asset or paid to transfer a liability in an orderly transaction between market participants at the measurement date. SFAS No. 157 establishes a fair value hierarchy that prioritizes the inputs to valuation techniques used to measure fair value. An asset or liability's classification is based on the lowest level of input that is significant to the fair value measurement. SFAS No. 157 requires that assets and liabilities carried at fair value be classified and disclosed in one of the following three categories:

- Level 1—Quoted market prices in active markets for identical assets or liabilities.
- Level 2—Observable market-based inputs or unobservable inputs that are corroborated by market data.
- Level 3—Unobservable inputs reflecting the reporting entity's own assumptions.

• • • • • •

The carrying values of cash and cash equivalents, accounts receivable and accounts payable approximate their fair values at June 30, 2009 and 2008, due to the short maturity and nature of those balances. See Note 11 for fair values of notes and loans payable and long-term debt.

TRADE ACCOUNTS PAYABLE

2.159 All the survey entities disclosed the existence of amounts owed to trade creditors. As shown in Table 2-23, such amounts were usually described as *Accounts Payable* or *Trade Accounts Payable*.

2.160 Under FASB ASC 825, *Financial Instruments*, fair value disclosure is not required for trade payables when the carrying amount of the trade payable approximates its fair value. 265 survey entities made 279 fair value disclosures. Carrying amount approximated fair value of trade payables for 258 disclosures.

2.161 Examples of trade accounts payable presentations follow.

2.162

TABLE 2-23: TRADE ACCOUNTS PAYABLE*

	2009	2008	2007	2006
Accounts payable................................	388	383	457	464
Trade accounts payable......................	65	68	85	79
Accounts payable combined with accrued liabilities or accrued expenses...	26	23	30	28
Other captions....................................	21	26	28	29
Total Entities....................................	**500**	**500**	**600**	**600**

* Appearing in either the balance sheet and/or the notes to financial statements.

2008–2009 based on 500 entities surveyed; 2006–2007 based on 600 entities surveyed.

2.163

CABOT CORPORATION (SEP)

(Dollars in millions)	2009	2008
Current liabilities:		
Notes payable to banks	$ 29	$ 91
Accounts payable and accrued liabilities	407	426
Income taxes payable	31	38
Deferred income taxes	5	7
Current portion of long-term debt	5	39
Total current liabilities	$477	$601

NOTES TO CONSOLIDATED FINANCIAL STATEMENTS

Note I (In Part): Accounts Payable, Accrued Liabilities and Other Liabilities

Accounts payable and accrued liabilities included in current liabilities consisted of the following:

(In millions)	2009	2008
Accounts payable	$269	$314
Accrued employee compensation	38	39
Accrued severance, termination and restructuring	34	4
Other accrued liabilities	66	69
Total	$407	$426

Note L. Fair Value of Financial Instruments

The carrying amounts and fair values of the Company's financial instruments at September 30, 2009 and 2008 are as follows:

	2009		2008	
(In millions)	Carrying Amount	Fair Value	Carrying Amount	Fair Value
Assets:				
Cash and cash equivalents	$304	$304	$129	$129
Short-term marketable securities	1	1	1	1
Accounts and notes receivable	452	452	646	646
Derivative instruments	1	1	2	2
Liabilities:				
Notes payable to banks—short-term	29	29	91	91
Accounts payable and accrued liabilities	407	407	426	426
Long-term debt—fixed rate	604	619	340	294
Long-term debt—floating rate	23	23	283	283
Derivative instruments	62	62	48	48

At September 30, 2009 and 2008, the fair values of cash, cash equivalents, accounts receivables, accounts payable and notes payable to banks approximated carrying values because of the short-term nature of these instruments. The estimated fair values of available for sale marketable securities are based on the market price at the respective year-ends. The estimated fair values of the derivative instruments are estimated based on the amount that Cabot would receive or pay to terminate the agreements at the respective year-ends. The fair value of Cabot's fixed rate long-term debt is estimated based on comparable quoted market prices at the respective year ends. The carrying amounts of Cabot's floating rate long-term debt approximates their fair value.

2.164

HARLEY-DAVIDSON, INC. (DEC)

(Dollars in thousands)	2009	2008
Current liabilities:		
Accounts payable	$ 162,515	$ 303,277
Accrued liabilities	514,084	503,466
Liabilities of discontinued operations	69,535	77,941
Short-term debt	189,999	1,738,649
Current portion of long-term debt	1,332,091	—
Total current liabilities	$2,268,224	$2,623,333

NOTES TO CONSOLIDATED FINANCIAL STATEMENTS

9 (In Part): Fair Value of Financial Instruments

The Company's financial instruments consist primarily of cash and cash equivalents, marketable securities, trade receivables, finance receivables held for investment, net, finance receivables held for sale, trade payables, debt, foreign currency contracts and interest rate swaps. Under U.S. GAAP certain of these items are required to be recorded in the financial statements at fair value, while others are required to be recorded at historical cost.

The following table summarizes the fair value and carrying value of the Company's financial instruments at December 31, 2009 (in thousands):

	2009		2008	
	Fair Value	Carrying Value	Fair Value	Carrying Value
Assets:				
Cash and cash equivalents	$1,630,433	$1,630,433	$ 568,894	$ 568,894
Marketable securities	39,685	39,685	—	—
Accounts receivable, net	269,371	269,371	265,319	265,319
Restricted cash	167,667	167,667	—	—
Derivatives	13,678	13,678	31,508	31,508
Finance receivables held for sale	—	—	2,443,965	2,443,965
Finance receivables held for investment	4,802,322	4,811,812	1,864,889	1,864,889
Investment in retained securitization interests	245,350	245,350	330,674	330,674
Liabilities:				
Accounts payable	162,515	162,515	303,272	303,272
Derivatives	16,293	16,293	23,503	23,503
Unsecured commercial paper	325,099	325,099	1,416,449	1,416,449
Asset-backed commercial paper conduit facility	—	—	500,000	500,000
Credit facilities	448,049	448,049	390,932	390,932
Medium-term notes	2,152,612	2,103,396	1,034,907	1,607,506
Senior unsecured notes	816,998	600,000	—	—
On-balance sheet securitization debt	2,166,056	2,159,585	—	—

Cash and Cash Equivalents, Restricted Cash, Accounts Receivable, Net and Accounts Payable

With the exception of certain money-market investments, these items are recorded in the financial statements at historical cost. The historical cost basis for these amounts is estimated to approximate their respective fair values due to the short maturity of these instruments.

EMPLOYEE-RELATED LIABILITIES

2.165 FASB ASC 715, *Compensation—Retirement Benefits,* requires that a business entity recognize the overfunded or underfunded status of a single-employer defined benefit postretirement plan as an asset or liability in its statement of financial position, recognize changes in that funded status in comprehensive income, and disclose in the notes to financial statements additional information about net periodic benefit cost. Examples of the funded status of a benefit plan recognized under FASB ASC 715 as asset or liability in the statement of financial position are presented in this section, the "Other Noncurrent Assets" section, and the "Other Noncurrent Liabilities" section. Additional examples can also be found in Section 3, under "Pensions and Other Postretirement Benefits."

2.166 Table 2-24 shows the nature of employee related liabilities disclosed by the survey companies as current liabilities. Examples of employee related liability presentations and disclosures follow.

2.167

TABLE 2-24: EMPLOYEE-RELATED LIABILITIES*

Description	2009	2008	2007	2006
Pension or profit-sharing contributions	239	191	214	150
Benefits	226	204	197	149
Salaries, wages, payrolls, commissions	219	220	273	271
Compensation	195	197	236	229
Other	57	50	45	69
Compensated absences	8	5	11	11
Total Presentations	**944**	**867**	**976**	**879**

	Number of Entities			
Disclosing employee related liabilities	450	450	538	524
Not disclosing	50	50	62	76
Total Entities	**500**	**500**	**600**	**600**

* Appearing in either the balance sheet and/or the notes to financial statements.

2008–2009 based on 500 entities surveyed; 2006–2007 based on 600 entities surveyed.

2.168

COLGATE-PALMOLIVE COMPANY (DEC)

(Dollars in millions)	2009	2008
Current liabilities		
Notes and loans payable	$ 35	$ 107
Current portion of long-term debt	326	91
Accounts payable	1,172	1,061
Accrued income taxes	387	272
Other accruals	1,679	1,421
Total current liabilities	$3,599	$2,952

NOTES TO CONSOLIDATED FINANCIAL STATEMENTS
(Dollars in millions)

10 (In Part): Retirement Plans and Other Retiree Benefits

Retirement Plans (In Part)

The Company and certain of its U.S. and overseas subsidiaries maintain defined benefit retirement plans. Benefits are based primarily on years of service and employees' career earnings. In the Company's principal U.S. plans and certain funded overseas plans, funds are contributed to trusts in accordance with regulatory limits to provide for current service and for any unfunded projected benefit obligation over a reasonable period.

• • • • • •

Other Retiree Benefits

The Company and certain of its subsidiaries provide health care and life insurance benefits for retired employees to the extent not provided by government-sponsored plans. The Company utilizes a portion of its leveraged ESOP to reduce its obligation to provide these other retiree benefits and to offset its current service cost.

The Company uses a December 31 measurement date for its defined benefit and other retiree benefit plans. Summarized information for the Company's defined benefit and other retiree benefit plans are as follows:

	Pension Benefits				Other Retiree Benefits	
	2009	2008	2009	2008	2009	2008
	United States		International			
Change in benefit obligations						
Benefit obligations at beginning of year	$1,570	$1,459	$ 604	$ 718	$ 542	$ 472
Service cost	42	40	15	15	3	1
Interest cost	95	95	37	37	36	34
Participants' contributions	1	2	3	3	—	—
Acquisitions/plan amendments	—	30	1	6	—	—
Actuarial loss (gain)	104	63	46	(24)	37	58
Foreign exchange impact	—	—	39	(97)	5	(11)
Termination benefits	—	1	—	1	—	—
Curtailments and settlements	—	—	(3)	(13)	—	—
Benefit payments	(109)	(120)	(36)	(42)	(20)	(12)
Benefit obligations at end of year	$1,703	$1,570	$ 706	$ 604	$ 603	$ 542
Change in plan assets						
Fair value of plan assets at beginning of year	$1,134	$1,452	$ 320	$ 442	$ 24	$ 32
Actual return on plan assets	189	(307)	43	(53)	4	(8)
Company contributions	85	108	45	41	20	12
Participants' contributions	1	1	3	3	—	—
Foreign exchange impact	—	—	29	(62)	—	—
Settlements	—	—	(3)	(9)	—	—
Benefit payments	(109)	(120)	(36)	(42)	(20)	(12)
Fair value of plan assets at end of year	$1,300	$1,134	$ 401	$ 320	$ 28	$ 24
Funded status						
Benefit obligations at end of year	$1,703	$1,570	$ 706	$ 604	$ 603	$ 542
Fair value of plan assets at end of year	1,300	1,134	401	320	28	24
Net amount recognized	$ (403)	$ (436)	$(305)	$(284)	$(575)	$(518)
Amounts recognized in balance sheet						
Noncurrent assets	$ —	$ —	$ 4	$ 5	$ —	$ —
Current liabilities	(12)	(15)	(14)	(13)	(35)	(28)
Noncurrent liabilities	(391)	(421)	(295)	(276)	(540)	(490)
Net amount recognized	$ (403)	$ (436)	$(305)	$(284)	$(575)	$(518)
Amounts recognized in accumulated other comprehensive income consist of						
Actuarial loss	$ 641	$ 687	$ 132	$ 113	$ 267	$ 246
Transition/prior service cost	29	32	8	11	2	1
	$ 670	$ 719	$ 140	$ 124	$ 269	$ 247
Accumulated benefit obligation	$1,645	$1,506	$ 635	$ 546	$ —	$ —

	Pension Benefits				Other Retiree Benefits	
	2009	2008	2009	2008	2009	2008
	United States		International			
Weighted-average assumptions used to determine benefit obligations						
Discount rate	5.75%	6.30%	5.41%	5.88%	5.75%	5.80%
Long-term rate of return on plan assets	8.00%	8.00%	6.58%	6.70%	8.00%	8.00%
Long-term rate of compensation increase	4.00%	4.00%	3.35%	3.33%	—	—
ESOP growth rate	—	—	—	—	10.00%	10.00%

The overall investment objective of the plans is to balance risk and return so that obligations to employees are met. The Company evaluates its long-term rate of return on plan assets on an annual basis. In determining the long-term rate of return, the Company considers the nature of the plans' investments, an expectation for the plans' investment strategies and the historical rates of return. The assumed rate of return for 2009 for the U.S. plans was 8%. Average annual rates of return for the U.S. plans for the most recent 1-year, 5-year, 10-year, 15-year and 25-year periods were 17%, 5%, 4%, 6%, and 9%, respectively. Similar assessments were performed in determining rates of return on international pension plan assets to arrive at the Company's 2009 weighted-average rate of return of 6.58%.

Plans with projected benefit obligations in excess of plan assets and plans with accumulated benefit obligations in excess of plan assets as of December 31 consist of the following:

	2009	2008
Benefit obligation exceeds fair value of plan assets		
Projected benefit obligation	$2,338	$2,085
Fair value of plan assets	1,629	1,361
Accumulated benefit obligation	2,170	1,967
Fair value of plan assets	1,579	1,346

• • • • • •

Expected Contributions & Benefit Payments

Management's best estimate of cash requirements to be paid directly from the Company's assets to its postretirement plans for the year ending December 31, 2010, is approximately $120, including approximately $35 for other retiree benefit plans. These estimated cash requirements include approximately $55 of projected contributions to the Company's postretirement plans, composed of $35 of voluntary contributions to our U.S. pension plans and approximately $20 of projected benefit payments made directly to participants of unfunded plans. Expected contributions are dependent on many variables, including the variability of the market value of the assets as compared to the obligation and other market or regulatory conditions. Accordingly, actual funding may differ from current estimates.

Total benefit payments expected to be paid to participants, which include payments directly from the Company's assets to participants of unfunded plans, as discussed above, as well as payments paid from the plans are as follows:

	Pension Benefits		Other
	United		Retiree
Years Ended December 31	States	International	Benefits
2010	$120	$ 41	$ 36
2011	120	51	38
2012	120	42	38
2013	122	43	38
2014	122	47	38
2015–2019	664	231	178

16 (In Part): Supplemental Balance Sheet Information

	2009	2008
Other accruals		
Accrued advertising	$ 538	$ 457
Accrued payroll and employee benefits	370	317
Accrued taxes other than income taxes	101	60
Restructuring accrual	15	33
Pension and other retiree benefits	61	56
Accrued interest	24	23
Derivatives	9	72
Other	561	403
Total other accruals	$1,679	$1,421

	2009	2008
Other liabilities		
Pension and other retiree benefits	$1,226	$1,187
Other	149	129
Total other liabilities	$1,375	$1,316

2.169

VALERO ENERGY CORPORATION (DEC)

(Millions of dollars)	2009	2008
Current liabilities		
Current portion of debt and capital lease obligations	$ 237	$ 312
Accounts payable	5,760	4,323
Accrued expenses	514	370
Taxes other than income taxes	725	592
Income taxes payable	95	—
Deferred income taxes	253	485
Liabilities related to discontinued operations	214	127
Total current liabilities	$7,798	$6,209

NOTES TO CONSOLIDATED FINANCIAL STATEMENTS

1 (In Part): Summary of Significant Accounting Policies

Defined Benefit Pension Plans

In December 2008, the FASB modified ASC Topic 715, "Compensation—Retirement Benefits," to require enhanced disclosures regarding (i) investment policies and strategies, (ii) categories of plan assets, (iii) fair value measurements of plan assets, and (iv) significant concentrations of risk. These disclosures are effective for fiscal years ending after December 15, 2009, with earlier application permitted. See Note 21 for the additional disclosures required by this accounting pronouncement. Since only disclosures are affected by these requirements, the adoption of these provisions effective December 31, 2009 did not affect our financial position or results of operations.

11. Accrued Expenses

Accrued expenses consisted of the following (in millions):

	2009	2008
Employee wage and benefit costs	$156	$165
Interest expense	100	66
Derivative liabilities	109	7
Environmental liabilities	41	42
Other	108	90
Accrued expenses	$514	$370

17 (In Part): Fair Value Measurements

A fair value hierarchy (Level 1, Level 2, or Level 3) is used to categorize fair value amounts based on the quality of inputs used to measure fair value. Accordingly, fair values determined by Level 1 inputs utilize quoted prices in active markets for identical assets or liabilities. Fair values determined by Level 2 inputs are based on quoted prices for similar assets and liabilities in active markets, and inputs other than quoted prices that are observable for the asset or liability. Level 3 inputs are unobservable inputs for the asset or liability, and include situations where there is little, if any, market activity for the asset or liability. We use appropriate valuation techniques based on the available inputs to measure the fair values of our applicable assets and liabilities. When available, we measure fair value using Level 1 inputs because they generally provide the most reliable evidence of fair value.

The tables below present information (dollars in millions) about our financial assets and liabilities measured and recorded at fair value on a recurring basis and indicate the fair value hierarchy of the inputs utilized by us to determine the fair values as of December 31, 2009 and 2008.

	Fair Value Measurements Using			
	Quoted Prices in Active Markets (Level 1)	Significant Other Observable Inputs (Level 2)	Significant Unobservable Inputs (Level 3)	Total as of December 31, 2009
Assets:				
Commodity derivative contracts	$ 10	$349	$—	$359
Nonqualified benefit plans	99	—	10	109
Liabilities:				
Commodity derivative contracts	100	9	—	109
Certain nonqualified benefit plans	34	—	—	34

	Fair Value Measurements Using			
	Quoted Prices in Active Markets (Level 1)	Significant Other Observable Inputs (Level 2)	Significant Unobservable Inputs (Level 3)	Total as of December 31, 2008
Assets:				
Commodity derivative contracts	$40	$610	$—	$650
Nonqualified benefit plans	98	—	—	98
Alon earn-out agreement	—	—	13	13
Liabilities:				
Commodity derivative contracts	—	7	—	7
Certain nonqualified benefit plans	26	—	—	26

The valuation methods used to measure our financial instruments at fair value are as follows:

- The nonqualified benefit plan assets and certain nonqualified benefit plan liabilities categorized in Level 1 of the fair value hierarchy are measured at fair value using a market approach based on quotations from national security exchanges. The nonqualified benefit plan assets categorized in Level 3 of the fair value hierarchy represent insurance contracts, the fair values of which are provided by the insurer.

21 (In Part): Employee Benefit Plans

Pension Plans and Postretirement Benefits Other Than Pensions

We have several qualified non-contributory defined benefit pension plans (collectively, the Qualified Plans), some of which are subject to collective bargaining agreements. The Qualified Plans cover substantially all employees in the United States and generally provide eligible employees with retirement income based on years of service and compensation during specific periods.

We also have several nonqualified supplemental executive retirement plans (Supplemental Plans), which provide additional pension benefits to executive officers and certain other employees. The Supplemental Plans and the Qualified Plans are collectively referred to as the Pension Plans.

We also provide certain health care and life insurance benefits for retired employees, referred to as other postretirement benefits. Substantially all of our employees may become eligible for these benefits if, while still working for us, they either reach normal retirement age or take early retirement. We offer health care benefits through a self-insured plan and, for certain locations, a health maintenance organization while life insurance benefits are provided through an insurance company. We fund our postretirement benefits other than pensions on a pay-as-you-go basis. Individuals who became our employees as a result of an acquisition became eligible for other postretirement benefits under our plan as determined by the terms of the relevant acquisition agreement.

The changes in benefit obligation, the changes in fair value of plan assets, and the funded status of our Pension Plans and other postretirement benefit plans as of and for the years ended December 31, 2009 and 2008 were as follows (in millions):

	Pension Plans		Other Postretirement Benefit Plans	
	2009	2008	2009	2008
Change in benefit obligation:				
Benefit obligation at beginning of year	$1,492	$1,292	$ 520	$ 477
Service cost	104	92	12	13
Interest cost	79	76	25	28
Participant contributions	—	—	9	7
Plan amendments	—	—	(51)	—
Special termination benefits	6	—	1	—
Medicare subsidy for prescription drugs	—	—	1	2
Benefits paid	(74)	(75)	(28)	(27)
Actuarial (gain) loss	(153)	107	(27)	26
Foreign currency exchange rate changes	—	—	4	(6)
Benefit obligation at end of year	$1,454	$1,492	$ 466	$ 520
Change in plan assets:				
Fair value of plan assets at beginning of year	$1,005	$1,358	$ —	$ —
Actual return on plan assets	228	(400)	—	—
Valero contributions	92	122	18	18
Participant contributions	—	—	9	7
Medicare subsidy for prescription drugs	—	—	1	2
Benefits paid	(74)	(75)	(28)	(27)
Fair value of plan assets at end of year	$1,251	$1,005	$ —	$ —
Reconciliation of funded status:				
Fair value of plan assets at end of year	$1,251	$1,005	$ —	$ —
Less: Benefit obligation at end of year	1,454	1,492	466	520
Funded status at end of year	$ (203)	$ (487)	$(466)	$(520)

The pre-tax amounts related to our Pension Plans and other postretirement benefit plans recognized in our consolidated balance sheets as of December 31, 2009 and 2008 were as follows (in millions):

	Pension Plans		Other Postretirement Benefit Plans	
	2009	2008	2009	2008
Accrued expenses	$ (19)	$ (13)	$ (25)	$ (22)
Other long-term liabilities	(184)	(474)	(441)	(498)
Accumulated other comprehensive (income) loss	358	645	(21)	43

As of both December 31, 2009 and 2008, the accumulated benefit obligation for our Pension Plans was $1.2 billion. With the exception of our main Qualified Plan as of December 31, 2009, the accumulated benefit obligation for each of our Pension Plans was in excess of the fair value of plan assets as of December 31, 2009 and 2008. Due to an increase in the fair value of the assets of our main Qualified Plan during 2009, the fair value of plan assets for our main Qualified Plan was in excess of the accumulated benefit obligation by $163 million as of December 31, 2009, thus resulting in the reduced amounts reflected in the table below. The aggregate projected benefit obligation, accumulated benefit obligation, and fair value of plan assets for our Pension Plans for which the accumulated benefit obligation exceeded the fair value of plan assets were as follows (in millions):

	2009	2008
Projected benefit obligation	$249	$1,492
Accumulated benefit obligation	221	1,201
Fair value of plan assets	81	1,005

There are no plan assets for our other postretirement benefit plans, and no assets related to our Supplemental Plans are included in the fair value of plan assets above. The assets of the Qualified Plans are measured at fair value using a market approach based on quotations from national securities exchanges and are categorized as Level 1 of the fair value hierarchy.

•   •   •   •   •   •

The following benefit payments, which reflect expected future service and anticipated Medicare subsidy, as appropriate, are expected to be paid (received) for the years ending December 31 (in millions):

	Pension Benefits	Other Benefits	Health Care Subsidy Receipts
2010	$ 73	$ 24	$ (2)
2011	78	27	(2)
2012	82	28	(3)
2013	93	29	(3)
2014	113	31	(3)
Years 2015–2019	682	171	(25)

INCOME TAX LIABILITY

2.170 Table 2-25 summarizes the descriptive balance sheet captions used to describe the current liability for income taxes.

2.171

TABLE 2-25: CURRENT INCOME TAX LIABILITY*

	2009	2008	2007	2006
Income taxes	243	261	330	330
Taxes—type not specified	44	46	53	61
U.S. and foreign income taxes	5	4	5	6
Federal and state income taxes	5	4	4	9
Federal, state, and foreign income taxes	3	3	3	6
Federal income taxes	—	3	1	1
Federal and foreign income taxes	2	2	3	2
Other captions	12	11	17	14
No current income tax liability	186	166	184	171
Total Entities	**500**	**500**	**600**	**600**

* Appearing in either the balance sheet and/or the notes to financial statements.

2008–2009 based on 500 entities surveyed; 2006–2007 based on 600 entities surveyed.

2.172

A. SCHULMAN, INC. (AUG)

(Dollars in thousands)	2009	2008
Current liabilities:		
Notes payable	$ 2,519	$ 9,540
Accounts payable	147,476	174,226
U.S. and foreign income taxes payable	8,858	3,212
Accrued payrolls, taxes and related benefits	36,207	37,686
Other accrued liabilities	32,562	34,566
Total current liabilities	$227,622	$259,230

2.173

SPECTRUM BRANDS, INC. (SEP)

(In thousands)	2009	2008
Current liabilities:		
Current maturities of long-term debt	$ 53,578	$ 48,637
Accounts payable	186,235	278,126
Accrued liabilities:		
Wages and benefits	88,443	72,299
Income taxes payable	21,950	10,272
Restructuring and related charges	26,203	34,559
Accrued interest	8,678	50,514
Other	109,981	87,672
Total current liabilities	$495,068	$582,079

CURRENT AMOUNT OF LONG-TERM DEBT

2.174 Table 2-26 summarizes the descriptive balance sheet captions used to describe the amount of long-term debt payable during the next year. FASB ASC 825, *Financial Instruments*, requires disclosure of both the fair value and the bases for estimating the fair value of the current amount of long-term debt unless it is not practicable to estimate that value.

2.175 FASB ASC 820, *Fair Value Measurements and Disclosures*, defines fair value, establishes a framework for measuring fair value, and requires certain disclosures about fair value measurements. FASB ASC 820 clarifies the definition of fair value as an exit price, i.e., a price that would be received to sell, as opposed to acquire, an asset or transfer a liability. FASB ASC 820 emphasizes that fair value is a market-based measurement. It establishes a fair value hierarchy that distinguishes between assumptions developed based on market data obtained from independent external sources and the reporting entity's own assumptions. Further, FASB ASC 820 specifies that fair value measurement should consider adjustment for risk, such as the risk inherent in a valuation technique or its inputs. For assets measured at fair value, whether on a recurring or a nonrecurring basis, FASB ASC 820 specifies the required disclosures concerning the inputs used to measure fair value. FASB Accounting Standards Update (ASU) No. 2010-06, *Improving Disclosures about Fair Value Measurements*, requires more robust disclosures about different classes of assets and liabilities measured at fair value, the valuation techniques and inputs used, the activity in Level 3 fair value measurements, and the transfers between Levels 1, 2, and 3. FASB ASU No. 2010-06 is effective for fiscal years beginning after December 15, 2009, except for the disclosures about certain Level 3 activity. Those disclosures are effective for fiscal years beginning after December 15, 2010. During 2009, 350 survey companies made 640 disclosures of fair value related to the current amount of long-term debt. 135 of those disclosures were based on the quoted price of the identical item in an active market (level 1 input). 202 of those disclosures were primarily based on other market-corroborated (level 2) inputs. 18 disclosures estimated fair value using nonmarket-corroborated (level 3) inputs. 86 disclosures presented carrying amounts which approximated fair value of the current amount of long-term debt. In addition, there were 8 disclosures in which carrying value was compared to fair value in an exposition or a table.

2.176 FASB ASC 825, *Financial Instruments*, permits entities to choose to measure many financial instruments and certain other items at fair value that are not currently required to be measured at fair value. Further, under FASB ASC 825 a business entity shall report unrealized gains and losses on eligible items for which the fair value option has been elected in earnings at each subsequent reporting date. The irrevocable election of the fair value option is made on an instrument by instrument basis, and applied to the entire instrument, not just a portion of it. FASB ASC 825 also establishes presentation and disclosure requirements designed to facilitate comparison between entities that choose different measurement attributes for similar types of assets and liabilities.

2.177

TABLE 2-26: CURRENT AMOUNT OF LONG-TERM DEBT*

	Number of Entities			
	2009	**2008**	**2007**	**2006**
Current portion of long-term debt.........	191	207	241	240
Current maturities of long-term debt....	129	137	160	160
Current amount of long-term leases....	48	44	54	41
Long-term debt due or payable within one year...	22	22	25	26
Current installment of long-term debt...	8	8	11	12
Other captions....................................	13	9	12	13

* Appearing in either the balance sheet and/or the notes to financial statements.

2008–2009 based on 500 entities surveyed; 2006–2007 based on 600 entities surveyed.

2.178

ADVANCED MICRO DEVICES, INC. (DEC)

(In millions)	2009	2008
Current liabilities:		
Accounts payable	$ 647	$ 631
Accrued liabilities	795	970
Deferred income on shipments to distributors	138	50
Other short-term obligations	171	86
Current portion of long-term debt and capital lease obligations	308	286
Other current liabilities	151	203
Total current liabilities	$2,210	$2,226

NOTES TO CONSOLIDATED FINANCIAL STATEMENTS

Note 7 (In Part): Financial Instruments

Fair Value of Other Financial Instruments

The fair value of the Company's long-term debt, except for the convertible notes issued by GF, is estimated based on the quoted market prices for the same or similar issues or on the current rates offered to the Company for debt of the same remaining maturities. The fair value of the convertible notes issued by GF is estimated based on a valuation model that incorporates relevant market inputs. The carrying amounts and estimated fair values of the Company's debt instruments are as follows:

(In millions)	Carrying Amount	Estimated Fair Value	Carrying Amount	Estimated Fair Value
Long-term debt (excluding capital leases)	$4,304	$4,046	$4,551	$2,071

Note 10 (In Part): Debt

Long-Term Borrowings and Obligations

The Company's long-term debt and capital lease obligations as of December 26, 2009 and December 27, 2008 consist of:

(In millions)	2009	2008
7.75% senior notes due 2012	$ —	$ 390
5.75% convertible senior notes due 2012	485	1,500
6.00% convertible senior notes due 2015	1,641	1,928
8.125% senior notes due 2017	449	—
Fab 36 term loan	460	705
Repurchase obligations to Fab 36 Partners	—	28
GF Class A subordinated convertible notes	254	—
GF Class B subordinated convertible notes	1,015	—
Capital lease obligations	256	225
	4,560	4,776
Less: current portion	308	286
Long-term debt and capital lease obligations, less current portion	$4,252	$4,490

Future Payments on Long Term Debt and Capital Lease Obligations

As of December 26, 2009, the Company's long term debt and capital lease payment obligations for each of the next five years and beyond, are:

(In millions)	Long Term Debt (Principal Only)	Capital Leases
2010	$ 290	$ 49
2011	170	49
2012	485	50
2013	—	50
2014	—	50
Beyond 2014	3,359	177
Total	4,304	425
Less: amount representing interest	—	169
Total	$4,304	$256

2.179

ARCHER DANIELS MIDLAND COMPANY (JUN)

(In millions)	2009	2008
Current liabilities		
Short-term debt	$ 356	$ 3,123
Accounts payable	5,786	6,544
Accrued expenses	2,695	4,722
Current maturities of long-term debt	48	232
Total current liabilities	$8,885	$14,621

NOTES TO CONSOLIDATED FINANCIAL STATEMENTS

Note 8 (In Part): Debt and Financing Arrangements

(In millions)	2009	2008
4.70% debentures $1,750 million face amount, due in 2041	$1,750	$1,750
0.875% convertible senior notes $1,150 million face amount, due in 2014	1,150	1,150
5.45% notes $700 million face amount, due in 2018	700	700
5.375% debentures $600 million face amount, due in 2035	586	586
6.45% debentures $500 million face amount, due in 2038	498	498
5.935% debentures $500 million face amount, due in 2032	494	494
7.0% debentures $400 million face amount, due in 2031	398	398
7.5% debentures $343 million face amount, due in 2027	341	341
6.625% debentures $298 million face amount, due in 2029	296	296
8.375% debentures $295 million face amount, due in 2017	292	292
6.95% debentures $250 million face amount, due in 2097	246	246
7.125% debentures $243 million face amount, due in 2013	243	243
6.75% debentures $200 million face amount, due in 2027	197	197
5.87% debentures $196 million face amount, due in 2010	177	164
8.125% debentures $103 million face amount, due in 2012	103	103
8.875% debentures $102 million face amount, due in 2011	102	102
Other	275	362
Total long-term debt including current maturities	7,848	7,922
Current maturities	(48)	(232)
Total long-term debt	$7,800	$7,690

• • • • • •

At June 30, 2009, the fair value of the Company's long-term debt exceeded the carrying value by $303 million, as estimated by using quoted market prices or discounted future cash flows based on the Company's current incremental borrowing rates for similar types of borrowing arrangements.

The aggregate maturities of long-term debt for the five years after June 30, 2009, are $48 million, $328 million, $151 million, $268 million, and $1,215 million, respectively.

OTHER CURRENT LIABILITIES

2.180   Table 2-27 summarizes other identified current liabilities. The most common types of other current liabilities are liabilities related to derivatives, discontinued operations, deferred revenue, accrued interest, and deferred taxes.

2.181

TABLE 2-27: OTHER CURRENT LIABILITIES*

| | Number of Entities | | | |
	2009	2008	2007	2006
Derivatives	253	88	76	70
Costs related to discontinued operations/restructuring	158	148	172	162
Deferred revenue	140	150	175	161
Interest	123	128	146	143
Deferred taxes	118	122	104	97
Taxes other than federal income taxes	116	122	135	139
Warranties	99	101	126	120
Insurance	86	83	97	101
Advertising	64	63	70	73
Dividends	59	62	75	68
Environmental costs	59	58	68	67
Rebates	55	54	54	59
Customer advances, deposits	54	57	65	68
Litigation	43	39	56	50
Tax uncertainties	33	29	N/C**	N/C**
Billings on uncompleted contracts	26	26	38	29
Due to affiliated companies	23	25	22	22
Royalties	19	20	23	21
Asset retirement obligations	15	18	24	20
Other—described	135	127	146	156

* Appearing in either the balance sheet and/or the notes to financial statements.

** N/C = Not compiled. Line item was not included in the table for the year shown.

2008–2009 based on 500 entities surveyed; 2006–2007 based on 600 entities surveyed.

Derivatives

2.182

CROWN HOLDINGS, INC. (DEC)

(In millions)	2009	2008
Current liabilities		
Short-term debt	$ 30	$ 59
Current maturities of long-term debt	29	31
Accounts payable and accrued liabilities—Note H	1,866	1,982
Total current liabilities	$1,925	$2,072

NOTES TO CONSOLIDATED FINANCIAL STATEMENTS
(In millions)

A (In Part): Summary of Significant Accounting Policies

Derivatives and Hedging

All outstanding derivative financial instruments are recognized in the balance sheet at their fair values. The impact on earnings from recognizing the fair values of these instruments depends on their intended use, their hedge designation and their effectiveness in offsetting changes in the fair values of the exposures they are hedging. Changes in the fair values of instruments designated to reduce or eliminate adverse fluctuations in the fair values of recognized assets and liabilities and unrecognized firm commitments are reported currently in earnings along with changes in the fair values of the hedged items. Changes in the effective portions of the fair values of instruments used to reduce or eliminate adverse fluctuations in cash flows of anticipated or forecasted transactions are reported in equity as a component of accumulated other comprehensive income. Amounts in accumulated other comprehensive income are reclassified to earnings when the related hedged items impact earnings or the anticipated transactions are no longer probable. Changes in the fair values of derivative instruments that are not designated as hedges or do not qualify for hedge accounting treatment are reported currently in earnings. Amounts reported in earnings are classified consistent with the item being hedged.

The effectiveness of derivative instruments in reducing risks associated with the hedged exposures is assessed at inception and on an ongoing basis. Any amounts excluded from the assessment of hedge effectiveness, and any ineffective portion of designated hedges, are reported currently in earnings. Time value, a component of an instrument's fair value, is excluded in assessing effectiveness for fair value hedges, except hedges of firm commitments, and included for cash flow hedges.

Hedge accounting is discontinued prospectively when (i) the derivative instrument is no longer effective in offsetting changes in fair value or cash flows of the underlying hedged item, (ii) the derivative instrument expires, is sold, terminated or exercised, or (iii) designating the derivative instrument as a hedge is no longer appropriate.

The Company formally documents all relationships between its hedging instruments and hedged items at inception, including its risk management objective and strategy for establishing various hedge relationships. Cash flows from hedging instruments are classified in the Consolidated Statements of Cash Flows consistent with the items being hedged.

required

H. Accounts Payable and Accrued Liabilities

	2009	2008
Trade accounts payable	$1,163	$1,266
Salaries, wages and other employee benefits, including pension and postretirement	192	194
Accrued taxes, other than on income	129	113
Fair value of derivatives	67	168
Accrued interest	20	34
Asbestos liabilities	25	25
Income taxes payable	25	18
Deferred taxes	14	10
Restructuring	25	12
Other	206	142
	$1,866	$1,982

R. Fair Value Measurements

Under GAAP a framework exists for measuring fair value, providing a three-tier fair value hierarchy of pricing inputs used to report assets and liabilities that are adjusted to fair value. Level 1 includes inputs such as quoted prices which are available in active markets for identical assets or liabilities as of the report date. Level 2 includes inputs other than quoted prices in active markets included in Level 1, which are either directly or indirectly observable as of the report date. Level 3 includes unobservable pricing inputs that are not corroborated by market data or other objective sources. The Company has no items valued using Level 3 inputs other than certain pension plan assets.

The following table sets forth the fair value hierarchy of the Company's financial assets and liabilities that were accounted for at fair value on a recurring basis as of December 31, 2009.

| | Assets/Liabilities at Fair Value | | Fair Value Measurements Using | | | |
| | | | Level 1 | | Level 2 | |
	2009	2008	2009	2008	2009	2008
Assets						
Derivative instruments	$45	$ 78	$31	$ 14	$14	$ 64
Liabilities						
Derivative instruments	$67	$210	$ 1	$104	$66	$106

The Company utilizes market data or assumptions that market participants would use in pricing the asset or liability. The Company's assessment of the significance of a particular input to the fair value measurement requires judgment and may affect the valuation of fair value assets and liabilities and their placement within the fair value hierarchy.

The Company applies a market approach to value its commodity price hedge contracts. Prices from observable markets are used to develop the fair value of these financial instruments and they are reported under Level 1. The Company uses an income approach to value its outstanding cross-currency swaps and foreign exchange forward contracts. These contracts are valued using a discounted cash flow model that calculates the present value of future cash flows under the terms of the contracts using market information as of the reporting date, such as prevailing interest rates and foreign exchange spot and forward rates, and are reported under Level 2 of the fair value hierarchy.

Refer to Note S for further discussion of the Company's use of derivative instruments and their fair values at December 31, 2009.

S (In Part): Derivative Financial Instruments

In the normal course of business the Company is subject to risk from adverse fluctuations in foreign exchange and interest rates and commodity prices. The Company manages these risks through a program that includes the use of derivative financial instruments, primarily swaps and forwards. Counterparties to these contracts are major financial institutions. The Company is exposed to credit loss in the event of nonperformance by these counterparties. The Company does not use derivative instruments for trading or speculative purposes.

The Company's objective in managing exposure to market risk is to limit the impact on earnings and cash flow. The extent to which the Company uses such instruments is dependent upon its access to these contracts in the financial markets and its success using other methods, such as netting exposures in the same currencies to mitigate foreign exchange risk and using sales agreements that permit the pass-through of commodity price and foreign exchange rate risk to customers.

For derivative financial instruments accounted for as hedging instruments, the Company formally designates and documents, at inception, the financial instrument as a hedge of a specific underlying exposure, the risk management objective and the manner in which effectiveness of the hedge will be assessed. The Company formally assesses, both at inception and at least quarterly thereafter, whether the derivative financial instruments used in hedging transactions are effective in offsetting changes in fair value or cash flows of the related underlying exposures. Any ineffective portion of the change in fair value of the instruments is recognized immediately in earnings.

Cash Flow Hedges

The Company designates certain derivative financial instruments as cash flow hedges. No components of the hedging instruments are excluded from the assessment of hedge effectiveness. All changes in fair value of outstanding derivatives in cash flow hedges, except any ineffective portion, are recorded in other comprehensive income until earnings are impacted by the hedged transaction. Classification of the gain or loss in the Consolidated Statements of Operations upon release from comprehensive income is the same as that of the underlying exposure. Contracts outstanding at December 31, 2009 mature between one and thirty-six months.

When the Company discontinues hedge accounting because it is no longer probable that an anticipated transaction will occur in the originally expected period or within an additional two-month period thereafter, changes to fair value accumulated in other comprehensive income are recognized immediately in earnings.

The Company may use cross-currency and interest rate swaps to manage its portfolio of fixed and variable debt, including foreign-currency denominated intercompany debt, and to manage the impact of debt on local cash flows. During 2005, the Company entered into four cross-currency swaps with an aggregate notional value of $700 that effectively convert fixed rate U.S. dollar intercompany debt to fixed rate euro intercompany debt. In November 2009, the third swap with a notional value of $225 matured and the Company paid $62. Currently the Company has only one swap outstanding, which matures in November 2010, with a notional value of $235 and a fair value loss of $49. The swaps have been and continue to be effective in mitigating the risk of changes in foreign exchange and interest rates because the critical terms of the swaps, including notional amounts, interest reset dates, maturity dates and underlying market indices, match those of the foreign-currency denominated debt.

The Company uses forwards to hedge anticipated purchases of various commodities, including aluminum, fuel oil and natural gas. Information about commodity price exposure is derived from supply forecasts submitted by customers and these exposures are hedged by a central treasury unit. The U.S. dollar-equivalent notional value of commodity contracts designated as cash flow hedges at December 31, 2009 was $167.

The Company also designates certain foreign exchange contracts as cash flow hedges of anticipated foreign currency-denominated sales or purchases. The Company manages these risks at the operating unit level. Often the hedging of foreign currency risk is performed in concert with related commodity price hedges. The U.S. dollar-equivalent notional value of foreign exchange contracts designated as cash flow hedges at December 31, 2009 was $283.

• • • • • •

Fair Value Hedges and Contracts Not Designated as Hedges

The Company designates certain derivative financial instruments as fair value hedges of recognized foreign-denominated assets and liabilities, which generally consist of trade accounts receivable and payable and unrecognized firm commitments. The notional values and maturity dates of the derivative instruments coincide with those of the hedged items. Changes in fair value of the derivative financial instruments, excluding time value, are offset by changes in fair value of the related hedged items. Other than for firm commitments, amounts related to time value are excluded from the assessment and measurement of hedge effectiveness and are reported in earnings, including $2 before income taxes for the twelve months ended December 31, 2009. The U.S. dollar-equivalent notional value of foreign exchange contracts designated as fair value hedges at December 31, 2009 was $114.

The Company does not designate foreign exchange contracts related to intercompany debt as fair value hedges. Although these derivative financial instruments were not designated or did not qualify for hedge accounting, they are effective economic hedges as the changes in their fair value, except for time value, are offset by changes in the fair value of the related intercompany debt. The Company's primary use of these derivative instruments is to offset the earnings impact that fluctuations in foreign exchange rates have on

intercompany debt denominated in nonfunctional currencies. Changes in fair value of these derivative instruments are immediately recognized in earnings as foreign exchange adjustments and their U.S dollar-equivalent notional value at December 31, 2009 was $575.

The impact on earnings of foreign exchange contracts designated as fair value hedges was a loss of $1 for the twelve months ended December 31, 2009. The impact on earnings of foreign exchange contracts not designated as hedges was a loss of $47. These items were reported as translation and foreign exchange in the Consolidated Statements of Operations and were offset by changes in the fair value of the related foreign currency exposure.

The fair values of outstanding derivative instruments in the Consolidated Balance Sheet at December 31, 2009 were:

Assets	
Derivatives designated as hedges:	
Foreign exchange	$ 4[1]
Commodities	31[2]
Derivatives not designated as hedges:	
Foreign exchange	10[1]
Total	$45
Liabilities	
Derivatives designated as hedges:	
Cross-currency swaps	$49[3]
Foreign exchange	4[3]
Commodities	1[3]
Derivatives not designated as hedges:	
Foreign exchange	13[3]
Total	$67

[1] Reported in other current assets.
[2] $14 reported in current assets and $17 reported in other non-current assets.
[3] Reported in accounts payable and accrued liabilities.

Restructuring

2.183

AIR PRODUCTS AND CHEMICALS, INC. (SEP)

(Millions of dollars)	2009	2008
Current liabilities		
Payables and accrued liabilities	$1,660.4	$1,665.6
Accrued income taxes	42.9	87.0
Short-term borrowings	333.8	419.3
Current portion of long-term debt	452.1	32.1
Current liabilities of discontinued operations	14.4	8.0
Total current liabilities	$2,503.6	$2,212.0

NOTES TO CONSOLIDATED FINANCIAL STATEMENTS (Millions of dollars)

3 (In Part): Global Cost Reduction Plan

2009

The 2009 results from continuing operations included a total charge of $298.2 ($200.3 after-tax, or $.94 per share) for the global cost reduction plan. In the first quarter of 2009, the Company announced the global cost reduction plan designed to lower its cost structure and better align its businesses to reflect rapidly declining economic conditions around the world. The first-quarter results included a charge of $174.2 ($116.1 after-tax, or $.55 per share). In the third quarter 2009, due to the continuing slow economic recovery, the Company committed to additional actions associated with its global cost reduction plan that resulted in a charge of $124.0 ($84.2 after-tax, or $.39 per share).

The total 2009 charge included $210.0 for severance and other benefits, including pension-related costs, associated with the elimination of approximately 2,550 positions from the Company's global workforce. The reductions are targeted at reducing overhead and infrastructure costs, reducing and refocusing elements of the Company's technology and business development spending, lowering its plant operating costs, and the closure of certain manufacturing facilities. The remainder of this charge, $88.2, was for business exits and asset management actions. Assets held for sale were written down to net realizable value, and an environmental liability of $16.0 was recognized. This environmental liability resulted from a decision to sell a production facility.

The planned actions associated with the global cost reduction plan are expected to be substantially completed within one year of when the related charges were recognized.

Business Segments

The charge recorded in 2009 was excluded from segment operating profit. The table below displays how this charge related to the businesses at the segment level:

	Severance and Other Benefits	Asset Impairments/ Other Costs	Total
Merchant Gases	$127.5	$ 7.2	$134.7
Tonnage Gases	14.2	—	14.2
Electronics and Performance Materials	30.6	58.9	89.5
Equipment and Energy	37.7	22.1	59.8
2009 Charge	$210.0	$88.2	$298.2

Accrual Balance

The following table summarizes changes to the carrying amount of the accrual for the global cost reduction plan:

	Severance and Other Benefits	Asset Impairments/ Other Costs	Total
First quarter 2009 charge	$120.0	$ 54.2	$174.2
Third quarter 2009 charge	90.0	34.0	124.0
Environmental charge(A)	—	(16.0)	(16.0)
Noncash expenses	(33.8)(B)	(66.1)	(99.9)
Cash expenditures	(75.3)	(.9)	(76.2)
Currency translation adjustment	4.3	—	4.3
30 September 2009	$105.2	$ 5.2	$110.4

(A) Reflected in accrual for environmental obligations.
(B) Primarily pension-related costs which are reflected in the accrual for pension benefits.

21 (In Part): Supplemental Information

Payables and Accrued Liabilities

	2009	2008
Trade creditors	$ 620.3	$ 755.2
Customer advances	72.6	122.0
Accrued payroll and employee benefits	137.9	203.7
Pension benefits	347.9	123.5
Dividends payable	95.1	92.1
Outstanding payments in excess of certain cash balances	25.2	56.1
Accrued interest expense	59.2	64.9
Derivative instruments	61.3	81.9
Global cost reduction plan accrual	110.4	—
Miscellaneous	130.5	166.2
	$1,660.4	$1,665.6

Deferred Revenue

2.184

CA, INC. (MAR)

(Dollars in millions)	2009	2008
Current liabilities		
Current portion of long-term debt and loans payable	$ 650	$ 361
Accounts payable	120	152
Accrued salaries, wages, and commissions	306	400
Accrued expenses and other current liabilities	362	439
Deferred revenue (billed or collected)— current	2,431	2,664
Taxes payable, other than income taxes payable	85	97
Federal, state, and foreign income taxes payable	84	59
Deferred income taxes—current	40	106
Total current liabilities	$4,078	$4,278

NOTES TO CONSOLIDATED FINANCIAL STATEMENTS

Note 1(In Part): Significant Accounting Policies

f (In Part): Revenue Recognition

The Company generates revenue from the following primary sources: (1) licensing software products; (2) providing customer technical support (referred to as "maintenance"); and (3) providing professional services, such as product implementation, consulting and education. Revenue is recorded net of applicable sales taxes.

The Company recognizes revenue pursuant to the requirements of Statement of Position (SOP) 97-2, "Software *Revenue Recognition*," issued by the American Institute of Certified Public Accountants, as amended by SOP 98-9, "Modification *of SOP 97-2, Software Revenue Recognition, With Respect to Certain Transactions.*" In accordance with SOP 97-2, the Company begins to recognize revenue from licensing and maintenance when all of the following criteria are met: (1) the Company has evidence of an arrangement with a customer; (2) the Company delivers the products; (3) license agreement terms are fixed or determinable and free of contingencies or uncertainties that may alter the agreement such that it may not be complete and final; and (4) collection is probable.

The Company's software licenses generally do not include acceptance provisions. An acceptance provision allows a customer to test the software for a defined period of time before committing to license the software. If a license agreement includes an acceptance provision, the Company does not recognize revenue until the earlier of the receipt of a written customer acceptance or, if not notified by the customer to cancel the license agreement, the expiration of the acceptance period.

Under the Company's subscription model, implemented in October 2000, software license agreements typically combine the right to use specified software products, the right to maintenance, and the right to receive unspecified future software products for no additional fee during the term of the agreement. Under these subscription licenses, once all four of the above-noted revenue recognition criteria are met, the Company is required under GAAP to recognize revenue ratably over the term of the license agreement.

For license agreements signed prior to October 2000, once all four of the above-noted revenue recognition criteria were met, software license fees were recognized as revenue generally when the software was delivered to the customer, or "up-front" (as the contracts did not include a right to unspecified future software products), and the maintenance fees were deferred and subsequently recognized as revenue over the term of the license. Currently, a relatively small amount of the Company's revenue from software licenses is recognized on an up-front basis, subject to meeting the same revenue recognition criteria in accordance with SOP 97-2 as described above. Software fees from such licenses are recognized up-front and are reported in the "Software fees and other" line item in the Consolidated Statements of Operations. Maintenance fees from such licenses are recognized ratably over the term of the license and are recorded on the "Subscription and maintenance revenue" line item in the Consolidated Statements of Operations. License agreements with software fees that are recognized up-front do not include the right to receive unspecified future software products. However, in the event such license agreements are executed within close proximity to or in contemplation of other license agreements that are signed under the Company's subscription model with the same customer, the licenses together may be considered a single multi-element agreement, and all such revenue is required to be recognized ratably and is recorded as "Subscription and maintenance revenue" in the Consolidated Statements of Operations.

Since the Company implemented its subscription model in October 2000, the Company's practice with respect to products of newly acquired businesses with established vendor specific objective evidence (VSOE) of fair value has been to record revenue initially on the acquired company's systems, generally under an up-front model; and, starting within the first fiscal year after the acquisition, to enter new licenses for such products under the Company's subscription model, following which revenue is recognized ratably and recorded as "Subscription and maintenance revenue." In some instances, the Company sells newly developed and recently acquired products on an up-front model. The software license fees from these contracts are presented as "Software fees and other." Selling such licenses under an up-front model may result in higher total revenue in a current reporting period than if such licenses were based on the Company's subscription model and the associated revenue recognized ratably.

Revenue from professional service arrangements is generally recognized as the services are performed. Revenue from committed professional services that are sold as part of a subscription license agreement is deferred and recognized on a ratable basis over the term of the related software license. If it is not probable that a project will be completed or the payment will be received, revenue recognition is deferred until the uncertainty is removed.

Revenue from sales to distributors, resellers, and value-added resellers commences when all four of the SOP 97-2 revenue recognition criteria noted above are met and when these entities sell the software product to their customers. This is commonly referred to as the sell-through method. Revenue from the sale of products to distributors, resellers and value-added resellers that include licensing terms that provide the right for the end-users to receive certain unspecified future software products is recognized on a ratable basis.

In the second quarter of fiscal year 2008, the Company decided that certain channel or "commercial" products sold through tier two distributors will no longer be licensed with terms entitling the customer to receive unspecified future software products. As such, license revenue from these sales where the Company has established VSOE for maintenance is recognized on a perpetual or up-front basis using the residual method and is reflected as "Software fees and other," with maintenance revenue being deferred and recognized ratably.

Subscription and Maintenance Revenue

Subscription and maintenance revenue is the amount of revenue recognized ratably during the reporting period from either: (i) subscription license agreements that were in effect during the period, which generally include maintenance that is bundled with and not separately identifiable from software usage fees or product sales, or (ii) maintenance agreements associated with providing customer technical support and access to software fixes and upgrades which are separately identifiable from software usage fees or product sales. Deferred revenue (billed or collected) is comprised of: (i) amounts received in advance of revenue recognition from the customer, (ii) amounts billed but not collected for which revenue has not yet been earned, and (iii) amounts received in advance of revenue recognition from financial institutions where the Company has transferred its interest in committed installments. Each of the categories is further differentiated by current or non-current classification depending on when the revenue is anticipated to be earned (i.e., within the next twelve months or subsequent to the next twelve months).

Software Fees and Other

Software fees and other revenue primarily consist of revenue that is recognized on an up-front basis. This includes revenue generated through transactions with distribution and original equipment manufacturer channel partners (sometimes referred to as the Company's "indirect" or "channel" revenue) and certain revenue associated with new or acquired products sold on an up-front basis. Also included is financing fee revenue, which results from the discounting of product sales recognized on an up-front basis with extended payment terms to present value. Revenue recognized on an up-front basis results in higher revenue for the period than if the same revenue had been recognized ratably under the Company's subscription model.

q. Deferred Revenue (Billed or Collected)

The Company accounts for unearned revenue on billed amounts due from customers on a "gross method" of presentation. Under the gross method, unearned revenue on billed installments (collected or uncollected) is reported as deferred revenue in the liability section of the balance sheet. The components of "Deferred revenue (billed or collected)—current" and "Deferred revenue (billed or collected)—noncurrent" as of March 31, 2009 and March 31, 2008 are as follows:

(In millions)	2009	2008
Current:		
Subscription and maintenance	$2,272	$2,455
Professional services	150	166
Financing obligations and other	9	43
Total deferred revenue (billed or collected)—current	2,431	2,664
Noncurrent:		
Subscription and maintenance	987	1,001
Professional services	10	22
Financing obligations and other	3	13
Total deferred revenue (billed or collected)—noncurrent	1,000	1,036
Total deferred revenue (billed or collected)	$3,431	$3,700

Deferred revenue (billed or collected) excludes unrealized revenue from contractual obligations that will be billed by the Company in future periods.

Interest

2.185

GANNETT CO., INC. (DEC)

(In thousands of dollars)	2009	2008
Current liabilities		
Accounts payable		
Trade	$216,721	$ 287,690
Other	35,864	36,883
Accrued liabilities		
Compensation	143,182	191,019
Interest	25,281	27,432
Other	201,711	250,271
Dividend payable	9,703	91,465
Income taxes	45,085	—
Deferred income	222,556	272,381
Total current liabilities	$900,103	$1,157,141

Deferred Taxes

2.186

ITT CORPORATION (DEC)

(In millions)	2009	2008
Current liabilities		
Accounts payable	$1,291.3	$1,234.6
Accrued expenses	1,034.7	991.2
Accrued taxes	105.0	30.2
Short-term debt and current maturities of long-term debt	75.0	1,679.0
Postretirement benefits	73.2	68.8
Deferred income taxes	36.4	26.7
Total current liabilities	$2,615.6	$4,030.5

NOTES TO CONSOLIDATED FINANCIAL STATEMENTS (Dollars in millions)

Note 1 (In Part): Summary of Significant Accounting Policies

Income Taxes

We determine the provision for income taxes using the asset and liability approach. Under this approach, deferred income taxes represent the expected future tax consequences of temporary differences between the carrying amounts and tax basis of assets and liabilities. We record a valuation allowance to reduce deferred tax assets when uncertainty regarding their realizability exists.

We recognize tax benefits from uncertain tax positions only if it is more likely than not that the tax position will be sustained on examination by the taxing authorities, based on the technical merits of the position. The tax benefits recognized in the Consolidated Financial Statements from such positions are measured based on the largest benefit that has a greater than 50% likelihood of being realized upon ultimate settlement.

Note 6 (In Part): Income Taxes

Deferred income taxes are established for temporary differences between the amount of assets and liabilities recognized for financial reporting purposes and for tax reporting purposes and for carryforwards.

Deferred tax assets and liabilities include the following:

	2009	2008
Deferred tax assets:		
Employee benefits	$ 736.0	$ 936.5
Accruals	281.3	198.3
Loss carryforwards	199.7	293.0
Uniform capitalization	13.0	11.7
State credit carryforwards	11.5	7.8
Foreign tax credit	—	1.1
Other	14.1	—
Subtotal	1,255.6	1,448.4
Valuation allowance	(149.9)	(265.4)
Net deferred tax assets	$1,105.7	$1,183.0
Deferred tax liabilities:		
Intangibles	$ 324.2	$ 322.4
Accelerated depreciation	46.7	6.3
Investment	15.7	108.5
Other	—	22.3
Total deferred tax liabilities	$ 386.6	$ 459.5

Deferred taxes in the Consolidated Balance Sheets consist of the following:

	2009	2008
Current assets	$234.1	$203.4
Non-current assets	583.2	608.5
Current liabilities	(36.4)	(26.7)
Other non-current liabilities	(61.8)	(61.7)
	$719.1	$723.5

No provision was made for U.S. taxes payable on accumulated undistributed foreign earnings of certain subsidiaries amounting to approximately $1,744.6 because these amounts are indefinitely reinvested. While the amount of federal income taxes, if such earnings are distributed in the future, cannot be determined, such taxes may be reduced by tax credits and other deductions. Taxes have not been provided for other basis differences since these differences are not expected to reverse in the foreseeable future.

We have the following attributes available for utilization:

Attribute	Amount	First Year of Expiration
U.S. net operating loss	$ 22.9	December 31, 2020
State net operating losses	3,041.2	December 31, 2010
Federal and state capital loss	109.0	December 31, 2012
State tax credits	11.5	December 31, 2012
Foreign net operating loss	309.7	December 31, 2010

As of December 31, 2009, a valuation allowance of approximately $149.9 had been established to reduce the deferred income tax asset related to certain U.S. state and foreign net operating losses and U.S. federal capital loss carryforwards. During 2009, the valuation allowance decreased by $115.5 resulting from the following: decrease of $9.8 attributable to foreign net operating loss carryforwards and foreign investments, decrease of $93.7 attributable to state net operating loss and credit carryforwards (see statement below for main components of this amount) and a decrease of $12.0 attributable to U.S. federal capital loss carryforwards that were utilized in 2009.

During 2009, the Company completed a study of its state tax attributes. As a result of the study, the Company determined that $21.6 of state deferred tax assets are unrecognized tax benefits, approximately $20.5 of state deferred tax assets are attributable to excess tax benefits on stock-based compensation that have not been realized, identified additional state net operating losses of $15.6 and refined the state tax attributable to minimum pension liability by $57.0 and has, accordingly, changed its valuation allowance. In addition, the Company, as a result of expected future income, has determined that it is more likely than not that a portion of its state deferred tax assets, in the amount of $13.7, will be realized and a valuation allowance is not necessary.

Taxes Other Than Federal Income Taxes

2.187

THE HOME DEPOT, INC. (JAN)

(Amounts in millions)	2009	2008
Current Liabilities:		
Short-term debt	$ —	$ 1,747
Accounts payable	4,822	5,732
Accrued salaries and related expenses	1,129	1,094
Sales taxes payable	337	445
Deferred revenue	1,165	1,474
Income taxes payable	289	60
Current Installments of long-term debt	1,767	300
Other accrued expenses	1,644	1,854
Total current liabilities	$11,153	$12,706

Product Warranties

2.188

MASCO CORPORATION (DEC)

(In millions)	2009	2008
Current liabilities		
Accounts payable	$ 578	$ 531
Notes payable	364	71
Accrued liabilities	839	945
Total current liabilities	$1,781	$1,547

NOTES TO CONSOLIDATED FINANCIAL STATEMENTS

A (In Part): Accounting Policies

Warranty

At the time of sale, the Company accrues a warranty liability for estimated costs to provide products, parts or services to repair or replace products in satisfaction of warranty obligations. The Company's estimate of costs to service its warranty obligations is based upon historical experience and expectations of future conditions.

A majority of the Company's business is at the consumer retail level through home centers and major retailers. A consumer may return a product to a retail outlet that is a warranty return. However, certain retail outlets do not distinguish between warranty and other types of returns when they claim a return deduction from the Company. The Company's revenue recognition policy takes into account this type of return when recognizing revenue, and deductions are recorded at the time of sale.

J. Accrued Liabilities

(In millions)	2009	2008
Insurance	$193	$198
Salaries, wages and commissions	193	183
Warranty (Note S)	109	119
Advertising and sales promotion	80	107
Interest	68	68
Employee retirement plans	36	34
Property, payroll and other taxes	33	29
Dividends payable	27	85
Litigation	7	14
Plant closures	3	10
Other	90	98
Total	$839	$945

S (In Part): Other Commitments and Contingencies

Warranty

Certain of the Company's products and product finishes and services are covered by a warranty to be free from defects in material and workmanship for periods ranging from one year to the life of the product. At the time of sale, the Company accrues a warranty liability for estimated costs to provide products, parts or services to repair or replace products in satisfaction of warranty obligations. The Company's estimate of costs to service its warranty obligations is based upon historical experience and expectations of future conditions. To the extent that the Company experiences any changes in warranty claim activity or costs associated with servicing those claims, its warranty liability is adjusted accordingly.

Changes in the Company's warranty liability were as follows, in millions:

(In millions)	2009	2008
Balance at January 1	$119	$133
Accruals for warranties issued during the year	32	42
Accruals related to pre-existing warranties	5	6
Settlements made (in cash or kind) during the year	(44)	(53)
Other, net (including currency translation)	(3)	(9)
Balance at December 31	$109	$119

Insurance

2.189

WALGREEN CO. (AUG)

(In millions)	2009	2008
Current liabilities		
Short-term borrowings	$ 15	$ 83
Trade accounts payable	4,308	4,289
Accrued expenses and other liabilities	2,406	2,272
Income taxes	40	—
Total current liabilities	$6,769	$6,644

NOTES TO CONSOLIDATED FINANCIAL STATEMENTS

1 (In Part): Summary of Major Accounting Policies

Insurance

The company obtains insurance coverage for catastrophic exposures as well as those risks required by law to be insured. It is the company's policy to retain a significant portion of certain losses related to workers' compensation, property, comprehensive general, pharmacist and vehicle liability. Liabilities for these losses are recorded based upon the company's estimates for claims incurred and are not discounted. The provisions are estimated in part by considering historical claims experience, demographic factors and other actuarial assumptions.

15 (In Part): Supplementary Financial Information

Included in the Consolidated Balance Sheets captions are the following assets and liabilities (in millions):

	2009	2008
Accrued expenses and other liabilities		
Accrued salaries	$ 687	$ 664
Taxes other than income taxes	408	406
Profit sharing	192	211
Insurance	164	128
Other	955	863
	$2,406	$2,272

Advertising and Promotion

2.190

ALTRIA GROUP, INC. (DEC)

(In millions of dollars)	2009	2008
Current portion of long-term debt	$ 775	$ 135
Accounts payable	494	510
Accrued liabilities:		
Marketing	467	374
Taxes, except income taxes	318	98
Employment costs	239	248
Settlement charges	3,635	3,984
Other	1,354	1,128
Dividends payable	710	665
Total current liabilities	$7,992	$7,142

NOTES TO CONSOLIDATED FINANCIAL STATEMENTS

Note 2 (In Part): Summary of Significant Accounting Policies

Marketing Costs

The consumer products businesses promote their products with advertising, consumer incentives and trade promotions. Such programs include, but are not limited to, discounts, coupons, rebates, in-store display incentives and volume-based incentives. Advertising costs are expensed as incurred. Consumer incentive and trade promotion activities are recorded as a reduction of revenues based on amounts estimated as being due to customers and consumers at the end of a period, based principally on historical utilization and redemption rates. For interim reporting purposes, advertising and certain consumer incentive expenses are charged to operations as a percentage of sales, based on estimated sales and related expenses for the full year.

Dividends

2.191

BALDOR ELECTRIC COMPANY (DEC)

(In thousands)	2009	2008
Current liabilities		
Accounts payable	$ 61,776	$ 98,046
Accrued employee compensation	7,436	11,165
Accrued profit sharing	7,815	16,554
Accrued warranty costs	9,330	9,477
Accrued insurance obligations	9,635	10,667
Accrued interest expense	27,782	22,830
Other accrued expenses	55,090	110,006
Dividends payable	7,924	7,863
Note payable	—	735
Current maturities of long-term obligations	7,108	7,609
Total current liabilities	$193,896	$294,952

Environmental Costs

2.192

PALL CORPORATION (JUL)

(In thousands)	2009	2008
Current liabilities:		
Notes payable	$ 42,371	$ 26,062
Accounts payable	171,956	200,744
Accrued liabilities	250,838	270,522
Income taxes payable	137,846	57,882
Current portion of long-term debt	97,432	3,252
Dividends payable	16,947	15,501
Total current liabilities	$717,390	$573,963

NOTES TO CONSOLIDATED FINANCIAL STATEMENTS (In thousands)

Note 1 (In Part): Accounting Policies and Related Matters

Environmental Matters

Accruals for environmental matters are recorded when it is probable that a liability has been incurred and the amount of the liability can be reasonably estimated, based on current law and existing technologies. These accruals are adjusted periodically as facts and circumstances change, assessment and remediation efforts progress or as additional technical or legal information becomes available. Costs of future expenditures for environmental remediation obligations are not discounted to their present value and are expected to be disbursed over an extended period of time. Accruals for environmental liabilities are included in "Accrued liabilities" and "Other non-current liabilities" in the Consolidated Balance Sheets.

Note 13. Accrued and Other Non-Current Liabilities

Accrued liabilities consist of the following:

	2009	2008
Payroll and related taxes	$113,401	$136,675
Benefits	16,490	18,075
Interest payable[a]	36,568	18,854
Environmental remediation[b]	5,530	5,180
Deferred income taxes	5,649	3,648
Other	73,200	88,090
	$250,838	$270,522

[a] Accrued liabilities include interest payable related to income taxes as of July 31, 2009 which was previously included in interest payable–non-current as of July 31, 2008; refer to Note 12, Income Taxes, for further discussion.

[b] For further discussion regarding environmental remediation liabilities refer to Note 15, Contingencies and Commitments.

Other non-current liabilities consist of the following:

	2009	2008
Retirement benefits[c]	$231,405	$167,737
Interest payable—non-current[a]	24,733	46,323
Deferred revenue[d]	11,667	13,821
Environmental remediation[b]	6,924	9,569
Other	13,217	14,648
	$287,946	$252,098

[a] Accrued liabilities include interest payable related to income taxes as of July 31, 2009 which was previously included in interest payable–non-current as of July 31, 2008; refer to Note 12, Income Taxes, for further discussion.

[b] For further discussion regarding environmental remediation liabilities refer to Note 15, Contingencies and Commitments.

[c] For discussion regarding retirement benefits refer to Note 14, Pension and Profit Sharing Plans and Arrangements.

[d] On December 16, 2005, the Company sold the rights to its Western Hemisphere commercial aerospace aftermarket distribution channel for the Company's products for a ten-year period to Satair. The proceeds received for the distribution rights were recorded as deferred revenue and are being amortized as an increase to sales over the life of the distribution agreement.

Note 15 (In Part): Contingencies and Commitments

Environmental Matters

Certain facilities of the Company are involved in environmental proceedings. The most significant matter pertains to the Company's subsidiary, Gelman Sciences Inc. ("Gelman"), which constitutes the majority of the $12,454 and $14,749 of accruals in the Company's Consolidated Balance Sheets at July 31, 2009, and July 31, 2008, respectively. The Company recorded charges of $2,179 and $1,275 in fiscal years 2009 and 2008, respectively, related to environmental matters. The increases recorded to the environmental liabilities represent management's best estimate of the cost to be incurred to perform remediation. The estimates are based upon the feasibility of the use of certain remediation technologies and processes as well as the facts known to management at the time the estimates are made. (Refer to Note 1, Accounting Policies and Related Matters).

In February 1988, an action was filed in the Circuit Court for Washtenaw County, Michigan (the "Court") by the State of Michigan (the "State") against Gelman Sciences Inc. ("Gelman"), a subsidiary acquired by the Company in February 1997. The action sought to compel Gelman to investigate and remediate contamination near Gelman's Ann Arbor facility and requested reimbursement of costs the State had expended in investigating the contamination, which the State alleged was caused by Gelman's disposal of waste water from its manufacturing process. Pursuant to a consent judgment entered into by Gelman and the State in October 1992 (amended September 1996 and October 1999) (the "Consent Judgment"), which resolved that litigation, Gelman is remediating the contamination without admitting wrongdoing. In February 2000, the State Assistant Attorney General filed a Motion to Enforce Consent Judgment in the Court seeking approximately $4,900 in stipulated penalties for the alleged violations of the Consent Judgment and additional injunctive relief. Gelman disputed these assertions. Following an evidentiary hearing in July 2000, the Court took the matter of penalties "under advisement." The Court issued a Remediation Enforcement Order (the "REO") requiring Gelman to submit and implement a detailed plan to reduce the contamination to acceptable levels within five years. Gelman's plan has been approved by both the Court and the State. Although groundwater concentrations remain above acceptable levels in much of the affected area, the Court has expressed its satisfaction with Gelman's progress during hearings both before and after the five-year period expired. Neither the State nor the Court has sought or suggested that Gelman should be penalized based on the continued presence of groundwater contamination at the site.

In February 2004, the Court instructed Gelman to submit its Final Feasibility Study describing how it intends to address an area of groundwater contamination not addressed by the previously approved plan. Gelman submitted its Feasibility Study as instructed. The State also submitted its plan for remediating this area of contamination to the Court. On December 17, 2004, the Court issued its Order and Opinion Regarding Remediation and Contamination of the Unit E Aquifer (the "Order") to address an area of groundwater contamination not addressed in the previously approved plan. Gelman is now in the process of implementing the requirements of the Order.

In correspondence dated June 5, 2001, the State asserted that stipulated penalties in the amount of $142 were owed for a separate alleged violation of the Consent Judgment. The Court found that a "substantial basis" for Gelman's position existed and again took the State's request "under advisement," pending the results of certain groundwater monitoring data. That data has been submitted to the Court, but no ruling has been issued.

On August 9, 2001, the State made a written demand for reimbursement of $227 it has allegedly incurred for groundwater monitoring. On October 23, 2006, the State made another written demand for reimbursement of these costs, which now total $494, with interest. In February 2007, the Company met with the State to discuss whether the State would be interested in a proposal for a "global settlement" to include, among other matters, the claim for past monitoring costs ($494). Gelman is engaged in discussion with the State with regard to this demand, however, Gelman considers this claim barred by the Consent Judgment.

By letter dated June 15, 2007, the Michigan Department of Environmental Quality ("DEQ") claimed Gelman was in violation of the Consent Judgment and related work plans due to its failure to operate a groundwater extraction well in the Evergreen Subdivision at the approved minimum purge rate. The DEQ sought to assess stipulated penalties. Gelman filed a Petition for Dispute Resolution with the Court on July 6, 2007 contesting these penalties. Prior to the hearing on Gelman's petition, the parties met and the DEQ agreed to waive these penalties in exchange for Gelman's agreement to perform additional investigations in the area. The Court entered a Stipulated Order to this effect on August 7, 2007. Since then, Gelman has installed several monitoring wells requested by the State. Representatives of Gelman and the State met on December 10, 2007 to discuss the data obtained from these wells and to plan further investigative activities. These discussions are ongoing. On April 15, 2008, Gelman submitted two reports summarizing the results of the investigation to date. Gelman also submitted a "capture zone analysis" that confirmed that Gelman was achieving the cleanup objective for the Evergreen Subdivision system. On June 23, 2008, the State provided its response to these reports. The response also addressed outstanding issues regarding several other areas of the site. In its response, the

State asked the Company to undertake additional investigation in the Evergreen Subdivision area and in other areas of the site to more fully delineate the extent of contamination. The State also asked the Company to capture additional contaminated groundwater in the Wagner Road area, near the Gelman property, unless the Company can show that it is not feasible to do so. Gelman proposed to the DEQ several modifications to the Consent Judgment on August 1, 2008 and met with the DEQ to discuss these modifications (and other outstanding issues) on September 15, 2008. The parties agreed that Gelman would prepare and submit to the DEQ an outline for modifications to the existing Consent Judgment (and Administrative Orders) by October 15, 2008 and that the parties would meet thereafter to discuss. On April 29, 2009, the Court issued an order that sets forth a schedule for the various steps that must be taken to implement agreed upon modifications to the cleanup program. Pursuant to that schedule, the Company submitted its Comprehensive Proposal to Modify Cleanup Program to the State on May 4, 2009. On June 15, 2009, the State refused to approve the Company's Proposal. Pursuant to the Court-imposed schedule, the Company filed pleadings identifying areas of dispute and motions seeking approval of its Proposal on August 18, 2009. The DEQ did not file any pleadings regarding the Company's Proposal, but did file a motion to enforce the existing Consent Judgment that asks the Court to order the Company to undertake additional response activities with regard to certain portions of the site. The DEQ's motion does not seek monetary damages. The Court has not indicated the exact process by which it will resolve these disputes.

In the opinion of management, the Company is in substantial compliance with applicable environmental laws and its accruals for environmental remediation are adequate at this time. Because regulatory standards under environmental laws are becoming increasingly stringent, there can be no assurance that future developments, additional information and experience gained will not cause the Company to incur material environmental liabilities or costs beyond those accrued in its consolidated financial statements.

Rebates

2.193

BELDEN INC. (DEC)

(In thousands)	2009	2008
Current liabilities		
Accounts payable	$169,763	$160,744
Accrued liabilities	141,922	180,801
Current maturities of long-term debt	46,268	—
Total current liabilities	$357,953	$341,545

NOTES TO CONSOLIDATED FINANCIAL STATEMENTS

Note 2 (In Part): Summary of Significant Accounting Policies

Accrued Sales Rebates

We grant incentive rebates to participating customers as part of our sales programs. The rebates are determined based on certain targeted sales volumes. Rebates are paid quarterly or annually in either cash or receivables credits. Until we can process these rebates through individual customer records, we estimate the amount of outstanding rebates and recognize them as accrued liabilities and reductions in our gross revenues. We base our estimates on both historical and anticipated sales demand and rebate program participation. We charge revisions to these estimates back to accrued liabilities and revenues in the period in which the facts that give rise to each revision become known. Future market conditions and product transitions might require us to take actions to increase sales rebates offered, possibly resulting in an incremental increase in accrued liabilities and an incremental reduction in revenues at the time the rebate is offered. Accrued sales rebates at December 31, 2009 and 2008 totaled $19.0 million and $20.5 million, respectively.

Note 11 (In Part): Accrued Liabilities

The carrying value of accrued liabilities was as follows:

(In thousands)	2009	2008
Wages, severance and related taxes	$ 46,786	$ 72,985
Employee benefits	17,274	25,429
Accrued rebates	19,045	20,496
Deferred revenue	19,249	17,507
Other (individual items less than 5% of total current liabilities)	39,568	44,384
Accrued liabilities	$141,922	$180,801

Advances/Deposits

2.194

ROCKWELL COLLINS, INC. (SEP)

(In millions)	2009	2008
Current liabilities		
Short-term debt	$ —	$ 287
Accounts payable	366	419
Compensation and benefits	199	295
Advance payments from customers	349	308
Product warranty costs	217	226
Other current liabilities	228	205
Total current liabilities	$1,359	$1,740

NOTES TO CONSOLIDATED FINANCIAL STATEMENTS

2 (In Part): Significant Accounting Policies

Advance Payments From Customers

Advance payments from customers represent cash collected from customers in advance of revenue recognition.

Litigation

2.195

HILL-ROM HOLDINGS, INC. (SEP)

(Dollars in millions)	2009	2008
Current liabilities		
Trade accounts payable	$ 81.3	$ 99.4
Short-term borrowings	102.2	122.6
Accrued compensation	72.7	84.8
Accrued litigation (Note 17)	21.2	21.2
Accrued product warranties	17.1	16.9
Other current liabilities	49.8	49.8
Total current liabilities	$344.3	$394.7

NOTES TO CONSOLIDATED FINANCIAL STATEMENTS
(Dollars in millions)

17 (In Part): Commitments and Contingencies

Legal Proceedings

Antitrust Settlement

In fiscal 2005, we entered into a definitive, court approved agreement with Spartanburg Regional Healthcare Systems and its attorneys to settle a purported antitrust class action lawsuit. The settlement resolved all of the claims of class members that did not opt out of the settlement, including the claims of all United States and Canadian purchasers or renters of Hill-Rom® products from 1990 through February 2, 2006 related to or arising out of the subject matter of the lawsuit, and the claims that may have resulted from the current or future effects of conduct or events occurring through February 2, 2006. The original settlement amount of $337.5 million was reduced by almost $21.2 million, to $316.3 million, reflecting the portion attributable to customers who opted out of the settlement. Opt-outs from the settlement account for roughly six percent of the total United States and Canadian revenue during the class period, and over 99 percent of that figure is attributable to the United States government's decision to opt out of the settlement. We believe we have meritorious defenses against any claims the United States government may choose to make, due to, among other reasons, pricing practices of government purchases that are different than the pricing practices primarily at issue in the lawsuit.

In connection with our assessment that it was probable that a settlement would be reached and finally approved by the Court during fiscal 2006, we recorded a litigation charge and established a litigation accrual in the amount of $358.6 million in the fourth quarter of fiscal 2005, which included certain legal and other costs associated with the proposed settlement. The Court entered the Order and Final Judgment in the third quarter of fiscal 2006, and we paid a total $316.3 million of the settlement amounts into escrow during that year. We also reversed $2.3 million of the $21.2 million of estimated legal and other costs originally provided as part of the litigation accrual as such amounts were not probable of payment in fiscal 2006 and subsequently reversed an additional $1.2 million in the fourth quarter of 2007. As of September 30, 2009 we have retained a $21.2 million litigation accrual associated with the opt-outs.

Tax Uncertainties

2.196

TERRA INDUSTRIES INC. (DEC)

(In thousands)	2009	2008
Accounts payable	$ 87,898	$ 99,893
Customer prepayments	39,238	111,592
Derivative hedge liabilities	281	125,925
Accrued and other current liabilities	78,792	127,770
Total current liabilities	$206,209	$465,180

NOTES TO CONSOLIDATED FINANCIAL STATEMENTS

11. Accrued and Other Current Liabilities

Accrued and other current liabilities consisted of the following at December 31:

(In thousands)	2009	2008
Payroll and benefit costs	$18,913	$ 27,104
Accrued CF defense costs	14,730	—
Income taxes payable	9,441	63,999
Accrued interest	8,898	9,748
Accrued property taxes	3,554	3,291
Current accrued phantom shares	3,449	4,341
Accrued consulting	1,972	1,390
Deferred revenue	1,530	3,346
Unrecognized tax benefit (see Note 21)	1,506	—
Other	14,799	14,551
Total	$78,792	$127,770

21. Unrecognized Tax Benefit

We adopted the provision of ASC 740, *Income Taxes* (previously referred to as FASB Interpretation No. 48, *Accounting for Uncertainty in Income Taxes* (FIN 48)), on January 1, 2007. Under ASC 740, tax benefits are recorded only for tax positions that are more likely than not to be sustained upon examination by tax authorities. The amount recognized is measured as the largest amount of benefit that is greater than 50 percent likely to be realized upon ultimate settlement. Unrecognized tax benefits are tax benefits claimed in our tax returns that do not meet these recognition and measurement standards.

The following table summarizes the activity related to our unrecognized tax benefits, interest and penalties:

(In thousands)	2009	2008	2007
Unrecognized tax benefits at January 1	$33,560	$33,560	$33,560
Gross increases (decreases)—tax positions in prior periods	27,415	—	—
Gross increases (decreases)—tax positions in current period	898	—	—
Decreases relating to settlements with tax authorities	—	—	—
Decreases from the lapse of applicable statute of limitations	(6,712)	—	—
Unrecognized tax benefits at December 31	$55,161	$33,560	$33,560
Accrued interest and penalties	7,249	2,389	—
Total ASC 740 liability	$62,410	$35,949	$33,560

The primary jurisdictions in which we or one of our subsidiaries files income tax returns are the United States including state and local jurisdictions and Canada. U.S. tax authorities have completed their federal income tax examinations for all years prior to 1998. With respect to state and local jurisdictions inside the United States, with limited exceptions, Terra and its subsidiaries are no longer subject to income tax audits for years before 2002. For Canada, income tax returns remain subject to examination by tax authorities for calendar years beginning in 2001. Although the outcome of tax audits is always uncertain, we believe that adequate amounts of tax, including interest and penalties, have been provided for any adjustments that are expected to result from those years.

The adoption of ASC 740 had no impact on our financial statements other than the reclassification of the unrecognized tax benefit. Other liabilities include a ASC 740 liability of $60.9 million and other current liability of $1.5 million, including accrued interest, at December 31, 2009. During the next twelve months we expect to settle an issue with Revenue Canada and have, therefore, classified $1.5 million as current. If recognized, $49.9 million of the ASC 740 liability would have an impact on the effective tax rate.

When applicable, we recognize accrued interest and penalties related to unrecognized tax benefits in income taxes on the statement of operations. Interest and penalties were recognized at December 31, 2009 in the amount of $5.9 million.

Billings in Excess of Uncompleted Contract Costs

2.197

URS CORPORATION (DEC)

(In thousands)	2009	2008
Current liabilities:		
Current portion of long-term debt	$115,261	$ 16,506
Accounts payable and subcontractors payable, including retentions of $51,475 and $85,097, respectively	586,783	712,552
Accrued salaries and employee benefits	435,456	430,938
Billings in excess of costs and accrued earnings on contracts	235,268	254,186
Other current liabilities	$156,746	$173,173

NOTES TO CONSOLIDATED FINANCIAL STATEMENTS

Note 1 (In Part): Accounting Policies

Billings in Excess of Costs and Accrued Earnings on Contracts

Billings in excess of costs and accrued earnings on contracts in the accompanying consolidated balance sheets is comprised of cash collected from clients and billings to clients on contracts in advance of work performed, advance payments negotiated as a contract condition, estimated losses on uncompleted contracts, normal profit liabilities, project-related legal liabilities; and other project-related reserves. The majority of the unearned project-related costs will be earned over the next twelve months.

We record provisions for estimated losses on uncompleted contracts in the period in which such losses become known. The cumulative effects of revisions to contract revenues and estimated completion costs are recorded in the accounting period in which the amounts become evident and can be reasonably estimated. These revisions can include such items as the effects of change orders and claims, warranty claims, liquidated damages or other contractual penalties, adjustments for audit findings on U.S. or other government contracts and contract closeout settlements.

Note 11. Billings in Excess of Costs and Accrued Earnings on Contracts

The following table summarizes the components of billings in excess of costs and accrued earnings on contracts:

(In millions)	2009	2008
Billings in excess of costs and accrued earnings on contracts	$195.6	$182.6
Advance payments negotiated as a contract condition	10.1	30.4
Estimated losses on uncompleted contracts	19.0	21.0
Normal profit liabilities	0.4	11.1
Project-related legal liabilities and other project-related reserves	5.9	4.0
Other	4.3	5.1
Total	$235.3	$254.2

Asset Retirement Obligations

2.198

CHEMTURA CORPORATION (DEC)

(In millions)	2009	2008
Current liabilities		
Short-term borrowings	$252	$ 3
Current portion of long-term debt	—	1,178
Accounts payable	128	243
Accrued expenses	184	361
Income taxes payable	5	28
Total current liabilities	$569	$1,813

NOTES TO CONSOLIDATED FINANCIAL STATEMENTS

20. Asset Retirement Obligations

The Company applies the provisions of guidance now codified under ASC Topic 410, *Asset Retirements and Environmental Obligations* ("ASC 410"), which require companies to make estimates regarding future events in order to record a liability for asset retirement obligations in the period in which a legal obligation is created. Such liabilities are recorded at fair value, with an offsetting increase to the carrying value of the related long-lived assets. The fair value is estimated by discounting projected cash flows over the estimated life of the assets using the Company's credit adjusted risk-free rate applicable at the time the obligation is initially recorded. In future periods, the liability is accreted to its present value and the capitalized cost is depreciated over the useful life of the related asset. The Company also adjusts the liability for changes resulting from revisions to the timing or the amount of the original estimate. Upon retirement of the long-lived asset, the Company either settles the obligation for its recorded amount or incurs a gain or loss.

The Company's asset retirement obligations include estimates for all asset retirement obligations identified for its worldwide facilities. The Company's asset retirement obligations are primarily the result of legal obligations for the removal of leasehold improvements and restoration of premises to their original condition upon termination of leases at approximately 22 facilities, legal obligations to close approximately 95 brine supply, brine disposal, waste disposal, and hazardous waste injection wells and the related pipelines at the end of their useful lives, and decommissioning and decontamination obligations that are legally required to be fulfilled upon closure of approximately 37 of the Company's manufacturing facilities.

The following is a summary of the change in the carrying amount of the asset retirement obligations during 2009 and 2008, the net book value of assets related to the asset retirement obligations at December 31, 2009 and 2008 and the related depreciation expense recorded in 2009 and 2008.

(In millions)	2009	2008
Asset retirement obligation balance at beginning of year	$23	$26
Liabilities assumed (includes purchase accounting adjustments)	—	2
Accretion expense—cost of goods sold[a]	4	4
Payments	(2)	(8)
Foreign currency translation	1	(1)
Asset retirement obligation balance at end of year	$26	$23
Net book value of asset retirement obligation assets at end of year	$ 2	$ 2
Depreciation expense	$ 1	$ 1

[a] The 2009 and 2008 accretion expense included $1 million and $3 million, respectively, primarily due to the acceleration of the recognition of asset retirement obligations for several of the Company's leased sites and manufacturing facilities resulting from revisions to the estimated lease termination or closure dates.

At December 31, 2009, $9 million of the asset retirement obligation balance was included in accrued expenses, $15 million was included in other liabilities and $2 million was included in liabilities subject to compromise on the Consolidated Balance Sheet. At December 31, 2008, $7 million was included in accrued expenses and $16 million was included in other liabilities on the Consolidated Balance Sheet.

LONG-TERM DEBT

2.199 Table 2-28 summarizes the types of long-term debt most frequently disclosed by the survey companies.

2.200 FASB ASC 470, *Debt*, requires that financial statements disclose for each of the five years following the date of the latest balance sheet presented the "aggregate amount of maturities and sinking fund requirements for all long-term borrowings." In addition, FASB ASC 440, *Commitments*, requires disclosure of terms and conditions provided in loan agreements, such as assets pledged as collateral, covenants to limit additional debt, maintain working capital, and restrict dividends.

2.201 FASB ASC 470, *Debt*, states that the current liability classification is intended to include long-term obligations that are or will be callable by the creditor either because the debtors' violation of a provision of the debt agreement at the balance sheet date makes the obligation callable or because the violation, if not cured within a specified grace period, will make the obligation callable. Accordingly, such callable obligations shall be classified as current liabilities unless one of the following conditions is met:

a. The creditor has waived or subsequently lost the right to demand payment for more than one year (or operating cycle, if longer) from the balance sheet date.

b. For long-term obligations containing a grace period within which the debtor may cure the violation, it is probable that the violation will be cured within that period, thus preventing the obligation from becoming callable. As part of long-term debt presentations there were seven disclosures of covenant violations.

2.202 FASB ASC 825, *Financial Instruments*, requires disclosure of both the fair value and the bases for estimating the fair value of long-term debt unless it is not practicable to estimate the value.

2.203 FASB ASC 820, *Fair Value Measurements and Disclosures*, defines fair value, establishes a framework for measuring fair value, and requires certain disclosures about fair value measurements. FASB ASC 820 clarifies the definition of fair value as an exit price, i.e., a price that would be received to sell, as opposed to acquire, an asset or transfer a liability. FASB ASC 820 emphasizes that fair value is a market-based measurement. It establishes a fair value hierarchy that distinguishes between assumptions developed based on market data obtained from independent external sources and the reporting entity's own assumptions. Further, FASB ASC 820 specifies that fair value measurement should consider adjustment for risk, such as the risk inherent in a valuation technique or its inputs. For assets measured at fair value, whether on a recurring or a nonrecurring basis, FASB ASC 820 specifies the required disclosures concerning the inputs used to measure fair value. FASB Accounting Standards Update (ASU) No. 2010-06, *Improving Disclosures about Fair Value Measurements*, requires more robust disclosures about different classes of assets and liabilities measured at fair value, the valuation techniques and inputs used, the activity in Level 3 fair value measurements, and the transfers between Levels 1, 2, and 3. FASB ASU No. 2010-06 is effective for fiscal years beginning after December 15, 2009, except for the disclosures about certain Level 3 activity. Those disclosures are effective for fiscal years beginning after December 15, 2010. During 2009, 429 survey companies made 825 disclosures of fair value related to long-term debt. 174 of those disclosures were based on the quoted price of the identical item in an active market (level 1 input). 258 of those disclosures were primarily based on other market-corroborated (level 2) inputs. 26 disclosures estimated fair value using nonmarket-corroborated (level 3) inputs. 89 disclosures presented carrying amounts which approximated fair value of long-term debt. In addition, there were 267 disclosures in which carrying value was compared to fair value in an exposition or a table.

2.204 FASB ASC 825, *Financial Instruments*, permits entities to choose to measure many financial instruments and certain other items at fair value that are not currently required to be measured at fair value. Further, under FASB ASC 825 a business entity shall report unrealized gains and losses on eligible items for which the fair value option has been elected in earnings at each subsequent reporting date. The irrevocable election of the fair value option is made on an instrument by instrument basis, and applied to the entire instrument, not just a portion of it. FASB ASC 825 also establishes presentation and disclosure requirements designed to facilitate comparison between entities that choose different measurement attributes for similar types of assets and liabilities.

2.205 Examples of long-term debt disclosures and presentations follow. Examples of long-term lease disclosures and presentations are presented under "Long-Term Leases" in this section.

2.206

TABLE 2-28: LONG-TERM DEBT*

| | Number of Entities | | | |
	2009	2008	2007	2006
Unsecured				
Notes	379	372	428	423
Debentures	106	106	134	140
Loans	74	83	79	87
Foreign	56	62	73	78
Commercial paper	25	32	51	43
Bonds	11	14	23	25
ESOP loans	8	12	14	11
Collateralized				
Capitalized leases	201	205	247	230
Notes or loans	75	65	111	100
Mortgages	29	29	45	47
Convertible				
Notes	69	62	80	68
Debentures	19	25	42	49

* Appearing in either the balance sheet and/or the notes to financial statements.

2008–2009 based on 500 entities surveyed; 2006–2007 based on 600 entities surveyed.

Unsecured

2.207

ANADARKO PETROLEUM CORPORATION (DEC)

(Millions)	2009	2008
Total current liabilities	$ 3,824	$5,536
Long-term debt	11,149	9,128
Midstream subsidiary note payable to a related party	1,599	1,739
Other long-term liabilities		
Deferred income taxes	9,925	9,974
Other	3,211	3,390

NOTES TO CONSOLIDATED FINANCIAL STATEMENTS

10. Debt and Interest Expense

(Millions)	2009 Principal	2009 Carrying Value	2009 Fair Value	2008 Principal	2008 Carrying Value	2008 Fair Value
7.30% notes due 2009	$ —	$ —	$ —	$ 52	$ 52	$ 52
Floating-rate notes due 2009	—	—	—	1,420	1,420	1,359
6.75% notes due 2011	950	940	1,004	950	934	950
6.875% notes due 2011	675	688	726	675	695	668
6.125% notes due 2012	170	169	180	170	169	168
5.00% notes due 2012	82	82	85	82	82	77
5.75% notes due 2014	275	274	296	—	—	—
7.625% notes due 2014	500	499	571	—	—	—
5.95% notes due 2016	1,750	1,744	1,893	1,750	1,744	1,546
7.05% debentures due 2018	114	108	120	114	108	107
6.95% notes due 2019	300	297	340	—	—	—
8.70% notes due 2019	600	598	749	—	—	—
6.95% notes due 2024	650	673	704	650	674	570
7.50% debentures due 2026	112	106	115	112	106	100
7.00% debentures due 2027	54	54	54	54	54	47
7.125% debentures due 2027	150	157	152	150	157	132
6.625% debentures due 2028	17	17	17	17	17	14
7.15% debentures due 2028	235	215	233	235	215	204
7.20% debentures due 2029	135	135	139	135	135	119
7.95% debentures due 2029	117	117	127	117	116	109
7.50% notes due 2031	900	858	1,010	900	856	796
7.875% notes due 2031	500	580	583	500	581	460
Zero-coupon notes due 2036	2,360	591	623	2,360	561	572
6.45% notes due 2036	1,750	1,742	1,827	1,750	1,742	1,380
7.95% notes due 2039	325	324	398	—	—	—
7.73% debentures due 2096	61	60	66	61	61	55
7.50% debentures due 2096	78	72	74	78	72	66
7.25% debentures due 2096	49	49	47	49	49	41
Midstream subsidiary note payable to a related party due 2012	1,599	1,599	1,599	1,739	1,739	1,739
Total debt	14,508	12,748	13,732	14,120	12,339	11,331
Less: current maturities	—	—	—	1,472	1,472	1,411
Total long-term debt	$14,508	$12,748	$13,732	$12,648	$10,867	$9,920

The fair value of debt is the estimated amount the Company would have to pay to repurchase its debt, including any premium or discount attributable to the difference between the stated interest rate and market rate of interest at the balance sheet date. Fair values are based on quoted market prices or average valuations of similar debt instruments at the balance sheet date for those debt instruments for which quoted market prices are not available.

Except for Anadarko's Midstream Subsidiary Note Payable to a Related Party (see following discussion), none of the Company's notes, debentures or credit agreements contain credit-rating-downgrade triggers that result in accelerating debt maturity. All of the Company's debt, with the exception of the WES credit facility, is senior unsecured debt of the Company. As of December 31, 2009, the Company had approximately $340 million in undrawn letters of credit.

The net unamortized debt discount, represented in the previous table, of $1.8 billion as of December 31, 2009 and 2008 is being amortized to interest expense over the terms of the related debt. See Note 6 for Anadarko's notes payable to certain investees that do not affect the reported debt balance.

The following table presents the debt activity of the Company for 2009 and 2008.

(Millions)	Activity	Principal	Carrying Value	Description
Balance as of December 31, 2007		$16,558	$14,747	
First quarter 2008				
	Repayments	(1,000)	(1,000)	Acquisition facility due 2008
	Other, net	—	7	Accretion and discount amortization
Second quarter 2008				
	Repayments	(350)	(350)	3.25% notes due 2008
	Repayments	(330)	(330)	Midstream subsidiary note payable to a related party
	Repayments	(47)	(46)	6.75% notes due 2008
	Other, net	—	7	Accretion and discount amortization
Third quarter 2008				
	Repayments	(344)	(344)	Floating-rate notes due 2009
	Other, net	—	7	Accretion and discount amortization
Fourth quarter 2008				
	Repayments	(236)	(236)	Floating-rate notes due 2009
	Repayments	(131)	(131)	Midstream subsidiary note payable to a related party
	Other, net	—	8	Accretion and discount amortization
Balance as of December 31, 2008		$14,120	$12,339	
First quarter 2009				
	Issuance	500	499	7.625% notes due 2014
	Issuance	600	598	8.70% notes due 2019
	Repayments	(452)	(452)	Floating-rate notes due 2009
	Other, net	—	6	Accretion and discount amortization
Second quarter 2009				
	Issuance	275	274	5.75% notes due 2014
	Issuance	300	297	6.95% notes due 2019
	Issuance	325	324	7.95% notes due 2039
	Repayments	(968)	(968)	Floating-rate notes due 2009
	Repayments	(52)	(52)	7.30% notes due 2009
	Other, net	—	8	Accretion and discount amortization
Third quarter 2009				
	Repayments	(100)	(100)	Midstream subsidiary note payable to a related party
	Other, net	—	7	Accretion and discount amortization
Fourth quarter 2009				
	Repayments	(40)	(40)	Midstream subsidiary note payable to a related party
	Other, net	—	8	Accretion and discount amortization
Balance as of December 31, 2009		$14,508	$12,748	

In October 2006, the Company received $500 million of proceeds from a private offering of Zero-Coupon Senior Notes due 2036 with an aggregate principal amount at maturity of $2.4 billion. The Company presents the note in long-term debt. The carrying amount as of December 31, 2009 includes $30 million, $28 million and $28 million related to accretion expense recognized in 2009, 2008 and 2007, respectively. The notes were issued with a yield to maturity of 5.24%, and the holder has an option to put the notes back to the Company annually, starting in 2010, at the accreted value, which approximates carrying value. If the put option is exercised in 2010, the Company intends to refinance the debt under its Revolving Credit Agreement (RCA).

Midstream Subsidiary Note Payable to a Related Party

In December 2007, Anadarko and the Investor formed Trinity, with initial capitalization totaling $2.3 billion. Note 6 provides additional information regarding Anadarko's interest in Trinity. Trinity extended a $2.2 billion loan to a wholly owned subsidiary of Anadarko, referred to herein as Midstream Hold-

ing, which holds and operates substantially all of Anadarko's midstream assets, directly and through its subsidiaries. The Company used all of the loan proceeds received by Midstream Holding to repay a portion of the Company's indebtedness related to the 2006 acquisitions.

The principal balance owed by Midstream Holding to Trinity is reflected in the accompanying consolidated balance sheet as Midstream Subsidiary Note Payable to a Related Party. The loan has an initial maturity date of December 27, 2012, subject to renewals for additional five-year periods on market terms at the time of renewal. Interest on the loan is based on three-month LIBOR plus a margin. The rate in effect at the beginning of 2010 is 1.32%.

Midstream Holding may repay the loan in whole or in part at any time prior to maturity. In December 2008, Anadarko provided a parental guaranty for the payment of principal and interest on the remaining balance of the Midstream Subsidiary Note Payable to a Related Party in exchange for the removal of various covenants in the loan agreement, including a ceiling on the maximum ratio of debt-to-earnings before interest, taxes, depreciation and amortization as defined in the loan agreement. Midstream Holding was in compliance with all previously existing covenants as of the date the Anadarko parental guaranty was provided. The amended loan agreement requires customary representations and warranties and affirmative and negative covenants, and includes the same financial covenants as the RCA discussed below. The Midstream Subsidiary Note Payable to a Related Party has the same priority with respect to the payment of principal and interest as Anadarko's other debt.

Following a sale or transfer of assets to third parties or other entities within the Anadarko consolidated group, Midstream Holding and/or its subsidiaries will be required to repay a portion of the loan principal. Further, maturity of the loan could be accelerated if Anadarko's senior unsecured credit rating were to be rated below "BB-" by Standard and Poor's (S&P) or "Ba3" by Moody's Investors Service (Moody's). As of December 31, 2009, the Company was in compliance with all covenants, and S&P and Moody's rated the Company's debt at "BBB-" and "Baa3", respectively.

Anadarko Revolving Credit Agreement

In March 2008, the Company entered into a $1.3 billion, five-year RCA with a syndicate of United States and foreign lenders. Under the terms of the RCA, the Company can, under certain conditions, request an increase in the borrowing capacity under the RCA up to a total available credit amount of $2.0 billion. The RCA has a maximum 65% debt-to-capitalization covenant. The RCA terminates in March 2013. As of December 31, 2009, the Company had no outstanding borrowings under the RCA. Anadarko was in compliance with existing covenants and the full amount of the RCA was available for borrowing at December 31, 2009.

WES Revolving Credit Facility

In October 2009, Anadarko's consolidated subsidiary, WES, entered into a three-year senior unsecured revolving credit facility (RCF) with a group of banks. The aggregate initial commitments of the lenders under the RCF are $350 million and are expandable to a maximum of $450 million.

The RCF matures in October 2012. The RCF contains various customary covenants including a limitation on debt to earnings before interest, taxes, depreciation and amortization and a minimum interest coverage requirement. As of December 31, 2009, WES had no outstanding borrowings under the RCF. WES was in compliance with existing covenants at December 31, 2009.

Scheduled Maturities

Total maturities related to debt for the five years ending December 31, 2014 are shown below.

(Millions)	
2010	$ —
2011	1,625
2012	1,850
2013	—
2014	775

Interest Expense

The following table summarizes the amounts included in interest expense.

(Millions)	2009	2008	2007
Interest expense			
Gross interest expense			
Current debt, long-term debt and other[1]	$732	$ 746	$1,203
Midstream subsidiary note payable to a related party	39	109	2
Capitalized interest[2]	(69)	(123)	(122)
Net interest expense	$702	$ 732	$1,083

[1] Included in 2009 is the reversal of the $78 million liability for unpaid interest related to the DWRRA dispute. See Note 14.
[2] Included in 2008 is additional capitalized interest related to a prior period of $16 million.

2.208

THE LUBRIZOL CORPORATION (DEC)

(In millions)	2009	2008
Total current liabilities	$ 637.2	$1,021.3
Long-term debt	1,390.3	954.6
Pension obligations	309.3	340.1
Other postretirement benefit obligations	92.7	83.1
Noncurrent liabilities	153.3	129.1
Deferred income taxes	57.4	37.7
Total liabilities	$2,640.2	$2,565.9

NOTES TO CONSOLIDATED FINANCIAL STATEMENTS

Note 7. Debt

The company's debt was comprised of the following at December 31, 2009 and 2008:

(In millions)	2009	2008
Short-term debt and current portion of long-term debt:		
Current portion of long-term debt	$ 0.3	$ 386.3
Other short-term debt	—	4.9
	$ 0.3	$ 391.2
Long-term debt:		
4.625% notes, due 2009, net of original issue discount of $0.1 million and fair value adjustment of $4.3 million for unrealized gains on derivative instruments at December 31, 2008	$ —	$ 386.0
5.5% notes, due 2014, net of original issue discount of $1.6 million and $1.9 million at December 31, 2009 and 2008, respectively, and fair value adjustments of $3.3 million for unrealized gains on derivative instruments at December 31, 2009	451.7	448.1
8.875% notes, due 2019, net of original issue discount of $3.5 million at December 31, 2009	496.5	—
7.25% debentures, due 2025	100.0	100.0
6.5% debentures, due 2034, net of original issue discount of $4.6 million and $4.7 million at December 31, 2009 and 2008, respectively	295.4	295.3
Debt supported by banking arrangements:		
U.S. revolving credit borrowing, at prime (3.25% at December 31, 2008)	—	75.0
Euro revolving credit borrowing, at EURIBOR plus 3.00% (3.625% at December 31, 2009) and EURIBOR plus .325% (3.036% at December 31, 2008)	45.8	34.9
Other	1.2	1.6
	1,390.6	1,340.9
Less: current portion of long-term debt	0.3	386.3
Total long-term debt	$1,390.3	$ 954.6

The scheduled principal payments for all outstanding debt are $0.3 million in 2010, $0.3 million in 2011, $46.2 million in 2012, $0.2 million in 2013, $450.0 million in 2014 and $900.0 million thereafter.

In July 2009, the company entered into a three-year, unsecured €150.0 million revolving credit facility maturing in July 2012. This new facility permits the company to borrow at variable rates based on EURIBOR for euro borrowings or LIBOR for dollar or pound sterling borrowings plus a specified credit spread. The company may elect to increase the facility amount once each year in increments of €10.0 million, up to an aggregate maximum of €200.0 million, subject to approval by the lenders. This new facility replaced the €250.0 million revolving credit facility that would have matured in September 2010. At December 31, 2009, the company had €118.0 million ($168.9 million) available under the revolving credit facility.

In March 2009, the company repurchased $177.0 million of the 4.625% notes due October 1, 2009, at a purchase price of 100.5% per note, resulting in a loss on retirement of $1.3 million. The loss on retirement resulting from the repurchase of the 4.625% notes was included in interest expense in the consolidated statements of operations.

In February 2009, the company entered into a $150.0 million term loan that it subsequently repaid in full in December 2009. The term loan was an unsecured, senior obligation of the company that bore interest based upon LIBOR plus a specified credit spread. The term loan was prepaid without penalty.

In January 2009, the company issued senior unsecured notes having an aggregate principal amount of $500.0 million at a price of 99.256%. The notes mature in February 2019 and bear interest at 8.875% per annum, payable semi-annually on February 1 and August 1 of each year. Including debt issuance costs, original issue discounts and losses on Treasury rate lock agreements, the notes have an effective annualized interest rate of approximately 9.2%. The notes include a step-up in interest payable in the event of certain ratings downgrades by credit rating agencies. Upon the occurrence of a change of control triggering event, as defined in the indenture, the company would be required to make an offer to repurchase the notes at 101% of their principal amount. The company used a portion of the net proceeds from these notes to repurchase $177.0 million of the 4.625% notes in March 2009 and repay in full on October 1, 2009, the remaining aggregate principal amount of the 4.625% notes.

In September 2006, the company entered into an amended five-year unsecured committed U.S. bank credit facility, which includes a $350.0 million revolving credit facility that matures in September 2011. This credit facility permits the company to borrow at variable rates based upon the U.S. prime rate or LIBOR plus a specified spread. The spread is dependent on the company's long-term unsecured senior debt rating from Standard and Poor's and Moody's Investor Services. At December 31, 2009, the company had $350.0 million available under the revolving credit facility.

In September 2004, the company issued senior unsecured notes and debentures having an aggregate principal amount of $1,150.0 million including: $400.0 million 4.625% notes due October 1, 2009; $450.0 million 5.5% notes due October 1, 2014; and $300.0 million 6.5% debentures due October 1, 2034. The price to the public was 99.911% per 2009 note, 99.339% per 2014 note and 98.341% per 2034 debenture. The resulting original issue discount from the issuance of these notes and debentures of $8.3 million was recorded as a reduction of the underlying debt issuances and is being amortized over the life of the debt using the effective interest method. Interest is payable semi-annually on April 1 and October 1 of each year, beginning April 1, 2005. The notes and debentures have no sinking fund requirements. Including debt issuance costs, original issue discounts and losses on Treasury rate lock agreements, the 2009 notes, 2014 notes and 2034 debentures have effective annualized interest rates of approximately 5.3%, 6.3% and 6.7%, respectively, with a weighted-average interest rate for the aggregate issuances of approximately 6.1%.

In June 1995, the company issued debentures in an aggregate principal amount of $100.0 million. These debentures are unsecured, senior obligations of the company that mature on June 15, 2025, and bear interest at an annualized rate of 7.25%, payable semi-annually on June 15 and December 15 of each year. The debentures are not redeemable prior to maturity and are not subject to any sinking fund requirements.

The U.S. and euro bank credit agreements contain customary affirmative covenants including, among others, compliance with laws, payment of taxes, maintenance of insurance, conduct of business, keeping of books and records, maintenance of properties and ensuring the credit facilities receive the same rights and privileges as any future senior unsecured debt. The agreements also contain customary negative covenants including, among others, restrictions on: liens and encumbrances, sale of assets and affiliate transactions. Additionally, the company is required to comply with financial ratios of debt to consolidated earnings before interest, income taxes, depreciation and amortization, extraordinary, unusual or non-recurring non-cash gains or losses, including the sale of property and equipment and goodwill impairments, and non-cash gains or losses from less than wholly owned subsidiaries and investments (Consolidated EBITDA), as defined in the credit agreements, and Consolidated EBITDA to interest expense. At December 31, 2009, the credit agreements required that the ratio of debt to Consolidated EBITDA be less than 3.5:1 and the ratio of Consolidated EBITDA to interest expense be greater than 3.5:1. At December 31, 2009, the company maintained a ratio of debt to Consolidated EBITDA of 1.4:1 and a ratio of Consolidated EBITDA to interest expense of 8.9:1.

The bank credit agreements also contain customary events of default including, among others, failure to make payment when due, materially incorrect representations and warranties, breach of covenants, events of bankruptcy, the occurrence of one or more unstayed judgments in excess of $25.0 million that is not covered by an acceptable policy of insurance, a party obtaining a beneficial ownership in excess of 20% of the company's voting stock, or the incurrence of $25.0 million of liabilities related to violations of employee benefit plan regulations or the withdrawal or termination of a multiemployer benefit plan. At December 31, 2009, the company was in compliance with all of its covenants and had not committed any acts of default.

The estimated fair value of the company's debt instruments at December 31, 2009 and 2008, approximated $1,561.8 million and $1,239.3 million, respectively, compared with a carrying value of $1,390.6 million and $1,345.8 million, respectively. The fair value of the company's debt instruments was estimated using prevailing market interest rates on long-term debt with similar creditworthiness, terms and maturities.

At December 31, 2009 and 2008, the company had $31.6 million and $39.8 million, respectively, of contingent obligations under standby letters of credit issued in the ordinary course of business to financial institutions, customers and insurance companies to secure short-term support for a variety of commercial transactions, insurance and benefit programs.

Interest paid, net of amounts capitalized, was $84.5 million, $71.4 million and $91.5 million during 2009, 2008 and 2007, respectively. The amount of interest capitalized during 2009, 2008 and 2007 was $2.5 million, $4.1 million and $1.7 million, respectively.

Collateralized

2.209

GARDNER DENVER, INC. (DEC)

(Dollars in thousands)	2009	2008
Total current liabilities	$323,530	$ 397,382
Long-term debt, less current maturities	330,935	506,700
Postretirement benefits other than pensions	15,269	17,481
Deferred income taxes	67,799	91,218
Other liabilities	137,506	117,601
Total liabilities	$875,039	$1,130,382

NOTES TO CONSOLIDATED FINANCIAL STATEMENTS
(Dollars in thousands)

Note 10. Debt

Debt as of December 31, 2009 and 2008 consists of the following:

	2009	2008
Short-term debt	$ 5,497	$ 11,786
Long-term debt:		
Credit line, due 2013[1]	$ 2,500	$ 37,000
Term loan denominated in U.S. dollars, due 2013[2]	113,000	177,750
Term loan denominated in euros, due 2013[3]	100,310	165,284
Senior subordinated notes at 8%, due 2013	125,000	125,000
Secured mortgages[4]	8,500	8,911
Variable rate industrial revenue bonds, due 2018	—	8,000
Capitalized leases and other long-term debt	9,709	9,937
Total long-term debt, including current maturities	359,019	531,882
Current maturities of long-term debt	28,084	25,182
Long-term debt, less current maturities	$330,935	$506,700

[1] The loans under this facility may be denominated in USD or several foreign currencies. At December 31, 2009, the outstanding balance consisted of only of USD borrowings. The interest rates under the facility are based on prime, federal funds and/or the London interbank offer rate ("LIBOR") for the applicable currency. The interest rate was 4.5% as of December 31, 2009.

[2] The interest rate for this loan varies with prime, federal funds and/or LIBOR. At December 31, 2009, this rate was 2.8% and averaged 3.0% for the twelve-month period ending December 31, 2009.

[3] The interest rate for this loan varies with LIBOR. At December 31, 2009, the rate was 2.9% and averaged 3.6% for the twelve-month period ending December 31, 2009.

[4] This amount consists of two fixed-rate commercial loans with an outstanding balance of €5,932 at December 31, 2009. The loans are secured by the Company's facility in Bad Neustadt, Germany.

On September 19, 2008, the Company entered into a credit agreement with a syndicate of lenders (the "2008 Credit Agreement") consisting of (i) a $310.0 million Revolving Line of Credit (the "Revolving Line of Credit"), (ii) a $180.0 million term loan ("U.S. Dollar Term Loan") and (iii) a €120.0 million term loan ("Euro Term Loan"). In addition, the 2008 Credit Agreement provides for a possible increase in the revolving credit facility of up to $200.0 million.

The U.S. Dollar and Euro Term Loans have a final maturity of October 15, 2013. The U.S. Dollar Term Loan requires quarterly principal payments aggregating approximately $13.7 million, $19.9 million, $33.6 million, and $45.8 million in 2010 through 2013, respectively. The Euro Term Loan requires quarterly principal payments aggregating approximately €8.5 million, €12.3 million, €20.8 million, and €28.4 million in 2010 through 2013, respectively.

The Revolving Line of Credit also matures on October 15, 2013. Loans under this facility may be denominated in USD or several foreign currencies and may be borrowed by the Company or two of its foreign subsidiaries as outlined in the 2008 Credit Agreement. On December 31, 2009, the Revolving Line of Credit had an outstanding principal balance of $2.5 million. In addition, letters of credit in the amount of $15.6 million were outstanding on the Revolving Line of

Credit at December 31, 2009, leaving $291.9 million available for future use, subject to the terms of the Revolving Line of Credit.

The interest rates per annum applicable to loans under the 2008 Credit Agreement are, at the Company's option, either a base rate plus an applicable margin percentage or a Eurocurrency rate plus an applicable margin. The base rate is the greater of (i) the prime rate or (ii) one-half of 1% over the weighted average of rates on overnight federal funds as published by the Federal Reserve Bank of New York. The Eurocurrency rate is LIBOR.

The initial applicable margin percentage over LIBOR under the 2008 Credit Agreement was 2.5% with respect to the term loans and 2.1% with respect to loans under the Revolving Line of Credit, and the initial applicable margin percentage over the base rate was 1.25%. After the Company's delivery of its financial statements and compliance certificate for each fiscal quarter, the applicable margin percentages are subject to adjustments based upon the ratio of the Company's Consolidated Total Debt to Consolidated Adjusted EBITDA (earnings before interest, taxes, depreciation and amortization) (each as defined in the 2008 Credit Agreement) being within certain defined ranges. The initial margins described above continued to be in effect through 2009. The Company periodically uses interest rate swaps to hedge some of its exposure to variability in future LIBOR-based interest payments on variable-rate debt (see Note 16 "Hedging Activities, Derivative Instruments and Credit Risk").

The obligations under the 2008 Credit Agreement are guaranteed by the Company's existing and future domestic subsidiaries. The obligations under the 2008 Credit Agreement are also secured by a pledge of the capital stock of each of the Company's existing and future material domestic subsidiaries, as well as 65% of the capital stock of each of the Company's existing and future first-tier material foreign subsidiaries.

The 2008 Credit Agreement includes customary covenants that are substantially similar to those contained in the Company's previous credit facilities. Subject to certain exceptions, these covenants restrict or limit the ability of the Company and its subsidiaries to, among other things: incur liens; engage in mergers, consolidations and sales of assets; incur additional indebtedness; pay dividends and redeem stock; make investments (including loans and advances); enter into transactions with affiliates, make capital expenditures and incur rental obligations. In addition, the 2008 Credit Agreement requires the Company to maintain compliance with certain financial ratios on a quarterly basis, including a maximum total leverage ratio test and a minimum interest coverage ratio test. As of December 31, 2009, the Company was in compliance with each of the financial ratio covenants under the 2008 Credit Agreement.

The 2008 Credit Agreement contains customary events of default, including upon a change of control. If an event of default occurs, the lenders under the 2008 Credit Agreement are entitled to take various actions, including the acceleration of amounts due under the 2008 Credit Agreement.

The Company issued $125.0 million of 8% Senior Subordinated Notes (the "Notes") in 2005. The Notes have a fixed annual interest rate of 8% and are guaranteed by certain of the Company's domestic subsidiaries (the "Guarantors"). The Company may redeem all or part of the Notes issued under the Indenture among the Company, the Guarantors and The Bank of New York Trust Company, N.A. (the "Indenture") at varying redemption prices, plus accrued and unpaid interest. The Company may also repurchase Notes from time to time in open market purchases or privately negotiated transactions. Upon a change of control, as defined in the Indenture, the Company is required to offer to purchase all of the Notes then outstanding at 101% of the principal amount thereof plus accrued and unpaid interest. The Indenture contains events of default and affirmative, negative and financial covenants customary for such financings, including, among other things, limits on incurring additional debt and restricted payments.

The Euro Term Loan has been designated as a hedge of net euro ("EUR") investments in foreign operations. As such, changes in the reported amount of these borrowings due to changes in currency exchange rates are included in accumulated other comprehensive income.

Total debt maturities for the five years subsequent to December 31, 2009 and thereafter are approximately $33.6 million, $39.1 million, $67.0 million, $214.7 million, $0.7 million and $9.4 million, respectively.

The rentals for all operating leases were $31.3 million, $24.7 million, and $20.5 million, in 2009, 2008 and 2007, respectively. Future minimum rental payments for operating leases for the five years subsequent to December 31, 2009 and thereafter are approximately $27.2 million, $21.6 million, $15.5 million, $10.2 million, $7.5 million, and $23.6 million, respectively.

Note 17 (In Part): Fair Value Measurements

A financial instrument is defined as a cash equivalent, evidence of an ownership interest in an entity, or a contract that creates a contractual obligation or right to deliver or receive cash or another financial instrument from another party. The Company's financial instruments consist primarily of cash equivalents, trade receivables, trade payables, deferred compensation obligations and debt instruments. The book values of these instruments, other than the Senior Subordinated Notes, are a reasonable estimate of their respective fair values. In addition, the Company selectively uses derivative financial instruments, including foreign currency forward contracts and interest rate swaps, to manage the risks from fluctuations in foreign currency exchange rates and interest rates.

The Senior Subordinated Notes outstanding are carried at cost. Their estimated fair value was approximately $122.8 million as of December 31, 2009 based upon non-binding market quotations that were corroborated by observable market data (Level 2). The estimated fair value is not indicative of the amount that the Company would have to pay to redeem these notes since they are infrequently traded and are not callable at this value.

2.210

QUANEX BUILDING PRODUCTS CORPORATION (OCT)

(In thousands)	2009	2008
Total current liabilities	$ 97,662	$118,191
Long-term debt	1,943	2,188
Deferred pension and postretirement benefits	6,655	3,092
Non-current environmental reserves	1,767	2,485
Other liabilities	13,047	7,063
Total liabilities	$121,074	$133,019

NOTES TO CONSOLIDATED FINANCIAL STATEMENTS

10 (In Part): Long-Term Debt and Financing Arrangements

Long-term debt consists of the following:

(In thousands)	2009	2008
Revolving credit facility	$ —	$ —
City of Richmond, Kentucky Industrial Building Revenue Bonds	1,100	1,250
Scott County, Iowa Industrial Waste Recycling Revenue Bonds	1,000	1,200
Capital lease obligations and other	166	101
Total debt	$2,266	$2,551
Less maturities due within one year included in current liabilities	323	363
Long-term debt	$1,943	$2,188

Other Debt Instruments

The City of Richmond, Kentucky Industrial Building Revenue Bonds were obtained as part of the acquisition of Mikron. These bonds are due in annual installments through October 2020. Interest is payable monthly at a variable rate. The average rate during fiscal 2009 and fiscal 2008 was 0.7% and 2.7%, respectively. These bonds are secured by the land, building and certain equipment of the Mikron East facility located in Richmond, Kentucky. In addition, a $1.1 million letter of credit under the Credit Facility serves as a conduit for making the scheduled payments.

In June 1999, the Company borrowed $3.0 million through Scott County, Iowa Variable Rate Demand Industrial Waste Recycling Revenue Bonds Series 1999. The bonds require 15 annual principal payments of $200,000 beginning on July 1, 2000. The variable interest rate is established by the re-marketing agent based on the lowest weekly rate of interest that would permit the sale of the bonds at par, on the basis of prevailing financial market conditions. Interest is payable on the first business day of each calendar month. Interest rates on these bonds during fiscal 2009 have ranged from 0.5% to 1.85%. These bonds are secured by a Letter of Credit.

Additional Debt Disclosures

The Company's consolidated debt had a weighted average interest rate of 1.1% and 2.3% as of October 31, 2009 and October 31, 2008, respectively. Approximately 93% and 96% of the total debt had a variable interest rate at October 31, 2009 and 2008, respectively. As of October 31, 2009 and

2008, the Company's debt of $2.3 million approximates fair value as nearly all the Company's debt is at a variable interest rate. As of October 31, 2009, the Company has $6.8 million in letters of credit, of which $5.8 million in letters of credit fall under the Credit Facility sublimit.

Convertible

2.211

ADC TELECOMMUNICATIONS, INC. (SEP)

(In millions)	2009	2008
Total current liabilities	$236.0	$ 278.0
Pension obligations and other long-term liabilities	100.4	78.1
Long-term notes payable	651.0	650.7
Total liabilities	$987.4	$1,006.8

NOTES TO CONSOLIDATED FINANCIAL STATEMENTS

Note 8. Notes Payable

Long-term debt as of September 30, 2009 and October 31, 2008 consist of the following:

(In millions)	2009	2008
Convertible subordinated notes, six-month LIBOR plus 0.375%, due June 15, 2013	$200.0	$200.0
Convertible subordinated notes, 3.5% fixed rate, due July 15, 2015	225.0	225.0
Convertible subordinated notes, 3.5% fixed rate, due July 15, 2017	225.0	225.0
Total convertible subordinated notes	650.0	650.0
Other, variable rate, various due dates	1.6	3.3
Total debt	651.6	653.3
Less: current portion of long-term debt	0.6	2.6
Long-term debt	$651.0	$650.7

On December 26, 2007, we issued $450.0 million of 3.5% fixed rate convertible unsecured subordinated notes. The notes were issued in two tranches of $225.0 million each. The first tranche matures on July 15, 2015 ("2015 notes"), and the second tranche matures on July 15, 2017 ("2017 notes"). The notes are convertible into shares of common stock of ADC, based on, in the case of the 2015 notes, an initial base conversion rate of 37.0336 shares of common stock per $1,000 principal amount and, in the case of the 2017 notes, an initial base conversion rate of 35.0318 shares of common stock per $1,000 principal amount, in each case subject to adjustment in certain circumstances. This represents an initial base conversion price of approximately $27.00 per share in the case of the 2015 notes and approximately $28.55 per share in the case of the 2017 notes, representing a 75% and 85% conversion premium, respectively, based on the closing price of $15.43 per share of ADC's common

stock on December 19, 2007. In addition, if at the time of conversion the applicable stock price of ADC's common stock exceeds the base conversion price, the conversion rate will be increased. The amount of the increase will be measured by a formula. The formula first calculates a fraction. The numerator of the fraction is the applicable stock price of ADC's common stock at the time of conversion less the initial base conversion price per share (i.e., approximately $27.00 in the case of the 2015 notes and approximately $28.55 in the case of the 2017 notes). The denominator of the fraction is the applicable stock price of ADC's common stock at the time of conversion. This fraction is then multiplied by an incremental share factor, which is 27.7752 shares of common stock per $1,000 principal amount of 2015 notes and 29.7770 shares of common stock per $1,000 principal amount of 2017 notes. The notes of each series are subordinated to existing and future senior indebtedness of ADC.

On June 4, 2003, we issued $400.0 million of convertible unsecured subordinated notes in two separate transactions. In the first transaction, we issued $200.0 million of 1.0% fixed rate convertible unsecured subordinated notes that matured on June 15, 2008. We paid the $200.0 million fixed rate notes in June 2008. In the second transaction, we issued $200.0 million of convertible unsecured subordinated notes that have a variable interest rate and mature on June 15, 2013. The interest rate for the variable rate notes is equal to 6-month LIBOR plus 0.375%. The holders of the variable rate notes may convert all or some of their notes into shares of our common stock at any time prior to maturity at a conversion price of $28.091 per share. We may redeem any or all of the variable rate notes at any time on or after June 23, 2008. A fixed interest rate swap was entered into for the variable rate note.

From time to time, we may use interest rate swaps to manage interest costs and the risk associated with changing interest rates. We do not enter into interest rate swaps for speculative purposes. On April 29, 2008, we entered into an interest rate swap effective June 15, 2008, for a notional amount of $200.0 million. The interest rate swap hedges the exposure to changes in interest rates of our $200.0 million of convertible unsecured subordinated notes that have a variable interest rate of six-month LIBOR plus 0.375% and a maturity date of June 15, 2013. We have designated the interest rate swap as a cash flow hedge for accounting purposes. The swap is structured so that we receive six-month LIBOR and pay a fixed rate of 4.0% (before the credit spread of 0.375%). The variable portion we receive resets semiannually and both sides of the swap are settled net semiannually based on the $200.0 million notional amount. The swap matures concurrently with the end of the debt obligation.

On January 30, 2009, we terminated the $200.0 million secured five-year revolving credit facility that we entered into in April 2008. This facility had no outstanding balances when it was terminated. As a consequence of terminating our revolving credit facility, we recorded a non-operating charge of $1.0 million to write-off the deferred financing costs associated with the facility.

The assets that secured the facility also served as collateral for our interest rate swap on our $200.0 million convertible unsecured floating rate notes that mature in 2013. As a result of the facility's termination, we were required to pledge cash collateral to secure the interest rate swap. As of September 30, 2009, we pledged $13.2 million of cash to secure the interest rate swap termination value, which is included in our restricted cash balance. This collateral amount could vary significantly as it fluctuates with the forward LIBOR.

We estimate the fair market value of our long-term notes payable to be approximately $475.0 million and $350.0 million at September 30, 2009 and October 31, 2008, respectively.

Concurrent with the issuance of our variable rate notes (due June 2013), we purchased ten-year call options on our common stock to reduce the potential dilution from conversion of the notes. Under the terms of these call options, which become exercisable upon conversion of the notes, we have the right to purchase from the counterparty at a purchase price of $28.091 per share the aggregate number of shares that we are obligated to issue upon conversion of the variable rate notes, which is a maximum of 7.1 million shares. We also have the option to settle the call options with the counterparty through a net share settlement or cash settlement, either of which would be based on the extent to which the then-current market price of our common stock exceeds $28.091 per share. The cost of the call options was partially offset by the sale of warrants to acquire shares of our common stock with a term of ten years to the same counterparty with whom we entered into the call options. The warrants are exercisable for an aggregate of 7.1 million shares at an exercise price of $36.96 per share. The warrants become exercisable upon conversion of the notes, and may be settled, at our option, either through a net share settlement or a net cash settlement, either of which would be based on the extent to which the then-current market price of our common stock exceeds $36.96 per share. The net effect of the call options and the warrants is either to reduce the potential dilution from the conversion of the notes (if we elect net share settlement) or to increase the net cash proceeds of the offering (if we elect net cash settlement) if the notes are converted at a time when the current market price of our common stock is greater than $28.091 per share.

Debt Covenant Violation

2.212

WENDY'S/ARBY'S GROUP, INC. (DEC)

NOTES TO CONSOLIDATED FINANCIAL STATEMENTS
(In thousands)

8 (In Part): Long-Term Debt

Long-term debt consisted of the following:

	2009	2008
10.00% senior notes, due 2016	$ 551,779	$ —
Senior secured term loan, average effective interest of 7.25% as of January 3, 2010	251,488	385,030
6.20% senior notes, due in 2014	204,303	199,111
6.25% senior notes, due in 2011	193,618	188,933
Sale-leaseback obligations due through 2029	125,176	123,829
Capitalized lease obligations due through 2036	89,886	106,841
7% debentures, due in 2025	80,081	78,974
6.54% Secured equipment term loan, due in 2013	18,901	19,790
Other	7,679	9,069
	1,522,911	1,111,577
Less amounts payable within one year	(22,127)	(30,426)
	$1,500,784	$1,081,151

A significant number of the underlying leases in the Arby's restaurants segment for sale-leaseback obligations and capitalized lease obligations, as well as the operating leases, require or required periodic financial reporting of certain subsidiary entities within ARG or of individual restaurants, which in many cases have not been prepared or reported. The Company has negotiated waivers and alternative covenants with its most significant lessors which substitute consolidated financial reporting of ARG for that of individual subsidiary entities and which modify restaurant level reporting requirements for more than half of the affected leases. Nevertheless, as of January 3, 2010, the Company was not in compliance, and remains not in compliance, with the reporting requirements under those leases for which waivers and alternative financial reporting covenants have not been negotiated. However, none of the lessors has asserted that the Company is in default of any of those lease agreements. The Company does not believe that such non-compliance will have a material adverse effect on its consolidated financial position or results of operations.

CREDIT AGREEMENTS

2.213 As shown in Table 2-29, many of the survey companies disclosed the existence of loan commitments from financial institutions for future loans. Examples of such loan commitment disclosures follow:

2.214

TABLE 2-29: CREDIT AGREEMENTS

	2009	2008	2007	2006
Disclosing credit agreements...............	447	451	551	548
Not disclosing credit agreements.........	53	49	49	52
Total Entities.....................................	**500**	**500**	**600**	**600**

2008–2009 based on 500 entities surveyed; 2006–2007 based on 600 entities surveyed.

2.215

AMKOR TECHNOLOGY, INC. (DEC)

(In thousands)	2009	2008
Total current liabilities	$ 605,837	$ 554,742
Long-term debt	1,095,241	1,338,751
Long-term debt, related party	250,000	100,000
Pension and severance obligations	83,067	116,789
Other non-current liabilities	9,063	30,548
Total liabilities	$2,043,208	$2,140,830

NOTES TO CONSOLIDATED FINANCIAL STATEMENTS

1 (In Part): Summary of Significant Accounting Policies

Risks and Uncertainties (In Part)

Our future results of operations involve a number of risks and uncertainties. Factors that could affect our business or future results and cause actual results to vary materially from historical results include, but are not limited to, dependence on the highly cyclical nature of the semiconductor industry, fluctuations in operating results, high fixed costs, our failure to meet guidance, declines in average selling prices, decisions by our integrated device manufacturer customers to curtail outsourcing, our substantial indebtedness, our ability to fund liquidity needs, our ability to draw on our current loan facilities, our restrictive covenants contained in the agreements governing our indebtedness, significant severance plan obligations, failure to maintain an effective system of internal controls, product return and liability risks, the absence of significant backlog in our business, our dependence on international operations and sales, proposed changes to U.S. tax laws, our management information systems may prove inadequate, attracting and retaining qualified employees, difficulties consolidating and evolving our operational capabilities, our dependence on materials and equipment suppliers, loss of customers, our need for significant capital expenditures, impairment charges, litigation incident to our business, adverse tax consequences, rapid technological change, complexity of packaging and test processes, competition, our need to comply with existing and future environmental regulations, the enforcement of intellectual property rights by or against us, fire, flood or other calamity and continued control by existing stockholders.

We believe that our cash flow from operating activities together with existing cash and cash equivalents will be sufficient to fund our working capital, capital expenditure and debt service requirements for at least the next twelve months. Thereafter, our liquidity will continue to be affected by, among other things, volatility in the global economy and credit markets, the performance of our business, our capital expenditure levels and our ability to either repay debt out of operating cash flow or refinance debt at or prior to maturity with the proceeds of debt or equity offerings.

12 (In Part): Debt

Following is a summary of short-term borrowings and long-term debt:

(In thousands)	2009	2008
Debt of Amkor Technology, Inc.		
Senior secured credit facilities:		
$100 million revolving credit facility, LIBOR plus 3.5%–4.0%, due April 2013	$ —	$ —
Senior notes:		
7.125% senior notes due March 2011	53,503	209,641
7.75% senior notes due May 2013	358,291	422,000
9.25% senior notes due June 2016	390,000	390,000
Senior subordinated notes:		
2.5% convertible senior subordinated notes due May 2011	42,579	111,566
6.0% convertible senior subordinated notes due April 2014, $150 million related party	250,000	—
Subordinated notes:		
6.25% convertible subordinated notes due December 2013, related party	100,000	100,000
Debt of subsidiaries:		
Secured loans:		
Term loan, Taiwan 90-day commercial paper primary market rate plus 1.2%, due November 2010	—	22,310
Term loan, bank base rate plus 0.5% due April 2014	192,852	235,708
Working capital facility, LIBOR + 1.7%, due February-March 2010	15,000	—
Revolving credit facilities	30,435	—
Secured equipment and property financing	1,525	2,135
	1,434,185	1,493,360
Less: short-term borrowings and current portion of long-term debt	(88,944)	(54,609)
Long-term debt (including related party)	$1,345,241	$1,438,751

Debt of Amkor Technology Inc. (In Part)

Senior Secured Credit Facilities

In April 2009, we amended our $100.0 million first lien revolving credit facility and extended its term to April 2013. The facility has a letter of credit sub-limit of $25.0 million. Interest is charged under the credit facility at a floating rate based on the base rate in effect from time to time plus the applicable margins which range from 2.0% to 2.5% for base rate revolving loans, or LIBOR plus 3.5% to 4.0% for LIBOR revolving loans. The LIBOR-based interest rate at December 31, 2009 was 3.73%. There have been no borrowings under this credit facility as of December 31, 2009; however, we have utilized $3.5 million of the available letter of credit sub-limit. The borrowing base for the revolving credit facility is based on the amount of our eligible accounts receivable, which exceeded $100.0 million as of December 31, 2009. In connection with amending and extending our $100.0 million facility, we incurred $3.0 million of debt issuance costs in 2009. We incur commitment fees on the unused amounts of the revolving credit facility ranging from 0.50% to 0.75%, based on our liquidity. This facility includes a number of affirmative and negative covenants, which could restrict our operations. If we were to default under the first lien revolving credit facility, we would not be permitted to draw additional amounts, and the banks could accelerate our obligation to pay all outstanding amounts.

Debt of Subsidiaries (In Part)

Revolving and Working Capital Credit Facilities

In January 2009, Amkor Assembly & Test (Shanghai) Co, Ltd., a Chinese subsidiary, entered into a $50.0 million U.S. dollar denominated working capital facility agreement with a Chinese bank maturing in January 2011. The facility is collateralized with certain real property and buildings in China. Principal amounts borrowed must be repaid within twelve months of the drawdown date and may be prepaid at any time without penalty. As of January 2010, no additional borrowings can be made according to the terms of the agreement. The working capital facility bears interest at LIBOR plus 1.7% which is payable in semi-annual payments. The borrowings outstanding as of December 31, 2009 were $15.0 million, and were due in February and March 2010. In January 2010, the maturity date of the outstanding balance was extended through January 2011. At December 31, 2009, the interest rate ranged from 2.38% to 2.59% based on the dates of borrowing.

Amkor Iwate Corporation, a Japanese subsidiary ("AIC"), has a revolving line of credit with a Japanese bank for 2.5 billion Japanese yen (approximately $27.6 million) that was renewed during 2009 and extended through September 2010. The line of credit accrues interest at the Tokyo Interbank Offering Rate ("TIBOR") plus 0.6%. The interest rate at December 31, 2009 and 2008 was 0.91% and 1.22%, respectively. The borrowing outstanding was $27.2 million and zero as of December 31, 2009 and 2008, respectively.

Additionally, AIC has a revolving line of credit at a Japanese bank for 300.0 million Japanese yen (approximately $3.3 million) that was renewed during 2009 and extended through June 2010. Borrowings under the line of credit bear interest at TIBOR plus 0.5%. The interest rate at December 31, 2009 and 2008 was 0.77% and 1.20%, respectively. The outstanding balance was $3.3 million and zero as of December 31, 2009 and 2008, respectively.

The working capital facility and lines of credit contain certain affirmative and negative covenants, which could restrict our operations. If we were to default on our obligations under any of these facilities, we would not be permitted to draw additional amounts, and the lenders could accelerate our obligation to pay all outstanding amounts.

Secured Equipment and Property Financing

Our secured equipment and property financing consists of loans secured with specific assets at our Japanese, Singaporean and Chinese subsidiaries. In May 2004, our Chinese subsidiary entered into a $5.5 million credit facility secured with buildings at one of our Chinese production facilities and is payable ratably through January 2012. The interest rate for the Chinese financing at December 31, 2009 and December 31, 2008, was 5.84% and 8.22%, respectively. Our Chinese subsidiary's financing agreement contains affirmative and negative covenants, which could restrict our operations, and, if we were to default on our obligations, the lender could accelerate our obligation to repay amounts borrowed under such facilities.

Compliance With Debt Covenants

Our secured bank debt agreements and the indentures governing our senior and senior subordinated notes restrict our ability to pay dividends. We were in compliance with all of our covenants as of December 31, 2009, 2008 and 2007.

2.216

NORTHROP GRUMMAN CORPORATION (DEC)

NOTES TO CONSOLIDATED FINANCIAL STATEMENTS

13 (In Part): Notes Payable to Banks and Long-Term Debt

Lines of Credit

The company has available uncommitted short-term credit lines in the form of money market facilities with several banks. The amount and conditions for borrowing under these credit lines depend on the availability and terms prevailing in the marketplace. No fees or compensating balances are required for these credit facilities.

Credit Facility

The company has a revolving credit facility in an aggregate principal amount of $2 billion that matures on August 10, 2012. The credit facility permits the company to request additional lending commitments of up to $500 million from the lenders under the agreement or other eligible lenders under certain circumstances. The agreement provides for swingline loans and letters of credit as sub-facilities for the credit facilities provided for in the agreement. Borrowings under the credit facility bear interest at various rates, including the London Interbank Offered Rate, adjusted based on the company's credit rating, or an alternate base rate plus an incremental margin. The credit facility also requires a facility fee based on the daily aggregate amount of commitments (whether or not utilized) and the company's credit rating level, and contains a financial covenant relating to a maximum debt to capitalization ratio, and certain restrictions on additional asset liens. There were no borrowings during 2009 and a maximum of $300 million borrowed under this facility during 2008. There was no balance outstanding under this facility at December 31, 2009, and 2008. As of December 31, 2009, the company was in compliance with all covenants.

LONG-TERM LEASES

2.217 FASB ASC 840, *Leases,* establishes standards for reporting leases on the financial statements of lessees and lessors.

2.218 Table 2-30, in addition to summarizing the number of survey entities reporting capitalized and/or noncapitalized lessee leases, shows the nature of information most frequently disclosed by the survey entities for capitalized and noncapitalized lessee leases. 42 survey entities reported lessor leases.

2.219 Examples of long-term lease presentations and disclosures follow.

2.220

TABLE 2-30: LONG-TERM LEASES

	Number of Entities			
	2009	2008	2007	2006
Information Disclosed as to Capitalized Leases				
Minimum lease payments.....................	127	131	150	151
Imputed interest..................................	84	84	92	96
Leased assets by major classifications.....................................	48	53	58	56
Executory costs....................................	5	4	4	4
Information Disclosed as to Noncapitalized Leases				
Rental expenses				
Basic..	470	474	566	565
Sublease....................................	70	61	79	57
Contingent.................................	54	51	53	42
Minimum rental payments				
Schedule of................................	460	473	559	561
Classified by major categories of property.................................	10	13	14	10
Summary of Capitalized and Noncapitalized Leases				
Noncapitalized leases only..................	238	260	311	315
Capitalized and noncapitalized leases...	247	229	274	271
Capitalized leases only.......................	3	6	6	5
No leases disclosed............................	12	5	9	9
Total Entities....................................	**500**	**500**	**600**	**600**

2008–2009 based on 500 entities surveyed; 2006–2007 based on 600 entities surveyed.

Lessee—Capital Leases

2.221

THE SHAW GROUP INC. (AUG)

(In thousands)	2009	2008
Assets		
Total current assets	$4,553,248	$2,489,128
Investments in and advances to unconsolidated entities, joint ventures and limited partnerships	21,295	19,535
Investment in Westinghouse	—	1,158,660
Property and equipment, at cost	636,402	519,305
Less accumulated depreciation	(250,796)	(233,755)
Property and equipment, net	385,606	285,550
Goodwill	501,305	507,355
Intangible assets	20,957	24,065
Deferred income taxes	—	3,245
Other assets	74,763	99,740
Total assets	$5,557,174	$4,587,278
Current liabilities:		
Accounts payable	$ 859,753	$ 731,074
Accrued salaries, wages and benefits	175,750	120,038
Other accrued liabilities	187,020	187,045
Advanced billings and billings in excess of costs and estimated earnings on uncompleted contracts	1,308,325	748,395
Japanese Yen-denominated bonds secured by Investment in Westinghouse	1,387,954	—
Interest rate swap contract on Japanese Yen-denominated bonds	31,369	—
Short-term debt and current maturities of long-term debt	15,399	6,004
Total current liabilities	$3,965,570	$1,792,556
Long-term debt, less current maturities	7,627	3,579
Japanese Yen-denominated long-term bonds secured by Investment in Westinghouse, net	—	1,162,007
Interest rate swap contract on Japanese Yen-denominated bonds	—	8,802
Deferred income taxes	26,152	—
Other liabilities	109,835	101,522
Minority interest	24,691	29,082

NOTES TO CONSOLIDATED FINANCIAL STATEMENTS

Note 5. Property and Equipment

Property and equipment consisted of the following (in thousands):

	2009	2008
Transportation equipment	$ 20,977	$ 31,252
Furniture, fixtures and software	146,905	142,311
Machinery and equipment	219,753	184,619
Buildings and improvements	151,708	130,018
Assets acquired under capital leases	5,651	9,102
Land	12,404	13,026
Construction in progress	79,004	8,977
	636,402	519,305
Less: accumulated depreciation	(250,796)	(233,755)
Property and equipment, net	$ 385,606	$ 285,550

Assets acquired under capital leases, net of accumulated depreciation, were $2.0 million and $2.3 million at August 31, 2009 and 2008, respectively. If the assets acquired under capital leases transfer title at the end of the lease term or contain a bargain purchase option, the assets are amortized over their estimated useful lives; otherwise, the assets are amortized over the respective lease term. Depreciation and amortization expense of $52.3 million, $43.7 million and $37.8 million for the fiscal years ended August 31, 2009, 2008, and 2007, respectively, is included in cost of revenues and general and administrative expenses in the accompanying consolidated statements of operations.

In fiscal year 2009, we recorded an increase of $64.4 million to construction in progress for our nuclear modular fabrication facility.

In fiscal year 2009, we recorded an asset impairment charge of $5.5 million for a consolidated joint venture. The impairment charge reduced the property, plant and equipment to its salvage value.

Note 8 (In Part): Debt and Revolving Lines of Credit

Our debt (including capital lease obligations) consisted of the following (in thousands):

	2009		2008	
	Short-Term	Long-Term	Short-Term	Long-Term
Notes payable on purchase of Gottlieb, Barnett & Bridges; 0% interest; due and paid on January 10, 2009	$ —	$ —	$2,716	$ —
Notes payable of Liquid Solutions LLC, a VIE; interest payable monthly at an average interest rate of 8.2% and 8.3% and monthly payments of $0.02 million and $0.08 million, through May and June 2011, respectively	1,197	1,269	946	2,466
Notes payable on purchases of equipment; 0% to 1.3% interest; payments discounted at imputed rate of 5.9% interest; due September through October 2010	10,610	2,146	—	—
Notes payable on purchases of equipment; 5.2% to 6.0% interest; due June 2011 through July 2012	1,188	1,824	—	—
Other notes payable	1,608	1,008	833	833
Capital lease obligations	796	1,380	1,509	280
Subtotal	15,399	7,627	6,004	3,579
Westinghouse bonds	1,387,954	—	—	1,162,007
Total	$1,403,353	$7,627	$6,004	$1,165,586

The notes payable on purchases of equipment are collateralized by the purchased equipment. The carrying amount of the equipment pledged as collateral was approximately $19.3 million at August 31, 2009.

Annual scheduled maturities of debt and minimum lease payments under capital lease obligations during each year ending August 31 are as follows (in thousands):

	Capital Lease Obligations	Debt
2010	$ 945	$ 14,603
2011	478	5,360
2012	401	887
2013	399	1,387,954
2014	266	—
Thereafter	—	—
Subtotal	2,489	1,408,804
Less: amount representing interest	(313)	—
Total	$2,176	$1,408,804

2.222

WAL-MART STORES, INC. (JAN)

(In millions)	2009	2008
Assets		
Total current assets	$ 48,949	$ 48,020
Property and equipment, at cost:		
Land	19,852	19,879
Buildings and improvements	73,810	72,141
Fixtures and equipment	29,851	28,026
Transportation equipment	2,307	2,210
Property and equipment, at cost	125,820	122,256
Less accumulated depreciation	(32,964)	(28,531)
Property and equipment, net	92,856	93,725
Property under capital lease:		
Property under capital lease	5,341	5,736
Less accumulated amortization	(2,544)	(2,594)
Property under capital lease, net	2,797	3,142
Goodwill	15,260	15,879
Other assets and deferred charges	3,567	2,748
Total assets	$163,429	$163,514
Current liabilities:		
Commercial paper	$ 1,506	$ 5,040
Accounts payable	28,849	30,344
Accrued liabilities	18,112	15,725
Accrued income taxes	677	1,000
Long-term debt due within one year	5,848	5,913
Obligations under capital leases due within one year		
Current liabilities of discontinued operations	83	140
Total current liabilities	$ 55,390	$ 58,478
Long-term debt	31,349	29,799
Long-term obligations under capital leases	3,200	3,603
Deferred income taxes and other	6,014	5,087
Minority interest	2,191	1,939

NOTES TO CONSOLIDATED FINANCIAL STATEMENTS

Note 1 (In Part): Significant Accounting Policies

Leases

The Company estimates the expected term of a lease by assuming the exercise of renewal options where an economic penalty exists that would preclude the abandonment of the lease at the end of the initial non-cancelable term and the exercise of such renewal is at the sole discretion of the Company. This expected term is used in the determination of whether a store lease is a capital or operating lease and in the calculation of straight-line rent expense. Additionally, the useful life of leasehold improvements is limited by the expected lease term or the economic life of the asset. If significant expenditures are made for leasehold improvements late in the expected term of a lease and renewal is reasonably assumed, the useful life of the leasehold improvement is limited to the end of the renewal period or economic life of the asset, whichever is shorter.

Rent abatements and escalations are considered in the calculation of minimum lease payments in the Company's capital lease tests and in determining straight-line rent expense for operating leases.

Depreciation and Amortization

Depreciation and amortization for financial statement purposes are provided on the straight-line method over the estimated useful lives of the various assets. Depreciation expense, including amortization of property under capital leases, for fiscal years 2009, 2008 and 2007 was $6.7 billion, $6.3 billion and $5.5 billion, respectively. For income tax purposes, accelerated methods of depreciation are used with recognition of deferred income taxes for the resulting temporary differences. Leasehold improvements are depreciated over the shorter of the estimated useful life of the asset or the remaining expected lease term. Estimated useful lives for financial statement purposes are as follows:

Buildings and improvements	5–50 years
Fixtures and equipment	3–20 years
Transportation equipment	4–15 years

9. Commitments

The Company and certain of its subsidiaries have long-term leases for stores and equipment. Rentals (including amounts applicable to taxes, insurance, maintenance, other operating expenses and contingent rentals) under operating leases and other short-term rental arrangements were $1.8 billion, $1.6 billion and $1.4 billion in 2009, 2008 and 2007, respectively. Aggregate minimum annual rentals at January 31, 2009, under non-cancelable leases are as follows (amounts in millions):

Fiscal Year	Operating Leases	Capital Leases
2010	$ 1,161	$ 569
2011	1,138	556
2012	997	527
2013	888	492
2014	816	460
Thereafter	7,830	2,914
Total minimum rentals	$12,830	$5,518
Less estimated executory costs		47
Net minimum lease payments		5,471
Less imputed interest at rates ranging from 3.0% to 13.6%		1,956
Present value of minimum lease payments		$3,515

Certain of the Company's leases provide for the payment of contingent rentals based on a percentage of sales. Such contingent rentals amounted to $21 million, $33 million and $41 million in 2009, 2008 and 2007, respectively. Substantially all of the Company's store leases have renewal options, some of which may trigger an escalation in rentals.

In connection with certain debt financing, we could be liable for early termination payments if certain unlikely events were to occur. At January 31, 2009, the aggregate termination payment would have been $153 million. The two arrangements pursuant to which these payments could be made expire in fiscal 2011 and fiscal 2019.

In connection with the development of our grocery distribution network in the United States, we have agreements with third parties which would require us to purchase or assume the leases on certain unique equipment in the event the agreements are terminated. These agreements, which can be terminated by either party at will, cover up to a five-year period and obligate the Company to pay up to approximately $66 million upon termination of some or all of these agreements.

The Company has potential future lease commitments for land and buildings for approximately 321 future locations. These lease commitments have lease terms ranging from 1 to 35 years and provide for certain minimum rentals. If executed, payments under operating leases would increase by $72 million for fiscal 2010, based on current cost estimates.

Lessee—Operating Leases

2.223

SUPERVALU INC. (FEB)

NOTES TO CONSOLIDATED FINANCIAL STATEMENTS
(Dollars in millions)

Note 8. Leases

The Company leases certain retail stores, distribution centers, office facilities and equipment from third parties. Many of these leases include renewal options and, to a limited extent, include options to purchase. Future minimum lease payments to be made by the Company for noncancellable operating leases and capital leases as of February 28, 2009 consist of the following:

	Lease Obligations	
Fiscal Year	Operating Leases	Capital Leases
2010	$ 426	$ 168
2011	415	164
2012	380	157
2013	335	154
2014	283	152
Thereafter	2,008	1,544
Total future minimum obligations	$3,847	2,339
Less interest		(1,005)
Present value of net future minimum obligations		1,334
Less current obligations		(69)
Long-term obligations		$ 1,265

Total future minimum obligations have not been reduced for future minimum subtenant rentals of $344 under certain operating subleases.

Rent expense and subtenant rentals under operating leases consisted of the following:

	2009	2008	2007
Operating leases:			
Minimum rent	$460	$450	$366
Contingent rent	8	7	5
	468	457	371
Subtenant rentals	(67)	(66)	(54)
	$401	$391	$317

The Company leases certain property to third parties under both operating and direct financing leases. Under the direct financing leases, the Company leases buildings to independent retail customers with terms ranging from five to 20 years. Future minimum lease and subtenant rentals under noncancellable leases as of February 28, 2009 consist of the following:

	Lease Receipts	
Fiscal Year	Operating Leases	Direct Financing Leases
2010	$ 24	$ 6
2011	22	5
2012	19	5
2013	18	4
2014	10	4
Thereafter	24	14
Total minimum lease receipts	$117	38
Less unearned income		(9)
Net investment in direct financing leases		29
Less current portion		(4)
Long-term portion		$25

The carrying value of owned property leased to third parties under operating leases was as follows:

	2009	2008
Property, plant and equipment	$22	$24
Less accumulated depreciation	(5)	(5)
Property, plant and equipment, net	$17	$19

2.224

THE GREAT ATLANTIC & PACIFIC TEA COMPANY, INC. (FEB)

NOTES TO CONSOLIDATED FINANCIAL STATEMENTS
(Dollars in thousands)

Note 11 (In Part): Lease Obligations

We operate primarily in leased facilities with lease terms generally ranging up to twenty-five years for store leases, with options to renew for additional periods. In addition, we lease certain store equipment and trucks. We recognize rent expense for operating leases with rent escalation clauses on a straight-line basis over the applicable lease term. The majority of the leases contain escalation clauses relating to real estate tax increases and certain store leases provide for increases in rentals when sales exceed specified levels. Our lease obligations consist of capital leases, operating leases and long-term real estate liabilities.

Rent expense recorded for our operating leases during the last three fiscal years consisted of the following:

Minimum Rentals	Fiscal 2008	Fiscal 2007	Fiscal 2006
Continuing operations	$174,232	$145,682	$125,704
Discontinued operations	—	20,452	44,629
	174,232	166,134	170,333
Contingent rentals			
Continuing operations	2,753	2,136	2,394
Discontinued operations	—	64	92
	2,753	2,200	2,486
Total rent expense	$176,985	$168,334	$172,819

Future minimum annual lease payments for capital leases and noncancelable operating leases in effect at February 28, 2009 are as follows:

		Operating Leases				
		Future Minimum Rental Payments			Future Minimum Sublease Rentals	Net Future Minimum Rental Payments
Fiscal	Capital Leases	Open Stores	Closed Sites	Total		
2009	$ 29,000	$ 195,285	$ 68,790	$ 264,075	$ 33,263	$ 230,812
2010	28,631	188,963	60,949	249,912	30,116	219,796
2011	26,901	176,729	55,522	232,251	26,552	205,699
2012	26,113	166,289	52,265	218,554	21,657	196,897
2013	22,711	148,212	50,214	198,426	17,752	180,674
2014 and thereafter	157,846	858,744	266,524	1,125,268	61,780	1,063,488
Net minimum rentals	291,202	$1,734,222	$554,264	$2,288,486	$191,120	$2,097,366
Less interest portion	(130,991)					
Present value of future minimum rentals	$ 160,211					

Included in the future minimum rental payments of closed sites of $554.3 million are amounts that are classified as current and non-current liabilities on our Consolidated Balance Sheets. These amounts represent estimated net cash flows based on our experience and knowledge of the market in which each closed store is located.

Lessor Leases

2.225

THE BOEING COMPANY (DEC)

(In millions)	2009	2008
Assets		
Cash and cash equivalents	$ 9,215	$ 3,268
Short-term investments	2,008	11
Accounts receivable, net	5,785	5,602
Current portion of customer financing, net	368	425
Deferred income taxes	966	1,046
Inventories, net of advances and progress billings	16,933	15,612
Total current assets	$35,275	$25,964
Customer financing, net	5,466	5,857
Property, plant and equipment, net	8,784	8,762
Goodwill	4,319	3,647
Other acquired intangibles, net	2,877	2,685
Deferred income taxes	3,062	4,114
Investments	1,030	1,328
Pension plan assets, net	16	16
Other assets, net of accumulated amortization of $492 and $400	1,224	1,406
Total assets	$62,053	$53,779

NOTES TO CONSOLIDATED FINANCIAL STATEMENTS
(Dollars in millions)

1 (In Part): Summary of Significant Accounting Policies

Financial Services Revenue

We record financial services revenue associated with sales-type finance leases, operating leases, and notes receivable.

Lease and financing revenue arrangements are included in Sales of services on the Consolidated Statements of Operations. For sales-type finance leases, we record an asset at lease inception. This asset is recorded at the aggregate future minimum lease payments, estimated residual value of the leased equipment, and deferred incremental direct costs less unearned income. Income is recognized over the life of the lease to approximate a level rate of return on the net investment. Residual values, which are reviewed periodically, represent the estimated amount we expect to receive at lease termination from the disposition of the leased equipment. Actual residual values realized could differ from these estimates. Declines in estimated residual value that are deemed other-than-temporary are recognized as Cost of services in the period in which the declines occur.

For operating leases, revenue on leased aircraft and equipment is recorded on a straight-line basis over the term of the lease. Operating lease assets, included in Customer financing, are recorded at cost and depreciated over the period that we project we will hold the asset to an estimated residual value, using the straight-line method. Prepayments received on operating lease contracts are classified as Other long-term liabilities on the Consolidated Statements of Financial Position. We periodically review our estimates of residual value and recognize forecasted changes by prospectively adjusting depreciation expense.

For notes receivable, notes are recorded net of any unamortized discounts and deferred incremental direct costs.

Interest income and amortization of any discounts are recorded ratably over the related term of the note.

Note 8. Customer Financing

Customer financing at December 31 consisted of the following:

	2009	2008
Aircraft financing		
Notes receivable	$ 779	$ 615
Investment in sales-type/finance leases	2,391	2,528
Operating lease equipment, at cost, less accumulated depreciation of $784 and $771	2,737	3,152
Other financing		
Notes receivable	229	256
Less allowance for losses on receivables	(302)	(269)
	$5,834	$6,282

The components of investment in sales-type/finance leases at December 31 were as follows:

	2009	2008
Minimum lease payments receivable	$ 3,147	$ 3,451
Estimated residual value of leased assets	677	735
Unearned income	(1,433)	(1,658)
	$ 2,391	$ 2,528

Aircraft financing operating lease equipment primarily includes jet and commuter aircraft. At December 31, 2009 and 2008, aircraft financing operating lease equipment included $385 and $685 of equipment available for sale or re-lease. At December 31, 2009 and 2008, we had firm lease commitments for $345 and $305 of this equipment.

When our Commercial Airplanes segment is unable to immediately sell used aircraft, it may place the aircraft under an operating lease. It may also provide customer financing with a note receivable. The carrying amount of the Commercial Airplanes segment used aircraft under operating leases and notes receivable included as a component of customer financing totaled $203 and $232 as of December 31, 2009 and 2008.

Impaired receivables and the allowance for losses on those receivables consisted of the following at December 31:

	2009	2008
Impaired receivables with no specific impairment allowance	$ 1	$163
Impaired receivables with specific impairment allowance	144	16
Allowance for losses on impaired receivables	2	8

The average recorded investment in impaired receivables as of December 31, 2009, 2008 and 2007, was $162, $197, and $589, respectively. Income recognition is generally suspended for receivables at the date full recovery of income and principal becomes not probable. Income is recognized when receivables become contractually current and performance is demonstrated by the customer. Interest income recognized on such receivables was $9, $14, and $50 for the years ended December 31, 2009, 2008 and 2007, respectively.

The change in the allowance for losses on receivables for the years ended December 31, 2009, 2008 and 2007, consisted of the following:

	Allowance for Losses
Beginning balance—January 1, 2007	$(254)
Customer financing valuation benefit/(provision)	60
Other	(1)
Ending balance—December 31, 2007	(195)
Customer financing valuation benefit/(provision)	(84)
Reduction in customer financing assets	10
Ending balance—December 31, 2008	(269)
Customer financing valuation benefit/(provision)	(45)
Reduction in customer financing assets	12
Ending balance—December 31, 2009	$(302)

Aircraft financing is collateralized by security in the related asset. The value of the collateral is closely tied to commercial airline performance and may be subject to reduced valuation with market decline. Our financing portfolio has a concentration of various model aircraft. Aircraft financing carrying values related to major aircraft concentrations at December 31 were as follows:

	2009	2008
717 Aircraft ($662 and $694 accounted for as operating leases)*	$2,262	$2,365
757 Aircraft ($708 and $780 accounted for as operating leases)*	902	991
737 Aircraft ($400 and $453 accounted for as operating leases)	553	464
767 Aircraft ($154 and $181 accounted for as operating leases)	465	540
MD-11 Aircraft ($384 and $536 accounted for as operating leases)*	384	536

* Out of production aircraft.

We recorded charges related to customer financing asset impairment in operating earnings, primarily as a result of declines in projected future cash flows. These charges for the years ended December 31 were as follows:

	2009	2008	2007
Boeing Capital Corporation	$91	$35	$33
Other Boeing	8		15
	$99	$35	$48

Scheduled receipts on customer financing are as follows:

Year	Principal Payments on Notes Receivable	Sales-Type/ Finance Lease Payments Receivable	Operating Lease Equipment Payments Receivable
2010	$284	$ 277	$349
2011	153	321	298
2012	129	316	239
2013	170	273	189
2014	55	273	140
Beyond 2014	220	1,687	343

Customer financing assets leased under capital leases and subleased to others were not significant in 2009 and 2008.

2.226

VERIZON COMMUNICATIONS INC. (DEC)

(In millions)	2008	2007
Assets		
Current assets		
Cash and cash equivalents	$ 2,009	$ 9,782
Short-term investments	490	509
Accounts receivable, net of allowances of $976 and $941	12,573	11,703
Inventories	2,289	2,092
Prepaid expenses and other	5,247	1,989
Total current assets	$ 22,608	$ 26,075
Plant, property and equipment	228,518	215,605
Less accumulated depreciation	137,052	129,059
	91,466	86,546
Investments in unconsolidated businesses	3,535	3,393
Wireless licenses	72,067	61,974
Goodwill	22,472	6,035
Other intangible assets, net	6,764	5,199
Other investments	—	4,781
Other assets	8,339	8,349
Total assets	$227,251	$202,352

NOTES TO FINANCIAL STATEMENTS

Note 8 (In Part): Leasing Arrangements

As Lessor

We are the lessor in leveraged and direct financing lease agreements for commercial aircraft and power generating facilities, which comprise the majority of the portfolio along with telecommunications equipment, real estate property and other equipment. These leases have remaining terms up to 41 years as of December 31, 2009. In addition, we lease space on certain of our cell towers to other wireless carriers. Minimum lease payments receivable represent unpaid rentals, less principal and interest on third-party nonrecourse debt relating to leveraged lease transactions. Since we have no general liability for this debt, which holds a senior security interest in the leased equipment and rentals, the related principal and interest have been offset against the minimum lease payments receivable in accordance with GAAP. All recourse debt is reflected in our consolidated balance sheets.

Finance lease receivables, which are included in Prepaid expenses and other and Other assets in our consolidated balance sheets are comprised of the following:

| | 2009 | | | 2008 | | |
| | Leveraged Leases | Direct Finance Leases | Total | Leveraged Leases | Direct Finance Leases | Total |
(Dollars in millions)						
Minimum lease payments receivable	$ 2,504	$166	$ 2,670	$ 2,734	$133	$ 2,867
Estimated residual value	1,410	12	1,422	1,501	12	1,513
Unearned income	(1,251)	(19)	(1,270)	(1,400)	(23)	(1,423)
Total	$ 2,663	$159	$ 2,822	$ 2,835	$122	$ 2,957
Allowance for doubtful accounts			(158)			(159)
Finance lease receivables, net			$ 2,664			$ 2,798
Current			$ 72			$ 46
Noncurrent			2,592			2,752
			$ 2,664			$ 2,798

Accumulated deferred taxes arising from leveraged leases, which are included in Deferred income taxes, amounted to $2,081 million at December 31, 2009 and $2,218 million at December 31, 2008.

The following table is a summary of the components of income from leveraged leases:

(Dollars in millions)	2009	2008	2007
Pretax lease income	$83	$74	$78
Income tax expense	34	30	30
Investment tax credits	4	4	4

The future minimum lease payments to be received from noncancelable capital leases (direct financing and leveraged leases), net of nonrecourse loan payments related to leveraged leases, along with payments relating to operating leases for the periods shown at December 31, 2009, are as follows:

(Dollars in millions)	Capital Leases	Operating Leases
2010	$ 228	$117
2011	169	96
2012	135	70
2013	136	41
2014	124	20
Thereafter	1,878	47
Total	$2,670	$391

OTHER NONCURRENT LIABILITIES

2.227   In addition to long-term debt, many of the survey entities presented captions for deferred taxes, minority interests, employee liabilities, estimated losses or expenses, and deferred credits. Table 2-31 summarizes the nature of such noncurrent liabilities and deferred credits. Examples of presentations and disclosures for noncurrent liabilities and deferred credits follow.

2.228

TABLE 2-31: OTHER NONCURRENT LIABILITIES*

	Number of Entities			
	2009	2008	2007	2006
Deferred income taxes	340	346	412	411
Tax uncertainties	155	151	80	N/C**
Derivatives	152	58	74	62
Redeemable noncontrolling/minority interest	65	154	174	185
Interest/penalties on tax uncertainties	33	N/C**	N/C**	N/C**
Preferred stock	13	14	13	16
Employee Liabilities				
Pension accruals	311	327	340	319
Benefits	268	203	276	264
Deferred compensation, bonus, etc.	65	71	81	87
Other—described	24	22	26	26
Estimated Losses or Expenses				
Environmental	70	70	72	83
Discontinued operations/ restructuring	58	55	71	82
Insurance	46	43	53	55
Asset retirement obligations	43	38	45	36
Warranties	28	24	31	30
Litigation	23	25	41	38
Other—described	72	63	76	67
Deferred Credits				
Payments received prior to rendering service	97	85	102	96
Deferred profits on sales	16	30	37	31
Other—described	6	5	2	6

* Appearing in either the balance sheet and/or the notes to financial statements.

** N/C = Not compiled. Line item was not included in the table for the year shown.

2008–2009 based on 500 entities surveyed; 2006–2007 based on 600 entities surveyed.

Deferred Income Taxes

2.229

AMETEK, INC. (DEC)

(In thousands)	2009	2008
Total current liabilities	$ 424,282	$ 447,513
Long-term debt	955,880	1,093,243
Deferred income taxes	206,354	144,941
Other long-term liabilities	92,492	82,073
Total liabilities	$1,679,008	$1,767,770

NOTES TO CONSOLIDATED FINANCIAL STATEMENTS

1 (In Part): Significant Accounting Policies

Income Taxes

The Company's annual provision for income taxes and determination of the related balance sheet accounts requires management to assess uncertainties, make judgments regarding outcomes and utilize estimates. The Company conducts a broad range of operations around the world and is therefore subject to complex tax regulations in numerous international taxing jurisdictions, resulting at times in tax audits, disputes and potential litigation, the outcome of which is uncertain. Management must make judgments currently about such uncertainties and determine estimates of the Company's tax assets and liabilities. To the extent the final outcome differs, future adjustments to the Company's tax assets and liabilities may be necessary. The Company recognizes interest and penalties accrued related to uncertain tax positions in income tax expense.

The Company also is required to assess the realizability of its deferred tax assets, taking into consideration the Company's forecast of future taxable income, the reversal of other existing temporary differences, available net operating loss carryforwards and available tax planning strategies that could be implemented to realize the deferred tax assets. Based on this assessment, management must evaluate the need for, and amount of, valuation allowances against the Company's deferred tax assets. To the extent facts and circumstances change in the future, adjustments to the valuation allowances may be required.

13 (In Part): Income Taxes

Significant components of deferred tax (asset) liability were as follows at December 31:

(In thousands)	2009	2008
Current deferred tax (asset) liability:		
Reserves not currently deductible	$ (19,437)	$ (20,885)
Share-based compensation	(3,870)	(1,984)
Net operating loss carryforwards	(2,829)	(1,107)
Foreign tax credit carryforwards	(3,360)	(3,360)
Other	(1,173)	(3,583)
Net current deferred tax asset	$ (30,669)	$ (30,919)
Noncurrent deferred tax (asset) liability:		
Differences in basis of property and accelerated depreciation	$ 22,285	$ 24,442
Reserves not currently deductible	(19,913)	(17,815)
Pensions	31,453	7,454
Differences in basis of intangible assets and accelerated amortization	188,045	136,417
Net operating loss carryforwards	(6,513)	(11,950)
Share-based compensation	(9,893)	(9,084)
Other	(3,578)	4,268
	201,886	133,732
Less: valuation allowance	4,468	11,209
Net noncurrent deferred tax liability	206,354	144,941
Net deferred tax liability	$175,685	$114,022

As of December 31, 2009, the Company had no provision for U.S. deferred income taxes on the undistributed earnings of its foreign subsidiaries, which total approximately $395 million. If the Company were to distribute those earnings to the United States, the Company would be subject to U.S. income taxes based on the excess of the U.S. statutory rate over statutory rates in the foreign jurisdiction and withholding taxes payable to the various foreign countries. Determination of the amount of the unrecognized deferred income tax liability on these undistributed earnings is not practicable.

At December 31, 2009, the Company had tax benefits of $9.3 million related to net operating loss carryforwards, which will be available to offset future income taxes payable, subject to certain annual or other limitations based on foreign and U.S. tax laws. This amount includes net operating loss carryforwards of $3.7 million for federal income tax purposes with a valuation allowance of $3.3 million, $3.6 million for state income tax purposes with a valuation allowance of $0.2 million, and $2.0 million for foreign locations with no valuation allowance. These net operating loss carryforwards, if not used, will expire between 2010 and 2032. As of December 31, 2009, the Company had $3.4 million of U.S. foreign tax credit carryforwards.

The Company maintains a valuation allowance to reduce certain deferred tax assets to amounts that are more likely than not to be realized. This allowance primarily relates to the deferred tax assets established for net operating loss carryforwards. In 2009, the Company recorded a decrease of $6.7 million in the valuation allowance primarily related to the utilization and expiration of net operating loss carryforwards.

2.230

CONOCOPHILLIPS (DEC)

(Millions of dollars)	2009	2008
Total current liabilities	$23,695	$21,780
Long-term debt	26,925	27,085
Asset retirement obligations and accrued environmental costs	8,713	7,163
Joint venture acquisition obligation—related party	5,009	5,669
Deferred income taxes	17,962	18,167
Employee benefit obligations	4,130	4,127
Other liabilities and deferred credits	3,097	2,609
Total liabilities	$89,531	$86,600

NOTES TO CONSOLIDATED FINANCIAL STATEMENTS

Note 1 (In Part): Accounting Policies

Income Taxes

Deferred income taxes are computed using the liability method and are provided on all temporary differences between the financial reporting basis and the tax basis of our assets and liabilities, except for deferred taxes on income considered to be permanently reinvested in certain foreign subsidiaries and foreign corporate joint ventures. Allowable tax credits are applied currently as reductions of the provision for income taxes. Interest related to unrecognized tax benefits is reflected in interest expense, and penalties in production and operating expenses.

Note 20 (In Part): Income Taxes

Deferred income taxes reflect the net tax effect of temporary differences between the carrying amounts of assets and liabilities for financial reporting purposes and the amounts used for tax purposes. Major components of deferred tax liabilities and assets at December 31 were:

(Millions of dollars)	2009	2008
Deferred tax liabilities		
Properties, plants and equipment, and intangibles	$21,281	$20,563
Investment in joint ventures	2,039	1,778
Inventory	13	283
Partnership income deferral	660	1,172
Other	813	564
Total deferred tax liabilities	24,806	24,360
Deferred tax assets		
Benefit plan accruals	1,802	1,819
Asset retirement obligations and accrued environmental costs	3,874	3,232
Deferred state income tax	251	289
Other financial accruals and deferrals	465	712
Loss and credit carryforwards	2,105	1,657
Other	484	338
Total deferred tax assets	8,981	8,047
Less valuation allowance	(1,540)	(1,340)
Net deferred tax assets	7,441	6,707
Net deferred tax liabilities	$17,365	$17,653

Current assets, long-term assets, current liabilities and long-term liabilities included deferred taxes of $581 million, $21 million, $5 million and $17,962 million, respectively, at December 31, 2009, and $457 million, $58 million, $1 million and $18,167 million, respectively, at December 31, 2008.

We have loss and credit carryovers in multiple taxing jurisdictions. These attributes generally expire between 2010 and 2029 with some carryovers having indefinite carryforward periods.

Valuation allowances have been established for certain loss and credit carryforwards that reduce deferred tax assets to an amount that will, more likely than not, be realized. During 2009, valuation allowances increased a total of $200 million. This reflects increases of $224 million primarily related to U.S. foreign tax credit and foreign and state tax loss carryforwards and currency effects, partially offset by decreases of $24 million related to utilization of loss carryforwards and asset relinquishment. Based on our historical taxable income, expectations for the future, and available tax-planning strategies, management expects remaining net deferred tax assets will be realized as offsets to reversing deferred tax liabilities and as offsets to the tax consequences of future taxable income.

At December 31, 2009 and 2008, income considered to be permanently reinvested in certain foreign subsidiaries and foreign corporate joint ventures totaled approximately $2,129 million and $3,871 million, respectively. Deferred income taxes have not been provided on this income, as we do not plan to initiate any action that would require the payment of income taxes. It is not practicable to estimate the amount of additional tax that might be payable on this foreign income if distributed.

Tax Uncertainties

2.231

POLARIS INDUSTRIES INC. (DEC)

(In thousands)	2009	2008
Total current liabilities	$343,074	$404,833
Long term income taxes payable	4,988	5,103
Deferred income taxes	11,050	4,185
Borrowings under credit agreement	200,000	200,000
Total liabilities	$559,112	$614,121

NOTES TO CONSOLIDATED FINANCIAL STATEMENTS

Note 4 (In Part): Income Taxes

The Company adopted the provisions of ASC Topic 740, (originally issued as FIN 48) in the first quarter 2007. Polaris had liabilities recorded related to unrecognized tax benefits totaling $4,988,000 and $5,103,000 at December 31, 2009 and 2008, respectively. The liabilities were classified as Long term taxes payable in the accompanying consolidated balance sheets in accordance with Topic 740. Polaris recognizes potential interest and penalties related to income tax positions as a component of the provision for income taxes on the consolidated statements of income. Polaris had potential interest of $612,000 and $481,000 recorded as a component of the liabilities at December 31, 2009 and 2008, respectively. The entire balance of unrecognized tax benefits at December 31, 2009, if recognized, would affect the Company's effective tax rate. The Company does not anticipate that total unrecognized tax benefits will materially change in the next twelve months. Tax years 2005 through 2008 remain open to examination by certain tax jurisdictions to which the Company is subject.

A reconciliation of the beginning and ending amount of unrecognized tax benefits is as follows (in thousands):

	2009	2008
Balance at January 1,	$5,103	$ 8,653
Gross increases for tax positions of prior years	94	—
Gross decreases for tax positions of prior years	(275)	(788)
Gross increases for tax positions of current year	985	1,236
Decreases due to settlements	(171)	(549)
Decreases for lapse of statute of limitations	(748)	(3,449)
Balance at December 31,	$4,988	$ 5,103

Derivatives

2.232

MOLSON COORS BREWING COMPANY (DEC)

(In millions)	2009	2008
Total current liabilities	$1,580.9	$ 986.1
Long-term debt	1,412.7	1,752.0
Pension and post-retirement benefits	823.8	581.0
Derivative hedging instruments	374.2	225.9
Deferred tax liabilities	468.0	399.4
Unrecognized tax benefits	65.0	230.4
Other liabilities	185.0	47.6
Discontinued operations	18.7	124.8
Total liabilities	$4,928.3	$4,347.2

NOTES TO CONSOLIDATED FINANCIAL STATEMENTS

19 (In Part): Derivative Instruments and Hedging Activities

Overview and Risk Management Policies

We use derivatives as a part of our normal business operations to manage our exposure to fluctuations in interest, foreign currency exchange, commodity, and production materials costs. We have established policies and procedures that govern the risk management of these exposures. We also occasionally transact derivatives for other strategic purposes, which includes our total return swaps. Our primary objective in managing these exposures is to decrease the volatility of our earnings and cash flows affected by changes in the underlying rates and prices.

To achieve this objective, we enter into a variety of financial derivatives, including foreign currency exchange, commodity, forward starting interest rate, and cross currency swaps, the values of which change in the opposite direction of the anticipated future cash flows. We also enter into physical hedging agreements directly with our suppliers as an added instrument to manage our exposure to certain commodities.

Counterparty Risk

While, by policy, the counterparties to any of the financial derivatives we enter into are major institutions with investment grade credit ratings of at least A- (Standard & Poor's), A3 (Moody's) or better, we are exposed to credit related losses in the event of non-performance by counterparties. This credit risk is generally limited to the unrealized gains in such contracts, should any of these counterparties fail to perform as contracted.

We have established counterparty credit policy and guidelines that are monitored and reported to management according to prescribed guidelines to assist in managing this risk. As an additional measure, we utilize a portfolio of institutions either headquartered or operating in the same countries that we conduct our business. In calculating the fair value of our derivative balances, we also record an adjustment to recognize the risk of counterparty credit and MCBC non-performance risk.

Liquidity Risk

We base the fair value of our derivative instruments upon market rates and prices. The volatility of these rates and prices are dependent on many factors that cannot be forecasted with reliable accuracy. The current fair values of our contracts could differ significantly from the cash settled values with our counterparties. As such, we are exposed to liquidity risk related to unfavorable changes in the fair value of our derivative contracts.

We may be forced to cash settle all or a portion of our derivative contracts before the expected settlement date upon the occurrence of certain contractual triggers including a change of control termination event or other breach of agreement. This could have a negative impact on our cash position. For derivative contracts that we have designated as hedging instruments, early cash settlement would result in the timing of our hedge settlement not being matched to the cash settlement of the forecasted transaction or firm commitment. We may also decide to cash settle all or a portion of our derivative contracts before the expected settlement date through negotiations with our counterparties, which could also impact our liquidity.

Due to the nature of our counterparty agreements, we are not able to net positions with the same counterparty across business units. Thus, in the event of default, we may be required to early settle all out-of-the-money contracts, without the benefit of netting the fair value of any in-the-money positions against this exposure.

Collateral

For the majority of our derivative transactions, we do not receive and are not required to post collateral unless a change of control event occurs. This termination event would give either party the right to early terminate all outstanding swap transactions in the event that the other party consolidates, merges with, or transfers all or substantially all its assets to, another entity, and the creditworthiness of the surviving entity that has assumed such party's obligations is "materially weaker" than that of such party.

We may also be required to post collateral with our counterparty if our total return swaps are in an out-of-the-money position. If our credit ratings with Moody's and Standard and Poor's with regard to our long-term debt remain at an investment grade level, we are required to post collateral for the portion of the out-of-the-money liability exceeding a pre-established threshold. If our credit ratings fall below investment grade with both ratings services, we must post collateral for the entire out-of-the-money liability. As of December 26, 2009, we did not have any collateral posted with our counterparty.

Derivative Accounting Policies

Overview

The majority of our derivative contracts qualifies and are designated as cash flow hedges. We have also elected the NPNS exemption for certain contracts. These contracts are typically transacted with our suppliers and include risk management features that allow us to fix the price on specific volumes of purchases for specified delivery periods. The Company also considers whether any provisions in our contracts represent "embedded" derivative instruments as defined in authoritative accounting guidance.

As of December 26, 2009, we have concluded that no "embedded" derivative instruments warrant separate fair value accounting.

Hedge Accounting Policies

We formally document all relationships between hedging instruments and hedged items, as well as the risk-management objective and strategy for undertaking hedge transactions. We also formally assess both at the hedge's inception and on an ongoing basis, specifically whether the derivatives that are used in hedging transactions have been highly effective in offsetting changes in the cash flows of hedged items and whether those derivatives may be expected to remain highly effective in future periods.

We discontinue hedge accounting prospectively when (1) the derivative is no longer highly effective in offsetting changes in the cash flows of a forecasted future transaction; (2) the derivative expires or is sold, terminated, or exercised; (3) it is no longer probable that the forecasted transaction will occur; (4) management determines that designating the derivative as a hedging instrument is no longer appropriate; or (5) management decides to cease hedge accounting.

When we discontinue hedge accounting prospectively, but it continues to be probable that the forecasted transaction will occur in the originally expected period, the existing gain or loss on the derivative remains in accumulated other comprehensive income ("AOCI") and is reclassified into earnings when the forecasted transaction affects earnings. However, if it is no longer probable that a forecasted transaction will occur by the end of the originally specified time period or within an additional two-month period of time thereafter, the gains and losses in AOCI are recognized immediately in earnings. In all situations in which hedge accounting is discontinued and the derivative remains outstanding, we carry the derivative at its fair value on the balance sheet until maturity, recognizing future changes in the fair value in current period earnings.

Presentation

Derivatives are recognized on the balance sheet at their fair value. See our discussion regarding fair value measurements below. In accordance with FASB issued guidance, we do not record the fair value of derivatives for which we have elected the Normal Purchase Normal Sales ("NPNS") exemption. We account for these contracts on an accrual basis, recording realized settlements related to these contracts to the same financial statement line items as the corresponding transaction.

For derivative contracts recorded on the balance sheet, MCBC allocates the current and non-current portion of each contract's fair value to the appropriate asset/liability line item. Unrealized gain positions are recorded as other current assets or other non-current assets. Unrealized loss positions are recorded as other current liabilities or other non-current liabilities. Our policy is to present all derivative balances on a gross basis, without regard to counterparty master netting agreements or similar arrangements.

We record realized gains and losses from derivative instruments to the same financial statement line item as the hedged item/forecasted transaction. Changes in unrealized gains and losses for derivatives not designated as either a cash flow hedge or fair value hedge are recorded directly in earnings each period and are recorded to the same financial statement line item as the associated realized (cash settled) gains and losses.

Changes in fair values (to the extent of hedge effectiveness) of outstanding cash flow hedges are recorded in OCI, until earnings are affected by the variability of cash flows of the underlying hedged transaction. The recognition of effective hedge results in the consolidated statement of income offsets the gains or losses on the underlying exposure. Any ineffectiveness is recorded directly into earnings each period.

Significant Derivative/Hedge Positions

Cross Currency Swaps

Simultaneous with the September 22, 2005, U.S. private debt placement, we entered into a cross currency swap transaction for the entire USD $300 million issue amount and for the same maturity of September 2010. In this transaction we exchanged our USD $300 million for a CAD $355.5 million obligation with a third party. The swaps also call for an exchange of fixed CAD interest payments for fixed USD interest receipts. We have designated this transaction as a hedge of the variability of the cash flows associated with the payment of interest and principal on the USD securities. Changes in the value of the transaction due to foreign exchange are recorded in earnings and are offset by a revaluation of the associated debt instrument. Changes in the value of the transaction due to interest rates are recorded to OCI.

On April 10, 2007, we entered into several cross currency swaps that mature in May 2012 to hedge the foreign currency impact of intercompany GBP debt in a CAD functional currency subsidiary. The cross currency swaps are designated as cash flow hedges of forecasted CAD cash flows related to GBP interest and principal payments on the intercompany loans. The notional amount of the swaps is GBP £530 million (CAD $1.2 billion at inception). The cross currency swaps have been designated as cash flow hedges of the changes in value of the future CAD interest and principal payments that results from changes in the GBP to CAD exchange rates on an intercompany loan between our U.K. and Corporate segments.

As of December 26, 2009, we are also a party to other cross currency swaps totaling GBP £530 million (USD $774 million at inception). The swaps call for an exchange of fixed GBP interest payments for fixed USD interest receipts. The cross currency swaps have been designated as cash flow hedges of the changes in value of the future GBP interest and principal receipts.

Forward Starting Interest Rate Swaps

In order to manage our exposure to the volatility of the interest rates associated with the future interest payments on a forecasted debt issuance, we have transacted forward starting interest rate swap contracts. These swaps have a total notional value of CAD $200 million with an average fixed rate of 3.3%. These forward starting interest rate swaps have an effective date starting in September 2010 and have a termination date in 2017, mirroring the term of the forecasted debt issuance. Under these agreements we are required to early terminate these swaps in 2010, at the time we expect to issue the forecasted debt. We have designated these contracts as cash flow hedges on a portion of the interest payments on a future forecasted debt issuance.

Foreign Currency Forwards

As of period end, we have financial foreign exchange forward contracts in place to manage our exposure to foreign currency fluctuations. We hedge foreign currency exposure related to certain royalty agreements, exposure associated with the purchase of production inputs and imports that are denominated in currencies other than the functional entity's local currency, and other foreign exchanges exposures. MCBC uses foreign currency forward contracts to hedge these future forecasted transactions with up to a thirty-six month horizon.

Commodity Swaps

As of period end, we had financial commodity swap contracts in place to hedge certain future expected purchases of natural gas. Essentially, these contracts allow us to swap our floating exposure to natural gas prices for a fixed rate. These contracts have been designated as cash flow hedges of forecasted natural gas purchases. The fair value of these swaps depends upon current market rates in relation to our fixed rate under the swap agreements at period end. MCBC uses these swaps to hedge forecasted purchases up to twenty-four months in advance.

Total Return Swaps

In 2008, we entered into a series of cash settled total return swap contracts. We transacted these swaps for the purpose of gaining exposure to Foster's, a major global brewer. These swaps are marked-to-market each period as these swaps do not qualify for hedge accounting. As such, all unrealized gains and losses related to these swaps are recorded directly to the income statement and are classified as other income (expense) in MCI and Corporate. Under the initial agreements, these total return swaps were scheduled to mature this year. However, during the second quarter of this year we amended these total return swap agreements with our counterparty to extend the maturity date by one year. As such, the current swaps are contracted to settle in 2010.

Derivative Fair Value Measurements

The fair values of our derivatives include credit risk adjustments to account for our counterparties' credit risk, as well as MCBC's own non-performance risk. These adjustments resulted in a $3 million net increase as of December 26, 2009 to other comprehensive income ("OCI"), as the fair value of these derivatives was in a net liability position. This represents a $4 million net decrease year to date, as these adjustments resulted in a $7 million net increase to OCI as of December 28, 2008.

The table below summarizes our derivative assets and liabilities that were measured at fair value as of December 26, 2009. We utilize market approaches to value derivative instruments.

| | | Fair Value Measurements at December 26, 2009 Using | | |
(In millions)	Total Carrying Value at December 26, 2009	Quoted Prices in Active Markets (Level 1)	Significant Other Observable Inputs (Level 2)	Significant Unobservable Inputs (Level 3)
Derivatives, net	$(417.9)	$—	$(417.9)	$—
Total	$(417.9)	$—	$(417.9)	$—

| | | Fair Value Measurements at December 28, 2008 Using | | |
(In millions)	Total Carrying Value at December 28, 2008	Quoted Prices in Active Markets (Level 1)	Significant Other Observable Inputs (Level 2)	Significant Unobservable Inputs (Level 3)
Derivatives, net	$(141.0)	$—	$(151.5)	$10.5
Total	$(141.0)	$—	$(151.5)	$10.5

The table below summarizes derivative valuation activity using significant unobservable inputs (Level 3) (In millions):

	Rollforward of Level 3 Inputs
Balance at December 31, 2007	$ —
Total gains or losses (realized/unrealized)	
Included in earnings (or change in net assets)	—
Included in AOCI	—
Purchases, issuances and settlements	—
Transfers in/out of Level 3	10.5
Balance at December 28, 2008	$ 10.5
Total gains or losses (realized/unrealized)	
Included in earnings (or change in net assets)	—
Included in AOCI	—
Purchases, issuances and settlements	—
Transfers in/out of Level 3	(10.5)
Balance at December 26, 2009	$ —

During the year we transferred $10.5 million of derivative liability related to one cross currency swap out of Level 3 and into Level 2 as the position's valuation became based upon observable market inputs with unobservable inputs no longer playing a significant role in the valuation.

Results of Period Derivative Activity

The tables below include the year to date results of our derivative activity in the Consolidated Balance Sheet as of December 26, 2009 and the Consolidated Statement of Operations for the year ended December 26, 2009.

Fair Value of Derivative Instruments in the Consolidated Balance Sheet (In millions)

		Notional Amount	Asset Derivatives		Liability Derivatives	
			Balance Sheet Location	Fair Value	Balance Sheet Location	Fair Value
2009						
Derivatives designated as hedging instruments:						
Cross currency swaps	USD	1,992.4	Other current assets	$ —	Accrued expenses	$ (46.9)
			Other assets	—	Long term derivative liability	(366.1)
Forward starting interest rate swaps	USD	190.5	Other current assets	6.3	Accrued expenses	—
Foreign currency forwards	USD	339.3	Other current assets	4.6	Accrued expenses	(6.1)
			Other assets	1.1	Long term derivative liability	(8.1)
Commodity swaps	Gigajoules	1.2	Other current assets	—	Accrued expenses	(0.9)
Total derivatives designated as hedging instruments				$12.0		$(428.1)
Derivatives not designated as hedging instruments:						
Total return swap	AUD	496.5	Other current assets	$ —	Accrued expenses	$ (1.8)
Total derivatives not designated as hedging instruments				$ —		$ (1.8)

MCBC allocates the current and non-current portion of each contract to the corresponding derivative account above.

Redeemable Noncontrolling Interest

2.233

CATERPILLAR INC. (DEC)

(Dollars in millions)	2009	2008
Total current liabilities	$19,292	$26,069
Long-term debt due after one year:		
Machinery and Engines	5,652	5,736
Financial Products	16,195	17,098
Liability for postemployment benefits	7,420	9,975
Other liabilities	2,179	2,190
Total liabilities	$50,738	$61,068
Commitments and contingencies		
Redeemable noncontrolling interest (Note 26)	477	524

NOTES TO CONSOLIDATED FINANCIAL STATEMENTS

26. Redeemable Noncontrolling Interest—Caterpillar Japan Ltd.

On August 1, 2008, SCM completed the first phase of a share redemption plan whereby SCM redeemed half of MHI's shares in SCM. This resulted in Caterpillar owning 67 percent of the outstanding shares of SCM and MHI owning the remaining 33 percent. As part of the share redemption, SCM was renamed Cat Japan. Both Cat Japan and MHI have options, exercisable after five years, to require the redemption of the remaining shares owned by MHI, which if exercised, would make Caterpillar the sole owner of Cat Japan.

The remaining 33 percent of Cat Japan owned by MHI has been reported as redeemable noncontrolling interest and classified as mezzanine equity (temporary equity) in Statement 2. The redeemable noncontrolling interest is reported at its estimated redemption value. Any adjustment to the redemption value impacts Profit employed in the business, but does not impact Profit. If the fair value of the redeemable noncontrolling interest falls below the redemption value, profit available to common stockholders would be reduced by the difference between the redemption value and the fair value. This would result in lower profit in the profit per common share computation in that period. Reductions impacting the profit per common share computation may be partially or fully reversed in subsequent periods if the fair value of the redeemable noncontrolling interest increases relative to the redemption value. Such increases in profit per common share would be limited to cumulative prior reductions. During 2009, the estimated redemption value decreased, resulting in adjustments to the carrying value of the redeemable noncontrolling interest. Profit employed in the business increased by $81 million due to these adjustments. There was no change to the estimated redemption value in 2008. As of December 31, 2009 and 2008, the fair value of the redeemable noncontrolling interest remained greater than the estimated redemption value.

We estimate the fair value of the redeemable noncontrolling interest using a discounted five year forecasted cash flow with a year-five residual value. If worldwide economic conditions deteriorate and Cat Japan's business forecast is negatively impacted, it is reasonably possible that the fair value of the redeemable noncontrolling interest may fall below the estimated redemption value in the near term. Should this occur, profit would be reduced in the profit per common share computation by the difference between the redemption value and the fair value. Lower long-term growth rates, reduced long-term profitability as well as changes in interest rates, costs, pricing, capital expenditures and general market conditions may reduce the fair value of the redeemable noncontrolling interest.

With the consolidation of Cat Japan's results of operations, 33 percent of Cat Japan's comprehensive income or loss is attributed to the redeemable noncontrolling interest, impacting its carrying value. Because the redeemable noncontrolling interest must be reported at its estimated future redemption value, the impact from attributing the comprehensive income or loss is offset by adjusting the carrying value to the redemption value. This adjustment impacts Profit employed in the business, but not Profit. In 2009 and 2008, the carrying value had decreased by $53 million and $2 million, respectively, due to Cat Japan's comprehensive loss. This resulted in an offsetting adjustment of $53 million in 2009 and $2 million in 2008 to increase the carrying value to the redemption value and a corresponding reduction to Profit employed in the business. As Cat Japan's functional currency is the Japanese yen, changes in exchange rates affect the reported amount of the redeemable noncontrolling interest. At December 31, 2009 and 2008, the redeemable noncontrolling interest was $477 million and $524 million, respectively.

Interest/Penalties on Tax Uncertainties

2.234

POLO RALPH LAUREN CORPORATION (MAR)

(Millions)	2009	2008
Total current liabilities	$674.1	$908.6
Long-term debt	406.4	472.8
Non-current liability for unrecognized tax benefits	154.8	155.2
Other non-current liabilities	386.1	439.2

NOTES TO CONSOLIDATED FINANCIAL STATEMENTS

3 (In Part): Summary of Significant Accounting Policies

Income Taxes (In Part)

Effective April 1, 2007, the Company adopted FIN No. 48, "Accounting for Uncertainty in Income Taxes—An Interpretation of FAS No. 109" ("FIN 48"). Upon the adoption of the provisions of FIN 48, the Company changed its policy related to the accounting for income tax uncertainties. If the Company considers that a tax position is "more-likely-than-not" of being sustained upon audit, based solely on the technical merits of the position, it recognizes the tax benefit. The Company measures the tax benefit by determining the largest amount that is greater than 50% likely of being realized upon settlement, presuming that the tax position is examined by the appropriate taxing authority that has full knowledge of all relevant information. These assessments can be complex and the Company often obtains assistance from external advisors. To the extent that the Company's estimates change or the final tax outcome of these matters is different than

the amounts recorded, such differences will impact the income tax provision in the period in which such determinations are made. If the initial assessment fails to result in the recognition of a tax benefit, the Company regularly monitors its position and subsequently recognizes the tax benefit if (i) there are changes in tax law or analogous case law that sufficiently raise the likelihood of prevailing on the technical merits of the position to "more-likely-than-not", (ii) the statute of limitations expires, or (iii) there is a completion of an audit resulting in a settlement of that tax year with the appropriate agency. Uncertain tax positions are classified as current only when the Company expects to pay cash within the next twelve months. Interest and penalties, if any, are recorded within the provision for income taxes in the Company's consolidated statements of operations and are classified on the consolidated balance sheets with the related liability for unrecognized tax benefits.

13 (In Part): Income Taxes

Uncertain Income Tax Benefits

Impact of FIN 48 Adoption

As a result of the adoption of FIN 48, the Company recognized a $62.5 million reduction in retained earnings as the cumulative effect to adjust its net liability for unrecognized tax benefits as of April 1, 2007. This adjustment consisted of a $99.9 million increase to the Company's liabilities for unrecognized tax benefits, offset in part by a $37.4 million increase to the Company's deferred tax assets principally representing the value of future tax benefits that could be realized at the U.S. federal level if the related liabilities for unrecognized tax benefits at the state and local levels ultimately are required to be settled. The total balance of unrecognized tax benefits, including interest and penalties, was $173.8 million as of April 1, 2007.

The Company classifies interest and penalties related to unrecognized tax benefits as part of its provision for income taxes. Accordingly, included in the liability for unrecognized tax benefits was a liability for interest and penalties in the amount of $45.7 million as of April 1, 2007.

Fiscal 2009 and Fiscal 2008 Activity (In Part)

A reconciliation of the beginning and ending amounts of unrecognized tax benefits, excluding interest and penalties, for Fiscal 2009 and Fiscal 2008 is presented below:

(Millions)	2009	2008
Unrecognized tax benefits beginning balance	$117.5	$128.1
Additions related to current period tax positions	5.4	11.5
Additions related to prior periods tax positions	19.4	15.5
Reductions related to prior periods tax positions	(17.8)	(22.2)
Reductions related to settlements with taxing authorities	(5.8)	(10.2)
Reductions related to expiration of statutes of limitations	—	(5.2)
Additions (reductions) charged to foreign currency translation	(5.0)	—
Unrecognized tax benefits ending balance	$113.7	$117.5

A reconciliation of the beginning and ending amounts of accrued interest and penalties related to unrecognized tax benefits for Fiscal 2009 and Fiscal 2008 is presented below:

(Millions)	2009	2008
Accrued interest and penalties beginning balance	$48.0	$45.7
Additions (reductions) charged to expense	(0.8)	7.6
Reductions related to settlements with taxing authorities	(5.1)	(5.1)
Reductions related to expiration of statutes of limitations	—	(1.4)
Additions (reductions) charged to foreign currency translation	(1.0)	1.2
Accrued interest and penalties ending balance	$41.1	$48.0

The total amount of unrecognized tax benefits, including interest and penalties, was $154.8 million as of March 28, 2009 and was included within non-current liability for unrecognized tax benefits in the consolidated balance sheet. The total amount of unrecognized tax benefits, including interest and penalties, was $165.5 million as of March 29, 2008, of which $10.3 was included within accrued expenses and other and $155.2 million was included within non-current liability for unrecognized tax benefits in the consolidated balance sheet. The total amount of unrecognized tax benefits that, if recognized, would affect the Company's effective tax rate was $117.1 million as of March 28, 2009 and $123.6 million as of March 29, 2008.

Preferred Stock

2.235

WHOLE FOODS MARKET, INC. (SEP)

(In thousands)	2009	2008
Total current liabilities	$ 684,024	$ 666,177
Long-term debt and capital lease obligations, less current installments	738,848	928,790
Deferred lease liabilities	250,326	199,635
Other long-term liabilities	69,262	80,110
Total liabilities	$1,742,460	$1,874,712
Series A redeemable preferred stock, $0.01 par value, 425 and no shares authorized, issued and outstanding in 2009 and 2008, respectively	413,052	—

NOTES TO CONSOLIDATED FINANCIAL STATEMENTS

12. Redeemable Preferred Stock

On December 2, 2008, the Company issued 425,000 shares of Series A 8% Redeemable, Convertible Exchangeable Participating Preferred Stock, $0.01 par value per share ("Series A Preferred Stock") to affiliates of Leonard Green & Partners, L.P., for approximately $413.1 million, net of approximately $11.9 million in closing and issuance costs. On April 12, 2009, the Company amended and restated the Statement of Designations governing the Series A Preferred Stock. This amendment limited the participation feature, as described below, of the Series A 8% Redeemable, Convertible Exchangeable Preferred Stock and provided for the mandatory payment of cash dividends in respect to the Series A Preferred Stock. The amendment also restricted the Company's ability to pay cash dividends on its common stock without the prior written consent of the holders representing at least a majority of the shares of Series A Preferred Stock then outstanding.

The Series A Preferred Stock was classified as temporary shareholders' equity at September 27, 2009 since the shares were (i) redeemable at the option of the holder and (ii) had conditions for redemption which are not solely within the control of the Company. During fiscal year 2009, the Company paid cash dividends on the Series A Preferred Stock totaling approximately $19.8 million.

Subsequent to year end, on October 23, 2009, the Company announced its intention to call all 425,000 outstanding shares of the Series A Preferred Stock for redemption in accordance with the terms governing the Series A Preferred Stock. Subject to conversion of the Series A Preferred Stock by its holders, the Company planned to redeem such Series A Preferred Stock on November 27, 2009 at a price per share equal to $1,000 plus accrued and unpaid dividends. In accordance with the terms governing the Series A Preferred Stock, at any time prior to the redemption date, the Series A Preferred Stock could be converted by the holders thereof. On November 26, 2009 the holders converted all 425,000 outstanding shares of Series A Preferred Stock into approximately 29.7 million shares of common stock of the Company.

On December 2, 2008, the Company announced that two partners of Leonard Green & Partners, L.P., were elected to the Board pursuant to the terms governing the Series A Preferred Stock. These two directors will continue to serve on the Board after November 26, 2009, the conversion date. Additionally, so long as the Leonard Green affiliates continue to hold 10% or more of the voting stock of the Company, the Company is obligated to nominate for election to the Board two individuals designated by the affiliates of Leonard Green & Partners; provided however, that if the affiliates of Leonard Green & Partners continue to hold 7% or more of the voting stock of the Company but less than 10%, the Company is obligated to nominate for election to the Board one individual designated by the affiliates of Leonard Green & Partners.

Description of Series A Preferred Stock During Period Outstanding

Each share of Series A Preferred Stock had an initial liquidation preference of $1,000, subject to adjustment. Subject to limited exceptions, the outstanding shares could not be transferred outside of the initial investor group prior to the third anniversary of share issuance. The holders of the Series A Preferred Stock were entitled to an 8% dividend, payable quarterly on the first day of each calendar quarter in cash. Beginning three years after issuance, the dividend would be reduced to (i) 6% if at any time the Company's common stock closes at or above $17.75 per share for at least 20 consecutive trading days, or (ii) 4% if at any time the Company's common stock closes at or above $23.13 per share for at least 20 consecutive trading days. Also, in the event a cash dividend or other distribution in cash was declared on the Company's common stock in an amount equal to or greater than the Company's stock price on the date of declaration, the holders of the Series A Preferred Stock were entitled to receive an additional amount equal to the cash amount per share distributed or to be distributed in respect of the common stock. To the extent the Company failed to pay dividends on the Series A Preferred Stock in cash, an amount equal to 12% of the liquidation preference of each share of the Series A Preferred Stock would be added to the liquidation preference of such share of Series A Preferred Stock.

The Series A Preferred Stock was convertible, under certain circumstances, to common stock based on the quotient of (i) the liquidation preference plus accrued dividends and (ii) 1,000, multiplied by the conversion rate, initially 68.9655. The conversion rate was subject to change based on certain customary antidilution provisions. The Series A Preferred Stock was convertible at any time, at the election of the holders, provided that at no time could any holder of the preferred shares beneficially own more than 19.99% of the Company's voting securities as a result of such conversion. The Company reserved, and kept available out of its authorized and unissued common stock, such number of shares that would be issued upon conversion of all Series A Preferred Stock then outstanding. Shares converted to common stock could not be transferred outside of the initial investor group prior to the third anniversary of the initial Preferred Stock issuance except under certain circumstances, including in the event that the Series A Preferred Stock was called for redemption by the Company.

The Company had the option to exchange the Series A Preferred Stock for subordinated convertible notes having economic terms similar to the preferred stock under certain circumstances.

The Company had the right to redeem the Series A Preferred Stock, in whole or in part, at any time after December 2, 2013, at a premium of 4%, declining ratably in annual increments to par on December 2, 2016, multiplied by the liquidation preference plus accrued dividends. Additionally, at any time, the Company could, upon 30 days notice, redeem the Series A Preferred Stock at par plus accrued dividends if the common stock closed at or above $28.50 per share for at least 20 consecutive trading days. On the redemption date, the redemption payment would become due and payable and the dividends on the Series A Preferred Stock would cease to accrue.

The holders of the Series A Preferred Stock had the right to require the Company to redeem their shares of Series A Preferred Stock, in whole or in part, at 101% of the liquidation preference plus accrued dividends upon the occurrence of certain fundamental changes to the Company, including a change of control and certain bankruptcy events. In addition, the holders of the Series A Preferred Stock had the right to require the Company to redeem their shares of Series A Preferred Stock at par any time on or after December 2, 2020.

In the event of any liquidation, dissolution or winding up of the affairs of the Company, whether voluntary or involuntary, holders of the Series A Preferred Stock were entitled to receive for each share, out of the assets of the Company or proceeds thereof (whether capital or surplus) available for distribution to shareholders of the Company, and after satisfaction of all liabilities and obligations to creditors of the Company, before any distribution of such assets or proceeds is made to or set aside for the holders of common stock, an amount equal to the greater of (i) the liquidation preference per share of Series A Preferred Stock plus accrued dividends and (ii) the per share amount of all cash and other property to be distributed in respect of the common stock such holder would have been entitled to had it converted such Series A Preferred Stock immediately prior to the date fixed for such liquidation, dissolution or winding up of the Company.

The holders of Series A Preferred Stock had the right to veto certain actions of the Company that might dilute, or alter the rights of, the Series A Preferred Stock. The Series A Preferred Stock voted together with the common stock on an as-converted basis, but no holder of Series A Preferred Stock could vote more than the equivalent of 19.99% of the Company's voting securities.

The holders of the Series A Preferred Stock, voting as a separate class, were entitled to elect two members of the Board of Directors of the Company. Additionally, the holders of the Series A Preferred Stock were entitled to designate one member to each of the committees of the Board of Directors and to appoint directors for election to the Board of Directors once the ability to elect directors ceases, subject to applicable government restrictions. Representation on the Board of Directors of the Company would be reduced based on certain dilution percentages of the Company's voting securities and would cease once the Series A Preferred Stock represented less than 7% of the Company's voting securities.

Employee-Related Liabilities

2.236

GOODRICH CORPORATION (DEC)

(Dollars in millions)	2009	2008
Total current liabilities	$1,613.1	$1,841.3
Long-term debt and capital lease obligations	2,008.1	1,410.4
Pension obligations	908.7	973.9
Postretirement benefits other than pensions	301.1	309.4
Long-term income taxes payable	171.1	172.3
Deferred income taxes	257.2	62.3
Other non-current liabilities	514.5	561.1

NOTES TO CONSOLIDATED FINANCIAL STATEMENTS

Note 1 (In Part): Significant Accounting Policies

Pension and Postretirement Benefits

The Company recognizes the funded status of the Company's pension plans and postretirement benefits plans other than pension (OPEB) on its consolidated balance sheet, with a corresponding adjustment to accumulated other comprehensive income (loss), net of tax. The measurement date used to determine the pension and OPEB obligations and assets for all plans was December 31. Plan assets have been valued at fair value. See Note 14, "Pensions and Postretirement Benefits."

Note 14 (In Part): Pensions and Postretirement Benefits

The Company has several defined benefit pension plans covering eligible employees. U.S. plans covering salaried and non-union hourly employees generally provide benefit payments using a formula that is based on an employee's compensation and length of service. Plans covering union employees generally provide benefit payments of stated amounts for each year of service. Plans outside of the U.S. generally provide benefit payments to eligible employees that relate to an employee's compensation and length of service. The Company also sponsors several unfunded defined benefit postretirement plans that provide certain health care and life insurance benefits to eligible employees in the U.S. and Canada. The health care plans are both contributory, with retiree contributions adjusted periodically, and non-contributory and can contain other cost-sharing features, such as deductibles and coinsurance. The life insurance plans are generally noncontributory.

Amortization of prior service cost is recognized on a straight-line basis over the average remaining service period of active employees. Amortization of actuarial gains and losses is recognized using the "corridor approach," which is the minimum amortization required. Under the corridor approach, actuarial net gain or loss in excess of 10% of the greater of the projected benefit obligation or the market-related value of the assets is amortized on a straight-line basis over the average remaining service period of the active employees.

Pension plans, defined contribution plans and postretirement benefits other than pensions include amounts related to divested and discontinued operations.

Amounts Recognized in Accumulated Other Comprehensive Income (Loss)

Following are the amounts included in accumulated other comprehensive income (loss) as of December 31, 2009 and 2008 and the amounts arising during 2009 and 2008. There are no transition obligations.

(Dollars in millions)	Net Actuarial Loss	Prior Service Cost	Total Before Tax	Tax	After Tax
Amounts recognized in accumulated other comprehensive income (loss):					
Unrecognized (loss) at December 31, 2007	$ (706.2)	$(12.2)	$ (718.4)	$285.6	$(432.8)
Amount recognized in net periodic benefit cost	52.2	4.4	56.6		
Amount due to January 1, 2008 valuation	(15.8)	—	(15.8)		
Amount due to plan changes	—	(12.2)	(12.2)		
Amount due to mid-year remeasurement	1.1	—	1.1		
Amount due to curtailment	11.2	(3.4)	7.8		
Amount due to settlement	(0.6)	—	(0.6)		
Foreign currency gain/(loss)	3.6	(3.0)	0.6		
Amount due to year end remeasurement	(711.7)	—	(711.7)		
Unrecognized (loss) at December 31, 2008	$(1,366.2)	$(26.4)	$(1,392.6)	$487.1	$(905.5)
Amount recognized in net periodic benefit cost	113.8	7.4	121.2		
Amount due to January 1, 2009 valuation	4.9	—	4.9		
Amount due to plan changes	—	(2.7)	(2.7)		
Amount due to settlement	(0.4)	—	(0.4)		
Foreign currency gain/(loss)	(18.0)	0.3	(17.7)		
Amount due to year end remeasurement	(105.2)	—	(105.2)		
Unrecognized (loss) at December 31, 2009	$(1,371.1)	$(21.4)	$(1,392.5)	$524.2	$(868.3)

The unrecognized loss at December 31, 2009 includes $0.9 million for the Company's share of the accumulated other comprehensive loss from a JV. This loss decreased our investment in the JV.

The amount of actuarial loss and prior service cost expected to be recognized in net periodic benefit cost during 2010 are approximately $120 million ($75 million after tax) and approximately $6 million ($4 million after tax) respectively.

Pensions

The following table sets forth the Company's defined benefit pension plans as of December 31, 2009 and 2008 and the amounts recorded in the consolidated balance sheet. Company contributions include amounts contributed directly to plan assets and indirectly as benefits are paid from the Company's assets. Benefit payments reflect the total benefits paid from the plan and the Company's assets. Information on the U.S. plans includes both the qualified and non-qualified plans. The fair value of assets for the U.S. plans excludes $61 million and $71 million held in a rabbi trust, which includes cash surrender value of life insurance policies, equity and fixed income mutual funds and cash and cash equivalents, designated for the non-qualified plans as of December 31, 2009 and 2008, respectively.

	U.S. Plans		U.K. Plans		Other Plans	
(Dollars in millions)	2009	2008	2009	2008	2009	2008
Change in projected benefit obligations						
Projected benefit obligation at beginning of year	$ 2,697.5	$ 2,678.7	$559.5	$ 776.7	$100.8	$121.7
Service cost	42.9	42.8	16.0	28.1	3.9	5.5
Interest cost	171.9	167.6	37.2	41.5	6.6	6.2
Amendments	13.1	2.4	—	—	(10.4)	10.2
Actuarial (gains) losses	168.3	2.6	18.2	(47.0)	9.2	(21.0)
Participant contributions	—	—	0.4	0.5	2.3	1.7
Curtailments	—	—	—	(11.2)	—	—
Settlements	—	(2.7)	—	—	(3.3)	—
Special termination benefits	—	—	1.2	—	—	—
Foreign currency translation	—	—	62.0	(220.6)	12.1	(19.7)
Benefits paid	(187.3)	(193.9)	(15.8)	(8.5)	(3.4)	(3.8)
Projected benefit obligation at end of year	$ 2,906.4	$ 2,697.5	$678.7	$ 559.5	$117.8	$100.8
Accumulated benefit obligation at end of year	$ 2,763.3	$ 2,575.9	$561.5	$ 467.8	$ 97.5	$ 84.3
Weighted average assumptions used to determine benefit obligations as of December 31						
Discount rate	5.90%	6.47%	5.88%	5.88%	5.75%	6.17%
Rate of compensation increase	4.10%	4.10%	3.75%	3.75%	3.38%	3.31%
Change in plan assets						
Fair value of plan assets at beginning of year	$ 1,856.3	$ 2,285.6	$458.2	$ 789.7	$ 58.6	$ 84.9
Actual return on plan assets	207.9	(420.5)	103.9	(148.0)	10.7	(15.1)
Settlements	—	(2.7)	—	—	(3.3)	—
Participant contributions	—	—	0.4	0.5	2.3	1.6
Company contributions	193.2	187.8	37.4	33.7	6.9	5.7
Foreign currency translation	—	—	49.4	(209.2)	8.7	(14.7)
Benefits paid	(187.3)	(193.9)	(15.8)	(8.5)	(3.4)	(3.8)
Fair value of plan assets at end of year	$ 2,070.1	$ 1,856.3	$633.5	$ 458.2	$ 80.5	$ 58.6
Funded status (underfunded)	$ (836.3)	$ (841.2)	$ (45.2)	$(101.3)	$ (37.3)	$ (42.2)
Amounts recognized in the balance sheet consist of:						
Prepaid pension	$ —	$ —	$ —	$ —	$ 0.8	$ 0.6
Accrued expenses—current liability	(10.2)	(10.4)	—	—	(0.7)	(1.0)
Pension obligation—non-current liability	(826.1)	(830.8)	(45.2)	(101.3)	(37.4)	(41.8)
Net asset (liability) recognized	$ (836.3)	$ (841.2)	$ (45.2)	$(101.3)	$ (37.3)	$ (42.2)
Accumulated other comprehensive income (loss)—before tax	$(1,245.7)	$(1,210.4)	$ (96.2)	$(130.0)	$ (27.4)	$ (31.5)

Defined benefit plans with an accumulated benefit obligation exceeding the fair value of plan assets had the following obligations and plan assets at December 31, 2009 and 2008:

	U.S. Plans		U.K. Plans		Other Plans	
(Dollars in millions)	2009	2008	2009	2008	2009	2008
Aggregate fair value of plan assets	$2,070.1	$1,856.3	$633.5	$458.2	$ 73.4	$54.4
Aggregate projected benefit obligation	2,906.4	2,697.5	678.7	559.5	111.5	97.1
Aggregate accumulated benefit obligations	2,763.3	2,575.9	561.5	467.8	91.5	80.8

• • • • • •

Pension assumptions were reevaluated on September 12, 2008 and on December 5, 2008 for the remeasurement of a U.S. nonqualified plan for retirement settlements resulting in a settlement loss of $0.6 million. On December 31, 2008, in connection with the formation of a JV as described in Note 5, "Other Income (Expense)—Net", the Company recorded a curtailment gain of $3.4 million in the U.K. Goodrich Pension Scheme. The curtailment and remeasurement decreased accumulated other comprehensive income by $7.8 million before tax or $5.1 million after tax. Also, a change to a French pension plan resulted in a settlement gain of $0.4 million and $1.2 million for 2009 and 2008 respectively.

On September 21, 2007, a definitive agreement to divest ATS was reached and assumptions for the U.S. qualified pension plans were reevaluated to remeasure the plan obligations and assets. In connection with the remeasurement, there was a curtailment loss of $6 million reported in discontinued operations for 2007. The remeasurement and curtailment increased accumulated other comprehensive income by $150.5 million before tax or $91.9 million after tax.

Postretirement Benefits Other Than Pensions

The following table sets forth the status of the Company's defined benefit postretirement plans other than pension as of December 31, 2009 and 2008, and the amounts recorded in the Company's consolidated balance sheet. The postretirement benefits related to divested and discontinued operations retained by the Company are included in the amounts below.

(Dollars in millions)	2009	2008
Change in projected benefit obligations		
Projected benefit obligation at beginning of year	$ 342.3	$ 394.1
Service cost	1.4	1.7
Interest cost	19.6	22.0
Amendments	—	(0.4)
Actuarial (gains) losses	2.3	(47.8)
Foreign currency translation/other	0.2	0.2
Gross benefits paid	(37.7)	(30.7)
Federal subsidy received	3.4	3.2
Projected benefit obligation at end of year	$ 331.5	$ 342.3
Weighted-average assumptions used to determine benefit obligations as of December 31		
Discount rate	5.55%	6.38%
Change in plan assets		
Fair value of plan assets at beginning of year	$ —	$ —
Company contributions	37.7	30.7
Gross benefits paid	(37.7)	(30.7)
Fair value of plan assets at end of year	$ —	$ —
Funded status (underfunded)	$(331.5)	$(342.3)
Amounts recognized in the balance sheet consist of:		
Accrued expenses—current liability	$ (30.4)	$ (32.9)
Postretirement benefits other than pensions—non-current liability	(301.1)	(309.4)
Net liability recognized	$(331.5)	$(342.3)
Accumulated other comprehensive income (loss)—before tax	$ (23.2)	$ (20.7)

2.237

V.F. CORPORATION (DEC)

(In thousands)	2009	2008
Total current liabilities	$1,092,583	$1,012,182
Long-term debt	938,494	1,141,546
Other liabilities	626,295	722,895

NOTES TO CONSOLIDATED FINANCIAL STATEMENTS

Note M (In Part): Other Liabilities

(In thousands)	2009	2008
Deferred compensation (Note N)	$182,965	$156,538
Pension liabilities (Note N)	247,583	405,517
Income taxes	18,269	47,773
Deferred income taxes	73,006	9,434
Deferred rent credits	46,970	42,057
Product warranty claims	29,710	28,693
Deferred credit—Majestic earnout	—	5,250
Other	27,792	27,633
Other liabilities	$626,295	$722,895

Note N (In Part): Retirement and Savings Benefit Plans

VF has several retirement and savings benefit plans covering eligible employees. VF retains the right to amend any aspect of the plans, or to curtail or discontinue any of the plans, subject to local regulations.

Defined Benefit Pension Plans

VF sponsors a noncontributory qualified defined benefit pension plan covering most full-time domestic employees initially employed before 2005 and an unfunded supplemental defined benefit pension plan that covers benefits earned that exceed limitations imposed by income tax regulations. VF also sponsors contributory defined benefit plans covering selected international employees. The defined benefit plans provide pension benefits based on compensation and years of service.

• • • • • •

The following provides a reconciliation of the changes in fair value of the pension plans' assets and projected benefit obligations for each year and the plans' funded status at the end of each year:

(In thousands)	2009	2008
Fair value of plan assets, beginning of year	$ 692,749	$1,066,980
Foreign plans*	50,018	—
Actual return on plan assets	132,295	(319,889)
VF contributions	212,128	15,579
Participant contributions	265	
Benefits paid	(58,653)	(69,921)
Currency translation	5,566	—
Fair value of plan assets, end of year	1,034,368	692,749
Projected benefit obligations, beginning of year	1,107,666	1,117,048
Foreign plans*	51,661	—
Service cost	17,200	16,473
Interest cost	75,242	69,043
Participant contributions	265	
Actuarial (gain) loss	73,569	(24,977)
Plan amendment	13,024	—
Benefits paid	(58,652)	(69,921)
Currency translation	5,278	—
Projected benefit obligations, end of year	1,285,253	1,107,666
Funded status, end of year	$ (250,885)	$ (414,917)
Amounts included in consolidated balance sheets:		
Current liabilities	$ (3,302)	$ (9,400)
Noncurrent liabilities	(247,583)	(405,517)
Funded status	$ (250,885)	$ (414,917)
Accumulated other comprehensive (income) loss:		
Deferred actuarial losses	$ 408,959	$ 459,569
Deferred prior service cost	22,577	13,818
	$ 431,536	$ 473,387
Accumulated benefit obligations	$1,225,213	$1,061,208
Assumptions used to determine benefit obligations:		
Discount rate	6.02%	6.50%
Rate of compensation increase	4.01%	4.00%

* Represents assets and projected benefit obligations, respectively, of foreign plans at the beginning in 2009. Amounts of assets, projected benefit obligations, funded status and deferred actuarial losses in prior years were not significant.

Accumulated benefit obligations at any pension plan measurement date are the present value of vested and unvested pension benefits earned through the measurement date, without projection to future periods. Projected benefit obligations are the present value of vested and unvested pension benefits earned, with projected future compensation increases.

Differences in any year between actual results and amounts estimated using actuarial assumptions are deferred and amortized as a component of future years' pension expense. These unrecognized actuarial gains and losses are amortized to pension expense as follows: amounts totaling less than 10% of the lower of plan assets or projected benefit obligations at the beginning of the year are not amortized; amounts totaling 10% to 20% of projected benefit obligations are amortized over the expected average remaining service of active participants; and amounts in excess of 20% of projected benefit obligations are amortized over five years. Deferred actuarial losses and deferred prior service costs are recorded in OCI. The estimated amounts of Accumulated OCI to be amortized to pension expense in 2010 are $45.5 million of deferred actuarial losses and $4.0 million of deferred prior service costs.

Deferred Compensation Plans

VF sponsors a nonqualified retirement savings plan for employees whose contributions to a tax qualified 401(k) plan would be limited by provisions of the Internal Revenue Code. This plan allows participants to defer receipt of a portion of their compensation and to receive matching contributions for a portion of the deferred amounts. Expense under this plan was $3.7 million in 2009, $4.4 million in 2008 and $4.3 million in 2007. Participants earn a return on their deferred compensation based on investment earnings of participant-selected mutual funds and VF Common Stock. Changes in the market value of the participants' investment selections are recorded as an adjustment to deferred compensation liabilities, with an offset to compensation expense in the Consolidated Statements of Income. Deferred compensation, including accumulated earnings on the participant-directed investment selections, is distributable in cash at participant-specified dates or upon retirement, death, disability or termination of employment. Similarly, under a separate nonqualified plan, nonemployee members of the Board of Directors may elect to defer their Board compensation and invest it in VF Common Stock equivalents. At December 2009, VF's liability to participants of the deferred compensation plans was $202.0 million, of which $19.0 million expected to be paid in 2009 was recorded in Accrued Liabilities and $183.0 million expected to be paid beyond one year was recorded in Other Liabilities (Note M).

VF has purchased (i) specific mutual funds and VF Common Stock in the same amounts as the participant-directed investment selections underlying the deferred compensation liabilities and (ii) variable life insurance contracts that, in turn, invest in mutual funds that are substantially the same as other participant-directed investment selections. These investment securities and earnings thereon, held in an irrevocable trust, are intended to provide (i) a source of funds to meet the deferred compensation obligations, subject to claims of creditors in the event of VF's insolvency, and (ii) an economic hedge of the financial impact of changes in deferred compensation liabilities based on changes in market value of the participant-selected investments underlying the liabilities. The mutual funds and life insurance investments are recorded at fair value. At December 2009, the fair value of the mutual fund and life insurance investments was $198.3 million, of which $19.0 million expected to be liquidated to fund payments to participants in 2010 was recorded in Other Current Assets and $179.3 million was recorded in Other Assets (Note I). The VF Common Stock purchased to match participant-directed investment selections is treated for financial reporting purposes as treasury stock (Note O), which is the primary reason for the difference in carrying value of the investment securities and the recorded deferred compensation liabilities. Realized and unrealized gains and losses on the mutual fund and life insurance investments (other than VF Common Stock) are recorded in compensation expense in the Consolidated Statements of Income and substantially offset losses and gains resulting from changes in deferred compensation liabilities to participants.

Other Retirement and Savings Plans

VF also sponsors defined contribution retirement and savings plans. For domestic employees not covered by VF's defined benefit plans or a collective bargaining agreement, VF contributes a specified percentage of an employee's gross earnings to a qualified retirement plan. VF also sponsors 401(k) and other retirement and savings plans for certain domestic and foreign employees where cash contributions are based on a specified percentage of employee contributions. Expense for these plans totaled $17.4 million in 2009, $16.0 million in 2008 and $14.2 million in 2007.

Note U (In Part): Fair Value Measurements

Fair value is the price that would be received from the sale of an asset or paid to transfer a liability (i.e., an exit price) in the principal or most advantageous market in an orderly transaction between market participants. In determining fair value, the accounting standards established a three-level hierarchy that distinguishes between (i) market data obtained or developed from independent sources (i.e., observable data inputs) and (ii) a reporting entity's own data and assumptions that market participants would use in pricing an asset or liability (i.e., unobservable data inputs). Financial assets and financial liabilities measured and reported at fair value are classified in one of the following categories, in order of priority of observability and objectivity of pricing inputs:

- Level 1—Fair value based on quoted prices in active markets for identical assets or liabilities.
- Level 2—Fair value based on significant directly observable data (other than Level 1 quoted prices) or significant indirectly observable data through corroboration with observable market data. Inputs would normally be (i) quoted prices in active markets for similar assets or liabilities, (ii) quoted prices in inactive markets for identical or similar assets or liabilities or (iii) information derived from or corroborated by observable market data.
- Level 3—Fair value based on prices or valuation techniques that require significant unobservable data inputs. Inputs would normally be a reporting entity's own data and judgments about assumptions that market participants would use in pricing the asset or liability.

The fair value measurement level for an asset or liability is based on the lowest level of any input that is significant to the fair value measurement. Valuation techniques should maximize the use of observable inputs and minimize the use of unobservable inputs.

Recurring Fair Value Measurements

The following table summarizes financial assets and financial liabilities measured at fair value on a recurring basis:

		Fair Value Measurement Using		
(In thousands)	Total Fair Value	Quoted Prices in Active Markets for Identical Assets (Level 1)	Significant Other Observable Inputs (Level 2)	Significant Unobservable Inputs (Level 3)
2009				
Financial assets:				
Cash equivalents	$454,070	$454,070	$ —	$—
Derivative instruments	8,536	—	8,536	—
Investment securities	182,306	140,872	41,434	—
Financial liabilities:				
Derivative instruments	13,587	—	13,587	—
Deferred compensation	199,831	—	199,831	—
2008				
Financial assets:				
Cash equivalents	$156,900	$156,900	$ —	$—
Derivative instruments	1,089	—	1,089	—
Investment securities	157,651	114,778	42,873	—
Financial liabilities:				
Derivative instruments	26,034	—	26,034	—
Deferred compensation	176,394	—	176,394	—

For the above financial assets and financial liabilities measured at fair value, cash equivalents represent funds held in institutional money market funds and time deposits at commercial banks. Derivative instruments represent net unrealized gains or losses on foreign currency forward exchange contracts, which are the net differences between (i) the functional currency value to be received or paid at the contracts' settlement date and (ii) the functional currency value to be sold or purchased at the current forward exchange rate. Investment securities, consisting primarily of mutual funds (classified as Level 1) and a separately managed fixed income fund (classified as Level 2), are purchased to offset a substantial portion of participant-directed investment selections representing underlying liabilities to participants in VF's deferred compensation plans. Liabilities under deferred compensation plans are recorded at amounts payable to participants, based on the fair value of participant-directed investment selections.

Environmental Costs

2.238

VALERO ENERGY CORPORATION (DEC)

(In millions)	2009	2008
Total current liabilities	$7,798	$6,209
Debt and capital lease obligations, less current portion	7,163	6,264
Deferred income taxes	4,063	3,829
Other long-term liabilities	1,869	2,158
Long-term liabilities related to discontinued operations	11	337

NOTES TO CONSOLIDATED FINANCIAL STATEMENTS

1 (In Part): Summary of Significant Accounting Policies

Environmental Matters

Liabilities for future remediation costs are recorded when environmental assessments and/or remedial efforts are probable and the costs can be reasonably estimated. Other than for assessments, the timing and magnitude of these accruals generally are based on the completion of investigations or other studies or a commitment to a formal plan of action. Environmental liabilities are based on best estimates of probable undiscounted future costs over a 20-year time period using currently available technology and applying current regulations, as well as our own internal environmental policies. Amounts recorded for environmental liabilities have not been reduced by possible recoveries from third parties.

13 (In Part): Other Long-Term Liabilities

Other long-term liabilities consisted of the following (in millions):

	2009	2008
Employee benefit plan liabilities	$ 703	$1,036
Tax liabilities for uncertain income tax positions	481	226
Environmental liabilities	238	255
Other tax liabilities	103	189
Insurance liabilities	84	90
Asset retirement obligations	76	72
Deferred gain on sale of assets to NuStar Energy L.P.	70	92
Unfavorable lease obligations	32	38
Other	82	160
Other long-term liabilities	$1,869	$2,158

Environmental liabilities reflect the long-term portion of our estimated remediation costs for environmental matters as discussed in Note 24.

24. Environmental Matters

Remediation Liabilities

Liabilities for future remediation costs are recorded when environmental assessments and/or remedial efforts are probable and the costs can be reasonably estimated. Other than for assessments, the timing and magnitude of these accruals

generally are based on the completion of investigations or other studies or a commitment to a formal plan of action. Environmental liabilities are based on best estimates of probable undiscounted future costs using currently available technology and applying current regulations, as well as our own internal environmental policies.

The balance of and changes in the accruals for environmental matters (excluding asset retirement obligations), which are principally included in other long-term liabilities described in Note 13, were as follows (in millions):

	2009	2008	2007
Balance as of beginning of year	$297	$285	$298
Adjustments to estimates, net	16	72	36
Payments, net of third-party recoveries	(40)	(51)	(55)
Foreign currency translation	6	(9)	6
Balance as of end of year	$279	$297	$285

The balance of accruals for environmental matters is included in the consolidated balance sheet as follows (in millions):

	2009	2008
Accrued expenses	$ 41	$ 42
Other long-term liabilities	238	255
Accruals for environmental matters	$279	$297

In connection with our various acquisitions, we assumed certain environmental liabilities including, but not limited to, certain remediation obligations, site restoration costs, and certain liabilities relating to soil and groundwater remediation. In addition, we have indemnified NuStar Energy L.P. for certain environmental liabilities related to assets we previously sold to NuStar Energy L.P. that were known on the date the assets were sold or are discovered within a specified number of years after the assets were sold and result from events occurring or conditions existing prior to the date of sale.

We believe that we have adequately provided for our environmental exposures with the accruals referred to above. These liabilities have not been reduced by potential future recoveries from third parties. Environmental liabilities are difficult to assess and estimate due to unknown factors such as the timing and extent of remediation, the determination of our obligation in proportion to other parties, improvements in remediation technologies, and the extent to which environmental laws and regulations may change in the future.

Discontinued Operations/Restructuring

2.239

SUN MICROSYSTEMS, INC. (JUN)

(In millions)	2009	2008
Total current liabilities	$5,621	$5,668
Long-term debt	695	1,265
Long-term deferred revenues	635	683
Other non-current obligations	976	1,136

NOTES TO CONSOLIDATED FINANCIAL STATEMENTS

5 (In Part): Balance Sheet Details

Other Non-Current Obligations

At June 30, Other non-current obligations, consisted of the following (in millions):

	2009	2008
Income taxes liabilities, net	$247	$ 316
Restructuring liabilities	140	163
Deferred settlement income from Microsoft	352	352
Other non-current obligations	237	305
	$976	$1,136

8. Restructuring Charges and Related Impairment of Long-Lived Assets

In accordance with SFAS 112, "Employers' Accounting for Post Employment Benefits" (SFAS 112) and SFAS 146, "Accounting for Costs Associated with Exit or Disposal Activities" (SFAS 146), we recognized a total of $395 million, $263 million and $97 million in restructuring and related impairment of long-lived assets for the fiscal years ended June 30, 2009, 2008 and 2007, respectively. The determination of when we accrue for severance costs and which standard applies depends on whether the termination benefits are provided under a one-time benefit arrangement as defined by SFAS 146 or under an on-going benefit arrangement as described in SFAS 112.

We estimated the cost of exiting and terminating our facility leases or acquired leases by referring to the contractual terms of the agreements and by evaluating the current real estate market conditions. In addition, we have estimated sublease income by evaluating the current real estate market conditions or, where applicable, by referring to amounts being negotiated. Our ability to generate this amount of sublease income, as well as our ability to terminate lease obligations at the amounts we have estimated, is highly dependent upon the commercial real estate market conditions in certain geographies at the time we perform our evaluations or negotiate the lease termination and sublease arrangements with third parties. The amounts we have accrued represent our best estimate of the obligations we expect to incur and could be subject to adjustment as market conditions change.

Restructuring Plan IX

In November 2008, we initiated a restructuring plan to further align our resources with our strategic business objectives through reducing our workforce by approximately 5,000 to 6,000 employees. Under this plan, we estimate in total that we will incur between $500 million to $700 million in severance and benefit costs. Through the end of fiscal year 2009, we notified approximately 4,200 employees and recognized total related severance and benefit costs of $303 million. The remainder of the estimated costs under this restructuring plan are expected to be incurred through the end of fiscal 2010.

Restructuring Plan VIII

In May 2008, we initiated a restructuring plan to further align our resources with our strategic business objectives. Under this plan, we estimate in total that we will incur between $170 million to $220 million in severance and benefit costs. Through the end of fiscal year 2009, we notified 1,950 employees and recognized total related severance and benefit costs of $167 million. All employees to be terminated under these plans have been notified and all facilities relating to the amounts accrued under these restructuring plans have been exited.

Restructuring Plan VII

In August 2007, we initiated a restructuring plan to further align our resources with our strategic business objectives (Restructuring Plan VII). Through the end of fiscal year 2009, we notified approximately 1,450 employees of their termination and recognized total related severance and benefit costs of $131 million. Additionally, we incurred $6 million in expenses related to facilities other restructuring related charges. All employees to be terminated under these plans have been notified and all facilities relating to the amounts accrued under these restructuring plans have been exited.

Restructuring Plans Prior to Phase VII

Prior to the initiation of Restructuring Plans VII, VIII and IX, we implemented certain workforce reduction and facilities exit actions. All employees to be terminated under these plans have been notified and all facilities relating to the amounts accrued under these restructuring plans have been exited.

The following table sets forth an analysis of our restructuring accrual activity (in millions):

			Restructuring Plans				
	IX	VIII		VII		Prior to VII	Total
	Severance and Benefits	Severance and Benefits	Facilities Related and Other	Severance and Benefits	Facilities Related and Other	Severance, Benefits, Facilities Related, and Other	
Balance as of June 30, 2006	—	—	—	—	—	$ 460	$ 460
Severance and benefits	—	—	—	—	—	68	68
Property and equipment impairment	—	—	—	—	—	19	19
Provision adjustments	—	—	—	—	—	10	10
Total restructuring charges	—	—	—	—	—	$ 97	$ 97
Cash paid	—	—	—	—	—	(253)	(253)
Non-cash	—	—	—	—	—	(29)	(29)
Balance as of June 30, 2007	—	—	—	—	—	$ 275	$ 275
Severance and benefits	—	$ 107	—	$ 141	—	—	248
Property and equipment impairment	—	—	—	—	$ 6	—	6
Provision adjustments	—	—	—	(6)	—	15	9
Total restructuring charges	$ —	$ 107	$—	$ 135	$ 6	$ 15	$ 263
Cash paid	—	—	—	(115)	(4)	(80)	(199)
Non-cash	—	—	—	—	—	(3)	(3)
Balance as of June 30, 2008	$ —	$ 107	$—	$ 20	$ 2	$ 207	$ 336
Severance and benefits	303	67	—	—	—	—	370
Accrued lease costs	—	—	18	—	—	18	36
Provision adjustments	—	(7)	—	(4)	—	—	(11)
Total restructuring charges	$ 303	$ 60	$18	$ (4)	$—	$ 18	$ 395
Cash paid	(212)	(158)	(3)	(16)	(1)	(46)	(436)
Translation Adjustments	2	(3)	—	—	—	(3)	(4)
Balance as of June 30, 2009	$ 93	$ 6	$15	$—	$ 1	$ 176	$ 291

The restructuring charges are based on estimates that are subject to change. Changes to the previous estimates have been reflected as "Provision adjustments" on the table in the period the changes in estimates were determined. As of June 30, 2009, our estimated sublease income to be generated from sublease contracts not yet negotiated approximated $17 million. Accrued lease costs include accretion expense associated with the passage of time.

The remaining cash expenditures relating to workforce reductions are expected to be paid through the end of fiscal 2010. Our accrual as of June 30, 2009, for facility-related leases (net of anticipated sublease proceeds), will be paid over their respective lease terms through fiscal 2024. As of June 30, 2009, of the total $291 million accrual for workforce reductions and facility-related leases, $151 million was classified as current accrued liabilities and other and the remaining $140 million was classified as other non-current obligations.

We anticipate recording additional charges related to our workforce and facilities reductions over the next several quarters, the timing of which will depend upon the timing of notification of the employees leaving as determined by local employment laws and as we exit facilities.

Insurance

2.240

CON-WAY INC. (DEC)

(Dollars in thousands)	2009	2008
Total current liabilities	$ 791,484	$ 658,077
Long-term liabilities		
Long-term debt and guarantees	719,501	926,224
Long-term obligations under capital leases	41,288	—
Self-insurance accruals	156,939	152,435
Employee benefits	439,899	659,508
Other liabilities and deferred credits	44,516	49,871
Deferred income taxes	15,861	—
Total liabilities	$2,209,488	$2,446,115

NOTES TO CONSOLIDATED FINANCIAL STATEMENTS

I (In Part): Principal Accounting Policies

Self-Insurance Accruals

Con-way uses a combination of purchased insurance and self-insurance programs to provide for the costs of medical, casualty, liability, vehicular, cargo and workers' compensation claims. The long-term portion of self-insurance accruals relates primarily to workers' compensation and vehicular claims that are expected to be payable over several years. Con-way periodically evaluates the level of insurance coverage and adjusts insurance levels based on risk tolerance and premium expense.

The measurement and classification of self-insured costs requires the consideration of historical cost experience, demographic and severity factors, and judgments about the current and expected levels of cost per claim and retention levels. These methods provide estimates of the undiscounted liability associated with claims incurred as of the balance sheet date, including claims not reported. Changes in these assumptions and factors can materially affect actual costs paid to settle the claims and those amounts may be different than estimates.

Con-way participates in a reinsurance pool to reinsure a portion of its workers' compensation and vehicular liabilities. Each participant in the pool cedes claims to the pool and assumes an equivalent amount of claims. Reinsurance does not relieve Con-way of its liabilities under the original policy. However, in the opinion of management, potential exposure to Con-way for non-payment is minimal. At December 31, 2009 and 2008, Con-way had recorded a liability related to assumed claims of $42.1 million and $36.1 million, respectively, and had recorded a receivable from the re-insurance pool of $35.8 million and $29.8 million, respectively. Revenues related to these reinsurance activities are reported net of the associated expenses and are classified as other operating expenses. In connection with its participation in the reinsurance pool, Con-way recognized operating income of $4.0 million in 2009, $1.7 million in 2008 and no net effect on operating results in 2007.

Asset Retirement Obligations

2.241

APACHE CORPORATION (DEC)

(In thousands)	2009	2008
Total current liabilities	$2,392,558	$2,520,435
Long-term debt	4,950,390	4,808,975
Deferred credits and other noncurrent liabilities:		
Income taxes	2,764,901	3,166,657
Asset retirement obligation	1,637,357	1,555,529
Other	661,916	626,168
	$5,064,174	$5,348,354

NOTES TO CONSOLIDATED FINANCIAL STATEMENTS

I (In Part): Summary of Significant Accounting Policies

Asset Retirement Obligation

The initial estimated asset retirement obligation (ARO) related to properties is recognized as a liability, with an associated increase in property and equipment for the asset retirement cost. Accretion expense is recognized over the estimated productive life of the related assets. If the fair value of the es-

timated ARO changes, an adjustment is recorded to both the ARO and the asset retirement cost. Revisions in estimated liabilities can result from changes in estimated inflation rates, changes in service and equipment costs and changes in the estimated timing of settling ARO.

4 (In Part): Asset Retirement Obligation

The following table describes changes to the Company's ARO liability for the years ended December 31, 2009 and 2008:

(In thousands)	2009	2008
Asset retirement obligation at beginning of year	$1,894,684	$1,866,686
Liabilities incurred	218,423	343,210
Liabilities settled	(508,426)	(587,246)
Accretion expense	104,815	101,348
Revisions in estimated liabilities	74,515	170,686
Asset retirement obligation at end of year	1,784,011	1,894,684
Less current portion	146,654	339,155
Asset retirement obligation, long-term	$1,637,357	$1,555,529

The ARO liability reflects the estimated present value of the amount of dismantlement, removal, site reclamation and similar activities associated with Apache's oil and gas properties. The Company utilizes current retirement costs to estimate the expected cash outflows for retirement obligations. The Company estimates the ultimate productive life of the properties, a risk-adjusted discount rate and an inflation factor in order to determine the current present value of this obligation. To the extent future revisions to these assumptions impact the present value of the existing ARO liability, a corresponding adjustment is made to the oil and gas property balance.

Liabilities settled primarily relate to individual properties plugged and abandoned during the period. Most of the activity in both periods was in the Gulf of Mexico, a portion of which relates to the continued abandonment activity on platforms toppled in 2005 during Hurricanes Katrina and Rita and in 2008 during Hurricane Ike.

10 (In Part): Fair Value Measurements

ASC 820-10-35 provides a hierarchy that prioritizes and defines the types of inputs used to measure fair value. The fair value hierarchy gives the highest priority to Level 1 inputs, which consist of unadjusted quoted prices for identical instruments in active markets. Level 2 inputs consist of quoted prices for similar instruments. Level 3 valuations are derived from inputs that are significant and unobservable, and these valuations have the lowest priority.

Assets and Liabilities Measured at Fair Value on a Nonrecurring Basis

Certain assets and liabilities are reported at fair value on a nonrecurring basis in Apache's Consolidated Balance Sheet. The following methods and assumptions were used to estimate fair values:

Asset Retirement Obligations Incurred in Current Period

Apache estimates the fair value of AROs based on discounted cash flow projections using numerous estimates, assumptions and judgments regarding such factors as the existence of a legal obligation for an ARO; estimated probabilities, amounts and timing of settlements; the credit-adjusted risk-free rate to be used; and inflation rates. AROs incurred in the current period were Level 3 fair value measurements. Note 4—Asset Retirement Obligation provides a summary of changes in the ARO liability.

Warranties

2.242

ALLERGAN, INC. (DEC)

(In millions)	2009	2008
Total current liabilities	$811.6	$697.0
Long-term debt	874.0	885.3
Long-term convertible notes	617.3	685.2
Deferred tax liabilities	1.4	69.0
Other liabilities	388.4	402.8

NOTES TO CONSOLIDATED FINANCIAL STATEMENTS

Note 5 (In Part): Composition of Certain Financial Statement Captions

(In millions)	2009	2008
Other liabilities		
Postretirement benefit plan	$ 41.0	$ 39.0
Qualified and non-qualified pension plans	117.7	156.2
Deferred executive compensation	59.8	51.6
Deferred income	95.0	80.8
Product warranties—breast implant products	22.7	23.2
Unrecognized tax benefit liabilities	23.2	22.4
Other	29.0	29.6
	$388.4	$402.8

Note 17. Product Warranties

The Company provides warranty programs for breast implant sales primarily in the United States, Europe and certain other countries. Management estimates the amount of potential future claims from these warranty programs based on actuarial analyses. Expected future obligations are determined based on the history of product shipments and claims and are discounted to a current value. The liability is included in both current and long-term liabilities in the Company's consolidated balance sheets. The U.S. programs include the *ConfidencePlus®* and *ConfidencePlus®* Premier warranty programs. The *ConfidencePlus®* program currently provides lifetime product replacement, $1,200 of financial assistance for surgical procedures within ten years of implantation and contralateral implant replacement. The *ConfidencePlus®* Premier program, which normally requires a low additional enrollment fee, generally provides lifetime product replacement, $2,400 of financial assistance for saline breast implants and $3,500 of financial assistance for silicone gel breast implants for surgical procedures within ten years of implantation and contralateral implant replacement. The

enrollment fee is deferred and recognized as income over the ten year warranty period for financial assistance. The warranty programs in non-U.S. markets have similar terms and conditions to the U.S. programs. The Company does not warrant any level of aesthetic result and, as required by government regulation, makes extensive disclosures concerning the risks of the use of its products and breast implant surgery. Changes to actual warranty claims incurred and interest rates could have a material impact on the actuarial analysis and the Company's estimated liabilities. A large majority of the product warranty liability arises from the U.S. warranty programs. The Company does not currently offer any similar warranty program on any other product.

The following table provides a reconciliation of the change in estimated product warranty liabilities for the years ended December 31, 2009 and 2008:

(In millions)	2009	2008
Balance, beginning of year	$29.5	$28.0
Provision for warranties issued during the year	5.5	6.5
Settlements made during the year	(5.6)	(5.8)
Increases in warranty estimates	—	0.8
Balance, end of year	$29.4	$29.5
Current portion	$ 6.7	$ 6.3
Non-current portion	22.7	23.2
Total	$29.4	$29.5

Litigation

2.243

DANA HOLDING CORPORATION (DEC)

(In millions)	2009	2008
Total current liabilities	$1,156	$1,446
Long-term debt	969	1,181
Deferred employee benefits and other non-current liabilities	1,160	845
Commitments and contingencies		
Total liabilities	$3,285	$3,472

NOTES TO CONSOLIDATED FINANCIAL STATEMENTS
(In millions)

Note 5 (In Part): Supplemental Balance Sheet and Cash Flow Information

	2009	2008
Other accrued liabilities (current)		
Warranty accruals, current portion	$ 56	$ 65
Non-income taxes payable	46	25
Dividends payable	43	11
Deferred income	25	11
Environmental	8	8
Workers compensation obligations	16	23
Asbestos personal injury liability	13	19
Accrued interest	11	14
Accrued legal fees	10	8
Payable under forward contracts	4	6
Accrued professional fees	4	3
Other expense accruals	52	81
Less: liabilities held for sale	(18)	(16)
Total	$ 270	$ 258
Deferred employee benefits and other non-current liabilities		
Pension obligations, net of related assets	$ 643	$ 352
Postretirement obligations other than pension	117	94
Deferred income tax liability	111	100
Asbestos personal injury liability	100	105
Non-current income tax liability	68	71
Workers compensation obligations	39	39
Warranty accruals	27	35
Other non-current liabilities	55	49
Total	$1,160	$845

Note 15 (In Part): Commitments and Contingencies

Asbestos Personal Injury Liabilities

We had approximately 31,000 active pending asbestos personal injury liability claims at December 31, 2009 and at December 31, 2008. For 2009, approximately 11,000 mostly inactive claims have been settled and are awaiting final documentation and dismissal, with or without payment. We have accrued $113 for indemnity and defense costs for settled, pending and future claims at December 31, 2009, compared to $124 at December 31, 2008. We use a fifteen year time horizon for our estimate of this liability.

At December 31, 2009, we had recorded $58 as an asset for probable recovery from our insurers for the pending and projected asbestos personal injury liability claims, compared to $63 recorded at December 31, 2008. The recorded asset reflects our assessment of the capacity of our current insurance agreements to provide for the payment of anticipated defense and indemnity costs for pending claims and projected future demands. The recorded asset does not represent the limits of our insurance coverage, but rather the amount we would expect to recover if we paid the accrued indemnity and defense costs.

As part of our reorganization, assets and liabilities associated with asbestos claims were retained in Prior Dana which was then merged into Dana Companies, LLC, a consolidated wholly-owned subsidiary of Dana. The assets of Dana Companies, LLC include insurance rights relating to coverage

against these liabilities and other assets which we believe are sufficient to satisfy its liabilities. Dana Companies, LLC continues to process asbestos personal injury claims in the normal course of business, is separately managed and has an independent board member. The independent board member is required to approve certain transactions including dividends or other transfers of $1 or more of value to Dana.

Other Liabilities Related to Asbestos Claims

After the Center for Claims Resolution (CCR) discontinued negotiating shared settlements for asbestos claims for its member companies in 2001, some former CCR members defaulted on the payment of their shares of some settlements and some settling claimants sought payment of the unpaid shares from other members of the CCR at the time of the settlements, including from us. We have been working with the CCR, other former CCR members, our insurers and the claimants over a period of several years in an effort to resolve these issues. Through December 31, 2009, we had collected the entire $47 paid to claimants with respect to these claims. Efforts to recover additional CCR-related payments from surety bonds and other claims are continuing. Additional recoveries are not assured and accordingly have not been recorded at December 31, 2009.

Deferred Credits

2.244

GENUINE PARTS COMPANY (DEC)

(In thousands)	2009	2008
Total current liabilities	$1,408,284	$1,287,103
Long-term debt	500,000	500,000
Pension and other post-retirement benefit liabilities	300,197	502,605
Other long-term liabilities	166,836	103,264

NOTES TO CONSOLIDATED FINANCIAL STATEMENTS

1 (In Part): Summary of Significant Accounting Policies

Other Long-Term Liabilities (In Part)

Other long-term liabilities are comprised of the following:

(In thousands)	2009	2008
Post-employment and other benefit liabilities	$ 26,311	$ 10,920
Obligations under capital and other leases	13,504	12,708
Insurance liabilities	46,423	43,019
Deferred gain on sale-leaseback	17,496	18,477
Other taxes payable	39,973	12,027
Other	23,129	6,113
Total other long-term liabilities	$166,836	$103,264

See Note 4 for further discussion of the Company's obligations under capital leases and the sale-leaseback transaction.

4 (In Part): Leased Properties

In October 2007, the Company entered into a sale-leaseback transaction with a financial institution. In connection with the transaction, the Company sold certain automotive retail store properties and immediately leased the properties back over a lease term of twenty years. The lease was classified as an operating lease. Net proceeds from the transaction amounted to approximately $56,000,000. The Company realized a net gain of approximately $20,000,000, which was deferred and is being amortized over the lease term. The unamortized portion of the deferred gain is included in other long-term liabilities in the accompanying consolidated balance sheets.

RESERVES—USE OF THE TERM "RESERVE"

2.245   Prior to being superseded by the APB, the Committee on Terminology of the AICPA issued four terminology bulletins. In Accounting Terminology Bulletin No. 1, *Review and Resume*, the Committee recommended that the term *reserve* be applied only to amounts of retained earnings appropriated for general or specific purposes. In practice, the term *reserve* is applied to amounts designated as valuation allowances deducted from assets or as accruals for estimated liabilities. Table 2-32 shows where the term *reserve* appears in the financial statements of the survey entities.

2.246

TABLE 2-32: USE OF TERM "RESERVE"

	Number of Entities			
	2009	2008	2007	2006
To Describe Deductions From Assets for				
Doubtful accounts	58	45	32	22
Reducing inventories to LIFO cost	52	41	38	46
Inventory obsolescence	46	46	58	42
Accumulated depreciation	2	2	2	2
Other—described	30	22	13	13
To Describe Accruals for				
Tax Contingency	77	74	90	77
Environmental costs	64	65	70	73
Insurance	63	63	59	56
Estimated expenses relating to property abandonments of discontinued operations	61	66	76	75
Litigation	60	60	57	43
Warranty	50	47	66	66
Employee benefits or compensation	9	7	8	9
Other—described	23	27	16	24

2008–2009 based on 500 entities surveyed; 2006–2007 based on 600 entities surveyed.

TITLE OF STOCKHOLDERS' EQUITY SECTION

2.247   Table 2-33 summarizes the titles used by the survey entities to identify the stockholders' equity section of the balance sheet.

2.248

TABLE 2-33: TITLE OF STOCKHOLDERS' EQUITY SECTION

	2009	2008	2007	2006
Stockholders' equity	256	258	307	299
Shareholders' equity	179	181	225	233
Shareowners' equity	16	17	17	16
Shareholders' investment	5	7	7	8
Common stockholders' equity	5	5	6	6
Common shareholders' equity	1	1	4	4
Term deficit or deficiency in title	22	18	24	27
Other or no title	16	13	10	7
Total Entities	**500**	**500**	**600**	**600**

2008–2009 based on 500 entities surveyed; 2006–2007 based on 600 entities surveyed.

CAPITAL STRUCTURES

2.249   FASB ASC 505, *Equity*, states the disclosure requirements for the capital structure of an entity.

2.250   Table 2-34 summarizes the capital structures disclosed on the balance sheets of the survey entities.

2.251

TABLE 2-34: CAPITAL STRUCTURES

	2009	2008	2007	2006
Common Stock With:				
No preferred stock	453	452	532	522
One class of preferred stock	39	38	58	70
Two classes of preferred stock	5	8	7	5
Three or more classes of preferred stock	3	2	3	3
Total Entities	**500**	**500**	**600**	**600**
Entities included above with two or more classes of common stock	54	46	57	58

2008–2009 based on 500 entities surveyed; 2006–2007 based on 600 entities surveyed.

COMMON STOCK

2.252 Table 2-35 summarizes the reporting bases of common stock. As in prior years, the majority of the survey entities show common stock at par value.

2.253

TABLE 2-35: COMMON STOCK

	2009	2008	2007	2006
Par value stock shown at:				
Par value	467	473	583	579
Amount in excess of par	11	11	13	9
Assigned per share amount	—	—	—	4
No par value stock shown at:				
Assigned per share amount	5	7	9	8
No assigned per share amount	47	40	51	55
Issues Outstanding	**530**	**531**	**656**	**655**

2008–2009 based on 500 entities surveyed; 2006–2007 based on 600 entities surveyed.

2.256

TABLE 2-36: PREFERRED STOCK

	Number of Entities			
	2009	2008	2007	2006
Par value stock shown at:				
Par value	12	9	13	18
Liquidation or redemption value	7	7	9	14
No assigned per share amount	3	1	—	—
Assigned per share amount	—	2	1	—
Fair value at issuance date	—	—	2	3
Other	—	—	3	1
No par value stock shown at:				
No assigned per share amount	7	4	4	4
Liquidation or redemption value	6	9	7	8
Assigned per share amount	3	4	6	5
Fair value at issuance date	—	—	—	1
Number of Entities				
Preferred stock outstanding	36	34	42	49
No preferred stock outstanding	464	466	558	551
Total Entities	**500**	**500**	**600**	**600**

2008–2009 based on 500 entities surveyed; 2006–2007 based on 600 entities surveyed.

PREFERRED STOCK

2.254 FASB ASC 505, *Equity*, provides reporting and disclosure requirements for preferred stock. FASB ASC 480, *Distinguishing Liabilities from Equity*, requires that an issuer classify certain financial instruments with characteristics of both liabilities and equity as liabilities. Some issuances of stock, such as mandatorily redeemable preferred stock, impose unconditional obligations requiring the issuer to transfer assets or issue its equity shares. FASB ASC 480 requires an issuer to classify such financial instruments as liabilities. Examples of preferred stock issues within the scope of FASB ASC 480 are included in the Other Noncurrent Liability section.

2.255 Table 2-36 summarizes the reporting bases of preferred stock. As with common stock, many of the survey entities present preferred stock at par value. Examples of preferred stock presentations and disclosures follow.

Preferred Stock Extended at Par Value

2.257

ALCOA INC. (DEC)

(In millions)	2009	2008
Shareholders' equity:		
Preferred stock (R)	$ 55	$ 55
Common stock	1,097	925
Additional capital	6,608	5,850
Retained earnings	11,020	12,400
Treasury stock, at cost	(4,268)	(4,326)
Accumulated other comprehensive loss	(2,092)	(3,169)
Total shareholders' equity	$12,420	$11,735

NOTES TO CONSOLIDATED FINANCIAL STATEMENTS (Dollars in millions)

R (In Part): Preferred and Common Stock

Preferred Stock

Alcoa has two classes of preferred stock. Serial preferred stock has 660,000 shares authorized at a par value of $100 per share with an annual $3.75 cumulative dividend preference per share. There were 546,024 of such shares outstanding at December 31, 2009 and 2008. Class B serial preferred stock has 10 million shares authorized (none issued) and a par value of $1 per share.

Preferred Stock Extended at Liquidating/ Redemption Value

2.258

RITE AID CORPORATION (FEB)

(In thousands)	2009	2008
Stockholders' (deficit) equity:		
Preferred stock—series G, par value $1 per share; liquidation value $100 per share; 2,000 shares authorized; shares issued .006 and 1,393	$ 1	$ 139,253
Preferred stock—series H, par value $1 per share; liquidation value $100 per share; 2,000 shares authorized; shares issued 1,435 and 1,352	143,498	135,202
Preferred stock—series I, par value $1 per share; liquidation value $25 per share; 5,200 shares authorized; shares issued 0 and 4,820	—	116,415
Common stock, par value $1 per share; 1,500,000 shares authorized; shares issued and outstanding 886,113 and 830,209	886,113	830,209
Additional paid-in capital	4,265,211	4,047,499
Accumulated deficit	(6,452,696)	(3,537,276)
Accumulated other comprehensive loss	(41,779)	(20,117)
Total stockholders' (deficit) equity	$(1,199,652)	$ 1,711,185

NOTES TO CONSOLIDATED FINANCIAL STATEMENTS (In thousands)

14 (In Part): Capital Stock

In fiscal 2006, the Company issued 4,820 shares of Series I Mandatory Convertible Preferred Stock ("Series I preferred stock") at an offering price of $25 per share. Dividends on the Series I preferred stock were $1.38 per share per year, and were due and payable on a quarterly basis in either cash or common stock or a combination of both at the Company's election. In the first quarter of fiscal 2009 the Company entered into agreements with several of the holders of the Series I preferred stock to convert 2,404 shares into Rite Aid common stock earlier than the mandatory conversion date, November 17, 2008, at a rate of 5.6561 which resulted in the issuance of 14,648 shares of Rite Aid common stock. On the mandatory conversion date, the remaining outstanding 2,416 shares of Series I preferred stock automatically converted at a rate of 5.6561 which resulted in the issuance of 13,665 shares of Rite Aid common stock.

The Company also has outstanding Series G and Series H preferred stock. The Series G preferred stock has a liquidation preference of $100 per share and pays quarterly dividends at 7% of liquidation preference. In the fourth quarter of 2009, at the election of the holder, substantially all of the Series G preferred stock was converted into 27,137 common shares, at a conversion rate of $5.50 per share. The remaining Series G preferred stock can be redeemed at the Company's election after January 2009. The Company has

not elected to redeem the remaining Series G preferred stock as of February 28, 2009.

The Series H preferred stock pays dividends of 6% of liquidation preference and can be redeemed at the Company's election after January 2010. All dividends can be paid in either cash or in additional shares of preferred stock, at the election of the Company. Any redemptions are at 105% of the liquidation preference of $100 per share, plus accrued and unpaid dividends. The Series H shares are convertible into common stock of the Company, at the holder's option, at a conversion rate of $5.50 per share.

ADDITIONAL PAID-IN CAPITAL

2.259 Table 2-37 lists the balance sheet captions used to describe additional paid-in capital. Examples of descriptive captions for additional paid-in capital are shown in this section in connection with discussions of the other components of stockholders' equity.

2.260

TABLE 2-37: ADDITIONAL PAID-IN CAPITAL—CAPTION TITLE

	2009	2008	2007	2006
Additional paid-in capital	285	280	338	339
Capital in excess of par or stated value	76	82	97	101
Paid-in capital	51	50	58	57
Additional capital, or other capital	14	17	20	23
Capital surplus	12	12	14	18
Other captions	14	12	14	11
	452	453	541	549
No additional paid-in capital account	48	47	59	51
Total Entities	**500**	**500**	**600**	**600**

2008–2009 based on 500 entities surveyed; 2006–2007 based on 600 entities surveyed.

RETAINED EARNINGS

2.261 Table 2-38 indicates that most of the survey entities use the term *retained earnings*. Examples of descriptive captions used for retained earnings are shown in connection with discussions of other components of stockholders' equity.

2.262

TABLE 2-38: RETAINED EARNINGS—CAPTION TITLE

	2009	2008	2007	2006
Retained earnings	385	393	473	474
Retained earnings with additional words	6	2	4	3
Earnings with additional words	17	18	21	22
Income with additional words	5	5	7	6
Retained earnings (deficit)	21	30	24	27
Accumulated deficit	64	50	69	66
Other	2	2	2	2
Total Entities	**500**	**500**	**600**	**600**

2008–2009 based on 500 entities surveyed; 2006–2007 based on 600 entities surveyed.

ACCUMULATED OTHER COMPREHENSIVE INCOME

2.263 FASB ASC 220, *Comprehensive Income*, requires that a separate caption for accumulated other comprehensive income be presented in the equity section of a balance sheet. Accumulated balances, by component, included in accumulated other comprehensive income must be disclosed either in the equity section of the balance sheet, or in a statement of changes of stockholders' equity, or in the notes to the financial statements.

2.264 Table 2-39 summarizes the captions used to describe comprehensive income in the stockholders' equity section of the balance sheet.

2.265 Table 2-40 shows where accumulated component balances are presented.

2.266 Examples showing the disclosure of accumulated balances for other comprehensive income items follow.

2.267

TABLE 2-39: ACCUMULATED OTHER COMPREHENSIVE INCOME—BALANCE SHEET CAPTION

	2009	2008	2007	2006
Accumulated other comprehensive income (loss)	133	168	137	121
Accumulated other comprehensive loss	228	162	200	227
Accumulated other comprehensive income	99	125	197	173
Accumulated other non-owner changes in equity	—	1	5	4
Other captions	2	3	4	9
	462	**459**	**543**	**534**
Accumulated balance by component presented	27	30	39	43
	489	**489**	**582**	**577**
No accumulated other comprehensive income	11	11	18	23
Total Entities	**500**	**500**	**600**	**600**
Accumulated Balances by Component Presented	**Number of Entities**			
Cumulative translation adjustments	23	27	32	33
Defined benefit postretirement plan adjustments	23	22	32	39
Unrealized losses/gains on certain investments	13	16	19	24
Changes in fair value of derivatives	14	16	19	20

2008–2009 based on 500 entities surveyed; 2006–2007 based on 600 entities surveyed.

2.268

TABLE 2-40: ACCUMULATED OTHER COMPREHENSIVE INCOME—PRESENTATION OF COMPONENT BALANCES

	2009	2008	2007	2006
Notes to financial statements	298	327	384	354
Statement of changes in stockholders' equity	90	68	76	85
Stockholders' equity section of the balance sheet	27	30	39	45
Statement of comprehensive income	1	1	1	3
Component balances not presented	73	63	82	90
	489	**489**	**582**	**577**
No accumulated other comprehensive income	11	11	18	23
Total Entities	**500**	**500**	**600**	**600**

2008–2009 based on 500 entities surveyed; 2006–2007 based on 600 entities surveyed.

Notes to Financial Statements

2.269

BRIGGS & STRATTON CORPORATION (JUN)

(In thousands, except per share data)	2009	2008
Shareholders' investment:		
Common stock—authorized 120,000 shares $.01 par value, issued 57,854 shares	$ 579	$ 579
Additional paid-in capital	77,522	76,667
Retained earnings	1,075,838	1,082,553
Accumulated other comprehensive income (loss)	(250,273)	(110,234)
Treasury stock at cost, 8,042 shares in 2009 and 8,154 shares in 2008	(208,982)	(212,042)
Total shareholders' investment	$ 694,684	$ 837,523

NOTES TO CONSOLIDATED FINANCIAL STATEMENTS

2 (In Part): Summary of Significant Accounting Policies

Comprehensive Income (Loss)

Comprehensive income (loss) is a more inclusive financial reporting method that includes disclosure of financial information that historically has not been recognized in the calculation of net income. The Company has chosen to report Comprehensive Income and Accumulated Other Comprehensive Income (Loss) which encompasses net income, cumulative translation adjustments, unrealized gain (loss) on derivatives and unrecognized pension and postretirement obligations in the Consolidated Statements of Shareholders' Investment. The Company's implementation of SFAS No. 158 on July 1, 2007 affected Accumulated Other Comprehensive Income (Loss) by recognizing the funded status of the Company's defined benefit pension and other postretirement plans. Information on Accumulated Other Comprehensive Income (Loss) is as follows (in thousands):

	Cumulative Translation Adjustments	Unrealized Gain (Loss) on Derivatives	Minimum Pension Liability Adjustment	Unrecognized Pension and Postretirement Obligation	Accumulated Other Comprehensive Income (Loss)
Balance at July 2, 2006	$ 7,524	$ (336)	$(2,228)	$ —	$ 4,960
Fiscal year change	4,275	(765)	2,228	(139,649)	(133,911)
Balance at July 1, 2007	11,799	(1,101)	—	(139,649)	(128,951)
Fiscal year change	10,846	5,550	—	2,321	18,717
Balance at June 29, 2008	22,645	4,449	—	(137,328)	(110,234)
Fiscal year change	(13,684)	(7,576)	—	(118,779)	(140,039)
Balance at June 28, 2009	$ 8,961	$(3,127)	$ —	$(256,107)	$(250,273)

2.270

SYSCO CORPORATION (JUN)

(In thousands except for share data)	2009	2008
Shareholders' equity		
Preferred stock, par value $1 per share		
Authorized 1,500,000 shares, issued none	$ —	$ —
Common stock, par value $1 per share		
Authorized 2,000,000,000 shares, issued 765,174,900 shares	765,175	765,175
Paid-in capital	760,352	712,208
Retained earnings	6,539,890	6,041,429
Accumulated other comprehensive loss	(277,986)	(68,768)
Treasury stock, 175,148,403 and 163,942,358 shares	(4,337,729)	(4,041,058)
Total shareholders' equity	$ 3,449,702	$ 3,408,986

NOTES TO CONSOLIDATED FINANCIAL STATEMENTS

15 (In Part): Comprehensive Income

The following table provides a summary of the changes in accumulated other comprehensive income (loss) for the years presented:

(In thousands)	Pension and Other Postretirement Benefit Plans, Net of Tax	Foreign Currency Translation	Interest Rate Swap, Net of Tax	Total
Balance as of July 1, 2006	$ (11,106,000)	$108,448,000	$(12,724,000)	$ 84,618,000
Minimum pension liability adjustment	3,469,000	—	—	3,469,000
Foreign currency translation adjustment	—	25,052,000	—	25,052,000
Amortization of cash flow hedge	—	—	428,000	428,000
Adoption of SFAS 158 recognition	(117,628,000)	—	—	(117,628,000)
Balance as of June 30, 2007	$(125,265,000)	$133,500,000	$(12,296,000)	$ (4,061,000)
Adoption of SFAS 158 measurement date	22,780,000	—	—	22,780,000
Foreign currency translation adjustment	—	30,514,000	—	30,514,000
Amortization of cash flow hedge	—	—	427,000	427,000
Amortization of prior service cost	3,777,000			3,777,000
Amortization of net actuarial loss (gain), net	2,003,000			2,003,000
Amortization of transition obligation	93,000	—	—	93,000
Prior service credit arising in current year	18,510,000			18,510,000
Net actuarial (loss) gain, net arising in current year	(142,811,000)			(142,811,000)
Balance as of June 28, 2008	$(220,913,000)	$164,014,000	$(11,869,000)	$ (68,768,000)
Foreign currency translation adjustment	—	(84,452,000)	—	(84,452,000)
Amortization of cash flow hedge	—	—	428,000	428,000
Amortization of prior service cost	2,418,000			2,418,000
Amortization of net actuarial loss (gain), net	10,824,000			10,824,000
Amortization of transition obligation	93,000	—	—	93,000
Pension liability assumption	(16,450,000)	—	—	(16,450,000)
Prior service cost arising in current year	(354,000)			(354,000)
Net actuarial (loss) gain, net arising in current year	(121,725,000)	—	—	(121,725,000)
Balance as of June 27, 2009	$(346,107,000)	$ 79,562,000	$(11,441,000)	$(277,986,000)

Statement of Changes in Stockholders' Equity

2.271

AMETEK, INC. (DEC)

Consolidated Statement of Stockholders' Equity

	2009		2008		2007	
(In thousands except share amounts)	Comprehensive Income	Stockholders' Equity	Comprehensive Income	Stockholders' Equity	Comprehensive Income	Stockholders' Equity
Capital stock						
Preferred Stock, $0.01 par value		$ —		$ —		$ —
Common Stock, $0.01 par value						
Balance at the beginning of the year		$ 1,102		$ 1,097		$ 1,085
Shares issued		8		5		12
Balance at the end of the year		$ 1,110		$ 1,102		$ 1,097
Capital in excess of par value						
Balance at the beginning of the year		$ 203,000		$ 174,450		$ 134,001
Issuance of common stock under employee stock plans		3,459		3,474		15,455
Share-based compensation costs		13,502		20,186		15,530
Excess tax benefits from exercise of stock options		4,096		4,890		9,464
Balance at the end of the year		$ 224,057		$ 203,000		$ 174,450
Retained earnings						
Balance at the beginning of the year		$1,320,470		$1,099,111		$ 902,379
Adoption of FIN 48		—		—		(5,901)
Net income	$205,770	205,770	$246,952	246,952	$228,020	228,020
Cash dividends paid		(25,579)		(25,685)		(25,748)
Other		(190)		92		361
Balance at the end of the year		$1,500,471		$1,320,470		$1,099,111
Accumulated other comprehensive (loss) income						
Foreign currency translation:						
Balance at the beginning of the year		$ (50,706)		$ 7,331		$ (1,137)
Translation adjustments	$ 38,357		$ (46,784)		$ 6,056	
Gain (loss) on net investment hedges, net of tax (expense) benefit of ($2,290), $6,058 and ($1,298) in 2009, 2008 and 2007, respectively	4,253		(11,253)		2,412	
	$ 42,610	42,610	$ (58,037)	(58,037)	$ 8,468	8,468
Balance at the end of the year		$ (8,096)		$ (50,706)		$ 7,331
Defined benefit pension plans:						
Balance at the beginning of the year		$ (93,360)		$ (3,040)		$ (33,213)
Change in pension plans, net of tax (expense) benefit of ($15,830), $56,344 and ($14,141) in 2009, 2008 and 2007, respectively	$ 26,239	26,239	$ (90,320)	(90,320)	$ 30,173	30,173
Balance at the end of the year		$ (67,121)		$ (93,360)		$ (3,040)

(continued)

(In thousands except share amounts)	2009 Comprehensive Income	2009 Stockholders' Equity	2008 Comprehensive Income	2008 Stockholders' Equity	2007 Comprehensive Income	2007 Stockholders' Equity
Unrealized holding gain (loss) on available-for-sale securities:						
Balance at the beginning of the year		$ (701)		$ 1,079		$ 798
Increase (decrease) during the year, net of tax benefit (expense) of $343, ($958) and $151 in 2009, 2008 and 2007, respectively	$ 637	637	$ (1,780)	(1,780)	$ 281	281
Balance at the end of the year		$ (64)		$ (701)		$ 1,079
Total other comprehensive income (loss) for the year	$ 69,486		$(150,137)		$ 38,922	
Total comprehensive income for the year	$275,256		$ 96,815		$266,942	
Accumulated other comprehensive (loss) income at the end of the year		$ (75,281)		$ (144,767)		$ 5,370
Treasury stock						
Balance at the beginning of the year		$ (92,033)		$ (39,321)		$ (37,241)
Issuance of common stock under employee stock plans		8,700		4,732		3,357
Purchase of treasury stock		—		(57,444)		(5,437)
Balance at the end of the year		$ (83,333)		$ (92,033)		$ (39,321)
Total stockholders' equity		$1,567,024		$1,287,772		$1,240,707

2.272

TARGET CORPORATION (JAN)

Consolidated Statement of Shareholders' Investment

(Millions)	Common Stock Shares	Stock Par Value	Additional Paid-In Capital	Retained Earnings	Accumulated Other Comprehensive Income/(Loss)		Total
					Pension and Other Benefit Liability Adjustments	Derivative Instruments and Other	
January 28, 2006	874.1	$73	$2,121	$12,013	$ (6)	$ 4	$14,205
Net earnings	—	—	—	2,787	—	—	2,787
Other comprehensive loss, net of taxes of $5	—	—	—	—	(7)	—	(7)
Total comprehensive income							2,780
Cumulative effect of adopting SFAS 158, net of taxes of $152	—	—	—	—	(234)	—	(234)
Dividends declared	—	—	—	(396)	—	—	(396)
Repurchase of stock	(19.5)	(2)	—	(987)	—	—	(989)
Stock options and awards	5.2	1	266	—	—	—	267
February 3, 2007	859.8	$72	$2,387	$13,417	$(247)	$ 4	$15,633
Net earnings	—	—	—	2,849	—	—	2,849
Other comprehensive income							
Pension and other benefit liability adjustments, net of taxes of $38	—	—	—	—	59	—	59
Unrealized losses on cash flow hedges, net of taxes of $31	—	—	—	—	—	(48)	(48)
Total comprehensive income							2,860
Cumulative effect of adopting new accounting pronouncements	—	—	—	(31)	54	—	23
Dividends declared	—	—	—	(454)	—	—	(454)
Repurchase of stock	(46.2)	(4)	—	(2,689)	—	—	(2,693)
Premiums on call options	—	—	—	(331)	—	—	(331)
Stock options and awards	5.1	—	269	—	—	—	269
February 2, 2008	818.7	$68	$2,656	$12,761	$(134)	$(44)	$15,307
Net earnings	—	—	—	2,214	—	—	2,214
Other comprehensive income							
Pension and other benefit liability adjustments, net of taxes of $242	—	—	—	—	(376)	—	(376)
Unrealized losses on cash flow hedges, net of taxes of $2	—	—	—	—	—	(2)	(2)
Total comprehensive income							1,836
Dividends declared	—	—	—	(471)	—	—	(471)
Repurchase of stock	(67.2)	(5)	—	(3,061)	—	—	(3,066)
Stock options and awards	1.2	—	106	—	—	—	106
January 31, 2009	752.7	$63	$2,762	$11,443	$(510)	$(46)	$13,712

Equity Section of Balance Sheet

2.273

BRUNSWICK CORPORATION (DEC)

(In millions, except share data)	2009	2008
Shareholders' equity		
Common stock; authorized: 200,000,000 shares, $0.75 par value; issued: 102,538,000 shares	$ 76.9	$ 76.9
Additional paid-in capital	415.1	412.3
Retained earnings	505.3	1,095.9
Treasury stock, at cost: 14,275,000 and 14,793,000 shares	(412.2)	(422.9)
Accumulated other comprehensive income (loss), net of tax:		
Foreign currency translation	39.7	28.8
Defined benefit plans:		
Prior service credits	15.5	1.9
Net actuarial losses	(438.8)	(462.9)
Unrealized investment gains (losses)	2.6	(2.5)
Unrealized gains on derivatives	6.2	2.4
Total accumulated other comprehensive loss	(374.8)	(432.3)
Shareholders' equity	$ 210.3	$ 729.9

2.274

WALTER ENERGY, INC. (DEC)

(In thousands, except share amounts)	2009	2008
Stockholders' equity:		
Common stock, $0.01 par value per share: Authorized—200,000,000 shares Issued—53,256,904 and 54,143,958 shares, respectively	$ 533	$ 541
Preferred stock, $0.01 par value per share: Authorized—20,000,000 shares, issued—0 shares	—	—
Capital in excess of par value	374,522	714,174
Retained earnings	50,852	50,990
Accumulated other comprehensive income (loss):		
Pension and other post-retirement benefit plans, net of tax	(167,037)	(137,364)
Unrealized gain on hedges, net of tax	525	1,928
Total stockholders' equity	$ 259,395	$ 630,269

TREASURY STOCK

2.275 FASB ASC 505-30, *Treasury Stock*, discusses the balance sheet presentation of treasury stock. As shown in Table 2-41, the prevalent balance sheet presentation of treasury stock is to show the cost of treasury stock as a reduction of stockholders' equity.

2.276 Examples of treasury stock presentations follow.

2.277

TABLE 2-41: TREASURY STOCK—BALANCE SHEET PRESENTATION

	2009	2008	2007	2006
Common Stock				
Cost of treasury stock shown as stockholders' equity deduction	316	318	371	381
Cost of treasury stock deducted from stock of the same class	5	10	6	8
Par or stated value of treasury stock deducted from issued stock of the same class	19	20	20	14
Other	—	2	1	2
Total Presentations	340	350	398	405
Preferred Stock				
Cost of treasury stock shown as stockholders' equity deduction	—	—	—	3
Other	—	—	1	2
Total Presentations	—	—	1	5
			Number of Entities	
Disclosing treasury stock	340	350	398	408
Not disclosing treasury stock	160	150	202	192
Total Entities	500	500	600	600

2008–2009 based on 500 entities surveyed; 2006–2007 based on 600 entities surveyed.

Cost of Treasury Stock Shown as Reduction of Stockholders' Equity

2.278

AMETEK, INC. (DEC)

(In thousands)	2009	2008
Stockholders' equity		
Preferred stock, $0.01 par value; authorized: 5,000,000 shares; none issued	$ —	$ —
Common stock, $0.01 par value; authorized: 400,000,000 shares; issued: 2009—111,000,578 shares; 2008—10,188,937 shares	1,110	1,102
Capital in excess of par value	224,057	203,000
Retained earnings	1,500,471	1,320,470
Accumulated other comprehensive (loss)	(75,281)	(144,767)
Treasury stock: 2009—3,116,579 shares; 2008—3,461,541 shares	(83,333)	(92,033)
Total stockholders' equity	$1,567,024	$1,287,772

NOTES TO CONSOLIDATED FINANCIAL STATEMENTS

10 (In Part): Stockholders' Equity

On both January 24, 2008 and July 23, 2008, the Board of Directors authorized increases of $50 million for the repurchase of common stock for a total of $100 million in 2008. These increases were added to the $25.9 million that remained available at December 31, 2007 from an existing $50 million authorization approved in March 2003. The Company did not repurchase shares in 2009. In 2008, the Company repurchased approximately 1,263,000 shares of common stock for $57.4 million in cash under its current share repurchase authorization. At December 31, 2009, $68.5 million of the current share repurchase authorization remained available. On January 28, 2010, the Board of Directors authorized an increase of $75 million in the authorization for the repurchase of its common stock. This increase was added to the $68.5 million that remained available from existing $100 million authorizations approved in 2008, for a total of $143.5 million available for repurchases of the Company's common stock. Subsequent to December 31, 2009, the Company repurchased 1,128,200 shares of its common stock for approximately $41.8 million. The remaining balance available for repurchases of the Company's common stock is $101.7 million as of the filing of this report.

At December 31, 2009, the Company held 3.1 million shares in its treasury at a cost of $83.3 million, compared with 3.5 million shares at a cost of $92.0 million at December 31, 2008. The number of shares outstanding at December 31, 2009 was 107.9 million shares, compared with 106.7 million shares at December 31, 2008.

2.279

JOHNSON & JOHNSON (DEC)

(Dollars in millions)	2009	2008
Shareholders' equity		
Preferred stock—without par value (authorized and unissued 2,000,000 shares)	$ —	$ —
Common stock—par value $1.00 per share (Note 12) (authorized 4,320,000,000 shares; issued 3,119,843,000 shares)	3,120	3,120
Accumulated other comprehensive income	(3,058)	(4,955)
Retained earnings	70,306	63,379
	70,368	61,544
Less: common stock held in treasury, at cost (Note 12) (365,522,000 shares and 350,665,000 shares)	19,780	19,033
Total shareholders' equity	$50,588	$42,511

NOTES TO CONSOLIDATED FINANCIAL STATEMENTS

12 (In Part): Capital and Treasury Stock

Changes in treasury stock were:

	Treasury Stock	
(Amounts in millions except treasury stock number of shares in thousands)	Shares	Amount
Balance at December 31, 2006	226,612	$10,974
Employee compensation and stock option plans	(33,296)	(2,180)
Conversion of subordinated debentures	(194)	(13)
Repurchase of common stock	86,498	5,607
Balance at December 30, 2007	279,620	14,388
Employee compensation and stock option plans	(29,906)	(2,005)
Conversion of subordinated debentures	(19)	(1)
Repurchase of common stock	100,970	6,651
Balance at December 28, 2008	350,665	19,033
Employee compensation and stock option plans	(22,161)	(1,377)
Conversion of subordinated debentures	(96)	(6)
Repurchase of common stock	37,114	2,130
Balance at January 3, 2010	365,522	$19,780

Par Value of Treasury Stock Deducted From Issued Stock

2.280

SERVICE CORPORATION INTERNATIONAL (DEC)

(In thousands)	2009	2008
Equity:		
Common stock, $1 per share par value, 500,000,000 shares authorized, 254,027,384 and 249,953,075 shares issued, respectively, and 254,017,384 and 249,472,075 shares outstanding, respectively	$ 254,017	$ 249,472
Capital in excess of par value	1,735,493	1,733,814
Accumulated deficit	(603,876)	(726,756)
Accumulated other comprehensive income	97,142	36,649
Total common stockholders' equity	$1,482,776	$1,293,179

NOTES TO CONSOLIDATED FINANCIAL STATEMENTS

2 (In Part): Summary of Significant Accounting Policies

Treasury Stock

We make treasury stock purchases in the open market or through privately negotiated transactions subject to market conditions and normal trading restrictions. We account for the repurchase of our common stock under the par value method. We use the average cost method upon the subsequent reissuance of treasury shares. On December 15, 2009, we cancelled 0.4 million shares of common stock held in our treasury. We cancelled 19.1 million and 36.5 million shares of common stock held in our treasury in 2008 and 2007, respectively. These retired treasury shares were changed to authorized but unissued status.

13 (In Part): Equity

Share Authorization

We are authorized to issue 1,000,000 shares of preferred stock, $1 per share par value. No preferred shares were issued as of December 31, 2009 or 2008. At December 31, 2009 and 2008, 500,000,000 common shares of $1 par value were authorized. We had 254,017,384 and 249,472,075 shares issued and outstanding, net of 10,000 and 481,000 shares held in treasury at par at December 31, 2009 and 2008, respectively.

Share Repurchase Program

Subject to market conditions, normal trading restrictions, and limitations in our debt covenants, we may make purchases in the open market or through privately negotiated transactions under our share repurchase program. During 2009, we did not repurchase any shares of our common stock. During 2008, we repurchased 17.7 million shares of common stock at an aggregate cost of $142.2 million including commissions, or an average cost per share of $8.03. During 2007, we repurchased 38.5 million shares of common stock at an aggregate cost of $505.1 million. In November 2008, our Board of Directors approved an increase in our share repurchase program authorizing the investment of up to an additional $120 million to repurchase our common stock. The remaining dollar value of shares authorized to be purchased under the share repurchase program was $123.4 million at December 31, 2009.

OTHER ACCOUNTS SHOWN IN STOCKHOLDERS' EQUITY SECTION

2.281 Many of the survey entities present accounts other than Capital Stock, Additional Paid-in Capital, Retained Earnings, Accumulated Other Comprehensive Income, and Treasury Stock in the stockholders' equity section of the balance sheet. Other stockholders' equity accounts appearing on the balance sheets of the survey entities include, but are not limited to, guarantees of ESOP debt, unearned or deferred compensation related to employee stock award plans, and amounts owed to an entity by employees for loans to buy company stock.

2.282 FASB ASC 810, *Consolidation*, establishes accounting and reporting standards for the noncontrolling interest in a subsidiary. It clarifies that a noncontrolling interest in a subsidiary is an ownership interest in the consolidated entity that should be reported as equity in the consolidated financial statements, but separate from the parent's equity. In addition, FASB ASC 810 requires expanded disclosures in the consolidated financial statements that clearly identify and distinguish between the interests of the parent's owners and the interests of the noncontrolling owners of a subsidiary. Those expanded disclosures include a reconciliation of the beginning and ending balances of the equity attributable to the parent and the noncontrolling owners and a schedule showing the effects of changes in a parent's ownership interest in a subsidiary on the equity attributable to the parent.

2.283 Table 2-42 shows the number of survey company balance sheets presenting other stockholders' equity accounts. Cumulative translation adjustments, unrealized losses/gains on certain investments, and changes in the funded status of defined benefit postretirement plans are all *other comprehensive income* items which are included in Table 2-40 under "Accumulated Other Comprehensive Income—Presentation of Component Balances."

2.284 107 survey entities disclosed that certain stock purchase rights have been distributed to common shareholders. A majority of the rights enable the holders to purchase additional equity in a company should an outside party acquire or tender for a substantial minority interest in the subject entity. Such rights usually do not appear on the balance sheet. Twelve survey entities either adopted a new plan or extended a plan that had or was about to expire. Seven survey entities either cancelled or chose not to extend a plan that expired.

2.285 Examples showing the presentation of other equity accounts follow.

2.286

TABLE 2-42: OTHER STOCKHOLDERS' EQUITY ACCOUNTS

	Number of Entities			
	2009	2008	2007	2006
Noncontrolling interests.........................	156	—	—	—
Warrants..	30	21	25	19
Unearned compensation.....................	17	20	30	73
Employee benefit trusts......................	11	13	13	19
Guarantees of ESOP debt...................	10	13	18	16
Receivables from sale of stock............	3	5	6	9

2008–2009 based on 500 entities surveyed; 2006–2007 based on 600 entities surveyed.

Noncontrolling Interests

2.287

KIMBERLY-CLARK CORPORATION (DEC)

(Millions of dollars except per share amounts)	2009	2008
Stockholders' equity		
Kimberly-Clark Corporation stockholders' equity:		
Preferred stock—no par value—authorized 20.0 million shares, none issued	$ —	$ —
Common stock—$1.25 par value—authorized 1.2 billion shares; issued 478.6 million shares at December 31, 2009 and 2008	598	598
Additional paid-in capital	399	486
Common stock held in treasury, at cost—61.6 million and 65.0 million shares at December 31, 2009 and 2008	(4,087)	(4,285)
Accumulated other comprehensive income (loss)	(1,833)	(2,386)
Retained earnings	10,329	9,465
Total Kimberly-Clark Corporation stockholders' equity	5,406	3,878
Noncontrolling interests	284	383
Total stockholders' equity	$ 5,690	$ 4,261

NOTES TO CONSOLIDATED FINANCIAL STATEMENTS

Note 11 (In Part): Stockholders' Equity

Effective January 1, 2009, as required, the following changes were made with respect to the classification of noncontrolling interests (formerly minority owners' interest in subsidiaries). In addition, prior year amounts in the Consolidated Financial Statements have been recast to conform to the new requirements.

- Noncontrolling interests, which are not redeemable at the option of the noncontrolling interests, were reclassified from the mezzanine to equity, separate from the parent's stockholders' equity, in the Consolidated Balance Sheet. Common securities, redeemable at the option of the noncontrolling interest and carried at redemption values of approximately $41 million and $35 million as of December 31, 2009 and 2008, respectively, are classified in a line item combined with redeemable preferred securities of subsidiary in the Consolidated Balance Sheet.

- Consolidated net income was recast to include net income attributable to both the Corporation and noncontrolling interests.

Set forth below are reconciliations for each of the three years ending December 31, 2009 of the carrying amount of total stockholders' equity from the beginning of the period to the end of the period and an allocation of this equity to the stockholders of the Corporation and Noncontrolling Interests. In addition, because a portion of net income is allocable to redeemable securities of subsidiaries, which is classified outside of stockholders' equity, each of the reconciliations displays the amount of net income allocable to redeemable securities of subsidiaries.

| (Millions of dollars) | Comprehensive Income | Stockholders' Equity Attributable to | | Redeemable Securities of Subsidiaries |
		The Corporation	Noncontrolling Interests	
Balance at December 31, 2008		$3,878	$ 383	$1,032
Comprehensive income:				
Net income	$1,994	1,884	54	56
Other comprehensive income, net of tax:				
Unrealized translation	625	619	6	—
Employee postretirement benefits	(34)	(32)	(2)	—
Other	3	3	—	—
Total comprehensive income	$2,588			
Stock-based awards		150	—	—
Income tax benefits on stock-based compensation		7	—	—
Shares repurchased		(7)	—	—
Recognition of stock-based compensation		86	—	—
Dividends declared		(996)	(45)	(1)
Additional investment in subsidiary and other		(186)	(111)	18
Return on redeemable preferred securities and noncontrolling interests		—	(1)	(53)
Balance at December 31, 2009		$5,406	$ 284	$1,052

GAAP requires that the purchase of additional ownership in an already controlled subsidiary be treated as an equity transaction with no gain or loss recognized in consolidated net income or comprehensive income. GAAP also requires the presentation of the below schedule displaying the effect of a change in ownership interest between the Corporation and a noncontrolling interest.

(Millions of dollars)	2009
Net Income attributable to Kimberly-Clark Corporation	$1,884
Decrease in Kimberly-Clark Corporation's additional paid-in capital for purchase of remaining shares in its Andean subsidiary[a]	(133)
Change from net income attributable to Kimberly-Clark Corporation and transfers to noncontrolling interests	$1,751

[a] During the first quarter of 2009, the Corporation acquired the remaining approximate 31 percent interest in its Andean region subsidiary, Colombiana Kimberly Colpapel S.A., for $289 million. The acquisition was recorded as an equity transaction that reduced noncontrolling interests, AOCI and additional paid-in capital by approximately $278 million and increased investments in equity companies by approximately $11 million.

Common Stock Warrants

2.288

VISTEON CORPORATION (DEC)

(Millions of dollars)	2009	2008
Shareholders' deficit		
Preferred stock (par value $1.00, 50 million shares authorized, none outstanding)	—	—
Common stock (par value $1.00, 500 million shares authorized, 131 million shares issued and 130 million shares outstanding)	$ 131	$ 131
Stock warrants	127	127
Additional paid-in capital	3,408	3,407
Accumulated deficit	(4,576)	(4,704)
Accumulated other comprehensive income	142	157
Other	(4)	(5)
Total Visteon Corporation shareholders' deficit	(772)	(887)
Noncontrolling interests	317	264
Total shareholders' deficit	$ (455)	$ (623)

NOTES TO CONSOLIDATED FINANCIAL STATEMENTS

Note 17 (In Part): Shareholders' Deficit

Stock Warrants and Other

In conjunction with the October 1, 2005 ACH Transactions, the Company granted warrants to Ford for the purchase of 25 million shares of the Company's common stock at an exercise price of $6.90. The warrants allow for either cash or share settlement at the sole discretion of the Company, were exercisable at any time after October 1, 2006 and before the expiration date on October 1, 2013. The warrants were valued at $127 million using a Black-Scholes pricing model, adjusted for the estimated impact on fair value of the restrictions relating to the warrants, and are recorded as permanent equity in the Company's consolidated balance sheets.

On May 17, 2007, Visteon entered into a letter agreement (the "Letter Agreement") with LB I Group, Inc., an affiliate of Lehman Brothers ("Lehman"), and Ford, pursuant to which, among other things, the Company consented to the transfer by Ford of the warrant to purchase 25 million shares of Visteon common stock and waived a provision of the Stockholder Agreement, dated as of October 1, 2005, between Visteon and Ford, that would have prohibited such transfer. The Letter Agreement also restricted Lehman's ability to enter into certain hedging transactions in respect of the shares underlying the Warrant for the first two years following such transfer. In addition, the warrant was modified so that it was not exercisable (except in the event of a change of control of Visteon) or transferable until May 17, 2009.

Treasury stock is carried at an average cost basis, is purchased for employee benefit plans, and consists of approximately 700,000 shares at December 31, 2009.

Unearned Compensation Relating to Stock Award Plans

2.289

UNITED PARCEL SERVICE, INC. (DEC)

(In millions)	2009	2008
Shareowners' equity:		
Class A common stock (285 and 314 shares issued in 2009 and 2008)	$ 3	$ 3
Class B common stock (711 and 684 shares issued in 2009 and 2008)	7	7
Additional paid-in capital	2	—
Retained earnings	12,745	12,412
Accumulated other comprehensive loss	(5,127)	(5,642)
Deferred compensation obligations	108	121
Less: treasury stock (2 shares in 2009 and 2008)	(108)	(121)
Total equity for controlling interests	7,630	6,780
Noncontrolling interests	66	—
Total shareowners' equity	$ 7,696	$ 6,780

NOTES TO CONSOLIDATED FINANCIAL STATEMENTS

Note 9 (In Part): Shareowners' Equity

Deferred Compensation Obligations and Treasury Stock

We maintain a deferred compensation plan whereby certain employees were previously able to elect to defer the gains on stock option exercises by deferring the shares received upon exercise into a rabbi trust. The shares held in this trust are classified as treasury stock, and the liability to participating employees is classified as "deferred compensation obligations" in the shareowners' equity section of the balance sheet. The number of shares needed to settle the liability for deferred compensation obligations is included in the denominator in both the basic and diluted earnings per share calculations. Employees are generally no longer able to defer the gains from stock options exercised subsequent to December 31, 2004. Activity in the deferred compensation program for the years ended December 31, 2009, 2008, and 2007 is as follows (in millions):

	2009		2008		2007	
	Shares	Dollars	Shares	Dollars	Shares	Dollars
Deferred compensation obligations						
Balance at beginning of year		$ 121		$ 137		$ 147
Reinvested dividends		3		5		4
Benefit payments		(16)		(21)		(14)
Balance at end of year		$ 108		$ 121		$ 137
Treasury stock						
Balance at beginning of year	(2)	$(121)	(2)	$(137)	(3)	$(147)
Reinvested dividends	—	(3)	—	(5)	—	(4)
Benefit payments	—	16	—	21	1	14
Balance at end of year	(2)	$(108)	(2)	$(121)	(2)	$(137)

Guarantees of ESOP Debt

2.290

SARA LEE CORPORATION (JUN)

(Dollars in millions)	2009	2008
Common stockholders' equity		
Common stock: (authorized 1,200,000,000 shares; $0.01 par value)		
Issued and outstanding—695,658,110 shares in 2009 and 706,358,624 shares in 2008	$ 7	$ 7
Capital surplus	17	7
Retained earnings	2,721	2,760
Unearned stock of ESOP	(104)	(112)
Accumulated other comprehensive income (loss)	(605)	149
Total common stockholders' equity	$2,036	$2,811

NOTES TO CONSOLIDATED FINANCIAL STATEMENTS

Note 9. Employee Stock Ownership Plans (ESOP)

The corporation maintains an ESOP that holds common stock of the corporation and provides a retirement benefit for nonunion domestic employees. During 2009, 2008 and 2007, the Sara Lee ESOP unallocated common stock received total dividends of $4 or $0.43 per share, $4 or $0.41 per share and $4 or $0.50 per share, respectively. The purchase of the original stock by the Sara Lee ESOP was funded both with debt guaranteed by the corporation and loans from the corporation. The debt guaranteed by the corporation was fully paid in 2004, and only loans from the corporation to the ESOP remain. Each year, the corporation makes contributions that, with the dividends on the common stock held by the Sara Lee ESOP, are used to pay loan interest and principal. Shares are allocated to participants based upon the ratio of the current year's debt service to the sum of the total principal and interest payments over the remaining life of the loan.

Sara Lee ESOP-related expenses amounted to $5 in 2009, $7 in 2008 and $11 in 2007. Payments to the Sara Lee ESOP were $11 in 2009, $16 in 2008 and $19 in 2007.

Employee Benefit Trust

2.291

KB HOME (NOV)

(In thousands, except share data)	2009	2008
Stockholders' equity:		
Preferred stock—$1.00 par value; authorized, 10,000,000 shares; none issued	—	—
Common stock—$1.00 par value; authorized, 290,000,000 shares at November 30, 2009 and 2008; and 115,120,305 shares issued at November 30, 2009 and 2008	$ 115,120	$ 115,120
Paid-in capital	860,772	865,123
Retained earnings	806,443	927,324
Accumulated other comprehensive loss	(22,244)	(17,402)
Grantor stock ownership trust, at cost: 11,228,951 and 11,901,382 shares at November 30, 2009 and 2008, respectively	(122,017)	(129,326)
Treasury stock, at cost: 27,047,379 and 25,512,386 shares at November 30, 2009 and 2008, respectively	(930,850)	(930,234)
Total stockholders' equity	$ 707,224	$ 830,605

NOTES TO CONSOLIDATED FINANCIAL STATEMENTS

Note 18 (In Part): Employee Benefit and Stock Plans

Grantor Stock Ownership Trust

On August 27, 1999, the Company established a grantor stock ownership trust (the "Trust") into which certain shares repurchased in 2000 and 1999 were transferred. The Trust, administered by a third-party trustee, holds and distributes the shares of common stock acquired to support certain employee compensation and employee benefit obligations of the Company under its existing stock option, 401(k) Plan and other employee benefit plans. The existence of the Trust has no impact on the amount of benefits or compensation that is paid under these plans.

For financial reporting purposes, the Trust is consolidated with the Company. Any dividend transactions between the Company and the Trust are eliminated. Acquired shares held by the Trust remain valued at the market price at the date of purchase and are shown as a reduction to stockholders' equity in the consolidated balance sheets. The difference between the Trust share value and the market value on the date shares are released from the Trust is included in paid-in capital. Common stock held in the Trust is not considered outstanding in the computations of earnings (loss) per share. The Trust held 11,228,951 and 11,901,382 shares of common stock at November 30, 2009 and 2008, respectively. The trustee votes shares held by the Trust in accordance with voting directions from eligible employees, as specified in a trust agreement with the trustee.

Receivables From Sale of Stock

2.292

DARDEN RESTAURANTS, INC. (MAY)

(In millions, except shares and per share amounts)	2009	2008
Stockholders' equity:		
Common stock and surplus, no par value; authorized 500.0 shares; issued 282.9 and 279.8 shares, respectively; outstanding 139.3 and 140.5 shares, respectively	$ 2,183.1	$ 2,074.9
Preferred stock, no par value; authorized 25.0 shares; none issued and outstanding	—	—
Retained earnings	2,357.4	2,096.0
Treasury stock, 143.6 and 139.3 shares, at cost, respectively	(2,864.2)	(2,724.0)
Accumulated other comprehensive income (loss)	(57.2)	(20.7)
Unearned compensation	(13.0)	(17.0)
Officer notes receivable	(0.1)	(0.1)
Total stockholders' equity	$ 1,606.0	$ 1,409.1

NOTES TO CONSOLIDATED FINANCIAL STATEMENTS

Note 13 (In Part): Stockholders' Equity

Stock Purchase/Loan Program

We have share ownership guidelines for our officers. To assist them in meeting these guidelines, we implemented the 1998 Stock Purchase/Option Award Loan Program (Loan Program) in conjunction with our Stock Option and Long-Term Incentive Plan of 1995. The Loan Program provided loans to our officers and awarded two options for every new share purchased, up to a maximum total share value equal to a designated percentage of the officer's base compensation. Loans are full recourse and interest bearing, with a maximum principal amount of 75 percent of the value of the stock purchased. The stock purchased is held on deposit with us until the loan is repaid. The interest rate for loans under the Loan Program is fixed and is equal to the applicable federal rate for midterm loans with semi-annual compounding for the month in which the loan originates. Interest is payable on a weekly basis. Loan principal is payable in installments with 25 percent, 25 percent and 50 percent of the total loan due at the end of the fifth, sixth and seventh years of the loan, respectively. Effective July 30, 2002, and in compliance with the Sarbanes-Oxley Act of 2002, we no longer issue new loans under the Loan Program. We account for outstanding officer notes receivable as a reduction of stockholders' equity.

Stock Purchase Rights

2.293

SMITH INTERNATIONAL, INC. (DEC)

NOTES TO CONSOLIDATED FINANCIAL STATEMENTS

12 (In Part): Stockholders' Equity

Stockholder Rights Plan

On June 8, 2000, the Company adopted a Stockholder Rights Plan (the "Rights Plan"). As part of the Rights Plan, the Company's Board of Directors declared a dividend of one junior participating preferred stock purchase right ("Right") for each share of the Company's common stock outstanding on June 20, 2000. The Board also authorized the issuance of one such Right for each share of the Company's common stock issued after June 20, 2000 until the occurrence of certain events. As further discussed in Note 19, the Company's Rights Plan was amended subsequent to December 31, 2009.

Except with respect to the contemplated business combination with Schlumberger, the Rights are exercisable upon the occurrence of certain events related to a person (an "Acquiring Person") acquiring or announcing the intention to acquire beneficial ownership of 20 percent or more of the Company's common stock. In the event any person becomes an Acquiring Person, each holder (except an Acquiring Person) will be entitled to purchase, at an effective exercise price of $87.50, subject to adjustment, shares of common stock having a market value of twice the Right's exercise price. The Acquiring Person will not be entitled to exercise these Rights. In addition, if at any time after a person has become an Acquiring Person, the Company is involved in a merger or other business combination transaction, or sells 50 percent or more of its assets or earning power to another entity, each Right will entitle its holder to purchase, at an effective exercise price of $87.50, subject to adjustment, shares of common stock of such other entity having a value of twice the Right's exercise price. After a person or group becomes an Acquiring Person, but before an Acquiring Person owns 50 percent or more of the Company's common stock, the Board may extinguish the Rights by exchanging one share of common stock, or an equivalent security, for each Right, other than Rights held by the Acquiring Person.

In the event the Rights become exercisable and sufficient shares of the Company's common stock are not authorized to permit the exercise of all outstanding Rights, the Company is required under the Rights Plan to take all necessary action including, if necessary, seeking stockholder approval to obtain additional authorized shares.

The Rights are subject to redemption at the option of the Board of Directors at a price of one-quarter of a cent per Right until the occurrence of certain events. The Rights currently trade with Smith common stock, have no voting or dividend rights and expire on June 8, 2010.

Section 3: Income Statement

INCOME STATEMENT TITLE

3.01 Table 3-1 summarizes the key words used in statement of income titles. Many of the survey entities which used the term "operations" showed a net loss in one or more of the years presented in the statement of income.

3.02

TABLE 3-1: INCOME STATEMENT TITLE

	2009	2008	2007	2006
Operations	242	227	264	252
Income	181	195	244	260
Earnings	70	74	89	87
Other	7	4	3	1
Total Entities	**500**	**500**	**600**	**600**

2008–2009 based on 500 entities surveyed; 2006–2007 based on 600 entities surveyed.

INCOME STATEMENT FORMAT

3.03 Either a single-step form or a multi-step form is acceptable for preparing a statement of income. Table 3-2 shows that the survey entities presented a multi-step income statement more frequently than a single-step income statement.

3.04 FASB *Accounting Standards Codification* (ASC) 220, *Comprehensive Income*, requires that comprehensive income and its components, as defined in the Statement, be reported in a financial statement. Comprehensive income and its components can be reported in an income statement, a separate statement of comprehensive income, or a statement of changes in stockholders' equity.

3.05 Examples of financial statement reporting comprehensive income and its components are presented in Section 4.

3.06 Occasionally the survey entities disclosed reclassifications of income statement amounts. Examples of such reclassifications follow.

3.07

TABLE 3-2: INCOME STATEMENT FORMAT

	2009	2008	2007	2006
Single-Step Form				
Income tax shown as separate last item	76	82	94	82
Multi-Step Form				
Costs deducted from sales to show gross margin	247	235	288	294
Costs and expenses deducted from sales to show operating income	177	183	218	224
Total Entities	**500**	**500**	**600**	**600**

2008–2009 based on 500 entities surveyed; 2006–2007 based on 600 entities surveyed.

Reclassifications

3.08

J. C. PENNEY COMPANY, INC. (JAN)

NOTES TO CONSOLIDATED FINANCIAL STATEMENTS

1 (In Part): Summary of Significant Accounting Policies

Reclassifications (In Part)
Certain reclassifications were made to prior year amounts to conform to the current period presentation. None of the reclassifications affected our net income in any period.

Pension (Income)/Expense

A significant decline in pension plan assets during 2008 will have a material negative impact on pension expense to be recorded beginning in 2009. The year-over-year swing in pension expense materially affects the year-to-year comparability of selling, general and administrative (SG&A) expenses. In order to present SG&A expenses on a more comparable basis and be more reflective of recent trends, the pension expense has been removed and reclassified to a separate line item on the Consolidated Statements of Operations.

For the year ended January 31, 2009, we reclassified $(90) million of pension (income) from SG&A expenses to the line item pension (income)/expense on the Consolidated Statements of Operations. This reclassification improves comparability of the components of SG&A, as well as provides transparency into pension (income)/expense reporting. The table below shows the reclassification as of 2007 and 2006.

($ in millions)	2007	2006
Selling, general and administrative (SG&A)—as previously reported	$5,357	$5,521
Pension (income)/expense	(45)	51
Selling, general and administrative (SG&A)—as reclassified	$5,402	$5,470

3.09

NETAPP, INC. (APR)

NOTES TO CONSOLIDATED FINANCIAL STATEMENTS
(Dollar amounts in thousands)

2 (In Part): Significant Accounting Policies

Reclassification

In the first quarter of fiscal 2009, we implemented a change in the reporting of warranty costs and reported these costs in cost of product revenues. These costs, which were included in cost of service revenues in previous periods, amounted to $26,997 and $22,082 for fiscal years 2008 and 2007, respectively, and have been reclassified on the accompanying financial statements to conform to current year classification. This change had no effect on the reported amounts of total costs of revenues, total gross margin, net income or cash flow from operations for any period presented.

REVENUES AND GAINS

3.10   Paragraphs 78 and 82 of Financial Accounting Standards Board (FASB) Statement of Financial Accounting Concepts (SFAC) No. 6, *Elements of Financial Statements*, define revenues and gains.

> 78. Revenues are inflows or other enhancements of assets of an entity or settlements of its liabilities (or a combination of both) from delivering or producing goods, rendering services, or other activities that constitute the entity's ongoing major or central operations.

> 82. Gains are increases in equity (net assets) from peripheral or incidental transactions of an entity and from all other transactions and other events and circumstances affecting the entity except those that result from revenues or investments by owners.

3.11   Table 3-3 summarizes the descriptive income statement captions used by the survey entities to describe revenue. Gains most frequently disclosed by the survey entities are listed in Table 3-4. Excluded from Table 3-4 are segment disposals, gains shown after the caption for income taxes (Table 3-17), and extraordinary gains (Table 3-18).

3.12   Examples of revenues and gains follow.

3.13

TABLE 3-3: REVENUE CAPTION TITLE

	2009	2008	2007	2006
Net Sales				
Net sales	213	218	262	259
Net sales and operating revenues	7	6	5	7
Sales				
Sales	50	54	61	71
Sales and operating revenues	11	11	12	12
Sales and services	2	1	3	3
Sales combined with other items	—	—	2	4
Other Captions				
Revenue	217	210	255	242
Shipments, rentals, fees, etc.	—	—	—	2
Total Entities	**500**	**500**	**600**	**600**

2008–2009 based on 500 entities surveyed; 2006–2007 based on 600 entities surveyed.

3.14

TABLE 3-4: GAINS*

	Number of Entities			
	2009	2008	2007	2006
Interest	318	327	389	384
Change in fair value of derivatives	202	90	90	95
Sale of assets	149	200	258	232
Equity in earnings of investees	108	111	136	154
Dividends	60	70	78	78
Liability accruals reduced	60	43	72	59
Foreign currency transactions	59	76	97	80
Debt extinguishments	33	26	8	6
Royalty, franchise and license fees	32	34	42	40
Litigation settlements	26	14	17	24
Insurance recoveries	15	22	32	39
Change in fair value of financial assets/liabilities	12	3	—	—
Employee benefit/pension related	8	5	10	10
Rentals	6	4	15	18
Noncontrolling interest in investee loss	6	4	11	14
Business combination adjustment gain	6	—	—	—

* Appearing in either the income statement and/or the notes to financial statements.

2008–2009 based on 500 entities surveyed; 2006–2007 based on 600 entities surveyed.

REVENUES

3.15

APPLE INC. (SEP)

(In millions)	2009	2008	2007
Net sales	$36,537	$32,479	$24,006
Cost of sales	23,397	21,334	15,852
Gross margin	13,140	11,145	8,154
Operating expenses:			
Research and development	1,333	1,109	782
Selling, general and administrative	4,149	3,761	2,963
Total operating expenses	5,482	4,870	3,745
Operating income	$ 7,658	$ 6,275	$ 4,409

NOTES TO CONSOLIDATED FINANCIAL STATEMENTS

Note 1 (In Part): Summary of Significant Accounting Policies

Revenue Recognition

Net sales consist primarily of revenue from the sale of hardware, software, digital content and applications, peripherals, and service and support contracts. For any product within these groups that either is software, or is considered software-related (e.g., Mac computers, iPhones and iPod portable digital music and video players), the Company accounts for such products in accordance with the specific industry accounting guidance for software and software related transactions. The Company applies various revenue-related GAAP for products that are not software or software-related, such as digital content sold on the iTunes Store and certain Mac, iPhone and iPod supplies and accessories, which is described below.

The Company recognizes revenue when persuasive evidence of an arrangement exists, delivery has occurred, the sales price is fixed or determinable, and collection is probable. Product is considered delivered to the customer once it has been shipped and title and risk of loss have been transferred. For most of the Company's product sales, these criteria are met at the time the product is shipped. For online sales to individuals, for some sales to education customers in the U.S., and for certain other sales, the Company defers revenue until the customer receives the product because the Company legally retains a portion of the risk of loss on these sales during transit. If at the outset of an arrangement the Company determines the arrangement fee is not, or is presumed not to be, fixed or determinable, revenue is deferred and subsequently recognized as amounts become due and payable and all other criteria for revenue recognition have been met.

Revenue from service and support contracts is deferred and recognized ratably over the service coverage periods. These contracts typically include extended phone support, repair services, web-based support resources, diagnostic tools, and extend the service coverage offered under the Company's standard limited warranty.

The Company sells software and peripheral products obtained from other companies. The Company generally establishes its own pricing and retains related inventory risk, is the primary obligor in sales transactions with its customers, and

assumes the credit risk for amounts billed to its customers. Accordingly, the Company generally recognizes revenue for the sale of products obtained from other companies based on the gross amount billed.

The Company accounts for multiple element arrangements that consist only of software or software-related products in accordance with industry specific accounting guidance for software and software related transactions. If a multiple-element arrangement includes deliverables that are neither software nor software-related, the Company applies various revenue-related GAAP to determine if those deliverables constitute separate units of accounting from the software or software-related deliverables. If the Company can separate the deliverables, the Company applies the industry specific accounting guidance to the software and software-related deliverables and applies other appropriate guidance to the non-software related deliverables. Revenue on arrangements that include multiple elements such as hardware, software and services is allocated to each element based on the relative fair value of each element. Each element's allocated revenue is recognized when the revenue recognition criteria for that element have been met. Fair value is generally determined by vendor specific objective evidence ("VSOE"), which is based on the price charged when each element is sold separately. If the Company cannot objectively determine the fair value of any undelivered element included in a multiple-element arrangement, the Company defers revenue until all elements are delivered and services have been performed, or until fair value can objectively be determined for any remaining undelivered elements. When the fair value of a delivered element has not been established, but fair value exists for the undelivered elements, the Company uses the residual method to recognize revenue if the fair value of all undelivered elements is determinable. Under the residual method, the fair value of the undelivered elements is deferred and the remaining portion of the arrangement fee is allocated to the delivered elements and is recognized as revenue.

For both iPhone and Apple TV, the Company has indicated it may from time-to-time provide future unspecified features and additional software products free of charge to customers. Accordingly, iPhone handsets and Apple TV sales are accounted for under subscription accounting in accordance with GAAP. As such, the revenue and associated cost of sales are deferred at the time of sale, and are both recognized on a straight-line basis over the currently estimated 24-month economic life of these products, with any loss recognized at the time of sale. Costs incurred by the Company for engineering, sales, marketing and warranty are expensed as incurred.

The Company records reductions to revenue for estimated commitments related to price protection and for customer incentive programs, including reseller and end-user rebates, and other sales programs and volume-based incentives. The estimated cost of these programs is accrued as a reduction to revenue in the period the Company has sold the product and committed to a plan. The Company also records reductions to revenue for expected future product returns based on the Company's historical experience. Revenue is recorded net of taxes collected from customers that are remitted to governmental authorities, with the collected taxes recorded as current liabilities until remitted to the relevant government authority.

Generally, the Company does not offer specified or unspecified upgrade rights to its customers in connection with software sales or the sale of extended warranty and support contracts. When the Company does offer specified upgrade rights, the Company defers revenue for the fair value of the specified upgrade right until the future obligation is fulfilled or the right to the specified upgrade expires. A limited number of the Company's software products are available with maintenance agreements that grant customers rights to unspecified future upgrades over the maintenance term on a when and if available basis. Revenue associated with such maintenance is recognized ratably over the maintenance term.

3.16

GOOGLE INC. (DEC)

(In thousands)	2007	2008	2009
Revenues	$16,593,986	$21,795,550	$23,650,563
Costs and expenses:			
Cost of revenues (including stock-based compensation expense of $22,335, $41,340, $47,051)	6,649,085	8,621,506	8,844,115
Research and development (including stock-based compensation expense of $569,797, $732,418, $725,342)	2,119,985	2,793,192	2,843,027
Sales and marketing (including stock-based compensation expense of $131,638, $206,020, $231,019)	1,461,266	1,946,244	1,983,941
General and administrative (including stock-based compensation expense of $144,876, $139,988, $160,642)	1,279,250	1,802,639	1,667,294
Total costs and expenses	11,509,586	15,163,581	15,338,377
Income from operations	$ 5,084,400	$ 6,631,969	$ 8,312,186

NOTES TO CONSOLIDATED FINANCIAL STATEMENTS

Note 1 (In Part): Summary of Significant Accounting Policies

Revenue Recognition
The following table presents our revenues by revenue source (in thousands):

	2007	2008	2009
Advertising revenues:			
Google web sites	$10,624,705	$14,413,826	$15,722,486
Google Network web sites	5,787,938	6,714,688	7,166,318
Total advertising revenues	16,412,643	21,128,514	22,888,804
Licensing and other revenues	181,343	667,036	761,759
Revenues	$16,593,986	$21,795,550	$23,650,563

Google AdWords is our automated online program that enables advertisers to place targeted text-based and display ads on our web sites and our Google Network members' web sites. Display advertising includes static or animated images as well as interactive audio or video media, such as the banner ads on the tops or sides of many popular web sites. Most of our AdWords customers pay us on a cost-per-click basis, which means that an advertiser pays us only when a user clicks on one of its ads. We also offer AdWords on a cost-per-impression basis that enables advertisers to pay us based on the number of times their ads appear on our web sites and our Google Network members' web sites as specified by the advertiser.

Google AdSense refers to the online programs through which we distribute our advertisers' AdWords ads for dis-

play on the web sites of our Google Network members as well as programs to deliver ads on television broadcasts.

We recognize as revenues the fees charged advertisers each time a user clicks on one of the text-based ads that are displayed next to the search results pages on our site or on the search results pages or content pages of our Google Network members' web sites and, for those advertisers who use our cost-per impression pricing, the fees charged advertisers each time an ad is displayed on our members' sites. We report our Google AdSense revenues on a gross basis principally because we are the primary obligor to our advertisers.

Google TV Ads enable advertisers, operators, and programmers to buy, schedule, deliver, and measure ads on television. We recognize as revenue the fees charged advertisers each time an ad is displayed on television in accordance with the terms of the related agreements.

We also offer display advertising management services such as media planning, buying, implementation, and measurement tools for advertisers and agencies and forecasting and reporting tools for publishers. We recognize the related fees as licensing and other revenues in the period advertising impressions are delivered.

Google Checkout is our online shopping payment processing system for both consumers and merchants. We recognize as revenues any fees charged to merchants on transactions processed through Google Checkout. Further, cash ultimately paid to merchants under Google Checkout promotions, including cash paid to merchants as a result of discounts provided to consumers on certain transactions processed through Google Checkout, are accounted for as an offset to revenues.

We generate fees from search services on a per-query basis. Our policy is to recognize revenues from per-query search fees in the period we provide the search results.

We also generate fees from the sale and license of our Search Appliance products, which include hardware, software, and post-contract support primarily for two years. As the deliverables are not sold separately, sufficient vendor-specific objective evidence does not exist for the allocation of revenue. As a result, we recognized the entire fee for the sale and license of these products ratably over the term of the post-contract support arrangement. Beginning the first quarter of 2010, we adopted the new accounting guidance which requires us to allocate the consideration of the arrangement to each of the deliverables based on our best estimate of their selling prices as there is no vendor-specific objective or third-party evidence of the selling prices. As a result, we now recognize revenue allocated to the hardware and software at the time of sale and revenue allocated to post-contract support ratably over the term of the service arrangement.

In addition, we generate fees through the license of our Google Apps products. We recognize as revenue the fees we charge customers for hosting the related enterprise applications and services ratably over the term of the service arrangement.

Revenues realized through display advertising management services, Google TV Ads, Google Checkout, search services, Search Appliance, and Google Apps were not material in any of the years presented.

We recognize revenues as described above because the services have been provided, the fees we charge are fixed or determinable, we and our advertisers or other customers understand the specific nature and terms of the agreed-upon transactions and collectability is reasonably assured.

We record deferred revenue when payments are received in advance of our performance in the underlying agreement on the accompanying Consolidated Balance Sheets.

GAINS

Interest

3.17

INTEL CORPORATION (DEC)

(In millions)	2009	2008	2007
Net revenue	$35,127	$37,586	$38,334
Cost of sales	15,566	16,742	18,430
Gross margin	19,561	20,844	19,904
Research and development	5,653	5,722	5,755
Marketing, general and administrative	7,931	5,452	5,401
Restructuring and asset impairment charges	231	710	516
Amortization of acquisition-related intangibles	35	6	16
Operating expenses	13,850	11,890	11,688
Operating income	5,711	8,954	8,216
Gains (losses) on equity method investments, net	(147)	(1,380)	3
Gains (losses) on other equity investments, net	(23)	(376)	154
Interest and other, net	163	488	793
Income before taxes	$ 5,704	$ 7,686	$ 9,166

NOTES TO CONSOLIDATED FINANCIAL STATEMENTS

Note 14. Interest and Other, Net

The components of interest and other, net were as follows:

(In millions)	2009	2008	2007
Interest income	$168	$592	$804
Interest expense	(1)	(8)	(15)
Other, net	(4)	(96)	4
Total interest and other, net	$163	$488	$793

Changes in Fair Value of Derivatives

3.18

BAKER HUGHES INCORPORATED (DEC)

(In millions)	2009	2008	2007
Revenues:			
Sales	$4,809	$ 5,734	$ 5,171
Services and rentals	4,855	6,130	5,257
Total revenues	9,664	11,864	10,428
Costs and expenses:			
Cost of sales	3,858	4,081	3,517
Cost of services and rentals	3,539	3,873	3,328
Research and engineering	397	426	372
Marketing, general and administrative	1,120	1,046	933
Acquisition-related costs	18	—	—
Litigation settlement	—	62	—
Total costs and expenses	8,932	9,488	8,150
Operating income	732	2,376	2,278
Equity in income of affiliates	—	2	1
Gain on sale of product line	—	28	—
Gain (loss) on investments	4	(25)	—
Interest expense	(131)	(89)	(66)
Interest and dividend income	6	27	44
Income before income taxes	$ 611	$ 2,319	$ 2,257

NOTES TO CONSOLIDATED FINANCIAL STATEMENTS
(Dollars in millions)

Note 1 (In Part): Summary of Significant Accounting Policies

Derivative Financial Instruments

We monitor our exposure to various business risks including commodity prices, foreign currency exchange rates and interest rates and occasionally use derivative financial instruments to manage these risks. Our policies do not permit the use of derivative financial instruments for speculative purposes. We use foreign currency forward contracts to hedge certain firm commitments and transactions denominated in foreign currencies. We use interest rate swaps to manage interest rate risk.

At the inception of any new derivative, we designate the derivative as a hedge as that term is defined in ASC 815, *Derivatives and Hedging*, or we determine the derivative to be undesignated as a hedging instrument as the facts dictate. We document all relationships between the hedging instruments and the hedged items, as well as our risk management objectives and strategy for undertaking various hedge transactions. We assess whether the derivatives that are used in hedging transactions are highly effective in offsetting changes in cash flows of the hedged item at both the inception of the hedge and on an ongoing basis.

Note 11 (In Part): Financial Instruments

Fair Value of Financial Instruments

Our financial instruments include cash and short-term investments, noncurrent investments in auction rate securities, accounts receivable, accounts payable, debt, foreign currency forward contracts, foreign currency option contracts and interest rate swaps. Except as described below, the estimated

fair value of such financial instruments at December 31, 2009 and 2008 approximates their carrying value as reflected in our consolidated balance sheets. The fair value of our debt, foreign currency forward contracts and interest rate swaps has been estimated based on quoted year end market prices.

The estimated fair value of total debt at December 31, 2009 and 2008 was $2,126 million and $2,471 million, respectively, which differs from the carrying amounts of $1,800 million and $2,333 million, respectively, included in our consolidated balance sheets.

Interest Rate Swaps

We are subject to interest rate risk on our debt and investment of cash and cash equivalents arising in the normal course of our business, as we do not engage in speculative trading strategies. We maintain an interest rate management strategy, which primarily uses a mix of fixed and variable rate debt that is intended to mitigate the exposure to changes in interest rates in the aggregate for our investment portfolio. In addition, we are currently using interest rate swaps to manage the economic effect of fixed rate obligations associated with our senior notes so that the interest payable on the senior notes effectively becomes linked to variable rates.

In June 2009, we entered into two interest rate swap agreements ("the Swap Agreements") for a notional amount of $250 million each in order to hedge changes in the fair market value of our $500 million 6.5% senior notes maturing on November 15, 2013. Under the Swap Agreements, we receive interest at a fixed rate of 6.5% and pay interest at a floating rate of one-month Libor plus a spread of 3.67% on one swap and three-month Libor plus a spread of 3.54% on the second swap both through November 15, 2013. The counterparties are primarily the lenders in our credit facilities. The Swap Agreements are designated and each qualifies as a fair value hedging instrument. The swap to three-month Libor is deemed to be 100 percent effective resulting in no gain or loss recorded in the consolidated statement of operations. The effectiveness of the swap to one-month Libor, which is highly effective, is calculated as of each period end and any ineffective portion is recognized in the consolidated statement of operations. The fair value of the Swap Agreements was determined using a model with Level 2 inputs including quoted market prices for contracts with similar terms and maturity dates.

Fair Value of Derivative Instruments (In Part)

The effects of derivative instruments in our consolidated statement of operations were as follows for the year ended December 31, 2009 (amounts exclude any income tax effects):

Derivative	Statement of Operations Location	Amount of Gain Recognized in Income
Foreign currency forward contracts	Marketing, general and administrative	$11
Interest rate swaps	Interest expense	6

Sale of Assets

3.19

TENET HEALTHCARE CORPORATION (DEC)

(Dollars in millions)	2009	2008	2007
Net operating revenues	$9,014	$8,585	$8,083
Operating expenses:			
Salaries, wages and benefits	3,857	3,779	3,617
Supplies	1,569	1,511	1,401
Provision for doubtful accounts	697	628	555
Other operating expenses, net	1,909	1,928	1,852
Depreciation and amortization	386	371	336
Impairment of long-lived assets and goodwill, and restructuring charges, net of insurance recoveries	27	16	36
Hurricane insurance recoveries, net of costs	—	—	(3)
Litigation and investigation costs, net of insurance recoveries	31	41	13
Operating income	538	311	276
Interest expense	(445)	(418)	(419)
Gain from early extinguishment of debt	97	—	—
Investment earnings	—	22	47
Net gain on sales of investments	15	139	—
Income (loss) from continuing operations, before income taxes	$ 205	$ 54	$ (96)

NOTES TO CONSOLIDATED FINANCIAL STATEMENTS

Note 1 (In Part): Significant Accounting Policies

Cash Equivalents (In Part)

In May 2009, we completed the sale of our 50% membership interest in Peoples Health Network, the company that administered the operations of Tenet Choices, Inc., our wholly owned Medicare Advantage HMO insurance subsidiary in Louisiana. The cash and cash equivalent balances of this insurance subsidiary were $53 million at December 31, 2008. The transaction resulted in a pretax gain in continuing operations of approximately $15 million during the year ended December 31, 2009 (see Note 17).

Note 17. Sales of Investments

During the year ended December 31, 2009, we recorded a gain on sale of investment of approximately $15 million in continuing operations related to the sale of our 50% membership interest in Peoples Health Network, the company that administered the operations of Tenet Choices, Inc., our wholly owned Medicare Advantage HMO insurance subsidiary in Louisiana.

During the year ended December 31, 2008, we recorded gains on sales of investments in continuing operations of $125 million from the sale of our entire interest in Broadlane, Inc. and $14 million from the sale of our interest in a joint venture with a real estate investment trust.

Equity in Earnings of Investees

3.20

ARROW ELECTRONICS, INC. (DEC)

(In thousands)	2009	2008	2007
Sales	$14,684,101	$16,761,009	$15,984,992
Costs and expenses:			
Cost of products sold	12,933,207	14,478,296	13,699,715
Selling, general and administrative expenses	1,305,566	1,607,261	1,519,908
Depreciation and amortization	67,027	69,286	66,719
Restructuring, integration, and other charges	105,514	80,955	11,745
Impairment charge	—	1,018,780	—
	14,411,314	17,254,578	15,298,087
Operating income (loss)	272,787	(493,569)	686,905
Equity in earnings of affiliated companies	4,731	6,549	6,906
Loss on prepayment of debt	5,312	—	—
Loss on the write-down of an investment	—	10,030	—
Interest and other financing expense, net	83,285	99,863	101,628
Income (loss) before income taxes	$ 188,921	$ (596,913)	$ 592,183

NOTES TO CONSOLIDATED FINANCIAL STATEMENTS

4. Investments in Affiliated Companies

The company owns a 50% interest in several joint ventures with Marubun Corporation (collectively "Marubun/Arrow") and a 50% interest in Altech Industries (Pty.) Ltd. ("Altech Industries"), a joint venture with Allied Technologies Limited. These investments are accounted for using the equity method.

The following table presents the company's investment in Marubun/Arrow, the company's investment and long-term note receivable in Altech Industries, and the company's other equity investments at December 31:

(In thousands)	2009	2008
Marubun/Arrow	$37,649	$34,881
Altech Industries	15,361	11,888
Other	—	19
	$53,010	$46,788

The equity in earnings (loss) of affiliated companies for the years ended December 31 consists of the following:

(In thousands)	2009	2008	2007
Marubun/Arrow	$3,745	$5,486	$5,440
Altech Industries	1,004	1,233	1,550
Other	(18)	(170)	(84)
	$4,731	$6,549	$6,906

Under the terms of various joint venture agreements, the company is required to pay its pro-rata share of the third party debt of the joint ventures in the event that the joint ventures are unable to meet their obligations. At December 31, 2009, the company's pro-rata share of this debt was approximately $6,100. The company believes that there is sufficient equity in the joint ventures to meet their obligations.

Dividends

3.21

WENDY'S/ARBY'S GROUP, INC. (DEC)

(In thousands)	2009	2008	2007
Revenues:			
Sales	$3,198,348	$1,662,291	$1,113,436
Franchise revenues	382,487	160,470	86,981
Asset management and related fees	—	—	63,300
	3,580,835	1,822,761	1,263,717
Costs and expenses:			
Cost of sales	2,728,484	1,415,534	894,450
Cost of services	—	—	25,183
General and administrative	452,713	248,718	205,375
Depreciation and amortization	190,251	88,315	66,277
Goodwill impairment	—	460,075	—
Impairment of other long-lived assets	82,132	19,203	7,045
Facilities relocation and corporate restructuring	11,024	3,913	85,417
Gain on sale of consolidated business	—	—	(40,193)
Other operating expense, net	4,255	653	263
	3,468,859	2,236,411	1,243,817
Operating profit (loss)	111,976	(413,650)	19,900
Interest expense	(126,708)	(67,009)	(61,331)
Investment (expense) income, net	(3,008)	9,438	62,110
Other than temporary losses on investments	(3,916)	(112,741)	(9,909)
Other income (expense), net	1,523	2,710	(4,038)
(Loss) income from continuing operations before income taxes	(20,133)	(581,252)	6,732
Benefit from income taxes	23,649	99,294	8,354
Income (loss) from continuing operations	$ 3,516	$ (481,958)	$ 15,086

NOTES TO CONSOLIDATED FINANCIAL STATEMENTS

16. Investment (Expense) Income, Net

(In thousands)	2009	2008	2007
Interest income	$ 249	$ 1,285	$ 9,100
Distributions, including dividends	205	2,818	1,784
Realized gains, net	2,948	8,460	49,829
Unrealized (losses) gains, net	—	(1,128)	1,578
Fee on early withdrawal of Equities Account	(5,500)	—	—
Other	(910)	(1,997)	(181)
	$(3,008)	$ 9,438	$62,110

Liability Accruals Reduced

3.22

ITT CORPORATION (DEC)

(In millions)	2009	2008	2007
Product revenue	$ 8,243.5	$ 9,181.2	$7,057.5
Service revenue	2,661.0	2,513.6	1,945.8
Total revenue	10,904.5	11,694.8	9,003.3
Costs of product revenue	5,527.6	6,255.1	4,746.4
Costs of service revenue	2,316.2	2,184.3	1,688.6
Total costs of revenue	7,843.8	8,439.4	6,435.0
Gross profit	3,060.7	3,255.4	2,568.3
Selling, general and administrative expenses	1,576.4	1,709.2	1,328.9
Research and development expenses	258.1	244.3	182.3
Asbestos-related costs, net	237.5	14.3	13.8
Restructuring and asset impairment charges, net	79.3	77.5	66.1
Operating income	$ 909.4	$ 1,210.1	$ 977.2

NOTES TO CONSOLIDATED FINANCIAL STATEMENTS
(Dollars in millions)

Note 4 (In Part): Restructuring and Asset Impairment Charges

2009 Restructuring Activities

During 2009, we recorded a net restructuring charge of $79.3, reflecting costs of $70.7 related to new actions and $11.4 related to prior years' plans, as well as the reversal of $2.8 of restructuring accruals that management determined would not be required. The charges associated with actions announced during 2009 primarily represent severance costs for reductions in headcount associated with the strategic relocation of certain production operations within our Fluid and Motion & Flow segments to lower cost regions, as well as other various planned reductions in headcount associated with our lean fulfillment initiative. Planned position eliminations total 1,092, including 528 factory workers, 530 office workers and 34 management employees. The costs recognized during 2009 related to prior years' plans of $11.4 primarily reflect additional severance and lease cancellation related costs. The following table details the components of restructuring charges recorded during 2009.

	2009 Actions						Prior Years' Plans	
Components of Charges	Severance	Other Employee-Related Costs	Lease Cancellation & Other Costs	Asset Write-Offs	Total	Planned Position Eliminations	Additional Costs	Reversal of Accruals
Fluid	$31.0	$0.4	$2.4	$0.4	$34.2	506	$ 3.9	$(1.3)
Motion & Flow	31.3	0.5	1.5	0.7	34.0	496	3.3	(0.7)
Defense	1.3	—	0.3	—	1.6	79	4.2	(0.6)
Corporate and other	0.6	0.2	0.1	—	0.9	11	—	(0.2)
	$64.2	$1.1	$4.3	$1.1	$70.7	1,092	$11.4	$(2.8)

Rollforward of Restructuring Accrual

	Fluid	Motion & Flow	Defense	Corporate and Other	Total
Balance, January 1, 2007	$ 22.4	$ 7.3	$ 3.3	$ 1.6	$ 34.6
Additional charges for prior year plans	3.5	1.0	2.9	—	7.4
Cash payments and other related to prior charges	(17.9)	(5.3)	(2.0)	(1.2)	(26.4)
Charges for 2007 actions	36.7	10.2	7.7	3.3	57.9
Reversal of prior charges	(1.1)	(0.5)	(0.9)	(1.7)	(4.2)
Cash payments and other related to 2007 charges	(20.5)	(3.2)	(3.1)	—	(26.8)
Asset write-offs	(2.1)	(0.4)	—	—	(2.5)
Balance, December 31, 2007	21.0	9.1	7.9	2.0	40.0
Additional charges for prior year plans	3.2	6.0	0.1	—	9.3
Cash payments and other related to prior charges	(20.8)	(10.4)	(5.1)	(1.5)	(37.8)
Charges for 2008 actions	32.1	22.3	10.9	1.6	66.9
Reversal of prior charges	(1.0)	(0.4)	(0.2)	—	(1.6)
Cash payments and other related to 2008 charges	(8.5)	(5.5)	(3.1)	(0.4)	(17.5)
Asset write-offs	(0.1)	(0.8)	—	—	(0.9)
Balance, December 31, 2008	25.9	20.3	10.5	1.7	58.4
Additional charges for prior year plans	3.9	3.3	4.2	—	11.4
Cash payments and other related to prior charges	(25.8)	(17.7)	(8.7)	(1.4)	(53.6)
Charges for 2009 actions	34.2	34.0	1.6	0.9	70.7
Reversal of prior charges	(1.3)	(0.7)	(0.6)	(0.2)	(2.8)
Cash payments and other related to 2009 charges	(18.3)	(7.7)	(2.7)	(0.5)	(29.2)
Asset write-offs	(0.4)	(0.7)	(0.5)	—	(1.6)
Balance, December 31, 2009	$ 18.2	$ 30.8	$ 3.8	$ 0.5	$ 53.3

The accrual balance as of December 31, 2009 of $53.3 includes $46.3 for severance and $7.0 for facility carrying costs and other. We expect that the remaining planned headcount reductions as of the end of 2009 from our past restructuring activities will be substantially completed by mid-2010.

As of the end of 2009, there are no planned facility closures remaining associated with the actions taken during 2009 or prior.

The following is a reconciliation of employee position eliminations associated with restructuring activities through 2009:

Planned reductions as of December 31, 2006	270
Planned reductions from 2007 actions	729
Actual reductions, January 1—December 31, 2007	(686)
Planned reductions as of December 31, 2007	313
Planned reductions from 2008 actions	1,360
Actual reductions, January 1—December 31, 2008	(1,163)
Planned reductions as of December 31, 2008	510
Planned reductions from 2009 actions	1,092
Actual reductions, January 1—December 31, 2009	(1,195)
Planned reductions as of December 31, 2009	407

Foreign Currency Transactions

3.23

LAM RESEARCH CORPORATION (JUN)

(In thousands)	2009	2008	2007
Total revenue	$1,115,946	$2,474,911	$2,566,576
Cost of goods sold	706,219	1,282,494	1,261,522
Cost of goods sold—restructuring and asset impairments	20,993	12,610	—
Cost of goods sold—409A expense	—	6,401	—
Total costs of goods sold	727,212	1,301,505	1,261,522
Gross margin	388,734	1,173,406	1,305,054
Research and development	288,269	323,759	285,348
Selling, general and administrative	233,061	287,282	241,046
Goodwill impairment	96,255	—	—
Restructuring and asset impairments	44,513	6,366	—
409A expense	3,232	44,494	—
Legal judgment	4,647	—	—
In-process research and development	—	2,074	—
Total operating expenses	669,977	663,975	526,394
Operating income (loss)	(281,243)	509,431	778,660
Other income (expense), net:			
Interest income	24,283	51,194	71,666
Interest expense	(6,497)	(12,674)	(17,817)
Foreign exchange gains (losses)	922	31,070	(1,512)
Favorable legal judgment	—	—	15,834
Other, net	(558)	(2,045)	892
Income (loss) before income taxes	$ (263,093)	$ 576,976	$ 847,723

NOTES TO CONSOLIDATED FINANCIAL STATEMENTS

Note 2 (In Part): Summary of Significant Accounting Policies

Derivative Financial Instruments

The Company carries derivative financial instruments (derivatives) on the balance sheet at their fair values in accordance with Statement of Financial Accounting Standards No. 133, "Accounting for Derivative Instruments and Hedging Activities" (SFAS No. 133), Statement of Financial Accounting Standards No. 149, "Amendment of Statement 133 on Derivative Instruments and Hedging Activities" ("SFAS No. 149"), and Statement of Financial Accounting Standards No. 161, "Disclosures about Derivative Instruments and Hedging Activities—An Amendment of FASB Statement 133" ("SFAS No. 161").

The Company has a policy that allows the use of derivative financial instruments, specifically foreign currency forward exchange rate contracts, to hedge foreign currency exchange rate fluctuations on forecasted revenue transactions denominated in Japanese yen and other foreign currency denominated assets. The Company does not use derivatives for trading or speculative purposes.

The Company's policy is to attempt to minimize short-term business exposure to foreign currency exchange rate risks using an effective and efficient method to eliminate or reduce such exposures. In the normal course of business, the Company's financial position is routinely subjected to market risk associated with foreign currency exchange rate fluctuations. To protect against the reduction in value of forecasted Japanese yen-denominated revenues, the Company has instituted a foreign currency cash flow hedging program. The Company enters into foreign currency forward exchange rate contracts that generally expire within 12 months, and no later than 24 months. These foreign currency forward exchange contracts are designated as cash flow hedges and are carried on the Company's balance sheet at fair value with the effective portion of the contracts' gains or losses included in accumulated other comprehensive income (loss) and subsequently recognized in revenue in the same period the hedged revenue is recognized.

Each period, hedges are tested for effectiveness using regression testing. Changes in the fair value of currency forwards due to changes in time value are excluded from the assessment of effectiveness and are recognized in revenue in the current period. To qualify for hedge accounting, the hedge relationship must meet criteria relating both to the derivative instrument and the hedged item. These include identification of the hedging instrument, the hedged item, the nature of the risk being hedged and how the hedging instrument's effectiveness in offsetting the exposure to changes in the hedged item's fair value or cash flows will be measured.

To receive hedge accounting treatment, all hedging relationships are formally documented at the inception of the hedge and the hedges must be highly effective in offsetting changes to future cash flows on hedged transactions. When derivative instruments are designated and qualify as effective cash flow hedges, the Company is able to defer changes in the fair value of the hedging instrument within accumulated other comprehensive income (loss) until the hedged exposure is realized. Consequently, with the exception of hedge ineffectiveness recognized, the Company's results of operations are not subject to fluctuation as a result of changes in the fair value of the derivative instruments. If hedges are not highly effective or if the Company does not believe that the underlying hedged forecasted transactions would occur, the Company may not be able to account for its investments in derivative instruments as cash flow hedges. If this were to occur, future changes in the fair values of the Company's derivative instruments would be recognized in earnings without the benefits of offsets or deferrals of changes in fair value arising from hedge accounting treatment.

The Company also enters into foreign exchange forward contracts to minimize the short-term impact of the foreign currency exchange rate fluctuations on Japanese yen-denominated assets and forecasted Japanese yen-denominated revenue and on net intercompany liability exposures denominated in Swiss francs, Euros and Taiwanese dollars. Under SFAS No. 133 and SFAS No. 149, these forward contracts are not designated for hedge accounting treatment. Therefore, the change in fair value of these derivatives is recorded into earnings as a component of other income and expense and offsets the change in fair value of the foreign currency denominated intercompany and trade receivables, recorded in other income and expense, assuming the hedge contract fully covers the intercompany and trade receivable balances.

To hedge foreign currency risks, the Company uses foreign currency exchange forward contracts, where possible and practical. These forward contracts are valued using standard valuation formulas with assumptions about future foreign currency exchange rates derived from existing exchange rates and interest rates observed in the market.

The Company considers its most current outlook in determining the level of foreign currency denominated intercompany revenues to hedge as cash flow hedges. The Company combines these forecasts with historical trends to establish the portion of its expected volume to be hedged. The revenues are hedged and designated as cash flow hedges to protect the Company from exposures to fluctuations in foreign currency exchange rates. In the event the underlying forecasted transaction does not occur, or it becomes probable that it will not occur, the related hedge gains and losses on the cash flow hedge are reclassified from accumulated other comprehensive income (loss) to interest and other income (expense) on the consolidated statement of operations at that time.

The Company does not believe that it is or was exposed to more than a nominal amount of credit risk in its interest rate and foreign currency hedges, as counterparties are established and well-capitalized financial institutions. The Company's exposures are in liquid currencies (Japanese yen and Euro), so there is minimal risk that appropriate derivatives to maintain the Company's hedging program would not be available in the future.

Note 8. Other Income (Expense), Net

The significant components of other income (expense), net, are as follows:

(In thousands)	2009	2008	2007
Interest income	$24,283	$ 51,194	$ 71,666
Interest expense	(6,497)	(12,674)	(17,817)
Foreign exchange gains (losses)	922	31,070	(1,512)
Favorable legal judgment	—	—	15,834
Other, net	(558)	(2,045)	892
	$18,150	$ 67,545	$ 69,063

Included in foreign exchange gains during the year ended June 29, 2008 are gains of $42.7 million relating primarily to the settlement of a hedge of the Swiss franc associated with the acquisition of SEZ. The legal judgment of $15.8 million in fiscal year 2007 was obtained in a lawsuit filed by the Company alleging breach of purchase order contracts by one of its customers.

Debt Extinguishments

3.24

MERITAGE HOMES CORPORATION (DEC)

(In thousands)	2009	2008	2007
Home closing revenue	$ 962,797	$ 1,505,117	$ 2,334,141
Land closing revenue	7,516	17,951	9,453
Total closing revenue	970,313	1,523,068	2,343,594
Cost of home closings	(832,614)	(1,304,882)	(1,981,776)
Cost of land closings	(7,432)	(17,662)	(8,414)
Home impairments	(111,490)	(194,955)	(327,230)
Land impairments	(14,726)	(42,484)	(13,128)
Total cost of closings and impairments	(966,262)	(1,559,983)	(2,330,548)
Home closing gross profit	18,693	5,280	25,135
Land closing gross loss	(14,642)	(42,195)	(12,089)
Total closing gross profit/(loss)	4,051	(36,915)	13,046
Commissions and other sales costs	(78,683)	(136,860)	(196,464)
General and administrative expenses	(63,148)	(68,231)	(106,161)
Goodwill and intangible asset impairments	—	(1,133)	(130,490)
Earnings/(loss) from unconsolidated entities, net	4,013	(17,038)	(40,229)
Interest expense	(36,531)	(23,653)	(6,745)
Gain on extinguishment of debt	9,390	—	—
Other income, net	6,109	7,864	10,561
Loss before income taxes	$(154,799)	$ (275,966)	$ (456,482)

NOTES TO CONSOLIDATED FINANCIAL STATEMENTS

Note 6 (In Part): Senior and Senior Subordinated Notes

Senior and senior subordinated notes consist of the following (in thousands):

	2009	2008
7.0% senior notes due 2014. At December 31, 2009 and 2008, there was approximately $38 and $47 in unamortized premium, respectively	$130,038	$130,047
6.25% senior notes due 2015. At December 31, 2009 and 2008, there was approximately $904 and $1,100 in unamortized discount, respectively	349,096	348,921
7.731% senior subordinated notes due 2017	125,875	150,000
	$605,009	$628,968

● ● ● ● ● ●

During 2009, we retired $24.1 million of our 7.731% senior subordinated notes maturing in 2017 by issuing approximately 783,000 shares of our common stock in a privately negotiated transaction. The transaction was completed at an average discount of 41% from the face value of the notes, resulting in a net $9.4 million gain on early extinguishment of debt which is reflected in our statement of operations for the year ending December 31, 2009. There were no such transactions during the year ending December 31, 2008.

Royalty, Franchise and License Fees

3.25

CLIFFS NATURAL RESOURCES INC. (DEC)

(In millions)	2009	2008	2007
Revenues from product sales and services			
Product	$ 2,216.2	$ 3,294.8	$ 1,997.3
Freight and venture partners' cost reimbursements	125.8	314.3	277.9
	2,342.0	3,609.1	2,275.2
Cost of goods sold and operating expenses	(2,033.1)	(2,449.4)	(1,813.2)
Sales margin	308.9	1,159.7	462.0
Other operating income (expense)			
Royalties and management fee revenue	4.8	21.7	14.5
Selling, general and administrative expenses	(120.7)	(188.6)	(114.2)
Terminated acquisition costs	—	(90.1)	—
Gain on sale of other assets—net	13.2	22.8	18.4
Casualty recoveries	—	10.5	3.2
Miscellaneous—net	24.0	2.9	(2.3)
	(78.7)	(220.8)	(80.4)
Operating income	$ 230.2	$ 938.9	$ 381.6

NOTES TO CONSOLIDATED FINANCIAL STATEMENTS

Note 1 (In Part): Significant Accounting Policies

Accounting Policies (In Part)

Revenue Recognition and Cost of Goods Sold and Operating Expenses (In Part)

North American Iron Ore

Where we are joint venture participants in the ownership of a mine, our contracts entitle us to receive royalties and/or management fees, which we earn as the pellets are produced. Revenue is recognized on the sale of services when the services are performed.

Litigation Settlement

3.26

ADVANCED MICRO DEVICES, INC. (DEC)

(In millions)	2009	2008	2007
Net revenue	$ 5,403	$ 5,808	$ 5,858
Cost of sales	3,131	3,488	3,669
Gross margin	2,272	2,320	2,189
Research and development	1,721	1,848	1,771
Marketing, general and administrative	994	1,304	1,360
Legal settlement	(1,242)	—	—
Amortization of acquired intangible assets and integration charges	70	137	236
Impairment of goodwill and acquired intangible assets	—	1,089	1,132
Restructuring charges	65	90	—
Gain on sale of 200 millimeter equipment	—	(193)	—
Operating income (loss)	$ 664	$(1,955)	$(2,310)

NOTES TO CONSOLIDATED FINANCIAL STATEMENTS

Note 12. Intel Settlement

On November 12, 2009, Intel Corporation and the Company entered into an agreement to end all outstanding legal disputes between the companies including antitrust litigation and patent cross license disputes. Under the terms of the agreement:

- The Company and Intel agreed to a new 5-year patent cross license agreement that gives the Company broad rights and the freedom to operate a business utilizing multiple foundries;
- Intel and the Company gave up any claims of breach from the previous license agreement;
- Intel paid the Company $1.25 billion;
- Intel agreed to abide by a set of business practice provisions going forward;
- The Company dropped all pending litigation, including the case in U.S. District Court in Delaware and two cases pending in Japan; and
- The Company withdrew all of its regulatory complaints worldwide.

This settlement satisfies all past antitrust litigation and disputes and there are no future obligations (e.g., the patent cross license agreement represents fully paid up licenses by both the Company and Intel for which no future payments or delivery is required) that the Company would need to perform to earn this settlement payment. Accordingly, the Company has recognized the entire settlement amount in its fiscal 2009 operating results.

Insurance Recoveries

3.27

CARLISLE COMPANIES INCORPORATED (DEC)

(In millions)	2009	2008	2007
Net sales	$2,379.5	$3,110.1	$2,812.1
Cost and expenses:			
Cost of goods sold	1,875.6	2,516.8	2,224.3
Selling and administrative expenses	289.0	316.3	276.1
Research and development expenses	16.6	16.2	15.8
Goodwill impairment charges	—	55.5	—
Gain related to fire settlement	(27.0)	—	—
Other expense (income), net	18.4	18.7	(46.5)
Earnings before interest and income taxes	$ 206.9	$ 186.6	$ 342.4

NOTES TO CONSOLIDATED FINANCIAL STATEMENTS

Note 2. Fire Gain

On November 16, 2008, a fire occurred at the tire and wheel plant in Bowdon, GA, and as a result the building and the majority of the machinery, equipment, records and other assets were destroyed. In order to service customers, partial operations were initiated at a facility in Heflin, AL, and some production was transferred to other tire and wheel plants or outsourced to third parties.

In the fourth quarter of 2008, while the Company was negotiating its claim, a pretax loss was recorded representing the deductible of $0.1 million. The net result of fire-related transactions in the first quarter of 2009 was a $2.5 million pretax gain, which included a $2.6 million pretax gain on the settlement of the inventory claim which was the difference between $8.9 million, representing the loss on inventory recorded in the fourth quarter of 2008 for which a receivable was recorded at December 31, 2008, and $11.5 million of cash proceeds received from the insurance carriers to settle the inventory claim in the first quarter of 2009. Total payments of $13.5 million were received from the insurance carriers in the first quarter of 2009.

The net result of fire-related transactions in the second quarter of 2009 was a $24.5 million pretax gain on the settlement of all other claims and that amount was reported as Gain related to fire settlement. This gain was the difference between the $41.0 million of cash proceeds received from the insurance carriers in settlement of all outstanding claims and the $11.2 million insurance claims receivable balance at March 31, 2009 included in Prepaid expenses and other current assets for a portion of the expected insurance reimbursements plus $5.3 million, representing fire-related cost in the second quarter of 2009.

From January 1, 2009 through June 30, 2009 cash proceeds of $54.5 million were received from the insurance carriers. Losses and cost incurred from November 16, 2008 through June 30, 2009 of $27.6 million included $8.9 million of inventory; $5.7 million of building, machinery, equipment and other assets; and $13.0 million of fire-related cost. The $26.9 million pretax gain from November 16, 2008 through June 30, 2009 was the difference between cash proceeds of $54.5 million and the losses of $27.6 million. On a quarterly basis, a loss of $0.1 million was recorded in the fourth quarter of 2008, a gain of $2.5 million was recorded in the first quarter of 2009, and a gain of $24.5 million was recorded in the second quarter of 2009.

A minimal amount of fire-related scrap was sold in the third quarter of 2009. Since all insurance claims due to this fire were settled with the carriers, there was no insurance claims receivable as of December 31, 2009 and no additional insurance proceeds are anticipated.

Change in Fair Value of Financial Assets/Liabilities

3.28

DEVON ENERGY CORPORATION (DEC)

(In millions)	2009	2008	2007
Revenues:			
Oil, gas and NGL sales	$6,097	$11,720	$8,225
Net gain (loss) on oil and gas derivative financial instruments	384	(154)	14
Marketing and midstream revenues	1,534	2,292	1,736
Total revenues	8,015	13,858	9,975
Expenses and other income, net:			
Lease operating expenses	1,670	1,851	1,532
Taxes other than income taxes	314	476	358
Marketing and midstream operating costs and expenses	1,022	1,611	1,217
Depreciation, depletion and amortization of oil and gas properties	1,832	2,948	2,412
Depreciation and amortization of non-oil and gas properties	276	255	201
Accretion of asset retirement obligations	91	80	70
General and administrative expenses	648	645	513
Restructuring costs	105	—	—
Interest expense	349	329	430
Change in fair value of other financial instruments	(106)	149	(34)
Reduction of carrying value of oil and gas properties	6,408	9,891	—
Other income, net	(68)	(217)	(51)
Total expenses and other income, net	12,541	18,018	6,648
Earnings (loss) from continuing operations before income taxes	$(4,526)	$(4,160)	$3,327

NOTES TO CONSOLIDATED FINANCIAL STATEMENTS

3 (In Part): Derivative Financial Instruments

The following table presents the cash settlements and unrealized gains and losses on fair value changes included in the accompanying statements of operations associated with these derivative financial instruments. None of Devon's derivative instruments included in the table have been designated as hedging instruments.

(In millions)	Statement of Operations Caption	2009	2008	2007
Cash settlements:				
Gas price collars	Net gain (loss) on oil and gas derivative financial instruments	$ 450	$(221)	$ 2
Gas price swaps	Net gain (loss) on oil and gas derivative financial instruments	55	(203)	38
Oil price collars	Net gain (loss) on oil and gas derivative financial instruments	—	27	—
Interest rate swaps	Change in fair value of other financial instruments	40	1	—
Total cash settlements		545	(396)	40
Unrealized (losses) gains:				
Gas price collars	Net gain (loss) on oil and gas derivative financial instruments	(255)	255	(4)
Gas price swaps	Net gain (loss) on oil and gas derivative financial instruments	169	(12)	(22)
Gas basis swaps	Net gain (loss) on oil and gas derivative financial instruments	3	—	—
Oil price collars	Net gain (loss) on oil and gas derivative financial instruments	(38)	—	—
Interest rate swaps	Change in fair value of other financial instruments	66	104	1
Embedded option	Change in fair value of other financial instruments	—	109	(248)
Total unrealized (losses) gains		(55)	456	(273)
Net gain (loss) recognized on statement of operations		$ 490	$ 60	$(233)

14. Other Financial Instruments

Until October 31, 2008, Devon owned 14.2 million shares of Chevron common stock. These shares were held in connection with debt owed by Devon that contained an exchange option. The exchange option allowed the debt holders, prior to the debt's maturity of August 15, 2008, to exchange the debt for shares of Chevron common stock owned by Devon. However, Devon had the option to settle any exchanges with cash equal to the market value of Chevron common stock at the time of the exchange. Devon settled exchange requests during 2008 and 2007 by paying $1.0 billion during 2008 and $0.2 billion during 2007. On October 31, 2008, Devon transferred its 14.2 million shares of Chevron common stock to Chevron. In exchange, Devon received Chevron's interest in the Drunkard's Wash coalbed natural gas field in east-central Utah and $280 million in cash.

The shares of Chevron common stock and the exchange option embedded in the debt were always recorded on Devon's balance sheet at fair value. However, pursuant to accounting rules prior to January 1, 2007, only the change in fair value of the embedded option had historically been included in Devon's results of operations. Conversely, the change in fair value of the Chevron common stock had not been included in Devon's results of operations, but instead had been recorded directly to stockholders' equity as part of "accumulated other comprehensive income." Effective January 1, 2007, under new accounting rules, Devon elected to begin recognizing the change in fair value of the Chevron common stock in its results of operations. Accordingly, beginning with the first quarter of 2007, the change in fair value of the Chevron common stock owned by Devon, along with the change in fair value of the related exchange option, were both included in Devon's results of operations. Also, as a result of

this change, Devon reclassified $364 million of after-tax unrealized gains related to Devon's investment in Chevron common stock from accumulated other comprehensive income to retained earnings in the first quarter of 2007.

The following table presents the changes in fair value and cash settlements related to Devon's other financial instruments, as well as its investment in Chevron Common Stock as presented in the accompanying consolidated statements of operations.

(In millions)	2009	2008	2007
(Gains) and losses from:			
Interest rate swaps—fair value changes (See Note 3)	$ (66)	$(104)	$ (1)
Interest rate swaps—settlements (See Note 3)	(40)	(1)	—
Chevron common stock	—	363	(281)
Option embedded in exchangeable debentures	—	(109)	248
Total	$(106)	$ 149	$ (34)

Employee Benefit/Pension Related

3.29

A. SCHULMAN, INC. (AUG)

(In thousands)	2009	2008	2007
Net sales	$1,279,248	$1,983,595	$1,786,892
Cost of sales	1,109,211	1,749,065	1,578,213
Selling, general and administrative expenses	148,143	169,275	149,393
Minority interest	349	872	1,027
Interest expense	4,785	7,814	8,118
Interest income	(2,348)	(2,338)	(2,306)
Foreign currency transaction (gains) losses	(5,645)	1,133	219
Other income	(1,826)	(9)	(1,832)
Curtailment gains	(2,805)	(4,009)	—
Goodwill impairment	—	964	—
Asset impairment	2,608	5,399	—
Restructuring expense	8,665	6,817	1,598
	1,261,137	1,934,983	1,734,430
Income from continuing operations before taxes	$ 18,111	$ 48,612	$ 52,462

NOTES TO CONSOLIDATED FINANCIAL STATEMENTS

Note 8 (In Part): Pensions

The components of net periodic benefit cost of the years ended August 31 are as follows:

(In thousands)	Pension Benefits			Other Postretirement Benefits		
	2009	2008	2007	2009	2008	2007
Service cost	$1,742	$ 2,492	$ 2,486	$ 42	$ 385	$1,306
Interest cost	4,429	4,640	3,728	847	1,077	1,509
Expected return on plan assets	(957)	(1,250)	(1,057)	—	—	—
Amortization of transition obligation	39	42	38	—	—	—
Amortization of prior service cost	48	279	497	(654)	(647)	(293)
Deferred asset gain	—	—	—	—	—	134
Recognized gains due to plan curtailments	(188)	(114)	—	(2,609)	(3,895)	—
Recognized net actuarial loss	250	189	582	—	—	—
	$5,363	$ 6,278	$ 6,274	$(2,374)	$(3,080)	$2,656

During the second quarter of fiscal 2009, the Company recorded a curtailment gain of $2.6 million as a result of a significant reduction in the expected years of future service, primarily due to its North American restructuring plan that was announced in December 2008. During the fourth quarter of fiscal 2009, the Company recorded a curtailment gain of $0.2 million as a result of a significant reduction in the expected years of future service, primarily due to the European restructuring plan which included the elimination of certain positions in the Company's Paris, France subsidiary as a result of the consolidation of back-office operations to the European shared service center.

During the second quarter of fiscal 2008, the Company announced that it planned to amend its U.S. postretirement health care coverage plan by eliminating post-65 retiree coverage as of March 24, 2008. During the second quarter of fiscal 2008, the Company reduced its postretirement health care benefit liability by approximately $5.0 million with a corresponding increase in accumulated other comprehensive income due to the negative plan amendment. During the third quarter of fiscal 2008, the Company recorded curtailment

gains of $2.3 million related to its U.S. postretirement health care coverage plan as a result of a significant reduction in the expected years of future service primarily due to the sale of the Orange, Texas facility and a change in the executive management. During the fourth quarter of fiscal 2008, the Company recorded a curtailment gain of $1.7 million as a result of the elimination of post retirement life insurance benefits under the U.S. postretirement health care coverage plan which eliminated the defined benefit for some or all of the future services of a significant number of plan participants. This U.S. postretirement health care benefit liability is included in accrued payrolls, taxes and related benefits and other long-term liabilities on the Company's consolidated balance sheet.

Rentals

3.30

ALLEGHENY TECHNOLOGIES INCORPORATED (DEC)

(In millions)	2009	2008	2007
Sales	$3,054.9	$5,309.7	$5,452.5
Costs and expenses:			
Cost of sales	2,646.5	4,157.8	4,003.1
Selling and administrative expenses	315.7	282.7	296.7
Income before interest, other income and income taxes	92.7	869.2	1,152.7
Interest expense, net	(19.3)	(3.5)	(4.8)
Debt extinguishment costs	(9.2)	—	—
Other income, net	0.7	2.0	6.2
Income before income taxes	$ 64.9	$ 867.7	$1,154.1

NOTES TO CONSOLIDATED FINANCIAL STATEMENTS

Note 5 (In Part): Supplemental Financial Statement Information

Other income (expense) for the years ended December 31, 2009, 2008, and 2007 was as follows:

(In millions)	2009	2008	2007
Rent, royalty income and other income	$ 0.9	$1.6	$1.3
Net gains (losses) on property and investments	(0.2)	0.1	2.5
Other	—	0.3	2.4
Total other income	$ 0.7	$2.0	$6.2

Business Combination Adjustment Gain

3.31

FLOWERS FOODS, INC. (DEC)

(Amounts in thousands)	2009	2008	2007
Sales	$2,600,849	$2,414,892	$2,036,674
Materials, supplies, labor and other production costs (exclusive of depreciation and amortization shown separately below)	1,390,183	1,263,962	1,039,011
Selling, marketing and administrative expenses	926,418	894,800	787,821
Depreciation and amortization	80,928	73,312	66,094
Gain on acquisition	(3,013)	—	—
Gain on sale of assets	—	(2,306)	—
Asset impairment	—	3,108	—
Gain on insurance recovery	—	(686)	(933)
Income from operations	$ 206,333	$ 182,702	$ 144,681

NOTES TO CONSOLIDATED FINANCIAL STATEMENTS

Note 3 (In Part): New Accounting Pronouncements

In December 2007, the FASB issued new guidance on business combinations. The new standard provides revised guidance on how acquirors recognize and measure the consideration transferred, identifiable assets acquired, liabilities assumed, noncontrolling interests, and goodwill acquired in a business combination. The new standard also expands required disclosures surrounding the nature and financial effects of business combinations. The standard was effective, on a prospective basis, for fiscal years beginning after December 15, 2008. Upon adoption on January 4, 2009, this standard did not have a material impact on our consolidated financial position and results of operations. We recorded the acquisition of a bakery mix operation in Cedar Rapids, Iowa on May 15, 2009 and the Leo's Foods acquisition on October 17, 2009 in accordance with this guidance as described in Note 9, *Acquisitions*.

Note 9 (In Part): Acquisitions

On May 15, 2009, the company acquired substantially all the assets of a bakery mix operation in Cedar Rapids, Iowa. Based on the purchase price allocation, the fair value of the identifiable assets acquired and liabilities assumed exceeded the fair value of the consideration paid. As a result, we recognized a gain of $3.0 million in the second quarter of fiscal 2009, which is included in the line item "Gain on acquisition" to derive income from operations in the consolidated statement of income for the fifty-two weeks ended January 2, 2010. We believe the gain on acquisition resulted from the seller's strategic intent to exit a non-core business operation. This acquisition is recorded in the company's warehouse delivery segment.

EXPENSES AND LOSSES

3.32   Paragraphs 80 and 83 of FASB *SFAC No. 6* define expenses and losses.

> 80. Expenses are outflows or other using up of assets or incurrences of liabilities (or a combination of both) from delivering or producing goods, rendering services, or carrying out other activities that constitute the entity's ongoing major or central operations.
>
> 83. Losses are decreases in equity (net assets) from peripheral or incidental transactions of an entity and from all other transactions and other events and circumstances affecting the entity except those that result from expenses or distributions to owners.

3.33   Table 3-5 reveals that most of the survey entities show a single caption and amount for cost of goods sold. Table 3-6 summarizes the nature of expenses, other than cost of goods sold. Excluded from Table 3-6 are rent (Table 2-30), employee benefits, depreciation (Table 3-14), and income taxes (Table 3-15). Table 3-7 lists losses most frequently disclosed by the survey entities. Excluded from Table 3-7 are losses shown after the caption for income taxes (Table 3-17), segment disposals, and extraordinary losses (Table 3-18).

3.34 Examples of expenses and losses follow.

3.35

TABLE 3-5: EXPENSES—COST OF GOODS SOLD CAPTIONS

	2009	2008	2007	2006
Single Amount				
Cost of sales	175	170	215	219
Cost of goods sold	78	80	94	92
Cost of products sold	51	50	66	72
Cost of revenues	32	30	43	38
Elements of cost	13	11	15	11
Other captions	80	79	74	79
	429	420	507	511
More than one amount	71	80	93	89
Total Entities	500	500	600	600

2008–2009 based on 500 entities surveyed; 2006–2007 based on 600 entities surveyed.

3.36

TABLE 3-6: EXPENSES—OTHER THAN COST OF GOODS SOLD*

	Number of Entities			
	2009	2008	2007	2006
Selling, general and administrative	300	298	347	348
Selling and administrative	70	70	96	107
General and/or administrative	98	94	122	109
Selling	40	33	44	39
Interest	453	457	551	548
Interest and penalty on income taxes	24	21	32	N/C**
Research, development, engineering, etc.	229	222	285	289
Advertising	173	188	221	209
Provision for doubtful accounts	122	130	131	116
Warranty	99	99	138	137
Shipping	62	58	65	61
Asset retirement obligation accretion	43	39	49	33
Taxes other than income taxes	17	18	18	19
Maintenance and repairs	14	12	18	13
Exploration, dry holes, abandonments	7	9	11	10

* Appearing in either the income statement and/or the notes to financial statements.

** N/C = Not compiled. Line item was not included in the table for the year shown.

2008–2009 based on 500 entities surveyed; 2006–2007 based on 600 entities surveyed.

3.37

TABLE 3-7: LOSSES*

	Number of Entities			
	2009	2008	2007	2006
Intangible asset amortization	276	280	344	324
Write-down of assets	248	234	234	197
Restructuring of operations	242	226	235	238
Change in fair value of derivatives	239	94	104	86
Impairment of intangibles	166	155	96	83
Foreign currency transactions	101	82	83	95
Sale of assets	84	75	69	66
Debt extinguishment	68	35	60	65
Litigation	49	52	50	69
Equity in losses of investees	47	40	42	24
Environmental cleanup	37	32	39	47
Sale of receivables	33	35	34	41
Merger costs	33	15	19	16
Software amortization	32	32	46	36
Fair value adjustments	23	8	2	N/C**
Minority interests	14	48	50	57
Start-up costs	11	8	9	10
Purchased R&D	10	15	20	21
Royalties	10	9	17	16
Business combination adjustment loss	4	N/C**	N/C**	N/C**
Distributions on preferred securities of subsidiary trust	—	1	—	1

* Appearing in either the income statement and/or the notes to financial statements.

** N/C = Not compiled. Line item was not included in the table for the year shown.

2008–2009 based on 500 entities surveyed; 2006–2007 based on 600 entities surveyed.

EXPENSES

Cost of Goods Sold

3.38

STANDEX INTERNATIONAL CORPORATION (JUN)

(In thousands)	2009	2008	2007
Net sales	$607,086	$697,541	$621,211
Cost of sales	431,111	495,694	448,407
Gross profit	175,975	201,847	172,804
Selling, general and administrative	140,776	162,328	142,421
Impairment of goodwill and intangible assets	21,339	—	—
Restructuring costs	7,839	590	286
Income from operations	$ 6,021	$ 38,929	$ 30,097

NOTES TO CONSOLIDATED FINANCIAL STATEMENTS

1 (In Part): Summary of Accounting Policies

Cost of Goods Sold and Selling, General and Administrative Expenses

The Company includes expenses in either cost of goods sold or selling, general and administrative categories based upon the natural classification of the expenses. Cost of goods sold includes expenses associated with the acquisition, inspection, manufacturing and receiving of materials for use in the manufacturing process. These costs include inbound freight charges, purchasing and receiving costs, inspection costs, warehousing costs, internal transfer costs as well as depreciation, amortization, wages, benefits and other costs that are incurred directly or indirectly to support the manufacturing process. Selling, general and administrative includes expenses associated with the distribution of our products, sales effort, administration costs and other costs that are not incurred to support the manufacturing process. The Company records distribution costs associated with the sale of inventory as a component of selling, general and administrative expenses in the Statements of Consolidated Income. These expenses include warehousing costs, outbound freight charges and costs associated with distribution personnel. Our gross profit margins may not be comparable to those of other entities due to different classifications of costs and expenses.

3.39

WOLVERINE WORLD WIDE, INC. (DEC)

(Thousands of dollars)	2009	2008	2007
Revenue	$1,101,056	$1,220,568	$1,198,972
Cost of goods sold	663,461	734,547	727,041
Restructuring and other transition costs	5,873	—	—
Gross profit	431,722	486,021	471,931
Selling, general and administrative expenses	316,378	345,183	333,151
Restructuring and other transition costs	29,723	—	—
Operating profit	$ 85,621	$ 140,838	$ 138,780

Interest and Penalty on Income Taxes

3.40

ALLERGAN, INC. (DEC)

(In millions)	2009	2008	2007
Revenues:			
Product net sales	$4,447.6	$4,339.7	$3,879.0
Other revenues	56.0	63.7	59.9
Total revenues	4,503.6	4,403.4	3,938.9
Operating costs and expenses:			
Cost of sales (excludes amortization of acquired intangible assets)	750.9	761.2	673.2
Selling, general and administrative	1,921.5	1,856.1	1,680.2
Research and development	706.0	797.9	718.1
Amortization of acquired intangible assets	146.3	150.9	121.3
Restructuring charges	50.9	41.3	26.8
Operating income	928.0	796.0	719.3
Non-operating income (expense):			
Interest income	7.0	33.5	65.3
Interest expense	(76.9)	(85.5)	(94.6)
Unrealized (loss) gain on derivative instruments, net	(13.6)	14.8	(0.4)
Gain on investments, net	24.6	—	—
Other, net	(20.6)	3.4	(25.2)
	(79.5)	(33.8)	(54.9)
Earnings from continuing operations before income taxes	$ 848.5	$ 762.2	$ 664.4

NOTES TO CONSOLIDATED FINANCIAL STATEMENTS

Note 9 (In Part): Income Taxes

Disclosures for Uncertainty in Income Taxes

The Company classifies interest expense related to uncertainty in income taxes in the consolidated statements of earnings as interest expense. Income tax penalties are recorded in income tax expense, and are not material.

A tabular reconciliation of the total amounts of unrecognized tax benefits at the beginning and end of 2009 and 2008 is as follows:

(In millions)	2009	2008
Balance, beginning of year	$ 47.5	$ 59.6
Gross increase as a result of positions taken in a prior year	20.5	24.0
Gross decrease as a result of positions taken in a prior year	(21.0)	(14.2)
Gross increase as a result of positions taken in current year	0.1	1.2
Decreases related to settlements	(7.8)	(23.1)
Balance, end of year	$ 39.3	$ 47.5

The total amount of unrecognized tax benefits at December 31, 2009 and December 31, 2008 that, if recognized, would affect the effective tax rate is $35.5 million and $42.0 million, respectively.

In 2009, the total amount of interest expense related to uncertainty in income taxes recognized in the Company's consolidated statement of earnings is $5.5 million. The total amount of accrued interest expense related to uncertainty in income taxes included in the Company's consolidated balance sheet is $11.1 million and $12.8 million at December 31, 2009 and 2008, respectively. The change to the accrued interest expense balance between December 31, 2009 and December 31, 2008 is primarily due to a decrease for an advance payment made during the year in connection with the ongoing 2005 and 2006 U.S. Internal Revenue Service income tax audit, partially offset by an increase for the current year interest expense.

The Company expects that during the next 12 months it is reasonably possible that unrecognized tax benefit liabilities related to various audit issues will decrease by approximately $18.0 million to $20.0 million primarily due to settlements of income tax audits in the United States.

3.41

DEAN FOODS COMPANY (DEC)

(Dollars in thousands)	2009	2008	2007
Net sales	$11,158,388	$12,454,613	$11,821,903
Cost of sales	8,042,401	9,509,359	9,084,318
Gross profit	3,115,987	2,945,254	2,737,585
Operating costs and expenses:			
Selling and distribution	1,826,935	1,817,690	1,721,617
General and administrative	627,132	486,280	419,518
Amortization of intangibles	9,637	9,836	6,744
Facility closing and reorganization costs	30,162	22,758	34,421
Other operating expense	—	—	1,688
Total operating costs and expenses	2,493,866	2,336,564	2,183,988
Operating income	622,121	608,690	553,597
Other (income) expense:			
Interest expense	246,494	308,080	333,202
Other (income) expense, net	(4,196)	933	5,926
Total other expense	242,298	309,013	339,128
Income from continuing operations before income taxes	379,823	299,677	214,469
Income taxes	152,065	114,837	84,007
Income from continuing operations	$ 227,758	$ 184,840	$ 130,462

NOTES TO CONSOLIDATED FINANCIAL STATEMENTS

1 (In Part): Summary of Significant Accounting Policies

Income Taxes (In Part)

We recognize the income tax benefit from an uncertain tax position when it is more likely than not that, based on technical merits, the position will be sustained upon examination, including resolutions of any related appeals or litigation processes. We recognize accrued interest related to uncertain tax positions as a component of income tax expense and penalties, if incurred, are recognized as a component of operating income.

8 (In Part): Income Taxes

We recognize accrued interest related to uncertain tax positions as a component of income tax expense. Penalties, if incurred, are recognized as a component of operating income. Income tax expense for 2009, 2008 and 2007 included interest expense, net of tax of $1.1 million, $(0.6) million and $2.8 million, respectively. Our liability for uncertain tax positions included accrued interest of $8.5 million and $8.2 million at December 31, 2009 and 2008, respectively.

Research and Development

3.42

COHERENT, INC. (SEP)

(In thousands)	2009	2008	2007
Net sales	$435,882	$599,262	$601,153
Cost of sales	274,772	347,356	351,145
Gross profit	161,110	251,906	250,008
Operating expenses:			
Research and development	61,417	74,287	74,590
In-process research and development	—	—	2,200
Selling, general and administrative	108,098	146,376	153,945
Impairment of goodwill	19,286	—	—
Amortization of intangible assets	7,466	8,651	8,152
Total operating expenses	196,267	229,314	238,887
Income (loss) from operations	$ (35,157)	$ 22,592	$ 11,121

NOTES TO CONSOLIDATED FINANCIAL STATEMENTS

Note 2 (In Part): Significant Accounting Policies

Research and Development

Research and development expenses include salaries, contractor and consultant fees, supplies and materials, as well as costs related to other overhead such as depreciation, facilities, utilities and other departmental expenses. The costs we incur with respect to internally developed technology and engineering services are included in research and development expenses as incurred as they do not directly relate to any particular licensee, license agreement or license fee.

We treat third party and government funding of our research and development activity, where we are the primary beneficiary of such work conducted, as a credit to research and development cost. Amounts offset against research and development costs were not material in any of the periods presented.

3.43

GOODRICH CORPORATION (DEC)

(Dollars in millions)	2009	2008	2007
Sales	$6,685.6	$7,061.7	$6,392.2
Operating costs and expenses:			
Cost of sales	4,724.1	4,906.2	4,483.3
Selling and administrative costs	1,032.3	1,054.6	1,027.6
	5,756.4	5,960.8	5,510.9
Operating income	$ 929.2	$1,100.9	$ 881.3

NOTES TO CONSOLIDATED FINANCIAL STATEMENTS

Note 1 (In Part): Significant Accounting Policies

Research and Development

The Company performs research and development under company-funded programs for commercial products and under contracts with others. Research and development under contracts with others is performed on both military and commercial products. Company-funded research and development programs are expensed as incurred and included in selling and administrative costs. Customer funding of the Company's research and development efforts is recorded as an offset to research and development expense. Total research and development expenditures from continuing operations in 2009, 2008 and 2007 were approximately $239 million, $284 million and $280 million, respectively. These amounts are net of approximately $101 million, $133 million and $124 million, respectively, which were funded by customers.

Advertising

3.44

HASBRO, INC. (DEC)

(Thousands of dollars)	2009	2008	2007
Net revenues	$4,067,947	$4,021,520	$3,837,557
Cost of sales	1,676,336	1,692,728	1,576,621
Gross profit	2,391,611	2,328,792	2,260,936
Expenses			
Amortization	85,029	78,265	67,716
Royalties	330,651	312,986	316,807
Research and product development	181,195	191,424	167,194
Advertising	412,580	454,612	434,742
Selling, distribution and administration	793,558	797,209	755,127
Total expenses	1,803,013	1,834,496	1,741,586
Operating profit	$ 588,598	$ 494,296	$ 519,350

NOTES TO CONSOLIDATED FINANCIAL STATEMENTS
(Thousands of dollars)

1 (In Part): Summary of Significant Accounting Policies

Advertising

Production costs of commercials are charged to operations in the fiscal year during which the production is first aired. The costs of other advertising, promotion and marketing programs are charged to operations in the fiscal year incurred.

Provision for Doubtful Accounts

3.45

GENUINE PARTS COMPANY (DEC)

(In thousands)	2009	2008	2007
Net sales	$10,057,512	$11,015,263	$10,843,195
Cost of goods sold	7,047,750	7,742,773	7,625,972
Gross margin	3,009,762	3,272,490	3,217,223
Operating expenses:			
Selling, administrative, and other expenses	2,219,935	2,359,829	2,278,155
Depreciation and amortization	90,411	88,698	87,702
Provision for doubtful accounts	28,463	23,883	13,514
Total operating expenses	2,338,809	2,472,410	2,379,371
Non-operating expenses (income):			
Interest expense	27,885	31,721	31,327
Other	(1,097)	(109)	(10,220)
Total non-operating expenses	26,788	31,612	21,107
Income before income taxes	$ 644,165	$ 768,468	$ 816,745

NOTES TO CONSOLIDATED FINANCIAL STATEMENTS

1 (In Part): Summary of Significant Accounting Policies

*Trade Accounts Receivable and the Allowance
for Doubtful Accounts*

The Company evaluates the collectability of trade accounts receivable based on a combination of factors. Initially, the Company estimates an allowance for doubtful accounts as a percentage of net sales based on historical bad debt experience. This initial estimate is periodically adjusted when the Company becomes aware of a specific customer's inability to meet its financial obligations (e.g., bankruptcy filing) or as a result of changes in the overall aging of accounts receivable. While the Company has a large customer base that is geographically dispersed, a general economic downturn in any of the industry segments in which the Company operates could result in higher than expected defaults, and, therefore, the need to revise estimates for bad debts. For the years ended December 31, 2009, 2008, and 2007, the Company recorded provisions for bad debts of approximately $28,463,000, $23,883,000, and $13,514,000, respectively. At December 31, 2009 and 2008, the allowance for doubtful accounts was approximately $16,590,000 and $18,588,000, respectively.

Warranty

3.46

CISCO SYSTEMS, INC. (JUL)

(In millions)	2009	2008	2007
Net sales:			
Product	$29,131	$33,099	$29,462
Service	6,986	6,441	5,460
Total net sales	36,117	39,540	34,922
Cost of sales:			
Product	10,481	11,660	10,567
Service	2,542	2,534	2,096
Total cost of sales	13,023	14,194	12,663
Gross margin	23,094	25,346	22,259
Operating expenses:			
Research and development	5,208	5,325	4,598
Sales and marketing	8,403	8,690	7,401
General and administrative	1,565	1,387	1,151
Amortization of purchased intangible assets	533	499	407
In-process research and development	63	3	81
Total operating expenses	15,772	15,904	13,638
Operating income	$ 7,322	$ 9,442	$ 8,621

NOTES TO CONSOLIDATED FINANCIAL STATEMENTS

11 (In Part): Commitments and Contingencies

e (In Part): Product Warranties and Guarantees

The following table summarizes the activity related to the product warranty liability during fiscal 2009 and 2008 (in millions):

	2009	2008
Balance at beginning of fiscal year	$ 399	$ 340
Provision for warranties issued	374	511
Payments	(452)	(455)
Fair value of warranty liability acquired	—	3
Balance at end of fiscal year	$ 321	$ 399

The Company accrues for warranty costs as part of its cost of sales based on associated material product costs, labor costs for technical support staff, and associated overhead. The products sold are generally covered by a warranty for periods ranging from 90 days to five years, and for some products the Company provides a limited lifetime warranty.

Shipping

3.47

BAXTER INTERNATIONAL INC. (DEC)

(In millions)	2009	2008	2007
Net sales	$12,562	$12,348	$11,263
Cost of sales	6,037	6,218	5,744
Gross margin	6,525	6,130	5,519
Marketing and administrative expenses	2,731	2,698	2,521
Research and development expenses	917	868	760
Restructuring charge	—	—	70
Net interest expense	98	76	22
Other expense, net	45	26	18
Income before income taxes	$ 2,734	$ 2,462	$ 2,128

NOTES TO CONSOLIDATED FINANCIAL STATEMENTS

Note 1 (In Part): Summary of Significant Accounting Policies

Shipping and Handling Costs

Shipping costs, which are costs incurred to physically move product from Baxter's premises to the customer's premises, are classified as marketing and administrative expenses. Handling costs, which are costs incurred to store, move and prepare products for shipment, are classified as cost of sales. Approximately $220 million in 2009, $237 million in 2008 and $231 million in 2007 of shipping costs were classified in marketing and administrative expenses.

LOSSES

Intangible Asset Amortization

3.48

JABIL CIRCUIT, INC. (AUG)

(In thousands)	2009	2008	2007
Net revenue	$11,684,538	$12,779,703	$12,290,592
Cost of revenue	10,965,723	11,911,902	11,478,562
Gross profit	718,815	867,801	812,030
Operating expenses:			
Selling, general and administrative	495,941	491,324	491,967
Research and development	27,321	32,984	36,381
Amortization of intangibles (note 6)	31,039	37,288	29,347
Restructuring and impairment charges	51,894	54,808	72,396
Goodwill impairment charges	1,022,821	—	—
Operating (loss) income	$ (910,201)	$ 251,397	$ 181,939

NOTES TO CONSOLIDATED FINANCIAL STATEMENTS

1 (In Part): Summary of Significant Accounting Policies

F (In Part): Goodwill and Other Intangible Assets

In accordance with Statement of Financial Accounting Standards No. 141, *Business Combinations* ("SFAS 141"), and SFAS 142, *Goodwill and Other Intangible Assets* ("SFAS 142") the Company accounts for goodwill in a purchase business combination as the excess of the cost over the fair value of net assets acquired. Business combinations can also result in other intangible assets being recognized. Amortization of intangible assets, if applicable, occurs over the estimated useful life. In accordance with SFAS 142, the Company tests goodwill for impairment at least annually or more frequently under certain circumstances, using a two-step method. The Company conducts this review during the fourth quarter of each fiscal year absent any triggering events. Furthermore, SFAS 142 also requires that an identifiable intangible asset that is determined to have an indefinite useful economic life not be amortized, but separately tested for impairment at least annually, using a one-step fair value based approach or when certain indicators of impairment are present.

6 (In Part): Goodwill and Other Intangible Assets

The Company reviews long-lived assets, including its intangible assets subject to amortization, which are contractual agreements, customer relationships and intellectual property, for impairment whenever events or changes in circumstances indicate that the carrying amount of such assets may not be recoverable. Recoverability of long-lived assets is measured by a comparison of the carrying amount of the asset group to the future undiscounted net cash flows expected to be generated by those assets. If such assets are considered to be impaired, the impairment charge recognized is the amount by which the carrying amounts of the assets exceeds the fair value of the assets. As a result of the impairment indicators described above, during the first quarter and again in the second quarter of fiscal year 2009, the Company tested its long-lived assets for impairment and determined that there was no impairment. There were no impairment indicators during the third or fourth quarters of fiscal year 2009.

•   •   •   •   •   •

Intangible assets consist primarily of contractual agreements and customer relationships, which are being amortized on a straight-line basis over periods of up to ten years, intellectual property which is being amortized on a straight-line basis over a period of up to five years and a trade name which has an indefinite life. No significant residual value is estimated for the amortizable intangible assets. The value of the Company's intangible assets purchased through business acquisitions is principally determined based on valuations of the net assets acquired. The following tables present the Company's total purchased intangible assets at August 31, 2009 and August 31, 2008 (in thousands):

	Gross Carrying Amount	Accumulated Amortization	Net Carrying Amount
2009			
Contractual agreements & customer relationships	$ 99,583	$(46,313)	$ 53,270
Intellectual property	83,729	(52,459)	31,270
Trade names	46,628	—	46,628
Total	$229,940	$(98,772)	$131,168
2008			
Contractual agreements & customer relationships	$121,855	$(53,636)	$ 68,219
Intellectual property	89,576	(33,606)	55,970
Trade names	48,646	—	48,646
Total	$260,077	$(87,242)	$172,835

The weighted-average amortization period for aggregate net intangible assets at August 31, 2009 is 6.9 years, which includes a weighted-average amortization period of 9.1 years for net contractual agreements and customer relationships and a weighted-average amortization period of 4.5 years for net intellectual property.

Intangible asset amortization for fiscal years 2009, 2008 and 2007 was approximately $31.0 million, $37.3 million, and $29.3 million, respectively. The decrease in the gross carrying amount of the Company's purchased intangible assets at August 31, 2009 was primarily the result of the write-off of certain fully amortized intangible assets. The estimated future amortization expense is as follows (in thousands):

Fiscal Year Ending August 31	Amount
2010	$25,718
2011	21,869
2012	13,965
2013	8,951
2014	7,668
Thereafter	6,369
Total	$84,540

Write-Down of Assets

3.49

ARVINMERITOR, INC. (SEP)

(In millions)	2009	2008	2007
Sales	$ 4,108	$ 6,390	$ 5,720
Cost of sales	(3,804)	(5,828)	(5,323)
Gross margin	304	562	397
Selling, general and administrative	(290)	(415)	(356)
Restructuring costs	(80)	(9)	(62)
Asset impairment charges	(153)	—	—
Goodwill impairment charge	(70)	—	—
Other operating expense, net	(1)	(3)	(1)
Operating income (loss)	$ (290)	$ 135	$ (22)

NOTES TO CONSOLIDATED FINANCIAL STATEMENTS

2 (In Part): Significant Accounting Policies

Impairment of Long-Lived Assets

Long-lived assets, excluding goodwill, to be held and used are reviewed for impairment whenever adverse events or changes in circumstances indicate a possible impairment. An impairment loss is recognized when a long-lived asset's carrying value exceeds the fair value. If business conditions or other factors cause the operating results and cash flows to decline, the company may be required to record impairment charges at that time (see Note 11).

Long-lived assets held for sale are recorded at the lower of their carrying amount or estimated fair value less cost to sell.

11 (In Part): Net Property and Impairments of Long-Lived Assets

In accordance with the FASB guidance on property, plant and equipment, the company reviews the carrying value of long-lived assets, excluding goodwill, to be held and used, for impairment whenever events or changes in circumstances indicate a possible impairment. An impairment loss is recognized when a long-lived asset's carrying value is not recoverable and exceeds estimated fair value.

At December 31, 2008, management determined certain impairment reviews were required due to declines in overall economic conditions including tightening credit markets, stock market declines and significant reductions in current and forecasted production volumes for light and commercial vehicles. As a result, the company recognized pre-tax, non-cash impairment charges of $209 million in the first quarter of fiscal year 2009, primarily related to the LVS segment. A portion of this non-cash charge relates to businesses presented in discontinued operations and accordingly, $56 million is included in loss from discontinued operations in the consolidated statement of operations (see Note 3). The estimated fair value of long-lived assets was calculated based on probability weighted cash flows taking into account current expectations for asset utilization and life expectancy. In addition, liquidation values were considered where appropriate, as well as indicated values from divestiture activities.

The following table describes the significant components of long-lived asset impairments recorded in continuing operations during the first quarter of fiscal year 2009.

(In millions)	Commercial Truck	Industrial	Aftermarket & Trailer	LVS	Total
Land and buildings	$5	$—	$—	$ 34	$ 39
Other (primarily machinery and equipment)	3	—	—	105	108
Total assets impaired[1]	$8	$—	$—	$139	$147

[1] The company also recognized $6 million of non-cash impairment charges associated with certain corporate long-lived assets.

Restructuring of Operations

3.50

MCCORMICK & COMPANY, INCORPORATED (NOV)

(Millions)	2009	2008	2007
Net sales	$3,192.1	$3,176.6	$2,916.2
Cost of goods sold	1,864.9	1,888.4	1,724.4
Gross profit	1,327.2	1,288.2	1,191.8
Selling, general and administrative expense	846.6	870.6	806.9
Impairment charge	—	29.0	—
Restructuring charges	13.7	12.1	30.7
Operating income	$ 466.9	$ 376.5	$ 354.2

NOTES TO CONSOLIDATED FINANCIAL STATEMENTS

11. Restructuring Activities

In November 2005, the Board of Directors approved a restructuring plan to consolidate our global manufacturing, rationalize our distribution facilities, improve our go-to-market strategy, eliminate administrative redundancies and rationalize our joint venture partnerships. From 2005 through 2009, we have recorded total pre-tax charges of $128.7 million for this program. Of these charges, we recorded $99.2 million of severance and other personnel costs and $49.4 million for other exit costs. Asset write-offs were $13.8 million, exclusive of the $33.7 million pre-tax gain on the redemption of our Signature Brands, L.L.C. joint venture (Signature) recorded in 2006. The cash related portion of these charges were $91.3 million through November 30, 2009, including the $14.4 million cash received from the Salinas sale in 2008 and $9.2 million cash received on redemption of our Signature investment in 2006. Another $12.2 million is expected to be paid in 2010.

The actions taken pursuant to the restructuring plan have eliminated approximately 1,300 positions as of November 30, 2009. As of November 30, 2009 this restructuring program was completed.

The following is a summary of restructuring activities:

(Millions)	2009	2008	2007
Pre-tax restructuring charges			
Other restructuring charges	$13.7	$12.1	$ 30.7
Recorded in cost of goods sold	2.5	4.5	3.3
Reduction in operating income	16.2	16.6	34.0
Income tax effect	(5.3)	(5.1)	(10.6)
Loss (gain) on sale of unconsolidated operations, net of tax	—	—	.8
Reduction in net income	$10.9	$11.5	$ 24.2

In 2009, we recorded $8.2 million of severance costs, primarily associated with the reduction of administrative personnel in Europe and to the planned closure of a manufacturing facility in The Netherlands. In addition, we recorded $2.5 million of other exit costs and $5.5 million for asset write-downs related to The Netherlands plant closure. The asset write-downs were for accelerated depreciation and inventory write-offs.

In 2008, we recorded $13.0 million of severance costs, primarily associated with the reduction of administrative personnel in Europe, the U.S. and Canada. In addition, we recorded $9.1 million of other exit costs related to the consolidation of production facilities in Europe and the reorganization of distribution networks in the U.S. and U.K. These restructuring charges were offset by a $5.5 million credit related to the disposal of assets. This credit was primarily the result of a gain on the disposal of our Salinas, California manufacturing facility, which was consolidated with other manufacturing facilities in 2007.

In 2007, we recorded $14.9 million of severance costs, primarily associated with the reduction of administrative personnel in the U.S. and Europe. In addition, we recorded $16.7 million of other exit costs resulting from the closure of manufacturing facilities in Salinas, California and Hunt Valley, Maryland and the consolidation of production facilities in Europe. The remaining $2.4 million of asset write-downs is comprised of inventory write-offs as a result of the closure of the manufacturing facilities in Salinas, California and Hunt Valley, Maryland and accelerated depreciation of assets, mostly offset by the asset gain from the sale of our manufacturing facility in Paisley, Scotland.

The business segment components of the restructuring charges recorded in 2009, 2008 and 2007 are as follows:

(Millions)	2009	2008	2007
Consumer	$12.3	$ 9.7	$23.8
Industrial	3.9	6.9	10.2
Total restructuring charges	$16.2	$16.6	$34.0

The restructuring charges recorded in the consumer business include severance costs and special early retirement benefits associated with our voluntary separation program in several functions in the U.S., Europe and Canada; consolidation of certain manufacturing facilities in Europe; the reorganization of distribution networks in the U.S. and the U.K.; and closure of manufacturing facilities in Salinas, California (offset by the asset gain); Sydney, Australia; Kerava, Finland and The Netherlands.

The restructuring charges recorded in the industrial business include severance costs and special early retirement benefits associated with our voluntary separation program in several functions in the U.S. and Europe; closures of manufacturing facilities in Hunt Valley, Maryland, and Paisley, Scotland (offset by the asset gain) including other exit and inventory write-off costs and accelerated depreciation of assets.

During 2009, 2008 and 2007, we spent $9.0 million, $0.8 million and $42.2 million, respectively, in cash on the restructuring plan.

The major components of the restructuring charges and the remaining accrual balance relating to the restructuring plan as of November 30, 2007, 2008 and 2009 follow:

(Millions)	Severance and Personnel Costs	Asset Write-Downs	Other Exit Costs	Total
Balance at Nov. 30, 2006	$ 20.3	—	$ 3.1	$ 23.4
2007				
Restructuring charges	$ 14.9	$ 2.4	$ 16.7	$ 34.0
Amounts utilized	(28.1)	(2.4)	(19.4)	(49.9)
	$ 7.1	—	$ .4	$ 7.5
2008				
Restructuring charges	$ 13.0	$(5.5)	$ 9.1	$ 16.6
Amounts utilized	(12.3)	5.5	(6.8)	(13.6)
	$ 7.8	—	$ 2.7	$ 10.5
2009				
Restructuring charges	$ 8.2	$ 5.5	$ 2.5	$ 16.2
Amounts utilized	(5.6)	(5.5)	(3.4)	(14.5)
	$ 10.4	—	$ 1.8	$ 12.2

Change in Fair Value of Derivatives

3.51

ANADARKO PETROLEUM CORPORATION (DEC)

(Millions)	2009	2008	2007
Revenues and other			
Gas sales	$2,924	$ 5,770	$ 4,043
Oil and condensate sales	4,022	6,425	5,407
Natural-gas-liquids sales	536	802	719
Gathering, processing and marketing sales	728	1,082	1,487
Gains (losses) on divestitures and other, net	133	1,083	4,760
Reversal of accrual for DWRRA dispute	657	—	—
Total	9,000	15,162	16,416
Costs and expenses			
Oil and gas operating	933	1,104	1,101
Oil and gas transportation and other	590	553	453
Exploration	1,107	1,369	905
Gathering, processing and marketing	617	800	1,025
General and administrative	983	866	936
Depreciation, depletion and amortization	3,532	3,194	2,840
Other taxes	746	1,452	1,234
Impairments	115	223	51
Total	8,623	9,561	8,545
Operating income	377	5,601	7,871
Other (income) expense			
Interest expense	702	732	1,083
(Gains) losses on commodity derivatives, net	408	(561)	524
(Gains) losses on other derivatives, net	(582)	10	9
Other (income) expense, net	(43)	52	(71)
Total	485	233	1,545
Income (loss) from continuing operations before income taxes	$ (108)	$ 5,368	$ 6,326

NOTES TO CONSOLIDATED FINANCIAL STATEMENTS

1 (In Part): Summary of Significant Accounting Policies

Derivative Instruments

Anadarko utilizes derivative instruments in its marketing and trading activities and to manage price risk attributable to the Company's forecasted sales of oil, natural-gas and NGLs production. Anadarko also periodically utilizes derivatives to manage its exposure associated with natural-gas processing, interest rates and foreign currency exchange rates. All derivatives that do not satisfy the normal purchases and sales exception criteria are carried on the balance sheet at fair value and are included in other current assets, other assets, accrued expenses or other long-term liabilities, depending on the derivative position and the expected timing of settlement. To the extent a legal right of offset with a counterparty exists, the Company reports derivative assets and liabilities on a net basis. Anadarko has exposure to credit risk to the extent the derivative-instrument counterparty is unable to satisfy its settlement commitment. The Company actively monitors the creditworthiness of each counterparty and assesses the impact, if any, on its derivative positions.

Through the end of 2006, Anadarko applied hedge accounting to certain commodity and interest-rate derivatives whereby gains and losses on these instruments were recognized in earnings in the same period in which the specifically identified hedged transactions affected earnings. Effective January 1, 2007, Anadarko discontinued its application of hedge accounting to all derivatives. As a result of this change, both realized and unrealized gains and losses on derivative instruments are recognized on a current basis. Net derivative losses attributable to derivatives previously subject to hedge accounting reside in accumulated other comprehensive income as of December 31, 2009 and will be reclassified to earnings in future periods as the economic transactions to which the derivatives relate affect earnings. See Note 8.

8 (In Part): Derivative Instruments

Objective and Strategy

The Company is exposed to commodity price and interest-rate risk, and management considers it prudent to periodically reduce the Company's exposure to cash flow variability resulting from commodity price changes and interest-rate fluctuations. Accordingly, the Company enters into certain derivative instruments in order to manage its exposure to these risks.

Futures, swaps and options are used to manage the Company's cash flow exposure to commodity price risk inherent in the Company's oil and gas production and gas-processing operations (Oil and Gas Production/Processing Derivative Activities). Futures contracts and commodity swap agreements are used to fix the price of expected future oil and gas sales at major industry trading locations, such as Henry Hub, Louisiana for gas and Cushing, Oklahoma for oil. Basis swaps are used to fix or float the price differential between the product price at one market location versus another. Options are used to establish a floor and a ceiling price (collar) for expected future oil and gas sales. Derivative instruments are also used to manage commodity price risk inherent in customer pricing requirements and to fix margins on the future sale of natural gas and NGLs from the Company's leased storage facilities (Marketing and Trading Derivative Activities).

The Company may also enter into physical-delivery sales contracts to manage cash flow variability. These contracts call for the receipt or delivery of physical product at a specified location and price, which may be fixed or market-based.

Interest-rate swaps are used to fix or float interest rates on existing or anticipated indebtedness. The purpose of these instruments is to mitigate the Company's existing or anticipated exposure to unfavorable interest-rate changes.

The Company does not apply hedge accounting to any of its derivative instruments. The application of hedge accounting was discontinued by the Company for periods beginning on or after January 1, 2007. As a result, both realized and unrealized gains and losses associated with derivative instruments are recognized in earnings. Net derivative losses attributable to derivatives previously subject to hedge accounting reside in accumulated other comprehensive income (loss) and are reclassified to earnings in future periods as the economic transactions to which the derivatives relate are recorded in earnings.

The accumulated other comprehensive loss balances related to commodity derivatives at December 31, 2009 and December 31, 2008, were $10 million ($7 million after tax) and $22 million ($14 million after tax), respectively. The accumulated other comprehensive loss balances related to interest-rate derivatives at December 31, 2009 and December 31, 2008, were $141 million ($89 million after tax) and $163 million ($104 million after tax), respectively.

Oil and Gas Production/Processing Derivative Activities

Below is a summary of the Company's derivative instruments related to its oil and gas production as of December 31, 2009. The natural-gas prices listed below are New York Mercantile Exchange (NYMEX) Henry Hub prices. The crude-oil prices listed below reflect a combination of NYMEX Cushing and London Brent Dated prices.

	2010	2011	2012
Natural gas			
Three-way collars (thousand MMBtu/d)	1,630	480	500
Average price per MMBtu			
Ceiling sold price (call)	$ 8.23	$ 8.29	$9.03
Floor purchased price (put)	$ 5.59	$ 6.50	$6.50
Floor sold price (put)	$ 4.22	$ 5.00	$5.00
Fixed-price contracts (thousand MMBtu/d)	90	90	—
Average price per MMBtu	$ 6.10	$ 6.17	$ —
Basis swaps (thousand MMBtu/d)	620	45	—
Price per MMBtu	$(0.98)	$(1.74)	$ —

MMBtu—million British thermal units.
MMBtu/d—million British thermal units per day.

	2010	2011	2012
Crude oil			
Three-way collars (MBbls/d)	129	3	2
Average price per barrel			
Ceiling sold price (call)	$90.73	$86.00	$92.50
Floor purchased price (put)	$64.34	$50.00	$50.00
Floor sold price (put)	$49.34	$35.00	$35.00

MBbls/d—thousand barrels per day.

A three-way collar is a combination of three options: a sold call, a purchased put and a sold put. The sold call establishes the maximum price that the Company will receive for the contracted commodity volumes. The purchased put establishes the minimum price that the Company will receive for the contracted volumes unless the market price for the commodity falls below the sold put strike price, at which point the minimum price equals the reference price (i.e., NYMEX) plus the excess of the purchased put strike price over the sold put strike price.

Marketing and Trading Derivative Activities

In addition to the positions in the above tables, the Company also engages in marketing and trading activities, which include physical product sales and derivative transactions entered into to reduce commodity price risk associated with certain physical product sales. At December 31, 2009 and December 31, 2008, the Company had outstanding physical transactions for 46 billion cubic feet (Bcf) and 51 Bcf, respectively, offset by derivative transactions for 17 Bcf and 34 Bcf, respectively, for net positions of 29 Bcf and 17 Bcf, respectively.

Interest-Rate Derivatives

As discussed in Note 10, during 2009, Anadarko issued fixed-rate senior notes in the aggregate principal amount of $2.0 billion. In advance of certain of these debt issuances, Anadarko entered into derivative financial instruments, effectively hedging the U.S. Treasury portion of the coupon rate on a portion of this debt. These derivative instruments were settled concurrently with the associated debt issuances, resulting in a realized loss of $16 million for the year ended December 31, 2009, reflected in (gains) losses on other derivatives, net.

As of December 31, 2009, the Company had scheduled debt maturities of approximately $3.5 billion in 2011 and 2012. In anticipation of refinancing a portion of these maturing debt obligations, in December 2008 and January 2009 Anadarko entered into interest-rate swap agreements to hedge a portion of the fixed interest rate it would pay on an aggregate notional principal amount of $3.0 billion, over a reference term of either 10 years or 30 years, beginning in 2011 and 2012. The swap instruments include a provision that requires both the termination of the swaps and cash settlement in full at the start of the reference period. A summary of the swaps detailing the outstanding notional principal amounts and the associated reference periods is shown in the table below.

Increases in the reference U.S. Treasury rates since contract inception have increased the value of this swap portfolio to Anadarko, the fixed-rate payor. During the second quarter of 2009, the Company revised the contractual terms of this swap portfolio to increase the weighted-average interest rate it is required to pay from approximately 3.25% to approximately 4.80%, and realized $552 million in cash. This realized gain was recorded to (gains) losses on other derivatives, net, as were unrealized gains of $57 million, for the year ended December 31, 2009, which were attributable to further fair-value changes of the Company's swap portfolio.

The Company's interest-rate derivative positions outstanding as of December 31, 2009, are as follows:

	Reference Period		
(Millions)	Start	End	Weighted-Average Interest Rate
Notional principal amount:			
$ 750	October 2011	October 2021	4.72%
$1,250	October 2011	October 2041	4.83%
$ 250	October 2012	October 2022	4.91%
$ 750	October 2012	October 2042	4.80%

Effect of Derivative Instruments—Balance Sheet

The fair value of all oil and gas and interest-rate derivative instruments not designated as hedging instruments (including physical-delivery sales contracts) is included in the table below.

(Millions)	Balance Sheet Classification	Gross Asset Derivatives		Gross Liability Derivatives	
		2009	2008	2009	2008
Derivatives					
Commodity	Other current assets	$140	$709	$ (63)	$(134)
	Other assets	82	156	(6)	(24)
	Accrued expenses	195	—	(417)	(14)
	Other liabilities	25	1	(52)	(28)
Total commodity derivatives		442	866	(538)	(200)
Interest rate	Other assets	53	3	—	—
	Accrued expenses	—	—	—	(10)
	Other liabilities	—	—	(3)	—
Total derivatives		$495	$869	$(541)	$(210)

Effect of Derivative Instruments—Statement of Income

The unrealized and realized gain or loss amounts and classification related to derivative instruments not designated as hedging instruments are as follows:

(Millions)	Classification of (Gain) Loss Recognized	Amount of (Gain) Loss Recognized		
		2009	2008	2007
Derivatives				
Commodity	Gathering, processing and marketing sales[*]	$ 37	$ (4)	$ 80
	(Gains) losses on commodity derivatives, net	408	(561)	524
Interest rate	(Gains) losses on other derivatives, net	(582)	10	9
Total derivative (gain) loss		$(137)	$(555)	$613

[*] Represents the effect of marketing and trading derivative activities.

ATT-SEC 3.51

The unrealized gain or loss amounts and classification related to derivative instruments included in the table above not designated as hedging instruments are as follows:

(Millions)	Classification of Unrealized (Gain) Loss Recognized	Amount of Unrealized (Gain) Loss Recognized		
		2009	2008	2007
Derivatives				
Commodity	Gathering, processing and marketing sales	$ 39	$ (29)	$ 52
	(Gains) losses on commodity derivatives, net	735	(900)	1,048
Interest rate	(Gains) losses on other derivatives, net	(57)	10	9
Total derivative unrealized (gain) loss		$717	$(919)	$1,109

Credit-Risk Considerations

The financial integrity of exchange-traded contracts are assured by NYMEX or the Intercontinental Exchange through their systems of financial safeguards and transaction guarantees and are subject to nominal credit risk. Over-the-counter traded swaps, options and futures contracts expose the Company to counterparty credit risk. The Company monitors the creditworthiness of each of its counterparties, establishes credit limits according to the Company's credit policies and guidelines, and assesses the impact, if any, of counterparties' creditworthiness on fair value. The Company has the ability to require cash collateral or letters of credit to mitigate credit-risk exposure. The Company also routinely exercises its contractual right to net realized gains against realized losses when settling with its counterparties.

The Company's net asset derivatives recorded at fair value on the balance sheet include amounts attributable to agreements entered into with financial institutions. Approximately $442 million of the Company's $495 million gross derivative asset balance at December 31, 2009 was attributable to open positions with financial institutions. The Company has netting and setoff agreements with each of these counterparties, which permit the net settlement of these gross derivative assets against gross derivative liabilities with this same group of counterparties. As of December 31, 2009, $321 million of the Company's $541 million gross derivative liability balance is permitted to offset the gross derivative asset balance. The table below includes the financial impact of our netting arrangements on the fair value of the Company's outstanding derivative positions.

Certain of the Company's derivative instruments contain provisions requiring either full or partial collateralization of the Company's obligations, or the immediate settlement of all such obligations in the event of a downgrade in the Company's credit rating to a level below investment grade from major credit rating agencies. The aggregate fair value of all derivative instruments with credit-risk-related contingent features for which a net liability position existed on December 31, 2009 was $146 million. This amount represents the amount that the Company would have to either collateralize or cash settle in the event the Company's credit rating was downgraded to a level below investment grade and the credit-risk-related features of such instruments were exercised.

Fair Value

The fair value of commodity-futures contracts are based on inputs that are quoted prices in active markets for identical assets or liabilities, resulting in Level 1 categorization of such measurements. The valuation of physical-delivery purchase and sale agreements, over-the-counter financial swaps and three-way collars are based on similar transactions observable in active markets or industry-standard models that primarily rely on market-observable inputs. Substantially all of the assumptions for industry-standard models are observable in active markets throughout the full term of the instrument. Therefore, the Company categorizes these measurements as Level 2.

The following tables set forth, by level within the fair-value hierarchy, the fair value of the Company's financial assets and liabilities.

(Millions)	Level 1	Level 2	Level 3	Netting and Collateral[1]	Total
2009					
Assets:					
Commodity derivatives	$ 4	$ 438	$—	$(289)	$ 153
Interest-rate derivatives	—	53	—	—	53
Total	$ 4	$ 491	$—	$(289)	$ 206
Liabilities:					
Commodity derivatives	$(6)	$(532)	$—	$ 333	$(205)
Interest-rate derivatives	—	(3)	—	—	(3)
Total	$(6)	$(535)	$—	$ 333	$(208)

[1] Represents the impact of netting assets, liabilities and collateral with counterparties with which the right of setoff exists. Cash collateral held by counterparties from Anadarko was $105 million at December 31, 2009. Anadarko held no cash collateral from counterparties at December 31, 2009.

Impairment of Intangibles

3.52

BEST BUY CO., INC. (FEB)

($ in millions)	2009	2008	2007
Revenue	$45,015	$40,023	$35,934
Cost of goods sold	34,017	30,477	27,165
Gross profit	10,998	9,546	8,769
Selling, general and administrative expenses	8,984	7,385	6,770
Restructuring charges	78	—	—
Goodwill and tradename impairment	66	—	—
Operating income	$ 1,870	$ 2,161	$ 1,999

NOTES TO CONSOLIDATED FINANCIAL STATEMENTS ($ in millions)

1 (In Part): Summary of Significant Accounting Policies

Goodwill and Intangible Assets (In Part)

Goodwill

Goodwill is the excess of the purchase price over the fair value of identifiable net assets acquired in business combinations accounted for under the purchase method. We do not amortize goodwill but test it for impairment annually in the fiscal fourth quarter, or when indications of potential impairment exist. These indicators would include a significant change in operating performance, the business climate, legal factors, competition, or a planned sale or disposition of a significant portion of the business, among other factors. We test for goodwill impairment utilizing a fair value approach at the reporting unit level. A reporting unit is an operating segment, or a business unit one level below that operating segment, for which discrete financial information is prepared and regularly reviewed by segment management. We have deemed our reporting units to be one level below our operating segments, Domestic and International, which is the level at which segment management regularly reviews operating results and makes resource allocation decisions.

Tradenames

We have indefinite-lived intangible assets related to our Pacific Sales, Speakeasy and Napster tradenames which are included in our Domestic segment. We also have indefinite-lived intangible assets related to our Future Shop and Five Star tradenames and definite-lived intangible assets related to our The Carphone Warehouse and The Phone House tradenames, which are included in our International segment.

Our valuation of identifiable intangible assets acquired is based on information and assumptions available to us at the time of acquisition, using income and market approaches to determine fair value. We test our tradenames annually for impairment, or when indications of potential impairment exist.

Our tradenames were as follows:

	2009	2008
Indefinite-lived	$104	$97
Definite-lived	69	—
Total	$173	$97

Impairment Testing

The impairment test for goodwill involves comparing the fair value of a reporting unit to its carrying amount, including goodwill. If the carrying amount of the reporting unit exceeds its fair value, a second step is required to measure the goodwill impairment loss. The second step includes hypothetically valuing all the tangible and intangible assets of the reporting unit as if the reporting unit had been acquired in a business combination. Then, the implied fair value of the reporting unit's goodwill is compared to the carrying amount of that goodwill. If the carrying amount of the reporting unit's goodwill exceeds the implied fair value of the goodwill, we recognize an impairment loss in an amount equal to the excess, not to exceed the carrying amount. We determine the fair values calculated in an impairment test using free cash flow models involving assumptions that are based upon what we believe a hypothetical marketplace participant would use in estimating fair value on the measurement date. The key assumptions relate to margins, growth rates, capital expenditures, terminal values and weighted-average cost of capital rates. In developing these assumptions, we compare the resulting estimated enterprise value derived by the aggregate fair values of our reporting units to our market enterprise value plus an estimated control premium.

The impairment test for tradenames involves comparing the fair value to its carrying amount. We derive fair value based on a discounted cash flow model (e.g., relief from royalty approach) using assumptions about revenue growth rates, royalty rates, the appropriate discount rates relative to risk and estimates of terminal values.

If changes in growth rates, estimated cash flows, economic conditions, discount rates or estimates of terminal values were to occur, goodwill or tradenames may become impaired.

During the fourth quarter of fiscal 2009, we completed our annual impairment testing of our goodwill and tradenames, using the valuation techniques described above, and recorded goodwill and tradename impairment charges of $62 and $4, respectively, related to our Speakeasy reporting unit. The decline in the fair value of our Speakeasy reporting unit below its book value was primarily the result of lower than expected revenue growth relative to the assumptions we made in the prior fiscal year, partially due to slower-than-anticipated synergies with Best Buy.

The changes in the carrying amount of goodwill and indefinite-lived tradenames by segment were as follows in fiscal 2009, 2008 and 2007:

	Goodwill			Tradenames		
	Domestic	International	Total	Domestic	International	Total
Balances at February 25, 2006	$ 6	$ 551	$ 557	$—	$ 44	$ 44
Acquisitions	369	27	396	17	21	38
Tax adjustment[1]	—	(21)	(21)	—	—	—
Changes in foreign currency exchange rates	—	(13)	(13)	—	(1)	(1)
Balances at March 3, 2007	375	544	919	17	64	81
Acquisitions	75	(4)	71	6	—	6
Tax adjustment[1]	—	(3)	(3)	—	—	—
Changes in foreign currency exchange rates	—	101	101	—	10	10
Balances at March 1, 2008	450	638	1,088	23	74	97
Acquisitions	46	1,641	1,687	13	8	21
Tax adjustment[1]	—	17	17	—	—	—
Impairments	(62)	—	(62)	(4)	—	(4)
Changes in foreign currency exchange rates	—	(527)	(527)	—	(10)	(10)
Balances at February 28, 2009	$434	$1,769	$2,203	$32	$ 72	$104

[1] Adjustment related to the resolution of certain tax matters associated with our acquisition of Future Shop and Five Star stores.

Foreign Currency Transactions

3.53

NEWMARKET CORPORATION (DEC)

(In thousands)	2009	2008	2007
Net sales	$1,530,122	$1,617,431	$1,374,874
Cost of goods sold	1,066,862	1,302,937	1,078,302
Gross profit	463,260	314,494	296,572
Selling, general, and administrative expenses	114,900	116,382	111,115
Research, development, and testing expenses	86,072	81,752	76,834
Operating profit	$ 262,288	$ 116,360	$ 108,623

NOTES TO CONSOLIDATED FINANCIAL STATEMENTS

22. Gains and Losses on Foreign Currency

Transactions conducted in a foreign currency resulted in a net loss of $8 million in 2009, a net gain of $3 million in 2008, and a net loss of $9 thousand in 2007. These amounts are reported in cost of sales.

Sale of Assets

3.54

THE MANITOWOC COMPANY, INC. (DEC)

(Millions of dollars)	2009	2008	2007
Operations			
Net sales	$3,782.6	$4,503.0	$3,684.0
Costs and expenses:			
Cost of sales	2,958.0	3,487.2	2,822.5
Engineering, selling and administrative expenses	549.7	455.1	377.9
Amortization expense	39.5	11.6	5.8
Gain on sale of parts line	—	—	(3.3)
Pension settlements	—	—	5.3
Goodwill impairment	548.8	—	—
Intangible asset impairment	151.2	—	—
Integration expense	3.6	7.6	—
Loss on sale of product lines	3.4	—	—
Restructuring expense	39.6	21.7	—
Total costs and expenses	4,293.8	3,983.2	3,208.2
Operating earnings (loss) from continuing operations	$ (511.2)	$ 519.8	$ 475.8

NOTES TO CONSOLIDATED FINANCIAL STATEMENTS

25 (In Part): Sale of Product and Parts Lines

During December of 2009, the company sold two product lines within its Foodservice segment for aggregate net proceeds of $15.0 million and recognized a loss on the sale of $3.4 million. The two product lines that were divested were the company's Lincoln Smallwares products and its Merco product category. The Smallwares products was sold to The Vollrath Company, L.L.C. and included products such as pots, pans, baking sheets and other cooking implements as well as manual food-preparation equipment (i.e. slicers, peelers). The Merco product category was sold to Hatco Corporation and included food warming equipment, merchandisers, toasters, and racking/dispensing systems. The company recorded a loss of $3.3 million for the sale of the Smallwares products and a loss of $0.1 million for the sale of the Merco products.

Debt Extinguishment

3.55

ARROW ELECTRONICS, INC. (DEC)

(In thousands)	2009	2008	2007
Sales	$14,684,101	$16,761,009	$15,984,992
Costs and expenses:			
Cost of products sold	12,933,207	14,478,296	13,699,715
Selling, general and administrative expenses	1,305,566	1,607,261	1,519,908
Depreciation and amortization	67,027	69,286	66,719
Restructuring, integration, and other charges	105,514	80,955	11,745
Impairment charge	—	1,018,780	—
	14,411,314	17,254,578	15,298,087
Operating income (loss)	272,787	(493,569)	686,905
Equity in earnings of affiliated companies	4,731	6,549	6,906
Loss on prepayment of debt	5,312	—	—
Loss on the write-down of an investment	—	10,030	—
Interest and other financing expense, net	83,285	99,863	101,628
Income (loss) before income taxes	$ 188,921	$ (596,913)	$ 592,183

NOTES TO CONSOLIDATED FINANCIAL STATEMENTS
(Dollars in thousands)

6 (In Part): Debt

Long-term debt consists of the following at December 31:

	2009	2008
9.15% senior notes, due 2010	$ —	$ 199,994
Bank term loan, due 2012	200,000	200,000
6.875% senior notes, due 2013	349,765	349,694
6.875% senior debentures, due 2018	198,241	198,032
6.00% notes, due 2020	299,909	—
7.5% senior debentures, due 2027	197,610	197,470
Cross-currency swap, due 2010	—	36,467
Cross-currency swap, due 2011	12,497	9,985
Interest rate swaps designated as fair value hedges	9,556	21,394
Other obligations with various interest rates and due dates	8,560	10,949
	$1,276,138	$1,223,985

The 7.5% senior debentures are not redeemable prior to their maturity. The 9.15% senior notes, 6.875% senior notes, 6.875% senior debentures, and 6.00% notes may be called at the option of the company subject to "make whole" clauses.

● ● ● ● ● ●

During 2009, the company repurchased $130,455 principal amount of its 9.15% senior notes due 2010. The related loss on the repurchase, including the premium paid and write-off of the deferred financing costs, offset by the gain for terminating a portion of the interest rate swaps aggregated $5,312 ($3,228 net of related taxes or $.03 per share on both a basic and diluted basis) and was recognized as a loss on prepayment of debt.

Litigation Settlement

3.56

LAM RESEARCH CORPORATION (JUN)

(In thousands)	2009	2008	2007
Total revenue	$1,115,946	$2,474,911	$2,566,576
Cost of goods sold	706,219	1,282,494	1,261,522
Cost of goods sold—restructuring and asset impairments	20,993	12,610	—
Cost of goods sold—409A expense	—	6,401	—
Total costs of goods sold	727,212	1,301,505	1,261,522
Gross margin	388,734	1,173,406	1,305,054
Research and development	288,269	323,759	285,348
Selling, general and administrative	233,061	287,282	241,046
Goodwill impairment	96,255	—	—
Restructuring and asset impairments	44,513	6,366	—
409A expense	3,232	44,494	—
Legal judgment	4,647	—	—
In-process research and development	—	2,074	—
Total operating expenses	669,977	663,975	526,394
Operating income (loss)	$ (281,243)	$ 509,431	$ 778,660

NOTES TO CONSOLIDATED FINANCIAL STATEMENTS

Note 20. Legal Proceedings

From time to time, the Company has received notices from third parties alleging infringement of such parties' patent or other intellectual property rights by the Company's products. In such cases it is the Company's policy to defend the claims, or if considered appropriate, negotiate licenses on commercially reasonable terms. However, no assurance can be given that the Company will be able in the future to negotiate necessary licenses on commercially reasonable terms, or at all, or that any litigation resulting from such claims would not have a material adverse effect on the Company's consolidated financial position or operating results.

Aspect Systems, Inc. ("Aspect") sued the Company for breach of contract and various business torts arising out of a transaction in which the Company licensed Aspect to sell certain of the Company's legacy Autoetch and Drytek products. The case went to trial in the United States District Court for the District of Arizona in December of 2008, resulting in a jury verdict in favor of Aspect. The Company filed an appeal from the ensuing judgment, which is now pending. The Company recorded the amount of the legal judgment of $4.6 million in its consolidated statement of operations for the year ended June 28, 2009.

Equity in Losses of Investee

3.57

TIME WARNER INC. (DEC)

(Millions)	2009	2008	2007
Revenues:			
Subscription	$ 8,859	$ 8,397	$ 7,838
Advertising	5,161	5,798	5,731
Content	11,020	11,435	11,709
Other	745	886	933
Total revenues	25,785	26,516	26,211
Costs of revenues	(14,438)	(14,953)	(15,393)
Selling, general and administrative	(6,153)	(6,692)	(6,203)
Amortization of intangible assets	(319)	(356)	(306)
Restructuring costs	(212)	(327)	(114)
Asset impairments	(85)	(7,213)	(34)
Gain (loss) on sale of assets	(33)	(3)	6
Operating income (loss)	4,545	(3,028)	4,167
Interest expense, net	(1,155)	(1,325)	(1,412)
Other loss, net	(107)	(44)	(9)
Income (loss) from continuing operations before income taxes	$ 3,283	$ (4,397)	$ 2,746

NOTES TO CONSOLIDATED FINANCIAL STATEMENTS

1 (In Part): Basis of Presentation and Summary of Significant Accounting Policies

Summary of Critical and Significant Accounting Policies (In Part)

Investments (In Part)

Investments in companies in which Time Warner has significant influence, but less than a controlling voting interest, are accounted for using the equity method. Significant influence is generally presumed to exist when Time Warner owns between 20% and 50% of the investee, holds substantial management rights or holds an interest of less than 20% where the investee is a limited liability partnership or limited liability corporation that is treated as a flow-through entity.

Under the equity method of accounting, only Time Warner's investment in and amounts due to and from the equity investee are included in the consolidated balance sheet; only Time Warner's share of the investee's earnings (losses) is included in the consolidated statement of operations; and only the dividends, cash distributions, loans or other cash received from the investee, additional cash investments, loan repayments or other cash paid to the investee are included in the consolidated statement of cash flows.

4 (In Part): Investments

The Company's investments consist of equity-method investments, fair-value and other investments, including available-for-sale securities, and cost-method investments. Time Warner's investments, by category, consist of (millions):

	2009	2008
Equity-method investments	$ 280	$ 313
Fair-value and other investments, including available-for-sale securities	578	608
Cost-method investments	323	106
Total	$1,181	$1,027

Equity-Method Investments

At December 31, 2009, investments accounted for using the equity method primarily represented certain network and filmed entertainment ventures which are generally 20–50% owned. No single investment individually or in the aggregate is considered significant for the periods presented.

17 (In Part): Additional Financial Information

Other Loss, Net

Other loss, net, consists of (millions):

	2009	2008	2007
Investment gains (losses), net	$ (21)	$(60)	$ 75
Amounts related to the separation of TWC	14	(11)	—
Costs related to the separation of AOL	(15)	—	—
Income (loss) on equity method investees	(63)	18	(24)
Losses on accounts receivable	(11)	(35)	(56)
Other	(11)	44	(4)
Total other loss, net	$(107)	$(44)	$ (9)

Environmental Clean-Up

3.58

THE SHERWIN-WILLIAMS COMPANY (DEC)

(Thousands of dollars)	2009	2008	2007
Net sales	$7,094,249	$7,979,727	$8,005,292
Cost of goods sold	3,831,080	4,480,927	4,406,365
Gross profit	3,263,169	3,498,800	3,598,927
Selling, general and administrative expenses	2,534,775	2,643,580	2,597,121
Other general expense—net	33,620	19,319	17,530
Impairments of trademarks and goodwill	14,144	54,604	16,123
Loss on dissolution of a foreign subsidiary	21,923		
Interest expense	40,026	65,684	71,630
Interest and net investment income	(2,393)	(3,930)	(14,099)
Other expense (income)—net	(1,743)	5,068	(2,321)
Income before income taxes	$ 622,817	$ 714,475	$ 912,943

NOTES TO CONSOLIDATED FINANCIAL STATEMENTS (Thousands of dollars)

Note 1 (In Part): Significant Accounting Policies

Environmental Matters

Capital expenditures for ongoing environmental compliance measures were recorded in Property, plant and equipment, and related expenses were included in the normal operating expenses of conducting business. The Company is involved with environmental investigation and remediation activities at some of its currently and formerly owned sites and at a number of third-party sites. The Company accrued for environmental-related activities for which commitments or clean-up plans have been developed and when such costs could be reasonably estimated based on industry standards and professional judgment. All accrued amounts were recorded on an undiscounted basis. Environmental-related expenses included direct costs of investigation and remediation and indirect costs such as compensation and benefits for employees directly involved in the investigation and remediation activities and fees paid to outside engineering, consulting and law firms. See Notes 9 and 14.

Note 9 (In Part): Other Long-Term Liabilities

The operations of the Company, like those of other companies in our industry, are subject to various domestic and foreign environmental laws and regulations. These laws and regulations not only govern current operations and products, but also impose potential liability on the Company for past operations. Management expects environmental laws and regulations to impose increasingly stringent requirements upon the Company and the industry in the future. Management believes that the Company conducts its operations in compliance with applicable environmental laws and regulations and has implemented various programs designed to protect the environment and promote continued compliance.

The Company is involved with environmental investigation and remediation activities at some of its currently and formerly owned sites (including sites which were previously owned and/or operated by businesses acquired by the Company). In addition, the Company, together with other parties, has been designated a potentially responsible party under federal and state environmental protection laws for the investigation and remediation of environmental contamination and hazardous waste at a number of third-party sites, primarily Superfund sites. In general, these laws provide that potentially responsible parties may be held jointly and severally liable for investigation and remediation costs regardless of fault. The Company may be similarly designated with respect to additional third-party sites in the future.

The Company initially provides for estimated costs of environmental-related activities relating to its past operations and third-party sites for which commitments or cleanup plans have been developed and when such costs can be reasonably estimated based on industry standards and professional judgment. These estimated costs are based on currently available facts regarding each site. If the best estimate of costs can only be identified as a range and no specific amount within that range can be determined more likely than any other amount within the range, the minimum of the range is provided. The Company continuously assesses its potential liability for investigation and remediation-related activities and adjusts its environmental-related accruals as information becomes available upon which more accurate costs can be reasonably estimated and as additional accounting guidelines are issued. Included in Other long-term liabilities at December 31, 2009, 2008, and 2007 were accruals for extended environmental-related activities of $106,168, $128,179 and $133,333, respectively. Included in Other accruals at December 31, 2009, 2008 and 2007 were accruals for estimated costs of current investigation and remediation activities of $64,685, $52,555 and $60,447, respectively.

Actual costs incurred may vary from the accrued estimates due to the inherent uncertainties involved including, among others, the number and financial condition of parties involved with respect to any given site, the volumetric contribution which may be attributed to the Company relative to that attributed to other parties, the nature and magnitude of the wastes involved, the various technologies that can be used for remediation and the determination of acceptable remediation with respect to a particular site. If the Company's future loss contingency is ultimately determined to be at the unaccrued maximum of the estimated range of possible outcomes for every site for which costs can be reasonably estimated, the Company's accrual for environmental-related activities would be $99,512 higher than the minimum accruals at December 31, 2009.

Four of the Company's currently and formerly owned manufacturing sites accounted for the majority of the accrual for environmental-related activities and the unaccrued maximum of the estimated range of possible outcomes at December 31, 2009. At December 31, 2009, $129,439, or 75.8 percent of the total accrual, related directly to these four sites. In the aggregate unaccrued maximum of $99,512 at December 31, 2009, $60,950, or 61.2 percent, related to these four sites. While environmental investigations and remedial actions are in different stages at these sites, additional investigations, remedial actions and monitoring will likely be required at each site.

Management cannot presently estimate the ultimate potential loss contingencies related to these sites or other less significant sites until such time as a substantial portion of the investigation at the sites is completed and remedial action plans are developed. In the event any future loss contingency significantly exceeds the current amount accrued, the recording of the ultimate liability may result in a material impact on net income for the annual or interim period during which the additional costs are accrued. Management does not believe that any potential liability ultimately attributed to the Company for its environmental-related matters will have a material adverse effect on the Company's financial condition, liquidity, or cash flow due to the extended period of time during which environmental investigation and remediation takes place. An estimate of the potential impact on the Company's operations cannot be made due to the aforementioned uncertainties.

Management expects these contingent environmental-related liabilities to be resolved over an extended period of time. Management is unable to provide a more specific time frame due to the indefinite amount of time to conduct investigation activities at any site, the indefinite amount of time to obtain environmental agency approval, as necessary, with respect to investigation and remediation activities, and the indefinite amount of time necessary to conduct remediation activities.

Note 14 (In Part): Other

Other General Expense—Net

Included in Other general expense—net were the following:

	2009	2008	2007
Provisions for environmental matters—net	$24,705	$ 6,947	$ 28,391
Loss (gain) on disposition of assets	972	6,440	(10,422)
Net expense (income) of exit or disposal activities	7,943	5,932	(439)
Total	$33,620	$19,319	$ 17,530

Provisions for environmental matters-net represent initial provisions for site-specific estimated costs of environmental investigation or remediation and increases or decreases to environmental-related accruals as information becomes available upon which more accurate costs can be reasonably estimated and as additional accounting guidelines are issued. Environmental-related accruals are not recorded net of insurance proceeds in accordance with the Offsetting Subtopic of the Balance Sheet Topic of the ASC. See Note 9 for further details on the Company's environmental-related activities.

Sale of Receivables

3.59

TENNECO INC. (DEC)

(Millions)	2009	2008	2007
Revenues			
Net sales and operating revenues	$4,649	$5,916	$6,184
Costs and expenses			
Cost of sales (exclusive of depreciation and amortization shown below)	3,875	5,063	5,210
Goodwill impairment charge	—	114	—
Engineering, research, and development	97	127	114
Selling, general, and administrative	344	392	399
Depreciation and amortization of intangibles	221	222	205
	4,537	5,918	5,928
Other income (expense)			
Loss on sale of receivables	(9)	(10)	(10)
Other income (expense)	(11)	9	6
	(20)	(1)	(4)
Income (loss) before interest expense, income taxes, and noncontrolling interests	$ 92	$ (3)	$ 252

NOTES TO CONSOLIDATED FINANCIAL STATEMENTS

1 (In Part): Summary of Accounting Policies

Sales of Accounts Receivable

We have an agreement to sell an interest in some of our U.S. trade accounts receivable to a third party. Receivables become eligible for the program on a daily basis, at which time the receivables are sold to the third party without recourse, net of a discount, through a wholly-owned subsidiary. Under this agreement, as well as individual agreements with third parties in Europe, we have accounts receivable of $137 million and $179 million at December 31, 2009 and 2008, respectively. We recognized a loss of $9 million, $10 million, and $10 million during 2009, 2008, and 2007 respectively, on these sales of trade accounts, representing the discount from book values at which these receivables were sold to the third party. The discount rate varies based on funding cost incurred by the third party, which has averaged approximately five percent during 2009. In the U.S. securitization program, we retain ownership of the remaining interest in the pool of receivables not sold to the third party. The retained interest represents a credit enhancement for the program. We record the retained interest based upon the amount we expect to collect from our customers, which approximates book value. In February 2010, the U.S. program was amended and extended to February 18, 2011 at a facility size of $100 million. As part of the renewal, the margin we pay the banks decreased.

Merger Costs

3.60

THE BLACK & DECKER CORPORATION (DEC)

(Dollars in millions)	2009	2008	2007
Sales	$4,775.1	$6,086.1	$6,563.2
Cost of goods sold	3,188.6	4,087.7	4,336.2
Selling, general, and administrative expenses	1,266.4	1,521.6	1,625.8
Merger-related expenses	58.8	—	—
Restructuring and exit costs	11.9	54.7	19.0
Operating income	$ 249.4	$ 422.1	$ 582.2

NOTES TO CONSOLIDATED FINANCIAL STATEMENTS

Note 2. Definitive Merger Agreement

On November 2, 2009, the Corporation announced that it had entered into a definitive merger agreement to create Stanley Black & Decker, Inc. in an all-stock transaction. Under the terms of the transaction, which has been approved by the Boards of Directors of both the Corporation and The Stanley Works, the Corporation's shareholders will receive a fixed ratio of 1.275 shares of The Stanley Works common stock for each share of the Corporation's common stock that they own. Consummation of the transaction is subject to customary closing conditions, including obtaining certain regulatory approvals as well as shareholder approval from the shareholders of both the Corporation and The Stanley Works.

On December 29, 2009, the Corporation announced that the Hart-Scott-Rodino antitrust review period had expired. The expiration of the Hart-Scott-Rodino antitrust review period satisfies one of the conditions to the closing of the transaction. On February 2, 2010, the Corporation and The Stanley Works announced that both companies will hold special shareholder meetings on March 12, 2010, to vote on the combination of their businesses. In connection with the proposed transaction, The Stanley Works has filed with the Securities and Exchange Commission (SEC) a Registration Statement on Form S-4 (File No. 333-163509) that includes a joint proxy statement of Stanley and the Corporation that also constitutes a prospectus of Stanley. The joint proxy statement of both the Corporation and The Stanley Works was mailed to shareholders commencing on or about Febuary 4, 2010. Investors and security holders are urged to read the joint proxy statement/prospectus and any other relevant documents filed with the SEC because they contain important information. The Corporation and The Stanley Works expect that closing of the proposed transaction will occur on March 12, 2010.

The provisions of the definitive merger agreement provide for a termination fee, in the amount of $125 million, to be paid by either the Corporation or by The Stanley Works under certain circumstances, including circumstances in which the Board of Directors of The Stanley Works or the Corporation withdraw or modify adversely their recommendation of the proposed transaction.

The Corporation recognized merger-related expenses of $58.8 million for the year ended December 31, 2009, for the matters described in the following paragraphs.

Approval of the definitive merger agreement by the Corporation's Board of Directors constituted a "change in control" as defined in certain agreements with employees. That "change in control" resulted in the following events, all of which were recognized in the Corporation's financial statements for the year ended December 31, 2009:

i. Under the terms of two restricted stock plans, all restrictions lapsed on outstanding, but non-vested, restricted stock and restricted stock units, except for those held by the Corporation's Chairman, President, and Chief Executive Officer. As a result of that lapse, the Corporation recognized previously unrecognized compensation expense in the amount of approximately $33.0 million, restrictions lapsed on 479,034 restricted shares, and the Corporation issued 311,963 shares in satisfaction of the restricted units (those 311,963 shares were net of 166,037 shares withheld to satisfy employee tax withholding requirements). In addition, the Corporation repurchased 186,326 shares, representing shares with a fair value equal to amounts necessary to satisfy employee tax withholding requirements on the 479,034 restricted shares on which restrictions lapsed.

ii. Under the terms of severance agreements with 19 of its key employees, all unvested stock options held by those individuals, aggregating approximately 1.1 million options, immediately vested. As a result, the Corporation recognized previously unrecognized compensation expense associated with those options in the amount of approximately $9.3 million.

iii. Under the terms of The Black & Decker Supplemental Executive Retirement Plan, which covers six key employees, the participants became fully vested. As a result, the Corporation recognized additional pension expense of approximately $5.3 million.

The events described in paragraphs i. through iii. above were recognized in the Corporation's financial statements for the year ended December 31, 2009, as the approval of the definitive merger agreement by the Corporation's Board of Directors on November 2, 2009, constituted a "change in control" under certain agreements with employees and resulted in the occurrence—irrespective of whether or not the proposed merger is ultimately consummated—of those events. Additional payments upon a change in control—that are solely payable upon consummation of the proposed merger or termination of certain employees—will not be recognized in the Corporation's financial statements until: (1) consummation of the proposed merger, which is subject to customary closing conditions, including obtaining certain regulatory approvals, as well as shareholder approval from the shareholders of both the Corporation and The Stanley Works, and therefore cannot be considered probable until such approvals are obtained; or (2) if prior to consummation of the proposed merger, the Corporation reaches a determination to terminate an affected employee, irrespective of whether the proposed merger is consummated.

On November 2, 2009, the Corporation's Board of Directors amended the terms of The Black & Decker 2008 Executive Long-Term Incentive/Retention Plan to remove the provision whereby cash payouts under the plan are adjusted upward or downward proportionately to the extent that the Corporation's common stock exceeds or is less than $67.78. As a result of this modification, the Corporation recognized additional compensation expense of $2.8 million in its financial statements for the year ended December 31, 2009.

The Corporation also expects that it will incur fees for various advisory, legal, and accounting services, as well as other expenses, associated with the proposed merger. The Corporation estimates that these outside service fees and other expenses, which will be expensed as incurred, will approximate $25 million, of which approximately $8.4 million of expenses were recognized in the year ended December 31, 2009. The anticipated $25 million of outside service fees includes approximately $10.5 million of fees that are only payable upon consummation of the proposed merger. The Corporation's estimate of outside service fees is based upon current forecasts of expected service activity. There is no assurance that the amount of these fees could not increase significantly in the future if circumstances change.

Software Amortization

3.61

FLOWERS FOODS, INC. (DEC)

(Amounts in thousands)	2009	2008	2007
Sales	$2,600,849	$2,414,892	$2,036,674
Materials, supplies, labor and other production costs (exclusive of depreciation and amortization shown separately below)	1,390,183	1,263,962	1,039,011
Selling, marketing and administrative expenses	926,418	894,800	787,821
Depreciation and amortization	80,928	73,312	66,094
Gain on acquisition	(3,013)	—	—
Gain on sale of assets	—	(2,306)	—
Asset impairment	—	3,108	—
Gain on insurance recovery	—	(686)	(933)
Income from operations	$ 206,333	$ 182,702	$ 144,681

NOTES TO CONSOLIDATED FINANCIAL STATEMENTS

Note 2 (In Part): Summary of Significant Accounting Policies

Software Development Cost

The company expenses software development costs incurred in the preliminary project stage, and, thereafter, capitalizes costs incurred in developing or obtaining internally used software. Certain costs, such as maintenance and training, are expensed as incurred. Capitalized costs are amortized over a period of three to eight years and are subject to impairment evaluation. The net balance of capitalized software development costs included in plant, property and equipment was $2.5 million and $3.1 million at January 2, 2010 and January 3, 2009, respectively. Amortization expense of capitalized software development costs, which is included in depreciation expense in the consolidated statements of income, was $1.1 million, $2.8 million and $4.2 million in fiscal years 2009, 2008 and 2007, respectively.

Fair Value Adjustments

3.62

APPLIED INDUSTRIAL TECHNOLOGIES, INC. (JUN)

(In thousands)	2009	2008	2007
Net sales	$1,923,148	$2,089,456	$2,014,109
Cost of Sales	1,403,138	1,520,173	1,466,057
	520,010	569,283	548,052
Selling, distribution and administrative, including depreciation	410,912	416,459	413,041
Goodwill impairment	36,605	—	—
Operating income	72,493	152,824	135,011
Interest expense	5,523	4,939	5,798
Interest income	(1,099)	(4,057)	(3,438)
Other expense (Income), net	2,255	227	(1,179)
	6,679	1,109	1,181
Income before income taxes	$ 65,814	$ 151,715	$ 133,830

NOTES TO CONSOLIDATED FINANCIAL STATEMENTS
(In thousands)

Note 1 (In Part): Business and Accounting Policies

Marketable Securities

The primary marketable security investments of the Company include money market and mutual funds. These are included in other assets, are classified as trading securities and reported at fair value, based on quoted market prices. Unrealized gains and losses are recorded in other expense (income), net in the statements of consolidated income and reflect changes in the fair value of the investment during the period.

Note 7 (In Part): Fair Value Measurements

Fair value as defined by SFAS No. 157, "Fair Value Measurements" ("SFAS 157"), is the price that would be received to sell an asset or be paid to transfer a liability in an orderly transaction between market participants at the measurement date. SFAS 157 classifies the inputs to measure fair value into three tiers. These tiers include: Level 1, defined as observable inputs such as quoted prices in active markets; Level 2, defined as inputs other than quoted prices in active markets that are either directly or indirectly observable; and Level 3, defined as unobservable inputs in which little or no market data exists, therefore requiring an entity to develop its own assumptions.

In February, 2008, the FASB finalized FASB Staff Position 157-2, "Effective Date of FASB Statement No. 157." This Staff Position delays the effective date of SFAS 157 for all non-financial assets and non-financial liabilities, except those that are recognized or disclosed at fair value in the financial statements on a recurring basis (at least annually). The effective date for Applied for items within the scope of this FASB Staff Position is July 1, 2009.

Financial assets and liabilities measured at fair value on a recurring basis are as follows at June 30, 2009:

| | | Fair Value Measurements | | |
	Recorded Value	Quoted Prices in Active Markets for Identical Instruments Level 1	Significant Other Observable Inputs Level 2	Significant Unobservable Inputs Level 3
Assets:				
Marketable securities	$8,211	$8,211		
Liabilities:				
Cross-currency swaps	$8,361		$8,361	
Interest rate swap	1,381		1,381	
Total liabilities	$9,742		$9,742	

Marketable securities in the above table are held in a rabbi trust for a non-qualified deferred compensation plan. The marketable securities are included in other assets in the consolidated balance sheets. The fair values were derived using quoted market prices. Marketable securities totaled $10,527 at June 30, 2008.

Note 14 (In Part): Other Expense (Income), Net

Other expense (income), net consists of the following:

	2009	2008	2007
Unrealized loss (gain) on assets held in rabbi trust for a nonqualified deferred compensation plan	$1,741	$ 327	$(1,397)
Foreign currency transaction losses (gains)	1,466	(384)	(27)
Unrealized (gain) loss on cross-currency swap	(947)	277	243
Other, net	(5)	7	2
Total other expense (income), net	$2,255	$ 227	$(1,179)

Business Combination Adjustment Loss

3.63

IRON MOUNTAIN INCORPORATED (DEC)

NOTES TO CONSOLIDATED FINANCIAL STATEMENTS
(In thousands)

6 (In Part): Acquisitions

In connection with some of our acquisitions, we have contingent earn-out obligations that become payable in the event the businesses we acquired achieve specified revenue targets and/or multiples of earnings before interest, taxes, depreciation and amortization (as defined in the purchase agreements). These payments are based on the future results of these operations and our estimate of the maximum contingent earn-out payments we may be required to make under all such agreements as of December 31, 2009 is approximately $9,610. These amounts are generally payable over periods ranging from 2010 through 2012 and all of these payments, if made, will be treated as additional consideration as part of the acquisition and will increase goodwill. We have recorded $535, $1,447 and $549 of compensation expense for the years ended December 31, 2007, 2008 and 2009, respectively, in the accompanying consolidated statements of operations related to contingent consideration arrangements. New accounting standards require that we must, for any acquisitions that we make on or any time after January 1, 2009, (i) estimate our contingent consideration payments at the time of the acquisition and include such amount as part of the initial purchase price allocation, and (ii) any subsequent changes in this estimate will directly impact the consolidated statement of operations.

PENSIONS AND OTHER POSTRETIREMENT BENEFITS

3.64 FASB ASC 715, *Compensation—Retirement Benefits*, states the disclosure requirements for pensions and other postretirement benefits including disclosures about the assets, obligations, cash flows, investment strategy, and net periodic benefit cost of defined pension and postretirement plans.

3.65 The disclosure requirements of FASB ASC 715 include, but are not limited to, disclosing the actuarial assumption rates used in accounting for pensions and other postretirement benefits. FASB ASC 715 also requires disclosure of the assumed health care cost trend rate for other postretirement benefits. In addition, FASB ASC 715 requires disclosure of the allocation by major category of plan assets, the inputs and valuation techniques used to measure the fair value of plan assets, the effect of fair value measurements using significant unobservable inputs (Level 3) on changes in plan assets for the period and significant concentrations of risk within plan assets. Tables 3-8, 3-9 and 3-10 show the actuarial assumption rates used by the survey entities in accounting for pension benefits. Table 3-11 shows the health care cost trend rate used by the survey entities in 2009 to

account for other postretirement benefits. Table 3-12 shows the asset allocations in 2009 of the 349 survey entities that disclosed the plan asset allocation of their defined benefit pension plan.

3.66 FASB ASC 715 requires that a business entity recognize the overfunded or underfunded status of a single-employer defined benefit postretirement plan as an asset or liability in its statement of financial position, recognize changes in that funded status in comprehensive income, and disclose in the notes to financial statements additional information about net periodic benefit cost. FASB ASC 715 requires a business entity to recognize as components of other comprehensive income the gains or losses and prior service costs or credits that arise during a period but are not recognized in the income statement as components of net periodic benefit cost of a period. Those amounts recognized in accumulated other comprehensive income are adjusted as they are subsequently recognized in the income statement as components of net periodic benefit cost. Additionally, FASB ASC 715 requires that a business entity measure plan assets and benefit obligations as of the date of its fiscal year-end statement of financial position. An employer whose equity securities are traded publicly is required to initially recognize the funded status of a defined benefit postretirement plan and to provide the required disclosures for their financial statements issued for fiscal years ending after December 15, 2006. The measurement-date requirement is effective for fiscal years ending after December 15, 2008, and shall not be applied retrospectively.

3.67 Examples of pension and other postretirement benefit presentations follow. Examples of the funded status of a benefit plan recognized under FASB ASC 715 as an asset or liability in the statement of financial position are presented in Section 2 under "Other Noncurrent Assets," "Employee-Related Liabilities," and "Other Noncurrent Liabilities."

3.68

TABLE 3-8: PENSION ACTUARIAL ASSUMPTION DISCOUNT RATE

%	2009	2008	2007	2006
4.5 or less	3	3	6	13
5	7	4	20	43
5.5	32	35	141	283
6	138	196	240	90
6.5	116	109	27	5
7	41	14	1	—
7.5	11	—	1	—
8	7	1	—	1
8.5	2	1	—	—
9	—	—	—	1
9.5	—	—	—	—
10	—	—	—	—
10.5	—	—	—	—
11 or greater	—	—	—	—
Not disclosed	8	7	9	5
Entities Disclosing Defined Benefit Plans	**365**	**370**	**441**	**441**

2008–2009 based on 500 entities surveyed; 2006–2007 based on 600 entities surveyed.

3.69

TABLE 3-9: PENSION ACTUARIAL ASSUMPTION RATE OF COMPENSATION INCREASE

%	2009	2008	2007	2006
4.5 or less	255	261	323	336
5	22	28	27	26
5.5	8	10	9	8
6	5	4	5	8
6.5	2	1	—	2
7	1	1	2	—
7.5	2	2	—	1
8	1	1	2	—
8.5	—	—	2	—
9	—	—	—	—
9.5	—	—	—	—
10	—	—	—	—
10.5	—	—	—	—
11 or greater	—	—	—	—
Not disclosed	69	62	75	60
Entities Disclosing Defined Benefit Plans	**365**	**370**	**445**	**441**

2008–2009 based on 500 entities surveyed; 2006–2007 based on 600 entities surveyed.

3.70

TABLE 3-10: PENSION ACTUARIAL ASSUMPTION EXPECTED RATE OF RETURN

%	2009	2008	2007	2006
4.5 or less	4	1	3	4
5	4	3	4	1
5.5	2	2	4	4
6	6	3	13	8
6.5	9	14	7	10
7	27	24	28	24
7.5	45	36	45	46
8	133	130	136	124
8.5	89	101	129	157
9	22	33	37	36
9.5	2	2	4	5
10	—	—	—	
10.5	—	—	—	—
11 or greater	—	—	—	—
Not disclosed	22	21	35	22
Entities Disclosing Defined Benefit Plans	**365**	**370**	**445**	**441**

2008–2009 based on 500 entities surveyed; 2006–2007 based on 600 entities surveyed.

3.71

TABLE 3-11: OTHER POSTRETIREMENT BENEFIT HEALTH CARE COST TREND RATE— 2009

%	All Participants	Participants Under Age 65	Participants Age 65 and Over
5.5 or less	12	1	1
6–6.5	9	—	2
7–7.5	42	7	4
8–8.5	114	8	6
9–9.5	53	5	8
10–10.5	16	1	—
11–11.5	—	1	1
12–12.5	—	—	—
13–13.5	—	—	—
14 or greater	—	—	—
Fixed amount (not subject to escalation)	6	—	1
Entities Disclosing Rate	**252**	**23**	**23**

3.72

TABLE 3-12: DEFINED BENEFIT PENSION PLAN ASSET ALLOCATION—2009

	Asset Category				
%	Equity	Debt	Real Estate	Cash & Equivalents	Other
81–100	11	7	—	1	3
61–80	118	8	—	1	1
41–60	152	59	1	2	8
21–40	45	215	—	7	23
1–20	14	44	122	163	146
None	9	16	226	175	168
Entities Disclosing Asset Allocation	**349**	**349**	**349**	**349**	**349**

Defined Benefit Plans

3.73

CAMERON INTERNATIONAL CORPORATION (DEC)

NOTES TO CONSOLIDATED FINANCIAL STATEMENTS

Note 8. Employee Benefit Plans

As of December 31, 2009, the Company sponsored separate defined benefit pension plans for employees of its United Kingdom (U.K.) and German subsidiaries as well as several unfunded defined benefit arrangements for various other employee groups. The U.K. defined benefit pension plan was frozen to new entrants effective June 14, 1996.

In June 2007, the Company notified employees and beneficiaries that it had elected to terminate the Cameron International Corporation Retirement Plan (Retirement Plan) as well as certain related unfunded supplemental plans, which covered the majority of salaried U.S. employees and certain domestic hourly employees at the time the Retirement Plan was frozen to new entrants, effective May 1, 2003. In addition, the Company curtailed future benefits from being earned under the Retirement Plan, effective December 31, 2007. The Company distributed the assets of the Retirement Plan in two phases. The first phase occurred during the fourth quarter of 2007 and included former employees who were participants in the Retirement Plan. In connection with this initial distribution of plan assets and the curtailment of future benefits from the Retirement Plan, the Company recorded a pre-tax settlement loss of $37,704,000 and a pre-tax curtailment gain of $1,979,000, for a net charge in 2007 of $35,725,000. During the fourth quarter of 2008, the Company recorded an additional settlement loss of $26,196,000 in connection with the final distribution of plan assets to current employees who were participants in the Retirement Plan and any others not covered by the initial distribution of plan assets during 2007. Following the final distribution, the excess remaining plan assets of approximately $5,117,000 became available to the Company to be used in meeting the cash funding obligations for matching contributions under the Cameron International Corporation Retirement Savings Plan, a defined contribution 401(k) plan available to the Company's eligible United States-based employees.

Certain of the Company's employees also participate in various domestic employee welfare benefit plans, including medical, dental and prescriptions. Additionally, certain employees receive retiree medical, prescription and life insurance benefits. All of the welfare benefit plans, including those providing postretirement benefits, are unfunded.

Total net benefit plan expense (income) associated with the Company's defined benefit pension and postretirement benefit plans consisted of the following:

(Dollars in thousands)	Pension Benefits			Postretirement Benefits		
	2009	2008	2007	2009	2008	2007
Service cost	$ 2,687	$ 3,867	$ 9,039	$ 8	$ 3	$ 5
Interest cost	14,068	20,315	25,129	534	1,075	1,211
Expected return on plan assets	(13,285)	(22,113)	(33,444)	—	—	—
Amortization of prior service cost (credit)	15	15	(540)	(890)	(382)	(383)
Amortization of losses (gains)	5,741	9,365	14,065	(1,915)	(1,484)	(1,078)
Net benefit plan expense (income) before settlement loss and curtailment gain	9,226	11,449	14,249	(2,263)	(788)	(245)
Settlement loss	235	26,196	37,704	—	—	—
Curtailment gain	—	—	(1,979)	—	—	—
Total net benefit plan expense (income)	$ 9,461	$ 37,645	$ 49,974	$(2,263)	$ (788)	$ (245)
Net benefit plan expense (income):						
U.S. plans	$ 361	$ 29,701	$ 42,065	$(2,263)	$ (788)	$ (245)
Foreign plans	9,100	7,944	7,909	—	—	—
Total net benefit plan expense (income)	$ 9,461	$ 37,645	$ 49,974	$(2,263)	$ (788)	$ (245)

Included in accumulated other elements of comprehensive income at December 31, 2009 and 2008 are the following amounts that have not yet been recognized in net periodic benefit plan cost, as well as the amounts that are expected to be recognized in net periodic benefit plan cost during the year ending December 31, 2010:

	December 31, 2009		December 31, 2008		Year Ending December 31, 2010
(Dollars in thousands)	Before Tax	After Tax	Before Tax	After Tax	Expected Amortization
Pension benefits:					
Prior service cost	$ (29)	$ (18)	$ (44)	$ (28)	$ —
Actuarial losses, net	(97,066)	(69,824)	(75,145)	(54,075)	6,913
Post retirement benefits:					
Prior service credit	4,926	3,110	5,816	3,664	(890)
Actuarial gains	11,348	7,208	18,018	11,351	(1,169)
	$(80,821)	$(59,524)	$(51,355)	$(39,088)	$4,854

The change in the projected benefit obligation associated with the Company's defined benefit pension plans and the change in the accumulated benefit obligation associated with the Company's postretirement benefit plans was as follows:

	Pension Benefits		Postretirement Benefits	
(Dollars in thousands)	2009	2008	2009	2008
Benefit obligation at beginning of year	$221,340	$389,820	$ 8,963	$17,825
Service cost	2,687	3,867	8	3
Interest cost	14,068	20,315	534	1,075
Plan participants' contributions	940	930	—	—
Actuarial losses (gains)	30,715	(20,588)	4,755	(4,639)
Exchange rate changes	21,182	(73,144)	—	—
Benefits and expenses paid from plan assets	(16,413)	(98,878)	—	—
Benefits paid directly by the Company	—	(3,679)	(1,601)	(1,571)
Plan amendments	—	—	—	(3,999)
Acquisitions	—	2,697	5,650	—
Change in plan measurement date	—	—	—	269
Benefit obligation at end of year	$274,519	$221,340	$18,309	$ 8,963
Benefit obligation at end of year:				
U.S. plans	$ 3,036	$ 12,872	$18,309	$ 8,963
Foreign plans	271,483	208,468	—	—
Benefit obligation at end of year	$274,519	$221,340	$18,309	$ 8,963

The total accumulated benefit obligation for the Company's defined benefit pension plans was $239,169,000 and $194,813,000 at December 31, 2009 and 2008, respectively.

The change in the plan assets associated with the Company's defined benefit pension and postretirement benefit plans was as follows:

	Pension Benefits		Postretirement Benefits	
(Dollars in thousands)	2009	2008	2009	2008
Fair value of plan assets at beginning of year	$195,129	$ 368,381	$ —	$—
Actual return on plan assets	23,509	(21,076)	—	—
Company contributions	25,428	12,225	1,601	—
Plan participants' contributions	940	930	—	—
Exchange rate changes	18,724	(65,359)	—	—
Acquisitions	—	2,585	—	—
Excess assets remitted to plan sponsor	(5,117)	—	—	—
Benefits and expenses paid from plan assets	(16,413)	(102,557)	(1,601)	—
Fair value of plan assets at end of year	$242,200	$ 195,129	$ —	$—
Fair value of plan assets at end of year:				
U.S. plans	$ —	$ 15,764	$ —	$—
Foreign plans	242,200	179,365	—	—
Fair value of plan assets at end of year	$242,200	$ 195,129	$ —	$—

The funded status of the Company's defined benefit pension and postretirement benefit plans was as follows:

	Pension Benefits		Postretirement Benefits	
(Dollars in thousands)	2009	2008	2009	2008
Overfunded plans	$ —	$ 5,328	$ —	$ —
Underfunded plans	(32,319)	(31,539)	(18,309)	(8,963)
Funded status	$(32,319)	$(26,211)	$(18,309)	$(8,963)
Funded status at end of year:				
Current	$ (207)	$ 5,125	$ (1,880)	$(1,169)
Non-current	(32,112)	(31,336)	(16,429)	(7,794)
Funded status at end of year	$(32,319)	$(26,211)	$(18,309)	$(8,963)

Actual asset investment allocations for the Company's main defined benefit pension plans in the United States and the United Kingdom, which account for approximately 97.0% of total plan assets, are as follows:

	Pension Benefits	
(Dollars in thousands)	2009	2008
U.S. plan:		
Equity securities	—	—
Fixed income debt securities, cash and other	—	100%
U.K. plan:		
Equity securities	56%	44%
Fixed income debt securities, cash and other	44%	56%

In each jurisdiction, the investment of plan assets is overseen by a plan asset committee whose members act as trustees of the plan and set investment policy. For the years ended December 31, 2009 and 2008, the investment strategy has been designed to approximate the performance of market indexes. The asset allocation for the U.S. plan at December 31, 2008 was heavily weighted towards fixed income debt securities, cash and other short-term investments due to the plan termination announced during 2007 as discussed above. The Company has modified its targeted allocation for the U.K. plan for 2010 and beyond to be approximately 55% in equities, 40% in fixed income debt securities and 5% in real estate and other.

During 2009, the Company made contributions totaling approximately $25,428,000 to the assets of its various defined benefit pension plans. Contributions to plan assets for 2010 are currently expected to approximate $9,380,000 assuming no change in the current discount rate or expected investment earnings.

The fair values of the Company's pension plan assets by asset category at December 31, 2009 were as follows:

(Dollars in thousands)	Fair Value Based on Quoted Prices in Active Markets for Identical Assets (Level 1)	Fair Value Based on Significant Other Observable Inputs (Level 2)	Fair Value Based on Significant Unobservable Inputs (Level 3)	Total
Cash and cash equivalents	$14,227	$ —	$ —	$ 14,277
Equity securities:				
U.S. equities	—	54,278	—	54,278
Other	22,919	53,438	—	76,357
Bonds:				
Non-U.S. government bonds	—	70,746	—	70,746
Non-U.S. corporate bonds	—	17,271	—	17,271
Alternative investments:				
Insurance contracts	—	—	7,172	7,172
Other	—	—	2,099	2,099
Total assets	$37,196	$195,733	$9,271	$242,200

Changes in the fair value of pension plan assets determined based on level 3 unobservable inputs were as follows (dollars in thousands):

(Dollars in thousands)	2009
Balance at beginning of the year	$ 8,622
Purchases/sales, net	479
Actual return on plan assets	(220)
Currency impact	390
Balance at end of the year	$9,271

The weighted-average assumptions associated with the Company's defined benefit pension and postretirement benefit plans were as follows:

	Pension Benefits		Postretirement Benefits	
	2009	2008	2009	2008
Assumptions related to net benefit costs:				
Domestic plans:				
Discount rate	5.08–6.52%	5.00–6.25%	4.88–6.52%	6.25%
Expected return on plan assets	5.25%	5.25%	—	—
Health care cost trend rate	—	—	9.00%	7.50%
Measurement date	1/1/2009	1/1/2008	1/1/2009	10/1/2007
International plans:				
Discount rate	5.75–6.25%	5.25–5.75%	—	—
Expected return on plan assets	5.50–6.75%	4.50–6.75%	—	—
Rate of compensation increase	3.00–4.50%	2.75–4.50%	—	—
Measurement date	1/1/2009	1/1/2008	—	—
Assumptions related to end-of-period benefit obligations:				
Domestic plans:				
Discount rate	5.03%	5.08–6.52%	5.03%	6.52%
Health care cost trend rate	—	—	9.00%	7.50%
Measurement date	12/31/2009	12/31/2008	12/31/2009	12/31/2008
International plans:				
Discount rate	5.50–5.75%	5.75–6.25%	—	—
Rate of compensation increase	3.00–4.50%	3.00–4.50%	—	—
Measurement date	12/31/2009	12/31/2008	—	—

The Company's discount rate assumptions for its U.S. postretirement benefits plan and its U.K. defined benefit pension plan are based on the average yield of a hypothetical high quality bond portfolio with maturities that approximately match the estimated cash flow needs of the plans.

The assumptions for expected long-term rates of return on assets are based on historical experience and estimated future investment returns, taking into consideration anticipated asset allocations, investment strategies and the views of various investment professionals.

The rate of compensation increase assumption for foreign plans reflect local economic conditions and the Company's compensation strategy in those locations.

The health care cost trend rate is assumed to decrease gradually from 9% to 5% by 2018 and remain at that level thereafter. A one-percentage-point change in the assumed health care cost trend rate would have the following effects:

(Dollars in thousands)	One-Percentage-Point Increase	One-Percentage-Point Decrease
Effect on total of service and interest cost components in 2009	$ 19	$ (18)
Effect on postretirement benefit obligation as of December 31, 2009	1,052	(945)

Year-end amounts applicable to the Company's pension plans with projected benefit obligations in excess of plan assets and accumulated benefit obligations in excess of plan assets were as follows:

(Dollars in thousands)	Projected Benefit Obligation in Excess of Plan Assets		Accumulated Benefit Obligation in Excess of Plan Assets	
	2009	2008	2009	2008
Fair value of applicable plan assets	$ 242,200	$ 179,761	$ 9,271	$ 7,005
Projected benefit obligation of applicable plans	(274,519)	(211,300)	—	—
Accumulated benefit obligation of applicable plans	—	—	(18,533)	(13,712)

Future expected benefit payments are as follows:

(Dollars in thousands)	Pension Benefits		Postretirement Benefits
	U.S. Unfunded Plans	Foreign Funded Plans	U.S. Unfunded Plans
Year ended December 31:			
2010	$ 212	$ 6,059	$1,926
2011	220	6,228	1,860
2012	214	6,420	1,828
2013	209	6,746	1,773
2014	205	6,914	1,719
2015–2019	1,243	38,634	7,190

The Company's United States-based employees who are not covered by a bargaining unit and certain others are also eligible to participate in the Cameron International Corporation Retirement Savings Plan. Under this plan, employees' savings deferrals are partially matched in cash and invested at the employees' discretion. In connection with the termination of the Retirement Plan, as described above, the Company modified the Retirement Savings Plan, effective January 1, 2008, to provide enhanced benefits to eligible employees.Beginning January 1, 2008, the Company provides nondiscretionary retirement contributions to the Retirement Savings Plan on behalf of each eligible employee equal to 3% of their defined pay (prior to January 1, 2008, the Company made cash contributions for hourly employees who were not covered under collective bargaining agreements and contributed 2% of pay for new employees hired after May 1, 2003, dependent on the Company meeting certain specified financial objectives). Eligible employees vest in the 3% retirement contributions plus any earnings after completing three years of service. In addition, the Company provides an immediately vested matching contribution of up to 100% of the first 6% of pay contributed by each eligible employee. Prior to January 1, 2008, the Company matched up to 100% of the first 3% of pay contributed by each eligible employee and up to 50% of the next 3% of eligible employee contributions. Employees may contribute amounts in excess of 6% of their pay to the Retirement Savings Plan, subject to certain United States Internal Revenue Service limitations. The Company's expense under this plan for the years ended December 31, 2009, 2008 and 2007 amounted to $20,575,000, $19,584,000 and $13,228,000, respectively. In addition, the Company provides savings or other benefit plans for employees under collective bargaining agreements and, in the case of certain international employees, as required by government mandate, which provide for, among other things, Company matching contributions in cash based on specified formulas. Expense with respect to these various defined contribution and government-mandated plans for the years ended December 31, 2009, 2008 and 2007 amounted to $34,295,000, $33,846,000 and $17,437,000, respectively.

3.74

CORNING INCORPORATED (DEC)

NOTES TO CONSOLIDATED FINANCIAL STATEMENTS
(In millions)

Note 13 (In Part): Employee Retirement Plans

Defined Benefit Plans

We have defined benefit pension plans covering certain domestic and international employees. Our funding policy has been to contribute, as necessary, an amount in excess of the minimum requirements in order to achieve the Company's long-term funding targets. In 2009, we made a voluntary contribution of $80 million to our domestic and international pension plans. In 2008, we made voluntary contributions of $52 million to our domestic and international pension plans.

In 2000, we amended our U.S. pension plan to include a cash balance pension feature. Certain salaried and non-union hourly employees remain in the traditional defined benefit plan. All salaried and non-union hourly employees hired after July 1, 2000, are automatically participants in the new cash balance plan. Under the cash balance plan, employee accounts are credited monthly with a percentage of eligible pay based on age and years of service. The Pension Protection Act of 2006 requires vesting after three years for cash balance plans by January 1, 2008. Corning adopted this measure on January 1, 2008.

Corning offers postretirement plans that provide health care and life insurance benefits for retirees and eligible dependents. Certain employees may become eligible for such postretirement benefits upon reaching retirement age. Prior to January 1, 2003, our principal retiree medical plans required retiree contributions each year equal to the excess of medical cost increases over general inflation rates. For current retirees (including surviving spouses) and active employees eligible for the salaried retiree medical program, we have placed a "cap" on the amount we will contribute toward retiree medical coverage in the future. The cap is equal to 120% of our 2005 contributions toward retiree medical benefits. Once our contributions toward salaried retiree medical costs reach this cap, impacted retirees will have to pay the excess amount in addition to their regular contributions for coverage. This cap was attained for post-65 retirees in 2008 and has impacted their contribution rate in 2009. The pre-65 retirees are expected to trigger the cap in 2011. Furthermore, employees hired or rehired on or after January 1, 2007 will be eligible for Corning retiree medical upon retirement; however, these employees will pay 100% of the cost.

In 2009, Corning recorded restructuring charges of $50 million for U.S. pension and postretirement benefit plans. This included a curtailment charge of $33 million for the qualified defined benefit plan (U.S. pension plan) and the U.S. postretirement benefit plan. Accordingly, we remeasured the U.S. pension and postretirement benefit plan as of March 31, 2009. The remeasurement resulted in an increase of $115 million to the Company's U.S. pension liability and a decrease of $12 million to the U.S. postretirement benefit plan liability. As part of the remeasurement, we updated the assumed discount rate for both plans to 6.25%, which reflected a 25 basis point increase from December 31, 2008.

Obligations and Funded Status

The change in benefit obligation and funded status of our employee retirement plans follow (in millions):

	Pension Benefits		Postretirement Benefits	
	2009	2008	2009	2008
Change in benefit obligation				
Benefit obligation at beginning of year	$ 2,601	$ 2,589	$ 843	$ 804
Service cost	46	51	11	12
Interest cost	157	150	51	47
Plan participants' contributions	1	2	7	5
Amendments		(5)		
Curtailment loss	19		11	
Actuarial losses (gains)	112	20	67	36
Special termination benefits	19	7	1	1
Other		5		
Benefits paid	(184)	(164)	(69)	(68)
Medicare subsidy received			6	6
Foreign currency translation	20	(54)		
Benefit obligation at end of year	$ 2,791	$ 2,601	$ 928	$ 843
Change in plan assets				
Fair value of plan assets at beginning of year	2,043	2,597		
Actual gain (loss) on plan assets	288	(398)		
Employer contributions	101	77		
Acquisition (divestitures)		(6)		
Plan participants' contributions	1	2		
Benefits paid	(184)	(164)		
Foreign currency translation	21	(65)		
Fair value of plan assets at end of year	$ 2,270	$ 2,043		
Funded status at end of year				
Fair value of plan assets	$ 2,270	$ 2,043		
Benefit obligations	(2,791)	(2,601)	$(928)	$(843)
Funded status of plans	$ (521)	$ (558)	$(928)	$(843)
Amounts recognized in the consolidated balance sheets consist of:				
Noncurrent asset		$ 16		
Current liability	$ (9)	(10)	$ (70)	$ (59)
Noncurrent liability	(512)	(564)	(858)	(784)
Recognized (liability) asset	$ (521)	$ (558)	$(928)	$(843)
Amounts recognized in accumulated other comprehensive income consist of:				
Net actuarial loss	$ 937	$ 967	$256	$ 201
Prior service cost (credit)	20	29	(16)	(20)
Transition asset	(1)	(1)		
Amount recognized at end of year	$ 956	$ 995	$ 240	$ 181

The accumulated benefit obligation for defined benefit pension plans was $2.7 billion and $2.5 billion at December 31, 2009 and 2008, respectively.

The following information is presented for pension plans where the projected benefit obligation and the accumulated benefit obligation as of December 31, 2009 and 2008 exceeded the fair value of plan assets (in millions):

	2009	2008
Projected benefit obligation	$2,791	$2,452
Accumulated benefit obligation	2,677	2,342
Fair value of plan assets	2,270	1,878

The components of net periodic benefit expense for our employee retirement plans follow (in millions):

	Pension Benefits			Postretirement Benefits		
	2009	2008	2007	2009	2008	2007
Service cost	$ 46	$ 51	$ 53	$ 11	$12	$12
Interest cost	157	150	145	51	47	44
Expected return on plan assets	(179)	(196)	(182)			
Amortization of net loss	31	14	12	11	8	6
Amortization of prior service cost (credit)	8	10	30	(3)	(3)	(3)
Total periodic benefit expense	$ 63	$ 29	$ 58	$ 70	$64	$59
Curtailment charge	22			10		
Total expense	$ 85	$ 29	$ 58	$ 80	$64	$59
Other changes in plan assets and benefit obligations recognized in other comprehensive income:						
Curtailment effects	$ (2)			$ 2		
Current year actuarial loss (gain)	2	$ 615	$(106)	66	$36	$ 6
Amortization of actuarial loss	(31)	(14)	(30)	(11)	(8)	(6)
Amortization of prior service (cost) credit	(9)	(10)	(12)	3	3	3
Total recognized in other comprehensive income	$ (40)	$ 591	$(148)	$ 60	$31	$ 3
Total recognized in net periodic benefit cost and other comprehensive income	$ 45	$ 620	$ (90)	$140	$95	$62

The Company expects to recognize $52 million of net loss and $8 million of net prior service cost as components of net periodic pension cost in 2010 for its defined benefit pension plans. The Company expects to recognize $15 million of net loss and $2 million of net prior service credit as components of net periodic postretirement benefit cost in 2010.

Corning uses a hypothetical yield curve and associated spot rate curve to discount the plan's projected benefit payments. Once the present value of projected benefit payments is calculated, the suggested discount rate is equal to the level rate that results in the same present value. The yield curve is based on actual high-quality corporate bonds across the full maturity spectrum, which also includes private placements as well as Eurobonds that are denominated in U.S. currency. The curve is developed from yields on approximately 550-600 bonds from four grading sources, Moody's, S&P, Fitch and the Dominion Bond Rating Service. A bond will be included if at least half of the grades from these sources are Aa, non-callable bonds. The very highest and lowest 10th percentile yields are excluded from the curve to eliminate outliers in the bond population.

Measurement of postretirement benefit expense is based on assumptions used to value the postretirement benefit obligation at the beginning of the year.

The weighted-average assumptions used to determine benefit obligations at December 31 follow:

	Pension Benefits						Postretirement Benefits		
	Domestic			International			Domestic		
	2009	2008	2007	2009	2008	2007	2009	2008	2007
Discount rate	5.75%	6.00%	6.00%	5.75%	5.12%	4.58%	5.75%	6.00%	6.00%
Rate of compensation increase	4.25%	5.00%	5.00%	4.04%	4.20%	3.99%			

The weighted-average assumptions used to determine net periodic benefit cost for years ended December 31 follow:

	Pension Benefits						Postretirement Benefits		
	Domestic			International			Domestic		
	2009	2008	2007	2009	2008	2007	2009	2008	2007
Discount rate	6.00/6.25%[1]	6.00%	5.75%	5.12%	4.58%	4.59%	6.00/6.25%[1]	6.00%	5.75%
Expected return on plan assets	7.75%	8.00%	8.00%	6.08%	6.73%	6.81%			
Rate of compensation increase	5.00%	5.00%	5.00%	4.20%	3.99%	3.89%			

[1] The discount rate at December 31, 2008 was 6.00%. At March 31, 2009 remeasurement date, the discount rate was changed to 6.25%.

The assumed rate of return was determined based on the current interest rate environment and historical market premiums relative to fixed income rates of equities and other asset classes. Reasonableness of the results is tested using models provided by investment consultants and the plan actuaries.

Assumed Health Care Trend Rates at December 31	2009	2008
Health care cost trend rate assumed for next year	8.5%	8.2%
Rate that the cost trend rate gradually declines to	5%	5%
Year that the rate reaches the ultimate trend rate	2017	2013

Assumed health care cost trend rates have a significant effect on the amounts reported for the health care plans. A one-percentage-point change in assumed health care cost trend rates would have the following effects (in millions):

	One-Percentage-Point Increase	One-Percentage-Point Decrease
Effect on annual total of service and interest cost	$ 4	$ (3)
Effect on postretirement benefit obligation	50	(41)

Plan Assets

The Company's overall investment strategy is to obtain sufficient return and provide adequate liquidity to meet the benefit obligations of the pension plan. Investments are made in public securities to ensure adequate liquidity to support benefit payments. Domestic and international stocks and bonds provide diversification to the portfolio. The target allocation for domestic equity investment is 12.5% which includes large, mid and small cap companies. The target allocation of international equities is 12.5%, which includes investments in both developed and emerging markets. The target allocation for bond investments is 55%, which predominately includes both government and corporate bonds. Long duration fixed income assets are utilized to mitigate the sensitivity of funding ratios to changes in interest rates. The target allocation for non-public investments in private equity and real estate is 15%, and is used to enhance returns and offer additional asset diversification. The target allocation for commodities is 5%, which provides some inflation protection to the portfolio.

The following table provides fair value measurement information for the Company's major categories of defined benefit plan assets (in millions):

	December 31, 2009	Quoted Prices in Active Markets for Identical Assets (Level 1)	Significant Other Observable Inputs (Level 2)	Significant Unobservable Inputs (Level 3)
Equity securities:				
U.S. companies	$ 270	$190	$ 80	
International companies	330	41	289	
Fixed income:				
U.S. treasuries/agencies	158		158	
U.S. corporate bonds	857		857	
International fixed income	194		194	
Other fixed income	19		19	
Private equity[1]	222			$222
Real estate[2]	61			61
Insurance contracts	5			5
Cash equivalents	47	11	36	
Commodities[3]	107		107	
Total	$2,270	$242	$1,740	$288

[1] This category includes venture capital, leverage buyouts and distressed debt limited partnerships invested primarily in the U.S. companies. The inputs are valued by internally generated Discounted Cash Flow Analysis and comparable sale analysis.
[2] This category includes industrial, office, apartments, hotels, infrastructure, and retail investments which are limited partnerships predominately in the U.S. The inputs are valued by internally generated Discounted Cash Flow Analysis; comparable sale analysis and periodic external appraisals.
[3] This category includes investments in energy, industrial metals, precious metals, agricultural and livestock primarily through futures, options, swaps, and exchange traded funds.

The table below sets forth a summary of changes in the fair value of the defined benefit plans Level 3 assets for the year ended December 31, 2009 (in millions):

| | Level 3 Assets | | |
| | 2009 | | |
	Private Equity	Real Estate	Insurance Contracts
Beginning balance at December 31, 2008	$225	$ 86	$5
Actual return on plan assets relating to assets still held at the reporting date	(14)	(32)	
Purchases, sales, and settlements			
Transfers in and/or out of level 3	11	7	
Ending balance at December 31, 2009	$222	$ 61	$5

Credit Risk

37% of plan assets are invested in long duration corporate bonds. The average rating for these bonds is A. These bonds are subject to credit risk, such that a decline in credit ratings for the underlying companies would result in a decline in the value of the bonds. These bonds are also subject to default risk.

Currency Risk

24% of assets are valued in non U.S. dollar denominated investments that are subject to currency fluctuations. The value of these securities will decline if the U.S. dollar increases in value relative to the value of the currencies in which these investments are denominated.

Liquidity Risk

13% of the securities are invested in Level 3 securities. These are long-term investments in private equity and private real estate investments that may not mature or be sellable in the near-term without significant loss.

At December 31, 2009 and 2008, the amount of Corning common stock included in equity securities was not significant.

Cash Flow Data

We anticipate making voluntary cash contributions of approximately $230 million to our domestic and international plans in 2010.

The following reflects the gross benefit payments which are expected to be paid for the domestic and international plans and the gross amount of annual Medicare Part D federal subsidy expected to be received (in millions):

| | Expected Benefit Payments | | Expected Federal Subsidy Payments Post Retirement Benefits |
	Pension Benefits	Postretirement Benefits	
2010	$ 187	$ 82	$ 7
2011	192	87	7
2012	199	92	8
2013	204	95	8
2014	210	99	9
2015–2019	1,161	538	49

Defined Contribution Plans

3.75

COMMERCIAL METALS COMPANY (AUG)

NOTES TO CONSOLIDATED FINANCIAL STATEMENTS

Note 11. Employees' Retirement Plans

Substantially all employees in the U.S. are covered by a defined contribution profit sharing and savings plan. This tax qualified plan is maintained and contributions made in accordance with ERISA. The Company also provides certain eligible executives' benefits pursuant to a nonqualified benefit restoration plan ("BRP Plan") equal to amounts that would have been available under the tax qualified ERISA plans, save for limitations of ERISA, tax laws and regulations. Company expenses, which are discretionary, for these plans were $20.8 million, $55.1 million and $70.8 million for 2009, 2008 and 2007, respectively.

The deferred compensation liability under the BRP Plan was $96.9 million and $93.0 million at August 31, 2009 and 2008, respectively, and recorded in other long-term liabilities. Though under no obligation to fund the plan, the Company has segregated assets in a trust with a current value at August 31, 2009 and 2008 of $55.6 million and $74.0 million, respectively, recorded in other long-term assets. The net holding gain (loss) on these segregated assets was $(12.2) million, $(6.5) million and $8.2 million for the years ended August 31, 2009, 2008 and 2007, respectively.

A certain number of employees outside of the U.S. participate in defined contribution plans maintained in accordance with local regulations. Company expenses for these international plans were $2.4 million, $4.3 million and $3.8 million for the years ended August 31, 2009, 2008 and 2007, respectively.

The Company provides and recognizes post retirement defined benefits to employees at certain divisions in accordance with SFAS No. 158, *Employers Accounting for Defined Benefit Pensions and Other Postretirement Plans (an amendment of FASB Statements No. 87, 88, 106, and 132R ("SFAS 158").* SFAS 158 requires the Company to recognize the unfunded status of defined benefit plans as a liability with a corresponding reduction to accumulated other comprehensive income, net of taxes. On August 31, 2007, the Company adopted the provisions of SFAS 158 and recognized the $0.9 million unfunded status of defined benefit plans as a liability with a corresponding reduction of $0.8 million to accumulated other comprehensive income, net of taxes. During 2009 and 2008, the Company recorded an additional liability of $0.5 million and $1.5 million, respectively, and a corresponding reduction to accumulated other comprehensive income, net of taxes of $0.4 million and $1.1 million, respectively, related to the unfunded status of the Company's defined benefit plans.

Supplemental Retirement Plans

3.76

ARROW ELECTRONICS, INC. (DEC)

NOTES TO CONSOLIDATED FINANCIAL STATEMENTS
(Dollars in thousands except per share data)

13 (In Part): Employee Benefit Plans

Supplemental Executive Retirement Plans ("SERP")
The company maintains an unfunded Arrow SERP under which the company will pay supplemental pension benefits to certain employees upon retirement. There are 12 current and 13 former corporate officers participating in this plan. The Board determines those employees who are eligible to participate in the Arrow SERP.

The Arrow SERP, as amended, provides for the pension benefits to be based on a percentage of average final compensation, based on years of participation in the Arrow SERP.

The Arrow SERP permits early retirement, with payments at a reduced rate, based on age and years of service subject to a minimum retirement age of 55. Participants whose accrued rights under the Arrow SERP, prior to the 2002 amendment, which were adversely affected by the amendment, will continue to be entitled to such greater rights.

The company acquired Wyle Electronics ("Wyle") in 2000. Wyle also sponsored an unfunded SERP for certain of its executives. Benefit accruals for the Wyle SERP were frozen as of December 31, 2000. There are 19 participants in this plan.

The company uses a December 31 measurement date for the Arrow SERP and the Wyle SERP. Pension information for the years ended December 31 is as follows:

	2009	2008
Accumulated benefit obligation	$ 49,058	$ 46,286
Changes in projected benefit obligation:		
Projected benefit obligation at beginning of year	$ 53,885	$ 53,065
Service cost (Arrow SERP)	2,320	2,587
Interest cost	3,017	2,929
Actuarial (gain)/loss	848	(1,768)
Benefits paid	(3,018)	(2,928)
Projected benefit obligation at end of year	$ 57,052	$ 53,885
Funded status	$(57,052)	$(53,885)
Components of net periodic pension cost:		
Service cost (Arrow SERP)	$ 2,320	$ 2,587
Interest cost	3,017	2,929
Amortization of net loss	(174)	321
Amortization of prior service cost (Arrow SERP)	591	549
Amortization of transition obligation (Arrow SERP)	410	411
Net periodic pension cost	$ 6,164	$ 6,797
Weighted average assumptions used to determine benefit obligation:		
Discount rate	5.50%	6.00%
Rate of compensation increase (Arrow SERP)	5.00%	5.00%

	2009	2008
Weighted average assumptions used to determine net periodic pension cost:		
Discount rate	6.00%	5.75%
Rate of compensation increase (Arrow SERP)	5.00%	5.00%

The amounts reported for net periodic pension cost and the respective benefit obligation amounts are dependent upon the actuarial assumptions used. The company reviews historical trends, future expectations, current market conditions, and external data to determine the assumptions. The discount rate represents the market rate for a high quality corporate bond. The rate of compensation increase is determined by the company, based upon its long-term plans for such increases. The actuarial assumptions used to determine the net periodic pension cost are based upon the prior year's assumptions used to determine the benefit obligation.

Benefit payments are expected to be paid as follows:

2010	$ 3,674
2011	3,656
2012	3,789
2013	3,820
2014	3,780
2015–2019	22,242

Multiemployer Plans

3.77

REPUBLIC SERVICES, INC. (DEC)

NOTES TO CONSOLIDATED FINANCIAL STATEMENTS

Note 11 (In Part): Employee Benefit Plans

Multiemployer Plans

We contribute to 25 multi-employer pension plans under collective bargaining agreements covering union-represented employees. Approximately 17% of our total current employees are participants in such multi-employer plans. These plans generally provide retirement benefits to participants based on their service to contributing employers. We do not administer these multi-employer plans. In general, these plans are managed by a board of trustees with the unions appointing certain trustees and other contributing employers of the plan appointing certain members. We generally are not represented on the board of trustees.

Based on the information available to us, we believe that some of the multi-employer plans to which we contribute are either "critical" or "endangered" as those terms are defined in the Pension Protection Act enacted in 2006 (the PPA). The PPA requires underfunded pension plans to improve their funding ratios within prescribed intervals based on the level of their underfunding. Until the plan trustees develop the funding improvement plans or rehabilitation plans as required by the PPA, we are unable to determine the amount of assessments we may be subject to, if any. Accordingly, we cannot determine at this time the impact that the PPA may have on our consolidated financial position, results of operations or cash flows.

Furthermore, under current law regarding multi-employer benefit plans, a plan's termination, our voluntary withdrawal (which we consider from time to time), or the mass withdrawal of all contributing employers from any under-funded, multi-employer pension plan would require us to make payments to the plan for our proportionate share of the multi-employer plan's unfunded vested liabilities. It is possible that there may be a mass withdrawal of employers contributing to these plans or plans may terminate in the near future. We could have adjustments to our estimates for these matters in the near term that could have a material effect on our consolidated financial condition, results of operations or cash flows.

Our pension expense for multi-employer plans was $43.0 million, $21.8 million and $18.9 million for the years ended December 31, 2009, 2008 and 2007, respectively.

Plan Amendment and Termination

3.78

POLYONE CORPORATION (DEC)

NOTES TO CONSOLIDATED FINANCIAL STATEMENTS

Note 1 (In Part): Summary of Significant Accounting Policies

Pension and Other Post-Retirement Plans

We account for our pensions and other post-retirement benefits in accordance with FASB ASC Topic 715, *Compensation—Retirement Benefits*. This standard requires us to (1) recognize the funded status of the benefit plans in our statement of financial position, (2) recognize as a component of other comprehensive income, net of tax, the gains or losses and prior service costs or credits that arise during the period but are not recognized as components of net periodic benefit cost, (3) measure defined benefit plan assets and obligations as of the date of the employer's fiscal year end statement of financial position and (4) disclose additional information in the notes to financial statements about certain effects on net periodic benefit costs for the next fiscal year that arise from delayed recognition of gains or losses, prior service costs or credits, and transition assets or obligations.

Note 11. Employee Benefit Plans

We have several pension plans; however, as of December 31, 2009, only certain foreign plans accrue benefits. The plans generally provide benefit payments using a formula that is based upon employee compensation and length of service. All U.S. defined benefit pension plans are frozen from accruing benefits and are closed to new participants.

On January 15, 2009, we adopted amendments to the Geon Pension Plan (Geon Plan), the Benefit Restoration Plan (BRP), the voluntary retirement savings plan (RSP) and the Supplemental Retirement Benefit Plan (SRP). Effective March 20, 2009, the amendments to the Geon Plan and the BRP permanently froze future benefit accruals and provide that participants will not receive credit under the Geon Plan or the BRP for any eligible earnings paid on or after that date. Additionally, certain benefits provided under the RSP and SRP were eliminated after March 20, 2009. These actions resulted in a reduction of our 2009 annual benefit expense of $3.7 million and are expected to reduce our future pension fund contribution requirements by approximately $20 million.

We also sponsor several unfunded defined benefit post-retirement plans that provide subsidized health care and life insurance benefits to certain retirees and a closed group of eligible employees. On September 1, 2009, we adopted changes to our U.S. postretirement healthcare plan whereby, effective January 1, 2010, the plan, for certain eligible retirees, will be discontinued, and benefits will be phased out through December 31, 2012. Only certain employees hired prior to December 31, 1999 are eligible to participate in our subsidized post-retirement health care and life insurance plans. These amendments resulted in a curtailment gain of $21.1 million in our 2009 results and decreased the accumulated pension benefit obligation by $58.1 million.

The following tables present the change in benefit obligation, change in plan assets and components of funded status for defined benefit pension and post-retirement health care benefit plans. Actuarial assumptions that were used are also included.

(In millions)	Pension Benefits		Health Care Benefits	
	2009	2008	2009	2008
Change in benefit obligation:				
Projected benefit obligation—beginning of year	$ 501.2	$ 487.1	$ 91.0	$ 91.5
Service cost	1.4	1.3	0.1	0.3
Interest cost	30.7	32.4	4.1	5.5
Participant contributions	0.1	—	5.9	6.0
Benefits paid	(38.9)	(37.0)	(10.9)	(12.1)
Plan amendments/settlements	(18.0)	2.2	(58.1)	6.1
Change in discount rate and other	22.2	15.2	(5.5)	(6.3)
Projected benefit obligation—end of year	$ 498.7	$ 501.2	$ 26.6	$ 91.0
Projected salary increases	2.1	19.9	—	—
Accumulated benefit obligation	$ 496.6	$ 481.3	$ 26.6	$ 91.0
Change in plan assets:				
Plan assets—beginning of year	$ 271.9	$ 401.3	$ —	$ —
Actual return on plan assets	63.7	(120.8)	—	—
Company contributions	23.5	29.8	5.0	6.1
Plan participants' contributions	0.1	—	5.9	6.0
Benefits paid	(38.9)	(37.0)	(10.9)	(12.1)
Other	0.3	(1.4)	—	—
Plan assets—end of year	$ 320.6	$ 271.9	$ —	$ —
Under-funded status at end of year	$(178.1)	$(229.3)	$(26.6)	$(91.0)

•   •   •   •   •   •

The following table summarizes the components of net period benefit cost that was recognized during each of the years in the three-year period ended December 31, 2009. Actuarial assumptions that were used are also included.

(In millions)	Pension Benefits			Health Care Benefits		
	2009	2008	2007	2009	2008	2007
Components of net periodic benefit costs:						
Service cost	$ 1.4	$ 1.3	$ 1.1	$ 0.1	$ 0.3	$ 0.4
Interest cost	30.7	32.4	30.1	4.1	5.5	5.2
Expected return on plan assets	(21.8)	(33.4)	(31.8)	—	—	—
Amortization of net loss	12.1	7.5	9.6	0.6	1.2	1.7
Curtailment (gain) loss and settlement charges	(0.8)	0.5	0.3	(21.1)	—	—
Amortization of prior service credit (cost)	0.8	0.2	(0.1)	(9.1)	(5.6)	(5.8)
	$ 22.4	$ 8.5	$ 9.2	$(25.4)	$ 1.4	$ 1.5

	Pension Benefits			Health Care Benefits		
	2009	2008	2007	2009	2008	2007
Weighted-average assumptions used to determine net periodic benefit cost for the years ended December 31:						
Discount rate	6.61%	6.78%	6.07%	6.50%	6.61%	6.02%
Expected long-term return on plan assets	8.50%	8.50%	8.50%	—	—	—
Rate of compensation increase	3.5%	3.5%	3.5%	—	—	—
Assumed health care cost trend rates at December 31:						
Health care cost trend rate assumed for next year	—	—	—	9.25%	9.25%	10.0%
Rate to which the cost trend rate is assumed to decline (the ultimate trend rate)	—	—	—	5.00%	5.00%	5.25%
Year that the rate reaches the ultimate trend rate	—	—	—	2015	2015	2013

The amounts in accumulated other comprehensive income that are expected to be amortized as net expense (income) during fiscal year 2010 are as follows:

(In millions)	Pension Benefits	Health Care Benefits
Amount of net prior service credit	$0.8	$(17.4)
Amount of net loss	9.3	0.7

• • • • • •

The estimated future benefit payments for our pension and health care plans are as follows:

(In millions)	Pension Benefits	Health Care Benefits	Medicare Part D Subsidy
2010	$ 37.6	$4.6	$0.2
2011	38.1	3.6	0.2
2012	37.8	2.9	0.1
2013	38.0	2.2	0.1
2014	38.2	2.1	0.1
2015 through 2019	195.1	9.1	0.6

We currently estimate that 2010 employer contributions will be $20.8 million to all qualified and nonqualified pension plans and $4.6 million to all health care benefit plans.

POSTEMPLOYMENT BENEFITS

3.79 FASB ASC 712, *Compensation—Nonretirement Postemployment Benefits*, requires that entities providing postemployment benefits to their employees accrue the cost of such benefits. FASB ASC 712 does not require that the amount of postemployment benefits be disclosed. Accordingly, many of the survey entities make little or no disclosure about postemployment benefits.

3.80 An example of a disclosure for postemployment benefits follows.

3.81

KELLOGG COMPANY (DEC)

NOTES TO CONSOLIDATED FINANCIAL STATEMENTS

Note 1 (In Part): Accounting Policies

Pension Benefits, Nonpension Postretirement and Postemployment Benefits

The Company sponsors a number of U.S. and foreign plans to provide pension, health care, and other welfare benefits to retired employees, as well as salary continuance, severance, and long-term disability to former or inactive employees.

The recognition of benefit expense is based on several actuarial assumptions, such as discount rate, long-term rate of compensation increase, long-term rate of return on plan assets and health care cost trend rate, and is reported within COGS and SGA expense on the Consolidated Statement of Income.

The Company recognizes the net overfunded or underfunded position of a defined postretirement benefit plan as a pension asset or pension liability on the Consolidated Balance Sheet. The change in funded status for the year is reported as a component of other comprehensive income (loss), net of tax, in equity.

Obligations associated with the Company's postemployment benefit plans, which are unfunded, are included in other current liabilities and other liabilities on the Consolidated Balance Sheet.

Note 9 (In Part): Nonpension Postretirement and Postemployment Benefits

Postemployment

Under certain conditions, the Company provides benefits to former or inactive employees in the United States and several foreign locations, including salary continuance, severance, and long-term disability. The Company recognizes an obligation for any of these benefits that vest or accumulate with service. Postemployment benefits that do not vest or accumulate with service (such as severance based solely on annual pay rather than years of service) or costs arising from actions that offer benefits to employees in excess of those specified in the respective plans are charged to expense when incurred. The Company's postemployment benefit plans are unfunded. Actuarial assumptions used are generally consistent with those presented for pension benefits in Note 8. The aggregate change in accumulated postemployment benefit obligation and the net amount recognized were:

(Millions)	2009	2008
Change in accumulated benefit obligation		
Beginning of year	$ 65	$ 63
Service cost	6	5
Interest cost	4	4
Actuarial loss	8	1
Benefits paid	(10)	(7)
Foreign currency adjustments	1	(1)
End of year	$ 74	$ 65
Funded status	$(74)	$(65)
Amounts recognized in the consolidated balance sheet consist of		
Other current liabilities	$ (7)	$ (6)
Other liabilities	(67)	(59)
Net amount recognized	$(74)	$(65)
Amounts recognized in accumulated other comprehensive income consist of		
Net experience loss	$ 39	$ 34
Net amount recognized	$ 39	$ 34

Components of postemployment benefit expense were:

(Millions)	2009	2008	2007
Service cost	$ 6	$ 5	$ 6
Interest cost	4	4	2
Recognized net loss	4	4	2
Postemployment benefit expense	$14	$13	$10

All gains and losses are recognized over the average remaining service period of active plan participants. The estimated net experience loss that will be amortized from accumulated other comprehensive income into postemployment benefit expense over the next fiscal year is approximately $4 million.

EMPLOYEE COMPENSATORY PLANS

3.82 FASB ASC 718, *Compensation—Stock Compensation*, establishes accounting and reporting standards for stock-based compensation plans. FASB ASC 718 requires for public entities that such share-based payment transactions be accounted for using a fair-value-based method. Thus public entities are required to recognize the cost of employee services received in exchange for award of equity instruments based on the grant-date fair value of those awards. FASB ASC 718 provides clarification and expanded guidance in several areas, including measuring fair value, classifying an award as equity or as a liability and attributing compensation cost to reporting periods.

3.83 Table 3-13 lists the types of employee compensatory plans disclosed by the survey entities. Compensatory plans may consist of stock awards or cash payments. The "stock award" caption in Table 3-13 represents restricted stock awards, performance awards, and bonuses paid by issuing stock.

3.84 Examples of employee compensatory plan disclosures follow.

3.85

TABLE 3-13: EMPLOYEE COMPENSATORY PLANS

	Number of Entities			
	2009	2008	2007	2006
Stock options	488	489	593	584
Stock award	427	439	475	401
Savings/investment	322	271	349	377
Stock purchase	155	155	196	179
Deferred compensation	124	119	140	146
Incentive compensation	63	63	57	58
Employee stock ownership	55	55	68	71
Profit-sharing	46	62	61	67

2008–2009 based on 500 entities surveyed; 2006–2007 based on 600 entities surveyed.

Stock Option Plans

3.86

EMC CORPORATION (DEC)

NOTES TO CONSOLIDATED FINANCIAL STATEMENTS (Dollar and share amounts in thousands, except per-share data)

A (In Part): Summary of Significant Accounting Policies

Accounting for Stock-Based Compensation

We have selected the Black-Scholes option-pricing model to determine the fair value of our stock option awards. For stock options, restricted stock and restricted stock units, we recognize compensation cost on a straight-line basis over the awards' vesting periods for those awards which contain only a service vesting feature. For awards with a performance condition vesting feature, when achievement of the performance condition is deemed probable, we recognize compensation cost on a graded-vesting basis over the awards' expected vesting periods.

P (In Part): Stock-Based Compensation

EMC Information Infrastructure Equity Plans

The EMC Corporation 2003 Stock Plan (the "2003 Plan") provides for the grant of stock options, stock appreciation rights, restricted stock and restricted stock units. The exercise price for a stock option shall not be less than 100% of the fair market value of our common stock on the date of grant. Options generally become exercisable in annual installments over a period of three to five years after the date of grant and expire ten years after the date of grant. Incentive stock options will expire no later than ten years after the date of grant. Restricted stock is common stock that is subject to a risk of forfeiture or other restrictions that will lapse upon satisfaction of specified conditions. Restricted stock units represent the right to receive shares of common stock in the future, with the right to future delivery of the shares subject to a risk of forfeiture or other restrictions that will lapse upon satisfaction of specified conditions. Grants of restricted stock awards or restricted stock units that vest only by the passage of time will not vest fully in less than three years after the date of grant, except for grants to non-employee Directors that are not subject to this minimum three-year vesting requirement. The 2003 Plan allows us to grant up to 300.0 million shares of common stock. Beginning in May 2007, we started recognizing restricted stock awards and restricted stock units against the 2003 Plan share reserve as two shares for every one share issued in connection with such awards.

In addition to the 2003 Plan, we have four other stock option plans (the "1985 Plan," the "1993 Plan," the "2001 Plan" and the "1992 Directors Plan"). In May 2007, these four plans were consolidated into the 2003 Plan such that all future grants will be granted under the 2003 Plan and shares that are not issued as a result of cancellations, expirations or forfeitures, will become available for grant under the 2003 Plan.

A total of 862.4 million shares of common stock have been reserved for issuance under the above five plans. At December 31, 2009, there were an aggregate of 60.8 million shares of common stock available for issuance pursuant to future grants under the 2003 Plan.

We have, in connection with the acquisition of various companies, assumed the stock option plans of these companies. We do not intend to make future grants under any of such plans.

EMC Information Infrastructure Stock Options

The following table summarizes our option activity under all equity plans in 2009, 2008 and 2007 (shares in thousands):

	Number of Shares	Weighted Average Exercise Price (Per Share)
Outstanding, January 1, 2007	303,184	$17.19
Options granted relating to business acquisitions	921	3.39
Granted	28,777	19.15
Forfeited	(9,640)	12.01
Expired	(4,321)	38.28
Exercised	(68,540)	9.66
Exchanged to VMware awards	(11,009)	12.19
Outstanding, December 31, 2007	239,372	19.60
Options granted relating to business acquisitions	1,200	12.43
Granted	36,208	14.95
Forfeited	(6,852)	14.43
Expired	(7,096)	33.98
Exercised	(12,713)	9.34
Outstanding, December 31, 2008	250,119	19.14
Options granted relating to business acquisitions	24,089	5.68
Granted	14,243	15.20
Forfeited	(10,178)	14.64
Expired	(14,953)	29.35
Exercised	(28,402)	8.85
Outstanding, December 31, 2009	234,918	18.31
Exercisable, December 31, 2009	154,191	20.62
Vested and expected to vest	227,398	18.48

At December 31, 2009, the weighted-average remaining contractual term was 3.9 years and the aggregate intrinsic value was $644.4 million for the 154,191 exercisable shares. For the 227,398 shares vested and expected to vest at December 31, 2009, the weighted-average remaining contractual term was 5.3 years and the aggregate intrinsic value was $925.1 million. The intrinsic value is based on our closing stock price of $17.47 as of December 31, 2009, which would have been received by the option holders had all in-the-money options been exercised as of that date. The total pre-tax intrinsic values of options exercised in 2009, 2008 and 2007 were $191.6 million, $77.2 million and $587.4 million, respectively. Cash proceeds from the exercise of stock options were $251.1 million, $118.7 million and $661.6 million in 2009, 2008 and 2007, respectively. Income tax benefits realized from the exercise of stock options in 2009, 2008 and 2007 were $53.6 million, $105.0 million and $160.7 million, respectively.

VMware Equity Plans

In June 2007, VMware adopted its 2007 Equity and Incentive Plan (the "2007 Plan"). In May 2009, VMware amended its 2007 Plan to increase the number of shares available for issuance by 20 million shares for total shares available for issuance of 100.0 million. Awards under the 2007 Plan may be in the form of stock options or other stock-based awards, including awards of restricted stock. The exercise price for a stock option awarded under the 2007 Plan shall not be less than 100% of the fair market value of VMware Class A common stock on the date of grant. Most options granted under the 2007 Plan vest 25% after the first year and then monthly thereafter over the following three years. All options granted pursuant to the 2007 Plan expire between six and seven years from the date of grant. Most restricted stock awards granted under the 2007 Plan have a three-year to four-year period over which they vest. VMware utilizes both authorized and unissued shares to satisfy all shares issued under the 2007 Plan.

2008 VMware Exchange Offer

In September 2008, VMware completed an offer to exchange certain employee stock options issued under VMware's 2007 Equity and Incentive Plan ("2008 Exchange Offer"). Certain previously granted options were exchanged for new, lower-priced stock options granted on a one-for-one basis. Executive officers and members of VMware's Board of Directors were excluded from participating in the 2008 Exchange Offer. Options for an aggregate of 4.1 million shares of VMware's Class A common stock were exchanged with a weighted-average exercise price per share of $71.60. Options granted pursuant to the 2008 Exchange Offer have an exercise price of $33.95 per share, vest pro rata over four years beginning September 10, 2008 with no credit for past vesting and have a new six-year option term. The 2008 Exchange Offer resulted in incremental stock-based compensation expense of $18.0 million to be recognized over the four-year vesting term.

VMware Stock Options

The following table summarizes activity since January 1, 2007 for VMware employees in VMware stock options (shares in thousands):

	Number of Shares	Weighted Average Exercise Price (Per Share)
Outstanding, January 1, 2007	—	$ —
Granted	39,271	27.88
Exchanged from EMC stock options	6,732	19.94
Forfeited	(539)	24.50
Expired	(5)	24.64
Exercised	(120)	23.00
Outstanding, December 31, 2007	45,339	26.76
Granted[1]	11,741	40.48
Forfeited[1]	(8,033)	51.74
Expired	(37)	24.26
Exercised	(6,574)	21.64
Outstanding, December 31, 2008	42,436	26.54
Granted	12,500	29.86
Forfeited	(3,736)	28.11
Expired	(177)	45.24
Exercised	(9,516)	22.01
Outstanding, December 31, 2009	41,507	28.34
Exercisable, December 31, 2009	13,398	26.85
Vested and expected to vest	39,994	27.98

[1] Includes options for 4,017 shares exchanged in the 2008 VMware Exchange Offer.

As of December 31, 2009, the weighted-average remaining contractual term was 3.9 years and the aggregate intrinsic value was $237.7 million for the 13.4 million exercisable shares. For the 40.0 million shares vested and expect to vest at December 31, 2009, the weighted-average remaining contractual term was 4.4 years and the aggregate intrinsic value was $625.3 million. These aggregate intrinsic values represent the total pre-tax intrinsic values based on VMware's closing stock price of $42.38 as of December 31, 2009, which would have been received by the option holders had all in-the-money options been exercised as of that date.

Cash proceeds from the exercise of VMware stock options for the years ended December 31, 2009, 2008 and 2007 were $209.4 million, $143.2 million and $2.8 million, respectively. The options exercised in 2009 and 2008 had a pre-tax intrinsic value of $132.6 million and $219.6 million, respectively, and income tax benefits realized from the exercise of stock options of $47.1 million and $71.4 million, respectively. There was no pre-tax intrinsic value to the options exercised or related income tax benefits realized in 2007.

In August 2009, VMware granted its President and Chief Executive Officer a stock option for the purchase of approximately 1.4 million shares of VMware's Class A common stock in exchange for a stock option he held for the purchase of shares of common stock of EMC Corporation. The exercise price of his new VMware grant was $31.59 per share, the closing trading price of VMware Class A common stock on the grant date of August 12, 2009. The option expires six years from the grant date. The new VMware grant preserves the 13 months of vesting that had been earned while serving as VMware's President and CEO since July 2008 and accordingly was vested with respect to 0.3 million of the shares on the date of grant. The remaining 1.1 million shares will vest ratably each month through March 2013 subject to his continued service to VMware. There is no incremental stock-based compensation expense as a result of modifying this award, and the original grant date fair value continues to be recognized over the requisite service period of the award.

Stock-Based Compensation Expense

The following tables summarize the components of total stock-based compensation expense included in our consolidated income statement in 2009, 2008 and 2007 (in thousands):

| | 2009 | | |
	Stock Options	Restricted Stock	Total Stock-Based Compensation
Cost of product sales	$ 33,423	$ 15,836	$ 49,259
Cost of services	35,004	15,130	50,134
Research and development	118,875	95,679	214,554
Selling, general and administrative	189,154	102,605	291,759
Restructuring charges	(1,015)	(306)	(1,321)
Stock-based compensation expense before income taxes	375,441	228,944	604,385
Income tax benefit	78,517	56,326	134,843
Total stock-based compensation, net of tax	$296,924	$172,618	$469,542

| | 2008 | | |
	Stock Options	Restricted Stock	Total Stock-Based Compensation
Cost of product sales	$ 23,092	$ 9,638	$ 32,730
Cost of services	35,350	12,046	47,396
Research and development	102,865	59,512	162,377
Selling, general and administrative	161,715	97,223	258,938
Restructuring charges	5,164	(1,740)	3,424
Stock-based compensation expense before income taxes	328,186	176,679	504,865
Income tax benefit	61,321	47,738	109,059
Total stock-based compensation, net of tax	$266,865	$128,941	$395,806

| | 2007 | | |
	Stock Options	Restricted Stock	Total Stock-Based Compensation
Cost of product sales	$ 22,886	$ 9,543	$ 32,429
Cost of services	20,493	4,303	24,796
Research and development	69,649	38,393	108,042
Selling, general and administrative	126,246	75,891	202,137
Restructuring charges	897	1,731	2,628
Stock-based compensation expense before income taxes	240,171	129,861	370,032
Income tax benefit	53,292	34,378	87,670
Total stock-based compensation, net of tax	$186,879	$ 95,483	$282,362

Stock option expense includes $46.5 million, $52.2 million and $36.7 million of expense associated with our employee stock purchase plans for 2009, 2008 and 2007, respectively.

The table below presents the net change in amounts capitalized or accrued in 2009 and 2008 for the following items (in thousands):

	Increased (Decreased) During the Year Ended December 31, 2009	Increased (Decreased) During the Year Ended December 31, 2008
Inventory	$ 1,254	$ 686
Other assets (capitalized software development costs)	1,435	16,749
Accrued expenses (accrued warranty expenses)	(1,835)	(4,730)

As of December 31, 2009, the total unrecognized after-tax compensation cost for stock options, restricted stock and restricted stock units was $955.0 million. This non-cash expense will be recognized through 2014 with a weighted average remaining period of 1.3 years.

Fair Value of EMC Information Infrastructure Options

The fair value of each option granted during 2009, 2008 and 2007 was estimated on the date of grant using the Black-Scholes option-pricing model with the following weighted-average assumptions:

EMC Stock Options	2009	2008	2007
Dividend yield	None	None	None
Expected volatility	35.4%	34.4%	33.8%
Risk-free interest rate	2.4%	2.8%	3.6%
Expected term (in years)	4.5	4.4	4.2
Weighted-average fair value at grant date	$ 5.04	$ 4.82	$ 6.29

EMC Employee Stock Purchase Plan	2009	2008	2007
Dividend yield	None	None	None
Expected volatility	58.1%	40.0%	25.5%
Risk-free interest rate	0.4%	2.6%	5.0%
Expected term (in years)	0.5	0.5	0.5
Weighted-average fair value at grant date	$ 3.16	$ 4.32	$ 3.53

Expected volatilities are based on our historical stock prices and implied volatilities from traded options in our stock. We use EMC historical data to estimate the expected term of options granted within the valuation model. The risk-free interest rate was based on a treasury instrument whose term is consistent with the expected life of the stock options. The assumptions for 2009 for the EMC Employee Stock Purchase Plan include only the January 1, 2009 grant due to the elimination of the look-back feature as of July 1, 2009.

Fair Value of VMware Options (In Part)

The fair value of each option to acquire VMware Class A common stock granted during the years ended December 31, 2009, 2008 and 2007 was estimated on the date of grant using the Black-Scholes option-pricing model with the following weighted-average assumptions:

VMware Stock Options	2009	2008	2007
Dividend yield	None	None	None
Expected volatility	36.1%	39.4%	39.2%
Risk-free interest rate	1.9%	2.5%	4.9%
Expected term (in years)	3.7	3.4	3.4
Weighted-average fair value at grant date	$12.18	$17.88	$27.88

For all equity awards granted in 2009, volatility was based on an analysis of historical stock prices and implied volatilities of publicly-traded companies with similar characteristics, including industry, stage of life cycle, size, financial leverage, as well as the implied volatilities of VMware's Class A common stock. The expected term was calculated based only upon the expected term of similar grants of comparable companies.

For all equity awards granted in 2008 and 2007, volatility was based on an analysis of historical stock prices and implied volatility of publicly-traded companies with similar characteristics, including industry, stage of life cycle, size and financial leverage. The expected term was calculated based on the historical experience that VMware employees have had with EMC stock option grants as well as the expected term of similar grants of comparable companies.

VMware's expected dividend yield input was zero as it has not historically paid, nor does it expect in the future to pay, cash dividends on its common stock. The risk-free interest rate was based on U.S. Treasury instrument whose term is consistent with the expected term of the stock options.

For the equity awards granted prior to VMware's IPO, VMware performed a contemporaneous valuation of their Class A common stock each time an equity grant of common stock was made. In determining the fair value of the equity, VMware analyzed general market data, including economic, governmental, and environmental factors; considered its historic, current, and future state of its operations; analyzed its operating and financial results; analyzed its forecasts; gathered and analyzed available financial data for publicly traded companies engaged in the same or similar lines of business to develop appropriate valuation multiples and operating comparisons and analyzed other facts and data considered pertinent to the valuation to arrive at an estimated fair value.

VMware utilized both the income approach and the market approach in estimating the value of the equity. The market approach estimates the fair value of a company by applying to the company's historical and/or projected financial metrics to market multiples of the corresponding financial metrics of publicly traded firms in similar lines of business. Due to the prospect of an imminent public offering, VMware did not apply a marketability discount in carrying out either approach. Further, VMware did not apply a minority interest discount in concluding on fair value.

In reaching its estimated valuation range, VMware considered the indicated values derived from each valuation approach in relation to the relative merits of each approach, the suitability of the information used, and the uncertainties involved. The results of the approaches overlapped, with the income approach results falling within a narrower range, which VMware ultimately relied on in its concluding estimate of value.

3.87

NETAPP, INC. (APR)

NOTES TO CONSOLIDATED FINANCIAL STATEMENTS
(Dollar and share amounts in thousands, except per-share data)

2 (In Part): Summary of Significant Accounting Policies

Stock-Based Compensation

We account for stock-based compensation expense in accordance with SFAS No. 123R, *"Share-Based Payment"* ("SFAS No. 123R"), which requires us to measure and recognize compensation expense for all stock-based payments awards, including employee stock options, restricted stock units and rights to purchase shares under our ESPP, based on their estimated fair value, and to recognize the costs in our financial statements over the employees' requisite service period. Total stock-based compensation expense recognized in fiscal 2009, 2008 and 2007 was $140,754, $147,964 and $163,033, respectively.

The fair value of employee restricted stock units is equal to the market value of our common stock on the date the award is granted. Calculating the fair value of employee stock options and the rights to purchase shares under the ESPP requires estimates and significant judgment. We use the Black-Scholes option pricing model to estimate the fair value of these awards, consistent with the provisions of SFAS No. 123R. The fair value of each option grant is estimated on the date of grant using the Black-Scholes option pricing model, and is not remeasured as a result of subsequent stock price fluctuations. Option-pricing models require the input of highly subjective assumptions, including the expected term of options, the expected price volatility of the stock underlying such options and forfeiture rate. Our expected term assumption is based primarily on historical exercise and post-vesting forfeiture experience. Our stock price volatility assumption is based on an implied volatility of call options and dealer quotes on call options, generally having a term of greater than twelve months. Changes in the subjective assumptions required in the valuation models may significantly affect the estimated value of our stock-based awards, the related stock-based compensation expense and, consequently, our results of operations. Likewise, the shortening of the contractual life of our options could change the estimated exercise behavior in a manner other than currently expected.

In addition, SFAS 123R requires that we estimate the number of stock-based awards that will be forfeited due to employee turnover. Our forfeiture assumption is based primarily on historical experience. Changes in the estimated forfeiture rate can have a significant effect on reported stock-based compensation expense, as the effect of adjusting the rate for all expense amortization after April 28, 2006 is recognized in the period the forfeiture estimate is changed. If the actual forfeiture rate is higher than the estimated forfeiture rate, then an adjustment will be made to increase the estimated forfeiture rate, which will result in a decrease to the expense recognized in the financial statements. If the actual forfeiture rate is lower than the estimated forfeiture rate, then an adjustment will be made to lower the estimated forfeiture rate, which will result in an increase to the expense recognized in our financial statements. The expense we recognize in future periods will be affected by changes in the estimated forfeiture rate and may differ significantly from amounts recognized in the current period and/or our forecasts.

5 (In Part): Stock-Based Compensation, Equity Incentive Programs and Stockholders' Equity

Stock-based compensation expenses included in the Consolidated Statements of Operations for fiscal 2009, 2008 and 2007 are as follows:

	2009	2008	2007
Cost of product revenues	$ 3,327	$ 3,384	$ 3,720
Cost of service revenues	12,289	10,442	10,088
Sales and marketing	65,085	65,399	71,701
Research and development	37,902	46,632	51,323
General and administrative	22,151	22,107	26,201
Total stock-based compensation expense before income taxes	$140,754	$147,964	$163,033

The following table summarizes stock-based compensation associated with each type of award:

	2009	2008	2007
Employee stock options and restricted stock units	$113,350	$131,410	$150,257
ESPP	27,411	16,513	13,099
Change in amounts capitalized in inventory	(7)	41	(323)
Total stock-based compensation expense before income taxes	$140,754	$147,964	$163,033

Valuation Assumptions

We estimated the fair value of stock options using the Black-Scholes model on the date of the grant. Assumptions used in the Black-Scholes valuation model were as follows:

	Stock Options			ESPP		
	2009	2008	2007	2009	2008	2007
Expected term in years[1]	4.0	4.0	4.0	1.3	1.3	1.3
Risk-free interest rate[2]	1.08%–3.69%	2.04%–5.02%	4.42%–5.05%	0.92%–2.52%	2.36%–4.95%	4.42%–5.06%
Volatility[3]	38%–69%	33%–55%	32%–38%	39%–76%	35%–49%	32%–38%
Expected dividend[4]	0%	0%	0%	0%	0%	0%

[1] The 4.0 years expected term of the options represent the estimated period of time until exercise and is based on historical experience with similar awards, giving consideration to the contractual terms, vesting schedules, and expectations of future employee behavior. The expected life for the ESPP rights was based on the term of the purchase period.

[2] The risk-free interest rate for the stock option awards was based upon United States ("U.S.") Treasury bills with equivalent expected terms. The risk-free interest rate for the employee stock purchase plan was based on the U.S. Treasury bills in effect at the time of grant for the expected term of the purchase period.

[3] We used the implied volatility of traded options to estimate our stock price volatility.

[4] The expected dividend was determined based on our history and expected dividend payouts.

We estimate our forfeiture rates based on historical termination behavior and recognize compensation expense only for those equity awards expected to vest.

Equity Incentive Programs

Stock Incentive Plans

The 1995 Plan

The 1995 Stock Incentive Plan ("the 1995 Plan") expired on August 31, 2008, and no further grants may be made from the plan.

Options granted under the 1995 Plan generally vested at a rate of 25% on the first anniversary of the vesting commencement date and then ratably over the following 36 months. Options expired as determined by the Board of Directors, but not more than 10 years after the date of grant. The 1999 Plan supplements the 1995 Plan.

The Nonofficer Plan

In April 1997, the Board of Directors adopted the Special Nonofficer Stock Option Plan ("the Nonofficer Plan") which provides for the grant of options and the issuance of common stock under terms substantially the same as those provided under the 1995 Plan, except that the Nonofficer Plan allows only for the issuance of nonqualified options to nonofficer employees. The Nonofficer Plan expired on December 31, 2007, and no further grants may be made from the plan.

The 1999 Plan

As amended through April 24, 2009, the 1999 Stock Option Plan ("the 1999 Plan") comprises five separate equity incentive programs: (i) the Discretionary Option Grant Program under which options may be granted to eligible individuals during the service period at a fixed price per share; (ii) the Stock Appreciation Rights Program under which eligible persons may be granted stock appreciation rights that allow individuals to receive the appreciation in Fair Market Value of the shares; (iii) the Stock Issuance Program under which eligible individuals may be issued shares of Common Stock directly; (iv) the Performance Share and Performance Unit Program (also known as restricted stock units or RSUs) under which eligible persons may be granted performance shares and performance units which result in payment to the participant only if performance goals or other vesting criteria are achieved; and (v) the Automatic Option Grant Program under which nonemployee board members automatically receive option grants at designated intervals over their period of board service.

Under the 1999 Plan, the Board of Directors may grant to employees, nonemployee directors, and consultants and other independent advisors options to purchase shares of our common stock during their period of service with us. The exercise price for an incentive stock option and a nonstatutory option cannot be less than 100% of the fair market value of the common stock on the grant date. Options granted under the 1999 Plan generally vest over a four-year period. Options granted prior to April 29, 2006, have a term of no more than 10 years after the date of grant and those granted after April 29, 2006 have a term of no more than seven years, subject to earlier termination upon the occurrence of certain events. The 1999 Plan prohibits the repricing of any outstanding stock option or stock appreciation right after it has been granted or to cancel any outstanding stock option or stock appreciation right and immediately replace it with a new stock option or stock appreciation right with a lower exercise price unless approved by stockholders. Restricted stock units granted under the 1999 Plan generally vest over a four-year period with 25% of the units vesting on each annual anniversary of the grant date. The 1999 Plan limits the percentage of Stock Issuance and Performance Shares or Performance Units that may be granted under the Plan to 30% of the shares reserved; limits the value of performance units a participant may receive during any calendar year to $2,000. The 1999 Plan expires on August 2019.

Acquisition Plans

In fiscal 2008, we assumed a stock incentive plan in connection with our acquisition of Onaro (see Note 11). Under the terms of the merger agreement, options and restricted stock units to purchase 1,000 shares were exchanged at certain exchange ratios. The options granted under this plan generally vest at a rate of 25% on the first anniversary of the vesting commencement date and then ratably over the following

36 months. The restricted stock units generally vest at a rate of 50% on the first and second annual anniversaries of the vesting commencement date.

In fiscal 2007, we assumed two stock incentive plans in connection with our acquisition of Topio (see Note 11.) Under the terms of the merger agreement, options and restricted stock units to purchase 858 shares were exchanged at certain exchange ratios. The options granted under these plans generally vest at a rate of 25% on the first anniversary of the

vesting commencement date and then ratably over the following 36 months. The restricted stock units generally vest at a rate of 50% on the first and second annual anniversaries of the vesting commencement date.

In fiscal 2009, 2008 and 2007, 1999 Plan was amended to increase the share reserved by an additional 6,600, 7,200, and 10,900 shares for issuance under the plan, respectively. As of April 24, 2009, 17,822 shares were available for grant under our equity incentive plans.

A summary of the combined activity under our stock option plans and agreements is as follows:

	Outstanding Options		Weighted Average	
	Numbers of Shares	Weighted Average Exercise Price	Remaining Contractual Term (Years)	Aggregate Intrinsic Value
Balances, April 28, 2006	64,861	$26.42		
Options granted	12,820	36.53		
Assumed Topio options issued (weighted average fair value of $39.33)	858	20.32		
Options exercised	(11,908)	14.97		
Options forfeitures and canceled	(3,039)	38.36		
Options expired	—	—		
Outstanding at April 27, 2007	63,592	$29.95		
Options granted	11,196	26.41		
Assumed Onaro options issued (weighted average fair value of $22.22)	808	13.82		
Options exercised	(5,343)	12.47		
Options forfeitures and cancellation	(4,639)	37.54		
Outstanding at April 25, 2008	65,614	$30.03		
Options granted	8,685	17.67		
Options exercised	(3,666)	11.20		
Options forfeitures and cancellations	(4,514)	32.61		
Outstanding at April 24, 2009	66,119	$29.27	4.43	$64,430
Options vested and expected to vest as of April 24, 2009	63,547	$29.49	4.37	$60,584
Exercisable at April 24, 2009	47,476	$31.01	3.88	$39,187

The intrinsic value of stock options represents the difference between the exercise price of stock options and the market price of our stock on that day for all in-the-money options. The weighted-average fair value of options granted during fiscal 2009, 2008 and 2007 was $7.28, $10.13 and $12.83, respectively. The total intrinsic value of options exercised

during fiscal 2009, 2008 and 2007 was $30,325, $83,129 and $267,165, respectively. We received $41,083, $66,614, and $178,241 from the exercise of stock options for fiscal 2009, 2008 and 2007, respectively. Total fair value of options vested during fiscal 2009 was $179,805.

The following table summarizes information about stock options outstanding under all option plans as of April 24, 2009:

Range of Exercise Prices		Options Outstanding			Options Exercisable	
		Number Outstanding at April 24, 2009	Weighted Average Remaining Contractual Life (In Years)	Weighted Average Exercise Price	Number Exercisable	Weighted Average Exercise Price
$ 0.55	$ 5.00	213	4.77	$ 1.93	168	$ 1.88
6.26	10.00	2,078	3.41	9.73	2,078	9.73
10.24	15.00	5,976	5.91	13.21	1,330	12.43
15.21	20.00	6,169	3.33	17.18	6,012	17.20
20.16	25.00	17,621	4.63	22.32	11,707	22.06
25.08	30.00	7,123	5.69	28.02	5,195	28.32
30.74	35.00	12,314	4.89	32.11	9,463	32.20
35.83	45.00	8,580	4.68	38.98	5,478	39.06
46.56	55.00	3,727	1.02	53.52	3,727	53.52
58.00	122.19	2,318	1.09	89.70	2,318	89.70
$ —	$122.19	66,119	4.43	$29.27	47,476	$31.01

The following table summarizes activity related to our restricted stock units:

	Numbers of Shares	Weighted Average Grant Date Fair Value	Weighted Average Remaining Contractual Term (Years)
Balances, April 28, 2006	848	$33.71	
Restricted stock units granted	753	37.58	
Restricted stock units vested	(120)	24.60	
Restricted stock units forfeitures and canceled	(30)	36.29	
Outstanding at April 27, 2007	1,451	$36.42	
Restricted stock units granted	3,373	23.11	
Assumed Onaro restricted stock units issued	192	22.83	
Restricted stock units vested	(309)	33.19	
Restricted stock units forfeitures and cancellation	(153)	33.65	
Outstanding at April 25, 2008	4,554	$26.30	
Restricted stock units granted	2,173	17.16	
Restricted stock units vested	(770)	28.81	
Restricted stock units forfeitures and cancellations	(504)	25.48	
Outstanding at April 24, 2009	5,453	$22.38	1.79

There was $256,745 of total unrecognized compensation expense as of April 24, 2009 related to options and restricted stock units. The unrecognized compensation expense will be amortized on a straight-line basis over a weighted-average remaining period of 2.5 years. For fiscal 2009, 2008 and 2007, total income tax benefit associated with employee stock transactions and recognized in the statement of stockholders equity was $43,855, $48,195 and $175,036, respectively.

Stock Award Plans

3.88

ADOBE SYSTEMS INCORPORATED (NOV)

NOTES TO CONSOLIDATED FINANCIAL STATEMENTS

Note 13 (In Part): Stock-Based Compensation

Restricted Stock Plan

We grant restricted stock awards and performance awards to officers and key employees under our Amended 1994 Performance and Restricted Stock Plan ("Restricted Stock Plan"). We can also grant restricted stock units to all eligible employees under the Restricted Stock Plan and the 2003 Plan. Restricted stock awards issued under these plans vest annually over three years. Performance awards and restricted stock units issued under these plans generally vest over four years, the majority of which vest 25% annually; certain other restricted stock units vest 50% on the second anniversary and 25% on each of the third and fourth anniversaries.

As of November 27, 2009, we had reserved 16.0 million shares of our common stock for issuance under the Restricted Stock Plan and approximately 0.3 million shares were available for grant.

Performance Share Programs

Effective January 26, 2009, the Executive Compensation Committee adopted the 2009 Performance Share Program (the "2009 Program"). The purpose of the 2009 Program is to align key management and senior leadership with stockholders' interests and to retain key employees. The measurement period for the 2009 Program is our fiscal 2009 year. All members of our executive management and other key senior leaders are participating in the 2009 Program. Awards granted under the 2009 Program were granted in the form of performance shares pursuant to the terms of our 2003 Equity Incentive Plan. If pre-determined performance goals are met, shares of stock will be granted to the recipient, with 25% vesting on the later of the date of certification of achievement or the first anniversary date of the grant, and the remaining 75% vesting evenly on the following three annual anniversary dates of the grant, contingent upon the recipient's continued service to Adobe. Participants in the 2009 Program have the ability to receive up to 115% of the target number of shares originally granted.

Issuance of Shares

Upon exercise of stock options, vesting of restricted stock and performance shares, and purchases of shares under the ESPP, we will issue treasury stock. If treasury stock is not available, common stock will be issued. In order to minimize the impact of on-going dilution from exercises of stock options and vesting of restricted stock and performance shares, we instituted a stock repurchase program.

Valuation of Stock-Based Compensation (In Part)

We recognize the estimated compensation cost of restricted stock awards and restricted stock units, net of estimated forfeitures, over the vesting term. The estimated compensation cost is based on the fair value of our common stock on the date of grant.

We recognize the estimated compensation cost of performance shares, net of estimated forfeitures. The awards are earned upon attainment of identified performance goals, some of which contain discretionary metrics. As such, these awards are re-valued based on our traded stock price at the end of each reporting period. If the discretion is removed, the award will be classified as a fixed equity award. The fair value of the awards will be based on the measurement date, which is the date the award becomes fixed. The awards will be subsequently amortized over the remaining performance period.

Summary of Restricted Stock

Restricted stock award activity for fiscal 2009, 2008 and 2007 was as follows (shares in thousands):

	2009 Non-Vested Shares	2009 Weighted Average Grant Date Fair Value	2008 Non-Vested Shares	2008 Weighted Average Grant Date Fair Value	2007 Non-Vested Shares	2007 Weighted Average Grant Date Fair Value
Beginning outstanding balance	4	$39.31	21	$36.41	501	$ 9.17
Awarded	—	—	—	—	5	40.03
Released	(1)	38.22	(15)	34.94	(92)	29.32
Forfeited	—	—	(2)	39.95	(393)	4.77
Ending outstanding balance	3	$40.01	4	$39.31	21	$36.41

The total fair value of restricted stock awards vested during fiscal 2009, 2008 and 2007 was $39.4 thousand, $0.5 million and $0.7 million, respectively.

Restricted stock awards are considered outstanding at the time of grant, as the stock award holders are entitled to dividends and voting rights. Unvested restricted stock awards are not considered outstanding in the computation of basic earnings per share.

Restricted stock unit activity for fiscal years 2009, 2008 and 2007 was as follows (in thousands):

	2009	2008	2007
Beginning outstanding balance	4,261	1,701	—
Awarded	6,176	3,177	1,771
Released	(1,162)	(422)	—
Forfeited	(401)	(195)	(70)
Increase due to acquisition	1,559	—	—
Ending outstanding balance	10,433	4,261	1,701

The weighted average grant date fair values of restricted stock units granted during fiscal 2009, 2008 and 2007 were $27.74, $33.55 and $39.67, respectively. The total fair value of restricted stock units vested during fiscal 2009 and 2008 was $27.1 million and $14.4 million, respectively.

Information regarding restricted stock units outstanding at the end of fiscal 2009, 2008 and 2007 is summarized below:

	Number of Shares (Thousands)	Weighted Average Remaining Contractual Life (Years)	Aggregate Intrinsic Value[*] (Millions)
2009			
Restricted stock units outstanding	10,433	1.82	$369.1
Restricted stock units vested and expected to vest	8,078	1.63	$285.7
2008			
Restricted stock units outstanding	4,261	1.73	$ 98.7
Restricted stock units vested and expected to vest	3,351	1.52	$ 77.6
2007			
Restricted stock units outstanding	1,701	1.88	$ 71.7
Restricted stock units vested and expected to vest	1,309	1.65	$ 55.2

[*] The intrinsic value is calculated as the market value as of end of the fiscal year. As reported by the NASDAQ Global Select Market, the market values as of November 27, 2009, November 28, 2008 and November 30, 2007 were $35.38, $23.16 and $42.14, respectively.

Summary of Performance Shares

The following table sets forth the summary of performance share activity under our 2009 Program for fiscal 2009 (in thousands):

	Shares Granted	Maximum Shares Eligible to Receive
Beginning outstanding balance	—	—
Awarded	559	643
Forfeited	(7)	(8)
Ending outstanding balance	552	635

However, the performance metrics under the 2009 program were not achieved and therefore no shares will be awarded under the grants noted above.

In the first quarter of fiscal 2009, the Executive Compensation Committee certified the actual performance achievement of participants in the 2008 Performance Share Program (the "2008 Program"). Based upon the achievement of goals outlined in the 2008 Program, participants had the ability to receive up to 200% of the target number of shares originally granted. Actual performance resulted in participants achieving approximately 124% of target or approximately 1.0 million shares for the 2008 Program. Shares under the 2008 Program vested 25% in the first quarter of fiscal 2009, and the remaining 75% vest evenly on the following three annual anniversary dates of the grant, contingent upon the recipient's continued service to Adobe.

The following table sets forth the summary of performance share activity under our 2006 through 2008 programs, based upon share awards actually achieved, for fiscal 2009 and fiscal 2008 (in thousands):

	2009	2008
Beginning outstanding balance	383	—
Achieved	1,022	993
Released	(382)	(480)
Forfeited	(73)	(130)
Ending outstanding balance	950	383

The total fair value of performance awards vested during fiscal 2009 and 2008 was $7.7 million and $16.7 million, respectively.

Information regarding performance shares outstanding at November 27, 2009 and November 28, 2008 is summarized below:

	Number of Shares (Thousands)	Weighted Average Remaining Contractual Life (Years)	Aggregate Intrinsic Value[*] (Millions)
2009			
Performance shares outstanding	950	1.05	$33.6
Performance shares vested and expected to vest	818	0.97	$28.8
2008			
Performance shares outstanding	383	1.20	$ 8.9
Performance shares vested and expected to vest	323	1.10	$ 7.4

[*] The intrinsic value is calculated as the market value as of end of the fiscal year. As reported by the NASDAQ Global Select Market, the market value as of November 27, 2009 and November 28, 2008 was $35.38 and $23.16, respectively.

Grants to Non-Employee Directors

The Directors Plan (and starting in fiscal 2008, the 2003 Plan) provides for the granting of nonqualified stock options to non-employee directors. Prior to fiscal 2009, option grants were limited to 25,000 shares per person in each fiscal year, except for a new non-employee director to whom 50,000 shares were granted upon election as a director. Options granted before November 29, 2008 vest over four years: 25% on the day preceding each of our next four annual meetings and have a ten-year term. Starting in fiscal 2009, the initial equity grant to a new non-employee director is a restricted stock unit award having an aggregate value of $0.5 million as based on the average stock price over the 30 calendar days ending on the day before the date of grant. The initial equity award vests over 2 years, 50% on the day preceding each of our next 2 annual meetings. For the annual equity grant, a non-employee director can elect to receive 100% options, 100% restricted stock units or 50% of each and shall have an aggregate value of $0.2 million as based on the average stock price over the 30 calendar days ending on the day before the date of grant. The target grant value of restricted stock units to stock options will be based on a 3:1 conversion ratio. Annual equity awards granted on or after November 29, 2008 vest 100% on the day preceding the next annual meeting. Options granted on or after November 29, 2008 have a seven-year term. The exercise price of the options that are issued is equal to the fair market value of our common stock on the date of grant.

Options granted to directors for fiscal 2009, 2008 and 2007 are as follows (shares in thousands):

	2009	2008	2007
Options granted to existing directors	175	250	250
Exercise price	$23.28	$37.09	$42.61

Restricted stock units granted to directors for fiscal 2009 are as follows (shares in thousands):

	2009
Restricted stock units granted to existing directors	27
Restricted stock units granted to new directors	20

Compensation Costs

With the exception of performance shares, stock-based compensation expense is recognized on a straight-line basis over the requisite service period of the entire award, which is generally the vesting period. For performance shares, expense is recognized on a straight-line basis over the requisite service period for each vesting portion of the award.

As of November 27, 2009, there was $305.0 million of unrecognized compensation cost, adjusted for estimated forfeitures, related to non-vested stock-based awards which will be recognized over a weighted average period of 2.4 years. Total unrecognized compensation cost will be adjusted for future changes in estimated forfeitures.

Total stock-based compensation costs that have been included in our Consolidated Statements of Income for fiscal 2009, 2008 and 2007 were as follows (in thousands):

| | Income Statement Classifications | | | | |
	Cost of Revenue—Services and Support	Research and Development	Sales and Marketing	General and Administrative	Total
Option grants and stock purchase rights[*]					
Fiscal 2009	$1,906	$45,535	$38,790	$24,595	$110,826
Fiscal 2008	$3,728	$55,653	$41,326	$24,521	$125,228
Fiscal 2007	$5,152	$58,579	$41,801	$24,467	$129,999
Restricted stock and performance share awards[*]					
Fiscal 2009	$ 639	$27,931	$19,818	$ 9,274	$ 57,662
Fiscal 2008	$ 570	$20,835	$17,928	$10,810	$ 50,143
Fiscal 2007	$ 346	$ 9,518	$ 6,084	$ 4,040	$ 19,988

[*] During fiscal 2009 and 2008, we recorded $0.9 million and $2.9 million, respectively, associated with cash recoveries of fringe benefit tax from employees in India.

Savings/Investment Plans

3.89

BE AEROSPACE, INC. (DEC)

NOTES TO CONSOLIDATED FINANCIAL STATEMENTS
(In millions, except share and per share data)

10. Employee Retirement Plans

The Company sponsors and contributes to a qualified, defined contribution savings and investment plan, covering substantially all U.S. employees. The BE Aerospace Savings and Investment Plan was established pursuant to Section 401(k) of the Internal Revenue Code. Under the terms of this plan, covered employees may contribute up to 100% of their pay, limited to certain statutory maximum contributions for 2009. Participants are vested in matching contributions immediately and the matching percentage is 100% of the first 3% of employee contributions and 50% on the next 2% of employee contributions. Total expense for the plan was $6.8, $6.9 and $5.6 for the calendar years ended December 31, 2009, 2008 and 2007, respectively. In addition, the Company contributes to the BE Aerospace, Inc. Hourly Tax-Sheltered Retirement Plan. This plan was established pursuant to Section 401(k) of the Internal Revenue Code and covers certain U.S. union employees. Total expense for the plan was $0.2,

$0.3 and $0.2 for the calendar years ended December 31, 2009, 2008 and 2007, respectively. The Company and its subsidiaries participate in government-sponsored programs in certain European countries. The Company funds these plans based on legal requirements, tax considerations, local practices and investment opportunities.

Stock Purchase Plans

3.90

HEWLETT-PACKARD COMPANY (OCT)

NOTES TO CONSOLIDATED FINANCIAL STATEMENTS

Note 2 (In Part): Stock-Based Compensation

Employee Stock Purchase Plan

HP sponsors the Hewlett-Packard Company 2000 Employee Stock Purchase Plan, also known as the Share Ownership Plan (the "ESPP"), pursuant to which eligible employees may contribute up to 10% of base compensation, subject to certain income limits, to purchase shares of HP's common stock. For purchases made on or before April 30, 2009, employees purchased stock pursuant to the ESPP semi-annually at a price equal to 85% of the fair market value on the purchase date, and HP recognized expense based on a 15% discount of the fair market value for those purchases. Effective May 1, 2009, HP modified the ESPP to eliminate the 15% discount applicable to purchases made under the ESPP.

The ESPP activity as of October 31 during each fiscal year was as follows:

(In millions, except weighted-average purchase price per share)	2009	2008	2007
Compensation expense, net of taxes	$ 24	$ 58	$ 56
Shares purchased	6.16	9.68	8.74
Weighted-average purchase price per share	$ 33	$ 36	$ 39

(In thousands)	2009	2008	2007
Employees eligible to participate	260	164	161
Employees who participated	49	50	51

Shares Reserved

Shares available for future grant and shares reserved for future issuance under the ESPP and incentive compensation plans were as follows:

(Shares in thousands)	2009	2008	2007
Shares available for future grant at October 31:			
HP plans	95,311[(1)]	117,655	136,392
Assumed Compaq and EDS plans	82,449[(2)]	73,147	45,312
	177,760	190,802	181,704
Shares reserved for future issuance under all stock-related benefit plans at October 31	410,977	498,574	549,045

(1) Includes 24,267,000 shares that expired in November 2009.

(2) In November 2009, HP retired the assumed Compaq and EDS plans for purposes of granting new awards. The shares that had been reserved for future awards under those plans were returned to HP's pool of authorized shares and will not be available for issuance under any other HP plans.

Deferred Compensation Plans

3.91

ABM INDUSTRIES INCORPORATED (OCT)

NOTES TO CONSOLIDATED FINANCIAL STATEMENTS

4 (In Part): Fair Value Measurements

As defined in ASC 820, fair value is determined based on inputs or assumptions that market participants would use in pricing an asset or a liability. These assumptions consist of (1) observable inputs—market data obtained from independent sources, or (2) unobservable inputs – market data determined using the Company's own assumptions about valuation. ASC 820 establishes a hierarchy to prioritize the inputs to valuation techniques, with the highest priority being given to Level 1 inputs and the lowest priority to Level 3 inputs, as described below:

- Level 1—Quoted prices for identical instruments in active markets;
- Level 2—Quoted prices for similar instruments in active markets; quoted prices for identical or similar instruments in markets that are not active; and model-derived valuations in which all significant inputs or significant value-drivers are observable in active markets; and
- Level 3—Unobservable inputs.

Effective May 1, 2009, the Company adopted further FASB guidance under ASC 820 on determining fair value when the volume and level of activity for the asset or liability have significantly decreased and identifying transactions that are not orderly. This guidance provides further directions on how to determine the fair value of assets and liabilities in the current economic environment and reemphasizes that the objective of a fair value measurement remains the determination of an exit price. If there has been a significant decrease in the volume and level of activity of the asset or liability in relation to normal market activities, quoted market values may not be representative of fair value and a change in valuation technique or the use of multiple valuation techniques may be appropriate. The adoption of this new guidance did not have an impact on the fair value of the Company's financial assets and liabilities.

Financial assets and liabilities measured at fair value on a recurring basis are summarized in the table below:

(In thousands)	Fair Value at October 31, 2009	Fair Value Measurements Using Inputs Considered as Level 1	Level 2	Level 3
Assets				
Assets held in funded deferred compensation plan[(1)]	$ 6,006	$6,006	$ —	$ —
Investment in auction rate securities[(2)]	19,531	—	—	19,531
Total assets	$25,537	$6,006	$ —	$19,531
Liabilities				
Interest rate swap[(3)]	$ 1,014	$ —	$1,014	$ —
Total liabilities	$ 1,014	$ —	$1,014	$ —

(1) The fair value of the assets held in the deferred compensation plan is based on quoted market prices.

(2) The fair value of the investments in auction rate securities is based on discounted cash flow valuation models, primarily utilizing unobservable inputs. See Note 5, "Auction Rate Securities."

(3) The fair value of the interest rate swap is estimated based on the difference between the present value of expected cash flows calculated at the contracted interest rates and at the current market interest rates using observable benchmarks for LIBOR forward rates at the end of the period. See Note 9, "Line of Credit Facility."

10 (In Part): Employee Benefit Plans

Deferred Compensation Plans

The Company accrues for deferred compensation and interest thereon for employees whom elect to participate in one of the following Company plans:

Employee Deferred Compensation Plan

This plan is available to executive, management, administrative, and sales employees whose annualized base salary equals or exceeds $135,000 for the year ended October 31, 2009. This plan allows employees to defer 1% to 20% of their pre-tax compensation. The average rate of interest earned by the employees in this plan was 3.31%, 5.09%, and 6.39% for the years ending October 31, 2009, 2008, and 2007 respectively.

Director Deferred Compensation Plan

This plan allows directors to defer receipt of all or any portion of the compensation that he or she would otherwise receive from the Company. The average rate of interest earned by the employees in this plan was 3.31%, 5.09%, and 7.03% for the years ending October 31, 2009, 2008, and 2007 respectively.

The deferred compensation under both the Employee and Director Deferred Compensation Plans earns interest equal to the prime interest rate on the last day of the calendar quarter. If the prime rate exceeds 6%, the interest rate is equal to 6% plus one half of the excess over 6%. Interest earned under both deferred compensation plans was capped at 120% of the long-term applicable federal rate (compounded quarterly).

OneSource Deferred Compensation Plan

The Company acquired OneSource on November 14, 2007, which sponsored a Deferred Compensation Plan. Under this deferred compensation plan a Rabbi Trust was created to fund the obligation in the event of employer bankruptcy. The plan requires the Company to contribute 50% of the Participant's deferred compensation contributions but only to the extent that the deferred contribution does not exceed 5%. This liability is adjusted, with a corresponding charge (or credit) to the deferred compensation cost, to reflect changes in the fair value. On December 31, 2008 the plan was amended to preclude new participants. The assets held in the rabbi trust are not available for general corporate purposes.

Aggregate expense recognized under these deferred compensation plans for the years ended October 31, 2009, 2008 and 2007 were $0.3 million, $0.5 million and $0.6 million, respectively. The total long-term liability of all deferred compensation plans at October 31, 2009 and 2008 was $15.0 million and $16.0 million, respectively, and is included in Retirement plans and other on the accompanying consolidated balance sheet.

Incentive Compensation Plans

3.92

ANADARKO PETROLEUM CORPORATION (DEC)

NOTES TO CONSOLIDATED FINANCIAL STATEMENTS

1 (In Part): Summary of Significant Accounting Policies

Stock-Based Compensation

The Company accounts for stock-based compensation at fair value. The Company grants various types of stock-based awards including stock options, non-vested equity shares (restricted stock awards and units) and performance-based awards. The fair value of stock option awards is determined using the Black-Scholes option-pricing model. Restricted stock awards and units are valued using the market price of Anadarko common stock on the grant date. For performance-based awards, the fair value of the market-condition portion of the award is measured using a Monte Carlo simulation, and the performance-condition portion is measured at the market price of Anadarko common stock on the grant date. Liability-classified awards are remeasured at estimated fair value at the end of each period based on the specifications of each plan. The Company records compensation cost, net of estimated forfeitures, for stock-based compensation awards over the requisite service period. As each award vests, an adjustment is made to compensation cost for any difference between the estimated forfeitures and the actual forfeitures related to the vested awards. For equity awards that contain service and market conditions, compensation cost is recorded using the straight-line method. If the requisite service period is satisfied, compensation cost is not adjusted unless the award contains a performance condition. If an award contains a performance condition, expense is recognized only for those shares that ultimately vest using the per-share fair value measured at the grant date. See Note 12.

12 (In Part): Stock-Based Compensation

Liability-Classified Awards

Value Creation Plan

As a part of its employee compensation program, the Company offers an incentive compensation program that generally provides non-officer employees the opportunity to earn cash bonus awards based on the Company's total shareholder return for the year, compared to the total shareholder return of a predetermined group of peer companies. As of December 31, 2009, the Company has accrued approximately $105 million for the 2009 performance period.

Performance-Based Unit Awards

In November 2008 and 2009, key officers of the Company were provided Performance Unit Award Agreements with a two-year performance period ending December 31, 2010 and 2011, respectively, and a three-year performance period ending December 31, 2011 and 2012, respectively. The vesting of these units is based solely on comparing the Company's total shareholder return to the total shareholder return of a predetermined group of peer companies over the specified performance period. Each performance unit represents the value of one share of the Company's common stock. At the end of each performance period, the value of the vested performance units, if any, will be paid in cash. As of December 31, 2009, the liability under Performance Unit Award Agreements was $16.7 million, and there was $38.4 million of total estimated unrecognized compensation cost related to these awards, which is expected to be recognized over a weighted-average period of two years.

Employee Stock Ownership Plans

3.93

COLGATE-PALMOLIVE COMPANY (DEC)

NOTES TO CONSOLIDATED FINANCIAL STATEMENTS
(Dollars in millions except per share amounts)

9. Employee Stock Ownership Plan

In 1989, the Company expanded its Employee Stock Ownership Plan (ESOP) through the introduction of a leveraged ESOP that funds certain benefits for employees who have met eligibility requirements. The ESOP issued $410 of long-term notes due through July 2009 bearing an average interest rate of 8.7%. The notes, which were guaranteed by the Company, were repaid in July 2009. The ESOP used the proceeds of the notes to purchase 6.3 million shares of Preference stock from the Company. The Preference stock, each share of which is convertible into eight shares of common stock, has a redemption price of $65 per share and pays semiannual dividends equal to the higher of $2.44 or the current dividend paid on eight common shares for the comparable six-month period. During 2000, the ESOP entered into a loan agreement with the Company under which the benefits of the ESOP may be extended through 2035.

Dividends on the Preference stock, as well as on the common stock also held by the ESOP, are paid to the ESOP trust and, together with cash contributions and advances from the Company, are used by the ESOP to repay principal and interest. Preference stock is released for allocation to participants based upon the ratio of the current year's debt service to the sum of total principal and interest payments over the life of the debt. As of December 31, 2009, 1,305,666 shares were released and allocated to participant accounts and 1,301,875 shares were available for future allocation.

Dividends on the Preference stock are deductible for income tax purposes and, accordingly, are reflected net of their tax benefit in the Consolidated Statements of Changes in Shareholders' Equity.

Annual expense related to the leveraged ESOP, determined as interest incurred on the original notes, plus the higher of either principal payments or the historical cost of Preference stock allocated, less dividends received on the shares held by the ESOP and advances from the Company, was $22 in 2009, $7 in 2008 and $12 in 2007. Unearned compensation, which is shown as a reduction in Shareholders' equity, represents the amount of ESOP debt due to the Company reduced by the difference between the cumulative cost of Preference stock allocated and the cumulative principal payments.

Interest incurred on the ESOP's notes was $2 in 2009, $8 in 2008 and $13 in 2007. The Company paid dividends on the shares held by the ESOP of $37 in 2009, $36 in 2008 and $36 in 2007. Company contributions to the ESOP were $22 in 2009, $7 in 2008 and $12 in 2007.

Profit Sharing Plans

3.94

LAM RESEARCH CORPORATION (JUN)

NOTES TO CONSOLIDATED FINANCIAL STATEMENTS

Note 12 (In Part): Profit Sharing and Benefit Plans

Profit sharing is awarded to certain employees based upon performance against specific corporate financial and operating goals. Distributions to employees by the Company are based upon a percentage of earned compensation, provided that a threshold level of the Company's financial and performance goals are met. In addition to profit sharing the Company has other bonus plans based on achievement of profitability and other specific performance criteria. Charges to expense under these plans were $16.2 million, $93.1 million, and $102.0 million during fiscal years 2009, 2008, and 2007, respectively.

Dividend Equivalent Plans

3.95

WAUSAU PAPER CORP. (DEC)

NOTES TO CONSOLIDATED FINANCIAL STATEMENTS

Note 9 (In Part): Stock Compensation Plans

Dividend Equivalents

We maintain a Dividend Equivalent Plan. Upon termination of employment, or at the time of exercise of options granted in tandem with the dividend equivalents, participants are entitled to receive the cash value of the dividend equivalent grant. The cash value is determined by the sum of the value of cash dividends that would have been paid on the stock covered by the grant had it been actual stock and assuming all such hypothetical dividends had been reinvested in Wausau Paper stock. All of the outstanding dividend equivalents were fully vested as of January 1, 2006.

The following table summarizes the activity relating to our dividend equivalent plan:

	2009	2008	2007
Outstanding at January 1 (number of shares)	151,750	151,750	151,750
Exercised	(91,668)	—	—
Outstanding and exercisable at December 31 (number of shares)	60,082	151,750	151,750

For the year ended December 31, 2009, $0.3 million was paid to a participant in settlement of outstanding dividend equivalent awards.

Share-based compensation provisions or credits related to stock appreciation rights and dividend equivalents are determined based upon a remeasurement to their fair value at each reporting period in accordance with the provisions of ASC 718-10. The (credit) provision for stock appreciation rights and dividend equivalents is shown in the following table.

(All dollar amounts in thousands)	2009	2008	2007
Stock appreciation rights	$ 30	$(108)	$(1,750)
Dividend equivalents	(262)	202	(224)
Total	$(232)	$ 94	$(1,974)

DEPRECIATION EXPENSE

3.96 FASB ASC 360, *Property, Plant, and Equipment*, stipulates that both the amount of depreciation expense and method or methods of depreciation should be disclosed in the financial statements or in notes thereto. FASB ASC 360 defines depreciation accounting (the process of allocating the cost of productive facilities over the expected useful lives of the facilities) as a "system of accounting which aims to distribute the cost or other basic value of tangible capital assets, less salvage (if any), over the estimated useful life of the unit (which may be a group of assets) in a systematic and rational manner. It is a process of allocation, not of valuation."

3.97 FASB ASC 250, *Accounting Changes and Error Corrections*, requires that a change in depreciation, amortization, or depletion method for long-lived, non-financial assets be accounted for as a change in accounting estimate effected by a change in accounting principle. Changes in accounting estimate are accounted for prospectively, not retrospectively as is required for changes in accounting principle.

3.98 Table 3-14 summarizes the methods of depreciation used to allocate the cost of productive facilities. There were eleven survey entities that allocated the cost of their natural resources using depletion. Examples of depreciation and depletion expense disclosures follow.

3.99

TABLE 3-14: DEPRECIATION METHODS

	Number of Entities			
	2009	2008	2007	2006
Straight-line	488	494	594	592
Declining-balance	10	10	13	16
Sum-of-the-years'-digits	3	3	4	5
Accelerated method—not specified	17	21	24	27
Units-of-production	16	14	20	23
Group/composite	10	7	11	9

2008–2009 based on 500 entities surveyed; 2006–2007 based on 600 entities surveyed.

Straight-Line Method

3.100

THE GOODYEAR TIRE & RUBBER COMPANY (DEC)

Consolidated Statements of Cash Flows

(In millions)	2009	2008	2007
Cash flows from operating activities:			
Net (loss) income	$(364)	$ (23)	$ 653
Less: discontinued operations	—	—	463
(Loss) income from continuing operations	(364)	(23)	190
Adjustments to reconcile net (loss) income from continuing operations to cash flows from operating activities:			
Depreciation and amortization	636	660	614
Amortization and write-off of debt issuance costs	20	26	47
Net rationalization charges	227	184	49
Net gains on asset sales	30	(53)	(15)
VEBA funding	—	(1,007)	—
Pension contributions and direct payments	(430)	(364)	(719)
Rationalization payments	(200)	(84)	(75)
Customer prepayments and government grants	14	105	9

NOTES TO CONSOLIDATED FINANCIAL STATEMENTS

Note 1 (In Part): Accounting Policies

Property, Plant and Equipment

Property, plant and equipment are stated at cost. Depreciation is computed using the straight-line method. Additions and improvements that substantially extend the useful life of property, plant and equipment, and interest costs incurred during the construction period of major projects are capitalized. Repair and maintenance costs are expensed as incurred. Property, plant and equipment are depreciated to their estimated residual values over their estimated useful lives, and reviewed for impairment whenever events or circumstances warrant such a review. Refer to Notes 9 and 16.

Note 9. Property, Plant and Equipment

(In millions)	2009 Owned	2009 Capital Leases	2009 Total	2008 Owned	2008 Capital Leases	2008 Total
Property, plant and equipment, at cost:						
Land	$ 409	$ 4	$ 413	$ 429	$ 4	$ 433
Buildings	1,807	53	1,860	1,847	62	1,909
Machinery and equipment	11,252	86	11,338	10,604	93	10,697
Construction in progress	692	—	692	748	—	748
	14,160	143	14,303	13,628	159	13,787
Accumulated depreciation	(8,528)	(98)	(8,626)	(8,213)	(97)	(8,310)
	5,632	45	5,677	5,415	62	5,477
Spare parts	166	—	166	157	—	157
	$ 5,798	$ 45	$ 5,843	$ 5,572	$ 62	$ 5,634

The range of useful lives of property used in arriving at the annual amount of depreciation provided are as follows: buildings and improvements, 5 to 45 years; machinery and equipment, 3 to 40 years.

Note 16. Interest Expense

Interest expense includes interest and amortization of debt discounts, less amounts capitalized as follows:

(In millions)	2009	2008	2007
Interest expense before capitalization	$325	$343	$478
Capitalized interest	(14)	(23)	(10)
	$311	$320	$468

Cash payments for interest, net of amounts capitalized were $290 million, $362 million and $482 million in 2009, 2008 and 2007, respectively.

3.101

PRIDE INTERNATIONAL, INC. (DEC)

(In millions)	2009	2008	2007
Revenues			
Revenues excluding reimbursable revenues	$1,563.5	$1,664.7	$1,294.2
Reimbursable revenues	30.7	37.9	34.8
	1,594.2	1,702.6	1,329.0
Costs and expenses			
Operating costs, excluding depreciation and amortization	828.3	766.5	618.6
Reimbursable costs	27.3	34.9	30.8
Depreciation and amortization	159.0	147.3	153.1
General and administrative, excluding depreciation and amortization	110.5	126.7	138.1
Department of Justice and Securities and Exchange Commission fines	56.2	—	—
Loss (gain) on sales of assets, net	(0.4)	0.1	(29.8)
	1,180.9	1,075.5	910.8
Earnings from operations	$ 413.3	$ 627.1	$ 418.2

NOTES TO CONSOLIDATED FINANCIAL STATEMENTS

Note 1 (In Part): Summary of Significant Accounting Policies

Property and Equipment

Property and equipment are carried at original cost or adjusted net realizable value, as applicable. Major renewals and improvements are capitalized and depreciated over the respective asset's remaining useful life. Maintenance and repair costs are charged to expense as incurred. When assets are sold or retired, the remaining costs and related accumulated depreciation are removed from the accounts and any resulting gain or loss is included in results of operations.

We depreciate property and equipment using the straight-line method based upon expected useful lives of each class of assets. The expected original useful lives of the assets for financial reporting purposes range from five to 35 years for rigs and rig equipment and three to 20 for other property and equipment. We evaluate our estimates of remaining useful lives and salvage value for our rigs when changes in market or economic conditions occur that may impact our estimates of the carrying value of these assets and when certain events occur that directly impact our assessment of the remaining useful lives of the rig and include changes in operating condition, functional capability, market and economic factors. In conducting this evaluation, the scope of work, age of the rig, general condition of the rig and design of the rig are factors that are considered in the evaluation. We also consider major capital upgrades required or rig refurbishment to perform certain contracts and the long-term impact of those upgrades on the future marketability when assessing the useful lives of individual rigs. During 2008, we reviewed the useful lives of certain rigs upon completion of shipyard projects, which resulted in extending the useful lives of the rigs, and as a re-

sult reduced depreciation expense by $2.4 million and $0.5 million for continuing and discontinued operations, respectively, and increased after-tax diluted earnings per share from continuing operations by $0.01. During 2007, we completed a technical evaluation of our offshore fleet. As a result of our evaluation, we increased our estimates of the remaining lives of certain semisubmersible and jackup rigs in our fleet between four and eight years, increased the expected useful lives of our drillships from 25 years to 35 years and our semisubmersibles from 25 years to 30 years, and updated our estimated salvage value for all of our offshore drilling rig fleet to 10% of the historical cost of the rigs. The effect for 2007 of these changes in estimates was a reduction to depreciation expense of approximately $19.3 million and $9.2 million for continuing and discontinued operations, respectively, and an after-tax increase to diluted earnings per share of $0.10 and $0.03 for continuing and discontinued operations, respectively.

Interest is capitalized on construction-in-progress at the weighted average cost of debt outstanding during the period of construction or at the interest rate on debt incurred for construction.

We assess the recoverability of the carrying amount of property and equipment if certain events or changes occur, such as a significant decrease in market value of the assets or a significant change in the business conditions in a particular market. In connection with the spin-off of Seahawk in August 2009, we conducted a fair value assessment of its long-lived assets. As a result of this assessment, we determined that the carrying value of these assets exceeded the fair value, resulting in an impairment loss of $33.4 million. We recorded the loss in income from discontinued operations for 2009. In 2008 and 2007, we recognized no impairment charges.

Note 4 (In Part): Property and Equipment

Property and equipment consisted of the following at December 31:

(In millions)	2009	2008
Rigs and rig equipment	$ 4,101.4	$ 4,873.6
Construction-in-progress—newbuild drillships	1,682.4	965.5
Construction-in-progress—other	222.8	165.7
Other	84.4	63.0
Property and equipment, cost	6,091.0	6,067.8
Accumulated depreciation and amortization	(1,200.7)	(1,474.9)
Property and equipment, net	$ 4,890.3	$ 4,592.9

Depreciation and amortization expense of property and equipment for 2009, 2008 and 2007 was $159.0 million, $147.3 million and $153.1 million, respectively.

During 2009, 2008 and 2007, maintenance and repair costs included in operating costs on the accompanying consolidated statements of operations were $129.1 million, $112.1 million and $63.8 million, respectively.

We capitalize interest applicable to the construction of significant additions to property and equipment. For 2009, 2008 and 2007, we capitalized interest of $74.7 million, $41.2 million and $11.2 million, respectively. For 2009, 2008 and 2007, total interest costs, including amortization of debt issuance costs, were $74.8 million, $61.2 million and $94.3 million, respectively.

Accelerated Methods

3.102

THE BOEING COMPANY (DEC)

Consolidated Statements of Cash Flows

(Dollars in millions)	2009	2008	2007
Cash flows—operating activities:			
Net earnings	$1,312	$2,672	$4,074
Adjustments to reconcile net earnings to net cash provided by operating activities:			
Non-cash items			
Share-based plans expense	238	209	287
Depreciation	1,459	1,325	1,334
Amortization of other acquired intangibles	207	166	152
Amortization of debt discount/premium and issuance costs	12	11	(1)
Investment/asset impairment charges, net	151	50	51
Customer financing valuation provision	45	84	(60)
(Gain)/loss on disposal of discontinued operations	36	(28)	(25)
(Gain)/loss on dispositions, net	24	(4)	(38)
Other charges and credits, net	214	116	197
Excess tax benefits from share-based payment arrangements	(5)	(100)	(144)

NOTES TO CONSOLIDATED FINANCIAL STATEMENTS
(Dollars in millions)

Note 1 (In Part): Summary of Significant Accounting Policies

Property, Plant and Equipment

Property, plant and equipment are recorded at cost, including applicable construction-period interest, less accumulated depreciation and are depreciated principally over the following estimated useful lives: new buildings and land improvements, from 10 to 40 years; and new machinery and equipment, from 3 to 20 years. The principal methods of depreciation are as follows: buildings and land improvements, 150% declining balance; and machinery and equipment, sum-of-the-years' digits. Capitalized internal use software is included in Other assets and amortized using the straight line method over five years. We periodically evaluate the appropriateness of remaining depreciable lives assigned to long-lived assets, including assets that may be subject to a management plan for disposition.

Long-lived assets held for sale are stated at the lower of cost or fair value less cost to sell. Long-lived assets held for use are subject to an impairment assessment whenever events or changes in circumstances indicate that the carrying amount may not be recoverable. If the carrying value is no longer recoverable based upon the undiscounted future cash flows of the asset, the amount of the impairment is the difference between the carrying amount and the fair value of the asset.

Note 9 (In Part): Property, Plant and Equipment

Property, plant and equipment at December 31 consisted of the following:

	2009	2008
Land	$ 539	$ 540
Buildings and land improvements	9,548	9,133
Machinery and equipment	10,383	9,990
Construction in progress	1,109	1,379
	21,579	21,042
Less accumulated depreciation	(12,795)	(12,280)
	$ 8,784	$ 8,762

Depreciation expense was $1,066, $1,013, and $978 for the years ended December 31, 2009, 2008 and 2007, respectively. Interest capitalized during the years ended December 31, 2009, 2008 and 2007 totaled $90, $99, and $117, respectively. At December 31, 2009 and 2008, we had $316 and $334 of operating lease properties, net of $262 and $242 of accumulated depreciation.

3.103

ALLIANT TECHSYSTEMS INC. (MAR)

Consolidated Statements of Cash Flows

(Amounts in thousands)	2009	2008	2007
Operating activities			
Net income	$155,119	$222,347	$184,128
Adjustments to net income to arrive at cash provided by operating activities:			
Depreciation	80,137	71,511	69,380
Amortization of intangible assets	5,616	5,975	6,772
Amortization of deferred financing costs	2,857	3,851	3,999
Impairment of goodwill	108,500	—	—
Write-off of debt issuance costs associated with convertible notes	—	5,600	—
Write-off of acquisition related costs	—	6,567	—
Deferred income taxes	113,999	(15,742)	81,725
Loss on disposal of property	9,030	2,505	9,295
Minority interest, net of income taxes	187	376	451
Share-based plans expense	18,952	23,415	38,076
Excess tax benefits from share-based plans	(3,287)	(9,459)	(3,539)

NOTES TO CONSOLIDATED FINANCIAL STATEMENTS
(Amounts in thousands)

6. Property, Plant, and Equipment

Property, plant, and equipment is stated at cost and depreciated over estimated useful lives. Machinery and test equipment is depreciated using the double declining balance method at most of ATK's facilities, and using the straight-line method at other ATK facilities. Other depreciable property is depreciated using the straight-line method. Machinery and equipment are depreciated over one to 23 years and buildings and improvements are depreciated over one to 45 years. Depreciation expense was $80,137 in fiscal 2009, $71,511 in fiscal 2008, and $69,380 in fiscal 2007.

ATK reviews property, plant, and equipment for impairment when indicators of potential impairment are present. When such impairment is identified, it is recorded as a loss in that period. During fiscal 2007, ATK recorded an impairment charge of approximately $9,300 related to the termination of an internal information systems project within general and administrative expense.

Maintenance and repairs are charged to expense as incurred. Major improvements that extend useful lives are capitalized and depreciated. The cost and accumulated depreciation of property, plant and equipment retired or otherwise disposed of are removed from the related accounts, and any residual values are charged or credited to income.

Property, plant, and equipment consists of the following:

	2009	2008
Land	$ 33,837	$ 33,115
Buildings and improvements	334,837	311,470
Machinery and equipment	826,640	740,773
Property not yet in service	48,703	50,424
Gross property, plant, and equipment	1,244,017	1,135,782
Less accumulated depreciation	(703,976)	(643,446)
Net property, plant, and equipment	$ 540,041	$ 492,336

Units-of-Production Method

3.104

OCCIDENTAL PETROLEUM CORPORATION (DEC)

(In millions)	2009	2008	2007
Revenues and other income			
Net sales	$15,403	$24,217	$18,784
Interest, dividends and other income	118	236	355
Gains on disposition of assets, net	10	27	874
	15,531	24,480	20,013
Costs and other deductions			
Cost of sales (excludes depreciation, depletion and amortization of $3,067 in 2009, $2,664 in 2008 and $2,338 in 2007)	5,360	7,423	6,454
Selling, general and administrative and other operating expenses	1,350	1,257	1,320
Depreciation, depletion and amortization	3,117	2,710	2,379
Taxes other than on income	433	588	414
Environmental remediation	25	28	107
Exploration expense	267	327	364
Charges for impairments	170	647	58
Interest and debt expense, net	140	129	339
	10,862	13,109	11,435
Income before income taxes and other items	$ 4,669	$11,371	$ 8,578

NOTES TO CONSOLIDATED FINANCIAL STATEMENTS

Note 1 (In Part): Summary of Significant Accounting Policies

Property, Plant and Equipment (In Part)

Chemical

The most critical accounting policy affecting Occidental's chemical assets is the determination of the estimated useful lives of the PP&E. Occidental's chemical plants are depreciated using either the unit-of-production or straight-line method, based upon the estimated useful lives of the facilities. The estimated useful lives of Occidental's chemical assets, which range from three years to 50 years, are also used for impairment tests. The estimated useful lives used for the chemical facilities are based on the assumption that Occidental will provide an appropriate level of annual expenditures to ensure productive capacity is sustained. Without these continued expenditures, the useful lives of these plants could decrease significantly. Other factors that could change the estimated useful lives of Occidental's chemical plants include sustained higher or lower product prices, which are particularly affected by both domestic and foreign competition, demand, feedstock costs, energy prices, environmental regulations and technological changes.

Occidental performs impairment tests on its chemical assets whenever events or changes in circumstances lead to a reduction in the estimated useful lives or estimated future cash flows that would indicate that the carrying amount may not be recoverable, or when management's plans change with respect to those assets. Any impairment loss would be calculated as the excess of the asset's net book value over its estimated fair value.

Midstream and Marketing

Occidental's midstream and marketing PP&E is depreciated over the estimated useful lives of the assets, using either the unit-of-production or straight-line method.

Occidental performs impairment tests on its midstream and marketing assets whenever events or changes in circumstances lead to a reduction in the estimated useful lives or estimated future cash flows that would indicate that the carrying amount may not be recoverable, or when management's plans change with respect to those assets. Any impairment loss would be calculated as the excess of the asset's net book value over its estimated fair value.

Composite Method

3.105

CYTEC INDUSTRIES INC. (DEC)

Consolidated Statements of Cash Flows

(Dollars in millions)	2009	2008	2007
Cash flows provided by (used in) operating activities			
Net (loss)/earnings	$ (0.9)	$(197.0)	$207.3
Non cash items included in net (loss)/earnings:			
Depreciation	135.9	113.7	100.9
Amortization	44.7	45.6	44.7
Share-based compensation	7.8	10.2	12.9
Deferred income taxes	(42.1)	(19.1)	27.2
Net gain on sales of assets	(0.2)	(3.9)	(13.6)
Non-cash gain on transfer of land	(8.9)	—	—
Non-cash pension settlement charge	12.2	—	—
Asset impairment charges	4.3	385.0	1.4
Net loss/(gain) on early extinguishment of debt	9.1	(1.9)	—
Unrealized (gain)/loss on derivative instruments	(5.7)	8.4	(1.7)
Other	1.0	0.7	1.9

NOTES TO CONSOLIDATED FINANCIAL STATEMENTS
(Currencies in millions)

1 (In Part): Summary of Significant Accounting Policies

D. Depreciation

Depreciation is provided on either the straight-line or the straight-line composite method. Assets in the United States acquired in conjunction with the Surface Specialties business (forming substantially all of our Coating Resins segment) of UCB SA ("UCB") and assets outside the United States and Canada are depreciated on a straight-line basis over the estimated useful lives of the assets. When these assets are retired or disposed of, the net book value of assets are removed from the consolidated balance sheet and the net gain or loss is included in the determination of earnings from operations. Depreciation for the remainder of our assets in the United States and Canada is recorded primarily on a straight-line composite method over the estimated useful lives of various classes of assets, with rates periodically reviewed and adjusted if necessary. When such depreciable assets are sold or otherwise retired from service, unless a major change in the composition of an asset class has occurred, their costs plus demolition costs less amounts realized on sale or salvage are charged or credited to the accumulated depreciation account. Expenditures for maintenance and repairs are charged to current operating expenses. Acquisitions, additions and betterments, either to provide necessary capacity, improve the efficiency of production units, modernize or replace older facilities or to install equipment for protection of the environment, are capitalized. We capitalize interest costs incurred during the period of construction of plants and equipment.

8. Plants, Equipment and Facilities

	2009	2008
Land and land improvements	$ 91.6	$ 88.4
Buildings	329.5	324.5
Machinery and equipment	1,653.8	1,570.7
Construction in progress	235.1	152.5
Plants, equipment and facilities, at cost	$2,310.0	$2,136.1

The average composite depreciation rates utilized in the U.S. and Canada, expressed as a percentage of the average depreciable property in service, were 4.6% in 2009, 4.5% in 2008, and 4.6% in 2007. Gross cost of the assets depreciated under the composite method in the U.S. and Canada totaled $1,260.7 and $1,232.3 as of December 31, 2009 and 2008, respectively. Depreciation is calculated using the straight line depreciation method for assets at the remainder of our locations.

Following are the depreciable lives for our assets under the composite and straight-line methods:

Category	Composite Depreciation	Straight-Line Depreciation
Buildings	31 years	20–33 years
Machinery and equipment	5–18 years	3–15 years

Depletion

3.106

CHESAPEAKE ENERGY CORPORATION (DEC)

($ in millions)	2009	2008	2007
Revenues:			
Natural gas and oil sales	$ 5,049	$ 7,858	$5,624
Marketing, gathering and compression sales	2,463	3,598	2,040
Service operations revenue	190	173	136
Total revenues	7,702	11,629	7,800
Operating costs:			
Production expenses	876	889	640
Production taxes	107	284	216
General and administrative expenses	349	377	243
Marketing, gathering and compression expenses	2,316	3,505	1,969
Service operations expense	182	143	94
Natural gas and oil depreciation, depletion and amortization	1,371	1,970	1,835
Depreciation and amortization of other assets	244	174	153
Impairment of natural gas and oil properties and other assets	11,130	2,830	—
Loss on sale of other property and equipment	38	—	—
Restructuring costs	34	—	—
Total operating costs	16,647	10,172	5,150
Income (loss) from operations	$(8,945)	$ 1,457	$2,650

NOTES TO CONSOLIDATED FINANCIAL STATEMENTS

1 (In Part): Summary of Significant Accounting Policies

Natural Gas and Oil Properties

Chesapeake follows the full-cost method of accounting under which all costs associated with property acquisition, exploration and development activities are capitalized. We capitalize internal costs that can be directly identified with our acquisition, exploration and development activities and do not include any costs related to production, general corporate overhead or similar activities (see Note 10). Capitalized costs are amortized on a composite unit-of-production method based on proved natural gas and oil reserves. Estimates of our proved reserves as of December 31, 2009 were prepared by both third party engineering firms and Chesapeake's internal staff. Approximately 83% of these proved reserves estimates (by volume) at year-end 2009 were prepared by independent engineering firms. In addition, our internal engineers review and update our reserves on a quarterly basis. The average composite rates used for depreciation, depletion and amortization were $1.51 per mcfe in 2009, $2.34 per mcfe in 2008 and $2.57 per mcfe in 2007.

Proceeds from the sale of properties are accounted for as reductions of capitalized costs unless such sales involve a significant change in the relationship between costs and the value of proved reserves or the underlying value of unproved properties, in which case a gain or loss is recognized.

The costs of unproved properties are excluded from amortization until the properties are evaluated. We review all of our unevaluated properties quarterly to determine whether or not and to what extent proved reserves have been assigned to the properties and otherwise if impairment has occurred. Unevaluated properties are grouped by major prospect area where individual property costs are not significant and are assessed individually when individual costs are significant.

We review the carrying value of our natural gas and oil properties under the full-cost accounting rules of the Securities and Exchange Commission on a quarterly basis. This quarterly review is referred to as a ceiling test. Under the ceiling test, capitalized costs, less accumulated amortization and related deferred income taxes, may not exceed an amount equal to the sum of the present value of estimated future net revenues (adjusted for cash flow hedges) less estimated future expenditures to be incurred in developing and producing the proved reserves, less any related income tax effects. In 2009, capitalized costs of natural gas and oil properties exceeded the estimated present value of future net revenues from our proved reserves, net of related income tax considerations, resulting in a write-down in the carrying value of natural gas and oil properties of $6.9 billion, net of tax. In calculating future net revenues, effective December 31, 2009, current prices are calculated as the average natural gas and oil prices during the preceding 12-month period prior to the end of the current reporting period, determined as the unweighted arithmetical average of prices on the first day of each month within the 12-month period and costs used are those as of the end of the appropriate quarterly period. Such prices are utilized except where different prices are fixed and determinable from applicable contracts for the remaining term of those contracts, including the effects of derivatives qualifying as cash flow hedges. Based on average prices for the prior 12-month period for natural gas and oil as of December 31, 2009, these cash flow hedges increased the full-cost ceiling by $1.1 billion, thereby reducing the ceiling

test write-down by the same amount. Our qualifying cash flow hedges as of December 31, 2009, which consisted of swaps and collars, covered 281 bcfe and 22 bcfe in 2010 and 2011, respectively. Our natural gas and oil hedging activities are discussed in Note 9 of these consolidated financial statements.

Two primary factors impacting the ceiling test are reserve levels and natural gas and oil prices, and their associated impact on the present value of estimated future net revenues. Revisions to estimates of natural gas and oil reserves and/or an increase or decrease in prices can have a material impact on the present value of estimated future net revenues. Any excess of the net book value, less deferred income taxes, is generally written off as an expense.

INCOME TAXES

PRESENTATION OF INCOME TAXES

3.107   FASB ASC 740, *Income Taxes*, sets forth standards for financial presentation and disclosure of income tax liabilities and expense. Further, FASB ASC 740, *Income Taxes*, clarifies the accounting for uncertainty in income taxes recognized in an enterprise's financial statements. FASB ASC 740 prescribes a more-likely-than-not recognition threshold and measurement attribute for the financial statement recognition and measurement of a tax position taken or expected to be taken. In addition, FASB ASC 740 provides guidance on derecognition, classification, disclosure and transition. Under FASB ASC 740, tax positions will be evaluated for recognition, derecognition, and measurement using consistent criteria. Finally, the disclosure provision of FASB ASC 740 will provide more information about the uncertainty in income tax assets and liabilities.

3.108   Table 3-15 summarizes the descriptive captions used by the survey entities to identify income tax expense. Examples of income tax expense presentation and disclosure follow.

3.109

TABLE 3-15: INCOME TAX EXPENSE

	2009	2008	2007	2006
Descriptive Terms				
Income taxes..	491	490	587	589
Federal income taxes............................	6	6	6	7
United States (U.S.) income taxes	2	2	2	2
	499	498	595	598
Other or no current year amount.........	1	2	5	2
Total Entities.......................................	**500**	**500**	**600**	**600**

2008–2009 based on 500 entities surveyed; 2006–2007 based on 600 entities surveyed.

Expense Provision

3.110

AUTOMATIC DATA PROCESSING, INC. (JUN)

(In millions)	2009	2008	2007
Revenues:			
Revenues, other than interest on funds held for clients and PEO revenues	$7,080.4	$7,038.9	$6,267.4
Interest on funds held for clients	609.8	684.5	653.6
PEO revenues	1,176.9	1,053.1	879.0
Total revenues	8,867.1	8,776.5	7,800.0
Expenses:			
Costs of revenues			
Operating expenses	4,102.0	3,915.7	3,392.3
Systems development and programming costs	499.7	525.9	486.1
Depreciation and amortization	237.8	238.5	208.9
Total costs of revenues	4,839.5	4,680.1	4,087.3
Selling, general and administrative expenses	2,197.6	2,370.4	2,206.2
Interest expense	33.3	80.5	94.9
Total expenses	7,070.4	7,131.0	6,388.4
Other income, net	(108.0)	(166.5)	(211.9)
Earnings from continuing operations before income taxes	1,904.7	1,812.0	1,623.5
Provision for income taxes	576.5	650.3	602.3
Net earnings from continuing operations	$1,328.2	$1,161.7	$1,021.2

NOTES TO CONSOLIDATED FINANCIAL STATEMENTS
(Dollars in millions)

Note 1 (In Part): Summary of Significant Accounting Policies

Income Taxes

The Company accounts for income taxes in accordance with SFAS No. 109, "Accounting for Income Taxes," which establishes financial accounting and reporting standards for the effect of income taxes. The objectives of accounting for income taxes are to recognize the amount of taxes payable or refundable for the current year and deferred tax liabilities and assets for the future tax consequences of events that have been recognized in an entity's financial statements or tax returns. The Company is subject to the continuous examination of our income tax returns by the Internal Revenue Service ("IRS") and other tax authorities.

The Company accounts for tax positions taken or expected to be taken in a tax return in accordance with the provisions of Financial Accounting Standards Board ("FASB") Interpretation No. 48 ("FIN 48"), which was adopted by the Company on July 1, 2007. As a result of the adoption, the Company recorded a net decrease to retained earnings of $11.7 million, as well as a corresponding increase to other liabilities on the Consolidated Balance Sheets. FIN 48 prescribes a financial statement recognition threshold and measurement attribute for tax positions taken or expected to be taken in a tax return. Specifically, it clarifies that an entity's tax benefits must be "more likely than not" of being sustained assuming that these positions will be examined by taxing authorities with full knowledge of all relevant information prior to recording the related tax benefit in the financial statements. If a tax position drops below the "more likely than not" standard, the benefit can no longer be recognized. Assumptions, judgment and the use of estimates are required in determining if the "more likely than not" standard has been met when develop-

ing the provision for income taxes. As of June 30, 2009 and 2008, the Company's liabilities for unrecognized tax benefits, which include interest and penalties, were $92.8 million and $404.2 million, respectively.

If certain pending tax matters settle within the next twelve months, the total amount of unrecognized tax benefits may increase or decrease for all open tax years and jurisdictions. Based on current estimates, settlements related to various jurisdictions and tax periods could increase earnings up to $20.5 million. Audit outcomes and the timing of audit settlements are subject to significant uncertainty. We continually assess the likelihood and amount of potential adjustments and adjust the income tax provision, the current tax liability and deferred taxes in the period in which the facts that give rise to a revision become known.

Note 15. Income Taxes

Earnings (loss) from continuing operations before income taxes shown below are based on the geographic location to which such earnings are attributable.

	2009	2008	2007
Earnings (loss) from continuing operations before income taxes:			
United States	$1,908.6	$1,618.6	$1,457.4
Foreign	(3.9)	193.4	166.1
	$1,904.7	$1,812.0	$1,623.5

The provision (benefit) for income taxes consists of the following components:

	2009	2008	2007
Current:			
Federal	$ 708.9	$632.3	$482.0
Foreign	(119.7)	79.2	70.3
State	35.2	31.5	34.9
Total current	624.4	743.0	587.2
Deferred:			
Federal	(63.3)	(75.7)	18.4
Foreign	26.2	(10.8)	(7.9)
State	(10.8)	(6.2)	4.6
Total deferred	(47.9)	(92.7)	15.1
Total provision for income taxes	$ 576.5	$650.3	$602.3

A reconciliation between the Company's effective tax rate and the U.S. federal statutory rate is as follows:

	2009	%	2008	%	2007	%
Provision for taxes at U.S. statutory rate	$ 666.6	35.0	$634.2	35.0	$568.2	35.0
Increase (decrease) in provision from:						
State taxes, net of federal tax	37.8	2.0	28.8	1.6	25.7	1.6
Non-deductible stock-based compensation expense	5.5	0.3	5.5	0.3	9.7	0.6
Tax on repatriated earnings	43.0	2.2	—	—	34.4	2.1
Utilization of foreign tax credits	(46.6)	(2.4)	—	—	(26.5)	(1.6)
Tax settlements	(120.0)	(6.3)	(12.4)	(0.7)	—	—
Other	(9.8)	(0.5)	(5.8)	(0.3)	(9.2)	(0.6)
	$ 576.5	30.3	$650.3	35.9	$602.3	37.1

The significant components of deferred income tax assets and liabilities and their balance sheet classifications are as follows:

	2009	2008
Deferred tax assets:		
Accrued expenses not currently deductible	$270.6	$190.1
Stock-based compensation expense	123.1	99.7
Accrued retirement benefits	41.7	—
Net operating losses	53.0	84.8
Other	6.1	25.7
	494.5	400.3
Less: valuation allowances	(51.7)	(44.4)
Deferred tax assets, net	$442.8	$355.9
Deferred tax liabilities:		
Prepaid retirement benefits	$ —	$ 44.1
Deferred revenue	103.4	86.3
Fixed and intangible assets	186.1	141.0
Prepaid expenses	40.2	27.4
Unrealized investment gains, net	154.6	46.2
Tax on unrepatriated earnings	30.4	42.1
Other	4.1	9.3
Deferred tax liabilities	$518.8	$396.4
Net deferred tax liabilities	$ 76.0	$ 40.5

There are $157.4 million and $92.3 million of current deferred tax assets included in other current assets on the Consolidated Balance Sheets at June 30, 2009 and 2008, respectively. There are $44.1 million and $44.8 million of long-term deferred tax assets included in other assets on the Consolidated Balance Sheets at June 30, 2009 and 2008, respectively. There are $23.0 million and $7.6 million of current deferred tax liabilities included in accrued expenses and other current liabilities on the Consolidated Balance Sheets at June 30, 2009 and 2008, respectively.

Income taxes have not been provided on undistributed earnings of certain foreign subsidiaries in an aggregate amount of approximately $793.0 million as of June 30, 2009, as the Company considers such earnings to be permanently reinvested outside of the United States. The additional U.S. income tax that would arise on repatriation of the remaining undistributed earnings could be offset, in part, by foreign tax credits on such repatriation. However, it is impractical to estimate the amount of net income and withholding tax that might be payable.

The Company has estimated foreign net operating loss carry-forwards of approximately $96.1 million as of June 30, 2009, of which $35.2 million expires in 2011 through 2023 and $60.9 million has an indefinite utilization period. In addition, the Company has estimated Federal net operating loss carry-forwards of acquired companies of approximately $35.6 million as of June 30, 2009, which expire in 2010 through 2027. There is an annual limitation pursuant to Internal Revenue Code section 382 on the utilization of the Federal net operating loss carry-forwards of approximately $17.4 million per year. The Company has estimated state net operating loss carry-forwards of approximately $235.6 million as of June 30, 2009, which expire in 2010 through 2028.

The Company has recorded valuation allowances of $51.7 million and $44.4 million at June 30, 2009 and 2008, respectively, to reflect the estimated amount of domestic and foreign deferred tax assets that may not be realized. A portion of the valuation allowances in the amounts of approximately $2.9 million and $4.7 million at June 30, 2009 and 2008, respectively, relate to net deferred tax assets which were recorded in purchase accounting. Any recognition of net deferred tax assets in future years will be a reduction to goodwill until the adoption of SFAS No. 141R. Subsequent to the adoption of SFAS No. 141R, any such adjustments in future years will be recorded to our provision for income taxes on the Statements of Consolidated Earnings.

Income tax payments were approximately $719.1 million, $755.7 million, and $718.2 million for fiscal 2009, 2008 and 2007, respectively.

As of June 30, 2009 and 2008, the Company's liabilities for unrecognized tax benefits, which include interest and penalties, were $92.8 million and $404.2 million, respectively. The amount that, if recognized, would impact the effective tax rate is $42.0 million and $171.2 million, respectively. The remainder, if recognized, would principally affect deferred taxes.

A reconciliation of the beginning and ending amounts of unrecognized tax benefits is as follows:

Unrecognized tax benefits at July 1, 2007	$ 350.2
Additions for tax positions of the fiscal year ended June 30, 2008	23.6
Reductions for tax positions of the fiscal year ended June 30, 2008	—
Additions for tax positions of periods prior to the fiscal year ended June 30, 2008	43.2
Reductions for tax positions of periods prior to the fiscal year ended June 30, 2008	(11.5)
Settlements with tax authorities	(1.1)
Expiration of the statute of limitations	(4.0)
Impact of foreign exchange rate fluctuations	3.8
Unrecognized tax benefits at June 30, 2008	$ 404.2
Unrecognized tax benefits at July 1, 2008	$ 404.2
Additions for tax positions of the fiscal year ended June 30, 2009	19.0
Reductions for tax positions of the fiscal year ended June 30, 2009	(6.4)
Additions for tax positions of periods prior to the fiscal year ended June 30, 2009	111.4
Reductions for tax positions of periods prior to the fiscal year ended June 30, 2009	(207.7)
Settlements with tax authorities	(216.9)
Expiration of the statute of limitations	(3.5)
Impact of foreign exchange rate fluctuations	(7.3)
Unrecognized tax benefits at June 30, 2009	$ 92.8

Subsequent to the adoption of FIN 48 on July 1, 2007, interest expense and penalties associated with uncertain tax positions have been recorded in the provision for income taxes on the Statements of Consolidated Earnings. Prior to the adoption of FIN 48 on July 1, 2007, interest expense was recorded in selling, general and administrative expenses. During the fiscal years ended June 30, 2009, 2008 and 2007, the Company recorded interest expense of $15.5 million, $18.4 million and $11.5 million, respectively. At June 30, 2009, the Company had accrued interest of $29.4 million recorded on the Consolidated Balance Sheets, all of which was recorded within other liabilities. At June 30, 2008, the Company had accrued interest of $117.6 million recorded on the Consolidated Balance Sheets, of which $53.5 million

was recorded within income taxes payable, and the remainder was recorded within other liabilities. At June 30, 2009, the Company had accrued penalties of $0.5 million recorded on the Consolidated Balance Sheets, all of which was recorded within other liabilities. At June 30, 2008, the Company had accrued penalties of $26.9 million, of which $23.8 million was recorded within income taxes payable, and the remainder was recorded within other liabilities on the Consolidated Balance Sheets.

The Company is routinely examined by the IRS and tax authorities in foreign countries in which it conducts business, as well as tax authorities in states in which it has significant business operations, such as California, Illinois, Minnesota and New Jersey. The tax years currently under examination vary by jurisdiction. Such examinations currently in progress are as follows:

Taxing Jurisdiction	Fiscal Years Under Examination
U.S. (IRS)	2007–2009
California	2004–2005
Illinois	2004–2005
Minnesota	1998–2004
New Jersey	2002–2006
France	2006–2008

Additionally, Canada has commenced a joint audit with the Province of Ontario for the fiscal years ended June 30, 2005 through June 30, 2007 in the fiscal year ending June 30, 2009 and the Province of Alberta is examining the 2007 tax return.

In June 2009, the Company reached an agreement with the IRS regarding all outstanding tax audit issues with the IRS in dispute for the tax years 1998 through 2006. As a result of the agreement, the Company expects to receive $264.2 million in refunds from the IRS and other tax jurisdictions and expects to pay $211.7 million to the IRS and other tax jurisdictions. Consequently, the agreement with the IRS will result in net cash receipts from the IRS and other tax jurisdictions of approximately $52.5 million during fiscal 2010. The Company had previously recorded a liability for unrecognized tax benefits of $317.6 million. During fiscal 2009, the Company recorded a benefit to the provision for income taxes of $99.7 million. The foreign loss from continuing operations before income taxes of $3.9 million for the fiscal year ended June 30, 2009 includes a cumulative adjustment between domestic and foreign earnings as a result of the IRS audit settlement described above and a related agreement with a foreign tax authority. The foreign benefit for income taxes of $119.7 million for the fiscal year ended June 30, 2009 reflects the corresponding income tax benefit due to the cumulative adjustment.

In April 2009, the Company settled a state tax matter, for which the Company had previously recorded a liability for unrecognized tax benefits of $14.2 million and a related deferred tax asset of $5.1 million. Accordingly, the Company recorded a reduction in the provision for income taxes of $9.2 million during the fourth quarter of fiscal 2009 related to the reversal of the liability for unrecognized tax benefits and the related deferred tax asset. In addition, the Company received a tax credit of $11.1 million related to the same matter, which further reduced the provision for income taxes during the fourth quarter of fiscal 2009.

During the fiscal year ended June 30, 2008, the Company recorded a reduction in the provision for income taxes of

$12.4 million, which was primarily related to the settlement of a state tax matter, for which the Company had previously recorded a liability for unrecognized tax benefits of $7.9 million and a related deferred tax asset of $2.9 million.

The Company regularly considers the likelihood of assessments resulting from examinations in each of the jurisdictions. The resolution of tax matters is not expected to have a material effect on the consolidated financial condition of the Company, although a resolution could have a material impact on the Company's Statements of Consolidated Earnings for a particular future period and on the Company's effective tax rate.

If certain pending tax matters settle within the next twelve months, the total amount of unrecognized tax benefits may increase or decrease for all open tax years and jurisdictions.

Based on current estimates, settlements related to various jurisdictions and tax periods could increase earnings up to $20.5 million in the next twelve months. We do not expect any cash payments related to unrecognized tax benefits in the next twelve months. Audit outcomes and the timing of audit settlements are subject to significant uncertainty. We continually assess the likelihood and amount of potential adjustments and adjust the income tax provision, the current tax liability and deferred taxes in the period in which the facts that give rise to a revision become known.

The Company acquired a business in May 1999 in a stock for stock transaction that was accounted for by the Company as a pooling of interests under Accounting Principles Board Opinion No. 16 "Business Combinations." During fiscal 2008, the Company recorded a tax-basis adjustment to capital in excess of par value on the Statements of Consolidated Stockholders' Equity.

3.111

BRIGGS & STRATTON CORPORATION (JUN)

(In thousands)	2009	2008	2007
Net sales	$2,092,189	$2,151,393	$2,156,833
Cost of goods sold	1,753,935	1,844,077	1,818,547
Impairment charge	4,575	—	43,088
Gross profit	333,679	307,316	295,198
Engineering, selling, general and administrative expenses	265,338	280,976	263,041
Income from operations	68,341	26,340	32,157
Interest expense	(31,147)	(38,123)	(43,691)
Other income, net	3,215	41,392	14,836
Income before provision (credit) for income taxes	40,409	29,609	3,302
Provision (credit) for income taxes	8,437	7,009	(3,399)
Net income	$ 31,972	$ 22,600	$ 6,701

NOTES TO CONSOLIDATED FINANCIAL STATEMENTS

1 (In Part): Summary of Significant Accounting Policies

Income Taxes

The Provision (Credit) for Income Taxes includes federal, state and foreign income taxes currently payable and those deferred because of temporary differences between the financial statement and tax bases of assets and liabilities. The Deferred Income Tax Asset (Liability) represents temporary differences relating to current assets and current liabilities, and the Long-Term Deferred Income Tax Asset (Liability) represents temporary differences related to noncurrent assets and liabilities.

6. Income Taxes

The provision (credit) for income taxes consists of the following (in thousands):

	2009	2008	2007
Current			
Federal	$(1,152)	$ (5,800)	$ 11,861
State	(336)	3	961
Foreign	2,557	2,300	1,226
	1,069	(3,497)	14,048
Deferred	7,368	10,506	(17,447)
	$ 8,437	$ 7,009	$ (3,399)

A reconciliation of the U.S. statutory tax rates to the effective tax rates on income follows:

	2009	2008	2007
U.S. statutory rate	35.0%	35.0%	35.0%
State Taxes, net of federal tax benefit	0.8%	2.4%	14.4%
Foreign tax benefits	(4.3%)	3.4%	(6.0%)
Benefit on dividends received	(1.5%)	(22.3%)	48.7%
Current year FIN 48 changes	(7.5%)	—	—
Other	(1.6%)	5.2%	10.8%
Effective tax rate	20.9%	23.7%	102.9%

The components of deferred income taxes were as follows (in thousands):

	2009	2008
Current asset (liability):		
Difference between book and tax related to:		
Inventory	$ 16,624	$ 16,674
Payroll related accruals	7,768	3,279
Warranty reserves	11,839	14,010
Workers compensation accruals	2,482	2,976
Other accrued liabilities	17,469	22,508
Pension cost	1,031	1,022
Miscellaneous	(5,555)	(6,973)
Deferred income tax asset	$ 51,658	$ 53,496
Long-term asset (liability):		
Difference between book and tax related to:		
Pension cost	$ 43,185	$(31,270)
Accumulated depreciation	(49,218)	(50,606)
Intangibles	(71,686)	(68,358)
Accrued employee benefits	28,472	25,836
Postretirement health care obligation	59,404	62,736
Warranty	4,530	5,707
Valuation allowance	(6,712)	(3,788)
Net operating loss carryforwards	7,073	3,788
Miscellaneous	8,117	8,689
Deferred income tax asset (liability)	$ 23,165	$(47,266)

The deferred tax assets that were generated as a result of foreign income tax loss carryforwards and tax incentives in the amount of $7.1 million are potentially not useable by certain foreign subsidiaries. If not utilized against taxable income, $6.9 million will expire from 2010 through 2020. The remaining $0.2 million has no expiration date. In addition, a deferred tax asset of $0.7 million was generated as a result of state income tax carryforwards. If not utilized against future taxable income, this amount will expire from 2010 through 2030. Realization of the deferred tax assets are contingent upon generating sufficient taxable income prior to expiration of these carryforwards. Management believes that realization of certain foreign deferred tax assets is unlikely, therefore valuation allowances were established in the amount of $6.7 million.

The Company has not recorded deferred income taxes applicable to undistributed earnings of foreign subsidiaries that are indefinitely reinvested in foreign operations. These undistributed earnings amounted to approximately $35.5 million at June 28, 2009. If these earnings were remitted to the U.S., they would be subject to U.S. income tax. However, this tax would be less than the U.S. statutory income tax because of available foreign tax credits.

The Company adopted FASB Interpretation No. 48, "Accounting for Uncertainty in Income Taxes" (FIN 48), at the beginning of fiscal year 2008. As a result of the implementation, the Company recognized a $4.0 million increase in the net liability for unrecognized tax benefits. This increase was accounted for as a decrease to the July 1, 2007 balance of retained earnings.

The change to the total unrecognized tax benefits of the Company during the fiscal year ended June 28, 2009 is reconciled as follows:

(In thousands)	
Uncertain tax positions:	
Beginning balance	$19,205
Changes based on tax positions related to prior year	(575)
Resolution of prior year tax matters	(2,664)
Additions based on tax positions related to current year	1,306
Settlements with taxing authorities	(827)
Impact of changes in foreign exchange rates and interest accruals	(312)
Balance at June 28, 2009	$16,133

As of June 28, 2009, the Company had $24.1 million of gross unrecognized tax benefits. Of this amount, $15.8 million represents the portion that, if recognized, would impact the effective tax rate. As of June 28, 2009, the Company had $6.3 million accrued for the payment of interest and penalties.

The Company is regularly audited by federal, state and foreign tax authorities. The Company's taxable years 2006, 2007 and 2008 are currently under IRS audit.

3.112

CRANE CO. (DEC)

(In thousands)	2009	2008	2007
Net sales	$2,196,343	$2,604,307	$2,619,171
Operating costs and expenses:			
Cost of sales	1,466,030	1,751,036	1,776,157
Asbestos charge	—	—	390,150
Environmental charge	—	24,342	18,912
Restructuring charge (gain)	5,243	40,703	(19,083)
Selling, general and administrative	516,801	590,737	560,691
	1,988,074	2,406,818	2,726,827
Operating profit (loss)	208,269	197,489	(107,656)
Other income (expense):			
Interest income	2,820	10,263	6,259
Interest expense	(27,139)	(25,799)	(27,404)
Miscellaneous income	976	1,694	10,013
	(23,343)	(13,842)	(11,132)
Income (loss) before income taxes	184,926	183,647	(118,788)
Provision (benefit) for income taxes	50,846	48,694	(56,553)
Net income (loss) before allocations to noncontrolling interests	$ 134,080	$ 134,953	$ (62,235)

NOTES TO CONSOLIDATED FINANCIAL STATEMENTS

A (In Part): Summary of Significant Accounting Policies

Income Taxes

The Company accounts for income taxes in accordance with Accounting Standards Codification ("ASC") 740 "Income Taxes" which requires an asset and liability approach for the financial accounting and reporting of income taxes. Under this method, deferred income taxes are recognized for the expected future tax consequences of differences between the tax bases of assets and liabilities and their reported amounts in the financial statements. These balances are measured using the enacted tax rates expected to apply in the year(s) in which these temporary differences are expected to reverse. The effect on deferred income taxes of a change in tax rates is recognized in income in the period when the change is enacted.

Based on consideration of all available evidence regarding their utilization, net deferred tax assets are recorded to the extent that it is more likely than not that they will be realized. Where, based on the weight of all available evidence, it is more likely than not that some amount of a deferred tax asset will not be realized, a valuation allowance is established for that amount that, in management's judgment, is sufficient to reduce the deferred tax asset to an amount that is more likely than not to be realized.

The Company accounts for unrecognized tax benefits in accordance with ASC Topic 740, which prescribes a minimum probability threshold that a tax position must meet before a financial statement benefit is recognized. The minimum threshold is defined as a tax position that is more likely than not to be sustained upon examination by the applicable taxing authority, including resolution of any related appeals or litigation, based solely on the technical merits of the position. The tax benefit to be recognized is measured as the largest amount of benefit that is greater than fifty percent likely of being realized upon ultimate settlement.

The Company recognizes interest and penalties related to unrecognized tax benefits within the income tax expense line of its Consolidated Statement of Operations, while accrued interest and penalties are included within the related tax liability line of its Consolidated Balance Sheets.

Note 3. Income Taxes

Income (loss) before taxes is as follows:

(In thousands)	2009	2008	2007
U.S. operations	$ 69,050	$ 14,107	$(286,826)
Non-U.S. operations	115,876	169,540	168,038
	$184,926	$183,647	$(118,788)

The provision (benefit) for income taxes consists of:

(In thousands)	2009	2008	2007
Current:			
U.S. federal tax	$ (4,187)	$ (8,498)	$ 28,020
State and local tax	5	1,050	(77)
Non-U.S. tax	28,744	42,846	42,356
	24,562	35,398	70,299
Deferred:			
U.S. federal tax	19,879	9,283	(124,684)
State and local tax	2,720	(11)	(96)
Non-U.S. tax	3,685	4,024	(2,072)
	26,284	13,296	(126,852)
Provision (benefit) for income taxes	$50,846	$48,694	$ (56,553)

The reconciliation of the statutory U.S. federal rate to the effective tax rate, is as follows:

(In thousands)	2009	2008	2007
Statutory U.S. federal tax at 35%	$64,646	$ 64,348	$(41,613)
Increase (reduction) from:			
Non-U.S. taxes	(9,205)	(13,159)	(20,019)
State and local tax, net of federal benefit	5,151	3,006	(15,575)
Valuation allowance on state deferred tax assets	(3,378)	(1,967)	15,463
U.S. domestic manufacturing deduction	(1,045)	(893)	(2,107)
Foreign dividend, net of credits	8,348	3,673	5,040
Deferred taxes on earnings of non-U.S. subsidiaries	(3,300)	200	10,400
Research and development tax credit	(4,177)	(6,656)	(3,512)
Tax benefit from sale of subsidiary	(5,238)	—	—
Other	(956)	142	(4,630)
Provision (benefit) for income taxes	$50,846	$ 48,694	$(56,553)
Effective tax rate	27.5%	26.5%	47.6%

As of December 31, 2009, the Company has recorded a deferred tax liability of $6.2 million which reflects the additional U.S. federal and state income tax due upon the ultimate repatriation of approximately $61 million of the undistributed earnings of its non-U.S. subsidiaries. Deferred taxes have not been provided on the remainder of the non-U.S. subsidiaries' undistributed earnings of approximately $216.8 million since these earnings have been, and under current plans will continue to be, indefinitely reinvested outside the U.S. If these earnings were distributed in the form of dividends or otherwise, the Company would be subject to U.S. income taxes and foreign withholding taxes; however, it is not practical to estimate the amount of taxes that would be payable upon remittance of these earnings because such tax, if any, is dependent on circumstances existing if and when remittance occurs.

In 2009, income tax benefits attributable to equity-based compensation transactions were less than the amounts recorded based on grant date fair value. As a result, a shortfall of $0.4 million was charged to equity. In 2008 and 2007, income tax benefits attributable to equity-based compensation transactions exceeded amounts recorded at grant date and, accordingly, were credited to equity in the amount of $0.7 million and $7.0 million, respectively.

Tax (expense)/benefit of $(0.7) million in 2009, $47.3 million in 2008 and $(13.1) million in 2007 related primarily to changes in pension and post-retirement plan assets and benefit obligations were included in accumulated other comprehensive income.

The components of deferred tax assets and liabilities included on the balance sheet are as follows:

(In thousands)	2009	2008
Deferred tax assets:		
Asbestos-related liabilities	$224,276	$247,543
Tax loss and credit carryforwards	76,954	37,566
Environmental	13,318	17,257
Inventories	17,946	16,873
Accrued bonus and stock-based compensation	13,234	10,948
Pension and post-retirement benefits	32,620	42,924
Restructuring reserves	3,737	13,701
Other	15,592	16,540
Total	397,677	403,352
Less: valuation allowance on non-U.S. and state deferred tax assets, tax loss and credit carryforwards	74,182	66,150
Total deferred tax assets, net	323,495	337,202
Deferred tax liabilities:		
Depreciation	(41,605)	(39,921)
Intangibles	(48,746)	(37,211)
Total deferred tax liabilities	(90,351)	(77,132)
Net deferred tax asset	$233,144	$260,070
Balance sheet classification:		
Current deferred tax assets	$ 58,856	$ 50,457
Long-term deferred tax assets	204,386	233,165
Accrued liabilities	(520)	(581)
Long-term deferred tax liability	(29,578)	(22,971)
Net deferred tax asset	$233,144	$260,070

As of December 31, 2009, the Company had U.S. federal, U.S. state and non-U.S. tax loss and credit carryforwards that will expire, if unused, as follows:

(In thousands)	U.S. Federal Tax Credits	U.S. State Tax Credits	U.S. State Tax Losses	Non-U.S. Tax Credits	Non-U.S. Tax Losses	Total
Year of expiration						
2010–2014	$ —	$ 1,482	$ 77,974	$ —	$11,326	
After 2014	30,879	3,474	307,257	—	21,688	
Indefinite	—	11,872	—	213	28,475	
Total	$30,879	$16,828	$385,231	$213	$61,489	
Deferred tax asset on tax carry forwards	$30,879	$10,938	$ 17,612	$213	$17,312	$76,954

Of the $76.9 million deferred tax asset for tax loss and credit carryforwards at December 31, 2009, $45.1 million has been offset by a valuation allowance due to the uncertainty of the Company ultimately realizing future tax benefits from these carryforwards. In addition, the Company considers it unlikely that a portion of the tax benefit related to various U.S. and non-U.S. deferred tax assets will be realized. Accordingly, a $29.1 million valuation allowance has been established against these U.S. and non-U.S. deferred tax assets. The Company's total valuation allowance at December 31, 2009 is approximately $74.2 million.

A reconciliation of the beginning and ending amount of the Company's gross unrecognized tax benefits, excluding interest and penalties, is as follows:

(In thousands)	2009	2008
Balance of liability as of January 1	$6,778	$4,402
Increase as a result of tax positions taken during a prior year	111	1,182
Decrease as a result of tax positions taken during a prior year	(816)	(164)
Increase as a result of tax positions taken during the current year	1,210	1,649
Decrease as a result of settlements with taxing authorities	(315)	(291)
Reduction as a result of a lapse of the statute of limitations	(31)	—
Balance of liability as of December 31	$6,937	$6,778

The total amount of unrecognized tax benefits that, if recognized, would affect the Company's effective tax rate was $7.3 million, $7.0 million and $4.3 million as of December 31, 2009, 2008 and 2007 respectively. The difference between these amounts for the years ended December 31, 2009 and 2008 and the amounts reflected in the tabular reconciliation above relates to (1) deferred U.S. federal income tax benefits on unrecognized tax benefits related to U.S. state income taxes, (2) interest expense, net of deferred federal, U.S. state and non-U.S. tax benefits, and (3) deferred non-U.S. income tax benefits on unrecognized tax benefits related to non-U.S. income taxes.

During the years ended December 31, 2009, December 31, 2008 and December 31, 2007, the Company recognized $0.1, $0.3 and $0.1 million, respectively, of interest expense related to unrecognized tax benefits in its consolidated statement of operations. At December 31, 2009 and December 31, 2008, the Company recognized $0.8 million and $0.7 million, respectively, of interest expense related to unrecognized tax benefits in its consolidated balance sheet.

The Company regularly assesses the potential outcomes of both ongoing examinations and future examinations for the current and prior years in order to ensure the Company's provision for income taxes is adequate. The Company believes that adequate accruals have been provided for all open years.

The Company's income tax returns are subject to examination by the Internal Revenue Service ("IRS") as well as U.S. state and local and non-U.S. taxing authorities. The IRS has completed its examinations of the Company's federal income tax returns for all years through 2005. During 2009, the IRS commenced an examination of the Company's 2007 and 2008 federal income tax returns.

With few exceptions, the Company is no longer subject to U.S. state and local or non-U.S. income tax examinations by taxing authorities for years before 2004. During 2009, certain U.S. state and non-U.S. income tax examinations were completed, and, as of December 31, 2009, the Company is currently under audit by various U.S. state and non-U.S. taxing authorities.

In the next twelve months, it is reasonably possible that the Company's unrecognized tax benefits could change by $5.3 million due to payments for, the expiration of the statute of limitation on, or resolution of federal, U.S. state and non-U.S. tax matters.

Credit Provision

3.113

VULCAN MATERIALS COMPANY (DEC)

(Dollars in thousands)	2009	2008	2007
Net sales	$2,543,707	$3,453,081	$3,090,133
Delivery revenues	146,783	198,357	237,654
Total revenues	2,690,490	3,651,438	3,327,787
Cost of goods sold	2,097,745	2,703,369	2,139,230
Delivery costs	146,783	198,357	237,654
Cost of revenues	2,244,528	2,901,726	2,376,884
Gross profit	445,962	749,712	950,903
Selling, administrative and general expenses	321,608	342,584	289,604
Goodwill impairment	0	252,664	0
Gain on sale of property, plant & equipment and businesses, net	27,104	94,227	58,659
Other operating income (expense), net	(3,006)	411	(5,541)
Operating earnings	148,452	249,102	714,417
Other income (expense), net	5,307	(4,357)	(5,322)
Interest income	2,282	3,126	6,625
Interest expense	175,262	172,813	48,218
Earnings (loss) from continuing operations before income taxes	(19,221)	75,058	667,502
Provision for income taxes			
Current	6,106	92,346	199,931
Deferred	(43,975)	(20,655)	4,485
Total provision for income taxes	(37,869)	71,691	204,416
Earnings from continuing operations	$ 18,648	$ 3,367	$ 463,086

NOTES TO CONSOLIDATED FINANCIAL STATEMENTS
(Dollars in thousands)

1 (In Part): Summary of Significant Accounting Policies

Income Taxes

We file various federal, state and foreign income tax returns, including some returns that are consolidated with subsidiaries. We account for the current and deferred tax effects of such returns using the asset and liability method. Our current and deferred tax assets and liabilities reflect our best assessment of estimated future taxes to be paid. Significant judgments and estimates are required in determining the current and deferred assets and liabilities.

Annually, we compare the liabilities calculated for our federal, state and foreign income tax returns to the estimated liabilities calculated as part of the year end income tax provision. Any adjustments are reflected in our current and deferred tax assets and liabilities.

We recognize deferred tax assets and liabilities based on the differences between the financial statement carrying amounts and the tax basis of assets and liabilities. Deferred tax assets represent items to be used as a tax deduction or credit in future tax returns for which we have already properly recorded the tax benefit in the income statement. At least quarterly, we assess the likelihood that the deferred tax asset balance will be recovered from future taxable income, and we will record a valuation allowance to reduce our deferred tax assets to the amount that is more likely than not to be realized. We take into account such factors as prior earnings history, expected future taxable income, mix of taxable income in the jurisdictions in which we operate, carryback and carryforward periods, and tax strategies that could potentially enhance the likelihood of realization of a deferred tax asset. If we were to determine that we would not be able to realize a portion of our deferred tax assets in the future for which there is currently no valuation allowance, an adjustment to the deferred tax assets would be charged to earnings in the period such determination was made. Conversely, if we were to make a determination that realization is more likely than not for deferred tax assets with a valuation allowance, the related valuation allowance would be reduced and a benefit to earnings would be recorded.

U.S. income taxes are not provided on foreign earnings when such earnings are indefinitely reinvested offshore. We periodically evaluate our investment strategies for each foreign tax jurisdiction in which we operate to determine whether foreign earnings will be indefinitely reinvested offshore and, accordingly, whether U.S. income taxes should be provided when such earnings are recorded.

We recognize a tax benefit associated with an uncertain tax position when, in our judgment, it is more likely than not that the position will be sustained upon examination by a taxing authority. For a tax position that meets the more-likely-than-not recognition threshold, we initially and subsequently measure the tax benefit as the largest amount that we judge to have a greater than 50% likelihood of being realized upon ultimate settlement with a taxing authority. Our liability associated with unrecognized tax benefits is adjusted periodically due to changing circumstances, such as the progress of tax audits, case law developments and new or emerging legislation. Such adjustments are recognized entirely in the period in which they are identified. Our effective tax rate includes the net impact of changes in the liability for unrecognized tax benefits and subsequent adjustments as considered appropriate by management.

A number of years may elapse before a particular matter for which we have recorded a liability related to an unrecognized tax benefit is audited and finally resolved. The number of years with open tax audits varies by jurisdiction. While it is often difficult to predict the final outcome or the timing of resolution of any particular tax matter, we believe our liability for unrecognized tax benefits is adequate. Favorable resolution of an unrecognized tax benefit could be recognized as a reduction in our tax provision and effective tax rate in the period of resolution. Unfavorable settlement of an unrecognized tax benefit could increase the tax provision and effective tax rate and may require the use of cash in the period of resolution. Our liability for unrecognized tax benefits is generally presented as noncurrent. However, if we anticipate paying cash within one year to settle an uncertain tax position, the liability is presented as current. We classify interest and penalties recognized on the liability for unrecognized tax benefits as income tax expense.

Our largest permanent item in computing both our effective tax rate and taxable income is the deduction allowed for statutory depletion. The impact of statutory depletion on the effective tax rate is presented in Note 9. The deduction for statutory depletion does not necessarily change proportionately to changes in pretax earnings.

The American Jobs Creation Act of 2004 created a new deduction for certain domestic production activities as described in Section 199 of the Internal Revenue Code. Generally, this deduction, subject to certain limitations, was set at 6% for 2007 through 2009 and increases to 9% in 2010

and thereafter. The estimated impact of this deduction on the 2009, 2008 and 2007 effective tax rates is presented in Note 9.

Note 9. Income Taxes

The components of earnings (loss) from continuing operations before income taxes are as follows (in thousands of dollars):

	2009	2008	2007
Domestic	$(43,180)	$45,445	$643,350
Foreign	23,959	29,613	24,152
Total	$(19,221)	$75,058	$667,502

Provision (benefit) for income taxes for continuing operations consists of the following (in thousands of dollars):

	2009	2008	2007
Current			
Federal	$ (3,965)	$ 64,428	$172,149
State and local	7,034	20,883	21,894
Foreign	3,037	7,035	5,888
Total	6,106	92,346	199,931
Deferred			
Federal	(37,790)	(18,978)	6,601
State and local	(5,794)	(1,724)	(488)
Foreign	(391)	47	(1,628)
Total	(43,975)	(20,655)	4,485
Total provision (benefit)	$(37,869)	$ 71,691	$204,416

The provision for income taxes differs from the amount computed by applying the federal statutory income tax rate to income before provision for income taxes. The sources and tax effects of the differences are as follows (in thousands of dollars):

	2009		2008		2007	
Income tax provision (benefit) at the federal statutory tax rate of 35%	$ (6,727)	35.0%	$ 26,272	35.0%	$233,630	35.0%
Increase (decrease) in income tax provision (benefit) resulting from statutory depletion	(19,464)	101.3%	(28,063)	−37.4%	(32,005)	−4.8%
State and local income taxes, net of federal income tax benefit	1,457	−7.6%	11,127	14.8%	18,235	2.7%
Nondeductible expense	1,694	−8.8%	1,619	2.2%	1,706	0.3%
Goodwill impairment	0	0.0%	65,031	86.6%	0	0.0%
ESOP dividend deduction	(2,408)	12.5%	(3,017)	−4.0%	(2,450)	−0.4%
U.S. production activities deduction	0	0.0%	(2,203)	−2.9%	(6,951)	−1.0%
Fair market value over tax basis of contributions	(2,931)	15.3%	(3,814)	−5.1%	(4,994)	−0.7%
Foreign tax rate differential	(4,461)	23.2%	(4,955)	−6.6%	(2,999)	−0.4%
Tax loss on sale of stock—divestiture	(4,143)	21.6%	0	0.0%	0	0.0%
Reversal cash surrender value—COLI plans	(412)	2.1%	(486)	−0.6%	0	0.0%
Prior year true up adjustments	375	−2.0%	1,932	2.5%	1,636	0.2%
Provision for uncertain tax positions	(451)	2.3%	1,516	2.0%	(1,363)	−0.3%
Gain on sale of goodwill on divested assets	0	0.0%	6,937	9.3%	0	0.0%
Other	(398)	2.1%	(205)	−0.3%	(29)	0.0%
Total income tax provision (benefit)	$(37,869)	197.0%	$ 71,691	95.5%	$204,416	30.6%

Deferred income taxes on the balance sheet result from temporary differences between the amount of assets and liabilities recognized for financial reporting and tax purposes. The components of the net deferred income tax liability at December 31 are as follows (in thousands of dollars):

	2009	2008
Deferred tax assets related to		
Pensions	$ 63,881	$ 57,323
Other postretirement benefits	46,718	43,741
Accruals for asset retirement obligations and environmental accruals	23,569	46,686
Accounts receivable, principally allowance for doubtful accounts	3,083	3,381
Deferred compensation, vacation pay and incentives	61,197	55,522
Interest rate swaps	34,468	38,734
Self-insurance reserves	24,551	22,343
Valuation allowance on net operating loss carryforwards	(10,768)	(6,057)
Other	37,343	24,453
Total deferred tax assets	284,042	286,126
Deferred tax liabilities related to		
Inventory	3,091	221
Fixed assets	848,923	873,999
Intangible assets	248,978	237,528
Other	12,351	23,648
Total deferred tax liabilities	1,113,343	1,135,396
Net deferred tax liability	$ 829,301	$ 849,270

The above amounts are reflected in the accompanying Consolidated Balance Sheets as of December 31 as follows (in thousands of dollars):

	2009	2008
Deferred income taxes		
Current assets	$ (57,967)	$ (71,205)
Deferred liabilities	887,268	920,475
Net deferred tax liability	$829,301	$849,270

Our determination of the realization of deferred tax assets is based upon management's judgment of various future events and uncertainties, including the timing, nature and amount of future income earned by certain subsidiaries and the implementation of various plans to maximize the realization of deferred tax assets. We believe that the subsidiaries will generate sufficient operating earnings to realize the deferred tax benefits. However, we do not believe that it is more likely than not that all of our state net operating loss carryforwards will be realized in future periods. Accordingly, valuation allowances amounting to $10,768,000 and $6,057,000 were established against the state net operating loss deferred tax assets as of December 31, 2009 and December 31, 2008, respectively. At December 31, 2009, we had $345,085,000 of net operating loss carryforwards in various state jurisdictions. The net operating losses relate to jurisdictions with either 15-year or 20-year carryforward periods, and relate to losses generated in years from 2007 forward. As a result, the vast majority of the loss carryforwards do not begin to expire until 2022.

Additionally, due to a significant decrease in 2009 earnings, along with a sizable dividend from our Mexican subsidiary, we generated a foreign tax credit carryforward of approximately $13,051,000. The carryforward period available for utilization is ten years, and we have concluded that it is more likely than not that the full credit carryforward will be utilized within the carryforward period. The primary factors projected over the ten-year carryforward period upon which we relied to reach this conclusion include (1) a return to more normal levels of earnings, (2) our ability to generate sufficient foreign source income, and (3) the reduction of our interest expense from corporate debt. As a result, no valuation allowance has been established against the foreign tax credit carryforward deferred tax asset.

Uncertain tax positions and the resulting unrecognized income tax benefits are discussed in our accounting policy for income taxes (See Note 1, caption Income Taxes). The change in the unrecognized income tax benefits for the years ended 2009, 2008 and 2007 is reconciled below (in thousands of dollars):

	2009	2008	2007
Unrecognized income tax benefits as of January 1	$18,131	$ 7,480	$ 9,700
Increases for tax positions related to			
Prior years	1,108	482	2,148
Current year	5,667	6,189	2,323
Acquisitions	0	5,250	0
Decreases for tax positions related to			
Prior years	(9)	(1,009)	(1,900)
Current year	0	0	0
Settlements with taxing authorities	(482)	(261)	(281)
Expiration of applicable statute of limitations	(3,441)	0	(4,510)
Unrecognized income tax benefits as of December 31	$20,974	$18,131	$ 7,480

We classify interest and penalties recognized on the liability for unrecognized income tax benefits as income tax expense. Interest and penalties recognized as income tax expense (benefit) were $472,000 in 2009, ($202,000) in 2008 and $1,990,000 in 2007. The balance of accrued interest and penalties included in our liability for unrecognized income tax benefits as of December 31 was $3,112,000 in 2009, $1,376,000 in 2008 and $4,050,000 in 2007.

Our unrecognized income tax benefits at December 31 in the table above include $12,181,000 in 2009, $12,724,000 in 2008 and $5,490,000 in 2007 that would affect the effective tax rate if recognized.

We are routinely examined by various taxing authorities. The U.S. federal statute of limitations for 2006 has been extended to March 31, 2011, with no anticipated significant tax increase or decrease to any single tax position. The U.S. federal statute of limitations for years prior to 2006 has expired. We anticipate no single tax position generating a significant increase or decrease in our liability for unrecognized tax benefits within 12 months of this reporting date.

We file income tax returns in the U.S. federal and various state and foreign jurisdictions. Generally, we are not subject to significant changes in income taxes by any taxing jurisdiction for the years prior to 2005.

We have not recognized deferred income taxes on $38,270,000 of undistributed earnings from one of our foreign subsidiaries, since we consider such earnings as indefinitely reinvested. If we distribute the earnings in the form of dividends, the distribution would be subject to U.S. income taxes. In this event, the amount of deferred income taxes to be recognized is $13,395,000.

OPERATING LOSS AND TAX CREDIT CARRYFORWARDS

3.114   FASB ASC 740, *Income Taxes*, states that amounts and expiration dates of operating loss and tax credit carryforwards for tax purposes should be disclosed. Examples of operating loss and tax credit carryforward disclosures follow.

3.115

AMPHENOL CORPORATION (DEC)

NOTES TO CONSOLIDATED FINANCIAL STATEMENTS
(Dollars in thousands)

Note 5 (In Part): Income Taxes

The components of income before income taxes and the provision for income taxes are as follows:

	2009	2008	2007
Income before income taxes:			
United States	$ 98,170	$179,292	$216,311
Foreign	348,357	413,288	295,191
	$446,527	$592,580	$511,502
Current provision:			
United States	$ 38,621	$ 63,052	$ 74,900
Foreign	89,969	100,744	64,137
	$128,590	$163,796	$139,037
Deferred provision:			
United States	$ (2,295)	$ 2,564	$ 11,829
Foreign	(6,984)	(3,357)	(3,076)
	$ (9,279)	$ (793)	$ 8,753
Total provision for income taxes	$119,311	$163,003	$147,790

At December 31, 2009, the Company had $49,182 and $3,429 of foreign tax loss and credit carryforwards, and state tax credit carryforwards net of federal benefit, respectively, of which $21,142 and $132, respectively, expire or will be refunded at various dates through 2024 and the balance can be carried forward indefinitely.

A valuation allowance of $13,816 and $9,946 at December 31, 2009 and 2008, respectively, has been recorded which relates to the foreign net operating loss carryforwards and state tax credits. The net change in the valuation allowance for deferred tax assets was an increase of $3,870 and $3,860 in 2009 and 2008, respectively, which was related to foreign net operating loss and foreign and state credit carryforwards.

Differences between the U.S. statutory federal tax rate and the Company's effective income tax rate are analyzed below:

	2009	2008	2007
U.S. statutory federal tax rate	35.0%	35.0%	35.0%
State and local taxes	.9	.6	1.1
Foreign earnings and dividends taxed at different rates	(9.6)	(8.4)	(7.3)
Valuation allowance	1.0	.4	—
Other	(.6)	(.1)	.1
Effective tax rate	26.7%	27.5%	28.9%

The Company's deferred tax assets and liabilities, excluding the valuation allowance, comprised the following:

	2009	2008
Deferred tax assets relating to:		
Accrued liabilities and reserves	$ 14,075	$10,138
Operating loss and tax credit carryforwards	16,758	10,683
Pensions, net	37,278	35,666
Interest rate derivatives	1,355	9,234
Inventory reserves	13,724	12,734
Employee benefits	18,463	14,275
	$101,653	$92,730
Deferred tax liabilities relating to:		
Goodwill	$ 45,657	$35,081
Depreciation	1,591	437
	$ 47,248	$35,518

3.116

XEROX CORPORATION (DEC)

NOTES TO CONSOLIDATED FINANCIAL STATEMENTS
(Dollars in millions)

Note 15 (In Part): Income and Other Taxes

Deferred Income Taxes (In Part)

The tax effects of temporary differences that give rise to significant portions of the deferred taxes at December 31, 2009 and 2008 were as follows:

	2009	2008
Tax effect of future tax deductions:		
Research and development	$ 752	$ 930
Post-retirement medical benefits	421	392
Depreciation	246	249
Net operating losses	576	486
Other operating reserves	261	249
Tax credit carryforwards	525	552
Deferred compensation	233	248
Allowance for doubtful accounts	93	84
Restructuring reserves	16	88
Pension	403	373
Other	132	182
Subtotal	3,658	3,833
Valuation allowance	(672)	(628)
Total	$ 2,986	$ 3,205
Tax effect of future taxable income:		
Unearned income and installment sales	$ (996)	$(1,119)
Intangibles and goodwill	(154)	(160)
Other	(38)	(53)
Total	$(1,188)	$(1,332)
Total deferred taxes, net	$ 1,798	$ 1,873

The above amounts are classified as current or long-term in the Consolidated Balance Sheets in accordance with the asset or liability to which they relate or, when applicable, based on the expected timing of the reversal. Current deferred tax assets at December 31, 2009 and 2008 amounted to $290 and $305, respectively.

The deferred tax assets for the respective periods were assessed for recoverability and, where applicable, a valuation allowance was recorded to reduce the total deferred tax asset to an amount that will, more-likely-than-not, be realized in the future. The net change in the total valuation allowance for the years ended December 31, 2009 and 2008 was an increase of $44 and a decrease of $119, respectively. The valuation allowance relates primarily to certain net operating loss carryforwards, tax credit carryforwards and deductible temporary differences for which we have concluded it is more-likely-than-not that these items will not be realized in the ordinary course of operations.

Although realization is not assured, we have concluded that it is more-likely-than-not that the deferred tax assets, for which a valuation allowance was determined to be unnecessary, will be realized in the ordinary course of operations based on the available positive and negative evidence, including scheduling of deferred tax liabilities and projected income from operating activities. The amount of the net deferred tax assets considered realizable, however, could be reduced in the near term if actual future income or income tax rates are lower than estimated, or if there are differences in the timing or amount of future reversals of existing taxable or deductible temporary differences.

At December 31, 2009, we had tax credit carryforwards of $525 available to offset future income taxes, of which $146 are available to carryforward indefinitely while the remaining $379 will expire 2010 through 2027 if not utilized. We also had net operating loss carryforwards for income tax purposes of $556 that will expire 2010 through 2029, if not utilized, and $2.5 billion available to offset future taxable income indefinitely.

TAXES ON UNDISTRIBUTED EARNINGS

3.117 FASB ASC 740, *Income Taxes*, requires, except in certain specified situations, that undistributed earnings of a subsidiary included in consolidated income be accounted for as a temporary difference. If a deferred tax liability is not recognized, FASB ASC 740 specifies what information should be disclosed. Examples of disclosures concerning undistributed earnings follow.

3.118

ELI LILLY AND COMPANY (DEC)

NOTES TO CONSOLIDATED FINANCIAL STATEMENTS
(Dollars in millions)

Note 1 (In Part): Summary of Significant Accounting Policies

Income Taxes (In Part)

Deferred taxes are recognized for the future tax effects of temporary differences between financial and income tax reporting based on enacted tax laws and rates. Federal income taxes are provided on the portion of the income of foreign subsidiaries that is expected to be remitted to the United States and be taxable.

Note 12 (In Part): Income Taxes

Significant components of our deferred tax assets and liabilities as of December 31 are as follows:

	2009	2008
Deferred tax assets		
Compensation and benefits	$ 1,153.2	$ 1,154.6
Tax credit carryforwards and carrybacks	738.2	755.0
Tax loss carryforwards and carrybacks	458.2	562.3
Intercompany profit in inventories	270.6	473.9
Asset purchases	253.4	251.5
Asset disposals	173.6	3.2
Contingencies	162.0	345.2
Sale of intangibles	122.6	117.9
Product return reserves	85.0	100.8
Debt	45.9	211.6
Other	510.2	310.4
	3,972.9	4,286.4
Valuation allowances	(836.8)	(845.4)
Total deferred tax assets	3,136.1	3,441.0
Deferred tax liabilities		
Intangibles	(818.4)	(860.2)
Property and equipment	(623.8)	(620.7)
Inventories	(544.4)	(431.6)
Unremitted earnings	(442.9)	(467.3)
Other	(195.4)	(287.8)
Total deferred tax liabilities	(2,624.9)	(2,667.6)
Deferred tax assets—net	$ 511.2	$ 773.4

• • • • • •

At December 31, 2009, we had an aggregate of $15.46 billion of unremitted earnings of foreign subsidiaries that have been or are intended to be permanently reinvested for continued use in foreign operations and that, if distributed, would result in additional income tax expense at approximately the U.S. statutory rate.

3.119

EXPRESS SCRIPTS, INC. (DEC)

NOTES TO CONSOLIDATED FINANCIAL STATEMENTS

Note 10 (In Part): Income Taxes

Income from continuing operations before income taxes of $1,309.3 million resulted in net tax expense of $482.8 million for 2009. We consider our Canadian earnings to be indefinitely reinvested and accordingly, have not recorded a provision for United States federal and state income taxes thereon. Cumulative undistributed Canadian earnings for which United States taxes have not been provided are included in consolidated retained earnings in the amount of $40.6 million, $31.5 million and $34.3 million as of December 31, 2009, 2008, and 2007, respectively. Upon distribution of such earnings, we would be subject to United States income taxes of approximately $14.6 million.

3.120

HALLIBURTON COMPANY (DEC)

NOTES TO CONSOLIDATED FINANCIAL STATEMENTS

Note 1 (In Part): Summary of Significant Accounting Policies

Income Taxes (In Part)

We generally do not provide income taxes on the undistributed earnings of non-United States subsidiaries because such earnings are intended to be reinvested indefinitely to finance foreign activities. These additional foreign earnings could be subject to additional tax if remitted, or deemed remitted, as a dividend; however, it is not practicable to estimate the additional amount, if any, of taxes payable. Taxes are provided as necessary with respect to earnings that are not permanently reinvested.

LONG-TERM CONTRACTS

3.121 Accounting and disclosure requirements for long-term contracts are discussed in FASB ASC 605–35, *Revenue Recognition—Construction-Type and Production-Type Contracts*.

3.122 Table 3-16 shows that usually the percentage of completion method or a modification of this method is used to recognize revenue on long-term contracts. Of the 500 survey entities, 86 had long-term contracts. Of the 63 entities using percentage-of-completion method based on an input measurement, 40 entities used cost-to-cost to measure progress towards completion. Of the 41 entities using percentage of completion method based on an output measurement, 23 used units-of-delivery to measure progress towards completion. Examples of disclosure for long-term contracts follow.

3.123

TABLE 3-16: METHOD OF ACCOUNTING FOR LONG-TERM CONTRACTS

	Number of Entities			
	2009	2008	2007	2006
Percentage-of-completion: input based	63	56	76	81
Percentage-of-completion: output based	41	40	43	55
Completed contract	20	17	24	9

2008–2009 based on 500 entities surveyed; 2006–2007 based on 600 entities surveyed.

3.124

NORTHROP GRUMMAN CORPORATION (DEC)

NOTES TO CONSOLIDATED FINANCIAL STATEMENTS

1 (In Part): Summary of Significant Accounting Policies

Revenue Recognition

As a defense contractor engaging in long-term contracts, the majority of the company's business is derived from long-term contracts for production of goods, and services provided to the federal government. In accounting for these contracts, the company extensively utilizes the cost-to-cost and the units-of-delivery measures of the percentage-of-completion method of accounting. Sales under cost-reimbursement contracts and construction-type contracts that provide for delivery at a low volume per year or a small number of units after a lengthy period of time over which a significant amount of costs have been incurred are accounted for using the cost-to-cost measure of the percentage-of-completion method of accounting. Under this method, sales, including estimated earned fees or profits, are recorded as costs are incurred. For most contracts, sales are calculated based on the percentage that total costs incurred bear to total estimated costs at completion. For certain contracts with large up-front purchases of material, primarily in the Shipbuilding segment, sales are calculated based on the percentage that direct labor costs incurred bear to total estimated direct labor costs. Sales under construction-type contracts that provide for delivery at a high volume per year are accounted for using the units-of-delivery measure of the percentage-of-completion method of accounting. Under this method, sales are recognized as deliveries are made to the customer generally using unit sales values for delivered units in accordance with the contract terms. The company estimates profit as the difference between total estimated revenue and total estimated cost of a contract and recognizes that profit over the life of the contract based on deliveries or as computed on the basis of the estimated final average unit costs plus profit. The company classifies contract revenues as product sales or service revenues depending upon the predominant attributes of the relevant underlying contracts.

Certain contracts contain provisions for price redetermination or for cost and/or performance incentives. Such redetermined amounts or incentives are included in sales when the amounts can reasonably be determined and estimated. Amounts representing contract change orders, claims, requests for equitable adjustment, or limitations in funding are included in sales only when they can be reliably estimated and realization is probable. In the period in which it is determined that a loss will result from the performance of a contract, the entire amount of the estimated ultimate loss is charged against income. Loss provisions are first offset against costs that are included in unbilled accounts receivable or inventoried costs, with any remaining amount reflected in liabilities. Changes in estimates of contract sales, costs, and profits are recognized using the cumulative catch-up method of accounting. This method recognizes in the current period the cumulative effect of the changes on current and prior periods. Hence, the effect of the changes on future periods of contract performance is recognized as if the revised estimate had been the original estimate. A significant change in an estimate on one or more contracts could have a material effect on the company's consolidated financial position or results of operations.

Revenue under contracts to provide services to non-federal government customers are generally recognized when services are performed. Service contracts include operations and maintenance contracts, and outsourcing-type arrangements, primarily in the Information Systems segment. Revenue under such contracts is generally recognized on a straight-line basis over the period of contract performance, unless evidence suggests that the revenue is earned or the obligations are fulfilled in a different pattern. Costs incurred under these service contracts are expensed as incurred, except that direct and incremental set-up costs are capitalized and amortized over the life of the agreement. Operating profit related to such service contracts may fluctuate from period to period, particularly in the earlier phases of the contract. For contracts that include more than one type of product or service, revenue recognition includes the proper identification of separate units of accounting and the allocation of revenue across all elements based on relative fair values.

Accounts Receivable

Accounts receivable include amounts billed and currently due from customers, amounts currently due but unbilled (primarily related to contracts accounted for under the cost-to-cost measure of the percentage-of-completion method of accounting), certain estimated contract change amounts, claims or requests for equitable adjustment in negotiation that are probable of recovery, and amounts retained by the customer pending contract completion.

Inventoried Costs

Inventoried costs primarily relate to work in process under fixed-price, units-of-delivery and fixed-priced-incentive contracts using labor dollars as the basis of the percentage-of-completion calculation. These costs represent accumulated contract costs less the portion of such costs allocated to delivered items. Accumulated contract costs include direct production costs, factory and engineering overhead, production tooling costs, and, for government contracts, allowable general and administrative expenses. According to the provisions of U.S. Government contracts, the customer asserts title to, or a security interest in, inventories related to such contracts as a result of contract advances, performance-based payments, and progress payments. In accordance with industry practice, inventoried costs are classified as a current asset and include amounts related to contracts having production cycles longer than one year. Product inventory primarily consists of raw materials and is stated at the lower of cost or market, generally using the average cost method. General corporate expenses and IR&D allocable to commercial contracts are expensed as incurred.

8. Accounts Receivable, Net

Unbilled amounts represent sales for which billings have not been presented to customers at year-end. These amounts are usually billed and collected within one year. Progress payments are received on a number of firm fixed-price contracts. Unbilled amounts are presented net of progress payments of $5.6 billion and $4.7 billion at December 31, 2009, and 2008, respectively.

Accounts receivable at December 31, 2009, are expected to be collected in 2010, except for approximately $76 million due in 2011 and $7 million due in 2012 and later.

Allowances for doubtful amounts mainly represent estimates of overhead costs which may not be successfully negotiated and collected.

Accounts receivable were composed of the following:

($ in millions)	2009	2008
Due from U.S. Government		
Amounts billed	$1,078	$1,177
Recoverable costs and accrued profit on progress completed—unbilled	1,980	1,747
	3,058	2,924
Due from other customers		
Amounts billed	318	419
Recoverable costs and accrued profit on progress completed—unbilled	342	658
	660	1,077
Total accounts receivable	3,718	4,001
Allowances for doubtful amounts	(324)	(300)
Total accounts receivable, net	$3,394	$3,701

9. Inventoried Costs, Net

Inventoried costs were composed of the following:

($ in millions)	2009	2008
Production costs of contracts in process	$ 2,698	$ 2,393
General and administrative expenses	175	221
	2,873	2,614
Progress payments received	(1,909)	(1,864)
	964	750
Product inventory	206	253
Total inventoried costs, net	$ 1,170	$ 1,003

3.125

RPM INTERNATIONAL INC. (MAY)

NOTES TO CONSOLIDATED FINANCIAL STATEMENTS

Note A (In Part): Summary of Significant Accounting Policies

12 (In Part): Revenue Recognition

We also record revenues generated under long-term construction contracts, mainly in connection with the installation of specialized roofing and flooring systems, and related services. Certain long-term construction contracts are accounted for under the percentage-of-completion method, and therefore we record contract revenues and related costs as our contracts progress. This method recognizes the economic results of contract performance on a timelier basis than does the completed-contract method; however, application of this method requires reasonably dependable estimates of progress toward completion, as well as other dependable estimates. When reasonably dependable estimates cannot be made, or if other factors make estimates doubtful,

the completed contract method is applied. Under the completed contract method, billings and costs are accumulated on the balance sheet as the contract progresses, but no revenue is recognized until the contract is complete or substantially complete.

3.126

TUTOR PERINI CORPORATION (DEC)

NOTES TO CONSOLIDATED FINANCIAL STATEMENTS

1 (In Part): Summary of Significant Accounting Policies

d. Method of Accounting for Contracts

Revenues and profits from the Company's contracts and construction joint venture contracts are generally recognized by applying percentages of completion for the period to the total estimated profits for the respective contracts. Percentage of completion is determined by relating the actual cost of the work performed to date to the current estimated total cost of the respective contracts. However, on construction management contracts, profit is generally recognized in accordance with the contract terms, usually on the as-billed method, which is generally consistent with the level of effort incurred over the contract period. When the estimate on a contract indicates a loss, the Company's policy is to record the entire loss during the accounting period in which it is estimable. In the ordinary course of business, at a minimum on a quarterly basis, the Company prepares updated estimates of the total forecasted revenue, cost and profit or loss for each contract. The cumulative effect of revisions in estimates of the total forecasted revenue and costs, including unapproved change orders and claims, during the course of the work is reflected in the accounting period in which the facts that caused the revision become known. The financial impact of these revisions to any one contract is a function of both the amount of the revision and the percentage of completion of the contract. An amount equal to the costs incurred which are attributable to unapproved change orders and claims is included in the total estimated revenue when realization is probable. Profit from unapproved change orders and claims is recorded in the period such amounts are resolved.

In accordance with normal practice in the construction industry, the Company includes in current assets and current liabilities amounts related to construction contracts realizable and payable over a period in excess of one year. Billings in excess of costs and estimated earnings represents the excess of contract billings to date over the amount of contract costs and profits (or contract revenue) recognized to date on the percentage of completion accounting method on certain contracts. Costs and estimated earnings in excess of billings represents the excess of contract costs and profits (or contract revenue) recognized to date on the percentage of completion accounting method over the amount of contract billings to date on the remaining contracts. Costs and estimated earnings in excess of billings results when (1) the appropriate contract revenue amount has been recognized in accordance with the percentage of completion accounting method, but a portion of the revenue recorded cannot be billed currently due to the billing terms defined in the contract and/or (2) costs, recorded at estimated realizable value, related to unapproved change orders or claims are incurred. Costs and estimated earnings in excess of billings related to the Company's contracts and joint venture contracts at December 31, 2009 and 2008, consisted of the following (in thousands):

	2009	2008
Unbilled costs and profits incurred to date(*)	$ 44,637	$ 30,623
Unapproved change orders	32,683	16,401
Claims	68,358	68,682
	$145,678	$115,706

(*) Represents the excess of contract costs and profits recognized to date on the percentage of completion accounting method over the amount of contract billings to date on certain contracts.

Of the balance of "Unapproved change orders" and "Claims" included above in costs and estimated earnings in excess of billings at December 31, 2009 and December 31, 2008, approximately $62.7 million and $56.6 million, respectively, are amounts subject to pending litigation or dispute resolution proceedings as described in Note 9. These amounts are management's estimate of the probable cost recovery from the disputed claims considering such factors as evaluation of entitlement, settlements reached to date and experience with the customer. In the event that future facts and circumstances, including the resolution of disputed claims, cause a reduction in the aggregate amount of the estimated probable cost recovery from the disputed claims, the amount of such reduction will be recorded against earnings in the relevant future period.

The prerequisite for billing "Unbilled costs and profits incurred to date" is provided in the defined billing terms of each of the applicable contracts. The prerequisite for billing "Unapproved change orders" or "Claims" is the final resolution and agreement between the parties. The amount of costs and estimated earnings in excess of billings at December 31, 2009 estimated by management to be collected beyond one year is approximately $30.0 million.

DISCONTINUED OPERATIONS

3.127 FASB ASC 205-20, *Discontinued Operations*, sets forth the financial accounting and reporting requirements for discontinued operations of a component of an entity. A component of an entity comprises operations and cash flows that can be clearly distinguished, operationally and for financial reporting purposes, from the rest of the entity. A component of an entity may be a reportable segment or operating segment, a reporting entity, or an asset group.

3.128 FASB ASC 205-20 uses a single accounting model to account for all long-lived assets to be disposed of (by sale, abandonment, or a distribution to owners). This includes asset disposal groups meeting the criteria for presentation as a discontinued operation as specified in FASB ASC 205-20. A long-lived asset group classified as held for sale shall be measured at the lower of its carrying amount or fair value less cost to sell. Additionally, in accordance with FASB ASC 360, *Property, Plant and Equipment*, a loss shall be recognized

for any write-down to fair value less cost to sell. A gain shall be recognized for any subsequent recovery of cost. Lastly, a gain or loss not previously recognized that results from the sale of the asset disposal group should be recognized at the date of sale. Accordingly, discontinued operations are no longer measured on a net realizable value basis, and future operating losses are no longer recognized before they occur.

3.129 The conditions for determining whether discontinued operation treatment is appropriate and the required income statement presentation are stated in FASB ASC 205-20 as follows:

The results of operations of a component of an entity that either has been disposed of or is classified as held for sale shall be reported in discontinued operations if both of the following conditions are met: (a) the operations and cash flow of the component have been (or will be) eliminated from the ongoing operations of the enterprise as a result of the disposal transaction and (b) the entity will not have any significant continuing involvement in the operations of the component after the disposal transaction.

In a period in which a component of an entity either has been disposed of or is classified as held for sale, the income statement of a business entity for current and prior periods shall report the results of operations of the component, including any gain or loss recognized, in discontinued operations. The results of operations of a component classified as held for sale shall be reported in discontinued operations in the period(s) in which they occur. The results of discontinued operations, less applicable income taxes (benefit), shall be reported as a separate component of income before extraordinary items (if applicable). For example, the results of discontinued operations may be reported in the income statement of a business entity as follows:

Income from continuing operations before income taxes	$XXXX	
Income taxes	XXX	
Income from continuing operations		$XXXX
Discontinued operations (Note X):		
Loss from operations of component X (including loss on disposal of $XXX)	$XXXX	
Income tax benefit	XXXX	
Loss on discontinued operations		XXXX
Net income		$XXXX

A gain or loss recognized on the disposal shall be disclosed either on the face of the income statement or in the notes to the financial statements.

3.130 Illustrations of transactions which should and should not be accounted for as business segment disposals are presented in the appendix of FASB ASC 205-20.

3.131 In 2009, 44 survey entities discontinued or planned to discontinue the operations of a component of an entity. 31 of the survey entities reported a gain or loss recognized on the disposal of a component of an entity. 21 of those survey entities presented the disposal gain or loss on the face of the income statement. Examples of discontinued operations accounted for separately from continuing operations follow.

Business Component Disposals

3.132

BRISTOL-MYERS SQUIBB COMPANY (DEC)

(Dollars in millions)	2009	2008	2007
Earnings from continuing operations before income taxes	$ 5,602	$4,776	$2,523
Provision for income taxes	1,182	1,090	471
Net earnings from continuing operations	4,420	3,686	2,052
Discontinued operations:			
Earnings, net of taxes	285	578	876
Gain on disposal, net of taxes	7,157	1,979	—
Net earnings from discontinued operations	7,442	2,557	876
Net earnings	11,862	6,243	2,928
Net earnings attributable to noncontrolling interest	1,250	996	763
Net earnings attributable to Bristol-Myers Squibb Company	$10,612	$5,247	$2,165
Amounts attributable to Bristol-Myers Squibb Company:			
Net earnings from continuing operations	$ 3,239	$2,697	$1,296
Net earnings from discontinued operations	7,373	2,550	869
Net earnings attributable to Bristol-Myers Squibb Company	$10,612	$5,247	$2,165

NOTES TO CONSOLIDATED FINANCIAL STATEMENTS

Note 7 (In Part): Discontinued Operations

Mead Johnson Nutrition Company Split-Off

The split-off of the remaining interest in Mead Johnson was completed on December 23, 2009. The split-off was effected through the exchange offer of previously held 170 million shares of Mead Johnson, after converting its Class B common stock to Class A common stock, for 269 million outstanding shares of the Company's stock resulting in a pre-tax gain of approximately $7.3 billion, $7.2 billion net of taxes.

The shares received in connection with the exchange were valued using the closing price on December 23, 2009 of $25.70 and reflected as treasury stock. The gain on the exchange was determined using the sum of the fair value of the shares received plus the net deficit of Mead Johnson attributable to the Company less taxes and other direct expenses related to the transaction, including a tax reserve of $244 million which was established.

Transitional Relationships With Discontinued Operations

Subsequent to the respective dispositions, cash flows and income associated with the Mead Johnson, ConvaTec and the Medical Imaging businesses continued to be generated relating to activities that are transitional in nature and generally result from agreements that are intended to facilitate the orderly transfer of business operations. The agreements include, among others, services for accounting, customer service, distribution and manufacturing and generally expire no later than 18 months from the date of the divestiture. The income generated from these transitional activities is included in other (income)/expense and are not expected to be material to the future results of operations or cash flows. Such activities related to ConvaTec and Medical Imaging businesses are substantially complete at December 31, 2009.

The following summarized financial information related to the Mead Johnson, ConvaTec and Medical Imaging businesses are segregated from continuing operations and

reported as discontinued operations through the date of disposition.

(Dollars in millions)	2009	2008	2007
Net sales:			
Mead Johnson	$2,826	$2,882	$2,576
ConvaTec	—	735	1,155
Medical Imaging	—	34	629
Net sales	$2,826	$3,651	$4,360
Earnings before income taxes:			
Mead Johnson	$ 674	$ 696	$ 663
ConvaTec	—	175	348
Medical Imaging	—	2	273
Earnings before income taxes	674	873	1,284
Provision for income taxes	(389)	(295)	(408)
Earnings, net of taxes	285	578	876
Gain on disposal:			
Mead Johnson	7,275	—	—
ConvaTec	—	3,387	—
Medical Imaging	—	25	—
Gain on disposal	7,275	3,412	—
Provision for income taxes	(118)	(1,433)	—
Gain on disposal, net of taxes	7,157	1,979	—
Net earnings from discontinued operations	7,442	2,557	876
Less net earnings from discontinued operations attributable to noncontrolling interest	(69)	(7)	(7)
Net earnings from discontinued operations attributable to Bristol-Myers Squibb Company	$7,373	$2,550	$ 869

3.133

PRECISION CASTPARTS CORP. (MAR)

(In millions)	2009	2008	2007
Income before income tax expense and minority interest	$1,577.5	$1,452.0	$904.5
Income tax expense	539.1	491.7	299.6
Minority interest	(0.3)	(1.2)	(1.4)
Net income from continuing operations	1,038.1	959.1	603.5
Net income from discontinued operations	6.4	28.2	29.6
Net income	$1,044.5	$ 987.3	$633.1

NOTES TO CONSOLIDATED STATEMENTS
(In millions)

4 (In Part): Discontinued Operations

Fiscal 2009

In the third quarter of fiscal 2009, we decided to dispose of two automotive fastener operations. The decision to discontinue these automotive fastener operations resulted from their non-core nature coupled with further erosion in the automotive market. These operations have been reclassified from the Fasteners Products segment to discontinued operations in the third quarter of fiscal 2009. In the first quarter of fiscal 2009, we sold the stock of our Technova entities, a foreign operation held for sale and previously recorded as discontinued from our former Flow Technologies pumps and valves business. The transaction resulted in a gain of approximately $3.0 million.

These businesses each meet the criteria as a component of an entity under SFAS No. 144, "Accounting for the Impairment or Disposal of Long-Lived Assets." Accordingly, any operating results of these businesses are presented in the Consolidated Statements of Income as discontinued operations, net of income tax, and all prior periods have been reclassified. The components of discontinued operations for the periods presented are as follows:

	2009	2008	2007
Net sales	$85.9	$166.6	$193.3
Cost of goods sold	85.7	140.2	155.1
Selling and administrative expenses	2.1	13.0	15.2
Interest (income) expense, net	(0.1)	—	0.7
Net (loss) income from operations before income taxes	(1.8)	13.4	22.3
Income tax expense	2.7	6.4	1.0
Net (loss) income from operations	(4.5)	7.0	21.3
Gain on disposal, net of tax (benefit) expense of $(1.3), $2.2, and $(1.4)	10.9	21.2	8.3
Net income from discontinued operations	$ 6.4	$ 28.2	$ 29.6

Included in the Consolidated Balance Sheets are the following major classes of assets and liabilities associated with the discontinued operations after adjustment for write-downs to fair value less cost to sell:

	2009	2008
Assets of discontinued operations:		
Current assets	$16.5	$46.9
Net property, plant and equipment	19.1	29.8
Other assets	1.9	0.6
	$37.5	$77.3
Liabilities of discontinued operations:		
Long term debt currently due	$ 0.3	$ 0.6
Other current liabilities	11.4	23.9
Long term debt	—	0.5
Other liabilities	3.4	3.4
	$15.1	$28.4

Adjustment of Gain/Loss Reported in Prior Period

3.134

GOODRICH CORPORATION (DEC)

(Dollars in millions)	2009	2008	2007
Income from continuing operations before income taxes	$ 784.1	$ 984.6	$ 737.4
Income tax expense	(207.8)	(293.0)	(220.9)
Income from continuing operations	576.3	691.6	516.5
Income (loss) from discontinued operations—net of income taxes	34.5	7.6	(13.4)
Consolidated net income	$ 610.8	$ 699.2	$ 503.1
Net income attributable to noncontrolling interests	(13.5)	(18.0)	(20.5)
Net income attributable to Goodrich	$ 597.3	$ 681.2	$ 482.6
Amounts attributable to Goodrich:			
Income from continuing operations	$ 562.8	$ 673.6	$ 496.0
Income (loss) from discontinued operations—net of income taxes	34.5	7.6	(13.4)
Net income attributable to Goodrich	$ 597.3	$ 681.2	$ 482.6

NOTES TO CONSOLIDATED FINANCIAL STATEMENTS

Note 6 (In Part): Discontinued Operations

The following summarizes the results of discontinued operations:

(Dollars in millions)	2009	2008	2007
Sales—ATS	$ —	$ —	$143.6
Operations—ATS—net of income tax expense of $1.6 in 2007	$ —	$ —	$2.8
Loss on the sale of ATS net of income tax benefit of $37.8 in 2007	—	—	(15.4)
Previously discontinued operations net of tax expense of $20.8 and $0.7 in 2009 and 2008, respectively and net of tax benefit of $0.6 in 2007	34.5	7.6	(0.8)
Income (loss) from discontinued operations—net of income taxes	$34.5	$7.6	$ (13.4)

During 2009, the income from discontinued operations related primarily to the resolution of litigation for an environmental matter at a divested business that had been previously reported as a discontinued operation and favorable resolution of other divestiture liabilities.

CHARGES OR CREDITS SHOWN AFTER INCOME TAX CAPTION

3.135   Table 3-17 indicates the nature of charges or credits, other than extraordinary items, positioned on an income statement after the caption for income taxes applicable to income from continuing operations. An example of a charge/credit shown after the caption for income taxes applicable to income from continuing operations follows.

3.136   FASB ASC 250, *Accounting Changes and Error Corrections*, specifies the requirements for the accounting for and reporting of a change in accounting principle. FASB ASC 250 requires, unless impracticable or otherwise specified by an applicable authoritative pronouncement, retrospective application to prior periods' financial statements of a change in accounting principle. Retrospective application is the application of a different accounting principle to prior accounting periods as if that principle had always been used. More specifically, retrospective application involves the following:

- The cumulative effect of the change on periods prior to those presented shall be reflected in the carrying amount of assets and liabilities as of the beginning of the first period presented.
- An offsetting adjustment, if any, shall be made to the opening balance of retained earnings (or other appropriate component of equity) for that period.
- Financial statements for each individual prior period presented shall be adjusted to reflect the period-specific effects of applying the new accounting principle.

3.137   FASB ASC 810, *Consolidation*, establishes accounting and reporting standards for the noncontrolling interest in a subsidiary. It clarifies that a noncontrolling interest in a subsidiary is an ownership interest in the consolidated entity that should be reported as equity in the consolidated financial statements. In addition, it changes the way the consolidated income statement is presented. The statement requires consolidated net income to be reported at amounts that include the amounts attributable to both the parent and the noncontrolling interest. It also requires disclosure, on the face of the consolidated statement of income, of the amounts of consolidated net income attributable to the parent and to the noncontrolling interest.

3.138

TABLE 3-17: CHARGES OR CREDITS SHOWN AFTER INCOME TAX CAPTION

	Number of Entities			
	2009	2008	2007	2006
Noncontrolling interest	188	123	142	130
Equity in earnings or losses of investees	34	40	44	42
Distributions on trust preferred securities	—	1	1	—
Cumulative effect of accounting change	—	—	3	53
Other	1	—	4	2

2008–2009 based on 500 entities surveyed; 2006–2007 based on 600 entities surveyed.

3.139

FREEPORT-MCMORAN COPPER & GOLD INC.
(DEC)

(In millions, except per share amounts)	2009	2008	2007
Income (loss) from continuing operations before income taxes and equity in affiliated companies' net earnings	$ 5,816	$(13,309)	$ 6,111
(Provision for) benefit from income taxes	(2,307)	2,844	(2,400)
Equity in affiliated companies' net earnings	25	15	22
Income (loss) from continuing operations	3,534	(10,450)	3,733
Income from discontinued operations, net of taxes	—	—	46
Net income (loss)	3,534	(10,450)	3,779
Net income attributable to noncontrolling interests	(785)	(617)	(802)
Preferred dividends and losses on induced conversions	(222)	(274)	(208)
Net income (loss) attributable to FCX common stockholders	$ 2,527	$(11,341)	$ 2,769
Basic net income (loss) per share attributable to FCX common stockholders:			
Continuing operations	$ 6.10	$ (29.72)	$ 8.02
Discontinued operations	—	—	0.10
Basic net income (loss)	$ 6.10	$ (29.72)	$ 8.12
Diluted net income (loss) per share attributable to FCX common stockholders:			
Continuing operations	$ 5.86	$ (29.72)	$ 7.41
Discontinued operations	—	—	0.09
Diluted net income (loss)	$ 5.86	$ (29.72)	$ 7.50
Weighted-average common shares outstanding:			
Basic	414	382	341
Diluted	469	382	397
Dividends declared per share of common stock	$ 0.15	$ 1.375	$ 1.375

EXTRAORDINARY ITEMS

3.140 FASB ASC 225-20, *Extraordinary and Unusual Items*, defines extraordinary items as events and transactions that are distinguished by their unusual nature and by the infrequency of their occurrence, and states that an event or transaction shall be presumed to be an ordinary and usual activity of the reporting entity, the effects of which should be included in income from operations, unless the evidence clearly supports its classification as an extraordinary item. FASB ASC 225-20 illustrates events and transactions which should and should not be classified as extraordinary items.

3.141 Table 3-18 shows the nature of items classified as extraordinary by the survey entities. An example of the presentation and disclosure of an extraordinary item follows.

3.142

TABLE 3-18: EXTRAORDINARY ITEMS

	2009	2008	2007	2006
Nature				
Recharacterization of debt	—	1	—	—
Negative goodwill	—	—	1	3
Expropriation	—	—	1	—
Other	3	1	2	1
Total Extraordinary Items	3	2	4	4
Number of Entities				
Presenting extraordinary items	3	2	4	4
Not presenting extraordinary items	497	498	596	596
Total Entities	500	500	600	600

2008–2009 based on 500 entities surveyed; 2006–2007 based on 600 entities surveyed.

Discontinuance of Regulatory Accounting

3.143

CENTURYTEL, INC. (DEC)

(Dollars in thousands)	2009	2008	2007
Income before income tax expense	$814,512	$561,387	$620,201
Income tax expense	301,881	194,357	200,572
Income before noncontrolling interests and extraordinary item	512,631	367,030	419,629
Noncontrolling interests	(1,377)	(1,298)	(1,259)
Net income before extraordinary item	511,254	365,732	418,370
Extraordinary item, net of income tax expense and noncontrolling interests (see Note 15)	135,957	—	—
Net income attributable to Centurytel, Inc.	$647,211	$365,732	$418,370

NOTES TO CONSOLIDATED FINANCIAL STATEMENTS

1 (In Part): Summary of Significant Accounting Policies

Regulatory Accounting

Through June 30, 2009, CenturyTel accounted for its regulated telephone operations (except for the properties acquired from Verizon in 2002) in accordance with the provisions of regulatory accounting under which actions by regulators can provide reasonable assurance of the recognition of an asset, reduce or eliminate the value of an asset and impose a liability on a regulated enterprise. Such regulatory assets and liabilities were required to be recorded and, accordingly, reflected in the balance sheet of an entity subject to regulatory accounting. On July 1, 2009, we discontinued the accounting requirements of regulatory accounting upon the conversion of substantially all of our rate-of-return study areas to federal price cap regulation (based on the FCC's approval of our petition to convert our study areas to price cap regulation). In the third quarter of 2009, upon the discontinuance of regulatory accounting, we recorded a non-cash extraordinary gain in our consolidated statements of income of $136.0 million after-tax. See Note 15 for additional information.

Subsequent to the July 1, 2009 discontinuance of regulatory accounting, all intercompany transactions with affiliates have been eliminated from the consolidated financial statements. Prior to July 1, 2009, intercompany transactions with regulated affiliates subject to regulatory accounting were not eliminated in connection with preparing the consolidated financial statements, as allowed by the provisions of regulatory accounting. The amount of intercompany revenues and costs that were not eliminated related to the first half of 2009 approximated $114 million.

15 (In Part): Discontinuance of Regulatory Accounting

Through June 30, 2009, CenturyTel accounted for its regulated telephone operations (except for its properties acquired from Verizon in 2002) in accordance with the provisions of regulatory accounting under which actions by regulators can provide reasonable assurance of the recognition of an asset, reduce or eliminate the value of an asset and impose a liability on a regulated enterprise. Such regulatory assets and liabilities were required to be recorded and, accordingly, reflected in the balance sheet of an entity subject to regulatory accounting.

As we previously disclosed, on July 1, 2009, we discontinued the accounting requirements of regulatory accounting upon the conversion of substantially all of our rate-of-return study areas to federal price cap regulation (based on the FCC's approval of our petition to convert our study areas to price cap regulation).

Upon the discontinuance of regulatory accounting, we were required to reverse previously established regulatory assets and liabilities. Depreciation rates of certain assets established by regulatory authorities for our telephone operations subject to regulatory accounting have historically included a component for removal costs in excess of the related salvage value. Notwithstanding the adoption of accounting guidance related to the accounting for asset retirement obligations, regulatory accounting required us to continue to reflect this accumulated liability for removal costs in excess of salvage value even though there was no legal obligation to remove the assets. Therefore, we did not adopt the asset retirement obligation provisions for our telephone operations that were subject to regulatory accounting. Upon the discontinuance of regulatory accounting, we eliminated such accumulated liability for removal costs included in accumulated depreciation and established an asset retirement obligation in a much smaller amount. Upon the discontinuance of regulatory accounting, we were required to adjust the carrying amounts of property, plant and equipment only to the extent the assets are impaired, as judged in the same manner applicable to nonregulated enterprises. We did not record an impairment charge related to the carrying value of the property, plant and equipment of our regulated telephone operations as a result of the discontinuance of regulatory accounting.

In the third quarter of 2009, upon the discontinuance of regulatory accounting, we recorded a non-cash extraordinary gain in our consolidated statements of income comprised of the following components (dollars, except per share amounts, in thousands):

	Gain (Loss)
Elimination of removal costs embedded in accumulated depreciation	$222,703
Establishment of asset retirement obligation	(1,556)
Elimination of other regulatory assets and liabilities	(2,585)
Net extraordinary gain before income tax expense and noncontrolling interests	218,562
Income tax expense associated with extraordinary gain	(81,060)
Net extraordinary gain before noncontrolling interests	137,502
Less: extraordinary gain attributable to noncontrolling interests	(1,545)
Extraordinary gain attributable to CenturyTel, Inc.	$135,957
Basic earnings per share of extraordinary gain	$ .68
Diluted earnings per share of extraordinary gain	.68

Historically, the depreciation rates we utilized for our telephone operations were based on rates established by regulatory authorities. Upon the discontinuance of regulatory accounting, we revised prospectively the lives of our property, plant and equipment to reflect the economic estimated remaining useful lives of the assets in accordance with generally accepted accounting principles. In general, the estimated remaining useful lives of our telephone property were lengthened as compared to the rates used that were established by regulatory authorities. Such lengthening of remaining useful lives reflects our expectations of future network utilization and capital expenditure levels required to provide service to our customers. Such revisions in remaining useful lives of our assets reduced depreciation expense by approximately $35 million in the last half of 2009 compared to what it would have been absent the change in remaining useful lives.

Upon the discontinuance of regulatory accounting, we also are eliminating certain intercompany transactions with regulated affiliates that previously were not eliminated under the application of regulatory accounting. This has caused our operating revenues and operating expenses to be lower by equivalent amounts (approximately $108 million) in the last half of 2009 as compared to the first half of 2009. For regulatory purposes, the accounting and reporting of our telephone subsidiaries will not be affected by the discontinued application of regulatory accounting.

EARNINGS PER SHARE

3.144 The reporting and disclosure requirements for earnings per share are stated in FASB ASC 260, *Earnings Per Share*. Examples of earnings per share presentations follow.

3.145

OWENS-ILLINOIS, INC. (DEC)

(Dollars in millions, except per share amounts)	2009	2008	2007
Earnings from continuing operations before income taxes	$ 325.3	$ 558.4	$ 506.6
Provision for income taxes	(127.5)	(236.7)	(147.8)
Earnings from continuing operations	197.8	321.7	358.8
Net earnings of discontinued operations			3.0
Gain on sale of discontinued operations		6.8	1,038.5
Net earnings	197.8	328.5	1,400.3
Net earnings attributable to noncontrolling interests	(36.0)	(70.2)	(59.7)
Net earnings attributable to the Company	$ 161.8	$ 258.3	$1,340.6
Convertible preferred stock dividends		(5.4)	(21.5)
Earnings available to common share owners	$ 161.8	$ 252.9	$1,319.1
Amounts attributable to the Company:			
Earnings from continuing operations	$ 161.8	$ 251.5	$ 299.3
Net earnings of discontinued operations			2.8
Gain on sale of discontinued operations		6.8	1,038.5
Net earnings	$ 161.8	$ 258.3	$1,340.6
Basic earnings per share:			
Earnings from continuing operations	$ 0.96	$ 1.49	$ 1.78
Net earnings of discontinued operations			0.02
Gain on sale of discontinued operations		0.04	6.66
Net earnings	$ 0.96	$ 1.53	$ 8.46
Diluted earnings per share:			
Earnings from continuing operations	$ 0.95	$ 1.48	$ 1.78
Net earnings of discontinued operations			0.02
Gain on sale of discontinued operations		0.04	6.19
Net earnings	$ 0.95	$ 1.52	$ 7.99

NOTES TO CONSOLIDATED FINANCIAL STATEMENTS
(Tabular data dollars in millions, except share and per share amount)

1 (In Part): Significant Accounting Policies

Newly Adopted Financial Statement Pronouncements (In Part)
Effective January 1, 2009, the Company adopted the provisions of a new accounting standard which required the Company to allocate earnings to unvested restricted shares outstanding during the period. Earnings per share for the years ended December 31, 2008 and 2007 were restated in accordance with the new provisions which are required to be applied retrospectively.

2. Earnings Per Share

The following table sets forth the computation of basic and diluted earnings per share:

	2009	2008	2007
Numerator:			
Net earnings attributable to the Company	$ 161.8	$ 258.3	$ 1,340.6
Convertible preferred stock dividends		(5.4)	(21.5)
Net earnings attributable to participating securities	(0.6)	(2.6)	(13.9)
Numerator for basic earnings per share—income available to common share owners	$ 161.2	$ 250.3	$ 1,305.2
Denominator:			
Denominator for basic earnings per share—weighted average shares outstanding	167,687,408	163,177,874	154,215,269
Effect of dilutive securities:			
Convertible preferred stock		2,147,339	8,589,355
Stock options and other	2,852,282	4,352,076	4,962,683
Denominator for diluted earnings per share—adjusted weighted average shares and assumed exchanges of preferred stock for common stock	170,539,690	169,677,289	167,767,307
Basic earnings per share:			
Earnings from continuing operations	$ 0.96	$ 1.49	$ 1.78
Net earnings of discontinued operations			0.02
Gain on sale of discontinued operations		0.04	6.66
Net earnings	$ 0.96	$ 1.53	$ 8.46
Diluted earnings per share:			
Earnings from continuing operations	$ 0.95	$ 1.48	$ 1.78
Net earnings of discontinued operations			0.02
Gain on sale of discontinued operations		0.04	6.19
Net earnings	$ 0.95	$ 1.52	$ 7.99

The convertible preferred stock was included in the computation of diluted earnings per share for 2008, to the extent outstanding during 2008, and 2007 on an "if converted" basis since the result was dilutive. For purposes of this computation, the preferred stock dividends were not subtracted from the numerator. Options to purchase 994,834, 241,711, and 862,906 weighted average shares of common stock which were outstanding during 2009, 2008, and 2007, respectively, were not included in the computation of diluted earnings per share because the options' exercise prices were greater than the average market price of the common shares.

Effective January 1, 2009, the Company adopted the provisions of a new accounting standard, which addresses whether instruments granted in share-based payment awards are participating securities prior to vesting and,

therefore, must be included in the earnings allocation in calculating earnings per share under the two-class method. The new provisions require that unvested share-based payment awards that contain non-forfeitable rights to dividends be treated as participating securities in calculating earnings per share. The Company was required to allocate earnings to unvested restricted shares outstanding during the period. Basic earnings per share for the years ended December 31, 2008 and 2007 were reduced by $0.02 and $0.09 per share, respectively, in accordance with the new provisions which require retrospective application. There was no impact on basic earnings per share for the year ended December 31, 2009 or diluted earnings per share in any period.

3.146

TEXTRON INC. (DEC)

(In millions, except per share data)	2009	2008	2007
Income (loss) from continuing operations before income taxes	$ (149)	$ 629	$1,234
Income tax expense (benefit)	(76)	305	368
Income (loss) from continuing operations	(73)	324	866
Income from discontinued operations, net of income taxes	42	162	51
Net income (loss)	$ (31)	$ 486	$ 917
Basic earnings per share			
Continuing operations	$(0.28)	$1.32	$ 3.47
Discontinued operations	0.16	0.65	0.20
Basic earnings per share	$(0.12)	$1.97	$ 3.67
Diluted earnings per share			
Continuing operations	$(0.28)	$1.29	$ 3.40
Discontinued operations	0.16	0.65	0.20
Diluted earnings per share	$(0.12)	$1.94	$ 3.60

NOTES TO CONSOLIDATED FINANCIAL STATEMENTS

Note 11 (In Part): Shareholders' Equity

Income Per Common Share

In the first quarter of 2009, we adopted the new accounting standard for determining whether instruments granted in share-based payment transactions are participating securities. This new standard requires us to include any unvested share-based payment awards that contain nonforfeitable rights to dividends or dividend equivalents (whether paid or unpaid) as participating securities in our basic earnings per share calculation. We have granted certain restricted stock units that are deemed participating securities under this new standard, and, as a result, prior period basic and diluted weighted-average shares outstanding have been recast to conform to the new calculation. The adoption of this standard reduced our basic and diluted earnings per share by $0.01 in 2008, and there was no impact in 2007.

We calculate basic and diluted earnings per share based on net income, which approximates income available to common shareholders for each period. Basic earnings per share is calculated using the two-class method, which includes the weighted-average number of common shares outstanding during the period and restricted stock units to be paid in stock that are deemed participating securities. Diluted earnings per share considers the dilutive effect of all potential future common stock, including convertible preferred shares, Convertible Notes, stock options and warrants and restricted stock units in the weighted-average number of common shares outstanding. The weighted-average shares outstanding for basic and diluted earnings per share are as follows:

(In thousands)	2009	2008	2007
Basic weighted-average shares outstanding	262,923	246,208	249,792
Dilutive effect of convertible preferred shares, stock options and restricted stock units	—	4,130	5,034
Diluted weighted-average shares outstanding	262,923	250,338	254,826

In 2009, the potential dilutive effect of 8 million weighted-average shares of restricted stock units, stock options and warrants, convertible preferred stock and Convertible Notes was excluded from the computation of diluted weighted-average shares outstanding as the shares would have an antidilutive effect on the loss from continuing operations. In addition, stock options to purchase 7 million shares of common stock outstanding are excluded from our calculation of diluted weighted-average shares outstanding in 2009 as the exercise prices were greater than the average market price of our common stock for those periods. These securities could potentially dilute earnings per share in the future.

3.147

THERMO FISHER SCIENTIFIC INC. (DEC)

(In millions except per share amounts)	2009	2008	2007
Income from continuing operations before provision for income taxes	$927.1	$1,128.0	$860.6
Provision for income taxes	(75.8)	(152.6)	(93.7)
Income from continuing operations	851.3	975.4	766.9
(Loss) gain on disposal of discontinued operations, net (net of income tax benefit of $0.6 in 2009 and income tax provision of $3.5 in 2008 and $4.2 in 2007)	(1.0)	5.5	(18.5)
Net income	$850.3	$ 980.9	$748.4
Earnings per share from continuing operations			
Basic	$ 2.06	$ 2.33	$ 1.82
Diluted	$ 2.01	$ 2.24	$ 1.73
Earnings per share			
Basic	$ 2.06	$ 2.34	$ 1.77
Diluted	$ 2.01	$ 2.25	$ 1.69
Weighted average shares			
Basic	412.4	418.2	421.5
Diluted	422.8	434.7	443.6

NOTES TO CONSOLIDATED FINANCIAL STATEMENTS

Note 1 (In Part): Summary of Significant Accounting Policies

Earnings Per Share

Basic earnings per share has been computed by dividing net income by the weighted average number of shares outstanding during the year. Except where the result would be antidilutive to income from continuing operations, diluted earnings per share has been computed using the treasury stock method for the convertible obligations, warrants and the exercise of stock options, as well as their related income tax effects.

Note 8. Earnings Per Share

(In millions except per share amounts)	2009	2008	2007
Income from continuing operations	$851.3	$975.4	$766.9
(Loss) gain on disposal of discontinued operations, net	(1.0)	5.5	(18.5)
Net income	850.3	980.9	748.4
Income allocable to participating securities	(0.6)	(1.5)	(0.5)
Net income for earnings per share	$849.7	$979.4	$747.9
Basic weighted average shares	412.4	418.2	421.5
Effect of:			
Convertible debentures	8.5	13.3	13.8
Stock options, restricted stock/units and warrants	1.9	3.2	8.3
Diluted weighted average shares	422.8	434.7	443.6
Basic earnings per share:			
Continuing operations	$ 2.06	$ 2.33	$ 1.82
Discontinued operations	—	.01	(.04)
	$ 2.06	$ 2.34	$ 1.77
Diluted earnings per share:			
Continuing operations	$ 2.01	$ 2.24	$ 1.73
Discontinued operations	—	.01	(.04)
	$ 2.01	$ 2.25	$ 1.69

Options to purchase 10.9 million, 3.6 million and 3.7 million shares of common stock were not included in the computation of diluted earnings per share for 2009, 2008 and 2007, respectively, because their effect would have been antidilutive.

Since the company must settle the par value of its convertible notes in cash, the company is not required to include any shares underlying the convertible notes in its diluted weighted average shares outstanding until the average stock price per share for the period exceeds the $23.73, $29.55, and $40.20 conversion price for the 2.50% Senior Convertible Notes due 2023, the Floating Rate Senior Convertible Debentures due 2033 and the 3.25% Senior Convertible Subordinated Notes due 2024, respectively, and only to the extent of the additional shares the company may be required to issue in the event the company's conversion obligation exceeds the principal amount of the notes or debentures converted (Note 9). At such time, only the number of shares that would be issuable (under the treasury stock method of accounting for share dilution) are included, which is based upon the amount by which the average stock price exceeds the conversion price.

The table below discloses the effect of changes in the company's stock price on the amount of shares to be included in the earnings per share calculation. The securities are convertible only if the common stock price equals or exceeds the trigger price. The table assumes normal conversion for the 2.50% Senior Convertible Notes due 2023, the Floating Rate Senior Convertible Debentures due 2033 and the 3.25% Senior Convertible Subordinated Notes due 2024 in which the principal amount is paid in cash, and the excess up to the conversion value is paid in shares of the company's stock as follows:

	2.50% Senior Convertible Notes	Floating Rate Senior Convertible Debentures	3.25% Senior Convertible Notes	Potential Share Increase
Principal outstanding (in millions)	$13.0	$326.5	$329.3	
Conversion price per share	23.73	29.55	40.20	
Trigger price	28.48	38.41	48.24	

(In millions)	Total Potential Shares			
Future common stock price				
$23.73	—	—	—	—
$24.73	—	—	—	—
$29.55	0.1	—	—	0.1
$30.55	0.1	0.4	—	0.5
$40.20	0.2	2.9	—	3.1
$41.20	0.2	3.1	0.2	3.5
$45.00	0.3	3.8	0.9	5.0
$50.00	0.3	4.5	1.6	6.4
$55.00	0.3	5.1	2.2	7.6
$60.00	0.3	5.6	2.7	8.6
$65.00	0.3	6.0	3.1	9.4
$70.00	0.4	6.4	3.5	10.3

Section 4: Comprehensive Income

PRESENTATION IN ANNUAL REPORT

4.01 FASB *Accounting Standards Codification* (ASC) 220, *Comprehensive Income*, requires that a full set of general-purpose financial statements report comprehensive income and its components. Comprehensive income includes net income, foreign currency items, defined benefit postretirement plan adjustments, changes in the fair value of certain derivatives, and unrealized gains and losses on certain investments in debt and equity securities. If an entity has only net income, it is not required to report comprehensive income. FASB ASC 220 encourages reporting comprehensive income in either a combined statement of income and comprehensive income or in a separate statement of comprehensive income.

4.02 FASB ASC 220 also states that an entity shall disclose the amount of income tax expense or benefit allocated to each component of other comprehensive income (including reclassification adjustments), either on the face of the statement in which those components are displayed or in the notes thereto.

4.03 Table 4-1 shows the statement in which comprehensive income and the related tax effect was presented.

4.04

TABLE 4-1: COMPREHENSIVE INCOME—REPORTING STATEMENT

	2009	2008	2007	2006
Reporting format:				
Included in statement of changes in stockholders' equity......................	405	415	488	485
Separate statement of comprehensive income................	76	62	76	75
Combined statement of income and comprehensive income................	11	15	20	21
	492	492	584	581
No comprehensive income reported....	8	8	16	19
Total Entities.......................................	**500**	**500**	**600**	**600**
Tax effect disclosure in any statement:				
Amount of tax effect allocated to each component............................	109	120	133	149
Amount of tax effect allocated to some, but not all, components......	136	133	167	130
Total amount of tax effect................	9	11	17	19
	254	264	317	298
Tax effect disclosure in notes:				
Amount of tax effect allocated to each component............................	76	77	74	75
Amount of tax effect allocated to some, but not all, components.........	41	25	39	66
Total amount of tax effect...................	7	11	9	10
	124	113	122	151
Tax effect not disclosed in any statement...	114	115	145	132
	492	492	584	581
No comprehensive income reported....	8	8	16	19
Total Entities.................................	**500**	**500**	**600**	**600**

2008–2009 based on 500 entities surveyed; 2006–2007 based on 600 entities surveyed.

4.05 Table 4-2 summarizes the titles used to describe comprehensive income.

4.06 Examples of comprehensive income reported in a statement of changes in stockholders' equity, in a separate statement of comprehensive income, and in a combined statement of income and comprehensive income follow.

4.07

TABLE 4-2: COMPREHENSIVE INCOME—REPORTING STATEMENT TITLE

	2009	2008	2007	2006
Comprehensive income reported in a statement of income and comprehensive income, or in a statement of comprehensive income				
Comprehensive income....................	50	51	73	69
Comprehensive income (loss)..........	35	21	16	15
Comprehensive loss.........................	2	1	3	2
Comprehensive earnings.................	2	3	1	2
Other title...	3	1	3	8
	92	**77**	**96**	**96**
Comprehensive income reported in a statement of changes in stockholders' equity				
Statement title does not refer to comprehensive income.................	307	319	388	393
Statement title does refer to comprehensive income................	93	96	100	92
	492	**492**	**488**	**485**
No comprehensive income reported....	8	8	16	19
Total Entities..	**500**	**500**	**600**	**600**

2008–2009 based on 500 entities surveyed; 2006–2007 based on 600 entities surveyed.

Included in Statement of Changes in Stockholders' Equity

4.08

ACUITY BRANDS, INC. (AUG)

Consolidated Statements of Stockholders' Equity and Comprehensive Income

(In thousands)	Comprehensive Income	Common Stock	Paid-In Capital	Retained Earnings	Pension Liability	Currency Translation Adjustment	Treasury Stock	Total
					Accumulated Other Comprehensive Income (Loss) Items			
Balance, August 31, 2006		$481	$560,973	$192,155	$(21,848)	$ 5,356	$(194,858)	$ 542,259
Comprehensive income:								
Net income	$148,054	—	—	148,054	—	—	—	148,054
Other comprehensive income (loss):								
Foreign currency translation adjustment (net of tax expense of $0)	4,550	—	—	—	—	4,550	—	4,550
Minimum pension liability adjustment (net of tax of $6,415)	11,404	—	—	—	11,404	—	—	11,404
Other comprehensive income	15,954							
Comprehensive income	$164,008							
Impact of adopting SFAS 158 (net of tax of $5,015)					(8,975)			(8,975)
Amortization, issuance, and forfeitures of restricted stock grants		(1)	8,884	—	—	—	—	8,884
Employee stock purchase plan issuances		—	741	—	—	—	—	741
Cash dividends of $0.60 per share paid on common stock		—	—	(26,359)	—	—	—	(26,359)
Stock options exercised		13	25,743	—	—	—	—	25,756
Repurchases of common stock		—	—	—	—	—	(49,707)	(49,707)
Tax effect on stock options and restricted stock		—	15,360	—	—	—	—	15,360
Balance, August 31, 2007		$493	$611,701	$313,850	$(19,419)	$ 9,906	$(244,565)	$ 671,966
Comprehensive income:								
Net income	$148,255	—	—	148,255	—	—	—	148,255
Other comprehensive income (loss):								
Foreign currency translation adjustment (net of tax expense of $0)	5,012	—	—	—	—	5,012	—	5,012
Minimum pension liability adjustment (net of tax of $2,457)	(6,508)	—	—	—	(6,508)	—	—	(6,508)
Other comprehensive loss	(1,496)							
Comprehensive income	$146,759							
Impact of spin-off of specialty products		—	—	(71,553)	—	(11,810)	—	(83,363)
Impact of adopting FIN 48		—	—	(1,182)	—	—	—	(1,182)
Amortization, issuance, and forfeitures of restricted stock grants		2	5,166	—	—	—	—	5,168
Employee stock purchase plan issuances		—	509	—	—	—	—	509
Cash dividends of $0.54 per share paid on common stock		—	—	(22,466)	—	—	—	(22,466)
Stock options exercised		2	4,037	—	—	—	—	4,039
Repurchases of common stock		—	—	—	—	—	(150,906)	(150,906)
Tax effect on stock options and restricted stock		—	5,022	—	—	—	—	5,022
Balance, August 31, 2008		$497	$626,435	$366,904	$(25,927)	$ 3,108	$(395,471)	$ 575,546

(continued)

| (In thousands) | Comprehensive Income | Common Stock | Paid-In Capital | Retained Earnings | Accumulated Other Comprehensive Income (Loss) Items | | Treasury Stock | Total |
					Pension Liability	Currency Translation Adjustment		
Balance, August 31, 2008		$497	$626,435	$366,904	$(25,927)	$ 3,108	$(395,471)	$ 575,546
Comprehensive income:								
Net income	$ 84,909	—	—	84,909	—	—	—	84,909
Other comprehensive income (loss):								
Foreign currency translation adjustment (net of tax expense of $0)	(18,474)	—	—	—	—	(18,474)	—	(18,474)
Pension liability adjustment (net of tax of $9,169)	(16,130)	—	—	—	(16,130)	—	—	(16,130)
Other comprehensive loss	(34,604)							
Comprehensive income	$ 50,305							
SFAS 158 adjustment (net of tax of $289)		—	—	(454)	—	—	—	(454)
Common Stock reissued from treasury shares for acquisition of businesses		—	7,175	(25,556)	—	—	73,155	54,774
Amortization, issuance, and forfeitures of restricted stock grants		1	10,182	—	—	—	—	10,183
Employee Stock Purchase Plan issuances		—	265	—	—	—	—	265
Cash dividends of $0.52 per share paid on common stock		—	—	(21,634)	—	—	—	(21,634)
Stock options exercised		1	2,773	—	—	—	—	2,774
Repurchases of common stock		—	—	—	—	—	—	—
Tax effect on stock options and restricted stock		—	381	—	—	—	—	381
Balance, August 31, 2009		$499	$647,211	$404,169	$(42,057)	$(15,366)	$(322,316)	$ 672,140

4.09

THERMO FISHER SCIENTIFIC INC. (DEC)

Consolidated Statement of Comprehensive Income and Shareholders' Equity

(In millions except share amounts)	2009	2008	2007
Comprehensive income			
Net income	$ 850.3	$ 980.9	$ 748.4
Other comprehensive items:			
Currency translation adjustment	198.8	(431.6)	200.9
Unrealized gains (losses) on available-for-sale investments, net of tax	2.2	(1.3)	1.5
Unrealized gains on hedging instruments, net of tax	0.2	0.2	0.3
Pension and other postretirement benefit liability adjustments, net of tax	36.6	(101.5)	35.5
	237.8	(534.2)	238.2
	$ 1,088.1	$ 446.7	$ 986.6
Shareholders' equity			
Common stock, $1 par value:			
Balance at beginning of year (421,791,009; 439,340,851 and 424,240,292 shares)	$ 421.8	$ 439.3	$ 424.2
Issuance of shares for conversion of debt (74,089 and 9,536 shares)	—	0.1	—
Retirement of treasury shares (25,000,000 shares)	—	(25.0)	—
Issuance of shares upon exercise of warrants (3,307,170 shares)	—	3.3	—
Issuance of shares under employees' and directors' stock plans (2,084,251; 4,068,899 and 15,091,023 shares)	2.1	4.1	15.1
Balance at end of year (423,875,260; 421,791,009 and 439,340,851 shares)	$ 423.9	$ 421.8	$ 439.3
Capital in excess of par value:			
Balance at beginning of year	$11,301.3	$12,273.6	$11,779.9
Settlement of convertible debt	(312.8)	(0.2)	0.4
Retirement of treasury shares	—	(1,193.2)	—
Issuance of shares upon exercise of warrants	—	12.7	—
Activity under employees' and directors' stock plans	63.4	88.2	316.6
Stock-based compensation	68.1	57.1	56.9
Tax benefit related to employees' and directors' stock plans	(1.6)	25.1	99.1
Reclassification from temporary equity	22.3	38.0	20.7
Balance at end of year	$11,140.7	$11,301.3	$12,273.6
Retained earnings			
Balance at beginning of year	$ 3,500.5	$ 2,519.6	$ 1,771.2
Net income	850.3	980.9	748.4
Balance at end of year	$ 4,350.8	$ 3,500.5	$ 2,519.6
Treasury stock:			
Balance at beginning of year (3,825,245; 24,102,880 and 7,635,184 shares)	$ (151.3)	$ (1,157.3)	$ (246.4)
Purchases of company common stock (10,463,757; 4,273,950 and 16,370,945 shares)	(414.6)	(187.4)	(898.0)
Retirement of treasury shares (25,000,000 shares)	—	1,218.2	—
Shares received for exercise of warrants (280,540 shares)	—	(16.0)	—
Activity under employees' and directors' stock plans (275,635; 167,875 and 96,751 shares)	(10.6)	(8.8)	(12.9)
Balance at end of year (14,564,637; 3,825,245 and 24,102,880 shares)	$ (576.5)	$ (151.3)	$ (1,157.3)
Accumulated other comprehensive items:			
Balance at beginning of year	$ (145.8)	$ 388.4	$ 150.2
Other comprehensive items	237.8	(534.2)	238.2
Balance at end of year	92.0	(145.8)	388.4
	$15,430.9	$14,926.5	$14,463.6

Separate Statement of Comprehensive Income

4.10

THE BRINK'S COMPANY (DEC)

Consolidated Statements of Comprehensive Income (Loss)

(In millions)	2009	2008	2007
Net income	$231.9	$ 223.1	$160.1
Other comprehensive income (loss):			
Benefit plan experience:			
Net experience gains (losses) arising during the year	68.2	(501.2)	112.6
Tax benefit (provision) related to net experience gains and losses arising during the year	(0.3)	32.7	(40.8)
Reclassification adjustment for amortization of prior net experience loss included in net income	28.2	11.8	27.1
Tax benefit related to reclassification adjustment	(9.5)	(0.7)	(8.9)
Benefit plan experience gain (loss), net of tax	86.6	(457.4)	90.0
Benefit plan prior service credit (cost):			
Prior service credit from plan amendment during the year	—	3.1	0.1
Tax provision related to prior service credit from plan amendment during the year	—	(0.5)	—
Reclassification adjustment for amortization of prior service cost (credit) included in net income	1.2	(0.3)	1.3
Tax provision (benefit) related to reclassification adjustment	(0.1)	0.6	—
Benefit plan prior service credit, net of tax	1.1	2.9	1.4
Foreign currency:			
Translation adjustments arising during the year	(92.4)	(47.0)	41.6
Tax benefit (provision) related to translation adjustments	(0.7)	0.8	(0.1)
Reclassification adjustment for dispositions of businesses	—	—	(0.1)
Foreign currency translation adjustments, net of tax	(93.1)	(46.2)	41.4
Marketable securities:			
Unrealized net gains (losses) on marketable securities arising during the year	2.1	(7.2)	1.1
Tax benefit (provision) related to unrealized net gains and losses on marketable securities	—	2.6	(0.4)
Reclassification adjustment for net (gains) losses realized in net income	—	6.2	(1.4)
Tax provision (benefit) related to reclassification adjustment	—	(2.2)	0.5
Unrealized net gains (losses) on marketable securities, net of tax	2.1	(0.6)	(0.2)
Other comprehensive income (loss)	(3.3)	(501.3)	132.6
Comprehensive income (loss)	$228.6	$(278.2)	$292.7
Amounts attributable to Brink's:			
Net income	$200.2	$ 183.3	$137.3
Benefit plan experience	86.6	(457.4)	90.0
Benefit plan prior service credit	1.1	2.9	1.4
Foreign currency	(40.3)	(43.9)	39.7
Marketable securities	2.6	(0.6)	(0.2)
Other comprehensive income (loss)	50.0	(499.0)	130.9
Comprehensive income (loss) attributable to Brink's	250.2	(315.7)	268.2
Amounts attributable to noncontrolling interests:			
Net income	31.7	39.8	22.8
Foreign currency	(52.8)	(2.3)	1.7
Marketable securities	(0.5)	—	—
Other comprehensive income (loss)	(53.3)	(2.3)	1.7
Comprehensive income (loss) attributable to noncontrolling interests	(21.6)	37.5	24.5
Comprehensive income (loss)	$228.6	$(278.2)	$292.7

4.11

EMC CORPORATION (DEC)

Consolidated Statements of Comprehensive Income

(In thousands)	2009	2008	2007
Net income	$1,121,801	$1,319,829	$1,614,420
Other comprehensive income (loss), net of taxes (benefit):			
Recognition of actuarial net gain (loss) from pension and other postretirement plans, net of taxes (benefit) of $13,092, $(55,680) and $10,501	21,877	(94,563)	17,960
Foreign currency translation adjustments	14,950	(38,080)	7,109
Changes in market value of investments, including unrealized gains (loss) and reclassification adjustments to net income, net of taxes (benefit) of $23,381, $(25,025) and $4,934	35,055	(37,715)	20,938
Changes in market value of derivatives, net of taxes (benefit) of $707, $(127) and $13	3,187	(1,145)	107
Other comprehensive income (loss)	75,069	(171,503)	46,114
Comprehensive income	1,196,870	1,148,326	1,660,534
Less: net income attributable to the non-controlling interest in VMware, Inc.	(33,724)	(44,725)	(15,455)
Less: other comprehensive income attributable to the non-controlling interest in VMware, Inc.	(839)	—	—
Comprehensive income attributable to EMC Corporation	$1,162,307	$1,103,601	$1,645,079

Combined Statement of Net Income and Comprehensive Income

4.12

CONVERGYS CORPORATION (DEC)

Consolidated Statements of Operations and Comprehensive Income (Loss)

(Amounts in millions)	2009	2008	2007
Revenues	$2,827.2	$2,785.8	$2,844.3
Operating costs and expenses:			
Cost of providing services and products sold	1,925.8	1,892.9	1,837.9
Selling, general and administrative expenses	648.8	593.8	554.9
Research and development costs	74.2	54.9	73.4
Depreciation	118.9	119.0	115.4
Amortization	11.7	13.5	9.0
Restructuring charges	47.0	34.4	3.4
Asset impairment	113.6	268.6	5.5
Total costs and expenses	2,940.0	2,977.1	2,599.5
Operating (loss) income	(112.8)	(191.3)	244.8
Equity in earnings of Cellular Partnerships	41.0	35.7	14.3
Other income (expense), net	(16.9)	14.3	4.0
Interest expense	(28.9)	(22.6)	(17.5)
(Loss) income before income taxes	(117.6)	(163.9)	245.6
Income tax (benefit) expense	(40.3)	(71.0)	76.1
Net (loss) income	$ (77.3)	$ (92.9)	$ 169.5
Other comprehensive (loss) income, net of tax:			
Foreign currency translation adjustments	$ 25.4	$ (59.4)	$ 12.9
Change related to pension liability (net of tax benefit (expense) of ($2.4), $12.2 and ($0.9))	2.2	(20.3)	1.6
Unrealized gain (loss) on hedging activities (net of tax benefit (expense) of ($27.9), $57.5 and ($17.3))	51.8	(107.0)	32.1
Total comprehensive income (loss)	$ 2.1	$ (279.6)	$ 216.1

TAX EFFECT DISCLOSURE

4.13

AIR PRODUCTS AND CHEMICALS, INC. (SEP)

Consolidated Statements of Shareholders' Equity

(Millions of dollars, except for share data)	2009	2008	2007
Number of common shares outstanding			
Balance, beginning of year	209,334,627	215,355,685	217,250,572
Purchase of treasury shares	—	(8,676,029)	(7,328,482)
Issuance of treasury shares for stock option and award plans	1,925,637	2,654,971	5,433,595
Balance, end of year	211,260,264	209,334,627	215,355,685
Common stock			
Balance, beginning and end of year	$ 249.4	$ 249.4	$ 249.4
Capital in excess of par value			
Balance, beginning of year	$ 811.7	$ 759.5	$ 682.5
Share-based compensation expense	59.3	62.5	66.6
Issuance of treasury shares for stock option and award plans	(71.9)	(74.2)	(70.3)
Tax benefit of stock option and award plans	23.8	63.9	80.7
Balance, end of year	$ 822.9	$ 811.7	$ 759.5
Retained earnings			
Balance, beginning of year	$ 6,990.2	$ 6,458.5	$ 5,743.5
Defined benefit plans measurement date change	(8.1)	—	—
Initial recording of accounting for uncertain tax positions	—	(13.3)	—
Adjusted balance, beginning of year	$ 6,982.1	$ 6,445.2	$ 5,743.5
Net income	631.3	909.7	1,035.6
Dividends on common stock (per share $1.79, $1.70, and $1.48)	(376.3)	(359.6)	(319.8)
Other	(2.5)	(5.1)	(.8)
Balance, end of year	$ 7,234.6	$ 6,990.2	$ 6,458.5
Accumulated other comprehensive income (loss)			
Balance, beginning of year	$ (549.3)	$ (142.9)	$ (221.7)
Defined benefit plans measurement date change, net of tax of $14.0	35.8	—	—
Adjusted balance, beginning of year	$ (513.5)	$ (142.9)	$ (221.7)
Translation adjustments, net of tax (benefit) of $(35.2), $7.9, and $(45.8)	(148.3)	(186.3)	272.8
Net (loss) on derivatives, net of tax (benefit) of $(1.8), $(30.2), and $(3.3)	(4.5)	(74.4)	(7.7)
Unrealized holding gain (loss) on available-for-sale securities, net of tax (benefit) of $1.4, $(2.4), and $4.2	2.4	(4.5)	8.1
Pension and postretirement benefits, net of tax (benefit) of $(287.4) and $(92.0)	(518.3)	(185.5)	—
Minimum pension liability adjustment, net of tax of $83.4	—	—	159.3
Reclassification adjustments:			
Currency translation adjustment	(3.2)	(53.7)	—
Derivatives, net of tax (benefit) of $(.8), $19.2, and $7.0	(.7)	50.7	15.9
Realized holding gains, net of tax of $20.1	—	—	(36.6)
Pension and postretirement benefits, net of tax of $9.8 and $24.5	24.3	47.3	—
Other comprehensive income (loss)	$ (648.3)	$ (406.4)	$ 411.8
Adjustment for initial recognition of funded status of benefit plans, net of tax (benefit) of $(169.6)	—	—	(333.0)
Balance, end of year	$ (1,161.8)	$ (549.3)	$ (142.9)
Treasury stock			
Balance, beginning of year	$ (2,471.3)	$ (1,828.9)	$ (1,529.7)
Purchase of treasury shares	—	(787.4)	(567.3)
Issuance of treasury shares for stock option and award plans	118.1	145.0	268.1
Balance, end of year	$ (2,353.2)	$ (2,471.3)	$ (1,828.9)
Total shareholders' equity	$ 4,791.9	$ 5,030.7	$ 5,495.6
Total comprehensive income (loss)			
Net income	$ 631.3	$ 909.7	$ 1,035.6
Other comprehensive income (loss)	(648.3)	(406.4)	411.8
Total comprehensive income (loss)	$ (17.0)	$ 503.3	$ 1,447.4

4.14

DEERE & COMPANY (OCT)

Statement of Changes in Consolidated Stockholders' Equity

(In millions of dollars)	Total Equity	Common Stock	Treasury Stock	Retained Earnings	Accumulated Other Comprehensive Income (Loss)
Balance October 31, 2006	$ 7,491.2	$2,203.5	$(2,673.4)	$ 7,886.8	$ 74.3
Comprehensive income					
Net income	1,821.7			1,821.7	
Other comprehensive income (loss)					
Minimum pension liability adjustment	65.8				65.8
Cumulative translation adjustment	329.1				329.1
Unrealized loss on derivatives	(14.4)				(14.4)
Unrealized loss on investments	(1.0)				(1.0)
Total comprehensive income	2,201.2				
Repurchases of common stock	(1,517.8)		(1,517.8)		
Treasury shares reissued	175.8		175.8		
Dividends declared	(408.4)			(408.4)	
Stock options and other	305.1	305.3		(.2)	
Adjustment to adopt FASB ASC 715 (FASB Statement No. 158), net of tax	(1,091.3)				(1,091.3)
Transfer for two-for-one stock split effective November 26, 2007		268.2		(268.2)	
Balance October 31, 2007	$ 7,155.8	$2,777.0	$(4,015.4)	$ 9,031.7	$ (637.5)
Comprehensive income					
Net income	2,052.8			2,052.8	
Other comprehensive income (loss)					
Retirement benefits adjustment	(305.3)				(305.3)
Cumulative translation adjustment	(406.0)				(406.0)
Unrealized loss on derivatives	(32.5)				(32.5)
Unrealized loss on investments	(6.0)				(6.0)
Total comprehensive income	1,303.0				
Adjustment to adopt FASB ASC 740 (FASB Interpretation No. 48)	(48.0)			(48.0)	
Repurchases of common stock	(1,677.6)		(1,677.6)		
Treasury shares reissued	98.4		98.4		
Dividends declared	(455.9)			(455.9)	
Stock options and other	157.0	157.0			
Balance October 31, 2008	$ 6,532.7	$2,934.0	$(5,594.6)	$10,580.6	$(1,387.3)
Comprehensive income					
Net income	873.5			873.5	
Other comprehensive income (loss)					
Retirement benefits adjustment	(2,536.6)				(2,536.6)
Cumulative translation adjustment	326.8				326.8
Unrealized loss on derivatives	(4.0)				(4.0)
Unrealized gain on investments	7.8				7.8
Total comprehensive income	(1,332.5)				
Repurchases of common stock	(3.2)		(3.2)		
Treasury shares reissued	33.1		33.1		
Dividends declared	(473.6)			(473.6)	
Stock options and other	62.2	62.2			
Balance October 31, 2009	$ 4,818.7	$2,996.2	$(5,564.7)	$10,980.5	$(3,593.3)

NOTES TO CONSOLIDATED FINANCIAL STATEMENTS

25. Other Comprehensive Income Items

Other comprehensive income items are transactions recorded in stockholders' equity during the year, excluding net income and transactions with stockholders. Following are the items included in other comprehensive income (loss) and the related tax effects in millions of dollars:

	Before Tax Amount	Tax (Expense) Credit	After Tax Amount
2007			
Minimum pension liability adjustment	$ 104	$ (38)	$ 66
Cumulative translation adjustment	325	4	329
Unrealized loss on derivatives:			
Hedging loss	(16)	6	(10)
Reclassification of realized gain to net income	(6)	2	(4)
Net unrealized loss	(22)	8	(14)
Unrealized loss on investments:			
Holding loss	(6)	2	(4)
Reclassification of realized loss to net income	4	(1)	3
Net unrealized loss	(2)	1	(1)
Total other comprehensive income (loss)	$ 405	$ (25)	$ 380
2008			
Retirement benefits adjustment:			
Net actuarial losses and prior service cost	$ (567)	$ 174	$ (393)
Reclassification of actuarial losses and prior service cost to net income	142	(54)	88
Net unrealized loss	(425)	120	(305)
Cumulative translation adjustment	(401)	(5)	(406)
Unrealized loss on derivatives:			
Hedging loss	(73)	24	(49)
Reclassification of realized loss to net income	24	(8)	16
Net unrealized loss	(49)	16	(33)
Unrealized loss on investments:			
Holding loss	(38)	13	(25)
Reclassification of realized loss to net income	29	(10)	19
Net unrealized loss	(9)	3	(6)
Total other comprehensive income (loss)	$ (884)	$ 134	$ (750)
2009			
Retirement benefits adjustment:			
Net actuarial losses and prior service cost	$(4,198)	$1,587	$(2,611)
Reclassification of actuarial losses and prior service cost to net income	105	(31)	74
Net unrealized loss	(4,093)	1,556	(2,537)
Cumulative translation adjustment	326	1	327
Unrealized loss on derivatives:			
Hedging loss	(90)	31	(59)
Reclassification of realized loss to net income	84	(29)	55
Net unrealized loss	(6)	2	(4)
Unrealized gain on investments:			
Holding loss	(793)	278	(515)
Reclassification of realized loss to net income	805	(282)	523
Net unrealized gain	12	(4)	8
Total other comprehensive income (loss)	$(3,761)	$1,555	$(2,206)

4.15

TEXAS INSTRUMENTS INCORPORATED (DEC)

Consolidated Statements of Comprehensive Income

(Millions of dollars)	2009	2008	2007
Income from continuing operations	$1,470	$1,920	$2,641
Other comprehensive income (loss):			
Available-for-sale investments:			
Unrealized gains (losses), net of tax benefit (expense) of ($9), $20 and ($3)	17	(38)	8
Reclassification of recognized transactions, net of tax benefit (expense) of ($3), $0 and $0	6	—	(1)
Net actuarial loss of defined benefit plans:			
Annual adjustment, net of tax benefit (expense) of ($38), $282 and ($19)	91	(476)	5
Reclassification of recognized transactions, net of tax benefit (expense) of ($27), ($17) and ($12)	62	32	28
Prior service cost of defined benefit plans:			
Annual adjustment, net of tax benefit (expense) of $1, $1 and $2	(1)	14	(2)
Reclassification of recognized transactions, net of tax benefit (expense) of $3, ($1) and $1	(6)	2	1
Total	169	(466)	39
Total comprehensive income from continuing operations	1,639	1,454	2,680
Income from discontinued operations, net of income taxes	—	—	16
Total comprehensive income	$1,639	$1,454	$2,696

COMPONENTS OF OTHER COMPREHENSIVE INCOME

4.16 FASB ASC 220, *Comprehensive Income*, requires that items included in other comprehensive income shall be classified based on their nature. For example, under existing pronouncements, other comprehensive income shall be classified separately into foreign currency items, defined benefit postretirement plan adjustments, changes in fair value of derivatives, and unrealized gains and losses on certain debt and equity securities.

4.17 FASB ASC 220 also requires that adjustments shall be made to avoid double counting, in comprehensive income, items that are displayed as part of net income for a period that also had been displayed as part of other comprehensive income in that period or earlier periods. For example, gains on investment securities that were realized and included in net income of the current period, that also had been included in other comprehensive income as unrealized holding gains in the period in which they arose, must be deducted through other comprehensive income of the period in which they are included in net income to avoid including them in comprehensive income twice. These adjustments are called reclassification adjustments. An entity may display reclassification adjustments on the face of the financial statement in which comprehensive income is reported or it may disclose them in the notes to the financial statements. During 2009, 133 survey entities reported reclassification adjustments.

4.18 Table 4-3 lists the components of other comprehensive income disclosed by survey entities in the statement used to present comprehensive income for the period reported.

4.19 Examples showing the presentation of components of other comprehensive income follow.

4.20

TABLE 4-3: OTHER COMPREHENSIVE INCOME—COMPONENTS*

	2009	2008	2007	2006
Cumulative translation adjustments.....	418	410	476	485
Defined benefit postretirement plan adjustments....................................	403	399	460	444
Changes in fair value of derivatives.....	304	316	318	321
Unrealized losses/gains on certain investments.....................................	226	228	254	263
Other..	6	6	7	6

* Appearing in the statement used to present comprehensive income.

2008–2009 based on 500 entities surveyed; 2006–2007 based on 600 entities surveyed.

Cumulative Translation Adjustments

4.21

HEWLETT-PACKARD COMPANY (OCT)

Consolidated Statements of Stockholders' Equity

(In millions, except number of shares in thousands)	Common Stock Number of Shares	Par Value	Additional Paid-In Capital	Prepaid Stock Repurchase	Retained Earnings	Accumulated Other Comprehensive (Loss) Income	Total
Balance October 31, 2006	2,732,034	$27	$17,966	$ (596)	$20,729	$ 18	$ 38,144
Net earnings					7,264		7,264
Net unrealized loss on available-for-sale securities						(12)	(12)
Net unrealized loss on cash flow hedges						(18)	(18)
Minimum pension liability						(3)	(3)
Cumulative translation adjustment						106	106
Comprehensive income							7,337
Issuance of common stock in connection with employee stock plans and other	116,661	1	3,134				3,135
Repurchases of common stock	(268,981)	(2)	(5,878)	596	(5,587)		(10,871)
Net excess tax benefits from employee stock plans			530				530
Dividends					(846)		(846)
Stock-based compensation expense			629				629
Cumulative effect of change in accounting principle						468	468
Balance October 31, 2007	2,579,714	$26	$16,381	$ —	$21,560	$ 559	$ 38,526
Net earnings					8,329		8,329
Net unrealized loss on available-for-sale securities						(16)	(16)
Net unrealized gain on cash flow hedges						866	866
Unrealized components of defined benefit pension plans						(538)	(538)
Cumulative translation adjustment						(936)	(936)
Comprehensive income							7,705
Issuance of common stock in connection with employee stock plans and other	65,235		2,034				2,034
Repurchases of common stock	(229,646)	(2)	(5,325)		(4,809)		(10,136)
Net excess tax benefits from employee stock plans			316				316
Dividends					(796)		(796)
Stock-based compensation expense			606				606
Cumulative effect of change in accounting principle					687		687
Balance October 31, 2008	2,415,303	$24	$14,012	$ —	$24,971	$ (65)	$ 38,942
Net earnings					7,660		7,660
Net unrealized gain on available-for-sale securities						16	16
Net unrealized loss on cash flow hedges						(971)	(971)
Unrealized components of defined benefit pension plans						(2,531)	(2,531)
Cumulative translation adjustment						304	304
Comprehensive income							4,478
Issuance of common stock in connection with employee stock plans and other	69,157	1	1,783				1,784
Repurchases of common stock	(119,651)	(1)	(2,789)		(1,922)		(4,712)
Net excess tax benefits from employee stock plans			163				163
Dividends					(766)		(766)
Stock-based compensation expense			635				635
Cumulative effect of change in accounting principle					(7)		(7)
	2,364,809	$24	$13,804	$ —	$29,936	$(3,247)	$ 40,517

NOTES TO CONSOLIDATED FINANCIAL STATEMENTS

Note 1 (In Part): Summary of Significant Accounting Policies

Foreign Currency Transactions

HP uses the U.S. dollar predominately as its functional currency. Assets and liabilities denominated in non-U.S. dollars are remeasured into U.S. dollars at current exchange rates for monetary assets and liabilities, and historical exchange rates for nonmonetary assets and liabilities. Net revenue, cost of sales and expenses are remeasured at average exchange rates in effect during each new reporting period, and net revenue, cost of sales and expenses related to the previously reported periods are remeasured at historical exchange rates. HP includes gains or losses from foreign currency remeasurement in net earnings. Certain foreign subsidiaries designate the local currency as their functional currency, and HP records the translation of their assets and liabilities into U.S. dollars at the balance sheet dates as translation adjustments and includes them as a component of accumulated other comprehensive loss.

Note 15 (In Part): Stockholders' Equity

Comprehensive Income

The changes in the components of other comprehensive income, net of taxes, were as follows for the following fiscal years ended October 31:

(In millions)	2009	2008	2007
Net earnings	$ 7,660	$8,329	$7,264
Net change in unrealized gains/losses on available-for-sale securities:			
Change in net unrealized gains (losses), net of tax of $11 million in fiscal 2009, net of tax benefit of $7 million in fiscal 2008 and net of tax of $2 million in fiscal 2007	17	(17)	2
Net unrealized (gains) losses reclassified into earnings, with no tax effect in fiscal 2009 and fiscal 2008, and net of tax benefit of $7 million in fiscal 2007	(1)	1	(14)
	16	(16)	(12)
Net change in unrealized gains/losses on cash flow hedges:			
Change in net unrealized (losses) gains, net of tax benefit of $94 million in fiscal 2009, net of tax of $468 million in fiscal 2008 and net of tax benefit of $37 million in fiscal 2007	(163)	808	(63)
Net unrealized (gains) losses reclassified into earnings, net of tax of $468 million in fiscal 2009, net of tax benefit of $34 million in fiscal 2008 and net of tax of $26 million in fiscal 2007	(808)	58	45
	(971)	866	(18)
Net change in cumulative translation adjustment, net of tax of $227 million in fiscal 2009, net of tax benefit of $476 million in fiscal 2008 and net of tax of $37 million in fiscal 2007	304	(936)	106
Net change in unrealized components of defined benefit plans, net of tax benefit of $905 million in fiscal 2009, $42 million in fiscal 2008 and $1 million in fiscal 2007	(2,531)	(538)	(3)
Comprehensive income	$ 4,478	$7,705	$7,337

The components of accumulated other comprehensive (loss) income, net of taxes, were as follows for the following fiscal years ended October 31:

(In millions)	2009	2008	2007
Net unrealized gain (loss) on available-for-sale securities	$ 4	$ (12)	$ 4
Net unrealized (loss) gain on cash flow hedges	(169)	802	(64)
Cumulative translation adjustment	(459)	(763)	173
Unrealized components of defined benefit plans	(2,623)	(92)	446
Accumulated other comprehensive (loss) income	$(3,247)	$ (65)	$559

4.22

QUIKSILVER, INC. (OCT)

Consolidated Statements of Comprehensive Loss

(In thousands)	2009	2008	2007
Net loss	$(192,042)	$(226,265)	$(121,119)
Other comprehensive income (loss):			
Foreign currency translation adjustment	99,798	(111,920)	116,882
Reclassification adjustment for foreign currency translation included in current period loss from discontinued operations	(47,850)	—	—
Net (loss) gain on derivative instruments, net of tax (benefit) provision of $(19,965) (2009), $26,322 (2008) and $(10,368) (2007) (2002)	(37,062)	44,313	(21,859)
Comprehensive loss	$(177,156)	$(293,872)	$ (26,096)

NOTES TO CONSOLIDATED FINANCIAL STATEMENTS

Note 1 (In Part): Significant Accounting Policies

Foreign Currency and Derivatives

The Company's reporting currency is the U.S. dollar, while Quiksilver Europe's functional currencies are primarily the euro and the British pound, and Quiksilver Asia/Pacific's functional currencies are primarily the Australian dollar and the Japanese yen. Assets and liabilities of the Company denominated in foreign currencies are translated at the rate of exchange on the balance sheet date. Revenues and expenses are translated using the average exchange rate for the period.

Derivative financial instruments are recognized as either assets or liabilities in the balance sheet and are measured at fair value. The accounting for changes in the fair value of a derivative depends on the use and type of the derivative. The Company's derivative financial instruments principally consist of foreign currency exchange contracts and interest rate swaps, which the Company uses to manage its exposure to the risk of foreign currency exchange rates and variable interest rates. The Company's objectives are to reduce the volatility of earnings and cash flows associated with changes in foreign currency exchange and interest rates. The Company does not enter into derivative financial instruments for speculative or trading purposes.

Comprehensive Loss

Comprehensive loss or income includes all changes in stockholders' equity except those resulting from investments by, and distributions to, stockholders. Accordingly, the Company's Consolidated Statements of Comprehensive Loss include its net loss and the foreign currency adjustments that arise from the translation of the financial statements of Quiksilver Europe, Quiksilver Asia/Pacific and the foreign entities within the Americas segment into U.S. dollars and fair value gains and losses on certain derivative instruments.

Defined Benefit Post Retirement Plan Adjustments

4.23

EL PASO CORPORATION (DEC)

Consolidated Statements of Comprehensive Income

(In millions)	2009	2008	2007
Net income (loss)	$(474)	$ (789)	$1,116
Pension and postretirement obligations:			
Unrealized actuarial gains (losses) arising during period (net of income taxes of $11 in 2009, $288 in 2008 and $91 in 2007)	36	(527)	181
Reclassifications of actuarial gains during period (net of income taxes of $16 in 2009, $8 in 2008 and $13 in 2007)	27	16	26
Cash flow hedging activities:			
Unrealized mark-to-market gains (losses) arising during period (net of income taxes of $6 in 2009, $106 in 2008 and $2 in 2007)	11	191	(3)
Reclassification adjustments for changes in initial value to the settlement date (net of income taxes of $146 in 2009, $31 in 2008 and $65 in 2007)	(260)	57	(112)
Investments available for sale:			
Unrealized gains on investments available for sale arising during period (net of income taxes of $2 in 2007)	—	—	3
Realized gains on investments available for sale arising during period (net of income taxes of $8 in 2007)	—	—	(15)
Other comprehensive income (loss)	(186)	(263)	80
Comprehensive income (loss)	(660)	(1,052)	1,196
Comprehensive income attributable to noncontrolling interests	(65)	(34)	(6)
Comprehensive income (loss) attributable to El Paso Corporation	$(725)	$(1,086)	$1,190

NOTES TO CONSOLIDATED FINANCIAL STATEMENTS

1 (In Part): Significant Accounting Policies

Pension and Other Postretirement Benefits

We maintain several pension and other postretirement benefit plans. We make contributions to our plans, if required, to fund the benefits to be paid out to participants and retirees. These contributions are invested until the benefits are paid out to plan participants. We record the net benefit cost related to these plans in our income statement. This net benefit cost is a function of many factors including benefits earned during the year by plan participants (which is a function of the employee's salary, the level of benefits provided under the plan, actuarial assumptions and the passage of time), expected returns on plan assets and amortization of certain deferred gains and losses. For a further discussion of our policies with respect to our pension and postretirement benefit plans, see Note 14.

In accounting for our pension and other postretirement benefit plans, we record an asset or liability based on the over funded or under funded status of each plan. Any deferred amounts related to unrecognized gains and losses or changes in actuarial assumptions are recorded either as a regulatory asset or liability for our regulated operations or in accumulated other comprehensive income (loss), a component of stockholders' equity, for all other operations until those gains and losses are recognized in the income statement.

14 (In Part): Retirement Benefits

Overview of Retirement Benefit Plans (In Part)

Pension Plans (In Part)

Our primary pension plan is a defined benefit plan that covers substantially all of our U.S. employees and provides benefits under a cash balance formula. Certain employees who participated in the prior pension plans of El Paso, Sonat, Inc. or The Coastal Corporation receive the greater of their cash balance benefits or their transition benefits under the prior plan formulas. Prior to December 31, 2008, we maintained two other frozen pension plans which provide benefits to former employees of our previously discontinued coal and convenience store operations. Effective December 31, 2008, these frozen plans were merged with our cash balance plan. We do not anticipate making any contributions to our cash balance pension plan in 2010.

In addition to our primary pension plan, we maintain a Supplemental Executive Retirement Plan (SERP) that provides additional benefits to selected officers and key management. The SERP provides benefits in excess of certain IRS limits that essentially mirror those in the primary pension plan. We expect to contribute $5 million to the SERP in 2010.

Other Postretirement Benefit Plans

We provide other postretirement benefits (OPEB), including medical benefits for closed groups of retired employees and limited postretirement life insurance benefits for current and retired employees. Medical benefits for these closed groups of retirees may be subject to deductibles, co-payment provisions, and other limitations and dollar caps on the amount of employer costs, and we reserve the right to change these benefits. OPEB for our regulated pipeline companies are prefunded to the extent such costs are recoverable through rates. To the extent OPEB costs for our regulated pipeline companies differ from the amounts recovered in rates, a regulatory asset or liability is recorded. We expect to contribute $48 million to our other postretirement benefit plans in 2010.

Benefit Obligation, Plan Assets and Funded Status

In accounting for our pension and other postretirement plans, we record an asset or liability based on the over funded or under funded status of each plan. Any deferred amounts related to unrecognized gains and losses or changes in actuarial assumptions are recorded either as a regulatory asset or liability for our regulated operations or in accumulated other comprehensive income (loss), a component of stockholders' equity, for all other operations until those gains and losses are recognized in the income statement.

The table below provides information about our pension and OPEB plans. In 2008, we adopted the revised measurement date provisions for accounting for retirement benefits and the information below for 2008 is presented and computed as of and for the fifteen months ended December 31, 2008. For 2009, the information is presented and computed as of and for the twelve months ended December 31, 2009.

(In millions)	Pension Benefits		Other Postretirement Benefits	
	2009	2008	2009	2008
Change in benefit obligation:[1]				
Benefit obligation—beginning of period	$1,989	$2,027	$ 673	$ 418
Service cost	19	18	—	—
Interest cost	121	150	38	44
Participant contributions	—	—	10	13
Actuarial (gain) loss	159	(12)	(28)	(12)
Benefits paid[2]	(171)	(209)	(51)	(72)
Case liability reclassification	—	—	—	282
Other	16	15	—	—
Benefit obligation—end of period	$2,133	$1,989	$ 642	$ 673
Change in plan assets:				
Fair value of plan assets—beginning of period	$1,773	$2,537	$ 210	$ 303
Actual return on plan assets[3]	373	(561)	37	(67)
Employer contributions	4	6	44	39
Participant contributions	—	—	9	13
Benefits paid	(171)	(209)	(57)	(78)
Fair value of plan assets—end of period	$1,979	$1,773	$ 243	$ 210
Reconciliation of funded status:				
Fair value of plan assets	$1,979	$1,773	$ 243	$ 210
Less: benefit obligation	2,133	1,989	642	673
Net liability at December 31	$ (154)	$ (216)	$(399)	$(463)

[1] The benefit obligation for our pension plans represents the projected benefit obligation, and the benefit obligation for our other postretirement benefit plans represents the accumulated postretirement benefit obligation.

[2] Amounts for other postretirement benefits are shown net of a subsidy of approximately $6 million for each of the years ended December 31, 2009 and 2008 related to the Medicare Prescription Drug, Improvement, and Modernization Act of 2003.

[3] We defer the difference between our actual return on plan assets and our expected return over a three year period, after which it is considered for inclusion in net benefit expense or income. Our deferred actuarial gains and losses are amortized only to the extent that our remaining unrecognized actual gains and losses exceed the greater of 10 percent of our benefit obligations or market related value of plan assets.

Components of Funded Status

The following table details the amounts recognized in our balance sheet at December 31, 2009 and 2008 related to our pension and other postretirement benefit plans.

(In millions)	Pension Benefits		Other Postretirement Benefits	
	2009	2008	2009	2008
Non-current benefit asset	$ —	$ —	$ 88	$ 42
Current benefit liability	(5)	(4)	(39)	(42)
Non-current benefit liability	(149)	(212)	(448)	(463)
Funded status	$(154)	$(216)	$(399)	$(463)

Components of Accumulated Other Comprehensive Income (Loss)

The following table details the amounts recognized in our accumulated other comprehensive income (loss), net of income taxes at December 31, 2009 and 2008 related to our pension and other postretirement benefit plans.

(In millions)	Pension Benefits		Other Postretirement Benefits	
	2009	2008	2009	2008
Unrecognized net gain (loss)	$(709)	$(765)	$43	$24
Unamortized prior service credit (cost)	(16)	(5)	—	1
Accumulated other comprehensive income (loss)	$(725)	$(770)	$43	$25

We anticipate that approximately $48 million of our accumulated other comprehensive loss, net of tax, will be recognized as part of our net periodic benefit cost in 2010.

Our accumulated benefit obligation for our defined benefit pension plans was $2.1 billion and $2.0 billion at December 31, 2009 and 2008. Our accumulated benefit obligation for our defined benefit pension plans, whose accumulated benefit obligations exceeded the fair value of plan assets, was $2.1 billion and $2.0 billion as of December 31, 2009 and 2008. The fair value of these plans' assets was approximately $2.0 billion and $1.8 billion at December 31, 2009 and 2008.

Our accumulated postretirement benefit obligation for our other postretirement benefit plans, whose accumulated postretirement benefit obligations exceeded the fair value of plan assets, was $542 million and $552 million as of December 31, 2009 and 2008. The fair value of these plans' assets was $55 million and $48 million at December 31, 2009 and 2008.

Components of Net Benefit Cost (Income)

For each of the years ended December 31, the components of net benefit cost (income) are as follows:

(In millions)	Pension Benefits			Other Postretirement Benefits		
	2009	2008	2007	2009	2008	2007
Service cost	$ 19	$ 15	$ 17	$ —	$ —	$ 1
Interest cost	121	120	119	38	38	26
Expected return on plan assets	(172)	(187)	(181)	(12)	(17)	(16)
Amortization of net actuarial (gain) loss	45	24	43	—	(5)	(1)
Amortization of prior service credit	(1)	(2)	(2)	(1)	(1)	(1)
Net benefit cost (income)	$ 12	$ (30)	$ (4)	$ 25	$ 15	$ 9

Components of Other Comprehensive Income (Loss)

The following table details the amounts recognized in our other comprehensive loss, net of income taxes, for the years ended December 31, 2009 and 2008 related to our pension and other postretirement benefit plans.

(In millions)	Pension Benefits		Other Postretirement Benefits	
	2009	2008	2009	2008
Prior service cost	$(10)	$ (11)	$—	$—
Net gain (loss)	27	(509)	19	(7)
Amortization of net actuarial (gain) loss	29	20	—	(1)
Amortization of prior service credit	(1)	(2)	(1)	(1)
Other comprehensive income (loss)	$ 45	$(502)	$18	$ (9)

4.24

TENET HEALTHCARE CORPORATION (DEC)

Consolidated Statements of Other Comprehensive Income (Loss)

(Dollars in millions)	2009	2008	2007
Net income (loss)	$197	$32	$(84)
Other comprehensive income (loss):			
Adjustments for supplemental executive retirement plans	(3)	(9)	17
Foreign currency translation adjustments	—	—	(2)
Unrealized gain (losses) on securities held as available-for-sale	3	(3)	—
Reclassification adjustments for realized losses included in net income (loss)	7	3	2
Other comprehensive income (loss) before income taxes	7	(9)	17
Income tax (expense) benefit related to items of other comprehensive income (loss)	(2)	—	—
Total other comprehensive income (loss), net of tax	5	(9)	17
Comprehensive income (loss)	202	23	(67)
Less: preferred stock dividends	6	—	—
Less: comprehensive income attributable to noncontrolling interests	10	7	5
Comprehensive income (loss) attributable to Tenet Healthcare Corporation common shareholders	$186	$16	$(72)

NOTES TO CONSOLIDATED FINANCIAL STATEMENTS

Note 7 (In Part): Employee Benefit Plans

Employee Retirement Plans (In Part)

We maintain one active and two frozen non-qualified defined benefit pension plans ("SERPs") that provide supplemental retirement benefits to certain of our current and former executives. The plans are not funded, and plan obligations are paid from our working capital. Pension benefits are generally based on years of service and compensation. The following tables summarize the balance sheet impact, as well as the benefit obligations, funded status and rate assumptions associated with the SERPs based on actuarial valuations prepared as of December 31, 2009 and 2008:

(Dollars in millions)	2009	2008
Reconciliation of funded status of plans and the amounts included in the consolidated balance sheets:		
Projected benefit obligations[1]		
Beginning obligations	$(245)	$(235)
Service cost	(1)	(2)
Interest cost	(14)	(14)
Actuarial loss	(7)	(12)
Benefits paid	18	18
Ending obligations	(249)	(245)
Fair value of plans' assets	—	—
Funded status of plans	$(249)	$(245)
Amounts recognized in the consolidated balance sheets consist of:		
Other current liability	$ (18)	$ (18)
Other long-term liability	(231)	(227)
Accumulated other comprehensive loss	29	26
	$(220)	$(219)
Assumptions:		
Discount rate	5.75%	5.75%
Compensation increase rate	3.00%	4.00%
Measurement date	December 31, 2009	December 31, 2008

[1] The accumulated benefit obligation at December 31, 2009 and 2008 was approximately $246 million and $242 million, respectively.

The components of net periodic benefit costs and related assumptions are as follows:

(Dollars in millions)	2009	2008	2007
Service costs	$ 1	$ 2	$ 2
Interest costs	14	14	14
Amortization of prior-year service costs	3	3	3
Amortization of net actuarial loss	1	—	—
Net periodic benefit cost	$19	$19	$19
Assumptions:			
Discount rate	5.75%	6.25%	5.75%
Long-term rate of return on assets	n/a	n/a	n/a
Compensation increase rate	4.00%	4.00%	4.00%
Measurement date	January 1, 2009	January 1, 2008	January 1, 2007
Census date	January 1, 2009	January 1, 2008	January 1, 2007

Net periodic benefit costs for the current year are based on assumptions determined at the valuation date of the prior year.

We recorded a $3 million loss adjustment, a $9 million loss adjustment and $17 million gain adjustment in other comprehensive income (loss) in the three months ended December 31, 2009, 2008 and 2007, respectively, to recognize changes in the funded status of our SERPs. Changes in the funded status are recorded as a direct increase or decrease to shareholders' equity through accumulated other comprehensive loss. Net actuarial gains (losses) of $(7) million, $(12) million and $14 million during the years ended December 31, 2009, 2008 and 2007, respectively, and the amortization of net prior service costs of $3 million for each of the years ended December 31, 2009, 2008 and 2007 were recognized in other comprehensive income (loss). Cumulative net actuarial losses of $29 million, $23 million and $11 million and unrecognized prior service costs of $0, $3 million and $6 million as of December 31, 2009, 2008 and 2007, respectively, have not yet been recognized as components of net periodic benefit costs. During the year ending December 31, 2010, no net prior service costs are expected to be recognized as components of net periodic benefit costs.

Changes in Fair Value of Derivatives

4.25

AK STEEL HOLDING CORPORATION (DEC)

Consolidated Statements of Comprehensive Income (Loss)

(Dollars in millions)	2009	2008	2007
Net income (loss) attributable to AK Steel Holding Corporation	$(74.6)	$ 4.0	$387.7
Other comprehensive income (loss), net of tax:			
Foreign currency translation adjustment	1.0	(4.0)	3.6
Derivative instrument hedges, mark to market:			
Losses arising in period	(12.4)	(20.5)	(8.6)
Less: Reclassification of (gains) losses included in net income	40.1	(10.5)	8.9
Unrealized gains (losses) on securities:			
Unrealized holding gains (losses) arising during period	2.3	(4.1)	—
Pension and OPEB adjustment	(22.7)	153.6	49.0
Comprehensive income (loss)	$(66.3)	$118.5	$440.6

NOTES TO CONSOLIDATED FINANCIAL STATEMENTS
(Dollars in millions)

Note 1 (In Part): Summary of Significant Accounting Policies

Financial Instruments (In Part)

The Company is a party to derivative instruments that are designated and qualify as hedges under ASC Topic 815, "Derivatives and Hedging." The Company may also enter into derivative instruments to which it does not apply hedge accounting treatment. The Company's objective in using these instruments is to protect its earnings and cash flows from fluctuations in the fair value of selected commodities and currencies.

In the ordinary course of business, the Company's income and cash flows may be affected by fluctuations in the price of certain commodities used in its production processes. The Company has implemented raw material and energy surcharges for its spot market customers and some of its contract customers. For certain commodities where such exposure exists, the Company uses cash settled commodity price swaps, collars and purchase options, with a duration of up to three years, to hedge the price of a portion of its natural gas, nickel, aluminum and zinc requirements. The Company designates the natural gas instruments as cash flow hedges and the effective portion of the changes in their fair value are recorded in other comprehensive income. Subsequent gains and losses are recognized into cost of products sold in the same period as the underlying physical transaction. The pre-tax net loss recognized in earnings during 2009 representing the component of the derivative instruments' current effectiveness and excluded from the assessment of hedge effectiveness was $9.4 and was recorded in cost of products sold. At December 31, 2009, currently valued outstanding commodity hedges would result in the reclassification into earnings of $1.3 in net-of-tax losses within the next twelve months. At December 31, 2008, currently valued outstanding commodity hedges would have resulted in the reclassification into earnings of $24.9 in net-of-tax losses within the next twelve months. The nickel, aluminum and zinc hedges are marked to market and recognized into cost of products sold with the offset recognized as current assets or accrued liabilities. At December 31, 2009, other current assets, other non-current assets and accrued liabilities included $1.9, $0.1 and $5.8, respectively, for the fair value of these commodity hedges.

• • • • • •

The Company formally documents all relationships between hedging instruments and hedged items, as well as its risk management objectives and strategies for undertaking various hedge transactions. In this documentation, the Company specifically identifies the asset, liability, firm commitment or forecasted transaction that has been designated as a hedged item and states how the hedging instrument is expected to hedge the risks related to that item. The Company formally measures effectiveness of its hedging relationships both at the hedge inception and on an ongoing basis. The Company discontinues hedge accounting prospectively when it determines that the derivative is no longer effective in offsetting changes in the fair value or cash flows of a hedged item; when the derivative expires or is sold, terminated or exercised; when it is probable that the forecasted transaction will not occur; when a hedged firm commitment no longer meets the definition of a firm commitment; or when management determines that designation of the derivative as a hedge instrument is no longer appropriate.

Comprehensive Income and Accumulated Other Comprehensive Income (Loss)

Comprehensive income in the Statement of Comprehensive Income (Loss) is presented net of an approximate 38% tax rate. The components of accumulated other comprehensive income (loss) at December 31 are as follows:

	2009	2008	2007
Foreign currency translation	$ 4.3	$ 3.3	$ 7.3
Derivative instrument hedges	(1.3)	(29.0)	2.0
Unrealized gain (loss) on investments	(1.6)	(3.9)	0.2
Employee benefit liability	166.5	189.2	38.3
Total	$167.9	$159.6	$47.8

Note 14 (In Part): Disclosures About Derivative Instruments and Hedging Activities

In the ordinary course of business, the Company is exposed to market risk for price fluctuations of raw materials and energy sources. The Company is also subject to risks of exchange rate fluctuations on a portion of inter-company receivables that are denominated in foreign currencies. The Company occasionally uses forward currency contracts to manage exposures to certain of these currency price fluctuations. As of December 31, 2009, the Company had entered into forward currency contracts in the amount of 16,300,000 euros.

The Company uses cash settled commodity price swaps and/or options to hedge the market risk associated with the purchase of certain of its raw materials and energy requirements. Such hedges routinely are used with respect to a portion of the Company's natural gas and nickel requirements and are sometimes used with respect to its aluminum and zinc requirements. The Company's hedging strategy is designed to protect it against normal volatility. However, abnormal price increases in any of these commodity markets could negatively impact operating costs. The effective portion of the gains and losses from the use of these instruments for natural gas are deferred in accumulated other comprehensive income on the consolidated balance sheets and recognized into cost of products sold in the same period as the underlying transaction. Gains and losses on the derivative representing either hedge ineffectiveness or hedge components excluded from the assessment of effectiveness are recognized in current earnings. All other commodity price swaps and options are marked to market and recognized into cost of products sold with the offset recognized as other current assets or other accrued liabilities.

Accounting guidance requires companies to recognize all derivative instruments as either assets or liabilities at fair value in the statement of financial position. In accordance with ASC Topic 815, "Derivatives and Hedging," the Company designates commodity price swaps and options as cash flow hedges of forecasted purchases of raw materials and energy sources.

Existing natural gas commodity hedges at December 31, 2009 have settlement dates ranging from January 2010 to December 2010. The amount of the existing losses expected to be reclassified into earnings within the next twelve months is $1.3.

As of December 31, 2009 the Company had the following outstanding commodity price swaps and/or options that were entered into to hedge forecasted purchases.

Commodity	Amount	Unit
Nickel	979,230	lbs
Natural gas	12,170,000	MMBTUs

• • • • • •

Effect of Derivative Instruments on the Consolidated Statement of Operations for the Year Ended December 31, 2009	Gain (Loss)
Derivatives in cash flow hedging relationships	
Commodity contracts	
Amount recognized in other comprehensive income ("OCI")	$(12.4)
Amount reclassified from accumulated OCI into cost of products sold (effective portion)	(40.1)
Amount recognized in cost of products sold (ineffective portion and amount excluded from effectiveness testing)	(9.4)
Derivatives not designated as hedging instruments	
Foreign exchange contracts	
Amount recognized in other income, net	2.3
Commodity contracts	
Amount recognized in cost of products sold	2.8

4.26

ANALOG DEVICES, INC. (OCT)

Consolidated Statements of Comprehensive Income

(Thousands)	2009	2008	2007
Income from continuing operations, net of tax	$247,408	$525,177	$502,123
Foreign currency translation adjustment	14,840	(42,370)	10,640
Net unrealized (losses) gains on securities:			
Net unrealized holding (losses) gains (net of taxes of $347 in 2009, $372 in 2008 and $2,746 in 2007) on securities classified as short-term investments	(2,456)	2,508	5,094
Net unrealized holding gains (losses) (net of taxes of $197 in 2009, $217 in 2008 and $100 in 2007) on securities classified as other investments	366	400	(185)
Net unrealized (losses) gains on securities	(2,090)	2,908	4,909
Derivative instruments designated as cash flow hedges:			
Changes in fair value of derivatives (net of taxes of $5,496 in 2009, $1,622 in 2008 and $846 in 2007)	35,529	(10,663)	5,282
Realized (gain) loss reclassification (net of taxes of $1,609 in 2009, $2,420 in 2008 and $107 in 2007)	(9,657)	(15,912)	665
Net change in derivative instruments designated as cash flow hedges	25,872	(26,575)	5,947
Minimum pension liability adjustment (net of taxes of $0 in 2009, $0 in 2008 and $640 in 2007)	—	—	1,495
Accumulated other comprehensive (loss) income—pension plans:			
Transition obligation (net of taxes of $1 in 2009 and $4 in 2008)	(34)	(43)	—
Net actuarial loss (net of taxes of $287 in 2009 and $1,971 in 2008)	(663)	(15,197)	—
Net prior service income (net of taxes of $1 in 2009 and $4 in 2008)	5	8	—
Net change in accumulated other comprehensive loss—pension plans (net of taxes of $286 in 2009 and $1,963 in 2008)	(692)	(15,232)	—
Other comprehensive income (loss)	37,930	(81,269)	22,991
Comprehensive income from continuing operations	285,338	443,908	525,114
Income (loss) from discontinued operations, net of tax	364	261,107	(5,216)
Comprehensive income	$285,702	$705,015	$519,898

NOTES TO CONSOLIDATED FINANCIAL STATEMENTS
(All tabular amounts in thousands)

2 (In Part): Summary of Significant Accounting Policies

i. Derivative Instruments and Hedging Agreements

Foreign Exchange Exposure Management

The Company enters into forward foreign currency exchange contracts to offset certain operational and balance sheet exposures from the impact of changes in foreign currency exchange rates. Such exposures result from the portion of the Company's operations, assets and liabilities that are denominated in currencies other than the U.S. dollar, primarily the Euro; other exposures include the Philippine Peso and the British Pound. These foreign currency exchange contracts are entered into to support transactions made in the normal course of business, and accordingly, are not speculative in nature. The contracts are for periods consistent with the terms of the underlying transactions, generally one year or less. Hedges related to anticipated transactions are designated and documented at the inception of the respective hedges as cash flow hedges and are evaluated for effectiveness monthly. Derivative instruments are employed to eliminate or minimize certain foreign currency exposures that can be confidently identified and quantified. As the terms of the contract and the underlying transaction are matched at inception, forward contract effectiveness is calculated by comparing the change in fair value of the contract to the change in the forward value of the anticipated transaction, with the effective portion of the gain or loss on the derivative instrument reported as a component of accumulated other comprehensive (loss) income (OCI) in shareholders' equity and reclassified into earnings in the same period during which the hedged transaction affects earnings. Any residual change in fair value of the instruments, or ineffectiveness, is recognized immediately in other income/expense. Additionally, the Company enters into forward foreign currency contracts that economically hedge the gains and losses generated by the remeasurement of certain recorded assets and liabilities in a non-functional currency. Changes in the fair value of these undesignated hedges are recognized in other income/expense immediately as an offset to the changes in the fair value of the asset or liability being hedged.

As of October 31, 2009, the total notional amount of these undesignated hedges was $38 million. The fair value of these hedging instruments in the Company's condensed consolidated balance sheet as of October 31, 2009 was immaterial.

Interest Rate Exposure Management

On June 30, 2009, the Company entered into interest rate swap transactions related to its outstanding notes where the Company swapped the notional amount of its $375 million of fixed rate debt at 5.0% into floating interest rate debt through July 1, 2014. Under the terms of the swaps, the Company will (i) receive on the $375 million notional amount a 5.0% annual interest payment that is paid in two installments on the 1st of every January and July, commencing January 1, 2010 through and ending on the maturity date; and (ii) pay on the $375 million notional amount an annual three-month LIBOR plus 2.05% (2.34% as of October 31, 2009) interest payment, payable in four installments on the 1st of every January, April, July and October, commencing on October 1, 2009 and ending on the maturity date. The LIBOR based

rate is set quarterly three months prior to the date of the interest payment. The Company designated these swaps as fair value hedges. The fair value of the swaps at inception were zero and subsequent changes in the fair value of the interest rate swaps were reflected in the carrying value of the interest rate swaps on the balance sheet. The carrying value of the debt on the balance sheet was adjusted by an equal and offsetting amount. The gain or loss on the hedged item (that is fixed-rate borrowings) attributable to the hedged benchmark interest rate risk and the offsetting gain or loss on the related interest rate swaps as of October 31, 2009 is as follows:

Income Statement Classification	Gain/(Loss) on Swaps	Gain/(Loss) on Note	Net Income Effect
Other income	$6,109	$(6,109)	$—

The amounts earned and owed under the swap agreements are accrued each period and are reported in interest expense. There was no ineffectiveness recognized in any of the periods presented.

The market risk associated with the Company's derivative instruments results from currency exchange rate or interest rate movements that are expected to offset the market risk of the underlying transactions, assets and liabilities being hedged. The counterparties to the agreements relating to the Company's derivative instruments consist of a number of major international financial institutions with high credit ratings. The Company does not believe that there is significant risk of nonperformance by these counterparties because the Company continually monitors the credit ratings of such counterparties. Furthermore, none of the Company's derivative transactions are subject to collateral or other security arrangements and none contain provisions that are dependent on the Company's credit ratings from any credit rating agency. While the contract or notional amounts of derivative financial instruments provide one measure of the volume of these transactions, they do not represent the amount of the Company's exposure to credit risk. The amounts potentially subject to credit risk (arising from the possible inability of counterparties to meet the terms of their contracts) are generally limited to the amounts, if any, by which the counterparties' obligations under the contracts exceed the obligations of the Company to the counterparties. As a result of the above considerations, the Company does not consider the risk of counterparty default to be significant.

The Company records the fair value of its derivative financial instruments in the consolidated financial statements in other current assets, other assets or accrued liabilities, depending on their net position, regardless of the purpose or intent for holding the derivative contract. Changes in the fair value of the derivative financial instruments are either recognized periodically in earnings or in shareholders' equity as a component of OCI. Changes in the fair value of cash flow hedges are recorded in OCI and reclassified into earnings when the underlying contract matures. Changes in the fair values of derivatives not qualifying for hedge accounting are reported in earnings as they occur.

The total notional amount of derivative instruments designated as hedging instruments as of October 31, 2009 is as follows: $375 million of interest rate swap agreements accounted as fair value hedges, and $128.0 million of cash flow hedges denominated in Euros, British Pounds and Philippine Pesos.

•   •   •   •   •   •

The effect of derivative instruments designated as cash flow hedges on our condensed consolidated statement of income for fiscal 2009 was as follows:

	2009
Gain recognized in OCI on derivatives, net of tax of $5,496	$35,529
Loss reclassified from OCI into income, net of tax of $1,609	$ (9,657)

The amounts reclassified into earnings before tax are recognized in cost of sales and operating expenses as follows: $4.9 million in cost of sales, $3.6 million in research and development and $2.8 million in selling, marketing, general and administrative. All derivative gains and losses included in OCI will be reclassified into earnings within the next 12 months. There was no ineffectiveness during the fiscal year ended October 31, 2009.

Accumulated Derivative Gains or Losses

The following table summarizes activity in accumulated other comprehensive (loss) income related to derivatives classified as cash flow hedges held by the Company during the period from November 4, 2007 through October 31, 2009:

	2009	2008
Balance at beginning of year	$(20,263)	$ 6,312
Changes in fair value of derivatives—gain (loss), net of tax	35,529	(10,663)
Reclassifications into earnings from other comprehensive loss, net of tax	(9,657)	(15,912)
Balance at end of year	$ 5,609	$(20,263)

All of the accumulated gain will be reclassified into earnings over the next twelve months.

Unrealized Losses/Gains on Certain Investments

4.27

ABM INDUSTRIES INCORPORATED (OCT)

Consolidated Statements of Stockholders' Equity and Comprehensive Income

(In thousands)	Common Stock Shares	Common Stock Amount	Treasury Stock Shares	Treasury Stock Amount	Additional Paid-In Capital	Accumulated Other Comprehensive Income (Loss)	Retained Earnings	Total
Balance October 31, 2006	55,663	$557	(7,028)	$(122,338)	$225,796	$149	$437,083	$541,247
Comprehensive income:								
Net income	—	—	—	—	—	—	52,440	52,440
Foreign currency translation	—	—	—	—	—	520	—	520
Comprehensive income	—	—	—	—	—	—	—	52,960
Adjustment to initially apply ASC 715, net of taxes	—	—	—	—	—	211	—	211
Dividends:								
Common stock	—	—	—	—	—	—	(23,805)	(23,805)
Tax benefit from exercise of stock options	—	—	—	—	4,046	—	—	4,046
Stock issued under employees' stock purchase and option plans	1,385	14	—	—	23,181	—	(255)	22,940
Share-based compensation expense	—	—	—	—	8,159	—	—	8,159
Balance October 31, 2007	57,048	$571	(7,028)	$(122,338)	$261,182	$880	$465,463	$605,758

(continued)

(In thousands)	Common Stock		Treasury Stock		Additional Paid-In Capital	Accumulated Other Comprehensive Income (Loss)	Retained Earnings	Total
	Shares	Amount	Shares	Amount				
Balance October 31, 2007	57,048	$571	(7,028)	$(122,338)	$ 261,182	$ 880	$465,463	$605,758
Comprehensive income:								
Net income	—	—	—	—	—	—	45,434	45,434
Unrealized loss on auction rate securities, net of taxes of $2,348	—	—	—	—	—	(3,621)	—	(3,621)
Foreign currency translation, net of taxes of $590	—	—	—	—	—	(909)	—	(909)
Actuarial gain—adjustments to pension & other post-retirement benefit plans, net of taxes of $148	—	—	—	—	—	228	—	228
Comprehensive income	—	—	—	—	—	—	—	41,132
Dividends:								
Common stock	—	—	—	—	—	—	(25,271)	(25,271)
Tax benefit from exercise of stock options	—	—	—	—	899	—	—	899
Stock issued under employees' stock purchase and option plans	944	10	—	—	14,818	—	(490)	14,338
Share-based compensation expense	—	—	—	—	7,195	—	—	7,195
Balance October 31, 2008	57,992	$581	(7,028)	$(122,338)	$ 284,094	$(3,422)	$485,136	$644,051
Comprehensive income:								
Net income	—	—	—	—	—	—	54,293	54,293
Unrealized gain on auction rate securities, net of taxes of $203	—	—	—	—	—	297	—	297
Reclass adjustment for credit losses recognized in earnings, net of taxes of $636	—	—	—	—	—	930	—	930
Foreign currency translation, net of taxes of $241	—	—	—	—	—	577	—	577
Actuarial loss—adjustments to pension & other post-retirement benefit plans, net of taxes of $139	—	—	—	—	—	(203)	—	(203)
Unrealized loss on interest rate swaps, net of taxes of $412	—	—	—	—	—	(602)	—	(602)
Comprehensive income	—	—	—	—	—	—	—	55,292
Dividends:								
Common stock	—	—	—	—	—	—	(26,727)	(26,727)
Tax benefit from exercise of stock options	—	—	—	—	(1,314)	—	—	(1,314)
Stock issued under employees' stock purchase and option plans	724	6	—	—	8,557	—	(226)	8,337
Share-based compensation expense	—	—	—	—	7,411	—	—	7,411
Treasury stock retirement	(7,028)	(70)	7,028	122,338	(122,268)	—	—	—
Balance October 31, 2009	51,688	$517	—	$ —	$ 176,480	$(2,423)	$512,476	$687,050

ATT-SEC 4.27

NOTES TO CONSOLIDATED FINANCIAL STATEMENTS

2 (In Part): Summary of Significant Accounting Policies

Significant Accounting Policies (In Part)

Investments in Auction Rate Securities

The Company considers its investments in auction rate securities as "available for sale." Accordingly, auction rate securities are presented at fair value with changes in fair value recorded within other comprehensive income, unless a decline in fair value is determined to be other-than-temporary. The credit loss component of an other-than-temporary decline in fair value is recorded in earnings in the period identified. See Note 5, "Auction Rate Securities," for additional information.

Accumulated Other Comprehensive Income (Loss)

Comprehensive income consists of net income and other related gains and losses affecting stockholders' equity that, under generally accepted accounting principles, are excluded from net income. For the Company, such other comprehensive income items consist primarily of unrealized foreign currency translation gains and losses, unrealized gains and losses on auction rate securities, unrealized losses on interest rate swap and actuarial adjustments to pension and other post-retirement benefit plans, net of tax effects.

5. Auction Rate Securities

As of October 31, 2009, the Company held investments in auction rate securities from five different issuers having an original principal amount of $5.0 million each (aggregating $25.0 million). At October 31, 2009 and October 31, 2008, the estimated fair value of these securities, in total, was approximately $19.5 million and $19.0 million, respectively. These auction rate securities are debt instruments with stated maturities ranging from 2025 to 2050, for which the interest rate is designed to be reset through Dutch auctions approximately every 30 days. However, due to events in the U.S. credit markets, auctions for these securities have not occurred since August 2007.

The Company continues to receive the scheduled interest payments from the issuers of the securities. During the first quarter of 2009, one issuer provided a notice of default. This default was cured on March 10, 2009 and all subsequent interest payments have been made by the issuer since that date. The scheduled interest and principal payments of that security are guaranteed by a U.K. financial guarantee insurance company, which made the guaranteed interest payments as scheduled during the first quarter of 2009. In July 2009, a rating agency downgraded its rating of this issuer to below investment grade. The remaining four securities are rated investment grade by rating agencies.

The Company estimates the fair values of auction rate securities it holds utilizing a discounted cash flow model, which considers, among other factors, assumptions about: (1) the underlying collateral; (2) credit risks associated with the issuer; (3) contractual maturity; (4) credit enhancements associated with any financial insurance guarantee, if any, which includes the rating of the associated guarantor, (where applicable); and (5) assumptions about when, if ever, the security might be re-financed by the issuer or have a successful auction (presently assumed to be approximately 4 to 8 years). Since there can be no assurance that auctions for these securities will be successful in the near future, the Company has classified its auction rate securities as long-term investments.

The Company's determination of whether impairments of its auction rate securities are other-than-temporary is based on an evaluation of several factors, circumstances and known or reasonably supportable trends including, but not limited to: (1) the Company's intent to not sell the securities; (2) the Company's assessment that it is not more likely than not that the Company will be required to sell the securities before recovering its costs; (3) expected defaults; (4) the decline in ratings for the auction rate securities or the underlying collateral; (5) the rating of the associated guarantor (where applicable); (6) the nature and value of the underlying collateral expected to service the investment; (7) actual historical performance of the security in servicing its obligations; and (8) actuarial experience of the underlying re-insurance arrangement (where applicable) which in certain circumstances may have preferential rights to the underlying collateral.

Based on the Company's analysis of the above factors, at July 31, 2009 the Company identified an other-than-temporary impairment of $3.6 million for the security whose rating was recently downgraded to below investment grade, of which a credit loss of $1.6 million was recognized in earnings with a corresponding reduction in the cost basis of that security. The credit loss was based upon the difference between the present value of the cash flows expected to be collected and its amortized cost basis. Significant assumptions used in estimating the credit loss include: (1) default rates (which were based on published historical default rates of similar securities and consideration of current market trends) and (2) the expected term of 8 years (which represents the Company's view of when market efficiency for that security may be restored). Adverse changes in any of these factors above could result in further material declines in fair value and additional other-than-temporary impairments in the future. No further other-than-temporary impairments were identified.

The following table provides the changes in the cost basis and fair value of the Company's auction rate securities for the years ended October 31, 2009 and 2008:

(In thousands)	Cost Basis	Fair Value (Level 3)
Balance at beginning of year	$25,000	$19,031
Unrealized gains	—	2,544
Unrealized losses	—	(2,044)
Other-than-temporary credit loss recognized in earnings	(1,566)	—
Balance at October 31, 2009	$23,434	$19,531
Balance at beginning of year	$25,000	$25,000
Unrealized gains	—	—
Unrealized losses	—	(5,969)
Balance at October 31, 2008	$25,000	$19,031

The other-than-temporary impairment ("OTTI") related to credit losses recognized in earnings for the year ended October 31, 2009 is as follows:

(In thousands)	Beginning Balance of OTTI Credit Losses Recognized for the Auction Rate Security Held at the Beginning of the Period for Which a Portion of OTTI Was Recognized in OCI	Additions for the Amount Related to Credit Loss for Which OTTI Was Not Previously Recognized	Additional Increases to the Amount Related to Credit Loss for Which an OTTI Was Previously Recognized	Reductions for Increases in Cash Flows Expected to Be Collected That Are Recognized Over the Remaining Life of the Security	Ending Balance of the Amount Related to Credit Losses Held at the End of the Period for Which a Portion of OTTI Was Recognized in OCI
OTTI credit loss recognized for auction rate security	$—	$1,566	$—	$—	$1,566

At October 31, 2009 and October 31, 2008, unrealized losses of $3.9 million ($2.3 million net of tax) and $6.0 million ($3.6 million net of tax) were recorded in accumulated other comprehensive loss, respectively.

ATT-SEC 4.27

4.28

INTERNATIONAL BUSINESS MACHINES CORPORATION (DEC)

Consolidated Statement of Changes in Equity

($ in millions)	Common Stock and Additional Paid-In Capital	Retained Earnings	Treasury Stock	Accumulated Other Comprehensive Income/(Loss)	Total IBM Stockholders' Equity	Non-Controlling Interests	Total Equity
2007							
Equity, January 1, 2007	$31,271	$52,432	$(46,296)	$(8,901)	$ 28,506	$129	$ 28,635
Cumulative effect of change in accounting principle		117			117		117
Net income plus other comprehensive income/(loss):							
Net income		10,418			$ 10,418		$ 10,418
Other comprehensive income/(loss), net of tax:							
Net unrealized gains/(losses) on cash flow hedge derivatives (net of tax benefit of $32)				(123)	(123)		(123)
Foreign currency translation adjustments (net of tax benefit of $553)				726	726		726
Retirement-related benefit plans:							
Prior service costs/(credits) (net of tax expense of $31)				44	44		44
Net gains/(losses) (net of tax expense of $1,913)				3,611	3,611		3,611
Amortization of prior service costs/(credits) (net of tax benefit of $50)				(85)	(85)		(85)
Amortization of net gains/(losses) (net of tax expense of $654)				1,110	1,110		1,110
Amortization of transition assets (net of tax benefit of $1)				(2)	(2)		(2)
Net unrealized gains/(losses) on marketable securities (net of tax expense of $132)				206	206		206
Total other comprehensive income/(loss)					5,487		5,487
Subtotal: net income plus other comprehensive income/(loss)					$ 15,905		$ 15,905
Cash dividends declared–common stock		(2,147)			(2,147)		(2,147)
Common stock issued under employee plans (49,137,038 shares)	4,332				4,332		4,332
Purchases (1,282,131 shares) and sales (9,282,055 shares) of treasury stock under employee plans–net		(179)	729		550		550
Other treasury shares purchased, not retired (178,385,436 shares)	(405)		(18,378)		(18,783)		(18,783)
Changes in other equity	(10)				(10)		(10)
Changes in noncontrolling interests						16	16
Equity, December 31, 2007	$35,188	$60,640	$(63,945)	$(3,414)	$ 28,470	$145	$ 28,615

($ in millions)	Common Stock and Additional Paid-In Capital	Retained Earnings	Treasury Stock	Accumulated Other Comprehensive Income/(Loss)	Total IBM Stockholders' Equity	Non-Controlling Interests	Total Equity
2008							
Equity, January 1, 2008	$35,188	$60,640	$(63,945)	$ (3,414)	$ 28,470	$145	$ 28,615
Net income plus other comprehensive income/(loss):							
Net income		12,334			$ 12,334		$ 12,334
Other comprehensive income/(loss), net of tax:							
Net unrealized gains/(losses) on cash flow hedge derivatives (net of tax expense of $79)				301	301		301
Foreign currency translation adjustments (net of tax benefit of $153)				(3,552)	(3,552)		(3,552)
Retirement-related benefit plans:							
Prior service (credits)/costs (net of tax benefit of $86)				(136)	(136)		(136)
Net (losses)/gains (net of tax benefit of $8,436)				(15,245)	(15,245)		(15,245)
Curtailments and settlements (net of tax expense of $9)				16	16		16
Amortization of prior service (credits)/costs (net of tax benefit of $73)				(132)	(132)		(132)
Amortization of net gains/(losses) (net of tax expense of $358)				640	640		640
Net unrealized gains/(losses) on marketable securities (net of tax benefit of $207)				(324)	(324)		(324)
Total other comprehensive income/(loss)					(18,431)		(18,431)
Subtotal: net income plus other comprehensive income/(loss)					$ (6,097)		$ (6,097)
Cash dividends declared–common stock		(2,585)			(2,585)		(2,585)
Common stock issued under employee plans (39,374,439 shares)	3,919				3,919		3,919
Purchases (1,505,107 shares) and sales (5,882,800 shares) of treasury stock under employee plans–net		(36)	391		355		355
Other treasury shares purchased, not retired (89,890,347 shares)	54		(10,618)		(10,563)		(10,563)
Changes in other equity	(33)				(33)		(33)
Changes in noncontrolling interests						(26)	(26)
Equity, December 31, 2008	$39,129	$70,353	$(74,171)	$(21,845)	$ 13,465	$119	$ 13,584

ATT-SEC 4.28

($ in millions)	Common Stock and Additional Paid-In Capital	Retained Earnings	Treasury Stock	Accumulated Other Comprehensive Income/(Loss)	Total IBM Stockholders' Equity	Non-Controlling Interests	Total Equity
2009							
Equity, January 1, 2009	$39,129	$70,353	$(74,171)	$(21,845)	$13,465	$119	$13,584
Net income plus other comprehensive income/(loss):							
Net income		13,425			$13,425		$13,425
Other comprehensive income/(loss), net of tax:							
Net unrealized gains/(losses) on cash flow hedge derivatives (net of tax benefit of $256)				(556)	(556)		(556)
Foreign currency translation adjustments (net of tax benefit of $57)				1,732	1,732		1,732
Retirement-related benefit plans:							
Prior service costs/(credits) (net of tax expense of $146)				229	229		229
Net (losses)/gains (net of tax expense of $439)				994	994		994
Curtailments and settlements (net of tax benefit of $33)				(93)	(93)		(93)
Amortization of prior service (credits)/costs (net of tax benefit of $55)				(107)	(107)		(107)
Amortization of net gains/(losses) (net of tax expense of $402)				704	704		704
Net unrealized gains/(losses) on marketable securities (net of tax expense of $71)				111	111		111
Total other comprehensive income/(loss)					3,015		3,015
Subtotal: net income plus other comprehensive income/(loss)					$16,440		$16,440
Cash dividends declared—common stock		(2,860)			(2,860)		(2,860)
Common stock issued under employee plans (30,034,808 shares)	3,011				3,011		3,011
Purchases (1,550,846 shares) and sales (6,408,265 shares) of treasury stock under employee plans—net		(19)	462		443		443
Other treasury shares purchased, not retired (68,650,727 shares)			(7,534)		(7,534)		(7,534)
Changes in other equity	(330)				(330)		(330)
Changes in noncontrolling interests						(1)	(1)
Equity, December 31, 2009	$41,810	$80,900	$(81,243)	$(18,830)	$22,637	$118	$22,755

NOTES TO CONSOLIDATED FINANCIAL STATEMENTS

Note A (In Part): Significant Accounting Policies

Financial Instruments

In determining the fair value of its financial instruments, the company uses a variety of methods and assumptions that are based on market conditions and risks existing at each balance sheet date. Refer to note E, "Financial Instruments (Excluding Derivatives)," for further information. All methods of assessing fair value result in a general approximation of value, and such value may never actually be realized.

Marketable Securities

Debt securities included in current assets represent securities that are expected to be realized in cash within one year of the balance sheet date. Long-term debt securities that are not expected to be realized in cash within one year and alliance equity securities are included in investments and sundry assets. Debt and marketable equity securities are considered available for sale and are reported at fair value with unrealized gains and losses, net of applicable taxes, recorded in other comprehensive income/(loss), a component of equity. The realized gains and losses for available for sale securities are included in other (income) and expense in the Consolidated Statement of Earnings. Realized gains and losses are calculated based on the specific identification method.

In determining whether an other-than-temporary decline in market value has occurred, the company considers the duration that, and extent to which, the fair value of the investment is below its cost, the financial condition and near-term prospects of the issuer or underlying collateral of a security; and the company's intent and ability to retain the security in order to allow for an anticipated recovery in fair value. Other-than-temporary declines in fair value from amortized cost for available for sale equity and debt securities that the company intends to sell or would more-likely-than-not be required to sell before the expected recovery of the amortized cost basis are charged to other (income) and expense in the period in which the loss occurs. For debt securities that the company has no intent to sell and believes that it more-likely-than-not will not be required to sell prior to recovery, only the credit loss component of the impairment is recognized in other (income) and expense, while the remaining loss is recognized in other comprehensive income/(loss). The credit loss component recognized in other (income) and expense is identified as the amount of the principal cash flows not expected to be received over the remaining term of the debt security as projected using the company's cash flow projections.

Note E (In Part): Financial Instruments (Excluding Derivatives)

Debt and Marketable Equity Securities

The following table summarizes the company's debt and marketable equity securities all of which are considered available-for-sale and recorded at fair value in the Consolidated Statement of Financial Position.

	Fair Value	
($ in millions)	2009	2008
Cash and cash equivalents:		
Time deposits and certificates of deposit	$4,324	$ 4,805
Commercial paper	2,099	3,194
Money market funds	2,780	1,950
Other securities	74	60
Total	$9,277	$10,009
Debt securities—current:		
Commercial paper	$1,491	$ 166
Securities of U.S. Federal government and its agencies	300	—
Total	$1,791	$ 166
Debt securities—noncurrent:		
Other securities	$ 9	$ 6
Total	$ 9	$ 6
Non-equity method alliance investments	$ 374	$ 165

Gross unrealized gains (before taxes) on debt securities were less than $1 million and $1 million at December 31, 2009 and 2008, respectively. Gross unrealized gains (before taxes) on marketable equity securities were $201 million and $31 million at December 31, 2009 and 2008, respectively. Gross unrealized losses (before taxes) on debt securities were less than $1 million at December 31, 2009 and 2008. Gross unrealized losses (before taxes) on marketable equity securities were $10 million and $27 million at December 31, 2009 and 2008, respectively. Based on an evaluation of available evidence as of December 31, 2009, the company believes that unrealized losses on marketable equity securities are temporary and do not represent a need for an other-than-temporary impairment. See note N, "Equity Activity," on pages 98 and 99 for net change in unrealized gains and losses on debt and marketable equity securities.

Proceeds from sales of debt securities and marketable equity securities were approximately $24 million and $787 million during 2009 and 2008, respectively. The gross realized gains and losses (before taxes) on these sales totaled $3 million and $40 million, respectively in 2009. The gross realized gains and losses (before taxes) on these sales totaled $182 million and $13 million, respectively, in 2008.

The contractual maturities of substantially all available-for-sale debt securities are due in less than one year at December 31, 2009.

Note N (In Part): Equity Activity

Accumulated Other Comprehensive Income/(Loss)
(Net of Tax)

($ in millions)	Net Unrealized Gains/(Losses) on Cash Flow Hedge Derivatives	Foreign Currency Translation Adjustments	Net Change Retirement-Related Benefit Plans	Net Unrealized Gains/(Losses) on Marketable Securities	Accumulated Other Comprehensive Income/(Loss)
December 31, 2007	$(227)	$ 3,655	$ (7,168)	$ 325	$ (3,414)
Change for period	301	(3,552)	(14,856)	(324)	(18,431)
December 31, 2008	74	103	(22,025)	2	(21,845)
Change for period	(556)	1,732	1,727	111	3,015
December 31, 2009	$(481)	$ 1,836	$(20,297)	$ 113	$(18,830)

Net Change in Unrealized Gains/(Losses) on Marketable Securities (Net of Tax)

($ in millions)	2009	2008
Net unrealized gains/(losses) arising during the period	$ 72	$(224)
Less: net (losses)/gains included in net income for the period*	(39)	100
Net change in unrealized gains/(losses) on marketable securities	$111	$(324)

* Includes writedowns of $16.2 million and $3.0 million in 2009 and 2008, respectively.

Reclassification Adjustments

4.29

PACTIV CORPORATION (DEC)

Consolidated Statement of Comprehensive Income (Loss)

(In millions)	2009	2008	2007
Net income	$324	$ 217	$246
Other comprehensive income (loss)			
Pension and postretirement plans	(40)	(795)	178
Net currency translation gain (loss)	13	(39)	16
Gain (loss) on derivatives	(1)	(1)	8
Total other comprehensive income (loss)	(28)	(835)	202
Consolidated comprehensive income (loss)	296	(618)	448
Comprehensive income (loss) attributable to the noncontrolling interest	1	2	3
Comprehensive income (loss) attributable to Pactiv	$295	$(620)	$445

NOTES TO FINANCIAL STATEMENTS

Note 2 (In Part): Summary of Accounting Policies

Risk Management

From time to time, we use derivative financial instruments to hedge our exposure to changes in foreign currency exchange rates, principally using foreign currency purchase and sale contracts with terms of less than 1 year. We do so to mitigate our exposure to exchange rate changes related to third-party trade receivables and accounts payable. Net gains or losses on such contracts are recognized in the statement of income as offsets to foreign currency exchange gains or losses on the underlying transactions. In the statement of cash flows, cash receipts and payments related to hedging contracts are classified in the same way as cash flows from the transactions being hedged. We had no open foreign currency contracts as of December 31, 2009.

Interest rate risk management is accomplished through the use of swaps. Interest rate swaps are booked at their fair value at each reporting date, with an equal offset recorded either in earnings or accumulated other comprehensive income depending on the designation (or lack thereof) of each swap as a hedging instrument.

From time to time, we employ commodity forward or other derivative contracts to hedge our exposure to adverse changes in the price of certain commodities used in our production processes. We do not use derivative financial instruments for speculative purposes. See Note 7 for additional information.

Note 7 (In Part): Financial Instruments

Instruments With Off-Balance Sheet Risk (Including Derivatives)

We use derivative instruments, principally swaps, forward contracts, and options, to manage our exposure to movements in foreign currency values, interest rates, and commodity prices.

Cash Flow Hedges

For derivative instruments that are designated and qualify as cash flow hedges, the effective portion of the gain or loss on the derivative is reported as a component of other comprehensive income (OCI) and reclassified into earnings in the same period or periods in which the hedged transaction affects earnings. Financial instruments designated as cash flow hedges are assessed both at inception and quarterly thereafter to ensure they are effective in offsetting changes in the cash flows of the related underlying exposures. The fair value of the hedge instruments are reclassified from OCI to earnings if the hedge ceases to be highly effective or if the hedged transaction is no longer probable.

Foreign Currency

From time to time, we use derivative financial instruments to hedge our exposure to changes in foreign currency exchange rates, principally using foreign currency purchase and sale contracts with terms of less than one year. We do so to mitigate our exposure to exchange rate changes related to third-party trade receivables and accounts payable. Net gains or losses on such contracts are recognized in the statement of income as offsets to foreign currency exchange gains or losses on the underlying transactions. In the statement of cash flows, cash receipts and payments related to hedging contracts are classified in the same way as cash flows from the transactions being hedged. We had no open foreign currency contracts as of December 31, 2009.

Interest Rates

We entered into interest rate swap agreements in connection with the acquisition of Prairie. The agreements were terminated on June 20, 2007, resulting in a gain of $9 million. This gain is being recorded as a reduction of interest expense over the average life of the underlying debt. Amounts recognized in earnings related to our hedging transactions were $1 million for the year ended December 31, 2009, and December 31, 2008.

Commodity

During the fourth quarter of 2009, we entered into natural gas purchase agreements with third parties, hedging a portion of the first half of 2010 purchases of natural gas used in the production processes at certain of our plants. These purchase agreements are marked to market, with the resulting gains or losses recognized in earnings when hedged transactions are recorded. The mark-to-market adjustments at December 31, 2009, were immaterial.

To minimize volatility in our margins due to large fluctuations in the price of commodities, in the second quarter of 2009 we entered into swap contracts to manage risks associated with market fluctuations in resin prices. These contracts were designated as cash flow hedges of forecasted commodity purchases. All monthly swap contracts entered into in the third quarter of 2009 have expired. There were no contracts outstanding as of December 31, 2009, and no gains are expected to be reclassified to earnings in the first quarter of 2010.

Fair Value Measurements (In Part)

There were no outstanding derivative instruments recorded in the consolidated balance sheet as of December 31, 2009, and as of December 31, 2008.

The following table indicates the amounts recognized in OCI for those derivatives designated as cash flow hedges for the years ended December 31, 2009, and 2008.

(In millions)	Gain or (Loss) Recognized in OCI (Effective Portion)		Location of Gain or (Loss) Reclassified From OCI Into Income (Effective Portion)	(Gain) or Loss Reclassified From OCI Into Income (Effective Portion)	
	2009	2008		2009	2008
Commodity contracts	$—	$—	Cost of sales	$(2)	$—
Interest rate contracts	$—	$—	Interest expense	$(1)	$(1)

There were no transactions that ceased to qualify as a cash flow hedge in the years ended December 31, 2009, or 2008.

4.30

ROCK-TENN COMPANY (SEP)

Consolidated Statements of Shareholders' Equity

(In millions, except share and per share data)	2009	2008	2007
Number of Class A common shares outstanding:			
Balance at beginning of year	38,228,523	37,988,779	37,688,522
Shares granted under restricted stock plan	194,885	25,000	165,497
Restricted stock grants forfeited	(26,499)	(59,499)	—
Issuance of Class A common stock, net of stock received for minimum tax withholdings	310,786	274,243	2,278,460
Purchases of Class A common stock	—	—	(2,143,700)
Balance at end of year	38,707,695	38,228,523	37,988,779
Class A common stock:			
Balance at beginning of year	$ 0.4	$ 0.4	$ 0.4
Balance at end of year	$ 0.4	$ 0.4	$ 0.4
Capital in excess of par value:			
Balance at beginning of year	$ 238.8	$ 222.6	$ 179.6
Income tax benefit from share-based plans	5.5	1.8	14.1
Compensation expense under share-based plans	11.9	9.2	7.3
Issuance of Class A common stock, net of stock received for minimum tax withholdings	8.3	5.2	33.6
Purchases of Class A common stock	—	—	(12.0)
Balance at end of year	$ 264.5	$ 238.8	$ 222.6
Retained earnings:			
Balance at beginning of year	$ 421.7	$ 357.8	$ 341.2
Net income	222.3	81.8	81.7
Impact of adopting certain provisions of ASC 740 (as hereinafter defined)	—	(1.8)	—
Cash dividends (per share—$0.40, $0.40 and $0.39)	(15.3)	(15.2)	(15.4)
Issuance of Class A common stock, net of stock received for minimum tax withholdings	(8.4)	(0.9)	(3.0)
Purchases of Class A common stock	—	—	(46.7)
Balance at end of year	$ 620.3	$ 421.7	$ 357.8
Accumulated other comprehensive (loss) income:			
Balance at beginning of year	$ (20.4)	$ 8.2	$ (12.6)
Foreign currency translation (loss) gain	(2.1)	(12.0)	14.0
Net deferred (loss) gain on cash flow hedge derivatives	(16.7)	1.9	(0.4)
Reclassification adjustment of net loss (gain) on cash flow hedge derivatives included in earnings	5.2	0.6	(2.5)
Pension liability adjustments, prior to adoption of certain provisions of ASC 715	—	—	24.0
Net actuarial loss arising during period	(78.6)	(21.2)	—
Amortization of net actuarial loss	4.5	2.0	—
Prior service cost arising during period	(1.0)	(0.1)	—
Amortization of prior service cost	0.7	0.2	—
Net other comprehensive (loss) income adjustments, net of tax	(88.0)	(28.6)	35.1
Impact of adopting certain provisions of ASC 715	—	—	(14.3)
Balance at end of year	$ (108.4)	$ (20.4)	$ 8.2
Total shareholders' equity	$ 776.8	$ 640.5	$ 589.0
Comprehensive income:			
Net income	$ 222.3	$ 81.8	$ 81.7
Net other comprehensive (loss) income adjustments, net of tax	(88.0)	(28.6)	35.1
Total comprehensive income	$ 134.3	$ 53.2	$ 116.8

NOTES TO CONSOLIDATED FINANCIAL STATEMENTS

Note 1 (In Part): Summary of Significant Accounting Policies

Derivatives

We are exposed to interest rate risk, commodity price risk, and foreign currency exchange risk. To manage these risks, from time-to-time and to varying degrees, we enter into a variety of financial derivative transactions and certain physical commodity transactions that are determined to be derivatives. Interest rate swaps may be entered into in order to manage the interest rate risk associated with a portion of our outstanding debt. Interest rate swaps are either designated as cash flow hedges of floating rate debt or fair value hedges of fixed rate debt, or we may elect not to treat them as accounting hedges. Forward contracts on certain commodities may be entered into to manage the price risk associated with forecasted purchases of those commodities. In addition, certain commodity derivative contracts and physical commodity contracts that are determined to be derivatives are not designated as accounting hedges because either they do not meet the criteria for treatment as accounting hedges under ASC 815, "Derivatives and Hedging," or we elect not to treat them as hedges under ASC 815. We may also enter into forward contracts to manage our exposure to fluctuations in Canadian foreign currency rates with respect to our receivables denominated in Canadian dollars.

Outstanding financial derivative instruments expose us to credit loss in the event of nonperformance by the counterparties to the agreements. However, we do not expect any of the counterparties to fail to meet their obligations. Our credit exposure related to these financial instruments is represented by the fair value of contracts reported as assets. We manage our exposure to counterparty credit risk through minimum credit standards, diversification of counterparties and procedures to monitor concentrations of credit risk.

For derivative instruments that are designated as a cash flow hedge, the effective portion of the gain or loss on the derivative instrument is reported as a component of other comprehensive income and reclassified into earnings in the same line item associated with the forecasted hedged transaction, and in the same period or periods during which the forecasted hedged transaction affects earnings. Gains and losses on the derivative representing either hedge ineffectiveness or hedge components excluded from the assessment of effectiveness are recognized in current earnings.

For derivative instruments that are designated and qualify as a fair value hedge, the gain or loss on the derivative instrument as well as the offsetting loss or gain on the hedged item attributable to the hedged risk are recognized in the same line item associated with the hedged item in current earnings. We amortize the adjustment to the carrying value of our fixed rate debt instruments that arose from previously terminated fair value hedges to interest expense using the effective interest method over the remaining life of the related debt.

For derivative instruments not designated as accounting hedges, the gain or loss is recognized in current earnings.

Note 3. Other Comprehensive (Loss) Income

Accumulated other comprehensive loss is comprised of the following, net of taxes (in millions):

	2009	2008
Foreign currency translation gain	$ 35.4	$ 37.5
Net deferred (loss) gain on cash flow hedge derivatives	(7.8)	3.7
Unrecognized pension net loss	(133.5)	(59.4)
Unrecognized pension prior service cost	(2.5)	(2.2)
Total accumulated other comprehensive loss	$(108.4)	$(20.4)

A summary of the components of other comprehensive (loss) income for the years ended September 30, 2009, 2008 and 2007, is as follows (in millions):

	Pre-Tax Amount	Tax	Net of Tax Amount
Fiscal 2009			
Foreign currency translation loss	$ (2.1)	$ —	$ (2.1)
Net deferred loss on cash flow hedge derivatives	(27.3)	10.6	(16.7)
Reclassification adjustment of net loss on cash flow hedge derivatives included in earnings	8.4	(3.2)	5.2
Net actuarial loss arising during period	(121.3)	42.7	(78.6)
Amortization of net actuarial loss	7.4	(2.9)	4.5
Prior service cost arising during period	(1.5)	0.5	(1.0)
Amortization of prior service cost	1.2	(0.5)	0.7
Other comprehensive loss	$(135.2)	$ 47.2	$(88.0)
Fiscal 2008			
Foreign currency translation loss	$ (12.0)	$ —	$(12.0)
Net deferred gain on cash flow hedge derivatives	3.2	(1.3)	1.9
Reclassification adjustment of net loss on cash flow hedge derivatives included in earnings	1.0	(0.4)	0.6
Net actuarial loss arising during period	(35.3)	14.1	(21.2)
Amortization of net actuarial loss	3.2	(1.2)	2.0
Prior service cost arising during period	(0.2)	0.1	(0.1)
Amortization of prior service cost	0.4	(0.2)	0.2
Other comprehensive loss	$ (39.7)	$ 11.1	$(28.6)
Fiscal 2007			
Foreign currency translation gain	$ 14.0	$ —	$14.0
Net deferred loss on cash flow hedge derivatives	(0.7)	0.3	(0.4)
Reclassification adjustment of net gain on cash flow hedge derivatives included in earnings	(4.0)	1.5	(2.5)
Pension liability adjustments, prior to adoption of certain provisions of ASC 715	39.1	(15.1)	24.0
Other comprehensive income	$ 48.4	$(13.3)	$ 35.1

Note 12 (In Part): Derivatives

Cash Flow Hedges

We have entered into interest rate swap agreements that effectively modify our exposure to interest rate risk by converting a portion of our floating rate debt to a fixed rate basis, thus reducing the impact of interest rate changes on future interest expense. These agreements involve the receipt of floating rate amounts in exchange for fixed interest rate payments over the life of the agreements without an exchange of the underlying principal amount. We have designated these swaps as cash flow hedges of the interest rate exposure on an equivalent amount of certain variable rate debt. In October 2007, we paid $3.5 million to terminate all of our then open interest rate swaps. In January 2008 we entered into floating-to-fixed interest rate swaps that we terminated in June 2008 and received proceeds of $10.4 million. As of September 30, 2009, our interest rate swap agreements, which terminate in April 2012, require that we pay fixed rates of approximately 4.00% and receive the one-month LIBOR rate on the notional amounts. As of September 30, 2009, the aggregate notional amount of outstanding debt related to these interest rate swaps was $452 million, declining at periodic intervals through April 2012 to an aggregate notional amount of $132 million. During fiscal 2008, we reclassified net pre-tax deferred losses of $1.2 million from accumulated other comprehensive income to earnings as a result of the discontinuance of certain commodity derivative cash flow hedges because it was probable the related forecasted transactions being hedged would not occur. During fiscal 2007, we recognized a net pre-tax loss of $1.2 million in earnings due to ineffectiveness of certain commodity derivative cash flow hedges; and we reclassified net pre-tax deferred gains of $4.0 million related to certain interest rate derivative cash flow hedges from accumulated other comprehensive income to earnings as a reduction of interest expense.

As of September 30, 2009 and September 30, 2008, we had the following outstanding commodity derivatives that were entered into to hedge forecasted sales:

Commodity	2009		2008	
	Notional Amount	Unit	Notional Amount	Unit
Paperboard, net	33,000	Tons	—	Tons

Fair Value Hedges

Prior to June 2005, we had a series of interest rate swaps that effectively converted our fixed rate debt to floating rates, thus hedging the fair value of the related fixed rate debt from changes in market interest rates. These interest rate swaps were terminated prior to maturity. The value at termination of these swaps is being amortized to interest expense over the remaining life of the related debt using the effective interest method. During each of fiscal 2009, 2008, and 2007, $1.9 million was amortized to earnings as a reduction of interest expense. In connection with our May 29, 2009 purchase of $93.3 million of tendered August 2011 Notes, $1.0 million, representing the proportionate amount of unamortized gain on previously terminated interest rate swaps associated with the extinguished debt, was reclassified to earnings as a component of loss on extinguishment of debt and related items.

• • • • • •

The following table summarizes the location and amount of gains and losses on derivative instruments in the Consolidated Statements of Income segregated by type of contract and designation for the year ended September 30, (in millions):

Derivatives in Cash Flow Hedging Relationships	Amount of Gain (Loss) Recognized in OCI on Derivative (Effective Portion)		Location of Gain (Loss) Reclassified From Accumulated OCI Into Income (Effective Portion)	Amount of Gain (Loss) Reclassified From Accumulated OCI Into Income (Effective Portion)		Location of Gain (Loss) Recognized in Income on Derivative (Ineffective Portion and Amount Excluded From Effectiveness Testing)	Amount of Gain (Loss) Recognized in Income on Derivative (Ineffective Portion and Amount Excluded From Effectiveness Testing)	
	2009	2008		2009	2008		2009	2008
Interest rate derivatives	$(27.8)	$2.1	Interest expense	$(8.4)	$ 0.3	N/A	$ —	$—
Commodity derivatives	—	—	Interest income and other income (expense)	—	(0.1)	N/A	—	—
Commodity derivatives	—	—	Cost of goods sold	—	(0.1)	N/A	—	—
Commodity derivatives	0.5	1.1	Net sales	—	(1.1)	Net sales	0.1	—
Total	$(27.3)	$3.2		$(8.4)	$(1.0)		$0.1	$—

• • • • • •

As of September 30, 2009, based on implied forward interest rates associated with our outstanding interest rate derivative cash flow hedges and the remaining amounts in accumulated other comprehensive income related to terminated interest rate swaps, we expect to reclassify net pre-tax deferred losses of approximately $9.6 million from accumulated other comprehensive income into earnings as an increase to interest expense within the next twelve months as the probable hedged interest payments occur. As of September 30, 2009, based on implied forward price curves associated with certain commodity derivative cash flow hedges, we expect to reclassify approximately $0.5 million from accumulated comprehensive income to earnings as an increase to net sales within the next twelve months as the probable hedged transactions occur. We believe amounts in accumulated other comprehensive income related to interest rate derivatives and commodity derivatives are appropriately recorded in accumulated other comprehensive income because the forecasted transactions related to those amounts are probable of occurring.

We enter into derivative contracts that may contain credit-risk-related contingent features which could result in a counterparty requesting immediate payment or demand immediate and ongoing full overnight collateralization on derivative instruments in net liability positions. Certain of our interest rate swap derivative contracts contain a provision whereby if we default on the Credit Facility, we may also be deemed in default of the interest rate swap obligation. The aggregate fair value of interest rate swaps under these agreements that are in a liability position at September 30, 2009 is approximately $18.3 million. These interest rate swaps share the same collateral as that of our Credit Facility and no other collateral has been posted against these interest rate swap obligations. If we were to default on these agreements, we may be required to settle our obligations at their termination value of approximately $18.6 million. Certain of our commodity derivative contracts contain contingent provisions that require us to provide the counterparty with collateral if the credit rating on our debt, as provided by major credit rating agencies, falls below certain specified minimums, or if the fair value of our obligation exceeds specified threshold amounts. The aggregate fair value of all commodity derivative instruments with credit-risk-related contingent features that are in a liability position at September 30, 2009, is approximately $0.7 million. We have posted collateral in the form of a letter of credit of approximately $1 million against one of these positions, which was triggered by the related obligation exceeding a specified threshold amount. If additional credit-risk-related contingent features underlying these commodity derivative agreements were triggered, we may be required to settle our obligations under the agreements at their termination value, which was $0.7 million at September 30, 2009.

Section 5: Stockholders' Equity

GENERAL

5.01   This section reviews the presentation of transactions, other than comprehensive income (loss) for the year, affecting stockholders' equity.

RETAINED EARNINGS

PRESENTATION OF CHANGES IN RETAINED EARNINGS

5.02   A statement of income and a statement of retained earnings are designed to reflect results of operations. As shown in Table 5-1, which summarizes the presentation formats used by the survey entities to present changes in retained earnings, changes in retained earnings are most frequently presented in a Statement of Stockholders' Equity. Examples of statements showing changes in retained earnings are presented throughout this section.

5.03

TABLE 5-1: PRESENTATION OF CHANGES IN RETAINED EARNINGS

	2009	2008	2007	2006
Statement of stockholders' equity	490	490	589	588
Separate statement of retained earnings	2	3	3	3
Combined statement of income and retained earnings	2	2	2	3
Schedule in notes	6	5	6	6
Total Entities	**500**	**500**	**600**	**600**

2008–2009 based on 500 entities surveyed; 2006–2007 based on 600 entities surveyed.

DIVIDENDS

5.04   Table 5-2 shows the nature of distributions made by the survey entities to their shareholders. Approximately 54% of the survey entities paying cash dividends to common stock shareholders indicate the per share amount of such dividends in the statement of retained earnings; approximately 32% of the survey entities made a similar disclosure for cash dividends paid to preferred stock shareholders.

5.05   Certain stock purchase rights enable the holders of such rights to purchase additional equity in an entity if an outside party acquires or tenders for a substantial minority interest in the subject entity.

5.06   Examples of distributions to shareholders follow.

5.07

TABLE 5-2: DIVIDENDS

	Number of Entities			
	2009	2008	2007	2006
Cash Dividends Paid to Common Stock Shareholders				
Per share amount disclosed in retained earnings statements	176	201	217	223
Per share amount not disclosed in retained earnings statements	152	145	175	176
Total	**328**	**346**	**392**	**399**
Cash Dividends Paid to Preferred Stock Shareholders				
Per share amount disclosed in retained earnings statements	7	9	12	13
Per share amount not disclosed in retained earnings statements	15	19	25	34
Total	**22**	**28**	**37**	**47**
Stock Dividends	—	—	1	3
Dividends in Kind	3	7	3	3
Stock Purchase Rights Plan Adopted/Extended	12	9	13	9

2008–2009 based on 500 entities surveyed; 2006–2007 based on 600 entities surveyed.

Cash Dividends

5.08

FMC CORPORATION (DEC)

(In millions except share data)	Common Stock, $0.10 Par Value	Capital in Excess of Par	Retained Earnings	Accumulated Other Comprehensive Income (Loss)	Treasury Stock	Noncontrolling Interest	Total Equity
	FMC Stockholders'						
Balance December 31, 2006	$9.3	$426.3	$1,157.1	$ (57.1)	$(525.4)	$ 59.0	$1,069.2
Net income			132.4			9.6	142.0
Stock compensation plans		(18.8)			37.3		18.5
Shares for benefit plan trust					(0.3)		(0.3)
Reclassification adjustments for losses (gains) included in net income, net of income tax expense of $11.4				17.6			17.6
Net unrealized pension and other benefit actuarial gains/(losses) and prior service cost credits, net of income tax benefit of $2.7				(2.6)			(2.6)
Net deferral of hedging gains (losses) and other, net of income tax benefit of $1.2				(1.4)			(1.4)
Foreign currency translation adjustments				33.6			33.6
Dividends ($0.405 per share)			(30.9)				(30.9)
Adjustment to initially apply new U.S. tax accounting guidance as of January 1, 2007			(2.8)				(2.8)
Repurchases of common stock					(110.0)		(110.0)
Distributions to noncontrolling interests						(10.2)	(10.2)
Balance December 31, 2007	$9.3	$407.5	$1,255.8	$ (9.9)	$(598.4)	$ 58.4	$1,122.7
Net income			304.6			17.0	321.6
Stock compensation plans		(12.0)			34.1		22.1
Shares for benefit plan trust					(1.0)		(1.0)
Reclassification adjustments for losses (gains) included in net income, net of income tax expense of $1.7				0.9			0.9
Net unrealized pension and other benefit actuarial gains/(losses) and prior service cost credits, net of income tax benefit of $116.6				(190.9)			(190.9)
Net deferral of hedging gains (losses) and other, net of income tax benefit of $17.8				(31.7)			(31.7)
Foreign currency translation adjustments				(44.5)		0.6	(43.9)
Dividends ($0.48 per share)			(35.7)				(35.7)
Repurchases of common stock					(185.2)		(185.2)
Distributions to noncontrolling interests						(12.5)	(12.5)
Balance December 31, 2008	$9.3	$395.5	$1,524.7	$(276.1)	$(750.5)	$ 63.5	$ 966.4

(continued)

(In millions except share data)	FMC Stockholders'						
	Common Stock, $0.10 Par Value	Capital in Excess of Par	Retained Earnings	Accumulated Other Comprehensive Income (Loss)	Treasury Stock	Noncontrolling Interest	Total Equity
Balance December 31, 2008	$9.3	$395.5	$1,524.7	$(276.1)	$(750.5)	$ 63.5	$ 966.4
Net income			228.5			10.3	238.8
Stock compensation plans		(7.3)			26.9		19.6
Shares for benefit plan trust					(0.6)		(0.6)
Reclassification adjustments for losses (gains) included in net income, net of income tax expense of $16.2				25.4			25.4
Net unrealized pension and other benefit actuarial gains/(losses) and prior service cost credits, net of income tax benefit of $28.6				(53.5)			(53.5)
Net deferral of hedging gains (losses) and other, net of income tax expense of $3.0				7.6			7.6
Acquisition of noncontrolling interest		0.4				(3.2)	(2.8)
Foreign currency translation adjustments				17.4		(0.5)	16.9
Dividends ($0.50 per share)			(36.3)				(36.3)
Repurchases of common stock					(35.0)		(35.0)
Distributions to noncontrolling interests						(13.4)	(13.4)
Balance December 31, 2009	$9.3	$388.6	$1,716.9	$(279.2)	$(759.2)	$ 56.7	$1,133.1

NOTES TO CONSOLIDATED FINANCIAL STATEMENTS

Note 15 (In Part): Equity

On January 21, 2010, we paid dividends aggregating $9.1 million to our shareholders of record as of December 31, 2009. This amount is included in "Accrued and other liabilities" on the consolidated balance sheets as of December 31, 2009. For the years ended December 31, 2009, 2008 and 2007, we paid $36.3 million, $34.4 million and $29.7 million in dividends, respectively.

5.09

THE MCGRAW-HILL COMPANIES, INC. (DEC)

(In thousands, except per share data)	Common Stock $1 Par	Additional Paid-In Capital	Retained Income	Accumulated Other Comprehensive Loss	Less Common Stock in Treasury at Cost	Noncontrolling Interests	Total
Balance at December 31, 2006	$411,709	$114,596	$4,821,118	$(115,212)	$2,552,593	$ 50,425	$ 2,730,043
Net income	—	—	1,013,559		—	13,799	1,027,358
Other comprehensive income:							
Foreign currency translation adjustment	—	—	—	28,618	—	5,915	34,533
Unrealized gain on investment, net of tax	—	—	—	3,747	—	—	3,747
Pension and other postretirement benefit plans, net of tax	—	—	—	70,224	—	—	70,224
Comprehensive income							1,135,862
Adjustment to initially apply FIN 48	—	—	(5,174)	—	—	—	(5,174)
Dividends	—	—	(277,746)	—	—	(3,747)	(281,493)
Share repurchases	—	—	—	—	2,212,655	—	(2,212,655)
Employee stock plans, net of tax benefit	—	54,683	—	—	(251,701)	—	306,384
Other	—	(92)	—	—	(167)	4,720	4,795
Balance at December 31, 2007	$411,709	$169,187	$5,551,757	$ (12,623)	$4,513,380	$ 71,112	$ 1,677,762
Net income	—	—	799,491		—	19,874	819,365
Other comprehensive loss:							
Foreign currency translation adjustment	—	—	—	(96,683)	—	(11,158)	(107,841)
Unrealized loss on investment, net of tax	—	—	—	(3,443)	—	—	(3,443)
Pension and other postretirement benefit plans, net of tax	—	—	—	(331,273)	—	65	(331,208)
Comprehensive income							376,873
Dividends	—	—	(280,455)	—	—	(9,297)	(289,752)
Share repurchases	—	—	—	—	447,233	—	(447,233)
Employee stock plans, net of tax benefit	—	(114,037)	—	—	(149,319)	—	35,282
Other	—	—	—	—	—	(61)	(61)
Balance at December 31, 2008	$411,709	$ 55,150	$6,070,793	$(444,022)	$4,811,294	$ 70,535	$ 1,352,871
Net income	—	—	730,502		—	19,259	749,761
Other comprehensive loss:							
Foreign currency translation adjustment	—	—	—	43,023	—	3,596	46,619
Unrealized gain on investment, net of tax	—	—	—	1,655	—	—	1,655
Pension and other postretirement benefit plans, net of tax	—	—	—	56,327	—	(96)	56,231
Comprehensive income							854,266
Dividends	—	—	(278,682)	—	—	(9,162)	(287,844)
Employee stock plans, net of tax benefit	—	(50,025)	—	—	(62,151)	—	12,126
Other	—	—	—	—	—	(2,242)	(2,242)
Balance at December 31, 2009	$411,709	$ 5,125	$6,522,613	$(343,017)	$4,749,143	$ 81,890	$ 1,929,177

NOTES TO CONSOLIDATED FINANCIAL STATEMENTS

7 (In Part): Equity

Capital Stock (In Part)

In 2009, dividends were paid at the quarterly rate of $0.225 per common share. Dividends were paid at an annualized rate of $0.90, $0.88 and $0.82 per common share in 2009, 2008 and 2007, respectively. Total dividends paid in 2009, 2008 and 2007 were $281.6 million, $280.5 million and $277.7 million, respectively. On January 20, 2010, the Board of Directors approved an increase in the dividends for 2010 to a quarterly rate of $0.235 per common share.

Dividends-in-Kind

5.10

WALTER ENERGY, INC. (DEC)

(In thousands)	Total	Common Stock	Capital in Excess of Par Value	Comprehensive Income	Retained Earnings (Deficit)	Treasury Stock	Accumulated Other Comprehensive Income (Loss)
Balance at December 31, 2006	$ 1,908	$ 728	$ 757,699		$(398,564)	$(259,317)	$(98,638)
Adjustment to initially apply FIN 48	(4,421)				(4,421)		
Adjusted balance at January 1, 2007	(2,513)	728	757,699		(402,985)	(259,317)	(98,638)
Comprehensive income:							
Net income	111,999			$111,999	111,999		
Other comprehensive income, net of tax:							
Change in pension and postretirement benefit plans, net of $9.7 million tax provision	15,231			15,231			15,231
Net unrealized loss on hedges, net of $4.3 million tax benefit	(8,446)			(8,446)			(8,446)
Comprehensive income				$118,784			
Retirement of treasury stock		(207)	(259,902)			260,109	
Purchases of stock under stock repurchase program	(5,627)	(1)	(5,626)				
Stock issued upon exercise of stock options	1,447		1,447				
Tax benefit on the exercise of stock options	2,015		2,015				
Dividends paid, $0.20 per share	(10,411)		(10,411)				
Stock based compensation	11,810		11,810				
Other	(792)					(792)	
Balance at December 31, 2007	$114,713	$ 520	$ 497,032		$(290,986)	$ —	$(91,853)

(continued)

(In thousands)	Total	Common Stock	Capital in Excess of Par Value	Comprehensive Income	Retained Earnings (Deficit)	Treasury Stock	Accumulated Other Comprehensive Income (Loss)
Balance at December 31, 2007	$ 114,713	$520	$ 497,032		$(290,986)	$—	$ (91,853)
Comprehensive income:							
Net income	346,580			$346,580	346,580		
Other comprehensive income, net of tax:							
Change in pension and postretirement benefit plans, net of $32.3 million tax benefit	(50,961)			(50,961)			(50,961)
Net unrealized gain on hedges, net of $4.5 million tax provision	6,710			6,710			6,710
Comprehensive income				$302,329			
Effects of changing the pension plan measurement date pursuant to FASB Statement No. 158:							
Service cost, interest cost, and expected return on plan assets for October 1—December 31, 2007, net of $3.0 million tax benefit	(4,604)				(4,604)		
Amortization of prior service cost and actuarial gain/loss for October 1—December 31, 2007, net of $0.5 million tax provision	668						668
Proceeds from public stock offering	280,464	32	280,432				
Purchases of stock under stock repurchase program	(64,644)	(16)	(64,628)				
Stock issued upon exercise of stock options	7,993	4	7,989				
Stock issued upon conversion of convertible notes	785	1	784				
Dividends paid, $0.30 per share	(16,233)		(16,233)				
Stock based compensation	10,439		10,439				
Other	(1,641)		(1,641)				
Balance at December 31, 2008	$ 630,269	$541	$ 714,174		$ 50,990	$—	$(135,436)
Comprehensive income:							
Net income	137,158			$137,158	137,158		
Other comprehensive income, net of tax:							
Change in pension and postretirement benefit plans, net of $44.2 million tax benefit	(28,513)			(28,513)			(28,513)
Change in unrealized gain (loss) on hedges, net of $0.4 million tax	(877)			(877)			(877)
Comprehensive income				$107,768			
Purchases of stock under stock repurchase program	(34,254)	(14)	(34,240)				
Stock issued upon the exercise of stock options	9,888	6	9,882				
Stock dividend for spin-off of Financing	(439,093)		(321,301)		(116,106)		(1,686)
Dividends paid, $0.40 per share	(21,190)				(21,190)		
Stock based compensation	6,703		6,703				
Other	(696)		(696)				
Balance at December 31, 2009	$ 259,395	$533	$ 374,522		$ 50,852	$—	$(166,512)

ATT-SEC 5.10

NOTES TO CONSOLIDATED FINANCIAL STATEMENTS

Note 3 (In Part): Discontinued Operations & Acquisitions

Spin-Off of Financing

On April 17, 2009, the Company completed the spin-off of its Financing business and the merger of that business with Hanover Capital Mortgage Holdings, Inc. to create Walter Investment Management Corp. ("Walter Investment"), which operates as a publicly traded real estate investment trust. The subsidiaries and assets that Walter Investment owned at the time of the spin-off included all assets of Financing except for those associated with the workers' compensation program and various other run-off insurance programs within Cardem Insurance Co., Ltd.

As a result of the distribution, the Company no longer has any ownership interest in Walter Investment. The Company and Walter Investment entered into several agreements to facilitate the spin-off. These include the following: (1) A Transition Services Agreement to provide certain services to each other, including tax, accounting, human resources and communication for a limited duration, in all cases not expected to exceed 24 months, with the precise term of each service set forth in the Transition Services Agreement; (2) A Tax Separation Agreement that sets forth the rights and obligations of the Company and Walter Investment with respect to taxes and other liabilities that could be imposed if Walter Investment is required to pay an additional dividend in order to maintain its REIT status for U.S. federal income tax purposes. If that need arises, the Company will be required to reimburse Walter Investment for a portion of such additional dividend; (3) A Joint Litigation Agreement that allocates responsibilities for pending and future litigation and claims, allocates insurance coverages and third-party indemnification rights, where appropriate, and provides that each party should cooperate with each other regarding such litigation claims and rights on a going forward basis, and; (4) A Trademark Licensing Agreement whereby the Company granted Walter Investment a paid-up, perpetual, non-exclusive, non-transferable (except to affiliates) license to use certain variations and/or acronyms of the "Walter," "Best Insurors" and "Mid-State" names in connection with mortgage finance, lending, insurance and reinsurance services, and financial services related thereto, in the United States.

In order to facilitate the successful spin-off of Financing, the Company entered into a Support Letter of Credit Agreement (the "L/C Agreement") and a revolving credit facility agreement with Walter Investment and certain of its subsidiaries on April 20, 2009. The L/C Agreement provides Walter Investments' financial lending institutions with a stand-by letter of credit totaling $15.7 million. This stand-by letter of credit was issued under the Company's 2005 Walter Credit Agreement and enabled Walter Investment to obtain third-party financing under a revolving credit agreement. The maximum amount of future payments that the Company could be required to make under the L/C Agreement is $15.7 million, plus any unreimbursed fees, in the event of a default. To date, no event of default has occurred that would trigger a draw under the stand-by letter of credit. The Company believes that the likelihood of a triggering event is remote. In addition, should a loss occur, sufficient collateral is available for the recovery of any loss the Company might suffer in the event of a default by Walter Investment. Under the terms of the L/C Agreement, Walter Investment agrees to reimburse the Company for all costs incurred in posting

the support letter of credit for Walter Investment's revolving credit agreement as well as any draws under bonds posted in support of Walter Investment and its subsidiaries. All obligations of the L/C Agreement will terminate on April 20, 2011.

In addition, the Company also entered into a revolving credit facility and security agreement with Walter Investment in which the Company has committed to make available up to $10.0 million in the event that a major hurricane occurs and causes projected losses greater than $2.5 million. A condition precedent to a draw under this facility is the granting of a security interest in certain collateral. Under the terms of the revolving credit facility and security agreement, Walter Investment will pay all fees and repay all loans made under the facility. Any obligations under the revolving credit facility and security agreement will be due and payable upon the termination of this agreement on April 20, 2011. There have been no loans made to Walter Investment pursuant to this arrangement.

As a result of the spin-off, amounts previously reported in the Financing segment are presented as discontinued operations for all periods presented.

Stock Purchase Rights Plan Adopted

5.11

KB HOME (NOV)

NOTES TO CONSOLIDATED FINANCIAL STATEMENTS

Note 17 (In Part): Stockholders' Equity

Preferred Stock

On January 22, 2009, the Company adopted a Rights Agreement between the Company and Mellon Investor Services LLC, as rights agent, dated as of that date (the "2009 Rights Agreement"), and declared a dividend distribution of one preferred share purchase right for each outstanding share of common stock that was payable to stockholders of record as of the close of business on March 5, 2009. Subject to the terms, provisions and conditions of the 2009 Rights Agreement, if these rights become exercisable, each right would initially represent the right to purchase from the Company 1/100th of a share of its Series A Participating Cumulative Preferred Stock for a purchase price of $85.00 (the "Purchase Price"). If issued, each fractional share of preferred stock would generally give a stockholder approximately the same dividend, voting and liquidation rights as does one share of the Company's common stock. However, prior to exercise, a right does not give its holder any rights as a stockholder, including without limitation any dividend, voting or liquidation rights. The rights will not be exercisable until the earlier of (i) 10 calendar days after a public announcement by the Company that a person or group has become an Acquiring Person (as defined under the 2009 Rights Agreement) and (ii) 10 business days after the commencement of a tender or exchange offer by a person or group if upon consummation of the offer the person or group would beneficially own 4.9% or more of the Company's outstanding common stock.

Until these rights become exercisable (the "Distribution Date"), common stock certificates will evidence the rights and may contain a notation to that effect. Any transfer of shares of the Company's common stock prior to the Distribution Date will constitute a transfer of the associated rights. After the Distribution Date, the rights may be transferred other than in connection with the transfer of the underlying shares of the Company's common stock. If there is an Acquiring Person on the Distribution Date or a person or group becomes an Acquiring Person after the Distribution Date, each holder of a right, other than rights that are or were beneficially owned by an Acquiring Person, which will be void, will thereafter have the right to receive upon exercise of a right and payment of the Purchase Price, that number of shares of the Company's common stock having a market value of two times the Purchase Price. After the later of the Distribution Date and the time the Company publicly announces that an Acquiring Person has become such, the Company's board of directors may exchange the rights, other than rights that are or were beneficially owned by an Acquiring Person, which will be void, in whole or in part, at an exchange ratio of one share of common stock per right, subject to adjustment.

At any time prior to the later of the Distribution Date and the time the Company publicly announces that an Acquiring Person becomes such, the Company's board of directors may redeem all of the then-outstanding rights in whole, but not in part, at a price of $0.001 per right, subject to adjustment (the "Redemption Price"). The redemption will be effective immediately upon the board of directors' action, unless the action provides that such redemption will be effective at a subsequent time or upon the occurrence or nonoccurrence of one or more specified events, in which case the redemption will be effective in accordance with the provisions of the action. Immediately upon the effectiveness of the redemption of the rights, the right to exercise the rights will terminate and the only right of the holders of rights will be to receive the Redemption Price, with interest thereon. The rights issued pursuant to the 2009 Rights Agreement will expire on the earliest of (a) the close of business on March 5, 2019, (b) the time at which the rights are redeemed, (c) the time at which the rights are exchanged, (d) the time at which the Company's board of directors determines that a related provision in the Company's Restated Certificate of Incorporation is no longer necessary, and (e) the close of business on the first day of a taxable year of the Company to which the Company's board of directors determines that no tax benefits may be carried forward. At the Company's annual meeting of stockholders on April 2, 2009, the Company's stockholders approved the 2009 Rights Agreement.

ADJUSTMENTS TO OPENING BALANCE OF RETAINED EARNINGS

5.12   Reasons for which the opening balance of retained earnings is properly restated include certain changes in accounting principles, changes in reporting entity, and corrections of an error in previously issued financial statements.

5.13   FASB ASC 250, *Accounting Changes and Error Corrections*, requires, unless impracticable or otherwise specified by applicable authoritative guidance, retrospective application to prior periods' financial statements of a change in accounting principle. Retrospective application is the application of a different accounting principle to prior account-

ing periods as if that principle had always been used. More specifically, retrospective application involves the following:
- The cumulative effect of the change on periods prior to those presented shall be reflected in the carrying amount of assets and liabilities as of the beginning of the first period presented.
- An offsetting adjustment, if any, shall be made to the opening balance of retained earnings (or other appropriate component of equity or net assets in the statement of financial position) for that period.
- Financial statements for each individual prior period presented shall be adjusted to reflect the period-specific effects of applying the new accounting principle.

5.14   FASB ASC 250 also requires any accounting error in the financial statements of a prior period discovered after the financial statements are issued or available to be issued shall be reported as an error correction, by restating the prior period financial statements. Restatement involves similar requirements as those specified for retrospective application of a change in accounting principle.

5.15   The Securities and Exchange Commission (SEC) materials codified at FASB ASC 250 provide guidance on the consideration of the effects of prior year misstatements in quantifying current year misstatements for the purpose of assessing materiality. FASB ASC 250 requires that registrant entities determine the quantitative effect of a financial statement misstatement using both an income statement ("rollover") and a balance sheet ("iron curtain") approach, and evaluate whether, under either approach, the error is material after considering all relevant quantitative and qualitative factors.

5.16   Table 5-3 summarizes the reasons disclosed by the survey entities as to why the opening balance of retained earnings was adjusted.

5.17

TABLE 5-3: ADJUSTMENTS TO OPENING BALANCE OF RETAINED EARNINGS

	Number of Entities			
	2009	2008	2007	2006
Accounting principle changes..............	93	226	232	27
Correction of an error/misstatement....	6	12	23	26
Other—described................................	—	1	2	1

2008–2009 based on 500 entities surveyed; 2006–2007 based on 600 entities surveyed.

Change in Accounting Principle

5.18

THE MOSAIC COMPANY (MAY)

| | | Shares | | | Dollars | | | |
(In millions, except per share data)	Preferred Stock	Class B Stock	Common Stock	Common Stock	Capital in Excess of Par Value	Retained Earnings	Accumulated Other Comprehensive Income (Loss)	Total Stockholders' Equity
Balance as of May 31, 2006	2.8	5.5	384.4	$3.9	$2,244.8	$ 982.9	$299.2	$3,530.8
Net earnings	—	—	—	—	—	419.7	—	419.7
Foreign currency translation adjustment, net of tax of $15.0 million	—	—	—	—	—	—	143.6	143.6
Minimum pension liability adjustment, net of tax of $0.2 million	—	—	—	—	—	—	0.4	0.4
Comprehensive income for 2007								563.7
Conversion of preferred stock and class B common stock	(2.8)	(5.5)	52.9	0.5	(0.5)	—	—	—
Stock option exercises	—	—	3.5	—	48.0	—	—	48.0
Amortization of stock based compensation	—	—	—	—	23.4	—	—	23.4
Adjustment to initially apply FASB Statement 158, net of tax of $7.1 million	—	—	—	—	—	—	15.7	15.7
Contributions from Cargill, Inc.	—	—	—	—	2.3	—	—	2.3
Balance as of May 31, 2007	—	—	440.8	$4.4	$2,318.0	$1,402.6	$458.9	$4,183.9
Net earnings	—	—	—	—	—	2,082.8	—	2,082.8
Foreign currency translation adjustment, net of tax of $7.2 million	—	—	—	—	—	—	318.5	318.5
Net actuarial gain, net of tax of $7.9 million	—	—	—	—	—	—	13.2	13.2
Comprehensive income for 2008								2,414.5
Stock option exercises	—	—	3.1	—	57.2	—	—	57.2
Amortization of stock based compensation	—	—	—	—	18.5	—	—	18.5
Contributions from Cargill, Inc.	—	—	—	—	4.6	—	—	4.6
Tax benefits related to stock option exercises	—	—	—	—	52.5	—	—	52.5
Balance as of May 31, 2008	—	—	443.9	$4.4	$2,450.8	$3,485.4	$790.6	$6,731.2

(continued)

(In millions, except per share data)	Shares			Dollars				
	Preferred Stock	Class B Stock	Common Stock	Common Stock	Capital in Excess of Par Value	Retained Earnings	Accumulated Other Comprehensive Income (Loss)	Total Stockholders' Equity
Balance as of May 31, 2008	—	—	443.9	$4.4	$2,450.8	$3,485.4	$ 790.6	$6,731.2
Adoption of FAS 158 measurement date, net of tax of $0.2 million	—	—	—	—	—	(0.5)	—	(0.5)
Beginning balance, as adjusted	—	—	443.9	$4.4	$2,450.8	$3,484.9	$ 790.6	$6,730.7
Net earnings	—	—	—	—	—	2,350.2	—	2,350.2
Foreign currency translation adjustment, net of tax of $13.3 million	—	—	—	—	—	—	(480.0)	(480.0)
Net actuarial loss, net of tax of $31.2 million	—	—	—	—	—	—	(52.0)	(52.0)
Comprehensive income for 2009								1,818.2
Stock option exercises	—	—	0.6	—	4.6	—	—	4.6
Amortization of stock based compensation	—	—	—	—	22.5	—	—	22.5
Distributions to Cargill, Inc.	—	—	—	—	(0.6)	—	—	(0.6)
Dividends paid ($0.20 per share)	—	—	—	—	—	(88.9)	—	(88.9)
Tax benefits related to stock option exercises	—	—	—	—	6.5	—	—	6.5
Balance as of May 31, 2009	—	—	444.5	$4.4	$2,483.8	$5,746.2	$ 258.6	$8,493.0

NOTES TO CONSOLIDATED FINANCIAL STATEMENTS

2 (In Part): Summary of Significant Accounting Policies

Pension and Other Postretirement Benefits

Mosaic offers a number of benefit plans that provide pension and other benefits to qualified employees. These plans include defined benefit pension plans, supplemental pension plans, defined contribution plans and other postretirement benefit plans.

We accrue, in accordance with the recognition provisions of SFAS No. 158, "Employers' Accounting for Defined Benefit Pension and Other Postretirement Plans," ("SFAS 158"), the funded status of our plans, which is representative of our obligations under employee benefit plans and the related costs, net of plan assets measured at fair value. The cost of pensions and other retirement benefits earned by employees is generally determined with the assistance of an actuary using the projected benefit method prorated on service and management's best estimate of expected plan investment performance, salary escalation, retirement ages of employees and expected healthcare costs.

4 (In Part): Recently Issued Accounting Guidance

In September 2006, the FASB issued SFAS 158. SFAS 158 requires the recognition of the funded status of pension and other postretirement benefit plans on the balance sheet. The overfunded or underfunded status would be recognized as an asset or liability on the balance sheet with changes occurring during the current year reflected through the comprehensive income portion of equity. SFAS 158 also requires the measurement of the funded status of a plan to match that of the date of our fiscal year-end financial statements, eliminating the use of earlier measurement dates previously permissible. We applied the recognition provision of SFAS 158 as of May 31, 2007. We adopted the measurement provision of SFAS 158 as of June 1, 2008, as described in Note 18.

18 (In Part): Pension Plans and Other Benefits

Accounting for Pension and Postretirement Plans

We adopted the measurement date provision of SFAS 158 as of June 1, 2008. Prior to fiscal 2009, we used a measurement date as of February 28. The adoption required us to record a $0.5 million reduction to retained earnings, a $36.3 million reduction of other non-current liabilities, a $12.5 million reduction to deferred tax assets and a $24.3 million increase to opening accumulated other comprehensive income.

5.19

WELLPOINT, INC. (DEC)

(In millions)	Common Stock Number of Shares	Par Value	Additional Paid-In Capital	Retained Earnings	Accumulated Other Comprehensive Income (Loss)	Total Shareholders' Equity
January 1, 2007	615.5	$ 6.1	$19,863.5	$ 4,656.1	$ 50.1	$24,575.8
Net income	—	—	—	3,345.4	—	3,345.4
Change in net unrealized gains/losses on investments	—	—	—	—	2.2	2.2
Change in net unrealized gains/losses on cash flow hedges	—	—	—	—	(2.4)	(2.4)
Change in net periodic pension and postretirement costs	—	—	—	—	106.2	106.2
Comprehensive income						3,451.4
Repurchase and retirement of common stock	(76.9)	(0.8)	(2,538.3)	(3,612.3)	—	(6,151.4)
Issuance of common stock under employee stock plans, net of related tax benefit	17.6	0.3	1,115.9	—	—	1,116.2
Adoption of FASB guidance on uncertain tax positions	—	—	—	(1.6)	—	(1.6)
December 31, 2007	556.2	$ 5.6	$18,441.1	$ 4,387.6	$ 156.1	$22,990.4
Net income	—	—	—	2,490.7	—	2,490.7
Change in net unrealized gains/losses on investments	—	—	—	—	(662.4)	(662.4)
Change in net unrealized gains/losses on cash flow hedges	—	—	—	—	(0.5)	(0.5)
Change in net periodic pension and postretirement costs	—	—	—	—	(388.1)	(388.1)
Adoption of FASB measurement date provisions	—	—	—	—	(0.8)	(0.8)
Comprehensive income						1,438.9
Repurchase and retirement of common stock	(56.4)	(0.6)	(1,879.1)	(1,396.5)	—	(3,276.2)
Issuance of common stock under employee stock plans, net of related tax benefit	3.4	—	281.0	—	—	281.0
Adoption of FASB retirement benefits guidance	—	—	—	(1.3)	—	(1.3)
Adoption of FASB measurement date provisions	—	—	—	(1.1)	—	(1.1)
December 31, 2008	503.2	$ 5.0	$16,843.0	$ 5,479.4	$(895.7)	$21,431.7
Cumulative effect of adoption of FASB OTTI guidance, net of taxes	—	—	—	88.9	(88.9)	—
Net income	—	—	—	4,745.9	—	4,745.9
Change in net unrealized gains/losses on investments	—	—	—	—	1,055.2	1,055.2
Non-credit component of other-than-temporary impairment losses on investments, net of taxes	—	—	—	—	(20.7)	(20.7)
Change in net unrealized gains/losses on cash flow hedges	—	—	—	—	(2.3)	(2.3)
Change in net periodic pension and postretirement costs	—	—	—	—	19.3	19.3
Foreign currency translation adjustments	—	—	—	—	1.2	1.2
Comprehensive income						5,798.6
Repurchase and retirement of common stock	(57.3)	(0.5)	(1,922.2)	(715.7)	—	(2,638.4)
Issuance of common stock under employee stock plans, net of related tax benefit	3.9	—	271.4	—	—	271.4
December 31, 2009	449.8	$ 4.5	$15,192.2	$ 9,598.5	$ 68.1	$24,863.3

NOTES TO CONSOLIDATED FINANCIAL STATEMENTS
(In millions)

2 (In Part): Significant Accounting Policies

Investments

In April 2009, the FASB issued guidance for recognition and presentation of other-than-temporary impairment, or FASB OTTI guidance. FASB OTTI guidance applies to fixed maturity securities only and provides new guidance on the recognition and presentation of other-than-temporary impairments. In addition, FASB OTTI guidance requires additional disclosures related to other-than-temporary impairments. Under this revised guidance, if a fixed maturity security is in an unrealized loss position and we have the intent to sell the fixed maturity security, or it is more likely than not that we will have to sell the fixed maturity security before recovery of its amortized cost basis, the decline in value is deemed to be other-than-temporary and is recorded to other-than-temporary impairment losses recognized in income in our consolidated income statements. For impaired fixed maturity securities that we do not intend to sell or it is more likely than not that we will not have to sell such securities, but we expect that we will not fully recover the amortized cost basis, the credit component of the other-than-temporary impairment is recognized in other-than-temporary impairment losses recognized in income in our consolidated income statements and the non-credit component of the other-than-temporary impairment is recognized in other comprehensive income. Furthermore, unrealized losses entirely caused by non-credit related factors related to fixed maturity securities for which we expect to fully recover the amortized cost basis continue to be recognized in accumulated other comprehensive income.

The credit component of an other-than-temporary impairment is determined by comparing the net present value of projected future cash flows with the amortized cost basis of the fixed maturity security. The net present value is calculated by discounting our best estimate of projected future cash flows at the effective interest rate implicit in the fixed maturity security at the date of acquisition. For mortgage-backed and asset-backed securities, cash flow estimates are based on assumptions regarding the underlying collateral including prepayment speeds, vintage, type of underlying asset, geographic concentrations, default rates, recoveries and changes in value. For all other debt securities, cash flow estimates are driven by assumptions regarding probability of default, including changes in credit ratings, and estimates regarding timing and amount of recoveries associated with a default.

Upon adoption of the FASB OTTI guidance on April 1, 2009, we recorded a cumulative-effect adjustment, net of taxes, of $88.9 as of the beginning of the period of adoption, April 1, 2009, to reclassify the non-credit component of previously recognized other-than-temporary impairments from retained earnings to accumulated other comprehensive income.

We classify the fixed maturity and equity securities in our investment portfolio as "available-for-sale" or "trading" and report those securities at fair value. Prior to the adoption of the FASB OTTI guidance, we classified our fixed maturity securities as current or noncurrent based on their contractual maturities. In connection with the adoption of the FASB OTTI guidance on April 1, 2009, we have determined that certain of these fixed maturity securities are available to support current operations and, accordingly, have classified such investments as current assets as of December 31, 2009 without regard to their contractual maturities. Investments used to satisfy contractual, regulatory or other requirements are classified as long-term, without regard to contractual maturity.

The unrealized gains or losses on our current and long-term equity securities classified as available-for-sale are included in accumulated other comprehensive income as a separate component of shareholders' equity, unless the decline in value is deemed to be other-than-temporary and we do not have the intent and ability to hold such equity securities until their full cost can be recovered, in which case such equity securities are written down to fair value and the loss is charged to other-than-temporary impairment losses recognized in income.

4 (In Part): Investments

A summary of current and long-term investments, available-for-sale, is as follows:

| | Cost or Amortized Cost | Gross Unrealized Gains | Gross Unrealized Losses | | Estimated Fair Value | Non-Credit Component of Other-Than-Temporary Impairments Recognized in AOCI |
			12 Months or Less	Greater Than 12 Months		
December 31, 2009:						
Fixed maturity securities:						
United States Government securities	$ 715.4	$ 14.8	$ (2.4)	$ (0.2)	$ 727.6	$ —
Government sponsored securities	632.8	8.3	(0.4)	—	640.7	—
States, municipalities and political subdivisions—tax-exempt	4,019.4	167.0	(5.7)	(34.4)	4,146.3	(0.5)
Corporate securities	6,219.3	352.2	(12.9)	(34.5)	6,524.1	(3.3)
Options embedded in convertible debt securities	88.3	—	—	—	88.3	—
Residential mortgage-backed securities	3,295.0	120.0	(7.9)	(47.0)	3,360.1	(9.0)
Commercial mortgage-backed securities	137.6	3.6	(0.1)	(4.9)	136.2	—
Other debt obligations	318.3	8.7	(1.1)	(21.9)	304.0	(5.7)
Total fixed maturity securities	15,426.1	674.6	(30.5)	(142.9)	15,927.3	$(18.5)
Equity securities	832.5	221.9	(11.2)	—	1,043.2	
Total investments, available-for-sale	$16,258.6	$896.5	$ (41.7)	$(142.9)	$16,970.5	
December 31, 2008:						
Fixed maturity securities:						
United States Government securities	$ 544.5	$ 46.2	$ (1.3)	$ —	$ 589.4	
Government sponsored securities	205.2	10.4	—	—	215.6	
States, municipalities and political subdivisions—tax-exempt	3,880.9	78.9	(86.1)	(58.6)	3,815.1	
Corporate securities	5,193.0	58.3	(355.7)	(121.9)	4,773.7	
Options embedded in convertible debt securities	39.9	—	—	—	39.9	
Residential mortgage-backed securities	3,527.3	114.1	(114.4)	(43.2)	3,483.8	
Commercial mortgage-backed securities	169.5	—	(9.2)	(7.5)	152.8	
Other debt obligations	379.6	0.2	(23.7)	(53.2)	302.9	
Total fixed maturity securities	13,939.9	308.1	(590.4)	(284.4)	13,373.2	
Equity securities	1,327.7	25.8	(234.8)	—	1,118.7	
Total investments, available-for-sale	$15,267.6	$333.9	$(825.2)	$(284.4)	$14,491.9	

At December 31, 2009, we owned $3,496.3 of mortgage-backed securities and $304.0 of asset-backed securities out of a total available-for-sale investment portfolio of $16,970.5. These securities included sub-prime and Alt-A securities with fair values of $107.5 and $285.9, respectively. These sub-prime and Alt-A securities had net unrealized losses of $14.8 and $38.1, respectively. The average credit rating of the sub-prime and Alt-A securities was "A" and "BBB," respectively.

The following table summarizes for fixed maturity securities and equity securities in an unrealized loss position at December 31, the aggregate fair value and gross unrealized loss by length of time those securities have been continuously in an unrealized loss position.

	12 Months or Less			Greater Than 12 Months		
(Securities are whole amounts)	Number of Securities	Fair Value	Gross Unrealized Loss	Number of Securities	Fair Value	Gross Unrealized Loss
December 31, 2009:						
Fixed maturity securities:						
United States Government securities	18	$ 286.8	$ (2.4)	3	$ 3.1	$ (0.2)
Government sponsored securities	17	149.3	(0.4)	—	—	—
States, municipalities and political subdivisions—tax-exempt	162	417.6	(5.7)	185	314.8	(34.4)
Corporate securities	462	914.5	(12.9)	233	404.3	(34.5)
Residential mortgage-backed securities	219	439.0	(7.9)	128	256.1	(47.0)
Commercial mortgage-backed securities	7	9.8	(0.1)	14	39.9	(4.9)
Other debt obligations	24	112.5	(1.1)	49	61.0	(21.9)
Total fixed maturity securities	909	2,329.5	(30.5)	612	1,079.2	(142.9)
Equity securities	788	99.0	(11.2)	—	—	—
Total fixed maturity and equity securities	1,697	$2,428.5	$ (41.7)	612	$1,079.2	$(142.9)
December 31, 2008:						
Fixed maturity securities:						
United States Government securities	8	$ 50.3	$ (1.3)	—	$ —	$ —
Government sponsored securities	3	8.1	—	1	—	—
States, municipalities and political subdivisions—tax-exempt	447	1,212.5	(86.1)	132	200.6	(58.6)
Corporate securities	1,686	2,899.4	(355.7)	325	450.4	(121.9)
Residential mortgage-backed securities	247	514.8	(114.4)	246	103.8	(43.2)
Commercial mortgage-backed securities	53	104.3	(9.2)	26	48.5	(7.5)
Other debt obligations	57	155.4	(23.7)	53	137.1	(53.2)
Total fixed maturity securities	2,501	4,944.8	(590.4)	783	940.4	(284.4)
Equity securities	2,098	633.1	(234.8)	—	—	—
Total fixed maturity and equity securities	4,599	$5,577.9	$(825.2)	783	$ 940.4	$(284.4)

The weighted average credit rating of our fixed maturity securities was "AA" as of December 31, 2009. We continue to review our investment portfolios under our impairment review policy. Given the significant judgments involved, there is a continuing risk that further declines in fair value may occur and additional material other-than-temporary impairments may be recorded in future periods.

The amortized cost and fair value of fixed maturity securities at December 31, 2009, by contractual maturity, are shown below. Expected maturities may be less than contractual maturities because the issuers of the securities may have the right to prepay obligations without prepayment penalties.

	Amortized Cost	Estimated Fair Value
Due in one year or less	$ 1,161.4	$ 1,168.3
Due after one year through five years	4,866.0	5,099.0
Due after five years through ten years	3,515.8	3,676.6
Due after ten years	2,450.3	2,487.1
Mortgage-backed securities	3,432.6	3,496.3
Total available-for-sale fixed maturity securities	$15,426.1	$15,927.3

ATT-SEC 5.19

Net realized investment gains/losses and net change in unrealized appreciation/depreciation in investments for the years ended December 31, are as follows:

	2009	2008	2007
Net realized gains/losses on investments:			
Fixed maturity securities:			
Gross realized gains from sales	$ 158.3	$ 37.7	$ 71.5
Gross realized losses from sales	(135.5)	(84.6)	(60.0)
Net realized gains/losses from sales of fixed maturity securities	22.8	(46.9)	11.5
Equity securities:			
Gross realized gains from sales	116.5	143.1	277.6
Gross realized losses from sales	(81.5)	(114.8)	(23.4)
Net realized gains from sales of equity securities	35.0	28.3	254.2
Other realized gains/losses on investments	(1.4)	47.3	5.2
Net realized gains on investments	56.4	28.7	270.9
Other-than-temporary impairment losses recognized in income:			
Fixed maturity securities	(217.6)	(479.8)	(154.1)
Equity securities	(232.6)	(728.1)	(105.6)
Other-than-temporary impairment losses recognized in income	(450.2)	(1,207.9)	(259.7)
Change in net unrealized gains/losses on investments:			
Cumulative effect of adoption of FASB OTTI guidance	(143.1)	—	—
Fixed maturity securities	1,209.1	(669.5)	151.1
Equity securities	419.7	(371.7)	(155.6)
Total change in net unrealized gains/losses on investments	1,485.7	(1,041.2)	(4.5)
Deferred income tax (expense) benefit	(540.1)	378.8	6.7
Net change in net unrealized gains/losses on investments	945.6	(662.4)	2.2
Net realized gains/losses on investments, other-than-temporary impairment losses recognized in income and net change in net unrealized gains/losses on investments	$ 551.8	$(1,841.6)	$ 13.4

During the year ended December 31, 2009, we sold $4,673.9 of fixed maturity and equity securities which resulted in gross realized losses of $217.0. In the ordinary course of business, we may sell securities at a loss for a number of reasons, including, but not limited to: (i) changes in the investment environment; (ii) expectation that the fair value could deteriorate further; (iii) desire to reduce exposure to an issuer or an industry; (iv) changes in credit quality; or (v) changes in expected cash flow.

A significant judgment in the valuation of investments is the determination of when an other-than-temporary decline in value has occurred. We follow a consistent and systematic process for recognizing impairments on securities that sustain other-than-temporary declines in value. We have established a committee responsible for the impairment review process. The decision to impair a security incorporates both quantitative criteria and qualitative information. The impairment review process considers a number of factors including, but not limited to: (i) the length of time and the extent to which the fair value has been less than book value, (ii) the financial condition and near term prospects of the issuer, (iii) our intent and ability to retain impaired investments for a period of time sufficient to allow for any anticipated recovery in value, (iv) whether the debtor is current on interest and principal payments, (v) the reasons for the decline in value (i.e., credit event compared to liquidity, general credit spread widening, currency exchange rate or interest rate factors) and (vi) general market conditions and industry or sector specific factors. For securities that are deemed to be other-than-temporarily impaired, the security is adjusted to fair value and the result-

ing losses are recognized in realized gains or losses in the consolidated statements of income. The new cost basis of the impaired securities is not increased for future recoveries in fair value.

Other-than-temporary impairments recorded in 2009 and 2007 were primarily the result of the continued credit deterioration on specific issuers in the bond markets and certain equity securities' fair value remaining below cost for an extended period of time. There were no individually significant other-than-temporary impairment losses on investments by issuer during 2009 or 2007.

The changes in the amount of the credit component of other-than-temporary impairment losses on fixed maturity securities recognized in income, for which a portion of the other-than-temporary impairment losses was recognized in other comprehensive income, was not material for the year ended December 31, 2009.

The significant other-than-temporary impairments recognized during 2008 primarily related to our investments in Federal Home Loan Mortgage Corporation, or Freddie Mac, Federal National Mortgage Association, or Fannie Mae, and Lehman Brothers Holdings Inc., or Lehman (or their respective subsidiaries, as appropriate), as discussed below.

Our equity securities at December 31, 2008 included investments in stock, largely preferred stock, of the U.S. government-sponsored enterprises Freddie Mac and Fannie Mae. Market concerns during the third quarter of 2008 related to those entities' financial condition and liquidity prompted the U.S. government to seize control of Freddie Mac and Fannie Mae. Any potential recovery of the fair value of these securities was dependent on a number of factors and was not expected in the near term. These facts, together with the significant declines in the fair value of these securities, led us to conclude that they were other-than-temporarily impaired. Accordingly, during 2008, we recorded $135.0 and $106.6 of realized losses from other-than-temporary impairments related to our equity security investments in Freddie Mac and Fannie Mae, respectively.

Our investments in fixed maturity securities included investments in Lehman at December 31, 2008. On September 15, 2008, Lehman filed for bankruptcy protection under Chapter 11 of the United States Bankruptcy Code. Accordingly, recovery of our investments, if any, was deemed remote and we recognized an other-than-temporary impairment of $90.2 during 2008.

In addition, other-than-temporary impairments recognized in 2008 included charges for fixed maturity securities and equity securities for which, due to credit downgrades and/or the extent and duration of their decline in fair value in light of the then current market conditions, we determined that the impairment was deemed other-than-temporary. These securities covered a number of industries, led by the banking and financial services sectors.

A primary objective in the management of the fixed maturity and equity portfolios is to maximize total return relative to underlying liabilities and respective liquidity needs. In achieving this goal, assets may be sold to take advantage of market conditions or other investment opportunities as well as tax considerations. Sales will generally produce realized gains and losses.

Investment securities are exposed to various risks, such as interest rate, market and credit. Due to the level of risk associated with certain investment securities and the level of uncertainty related to changes in the value of investment securities, it is possible that changes in these risk factors in the near term could have an adverse material impact on our results of operations or shareholders' equity.

At December 31, 2009 and 2008, no investments, other than investments in U.S. government agency securities, exceeded 10% of shareholders' equity.

The carrying value of fixed maturity investments that did not produce income during 2009 and 2008 was $22.4 and $0.0 at December 31, 2009 and 2008, respectively.

Correction of an Error/Misstatement

5.20

SEALY CORPORATION (NOV)

(In thousands)	Comprehensive Income (Loss)	Common Stock		Additional Paid-In Capital	Accumulated Deficit	Accumulated Other Comprehensive Income (Loss)	Total
		Shares	Amount				
Balance at November 26, 2006	$79,122	90,983	$904	$664,609	$(846,455)	$7,793	$(173,149)
Net income	77,321				77,321		77,321
Foreign currency translation adjustment	11,146					11,146	11,146
Excess of additional pension liability over unrecognized prior service cost, net of tax of $568	(1,160)					(1,160)	(1,160)
Adjustment to adopt certain provisions of ASC Topic 715, net of income taxes of $699						(1,028)	(1,028)
Change in fair value of cash flow hedge, net of tax of $4,667	(7,549)					(7,549)	(7,549)
Share-based compensation:							
Compensation associated with stock option grants				2,124			2,124
Directors' deferred stock compensation				281			281
Cash dividend					(27,389)		(27,389)
Repurchase of common stock		(1,057)	(11)	(16,242)			(16,253)
Exercise of stock options		888	9	(6,888)			(6,879)
Excess tax benefit on options exercised				6,585			6,585
Adjustment of temporary equity subject to redemption				4,107			4,107
Other				50			50
Balance at December 2, 2007	$79,758	90,814	$902	$654,626	$(796,523)	$9,202	$(131,793)

(continued)

(In thousands)	Comprehensive Income (Loss)	Common Stock		Additional Paid-In Capital	Accumulated Deficit	Accumulated Other Comprehensive Income (Loss)	Total
		Shares	Amount				
Balance at December 2, 2007	$ 79,758	90,814	$902	$654,626	$(796,523)	$ 9,202	$(131,793)
Net loss	(3,803)				(3,803)		(3,803)
Foreign currency translation adjustment	(24,731)					(24,731)	(24,731)
Adjustment to defined benefit plan liability, net of tax of $1,045	(1,644)					(1,644)	(1,644)
Change in fair value of cash flow hedge, net of tax of $1,559	(2,538)					(2,538)	(2,538)
Cumulative effect of a change in accounting principle—adoption of certain provisions of ASC Topic 740					(10,460)		(10,460)
Share-based compensation:							—
Compensation associated with stock option grants				2,981			2,981
Directors' deferred stock compensation				26			26
Current period expense from restricted stock awards				222			222
Cash dividend					(6,811)		(6,811)
Repurchase of common stock							—
Exercise of stock options		986	14	(882)			(868)
Excess tax benefit on options exercised				407			407
Reversal of retiree put liability				2,372			2,372
Adjustment of common stock and options subject to redemption			1	8,795			8,796
Balance at November 30, 2008	$(32,716)	91,800	$917	$668,547	$(817,597)	$(19,711)	$(167,844)
Net income	13,485				13,485		13,485
Foreign currency translation adjustment	11,164					11,164	11,164
Adjustment to defined benefit plan liability, net of tax of $680	(1,814)					(1,814)	(1,814)
Change in fair value of cash flow hedges, net of tax of $44	(136)					(136)	(136)
Loss on termination of interest rate swaps, net of tax of $5,834	9,444					9,444	9,444
Share-based compensation:							
Compensation associated with stock option grants				4,819			4,819
Directors' deferred stock compensation				371			371
Compensation associated with restricted stock awards				667			667
Compensation associated with restricted stock units				6,776			6,776
Exercise of stock options		271	4	23			27
Excess tax deficiency on options exercised				(647)			(647)
Distribution of rights to purchase convertible notes					(188,838)		(188,838)
Settlement of rights to purchase convertible notes				193,388			193,388
Conversion of convertible notes		2,346	23	2,267			2,290
Adjustment of common stock and options subject to redemption			3	8,853			8,856
Balance at November 29, 2009	$ 32,143	94,417	$947	$885,064	$(992,950)	$ (1,053)	$(107,992)

NOTES TO CONSOLIDATED FINANCIAL STATEMENTS

Note 2. Restatement of Previous Periods

During the year-end financial close process of fiscal 2009, the Company discovered an error related to the depreciation of the assets acquired through the purchase of certain of its European subsidiaries in fiscal 2001. The Company also discovered an error related to the deferred income tax liabilities recorded on these assets. The errors, which were immaterial to the prior periods, resulted in an understatement of depreciation expense, recorded as a component of cost of goods sold and an overstatement of the income tax provision in the Consolidated Statement of Operations for prior periods. The recorded balances of accumulated depreciation and deferred tax liabilities were likewise understated and overstated, respectively in the Consolidated Balance Sheets for prior periods. The Company evaluated the effects of these errors on prior periods' consolidated financial statements, individually and in the aggregate, in accordance with the guidance provided by SEC Staff Accounting Bulletin No. 108, codified as Topic 1.N, "Considering the Effects of Prior Year Misstatements When Quantifying Misstatements in Current Year Financial Statements," and concluded that no prior period is materially misstated. However, in accordance with the provisions of this SAB Topic, the Company is restating its Consolidated Financial Statements as of and for the years ended November 30, 2008 and December 2, 2007 as follows (in thousands):

	Consolidated Balance Sheet Information as of November 30, 2008		
	As Previously Reported	Adjustments	Restated
Accumulated depreciation	$(218,560)	$(7,398)	$(225,958)
Deferred income tax liabilities	4,962	(4,378)	584
Accumulated deficit	(814,298)	(3,299)	(817,597)
Accumulated other comprehensive income	(19,990)	279	(19,711)

	Consolidated Statements of Operations Information for the Years Ended					
	2008			2007		
	As Previously Reported	Adjustments	Restated	As Previously Reported	Adjustments	Restated
Cost of goods sold	$913,982	$ 1,995	$915,977	$992,455	$ 2,245	$994,700
Gross profit	584,041	(1,995)	582,046	709,610	(2,245)	707,365
Income from operations	84,509	(1,995)	82,514	179,208	(2,245)	176,963
Income before income taxes	19,064	(1,995)	17,069	114,431	(2,245)	112,186
Income tax provision	21,931	(1,059)	20,872	35,058	(193)	34,865
Net income (loss)	(2,867)	(936)	(3,803)	79,373	(2,052)	77,321
Earnings (loss) per common share—Basic	(0.03)	(0.01)	(0.04)	0.87	(0.02)	0.85
Earnings (loss) per common share—Diluted	(0.03)	(0.01)	(0.04)	0.82	(0.02)	0.80

	Consolidated Statements of Stockholders' Deficit for the Years Ended December 2, 2007 and November 30, 2008					
	Accumulated Deficit			Accumulated Other Comprehensive Income (Loss)		
	As Previously Reported	Adjustments	Restated	As Previously Reported	Adjustments	Restated
Balance—November 26, 2006	$(846,144)	$ (311)	$(846,455)	$ 7,793	$ —	$ 7,793
Net income (for the year ended December 2, 2007)	79,373	(2,052)	77,321			
Foreign currency translation adjustment (for the year ended December 2, 2007)	—	—	—	11,183	(37)	11,146
Balance—December 2, 2007	(794,160)	(2,363)	(796,523)	9,239	(37)	9,202
Net loss (for the year ended November 30, 2008)	(2,867)	(936)	(3,803)			
Foreign currency translation adjustment (for the year ended November 30, 2008)	—	—	—	(25,047)	316	(24,731)
Balance—November 30, 2008	$(814,298)	$(3,299)	$(817,597)	$(19,990)	$279	$(19,711)

| | Consolidated Statements of Cash Flow for the Years Ended | | | | | |
| | 2008 | | | 2007 | | |
	As Previously Reported	Adjustments	Restated	As Previously Reported	Adjustments	Restated
Net income (loss)	$ (2,867)	$ (936)	$ (3,803)	$79,373	$(2,052)	$77,321
Adjustments to reconcile net income (loss) to cash provided by operating activities:						
Depreciation and amortization	33,954	1,995	35,949	30,493	2,245	32,738
Deferred income taxes	8,317	(1,059)	7,258	(5,207)	(193)	(5,400)
Net cash provided by operating activities	53,713	—	53,713	94,382	—	94,382

| | Segment Information for the Years Ended | | | | | |
| | 2008 | | | 2007 | | |
	As Previously Reported	Adjustments	Restated	As Previously Reported	Adjustments	Restated
Total assets:						
Europe	$ 69,784	$(7,398)	$ 62,386	$ 122,630	$(6,223)	$ 116,407
Total assets	920,874	(7,398)	913,476	1,025,079	(6,223)	1,018,856

OTHER CHANGES IN RETAINED EARNINGS

5.21   In addition to opening balance adjustments, the retained earnings account is affected by direct charges and credits. The most frequent direct charges to retained earnings are net loss for the year, losses on treasury stock transactions, and cash or stock dividends. The most common direct credit to retained earnings is net income for the year. Direct charges and credits—other than net loss, net income, dividends, and stock splits—are summarized in Table 5-4. Examples of such charges and credits follow.

5.22

TABLE 5-4: OTHER CHANGES IN RETAINED EARNINGS*

| | Number of Entities | | | |
	2009	2008	2007	2006
Charges				
Purchase or retirement of capital stock	55	91	98	78
Treasury stock issued for less than cost.................	36	31	31	28
Share based awards subject to redemption.........................	10	5	7	2
Preferred stock accretion...................	3	1	—	—
Other—described...............................	21	14	58	21
Credits				
Tax benefit on stock option exercise...	6	7	6	6
Tax benefit on dividends paid to ESOP	4	3	6	6
Other—described...............................	21	18	45	23

* Appearing in either the statement of stockholders' equity and/or the notes to financial statements.

2008–2009 based on 500 entities surveyed; 2006–2007 based on 600 entities surveyed.

Treasury Stock Transactions

5.23

ABBOTT LABORATORIES (DEC)

(Dollars in thousands except per share data)	2009	2008	2007
Common shares:			
Beginning of year			
Shares: 2009: 1,601,580,899; 2008: 1,580,854,677; 2007: 1,550,590,438	7,444,411	6,104,102	4,290,929
Issued under incentive stock programs			
Shares: 2009: 11,103,088; 2008: 20,726,222; 2007: 30,264,239	530,373	1,001,507	1,316,294
Tax benefit from option shares and vesting of restricted stock awards			
(no share effect)	15,351	64,714	163,808
Share-based compensation	366,128	342,315	433,319
Issuance of restricted stock awards	(98,390)	(68,227)	(100,248)
End of year			
Shares 2009: 1,612,683,987; 2008: 1,601,580,899; 2007: 1,580,854,677	8,257,873	7,444,411	6,104,102
Common shares held in treasury:			
Beginning of year			
Shares: 2009: 49,147,968; 2008: 30,944,537; 2007: 13,347,272	(2,626,404)	(1,213,134)	(195,237)
Private transaction			
Shares purchased: 15,176,500;			
shares issued: 14,870,195	—	(378,931)	—
Issued under incentive stock programs			
Shares: 2009: 2,477,853; 2008: 1,607,326; 2007: 2,063,123	133,042	40,946	37,080
Purchased			
Shares: 2009: 14,846,283; 2008: 19,504,452; 2007: 19,660,388	(816,985)	(1,075,285)	(1,054,977)
End of year			
Shares: 2009: 61,516,398; 2008: 49,147,968; 2007: 30,944,537	(3,310,347)	(2,626,404)	(1,213,134)
Earnings employed in the business:			
Beginning of year	$13,825,383	$10,805,809	$9,568,728
Net earnings	5,745,838	4,880,719	3,606,314
Cash dividends declared on common shares (per share—2009: $1.60;			
2008: $1.44; 2007: $1.30)	(2,476,036)	(2,228,776)	(2,009,696)
Reclassification resulting from the application of the fair value option			
to Boston Scientific common stock, net of tax	—	—	(188,534)
Cost of common shares retired in excess of stated capital amount	(25,040)	(70,590)	(237,958)
Cost of treasury shares issued (above) below market value	(16,118)	438,221	66,955
End of year	$17,054,027	$13,825,383	$10,805,809
Accumulated other comprehensive income (loss):			
Beginning of year	$ (1,163,839)	$ 2,081,763	$ 389,766
Reclassification resulting from the application of the fair value option			
to Boston Scientific common stock, net of tax	—	—	181,834
Other comprehensive income (loss)	2,017,913	(3,245,602)	1,510,163
End of year	$ 854,074	$ (1,163,839)	$ 2,081,763
Comprehensive income	$ 7,763,751	$ 1,635,117	$ 5,116,477
Noncontrolling interests in subsidiaries:			
Beginning of year	$ 39,140	$ 45,405	$ 43,945
Noncontrolling interests' share of income, net of distributions			
and share repurchases	3,962	(6,265)	1,460
End of year	$ 43,102	$ 39,140	$ 45,405

NOTES TO CONSOLIDATED FINANCIAL STATEMENTS

Note 9 (In Part): Incentive Stock Program

The 2009 Incentive Stock Program authorizes the granting of nonqualified stock options, replacement stock options, restricted stock awards, restricted stock units, performance awards, foreign benefits and other share-based awards. Stock options, replacement stock options and restricted stock awards and units comprise the majority of benefits that have been granted and are currently outstanding under this program and a prior program. In 2009, Abbott granted 1,783,300 stock options, 1,449,301 replacement stock options, 1,278,467 restricted stock awards and 5,677,322 restricted stock units under this program. In addition, 2,899,411 options were issued in connection with the conversion of Advanced Medical Optics, Inc. options to Abbott options. The purchase price of shares under option must be at least equal to the fair market value of the common stock on the date of grant, and the maximum term of an option is 10 years. Options vest equally over three years except for replacement options, which vest in six months. Options granted before January 1, 2005 included a replacement feature. Except for options outstanding that have a replacement feature, options granted after December 31, 2004 do not include a replacement feature. When an employee tenders mature shares to Abbott upon exercise of a stock option, a replacement stock option may be granted equal to the amount of shares tendered. Replacement options are granted at the then current market price for a term that expires on the date of the underlying option grant. Upon a change in control of Abbott, all outstanding stock options become fully exercisable, and all terms and conditions of all restricted stock awards and units are deemed satisfied. Restricted stock awards generally vest between 3 and 5 years and for restricted stock awards that vest over 5 years, no more than one-third of the award vests in any one year upon Abbott reaching a minimum return on equity target. Restricted stock units vest over three years and upon vesting, the recipient receives one share of Abbott stock for each vested restricted stock unit. The aggregate fair market value of restricted stock awards and units is recognized as expense over the service period. Restricted stock awards and settlement of vested restricted stock units are issued out of treasury shares. Abbott generally issues new shares for exercises of stock options. Abbott does not have a policy of purchasing its shares relating to its share-based programs. At December 31, 2009, approximately 220 million shares were reserved for future grants, including 175 million shares authorized by Abbott's shareholders in April 2009. Subsequent to year-end, the reserve was reduced by approximately 23 million shares for stock options and restricted stock awards and units granted by the Board of Directors.

The number of restricted stock awards and units outstanding and the weighted-average grant-date fair value at December 31, 2008 and December 31, 2009 was 3,574,445 and $52.21 and 8,703,247 and $53.64, respectively. The number of restricted stock awards and units, and the weighted-average grant-date fair value, that were granted, vested and lapsed during 2009 were 6,955,789 and $53.54, 1,556,472 and $49.98 and 270,515 and $53.39, respectively. The fair market value of restricted stock awards and units vested in 2009, 2008 and 2007 was $81 million, $76 million and $114 million, respectively.

	Options Outstanding			Exercisable Options		
	Shares	Weighted Average Exercise Price	Weighted Average Remaining Life (Years)	Shares	Weighted Average Exercise Price	Weighted Average Remaining Life (Years)
December 31, 2008	128,827,135	$49.16	6.4	87,770,715	$47.39	5.4
Granted	6,132,012	58.50				
Exercised	(13,281,445)	43.91				
Lapsed	(2,817,581)	54.94				
December 31, 2009	118,860,121	$50.09	5.7	98,251,406	$49.16	5.2

5.24

THE TORO COMPANY (OCT)

(Dollars in thousands, except per share data)	Common Stock	Retained Earnings	Accumulated Other Comprehensive Loss	Total Stockholders' Equity	Comprehensive Income
Balance as of October 31, 2006	$40,356	$ 358,522	$ (6,849)	$ 392,029	
Cash dividends paid on common stock—$0.48 per share	—	(19,459)	—	(19,459)	
Issuance of 937,846 shares under stock-based compensation plans	938	18,862	—	19,800	
Contribution of stock to a deferred compensation trust	—	748	—	748	
Purchase of 3,342,729 shares of common stock	(3,343)	(179,500)	—	(182,843)	
Excess tax benefits from stock options	—	13,775	—	13,775	
Adjustment related to adoption of SFAS No. 158, net of tax	—	—	(1,484)	(1,484)	
Minimum pension liability adjustment, net of tax	—	—	41	41	$ 41
Foreign currency translation adjustments	—	—	9,757	9,757	9,757
Unrealized loss on derivative instruments, net of tax	—	—	(4,362)	(4,362)	(4,362)
Net earnings	—	142,436	—	142,436	142,436
Total comprehensive income					$147,872
Balance as of October 31, 2007	$37,951	$ 335,384	$ (2,897)	$ 370,438	
Cash dividends paid on common stock—$0.60 per share	—	(22,615)	—	(22,615)	
Issuance of 343,862 shares under stock-based compensation plans	344	9,035	—	9,379	
Contribution of stock to a deferred compensation trust	—	302	—	302	
Purchase of 2,809,927 shares of common stock	(2,810)	(107,545)	—	(110,355)	
Excess tax benefits from stock options	—	3,522	—	3,522	
Pension liability adjustment, net of tax	—	—	359	359	$ 359
Foreign currency translation adjustments	—	—	(18,367)	(18,367)	(18,367)
Unrealized gain on derivative instruments, net of tax	—	—	12,361	12,361	12,361
Net earnings	—	119,651	—	119,651	119,651
Total comprehensive income					$114,004
Balance as of October 31, 2008	$35,485	$ 337,734	$ (8,544)	$ 364,675	
Cash dividends paid on common stock—$0.60 per share	—	(21,403)	—	(21,403)	
Issuance of 1,201,256 shares under stock-based compensation plans	1,201	16,524	—	17,725	
Contribution of stock to a deferred compensation trust	—	118	—	118	
Purchase of 3,316,536 shares of common stock	(3,317)	(111,967)	—	(115,284)	
Excess tax benefits from stock options	—	7,403	—	7,403	
Pension liability adjustment, net of tax	—	—	(2,633)	(2,633)	$ (2,633)
Foreign currency translation adjustments	—	—	13,286	13,286	13,286
Unrealized loss on derivative instruments, net of tax	—	—	(11,512)	(11,512)	(11,512)
Net earnings	—	62,837	—	62,837	62,837
Total comprehensive income					$ 61,978
Balance as of October 31, 2009	$33,369	$ 291,246	$ (9,403)	$ 315,212	

NOTES TO CONSOLIDATED FINANCIAL STATEMENTS

8 (In Part): Stockholders' Equity

Stock Repurchase Program

The company's Board of Directors authorized the repurchase of shares of the company's common stock as follows:
- In July 2006, 3,000,000 shares
- In May 2007, 3,000,000 shares
- In May 2008, 4,000,000 shares
- In July 2009, 5,000,000 shares

During fiscal 2009, 2008, and 2007, the company paid $115,283, $110,355, and $182,843 to repurchase an aggre-gate of 3,316,536, 2,809,927 shares, and 3,342,729 shares, respectively. As of October 31, 2009, 4,007,712 shares remained authorized for repurchase.

Treasury Shares

As of October 31, 2009, the company had 20,662,734 treasury shares at a cost of $764,015. As of October 31, 2008, the company had 18,547,454 treasury shares at a cost of $688,015.

Tax Benefit From ESOP Dividends

5.25

CHEVRON CORPORATION (DEC)

(Shares in thousands; amounts in millions of dollars)	2009 Shares	2009 Amount	2008 Shares	2008 Amount	2007 Shares	2007 Amount
Preferred stock	—	$ —	—	$ —	—	$ —
Common stock	2,442,677	$ 1,832	2,442,677	$ 1,832	2,442,677	$ 1,832
Capital in excess of par						
Balance at January 1		$ 14,448		$ 14,289		$ 14,126
Treasury stock transactions		183		159		163
Balance at December 31		$ 14,631		$ 14,448		$ 14,289
Retained earnings						
Balance at January 1		$101,102		$ 82,329		$ 68,464
Net income attributable to Chevron Corporation		10,483		23,931		18,688
Cash dividends on common stock		(5,302)		(5,162)		(4,791)
Adoption of new accounting standard for uncertain income tax positions		—		—		(35)
Tax benefit from dividends paid on unallocated ESOP shares and other		6		4		3
Balance at December 31		$106,289		$101,102		$ 82,329
Notes receivable—key employees		$ —		$ —		$ (1)
Accumulated other comprehensive loss						
Currency translation adjustment						
Balance at January 1		$ (171)		$ (59)		$ (90)
Change during year		60		(112)		31
Balance at December 31		$ (111)		$ (171)		$ (59)
Pension and other postretirement benefit plans						
Balance at January 1		$ (3,909)		$ (2,008)		$ (2,585)
Change to defined benefit plans during year		(399)		(1,901)		685
Adoption of new accounting standard for defined benefit pension and other postretirement plans		—		—		(108)
Balance at December 31		$ (4,308)		$ (3,909)		$ (2,008)
Unrealized net holding gain on securities						
Balance at January 1		$ 13		$ 19		$ —
Change during year		2		(6)		19
Balance at December 31		$ 15		$ 13		$ 19
Net derivatives gain (loss) on hedge transactions						
Balance at January 1		$ 143		$ 33		$ 39
Change during year		(60)		110		(6)
Balance at December 31		$ 83		$ 143		$ 33
Balance at December 31		$ (4,321)		$ (3,924)		$ (2,015)
Deferred compensation and benefit plan trust						
Deferred compensation						
Balance at January 1		$ (194)		$ (214)		$ (214)
Net reduction of ESOP debt and other		85		20		—
Balance at December 31		(109)		(194)		(214)
Benefit Plan Trust (common stock)	14,168	(240)	14,168	(240)	14,168	(240)
Balance at December 31	14,168	$ (349)	14,168	$ (434)	14,168	$ (454)
Treasury stock at cost						
Balance at January 1	438,445	$ (26,376)	352,243	$ (18,892)	278,118	$(12,395)
Purchases	85	(6)	95,631	(8,011)	85,429	(7,036)
Issuances—mainly employee benefit plans	(3,575)	214	(9,429)	527	(11,304)	539
Balance at December 31	434,955	$ (26,168)	438,445	$ (26,376)	352,243	$(18,892)
Total Chevron Corporation stockholders' equity at December 31		$ 91,914		$ 86,648		$ 77,088
Noncontrolling interests		$ 647		$ 469		$ 204
Total equity		$ 92,561		$ 87,117		$ 77,292

NOTES TO CONSOLIDATED FINANCIAL STATEMENTS

Note 21 (In Part): Employee Benefit Plans

Employee Stock Ownership Plan

Within the Chevron ESIP is an employee stock ownership plan (ESOP). In 1989, Chevron established a LESOP as a constituent part of the ESOP. The LESOP provides partial prefunding of the company's future commitments to the ESIP.

As permitted by accounting standards for share-based compensation (ASC 718), the debt of the LESOP is recorded as debt, and shares pledged as collateral are reported as "Deferred compensation and benefit plan trust" on the Consolidated Balance Sheet and the Consolidated Statement of Equity.

The company reports compensation expense equal to LESOP debt principal repayments less dividends received and used by the LESOP for debt service. Interest accrued on LESOP debt is recorded as interest expense. Dividends paid on LESOP shares are reflected as a reduction of retained earnings. All LESOP shares are considered outstanding for earnings-per-share computations.

Total credits to expense for the LESOP were $3, $1 and $1 in 2009, 2008 and 2007, respectively. The net credit for the respective years was composed of credits to compensation expense of $15, $15 and $17 and charges to interest expense for LESOP debt of $12, $14 and $16.

Of the dividends paid on the LESOP shares, $110, $35 and $8 were used in 2009, 2008 and 2007, respectively, to service LESOP debt. No contributions were required in 2009, 2008 or 2007 as dividends received by the LESOP were sufficient to satisfy LESOP debt service.

Shares held in the LESOP are released and allocated to the accounts of plan participants based on debt service deemed to be paid in the year in proportion to the total of current-year and remaining debt service. LESOP shares as of December 31, 2009 and 2008, were as follows:

(Thousands)	2009	2008
Allocated shares	21,211	19,651
Unallocated shares	3,636	6,366
Total LESOP shares	24,847	26,017

ADDITIONAL PAID-IN CAPITAL

PRESENTATION OF CHANGES IN ADDITIONAL PAID-IN CAPITAL

5.26 FASB ASC 505, *Equity*, states if both financial position and results of operations are presented, disclosure of changes in the separate accounts comprising stockholders' equity (in addition to retained earnings) and of the changes in the number of shares of equity securities during at least the most recent annual fiscal period and any subsequent interim period presented is required to make the financial statements sufficiently informative. Disclosure of such changes may take the form of separate statements or may be made in the basic financial statements or notes thereto.

5.27 Table 5-5 summarizes the presentation formats used by the survey entities to present changes in additional paid-in capital.

5.28

TABLE 5-5: PRESENTATION OF CHANGES IN ADDITIONAL PAID-IN CAPITAL

	2009	2008	2007	2006
Statement of stockholders' equity	446	449	539	532
Schedule in notes	8	7	10	9
No statement or schedule but changes disclosed	—	—	1	2
Balance unchanged during year	1	3	3	3
	455	459	553	546
Additional paid-in capital account not presented	45	41	47	54
Total Entities	**500**	**500**	**600**	**600**

2008–2009 based on 500 entities surveyed; 2006–2007 based on 600 entities surveyed.

STOCK SPLITS

5.29 Table 5-6 shows the number of survey entities disclosing stock splits and summarizes the accounting treatments for stock splits. Examples of disclosures of stock splits follow.

5.30

TABLE 5-6: STOCK SPLITS

	2009	2008	2007	2006
Ratio				
Less than three-for-two	1	—	2	1
Three-for-two (50%) to two-for-one	—	2	7	9
Two-for-one (100%)	1	8	26	29
Greater than two-for-one	—	—	—	2
	2	10	35	41
Reverse Ratio				
One-for-two	—	—	—	—
One-for-three	1	—	—	—
One-for-four	—	—	—	—
Other	3	—	3	1
Total Entities	**6**	**10**	**38**	**42**
Account(s) Charged				
Additional paid-in capital	2	—	13	12
Retained earnings	2	1	2	2
Both additional paid-in capital and retained earnings	—	—	2	—
No charge	2	9	21	28
Total Entities	**6**	**10**	**38**	**42**

2008–2009 based on 500 entities surveyed; 2006–2007 based on 600 entities surveyed.

5.31

BROWN-FORMAN CORPORATION (APR)

(Dollars in millions, except per share amounts)	2007	2008	2009
Class A common stock	$ 9	$ 9	$ 9
Class B common stock:			
Balance at beginning of year	10	10	10
Stock distribution (Note 1)	—	—	5
Balance at end of year	10	10	15
Additional paid-in capital:			
Balance at beginning of year	47	64	74
Stock issued under compensation plans	2	3	—
Stock-based compensation expense	6	6	5
Adjustment for stock option exercises	1	(9)	(16)
Excess tax benefits from stock options	8	10	4
Balance at end of year	64	74	67
Retained earnings:			
Balance at beginning of year	1,607	1,649	1,931
Net income	389	440	435
Cash dividends ($0.93, $1.03, and $1.12 per share in 2007, 2008, and 2009, respectively)	(143)	(158)	(169)
Special cash distribution to stockholders ($1.32 per share in 2007)	(204)	—	—
Stock distribution (Note 1)	—	—	(5)
Adoption of SFAS 158 measurement date provision, net of tax of $2	—	—	(3)
Balance at end of year	1,649	1,931	2,189
Treasury stock, at cost:			
Balance at beginning of year	(128)	(102)	(304)
Acquisition of treasury stock	—	(223)	(39)
Stock issued under compensation plans	24	17	10
Stock-based compensation expense	2	4	2
Balance at end of year	(102)	(304)	(331)
Accumulated other comprehensive income (loss):			
Balance at beginning of year	18	(57)	5
Net other comprehensive income (loss)	19	62	(147)
Adjustment to initially apply SFAS 158, net of tax of $60	(94)	—	—
Adoption of SFAS 158 measurement date provision, net of tax of $(6)	—	—	9
Balance at end of year	(57)	5	(133)
Total stockholders' equity	$ 1,573	$ 1,725	$ 1,816
Class A common shares outstanding (in thousands):			
Balance at beginning of year	56,829	56,870	56,573
Acquisition of treasury stock	—	(340)	(22)
Stock issued under compensation plans	41	43	39
Balance at end of year	56,870	56,573	56,590
Class B common shares outstanding (in thousands):			
Balance at beginning of year	65,636	66,367	64,019
Stock distribution (Note 1)	—	—	30,175
Acquisition of treasury stock	—	(2,937)	(843)
Stock issued under compensation plans	731	589	186
Balance at end of year	66,367	64,019	93,537
Total common shares outstanding (in thousands)	123,237	120,592	150,127

NOTES TO CONSOLIDATED FINANCIAL STATEMENTS
(Dollars in millions, except per share amounts)

1 (In Part): Accounting Policies

Stock Distribution

In September 2008, our Board of Directors authorized a stock split, effected as a stock dividend, of one share of Class B common stock for every four shares of either Class A or Class B common stock held by stockholders of record as of the close of business on October 6, 2008, with fractional shares paid in cash. The distribution took place on October 27, 2008.

As a result of the stock distribution, we reclassified approximately $5 from the company's retained earnings account to its common stock account. The $5 represents the $0.15 par value per share of the shares issued in the stock distribution.

All previously reported per share and Class B share amounts in the accompanying financial statements and related notes have been restated to reflect the stock distribution.

5.32

SANMINA-SCI CORPORATION (SEP)

NOTES TO CONSOLIDATED FINANCIAL STATEMENTS

11 (In Part): Stockholders' Equity

Reverse Stock Split

On July 20, 2009, the Board of Directors of the Company authorized a reverse split of its common stock at a ratio of one for six, effective August 14, 2009. The Company's stockholders previously approved the reverse split in September 2008. As a result of the reverse split, every six shares of common stock outstanding were combined into one share of common stock. The reverse split did not affect the amount of equity the Company has nor did it affect the Company's market capitalization.

CHANGES IN ADDITIONAL PAID-IN CAPITAL

5.33   Table 5-7 summarizes credits and charges to additional paid-in capital. Examples of such credits and charges follow.

5.34

TABLE 5-7: CHANGES IN ADDITIONAL PAID-IN CAPITAL*

| | Number of Entities | | | |
	2009	2008	2007	2006
Credits				
Common stock issued				
Employee benefits	303	369	440	442
Public offerings	38	27	29	36
Business combinations	20	27	24	41
Debt conversions/ extinguishments	14	15	22	20
Preferred stock conversions	8	9	7	15
Compensation recognized	310	291	352	307
Stock compensation tax benefits	137	201	265	249
Warrants issued or exercised	6	—	1	2
Other—described	70	59	65	80
Charges				
Treasury stock issued for less than cost	86	79	60	75
Purchase or retirement of capital stock	84	120	166	128
Stock compensation tax benefits	66	N/C**	N/C**	N/C**
Restricted stock	64	61	64	69
Other employee benefits	52	48	45	82
Conversion of preferred stock	4	4	6	6
Other—described	59	50	46	74

* Appearing in either the statement of stockholders' equity and/or the notes to financial statements.

** N/C = Not compiled. Line item was not included in the table for the year shown.

2008–2009 based on 500 entities surveyed; 2006–2007 based on 600 entities surveyed.

Common Stock Issued in Connection With Employee Benefit Plans

5.35

AVNET, INC. (JUN)

(In thousands)	Common Stock	Additional Paid-In Capital	Retained Earnings	Accumulated Other Comprehensive Income	Treasury Stock	Total Shareholders' Equity
Balance at July 1, 2006	146,667	$1,010,336	$ 1,487,575	$ 186,876	$(271)	$ 2,831,183
Net income	—	—	393,067	—	—	393,067
Translation adjustments	—	—	—	83,094	—	83,094
Pension liability adjustment, net of tax of $4,181	—	—	—	6,539	—	6,539
Comprehensive income						482,700
Stock option and incentive programs, including related tax benefits of $15,597	3,159	83,874	—	—	(271)	86,762
Balance, June 30, 2007	149,826	$1,094,210	$ 1,880,642	$ 276,509	$(542)	$ 3,400,645
Net income	—	—	499,081	—	—	499,081
Translation adjustments	—	—	—	222,551	—	222,551
Pension liability adjustment, net of tax of $10,901	—	—	—	(16,882)	—	(16,882)
Comprehensive income						704,750
Stock option and incentive programs, including related tax benefits of $3,840	591	28,642	—	—	63	29,296
Balance, June 28, 2008	150,417	$1,122,852	$ 2,379,723	$ 482,178	$(479)	$ 4,134,691
Net loss	—	—	(1,122,462)	—	—	(1,122,462)
Translation adjustments	—	—	—	(237,903)	—	(237,903)
Pension liability adjustment, net of tax of $16,767	—	—	—	(26,181)	—	(26,181)
Comprehensive loss						(1,386,546)
Stock option and incentive programs, including related tax benefits of $653	682	12,482	—	—	(452)	12,712
Balance, June 27, 2009	151,099	$1,135,334	$ 1,257,261	$ 218,094	$(931)	$ 2,760,857

NOTES TO CONSOLIDATED FINANCIAL STATEMENTS

Note 1 (In Part): Summary of Significant Accounting Policies

Stock-Based Compensation

The Company measures share-based payments, including grants of employee stock options, at fair value and recognizes the associated expense in the consolidated statement of operations over the service period.

Note 13 (In Part): Stock-Based Compensation

Stock Plan

The Company has one stock compensation plan, the 2006 Stock Compensation Plan ("2006 Plan") which was approved by the shareholders in fiscal 2007. The 2006 Plan has a termination date of November 8, 2016 and 2,530,617 shares were available for grant at June 27, 2009. At June 27, 2009, the Company had 8,357,205 shares of common stock reserved for stock option and stock incentive programs.

Stock Options

Option grants under the 2006 Plan have a contractual life of ten years, vest 25% on each anniversary of the grant date, commencing with the first anniversary, and provide for a mini-

mum exercise price of 100% of fair market value at the date of grant. Pre-tax compensation expense associated with stock options during fiscal 2009, 2008 and 2007 were $4,245,000, $6,155,000 and $8,356,000, respectively.

The fair value of options granted is estimated on the date of grant using the Black-Scholes model based on the assumptions in the following table. The assumption for the expected term is based on evaluations of historical and expected future employee exercise behavior. The risk-free interest rate is based on the US Treasury rates at the date of grant with maturity dates approximately equal to the expected term at the grant date. The historical volatility of Avnet's stock is used as the basis for the volatility assumption.

	2009	2008	2007
Expected term (years)	5.75	6.0	6.0
Risk-free interest rate	3.4%	4.6%	4.8%
Weighted average volatility	30.7%	35.9%	40.1%
Dividend yield	—	—	—

The following is a summary of the changes in outstanding options for fiscal 2009:

(In thousands)	Shares	Weighted Average Exercise Price	Weighted Average Remaining Contractual Life	Aggregate Intrinsic Value
Outstanding at June 28, 2008	3,585,679	$20.21	61 Months	
Granted	405,716	$28.47	110 Months	
Exercised	(31,297)	$17.99	40 Months	
Forfeited or expired	(78,292)	$21.94	18 Months	
Outstanding at June 27, 2009	3,881,806	$21.06	56 Months	$26,579
Exercisable at June 27, 2009	3,060,138	$19.28	45 Months	$26,579

The weighted-average grant-date fair values of stock options granted during fiscal 2009, 2008, and 2007 were $10.21, $14.90, and $8.88, respectively. The total intrinsic values of share options exercised during fiscal 2009, 2008 and 2007 were $3,000, $109,000 and $524,000, respectively.

The following is a summary of the changes in non-vested stock options for the fiscal year ended June 27, 2009:

	Shares	Weighted Average Grant-Date Fair Value
Non-vested stock options at June 28, 2008	816,541	$12.95
Granted	405,716	$10.21
Vested	(399,149)	$13.92
Forfeited	(1,440)	$ 8.35
Non-vested stock options at June 27, 2009	821,668	$11.14

As of June 27, 2009, there was $9,152,000 of total unrecognized compensation cost related to non-vested awards granted under the option plans, which is expected to be recognized over a weighted-average period of 3.3 years. The total fair values of shares vested during fiscal 2009, 2008 and 2007 were $5,555,000, $4,969,000 and $7,901,000, respectively.

Cash received from option exercises during fiscal 2009, 2008 and 2007 totaled $563,000, $5,111,000 and $54,357,000, respectively. The impact of these cash receipts is included in "Other, net" in financing activities in the accompanying consolidated statements of cash flows.

Incentive Shares

Delivery of incentive shares, and the associated compensation expense, is spread equally over a five-year period and is subject to the employee's continued employment by the Company. As of June 27, 2009, 1,139,243 shares previously awarded have not yet been delivered. Pre-tax compensation expense associated with this program was $15,843,000, $12,074,000 and $8,231,000 for fiscal years 2009, 2008 and 2007, respectively.

The following is a summary of the changes in non-vested incentive shares for the fiscal year ended June 27, 2009:

	Shares	Weighted Average Grant-Date Fair Value
Non-vested incentive shares at June 28, 2008	1,035,148	$25.06
Granted	697,805	$28.80
Vested	(503,961)	$24.98
Forfeited	(89,749)	$27.14
Non-vested incentive shares at June 27, 2009	1,139,243	$27.22

As of June 27, 2009, there was $29,372,000 of total unrecognized compensation cost related to non-vested incentive shares, which is expected to be recognized over a weighted-average period of 2.6 years. The total fair values of shares vested during fiscal 2009, 2008 and 2007 were $12,588,000, $9,097,000 and $6,027,000, respectively.

Performance Shares

Eligible employees, including Avnet's executive officers, may receive a portion of their long-term equity-based incentive compensation through the performance share program, which allows for the award of shares of stock based upon performance-based criteria ("Performance Shares"). The Performance Shares will provide for the issuance to each grantee of a number of shares of Avnet's common stock at the end of a three-year period based upon the Company's achievement of performance goals established by the Compensation Committee of the Board of Directors for each three-year period. These performance goals are based upon a three-year cumulative increase in the Company's absolute economic profit, as defined, over the prior three-year period and the increase in the Company's economic profit relative to the increase in the economic profit of a peer group of companies. During fiscal 2009, 2008 and 2007, the Company granted 246,650, 170,630 and 238,795 performance shares, respectively, to be awarded to participants in the Performance Share program, of which 38,740 have been forfeited. The actual amount of Performance Shares issued at the end of the three year period is determined based upon the level of achievement of the defined performance goals and can range from 0% to 200% of the initial award. The Company anticipates issuing 113,130 shares in the first quarter of fiscal 2010 based upon the goals achieved at the end of the 2007 Performance Share plan three-year period which ended June 27,

2009. During fiscal 2009, the Company recorded a pre-tax net credit of $1,819,000 in "selling, general and administrative expenses" associated with the Performance Share plans based upon actual performance under the 2007 plan and based upon the probability assessment of the remaining plans. During fiscal 2008 and 2007, the Company recognized pre-tax compensation expense associated with the Performance Shares of $6,380,000 and $7,025,000, respectively.

Outside Director Stock Bonus Plan

Non-employee directors are awarded shares equal to a fixed dollar amount of Avnet common stock upon their re-election each year, as part of their director compensation package. Directors may elect to receive this compensation in the form of common stock under the Outside Director Stock Bonus Plan or they may elect to defer their compensation to be paid in common stock at a later date. During fiscal 2009, 2008 and 2007, pre-tax compensation cost associated with the outside director stock bonus plan was $960,000, $780,000 and $638,000, respectively.

Employee Stock Purchase Plan

The Company has an Employee Stock Purchase Plan ("ESPP") under the terms of which eligible employees of the Company are offered options to purchase shares of Avnet common stock at a price equal to 95% of the fair market value on the last day of each monthly offering period. Based on the terms of the ESPP, Avnet is not required to record expense in the consolidated statements of operations related to the ESPP.

The Company has a policy of repurchasing shares on the open market to satisfy shares purchased under the ESPP, and expects future repurchases during fiscal 2010 to be similar to the number of shares repurchased during fiscal 2009, based on current estimates of participation in the program. During fiscal 2009, 2008 and 2007, there were 100,206, 70,553 and 96,013 shares, respectively, of common stock issued under the ESPP program.

5.36

ABM INDUSTRIES INCORPORATED (OCT)

(In thousands)	Common Stock		Treasury Stock		Additional Paid-In Capital	Accumulated Other Comprehensive Income (Loss)	Retained Earnings	Total
	Shares	Amount	Shares	Amount				
Balance October 31, 2006	55,663	$557	(7,028)	$(122,338)	$225,796	$149	$437,083	$541,247
Comprehensive income:								
Net income	—	—	—	—	—	—	52,440	52,440
Foreign currency translation	—	—	—	—	—	520	—	520
Comprehensive income	—	—	—	—	—	—	—	52,960
Adjustment to initially apply ASC 715, net of taxes	—	—	—	—	—	211	—	211
Dividends:								
Common stock	—	—	—	—	—	—	(23,805)	(23,805)
Tax benefit from exercise of stock options	—	—	—	—	4,046	—	—	4,046
Stock issued under employees' stock purchase and option plans	1,385	14	—	—	23,181	—	(255)	22,940
Share-based compensation expense	—	—	—	—	8,159	—	—	8,159
Balance October 31, 2007	57,048	$571	(7,028)	$(122,338)	$261,182	$880	$465,463	$605,758

(continued)

(In thousands)	Common Stock		Treasury Stock		Additional Paid-In Capital	Accumulated Other Comprehensive Income (Loss)	Retained Earnings	Total
	Shares	Amount	Shares	Amount				
Balance October 31, 2007	57,048	$571	(7,028)	$(122,338)	$ 261,182	$ 880	$465,463	$605,758
Comprehensive income:								
Net income	—	—	—	—	—	—	45,434	45,434
Unrealized loss on auction rate securities, net of taxes of $2,348	—	—	—	—	—	(3,621)	—	(3,621)
Foreign currency translation, net of taxes of $590	—	—	—	—	—	(909)	—	(909)
Actuarial gain—adjustments to pension & other post-retirement benefit plans, net of taxes of $148	—	—	—	—	—	228	—	228
Comprehensive income	—	—	—	—	—	—	—	41,132
Dividends:								
Common stock	—	—	—	—	—	—	(25,271)	(25,271)
Tax benefit from exercise of stock options	—	—	—	—	899	—	—	899
Stock issued under employees' stock purchase and option plans	944	10	—	—	14,818	—	(490)	14,338
Share-based compensation expense	—	—	—	—	7,195	—	—	7,195
Balance October 31, 2008	57,992	$581	(7,028)	$(122,338)	$ 284,094	$(3,422)	$485,136	$644,051
Comprehensive income:								
Net income	—	—	—	—	—	—	54,293	54,293
Unrealized gain on auction rate securities, net of taxes of $203	—	—	—	—	—	297	—	297
Reclass adjustment for credit losses recognized in earnings, net of taxes of $636	—	—	—	—	—	930	—	930
Foreign currency translation, net of taxes of $241	—	—	—	—	—	577	—	577
Actuarial loss—adjustments to pension & other post-retirement benefit plans, net of taxes of $139	—	—	—	—	—	(203)	—	(203)
Unrealized loss on interest rate swaps, net of taxes of $412	—	—	—	—	—	(602)	—	(602)
Comprehensive income	—	—	—	—	—	—	—	55,292
Dividends:								
Common stock	—	—	—	—	—	—	(26,727)	(26,727)
Tax benefit from exercise of stock options	—	—	—	—	(1,314)	—	—	(1,314)
Stock issued under employees' stock purchase and option plans	724	6	—	—	8,557	—	(226)	8,337
Share-based compensation expense	—	—	—	—	7,411	—	—	7,411
Treasury stock retirement	(7,028)	(70)	7,028	122,338	(122,268)	—	—	—
Balance October 31, 2009	51,688	$517	—	$ —	$ 176,480	$(2,423)	$512,476	$687,050

ATT-SEC 5.36

NOTES TO CONSOLIDATED FINANCIAL STATEMENTS

Note 1 (In Part): Summary of Significant Accounting Policies

Share-Based Compensation

Share-based compensation expense is measured at the grant date, based on the fair value of the award, and is recognized as an expense over the requisite employee service period (generally the vesting period) for awards expected to vest (considering estimated forfeitures). The Company estimates the fair value of stock options using the Black-Scholes option-pricing model. The fair value of restricted stock and performance awards is determined based on the number of shares granted and the grant date fair value of the award. The estimation of stock awards that will ultimately vest requires judgment, and to the extent actual results or updated estimates differ from the Company's current estimates, such amounts will be recorded as a cumulative adjustment in the period estimates are revised. The Company considers many factors when estimating expected forfeitures, including types of awards, employee class, and historical experience. Stock option exercises and restricted stock and performance award issuances are expected to be fulfilled with new shares of common stock. The compensation cost is included in selling, general and administrative expenses and is amortized on a straight-line basis over the vesting term.

13. Share Based Compensation Plans

Compensation expense and related income tax benefit in connection with the Company's share-based compensation plans for the years ended October 31, 2009, 2008 and 2007 were as follows:

(In thousands)	2009	2008	2007
Share-based compensation expense recognized in selling, general and administrative expenses before income taxes	$ 7,411	$ 7,195	$ 8,159
Income tax benefit	(3,025)	(2,764)	(3,136)
Total share-based compensation expense after income taxes	$ 4,386	$ 4,431	$ 5,023

The total intrinsic value of the 494,843, 728,332, and 1,137,864 shares exercised for all share based compensation plans during the years ended October 31, 2009, 2008,

and 2007, was $3.0 million, $6.3 million, and $12.5 million, respectively. The total fair value of shares that vested during the years ended October 31, 2009, 2008 and 2007 was $3.8 million, $3.1 million and $11.8 million, respectively.

The Company has five share-based compensation plans and an employee stock purchase plan which are described below.

2006 Equity Incentive Plan

On May 2, 2006, the stockholders of the Company approved the 2006 Equity Incentive Plan (the "2006 Equity Plan"). Prior to the adoption of the 2006 Equity Plan, stock option awards were made under the Time-Vested Incentive Stock Option Plan (the "Time-Vested Plan"), the 1996 Price-Vested Performance Stock Option Plan (the "1996 Price-Vested Plan") and the 2002 Price-Vested Performance Stock Option Plan (the "2002 Price-Vested Plan" and collectively with the Time-Vested Plan and the 1996 Price-Vested Plan, the "Prior Plans"). The 2006 Equity Plan provides for the issuance of awards for 2,500,000 shares of the Company's common stock plus the remaining shares authorized but not issued under the Prior Plans as of May 2, 2006, plus forfeitures under the Prior Plans after that date. No further grants can be made under the Prior Plans. On March 3, 2009, the shareholders authorized an additional 2,750,000 shares to be issued under the 2006 Equity Plan. At October 31, 2009, 3,247,423 shares were available for award under the 2006 Equity Plan. The terms and conditions governing existing options under the Prior Plans will continue to apply to the options outstanding under those plans. The 2006 Equity Plan is an "omnibus" plan that provides for a variety of equity and equity-based award vehicles, including stock options, stock appreciation rights, restricted stock, RSUs awards, performance shares, and other share-based awards. Shares subject to awards that terminate without vesting or exercise may be reissued. Certain of the awards available under the 2006 Equity Plan may qualify as "performance-based" compensation under Internal Revenue Code Section 162(m) ("Section 162(m)"). The status of the stock options, RSUs and performance shares granted under the 2006 Equity Plan as of October 31, 2009 are summarized below.

Stock Options

The nonqualified stock options issued under the 2006 Equity Plan vest and become exercisable at a rate of 25% per year beginning one year after date of grant and expire seven years and one month after the date of grant.

Stock option activity in the year ended October 31, 2009 is summarized below:

	Number of Shares (In Thousands)	Weighted-Average Exercise Price per Share	Weighted-Average Remaining Contractual Term (In Years)	Aggregate Intrinsic Value (In Thousands)
Outstanding at October 31, 2008	597	$20.23		
Granted	120	17.90		
Forfeited or expired	7	18.97		
Outstanding at October 31, 2009	710	$19.85	5.04	$114
Vested and exercisable at October 31, 2009	234	$20.40	4.54	$ 6

As of October 31, 2009, there was $1.8 million of total un-recognized compensation cost (net of estimated forfeitures) related to unvested stock options under the 2006 Equity Plan. The cost is expected to be recognized on a straight-line ba-sis over a weighted-average vesting period of 1.27 years. The exercise prices of the outstanding and vested stock options exceeded the October 31, 2009 closing price of the Com-pany's stock, resulting in zero aggregate intrinsic value.

The Company estimates the fair value of each option award on the date of grant using the Black-Scholes option valuation model. The Company estimates forfeiture rates based on his-torical data and adjusts the rates periodically or as needed. The adjustment of the forfeiture rate may result in a cumu-lative adjustment in any period the forfeiture rate estimate is changed. During 2009, the Company adjusted its forfeiture rate to align the estimate with expected forfeitures, and the effect of such adjustment was immaterial.

The assumptions used in the option valuation model for the years ended October 31, 2009, 2008 and 2007 are shown in the table below:

	2009	2008	2007
Expected life from the date of grant[1]	5.7 years	5.7 years	5.2 years
Expected stock price volatility[2]	35.2%	30.4%	25.3%
Expected dividend yield[3]	2.5%	2.4%	2.1%
Risk-free interest rate[4]	1.7%	3.2%	4.3%
Weighted average fair value of option grants	$4.82	$5.06	$6.05

[1] The expected life for options granted under the 2006 Equity Plan is based on observed historical exercise patterns of the previously granted Time-Vested Plan options adjusted to reflect the change in vesting and expiration dates.
[2] The expected volatility is based on considerations of implied volatility from publicly traded and quoted options on the Com-pany's common stock and the historical volatility of the Com-pany's common stock.
[3] The dividend yield is based on the historical dividend yield over the expected term of the options granted.
[4] The risk-free interest rate is based on the continuous com-pounded yield on U.S. Treasury Constant Maturity Rates with a remaining term equal to the expected term of the option.

Restricted Stock Units

RSUs granted to directors will be settled in shares of the Company's common stock with respect to one-third of the underlying shares on the first, second and third anniversaries of the annual shareholders' meeting, which in several cases vary from the anniversaries of the award. RSUs granted to persons other than directors will be settled in shares of the Company's common stock with respect to 50% of the un-derlying shares on the second anniversary of the award and 50% on the fourth anniversary of the award.

RSU activity in the year ended October 31, 2009 is sum-marized below:

	Number of Shares (In Thousands)	Weighted-Average Grant Date Fair Value per Share
Outstanding at October 31, 2008	532	$20.88
Granted	229	17.43
Issued (including 11 shares withheld for income taxes)	50	25.08
Forfeited	23	18.84
Outstanding at October 31, 2009	688	$19.50
Vested at October 31, 2009	50	$25.08

As of October 31, 2009, there was $7.7 million of total un-recognized compensation cost (net of estimated forfeitures) related to RSUs under the 2006 Equity Plan. The cost is expected to be recognized on a straight-line basis over a weighted-average vesting period of 1.59 years.

Performance Shares

Performance shares consist of a contingent right to acquire shares of the Company's common stock based on perfor-mance targets adopted by the Compensation Committee. The number of performance shares will vest based on pre-established financial performance targets for either one year, two year or three year periods ending October 31, 2009, Oc-tober 31, 2010, or October 31, 2011. Vesting of 0% to 125% of the indicated shares will occur depending on the achieved targets.

Performance share activity in the year ended October 31, 2009 is summarized below:

	Number of Shares (In Thousands)	Weighted-Average Grant Date Fair Value per Share
Outstanding at October 31, 2008	432	$19.64
Granted	107	17.90
Issued (including 35 shares withheld for income taxes)	100	18.71
Forfeited	32	19.48
Outstanding at October 31, 2009	407	$19.34
Vested at October 31, 2009	37	$24.38

As of October 31, 2009, there was $2.8 million of total un-recognized compensation cost (net of estimated forfeitures) related to performance shares. The cost is expected to be recognized on a straight-line basis over a weighted average vesting period of 1.22 years. These costs are based on es-timated achievement of performance criteria and estimated costs will be reevaluated periodically.

Dividend Equivalent Rights

RSUs and performance shares granted prior to January 13, 2009 are credited with dividend equivalent rights which will be converted to RSUs or performance shares, as applicable, at the fair market value of the Company's common stock on the dates the dividend payments are declared and are subject to the same terms and conditions as the underlying award. Performance shares granted on or after January 13, 2009 are credited with dividend equivalent rights which will be converted to performance shares at the fair market value of the Company's common stock beginning after the performance targets have been satisfied and are subject to the same terms and conditions as the underlying award.

Time-Vested Plan

Under the Time-Vested Plan, the options become exercisable at a rate of 20% of the shares per year beginning one year after the date of grant and expire ten years plus one month after the date of grant.

The Time-Vested Plan activity in the year ended October 31, 2009 is summarized below:

	Number of Shares (In Thousands)	Weighted-Average Exercise Price per Share	Weighted-Average Remaining Contractual Term (In Years)	Aggregate Intrinsic Value (In Thousands)
Outstanding at October 31, 2008	1,321	$17.04		
Exercised	185	14.02		
Forfeited or expired	71	18.40		
Outstanding at October 31, 2009	1,065	$17.47	3.73	$2,280
Vested and exercisable at October 31, 2009	939	$17.05	3.45	$2,280

As of October 31, 2009, there was $0.4 million of total unrecognized compensation cost (net of estimated forfeitures) related to unvested stock options under the Time-Vested Plan. The cost is expected to be recognized on a straight-line basis over a weighted-average vesting period of 0.54 years.

1996 and 2002 Price-Vested Plans

The Company has two Price-Vested Plans: (1) the 1996 Price-Vested Plan; and (2) the 2002 Price-Vested Plan. The two plans are substantially similar as each plan has pre-defined vesting prices that provide for accelerated vesting. Under each form of option agreement, if, at the end of four years, any of the stock price performance targets are not achieved, then the remaining options vest at the end of eight years from the date the options were granted. Options vesting during the first year following grant do not become exercisable until after the first anniversary of grant. The options expire ten years after the date of grant.

Share-based compensation expense in the year ended October 31, 2007 included $4.0 million of expense attributable to the accelerated vesting of stock options under the Price-Vested Performance Stock Option Plans. When the Company's stock price achieved $22.50 and $23.00 target prices for ten trading days within a 30 consecutive trading day period during the first quarter of 2007, options for 481,638 shares vested in full. When the Company's stock price achieved $25.00 and $26.00 target prices for ten trading days within a 30 consecutive trading day period during the second quarter of 2007, options for 452,566 shares vested in full. When the Company's stock price achieved a $27.50 target price for ten trading days within a 30 consecutive trading day period during the third quarter of 2007, options for 36,938 shares vested in full.

On May 2, 2006, the remaining 2,350,963 shares authorized under these plans became available for grant under the 2006 Equity Plan, as will forfeitures after this date. There have been no grants under these plans since 2005.

The 1996 and 2002 Price-Vested Plan's activity in the year ended October 31, 2009 is summarized below:

	Number of Shares (In Thousands)	Weighted-Average Exercise Price per Share	Weighted-Average Remaining Contractual Term (In Years)	Aggregate Intrinsic Value (In Thousands)
Outstanding at October 31, 2008	1,372	$17.14		
Exercised	69	17.74		
Forfeited or expired	54	16.56		
Outstanding at October 31, 2009	1,249	$17.13	3.69	$2,089
Vested and exercisable at October 31, 2009	840	$17.36	4.07	$1,225

As of October 31, 2009, there was $0.3 million of total unrecognized compensation cost (net of estimated forfeitures) related to unvested stock options under the Price-Vested Plans. The cost is expected to be recognized on a straight-line basis over a weighted-average vesting period of 0.90 years.

Executive Stock Option Plan ("Age-Vested Plan")

Under the Age-Vested Plan, options are exercisable for 50% of the shares when the option holders reach their 61st birthdays and the remaining 50% become exercisable on their 64th birthdays. To the extent vested, the options may be exercised at any time prior to one year after termination of employment. Effective as of December 9, 2003, no further grants may be made under the plan.

The Age-Vested Plan activity in the year ended October 31, 2009, is summarized below:

	Number of Shares (In Thousands)	Weighted-Average Exercise Price per Share	Weighted-Average Remaining Contractual Term (In Years)	Aggregate Intrinsic Value (In Thousands)
Outstanding at October 31, 2008	533	$13.27		
Exercised	92	11.13		
Forfeited or expired	18	14.08		
Outstanding at October 31, 2009	423	$13.70	44.60	$2,153
Vested and exercisable at October 31, 2009	58	$ 9.98	38.19	$ 506

As of October 31, 2009, there was $0.7 million of total unrecognized compensation cost (net of estimated forfeitures) related to unvested stock options under the Age-Vested Plan which is expected to be recognized on a straight-lined basis over a weighted-average vesting period of 8.69 years.

Employee Stock Purchase Plan

On March 9, 2004, the stockholders of the Company approved the 2004 Employee Stock Purchase Plan under which an aggregate of 2,000,000 shares may be issued. Effective May 1, 2006, the purchase price became 95% (from 85%) of the fair market value of the Company's common stock on the last trading day of the month. After that date, the plan is no longer considered compensatory and the value of the awards are no longer treated as share-based compensation expense. Employees may designate up to 10% of their compensation for the purchase of stock, subject to a $25,000 annual limit. Employees are required to hold their shares for a minimum of six months from the date of purchase.

The weighted average fair values of the purchase rights granted in the years ended October 31, 2009, 2008 and 2007 under the new plan were $0.86, $1.05, and $1.23, respectively. During the years ended October 31, 2009, 2008 and 2007, 219,067, 222,648, and 215,376 shares of stock were issued under the plan at a weighted average price of $16.29, $20.00, and $23.33, respectively. The aggregate purchases in the years ended October 31, 2009, 2008 and 2007 were $3.6 million, $4.5 million and $5.0 million, respectively. At October 31, 2009, 293,174 shares remained unissued under the plan.

Public Offering

5.37

VALERO ENERGY CORPORATION (DEC)

(Dollars in millions)	Common Stock	Additional Paid-In Capital	Treasury Stock	Retained Earnings	Accumulated Other Comprehensive Income (Loss)
Balance as of December 31, 2006	$ 6	$7,779	$(1,396)	$11,951	$ 265
Net income	—	—	—	5,234	—
Dividends on common stock	—	—	—	(271)	—
Stock-based compensation expense	—	89	—	—	—
Shares repurchased under $6 billion common stock purchase program	—	—	(4,873)	—	—
Shares issued, net of shares repurchased, in connection with employee stock plans and other	—	(757)	172	—	—
Other comprehensive income	—	—	—	—	308
Balance as of December 31, 2007	$ 6	$7,111	$(6,097)	$16,914	$ 573
Net loss	—	—	—	(1,131)	—
Dividends on common stock	—	—	—	(299)	—
Stock-based compensation expense	—	62	—	—	—
Shares repurchased under $6 billion common stock purchase program	—	—	(667)	—	—
Shares repurchased, net of shares issued, in connection with employee stock plans and other	—	17	(120)	—	—
Other comprehensive loss	—	—	—	—	(749)
Balance as of December 31, 2008	$ 6	$7,190	$(6,884)	$15,484	$(176)
Net loss	—	—	—	(1,982)	—
Dividends on common stock	—	—	—	(324)	—
Sale of common stock	1	798	—	—	—
Stock-based compensation expense	—	68	—	—	—
Shares issued, net of shares repurchased, in connection with employee stock plans and other	—	(160)	163	—	—
Other comprehensive income	—	—	—	—	541
Balance as of December 31, 2009	$ 7	$7,896	$(6,721)	$13,178	$ 365

NOTES TO CONSOLIDATED FINANCIAL STATEMENTS

14 (In Part): Stockholders' Equity

Share Activity

For the years ended December 31, 2009, 2008, and 2007, activity in the number of shares of common stock and treasury stock was as follows (in millions):

	Common Stock	Treasury Stock
Balance as of December 31, 2006	627	(24)
Shares repurchased under $6 billion common stock purchase program	—	(70)
Shares issued, net of shares repurchased, in connection with employee stock plans and other	—	3
Balance as of December 31, 2007	627	(91)
Shares repurchased under $6 billion common stock purchase program	—	(18)
Shares repurchased, net of shares issued, in connection with employee stock plans and other	—	(2)
Balance as of December 31, 2008	627	(111)
Sale of common stock	46	—
Shares issued, net of shares repurchased, in connection with employee stock plans and other	—	2
Balance as of December 31, 2009	673	(109)

Common Stock Offering

On June 3, 2009, we sold in a public offering 46 million shares of our common stock, which included 6 million shares related to an overallotment option exercised by the underwriters, at a price of $18.00 per share and received proceeds, net of underwriting discounts and commissions and other issuance costs, of $799 million.

Business Combination

5.38

CENTURYTEL, INC. (DEC)

(Dollars, except per share amounts, and shares in thousands)	2009	2008	2007
Common stock (represents dollars and shares)			
Balance at beginning of year	$ 100,277	$ 108,492	$ 113,254
Issuance of common stock to acquire Embarq Corporation	196,083	—	—
Repurchase of common stock	—	(9,626)	(10,172)
Conversion of debt into common stock	—	—	3,699
Conversion of preferred stock into common stock	—	367	26
Shares withheld to satisfy tax withholdings	(503)	(50)	(41)
Issuance of common stock through dividend reinvestment, incentive and benefit plans	3,332	1,094	1,726
Balance at end of year	$ 299,189	$ 100,277	$ 108,492
Paid-in capital			
Balance at beginning of year	$ 39,961	$ 91,147	$ 24,256
Issuance of common stock to acquire Embarq Corporation, including portion of share-based compensation awards assumed by CenturyTel	5,873,904	—	—
Repurchase of common stock	—	(91,408)	(154,970)
Shares withheld to satisfy tax withholdings	(15,060)	(1,667)	(66)
Conversion of debt into common stock	—	—	142,732
Conversion of preferred stock into common stock	—	6,368	453
Issuance of common stock through dividend reinvestment, incentive and benefit plans	53,491	13,505	47,678
Excess tax benefits from share-based compensation	4,194	1,123	6,427
Share-based compensation	55,153	16,390	19,962
Other	2,408	4,503	4,675
Balance at end of year	$6,014,051	$ 39,961	$ 91,147
Accumulated other comprehensive loss, net of tax			
Balance at beginning of year	$ (123,489)	$ (42,707)	$ (104,942)
Net change in other comprehensive loss (net of reclassification adjustment), net of tax	38,183	(80,782)	62,235
Balance at end of year	$ (85,306)	$ (123,489)	$ (42,707)
Retained earnings			
Balance at beginning of year	$3,146,255	$3,245,302	$3,150,933
Net income attributable to CenturyTel, Inc.	647,211	365,732	418,370
Repurchase of common stock	—	(244,513)	(293,728)
Shares withheld to satisfy tax withholdings	—	—	(1,699)
Cumulative effect of adoption of FIN 48	—	—	478
Cash dividends declared			
Common stock—$2.80, $2.1675 and $.26 per share	(560,685)	(220,086)	(28,684)
Preferred stock	(12)	(180)	(368)
Balance at end of year	$3,232,769	$3,146,255	$3,245,302

(continued)

(Dollars, except per share amounts, and shares in thousands)	2009	2008	2007
Preferred stock—non-redeemable			
Balance at beginning of year	$ 236	$ 6,971	$ 7,450
Conversion of preferred stock into common stock	—	(6,735)	(479)
Balance at end of year	$ 236	$ 236	$ 6,971
Noncontrolling interests			
Balance at beginning of period	$ 4,568	$ 6,605	$ 8,013
Net income attributable to noncontrolling interests	1,377	1,298	1,259
Extraordinary gain attributable to noncontrolling interests	1,545	—	—
Distributions to noncontrolling interests	(1,630)	(3,335)	(2,667)
Balance at end of period	$ 5,860	$ 4,568	$ 6,605
Total stockholders' equity	$9,466,799	$3,167,808	$3,415,810

NOTES TO CONSOLIDATED FINANCIAL STATEMENTS

2 (In Part): Acquisitions

On July 1, 2009, pursuant to the terms and conditions of the Merger Agreement, we acquired Embarq through a merger transaction, with Embarq surviving the merger as a wholly-owned subsidiary of CenturyTel. Such acquisition was recorded pursuant to Financial Accounting Standards Board guidance on business combinations, which was effective for all business combinations consummated on or after January 1, 2009, as more fully described below.

As a result of the acquisition, each outstanding share of Embarq common stock was converted into the right to receive 1.37 shares of CenturyTel common stock ("CTL common stock"), with cash paid in lieu of fractional shares. Based on the number of CenturyTel common shares issued to consummate the merger (196.1 million), the closing stock price of CTL common stock as of June 30, 2009 ($30.70) and the precombination portion of share-based compensation awards assumed by CenturyTel ($50.2 million), the aggregate merger consideration approximated $6.1 billion. The premium paid by us in this transaction is attributable to strategic benefits, including enhanced financial and operational scale, market diversification, leveraged combined networks and improved competitive positioning. None of the goodwill associated with this transaction is deductible for income tax purposes.

The results of operations of Embarq are included in our consolidated results of operations beginning July 1, 2009. Approximately $2.563 billion of operating revenues of Embarq are included in our consolidated results of operations for 2009. CenturyTel was the accounting acquirer in this transaction. We have recognized Embarq's assets and liabilities at their acquisition date estimated fair values pursuant to business combination accounting rules that were effective for acquisitions consummated on or after January 1, 2009. The assignment of a fair value to the assets acquired and liabilities assumed of Embarq (and the related estimated lives of depreciable tangible and identifiable intangible assets) require a significant amount of judgment. The fair value of property, plant and equipment and identifiable intangible assets were determined based upon analysis performed by an independent valuation firm. The fair value of pension and postretirement obligations was determined by independent actuaries. The fair value of long-term debt was determined by management based on a discounted cash flow analysis, using the rates and maturities of these obligations compared to terms and rates currently available in the long-term financing markets. All other fair value determinations, which consisted primarily of current assets, current liabilities and deferred income taxes, were made by management. The following is a preliminary assignment of the fair value of the assets acquired and liabilities assumed based on currently available information.

(Dollars in thousands)	Fair Value as of July 1, 2009
Current assets*	$ 675,720
Net property, plant and equipment	6,077,672
Identifiable intangible assets	
Customer list	1,098,000
Rights of way	268,472
Other (trademarks, internally developed software, licenses)	26,817
Other non-current assets	24,131
Current liabilities	(828,385)
Long-term debt, including current maturities	(4,886,708)
Other long-term liabilities	(2,621,358)
Goodwill	6,236,084
Total purchase price	$ 6,070,445

* Includes a fair value of $440 million assigned to accounts receivable which had a gross contractual value of $492 million as of July 1, 2009. The $52 million difference represents our best estimate of the contractual cash flows that will not be collected.

We recognized approximately $64 million of liabilities arising from contingencies as of the acquisition date on the basis that it was probable that a liability had been incurred and the amount could be reasonably estimated. Such contingencies primarily relate to transaction and property tax contingencies and contingencies arising from billing disputes with various parties in the communications industry. The assignment of fair values to Embarq's assets and liabilities has not been finalized as of December 31, 2009. Further adjustments may be necessary prior to June 30, 2010, particularly as it relates to contingent liabilities and other long-term liabilities (including deferred income taxes).

The following unaudited pro forma financial information presents the combined results of CenturyTel and Embarq as though the acquisition had been consummated as of January 1, 2009 and 2008, respectively, for the two periods presented below.

(Dollars in thousands)	2009	2008
Operating revenues	$7,645	$8,289
Income before extraordinary item	895	1,087
Basic earnings per share before extraordinary item	3.00	3.55
Diluted earnings per share before extraordinary item	2.99	3.53

These results include certain adjustments, primarily due to increased depreciation and amortization associated with the property, plant and equipment and identifiable intangible assets, increased retiree benefit costs due to the remeasurement of the benefit obligations, and the related income tax effects. The pro forma information does not necessarily reflect the actual results of operations had the acquisition been consummated at the beginning of the periods indicated nor is it necessarily indicative of future operating results. Other than those actually realized subsequent to the July 1, 2009 acquisition date, the pro forma information does not give effect to any potential revenue enhancements or cost synergies or other operating efficiencies that could result from the acquisition.

During 2009, we recognized an aggregate of approximately $253.7 million of integration, transaction and other costs related to the Embarq acquisition. Of the $253.7 million, approximately $47.2 million related to closing costs, including investment banker and legal fees, in connection with consummation of the merger and is reflected as an operating expense. In addition, we incurred approximately $206.5 million of integration-related operating expenses related to system and customer conversions, employee-related severance and benefit costs and branding costs associated with changing our trade name to CenturyLink.

On July 1, 2009, in connection with the Merger Agreement, and as approved by our shareholders on January 27, 2009, we filed Amended and Restated Articles of Incorporation to (i) eliminate our time-phase voting structure, which previously entitled persons who beneficially owned shares of our common stock continuously since May 30, 1987 to ten votes per share, and (ii) increase the authorized number of shares of our common stock from 350 million to 800 million. As so amended and restated, our Articles of Incorporation provide that each share of our common stock is entitled to one vote per share with respect to each matter properly submitted to shareholders for their vote, consent, waiver, release or other action. These amendments reflect changes contemplated or necessitated by the Merger Agreement and are described in detail in our joint proxy statement-prospectus filed with the Securities and Exchange Commission and first mailed to shareholders of CenturyTel and Embarq on or about December 22, 2008. In Robert M. Garst, Sr. et al. v. CenturyTel, Inc. et al., filed March 13, 2009 in the 142nd Judicial District Court of Texas, Midland County (Case No. CV-46861), certain of our former ten-vote shareholders challenged the effectiveness of the vote to eliminate our time-phase voting structure. We believe we followed all necessary steps to properly effect the amendments described above and are defending the case accordingly.

On January 23, 2009, Embarq amended its Credit Agreement to effect, upon completion of the merger, a waiver of the event of default that would have arisen under the Credit Agreement solely as a result of the merger and enabled the Credit Agreement, as amended, to remain in place after the merger. Previously, in connection with the Merger Agreement, we had entered into a commitment letter with various lenders which provided for an $800 million bridge facility that would be available to, among other things, refinance borrowings under the Credit Agreement in the event a waiver of the event of default arising from the consummation of the merger could not have been obtained and other financing was unavailable. On January 23, 2009, we terminated the commitment letter and paid an aggregate of $8.0 million to the lenders. Such amount has been reflected as an expense (in Other income (expense)) in 2009.

9 (In Part): Stockholders' Equity

Common Stock (In Part)

On July 1, 2009, we issued 196.1 million shares of CenturyTel common stock in connection with the acquisition of Embarq. See Note 2 for additional information.

Debt Conversion

5.39

COSTCO WHOLESALE CORPORATION (AUG)

(Dollars in millions, except share data)	Common Stock		Additional Paid-In Capital	Accumulated Other Comprehensive Income	Retained Earnings	Total
	Shares	Amount				
Balance at September 3, 2006	462,279	$ 2	$2,823	$ 278	$ 6,041	$ 9,144
Comprehensive Income:						
Net income	—	—	—	—	1,083	1,083
Foreign currency translation adjustment and other	—	—	—	93	—	93
Comprehensive income						1,176
Stock options exercised and vesting of restricted stock units, including income tax benefits and other	9,735	—	351	—	—	351
Conversion of convertible notes	1,389	—	42	—	—	42
Stock repurchase	(36,390)	—	(233)	—	(1,746)	(1,979)
Stock-based compensation	—	—	135	—	—	135
Cash dividends	—	—	—	—	(246)	(246)
Balance at September 2, 2007	437,013	$ 2	$3,118	$ 371	$ 5,132	$ 8,623
Cumulative effect of adjustments resulting from the adoption of FIN 48, net of tax	—	—	—	—	(6)	(6)
Adjusted balance at September 2, 2007	437,013	$ 2	$3,118	$ 371	$ 5,126	$ 8,617
Comprehensive Income:						
Net income	—	—	—	—	1,283	1,283
Foreign currency translation adjustment and other	—	—	—	(85)	—	(85)
Comprehensive income						1,198
Stock options exercised and vesting of restricted stock units, including income tax benefits and other	9,299	—	363	—	—	363
Conversion of convertible notes	13	—	—	—	—	—
Stock repurchase	(13,812)	—	(104)	—	(783)	(887)
Stock-based compensation	—	—	166	—	—	166
Cash dividends	—	—	—	—	(265)	(265)
Balance at August 31, 2008	432,513	$ 2	$3,543	$ 286	$ 5,361	$ 9,192
Comprehensive Income:						
Net income	—	—	—	—	1,086	1,086
Foreign currency translation adjustment and other	—	—	—	(182)	—	(182)
Comprehensive income						904
Stock options exercised and vesting of restricted stock units, including income tax benefits and other	3,794	—	75	—	—	75
Conversion of convertible notes	562	—	19	—	—	19
Stock repurchase	(895)	—	(7)	—	(50)	(57)
Stock-based compensation	—	—	181	—	—	181
Cash dividends	—	—	—	—	(296)	(296)
Balance at August 30, 2009	435,974	$ 2	$3,811	$ 104	$ 6,101	$10,018

NOTES TO CONSOLIDATED FINANCIAL STATEMENTS
(Dollars in millions, except share data)

Note 4 (In Part): Debt

Long-Term Debt (In Part)

Long-term debt at August 30, 2009 and August 31, 2008 consisted of the following:

	2009	2008
5.5% senior notes due March 2017	$1,096	$1,095
5.3% senior notes due March 2012	899	898
2.695% promissory notes due October 2017	69	60
0.92% promissory notes due April 2010	43	37
3.5% zero coupon convertible subordinated notes due August 2017	32	49
0.35% over yen tibor (6-month) term loan due June 2018	32	28
0.88% promissory notes due November 2009	32	28
Capital lease obligations and other	84	17
Total long-term debt	2,287	2,212
Less current portion	81	6
Long-term debt, excluding current portion	$2,206	$2,206

• • • • • •

In August 1997, the Company sold $900 principal amount at maturity 3.5% Zero Coupon Convertible Subordinated Notes (Zero Coupon Notes) due in August 2017. The Zero Coupon Notes were priced with a yield to maturity of 3.5%, resulting in gross proceeds to the Company of $450. The current Zero Coupon Notes outstanding are convertible into a maximum of 961,000 shares of Costco Common Stock shares at an initial conversion price of $22.71. Holders of the Zero Coupon Notes may require the Company to purchase the Zero Coupon Notes (at the discounted issue price plus accrued interest to date of purchase) in August 2012. The Company, at its option, may redeem the Zero Coupon Notes (at the discounted issue price plus accrued interest to date of redemption) any time after August 2002. As of August 30, 2009, $858 in principal amount of the Zero Coupon Notes had been converted by note holders to shares of Costco Common Stock, of which $25, $1, and $61 in principal were converted in 2009, 2008, and 2007, respectively, or $19 and $42 in 2009 and 2007, respectively, after factoring in the related debt discount. In 2008, the conversion of principle for Zero Coupon Notes after factoring the related debt discount was not significant.

At August 30, 2009, the fair value of the Zero Coupon Notes, based on market quotes, was approximately $44, the fair value of the 2012 Notes and 2017 Notes was $973 and $1,213, respectively, and the fair value of other long-term debt approximated its carrying value. The fair value of the Zero Coupon Notes and the 2007 Senior Notes are based on quoted market prices of similar types of borrowing arrangements or the Company's current incremental borrowing rate, if applicable.

Preferred Stock Conversion

5.40

MERCK & CO., INC. (DEC)

($ in millions except per share amounts)	Common Stock	Other Paid-In Capital	Retained Earnings	Accumulated Other Comprehensive Loss	Treasury Stock	Non-controlling Interests	Total
Balance at January 1, 2007	$ 29.8	$ 7,166.5	$ 39,095.1	$(1,164.3)	$(27,567.4)	$2,406.1	$19,965.8
Net income attributable to Merck & Co., Inc.			3,275.4				3,275.4
Total other comprehensive income, net of tax				338.2			338.2
Comprehensive income, net of tax							3,613.6
Cumulative effect of adoption of guidance on accounting for unrecognized tax benefits			81.0				81.0
Cash dividends declared on common stock ($1.52 per share)			(3,310.7)				(3,310.7)
Treasury stock shares purchased					(1,429.7)		(1,429.7)
Acquisition of NovaCardia, Inc.		366.4					366.4
Net income attributable to noncontrolling interests						121.4	121.4
Distributions attributable to noncontrolling interests						(120.8)	(120.8)
Share-based compensation plans and other		482.0			822.4		1,304.4
Balance at December 31, 2007	$ 29.8	$ 8,014.9	$ 39,140.8	$ (826.1)	$(28,174.7)	$2,406.7	$20,591.4

(continued)

($ in millions except per share amounts)	Common Stock	Other Paid-In Capital	Retained Earnings	Accumulated Other Comprehensive Loss	Treasury Stock	Non-controlling Interests	Total
Balance at December 31, 2007	$ 29.8	$ 8,014.9	$ 39,140.8	$ (826.1)	$(28,174.7)	$2,406.7	$20,591.4
Net income attributable to Merck & Co., Inc.			7,808.4				7,808.4
Total other comprehensive loss, net of tax				(1,727.8)			(1,727.8)
Comprehensive income, net of tax							6,080.6
Cash dividends declared on common stock ($1.52 per share)			(3,250.4)				(3,250.4)
Treasury stock shares purchased					(2,725.0)		(2,725.0)
Net income attributable to noncontrolling interests						123.9	123.9
Distributions attributable to noncontrolling interests						(121.8)	(121.8)
Share-based compensation plans and other		304.2			164.2		468.4
Balance at December 31, 2008	$ 29.8	$ 8,319.1	$ 43,698.8	$(2,553.9)	$(30,735.5)	$2,408.8	$21,167.1
Net income attributable to Merck & Co., Inc.			12,901.3				12,901.3
Total other comprehensive loss, net of tax				(212.6)			(212.6)
Comprehensive income, net of tax							12,688.7
Schering-Plough merger	1,752.0	30,860.7			(1,964.1)	22.3	30,670.9
Cancellations of treasury stock	(4.9)		(11,595.4)		11,600.3		—
Preferred stock conversions	0.1	5.4					5.5
Cash dividends declared on common stock ($1.52 per share)			(3,597.7)				(3,597.7)
Net income attributable to noncontrolling interests						122.9	122.9
Distributions attributable to noncontrolling interests						(119.4)	(119.4)
Share-based compensation plans and other	4.3	497.4	(2.1)		55.0		554.6
Balance at December 31, 2009	$1,781.3	$39,682.6	$ 41,404.9	$(2,766.5)	$(21,044.3)	$2,434.6	$61,492.6

NOTES TO CONSOLIDATED FINANCIAL STATEMENTS
($ in millions except per share amounts)

Note 13 (In Part): Equity

In accordance with the New Merck certificate of incorporation there are 6,500,000,000 shares of common stock and 20,000,000 shares of preferred stock authorized. Of the authorized shares of preferred stock, there is a series of 11,500,000 shares which is designated as 6% mandatory convertible preferred stock.

6% Mandatory Convertible Preferred Stock

Prior to the Merger, on August 15, 2007, Schering-Plough issued 10,000,000 shares of Schering-Plough 6% preferred stock. In connection with the Merger, holders of the Schering-Plough 6% preferred stock received 6% preferred stock (which rights were substantially similar to the rights of the Schering-Plough 6% preferred stock) in accordance with the New Merck Restated Certificate of Incorporation. As a result of the Merger, the 6% preferred stock became subject to the "make-whole" acquisition provisions of the preferred stock effective as of November 3, 2009. During the make-whole acquisition conversion period that ended on November 19, 2009, the 6% preferred stock was convertible at a make-whole conversion rate of 8.2021. For each share of preferred stock that was converted during this period, the holder received $86.12 in cash and 4.7302 New Merck common shares. Holders also received a dividend make-whole payment of between $10.79 and $10.82 depending on the date of the conversion. A total of 9,110,423 shares of 6% preferred stock were converted into 43,093,881 shares of New Merck common stock and cash payments of approximately $785 million were made to those holders who converted. In addition, make-whole dividend payments of $98.5 million were made to those holders who converted representing the present value of all remaining future dividend payments from the conversion date through the mandatory conversion date on August 13, 2010 using the discount rate as stipulated in the preferred stock designations.

As of December 31, 2009, 855,422 shares of 6% preferred stock remained issued and outstanding. These outstanding shares will automatically convert into common shares of the Company and cash on August 13, 2010, pursuant to the provisions of the New Merck Restated Certificate of Incorporation. The holders may also elect to convert at any time prior to August 13, 2010. The 6% preferred stock of $206.6 million at December 31, 2009 has been classified as a current liability because all conversions will be settled as a combination of cash and common stock. Additionally, under certain conditions, the Company may elect to cause the conversion of all, but not less than all, of the Merck 6% preferred stock then outstanding.

The 6% preferred stock accrues dividends at an annual rate of 6% on shares outstanding. The dividends are cumulative from the date of issuance and, to the extent the Company is legally permitted to pay dividends and the Board of

Directors declares a dividend payable, the Company will pay dividends on each dividend payment date. The remaining dividend payment dates are February 15, May 15 and August 13, 2010.

Compensation Recognized

5.41

HEWITT ASSOCIATES, INC. (SEP)

(In thousands)	Class A Common Shares		Additional Paid-In Capital	Treasury Stock, at Cost		Retained Earnings	Accumulated Other Comprehensive Income	Total
	Shares	Amount		Shares	Amount			
Balance at September 30, 2006	124,932,189	$1,249	$1,368,189	14,109,780	$(401,365)	$ 213,224	$ 75,072	$1,256,369
Comprehensive loss:								
Net loss	—	—	—	—	—	(175,080)	—	(175,080)
Other comprehensive income:								
Unrealized gains on short-term investments, net of tax	—	—	—	—	—	—	8	8
Foreign currency translation adjustments, net of tax	—	—	—	—	—	—	49,827	49,827
Total other comprehensive income							49,835	49,835
Total comprehensive loss								(125,245)
Share-based compensation expense	—	—	40,925	—	—	—	—	40,925
Excess tax benefits from stock plans	—	—	9,140	—	—	—	—	9,140
Restricted stock unit vesting	613,678	6	(6)	—	—	—	—	—
Purchase of Class A common shares for treasury	—	—	—	6,436,164	(195,835)	—	—	(195,835)
Issuance of Class A common shares:								
Employee stock options	2,377,618	24	54,159	—	—	—	—	54,183
Outside Directors	3,508	—	—	—	—	—	—	—
Net forfeiture of restricted common stock pursuant to the global stock plan	(254,740)	(2)	2	—	—	—	—	—
Adoption of FASB ASC 715-30 recognition provisions (formerly SFAS No. 158) (net of tax)	—	—	—	—	—	—	(1,525)	(1,525)
Balance at September 30, 2007	127,672,253	$1,277	$1,472,409	20,545,944	$(597,200)	$ 38,144	$123,382	$1,038,012

(continued)

(In thousands)	Class A Common Shares		Additional Paid-In Capital	Treasury Stock, at Cost		Retained Earnings	Accumulated Other Comprehensive Income	Total
	Shares	Amount		Shares	Amount			
Balance at September 30, 2007	127,672,253	$1,277	$1,472,409	20,545,944	$ (597,200)	$ 38,144	$123,382	$1,038,012
Comprehensive income:								
Net income	—	—	—	—	—	188,142	—	188,142
Other comprehensive loss:								
Unrealized losses on investments, net of tax	—	—	—	—	—	—	(4,273)	(4,273)
Retirement plans, net of tax							(23,834)	(23,834)
Unrealized losses on hedging transactions, net of tax	—	—	—	—	—	—	(6,412)	(6,412)
Foreign currency translation adjustments, net of tax	—	—	—	—	—	—	(42,173)	(42,173)
Total other comprehensive loss							(76,692)	(76,692)
Total comprehensive income								111,450
Share-based compensation expense	—	—	48,345	—	—	—	—	48,345
Excess tax benefits from stock plans	—	—	14,744	—	—	—	—	14,744
Restricted stock unit vesting	938,872	9	(9)	—	—	—	—	—
Purchase of Class A common shares for treasury	—	—	—	15,617,816	(586,227)	—	—	(586,227)
Issuance of Class A common shares:								
Employee stock options	1,847,653	18	43,588	—	—	—	—	43,606
Net forfeiture of restricted common stock pursuant to the global stock plan	(67,898)	—	—	—	—	—	—	—
Adoption of certain provisions of FASB ASC 740-10 (formerly FIN 48)	—	—	—	—	—	(7,036)	—	(7,036)
Adoption of FASB ASC 710-10-25-4 (formerly EITF 06-02) (net of tax)	—	—	—	—	—	(12,692)	—	(12,692)
Balance at September 30, 2008	130,390,880	$1,304	$1,579,077	36,163,760	$(1,183,427)	$206,558	$ 46,690	$ 650,202

(continued)

(In thousands)	Class A Common Shares		Additional Paid-In Capital	Treasury Stock, at Cost		Retained Earnings	Accumulated Other Comprehensive Income	Total
	Shares	Amount		Shares	Amount			
Balance at September 30, 2008	130,390,880	$1,304	$1,579,077	36,163,760	$(1,183,427)	$206,558	$46,690	$650,202
Comprehensive income:								
Net income	—	—	—	—	—	265,125	—	265,125
Other comprehensive loss:								
Unrealized gains on investments, net of tax	—	—	—	—	—	—	1,438	1,438
Retirement plans, net of tax							(10,732)	(10,732)
Unrealized gains on hedging transactions, net of tax	—	—	—	—	—	—	4,189	4,189
Foreign currency translation adjustments, net of tax	—	—	—	—	—	—	(37,448)	(37,448)
Total other comprehensive loss							(42,553)	(42,553)
Total comprehensive income								222,572
Share-based compensation expense	—	—	54,329	—	—	—	—	54,329
Excess tax benefits from stock plans	—	—	9,253	—	—	—	—	9,253
Restricted stock unit vesting	1,613,745	16	(16)	—	—	—	—	—
Purchase of Class A common shares for treasury	—	—	—	3,145,239	(94,388)	—	—	(94,388)
Issuance of Class A common shares:								
Employee stock options	866,871	9	20,043	—	—	—	—	20,052
Net forfeiture of restricted common stock pursuant to the global stock plan	(27,227)	(1)	1	—	—	—	—	—
Adoption of FASB ASC 715-30 measurement date provision (formerly SFAS No. 158) (net of tax)	—	—	—	—	—	(1,906)	188	(1,718)
Balance at September 30, 2009	132,844,269	$1,328	$1,662,687	39,308,999	$(1,277,815)	$469,777	$ 4,325	$860,302

NOTES TO CONSOLIDATED FINANCIAL STATEMENTS (In thousands except for share and per share amounts unless otherwise noted)

Note 2 (In Part): Summary of Significant Accounting Policies

Share-Based Compensation

Restricted stock awards, including restricted stock and restricted stock units, are measured using the fair market value of the stock as of the grant date. The Company recognizes compensation expense, net of estimated forfeitures, on a straight-line basis over the vesting period. Compensation cost of all share-based awards with performance conditions are recognized on a straight-line basis (if cliff-vesting) or on an accelerated-attribution basis (if graded-vesting) over the requisite service period or the implicit service period, if it is probable that the performance conditions will be met. Estimated forfeitures are reviewed periodically and changes to the estimated forfeiture rate are recorded in current period earnings. Employer payroll taxes are also recorded as expense over the vesting period. The remaining unvested shares are subject to forfeiture and restrictions on sale or transfer based on vesting dates.

The Company also grants nonqualified stock options at an exercise price equal to the fair market value of the Company's stock on the grant date. The Company applies the Black-Scholes valuation method to compute the estimated fair value of the stock options and recognizes compensation expense, net of estimated forfeitures, on a straight-line basis so that the award is fully expensed at the vesting date. Generally, stock options vest 25 percent on each anniversary of the grant date, are fully vested four years from the grant date and have a term of ten years.

The Company uses the simplified method to determine the expected life assumption for all of its options. The Company continues to use the simplified method as it does not believe that it has sufficient historical exercise data to provide a reasonable basis upon which to estimate expected life due to the limited time its equity shares have been publicly traded.

18. Share-Based Compensation Plans

During the years ended September 30, 2009, 2008 and 2007, the Company recorded pretax share-based compensation expense of $54,329, $48,345 and $40,937, respectively, related to the Company's stock options, restricted stock, restricted stock units and performance share units. During fiscal 2007, the Company reduced share-based compensation expense by $4,505 related to adjustments in the forfeiture rate used to record share-based compensation.

For the years ended September 30, 2009, 2008 and 2007, the excess tax benefits of $7,002, $10,227 and $4,912, respectively, were recorded as cash flows from financing activities in the consolidated statement of cash flows. The total compensation cost related to non-vested restricted stock and stock option awards not yet recognized as of September 30, 2009 was approximately $67,486, which is expected to be recognized over a weighted average period of 2.3 years.

Under the Company's Global Stock and Incentive Compensation Plan (the "Plan"), which was adopted in fiscal 2002 and is administered by the Compensation and Leadership Committee (the "Committee") of the Company's Board of Directors, employees and directors may receive awards of stock options, stock appreciation rights, restricted stock, restricted stock units, performance shares, performance share units and cash-based awards; employees can also receive incentive stock options. The Plan was amended in January 2008 to increase the number of shares of Class A common stock authorized and reserved for issuance by 7,000,000 shares. As of September 30, 2009, only restricted stock, restricted stock units, performance share units and stock options have been granted. A total of 32,000,000 shares of Class A common stock have been reserved for issuance under the Plan. As of September 30, 2009, there were 5,551,885 shares available for grant under the Plan.

Restricted Stock and Restricted Stock Units

The following table summarizes restricted stock activity during 2009, 2008 and 2007:

	2009		2008		2007	
	Restricted Stock	Weighted Average Grant Date Fair Value	Restricted Stock	Weighted Average Grant Date Fair Value	Restricted Stock	Weighted Average Grant Date Fair Value
Outstanding at beginning of fiscal year	315,921	$26.94	1,190,808	$25.45	2,076,201	$26.00
Vested	(237,583)	$27.21	(781,989)	$24.66	(603,153)	$26.89
Forfeited	(78,338)	$26.10	(92,898)	$27.11	(282,240)	$26.41
Outstanding at end of fiscal year	—	$ —	315,921	$26.94	1,190,808	$25.45

The following table summarizes restricted stock units activity during 2009, 2008 and 2007:

	2009		2008		2007	
	Restricted Stock Units	Weighted Average Grant Date Fair Value	Restricted Stock Units	Weighted Average Grant Date Fair Value	Restricted Stock Units	Weighted Average Grant Date Fair Value
Outstanding at beginning of fiscal year	2,263,986	$31.36	1,945,014	$25.72	294,657	$25.56
Granted	2,109,868	$27.24	1,623,680	$36.75	2,591,352	$25.59
Vested	(1,599,075)	$29.12	(971,149)	$29.84	(625,167)	$25.20
Forfeited	(354,947)	$30.15	(333,559)	$29.14	(315,828)	$25.50
Outstanding at end of fiscal year	2,419,832	$29.42	2,263,986	$31.36	1,945,014	$25.72

Performance share units ("PSUs") are intended to provide an incentive for achieving specific performance objectives over a defined period. PSUs represent an obligation of the Company to deliver a number of shares ranging from zero to 200% of the initial number of units granted, depending on performance against objective, pre-established financial metrics at the end of the performance period. The Company believes it is probable that such goals will be achieved for shares which vest upon meeting certain financial performance conditions, and these goals are evaluated quarterly. If such goals are not met or it is probable the goals will not be met, no compensation cost is recognized and any recognized compensation cost is reversed.

During fiscal 2009, 197,200 PSUs were granted to certain Hewitt leadership which are included in the restricted stock unit information disclosed above. The financial metrics for these grants are based on Hewitt's corporate performance in fiscal 2009 and are calculated to be paid out at a rate of 104%. These grants are scheduled to vest in one-third increments on September 30, 2009, 2010 and 2011. During fiscal 2008, 112,900 PSUs were granted to certain Hewitt leadership which are included in the restricted stock unit information disclosed above. The financial metrics for these grants were based on Hewitt's corporate performance in fiscal 2008 and are to be paid out at a rate of 195%. These grants are scheduled to vest in one-third increments on September 30, 2008, 2009 and 2010. During fiscal 2007, 137,000 PSUs were granted to certain Hewitt leadership, which are included in the restricted stock unit information disclosed above. The financial metrics for these grants were based on Hewitt's fiscal

2007 corporate performance and are to be paid out at a rate of 180%. The fiscal 2007 grants are scheduled to cliff vest on September 30, 2010.

Stock Options

The Committee may grant both incentive stock options and stock options to purchase shares of Class A common stock. Subject to the terms and provisions of the Plan, options may be granted to participants, as determined by the Committee, provided that incentive stock options may not be granted to non-employee directors. The option price is determined by the Committee, provided that for options issued to participants in the U.S., the option price may not be less than 100% of the fair market value of the shares on the date the option is granted and no option may be exercisable later than the tenth anniversary of its grant. The stock options generally vest in equal annual installments over a period of four years.

The fair value used to determine compensation expense for the years ended September 30, 2009, 2008 and 2007 was estimated at the date of grant using a Black-Scholes option pricing model. The following table summarizes the weighted-average assumptions used to determine fair value for options granted during the years ended September 30, 2009, 2008 and 2007:

	2009	2008	2007
Expected volatility	29.30%	26.61%	28.15%
Risk-free interest rate	2.13%	3.83%	4.42%
Expected life (in years)	6.17	6.03	6.23
Dividend yield	0%	0%	0%

The Company uses the simplified method to determine the expected life assumption for all of its options. The Company continues to use the simplified method as it does not believe that it has sufficient historical exercise data to provide a reasonable basis upon which to estimate expected life due to the limited time its equity shares have been publicly traded.

The following table summarizes stock option activity during 2009, 2008 and 2007:

	2009 Options	2009 Weighted Average Exercise Price	2008 Options	2008 Weighted Average Exercise Price	2007 Options	2007 Weighted Average Exercise Price
Outstanding at beginning of fiscal year	6,283,927	$25.68	7,611,095	$24.06	9,664,292	$23.69
Granted	1,098,790	$26.49	772,620	$37.53	937,650	$25.66
Exercised	(866,871)	$23.13	(1,847,653)	$23.61	(2,377,618)	$22.78
Forfeited	(124,710)	$30.79	(199,426)	$29.65	(197,847)	$24.95
Expired	(92,815)	$27.90	(52,709)	$23.69	(415,382)	$25.79
Outstanding at end of fiscal year	6,298,321	$26.04	6,283,927	$25.68	7,611,095	$24.06
Exercisable options at end of fiscal year	4,969,290	$25.27	5,271,903	$24.53	6,758,976	$23.94

The weighted average estimated fair value of employee stock options granted during 2009, 2008 and 2007 was $8.80, $12.81 and $9.74 per share, respectively. These stock options were granted at exercise prices equal to the current fair market value of the underlying stock on the grant date.

The following table summarizes information about stock options outstanding at September 30, 2009:

	Outstanding Options Number Outstanding	Outstanding Options Weighted Average Exercise Price	Outstanding Options Aggregate Intrinsic Value	Outstanding Options Weighted Average Term (Years)	Exercisable Options Number Outstanding	Exercisable Options Weighted Average Exercise Price	Exercisable Options Aggregate Intrinsic Value
Summary price range groupings							
$19.00	895,943	$19.00	$15,616	2.7	895,943	$19.00	$15,616
$19.01–$25.00	1,679,753	$23.80	21,208	4.2	1,619,887	$23.84	20,392
$25.01–$30.00	3,016,708	$26.80	29,060	6.7	2,073,377	$27.00	19,555
$30.01–$40.00	705,917	$37.02	336	7.9	380,083	$36.65	273
	6,298,321	$26.04	$66,220	5.6	4,969,290	$25.27	$55,836

The total intrinsic value of options exercised during the years ended September 30, 2009, 2008 and 2007, based upon the average market price during the period, was approximately $8,065, $28,265 and $18,027, respectively.

Stock Compensation Tax Benefit

5.42

UNIVERSAL FOREST PRODUCTS, INC. (DEC)

(In thousands, except share and per share data)	Controlling Interest Shareholders' Equity					Noncontrolling Interest	Total
	Common Stock	Additional Paid-In Capital	Retained Earnings	Accumulated Other Comprehensive Earnings	Employees Stock Notes Receivable		
Balance at December 30, 2006	$18,859	$113,754	$380,931	$ 2,451	$(1,253)	$10,819	$525,561
Comprehensive earnings:							
Net earnings			21,045			2,168	
Foreign currency translation adjustment				2,253		45	
Total comprehensive earnings							25,511
Purchase of additional noncontrolling interest						(859)	(859)
Distributions to noncontrolling interest						(1,797)	(1,797)
Cash dividends—$0.115 per share			(2,185)				(2,185)
Issuance of 220,345 shares under employee stock plans	220	3,683					3,903
Issuance of 3,961 shares under stock grant programs	4	170					174
Issuance of 69,777 shares under deferred compensation plans	70	(70)					—
Repurchase of 239,400 shares	(239)		(8,538)				(8,777)
Received 15,866 shares for the exercise of stock options	(16)	(766)					(782)
Tax benefits from non-qualified stock options exercised		1,867					1,867
Expense associated with share-based compensation arrangements		505					505
Accrued expense under deferred compensation plans		3,733					3,733
Issuance of 10,132 shares in exchange for employee stock notes receivable	10	492			(502)		—
Payments received on employee stock notes receivable					190		190
Balance at December 29, 2007	$18,908	$123,368	$391,253	$ 4,704	$(1,565)	$10,376	$547,044

(continued)

(In thousands, except share and per share data)	Controlling Interest Shareholders' Equity					Noncontrolling Interest	Total
	Common Stock	Additional Paid-In Capital	Retained Earnings	Accumulated Other Comprehensive Earnings	Employees Stock Notes Receivable		
Balance at December 29, 2007	$18,908	$123,368	$391,253	$ 4,704	$(1,565)	$10,376	$547,044
Comprehensive earnings:							
Net earnings			4,343			1,117	
Foreign currency translation adjustment				(2,351)		(1,071)	
Total comprehensive earnings							2,038
Capital contribution from noncontrolling interest						419	419
Purchase of additional noncontrolling interest						(844)	(844)
Distributions to noncontrolling interest						(3,654)	(3,654)
Cash dividends—$0.120 per share			(2,284)				(2,284)
Issuance of 174,528 shares under employee stock plans	175	3,030					3,205
Issuance of 3,706 shares under stock grant programs	4	100					104
Issuance of 15,288 shares under deferred compensation plans	15	(15)					—
Received 19,857 shares for the exercise of stock options	(20)	(622)					(642)
Tax benefits from non-qualified stock options exercised		878					878
Expense associated with share-based compensation arrangements		1,136					1,136
Accrued expense under deferred compensation plans		725					725
Issuance of 7,374 shares in exchange for employee stock notes receivable	7	230			(237)		—
Payments received on employee stock notes receivable					101		101
Balance at December 27, 2008	$19,089	$128,830	$393,312	$ 2,353	$(1,701)	$ 6,343	$548,226
Comprehensive earnings:							
Net earnings			24,272			473	
Foreign currency translation adjustment				1,280		85	
Total comprehensive earnings							26,110
Capital contribution from noncontrolling interest						14	14
Purchase of additional noncontrolling interest		(853)				(917)	(1,770)
Distributions to noncontrolling interest						(270)	(270)
Cash dividends—$0.260 per share			(5,017)				(5,017)
Issuance of 130,265 shares under employee stock plans	130	2,290					2,420
Issuance of 79,216 shares under stock grant programs	80	29					109
Issuance of 74,229 shares under deferred compensation plans	74	(74)					—
Repurchase of 90,122 shares	(90)		(3,289)				(3,379)
Received 1,602 shares for the exercise of stock options	(2)	(33)					(35)
Tax benefits from non-qualified stock options exercised		730					730
Deferred income tax asset reversal for deferred compensation plans		(518)					(518)
Expense associated with share-based compensation arrangements		1,597					1,597
Accrued expense under deferred compensation plans		646					646
Issuance of 3,721 shares in exchange for employee stock notes receivable	4	121			(125)		—
Payments received on employee stock notes receivable					83		83
Balance at December 26, 2009	$19,285	$132,765	$409,278	$ 3,633	$(1,743)	$ 5,728	$568,946

ATT-SEC 5.42

NOTES TO CONSOLIDATED FINANCIAL STATEMENTS

K (In Part): Stock-Based Compensation

All Share-Based Payment Arrangements

The total share-based compensation cost and the related total income tax benefit that has been recognized in results of operations was approximately $1,252,000 and $724,000, respectively in 2009. The total share-based compensation cost and the related total income tax benefit that has been recog-

nized in results of operations was approximately $820,000 and $255,000, respectively in 2008. The total share-based compensation cost and the related total income tax benefit that has been recognized in results of operations was approximately $892,000 and $299,000, respectively in 2007.

In 2009, 2008 and 2007, cash received from option exercises and share issuances under our plans was $2.4 million, $3.0 million and $3.5 million, respectively. The actual tax benefit realized in 2009, 2008 and 2007 for the tax deductions from option exercises totaled $0.7 million, $0.9 million and $1.9 million, respectively.

Warrants Issued or Exercised

5.43

SMITHFIELD FOODS, INC. (APR)

(In millions)	2009	2008	2007
Common stock—shares:			
Balance, beginning of year	134.4	112.4	111.2
Common stock issued	9.2	21.7	—
Exercise of stock options	—	0.3	1.2
Balance, end of year	143.6	134.4	112.4
Common stock—par value:			
Balance, beginning of year	$ 67.2	$ 56.2	$ 55.6
Common stock issued	4.6	10.8	—
Exercise of stock options	—	0.2	0.6
Balance, end of year	$ 71.8	$ 67.2	$ 56.2
Additional paid-in capital:			
Balance, beginning of year	$1,130.2	$ 510.1	$ 494.1
Common stock issued	177.7	609.4	—
Exercise of stock options	0.2	2.7	4.2
Stock option expense	3.8	2.0	1.3
Tax benefit of stock option exercises	—	1.3	10.5
Equity method investee acquisitions of treasury shares	—	4.7	—
Purchase of call options	(53.9)	—	—
Sale of warrants	36.7	—	—
Balance, end of year	$1,294.7	$1,130.2	$ 510.1
Stock held in trust:			
Balance, beginning of year	(53.1)	(52.5)	(51.8)
Purchase of stock for trust	(0.6)	(0.6)	(0.7)
Purchase of stock for supplemental employee retirement plan	(11.1)	—	—
Balance, end of year	$ (64.8)	$ (53.1)	$ (52.5)
Retained earnings:			
Balance, beginning of year	$1,838.5	$1,724.8	$1,558.0
Adoption of FIN 48	—	(15.2)	—
Net income (a)	(190.3)	128.9	166.8
Balance, end of year	$1,648.2	$1,838.5	$1,724.8
Accumulated other comprehensive income (loss):			
Balance, beginning of year (b)	$ 65.4	$ 2.2	$ (27.7)
Pension and other post-retirement benefits, net of tax of $(73.8), $(5.4) and $0.5	(125.4)	(8.5)	0.7
Adjustment to initially apply SFAS 158, net of tax of $(4.3) (d)	—	—	(6.7)
Hedge accounting, net of tax of $(78.4), $0.1 and $11.4	(173.2)	0.2	18.7
Foreign currency translation	(261.0)	85.7	19.3
Reclassification adjustments:			
Pension and other post-retirement benefits, net of tax of $2.2 and $2.8	3.5	4.5	—
Hedge accounting, net of tax of $45.6, $(11.4) and $(1.3)	101.2	(18.7)	(2.1)
Foreign currency translation	1.0	—	—
Balance, end of year (c)	$ (388.5)	$ 65.4	$ 2.2
Total shareholders' equity	$2,561.4	$3,048.2	$2,240.8
Total comprehensive income (loss) (a−b+c−d)	$ (644.2)	$ 192.1	$ 203.4

NOTES TO CONSOLIDATED FINANCIAL STATEMENTS

Note 12 (In Part): Shareholders' Equity

Call Spread Transactions

In connection with the issuance of the Convertible Notes (see Note 8—Debt), we entered into separate convertible note hedge transactions with respect to our common stock to minimize the impact of potential economic dilution upon conversion of the Convertible Notes, and separate warrant transactions.

We purchased call options in private transactions that permit us to acquire up to approximately 17.6 million shares of our common stock at an initial strike price of $22.68 per share, subject to adjustment, for $88.2 million. In general, the call options allow us to acquire a number of shares of our common stock initially equal to the number of shares of common stock issuable to the holders of the Convertible Notes upon conversion. These call options will terminate upon the maturity of the Convertible Notes.

We also sold warrants in private transactions for total proceeds of approximately $36.7 million. The warrants permit the purchasers to acquire up to approximately 17.6 million shares of our common stock at an initial exercise price of $30.54 per share, subject to adjustment. The warrants expire on various dates from October 2013 (fiscal 2014) to December 2013 (fiscal 2014).

The Call Spread Transactions, in effect, increase the initial conversion price of the Convertible Notes from $22.68 per share to $30.54 per share, thus reducing the potential future economic dilution associated with conversion of the notes. The Convertible Notes and the warrants could have a dilutive effect on our earnings per share to the extent that the price of our common stock during a given measurement period exceeds the respective exercise prices of those instruments. The call options are excluded from the calculation of diluted earnings per share as their impact is anti-dilutive.

Under EITF 00-19 and other relevant literature, the Call Spread Transactions meet the criteria for classification as equity instruments. As a result, we recorded the purchase of the call options as a reduction to additional paid-in capital and the proceeds of the warrants as an increase to additional paid-in capital. In accordance with EITF 00-19, subsequent changes in fair value of those instruments are not recognized in the financial statements as long as the instruments continue to meet the criteria for equity classification.

Reclassification of Redeemable Common Stock

5.44

GENCORP INC. (NOV)

(In millions, except share amounts)	Comprehensive Income (Loss)	Common Stock		Other Capital	Accumulated Deficit	Accumulated Other Comprehensive Loss	Total Shareholders' Deficit
		Shares	Amount				
November 30, 2006		55,815,828	$5.6	$194.8	$(296.4)	$ —	$ (96.0)
Net income	$ 69.0	—	—	—	69.0	—	69.0
New defined benefit pension plan accounting standards transition amount	—	—	—	—	—	(35.5)	(35.5)
Stock-based compensation	—	—	—	1.0	—	—	1.0
Shares issued under stock option and stock incentive plans	—	770,892	0.1	9.4	—	—	9.5
November 30, 2007	$ 69.0	56,586,720	$5.7	$205.2	$(227.4)	$ (35.5)	$ (52.0)
Net income	1.5	—	—	—	1.5	—	1.5
Amortization of net actuarial losses	7.9	—	—	—	—	7.9	7.9
Actuarial losses arising during the period, net	(51.8)	—	—	—	—	(51.8)	(51.8)
Amortization of prior service costs	2.1	—	—	—	—	2.1	2.1
Prior service costs arising during the period, net	(5.3)	—	—	—	—	(5.3)	(5.3)
Curtailment	50.9	—	—	—	—	50.9	50.9
Cumulative effect adjustment related to the adoption of new income tax related accounting standards	—	—	—	—	9.1	—	9.1
Reclassification to redeemable common stock	—	(754,863)	(0.1)	(7.5)	—	—	(7.6)
Stock-based compensation	—	—	—	1.6	—	—	1.6
Shares issued under stock option and stock incentive plans, net	—	1,421,544	0.1	8.4	—	—	8.5
November 30, 2008	$ 5.3	57,253,401	$5.7	$207.7	$(216.8)	$ (31.7)	$ (35.1)

(continued)

(In millions, except share amounts)	Comprehensive Income (Loss)	Common Stock		Other Capital	Accumulated Deficit	Accumulated Other Comprehensive Loss	Total Shareholders' Deficit
		Shares	Amount				
November 30, 2008	$ 5.3	57,253,401	$5.7	$207.7	$(216.8)	$ (31.7)	$ (35.1)
Net income	59.3	—	—	—	59.3	—	59.3
Amortization of net actuarial gains	(9.0)	—	—	—	—	(9.0)	(9.0)
Actuarial losses arising during the period, net	(313.4)	—	—	—	—	(313.4)	(313.4)
Amortization of prior service costs	0.1	—	—	—	—	0.1	0.1
Reclassification from redeemable common stock	—	183,105	0.1	1.5	—	—	1.6
Stock-based compensation	—	—	—	0.1	—	—	0.1
Cumulative effect adjustment related to the adoption of defined benefit pension plan accounting standards	—	—	—	—	(0.4)	0.2	(0.2)
Shares issued under stock option and stock incentive plans, net	—	487,257	0.1	1.4	—	—	1.5
November 30, 2009	$(263.0)	57,923,763	$5.9	$210.7	$(157.9)	$(353.8)	$(295.1)

NOTES TO CONSOLIDATED FINANCIAL STATEMENTS

8. Redeemable Common Stock

The Company inadvertently failed to register with the SEC the issuance of certain of its common shares in its defined contribution 401(k) employee benefit plan (the "Plan"). As a result, certain Plan participants who purchased such securities pursuant to the Plan may have the right to rescind certain of their purchases for consideration equal to the purchase price paid for the securities (or if such security has been sold, to receive consideration with respect to any loss incurred on such sale) plus interest from the date of purchase. As of November 30, 2009 and 2008, the Company has classified 0.6 million and 0.8 million shares, respectively, as redeemable common stock because the redemption features are not within the control of the Company. The Company may also be subject to civil and other penalties by regulatory authorities as a result of the failure to register these shares. These shares have always been treated as outstanding for financial reporting purposes. In June 2008, the Company filed a registration statement on Form S-8 to register future transactions in the GenCorp Stock Fund in the Plan. The Company intends to make a registered rescission offer to eligible plan participants which will require an amendment to the Company's Senior Credit Facility. The Company is seeking an amendment to the Senior Credit Facility. During fiscal 2009 and 2008, the Company recorded a charge of $1.3 million and $1.7 million, respectively, for realized losses and interest associated with this matter.

9 (In Part): Shareholders' Deficit

b. Common Stock

As of November 30, 2009, the Company had 150.0 million authorized shares of common stock, par value $0.10 per share, of which 57.9 million shares were issued and outstanding, and 24.7 million shares were reserved for future issuance for discretionary payments of the Company's portion of retirement savings plan contributions, exercise of stock options (ten year contractual life) and restricted stock (no maximum contractual life), payment of awards under stock-based compensation plans, and conversion of the Company's Notes. See Note 8 for information about the Company's redeemable common stock.

Equity Component of Convertible Debt Issuance

5.45

TEREX CORPORATION (DEC)

(In millions)	Outstanding Shares	Common Stock	Additional Paid-In Capital	Retained Earnings	Accumulated Other Comprehensive Income (Loss)	Common Stock in Treasury	Noncontrolling Interest	Total
Balance at January 1, 2007	101.1	$1.0	$ 923.7	$ 707.3	$ 155.2	$ (36.2)	$ 9.4	$1,760.4
Net income	—	—	—	613.9	—	—	4.3	618.2
Other comprehensive income (loss)—net of tax:								
Translation adjustment	—	—	—	—	96.9	—	0.5	97.4
Pension liability adjustment	—	—	—	—	10.5	—	—	10.5
Derivative hedging adjustment	—	—	—	—	(6.0)	—	—	(6.0)
Comprehensive loss								720.1
Impact of adoption of new accounting pronouncement	—	—	—	(36.5)	—	—	—	(36.5)
Issuance of common stock	1.5	0.1	42.6	—	—	—	—	42.7
Compensation under stock-based plans—net	—	—	37.8	—	—	1.3	—	39.1
Acquisition	—	—	—	—	—	—	3.4	3.4
Sale of equity interest	—	—	—	—	—	—	2.2	2.2
Acquisition of treasury stock	(2.3)	—	—	—	—	(168.4)	—	(168.4)
Balance at December 31, 2007	100.3	$1.1	$1,004.1	$1,284.7	$ 256.6	$(203.3)	$19.8	$2,363.0
Net income	—	—	—	71.9	—	—	3.7	75.6
Other comprehensive income (loss)—net of tax:								
Translation adjustment	—	—	—	—	(332.2)	—	0.3	(331.9)
Pension liability adjustment	—	—	—	—	(10.7)	—	—	(10.7)
Derivative hedging adjustment	—	—	—	—	4.0	—	—	4.0
Comprehensive loss								(263.0)
Issuance of common stock	0.9	—	44.0	—	—	—	—	44.0
Compensation under stock-based plans—net	0.2	—	(2.3)	—	—	3.6	—	1.3
Capital contributed	—	—	—	—	—	—	1.0	1.0
Distributions to noncontrolling interest	—	—	—	—	—	—	(2.6)	(2.6)
Acquisition of treasury stock	(7.4)	—	0.4	—	—	(400.2)	—	(399.8)
Balance at December 31, 2008	94.0	$1.1	$1,046.2	$1,356.6	$ (82.3)	$(599.9)	$22.2	$1,743.9
Net (loss) income	—	—	—	(398.4)	—	—	2.3	(396.1)
Other comprehensive income (loss)—net of tax:								
Translation adjustment	—	—	—	—	139.6	—	—	139.6
Pension liability adjustment	—	—	—	—	(18.7)	—	—	(18.7)
Derivative hedging adjustment	—	—	—	—	(2.6)	—	—	(2.6)
Comprehensive loss								(277.8)
Issuance of common stock	13.3	0.1	186.5	—	—	—	—	186.6
Compensation under stock-based plans—net	—	—	(15.4)	—	—	1.4	—	(14.0)
Acquisition	—	—	—	—	—	—	9.7	9.7
Purchase of noncontrolling interest	—	—	1.2	—	—	—	(2.9)	(1.7)
Distributions to noncontrolling interest	—	—	—	—	—	—	(7.1)	(7.1)
Issuance of convertible debt—net of tax	—	—	35.0	—	—	—	—	35.0
Acquisition of treasury stock	—	—	—	—	—	(0.2)	—	(0.2)
Balance at December 31, 2009	107.3	$1.2	$1,253.5	$ 958.2	$ 36.0	$(598.7)	$24.2	$1,674.4

NOTES TO CONSOLIDATED FINANCIAL STATEMENTS

Note N (In Part): Long Term Obligations

4% Convertible Senior Subordinated Notes

On June 3, 2009, the Company sold and issued $172.5 million aggregate principal amount of 4% Convertible Notes. In certain circumstances and during certain periods, the 4% Convertible Notes will be convertible at an initial conversion rate of 61.5385 shares of Common Stock per $1,000 principal amount of convertible notes, equivalent to an initial conversion price of approximately $16.25 per share of Common Stock, subject to adjustment in some events. Upon conversion, Terex will deliver cash up to the aggregate principal amount of the 4% Convertible Notes to be converted and shares of Common Stock with respect to the remainder, if any, of Terex's convertible obligation in excess of the aggregate principal amount of the 4% Convertible Notes being converted. The 4% Convertible Notes are not currently guaranteed by any of the Company's subsidiaries, but under specified limited circumstances, along with the 10-7/8% Notes and 8% Senior Subordinated Notes, could be guaranteed by certain domestic subsidiaries of the Company in the future.

The Company, as issuer of the 4% Convertible Notes, must separately account for the liability and equity components of the 4% Convertible Notes in a manner that reflects the Company's nonconvertible debt borrowing rate at the date of issuance when interest cost is recognized in subsequent periods. The Company allocated $54.3 million of the $172.5 million principal amount of the 4% Convertible Notes to the equity component, which represents a discount to the debt and will be amortized into interest expense using the effective interest method through June 2015. The Company recorded a related deferred tax liability of $19.4 million on the equity component. The balance of the 4% Convertible Notes was $122.1 million at December 31, 2009. Accordingly, the Company's effective interest rate on the 4% Convertible Notes will be 11.375%, so the Company will recognize interest expense during the twelve months ended June 2010 on the 4% Convertible Notes in an amount that approximates 11.375% of $118.2 million, the liability component of the 4% Convertible Notes at the date of issuance. The Company recognized interest expense of $7.8 million on the 4% Convertible Notes for the year ended December 31, 2009. The interest expense recognized for the 4% Convertible Notes will increase as the discount is amortized using the effective interest method, which accretes the debt balance over its term to $172.5 million at maturity. Interest expense on the 4% Convertible Notes throughout its term includes 4% annually of cash interest on the maturity balance of $172.5 million plus non-cash interest expense accreted to the debt balance as described. The 4% Convertible Notes are classified as long-term debt in the Company's Consolidated Balance Sheet at December 31, 2009 based on their June 2015 maturity date.

Treasury Stock Issued

5.46

CAMERON INTERNATIONAL CORPORATION (DEC)

(Dollars in thousands)	Common Stock	Capital in Excess of Par Value	Retained Earnings	Accumulated Other Elements of Comprehensive Income	Treasury Stock	Total
Balance—December 31, 2006	$1,162	$1,207,281	$ 745,829	$ 16,326	$(177,772)	$1,792,826
Net income			488,181			488,181
Foreign currency translation				59,686		59,686
Change in fair value of derivatives accounted for as cash flow hedges, net of $2,803 in taxes				5,011		5,011
Other comprehensive income from derivative transactions recognized in current year earnings, net of $2,225 in taxes				(4,583)		(4,583)
Pension settlement loss, net of $14,422 in taxes				23,282		23,282
Pension curtailment gain, net of $757 in taxes				(1,222)		(1,222)
Actuarial loss, net of amortization				2,504		2,504
Comprehensive income						572,859
Adjustment to initially apply FIN 48		(2,000)	(4,996)			(6,996)
Non-cash stock compensation expense		31,383				31,383
Purchase of treasury stock					(341,423)	(341,423)
Common and treasury stock issued under stock option and other employee benefit plans		(40,411)			93,195	52,784
Tax benefit of employee stock compensation plan transactions		32,239				32,239
Stock split	1,162	(1,162)				—
Balance—December 31, 2007	$2,324	$1,227,330	$1,229,014	$101,004	$(426,000)	$2,133,672

(continued)

(Dollars in thousands)	Common Stock	Capital in Excess of Par Value	Retained Earnings	Accumulated Other Elements of Comprehensive Income	Treasury Stock	Total
Balance—December 31, 2007	$2,324	$1,227,330	$1,229,014	$ 101,004	$(426,000)	$2,133,672
Net income			580,703			580,703
Foreign currency translation				(169,378)		(169,378)
Loss on treasury locks, net of amortization and taxes				(1,192)		(1,192)
Change in fair value of derivatives accounted for as cash flow hedges, net of $26,920 in taxes				(47,245)		(47,245)
Other comprehensive income from derivative transactions recognized in current year earnings, net of $1,421 in taxes				3,254		3,254
Pension settlement loss, net of $9,693 in taxes				16,503		16,503
Impact after currency effects of actuarial gains/losses and plan amendments, net of $3,917 in taxes				7,911		7,911
Amortization of net actuarial losses and prior service credits, net of $2,295 in taxes				5,219		5,219
Comprehensive income						395,775
Adjustment for change in measurement date for post-retirement benefit plans			196	(294)		(98)
Non-cash stock compensation expense		35,627				35,627
Purchase of treasury stock					(259,883)	(259,883)
Treasury stock issued under stock option and other employee benefit plans		(30,159)			47,759	17,600
Tax benefit of employee stock compensation plan transactions		22,548				22,548
Stock issued for conversion of convertible debt	39	(39)				—
Adjustment to conversion option resulting from conversion of convertible debt, net of taxes		(714)				(714)
Balance—December 31, 2008	$2,363	$1,254,593	$1,809,913	$ (84,218)	$(638,124)	$2,344,527
Net income			475,519			475,519
Foreign currency translation				86,649		86,649
Amortization of treasury locks, net of taxes				26		26
Change in fair value of derivatives accounted for as cash flow hedges, net of $6,664 in taxes				11,256		11,256
Other comprehensive income from derivative transactions recognized in current year earnings, net of $9,601 in taxes				16,215		16,215
Impact after currency effects of actuarial gains/losses, net of $9,697 in taxes				(22,955)		(22,955)
Amortization of net actuarial losses and prior service credits, net of $580 in taxes				2,371		2,371
Pension settlement loss				148		148
Comprehensive income						569,229
Equity securities issued for purchase of NATCO	236	982,082			6,207	988,525
Non-cash stock compensation expense		27,701				27,701
Purchase of treasury stock					(29,175)	(29,175)
Treasury stock issued under stock option and other employee benefit plans		(30,062)			39,297	9,235
Tax benefit of employee stock compensation plan transactions		9,718				9,718
Stock issued for conversion of convertible debt	32	(32)				—
Balance—December 31, 2009	$2,631	$2,244,000	$2,285,432	$ 9,492	$(621,795)	$3,919,760

ATT-SEC 5.46

NOTES TO CONSOLIDATED FINANCIAL STATEMENTS

Note 9 (In Part): Stock-Based Compensation Plans

The Company has grants outstanding under four equity compensation plans, only one of which, the 2005 Equity Incentive Plan (2005 EQIP), is currently available for future grants of equity compensation awards to employees and non-employee directors. The other three plans, which continue to have options outstanding at December 31, 2009, are the Company's Long-Term Incentive Plan, as Amended and Restated as of November 2002, the Broadbased 2000 Incentive Plan and the Second Amended and Restated 1995 Stock Option Plan for Non-Employee Directors. Options granted under the Company's four equity compensation plans had an exercise price equal to the market value of the underlying common stock on the date of grant and all terms were fixed.

Stock-based compensation expense recognized was as follows:

(Dollars in thousands)	2009	2008	2007
Outstanding restricted and deferred stock unit and award grants	$18,505	$20,084	$15,610
Unvested outstanding stock option grants	9,196	15,543	15,773
Total stock-based compensation expense	$27,701	$35,627	$31,383

The total income statement tax benefit recognized from stock-based compensation arrangements during the years ended December 31, 2009, 2008 and 2007 totaled approximately $10,208,000, $13,182,000, $12,004,000, respectively.

Stock Options

Options with terms of seven years are granted to officers and other key employees of the Company under the 2005 EQIP plan at a fixed exercise price equal to the fair value of the Company's common stock on the date of grant. The options vest in one-third increments each year on the anniversary date following the date of grant, based on continued employment. Grants made in previous years to officers and other key employees under the Long-Term and Broadbased Incentive Plans provide similar terms, except that the options terminate after ten years rather than seven.

In connection with the acquisition of NATCO, effective November 18, 2009, the Company issued 811,727 vested and 132,793 unvested options for the Company's common stock to certain former NATCO employees in exchange for similar options in NATCO common stock held by those employees immediately prior to the acquisition date. The terms, conditions and value of the options issued by the Company were similar to the NATCO options and thus, no option modification accounting was required at the date of the exchange.

A summary of option activity under the Company's stock compensation plans as of and for the year ended December 31, 2009 is presented below:

Options	Shares	Weighted-Average Exercise Price	Weighted-Average Remaining Contractual Term (In Years)	Aggregate Intrinsic Value (Dollars in Thousands)
Outstanding at January 1, 2009	7,368,776	$26.52		
Granted	827,000	39.24		
Added through acquisitions	944,520	27.26		
Exercised	(1,220,531)	17.17		
Forfeited	(88,043)	30.42		
Expired	(31,734)	32.96		
Outstanding at December 31, 2009	7,799,988	$29.35	4.49	$100,973
Vested at December 31, 2009 or expected to vest in the future	7,775,983	$29.34	4.48	$100,761
Exercisable at December 31, 2009	5,293,918	$27.52	3.83	$ 78,197

At December 31, 2009:	
Stock-based compensation cost not yet recognized under the straight-line method (dollars in thousands)	$12,720
Weighted-average remaining expense recognition period (in years)	2.02

The fair values per share of option grants for the years ended December 31, 2009, 2008 and 2007 were estimated using the Black-Scholes-Merton option pricing formula with the following weighted-average assumptions:

	2009	2008	2007
Expected life (in years)	2.4	3.3	2.6
Risk-free interest rate	1.1%	1.7%	3.4%
Volatility	32.0%	36.8%	31.2%
Expected dividend yield	0.0%	0.0%	0.0%

The Company determined the assumptions involving the expected life of its options and volatility rates based primarily on historical data and consideration of expectations for the future.

The above assumptions and market prices of the Company's common stock at the date of option exercises resulted in the following values:

	2009	2008	2007
Grant-date fair value per option	$ 8.10	$ 6.31	$ 10.32
Intrinsic value of options exercised (dollars in thousands)	$23,511	$59,921	$95,203
Average intrinsic value per share of options exercised	$ 19.26	$ 35.08	$ 23.69

Restricted and Deferred Stock Units and Awards

During 2005, the Company began issuing restricted stock units with no exercise price to key employees in place of stock options. During 2009, 2008 and 2007, grants of restricted stock units were made to officers and key employees. Approximately 72,634 and 235,433 of the restricted stock unit grants during 2008 and 2007, respectively, contained performance-based conditions which were fully satisfied based on the Company's full-year 2008 and 2007 financial performance against certain targets. No 2009 restricted stock unit grants contained performance-based conditions. The restricted stock units granted to officers and other key employees generally provided for three-year 100% cliff vesting on the third anniversary of the date of grant, based on continued employment.

In connection with the acquisition of NATCO, effective November 18, 2009, the Company issued 68,881 unvested Cameron restricted common stock awards to certain former NATCO employees in exchange for similar shares of NATCO restricted stock held by those employees immediately prior to the acquisition date. The terms, conditions and value of the restricted stock awards issued by the Company were similar to the NATCO restricted stock awards and thus, no restricted stock modification accounting was required at the date of the exchange (see Note 2 of the Notes to Consolidated Financial Statements for further information).

Under an update to the Compensation Program for Non-Employee Directors approved by the Board of Directors in May 2008, non-employee directors are entitled to receive an annual number of deferred stock units that is equal to a value of $250,000 determined on the day following the Company's annual meeting of stockholders or, if a director's election to the Board occurs between annual meetings of stockholders, the initial grant of deferred stock units is based on a pro-rata portion of the annual grant amount equal to the remaining number of months in the board year until the next annual meeting of stockholders. These units, which have no exercise price and no expiration date, vest in one-fourth increments quarterly over the following year but cannot be converted into common stock until the earlier of termination of Board service or three years, although Board members have the ability to voluntarily defer conversion for a longer period of time.

A summary of restricted stock unit and restricted stock award activity under the Company's stock compensation plans as of and for the year ended December 31, 2009 is presented below:

Restricted Stock Units and Awards	Number	Weighted-Average Grant Date Fair Value
Nonvested at January 1, 2009	1,799,869	$30.16
Granted	616,904	25.44
Added through acquisitions	68,881	40.59
Vested	(525,160)	21.57
Forfeited	(48,407)	27.46
Nonvested at December 31, 2009	1,912,087	$31.56

At December 31, 2009	
Stock-based compensation cost not yet recognized under the straight-line method (dollars in thousands)	$19,447
Weighted-average remaining expense recognition period (in years)	1.28

The intrinsic value of restricted stock units vesting during the years ended December 31, 2009, 2008 and 2007 was $10,980,000, $19,278,000 and $5,277,000, respectively.

During the years ended December 31, 2009, 2008 and 2007, respectively, a total of 616,904, 639,799 and 708,042 restricted stock units (post-split) at a weighted-average grant date fair value of $25.44, $36.40 and $29.04 per share (post-split) were granted. The fair value of restricted stock units is determined based on the closing trading price of the Company's common stock on the grant date.

At December 31, 2009, 8,340,040 shares were reserved for future grants of options, deferred stock units, restricted stock units and other awards. The Company may issue either treasury shares or newly issued shares of its common stock in satisfaction of these awards.

Note 13 (In Part): Stockholders' Equity

Common Stock

On December 7, 2007, stockholders of the Company approved an amendment to the Company's Amended and Restated Certificate of Incorporation to increase the number of authorized shares of common stock from 150,000,000 to 400,000,000. Additionally, effective December 28, 2007, the Company implemented a 2-for-1 stock split in the form of a stock dividend at that date.

In February 2006, the Company's Board of Directors changed the number of shares of the Company's common stock authorized for repurchase from the 5,000,000 shares authorized in August 2004 to 10,000,000 shares in order to reflect the 2-for-1 stock split effective December 15, 2005. This authorization was subsequently increased to 20,000,000 in connection with the 2-for-1 stock split effective December 28, 2007 and eventually to 30,000,000 by a resolution adopted by the Board of Directors on February 21, 2008. Additionally, on May 22, 2006, the Company's Board of Directors approved repurchasing shares of the Company's common stock with the proceeds remaining from the Company's 2.5% Convertible Debenture offering, after taking into account a planned repayment of $200,000,000 principal amount of the Company's outstanding 2.65% Senior Notes due 2007. This authorization is in addition to the 30,000,000 shares described above.

Purchases pursuant to the 30,000,000-share Board authorization may be made by way of open market purchases, directly or indirectly, for the Company's own account or through commercial banks or financial institutions and by the use of derivatives such as a sale or put on the Company's common stock or by forward or economically equivalent transactions.

Changes in the number of shares of the Company's outstanding stock for the last three years were as follows:

	Common Stock	Treasury Stock	Shares Outstanding
Balance—December 31, 2006	116,170,863	(3,881,236)	112,289,627
Purchase of treasury stock before stock split	—	(5,284,256)	(5,284,256)
Stock issued under stock option and other employee benefit plans before stock split	—	2,074,029	2,074,029
Effect of stock split on shares outstanding	116,170,863	(7,091,464)	109,079,399
Purchase of treasury stock after stock split	—	(150,000)	(150,000)
Balance—December 31, 2007	232,341,726	(14,332,927)	218,008,799
Purchase of treasury stock	—	(6,968,363)	(6,968,363)
Stock issued under stock option and other employee benefit plans	—	1,877,170	1,877,170
Stock issued upon conversion of the 1.5% convertible debentures	3,975,147	—	3,975,147
Balance—December 31, 2008	236,316,873	(19,424,120)	216,892,753
Purchase of treasury stock	—	(935,178)	(935,178)
Stock issued related to NATCO acquisition	23,637,708	237,323	23,875,031
Stock issued under stock option and other employee benefit plans	—	1,668,217	1,668,217
Stock issued upon conversion of the 1.5% convertible debentures	3,156,891	—	3,156,891
Balance—December 31, 2009	263,111,472	(18,453,758)	244,657,714

At December 31, 2009, 17,204,156 shares of unissued common stock were reserved for future issuance under various employee benefit plans.

Treasury Stock Purchased

5.47

NATIONAL SEMICONDUCTOR CORPORATION (MAY)

(In millions, except per share amount)	Common Stock		Additional Paid-In Capital	Retained Earnings	Unearned Compensation	Accumulated Other Comprehensive Loss	Total
	Shares	Par Value					
Balance at May 28, 2006	335.7	$167.8	$ 504.2	$ 1,417.7	$(8.6)	$(113.5)	$ 1,967.6
Net income	—	—	—	375.3	—	—	375.3
Cash dividend declared and paid ($0.14 per share)	—	—	—	(45.1)	—	—	(45.1)
Issuance of common stock under option and purchase plans	7.3	3.7	99.3	—	—	—	103.0
Issuance of restricted stock	0.2	0.1	(0.1)	—	—	—	—
Cancellation of restricted stock	—	—	(1.4)	—	—	—	(1.4)
Share-based compensation cost	—	—	113.8	—	—	—	113.8
Elimination of unearned compensation upon adoption of SFAS No. 123R	—	—	(8.6)	—	8.6	—	—
Tax benefit associated with stock options	—	—	29.6	—	—	—	29.6
Purchase and retirement of treasury stock	(32.9)	(16.5)	(736.8)	(20.7)	—	—	(774.0)
Other comprehensive income	—	—	—	—	—	20.0	20.0
Unadjusted balance at May 27, 2007	310.3	$155.1	$ —	$ 1,727.2	$ —	$ (93.5)	$ 1,788.8
Effect upon the adoption of SFAS No. 158, net of tax	—	—	—	—	—	(20.3)	(20.3)
Balance at May 27, 2007	310.3	$155.1	$ —	$ 1,727.2	$ —	$(113.8)	$ 1,768.5
Cumulative effect adjustment upon adoption of FIN 48	—	—	—	37.1	—	—	37.1
Net income	—	—	—	332.3	—	—	332.3
Cash dividend declared and paid ($0.20 per share)	—	—	—	(50.6)	—	—	(50.6)
Issuance of common stock under option and purchase plans	7.6	3.9	99.8	—	—	—	103.7
Issuance of stock under Executive Officer Equity Plan	1.0	0.5	(0.5)	—	—	—	—
Cancellation of restricted stock	(0.4)	(0.2)	(14.4)	—	—	—	(14.6)
Share-based compensation cost	—	—	89.4	—	—	—	89.4
Tax benefit associated with stock options	—	—	27.6	—	—	—	27.6
Purchase and retirement of treasury stock	(85.9)	(43.0)	(201.9)	(1,878.6)	—	—	(2,123.5)
Other comprehensive income	—	—	—	—	—	27.0	27.0
Balance at May 25, 2008	232.6	$116.3	$ —	$ 167.4	$ —	$ (86.8)	$ 196.9
Effect upon the adoption of SFAS No. 158 for change in measurement date, net of tax	—	—	—	(0.6)	—	—	(0.6)
Net income	—	—	—	73.3	—	—	73.3
Cash dividend declared and paid ($0.28 per share)	—	—	—	(64.4)	—	—	(64.4)
Issuance of common stock under option and purchase plans	6.2	3.1	59.1	—	—	—	62.2
Cancellation of restricted stock	—	—	(0.4)	—	—	—	(0.4)
Share-based compensation cost	—	—	67.2	—	—	—	67.2
Tax benefit associated with stock options	—	—	8.1	—	—	—	8.1
Purchase and retirement of treasury stock	(6.2)	(3.1)	(125.3)	—	—	—	(128.4)
Treasury stock retirement in excess of additional paid-in capital	—	—	58.9	(58.9)	—	—	—
Other comprehensive income	—	—	—	—	—	(36.9)	(36.9)
Balance at May 31, 2009	232.6	$116.3	$ 67.6	$ 116.8	$ —	$(123.7)	$ 177.0

NOTES TO CONSOLIDATED FINANCIAL STATEMENTS

Note 13 (In Part): Shareholders' Equity

Stock Repurchase Programs

Fiscal 2009

The following table provides a summary of the activity under our stock repurchase program in fiscal 2009 and related amount remaining available for future common stock repurchases at May 31, 2009:

(In millions)	Stock Repurchase Program June 2007
Balance at May 25, 2008	$ 255.8
Common stock repurchases	(128.4)
Balance at May 31, 2009	$ 127.4

We repurchased a total of 6.2 million shares of our common stock during fiscal 2009 for $128.4 million as part of the $500 million stock repurchase program announced in June 2007. All of these shares were repurchased in the open market and have been cancelled as of May 31, 2009. There is no expiration date for the current repurchase program.

Fiscal 2008

In June 2007, our Board of Directors approved (i) a $1.5 billion accelerated stock repurchase program; and (ii) an additional $500 million stock repurchase program similar to our existing stock repurchase program announced in March 2007. We entered into two separate agreements with Goldman Sachs to conduct the accelerated stock repurchase program. Under one of the agreements, we repurchased from Goldman Sachs, for $1.0 billion, a number of shares of our common stock determined by the volume-weighted average price of the stock during a six month period, subject to provisions establishing minimum and maximum numbers of shares. Under the other agreement, we repurchased shares of our common stock from Goldman Sachs immediately for an initial amount of $500 million. Goldman Sachs purchased an equivalent number of shares of our common stock in the open market over the next six months, and at the end of that period, the initial price was adjusted down based on the volume-weighted average price during the same period. The price adjustment was settled by us, at our option, in shares of our common stock. The $1.5 billion accelerated stock repurchase program was completed in December 2007 with a total 58.0 million shares repurchased.

In addition to the accelerated stock repurchase program, we repurchased an additional 27.9 million shares of our common stock during fiscal 2008 for $623.5 million as part of two $500 million stock repurchase programs: (i) the $500 million stock repurchase program announced in March 2007, which was completed during the third quarter of fiscal 2008, and (ii) the $500 million stock repurchase program announced in June 2007. All of these shares were repurchased in the open market. For all of fiscal 2008, we repurchased a total of 85.9 million shares of our common stock for $2,123.5 million through both the $1.5 billion accelerated stock repurchase program and the two $500 million stock repurchase programs. All shares of common stock that were repurchased had been cancelled as of the end of fiscal 2008.

Fiscal 2007

We repurchased a total of 32.9 million shares of our common stock during fiscal 2007 for $774.0 million as part of three programs: (i) the $400 million stock repurchase program announced in December 2005, which was completed during the first quarter of fiscal 2007, (ii) the $500 million stock repurchase program announced in June 2006, which was completed during the fourth quarter of fiscal 2007 and (iii) the $500 million stock repurchase program announced in March 2007. All of these shares were repurchased in the open market.

Restricted Stock

5.48

MATTEL, INC. (DEC)

(In thousands)	Common Stock	Additional Paid-In Capital	Treasury Stock	Retained Earnings	Accumulated Other Comprehensive (Loss) Income	Total Stockholders' Equity
Balance, December 31, 2006	$441,369	$1,613,307	$ (996,981)	$1,652,140	$(276,861)	$2,432,974
Comprehensive income:						
Net income				599,993		599,993
Change in net unrealized (loss) on derivative instruments					(13,918)	(13,918)
Defined benefit pension plans, net prior service cost, and net actuarial loss					28,316	28,316
Currency translation adjustments					86,653	86,653
Comprehensive income				599,993	101,051	701,044
Purchase of treasury stock			(806,349)			(806,349)
Issuance of treasury stock for stock option exercises		(5,395)	225,467			220,072
Other issuance of treasury stock		25	40			65
Restricted stock units		(275)	266			(9)
Deferred compensation			6,046			6,046
Share-based compensation		21,870				21,870
Tax benefits from share-based payment arrangements		5,706				5,706
Dividend equivalents for restricted stock units				(2,334)		(2,334)
Dividends				(272,343)		(272,343)
Balance, December 31, 2007	$441,369	$1,635,238	$(1,571,511)	$1,977,456	$(175,810)	$2,306,742
Comprehensive income:						
Net income				379,636		379,636
Change in net unrealized gain on derivative instruments					25,388	25,388
Defined benefit pension plans, net prior service cost, and net actuarial loss					(87,636)	(87,636)
Currency translation adjustments					(192,577)	(192,577)
Comprehensive income				379,636	(254,825)	124,811
Purchase of treasury stock			(90,570)			(90,570)
Issuance of treasury stock for stock option exercises		(10,334)	28,453			18,119
Other issuance of treasury stock		(1)	151			150
Restricted stock units		(16,147)	10,799			(5,348)
Deferred compensation			1,414			1,414
Share-based compensation		35,639				35,639
Tax benefits from share-based payment arrangements		(2,303)				(2,303)
Dividend equivalents for restricted stock units				(2,665)		(2,665)
Dividends				(268,854)		(268,854)
Balance, December 31, 2008	$441,369	$1,642,092	$(1,621,264)	$2,085,573	$(430,635)	$2,117,135
Comprehensive income:						
Net income				528,704		528,704
Change in net unrealized (loss) on derivative instruments					(19,805)	(19,805)
Defined benefit pension plans, net prior service cost, and net actuarial loss					18,696	18,696
Currency translation adjustments					52,210	52,210
Comprehensive income				528,704	51,101	579,805
Issuance of treasury stock for stock option exercises		(17,219)	48,115			30,896
Other issuance of treasury stock		(209)	209			0
Restricted stock units		(26,658)	18,566			(8,092)
Deferred compensation			(672)	(323)		(995)
Share-based compensation		49,962				49,962
Tax benefits from share-based payment arrangements		36,726				36,726
Dividend equivalents for restricted stock units				(3,095)		(3,095)
Dividends				(271,353)		(271,353)
Balance, December 31, 2009	$441,369	$1,684,694	$(1,555,046)	$2,339,506	$(379,534)	$2,530,989

NOTES TO CONSOLIDATED FINANCIAL STATEMENTS

Note 10 (In Part): Share-Based Payments

Mattel Stock Option Plans

In May 2005, Mattel's stockholders approved the Mattel, Inc. 2005 Equity Compensation Plan (the "2005 Plan"). Upon approval of the 2005 Plan, Mattel terminated its Amended and Restated 1996 Stock Option Plan (the "1996 Plan") and its 1999 Stock Option Plan (the "1999 Plan"), except with respect to grants then outstanding under the 1996 Plan and the 1999 Plan. Restricted stock awards made under the 1996 Plan continue to vest pursuant to the terms of their respective grant agreements. Outstanding stock option grants under plans that have expired or have been terminated continue to be exercisable under the terms of their respective grant agreements. All such stock options expire no later than ten years from the date of grant and generally provide for vesting over a period of three years from the date of grant. Stock options generally were granted with exercise prices equal to the fair market value of Mattel's common stock on the date of grant, although there are some outstanding stock options that were granted with an exercise price in excess of the fair market value of Mattel's common stock on the date of grant, as to which vesting was dependent upon Mattel's common stock achieving a specified fair market value during a specified time period. Options were granted to non-employee members of Mattel's Board of Directors under the 1996 Plan with exercise prices equal to the fair market value of Mattel's common stock on the date of grant; such options expire no later than ten years from the date of grant and vest over a period of four years from the date of grant.

Under the 2005 Plan, Mattel has the ability to grant non-qualified stock options, incentive stock options, stock appreciation rights, restricted stock, RSUs, dividend equivalent rights, and shares of common stock to officers, employees, and other persons providing services to Mattel. Generally, options vest and become exercisable contingent upon the grantees' continued employment or service with Mattel. Non-qualified stock options are granted at not less than 100% of the fair market value of Mattel's common stock on the date of grant, expire no later than ten years from the date of grant, and vest on a schedule determined by the Compensation Committee of the Board of Directors, generally during a period of three years from the date of grant. In the event of a retirement of an employee aged 55 years or greater with 5 or more years of service that occurs at least 6 months after the grant date, nonqualified stock options become fully vested. With regard to grants of stock options in the 2007 annual grant and later, death and disability at least 6 months after the grant date also result in accelerated vesting. With regard to grants of stock options before the 2007 annual grant, there is no accelerated vesting for death or disability. Similar provisions exist for non-employee directors. RSUs granted under the 2005 Plan are generally accompanied by dividend equivalent rights and generally vest over a period of three years from the date of grant. In the event of the involuntary termination of an employee aged 55 years or greater with 5 or more years of service, or the death or disability of an employee, that occurs at least 6 months after the grant date, RSUs receive accelerated vesting as to some or all of the RSUs. The 2005 Plan also contains provisions regarding grants of equity compensation to the non-employee members of the Board of Directors. The 2005 Plan expires on May 18, 2015, except as to any grants then outstanding.

The number of shares of common stock available for grant under the 2005 Plan is subject to an aggregate limit of 50 million shares and is further subject to share-counting rules as provided in the 2005 Plan. As a result of such share-counting rules, full-value grants such as grants of restricted stock or RSUs count against shares remaining available for grant at a higher rate than grants of stock options and stock appreciation rights. Each stock option or stock appreciation right grant is treated as using one available share for each share actually subject to such grant, whereas each full-value grant is treated as using three available shares for each share actually subject to such full-value grant. The 2005 Plan contains detailed provisions with regard to share-counting. At December 31, 2009, there were approximately 8 million shares of common stock available for grant remaining under the 2005 Plan.

As of December 31, 2009, total unrecognized compensation cost related to unvested share-based payments totaled $69.8 million and is expected to be recognized over a weighted-average period of 2.0 years.

Restricted Stock and Restricted Stock Units

RSUs are valued at the market value on the date of grant and the expense is evenly attributed to the periods in which the restrictions lapse, which is three years from the date of grant.

Compensation expense recognized related to grants of RSUs was $31.7 million, $24.7 million, and $14.8 million in 2009, 2008, and 2007, respectively, and is included within other selling and administrative expenses. Income tax benefits related to RSU compensation expense recognized in the consolidated statements of operations during 2009, 2008, and 2007 totaled $9.5 million, $7.9 million, and $4.6 million, respectively.

The following table summarizes the number and weighted average grant date fair value of Mattel's unvested RSUs during the year (amounts in thousands, except weighted average grant date fair value):

| | 2009 | | 2008 | | 2007 | |
	Shares	Weighted Average Grant Date Fair Value	Shares	Weighted Average Grant Date Fair Value	Shares	Weighted Average Grant Date Fair Value
Unvested at January 1	3,927	$21.03	3,452	$20.38	1,811	$17.28
Granted	2,113	17.41	1,873	20.09	1,744	23.60
Vested	(1,408)	20.96	(990)	16.91	(15)	28.10
Forfeited	(183)	20.53	(408)	21.16	(88)	19.27
Unvested at December 31	4,449	$19.36	3,927	$21.03	3,452	$20.38

At December 31, 2009, total RSUs expected to vest totaled 4.1 million shares, with a weighted average grant date fair value of $19.42. The total grant date fair value of RSUs vested during 2009, 2008, and 2007 totaled $29.5 million, $16.7 million, and $0.4 million, respectively.

In addition to the expense and share amounts described above, Mattel recognized compensation expense of $5.3 million and $1.5 million, during 2009 and 2008, respectively, for performance RSUs granted in connection with its January 1, 2008–December 31, 2010 Long-Term Incentive Program.

Purchase of Noncontrolling Interest

5.49

KIMBERLY-CLARK CORPORATION (DEC)

(Dollars in millions, shares in thousands)	Common Stock Issued Shares	Amount	Additional Paid-In Capital	Treasury Stock Shares	Amount	Retained Earnings	Accumulated Other Comprehensive Income (Loss)	Noncontrolling Interests
Balance at December 31, 2006	478,597	$598	$ 428	22,978	$(1,392)	$ 7,896	$(1,432)	$ 404
Net income in stockholders' equity	—	—	—	—	—	1,823	—	85
Other comprehensive income:								
Unrealized translation	—	—	—	—	—	—	365	12
Employee postretirement benefits, net of tax	—	—	—	—	—	—	266	—
Other	—	—	—	—	—	—	10	—
Stock-based awards exercised or vested	—	—	(40)	(6,646)	389	(4)	—	—
Income tax benefits on stock-based compensation	—	—	32	—	—	—	—	—
Shares repurchased	—	—	—	41,344	(2,811)	—	—	—
Recognition of stock-based compensation	—	—	63	—	—	—	—	—
Dividends declared	—	—	—	—	—	(933)	—	(30)
Additional investment in subsidiary and other	—	—	—	—	—	—	—	(8)
Adoption of uncertain tax positions accounting standard	—	—	—	—	—	(34)	—	—
Balance at December 31, 2007	478,597	$598	$ 483	57,676	$(3,814)	$ 8,748	$ (791)	$ 463
Net income in stockholders' equity	—	—	—	—	—	1,690	—	82
Other comprehensive income:								
Unrealized translation	—	—	—	—	—	—	(900)	(81)
Employee postretirement benefits, net of tax	—	—	—	—	—	—	(687)	(2)
Other	—	—	—	—	—	—	(8)	—
Stock-based awards exercised or vested	—	—	(59)	(2,870)	170	(7)	—	—
Income tax benefits on stock-based compensation	—	—	10	—	—	—	—	—
Shares repurchased	—	—	5	10,232	(641)	—	—	—
Recognition of stock-based compensation	—	—	47	—	—	—	—	—
Dividends declared	—	—	—	—	—	(966)	—	(51)
Additional investment in subsidiary and other	—	—	—	—	—	—	—	(28)
Balance at December 31, 2008	478,597	$598	$ 486	65,038	$(4,285)	$ 9,465	$(2,386)	$ 383
Net income in stockholders' equity	—	—	—	—	—	1,884	—	54
Other comprehensive income:								
Unrealized translation	—	—	—	—	—	—	619	6
Employee postretirement benefits, net of tax	—	—	—	—	—	—	(32)	(2)
Other	—	—	—	—	—	—	3	—
Stock-based awards exercised or vested	—	—	(47)	(3,519)	204	(7)	—	—
Income tax benefits on stock-based compensation	—	—	7	—	—	—	—	—
Shares repurchased	—	—	—	130	(7)	—	—	—
Recognition of stock-based compensation	—	—	86	—	—	—	—	—
Dividends declared	—	—	—	—	—	(996)	—	(45)
Additional investment in subsidiary and other	—	—	(133)	—	1	(17)	(37)	(112)
Balance at December 31, 2009	478,597	$598	$ 399	61,649	$(4,087)	$10,329	$(1,833)	$ 284

NOTES TO CONSOLIDATED FINANCIAL STATEMENTS

Note 6 (In Part): Acquisitions and Intangible Assets

Acquisitions (In Part)

During the first quarter of 2009, the Corporation acquired the remaining approximate 31 percent interest in its Andean region subsidiary, Colombiana Kimberly Colpapel S.A. ("CKC"), for $289 million. The acquisition was recorded as an equity transaction that reduced noncontrolling interests, accumulated other comprehensive income ("AOCI") and additional paid-in capital by approximately $278 million and increased investments in equity companies by approximately $11 million.

Note 11 (In Part): Stockholders' Equity

GAAP requires that the purchase of additional ownership in an already controlled subsidiary be treated as an equity transaction with no gain or loss recognized in consolidated net income or comprehensive income. GAAP also requires the presentation of the below schedule displaying the effect of a change in ownership interest between the Corporation and a noncontrolling interest.

(Millions of dollars)	2009
Net income attributable to Kimberly-Clark Corporation	$1,884
Decrease in Kimberly-Clark Corporation's additional paid-in capital for purchase of remaining shares in its Andean subsidiary[a]	(133)
Change from net income attributable to Kimberly-Clark Corporation and transfers to noncontrolling interests	$1,751

[a] During the first quarter of 2009, the Corporation acquired the remaining approximate 31 percent interest in its Andean region subsidiary, Colombiana Kimberly Colpapel S.A., for $289 million. The acquisition was recorded as an equity transaction that reduced noncontrolling interests, AOCI and additional paid-in capital by approximately $278 million and increased investments in equity companies by approximately $11 million.

OTHER COMPONENTS OF STOCKHOLDERS' EQUITY

5.50 Certain items such as receivables from the sale of stock, and employee stock ownership plans are presented as separate components of stockholders' equity. Other items such as foreign currency translation adjustments, unrealized gains and losses on certain investments in debt and equity securities, and defined benefit postretirement plan adjustments are considered components of other comprehensive income. FASB ASC 220, *Comprehensive Income*, permits presentation of components of other comprehensive income and total comprehensive income in a statement of changes in stockholders' equity. In addition, the Standard allows disclosure of accumulated balances, by component, included in accumulated other comprehensive income in a statement of changes in stockholders' equity.

5.51 FASB ASC 810, *Consolidation*, establishes accounting and reporting standards for the noncontrolling interest in a subsidiary. It clarifies that a noncontrolling interest in a subsidiary is an ownership interest in the consolidated entity that should be reported as equity in the consolidated financial statements, but separate from the parent's equity. In addition, FASB ASC 810 requires expanded disclosures in the consolidated financial statements that clearly identify and distinguish between the interests of the parent's owners and the interests of the noncontrolling owners of a subsidiary. Those expanded disclosures include a reconciliation of the beginning and ending balances of the equity attributable to the parent and the noncontrolling owners and a schedule showing the effects of changes in a parent's ownership interest in a subsidiary on the equity attributable to the parent.

5.52 Examples of statements reporting changes in separate components of stockholders' equity, other than those classified as components of other comprehensive income, follow. See Sections 2 and 4 for examples of presentation of other comprehensive income and related accumulated balances in statements of changes in stockholders' equity.

Unearned Compensation Expense

5.53

DONALDSON COMPANY, INC. (JUL)

(Thousands of dollars)	Common Stock	Additional Paid-In Capital	Retained Earnings	Stock Compensation Plans	Accumulated Other Comprehensive Income (Loss)	Treasury Stock	Total
Balance July 31, 2006	$443,216	$ —	$275,598	$20,535	$ 51,194	$(243,741)	$546,802
Comprehensive income							
Net earnings			150,717				150,717
Foreign currency translation					28,615		28,615
Additional minimum pension liability, net of tax					312		312
Net loss on cash flow hedging derivatives					118		118
Comprehensive income							179,762
Treasury stock acquired						(76,898)	(76,898)
Stock options exercised		(7,700)	(9,499)	1,513		19,133	3,447
Deferred stock and other activity			(2,273)	541		3,276	1,544
Performance awards			(1,163)	(1,768)		1,626	(1,305)
Stock option expense			3,422				3,422
Tax reduction—employee plans		7,700					7,700
Adjustment to adopt SFAS 158, net of tax					(10,231)		(10,231)
Dividends ($.370 per share)			(29,545)				(29,545)
Balance July 31, 2007	$443,216	$ —	$387,257	$20,821	$ 70,008	$(296,604)	$624,698
Comprehensive income							
Net earnings			171,953				171,953
Foreign currency translation					57,151		57,151
Additional minimum pension liability, net of tax					(14,671)		(14,671)
Net gain on cash flow hedging derivatives					395		395
Comprehensive income							214,828
Treasury stock acquired						(92,202)	(92,202)
Stock options exercised		(7,827)	(9,810)	4,223		20,883	7,469
Deferred stock and other activity		(2,981)	2,564	3,474		1,363	4,420
Performance awards		(675)	279	(1,453)		955	(894)
Stock option expense			4,214				4,214
Tax reduction—employee plans		11,483					11,483
Adjustment to adopt FIN 48			(336)				(336)
Dividends ($.430 per share)			(33,645)				(33,645)
Balance July 31, 2008	$443,216	$ —	$522,476	$27,065	$112,883	$(365,605)	$740,035
Comprehensive income							
Net earnings			131,907				131,907
Foreign currency translation					(63,385)		(63,385)
Pension liability adjustment, net of tax					(58,593)		(58,593)
Net gain on cash flow hedging derivatives					(582)		(582)
Comprehensive income							9,347
Treasury stock acquired						(32,773)	(32,773)
Stock options exercised		(2,998)	(6,151)			12,104	2,955
Deferred stock and other activity		(529)	(88)	(4,344)		3,710	(1,251)
Performance awards		(266)	(60)	(2,827)		1,932	(1,221)
Stock option expense			4,143				4,143
Tax reduction—employee plans		3,793					3,793
Adjustment to adopt FAS 158 measurement date provision, net of tax			(887)				(887)
Dividends ($.460 per share)			(35,523)				(35,523)
Balance July 31, 2009	$443,216	$ —	$615,817	$19,894	$ (9,677)	$(380,632)	$688,618

NOTES TO CONSOLIDATED FINANCIAL STATEMENTS

Note F (In Part): Employee Benefit Plans

Deferred Compensation and Other Benefit Plans

The Company provides various deferred compensation and other benefit plans to certain executives. The deferred compensation plan allows these employees to defer the receipt of all of their bonus and other stock related compensation and up to 75 percent of their salary to future periods. Other benefit plans are provided to supplement the benefits for a select group of highly compensated individuals which are reduced because of compensation limitations set by the Internal Revenue Code. The Company has recorded a liability in the amount of $10.0 million and $10.6 million as of the year ended July 31, 2009 and July 31, 2008, respectively, related primarily to its deferred compensation plans.

Note G (In Part): Shareholders' Equity

Stock Compensation Plans

The Stock Compensation Plans in the Consolidated Statements of Changes in Shareholders' Equity consist of the balance of amounts payable to eligible participants for stock compensation that was deferred to a Rabbi Trust pursuant to the provisions of the 2001 Master Stock Incentive Plan, as well as performance awards payable in common stock discussed further in Note H.

Note H (In Part): Stock Option Plans

Employee Incentive Plans (In Part)

In November 2001, shareholders approved the 2001 Master Stock Incentive Plan (the "Plan") that replaced the 1991 Plan that expired on December 31, 2001, and provided for similar awards. The Plan extends through December 2011 and allows for the granting of nonqualified stock options, incentive stock options, restricted stock, stock appreciation rights ("SAR"), dividend equivalents, dollar-denominated awards and other stock-based awards. Options under the Plan are granted to key employees at market price at the date of grant. Options are exercisable for up to 10 years from the date of grant. The Plan also allows for the granting of performance awards to a limited number of key executives. As administered by the Human Resources Committee of the Company's Board of Directors, these performance awards are payable in common stock and are based on a formula which measures performance of the Company over a three-year period. The Company recorded a net reversal of performance award expense in Fiscal 2009 of $3.1 million. The net benefit is due to the reversal of $3.6 million of Long-Term Compensation Plan expense recognized in prior periods. This reversal reflects an adjustment in the expected payouts for the three-year cycles ending July 31, 2009, and July 31, 2010, to zero based upon actual and forecasted results. Performance award expense under these plans totaled $4.2 million and $2.7 million in Fiscal 2008 and 2007, respectively.

Employee Stock Ownership Plan

5.54

THE J. M. SMUCKER COMPANY (APR)

(Dollars in thousands, except per share data)	Common Shares Outstanding	Common Shares	Additional Capital	Retained Income	Deferred Compensation	Amount Due From ESOP Trust	Accumulated Other Comprehensive Income (Loss)	Total Shareholders' Equity
Balance at May 1, 2006	56,949,044	$14,237	$1,212,598	$489,067	$(8,527)	$(6,525)	$27,209	$1,728,059
Net income				157,219				157,219
Foreign currency translation adjustment							2,437	2,437
Minimum pension liability adjustment							427	427
Unrealized gain on available-for-sale securities							1,644	1,644
Unrealized gain on cash flow hedging derivatives							138	138
Comprehensive income								161,865
Purchase of treasury shares	(1,100,194)	(275)	(23,915)	(27,935)				(52,125)
Stock plans	931,000	233	24,247		8,527			33,007
Cash dividends declared— $1.14 per share				(64,720)				(64,720)
Adjustments to initially apply Statement of Financial Accounting Standards No. 158, net of tax of $7,377							(14,098)	(14,098)
Tax benefit of stock plans			3,161					3,161
Other						508		508
Balance at April 30, 2007	56,779,850	$14,195	$1,216,091	$553,631	$ —	$(6,017)	$17,757	$1,795,657

(continued)

(Dollars in thousands, except per share data)	Common Shares Outstanding	Common Shares	Additional Capital	Retained Income	Deferred Compensation	Amount Due From ESOP Trust	Accumulated Other Comprehensive Income (Loss)	Total Shareholders' Equity
Balance at April 30, 2007	56,779,850	$14,195	$1,216,091	$553,631	$—	$(6,017)	$ 17,757	$1,795,657
Net income				170,379				170,379
Foreign currency translation adjustment							20,861	20,861
Pensions and other postretirement liabilities							(2,920)	(2,920)
Unrealized loss on available-for-sale securities							(379)	(379)
Unrealized gain on cash flow hedging derivatives							7,293	7,293
Comprehensive income								195,234
Purchase of treasury shares	(2,991,920)	(748)	(66,075)	(85,698)				(152,521)
Stock plans	834,682	209	20,398					20,607
Cash dividends declared— $1.22 per share				(68,519)				(68,519)
Adjustments to initially apply Financial Accounting Standards Board Interpretation No. 48				(2,374)				(2,374)
Tax benefit of stock plans			11,231					11,231
Other						538		538
Balance at April 30, 2008	54,622,612	$13,656	$1,181,645	$567,419	$—	$(5,479)	$ 42,612	$1,799,853
Net income				265,953				265,953
Foreign currency translation adjustment							(47,024)	(47,024)
Pensions and other postretirement liabilities							(43,479)	(43,479)
Unrealized loss on available-for-sale securities							(2,798)	(2,798)
Unrealized loss on cash flow hedging derivatives							(6,581)	(6,581)
Comprehensive income								166,071
Purchase of treasury shares	(81,685)	(20)	(3,982)	(23)				(4,025)
Purchase business combination	63,166,532	15,792	3,350,561					3,366,353
Stock plans	714,664	178	17,344					17,522
Cash dividends declared— $6.31 per share				(408,845)				(408,845)
Tax benefit of stock plans			2,353					2,353
Other						649		649
Balance at April 30, 2009	118,422,123	$29,606	$4,547,921	$424,504	$—	$(4,830)	$(57,270)	$4,939,931

NOTES TO CONSOLIDATED FINANCIAL STATEMENTS
(Dollars in thousands)

Note I (In Part): Savings Plans

ESOP

The Company sponsors an Employee Stock Ownership Plan and Trust ("ESOP") for certain domestic, nonrepresented employees. The Company has entered into loan agreements with the Trustee of the ESOP for purchases by the ESOP of the Company's common shares in amounts not to exceed a total of 1,134,120 unallocated common shares of the Company at any one time. These shares are to be allocated to participants over a period of not less than 20 years.

ESOP loans bear interest at one-half percentage point over prime, are secured by the unallocated shares of the plan, and are payable as a condition of allocating shares to participants. Interest expense incurred on ESOP debt was $261, $376, and $530 in 2009, 2008, and 2007, respectively. Contributions to the plan, representing compensation expense, are made annually in amounts sufficient to fund ESOP debt repayment and were $614, $690, and $684 in 2009, 2008, and 2007, respectively. Dividends on unallocated shares are used to reduce expense and were $1,461, $334, and $356 in 2009, 2008, and 2007, respectively. The principal payments received from the ESOP in 2009, 2008, and 2007 were $649, $538, and $508, respectively.

Dividends on allocated shares are credited to participant accounts and are used to purchase additional common shares for participant accounts. Dividends on allocated and unallocated shares are charged to retained income by the Company.

As permitted by Statement of Position 93-6, *Employers' Accounting for Employee Stock Ownership Plans,* the Company will continue to recognize future compensation using the cost basis as all shares currently held by the ESOP were acquired prior to 1993. At April 30, 2009, the ESOP held 231,594 unallocated and 818,552 allocated shares. All shares held by the ESOP were considered outstanding in earnings per share calculations for all periods presented.

Stock Subscriptions Receivable

5.55

UNIVERSAL FOREST PRODUCTS, INC. (DEC)

	Controlling Interest Shareholders' Equity						
(In thousands)	Common Stock	Additional Paid-In Capital	Retained Earnings	Accumulated Other Comprehensive Earnings	Employees Stock Notes Receivable	Noncontrolling Interest	Total
Balance at December 30, 2006	$18,859	$113,754	$380,931	$2,451	$(1,253)	$10,819	$525,561
Comprehensive earnings:							
Net earnings			21,045			2,168	
Foreign currency translation adjustment				2,253		45	
Total comprehensive earnings							25,511
Purchase of additional noncontrolling interest						(859)	(859)
Distributions to noncontrolling interest						(1,797)	(1,797)
Cash dividends—$0.115 per share			(2,185)				(2,185)
Issuance of 220,345 shares under employee stock plans	220	3,683					3,903
Issuance of 3,961 shares under stock grant programs	4	170					174
Issuance of 69,777 shares under deferred compensation plans	70	(70)					—
Repurchase of 239,400 shares	(239)		(8,538)				(8,777)
Received 15,866 shares for the exercise of stock options	(16)	(766)					(782)
Tax benefits from non-qualified stock options exercised		1,867					1,867
Expense associated with share-based compensation arrangements		505					505
Accrued expense under deferred compensation plans		3,733					3,733
Issuance of 10,132 shares in exchange for employee stock notes receivable	10	492			(502)		—
Payments received on employee stock notes receivable					190		190
Balance at December 29, 2007	$18,908	$123,368	$391,253	$4,704	$(1,565)	$10,376	$547,044

(continued)

| (In thousands) | Controlling Interest Shareholders' Equity | | | | | | |
	Common Stock	Additional Paid-In Capital	Retained Earnings	Accumulated Other Comprehensive Earnings	Employees Stock Notes Receivable	Noncontrolling Interest	Total
Balance at December 29, 2007	$18,908	$123,368	$391,253	$ 4,704	$(1,565)	$10,376	$547,044
Comprehensive earnings:							
Net earnings			4,343			1,117	
Foreign currency translation adjustment				(2,351)		(1,071)	
Total comprehensive earnings							2,038
Capital contribution from noncontrolling interest						419	419
Purchase of additional noncontrolling interest						(844)	(844)
Distributions to noncontrolling interest						(3,654)	(3,654)
Cash dividends—$0.120 per share			(2,284)				(2,284)
Issuance of 174,528 shares under employee stock plans	175	3,030					3,205
Issuance of 3,706 shares under stock grant programs	4	100					104
Issuance of 15,288 shares under deferred compensation plans	15	(15)					—
Received 19,857 shares for the exercise of stock options	(20)	(622)					(642)
Tax benefits from non-qualified stock options exercised		878					878
Expense associated with share-based compensation arrangements		1,136					1,136
Accrued expense under deferred compensation plans		725					725
Issuance of 7,374 shares in exchange for employee stock notes receivable	7	230			(237)		—
Payments received on employee stock notes receivable					101		101
Balance at December 27, 2008	$19,089	$128,830	$393,312	$ 2,353	$(1,701)	$ 6,343	$548,226
Comprehensive earnings:							
Net earnings			24,272			473	
Foreign currency translation adjustment				1,280		85	
Total comprehensive earnings							26,110
Capital contribution from noncontrolling interest						14	14
Purchase of additional noncontrolling interest		(853)				(917)	(1,770)
Distributions to noncontrolling interest						(270)	(270)
Cash dividends—$0.260 per share			(5,017)				(5,017)
Issuance of 130,265 shares under employee stock plans	130	2,290					2,420
Issuance of 79,216 shares under stock grant programs	80	29					109
Issuance of 74,229 shares under deferred compensation plans	74	(74)					—
Repurchase of 90,122 shares	(90)		(3,289)				(3,379)
Received 1,602 shares for the exercise of stock options	(2)	(33)					(35)
Tax benefits from non-qualified stock options exercised		730					730
Deferred income tax asset reversal for deferred compensation plans		(518)					(518)
Expense associated with share-based compensation arrangements		1,597					1,597
Accrued expense under deferred compensation plans		646					646
Issuance of 3,721 shares in exchange for employee stock notes receivable	4	121			(125)		—
Payments received on employee stock notes receivable					83		83
Balance at December 26, 2009	$19,285	$132,765	$409,278	$ 3,633	$(1,743)	$ 5,728	$568,946

ATT-SEC 5.55

Warrants

5.56

RETAIL VENTURES, INC. (JAN)

(In thousands)	Number of Shares								
	Common Shares	Common Shares in Treasury	Common Shares	Warrants	Retained Earnings (Accumulated Deficit)	Deferred Compensation Expense	Treasury Shares	Total Accumulated Other Comprehensive Loss	Total
Balance, January 28, 2006	39,865	8	$159,617	$	$ (36,082)	$(1)	$(59)	$(6,929)	$ 116,546
Loss from continuing operations					(122,880)				(122,880)
Loss from discontinued operations					(28,033)				(28,033)
Change in minimum pension liability, net of income tax expense of $44								500	500
Change in minimum pension liability, net of income tax expense of $109, discontinued operations								692	692
Total comprehensive loss									(149,721)
Capital transactions of subsidiary					2,534				2,534
Stock based compensation expense, before related tax effects			634						634
Exercise of stock options	406		2,934						2,934
Exercise of warrants	7,000		110,317						110,317
Deferred income tax adjustment			3,189						3,189
Reclassification of unamortized deferred compensation			(1)			1			
Adjustment to initially apply FASB Statement No. 158, net of tax expense of $1,543								2,403	2,403
Adjustment to initially apply FASB Statement No. 158, net of tax expense of $1,787, discontinued operations								2,784	2,784
Balance, February 3, 2007	47,271	8	$276,690	$	$(184,461)	$	$(59)	$ (550)	$ 91,620

(continued)

(In thousands)	Number of Shares				Retained Earnings (Accu-mulated Deficit)	Deferred Compen-sation Expense	Treasury Shares	Total Accumulated Other Compre-hensive Loss	Total
	Common Shares	Common Shares in Treasury	Common Shares	Warrants					
Balance, February 3, 2007	47,271	8	$276,690	$	$(184,461)	$	$(59)	$ (550)	$ 91,620
Income from continuing operations					241,967				241,967
Loss from discontinued operations					(190,525)				(190,525)
Change in minimum pension liability, net of income tax expense of $1,004								(1,269)	(1,269)
Total comprehensive income									50,173
Capital transactions of subsidiary					3,083				3,083
Cumulative effect of FIN 48 adoption for discontinued operations					(641)				(641)
Reclassification of stock appreciation rights			1,934						1,934
Stock based compensation expense, before related tax effects			947						947
Exercise of stock options	19		71						71
Exercise of warrants	1,333		25,612						25,612
Issuance of warrants				124					124
Balance, February 2, 2008	48,623	8	$305,254	$124	$(130,577)	$	$(59)	$(1,819)	$ 172,923
Income from continuing operations					99,220				99,220
Loss from discontinued operations					(48,379)				(48,379)
Change in minimum pension liability								(2,245)	(2,245)
Valuation allowance on pension deferred tax asset								(2,670)	(2,670)
Unrealized loss on available-for-sale securities								(655)	(655)
Total comprehensive income									45,271
Capital transactions of subsidiary					2,806				2,806
Stock based compensation expense, before related tax effects			1,407						1,407
Exercise of stock options	68		207						207
Balance, January 31, 2009	48,691	8	$306,868	$124	$ (76,930)	$	$(59)	$(7,389)	$ 222,614

ATT-SEC 5.56

NOTES TO CONSOLIDATED FINANCIAL STATEMENTS

12 (In Part): Warrants

VCHI Acquisition Co. Warrants

On January 23, 2008, Retail Ventures disposed of an 81% ownership interest in its Value City Department Stores business to VCHI Acquisition Co., a newly formed entity owned by VCDS Acquisition Holdings, LLC, Emerald Capital Management LLC and Crystal Value, LLC. As part of the transaction, Retail Ventures issued warrants ("the VCHI Warrants") to VCHI Acquisition Co. to purchase 150,000 RVI Common Shares, at an exercise price of $10.00 per share, and exercis-

able within 18 months of January 23, 2008. Upon exercise of the VCHI Warrants, Retail Ventures will deliver the shares via net-share or physical settlement at the election of the warrant holder.

The VCHI Warrants are not derivative instruments as defined under SFAS 133. The warrants were measured at fair value on the date of the transaction, January 23, 2008, and recorded within equity. The $0.1 million value ascribed to the VCHI Warrants was estimated as of January 23, 2008 using the Black-Scholes Pricing Model with the following assumptions: risk-free interest rate of 2.1%; expected life of 1.5 years; expected volatility of 58.4% and an expected dividend yield of 0.0%.

Section 6: Statement of Cash Flows

GENERAL

6.01 FASB *Accounting Standards Codification* (ASC) 230, *Statement of Cash Flows*, requires entities to present a Statement of Cash Flows which classifies cash receipts and payments by operating, investing, and financing activities.

6.02 This section reviews the format and content of the Statement of Cash Flows.

PRESENTATION IN ANNUAL REPORT

6.03 Table 6-1 shows where in relation to other financial statements a Statement of Cash Flows is presented in an annual report. As shown in Table 6-1, a Statement of Cash Flows is usually presented as the last financial statement or after the income statement and balance sheet but before the statement of changes in stockholders' equity.

6.04

TABLE 6-1: PRESENTATION OF STATEMENT OF CASH FLOWS IN ANNUAL REPORT

	2009	2008	2007	2006
Final statement	239	244	296	296
Follows income statement and balance sheet	246	240	286	287
Between income statement and balance sheet	14	15	17	16
First statement	1	1	1	1
Total Entities	**500**	**500**	**600**	**600**

2008–2009 based on 500 entities surveyed; 2006–2007 based on 600 entities surveyed.

CASH FLOWS FROM OPERATING ACTIVITIES

6.05 FASB ASC 230 defines those transactions and events that constitute operating cash receipts and payments. FASB ASC 230 recommends that the direct method be used to report net cash flow from operating activities. Most of the survey entities used the indirect method (reconciling net income to net cash flow from operating activities) to report net cash flow from operating activities. Regardless of whether the direct or indirect method is used, FASB ASC 230 requires that a reconciliation of net income to net cash flow from operat-

ing activities be presented and that interest and income tax payments be disclosed.

6.06 Table 6-2 shows the methods used to report cash flows from operating activities. Entities using the direct method usually present the reconciliation of net income to net cash flow from operating activities as a schedule at the bottom of the Statement of Cash Flows or on the page adjacent to the Statement. Companies using the indirect method usually present the reconciliation within the Statement of Cash Flows.

6.07 FASB ASC 230 states that the reconciliation of net income to net cash flow from operating activities shall separately report all major classes of reconciling items. For example, major classes of deferrals of past operating cash receipts and payments, and accruals of expected future operating cash receipts and payments, including at a minimum changes during the period in receivables pertaining to operating activities, in inventory, and in payables pertaining to operating activities, shall be separately reported. Table 6-3 lists the major types of items used by the survey entities to reconcile net income to net cash flow from operating activities. Depreciation and amortization expense is the most frequently presented reconciling item, followed by deferred taxes.

6.08 Table 6-4 shows where in the financial statements interest and income tax payments are disclosed. Those survey entities disclosing the amount of interest payments in the notes to financial statements did so usually in a note discussing debt or in a note discussing details about the Statement of Cash Flows. Those survey entities disclosing the amount of income tax payments in the notes to financial statements did so usually in a note discussing income taxes or in a note discussing details about the Statement of Cash Flows.

6.09 Examples of reporting cash flows from operating activities and related interest and income tax payment disclosures follow.

6.10

TABLE 6-2: METHOD OF REPORTING CASH FLOWS FROM OPERATING ACTIVITIES

	2009	2008	2007	2006
Indirect method	495	495	594	594
Direct method	5	5	6	6
Total Entities	**500**	**500**	**600**	**600**

2008–2009 based on 500 entities surveyed; 2006–2007 based on 600 entities surveyed.

6.11

TABLE 6-3: CASH FLOWS FROM OPERATING ACTIVITIES—RECONCILING ITEMS

	2009	2008	2007	2006
Income Statement Items				
Depreciation and/or amortization.........	498	499	597	600
Deferred taxes.....................................	438	438	529	512
Employee related costs........................	422	405	490	442
Write-down of assets...........................	189	155	140	116
Gain or loss on sale of property...........	173	162	203	208
Tax benefit from share-based compensation plans..........................	153	164	199	197
Equity in investee's earnings...............	137	142	165	179
Gain or loss on sale of assets other than property....................................	128	175	229	192
Provision for doubtful accounts............	128	116	155	145
Intangible asset impairment.................	114	113	81	72
Intangible asset amortization...............	111	120	154	144
Gain or loss from discontinued operations......................................	111	110	148	145
Restructuring.......................................	101	95	96	109
Changes in Operating Assets and Liabilities				
Accounts receivable.............................	460	467	544	556
Inventories..	423	423	492	497
Accounts receivable combined with inventories and/or other items..........	27	26	48	40
Accounts payable................................	275	266	322	333
Accounts payable combined with other items...	207	213	252	241
Income taxes payable..........................	205	211	255	247
Employee related liabilities.................	112	107	137	136

2008–2009 based on 500 entities surveyed; 2006–2007 based on 600 entities surveyed.

6.12

TABLE 6-4: PRESENTATION OF INTEREST AND INCOME TAX PAYMENTS

	2009	2008	2007	2006
Interest Payments				
Notes to financial statements...............	244	250	292	298
Bottom of statement of cash flows.......	235	237	285	282
Within statement of cash flows............	6	5	6	6
Amount not disclosed...........................	15	8	17	14
Total Entities....................................	**500**	**500**	**600**	**600**
Income Tax Payments				
Notes to financial statements...............	252	252	296	303
Bottom of statement of cash flows.......	241	240	291	288
Within statement of cash flows............	7	6	7	7
Amount not disclosed...........................	—	2	6	2
Total Entities....................................	**500**	**500**	**600**	**600**

2008–2009 based on 500 entities surveyed; 2006–2007 based on 600 entities surveyed.

DIRECT METHOD

6.13

ARDEN GROUP, INC. (DEC)

(In thousands)	2009	2008	2007
Cash flows from operating activities:			
Cash received from customers	$ 431,108	$ 479,578	$ 485,819
Cash paid to suppliers and employees	(391,957)	(437,970)	(438,044)
Interest and dividends received	565	2,513	3,186
Interest paid	(87)	(109)	(99)
Income taxes paid	(13,895)	(15,545)	(20,660)
Net cash provided by operating activities	25,734	28,467	30,202
Cash flows from investing activities:			
Capital expenditures	(2,890)	(5,159)	(3,824)
Purchases of investments	(30,164)	(25,130)	(945)
Sales of investments	13,127	35,556	2
Proceeds from the sale of property, plant and equipment	48	21	28
Net cash provided by (used in) investing activities	(19,879)	5,288	(4,739)
Cash flows from financing activities:			
Principal payments under capital lease obligations	—	—	(225)
Cash dividends paid	(3,161)	(82,188)	(3,161)
Net cash used in financing activities	(3,161)	(82,188)	(3,386)
Net increase (decrease) in cash and cash equivalents	2,694	(48,433)	22,077
Cash and cash equivalents at beginning of year	10,486	58,919	36,842
Cash and cash equivalents at end of year	$ 13,180	$ 10,486	$ 58,919

(In thousands)	2009	2008	2007
Reconciliation of net income to net cash provided by operating activities:			
Net income	$21,624	$24,667	$29,207
Adjustments to reconcile net income to net cash provided by operating activities:			
Depreciation and amortization	5,599	6,110	6,685
Provision for losses on accounts receivable	94	169	45
Deferred income taxes	108	1,923	798
Net loss from the disposal of property, plant and equipment	54	89	30
Realized (gain) loss on investments, net	—	907	(64)
Amortization of premium on investments	472	259	0
Stock appreciation rights compensation expense (income)	(273)	1,823	2,908
Changes in assets and liabilities net of effects from noncash investing and financing activities:			
(Increase) decrease in assets:			
Accounts and notes receivable	(246)	527	(263)
Inventories	972	3,712	(1,677)
Other current assets	204	(281)	28
Other assets	16	(69)	299
Increase (decrease) in liabilities:			
Accounts payable, trade and other current liabilities	(2,402)	(9,148)	(4,621)
Federal and state income taxes payable	668	(608)	(2,411)
Deferred rent	99	154	74
Other liabilities	(1,255)	(1,767)	(836)
Net cash provided by operating activities	$25,734	$28,467	$30,202

6.14

CVS CAREMARK CORPORATION (DEC)

(In millions)	2009	2008	2007
Cash flows from operating activities:			
Cash receipts from revenues	$ 93,568	$ 82,250	$ 72,533
Cash paid for inventory and prescriptions dispensed by retail network pharmacies	(73,536)	(64,131)	(56,319)
Cash paid to other suppliers and employees	(13,121)	(11,832)	(10,769)
Interest and dividends received	5	20	34
Interest paid	(542)	(574)	(468)
Income taxes paid	(2,339)	(1,786)	(1,781)
Net cash provided by operating activities	4,035	3,947	3,230
Cash flows from investing activities:			
Additions to property and equipment	(2,548)	(2,180)	(1,805)
Proceeds from sale-leaseback transactions	1,562	204	601
Acquisitions (net of cash acquired) and other investments	(101)	(2,651)	(1,984)
Purchase of short-term investments	(5)	—	—
Sale of short-term investments	—	28	—
Proceeds from sale or disposal of assets	23	19	106
Net cash used in investing activities	(1,069)	(4,580)	(3,082)
Cash flows from financing activities:			
Increase (decrease) in short-term debt	(2,729)	959	242
Repayment of debt assumed in acquisition	—	(353)	—
Issuance of long-term debt	2,800	350	6,000
Repayments of long-term debt	(653)	(2)	(822)
Dividends paid	(439)	(383)	(323)
Derivative settlements	(3)	—	—
Proceeds from exercise of stock options	250	328	553
Excess tax benefits from stock-based compensation	19	53	98
Repurchase of common stock	(2,477)	(23)	(5,370)
Net cash provided by (used in) financing activities	(3,232)	929	378
Net increase (decrease) in cash and cash equivalents	(266)	296	526
Cash and cash equivalents at beginning of year	1,352	1,056	530
Cash and cash equivalents at end of year	$ 1,086	$ 1,352	$ 1,056
Reconciliation of net income to net cash provided by operating activities:			
Net income	$ 3,696	$ 3,212	$ 2,637
Adjustments required to reconcile net income to net cash provided by operating activities:			
Depreciation and amortization	1,389	1,274	1,095
Stock-based compensation	165	92	78
Deferred income taxes and other non-cash items	48	(3)	39
Change in operating assets and liabilities, net of effects from acquisitions:			
Accounts receivable, net	(86)	(291)	280
Inventories	(1,199)	(488)	(448)
Other current assets	48	12	(59)
Other assets	(2)	19	(26)
Accounts payable	4	(64)	(181)
Accrued expenses	(66)	183	(168)
Other long-term liabilities	38	1	(17)
Net cash provided by operating activities	$ 4,035	$ 3,947	$ 3,230

INDIRECT/RECONCILIATION METHOD

6.15

MANPOWER INC. (DEC)

(In millions)	2009	2008	2007
Cash flows from operating activities			
Net (loss) earnings	$ (9.2)	$ 205.5	$ 473.7
Adjustments to reconcile net (loss) earnings to net cash provided by operating activities:			
Depreciation and amortization	97.2	107.1	99.0
Non-cash goodwill and intangible asset impairment charges	61.0	163.1	—
Deferred income taxes	(29.2)	(32.8)	22.2
Provision for doubtful accounts	27.8	23.4	21.8
Loss from sale of an equity investment	10.3	—	—
Share-based compensation	17.5	21.1	26.0
Excess tax benefit on exercise of stock options	(0.5)	(0.5)	(4.6)
Change in operating assets and liabilities, excluding the impact of acquisitions:			
Accounts receivable	663.6	575.0	(316.0)
Other assets	(71.5)	2.9	(3.5)
Other liabilities	(352.7)	(272.8)	113.6
Cash provided by operating activities	414.3	792.0	432.2
Cash flows from investing activities			
Capital expenditures	(35.1)	(93.1)	(91.6)
Acquisitions of businesses, net of cash acquired	(21.6)	(242.0)	(122.8)
Proceeds from the sale of an equity investment	13.3	—	—
Proceeds from the sale of property and equipment	3.6	5.9	12.9
Cash used in investing activities	(39.8)	(329.2)	(201.5)
Cash flows from financing activities			
Net change in short-term borrowings	(14.6)	16.0	6.1
Proceeds from long-term debt	146.5	233.7	1.0
Repayments of long-term debt	(359.3)	(170.7)	(2.2)
Proceeds from stock option and purchase plans	14.2	12.2	35.0
Excess tax benefit on exercise of stock options	0.5	0.5	4.6
Repurchases of common stock	—	(125.4)	(419.2)
Dividends paid	(58.0)	(58.1)	(57.1)
Cash used in financing activities	(270.7)	(91.8)	(431.8)
Effect of exchange rate changes on cash	36.8	(34.5)	50.7
Net increase (decrease) in cash and cash equivalents	140.6	336.5	(150.4)
Cash and cash equivalents, beginning of year	874.0	537.5	687.9
Cash and cash equivalents, end of year	$1,014.6	$ 874.0	$ 537.5
Supplemental cash flow information			
Interest paid	$ 62.0	$ 64.8	$ 50.5
Income taxes paid	$ 75.2	$ 293.5	$ 248.5

6.16

WORTHINGTON INDUSTRIES, INC. (MAY)

(Dollars in thousands)	2009	2008	2007
Operating activities:			
Net earnings (loss)	$(108,214)	$ 107,077	$ 113,905
Adjustments to reconcile net earnings (loss) to net cash provided by operating activities:			
Bad debt expense	8,307	1,398	(903)
Depreciation and amortization	64,073	63,413	61,469
Goodwill impairment	96,943	—	—
Restructuring charges, non-cash	8,925	5,169	—
Provision for deferred income taxes	(25,479)	(3,228)	(3,068)
Equity in net income of unconsolidated affiliates, net of distributions	8,491	(8,539)	68,510
Minority interest in net income of consolidated subsidiaries	4,529	6,969	5,409
Net loss on sale of assets	1,317	3,756	826
Stock-based compensation	5,767	4,173	3,480
Excess tax benefits—stock-based compensation	(433)	(2,035)	(2,370)
Gain on sale of Aegis	(8,331)	—	—
Changes in assets and liabilities:			
Receivables	226,690	5,569	8,312
Inventories	329,892	(144,474)	20,491
Prepaid expenses and other current assets	(20,805)	8,252	(2,078)
Other assets	(643)	(1,546)	4,898
Accounts payable and accrued expenses	(321,798)	138,822	(99,283)
Other liabilities	(14,905)	(4,255)	833
Net cash provided by operating activities	254,326	180,521	180,431
Investing activities:			
Investment in property, plant and equipment, net	(64,154)	(47,520)	(57,691)
Acquisitions, net of cash acquired	(42,199)	(2,225)	(31,727)
Distributions from (investments in) unconsolidated affiliates, net	20,362	(47,598)	(1,000)
Proceeds from sale of assets	6,883	1,025	18,237
Proceeds from sale of unconsolidated affiliates	25,863	—	—
Purchases of short-term investments	—	—	(25,562)
Sales of short-term investments	—	25,562	2,173
Net cash used by investing activities	(53,245)	(70,756)	(95,570)
Financing activities:			
Net proceeds from (payments on) short-term borrowings	(142,385)	103,800	31,650
Principal payments on long-term debt	(7,241)	—	(7,691)
Proceeds from issuance of common shares	3,899	13,171	9,866
Excess tax benefits—stock-based compensation	433	2,035	2,370
Payments to minority interest	(7,152)	(11,904)	(3,360)
Repurchase of common shares	(12,402)	(125,785)	(76,617)
Dividends paid	(53,686)	(55,587)	(59,018)
Net cash used by financing activities	(218,534)	(74,270)	(102,800)
Increase (decrease) in cash and cash equivalents	(17,453)	35,495	(17,939)
Cash and cash equivalents at beginning of year	73,772	38,277	56,216
Cash and cash equivalents at end of year	$ 56,319	$ 73,772	$ 38,277

ADJUSTMENTS TO RECONCILE NET INCOME TO OPERATING CASH FLOWS

Employee Related Costs

6.17

WOLVERINE WORLD WIDE, INC. (DEC)

(Thousands of dollars)	2009	2008	2007
Operating activities			
Net earnings	$ 61,912	$ 95,821	$ 92,886
Adjustments necessary to reconcile net earnings to net cash provided by operating activities:			
Depreciation	15,932	18,460	20,223
Amortization	1,689	2,236	2,568
Deferred income taxes	(7,845)	(43)	(5,660)
Stock-based compensation expense	8,935	8,164	8,316
Excess tax benefits from stock-based compensation	(462)	(1,610)	(2,620)
Pension expense	11,177	1,252	2,884
Restructuring and other transition costs	35,596	—	—
Cash payments related to restructuring and other transition costs	(20,653)	—	—
Other	(7,921)	13,966	4,339
Changes in operating assets and liabilities:			
Accounts receivable	9,817	3,419	(21,530)
Inventories	44,500	(39,201)	22,450
Other operating assets	3,103	(386)	3,141
Accounts payable	(7,326)	(5,064)	3,140
Income taxes	17,070	(2,094)	(2,524)
Other operating liabilities	3,085	(1,450)	(4,325)
Net cash provided by operating activities	$168,609	$93,470	$123,288

Write-Down of Assets

6.18

THE L.S. STARRETT COMPANY (JUN)

(In thousands of dollars)	2009	2008	2007
Cash flows from operating activities:			
Net (loss) income	$(3,220)	$10,831	$ 6,653
Noncash operating activities:			
Gain from sale of real estate	—	(1,703)	(299)
Depreciation	8,649	9,535	10,047
Amortization	1,247	1,240	1,103
Impairment of fixed assets	52	95	724
Goodwill impairment	5,260	—	—
Net long-term tax payable	604	847	—
Deferred taxes	(6,145)	1,221	1,646
Unrealized transaction gains	1,077	(990)	(592)
Retirement benefits	(2,088)	(3,332)	(1,519)
Working capital changes:			
Receivables	7,170	893	(2,720)
Inventories	(4,233)	(45)	2,252
Other current assets	(2,759)	(157)	(689)
Other current liabilities	(7,313)	478	(3,127)
Prepaid pension cost and other	2,358	99	(630)
Net cash provided by operating activities	$ 659	$19,012	$12,849

Sale of Property

6.19

NCR CORPORATION (DEC)

(In millions)	2009	2008	2007
Operating activities			
Net (loss) income	$ (30)	$227	$ 274
Adjustments to reconcile net income (loss) to net cash provided by operating activities:			
Loss (income) from discontinued operations	—	3	(103)
Depreciation and amortization	124	109	110
Stock-based compensation expense	12	41	42
Excess tax benefit from stock-based compensation	—	(2)	(9)
Deferred income taxes	(132)	—	(7)
Gains on sale of property, plant, and equipment, net	(9)	(27)	(2)
Impairment of equity investments and related assets	39	—	—
Changes in operating assets and liabilities:			
Receivables	27	249	(166)
Inventories	5	25	(76)
Current payables and accrued expenses	(28)	(56)	52
Deferred service revenue and customer deposits	18	(42)	43
Employee severance and pension	49	(43)	(31)
Environmental liabilities	109	1	9
Other assets and liabilities	39	(70)	15
Net cash provided by operating activities	$ 223	$415	$ 151

Tax Benefit From Share-Based Compensation Plans

6.20

ROCKWELL AUTOMATION, INC. (SEP)

(In millions)	2009	2008	2007
Continuing operations:			
Operating activities:			
Net income	$ 220.7	$577.6	$1,487.8
Income from discontinued operations	(2.8)	—	(918.5)
Income from continuing operations	217.9	577.6	569.3
Adjustments to arrive at cash provided by operating activities:			
Depreciation	101.7	101.3	93.5
Amortization of intangible assets	32.4	35.2	24.4
Share-based compensation expense	27.8	32.5	29.0
Retirement benefit expense	48.5	44.0	59.3
Pension trust contributions	(28.8)	(39.2)	(49.1)
Deferred income taxes	14.7	(16.1)	(43.7)
Net loss (gain) on dispositions of securities and property	4.4	(5.0)	(5.4)
Income tax benefit from the exercise of stock options	0.1	0.2	1.3
Excess income tax benefit from the exercise of stock options	(2.4)	(4.6)	(27.1)
Changes in assets and liabilities, excluding effects of acquisitions, divestitures, and foreign currency adjustments:			
Receivables	228.2	(16.0)	(95.1)
Inventories	127.5	(76.2)	(67.7)
Accounts payable	(101.1)	(49.0)	68.4
Compensation and benefits	(56.7)	15.4	7.8
Income taxes	(55.5)	(17.5)	(161.0)
Other assets and liabilities	(32.3)	14.2	41.0
Cash provided by operating activities	$ 526.4	$596.8	$ 444.9

Equity Earnings/(Loss)

6.21

NUCOR CORPORATION (DEC)

(In thousands)	2009	2008	2007
Operating activities:			
Net earnings (loss)	$ (237,178)	$2,144,911	$1,765,448
Adjustments:			
Depreciation	494,035	479,484	403,172
Amortization	72,388	69,423	24,384
Stock-based compensation	54,665	49,873	44,001
Deferred income taxes	88,546	(293,476)	(81,206)
Equity in losses of unconsolidated affiliates	82,341	36,920	24,618
Impairment of non-current assets	2,800	105,183	—
Changes in assets and liabilities (exclusive of acquisitions):			
Accounts receivable	141,104	855,572	(174,326)
Inventories	1,117,600	(364,280)	(102,490)
Accounts payable	170,229	(861,334)	57,259
Federal income taxes	(422,116)	278,663	13,332
Salaries, wages and related accruals	(419,800)	129,927	(42,931)
Other	37,683	(132,138)	4,045
Cash provided by operating activities	$1,182,297	$2,498,728	$1,935,306

Sale of Assets Other Than Property

6.22

THE RYLAND GROUP, INC. (DEC)

(In thousands)	2009	2008	2007
Cash flows from operating activities			
Net loss	$(162,474)	$(396,585)	$(333,526)
Adjustments to reconcile net loss to net cash provided by operating activities:			
Depreciation and amortization	25,068	51,611	54,320
Stock-based compensation expense	10,222	9,048	12,257
(Gain) loss on early extinguishment of debt, net	(10,573)	604	490
Gain on sale of marketable securities	(963)	—	—
Inventory and other asset impairments and write-offs	201,975	325,480	583,363
Deferred tax valuation allowance	2,132	143,784	75,166
Changes in assets and liabilities:			
Decrease in inventories	214,086	383,237	272,271
Net change in other assets, payables and other liabilities	14,931	(239,362)	(411,841)
Excess tax benefits from stock-based compensation	(580)	(3,138)	(6,714)
Other operating activities, net	1,859	(26,227)	(17,271)
Net cash provided by operating activities	$ 295,683	$ 248,452	$ 228,515

Provision for Doubtful Accounts

6.23

VALASSIS COMMUNICATIONS, INC. (DEC)

(In thousands of U.S. dollars)	2009	2008	2007
Cash flows from operating activities:			
Net earnings (loss)	$ 66,768	$(209,652)	$ 52,240
Adjustments to reconcile net earnings to net cash provided by operating activities:			
Depreciation	55,224	60,145	54,592
Amortization of intangibles	12,624	9,223	7,915
Amortization of bond discount	3,281	6,564	12,348
Provision for losses on accounts receivable	5,732	8,602	5,290
Gain on debt extinguishment, net of taxes	(10,028)	—	—
Writedown of impaired assets	—	245,700	3,063
Loss on termination of cash flow hedges, net	2,513	—	—
(Gain) loss on equity investments	(4,561)	2,172	(2,040)
Stock-based compensation expense	7,109	7,043	7,258
(Gain) loss on sale of property, plant and equipment	(228)	3,326	246
Deferred income taxes	(10,965)	(26,467)	546
Changes in assets and liabilities which increase (decrease) cash flow:			
Accounts receivable	45,181	25,045	3,411
Inventories	7,701	(4,582)	(11,613)
Prepaid expenses and other	(5,810)	(11,856)	9,013
Other assets	7,360	5,735	25,946
Other liabilities	10,571	(1,630)	(17,993)
Accounts payable	1,059	2,365	29,023
Accrued interest and expenses	4,958	(15,275)	(8,702)
Income taxes	2,931	(9,124)	249
Progress billings	(4,007)	(1,077)	(13,960)
Total adjustments	130,645	305,909	104,592
Cash flows provided by operating activities	$197,413	$ 96,257	$156,832

Intangible Asset Impairment

6.24

MOLEX INCORPORATED (JUN)

(In thousands)	2009	2008	2007
Operating activities:			
Net (loss) income	$(321,287)	$215,437	$240,768
Add (deduct) non-cash items included in net income (loss):			
Depreciation and amortization	251,902	252,344	237,912
Goodwill impairment	264,140		
Asset write-downs included in restructuring costs	41,376	13,599	8,667
(Gain) loss on investments	(143)	111	(1,154)
Deferred income taxes	(26,606)	31,096	20,998
Loss on sale of property, plant and equipment	2,478	296	1,800
Share-based compensation	26,508	24,249	27,524
Other non-cash items	(8,124)	(6,778)	23,373
Changes in assets and liabilities, excluding effects of foreign currency adjustments and acquisitions:			
Accounts receivable	201,080	478	27,913
Inventories	95,529	(26,240)	(16,514)
Accounts payable	(84,502)	34,197	(57,479)
Other current assets and liabilities	(24,967)	(45,798)	(60,421)
Other assets and liabilities	(47,486)	(13,857)	(1,953)
Cash provided from operating activities	$ 369,898	$479,134	$451,434

Intangible Asset Amortization

6.25

LEGGETT & PLATT, INCORPORATED (DEC)

(Amounts in millions)	2009	2008	2007
Operating activities			
Net earnings (loss)	$115.0	$109.0	$ (5.7)
Adjustments to reconcile net earnings (loss) to net cash provided by operating activities:			
Depreciation	109.6	115.9	156.9
Amortization	20.7	24.5	26.5
Impairment charges:			
Goodwill	3.0	25.6	243.0
Other long-lived assets	2.8	19.2	44.1
Provision for losses on accounts and notes receivable	29.5	23.4	8.5
Writedown of inventories	16.2	27.1	22.5
Net (gain) loss from sales of assets	(3.0)	2.3	(35.8)
Deferred income tax expense (benefit)	44.0	25.5	(56.1)
Stock-based compensation	38.0	41.6	49.0
Other	3.9	(10.7)	(12.4)
Other changes, excluding effects from acquisitions and divestitures:			
Decrease in accounts and other receivables	105.7	36.5	90.4
Decrease in inventories	87.6	49.9	65.5
Decrease in other current assets	1.4	9.5	10.5
Increase (decrease) in accounts payable	18.4	(46.8)	13.0
Decrease in accrued expenses and other current liabilities	(27.5)	(16.3)	(6.2)
Net cash provided by operating activities	$565.3	$436.2	$613.7

Restructuring Charges

6.26

MOHAWK INDUSTRIES, INC. (DEC)

(In thousands)	2009	2008	2007
Cash flows from operating activities:			
Net (loss) earnings	$ (1,019)	$(1,452,534)	$ 714,413
Adjustments to reconcile net (loss) income to net cash provided by operating activities:			
Impairment of goodwill and other intangibles	—	1,543,397	—
Restructuring	57,412	29,617	—
Depreciation and amortization	303,004	295,054	306,437
Deferred income taxes	(20,579)	69,842	(289,902)
Loss on disposal of property, plant and equipment	1,481	2,272	7,689
Excess tax deficit (benefit) from stock-based compensation	342	(334)	(6,828)
Stock-based compensation expense	9,653	11,991	13,594
Changes in operating assets and liabilities, net of acquisitions:			
Receivables	102,799	118,199	127,475
Income tax receivable	(72,515)	—	—
Inventories	276,169	102,706	20,976
Accounts payable and accrued expenses	11,510	(127,905)	(58,776)
Other assets and prepaid expenses	17,320	(23,774)	31,007
Other liabilities	(13,372)	7,555	14,310
Net cash provided by operating activities	$672,205	$ 576,086	$ 880,395

Changes in Assets and Liabilities

6.27

MEREDITH CORPORATION (JUN)

(In thousands)	2009	2008	2007
Cash flows from operating activities			
Net earnings (loss)	$(107,084)	$134,672	$162,346
Adjustments to reconcile net earnings (loss) to net cash provided by operating activities:			
Depreciation	32,941	35,370	31,840
Amortization	9,648	14,192	13,948
Share-based compensation	10,220	7,885	11,108
Deferred income taxes	(53,333)	20,527	24,638
Amortization of broadcast rights	25,121	26,511	27,990
Payments for broadcast rights	(25,275)	(26,672)	(28,516)
Net gain from dispositions of assets, net of taxes	(1,205)	(2,340)	(2,403)
Provision for write-down of impaired assets	300,131	9,666	10,829
Excess tax benefits from share-based payments	(906)	(1,475)	(3,514)
Changes in assets and liabilities, net of acquisitions/dispositions			
Accounts receivable	38,778	38,128	(19,911)
Inventories	15,305	3,185	1,846
Other current assets	(5,851)	(36)	2,977
Subscription acquisition costs	(7,537)	15,965	12,064
Other assets	(2,742)	(87)	(20,124)
Accounts payable	(4,408)	(2,836)	(6,555)
Accrued expenses and other liabilities	(31,287)	(11,261)	5,611
Unearned subscription revenues	(14,009)	(26,185)	(10,756)
Other noncurrent liabilities	2,413	20,755	(2,896)
Net cash provided by operating activities	$ 180,920	$255,964	$210,522

6.28

PRIDE INTERNATIONAL, INC. (DEC)

(In millions)	2009	2008	2007
Cash flows from (used in) operating activities:			
Net income	$285.8	$ 851.1	$ 778.3
Adjustments to reconcile net income to net cash from operating activities:			
Gain on sale of Eastern Hemisphere land rigs	(5.4)	(6.2)	—
Gain on sale of tender-assist rigs	—	(121.4)	—
Gain on sale of Latin America and E&P Services segments	—	(56.8)	(268.6)
Gain on sale of equity method investment	—	(11.4)	—
Depreciation and amortization	196.5	210.8	269.7
Amortization and write-offs of deferred financing costs	2.4	5.2	4.0
Amortization of deferred contract liabilities	(53.8)	(59.0)	(57.3)
Impairment charges	33.4	—	—
Gain on sales of assets, net	(0.4)	(24.0)	(31.5)
Deferred income taxes	(13.2)	78.1	49.8
Excess tax benefits from stock-based compensation	(1.5)	(7.7)	(7.2)
Stock-based compensation	35.9	24.8	23.0
Other, net	0.9	2.2	16.5
Net effect of changes in operating accounts (see note 15)	142.8	(26.9)	(152.0)
Change in deferred gain on asset sales and retirements	4.9	(12.3)	—
Increase (decrease) in deferred revenue	13.8	(8.7)	35.3
Decrease (increase) in deferred expense	(15.0)	6.3	25.0
Net cash flows from (used in) operating activities	$627.1	$ 844.1	$ 685.0

NOTES TO CONSOLIDATED FINANCIAL STATEMENTS

Note 15 (In Part): Other Supplemental Information

Supplemental cash flows and non-cash transactions were as follows for the years ended December 31:

(In millions)	2009	2008	2007
Decrease (increase) in:			
Trade receivables	$118.4	$(101.2)	$ (78.5)
Prepaid expenses and other current assets	7.6	9.4	(0.7)
Other assets	(18.3)	(2.5)	(19.0)
Increase (decrease) in:			
Accounts payable	(14.9)	58.8	(53.5)
Accrued expenses	44.1	(15.9)	(15.6)
Other liabilities	5.9	24.5	15.3
Net effect of changes in operating accounts	$142.8	$ (26.9)	$(152.0)
Cash paid during the year for:			
Interest	$ 70.2	$ 56.1	$ 77.6
Income taxes—U.S., net	0.6	2.4	8.6
Income taxes—foreign, net	123.7	145.8	127.6
Change in capital expenditures in accounts payable	24.0	(54.6)	(50.6)

INTEREST AND INCOME TAX PAYMENTS

6.29

CYTEC INDUSTRIES INC. (DEC)

NOTES TO CONSOLIDATED FINANCIAL STATEMENTS
(Currencies in millions)

10 (In Part): Debt

Cash payments during the years ended December 31, 2009, 2008 and 2007, included interest of $34.7, $42.7 and $44.5, respectively. Included in interest expense, net, for the years ended December 31, 2009, 2008 and 2007, is interest income of $7.4, $3.5 and $2.1, respectively. Capitalized interest for the years ended 2009 and 2008 was $8.3 and $3.0, respectively.

12 (In Part): Income Taxes

Income taxes paid in 2009, 2008 and 2007 were $30.0, $72.7 and $59.7, respectively, and include non-U.S. taxes of $28.9, $45.2 and $45.8 in 2009, 2008 and 2007, respectively. Income taxes paid related to the pre-acquisition tax period of the Surface Specialties entities in 2009, 2008 and 2007 were $2.1, $0.0 and $0.0, respectively, in which $2.1, $0.8 and $0.1 in 2009, 2008, and 2007, respectively, has been reimbursed to us thus far from UCB pursuant to the Stock and Asset Purchase Agreement.

6.30

HUNTSMAN CORPORATION (DEC)

(Dollars in millions)	2009	2008	2007
Increase (decrease) in cash and cash equivalents	$1,088	$503	$(109)
Cash and cash equivalents at beginning of period	657	154	263
Cash and cash equivalents at end of period	$1,745	$657	$ 154
Supplemental cash flow information:			
Cash paid for interest	$ 227	$265	$ 301
Cash paid for income taxes	155	34	73

6.31

QUANEX BUILDING PRODUCTS CORPORATION (OCT)

NOTES TO CONSOLIDATED FINANCIAL STATEMENTS

1 (In Part): Significant Accounting Policies

Statements of Cash Flows

The Company generally considers all highly liquid debt instruments purchased with a maturity of three months or less to be cash equivalents. Similar investments with original maturities beyond three months are considered short-term investments.

Supplemental cash flow information is as follows:

(In thousands)	2009	2008	2007
Cash paid for interest	$ 396	$ 408	$ 563
Cash paid for income taxes	2,693	14,089	30,085
Cash received for income tax refunds	1,120	—	3

CASH FLOWS FROM INVESTING ACTIVITIES

6.32 FASB ASC 230, *Statement of Cash Flows*, defines those transactions and events which constitute investing cash receipts and payments. Generally, cash receipts and payments should be reported separately and not netted. Examples of reporting cash flows from investing activities follow.

Property Acquisitions/Disposals

6.33

BALL CORPORATION (DEC)

($ in millions)	2009	2008	2007
Cash flows from investing activities			
Additions to property, plant and equipment	$(187.1)	$(306.9)	$(308.5)
Cash collateral, net	105.3	(105.5)	—
Business acquisitions, net of cash acquired	(574.7)	(2.3)	—
Proceeds from dispositions, net of cash sold	69.0	8.7	—
Property insurance proceeds	—	—	48.6
Other, net	6.1	(12.0)	(5.9)
Cash used in investing activities	$(581.4)	$(418.0)	$(265.8)

6.34

PFIZER INC. (DEC)

(Millions of dollars)	2009	2008	2007
Investing activities			
Purchases of property, plant and equipment	$ (1,205)	$ (1,701)	$ (1,880)
Purchases of short-term investments with original maturities greater than 90 days	(35,331)	(35,705)	(25,426)
Proceeds from redemptions and sales of short-term investments with original maturities greater than 90 days	42,364	27,883	23,053
Proceeds from redemptions and sales of short-term investments with original maturities of 90 days or less—net	5,775	7,913	7,235
Purchases of long-term investments	(6,888)	(9,357)	(1,635)
Proceeds from redemptions and sales of long-term investments	6,504	1,009	172
Acquisitions, net of cash acquired	(43,123)	(1,184)	(464)
Other investing activities	632	(1,693)	(260)
Net cash (used in)/provided by investing activities	$(31,272)	$(12,835)	$ 795

Investments

6.35

LEE ENTERPRISES, INCORPORATED (SEP)

(Thousands)	2009	2008	2007
Cash provided by (required for) investing activities of continuing operations:			
Purchases of marketable securities	$(47,777)	$(115,555)	$(90,005)
Sales or maturities of marketable securities	166,109	87,873	78,018
Purchases of property and equipment	(11,555)	(20,606)	(34,381)
Proceeds from sale of assets	1,418	12,685	1,334
Acquisitions, net	—	(1,624)	(1,065)
Decrease (increase) in restricted cash	(2,291)	13,771	(1,165)
Other	3,081	8,493	8,741
Net cash provided by (required for) investing activities of continuing operations	$108,985	$ (14,963)	$(38,523)

NOTES TO CONSOLIDATED FINANCIAL STATEMENTS

5. Marketable Securities Available-For-Sale

Marketable securities, which are comprised of debt securities issued by the U.S. government and agencies, and which include certain of the Company's restricted cash and investments, are classified as available-for-sale securities at September 28, 2008, and consisted of the following:

(Thousands)	2008
Amortized cost	$118,347
Gross unrealized gains	899
Gross unrealized losses	(219)
Fair value	$119,027

In 2009, the Company sold its available for sale securities and used the proceeds primarily to reduce debt. See Note 7.

Proceeds from the sale of such securities total $166,109,000 in 2009, $87,873,000 in 2008, and $78,018,000 in 2007. The Company recognized gross realized gains of $1,856,000 and gross unrealized losses of $46,000 in 2009. No significant gross realized gains or losses were realized in 2008 and 2007.

6.36

THE J. M. SMUCKER COMPANY (APR)

(Dollars in thousands)	2009	2008	2007
Investing activities			
Businesses acquired, net of cash acquired	$ (77,335)	$(220,949)	$(60,488)
Additions to property, plant, and equipment	(108,907)	(76,430)	(57,002)
Proceeds from sale of businesses	—	3,407	84,054
Purchase of marketable securities	—	(229,405)	(20,000)
Sale and maturities of marketable securities	3,013	257,536	26,272
Disposal of property, plant, and equipment	2,965	3,532	2,313
Other—net	5,448	(177)	(2,190)
Net cash used for investing activities	$(174,816)	$(262,486)	$(27,041)

NOTES TO CONSOLIDATED FINANCIAL STATEMENTS
(Dollars in thousands)

Note F. Marketable Securities

Under the Company's investment policy, it may invest in debt securities deemed to be investment grade at the time of purchase. Currently, these investments are defined as mortgage-backed obligations, corporate bonds, municipal bonds, federal agency notes, and commercial paper. However, in light of current market conditions, the Company has limited recent investments primarily to high-quality money market funds. The Company determines the appropriate categorization of debt securities at the time of purchase and reevaluates such designation at each balance sheet date. The Company has categorized all debt securities as available for sale because it currently has the intent to convert these investments into cash if and when needed. Classification of these available-for-sale marketable securities as current or noncurrent is based on whether the conversion to cash is expected to be necessary for current operations, which is currently consistent with the security's maturity date.

Securities categorized as available for sale are stated at fair value, with unrealized gains and losses reported as a component of other comprehensive income. Approximately $3,013, $257,536, and $26,272 of proceeds have been realized upon maturity or sale of available-for-sale marketable securities in 2009, 2008, and 2007, respectively. The Company uses specific identification to determine the basis on which securities are sold.

The following table is a summary of available-for-sale marketable securities, consisting entirely of mortgage-backed securities, at April 30, 2009 and 2008.

	2009	2008
Cost	$13,519	$16,532
Gross unrealized losses	(706)	(489)
Estimated fair value	$12,813	$16,043

There were two marketable securities in an unrealized loss position for greater than twelve months at April 30, 2009. Based on management's evaluation at April 30, 2009, considering the nature of the investments, the credit worthiness of the issuers, and the intent and ability of the Company to hold the securities for the period necessary to recover the cost of the securities, the decline in the fair values was determined to be temporary.

Business Combinations

6.37

AMETEK, INC. (DEC)

(In thousands)	2009	2008	2007
Investing activities:			
Additions to property, plant and equipment	$ (33,062)	$ (44,215)	$ (37,620)
Purchases of businesses, net of cash acquired	(72,919)	(463,012)	(300,569)
(Increase) decrease in marketable securities	(638)	6,323	(1,700)
Other	275	4,282	5,228
Total investing activities	$(106,344)	$(496,622)	$(334,661)

NOTES TO CONSOLIDATED FINANCIAL STATEMENTS

Note 6 (In Part): Acquisitions

The Company spent approximately $72.9 million in cash, net of cash acquired, to acquire High Standard Aviation in January 2009, a small acquisition of two businesses in India, Unispec Marketing Pvt. Ltd. and Thelsha Technical Services Pvt. Ltd., in September 2009 and Ameron Global in December 2009. High Standard Aviation is a provider of electrical and electromechanical, hydraulic and pneumatic repair services to the aerospace industry. Ameron Global is a manufacturer of highly engineered pressurized gas components and systems for commercial and aerospace customers and is also a leader in maintenance, repair and overhaul of fire suppression and oxygen supply systems. High Standard Aviation and Ameron Global are a part of EMG.

●   ●   ●   ●   ●   ●

In 2008, the Company spent a total of approximately $463.0 million in cash, net of cash acquired, for six acquisitions and one small technology line. The acquisitions include Drake Air ("Drake") and Motion Control Group ("MCG") in February 2008, Reading Alloys in April 2008, Vision Research, Inc. in June 2008, the programmable power business of Xantrex Technology, Inc. ("Xantrex Programmable") in August 2008 and Muirhead Aerospace Limited ("Muirhead") in November 2008. Drake is a provider of heat-transfer repair services to the commercial aerospace industry and further expands the Company's presence in the global aerospace maintenance, repair and overhaul ("MRO") services industry. MCG is a leading global manufacturer of highly customized motors and motion control solutions for the medical, life sciences, industrial automation, semiconductor and aviation markets. MCG enhances the Company's capability in providing precision motion technology solutions. Reading Alloys is a global leader in specialty titanium master alloys and highly engineered metal powders used in the aerospace, medical implant, military and electronics markets. Vision Research is a leading manufacturer of high-speed digital imaging systems used for motion capture and analysis in numerous test and measurement applications. Xantrex Programmable is a leader in alternating current and direct current programmable power supplies used to test electrical and electronic products. Muirhead is a leading manufacturer of motion technology products and a provider of avionics repair and overhaul services for the aerospace and defense markets. Drake, MCG, Reading Alloys and Muirhead are part of EMG and Vision Research and Xantrex Programmable are part of EIG.

●   ●   ●   ●   ●   ●

In 2007, the Company spent $300.6 million in cash, net of cash acquired, for seven acquisitions and one small technology line. The acquisitions include Seacon Phoenix, subsequently renamed AMETEK SCP, Inc. ("SCP"), in April 2007, Advanced Industries, Inc. ("Advanced"), B&S Aircraft Parts and Accessories ("B&S") and Hamilton Precision Metals ("Hamilton") in June 2007, Cameca SAS ("Cameca") in August 2007, the Repair & Overhaul Division of Umeco plc ("Umeco R&O") in November 2007 and California Instruments Corporation ("California Instruments") in December 2007. SCP provides undersea electrical interconnect subsystems to the global submarine market. Advanced manufactures starter generators, brush and brushless motors, vane-axial centrifugal blowers for cabin ventilation and linear actuators for the business jet, light jet and helicopter markets. B&S provides third-party MRO services, primarily for starter generators and hydraulic and fuel system components, for a variety of business aircraft and helicopter applications. Hamilton produces highly differentiated niche specialty metals used in medical implant devices and surgical instruments, electronic components and measurement devices for aerospace and other industrial markets. Cameca is

a manufacturer of high-end elemental analysis systems used in advanced laboratory research, semiconductor and nanotechnology applications. Umeco R&O provides third-party MRO services for a variety of helicopters and commercial and regional aircraft throughout Europe. California Instruments is a leader in the niche market for programmable alternating current power sources used to test electrical and electronic products, with an especially strong position in the high-power segment. Advanced, B&S, Cameca and California Instruments are part of EIG and SCP, Hamilton and Umeco R&O are part of EMG.

Sale of Discontinued Operations

6.38

BECTON, DICKINSON AND COMPANY (SEP)

(Thousands of dollars)	2009	2008	2007
Investing activities			
Capital expenditures	$ (591,103)	$(601,684)	$ (556,287)
Capitalized software	(109,588)	(49,306)	(22,334)
Change in short-term investments	(338,228)	(46,321)	(30,167)
Proceeds (purchases) of long-term investments	840	(5,666)	(3,881)
Acquisitions of businesses, net of cash acquired	—	(41,259)	(339,528)
Divestiture of businesses	51,022	—	19,971
Other, net	(85,900)	(38,491)	(85,922)
Net cash used for continuing investing activities	$(1,072,957)	$(782,727)	$(1,018,148)

NOTES TO CONSOLIDATED FINANCIAL STATEMENTS (Thousands of dollars)

Note 4 (In Part): Divestitures

On July 8, 2009, the Company sold certain assets and liabilities related to the elastics and thermometer components of the Home Healthcare product line of the Medical segment for $51,022. The Company recognized a pre-tax gain on sale of $18,145. Concurrent with the sale, the Company exited the remaining portion of the Home Healthcare product line. The results of operations associated with the Home Healthcare product line are reported as discontinued operations for all periods presented in the accompanying Condensed Consolidated Statements of Income and Cash Flows and related disclosures.

On December 11, 2006, the Company sold the blood glucose monitoring ("BGM") product line for $19,971 and recognized a pre-tax gain on sale of $15,226. During 2007, adjustments of $9,319 were made to reduce sales returns and other accruals related to obligations that remained with the Company upon divestiture of the product line. Additionally, the Company received a payment of $4,675, which represented the resolution of a contingency with a former supplier. Following the sale, the Company's prior period Consolidated Statements of Income and Cash Flows and related disclosures have been restated to separately present the results of the BGM product line as discontinued operations.

Notes Receivable

6.39

THE WESTERN UNION COMPANY (DEC)

(In millions)	2009	2008	2007
Cash flows from investing activities			
Capitalization of contract costs	$ (27.3)	$ (82.8)	$ (80.9)
Capitalization of purchased and developed software	(11.9)	(17.0)	(27.7)
Purchases of property and equipment	(59.7)	(53.9)	(83.5)
Acquisition of businesses, net of cash acquired	(515.9)	(42.8)	—
Proceeds from/(increase in) receivable for securities sold	255.5	(298.1)	—
Notes receivable issued to agents	—	(1.0)	(6.1)
Repayments of notes receivable issued to agents	35.2	41.9	32.0
Purchase of equity method investments	—	—	(35.8)
Net cash used in investing activities	$(324.1)	$(453.7)	$(202.0)

NOTES TO CONSOLIDATED FINANCIAL STATEMENTS

2 (In Part): Summary of Significant Accounting Policies

Settlement Assets and Obligations (In Part)

Settlement assets represent funds received or to be received from agents for unsettled money transfers, money orders and consumer payments. Western Union records corresponding settlement obligations relating to amounts payable under money transfers, money orders and consumer payment service arrangements. Settlement assets and obligations also include amounts receivable from and payable to businesses for the value of customer cross-currency payment transactions related to the global business payments segment.

Settlement assets consist of cash and cash equivalents, receivables from selling agents and business-to-business customers and investment securities. Cash received by Western Union agents generally becomes available to Western Union within one week after initial receipt by the agent. Cash equivalents consist of short-term time deposits, commercial paper and other highly liquid investments. Receivables from selling agents represent funds collected by such agents, but in transit to Western Union. Western Union has a large and diverse agent base, thereby reducing the credit risk of the Company from any one agent. In addition, Western Union performs ongoing credit evaluations of its agents' financial condition and credit worthiness.

Receivables from business-to-business customers arise from cross-currency payment transactions in the global business payments segment. Receivables (for currency to be received) and payables (for the cross-currency payments to be made) are recognized at trade date for these transactions. The credit risk arising from these spot foreign currency exchange contracts is largely mitigated, as in most cases Custom House requires the receipt of funds from customers before releasing the associated cross-currency payment.

• • • • • •

Settlement assets and obligations consisted of the following (in millions):

	2009	2008
Settlement assets:		
Cash and cash equivalents	$ 161.9	$ 42.3
Receivables from selling agents and business-to-business customers	1,004.4	759.6
Investment securities	1,222.8	405.6
	$2,389.1	$1,207.5
Settlement obligations:		
Money transfer, money order and payment service payables	$1,954.8	$ 799.5
Payables to agents	434.3	408.0
	$2,389.1	$1,207.5

Capitalized Software

6.40

EASTMAN CHEMICAL COMPANY (DEC)

(Dollars in millions)	2009	2008	2007
Cash flows from investing activities			
Additions to properties and equipment	$(310)	$(634)	$(518)
Proceeds from sale of assets and investments	30	337	202
Acquisitions of and investments in joint ventures	(68)	(38)	(40)
Additions to capitalized software	(8)	(10)	(11)
Other items, net	(13)	(31)	32
Net cash used in investing activities	$(369)	$(376)	$(335)

NOTES TO CONSOLIDATED FINANCIAL STATEMENTS

1 (In Part): Significant Accounting Policies

Computer Software Costs

Capitalized software costs are amortized primarily on a straight-line basis over three years, the expected useful life of such assets, beginning when the software project is substantially complete and placed in service. Capitalized software in 2009, 2008, and 2007 was approximately $8 million, $10 million, and $11 million, respectively. During those same periods, approximately $11 million, $11 million, and $13 million, respectively, of previously capitalized costs were amortized. At December 31, 2009 and 2008, the unamortized capitalized software costs were $21 million and $24 million, respectively. Capitalized software costs are reflected in other noncurrent assets.

Restricted Cash

6.41

RYDER SYSTEM, INC. (DEC)

(In thousands)	2009	2008	2007
Cash flows from investing activities of continuing operations:			
Purchases of property and revenue earning equipment	$(651,953)	$(1,230,401)	$(1,304,033)
Sales of revenue earning equipment	211,002	257,679	354,736
Sales of operating property and equipment	4,634	3,727	18,725
Sale and leaseback of revenue earning equipment	—	—	150,348
Acquisitions	(88,873)	(246,993)	(75,226)
Collections on direct finance leases	65,242	61,096	62,346
Changes in restricted cash	11,129	51,029	(19,686)
Other, net	209	395	1,588
Net cash used in investing activities of continuing operations	$(448,610)	$(1,103,468)	$ (811,202)

NOTES TO CONSOLIDATED FINANCIAL STATEMENTS

1 (In Part): Summary of Significant Accounting Policies

Restricted Cash

Restricted cash primarily consists of cash proceeds from the sale of eligible vehicles or operating property set aside for the acquisition of replacement vehicles or operating property under our like-kind exchange tax programs. See Note 14, "Income Taxes," for a complete discussion of the vehicle like-kind exchange tax program. We classify restricted cash within "Prepaid expenses and other current assets" if the restriction is expected to expire in the twelve months following the balance sheet date or within "Direct financing leases and other assets" if the restriction is expected to expire more than twelve months after the balance sheet date. The changes in restricted cash balances are reflected as an investing activity in our Consolidated Statements of Cash Flows as they relate to the sales and purchases of revenue earning equipment and operating property and equipment.

Insurance Proceeds

6.42

SPECTRUM CONTROL, INC. (NOV)

(Dollar amounts in thousands)	2009	2008	2007
Cash flows from investing activities:			
Payments for acquired businesses, net of cash received	$(12,938)	$ (5,587)	$(2,365)
Insurance proceeds related to property, plant and equipment	1,180	—	1,748
Purchase of property, plant and equipment	(3,952)	(4,440)	(5,810)
Net cash used in investing activities	$(15,710)	$(10,027)	$(6,427)

NOTES TO CONSOLIDATED FINANCIAL STATEMENTS

14. Insurance Recoveries

The Company conducts its operations in numerous locations, including a leased facility in Marlborough, Massachusetts (the "Marlborough Facility") and an owned facility in Wesson, Mississippi (the "Wesson Facility"). In January 2009, the Marlborough Facility sustained wind damage to its roof which, in turn, resulted in water damage to certain machinery, equipment, and leasehold improvements. Also in January 2009, a small outbuilding at the Wesson Facility sustained a fire, destroying the outbuilding and certain plating equipment contained inside. The aggregate book value of the assets damaged or destroyed by these two involuntary conversions amounted to $652,000. In addition, the Company incurred costs of $106,000 for various clean-up, repairs and related outside services. Upon the settlement of all related insurance claims, the Company received aggregate insurance recoveries of $1,286,000. Accordingly, the Company recorded a net gain of $528,000 representing the excess of the insurance recoveries over the carrying value of the assets destroyed and related costs incurred. This credit has been included in selling, general and administrative expense in the Company's consolidated statement of income for the year ended November 30, 2009.

In-Process Research and Development

6.43

ELI LILLY AND COMPANY (DEC)

(Dollars in millions)	2009	2008	2007
Cash flows from investing activities			
Purchases of property and equipment	$ (765.0)	$ (947.2)	$(1,082.4)
Disposals of property and equipment	17.7	25.7	32.3
Net change in short-term investments	399.1	957.6	(376.9)
Proceeds from sales and maturities of noncurrent investments	1,107.8	1,597.3	800.1
Purchases of noncurrent investments	(432.3)	(2,412.4)	(750.7)
Purchases of in-process research and development	(90.0)	(122.0)	(111.0)
Cash paid for acquisitions, net of cash acquired	—	(6,083.0)	(2,673.2)
Other, net	(94.5)	(284.8)	(166.3)
Net cash provided by (used for) investing activities	$ 142.8	$(7,268.8)	$(4,328.1)

NOTES TO CONSOLIDATED FINANCIAL STATEMENTS
(Dollars in millions)

Note 1 (In Part): Summary of Significant Accounting Policies

Acquired Research and Development

We recognize as incurred the cost of directly acquiring assets to be used in the research and development process that have not yet received regulatory approval for marketing and for which no alternative future use has been identified. Beginning in 2009, in process research and development acquired in a business combination is capitalized at the fair value as of the time of the acquisition. For in-process research and development assets acquired in both direct acquisitions and business combinations, once the product has obtained regulatory approval, we capitalize any milestones paid and amortize them over the period benefited. Milestones paid prior to regulatory approval of the product are generally expensed when the event requiring payment of the milestone occurs.

Note 3 (In Part): Acquisitions

In addition to the acquisitions of businesses, we also acquired several products in development. The acquired IPR&D related to these products of $90.0 million, $122.0 million, and $405.1 million in 2009, 2008, and 2007, respectively, was also written off by a charge to income immediately upon acquisition because the products had no alternative future use.

CASH FLOWS FROM FINANCING ACTIVITIES

6.44 FASB ASC 230, *Statement of Cash Flows*, defines those transactions and events which constitute financing cash receipts and payments. Generally, cash receipts and payments should be reported separately and not netted. Examples of reporting cash flows from financing activities follow.

Debt Proceeds/Repayments

6.45

AK STEEL HOLDING CORPORATION (DEC)

(Dollars in millions)	2009	2008	2007
Cash flows from financing activities:			
Redemption of long-term debt	$(23.5)	$(26.9)	$(450.0)
Fees related to new credit facility or new debt	—	—	(2.6)
Proceeds from exercise of stock options	0.5	3.4	9.2
Purchase of treasury stock	(11.4)	(24.0)	(2.4)
Excess tax benefits from stock-based compensation	—	12.2	6.5
Common stock dividends paid	(22.0)	(22.4)	—
Advances from noncontrolling interest owner to Middletown Coke	29.0	45.5	—
Other financing items, net	1.0	(4.0)	3.6
Net cash flows from financing activities	$(26.4)	$(16.2)	$(435.7)

NOTES TO CONSOLIDATED FINANCIAL STATEMENTS
(Dollars in millions)

Note 5 (In Part): Long-Term Debt and Other Financing

At December 31, 2009 and 2008, the Company's long-term debt balances were as follows:

	2009	2008
7 3/4% senior notes due June 2012	$504.0	$530.4
Tax exempt financing due 2010 through 2029 (variable rates of 0.25% to 4.0% in 2009)	103.0	103.7
Unamortized discount	(0.5)	(0.8)
Total debt	$606.5	$633.3

During the fourth quarter of 2008, the Company repurchased $19.6 of the $550.0 original par value of the Company's $7^3/_4$% senior notes due in 2012 with cash payments totaling $14.2. In connection with the 2008 repurchases, the Company incurred non-cash, pre-tax gains of approximately $5.4 in 2008. During 2009, the Company repurchased an additional $26.4 of those senior notes, with cash payments totaling $22.8. In connection with the 2009 repurchases, the Company incurred non-cash, pre-tax gains of approximately $3.6 in 2009. The repurchases were funded from the Company's existing cash balances.

6.46

HONEYWELL INTERNATIONAL INC. (DEC)

(Dollars in millions)	2009	2008	2007
Cash flows from financing activities:			
Net (decrease)/increase in commercial paper	$(1,133)	$ (325)	$ 1,078
Net decrease in short-term borrowings	(521)	(1)	(3)
Payments of debt assumed with acquisitions	—	—	(40)
Proceeds from issuance of common stock	37	146	603
Proceeds from issuance of long-term debt	1,488	1,487	1,885
Payments of long-term debt	(1,106)	(428)	(430)
Excess tax benefits from share based payment arrangements	1	21	86
Repurchases of common stock	—	(1,459)	(3,986)
Cash dividends paid	(918)	(811)	(767)
Net cash used for financing activities	$(2,152)	$(1,370)	$(1,574)

NOTES TO FINANCIAL STATEMENTS
(Dollars in millions)

Note 14 (In Part): Long-Term Debt and Credit Agreements

	2009	2008
Floating rate notes due 2009	$ —	$ 300
Floating rate notes due 2009	—	500
Zero coupon bonds and money multiplier notes, 13.0%–14.26%, due 2009	—	100
Floating rate notes due 2009–2011	—	193
7.50% notes due 2010	1,000	1,000
6.125% notes due 2011	500	500
5.625% notes due 2012	400	400
4.25% notes due 2013	600	600
3.875% notes due 2014	600	—
5.40% notes due 2016	400	400
5.30% notes due 2017	400	400
5.30% notes due 2018	900	900
5.00% notes due 2019	900	—
Industrial development bond obligations, floating rate maturing at various dates through 2037	47	60
6.625 % debentures due 2028	216	216
9.065% debentures due 2033	51	51
5.70% notes due 2036	550	550
5.70% notes due 2037	600	600
Other (including capitalized leases), 0.62%–15.5%, maturing at various dates through 2017	100	118
	7,264	6,888
Less—current portion	(1,018)	(1,023)
	$ 6,246	$ 5,865

In February 2009, the Company issued $600 million 3.875% Senior Notes due 2014 and $900 million 5.00% Senior Notes due 2019 (collectively, the "2009 Senior Notes"). The 2009 Senior Notes are senior unsecured and unsubordinated obligations of Honeywell and rank equally with all of Honeywell's existing and future senior unsecured debt and senior to all of Honeywell's subordinated debt. The offering resulted in gross proceeds of $1.5 billion, offset by $12 million in discount and issuance costs.

In the first quarter of 2009, the Company repaid $493 million of its floating rate notes. In the third quarter of 2009, the Company repaid $500 million of its floating rate notes and $100 million of its zero coupon bonds and money multiplier notes.

Capital Stock Proceeds/Payments

6.47

DIRECTV (DEC)

(Dollars in millions)	2009	2008	2007
Cash flows from financing activities			
Cash proceeds from debt issuance	$ 1,990	$2,490	$ —
Debt issuance costs	(14)	(19)	—
Repayment of long-term debt	(1,018)	(53)	(220)
Repayment of collar loan	(751)	—	—
Net increase in short-term borrowings	—	—	2
Repayment of other long-term obligations	(116)	(117)	(121)
Common shares repurchased and retired	(1,696)	(3,174)	(2,025)
Capital contribution	—	160	—
Stock options exercised	35	105	118
Taxes paid in lieu of shares issued for share-based compensation	(72)	—	—
Excess tax benefit from share-based compensation	5	8	7
Net cash used in financing activities	$(1,637)	$ (600)	$(2,239)

NOTES TO CONSOLIDATED FINANCIAL STATEMENTS

Note 13 (In Part): Stockholders' Equity

Share Repurchase Program

Since 2006 our Board of Directors has approved multiple authorizations for the repurchase of our common stock, the most recent of which was announced in February 2010, authorizing share repurchases of $3.5 billion. The authorizations allow us to repurchase our common stock from time to time through open market purchases and negotiated transactions, or otherwise. The timing, nature and amount of such transactions will depend on a variety of factors, including market conditions, and the program may be suspended, discontinued or accelerated at any time. The sources of funds for the purchases under the remaining authorizations are our existing cash on hand, cash from operations and potential additional borrowings. Purchases are made in the open market, through block trades and other negotiated transactions. Repurchased shares are retired but remain authorized for registration and issuance in the future.

The following table sets forth information regarding shares repurchased and retired for the years ended December 31:

(Amounts in millions, except per share amounts)	2009	2008	2007
Total cost of repurchased and retired shares	$1,696	$3,174	$2,025
Average price per share	23.79	24.12	23.48
Number of shares repurchased and retired	71	131	86

For the year ended December 31, 2009, we recorded the $1,696 million in repurchases as a decrease of $591 million to "Common stock and additional paid in capital" and an increase of $1,105 million to "Accumulated deficit" in the Consolidated Balance Sheets. For the year ended December 31, 2008, we recorded the $3,174 million in repurchases as a decrease of $1,089 million to "Common stock and additional paid in capital" and an increase of $2,085 million to "Accumulated deficit" in the Consolidated Balance Sheets. For the year ended December 31, 2007, we recorded the $2,025 million in repurchases as a decrease of $692 million to "Common stock and additional paid in capital" and an increase of $1,333 million to "Accumulated deficit" in the Consolidated Balance Sheets.

6.48

FREEPORT-MCMORAN COPPER & GOLD INC. (DEC)

(In millions)	2009	2008	2007
Cash flow from financing activities:			
Proceeds from term loans under bank credit facility	$ —	$ —	$ 12,450
Repayments of term loans under bank credit facility	—	—	(12,450)
Net proceeds from sales of senior notes	—	—	5,880
Net proceeds from sale of 6³/₄% mandatory convertible preferred stock	—	—	2,803
Net proceeds from sale of common stock	740	—	2,816
Proceeds from revolving credit facility and other debt	330	890	744
Repayments of revolving credit facility and other debt	(1,380)	(766)	(1,069)
Purchases of FCX common stock	—	(500)	—
Cash dividends and distributions paid:			
Common stock	—	(693)	(421)
Preferred stock	(229)	(255)	(175)
Noncontrolling interests	(535)	(730)	(967)
Contributions from noncontrolling interests	57	201	4
Net proceeds from (payments for) stock-based awards	6	22	(14)
Excess tax benefit from stock-based awards	3	25	16
Bank credit facilities fees and other, net	(4)	—	(262)
Net cash (used in) provided by financing activities	$(1,012)	$(1,806)	$ 9,355

NOTES TO CONSOLIDATED FINANCIAL STATEMENTS

Note 12 (In Part): Stockholders' Equity and Stock-Based Compensation

Common Stock (In Part)

In February 2009, FCX completed a public offering of 26.8 million shares of FCX common stock at an average price of $28.00 per share, which generated gross proceeds of $750 million (net proceeds of approximately $740 million).

Exercise of Stock Options and Related Tax Effect

6.49

GENERAL CABLE CORPORATION (DEC)

(In millions)	2009	2008	2007
Cash flows of financing activities:			
Preferred stock dividends paid	$ (0.3)	$ (0.3)	$ (0.3)
Settlement of net investment hedge	—	—	(30.5)
Excess tax benefits from stock-based compensation	0.7	6.1	11.1
Proceeds from revolving credit borrowings	96.5	124.7	100.0
Repayments of revolving credit borrowings	(96.5)	(184.7)	(40.0)
Proceeds (repayments) of other debt	(160.0)	93.3	7.3
Issuance of long-term debt	—	—	800.0
Payment of deferred financing fees	(14.5)	—	(19.0)
Settlement of long-term debt	—	—	(305.5)
Purchase of treasury shares	—	(11.7)	—
Proceeds from exercise of stock options	0.4	2.2	5.0
Net cash flows of financing activities	$(173.7)	$ 29.6	$ 528.1

NOTES TO CONSOLIDATED FINANCIAL STATEMENTS

14 (In Part): Share-Based Compensation

General Cable has various plans which provide for granting options and common stock to certain employees and independent directors of the Company and its subsidiaries. The Company recognizes compensation expense for share-based payments based on the fair value of the awards at the grant date. The table below summarizes compensation expense for the Company's non-qualified stock options, nonvested stock awards and performance-based nonvested stock awards based on the fair value method as estimated using the Black-Scholes valuation model for the years ended December 31, 2009, 2008 and 2007. The Company records compensation expense related to non-vested stock awards as a component of selling, general and administrative expense.

(In millions)	2009	2008	2007
Non-qualified stock option expense	$ 5.0	$ 4.8	$ 2.0
Non-vested stock awards expense	4.1	4.2	3.5
Stock unit awards	1.8	1.6	0.5
Performance-based non-vested stock awards expense	—	—	0.3
Total pre-tax share-based compensation expense	$10.9	$10.6	$ 6.3
Excess tax benefit on share-based compensation[1]	$ 0.7	$ 6.1	$11.1

[1] Cash inflows recognized as financing activities in the Company's consolidated statement of cash flows.

During the years ended December 31, 2009, 2008 and 2007, cash received from stock option exercises was $0.4 million, $2.2 million and $5.0 million, respectively. The total tax benefit to be realized for tax deductions from these option exercises was $0.8 million, $4.6 million and $7.4 million, respectively. The $3.8 million and $18.1 million tax deductions for all share-based compensation for the years ended December 31, 2009 and 2008, respectively, includes $0.7 million and $6.1 million of excess tax benefits that are classified as a financing cash flow and would have been classified as an operating cash inflow prior to the adoption of ASC 718. The

Company has elected the alternative method to calculate the pool of excess tax benefits available to absorb tax deficiencies recognized subsequent to the adoption of ASC 718.

Stock Options (In Part)

A summary of stock option activity for the year ended December 31, 2009, is as follows (options in thousands and aggregate intrinsic value in millions):

	Options Outstanding	Weighted Average Exercise Price	Weighted Average Remaining Contractual Term	Aggregate Intrinsic Value
Outstanding at December 31, 2008	806.8	$35.40	6.6 years	$ 2.6
Granted	480.0	19.59		
Exercised	(65.0)	6.64		
Forfeited or expired	(18.5)	41.58		
Outstanding at December 31, 2009	1,203.3	$30.55	7.2 years	$10.3
Exercisable at December 31, 2009	486.9	$27.45	5.1 years	$ 5.6
Options expected to vest in the next twelve months	337.0	$39.88	8.3 years	$ 1.6

Dividends Paid

6.50

WHOLE FOODS MARKET, INC. (SEP)

(In thousands)	2009	2008	2007
Cash flows from financing activities			
Common stock dividends paid	$ —	$(109,072)	$ (96,742)
Preferred stock dividends paid	(19,833)	—	—
Issuance of common stock	4,286	18,019	54,383
Purchase of treasury stock	—	—	(99,997)
Excess tax benefit related to exercise of team member stock options	42	5,686	12,839
Proceeds from issuance of redeemable preferred stock, net	413,052	—	—
Proceeds from long-term borrowings	123,000	317,000	717,000
Payments on long-term debt and capital lease obligations	(318,370)	(161,151)	(93,360)
Other financing activities	(2,722)	(652)	—
Net cash provided by financing activities	$199,455	$ 69,830	$494,123

NOTES TO CONSOLIDATED FINANCIAL STATEMENTS

12 (In Part): Redeemable Preferred Stock

On December 2, 2008, the Company issued 425,000 shares of Series A 8% Redeemable, Convertible Exchangeable Participating Preferred Stock, $0.01 par value per share ("Series A Preferred Stock") to affiliates of Leonard Green & Partners, L.P., for approximately $413.1 million, net of approximately $11.9 million in closing and issuance costs. On April 12, 2009, the Company amended and restated the Statement of Designations governing the Series A Preferred Stock. This amendment limited the participation feature, as described below, of the Series A 8% Redeemable, Convertible Exchangeable Preferred Stock and provided for the mandatory payment of cash dividends in respect to the Series A Preferred Stock. The amendment also restricted the Company's ability to pay cash dividends on its common stock without the prior written consent of the holders representing at least a majority of the shares of Series A Preferred Stock then outstanding.

The Series A Preferred Stock was classified as temporary shareholders' equity at September 27, 2009 since the shares were (i) redeemable at the option of the holder and (ii) had conditions for redemption which are not solely within the control of the Company. During fiscal year 2009, the Company paid cash dividends on the Series A Preferred Stock totaling approximately $19.8 million.

Debt Issuance Costs

6.51

SEALY CORPORATION (NOV)

(In thousands)	2009	2008	2007
Financing activities:			
Cash dividends	$ —	$ (6,811)	$ (27,389)
Proceeds from issuance of long-term obligations	6,280	9,305	—
Repayments of long-term obligations, including discounts taken of $460 in 2007	(18,285)	(44,455)	(79,202)
Repayment of senior term loans	(377,181)	—	—
Proceeds from issuance of new senior secured notes	335,916	—	—
Proceeds from issuance of related party notes	177,132	—	—
Repayment of related party notes	(83,284)	—	—
Proceeds from issuance of convertible notes, net	83,284	—	—
Repayment of subordinated notes, including discounts taken of $47	(4,953)	—	—
Borrowings under revolving credit facilities	141,158	283,527	233,990
Repayments under revolving credit facilities	(205,558)	(260,617)	(206,643)
Repurchase of common stock	—	—	(16,253)
Exercise of employee stock options, including related excess tax benefits	30	482	7,166
Debt issuance costs	(27,617)	(100)	—
Other	(428)	—	2,113
Net cash provided by (used in) financing activities	$ 26,494	$ (18,669)	$ (86,218)

NOTES TO CONSOLIDATED FINANCIAL STATEMENTS

Note 1 (In Part): Significant Accounting Policies

Debt Issuance Costs

The Company capitalizes costs associated with the issuance of debt and amortizes them as additional interest expense over the lives of the debt on a straight-line basis which approximates the effective interest method. Upon the prepayment of the related debt, the Company accelerates the recognition of an appropriate amount of the costs as interest expense. Additional interest expense arising from such prepayments during fiscal 2009, 2008 and 2007 was $0.1 million, $0.0 million and $0.1 million, respectively.

In connection with the refinancing of the Company's senior secured credit facilities in May 2009, the Company recorded fees in the amount of $27.6 million which were deferred and will be amortized over the life of the new agreements. Since the old senior secured term loans are considered terminated, the remaining unamortized debt issuance costs of $2.1 million were expensed and recognized as a component of refinancing and extinguishment of debt and interest rate derivatives in the Consolidated Statements of Operations. The remaining unamortized debt issuance costs associated with the old senior revolving credit facility will continue to be amortized over the life of the Company's new asset-based revolving credit facility as such credit facility met the criteria for modification treatment rather than extinguishment.

In connection with the Second Amendment to the Third Amended and Restated Credit Agreement entered into in November 2008, the Company paid fees to the creditor in the amount of $5.4 million, which were recorded as a component of refinancing and extinguishment of debt and interest rate derivatives in the Consolidated Statements of Operations. In accordance with the FASB's authoritative guidance surrounding a debtor's accounting for a modification or exchange of debt instruments, these costs were expensed as incurred. The Company also paid approximately $0.1 million of fees to third parties that were deferred and will be amortized over the life of the amended agreement. The Company has the following amounts recorded in debt issuance costs, net, and other assets (in thousands):

	2009	2008
Gross cost	$34,008	$11,035
Accumulated amortization	(4,783)	(2,395)
Net deferred debt issuance costs	$29,225	$ 8,640

Lease Obligation Payments

6.52

CAMERON INTERNATIONAL CORPORATION (DEC)

(Dollars in thousands)	2009	2008	2007
Cash flows from financing activities:			
Short-term loan borrowings (repayments), net	$ (18,908)	$ 31,859	$(200,707)
Redemption of convertible debt securities	(131,109)	(106,891)	—
Issuance of long-term senior notes	—	747,922	—
Debt issuance costs	—	(5,550)	—
Purchase of treasury stock	(29,175)	(279,393)	(321,913)
Proceeds from stock option exercises	10,193	17,628	52,784
Excess tax benefits from employee stock compensation plans transactions	6,446	16,986	28,034
Principal payments on capital leases	(6,737)	(7,434)	(5,312)
Net cash provided by (used for) financing activities	$(169,290)	$ 415,127	$(447,114)

NOTES TO CONSOLIDATED FINANCIAL STATEMENTS

Note 11. Leases

The Company leases certain facilities, office space, vehicles and office, data processing and other equipment under capital and operating leases. Rental expenses for the years ended December 31, 2009, 2008 and 2007 were $57,419,000, $49,582,000 and $42,709,000, respectively. Future minimum lease payments with respect to capital leases and operating leases with noncancelable terms in excess of one year were as follows:

(Dollars in thousands)	Capital Lease Payments	Operating Lease Payments
Year ended December 31:		
2010	$ 5,553	$ 32,140
2011	4,165	32,234
2012	2,407	20,716
2013	520	17,938
2014	16	20,842
Thereafter	—	36,260
Future minimum lease payments	12,661	160,130
Less: amount representing interest	(241)	—
Lease obligations at December 31, 2009	$12,420	$160,130

Financial Instrument Settlements

6.53

THE WARNACO GROUP, INC. (DEC)

(Dollars in thousands)	2009	2008	2007
Cash flows from financing activities:			
Payment of deferred financing costs	$ (515)	$ (3,934)	$ (480)
Repayments of senior note due 2013	—	(46,185)	—
Repayments of Term B note	—	(107,300)	(61,800)
Proceeds from the exercise of employee stock options	4,034	28,496	16,149
Purchase of treasury stock	(1,498)	(20,532)	(57,691)
Premium on cancellation of interest rate swaps	2,218	—	—
Increase (decrease) in short-term notes payable	(23,985)	16,593	(17,493)
Borrowings (repayments) under revolving credit facility	(11,805)	12,000	—
Payment of dividend to non-controlling interest	(4,018)	—	—
Cost to purchase non-controlling interest in an equity transaction	(5,339)	—	—
Other	—	170	(373)
Net cash (used in) financing activities from continuing operations	(40,908)	(120,692)	(121,688)
Net cash (used in) financing activities from discontinued operations	—	—	—
Net cash (used in) financing activities	$(40,908)	$(120,692)	$(121,688)

NOTES TO CONSOLIDATED FINANCIAL STATEMENTS
(Dollars in thousands)

Note 12 (In Part): Debt

Interest Rate Swap Agreements

The Company entered into interest rate swap agreements on September 18, 2003 (the "2003 Swap Agreement") and November 5, 2004 (the "2004 Swap Agreement") with respect to the Senior Notes for a total notional amount of $75 million. In June 2009, the 2004 Swap Agreement was called by the issuer and the Company received a debt premium of $740. On July 15, 2009, the 2003 Swap Agreement was called by the issuer and the Company received a debt premium of $1,479. Both debt premiums are being amortized as reductions to interest expense through June 15, 2013 (the date on which the Senior Notes mature). During Fiscal 2009, $273 was amortized. The 2003 Swap Agreement and the 2004

Swap Agreement provided that the Company would receive interest at 8 7 / 8 % and pay variable rates of interest based upon six month LIBOR plus 4.11% and 4.34%, respectively. As a result of the 2003 Swap Agreement, the 2004 Swap Agreement and the amortization of the debt premiums, the weighted average effective interest rate of the Senior Notes was 8.53% as of January 2, 2010 and 7.77% as of January 3, 2009.

The fair values of the Company's interest rate swap agreements reflect the termination premium or termination discount that the Company would have realized if such swaps had been terminated on the valuation dates. Since the provisions of the Company's 2003 Swap Agreement and 2004 Swap Agreement matched the provisions of the Company's outstanding Senior Notes (the "Hedged Debt"), changes in the fair values of the swaps did not have any effect on the Company's results of operations but were recorded in the Company's Consolidated Balance Sheets. Unrealized gains on the interest rate swap agreements were included in other assets with a corresponding increase in the Hedged Debt. Unrealized losses on the interest rate swap agreements were included as a component of long-term debt with a corresponding decrease in the Hedged Debt.

As of January 2, 2010, the Company had no outstanding interest rate swap agreements. The table below summarizes the unrealized gain of the Company's swap agreements at January 3, 2009:

	2009
Unrealized gain:	
2003 swap agreement	$1,972
2004 swap agreement	932
Net unrealized gain	$2,904

Acquisition of Noncontrolling Interest

6.54

ZIMMER HOLDINGS, INC. (DEC)

(In millions)	2009	2008	2007
Cash flows provided by (used in) financing activities:			
Net proceeds (payments) under revolving credit facility	$(330.0)	$ 330.0	$ —
Debt issuance costs	(8.5)	—	—
Proceeds from employee stock compensation plans	9.5	57.0	149.8
Excess income tax benefit from stock option exercises	0.4	6.5	27.0
Repurchase of common stock	(923.7)	(737.0)	(576.3)
Proceeds from issuance of notes	998.8	—	—
Acquisition of noncontrolling interest	(8.6)	—	—
Net cash used in financing activities	$(262.1)	$(343.5)	$(399.5)

NOTES TO CONSOLIDATED FINANCIAL STATEMENTS

Note 2 (In Part): Significant Accounting Policies

Noncontrolling Interest

On January 1, 2009, we adopted the FASB's newly issued guidance related to noncontrolling interests. This new guidance changes the accounting and reporting for minority interests, which are now recharacterized as noncontrolling interests and classified as a component of equity. This new guidance requires retroactive adoption of the presentation and disclosure requirements for existing noncontrolling interests. This adoption did not have a material impact on our consolidated financial statements or results of operations. During the year ended December 31, 2009, we acquired 100 percent ownership of our only outstanding noncontrolling interest for approximately $8.6 million. This purchase was recorded as an equity transaction and is reflected as a financing activity in our consolidated statement of cash flows. As a result, the carrying balance of the noncontrolling interests of $3.6 million was eliminated, and the remaining $5.0 million, representing the difference between the purchase price and carrying balance, was recorded as a reduction in paid-in capital. Transactions with noncontrolling interests had the following effect on equity attributable to Zimmer Holdings, Inc. (in millions):

	2009	2008
Net earnings of Zimmer Holdings, Inc.	$717.4	$848.6
Transfers to noncontrolling interests:		
Decrease in equity related to the purchase of noncontrolling interests	(5.0)	—
Change from net earnings of Zimmer Holdings, Inc. and transfers to noncontrolling interests	$712.4	$848.6

FOREIGN CURRENCY CASH FLOWS

6.55   FASB ASC 830-230, *Foreign Currency Matters— Statement of Cash Flows*, specifies the effect of exchange rate changes on cash balances held in foreign currencies be reported as a separate part of the Statement of Cash Flows. Examples of reporting foreign currency cash flows follow.

6.56

AVIS BUDGET GROUP, INC. (DEC)

(In millions)	2009	2008	2007
Operating activities			
Net loss	$ (47)	$(1,124)	$ (916)
Adjustments to arrive at loss from continuing operations	—	—	(31)
Loss from continuing operations	(47)	(1,124)	(947)
Adjustments to reconcile loss from continuing operations to net cash provided by operating activities exclusive of vehicle programs:			
Non-vehicle related depreciation and amortization	96	88	84
Deferred income taxes	(60)	(241)	(57)
Impairment	33	1,262	1,195
Net change in assets and liabilities, excluding the impact of acquisitions and dispositions:			
Receivables	52	50	(6)
Income taxes	10	7	38
Accounts payable and other current liabilities	(19)	(40)	(120)
Other, net	35	63	(38)
Net cash provided by operating activities exclusive of vehicle programs	100	65	149
Vehicle programs:			
Vehicle depreciation	1,391	1,639	1,565
	1,391	1,639	1,565
Net cash provided by operating activities	1,491	1,704	1,714
Investing activities			
Property and equipment additions	(39)	(83)	(94)
Proceeds received on asset sales	14	17	19
Payments received from (made to) Realogy and Wyndham, net	2	(3)	(108)
Net assets acquired (net of cash acquired) and acquisition-related payments	—	(88)	(11)
Proceeds from sale of investment	—	—	106
Purchase of equity investment	—	—	(60)
Other, net	(2)	(14)	(13)
Net cash used in investing activities exclusive of vehicle programs	(25)	(171)	(161)
Vehicle programs:			
Decrease (increase) in program cash	(145)	(11)	13
Investment in vehicles	(6,775)	(8,608)	(10,633)
Proceeds received on disposition of vehicles	7,144	6,722	8,864
Other, net	(33)	(28)	—
	191	(1,925)	(1,756)
Net cash provided by (used in) investing activities	166	(2,096)	(1,917)
Financing activities			
Proceeds from borrowings	445	—	—
Principal payments on borrowings	(111)	(10)	(45)
Proceeds from warrant issuance	62	—	—
Purchase of call options	(95)	—	—
Repurchases of common stock	—	(33)	—
Issuances of common stock	—	—	50
Other, net	(13)	(28)	(1)
Net cash provided by (used in) financing activities exclusive of vehicle programs	288	(71)	4
Vehicle programs:			
Proceeds from borrowings	7,527	8,476	10,565
Principal payments on borrowings	(9,147)	(8,060)	(10,236)
Net change in short-term borrowings	(107)	152	(86)
Other, net	(26)	(34)	(8)
	(1,753)	534	235
Net cash provided by (used in) financing activities	(1,465)	463	239
Effect of changes in exchange rates on cash and cash equivalents	32	(27)	6
Net increase in cash and cash equivalents	224	44	42
Cash and cash equivalents, beginning of period	258	214	172
Cash and cash equivalents, end of period	$ 482	$ 258	$ 214
Supplemental disclosure			
Interest payments	$ 461	$ 468	$ 461
Income tax payments (refunds), net	$ 20	$ 15	$ (26)

6.57

NEWS CORPORATION (JUN)

(In millions)	2009	2008	2007
Operating activities:			
Net (loss) income	$(3,378)	$ 5,387	$ 3,426
Adjustments to reconcile net (loss) income to cash provided by operating activities:			
Depreciation and amortization	1,138	1,207	879
Amortization of cable distribution investments	88	80	77
Equity losses (earnings) of affiliates	309	(327)	(1,019)
Cash distributions received from affiliates	298	350	255
Impairment charges (net of tax of $1.7 billion)	7,189	—	—
Other, net	(1,256)	(2,293)	(359)
Minority interest in subsidiaries, net of tax	68	131	66
Change in operating assets and liabilities, net of acquisitions:			
Receivables and other assets	194	(923)	(169)
Inventories, net	(485)	(587)	(360)
Accounts payable and other liabilities	(1,917)	900	1,314
Net cash provided by operating activities	2,248	3,925	4,110
Investing activities:			
Property, plant and equipment, net of acquisitions	(1,101)	(1,443)	(1,308)
Acquisitions, net of cash acquired	(847)	(5,567)	(1,059)
Investments in equity affiliates	(403)	(799)	(121)
Other investments	(76)	(125)	(328)
Proceeds from sale of investments, other non-current assets and business disposals	1,762	1,580	740
Net cash used in investing activities	(665)	(6,354)	(2,076)
Financing activities:			
Borrowings	1,040	1,292	1,196
Repayment of borrowings	(343)	(728)	(198)
Issuance of shares	4	90	392
Repurchase of shares	—	(939)	(1,294)
Dividends paid	(366)	(373)	(369)
Other, net	18	22	—
Net cash provided by (used in) financing activities	353	(636)	(273)
Net increase (decrease) in cash and cash equivalents	1,936	(3,065)	1,761
Cash and cash equivalents, beginning of year	4,662	7,654	5,783
Exchange movement of opening cash balance	(58)	73	110
Cash and cash equivalents, end of year	$ 6,540	$ 4,662	$ 7,654

NONCASH ACTIVITIES

6.58   FASB ASC 230, *Statement of Cash Flows*, requires the disclosure of information about noncash investing and financing activities. Examples of the disclosure of noncash activities follow.

6.59

BALDOR ELECTRIC COMPANY (DEC)

(In thousands)	2009	2008	2007
Net increase (decrease) in cash and cash equivalents	$ 2,172	$(24,659)	$25,020
Beginning cash and cash equivalents	13,098	37,757	12,737
Ending cash and cash equivalents	$15,270	$ 13,098	$37,757

Noncash items:

- Additional paid-in capital resulting from shares traded for option exercises and taxes amounted to $1,566, $1,411, and $3,040 in 2009, 2008, and 2007, respectively.
- Common stock valued at $50,932 was issued January 31, 2007, in conjunction with the acquisition of Reliance Electric (see NOTE B).
- Treasury shares amounting to $3,487 and $3,284 were issued in March 2009 and 2008 to fund the 2008 and 2007 accrued profit sharing contributions, respectively.

NOTES TO CONSOLIDATED FINANCIAL STATEMENTS

Note B (In Part): Acquisitions

On January 31, 2007, Baldor acquired all of the equity of Reliance Electric from Rockwell and certain of its affiliates. Reliance was a leading manufacturer of industrial electric motors and other mechancial power transmission products. The acquisition extended Baldor's product offerings, provided a manufacturing base in China for the Asian markets, increased the Company's manufacturing capabilities and flexibility, strengthened the management team, and provided strong opportunities for synergies and cost savings. The purchase price was $1.83 billion, consisting of $1.78 billion in cash and 1.58 million shares of Baldor common stock valued at $50.93 million, based on the average closing price per share of Baldor's common stock on the New York Stock Exchange for the three days preceding and the three days subsequent to November 6, 2006, the date of the definitive purchase agreement. The cash portion of the purchase price was funded with proceeds from the issuance of 10,294,118 shares of Baldor common stock at a price of $34.00 per common share, proceeds from the issuance of $550.0 million of 8.625% senior notes due 2017, and borrowings of $1.00 billion under a new $1.20 billion senior secured credit facility. In conjunction with an over-allotment option in the common stock offering, 1,430,882 additional common shares were issued at a price of $34.00 per share. Proceeds from the over-allotment offering of approximately $46.5 million were utilized to reduce borrowings under the senior secured credit facility. Reliance's results of operations are included in the consolidated financial statements beginning February 1, 2007.

6.60

H.J. HEINZ COMPANY (APR)

NOTES TO CONSOLIDATED FINANCIAL STATEMENTS

4 (In Part): Acquisitions

During the second quarter of Fiscal 2009, the Company acquired Bénédicta, a sauce business in France for approximately $116 million. During the third quarter of Fiscal 2009, the Company acquired Golden Circle Limited, a fruit and juice business in Australia for approximately $211 million, including the assumption of $68 million of debt that was immediately refinanced by the Company. Additionally, the Company acquired La Bonne Cuisine, a chilled dip business in New Zealand for approximately $28 million in the third quarter of Fiscal 2009. During the fourth quarter of Fiscal 2009, the Company acquired Papillon, a South African producer of chilled products for approximately $6 million. The Company also made payments during Fiscal 2009 related to acquisitions completed in prior fiscal years, none of which were significant.

8. Supplemental Cash Flows Information

(Dollars in thousands)	2009	2008	2007
Cash paid during the year for:			
Interest	$310,047	$360,698	$268,781
Income taxes	$203,298	$261,283	$283,431
Details of acquisitions:			
Fair value of assets	$478,440	$165,093	$108,438
Liabilities[*]	181,093	13,489	19,442
Cash paid	297,347	151,604	88,996
Less cash acquired	3,449	—	—
Net cash paid for acquisitions	$293,898	$151,604	$ 88,996

[*] Includes obligations to sellers of $11.5 million and $2.0 million in 2008 and 2007, respectively.

A capital lease obligation of $51.0 million was incurred when the Company entered into a lease for equipment during the first quarter of Fiscal 2007. This equipment was previously under an operating lease. This non-cash transaction has been excluded from the consolidated statement of cash flows for the year ended May 2, 2007.

6.61

PFIZER INC. (DEC)

(Millions of dollars)	2009	2008	2007
Net (decrease)/ increase in cash and cash equivalents	$ (144)	$(1,284)	$1,579
Cash and cash equivalents at beginning of year	2,122	3,406	1,827
Cash and cash equivalents at end of year	$ 1,978	$ 2,122	$3,406
Supplemental cash flow information Non-cash transactions:			
Acquisition of Wyeth, treasury stock issued	$23,303	$ —	$ —
Cash paid during the period for:			
Income taxes	$ 2,300	$ 2,252	$5,617
Interest	935	782	643

NOTES TO CONSOLIDATED FINANCIAL STATEMENTS

2 (In Part): Acquisition of Wyeth

A (In Part): Description of the Transaction

On October 15, 2009 (the acquisition date), we acquired all of the outstanding equity of Wyeth in a cash-and-stock transaction, valued at approximately $68 billion, in which each share of Wyeth common stock outstanding, with certain limited exceptions, was canceled and converted into the right to receive $33.00 in cash without interest and 0.985 of a share of Pfizer common stock. The stock component was valued at $17.40 per share of Wyeth common stock based on the closing market price of Pfizer's common stock on the acquisition date, resulting in a total merger consideration value of $50.40 per share of Wyeth common stock. While Wyeth now is a wholly owned subsidiary of Pfizer, the merger of local Pfizer and Wyeth entities may be pending or delayed in various jurisdictions and integration in these jurisdictions is subject to completion of various local legal and regulatory obligations.

B. Fair Value of Consideration Transferred

The table below details the consideration transferred to acquire Wyeth:

(In millions, except per share amounts)	Conversion Calculation	Fair Value	Form of Consideration
Wyeth common stock outstanding as of the acquisition date	1,339.6		
Multiplied by Pfizer's stock price as of the acquisition date multiplied by the exchange ratio of 0.985 ($17.66 (a) × 0.985)	$ 17.40	$23,303	Pfizer common stock[a],[b]
Wyeth common stock outstanding as of the acquisition date	1,339.6		
Multiplied by cash consideration per common share outstanding	$ 33.00	44,208	Cash
Wyeth stock options canceled for a cash payment[c]		405	Cash
Wyeth restricted stock/restricted stock units and other equity-based awards canceled for a cash payment		320	Cash
Total fair value of consideration transferred		$68,236	

[a] The fair value of Pfizer's common stock used in the conversion calculation represents the closing market price of Pfizer's common stock on the acquisition date.

[b] Approximately 1.3 billion shares of Pfizer common stock, previously held as Pfizer treasury stock, were issued to former Wyeth shareholders. The excess of the average cost of Pfizer treasury stock issued over the fair value of the stock portion of the consideration transferred to acquire Wyeth was recorded as a reduction to *Retained earnings*.

[c] Each Wyeth stock option, whether or not vested and exercisable on the acquisition date, was canceled for a cash payment equal to the excess of the per share value of the merger consideration (calculated on the basis of the volume-weighted average of the per share price of Pfizer common stock on the New York Stock Exchange Transaction Reporting System for the five consecutive trading days ending two days prior to the acquisition date) over the per share exercise price of the Wyeth stock option.

CASH AND CASH EQUIVALENTS

6.62 A Statement of Cash Flows explains the change during a period in cash and cash equivalents. The amount of cash and cash equivalents reported on a Statement of Cash Flows should agree with the amount of cash and cash equivalents reported on a Statement of Financial Position. FASB ASC 230, *Statement of Cash Flows*, requires that an entity disclose what items are treated as cash equivalents. Table 6-5 shows the descriptive terms used by the survey entities to describe a change in cash and cash equivalents. Examples of cash and cash equivalents disclosure follow.

6.63

TABLE 6-5: DESCRIPTIVE TERM USED TO DESCRIBE CASH AND CASH EQUIVALENTS

	2009	2008	2007	2006
Cash and cash equivalents..................	438	441	526	527
Cash and equivalents...........................	35	34	43	42
Cash..	19	15	21	19
Cash and short-term cash investments......................	5	5	5	6
Cash and short-term investments........	1	3	4	5
Cash and temporary investments........	1	1	1	1
Other descriptive captions..................	1	1	—	—
Total Entities.....................................	**500**	**500**	**600**	**600**

2008–2009 based on 500 entities surveyed; 2006–2007 based on 600 entities surveyed.

6.64

AIRGAS, INC. (MAR)

Consolidated Balance Sheets

(In thousands)	2009	2008
Current assets		
Cash	$ 47,188	$ 43,048
Trade receivables, less allowances for doubtful accounts of $27,572 in 2009 and $22,624 in 2008	184,739	183,569
Inventories, net	390,445	330,732
Deferred income tax asset, net	34,760	22,258
Prepaid expenses and other current assets	60,838	67,110
Total current assets	$717,970	$646,717

Consolidated Statements of Cash Flows

(In thousands)	2009	2008	2007
Change in cash	$ 4,140	$17,117	$(9,054)
Cash—beginning of year	43,048	25,931	34,985
Cash—end of year	$47,188	$43,048	$25,931

NOTES TO CONSOLIDATED FINANCIAL STATEMENTS

1 (In Part): Summary of Significant Accounting Policies

d. Cash and Cash Overdraft

On a daily basis, all available funds are swept from depository accounts into a concentration account and used to repay debt under the Company's revolving credit facilities. Cash principally represents the balance of customer checks that have not yet cleared through the banking system and become available to be swept into the concentration account, and deposits made subsequent to the daily cash sweep. The Company does not fund its disbursement accounts for checks it has written until the checks are presented to the bank for payment. Cash overdrafts represent the balance of outstanding checks and are classified with other current liabilities. There are no compensating balance requirements or other restrictions on the transfer of cash associated with the Company's depository accounts.

6.65

EMERSON ELECTRIC CO. (SEP)

Consolidated Balance Sheets

(Dollars in millions)	2008	2009
Current assets		
Cash and equivalents	$1,777	$1,560
Receivables, less allowances of $90 in 2008 and $93 in 2009	4,618	3,623
Inventories:		
Finished products	884	697
Raw materials and work in process	1,464	1,158
Total inventories	2,348	1,855
Other current assets	588	615
Total current assets	$9,331	$7,653

Consolidated Statements of Cash Flows

(Dollars in millions)	2007	2008	2009
Increase (decrease) in cash and equivalents	$ 198	$ 769	$ (217)
Beginning cash and equivalents	810	1,008	1,777
Ending cash and equivalents	$1,008	$1,777	$1,560

NOTES TO CONSOLIDATED FINANCIAL STATEMENTS

1 (In Part): Summary of Significant Accounting Policies

Cash Equivalents

Cash equivalents consist of highly liquid investments with original maturities of three months or less.

6.66

RPM INTERNATIONAL INC. (MAY)

Consolidated Balance Sheets

(In thousands)	2009	2008
Current assets		
Cash and cash equivalents	$ 253,387	$ 231,251
Trade accounts receivable (less allowances of $22,934 in 2009 and $24,554 in 2008)	638,659	817,241
Inventories	406,175	476,149
Deferred income taxes	44,540	37,644
Prepaid expenses and other current assets	210,155	221,690
Total current assets	$1,552,916	$1,783,975

Consolidated Statements of Cash Flows

(In thousands)	2009	2008	2007
Net change in cash and cash equivalents	$ 22,136	$ 72,235	$ 50,400
Cash and cash equivalents at beginning of year	231,251	159,016	108,616
Cash and cash equivalents at end of year	$253,387	$231,251	$159,016

NOTES TO CONSOLIDATED FINANCIAL STATEMENTS

Note A (In Part): Summary of Significant Accounting Policies

6. Cash and Cash Equivalents

For purposes of the statement of cash flows, we consider all highly liquid debt instruments purchased with a maturity of three months or less to be cash equivalents. We do not believe we are exposed to any significant credit risk on cash and cash equivalents. The carrying amounts of cash and cash equivalents approximate fair value.

Section 7: Independent Auditors' Report

PRESENTATION IN ANNUAL REPORT

7.01 This section reviews the format and content of Independent Auditors' Reports appearing in the annual reports of the 500 survey entities. Codification of Statements on Auditing Standards (AU) section 508, *Reports on Audited Financial Statements*, and its amendments, applies to auditors' reports issued in connection with audits of historical financial statements that are intended to present financial position, results of operations, and cash flows in conformity with generally accepted accounting principles.

7.02 Commencing with auditors' reports issued or reissued on or after May 24, 2004, the format and content of independent auditors' reports appearing in the annual reports of public entities are determined by the auditing standards set by the Public Company Accounting Oversight Board (PCAOB). The Sarbanes-Oxley Act of 2002 established the PCAOB. The PCAOB is appointed by the Securities and Exchange Commission (SEC), and provides oversight for auditors of public entities. Section 103(a) of the Sarbanes-Oxley Act authorized the PCAOB to establish auditing and related professional practice standards to be used by public accounting firms registered with the PCAOB. PCAOB Rule 3100, *Compliance With Auditing and Related Professional Practice Standards*, requires auditors to comply with all applicable auditing and related professional practice standards of the PCAOB. On an initial, transitional basis, the PCAOB adopted, as interim standards, the generally accepted auditing standards described in the American Institute of Certified Public Accountants' (AICPA) AU section 150, *Generally Accepted Auditing Standards*, in existence on April 16, 2003, to the extent not superseded or amended by the PCAOB.

7.03 Table 7-1 shows where, in relation to the financial statements and notes thereto, the Independent Auditors' Reports were presented in the annual reports to stockholders.

7.04

TABLE 7-1: PRESENTATION OF INDEPENDENT AUDITORS' REPORT IN ANNUAL REPORT

	2009	2008	2007	2006
Precedes financial statements and notes	377	368	443	420
Follows financial statements and notes	123	132	157	179
Between financial statements and notes	—	—	—	1
Total Entities	**500**	**500**	**600**	**600**

2008–2009 based on 500 entities surveyed; 2006–2007 based on 600 entities surveyed.

TITLE

7.05 Paragraph 8a of *AU section 508* states that the title of an auditors' report should include the word *independent*. For all but four of the entities surveyed, the auditors' report is entitled "*Report of Independent Registered Public Accounting Firm.*"

ADDRESSEE

7.06 Paragraph 9 of *AU section 508* states:

> The report may be addressed to the Company whose financial statements are being audited or to its board of directors or stockholders. A report on the financial statements of an unincorporated entity should be addressed as circumstances dictate, for example, to the partners, to the general partner, or to the proprietor. Occasionally, an auditor is retained to audit the financial statements of a Company that is not his client; in such a case, the report is customarily addressed to the client and not to the directors or stockholders of the Company whose financial statements are being audited.

7.07 Table 7-2 summarizes the addressee mentioned in the auditors' reports of the survey entities.

7.08

TABLE 7-2: ADDRESSEE OF AUDITORS' REPORTS

	2009	2008	2007	2006
Board of Directors and Stockholders	488	484	576	572
Board of Directors	4	8	12	17
Stockholders	5	5	7	7
Company	2	2	4	3
Other or no addressee	1	1	1	1
Total Entities	**500**	**500**	**600**	**600**

2008–2009 based on 500 entities surveyed; 2006–2007 based on 600 entities surveyed.

AUDITORS' STANDARD REPORT

7.09   Paragraph 8 of *AU section 508* presents examples of auditors' standard reports for single-year financial statements and for comparative two-year financial statements. The examples presented in Paragraph 8 of *AU section 508*, as amended, follow:

INDEPENDENT AUDITORS' REPORT

We have audited the accompanying balance sheet of X Company as of December 31, 20XX, and the related statements of income, retained earnings, and cash flows for the year then ended. These financial statements are the responsibility of the Company's management. Our responsibility is to express an opinion on these financial statements based on our audit.

We conducted our audit in accordance with auditing standards generally accepted in the United States of America. Those standards require that we plan and perform the audit to obtain reasonable assurance about whether the financial statements are free of material misstatement. An audit includes examining, on a test basis, evidence supporting the amounts and disclosures in the financial statements. An audit also includes assessing the accounting principles used and significant estimates made by management, as well as evaluating the overall financial statement presentation. We believe that our audit provides a reasonable basis for our opinion.

In our opinion, the financial statements referred to above present fairly, in all material respects, the financial position of X Company as of [at] December 31, 20XX, and the results of its operations and its cash flows for the year then ended in conformity with accounting principles generally accepted in the United States of America.

INDEPENDENT AUDITORS' REPORT

We have audited the accompanying balance sheet of X Company as of December 31, 20X2 and 20X1, and the related statements of income, retained earnings, and cash flows for the years then ended. These financial statements are the responsibility of the Company's management. Our responsibility is to express an opinion on these financial statements based on our audits.

We conducted our audits in accordance with auditing standards generally accepted in the United States of America. Those standards require that we plan and perform the audit to obtain reasonable assurance about whether the financial statements are free of material misstatement. An audit includes examining, on a test basis, evidence supporting the amounts and disclosures in the financial statements. An audit also includes assessing the accounting principles used and significant estimates made by management, as well as evaluating the overall financial statement presentation. We believe that our audits provide a reasonable basis for our opinion.

In our opinion, the financial statements referred to above present fairly, in all material respects, the financial position of X Company as of [at] December 31, 20X2 and 20X1, and the results of its operations and

its cash flows for the years then ended in conformity with accounting principles generally accepted in the United States of America.

7.10   Most of the survey entities present a balance sheet for 2 years and the other basic financial statements for 3 years. Appropriate wording in this situation is stated in footnote 8 to paragraph 8 of *AU section 508*.

7.11   As permitted by FASB ASC 220, *Comprehensive Income*, 92 survey entities reported components of comprehensive income in either a separate financial statement or a combined statement of income and comprehensive income. Alternatively, FASB ASC 220 allows components of comprehensive income to be reported in a statement of stockholders' equity. Although an entity may include the term "comprehensive income" in the title of the statement in which it is presented, FASB ASC 220 does not require the use of the term in an entity's financial statements. FASB ASC 220 acknowledges the use of equivalent terms. Standard auditors' reports for each situation follow.

Statement of Comprehensive Income

7.12

REPORT OF INDEPENDENT REGISTERED PUBLIC ACCOUNTING FIRM

The Board of Directors
Texas Instruments Incorporated

We have audited the accompanying consolidated balance sheets of Texas Instruments Incorporated and subsidiaries (the Company) as of December 31, 2009 and 2008, and the related consolidated statements of income, comprehensive income, stockholders' equity, and cash flows for each of the three years in the period ended December 31, 2009. These financial statements are the responsibility of the Company's management. Our responsibility is to express an opinion on these financial statements based on our audits.

We conducted our audits in accordance with the standards of the Public Company Accounting Oversight Board (United States). Those standards require that we plan and perform the audit to obtain reasonable assurance about whether the financial statements are free of material misstatement. An audit includes examining, on a test basis, evidence supporting the amounts and disclosures in the financial statements. An audit also includes assessing the accounting principles used and significant estimates made by management, as well as evaluating the overall financial statement presentation. We believe that our audits provide a reasonable basis for our opinion.

In our opinion, the financial statements referred to above present fairly, in all material respects, the consolidated financial position of Texas Instruments Incorporated and subsidiaries at December 31, 2009 and 2008, and the consolidated results of their operations and their cash flows for each of the three years in the period ended December 31, 2009, in conformity with U.S. generally accepted accounting principles.

We also have audited, in accordance with the standards of the Public Company Accounting Oversight Board (United

States), the Company's internal control over financial reporting as of December 31, 2009, based on criteria established in Internal Control—Integrated Framework issued by the Committee of Sponsoring Organizations of the Treadway Commission and our report dated February 23, 2010 expressed an unqualified opinion thereon.

Statement of Operations and Comprehensive Income

7.13

REPORT OF INDEPENDENT REGISTERED PUBLIC ACCOUNTING FIRM

Board of Directors and Shareholders
The Standard Register Company

We have audited the accompanying consolidated balance sheet of The Standard Register Company and subsidiaries as of January 3, 2010 and December 28, 2008, and the related consolidated statements of income and comprehensive income, cash flows, and shareholders' equity for each of the three years in the period ended January 3, 2010. These financial statements are the responsibility of the Company's management. Our responsibility is to express an opinion on these financial statements based on our audits.

We conducted our audits in accordance with the standards of the Public Company Accounting Oversight Board (United States). Those standards require that we plan and perform the audit to obtain reasonable assurance about whether the financial statements are free of material misstatement. An audit includes examining, on a test basis, evidence supporting the amounts and disclosures in the financial statements. An audit also includes assessing the accounting principles used and significant estimates made by management, as well as evaluating the overall financial statement presentation. We believe that our audits provide a reasonable basis for our opinion.

In our opinion, the consolidated financial statements referred to above present fairly, in all material respects, the financial position of The Standard Register Company and subsidiaries as of January 3, 2010 and December 28, 2008, and the results of their operations and their cash flows for each of the three years in the period ended January 3, 2010, in conformity with accounting principles generally accepted in the United States of America.

We have also audited, in accordance with the standards of the Public Company Accounting Oversight Board (United States), The Standard Register Company and subsidiaries' internal control over financial reporting as of January 3, 2010, based on criteria established in *Internal Control—Integrated Framework* issued by the Committee of Sponsoring Organizations of the Treadway Commission, and our report dated March 11, 2010 expressed an unqualified opinion on the effectiveness of The Standard Register Company and subsidiaries' internal control over financial reporting.

Statement of Changes in Shareholders' Equity

7.14

REPORT OF INDEPENDENT REGISTERED PUBLIC ACCOUNTING FIRM

To the Board of Directors and Shareholders
CSP Inc.

We have audited the accompanying consolidated balance sheets of CSP Inc. and Subsidiaries as of September 30, 2009 and 2008, and the related consolidated statements of operations, shareholders' equity and comprehensive income (loss), and cash flows for the years then ended. These financial statements are the responsibility of the Company's management. Our responsibility is to express an opinion on these financial statements based on our audits.

We conducted our audits in accordance with the standards of the Public Company Accounting Oversight Board (United States). Those standards require that we plan and perform the audit to obtain reasonable assurance about whether the financial statements are free of material misstatement. An audit includes examining, on a test basis, evidence supporting the amounts and disclosures in the financial statements. An audit also includes assessing the accounting principles used and significant estimates made by management, as well as evaluating the overall financial statement presentation. We believe that our audits provide a reasonable basis for our opinion.

In our opinion, the consolidated financial statements referred to above present fairly, in all material respects, the financial position of CSP Inc. and Subsidiaries as of September 30, 2009 and 2008, and the results of their operations and their cash flows for the years then ended in conformity with U.S. generally accepted accounting principles.

We were not engaged to examine management's assessment of the effectiveness of CSP Inc. and Subsidiaries' internal control over financial reporting as of September 30, 2009, included in the accompanying Management's Report on Internal Control Over Financial Reporting in Item 9A(T), and, accordingly, we do not express an opinion thereon.

AUDITORS' STANDARD REPORT OF A PUBLIC COMPANY

7.15 For audits of public entities (i.e., issuers as defined by the Sarbanes-Oxley Act of 2002, and other entities when prescribed by the rules of the SEC), PCAOB Auditing Standard (AS) No. 1, *References in Auditors' Reports to the Standards of the Public Company Accounting Oversight Board*, directs auditors to state that the engagement was conducted in accordance with "the standards of the Public Company Accounting Oversight Board (United States)" whenever the auditor has performed the engagement in accordance with the PCAOB's standards. *AS No. 1* is effective for auditors' reports issued or reissued after May 24, 2004. In addition, the PCAOB adopted as interim standards the generally accepted auditing standards of the AICPA as they existed on April 16, 2003. Consequently, reference to "the standards of the Public Company Accounting Oversight Board" with respect to audits performed prior to the effective date of this standard is equivalent to the previously required reference to generally accepted auditing standards. Accordingly, upon adoption of *AS No. 1*, reference to "generally accepted auditing standards" is no longer appropriate or necessary.

7.16   An example of a standard independent registered auditor's report presented in the Appendix to *AS No. 1* follows.

REPORT OF INDEPENDENT REGISTERED PUBLIC ACCOUNTING FIRM

We have audited the accompanying balance sheets of X Company as of December 31, 20X3 and 20X2, and related statements of operations, stockholders' equity, and cash flows for each of the three years in the period ended December 31, 20X3. These financial statements are the responsibility of the Company's management. Our responsibility is to express an opinion on these financial statements based on our audits.

We conducted our audits in accordance with the standards of the Public Company Accounting Oversight Board (United States). Those standards require that we plan and perform the audit to obtain reasonable assurance about whether the financial statements are free of material misstatement. An audit includes examining, on a test basis, evidence supporting the amounts and disclosures in the financial statements. An audit also includes assessing the accounting principles used and significant estimates made by management, as well as evaluating the overall financial statement presentation. We believe that our audits provide a reasonable basis for our opinion.

In our opinion, the financial statements referred to above present fairly, in all material respects, the financial position of the company as of December 31, 20X3 and 20X2, and the results of its operations and its cash flows for each of the three years in the period ended December 31, 20X3, in conformity with U.S. generally accepted accounting principles.

REFERENCE TO REPORT OF OTHER AUDITORS

7.17   When the opinion of a principal auditor is based in part on the report of another auditor, AU section 543, *Part of Audit Performed by Other Independent Auditors*, as amended, provides guidance to the principal auditor. Paragraph 7 of *AU section 543* states:

> When the principal auditor decides that he will make reference to the audit of the other auditor, his report should indicate clearly, in both the introductory, scope and opinion paragraphs, the division of responsibility as between that portion of the financial statements covered by his own audit and that covered by the audit of the other auditor. The report should disclose the magnitude of the portion of the financial statements audited by the other auditor. This may be done by stating the dollar amounts or percentages of one or more of the following: total assets, total revenues, or other

appropriate criteria, whichever most clearly reveals the portion of the financial statements audited by the other auditor. The other auditor may be named but only with his express permission and provided his report is presented together with that of the principal auditor.

7.18   Paragraphs 12 and 13 of *AU section 508* reaffirm the requirements of *AU section 543*. Paragraph 13 presents an example of an auditors' report referring to the report of other auditors.

7.19   The auditors' report for seven survey entities made reference to the report of other auditors. The reference to other auditors in one of these reports related to prior year financial statements. An example of an auditors' report making reference to a report of other auditors follows.

7.20

REPORT OF INDEPENDENT REGISTERED PUBLIC ACCOUNTING FIRM

The Board of Directors and Stockholders of
El Paso Corporation

We have audited the accompanying consolidated balance sheets of El Paso Corporation as of December 31, 2009 and 2008, and the related consolidated statements of income, comprehensive income, equity, and cash flows for each of the three years in the period ended December 31, 2009. Our audits also included the financial statement schedule listed in the Index at Item 15(a). These financial statements and schedule are the responsibility of the Company's management. Our responsibility is to express an opinion on these financial statements and schedule based on our audits. The financial statements of Citrus Corp. and Subsidiaries (a corporation in which the Company has a 50% interest) as of December 31, 2009 and 2008 and for the three years in the period ended December 31, 2009 and Four Star Oil & Gas Company (a corporation in which the Company has approximately a 49% interest) as of December 31, 2008 and for the two years in the period ended December 31, 2008 have been audited by other auditors whose reports have been furnished to us, and our opinion on the consolidated financial statements, insofar as it relates to the amounts included from Citrus Corp. and Subsidiaries and Four Star Oil & Gas Company, is based solely on the reports of the other auditors. In the consolidated financial statements, the Company's investments in unconsolidated affiliates includes approximately $674 million from Citrus Corp. and Subsidiaries as of December 31, 2009 and approximately $744 million from Citrus Corp. and Subsidiaries and Four Star Oil & Gas Company combined at December 31, 2008, and the Company's earnings from unconsolidated affiliates includes approximately $65 million for the year ended December 31, 2009 from Citrus Corp. and approximately $147 million and $149 million for the years ended December 31, 2008 and 2007, respectively, from Citrus Corp. and Subsidiaries and Four Star Oil & Gas Company combined, all of which were audited by other auditors.

We conducted our audits in accordance with the standards of the Public Company Accounting Oversight Board (United

States). Those standards require that we plan and perform the audit to obtain reasonable assurance about whether the financial statements are free of material misstatement. An audit includes examining, on a test basis, evidence supporting the amounts and disclosures in the financial statements. An audit also includes assessing the accounting principles used and significant estimates made by management, as well as evaluating the overall financial statement presentation. We believe that our audits and the reports of other auditors provide a reasonable basis for our opinion.

In our opinion, based on our audits and the reports of other auditors, the financial statements referred to above present fairly, in all material respects, the consolidated financial position of El Paso Corporation at December 31, 2009 and 2008, and the consolidated results of its operations and its cash flows for each of the three years in the period ended December 31, 2009 in conformity with U.S. generally accepted accounting principles. Also, in our opinion, the related financial statement schedule, when considered in relation to the basic financial statements taken as a whole, presents fairly in all material respects the information set forth therein.

As discussed in Note 1 to the consolidated financial statements, effective December 31, 2009 the Company has changed its reserve estimates and related disclosures as a result of adopting new oil and gas reserve estimation and disclosure requirements, effective January 1, 2009 the Company adopted accounting standards for the presentation and disclosure of noncontrolling interests in the financial statements, effective January 1, 2008 the Company adopted the measurement provisions of the accounting standards for retirement benefits, and effective January 1, 2007 the Company adopted the accounting standards related to income tax contingencies.

We also have audited, in accordance with the standards of the Public Company Accounting Oversight Board (United States), El Paso Corporation's internal control over financial reporting as of December 31, 2009, based on criteria established in Internal Control-Integrated Framework issued by the Committee of Sponsoring Organizations of the Treadway Commission and our report dated March 1, 2010 expressed an unqualified opinion thereon.

UNCERTAINTIES

7.21 *AU section 508*, as amended, does not require an explanatory paragraph for uncertainties as defined in paragraphs 29 and 30 of *AU section 508*. This does not apply to uncertainties related to going concern situations for which AU section 341, *The Auditor's Consideration of an Entity's Ability to Continue as a Going Concern*, as amended, provides guidance.

7.22 Table 7-3 summarizes the nature of uncertainties for which an explanatory paragraph was included in an auditors' report. Examples of explanatory language for an uncertainty follow.

7.23

TABLE 7-3: REFERENCES TO UNCERTAINTIES IN AUDITORS' REPORT

	2009	2008	2007	2006
Going concern	8	12	4	9
Other	—	1	—	—
Total Uncertainties	**8**	**13**	**4**	**9**
Total Entities	**8**	**13**	**4**	**9**

2008–2009 based on 500 entities surveyed; 2006–2007 based on 600 entities surveyed.

7.24

REPORT OF INDEPENDENT REGISTERED PUBLIC ACCOUNTING FIRM

The Board of Directors and Stockholders
Chemtura Corporation

We have audited the accompanying consolidated balance sheets of Chemtura Corporation and subsidiaries (Debtor-In Possession) (the "Company") as of December 31, 2009 and 2008, and the related consolidated statements of operations, stockholders' equity, and cash flows for each of the years in the three-year period ended December 31, 2009. In connection with our audits of the consolidated financial statements, we also have audited the financial statement Schedule II, Valuation and Qualifying Accounts. We also have audited Chemtura Corporation's internal control over financial reporting as of December 31, 2009, based on criteria established in *Internal Control—Integrated Framework* issued by the Committee of Sponsoring Organizations of the Treadway Commission (COSO). The Company's management is responsible for these consolidated financial statements and financial statement schedule, for maintaining effective internal control over financial reporting, and for its assessment of the effectiveness of internal control over financial reporting, included in the accompanying Management's Annual Report on Internal Control over Financial Reporting (Item 9A(b)). Our responsibility is to express an opinion on these consolidated financial statements and financial statement schedule and an opinion on the Company's internal control over financial reporting based on our audits.

We conducted our audits in accordance with the standards of the Public Company Accounting Oversight Board (United States). Those standards require that we plan and perform the audits to obtain reasonable assurance about whether the financial statements are free of material misstatement and whether effective internal control over financial reporting was maintained in all material respects. Our audits of the consolidated financial statements included examining, on a test basis, evidence supporting the amounts and disclosures in the financial statements, assessing the accounting principles used and significant estimates made by management, and evaluating the overall financial statement presentation.

Our audit of internal control over financial reporting included obtaining an understanding of internal control over financial reporting, assessing the risk that a material weakness exists, and testing and evaluating the design and operating effectiveness of internal control based on the assessed risk. Our audits also included performing such other procedures as we considered necessary in the circumstances. We believe that our audits provide a reasonable basis for our opinions.

A company's internal control over financial reporting is a process designed to provide reasonable assurance regarding the reliability of financial reporting and the preparation of financial statements for external purposes in accordance with generally accepted accounting principles. A company's internal control over financial reporting includes those policies and procedures that (1) pertain to the maintenance of records that, in reasonable detail, accurately and fairly reflect the transactions and dispositions of the assets of the company; (2) provide reasonable assurance that transactions are recorded as necessary to permit preparation of financial statements in accordance with generally accepted accounting principles, and that receipts and expenditures of the company are being made only in accordance with authorizations of management and directors of the company; and (3) provide reasonable assurance regarding prevention or timely detection of unauthorized acquisition, use, or disposition of the company's assets that could have a material effect on the financial statements.

Because of its inherent limitations, internal control over financial reporting may not prevent or detect misstatements. Also, projections of any evaluation of effectiveness to future periods are subject to the risk that controls may become inadequate because of changes in conditions, or that the degree of compliance with the policies or procedures may deteriorate.

In our opinion, the consolidated financial statements referred to above present fairly, in all material respects, the financial position of Chemtura Corporation and subsidiaries as of December 31, 2009 and 2008, and the results of their operations and their cash flows for each of the years in the three-year period ended December 31, 2009, in conformity with U.S. generally accepted accounting principles. Also, in our opinion, the related financial statement schedule, when considered in relation to the basic consolidated financial statements taken as a whole, presents fairly, in all material respects the information set forth therein. Also, in our opinion, Chemtura Corporation maintained, in all material respects, effective internal control over financial reporting as of December 31, 2009, based on criteria established in *Internal Control—Integrated Framework* issued by COSO.

The accompanying consolidated financial statements and financial statement schedule have been prepared assuming that the Company will continue as a going concern. As discussed in Note 1 to the consolidated financial statements, on March 18, 2009, Chemtura Corporation and 26 of its subsidiaries organized in the United States filed for relief under Chapter 11 of Title 11 of the United States Bankruptcy Code and there are uncertainties inherent in the bankruptcy process. The Company also has suffered recurring losses from continuing operations. These factors raise substantial doubt about the Company's ability to continue as a going concern. Management's plans in regard to these matters are also described in Note 1. The consolidated financial statements and financial statement schedule do not include any adjustments that might result from the outcome of this uncertainty.

As discussed in Note 2 to Notes to Consolidated Financial Statements, the Company, due to the adoption of new accounting principles, in 2009, changed its method of accounting for fair value measurements for non-financial assets and liabilities, and non-controlling interests; in 2008, changed its method of accounting for fair value measurements for financial assets and liabilities; and in 2007, changed its method of accounting for uncertainty in income taxes.

NOTES TO CONSOLIDATED FINANCIAL STATEMENTS

1 (In Part): Nature of Operations and Bankruptcy Proceedings

Liquidity and Bankruptcy Proceedings

The Company entered 2009 with significantly constrained liquidity. The fourth quarter of 2008 saw an unprecedented reduction in orders for the Company's products as the global recession deepened and customers saw or anticipated reductions in demand in the industries they served. The impact was more pronounced on those business segments that served cyclically exposed industries. As a result, the Company's sales and overall financial performance deteriorated resulting in the Company's non-compliance with the two financial maintenance covenants under its Amended and Restated Credit Agreement, dated as of July 31, 2007 (the "2007 Credit Facility") as of December 31, 2008. On December 30, 2008, the Company obtained a 90-day waiver of compliance with these covenants from the lenders under the 2007 Credit Facility.

The Company's liquidity was further constrained in the fourth quarter of 2008 by changes in the availability under its accounts receivable financing facilities in the United States and Europe. The eligibility criteria and reserve requirements under the Company's prior U.S. accounts receivable facility (the "U.S. Facility") tightened in the fourth quarter of 2008 following a credit rating downgrade, significantly reducing the value of accounts receivable that could be sold under the U.S. Facility compared with the third quarter of 2008. Additionally, the availability and access to the Company's European accounts receivable financing facility (the "European Facility") was restricted in late December 2008 because of the Company's financial performance resulting in the Company's inability to sell additional receivables under the European Facility.

The crisis in the credit markets compounded the liquidity challenges faced by the Company. Under normal market conditions, the Company believed it would have been able to refinance its $370 million notes maturing on July 15, 2009 (the "2009 Notes") in the debt capital markets. However, with the deterioration of the credit market in the late summer of 2008 combined with the Company's deteriorating financial performance, the Company did not believe it would be able to refinance the 2009 Notes on commercially reasonable terms, if at all. As a result, the Company sought to refinance the 2009 Notes through the sale of one of its businesses.

On January 23, 2009, a special-purpose subsidiary of the Company entered into a new three-year U.S. accounts receivable financing facility (the "2009 U.S. Facility") that restored most of the liquidity that the Company had available to it under the prior U.S. accounts receivable facility before the fourth quarter of 2008 events described above. However, despite good faith discussions, the Company was unable to agree to terms under which it could resume the sale of accounts receivable under its European Facility during the first quarter of 2009. The balance of accounts receivable previously sold under the facility continued to decline, offsetting much of the benefit to liquidity gained by the new 2009 U.S. Facility. During the second quarter of 2009, with no agreement to restart the European Facility, the remaining balance of the accounts receivable previously sold under the facility were settled and the European Facility was terminated.

January 2009 saw no improvement in customer demand from the depressed levels in December 2008 and some business segments experienced further deterioration. Although February and March of 2009 saw incremental improvement in net sales compared to January 2009, overall business conditions remained difficult as sales declined by 43% in the first quarter of 2009 compared to the first quarter of 2008. As awareness grew of the Company's constrained liquidity and deteriorating financial performance, suppliers began restricting trade credit and, as a result, liquidity dwindled further. Despite moderate cash generation through inventory reductions and restrictions on discretionary expenditures, the Company's trade credit continued to tighten, resulting in unprecedented restrictions on its ability to procure raw materials.

In January and February of 2009, the Company was in the midst of the asset sale process with the objective of closing a transaction prior to the July 15, 2009 maturity of the 2009 Notes. Potential buyers conducted due diligence and worked towards submitting their final offers on several of the Company's businesses. However, with the continuing recession and speculation about the financial condition of the Company, potential buyers became progressively more cautious. Certain potential buyers expressed concern about the Company's ability to perform its obligations under a sale agreement. They increased their due diligence requirements or decided not to proceed with a transaction. In March 2009, the Company concluded that although there were potential buyers of its businesses, a sale was unlikely to be closed in sufficient time to offset the continued deterioration in liquidity or at a value that would provide sufficient liquidity to both operate the business and meet the Company's impending debt maturities.

By March 2009, dwindling liquidity and growing restrictions on available trade credit resulted in production stoppages as raw materials could not be purchased on a timely basis. At the same time, the Company concluded that it was improbable that it could resume sales of accounts receivable under its European Facility or complete the sale of a business in sufficient time to provide the immediate liquidity it needed to operate. Absent such an infusion of liquidity, the Company would likely experience increased production stoppages or sustained limitations on its business operations that ultimately would have a detrimental effect on the value of the Company's business as a whole. Specifically, the inability to maintain and stabilize its business operations would result in depleted inventories, missed supply obligations and damaged customer relationships.

Having carefully explored and exhausted all possibilities to gain near-term access to liquidity, the Company determined that debtor-in-possession financing presented the best available alternative for the Company to meet its immediate and ongoing liquidity needs and preserve the value of the business. As a result, having obtained the commitment of a $400 million senior secured super-priority debtor-in-possession credit facility agreement (the "DIP Credit Facility"), Chem-

tura and 26 of its subsidiaries organized in the United States (collectively, the "Debtors") filed for relief under Chapter 11 of Title 11 of the United States Bankruptcy Code (the "Bankruptcy Code") on March 18, 2009 (the "Petition Date") in the United States Bankruptcy Court for the Southern District of New York (the "Bankruptcy Court"). The Chapter 11 cases are being jointly administered by the Bankruptcy Court. The Company's non-U.S. subsidiaries and certain U.S. subsidiaries were not included in the filing and are not subject to the requirements of the Bankruptcy Code. The Company's U.S. and worldwide operations are expected to continue without interruption during the Chapter 11 reorganization process.

The Debtors own substantially all of the Company's U.S. assets. The Debtors consist of Chemtura and the following subsidiaries:

- A&M Cleaning Products LLC
- Aqua Clear Industries, LLC
- ASEPSIS, Inc.
- ASCK, Inc.
- BioLab, Inc.
- BioLab Company Store, LLC
- Biolab Franchise Company, LLC
- BioLab Textile Additives, LLC
- CNK Chemical Realty Corporation
- Crompton Colors Incorporated
- Crompton Holding Corporation
- Crompton Monochem, Inc.
- GLCC Laurel, LLC
- Great Lakes Chemical Corporation
- Great Lakes Chemical Global, Inc.
- GT Seed Treatment, Inc.
- HomeCare Labs, Inc
- ISCI, Inc.
- Kem Manufacturing Corporation
- Laurel Industries Holdings, Inc.
- Monochem, Inc.
- Naugatuck Treatment Company
- Recreational Water Products, Inc.
- Uniroyal Chemical Company Limited
- Weber City Road LLC
- WRL of Indiana, Inc.

The principal U.S. assets and business operations of the Debtors are owned by Chemtura, BioLab, Inc. and Great Lakes Chemical Corporation.

On March 18, 2009, Raymond E. Dombrowski, Jr. was appointed Chief Restructuring Officer. In connection with this appointment, the Company entered into an agreement with Alvarez & Marsal North America, LLC ("A&M") to compensate A&M for Mr. Dombrowski's services as Chief Restructuring Officer on a monthly basis at a rate of $150 thousand per month and incentive compensation in the amount of $3 million payable upon the earlier of (a) the consummation of a Chapter 11 plan of reorganization ("Plan") or (b) the sale, transfer, or other disposition of all or a substantial portion of the assets or equity of the Company. Mr. Dombrowski is independently compensated pursuant to arrangements with A&M, a financial advisory and consulting firm specializing in corporate restructuring. Mr. Dombrowski will not receive any compensation directly from the Company and will not participate in any of the Company's employee benefit plans.

The Chapter 11 cases were filed to gain liquidity for continuing operations while the Debtors restructure their balance sheets to allow the Company to continue as a viable going concern. While the Company believes it will be able to achieve these objectives through the Chapter 11 reorganization process, there can be no certainty that it will be successful in doing so.

Under Chapter 11 of the Bankruptcy Code, the Debtors are operating their U.S. businesses as a debtor-in-possession ("DIP") under the protection of the Bankruptcy Court from their pre-filing creditors and claimants. Since the filing, all orders of the Bankruptcy Court sufficient to enable the Debtors to conduct normal business activities, including "first day" motions and the interim and final approval of the DIP Credit Facility and amendments thereto, have been entered by the Bankruptcy Court. While the Debtors are subject to Chapter 11, all transactions outside the ordinary course of business will require the prior approval of the Bankruptcy Court.

On March 20, 2009, the Bankruptcy Court approved the Debtors' "first day" motions. Specifically, the Bankruptcy Court granted the Debtors, among other things, interim approval to access $190 million of its $400 million DIP Credit Facility, approval to pay outstanding employee wages, health benefits, and certain other employee obligations and authority to continue to honor their current customer policies and programs, in order to ensure the reorganization process will not adversely impact their customers. On April 29, 2009, the Bankruptcy Court entered a final order providing full access to the $400 million DIP Credit Facility. The Bankruptcy Court also approved Amendment No. 1 to the DIP Credit Facility which provided for, among other things: (i) an increase in the outstanding amount of inter-company loans the Debtors could make to the non-debtor foreign subsidiaries of the Company from $8 million to $40 million; (ii) a reduction in the required level of borrowing availability under the minimum availability covenant; and (iii) the elimination of the requirement to pay additional interest expense if a specified level of accounts receivable financing was not available to the Company's European subsidiaries.

On July 13, 2009, the Company and the parties to the DIP Credit Facility entered into Amendment No. 2 to the DIP Credit Facility subject to approvals by the Bankruptcy Court and the Company's Board of Directors which approvals were obtained on July 14 and July 15, 2009, respectively. Amendment No. 2 amended the DIP Credit Facility to provide for, among other things, an option by the Company to extend the maturity of the DIP Credit Facility for two consecutive three month periods subject to the satisfaction of certain conditions. Prior to Amendment No. 2, the DIP Credit Facility matured on the earlier of 364 days (from the Petition Date), the effective date of a Plan or the date of termination in whole of the Commitments (as defined in the DIP Credit Facility).

As a consequence of the Chapter 11 cases, substantially all pre-petition litigation and claims against the Debtors have been stayed. Accordingly, no party may take any action to collect pre-petition claims or to pursue litigation arising as a result of pre-petition acts or omissions except pursuant to an order of the Bankruptcy Court.

On August 21, 2009, the Bankruptcy Court established October 30, 2009 as the deadline for the filing of proofs of claim against the Debtors (the "Bar Date"). Under certain limited circumstances, some creditors may be permitted to file proofs of claim after the Bar Date. Accordingly, it is possible that not all potential proofs of claim were filed as of the filing of this Annual Report.

The Debtors have received approximately 15,300 proofs of claim covering a broad array of areas. Approximately 8,000 proofs of claim have been asserted in "unliquidated" amounts or contain an unliquidated component that are treated as being asserted in "unliquidated" amounts. Excluding proofs of claim in "unliquidated" amounts, the aggregate amount of proofs of claim filed totaled approximately $23.6 billion.

The Company is in the process of evaluating the amounts asserted in and the factual and legal basis of the proofs of claim filed against the Debtors. Based upon the Company's initial review and evaluation, which is continuing, a significant number of proofs of claim are duplicative and/or legally or factually without merit. As to those claims, the Company has filed and intends to file objections with the Bankruptcy Court. However, there can be no assurance that these claims will not be allowed in full.

Further, while the Debtors believe they have insurance to cover certain asserted claims, there can be no assurance that material uninsured obligations will not be allowed as claims in the Chapter 11 cases. Because of the substantial number of asserted contested claims, as to which review and analysis is ongoing, there is no assurance as to the ultimate value of claims that will be allowed in the Chapter 11 cases, nor is there any assurance as to the ultimate recoveries for the Debtors' stakeholders, including the Debtors' bondholders and the Company's shareholders. The differences between amounts recorded by the Debtors and proofs of claim filed by the creditors will continue to be investigated and resolved through the claims reconciliation process.

The Company has recognized certain charges related to expected allowed claims. As the Company completes the process of evaluating and resolving the proofs of claim, appropriate adjustments to the Company's Consolidated Financial Statements will be made. Adjustments may also result from actions of the Bankruptcy Court, settlement negotiations, rejection of executory contracts and real property leases, determination as to the value of any collateral securing claims and other events. Any such adjustments could be material to the Company's results of operations and financial condition in any given period. For additional information on liabilities subject to compromise, see Note 4—Liabilities Subject to Compromise and Reorganization Items, Net.

As provided by the Bankruptcy Code, the Debtors have the exclusive right to file and solicit acceptance of a Plan for 120 days after the Petition Date with the possibility of extensions thereafter. On February 23, 2010, the Bankruptcy Court granted the Company's application for extensions of the period during which it has the exclusive right to file a Plan from February 11, 2010 to June 11, 2010. The Bankruptcy Court had previously granted the Company's application for an extension of the exclusivity period on July 28, 2009 and October 27, 2009. There can be no assurance that a Plan will be filed by the Debtors or confirmed by the Bankruptcy Court, or that any such Plan will be consummated. After a Plan has been filed with the Bankruptcy Court, the Plan, along with a disclosure statement approved by the Bankruptcy Court, will be sent to all creditors and other parties entitled to vote to accept or reject the Plan. Following the solicitation period, the Bankruptcy Court will consider whether to confirm the Plan. In order to confirm a Plan, the Bankruptcy Court must make certain findings as required by the Bankruptcy Code. The Bankruptcy Court may confirm a Plan notwithstanding the non-acceptance of the Plan by an impaired class of creditors or equity security holders if certain requirements of the Bankruptcy Code are met.

On January 15, 2010 the Company entered into Amendment No. 3 of the DIP Credit Facility that provided for, among other things, the consent of the Company's DIP lenders to the sale of the PVC additives business.

On February 9, 2010, the Court gave interim approval of an Amended and Restated Senior Secured Super-Priority Debtor-in-Possession Credit Agreement (the "Amended and Restated DIP Credit Agreement") by and among the Debtors, Citibank N.A. and the other lenders party thereto. The Amended and Restated DIP Credit Agreement provides for a first priority and priming secured revolving and term loan credit commitment of up to an aggregate of $450 million. The proceeds of the loans and other financial accommodations incurred under the Amended and Restated DIP Credit Agreement were used to, among other things, refinance the obligations outstanding under the DIP Credit Facility and provide working capital for general corporate purposes. The Amended and Restated DIP Credit Agreement provided a substantial reduction in the Company's financing costs through interest rate reductions and the avoidance of the extension fees that would have been payable under the DIP Credit Facility in February and May 2010. The Amended and Restated DIP Credit Agreement closed on February 12, 2010 with the drawing of the $300 million term loan. On February 18, 2010, the Bankruptcy Court entered a final order providing full access to the Amended and Restated DIP Credit Agreement. The Amended and Restated DIP Credit Agreement matures on the earlier of 364 days after the closing, the effective date of a Plan or the date of termination in whole of the Commitments (as defined in the Amended and Restated DIP Credit Agreement).

The ultimate recovery by the Debtors' creditors and the Company's shareholders, if any, will not be determined until confirmation and implementation of a Plan. No assurance can be given as to what recoveries, if any, will be assigned in the Chapter 11 cases to each of these constituencies. A Plan could result in the Company's shareholders receiving little or no value for their interests and holders of the Debtors' unsecured debt, including trade debt and other general unsecured creditors, receiving less, and potentially substantially less, than payment in full for their claims. Because of such possibilities, the value of the Company's common stock and unsecured debt is highly speculative. Accordingly, the Company urges that appropriate caution be exercised with respect to existing and future investments in any of these securities. Although the shares of the Company's common stock continue to trade on the Pink Sheets Electronic Quotation Service ("Pink Sheets") under the symbol "CEMJQ," the trading prices may have little or no relationship to the actual recovery, if any, by the holders under any eventual Bankruptcy Court-approved Plan. The opportunity for any recovery by holders of the Company's common stock under such Plan is uncertain as all creditors' claims must be met in full, with interest where due, before value can be attributed to the common stock and, therefore, the shares of the Company's common stock may be cancelled without any compensation pursuant to such Plan.

Continuation of the Company as a going concern is contingent upon, among other things, the Company's and/or Debtors' ability (i) to comply with the terms and conditions of the Amended and Restated DIP Credit Agreement; (ii) to obtain confirmation of a Plan under the Bankruptcy Code; (iii) to return to profitability; (iv) to generate sufficient cash flow from operations; and (v) to obtain financing sources to meet the Company's future obligations. These matters raise substantial doubt about the Company's ability to continue as a going concern. The Consolidated Financial Statements

do not reflect any adjustments relating to the recoverability and classification of recorded asset amounts or the amounts and classification of liabilities that might result from the outcome of these uncertainties. Additionally, a Plan could materially change amounts reported in the Consolidated Financial Statements, which do not give effect to all adjustments of the carrying value of assets and liabilities that may be necessary as a consequence of completing a reorganization under Chapter 11 of the Bankruptcy Code.

In addition, as part of the Company's emergence from bankruptcy protection, the Company may be required to adopt fresh start accounting in a future period. If fresh start accounting is applicable, our assets and liabilities will be recorded at fair value as of the fresh start reporting date. The fair value of our assets and liabilities as of such fresh start reporting date may differ materially from the recorded values of assets and liabilities on our Consolidated Balance Sheets. Further, if fresh start accounting is required, the financial results of the Company after the application of fresh start accounting may not be comparable to historical trends.

2 (In Part): Basis of Presentation and Summary of Significant Accounting Policies

The Consolidated Financial Statements have been prepared in accordance with Accounting Standards Codification ("ASC") Section 852-10-45, *Reorganizations—Other Presentation Matters* ("ASC 852-10-45"). ASC 852-10-45 does not ordinarily affect or change the application of U.S. generally accepted accounting principles ("GAAP"). However, it does require the Company to distinguish transactions and events that are directly associated with the reorganization in connection with the Chapter 11 cases from the ongoing operations of the business. Expenses incurred and settlement impacts due to the Chapter 11 cases are reported separately as reorganization items, net on the Consolidated Statements of Operations for the year ended December 31, 2009. Interest expense related to pre-petition indebtedness has been reported only to the extent that it will be paid during the pendency of the Chapter 11 cases or is permitted by Bankruptcy Court approval or is expected to be an allowed claim. The pre-petition liabilities subject to compromise are disclosed separately on the December 31, 2009 Consolidated Balance Sheet. These liabilities are reported at the amounts expected to be allowed by the Bankruptcy Court, even if they may be settled for a lesser amount. These expected allowed claims require management to estimate the likely claim amount that will be allowed by the Bankruptcy Court prior to its ruling on the individual claims. These estimates are based on reviews of claimants' supporting material, obligations to mitigate such claims, and assessments by management and third-party advisors. The Company expects that its estimates, although based on the best available information, will change as the claims are resolved by the Bankruptcy Court.

LACK OF CONSISTENCY

7.25 Table 7-4 summarizes the accounting changes for which auditors expressed unqualified opinions but included explanatory language in their reports as required by paragraphs 16–18 of *AU section 508*, as amended. Of the 500 references to lack of consistency, 311 relate to changes made in years prior to 2009. Examples of references to lack of consistency follow.

7.26

TABLE 7-4: REFERENCES TO LACK OF CONSISTENCY IN AUDITORS' REPORT

	2009	2008	2007	2006
Income tax uncertainties	185	338	291	1
Employee benefits	107	247	368	259
Consolidations/noncontrolling interests	66	N/C*	N/C*	N/C*
Business Combinations	38	N/C*	N/C*	N/C*
Fair value measurements	24	27	4	—
Convertible instruments	21	N/C*	N/C*	N/C*
Stock-based compensation	11	85	353	361
Earnings per share	9	N/C*	N/C*	N/C*
Accounting errors/misstatements	8	23	32	18
Inventories	3	7	5	9
Impairment of long-lived assets	2	1	1	1
Variable interest entities	2	—	—	13
Derivative financial instruments	2	—	—	—
Revenue recognition	2	—	—	—
Transfer of financial assets	1	N/C*	N/C*	N/C*
Asset retirement obligations	—	6	31	41
Goodwill not amortized	—	—	—	3
Other—described	19	27	29	23
Total References	**500**	**761**	**1114**	**729**
Total Entities	**290**	**402**	**529**	**439**

* N/C = Not compiled. Line item was not included in the table for the year shown.

2008–2009 based on 500 entities surveyed; 2006–2007 based on 600 entities surveyed.

Employee Benefits

7.27

REPORT OF INDEPENDENT REGISTERED PUBLIC ACCOUNTING FIRM

To the Board of Directors and Stockholders of Ameron International Corporation

In our opinion, the accompanying consolidated balance sheets and the related consolidated statements of income, of stockholders' equity, of comprehensive income, and of cash flows present fairly, in all material respects, the financial position of Ameron International Corporation and its subsidiaries at November 30, 2009 and 2008, and the results of their operations and their cash flows for each of the three years in the period ended November 30, 2009 in conformity with accounting principles generally accepted in the United States of America. In addition, in our opinion, the financial statement schedule listed in the accompanying index appearing under Item 15(a)(2) presents fairly, in all material respects, the information set forth therein when read in conjunction with the related consolidated financial statements. Also in our opinion, the Company maintained, in all material respects, effective internal control over financial reporting as of November 30, 2009, based on criteria established in *Internal Control—Integrated Framework* issued by the Committee of Sponsoring Organizations of the Treadway Commission (COSO). The Company's management is responsible for these financial statements and financial statement schedule, for maintaining effective internal control over financial reporting and for its assessment of the effectiveness of internal control over financial reporting, included in the accompanying Management's Report on Internal Control over Financial Reporting. Our responsibility is to express opinions on these financial statements, on the financial statement schedule, and on the Company's internal control over financial reporting based on our integrated audits. We conducted our audits in accordance with the standards of the Public Company Accounting Oversight Board (United States). Those standards require that we plan and perform the audits to obtain reasonable assurance about whether the financial statements are free of material misstatement and whether effective internal control over financial reporting was maintained in all material respects. Our audits of the financial statements included examining, on a test basis, evidence supporting the amounts and disclosures in the financial statements, assessing the accounting principles used and significant estimates made by management, and evaluating the overall financial statement presentation. Our audit of internal control over financial reporting included obtaining an understanding of internal control over financial reporting, assessing the risk that a material weakness exists, and testing and evaluating the design and operating effectiveness of internal control based on the assessed risk. Our audits also included performing such other procedures as we considered necessary in the circumstances. We believe that our audits provide a reasonable basis for our opinions.

As discussed in Note 1 and Note 10 to the consolidated financial statements, the Company changed the manner in which it accounts for income taxes in 2008. As discussed in Note 1 and Note 16 to the consolidated financial statements, the Company changed the manner in which it accounts for defined benefit pension and other postretirement benefit plans in 2007 and 2009.

A company's internal control over financial reporting is a process designed to provide reasonable assurance regarding the reliability of financial reporting and the preparation of financial statements for external purposes in accordance with generally accepted accounting principles. A company's internal control over financial reporting includes those policies and procedures that (i) pertain to the maintenance of records that, in reasonable detail, accurately and fairly reflect the transactions and dispositions of the assets of the company; (ii) provide reasonable assurance that transactions are recorded as necessary to permit preparation of financial statements in accordance with generally accepted accounting principles, and that receipts and expenditures of the company are being made only in accordance with authorizations of management and directors of the company; and (iii) provide reasonable assurance regarding prevention or timely detection of unauthorized acquisition, use, or disposition of the company's assets that could have a material effect on the financial statements.

Because of its inherent limitations, internal control over financial reporting may not prevent or detect misstatements. Also, projections of any evaluation of effectiveness to future periods are subject to the risk that controls may become inadequate because of changes in conditions, or that the degree of compliance with the policies or procedures may deteriorate.

NOTES TO CONSOLIDATED FINANCIAL STATEMENTS

Note 1 (In Part): Summary of Significant Accounting Policies

New Accounting Pronouncements (In Part)

In September 2006, the FASB required companies to recognize the overfunded or underfunded status of a defined benefit postretirement plan (other than a multiemployer plan) as an asset or liability in its financial statements and to recognize changes in that status in the year in which the changes occur. The guidance also requires a company to measure the funded status of a plan as of the date of its year-end financial statements. The Company adopted the recognition provisions in 2008 and the measurement provisions in 2009.

Note 16 (In Part): Employee Benefit Plans

Pension Benefits (In Part)

The following sets forth the change in benefit obligation, change in plan assets, funded status and amounts recognized in the balance sheets as of November 30, 2009 and 2008 for the Company's U.S. and non-U.S. defined benefit retirement plans:

(In thousands)	U.S. Pension Benefits		Non-U.S. Pension Benefits	
	2009	2008	2009	2008
Change in benefit obligation				
Projected benefit obligation—beginning of year	$ 175,373	$192,410	$34,111	$45,908
Service cost	3,439	2,974	342	439
Interest cost	14,706	11,553	2,335	2,541
Participant contributions	—	—	188	185
Amendments	—	46	—	—
Actuarial loss/(gain)	31,393	(19,861)	6,590	(7,429)
Foreign currency exchange rate changes	—	—	6,430	(6,039
Benefit payments	(14,049)	(11,749)	(1,165)	(1,494)
Projected benefit obligation—end of year	$ 210,862	$175,373	$48,831	$34,111
Accumulated benefit obligation	$ 202,227	$167,318	$46,545	$33,663
Change in plan assets				
Plan assets at fair value—beginning of year	$ 140,447	$183,940	$32,554	$34,310
Actual return on plan assets	(766)	(34,775)	3,181	4,423
Foreign currency exchange rate changes	—	—	5,860	(5,810)
Employer contributions	8,536	3,031	1,738	940
Participant contributions	—	—	188	185
Benefit payments	(14,049)	(11,749)	(1,165)	(1,494)
Plan assets at fair value—end of year	$(134,168)	$140,447	$42,356	$32,554
Funded status	$ (76,694)	$ (34,926)	$ (6,475)	$ (1,557)
Balance sheet amounts				
Noncurrent assets	$ —	$ —	$ —	$ —
Current liabilities	(30)	(30)	—	—
Noncurrent liabilities	(76,664)	(34,896)	(6,475)	(1,557)
Net amount recognized	$ (76,694)	$ (34,926)	$ (6,475)	$ (1,557)

In 2009, the Company changed the U.S. defined benefit plan measurement date from October 1 to November 30 to match its fiscal year-end. The changes shown above for 2008 include 12 months, while the changes for 2009 include 14 months.

• • • • • •

Net periodic benefit costs for the Company's defined benefit retirement plans for 2009, 2008 and 2007 included the following components:

(In thousands)	U.S. Pension Benefits			Non-U.S. Pension Benefits		
	2009	2008	2007	2009	2008	2007
Service cost	$ 3,439	$ 2,974	$ 2,928	$ 342	$ 439	$ 529
Interest cost	14,706	11,553	11,178	2,335	2,541	2,260
Expected return on plan assets	(13,768)	(15,713)	(14,172)	(1,571)	(1,692)	(1,680)
Amortization of unrecognized prior service cost	81	117	113	286	306	281
Amortization of unrecognized net transition obligation	—	—	—	—	—	151
Amortization of accumulated loss/(gain)	7,010	1,134	3,904	(439)	—	—
Net periodic cost adjustment to retained earnings, pre-tax	(1,631)	—	—	—	—	—
Net periodic cost	$ 9,837	$ 65	$ 3,951	$ 953	$ 1,594	$ 1,541

The above table includes net periodic costs for 12 months for all periods. Additionally in 2009, the Company recorded to retained earnings two months of net periodic costs of $1,631,000 ($993,000 net of tax) relating to the change in measurement date for the Company's U.S. defined benefit plan.

Noncontrolling Interests

7.28

REPORT OF INDEPENDENT REGISTERED PUBLIC ACCOUNTING FIRM

To the Board of Directors and Shareowners of Honeywell International Inc.

In our opinion, the consolidated financial statements listed in the index appearing under Item 15(a)(1.) present fairly, in all material respects, the financial position of Honeywell International Inc. and its subsidiaries at December 31, 2009 and 2008, and the results of their operations and their cash flows for each of the three years in the period ended December 31, 2009 in conformity with accounting principles generally accepted in the United States of America. In addition, in our opinion, the financial statement schedule listed in the index appearing under Item 15(a)(2.) presents fairly, in all material respects, the information set forth therein when read in conjunction with the related consolidated financial statements. Also in our opinion, the Company maintained, in all material respects, effective internal control over financial reporting as of December 31, 2009, based on criteria established in *Internal Control—Integrated Framework* issued by the Committee of Sponsoring Organizations of the Treadway Commission (COSO). The Company's management is responsible for these financial statements and financial statement schedule, for maintaining effective internal control over financial reporting and for its assessment of the effectiveness of internal control over financial reporting, included in Management's Report on Internal Control Over Financial Reporting appearing under Item 9A. Our responsibility is to express opinions on these financial statements, on the financial statement schedule, and on the Company's internal control over financial reporting based on our integrated audits. We conducted our audits in accordance with the standards of the Public Company Accounting Oversight Board (United States). Those standards require that we plan and perform the audits to obtain reasonable assurance about whether the financial statements are free of material misstatement and whether effective internal control over financial reporting was maintained in all material respects. Our audits of the financial statements included examining, on a test basis, evidence supporting the amounts and disclosures in the financial statements, assessing the accounting principles used and significant estimates made by management, and evaluating the overall financial statement presentation. Our audit of internal control over financial reporting included obtaining an understanding of internal control over financial reporting, assessing the risk that a material weakness exists, and testing and evaluating the design and operating effectiveness of internal control based on the assessed risk. Our audits also included performing such other procedures as we considered necessary in the circumstances. We believe that our audits provide a reasonable basis for our opinions.

As discussed in Note 1 to the accompanying consolidated financial statements, in 2009 the Company retrospectively applied the accounting for noncontrolling interests and in 2007 changed the manner in which it accounts for income tax uncertainties.

A company's internal control over financial reporting is a process designed to provide reasonable assurance regarding the reliability of financial reporting and the preparation of financial statements for external purposes in accordance with generally accepted accounting principles. A company's internal control over financial reporting includes those policies and procedures that (i) pertain to the maintenance of records that, in reasonable detail, accurately and fairly reflect the transactions and dispositions of the assets of the company; (ii) provide reasonable assurance that transactions are recorded as necessary to permit preparation of financial statements in accordance with generally accepted accounting principles, and that receipts and expenditures of the company are being made only in accordance with authorizations of management and directors of the company; and (iii) provide reasonable assurance regarding prevention or timely detection of unauthorized acquisition, use, or disposition of the company's assets that could have a material effect on the financial statements.

Because of its inherent limitations, internal control over financial reporting may not prevent or detect misstatements. Also, projections of any evaluation of effectiveness to future periods are subject to the risk that controls may become inadequate because of changes in conditions, or that the degree of compliance with the policies or procedures may deteriorate.

NOTES TO FINANCIAL STATEMENTS
(Dollars in millions)

Note 1 (In Part): Summary of Significant Accounting Policies

Recent Accounting Pronouncements (In Part)

In December 2007, the FASB issued new guidance on noncontrolling interests which establishes requirements for ownership interests in subsidiaries held by parties other than the Company (sometimes called "minority interests") be clearly identified, presented, and disclosed in the consolidated statement of financial position within equity, but separate from the parent's equity. All changes in the parent's ownership interests are required to be accounted for consistently as equity transactions and any noncontrolling equity investments in unconsolidated subsidiaries must be measured initially at fair value. The new guidance is effective, on a prospective basis, for fiscal years beginning after December 15, 2008. However, presentation and disclosure requirements must be retrospectively applied to comparative financial statements. Upon adoption of the new guidance on noncontrolling interest the Company reclassified $82 million and $71 million of noncontrolling interest from other liabilities to noncontrolling interest as a separate component of shareholders equity in our consolidated balance sheet as of December 31, 2008 and 2007, respectively and $20 million and $16 million of noncontrolling interest expense to net income attributable to noncontrolling interest in our statement of operations for the years ended December 31, 2008 and 2007, respectively. See statement of shareholders' equity for additional disclosures regarding noncontrolling interest components of other comprehensive income. The implementation of this standard did not have a material impact on our consolidated financial position and results of operations.

Business Combinations

7.29

REPORT OF INDEPENDENT REGISTERED PUBLIC ACCOUNTING FIRM

To the Shareholders and Board of Directors of
Alcoa Inc.

In our opinion, the accompanying consolidated balance sheets and the related statements of consolidated operations, changes in consolidated equity, consolidated comprehensive income (loss), and consolidated cash flows present fairly, in all material respects, the financial position of Alcoa Inc. and its subsidiaries (the "Company") at December 31, 2009 and 2008, and the results of their operations and their cash flows for each of the three years in the period ended December 31, 2009 in conformity with accounting principles generally accepted in the United States of America. Also in our opinion, the Company maintained, in all material respects, effective internal control over financial reporting as of December 31, 2009, based on criteria established in *Internal Control—Integrated Framework* issued by the Committee of Sponsoring Organizations of the Treadway Commission (COSO). The Company's management is responsible for these financial statements, for maintaining effective internal control over financial reporting and for its assessment of the effectiveness of internal control over financial reporting, included in the accompanying Management's Report on Internal Control over Financial Reporting. Our responsibility is to express opinions on these financial statements and on the Company's internal control over financial reporting based on our integrated audits. We conducted our audits in accordance with the standards of the Public Company Accounting Oversight Board (United States). Those standards require that we plan and perform the audits to obtain reasonable assurance about whether the financial statements are free of material misstatement and whether effective internal control over financial reporting was maintained in all material respects. Our audits of the financial statements included examining, on a test basis, evidence supporting the amounts and disclosures in the financial statements, assessing the accounting principles used and significant estimates made by management, and evaluating the overall financial statement presentation. Our audit of internal control over financial reporting included obtaining an understanding of internal control over financial reporting, assessing the risk that a material weakness exists, and testing and evaluating the design and operating effectiveness of internal control based on the assessed risk. Our audits also included performing such other procedures as we considered necessary in the circumstances. We believe that our audits provide a reasonable basis for our opinions.

As discussed in Note A to the accompanying consolidated financial statements, effective January 1, 2009, the Company changed its accounting and reporting for noncontrolling interests, business combinations, and earnings per share.

A company's internal control over financial reporting is a process designed to provide reasonable assurance regarding the reliability of financial reporting and the preparation of financial statements for external purposes in accordance with generally accepted accounting principles. A company's internal control over financial reporting includes those policies and procedures that (i) pertain to the maintenance of records that, in reasonable detail, accurately and fairly reflect the transactions and dispositions of the assets of the company; (ii) provide reasonable assurance that transactions are recorded as necessary to permit preparation of financial statements in accordance with generally accepted accounting principles, and that receipts and expenditures of the company are being made only in accordance with authorizations of management and directors of the company; and (iii) provide reasonable assurance regarding prevention or timely detection of unauthorized acquisition, use, or disposition of the company's assets that could have a material effect on the financial statements.

Because of its inherent limitations, internal control over financial reporting may not prevent or detect misstatements. Also, projections of any evaluation of effectiveness to future periods are subject to the risk that controls may become inadequate because of changes in conditions, or that the degree of compliance with the policies or procedures may deteriorate.

NOTES TO CONSOLIDATED FINANCIAL STATEMENTS

A (In Part): Summary of Significant Accounting Policies

Business Combinations and Consolidation Accounting (In Part)

On January 1, 2009, Alcoa adopted changes issued by the FASB to accounting for business combinations. While retaining the fundamental requirements of accounting for business combinations, including that the purchase method be used for all business combinations and for an acquirer to be identified for each business combination, these changes define the acquirer as the entity that obtains control of one or more businesses in the business combination and establishes the acquisition date as the date that the acquirer achieves control instead of the date that the consideration is transferred. These changes require an acquirer in a business combination, including business combinations achieved in stages (step acquisition), to recognize the assets acquired, liabilities assumed, and any noncontrolling interest in the acquiree at the acquisition date, measured at their fair values as of that date, with limited exceptions. This guidance also requires the recognition of assets acquired and liabilities assumed arising from certain contractual contingencies as of the acquisition date, measured at their acquisition-date fair values. Additionally, these changes require acquisition-related costs to be expensed in the period in which the costs are incurred and the services are received instead of including such costs as part of the acquisition price. The adoption of these changes resulted in a charge of $18 ($12 after-tax) in Restructuring and other charges on the accompanying Statement of Consolidated Operations for the write off of previously capitalized third-party costs related to potential business acquisitions. Also, this guidance was applied to an acquisition completed on March 31, 2009 (see Note F).

Effective January 1, 2009, Alcoa adopted changes issued by the FASB on April 1, 2009 to accounting for business combinations. These changes apply to all assets acquired and liabilities assumed in a business combination that arise from certain contingencies and requires (i) an acquirer to recognize at fair value, at the acquisition date, an asset acquired or liability assumed in a business combination that arises from a contingency if the acquisition-date fair value of that asset or liability can be determined during the measurement pe-

riod otherwise the asset or liability should be recognized at the acquisition date if certain defined criteria are met; (ii) contingent consideration arrangements of an acquiree assumed by the acquirer in a business combination be recognized initially at fair value; (iii) subsequent measurements of assets and liabilities arising from contingencies be based on a systematic and rational method depending on their nature and contingent consideration arrangements be measured subsequently; and (iv) disclosures of the amounts and measurement basis of such assets and liabilities and the nature of the contingencies. These changes were applied to an acquisition completed on March 31, 2009 (see Note F).

F (In Part): Acquisitions and Divestitures

2009 Acquisitions

In March 2009, Alcoa completed a non-cash exchange of its 45.45% stake in the Sapa AB joint venture for Orkla ASA's (Orkla) 50% stake in the Elkem Aluminium ANS joint venture (Elkem). As a result of this transaction, Elkem is now owned 100% by Alcoa and Sapa AB is now owned 100% by Orkla. Prior to the completion of the exchange transaction, Alcoa accounted for its investments in Sapa AB and Elkem on the equity method and the carrying values were $475 and $435, respectively, at December 31, 2008. Elkem includes aluminum smelters in Lista and Mosjøen, Norway with a combined output of 282 kmt and the anode plant in Mosjøen in which Alcoa already held an 82% stake. These three facilities employed approximately 700 workers combined. The addition of the two smelters and anode plant (supports Norway and Iceland operations) strengthens Alcoa's leadership position within the aluminum industry. The assets and liabilities of Elkem were included in the Primary Metals segment beginning March 31, 2009 (the final amounts to be recorded will be based on valuation and other studies that have not yet been completed) and Elkem's results of operations were reflected in this segment starting on April 1, 2009 (prior to this transaction, Alcoa's existing 50% stake in Elkem was reflected as equity income in this segment). The exchange transaction resulted in the recognition of a $188 gain ($133 after-tax), comprised of a $156 adjustment to the carrying value of Alcoa's existing 50% interest in Elkem in accordance with fair value accounting and a $32 adjustment for the finalization of the estimated fair value of the Sapa AB joint venture. The $188 gain was reflected in Other income, net on the accompanying Statement of Consolidated Operations, of which $156 ($112 after-tax) was reflected in the Primary Metals segment and $32 ($21 after-tax) was reflected in Corporate. The portion of the gain reflected in Corporate was because the original write-down of the 45.45% Sapa AB investment to its estimated fair value in December 2008 was reflected in Corporate (see Note D and I). At the time the exchange transaction was completed, Elkem had $18 in cash, which was reflected in the accompanying Statement of Consolidated Cash Flows as a cash inflow on the acquisitions line.

In June 2009, Alcoa completed an acquisition of a fasteners business located in Mexico for $3. This transaction did not have a material impact on Alcoa's Consolidated Financial Statements.

In July 2009, Alcoa World Alumina LLC (AWA LLC), a majority-owned subsidiary of Alcoa and part of Alcoa World Alumina and Chemicals, acquired a BHP Billiton (BHP) subsidiary that holds interests in four bauxite mines and one refining facility in the Republic of Suriname. These interests were part of joint ventures between AWA LLC's wholly-owned subsidiary in Suriname (Suriname Aluminum Company LLC (Suralco)) and BHP's subsidiary in which Suralco held a 55% stake and BHP's subsidiary held a 45% stake. This acquisition strengthens Alcoa's presence in Suriname and supports its overall growth strategy. In this transaction, in exchange for relinquishing BHP of any further obligations, liabilities, and responsibilities related to the joint ventures (certain of which could result in the recognition of charges in future periods), AWA LLC received direct ownership of the BHP subsidiary. This transaction was accounted for as an asset acquisition as it did meet the requirements to be accounted for as a business combination. Prior to the completion of this transaction, Suralco accounted for its 55% interest in the Suriname operations on the proportional consolidation method. The assets and liabilities of the former BHP subsidiary were included in the Alumina segment beginning July 31, 2009 and 100% of the results of the Suriname operations were reflected in this segment starting on August 1, 2009. This acquisition resulted in the addition of 993 kmt of alumina refining capacity (2,207 kmt is total refinery capacity—approximately 870 kmt is curtailed) to Alcoa's global refining system. Alcoa recorded a gain of $92 ($36 after-tax and noncontrolling interest), which was reflected in Other income, net on the accompanying Statement of Consolidated Operations and was reflected in the Alumina segment's results ($60 after-tax). At the time this transaction was completed, the BHP subsidiary had $97 in cash, which was reflected in the accompanying Statement of Consolidated Cash Flows as a cash inflow on the acquisitions line.

Fair Value Measurements

7.30

REPORT OF INDEPENDENT REGISTERED PUBLIC ACCOUNTING FIRM

Shareholders and Board of Directors
WellPoint, Inc.

We have audited the accompanying consolidated balance sheets of WellPoint, Inc. (the "Company") as of December 31, 2009 and 2008, and the related consolidated statements of income, shareholders' equity, and cash flows for each of the three years in the period ended December 31, 2009. Our audits also included the financial statement schedule listed in the Index at Item 15(a). These financial statements and schedule are the responsibility of the Company's management. Our responsibility is to express an opinion on these financial statements and schedule based on our audits.

We conducted our audits in accordance with the standards of the Public Company Accounting Oversight Board (United States). Those standards require that we plan and perform the audit to obtain reasonable assurance about whether the financial statements are free of material misstatement. An audit includes examining, on a test basis, evidence supporting the amounts and disclosures in the financial statements. An audit also includes assessing the accounting principles used and significant estimates made by management, as well as evaluating the overall financial statement presentation. We believe that our audits provide a reasonable basis for our opinion.

In our opinion, the financial statements referred to above present fairly, in all material respects, the consolidated financial position of WellPoint, Inc. at December 31, 2009 and 2008, and the consolidated results of its operations and its cash flows for each of the three years in the period ended December 31, 2009, in conformity with U.S. generally accepted accounting principles. Also, in our opinion, the related financial statement schedule, when considered in relation to the basic financial statements taken as a whole, presents fairly in all material respects the information set forth therein.

As discussed in Note 2 to the consolidated financial statements, during 2009, the Company changed its method of accounting for the recognition of other-than-temporary impairments related to its fixed maturity securities.

We also have audited, in accordance with the standards of the Public Company Accounting Oversight Board (United States), WellPoint, Inc.'s internal control over financial reporting as of December 31, 2009, based on criteria established in Internal Control—Integrated Framework issued by the Committee of Sponsoring Organizations of the Treadway Commission and our report dated February 18, 2010 expressed an unqualified opinion thereon.

NOTES TO CONSOLIDATED FINANCIAL STATEMENTS (In millions)

2 (In Part): Significant Accounting Policies

Investments (In Part)

In April 2009, the FASB issued guidance for recognition and presentation of other-than-temporary impairment, or FASB OTTI guidance. FASB OTTI guidance applies to fixed maturity securities only and provides new guidance on the recognition and presentation of other-than-temporary impairments. In addition, FASB OTTI guidance requires additional disclosures related to other-than-temporary impairments. Under this revised guidance, if a fixed maturity security is in an unrealized loss position and we have the intent to sell the fixed maturity security, or it is more likely than not that we will have to sell the fixed maturity security before recovery of its amortized cost basis, the decline in value is deemed to be other-than-temporary and is recorded to other-than-temporary impairment losses recognized in income in our consolidated income statements. For impaired fixed maturity securities that we do not intend to sell or it is more likely than not that we will not have to sell such securities, but we expect that we will not fully recover the amortized cost basis, the credit component of the other-than-temporary impairment is recognized in other-than-temporary impairment losses recognized in income in our consolidated income statements and the non-credit component of the other-than-temporary impairment is recognized in other comprehensive income. Furthermore, unrealized losses entirely caused by non-credit related factors related to fixed maturity securities for which we expect to fully recover the amortized cost basis continue to be recognized in accumulated other comprehensive income.

The credit component of an other-than-temporary impairment is determined by comparing the net present value of projected future cash flows with the amortized cost basis of the fixed maturity security. The net present value is calculated by discounting our best estimate of projected future cash flows at the effective interest rate implicit in the fixed maturity security at the date of acquisition. For mortgage-backed and asset-backed securities, cash flow estimates are based on assumptions regarding the underlying collateral including prepayment speeds, vintage, type of underlying asset, geographic concentrations, default rates, recoveries and changes in value. For all other debt securities, cash flow estimates are driven by assumptions regarding probability of default, including changes in credit ratings, and estimates regarding timing and amount of recoveries associated with a default.

Upon adoption of the FASB OTTI guidance on April 1, 2009, we recorded a cumulative-effect adjustment, net of taxes, of $88.9 as of the beginning of the period of adoption, April 1, 2009, to reclassify the non-credit component of previously recognized other-than-temporary impairments from retained earnings to accumulated other comprehensive income.

We classify the fixed maturity and equity securities in our investment portfolio as "available-for-sale" or "trading" and report those securities at fair value. Prior to the adoption of the FASB OTTI guidance, we classified our fixed maturity securities as current or noncurrent based on their contractual maturities. In connection with the adoption of the FASB OTTI

guidance on April 1, 2009, we have determined that certain of these fixed maturity securities are available to support current operations and, accordingly, have classified such investments as current assets as of December 31, 2009 without regard to their contractual maturities. Investments used to satisfy contractual, regulatory or other requirements are classified as long-term, without regard to contractual maturity.

The unrealized gains or losses on our current and long-term equity securities classified as available-for-sale are included in accumulated other comprehensive income as a separate component of shareholders' equity, unless the decline in value is deemed to be other-than-temporary and we do not have the intent and ability to hold such equity securities until their full cost can be recovered, in which case such equity securities are written down to fair value and the loss is charged to other-than-temporary impairment losses recognized in income.

4 (In Part): Investments

A summary of current and long-term investments, available-for-sale, is as follows:

	Cost or Amortized Cost	Gross Unrealized Gains	Gross Unrealized Losses		Estimated Fair Value	Non-Credit Component of Other-Than-Temporary Impairments Recognized in AOCI
			12 Months or Less	Greater Than 12 Months		
December 31, 2009:						
Fixed maturity securities:						
United States Government securities	$ 715.4	$ 14.8	$ (2.4)	$ (0.2)	$ 727.6	$ —
Government sponsored securities	632.8	8.3	(0.4)	—	640.7	—
States, municipalities and political subdivisions—tax-exempt	4,019.4	167.0	(5.7)	(34.4)	4,146.3	(0.5)
Corporate securities	6,219.3	352.2	(12.9)	(34.5)	6,524.1	(3.3)
Options embedded in convertible debt securities	88.3	—	—	—	88.3	—
Residential mortgage-backed securities	3,295.0	120.0	(7.9)	(47.0)	3,360.1	(9.0)
Commercial mortgage-backed securities	137.6	3.6	(0.1)	(4.9)	136.2	—
Other debt obligations	318.3	8.7	(1.1)	(21.9)	304.0	(5.7)
Total fixed maturity securities	15,426.1	674.6	(30.5)	(142.9)	15,927.3	$(18.5)
Equity securities	832.5	221.9	(11.2)	—	1,043.2	
Total investments, available-for-sale	$16,258.6	$896.5	$ (41.7)	$(142.9)	$16,970.5	
December 31, 2008:						
Fixed maturity securities:						
United States Government securities	$ 544.5	$ 46.2	$ (1.3)	$ —	$ 589.4	
Government sponsored securities	205.2	10.4	—	—	215.6	
States, municipalities and political subdivisions—tax-exempt	3,880.9	78.9	(86.1)	(58.6)	3,815.1	
Corporate securities	5,193.0	58.3	(355.7)	(121.9)	4,773.7	
Options embedded in convertible debt securities	39.9	—	—	—	39.9	
Residential mortgage-backed securities	3,527.3	114.1	(114.4)	(43.2)	3,483.8	
Commercial mortgage-backed securities	169.5	—	(9.2)	(7.5)	152.8	
Other debt obligations	379.6	0.2	(23.7)	(53.2)	302.9	
Total fixed maturity securities	13,939.9	308.1	(590.4)	(284.4)	13,373.2	
Equity securities	1,327.7	25.8	(234.8)	—	1,118.7	
Total investments, available-for-sale	$15,267.6	$333.9	$(825.2)	$(284.4)	$14,491.9	

At December 31, 2009, we owned $3,496.3 of mortgage-backed securities and $304.0 of asset-backed securities out of a total available-for-sale investment portfolio of $16,970.5. These securities included sub-prime and Alt-A securities with fair values of $107.5 and $285.9, respectively. These sub-prime and Alt-A securities had net unrealized losses of $14.8 and $38.1, respectively. The average credit rating of the sub-prime and Alt-A securities was "A" and "BBB", respectively.

●   ●   ●   ●   ●   ●

Net realized investment gains/losses and net change in unrealized appreciation/depreciation in investments for the years ended December 31, are as follows:

	2009	2008	2007
Net realized gains/losses on investments:			
Fixed maturity securities:			
Gross realized gains from sales	$ 158.3	$ 37.7	$ 71.5
Gross realized losses from sales	(135.5)	(84.6)	(60.0)
Net realized gains/losses from sales of fixed maturity securities	22.8	(46.9)	11.5
Equity securities:			
Gross realized gains from sales	116.5	143.1	277.6
Gross realized losses from sales	(81.5)	(114.8)	(23.4)
Net realized gains from sales of equity securities	35.0	28.3	254.2
Other realized gains/losses on investments	(1.4)	47.3	5.2
Net realized gains on investments	56.4	28.7	270.9
Other-than-temporary impairment losses recognized in income:			
Fixed maturity securities	(217.6)	(479.8)	(154.1)
Equity securities	(232.6)	(728.1)	(105.6)
Other-than-temporary impairment losses recognized in income	(450.2)	(1,207.9)	(259.7)
Change in net unrealized gains/losses on investments:			
Cumulative effect of adoption of FASB OTTI guidance	(143.1)	—	—
Fixed maturity securities	1,209.1	(669.5)	151.1
Equity securities	419.7	(371.7)	(155.6)
Total change in net unrealized gains/losses on investments	1,485.7	(1,041.2)	(4.5)
Deferred income tax (expense) benefit	(540.1)	378.8	6.7
Net change in net unrealized gains/losses on investments	945.6	(662.4)	2.2
Net realized gains/losses on investments, other-than-temporary impairment losses recognized in income and net change in net unrealized gains/losses on investments	$ 551.8	$(1,841.6)	$ 13.4

During the year ended December 31, 2009, we sold $4,673.9 of fixed maturity and equity securities which resulted in gross realized losses of $217.0. In the ordinary course of business, we may sell securities at a loss for a number of reasons, including, but not limited to: (i) changes in the investment environment; (ii) expectation that the fair value could deteriorate further; (iii) desire to reduce exposure to an issuer or an industry; (iv) changes in credit quality; or (v) changes in expected cash flow.

A significant judgment in the valuation of investments is the determination of when an other-than-temporary decline in value has occurred. We follow a consistent and systematic process for recognizing impairments on securities that sustain other-than-temporary declines in value. We have established a committee responsible for the impairment review process. The decision to impair a security incorporates both quantitative criteria and qualitative information. The impairment review process considers a number of factors including, but not limited to: (i) the length of time and the extent to which the fair value has been less than book value, (ii) the financial condition and near term prospects of the issuer, (iii) our in-

tent and ability to retain impaired investments for a period of time sufficient to allow for any anticipated recovery in value, (iv) whether the debtor is current on interest and principal payments, (v) the reasons for the decline in value (i.e., credit event compared to liquidity, general credit spread widening, currency exchange rate or interest rate factors) and (vi) general market conditions and industry or sector specific factors. For securities that are deemed to be other-than-temporarily impaired, the security is adjusted to fair value and the resulting losses are recognized in realized gains or losses in the consolidated statements of income. The new cost basis of the impaired securities is not increased for future recoveries in fair value.

Other-than-temporary impairments recorded in 2009 and 2007 were primarily the result of the continued credit deterioration on specific issuers in the bond markets and certain equity securities' fair value remaining below cost for an extended period of time. There were no individually significant other-than-temporary impairment losses on investments by issuer during 2009 or 2007.

The changes in the amount of the credit component of other-than-temporary impairment losses on fixed maturity securities recognized in income, for which a portion of the other-than-temporary impairment losses was recognized in other comprehensive income, was not material for the year ended December 31, 2009.

Convertible Instruments

7.31

REPORT OF INDEPENDENT REGISTERED PUBLIC ACCOUNTING FIRM

To the Stockholders and Board of Directors of
3M Company

In our opinion, the consolidated financial statements listed in the accompanying index present fairly, in all material respects, the financial position of 3M Company and its subsidiaries (the "Company") at December 31, 2009 and 2008, and the results of their operations and their cash flows for each of the three years in the period ended December 31, 2009 in conformity with accounting principles generally accepted in the United States of America. Also in our opinion, the Company maintained, in all material respects, effective internal control over financial reporting as of December 31, 2009, based on criteria established in Internal Control—Integrated Framework issued by the Committee of Sponsoring Organizations of the Treadway Commission (COSO). The Company's management is responsible for these financial statements, for maintaining effective internal control over financial reporting and for its assessment of the effectiveness of internal control over financial reporting, included in "Management's Report on Internal Control Over Financial Reporting" in the accompanying index. Our responsibility is to express opinions on these financial statements and on the Company's internal control over financial reporting based on our integrated audits. We conducted our audits in accordance with the standards of the Public Company Accounting Oversight Board (United States). Those standards require that we plan and perform the audits to obtain reasonable assurance about whether the financial statements are free of material misstatement and whether effective internal control over financial reporting was maintained in all material respects. Our audits of the financial statements included examining, on a test basis, evidence supporting the amounts and disclosures in the financial statements, assessing the accounting principles used and significant estimates made by management, and evaluating the overall financial statement presentation. Our audit of internal control over financial reporting included obtaining an understanding of internal control over financial reporting, assessing the risk that a material weakness exists, and testing and evaluating the design and operating effectiveness of internal control based on the assessed risk. Our audits also included performing such other procedures as we considered necessary in the circumstances. We believe that our audits provide a reasonable basis for our opinions.

As discussed in Note 1 to the consolidated financial statements, the Company changed the manner in which it accounts for uncertain tax positions in 2007. Also as discussed in Note 1 to the consolidated financial statements, the Company retrospectively changed the manner in which it accounts for noncontrolling interests in consolidated subsidiaries and certain convertible debt instruments in 2009.

A company's internal control over financial reporting is a process designed to provide reasonable assurance regarding the reliability of financial reporting and the preparation of financial statements for external purposes in accordance with generally accepted accounting principles. A company's internal control over financial reporting includes those policies and procedures that (i) pertain to the maintenance of records that, in reasonable detail, accurately and fairly reflect the transactions and dispositions of the assets of the company; (ii) provide reasonable assurance that transactions are recorded as necessary to permit preparation of financial statements in accordance with generally accepted accounting principles, and that receipts and expenditures of the company are being made only in accordance with authorizations of management and directors of the company; and (iii) provide reasonable assurance regarding prevention or timely detection of unauthorized acquisition, use, or disposition of the company's assets that could have a material effect on the financial statements.

Because of its inherent limitations, internal control over financial reporting may not prevent or detect misstatements. Also, projections of any evaluation of effectiveness to future periods are subject to the risk that controls may become inadequate because of changes in conditions, or that the degree of compliance with the policies or procedures may deteriorate.

NOTES TO CONSOLIDATED FINANCIAL STATEMENTS

Note 1 (In Part): Significant Accounting Policies

New Accounting Pronouncements (In Part)
In May 2008, the FASB issued an accounting standard which addresses convertible debt securities that, upon conversion by the holder, may be settled by the issuer fully or partially in cash (rather than settled fully in shares) and specifies that issuers of such instruments should separately account for the liability and equity components in a manner that reflects the issuer's nonconvertible debt borrowing rate when related interest cost is recognized. This standard was effective for 3M beginning January 1, 2009 with retrospective application to all periods presented. This standard impacted the Company's "Convertible Notes" (refer to Note 10 to the Consolidated Financial Statements for more detail), and required that additional interest expense essentially equivalent to the portion of issuance proceeds be retroactively allocated to the instrument's equity component and be recognized over the period from the Convertible Notes' issuance on November 15, 2002 through November 15, 2005 (the first date holders of these Notes had the ability to put them back to 3M). 3M adopted this standard in January 2009. Its retrospective application had no impact on results of operations for periods following 2005, but on post-2005 consolidated balance sheets, it resulted in an increase of approximately $22 million in previously reported opening additional paid in capital and a corresponding decrease in previously reported opening retained earnings.

Note 10 (In Part): Long-Term Debt and Short-Term Borrowings

3M may redeem its 30-year zero-coupon senior notes (the "Convertible Notes") at any time in whole or in part at the accreted conversion price; however, bondholders may convert upon notification of redemption each of the notes into 9.4602 shares of 3M common stock (which 3M would intend to payout in cash). Holders of the 30-year zero-coupon senior notes have the option to require 3M to purchase their notes at accreted value on November 21 in the years 2005, 2007, 2012, 2017, 2022 and 2027. In November 2005, 22,506 of the 639,000 in outstanding bonds were redeemed, resulting in a payout from 3M of approximately $20 million. In November 2007, an additional 364,598 outstanding bonds were redeemed resulting in a payout from 3M of approximately $322 million. These payouts reduced the Convertible Notes' face value at maturity to $252 million, which equates to a book value of approximately $225 million at December 31, 2009. As disclosed in a Form 8-K in November 2005, 3M amended the terms of these securities to pay cash at a rate of 2.40% per annum of the principal amount at maturity of the Company's Convertible Notes, which equated to 2.75% per annum of the notes' accreted value on November 21, 2005. The cash interest payments were made semiannually in arrears on May 22, 2006, November 22, 2006, May 22, 2007 and November 22, 2007 to holders of record on the 15th calendar day preceding each such interest payment date. Effective November 22, 2007, the effective interest rate reverted back to the original yield of 0.50%.

3M originally sold $639 million in aggregate face amount of these "Convertible Notes" on November 15, 2002, which are convertible into shares of 3M common stock. The gross proceeds from the offering, to be used for general corporate purposes, were $550 million ($540 million net of issuance costs). As discussed in Note 1, 3M adopted changes to accounting for convertible debt instruments that may be settled in cash upon conversion (including partial cash settlement), effective January 1, 2009, with retrospective application to all periods presented. As such, additional interest expense essentially equivalent to the portion of issuance proceeds retroactively allocated to the instrument's equity component was recognized over the period from the Convertible Notes' issuance on November 15, 2002 through November 15, 2005 (the first date holders of these Notes had the ability to put them back to 3M). Debt issuance costs were amortized on a straight-line basis over a three-year period beginning in November 2002. Debt issue costs allocated to the Notes' equity component were not material. On February 14, 2003, 3M registered these Convertible Notes in a registration statement filed with the Securities and Exchange Commission. The terms of the Convertible Notes include a yield to maturity of 0.50% and an initial conversion premium of 40 percent over the $65.00 (split-adjusted) closing price of 3M common stock on November 14, 2002. If certain conditions for conversion (relating to the closing common stock prices of 3M exceeding the conversion trigger price for specified periods) are met, holders may convert each of the 30-year zero-coupon senior notes into 9.4602 shares of 3M common stock in any calendar quarter commencing after March 31, 2003. The conversion trigger price for the fourth quarter of 2009 was $122.42 per share. If the conditions for conversion are met, and 3M elects not to settle in cash, the 30-year zero-coupon senior notes will be convertible in the aggregate into approximately 2.4 million shares of 3M common stock. The conditions for conversion related to the Company's Convertible Notes have never been met. If the conditions for conversion are met, 3M may choose to pay in cash and/or common stock; however, if this occurs, the Company has the intent and ability to settle this debt security in cash. Accordingly, there was no impact on 3M's diluted earnings per share.

Earnings Per Share

7.32

REPORT OF INDEPENDENT REGISTERED PUBLIC ACCOUNTING FIRM

The Board of Directors and Shareholders
W.W. Grainger, Inc.

We have audited the accompanying consolidated balance sheets of W.W Grainger, Inc. and subsidiaries as of December 31, 2009, 2008, and 2007, and the related consolidated statements of earnings, comprehensive earnings, shareholders' equity, and cash flows for each of the three years in the period ended December 31, 2009. These financial statements are the responsibility of the Company's management. Our responsibility is to express an opinion on these financial statements based on our audits.

We conducted our audits in accordance with the standards of the Public Company Accounting Oversight Board (United States). Those standards require that we plan and perform the audit to obtain reasonable assurance about whether the financial statements are free of material misstatement. An audit includes examining, on a test basis, evidence supporting the amounts and disclosures in the financial statements. An audit also includes assessing the accounting principles used and significant estimates made by management, as well as evaluating the overall financial statement presentation. We believe that our audits provide a reasonable basis for our opinion.

In our opinion, the financial statements referred to above present fairly, in all material respects, the consolidated financial position of W.W. Grainger, Inc. and subsidiaries at December 31, 2009, 2008 and 2007, and the consolidated results of their operations and their cash flows for each of the three years in the period ended December 31, 2009, in conformity with U.S. generally accepted accounting principles.

As described in Note 16 to the consolidated financial statements, effective January 1, 2007, the Company changed its method of accounting for uncertain tax positions to conform with ASC 740.

As described in Note 17 to the consolidated financial statements, effective January 1, 2009, the Company changed its method of computing earnings per share to the two-class method from the treasury stock method to conform with ASC 260.

We also have audited, in accordance with the standards of the Public Company Accounting Oversight Board (United States), W.W. Grainger, Inc.'s internal control over financial reporting as of December 31, 2009, based on criteria established in Internal Control—Integrated Framework issued by the Committee of Sponsoring Organizations of the Treadway Commission and our report dated February 25, 2010, expressed an unqualified opinion thereon.

NOTES TO CONSOLIDATED FINANCIAL STATEMENTS

Note 17. Earnings Per Share

In June 2008, the FASB issued authoritative guidance which states that unvested share-based payment awards that contain nonforfeitable rights to dividends or dividend equivalents (whether paid or unpaid) are participating securities and shall be included in the computation of earnings per share pursuant to the two-class method.

Effective January 1, 2009, the Company adopted the authoritative guidance. The Company's unvested share-based payment awards, such as certain Performance Shares, Restricted Stock and Restricted Stock Units that contain nonforfeitable rights to dividends, meet the criteria of a participating security. The adoption has changed the methodology of computing the Company's earnings per share to the two-class method from the treasury stock method. As a result, the Company has restated previously reported earnings per share. This change has not affected previously reported consolidated net earnings or net cash flows from operations. Under the two-class method, earnings are allocated between common stock and participating securities. Under the authoritative guidance the presentation of basic and diluted earnings per share is required only for each class of common stock and not for participating securities. As such, the Company will present basic and diluted earnings per share for its one class of common stock.

The two-class method includes an earnings allocation formula that determines earnings per share for each class of common stock according to dividends declared and undistributed earnings for the period. The Company's reported net earnings is reduced by the amount allocated to participating securities to arrive at the earnings allocated to common stock shareholders for purposes of calculating earnings per share.

The dilutive effect of participating securities is calculated using the more dilutive of the treasury stock or the two-class method. The Company has determined the two-class method to be the more dilutive. As such, the earnings allocated to common stock shareholders in the basic earnings per share calculation is adjusted for the reallocation of undistributed earnings to participating securities as prescribed by the authoritative guidance to arrive at the earnings allocated to common stock shareholders for calculating the diluted earnings per share.

The Company had additional outstanding stock options of 2.6 million for the year ended December 31, 2008 that were excluded from the computation of diluted earnings per share because the options' exercise price was greater than the average market price of the common stock.

The following table sets forth the computation of basic and diluted earnings per share under the two-class method (in thousands of dollars, except for share and per share amounts):

	2009	2008	2007
Net earnings attributable to W.W. Grainger, Inc. as reported	$ 430,466	$ 475,355	$ 420,120
Less: distributed earnings available to participating securities	(2,990)	(2,560)	(1,707)
Less: undistributed earnings available to participating securities	(7,059)	(7,935)	(5,428)
Numerator for basic earnings per share:			
Undistributed and distributed earnings available to common shareholders	420,417	464,860	412,985
Add: undistributed earnings allocated to participating securities	7,059	7,935	5,428
Less: undistributed earnings reallocated to participating securities	(6,957)	(7,804)	(5,316)
Numerator for diluted earnings per share:			
Undistributed and distributed earnings available to common shareholders	$ 420,519	$ 464,991	$ 413,097
Denominator for basic earnings per share—weighted average shares	73,786,346	76,579,856	82,403,958
Effect of dilutive securities	1,105,506	1,307,764	1,769,423
Denominator for diluted earnings per share—weighted average shares adjusted for dilutive securities	74,891,852	77,887,620	84,173,381
Earnings per share two-class method			
Basic	$ 5.70	$ 6.07	$ 5.01
Diluted	$ 5.62	$ 5.97	$ 4.91

Inventories

7.33

REPORT OF INDEPENDENT REGISTERED PUBLIC ACCOUNTING FIRM

The Board of Directors and Shareholders of
Pactiv Corporation

We have audited the accompanying consolidated statement of financial position of Pactiv Corporation (the Company) as of December 31, 2009 and 2008, and the related consoli-dated statements of income, changes in equity, comprehensive income (loss), and cash flows for each of the three years in the period ended December 31, 2009. Our audits also included the financial statement schedule listed in the Index at Item 15. These financial statements and schedule are the responsibility of the Company's management. Our responsibility is to express an opinion on these financial statements and schedule based on our audits.

We conducted our audits in accordance with the standards of the Public Company Accounting Oversight Board (United States). Those standards require that we plan and perform the audit to obtain reasonable assurance about whether the financial statements are free of material misstatement. An audit includes examining, on a test basis, evidence supporting the amounts and disclosures in the financial statements. An audit also includes assessing the accounting principles used and significant estimates made by management, as well as evaluating the overall financial statement presentation. We believe that our audits provide a reasonable basis for our opinion.

In our opinion, the financial statements referred to above present fairly, in all material respects, the consolidated financial position of Pactiv Corporation at December 31, 2009 and 2008, and the consolidated results of its operations and its cash flows for each of the three years in the period ended December 31, 2009, in conformity with U.S. generally accepted accounting principles. Also, in our opinion, the related financial statement schedule, when considered in relation to the basic financial statements taken as a whole, presents fairly in all material respects the information set forth therein.

As discussed in Note 2 to the consolidated financial statements, in 2009 the Company changed its method of accounting for inventory and in 2008 the Company adopted the requirement to measure the funded status of its defined benefit pension and postretirement healthcare plans as of the date of the year-end statement of financial position.

We also have audited, in accordance with the standards of the Public Company Accounting Oversight Board (United States), Pactiv Corporation's internal control over financial reporting as of December 31, 2009, based on criteria established in Internal Control—Integrated Framework issued by the Committee of Sponsoring Organizations of the Tread-

way Commission and our report dated February 26, 2010 expressed an unqualified opinion thereon.

NOTES TO FINANCIAL STATEMENTS

Note 2 (In Part): Summary of Accounting Policies

Inventories

Our inventories are stated at the lower of cost or market using the FIFO method. We periodically review inventory balances to identify slow-moving and/or obsolete items. This determination is based on a number of factors, including new product introductions, changes in consumer demand patterns, and historical usage trends.

In 2009, we changed our method of accounting for inventory from a combination of the LIFO method and the FIFO method to the FIFO method. All of our businesses now use the FIFO method of accounting for inventory. We believe the new method of accounting for inventory is preferable because the FIFO method better reflects the current value of inventories on the Consolidated Statement of Financial Position, provides better matching of revenue and expenses under our business model, and provides uniformity across our operations with respect to the method of inventory accounting for financial reporting.

In accordance with ASC 250-10 "Accounting Changes and Error Corrections," all prior periods presented have been retrospectively adjusted to apply the new method of accounting.

The following table presents the line items on the statement of income that were impacted by the accounting change for the years ended December 31, 2008, and 2007.

(In millions, except per share data)	2008 As Originally Reported	2008 As Adjusted	2007 As Originally Reported	2007 As Adjusted
Cost of sales, excluding depreciation and amortization	$2,636	$2,638	$2,322	$2,325
Operating income	446	444	472	469
Income tax expense	120	119	135	133
Income from continuing operations	222	221	246	245
Net income attributable to Pactiv	217	216	245	244
Earnings (loss) per share of common stock:				
Basic	$ 1.66	$ 1.65	$ 1.87	$ 1.86
Diluted	$ 1.64	$ 1.63	$ 1.85	$ 1.84

The following table presents the line items on the statement of financial position that were impacted by the accounting change as of December 31, 2008.

(In millions)	2008 As Originally Reported	As Adjusted
Inventories	$ 344	$ 391
Deferred income tax assets	14	—
Goodwill	1,124	1,128
Other current liabilities	50	55
Retained earnings	1,626	1,658

The following table presents the line items on the statement of cash flows that were impacted by the accounting change for the years ended December 31, 2008, and 2007.

| | 2008 | | 2007 | |
| | As Originally | | As Originally | |
(In millions)	Reported	As Adjusted	Reported	As Adjusted
Net income	$218	$217	$247	$246
Deferred income taxes	113	112	38	37
(Increase) decrease in inventories	20	22	1	4

The following table presents the segment information line items that were impacted by the accounting change for the years ended December 31, 2008, and 2007.

| | 2008 | | 2007 | |
| | As Originally | | As Originally | |
(In millions)	Reported	As Adjusted	Reported	As Adjusted
Operating income (loss)				
Consumer products	$ 207	$ 207	$ 227	$ 226
Foodservice/Food packaging	236	234	247	245
Other	3	3	(2)	(2)
Total operating income (loss)	$ 446	$ 444	$ 472	$ 469
Total assets				
Consumer products	$1,307	$1,326	$1,345	$1,365
Foodservice/Food packaging	2,070	2,102	2,125	2,159
Other	348	333	295	274
Total assets	$3,725	$3,761	$3,765	$3,798

EMPHASIS OF A MATTER

7.34   Paragraph 19 of *AU section 508*, as amended, states:

19. In any report on financial statements, the auditor may emphasize a matter regarding the financial statements. Such explanatory information should be presented in a separate paragraph of the auditors' report. Phrases such as "with the foregoing (following) explanation" should not be used in the opinion paragraph if an emphasis paragraph is included in the auditors' report. Emphasis paragraphs are never required; they may be added solely at the auditors' discretion. Examples of matters the auditor may wish to emphasize are—

- That the entity is a component of a larger business enterprise.
- That the entity has had significant transactions with related parties.
- Unusually important subsequent events.
- Accounting matters, other than those involving a change or changes in accounting principles, affecting the comparability of the financial statements with those of the preceding period.

7.35   The auditors' reports for four survey entities included explanatory information emphasizing a matter regarding the financial statements. Examples of such explanatory information follow.

7.36

REPORT OF INDEPENDENT REGISTERED PUBLIC ACCOUNTING FIRM

The Board of Directors and Stockholders
Fidelity National Information Services, Inc.

We have audited the accompanying consolidated balance sheets of Fidelity National Information Services, Inc. and subsidiaries (the "Company") as of December 31, 2009 and 2008, and the related consolidated statements of earnings, equity and comprehensive earnings and cash flows for each of the years in the three-year period ended December 31, 2009. These consolidated financial statements are the responsibility of the Company's management. Our responsibility is to express an opinion on these consolidated financial statements based on our audits.

We conducted our audits in accordance with the standards of the Public Company Accounting Oversight Board (United States). Those standards require that we plan and perform the audit to obtain reasonable assurance about whether the financial statements are free of material misstatement. An audit includes examining, on a test basis, evidence supporting the amounts and disclosures in the financial statements. An audit also includes assessing the accounting principles used and significant estimates made by management, as well as evaluating the overall financial statement presentation.

We believe that our audits provide a reasonable basis for our opinion.

In our opinion, the consolidated financial statements referred to above present fairly, in all material respects, the financial position of Fidelity National Information Services, Inc. and subsidiaries as of December 31, 2009 and 2008, and the results of their operations and their cash flows for each of the years in the three-year period ended December 31, 2009, in conformity with U.S. generally accepted accounting principles.

We also have audited, in accordance with the standards of the Public Accounting Oversight Board (United States), Fidelity National Information Services, Inc.'s and subsidiaries' internal control over financial reporting as of December 31, 2009, based on criteria established in Internal Control—Integrated Framework issued by the Committee of Sponsoring Organizations of the Treadway Commission (COSO), and our report dated February 26, 2010 expressed an unqualified opinion on the effectiveness of the Company's internal control over financial reporting.

As discussed in note 6 to the consolidated financial statements, the Company completed a merger with Metavante Technologies, Inc. on October 1, 2009.

NOTES TO CONSOLIDATED FINANCIAL STATEMENTS

1 (In Part): Basis of Presentation

FIS is a leading global provider of banking and payments technology solutions, processing services and information-based services. On February 1, 2006, the Company completed a merger with Certegy (the "Certegy Merger") which was accounted for as a reverse acquisition and purchase accounting was applied to the acquired assets and assumed liabilities of Certegy. In form, Certegy was the legal acquirer in the Certegy Merger and the continuing registrant for Securities and Exchange Commission (the "SEC") reporting purposes. However, due to the majority ownership in the combined entity held by FIS shareholders, FIS was designated the acquirer for accounting purposes and, effective on the Certegy Merger date, the historical financial statements of FIS became the historical financial statements of the continuing registrant for all periods prior to the Certegy Merger. Immediately after the Certegy Merger, the name of the SEC registrant was changed to Fidelity National Information Services, Inc.

6 (In Part): Acquisitions and Dispositions

The results of operations and financial position of the entities acquired during the years ended December 31, 2009, 2008, and 2007 are included in the Consolidated Financial Statements from and after the date of acquisition. There were no significant acquisitions in 2008.

2009 Significant Acquisition

Metavante

On October 1, 2009, we completed the acquisition of Metavante (the "Metavante Acquisition"). Metavante expands the scale of FIS core processing and payment capabilities, adds trust and wealth management services and includes the NYCE Network, a leading national EFT network. In addition, Metavante adds significant scale to treasury and cash management offerings and provides an entry into the emerging

markets of healthcare and government payments. Pursuant to the Agreement and Plan of Merger (the "Metavante Merger Agreement") dated as of March 31, 2009, Metavante became a wholly-owned subsidiary of FIS. Each issued and outstanding share of Metavante common stock, par value $0.01 per share, was converted into 1.35 shares of FIS common stock. In addition, outstanding Metavante stock options and other stock-based awards converted into comparable FIS stock options and other stock-based awards at the same conversion ratio.

The total purchase price was as follows (in millions):

Value of Metavante common stock	$4,066.4
Value of Metavante stock awards	121.4
Total purchase price	$4,187.8

We have recorded a preliminary allocation of the purchase price to Metavante tangible and identifiable intangible assets acquired and liabilities assumed based on their fair values as of October 1, 2009. Goodwill has been recorded based on the amount by which the purchase price exceeds the fair value of the net assets acquired. The preliminary purchase price allocation is as follows (in millions):

Cash	$ 439.7
Trade and other receivables	237.9
Land, buildings, and equipment	119.8
Other assets	144.4
Computer software	287.7
Intangible assets	1,572.0
Goodwill	4,083.1
Liabilities assumed	(2,673.4)
Noncontrolling interest	(23.4)
Total purchase price	$ 4,187.8

The preliminary allocation of the purchase price to intangible assets, including computer software and customer relationships, is based on valuations performed to determine the fair value of such assets as of the merger date. The Company is still assessing the economic characteristics of certain software projects and customer relationships. The Company expects to substantially complete this assessment during the first quarter of 2010 and may adjust the amounts recorded as of December 31, 2009 to reflect any revised evaluations. Land and building valuations are based upon appraisals performed by certified property appraisers.

The following table summarizes the liabilities assumed in the Metavante Acquisition (in millions):

Long-term debt including current portion	$1,720.1
Deferred income taxes	544.4
Other liabilities	408.9
	$2,673.4

In connection with the Metavante Acquisition, we also acquired Metavante stock option plans and registered approximately 12.2 million options and 0.6 million restricted stock units in replacement of similar outstanding awards held by Metavante employees. The amounts attributable to vested options are included as an adjustment to the purchase price, and the amounts attributable to unvested options and restricted stock units will be expensed over the remaining vesting period based on a valuation as of the date of closing.

As of the acquisition date, WPM, L.P., a Delaware limited partnership affiliated with Warburg Pincus Private Equity IX, L.P. (collectively "Warburg Pincus") owned 25% of the outstanding shares of Metavante common stock, and was a party to a purchase right agreement with Metavante which granted Warburg Pincus the right to purchase additional shares of Metavante common stock under certain conditions in order to maintain its interest. The Company and Warburg Pincus entered into a replacement stock purchase right agreement effective upon consummation of the merger, granting Warburg Pincus the right to purchase comparable FIS shares in lieu of Metavante shares. The purchase right agreement relates to Metavante employee stock options that were outstanding as of the date of Warburg Pincus' initial investment in Metavante. The stock purchase right may be exercised quarterly for the difference between one-third of the number of said employee stock options exercised during the preceding quarter and the quotient of one-third of the aggregate exercise prices of such options exercised divided by the quoted closing price of a common share on the day immediately before exercise of the purchase right. As of October 1, 2009, approximately 7.0 million options remained outstanding that were subject to this purchase right, and approximately 0.5 million were exercised during the fourth quarter of 2009.

Pro Forma Results

Metavante's revenues of $404.1 million for the fourth quarter of 2009 are included in the Consolidated Statements of Earnings. Disclosure of the earnings of Metavante since the acquisition date is not practicable as it is not being operated as a standalone subsidiary.

Selected unaudited pro forma results of operations for the years ended December 31, 2009 and 2008, assuming the Metavante Acquisition had occurred as of January 1 of each respective year, are presented for comparative purposes below (in millions, except per share amounts):

	2009	2008
Total revenues	$4,983.1	$5,020.8
Net earnings from continuing operations attributable to FIS common stockholders	155.1	131.6
Pro forma earnings per share—basic from continuing operations attributable to FIS common stockholders	0.41	0.36
Pro forma earnings per share—diluted from continuing operations attributable to FIS common stockholders	0.40	0.35

Pro forma results include impairment charges of $136.9 million and Metavante merger and integration related costs of approximately $143.2 million, on a pre-tax basis. Excluding the impact of deferred revenue adjustments, total pro forma revenues would be $5,051.9 million and $5,092.0 million for 2009 and 2008, respectively.

DEPARTURES FROM UNQUALIFIED OPINIONS

7.37 *AU section 508* does not require auditors to express qualified opinions as to the effects of uncertainties or as to lack of consistency. Under *AU section 508*, departures from unqualified opinions include opinions qualified because of a scope limitation or a departure from generally accepted accounting principles, adverse opinions, and disclaimers of opinion. Paragraphs 20–63 of *AU section 508*, as amended, discuss these departures. None of the auditors' reports issued in connection with the financial statements of the survey entities contained a departure as defined by *AU section 508*.

REPORTS ON COMPARATIVE FINANCIAL STATEMENTS

7.38 Paragraphs 65–74 of *AU section 508*, as amended, discuss Reports on Comparative Financial Statements. None of the auditors' reports for the survey entities expressed an opinion on prior year financial statements that differed from the opinion originally expressed.

7.39 In 2009, four auditor reports indicated that a change in auditors had occurred in the current year. An example of such a report follows.

7.40

REPORT OF INDEPENDENT REGISTERED PUBLIC ACCOUNTING FIRM

To the Board of Directors and Stockholders of Polo Ralph Lauren Corporation

We have audited the accompanying consolidated balance sheet of Polo Ralph Lauren Corporation and subsidiaries (the "Company") as of March 28, 2009, and the related consolidated statement of operations, stockholders' equity, and cash flows for the fiscal year then ended. These financial statements are the responsibility of the Company's management. Our responsibility is to express an opinion on the financial statements based on our audit.

We conducted our audit in accordance with the standards of the Public Company Accounting Oversight Board (United States). Those standards require that we plan and perform the audit to obtain reasonable assurance about whether the financial statements are free of material misstatement. An audit includes examining, on a test basis, evidence supporting the amounts and disclosures in the financial statements. An audit also includes assessing the accounting principles used and significant estimates made by management, as well as evaluating the overall financial statement presentation. We believe that our audit provides a reasonable basis for our opinion.

In our opinion, the financial statements referred to above present fairly, in all material respects, the consolidated financial position of the Company at March 28, 2009, and the consolidated results of its operations and its cash flows for the fiscal year then ended, in conformity with U.S. generally accepted accounting principles.

We also have audited, in accordance with the standards of the Public Company Accounting Oversight Board (United States), the Company's internal control over financial reporting as of March 28, 2009, based on the criteria established in Internal Control—Integrated Framework issued by the Committee of Sponsoring Organizations of the Treadway Commission and our report dated May 26, 2009 expressed an unqualified opinion thereon.

REPORT OF INDEPENDENT REGISTERED PUBLIC ACCOUNTING FIRM

To the Board of Directors and Stockholders of
Polo Ralph Lauren Corporation

We have audited the accompanying consolidated balance sheet of Polo Ralph Lauren Corporation and subsidiaries (the "Company") as of March 29, 2008, and the related consolidated statements of operations, stockholders' equity, and cash flows for each of the two fiscal years in the period ended March 29, 2008. These financial statements are the responsibility of the Company's management. Our responsibility is to express an opinion on the financial statements based on our audits.

We conducted our audits in accordance with the standards of the Public Company Accounting Oversight Board (United States). Those standards require that we plan and perform the audit to obtain reasonable assurance about whether the financial statements are free of material misstatement. An audit includes examining, on a test basis, evidence supporting the amounts and disclosures in the financial statements. An audit also includes assessing the accounting principles used and significant estimates made by management, as well as evaluating the overall financial statement presentation. We believe that our audits provide a reasonable basis for our opinion.

In our opinion, such consolidated financial statements present fairly, in all material respects, the financial position of the Company as of March 29, 2008, and the results of its operations and its cash flows for each of the two fiscal years in the period ended March 29, 2008, in conformity with accounting principles generally accepted in the United States of America.

As discussed in Note 3 to the notes to consolidated financial statements, the Company adopted Financial Accounting Standards Board Interpretation No. 48, "Accounting for Uncertainty in Income Taxes," effective April 1, 2007. Also, as discussed in Note 4 to the notes to consolidated financial statements, the Company elected application of Staff Accounting Bulletin No. 108, "Considering the Effects of Prior Year Misstatements when Quantifying Misstatements in Current Year Financial Statements," effective April 2, 2006.

OPINION EXPRESSED ON SUPPLEMENTARY FINANCIAL INFORMATION

7.41   Many survey entities provide to stockholders a copy of the Securities and Exchange Commission Form 10-K in lieu of the annual report. The auditors' report included in the Form 10-K generally expresses an opinion on supplementary financial information to the basic financial statements, such as valuation account schedules. During 2009, 220 survey entities expressed an opinion on supplementary financial information. An example of such a report follows.

7.42

REPORT OF INDEPENDENT REGISTERED PUBLIC ACCOUNTING FIRM

To the Board of Directors and Shareholders of
Avon Products, Inc.

In our opinion, the accompanying consolidated balance sheets and the related consolidated statements of income, cash flows and changes in shareholders' equity present fairly, in all material respects, the financial position of Avon Products, Inc. and its subsidiaries at December 31, 2009 and December 31, 2008, and the results of their operations and their cash flows for each of the three years in the period ended December 31, 2009 in conformity with accounting principles generally accepted in the United States of America. In addition, in our opinion, the financial statement schedule listed in Item 15(a)(2) presents fairly, in all material respects, the information set forth therein when read in conjunction with the related consolidated financial statements. Also in our opinion, the Company maintained, in all material respects, effective internal control over financial reporting as of December 31, 2009, based on criteria established in Internal Control—Integrated Framework issued by the Committee of Sponsoring Organizations of the Treadway Commission (COSO). The Company's management is responsible for these financial statements and financial statement schedule, for maintaining effective internal control over financial reporting and for its assessment of the effectiveness of internal control over financial reporting, included in Management's Report on Internal Control over Financial Reporting, appearing in Item 9A. Our responsibility is to express opinions on these financial statements, on the financial statement schedule, and on the Company's internal control over financial reporting based on our integrated audits. We conducted our audits in accordance with the standards of the Public Company Accounting Oversight Board (United States). Those standards require that we plan and perform the audits to obtain reasonable assurance about whether the financial statements are free of material misstatement and whether effective internal control over financial reporting was maintained in all material respects. Our audits of the financial statements included examining, on a test basis, evidence supporting the amounts and disclosures in the financial statements, assessing the accounting principles used and significant estimates made by management, and evaluating the overall financial statement presentation.

Our audit of internal control over financial reporting included obtaining an understanding of internal control over financial reporting, assessing the risk that a material weakness exists, and testing and evaluating the design and operating effectiveness of internal control based on the assessed risk. Our audits also included performing such other procedures as we considered necessary in the circumstances. We believe that our audits provide a reasonable basis for our opinions.

As discussed in Note 2 to the consolidated financial statements, in 2009 the Company changed the manner in which it accounts for noncontrolling interests in subsidiaries. In 2007 the Company changed the manner in which it accounts for uncertain tax positions.

A company's internal control over financial reporting is a process designed to provide reasonable assurance regarding the reliability of financial reporting and the preparation of financial statements for external purposes in accordance with generally accepted accounting principles. A company's internal control over financial reporting includes those policies and procedures that (i) pertain to the maintenance of records that, in reasonable detail, accurately and fairly reflect the transactions and dispositions of the assets of the company; (ii) provide reasonable assurance that transactions are recorded as necessary to permit preparation of financial statements in accordance with generally accepted accounting principles, and that receipts and expenditures of the company are being made only in accordance with authorizations of management and directors of the company; and (iii) provide reasonable assurance regarding prevention or timely detection of unauthorized acquisition, use, or disposition of the company's assets that could have a material effect on the financial statements.

Because of its inherent limitations, internal control over financial reporting may not prevent or detect misstatements. Also, projections of any evaluation of effectiveness to future periods are subject to the risk that controls may become inadequate because of changes in conditions, or that the degree of compliance with the policies or procedures may deteriorate.

SCHEDULE II

VALUATION AND QUALIFYING ACCOUNTS

(In millions)	Balance at Beginning of Period	Additions Charged to Costs and Expenses	Additions Charged to Revenue	Deductions	Balance at End of Period
2009					
Allowance for doubtful accounts receivable	$102.0	$221.7	$ —	$191.1[1]	$132.6
Allowance for sales returns	25.8	—	374.1	367.0[2]	32.9
Allowance for inventory obsolescence	98.2	122.9[4]	—	105.1[3]	116.0
Deferred tax asset valuation allowance	284.1	110.0	—	—	394.1
2008					
Allowance for doubtful accounts receivable	$109.0	$195.5	$ —	$202.5[1]	$102.0
Allowance for sales returns	32.1	—	369.3	375.6[2]	25.8
Allowance for inventory obsolescence	216.9	80.8[4]	—	199.5[3]	98.2
Deferred tax asset valuation allowance	278.3	5.8	—	—	284.1
2007					
Allowance for doubtful accounts receivable	$ 91.1	$164.1	$ —	$146.2[1]	$109.0
Allowance for sales returns	28.0	—	338.1	334.0[2]	32.1
Allowance for inventory obsolescence	125.0	280.6[4]	—	188.7[3]	216.9
Deferred tax asset valuation allowance	234.1	62.9	—	18.7[5]	278.3

[1] Accounts written off, net of recoveries and foreign currency translation adjustment.

[2] Returned product destroyed and foreign currency translation adjustment.

[3] Obsolete inventory destroyed and foreign currency translation adjustment.

[4] Increase in valuation allowance for tax loss carryforward benefits is because it is more likely than not that some or all of the deferred tax assets will not be realized in the future.

[5] Release of valuation allowance on deferred tax assets that are more likely than not to be realized in the future.

DATING OF REPORT

7.43 AU section 530, *Dating of the Independent Auditor's Report*, as amended, discusses dating of the independent auditor's report. Paragraphs 1 and 5 of *AU section 530* state:

1. The auditor's report should not be dated earlier than the date on which the auditor has obtained sufficient appropriate audit evidence to support the opinion. Paragraph.05 describes the procedure to be followed when a subsequent event occurring after the date of the auditor's report is disclosed in the financial statements.

5. The independent auditor has two methods available for dating his report when a subsequent event disclosed in the financial statements occurs after the original date of the auditor's report but before issuance of the related financial statements. The auditor may use "dual dating," for example, "February 16, 20___, except for Note___, as to which the date is March 1, 20___," or may date the report as of the later date. In the former instance, his responsibility for events occurring subsequent to the original report date is limited to the specific event referred to in the note (or otherwise disclosed). In the latter instance, the independent auditor's responsibility for subsequent events extends to the date of the report and, accordingly, the procedures outlined in Section 560.12 generally should be extended to that date.

7.44 None of the survey entities' auditor's reports used dual dating.

AUDITORS' REPORT ON INTERNAL CONTROL OVER FINANCIAL REPORTING

7.45 Section 404(a) of the Sarbanes-Oxley Act of 2002 requires that management of a public entity assess the effectiveness of the entity's internal control over financial reporting as of the end of the entity's most recent fiscal year, and to include in the entity's annual report management's conclusions as to the effectiveness of the entity's internal control structure and procedures. Management is required to state a direct conclusion about whether the entity's internal control over financial reporting is effective. Management's report on internal control over financial reporting is required to include the following:

- A statement of management's responsibility for establishing and maintaining adequate internal control over financial reporting for the entity;
- A statement identifying the framework used by management to conduct the required assessment of the effectiveness of the entity's internal control over financial reporting;
- An assessment of the effectiveness of the entity's internal control over financial reporting as of the end of the entity's most recent fiscal year, including an explicit statement as to whether that internal control over financial reporting is effective; and
- A statement that the registered public accounting firm that audited the financial statements included in the an-

nual report has issued an attestation report on management's assessment of the entity's internal control over financial reporting.

7.46 Under section 404(b) of the Sarbanes-Oxley Act of 2002, the auditor that audits the public entity's financial statements included in the annual report is required to audit the entity's internal control over financial reporting. In addition, the auditor is required to audit and report on management's assessment of the effectiveness of internal control over financial reporting. AS No. 2, *An Audit of Internal Control Over Financial Reporting Performed in Conjunction With an Audit of Financial Statements*, establishes professional standards governing the auditor's attestation. In July 2007, the SEC approved AS No. 5, *An Audit of Internal Control Over Financial Reporting That is Integrated With an Audit of Financial Statements*. *AS No. 5* supersedes *AS No. 2* and is effective for audits of internal control over financial reporting required by section 404(b) of the Sarbanes-Oxley Act of 2002 for fiscal years ending on or after November 15, 2007. Under *AS No. 5*, the auditor's objective in an audit of internal control over financial reporting is to express an opinion on the effectiveness of the entity's internal control over financial reporting. The audit of internal control over financial reporting should be integrated with the audit of the financial statements. Accordingly, independent auditors engaged to audit the financial statements of such entities also are required to audit and report on the entity's internal control over financial reporting as of the end of such fiscal year. Further, if the auditor determines that elements of management's annual report on internal control over financial reporting are incomplete or improperly presented, the auditor should modify the report to include an explanatory paragraph describing the reasons for this determination, and identify and fairly describe any material weakness. Paragraph 86 of *AS No. 5* allows the auditor to issue a combined report (i.e., one report containing both an opinion on the financial statements and an opinion on internal control over financial reporting), or separate reports on the entity's financial statements and on internal control over financial reporting.

7.47 During 2009, 496 of the entities surveyed presented a management's report on internal control over financial reporting. 457 of those entities presented the management report on internal control over financial reporting separate from the general report of management. Also, 493 of the entities surveyed presented an auditor's report on internal control over financial reporting. 178 of those entities had the auditor's report on internal control over financial reporting combined with the auditor's report on financial statements. The auditor's report on internal control over financial reporting for four of the entities surveyed indicated internal control was not effective. Examples of auditors' reports on internal control over financial reporting and their related management reports follow.

Separate Report on Internal Control

7.48

*REPORT OF INDEPENDENT REGISTERED
PUBLIC ACCOUNTING FIRM ON INTERNAL
CONTROL OVER FINANCIAL REPORTING*

To the Board of Directors and Shareholders of
Best Buy Co., Inc.

We have audited the internal control over financial reporting
of Best Buy Co., Inc. and subsidiaries (the "Company") as of
February 28, 2009, based on criteria established in Internal
Control—Integrated Framework issued by the Committee of
Sponsoring Organizations of the Treadway Commission. As
described in Management's Report on Internal Control Over
Financial Reporting, management excluded from its assessment the internal control over financial reporting at Best Buy
Europe, which was acquired on June 28, 2008, and whose
financial statements reflect total assets and total revenues
constituting 26% and 7%, respectively, of the consolidated
financial statement amounts as of and for the year ended
February 28, 2009. Management has also excluded from
its assessment the internal control over financial reporting
at Napster, which was acquired on October 25, 2008, and
whose financial statements reflect total assets and total revenues that constitute less than 1% of the consolidated financial statement amounts as of and for the year ended February
28, 2009. Accordingly, our audit did not include the internal control over financial reporting at Best Buy Europe and
Napster. The Company's management is responsible for
maintaining effective internal control over financial reporting
and for its assessment of the effectiveness of internal control over financial reporting, included in the accompanying
Management's Report on Internal Control Over Financial Reporting. Our responsibility is to express an opinion on the
Company's internal control over financial reporting based on
our audit.

We conducted our audit in accordance with the standards
of the Public Company Accounting Oversight Board (United
States). Those standards require that we plan and perform
the audit to obtain reasonable assurance about whether effective internal control over financial reporting was maintained in all material respects. Our audit included obtaining
an understanding of internal control over financial reporting,
assessing the risk that a material weakness exists, testing
and evaluating the design and operating effectiveness of internal control based on the assessed risk, and performing
such other procedures as we considered necessary in the
circumstances. We believe that our audit provides a reasonable basis for our opinion.

A company's internal control over financial reporting is a
process designed by, or under the supervision of, the company's principal executive and principal financial officers, or
persons performing similar functions, and effected by the
company's board of directors, management, and other personnel to provide reasonable assurance regarding the reliability of financial reporting and the preparation of financial statements for external purposes in accordance with
generally accepted accounting principles. A company's internal control over financial reporting includes those policies and procedures that (1) pertain to the maintenance of
records that, in reasonable detail, accurately and fairly reflect
the transactions and dispositions of the assets of the company; (2) provide reasonable assurance that transactions
are recorded as necessary to permit preparation of financial statements in accordance with generally accepted accounting principles, and that receipts and expenditures of
the company are being made only in accordance with authorizations of management and directors of the company;
and (3) provide reasonable assurance regarding prevention
or timely detection of unauthorized acquisition, use, or disposition of the company's assets that could have a material
effect on the financial statements.

Because of the inherent limitations of internal control over
financial reporting, including the possibility of collusion or improper management override of controls, material misstatements due to error or fraud may not be prevented or detected
on a timely basis. Also, projections of any evaluation of the
effectiveness of the internal control over financial reporting to
future periods are subject to the risk that the controls may become inadequate because of changes in conditions, or that
the degree of compliance with the policies or procedures may
deteriorate.

In our opinion, the Company maintained, in all material respects, effective internal control over financial reporting as of
February 28, 2009, based on the criteria established in Internal Control—Integrated Framework issued by the Committee
of Sponsoring Organizations of the Treadway Commission.

We have also audited, in accordance with the standards
of the Public Company Accounting Oversight Board (United
States), the consolidated financial statements and financial
statement schedule as of and for the year ended February 28,
2009 of the Company and our report dated April 24, 2009, expressed an unqualified opinion on those financial statements
and financial statement schedule and included an explanatory paragraph relating to the Company's change effective
March 4, 2007, in its method of accounting for uncertain tax
benefits.

*MANAGEMENT'S REPORT ON INTERNAL
CONTROL OVER FINANCIAL REPORTING*

Our management is responsible for establishing and maintaining adequate internal control over financial reporting as
defined in Rule 13a-15(f) under the Exchange Act. Our internal control over financial reporting is designed under the
supervision of our principal executive officer and principal financial officer, and effected by our Board, management and
other personnel, to provide reasonable assurance regarding
the reliability of financial reporting and the preparation of financial statements for external purposes in accordance with
GAAP and include those policies and procedures that:

(1) Pertain to the maintenance of records that in reason-
    able detail accurately and fairly reflect our transactions
    and the dispositions of our assets;
(2) Provide reasonable assurance that our transactions
    are recorded as necessary to permit preparation of fi-
    nancial statements in accordance with GAAP, and that
    our receipts and expenditures are being made only in
    accordance with authorizations of our management
    and Board; and
(3) Provide reasonable assurance regarding prevention or
    timely detection of unauthorized acquisition, use or
    disposition of our assets that could have a material
    effect on our financial statements.

Because of its inherent limitations, internal control over financial reporting may not prevent or detect misstatements. Therefore, even those systems determined to be effective can provide only reasonable assurance with respect to financial statement preparation and presentation.

Under the supervision and with the participation of our management, including our principal executive officer and principal financial officer, we assessed the effectiveness of our internal control over financial reporting as of February 28, 2009, using the criteria set forth by the Committee of Sponsoring Organizations of the Treadway Commission (COSO) in Internal Control—Integrated Framework. Based on our assessment, we have concluded that our internal control over financial reporting was effective as of February 28, 2009. During our assessment, we did not identify any material weaknesses in our internal control over financial reporting. We have excluded from our assessment the internal control over financial reporting at Best Buy Europe, which was acquired on June 28, 2008, and whose financial statements reflect total assets and total revenue constituting 26% and 7%, respectively, of our consolidated financial statement amounts as of and for the year ended February 28, 2009. We have also excluded from our assessment the internal control over financial reporting at Napster, which was acquired on October 25, 2008, and whose financial statements reflect total assets and total revenue that constitute less than 1% of our consolidated financial statement amounts as of and for the year ended February 28, 2009. Deloitte & Touche LLP, the independent registered public accounting firm that audited our consolidated financial statements for the year ended February 28, 2009, included in Item 8, Financial Statements and Supplementary Data, of this Annual Report on Form 10-K, has issued an unqualified attestation report on the effectiveness of our internal control over financial reporting as of February 28, 2009.

7.49

REPORT OF INDEPENDENT REGISTERED PUBLIC ACCOUNTING FIRM

To the Board of Directors and Stockholders of
The L.S. Starrett Company

We have audited The L.S. Starrett Company and subsidiaries' (the "Company") internal control over financial reporting as of June 27, 2009, based on criteria established in Internal Control—Integrated Framework issued by the Committee of Sponsoring Organizations of the Treadway Commission (COSO). The Company's management is responsible for maintaining effective internal control over financial reporting and for its assessment of the effectiveness of internal control over financial reporting, and for its assertion of the effectiveness of internal control over financial reporting included in the accompanying "Management's Report on Internal Control Over Financial Reporting" ("Management's Report"). Our responsibility is to express an opinion on the Company's internal control over financial reporting based on our audit.

We conducted our audit in accordance with attestation standards established by the American Institute of Certified Public Accountants. Those standards require that we plan and perform the audit to obtain reasonable assurance about whether effective internal control over financial reporting was maintained in all material respects. Our audit included obtaining an understanding of internal control over financial reporting, assessing the risk that a material weakness exists, testing and evaluating the design and operating effectiveness of internal control based on the assessed risk, and performing such other procedures as we considered necessary in the circumstances. We believe that our audit provides a reasonable basis for our opinion.

A Company's internal control over financial reporting is a process effected by those charged with governance, management, and other personnel, designed to provide reasonable assurance regarding the preparation of reliable financial statements in accordance with generally accepted accounting principles. A company's internal control over financial reporting includes those policies and procedures that (1) pertain to the maintenance of records that, in reasonable detail, accurately and fairly reflect the transactions and dispositions of the assets of the company; (2) provide reasonable assurance that transactions are recorded as necessary to permit preparation of financial statements in accordance with generally accepted accounting principles, and that receipts and expenditures of the company are being made only in accordance with authorizations of management and those charged with governance; and (3) provide reasonable assurance regarding prevention, or timely detection and correction of unauthorized acquisition, use, or disposition of the company's assets that could have a material effect on the financial statements.

Because of its inherent limitations, internal control over financial reporting may not prevent, or detect and correct misstatements. Also, projections of any evaluation of effectiveness to future periods are subject to the risk that controls may become inadequate because of changes in conditions, or that the degree of compliance with the policies or procedures may deteriorate.

A material weakness is a deficiency, or combination of deficiencies, in internal control over financial reporting, such that there is a reasonable possibility that a material misstatement of the Company's financial statements will not be prevented, or detected and corrected on a timely basis. The following material weakness has been identified and included in Management's Report: a weakness related to financial reporting resources at both the corporate and subsidiary level. This weakness resulted in material adjustments to the consolidated financial statements.

In our opinion, because of the effect of the material weakness described above on the achievement of the objectives of the control criteria, the Company has not maintained effective internal control over financial reporting as of June 27, 2009 based on criteria established in Internal Control—Integrated Framework issued by COSO.

We also have audited, in accordance with the auditing standards generally accepted in the United States of America as established by the American Institute of Certified Public Accountants, the consolidated balance sheets of the Company as of June 27, 2009 and June 28, 2008, and the related consolidated statements of operations, shareholders' equity, and cash flows for each of the three years in the period ended June 27, 2009. The material weakness identified above was considered in determining the nature, timing, and extent of audit tests applied in our audit of the fiscal 2009 financial statements, and this report does not affect our report dated

September 10, 2009 expressing an unqualified opinion on those financial statements.

We do not express an opinion or any other form of assurance on management's remediation plans with respect to the material weakness included in Management's Report.

MANAGEMENT'S ANNUAL REPORT ON INTERNAL CONTROL OVER FINANCIAL REPORTING

Management of the Company is responsible for establishing and maintaining adequate internal control over financial reporting as defined in Rules 13a-15(f) and 15d-15(f) under the Securities Exchange Act of 1934. The Company's internal control over financial reporting is a process designed to provide reasonable assurance regarding the reliability of financial reporting and the preparation of financial statements for external purposes in accordance with accounting principles generally accepted in the United States of America. Internal control over financial reporting includes those written policies and procedures that:

- Pertain to the maintenance of records that, in reasonable detail, accurately and fairly reflect the transactions and acquisitions and dispositions of the assets of the Company;
- Provide reasonable assurance that transactions are recorded as necessary to permit preparation of financial statements in accordance with accounting principles generally accepted in the United States of America;
- Provide reasonable assurance that receipts and expenditures of the Company are being made only in accordance with authorization of management and directors of the Company; and
- Provide reasonable assurance regarding prevention or timely detection of unauthorized acquisition, use or disposition of assets that could have a material effect on the consolidated financial statements.

Internal control over financial reporting includes the controls themselves, monitoring and internal auditing practices and actions taken to correct deficiencies as identified.

A deficiency in internal control exists when the design or operation of a control does not allow management or employees, in the normal course of performing their assigned functions, to prevent or detect misstatements on a timely basis.

A material weakness is a deficiency, or a combination of deficiencies, in internal control over financial reporting, such that there is a reasonable possibility that a material misstatement of the Company's annual or interim financial statements will not be prevented or detected on a timely basis. A significant deficiency is a deficiency, or a combination of deficiencies, in internal control over financial reporting that is less severe than a material weakness, yet important enough to merit attention by those responsible for oversight of the company's financial reporting (also referred to as those charged with governance).

Because of its inherent limitations, internal control over financial reporting may not prevent or detect all misstatements. Also, projections of any evaluation of effectiveness to future periods are subject to the risk that controls may become inadequate because of changes in conditions, or that the degree of compliance with the policies or procedures may deteriorate.

Management assessed the effectiveness of the Company's internal control over financial reporting as of June 27, 2009.

Management based this assessment on criteria for effective internal control over financial reporting described in "Internal Control—Integrated Framework" issued by the Committee of Sponsoring Organizations of the Treadway Commission. Management's assessment included an evaluation of the design of the Company's internal control over financial reporting and testing of the operational effectiveness of its internal control over financial reporting. Management reviewed the results of its assessment with the Audit Committee of the Board of Directors.

Based on this assessment, we consider the following identified control deficiencies to aggregate to a material weakness around the operating effectiveness of certain financial reporting controls: financial reporting resources and oversight of subsidiary operations. Subsidiary financial reporting resources failed to identify certain significant accounting issues and the corporate financial reporting resources failed to detect the related errors during the close process. In light of these matters, management has taken additional steps to ensure the accuracy of the Form 10-K.

Planned remediation efforts regarding this material weakness include the following: 1) hiring of appropriate financial reporting resources and additional training of existing resources to ensure proper accounting at the subsidiary level and adequate oversight at Corporate; 2) enhancement of accounting policies and procedures with country specific translations for a global rollout during the first half of fiscal year 2010; 3) affirmation of subsidiary reporting responsibility to the Corporate CFO including monthly written representations; 4) improved subsidiary and corporate-level analysis of all significant financial statement accounts and changes monthly; and 5) more frequent visits to subsidiary locations by Corporate Accounting and Internal Audit during the year.

Management believes that the efforts described above, when fully implemented, will be effective in remediation of the material weaknesses.

The effectiveness of our internal control over financial reporting as of June 27, 2009 has been audited by Grant Thornton LLP, our independent registered public accounting firm, as stated in their report, which is included as Item 9A(e) of this Form 10-K.

Combined Report on Financial Statements and Internal Control

7.50

REPORT OF INDEPENDENT REGISTERED PUBLIC ACCOUNTING FIRM

To the Board of Directors and Shareholders of Leggett & Platt, Incorporated

In our opinion, the consolidated financial statements listed in the index appearing under Item 15(a) present fairly, in all material respects, the financial position of Leggett & Platt, Incorporated and its subsidiaries at December 31, 2009 and 2008, and the results of their operations and their cash flows for each of the three years in the period ended December 31, 2009 in conformity with accounting principles generally accepted in the United States of America. In addition, in our opinion, the financial statement schedule listed in the index appearing under Item 15(a) presents fairly, in all material respects, the information set forth therein when read in conjunction with the related consolidated financial statements. Also in our opinion, the Company maintained, in all material respects, effective internal control over financial reporting as of December 31, 2009, based on criteria established in Internal Control—Integrated Framework issued by the Committee of Sponsoring Organizations of the Treadway Commission (COSO). The Company's management is responsible for these financial statements and financial statement schedule, for maintaining effective internal control over financial reporting and for its assessment of the effectiveness of internal control over financial reporting, included in the accompanying Management's Annual Report on Internal Control over Financial Reporting. Our responsibility is to express opinions on these financial statements, on the financial statement schedule, and on the Company's internal control over financial reporting based on our integrated audits. We conducted our audits in accordance with the standards of the Public Company Accounting Oversight Board (United States). Those standards require that we plan and perform the audits to obtain reasonable assurance about whether the financial statements are free of material misstatement and whether effective internal control over financial reporting was maintained in all material respects. Our audits of the financial statements included examining, on a test basis, evidence supporting the amounts and disclosures in the financial statements, assessing the accounting principles used and significant estimates made by management, and evaluating the overall financial statement presentation. Our audit of internal control over financial reporting included obtaining an understanding of internal control over financial reporting, assessing the risk that a material weakness exists, and testing and evaluating the design and operating effectiveness of internal control based on the assessed risk. Our audits also included performing such other procedures as we considered necessary in the circumstances. We believe that our audits provide a reasonable basis for our opinions.

A company's internal control over financial reporting is a process designed to provide reasonable assurance regarding the reliability of financial reporting and the preparation of financial statements for external purposes in accordance with generally accepted accounting principles. A company's internal control over financial reporting includes those policies and procedures that (i) pertain to the maintenance of records that, in reasonable detail, accurately and fairly reflect the transactions and dispositions of the assets of the company; (ii) provide reasonable assurance that transactions are recorded as necessary to permit preparation of financial statements in accordance with generally accepted accounting principles, and that receipts and expenditures of the company are being made only in accordance with authorizations of management and directors of the company; and (iii) provide reasonable assurance regarding prevention or timely detection of unauthorized acquisition, use, or disposition of the company's assets that could have a material effect on the financial statements.

Because of its inherent limitations, internal control over financial reporting may not prevent or detect misstatements. Also, projections of any evaluation of effectiveness to future periods are subject to the risk that controls may become inadequate because of changes in conditions, or that the degree of compliance with the policies or procedures may deteriorate.

MANAGEMENT'S REPORT ON INTERNAL CONTROL OVER FINANCIAL REPORTING

Management of Leggett & Platt, Incorporated is responsible for establishing and maintaining adequate internal control over financial reporting as defined in Exchange Act Rule 13a-15(f). Leggett & Platt's internal control over financial reporting is a process designed to provide reasonable assurance regarding the reliability of financial reporting and the preparation of financial statements for external purposes in accordance with accounting principles generally accepted in the United States of America. The Company's internal control over financial reporting includes those policies and procedures that:

- Pertain to the maintenance of records that, in reasonable detail, accurately and fairly reflect the transactions and dispositions of the assets of Leggett & Platt;
- Provide reasonable assurance that transactions are recorded as necessary to permit preparation of financial statements in accordance with accounting principles generally accepted in the United States of America, and that receipts and expenditures of Leggett & Platt are being made only in accordance with authorizations of management and directors of Leggett & Platt; and
- Provide reasonable assurance regarding prevention or timely detection of unauthorized acquisition, use or disposition of Leggett & Platt assets that could have a material effect on the financial statements.

Because of its inherent limitations, internal control over financial reporting may not prevent or detect misstatements. Also, projections of any evaluation of effectiveness to future periods are subject to the risk that controls may become inadequate because of changes in conditions, or that the degree of compliance with the policies or procedures may deteriorate.

Under the supervision and with the participation of management (including ourselves), we conducted an evaluation of the effectiveness of Leggett & Platt's internal control over financial reporting, as of December 31, 2009, based on the criteria in Internal Control—Integrated Framework issued by the Committee of Sponsoring Organizations of the Treadway Commission. Based on the evaluation under this framework, we concluded that Leggett & Platt's internal control over financial reporting was effective as of December 31, 2009.

Leggett & Platt's internal control over financial reporting, as of December 31, 2009, has been audited by PricewaterhouseCoopers LLP, an independent registered public accounting firm, as stated in their report.

GENERAL MANAGEMENT AND SPECIAL PURPOSE COMMITTEE REPORTS

7.51 There were 166 survey entities that presented a Report of Management on Financial Statements. These reports may include:

- Description of management's responsibility for preparing the financial statements,
- Identification of independent auditors,
- Statement about management's representations to the independent auditors,

- Statement about financial records and related data made available to the independent auditors,
- Description of special purpose committees of the Board of Directors,
- General description of the entity's system of internal control, and
- Description of the entity's code of conduct.

Occasionally, survey entities presented a report of a special purpose committee, such as the Audit Committee or the Compensation Committee.

7.52 Examples of a Report of Management on Financial Statements and certain special purpose committee reports follow.

Report of Management on Financial Statements

7.53

ELI LILLY AND COMPANY (DEC)

MANAGEMENT'S REPORT FOR FINANCIAL STATEMENTS

Management of Eli Lilly and Company and subsidiaries is responsible for the accuracy, integrity, and fair presentation of the financial statements. The statements have been prepared in accordance with generally accepted accounting principles in the United States and include amounts based on judgments and estimates by management. In management's opinion, the consolidated financial statements present fairly our financial position, results of operations, and cash flows.

In addition to the system of internal accounting controls, we maintain a code of conduct (known as *The Red Book*) that applies to all employees worldwide, requiring proper overall business conduct, avoidance of conflicts of interest, compliance with laws, and confidentiality of proprietary information. *The Red Book* is reviewed on a periodic basis with employees worldwide, and all employees are required to report suspected violations. A hotline number is published in *The Red Book* to enable employees to report suspected violations anonymously. Employees who report suspected violations are protected from discrimination or retaliation by the company. In addition to *The Red Book*, the CEO, and all financial management must sign a financial code of ethics, which further reinforces their fiduciary responsibilities.

The consolidated financial statements have been audited by Ernst & Young LLP, an independent registered public accounting firm. Their responsibility is to examine our consolidated financial statements in accordance with generally accepted auditing standards of the Public Company Accounting Oversight Board (United States). Ernst & Young's opinion with respect to the fairness of the presentation of the statements is included in Item 8 of our annual report on Form 10-K. Ernst & Young reports directly to the audit committee of the board of directors.

Our audit committee includes five nonemployee members of the board of directors, all of whom are independent from our company. The committee charter, which is available on our web site, outlines the members' roles and responsibilities and is consistent with enacted corporate reform laws and regulations. It is the audit committee's responsibility to appoint an independent registered public accounting firm subject to shareholder ratification, approve both audit and nonaudit services performed by the independent registered public accounting firm, and review the reports submitted by the firm. The audit committee meets several times during the year with management, the internal auditors, and the independent public accounting firm to discuss audit activities, internal controls, and financial reporting matters, including reviews of our externally published financial results. The internal auditors and the independent registered public accounting firm have full and free access to the committee.

We are dedicated to ensuring that we maintain the high standards of financial accounting and reporting that we have established. We are committed to providing financial information that is transparent, timely, complete, relevant, and accurate. Our culture demands integrity and an unyielding commitment to strong internal practices and policies. Finally, we have the highest confidence in our financial reporting, our underlying system of internal controls, and our people, who are objective in their responsibilities and operate under a code of conduct and the highest level of ethical standards.

Chairman, President, and Chief Executive Officer

Executive Vice President, Global Services and Chief Financial Officer

Audit Committee Report

7.54

AUTOMATIC DATA PROCESSING, INC. (JUN)

AUDIT COMMITTEE REPORT

The audit committee oversees the financial management of the company, the company's independent auditors and financial reporting procedures of the company on behalf of the board of directors. In fulfilling its oversight responsibilities, the committee reviewed and discussed the company's audited financial statements with management, which has primary responsibility for the preparation of the financial statements. In performing its review, the committee discussed the propriety of the application of accounting principles by the company, the reasonableness of significant judgments and estimates used in the preparation of the financial statements, and the clarity of disclosures in the financial statements. Management represented to the audit committee that the company's financial statements were prepared in accordance with generally accepted accounting principles. The committee also reviewed and discussed the company's audited financial statements with Deloitte & Touche LLP, an independent registered public accounting firm, the company's independent auditors for the fiscal year 2009, which is responsible for expressing an opinion on the conformity of the company's audited financial statements with generally accepted accounting principles.

During the course of fiscal year 2009, management completed the documentation, testing and evaluation of the company's system of internal control over financial reporting in response to the requirements set forth in Section 404 of the Sarbanes-Oxley Act of 2002 and related regulations. The audit committee was kept apprised of the progress of the evaluation and provided oversight and advice to management during the process. In connection with this oversight, the audit committee received periodic updates provided by management and Deloitte & Touche LLP at each audit committee meeting. At the conclusion of the process, management provided the audit committee with, and the audit committee reviewed, a report on the effectiveness of the company's internal control over financial reporting. The audit committee also reviewed the report of management contained in the annual report on Form 10-K for the fiscal year ended June 30, 2009 filed with the SEC, as well as Deloitte & Touche LLP's Report of Independent Registered Public Accounting Firm included in the annual report on Form 10-K for the fiscal year ended June 30, 2009 related to its audit of the consolidated financial statements and financial statement schedule, and the effectiveness of internal control over financial reporting. The audit committee continues to oversee the company's efforts related to its internal control over financial reporting and management's preparations for the evaluation in fiscal year 2010.

The audit committee has discussed with Deloitte & Touche LLP the matters that are required to be discussed by Statement on Auditing Standards No. 61 (Communication with Audit Committees), as amended. Deloitte & Touche LLP has provided to the committee the written disclosures and the letter required by applicable requirements of the Public Company Accounting Oversight Board regarding Deloitte & Touche LLP's communications with the audit committee concerning independence, and the committee discussed with Deloitte & Touche LLP the firm's independence, including the matters in those written disclosures. The committee also considered whether Deloitte & Touche LLP's provision of non-audit services to the company and its affiliates and the fees and costs billed and expected to be billed by Deloitte & Touche LLP for those services, is compatible with Deloitte & Touche LLP's independence. The audit committee has discussed with the company's internal auditors and with Deloitte & Touche LLP, with and without management present, their respective evaluations of the company's internal accounting controls and the overall quality of the company's financial reporting. In addition, the committee discussed with management, and took into consideration when issuing this report, the Auditor Independence Policy, which prohibits the company or any of its affiliates from entering into most non-audit related consulting arrangements with its independent auditors. The Auditor Independence Policy is discussed in further detail below under "Independent Registered Public Accounting Firm's Fees."

Based on the considerations referred to above, the audit committee recommended to the board of directors that the audited financial statements be included in our annual report on Form 10-K for the fiscal year ended June 30, 2009. In addition, the committee appointed Deloitte & Touche LLP as the independent auditors for the company for the fiscal year

2010, subject to the ratification by the stockholders at the 2009 Annual Meeting of Stockholders.

Audit Committee of the Board of Directors

Chairman

Compensation Committee Report

7.55

HASBRO, INC. (DEC)

COMPENSATION COMMITTEE REPORT

The Compensation Committee (the "Committee") of the Company's Board is responsible for reviewing, approving and overseeing the compensation and benefits for the Company's senior management, including all of the Company's executive officers, and is authorized to make grants and awards under the Company's employee stock equity plans. The Committee operates under a written charter which has been established by the Company's Board. The current Committee charter is available on the Company's website at www.hasbro.com, under "Corporate—Investor Relations—Corporate Governance."

The Committee is composed solely of persons who are both "Non-Employee Directors," as defined in Rule 16b-3 of the rules and regulations of the United States Securities and Exchange Commission, and "outside directors," as defined in Section 162(m) of the Internal Revenue Code of 1986, as amended (the "Code"). The Board has determined that each member of the Committee is independent under the Company's Independence Standards and the requirements of the New York Stock Exchange's corporate governance listing standards.

The following section of this proxy statement, entitled "Compensation Discussion and Analysis", contains disclosure regarding the philosophy, policies and processes utilized by the Committee in reviewing and approving the compensation and benefits of the Company's executive officers.

The Committee has reviewed and discussed with management the Compensation Discussion and Analysis which follows this report.

Based on its review and discussions with management, the Committee recommended to the Company's full Board and the Board has approved the inclusion of the Compensation Discussion and Analysis in this proxy statement for the Meeting and, by incorporation by reference, in the Company's Annual Report on Form 10-K for the year ended December 27, 2009.

Report issued by the Chair
and the members of the Committee
as of the 2009 fiscal year end

Appendix of 500 Entities

List of 500 Survey Entities and Where in the Text Excerpts From Their Annual Reports Can Be Found

The following table lists the 500 entities surveyed in this edition of *Accounting Trends & Techniques* (*Trends*) in alphabetical order, as well as where in the text their annual reports are excerpted. A list of the companies included in the 2009 edition but not included in this edition follows the table.

Company Name	Month of Fiscal Year End*	Replacement Company	Accounting Technique Illustration
3Com Corporation	5	New	2.24
3M Company	12		1.46, 2.116, 7.31
A. O. Smith Corporation	12		
A. Schulman, Inc.	8		2.172, 3.29
Abbott Laboratories	12		1.58, 5.23
ABM Industries Incorporated	10		1.124, 3.91, 4.27, 5.36
Acuity Brands, Inc.	8		4.08
ADC Telecommunications, Inc.	9		1.32, 2.211
Administaff, Inc.	12		2.76
Adobe Systems Incorporated	11		3.88
Advanced Micro Devices, Inc.	12		2.178, 3.26
AGCO Corporation	12		
Air Products and Chemicals, Inc.	9		1.92, 2.183, 4.13
Airgas, Inc.	3		6.64
AK Steel Holding Corporation	12		1.170, 4.25, 6.45
Alberto-Culver Company	9	New	1.14
Alcoa Inc.	12		2.257, 7.29
Allegheny Technologies Incorporated	12		3.30
Allergan, Inc.	12		2.242, 3.40
Alliance One International, Inc.	3		2.78
Alliant Techsystems Inc.	3		2.33, 3.103
Altria Group, Inc.	12		2.190
Amazon.com, Inc.	12		
American Greetings Corporation	2		1.109
Ameron International Corporation	11		7.27
AMETEK, Inc.	12		2.229, 2.271, 2.278, 6.37
Amgen Inc.	12		2.134
Amkor Technology, Inc.	12		2.215
Ampco-Pittsburgh Corporation	12		
Amphenol Corporation	12		1.180, 3.115
Anadarko Petroleum Corporation	12		1.134, 2.133, 2.207, 3.51, 3.92
Analog Devices, Inc.	10		1.99, 1.144, 4.26
Apache Corporation	12		2.241
Apple Inc.	9		2.37, 3.15
Applied Industrial Technologies, Inc.	6		3.62
Applied Materials, Inc.	10		
Archer Daniels Midland Company	6		2.32, 2.179
Arden Group, Inc.	12		1.125, 6.13
Arkansas Best Corporation	12		
Armstrong World Industries, Inc.	12		
Arrow Electronics, Inc.	12		3.20, 3.55, 3.76
ArvinMeritor, Inc.	9		2.38, 3.49
Ashland Inc.	9		1.107, 2.126
AT&T Inc.	12		1.15, 2.104
Atmel Corporation	12		

* Months are numbered in calendar-year sequence, January through December (e.g., January = 1 and February = 2).

Company Name	Month of Fiscal Year End*	Replacement Company	Accounting Technique Illustration
Autodesk, Inc.	1		
Automatic Data Processing, Inc.	6		1.18, 2.80, 3.110, 7.54
AutoNation, Inc.	12		
AutoZone, Inc.	8		
Avery Dennison Corporation	12		
Avis Budget Group, Inc.	12		2.137, 6.56
Avnet, Inc.	6		5.35
Avon Products, Inc.	12		2.63, 7.42
Badger Meter, Inc.	12		
Baker Hughes Incorporated	12		1.152, 3.18
Baldor Electric Company	12		2.191, 6.59
Ball Corporation	12		2.124, 2.141, 6.33
Barnes & Noble, Inc.	1		
Bassett Furniture Industries, Incorporated	11		
Baxter International Inc.	12		1.59, 3.47
BE Aerospace, Inc.	12		3.89
Beckman Coulter, Inc.	12		
Becton, Dickinson and Company	9		6.38
Belden Inc.	12		1.33, 2.193
Bemis Company, Inc.	12		
Best Buy Co., Inc.	2		2.157, 3.52, 7.48
BJ Services Company	9		1.88
The Black & Decker Corporation	12		3.60
BMC Software, Inc.	3		2.143
The Boeing Company	12		1.122, 1.137, 2.69, 2.225, 3.102
The Bon-Ton Stores, Inc.	1		
Boston Scientific Corporation	12		1.95, 1.159
Boyd Gaming Corporation	12		
Breeze-Eastern Corporation	3		
Briggs & Stratton Corporation	6		2.269, 3.111
Brinker International, Inc.	6		
The Brink's Company	12		4.10
Bristol-Myers Squibb Company	12		1.75, 2.106, 3.132
Brown Shoe Company, Inc.	1		
Brown-Forman Corporation	4		5.31
Brunswick Corporation	12		2.273
C. R. Bard, Inc.	12		1.145, 1.181
CA, Inc.	3		2.184
Cablevision Systems Corporation	12		
Cabot Corporation	9		2.163
CACI International Inc.	6		
Cameron International Corporation	12		3.73, 5.46, 6.52
Campbell Soup Company	7		1.135
Cardinal Health, Inc.	6		
Career Education Corporation	12		
Carlisle Companies Incorporated	12		3.27
Carpenter Technology Corporation	6		
Caterpillar Inc.	12		1.102, 2.233
CBS Corporation	12		
Centex Corporation	3		
CenturyTel, Inc.	12		2.144, 3.143, 5.38
Cenveo, Inc.	12		
Chemtura Corporation	12		2.198, 7.24
Chesapeake Energy Corporation	12		3.106
Chevron Corporation	12		5.25
Chiquita Brands International, Inc.	12		1.56
Church & Dwight Co., Inc.	12		
Cintas Corporation	5		
Cisco Systems, Inc.	7		3.46

* Months are numbered in calendar-year sequence, January through December (e.g., January = 1 and February = 2).

Company Name	Month of Fiscal Year End*	Replacement Company	Accounting Technique Illustration
Cliffs Natural Resources Inc.	12		1.60, 1.121, 1.142, 2.25, 3.25
The Clorox Company	6		2.158
The Coca-Cola Company	12		
Coca-Cola Enterprises Inc.	12		
Coherent, Inc.	9	New	3.42
Colgate-Palmolive Company	12		2.168, 3.93
Collective Brands, Inc.	1		
Comcast Corporation	12		
Commercial Metals Company	8		2.47, 3.75
Computer Sciences Corporation	3		
ConAgra Foods, Inc.	5		
ConocoPhillips	12		2.230
Constellation Brands, Inc.	2		
Convergys Corporation	12		1.24, 4.12
Con-way Inc.	12		2.240
Cooper Tire & Rubber Company	12		1.136
Corn Products International, Inc.	12		
Corning Incorporated	12		3.74
Costco Wholesale Corporation	8		2.22, 5.39
Covance Inc.	12		2.129
Cracker Barrel Old Country Store, Inc.	7		
Crane Co.	12		1.90, 1.182, 2.36, 3.112
Crown Holdings, Inc.	12		2.182
CSP Inc.	9	New	7.14
Cummins Inc.	12		
CVS Caremark Corporation	12		1.10, 6.14
Cytec Industries Inc.	12		3.105, 6.29
D.R. Horton, Inc.	9		
Dana Holding Corporation	12		2.146, 2.243
Danaher Corporation	12		
Darden Restaurants, Inc.	5		2.292
Dean Foods Company	12		1.116, 3.41
Deere & Company	10		1.164, 4.14
Del Monte Foods Company	4		
Dell Inc.	1		
Devon Energy Corporation	12		3.28
Dillard's, Inc.	1		
DIRECTV	12		6.47
Domino's Pizza, Inc.	12	New	
Donaldson Company, Inc.	7		5.53
Dover Corporation	12		
The Dow Chemical Company	12		1.76, 2.132
The Dun & Bradstreet Corporation	12		
E. I. du Pont de Nemours and Company	12		1.138
The E. W. Scripps Company	12		
Eastman Chemical Company	12		6.40
Eastman Kodak Company	12		
Eaton Corporation	12		
eBay Inc.	12		
Ecolab Inc.	12		
El Paso Corporation	12		4.23, 7.20
Electronic Arts Inc.	3		
Eli Lilly and Company	12		1.97, 3.118, 6.43, 7.53
EMC Corporation	12		1.54, 1.156, 3.86, 4.11
EMCOR Group, Inc.	12		2.81
Emerson Electric Co.	9		6.65
Energizer Holdings, Inc.	9		
Equifax Inc.	12		
The Estee Lauder Companies Inc.	6		2.127

* Months are numbered in calendar-year sequence, January through December (e.g., January = 1 and February = 2).

Company Name	Month of Fiscal Year End*	Replacement Company	Accounting Technique Illustration
Exide Technologies	3		
Express Scripts, Inc.	12		3.119
Exxon Mobil Corporation	12		
Family Dollar Stores, Inc.	8		
Federal-Mogul Corporation	12		
FedEx Corporation	5		
Fidelity National Information Services, Inc.	12		1.82, 2.148, 7.36
Fiserv, Inc.	12		
Flowers Foods, Inc.	12		2.79, 3.31, 3.61
Fluor Corporation	12		
FMC Corporation	12		5.08
Foot Locker, Inc.	1		
Ford Motor Company	12		
Fortune Brands, Inc.	12		1.19, 1.25, 2.64
Freds Inc.	1		
Freeport-McMoRan Copper & Gold Inc.	12		2.12, 3.139, 6.48
Frontier Communications Corporation	12		
Furniture Brands International, Inc.	12		
GameStop Corp.	1		
Gannett Co., Inc.	12		2.185
The Gap, Inc.	1		
Gardner Denver, Inc.	12		2.209
GenCorp Inc.	11		1.150, 5.44
General Cable Corporation	12		6.49
General Dynamics Corporation	12		
General Electric Company	12		
General Mills, Inc.	5		1.105
Genuine Parts Company	12		2.244, 3.45
Georgia Gulf Corporation	12		
Goodrich Corporation	12		1.93, 2.236, 3.43, 3.134
The Goodyear Tire & Rubber Company	12		3.100
Google Inc.	12		2.23, 3.16
The Great Atlantic & Pacific Tea Company, Inc.	2		2.224
Greif, Inc.	10		1.183
Griffon Corporation	9	New	
H.J. Heinz Company	4		6.60
Halliburton Company	12		3.120
Hanesbrands Inc.	12		
Harley-Davidson, Inc.	12		2.164
Harman International Industries, Incorporated	6		
Harris Corporation	6		2.07
Harsco Corporation	12		
Hasbro, Inc.	12		1.84, 3.44, 7.55
Health Net, Inc.	12		
Herman Miller, Inc.	5		
The Hershey Company	12		
Hess Corporation	12		1.16
Hewitt Associates, Inc.	9		5.41
Hewlett-Packard Company	10		1.66, 1.110, 3.90, 4.21
Hill-Rom Holdings, Inc.	9		2.195
HNI Corporation	12		2.77
The Home Depot, Inc.	1		2.187
Honeywell International Inc.	12		6.46, 7.28
Hormel Foods Corporation	10		1.63
Hovnanian Enterprises, Inc.	10		
Hubbell Incorporated	12		
Huntsman Corporation	12		6.30
IAC/InterActiveCorp	12		
IDT Corporation	7		

* Months are numbered in calendar-year sequence, January through December (e.g., January = 1 and February = 2).

ATT-APP

Company Name	Month of Fiscal Year End*	Replacement Company	Accounting Technique Illustration
Illinois Tool Works Inc.	12		1.157
Ingram Micro Inc.	12		
Intel Corporation	12		1.62, 3.17
International Business Machines Corporation	12		4.28
International Flavors & Fragrances Inc.	12		1.12
International Paper Company	12		
The Interpublic Group of Companies, Inc.	12		
Intuit Inc.	7		
Iron Mountain Incorporated	12		2.91, 2.128, 3.63
ITT Corporation	12		2.186, 3.22
J. C. Penney Company, Inc.	1		3.08
The J. M. Smucker Company	4		1.160, 5.54, 6.36
Jabil Circuit, Inc.	8		3.48
Jack in the Box Inc.	9		
Jacobs Engineering Group Inc.	9		
Jarden Corporation	12		
JDS Uniphase Corporation	6		
Johnson & Johnson	12		1.106, 2.279
Johnson Controls, Inc.	9		
Jones Apparel Group, Inc.	12		
Joy Global Inc.	10		2.131
Juniper Networks, Inc.	12		1.158, 2.142
KB Home	11		2.291, 5.11
Kellogg Company	12		1.143, 3.81
Kelly Services, Inc.	12		
Kimball International, Inc.	6		1.68, 1.146
Kimberly-Clark Corporation	12		1.55, 1.168, 2.65, 2.287, 5.49
KLA-Tencor Corporation	6		
Kohl's Corporation	1		
The Kroger Co.	1		
The L.S. Starrett Company	6		1.117, 6.18, 7.49
L-3 Communications Holdings, Inc.	12		
Lam Research Corporation	6		3.23, 3.56, 3.94
Lance, Inc.	12	New	
Las Vegas Sands Corp.	12		
La-Z-Boy Incorporated	4		
Lear Corporation	12		
Lee Enterprises, Incorporated	9		6.35
Leggett & Platt, Incorporated	12		2.08, 2.139, 6.25, 7.50
Lennar Corporation	11		
Lennox International Inc.	12		
Lexmark International, Inc.	12		2.46
Liberty Media Corporation	12		
Liz Claiborne, Inc.	12		
Lockheed Martin Corporation	12		
Louisiana-Pacific Corporation	12		1.103
Lowe's Companies, Inc.	1		2.107
LSI Corporation	12		
The Lubrizol Corporation	12		2.208
Macy's, Inc.	1		
The Manitowoc Company, Inc.	12		3.54
Manpower Inc.	12		6.15
Marriott International, Inc.	12		
Martin Marietta Materials, Inc.	12		
Masco Corporation	12		2.188
Mattel, Inc.	12		5.48
The McClatchy Company	12		1.151
McCormick & Company, Incorporated	11		3.50
McDonald's Corporation	12		

* Months are numbered in calendar-year sequence, January through December (e.g., January = 1 and February = 2).

AICPA Accounting Trends & Techniques   **ATT-APP**

Company Name	Month of Fiscal Year End*	Replacement Company	Accounting Technique Illustration
The McGraw-Hill Companies, Inc.	12		5.09
McKesson Corporation	3		
MeadWestvaco Corporation	12		2.140
Medtronic, Inc.	4		
Merck & Co., Inc.	12		1.11, 5.40
Meredith Corporation	6		6.27
Meritage Homes Corporation	12		3.24
Mettler-Toledo International Inc.	12		
Micron Technology, Inc.	8		
Microsoft Corporation	6		
Mohawk Industries, Inc.	12		6.26
Molex Incorporated	6		6.24
Molson Coors Brewing Company	12		2.232
Monsanto Company	8		1.141, 2.45
The Mosaic Company	5		1.166, 5.18
Motorola, Inc.	12		
Mueller Industries, Inc.	12		
Murphy Oil Corporation	12		
NACCO Industries, Inc.	12		
Nash-Finch Company	12		
National Oilwell Varco, Inc.	12		
National Semiconductor Corporation	5		5.47
NCR Corporation	12		6.19
NetApp, Inc.	4		1.139, 2.130, 3.09, 3.87
The New York Times Company	12		
Newell Rubbermaid Inc.	12		
NewMarket Corporation	12	New	2.72, 2.145, 3.53
Newmont Mining Corporation	12		
News Corporation	6		1.167, 6.57
NIKE, Inc.	5		1.13
Noble Energy, Inc.	12		
Nordstrom, Inc.	1		2.92
Northrop Grumman Corporation	12		2.216, 3.124
Novell, Inc.	10	New	
Nucor Corporation	12		6.21
NVR, Inc.	12		
Occidental Petroleum Corporation	12		3.104
Office Depot, Inc.	12		
Olin Corporation	12		1.17
Omnicom Group Inc.	12		
Oracle Corporation	5		
Owens-Illinois, Inc.	12		3.145
PACCAR Inc	12		
Pactiv Corporation	12		4.29, 7.33
Pall Corporation	7		1.83, 2.192
Parker-Hannifin Corporation	6		
Paychex, Inc.	5		
Peabody Energy Corporation	12		
Pentair, Inc.	12		
The Pepsi Bottling Group, Inc.	12		
PepsiAmericas, Inc.	12		
PepsiCo, Inc.	12		
PerkinElmer, Inc.	12		
Pfizer Inc.	12		6.34, 6.61
Phillips-Van Heusen Corporation	1		
Pilgrim's Pride Corporation	9		
Pitney Bowes Inc.	12		
Plum Creek Timber Company, Inc.	12		
Polaris Industries Inc.	12		2.231

* Months are numbered in calendar-year sequence, January through December (e.g., January = 1 and February = 2).

Company Name	Month of Fiscal Year End*	Replacement Company	Accounting Technique Illustration
Polo Ralph Lauren Corporation	3		1.126, 2.234, 7.40
PolyOne Corporation	12		2.35, 3.78
Potlatch Corporation	12		1.118
PPG Industries, Inc.	12		
Praxair, Inc.	12		1.119
Precision Castparts Corp.	3		3.133
Pride International, Inc.	12		3.101, 6.28
The Procter & Gamble Company	6		
Pulte Homes, Inc.	12		
QUALCOMM Incorporated	9		
Quanex Building Products Corporation	10		2.210, 6.31
Quantum Corporation	3		
Quiksilver, Inc.	10		4.22
Qwest Communications International Inc.	12		
R.R. Donnelley & Sons Company	12		
RadioShack Corporation	12		
Raytheon Company	12		1.64
Regal Beloit Corporation	12		
Regal Entertainment Group	12		
Republic Services, Inc.	12		3.77
Retail Ventures, Inc.	1		5.56
Reynolds American Inc.	12		
Rite Aid Corporation	2		2.258
Robbins & Myers, Inc.	8	New	
Robert Half International Inc.	12		
Rock-Tenn Company	9		1.26, 1.94, 4.30
Rockwell Automation, Inc.	9		6.20
Rockwell Collins, Inc.	9		1.111, 2.194
RPM International Inc.	5		3.125, 6.66
Ruddick Corporation	9		
Ryder System, Inc.	12		2.117, 6.41
The Ryland Group, Inc.	12		6.22
Safeway Inc.	12		
Sanmina-SCI Corporation	9		5.32
Sara Lee Corporation	6		1.96, 2.290
Schnitzer Steel Industries, Inc.	8		2.68
Scholastic Corporation	5		
The Scotts Miracle-Gro Company	9		
Seaboard Corporation	12		1.123
Sealed Air Corporation	12		
Sealy Corporation	11		5.20, 6.51
Sears Holdings Corporation	1		
Service Corporation International	12		2.280
SFN Group, Inc.	12		
The Shaw Group Inc.	8		2.221
The Sherwin-Williams Company	12		3.58
Silgan Holdings Inc.	12		1.65, 2.13
Smith International, Inc.	12		2.293
Smithfield Foods, Inc.	4		5.43
Smurfit-Stone Container Corporation	12		
Snap-on Incorporated	12		1.34, 1.77, 2.34
Sonic Automotive, Inc.	12		
Sonoco Products Company	12		
Span-America Medical Systems, Inc.	9	New	1.174
Sparton Corporation	6		
Spectrum Brands, Inc.	9		2.173
Spectrum Control, Inc.	11	New	6.42
Sprint Nextel Corporation	12		
SPX Corporation	12		

* Months are numbered in calendar-year sequence, January through December (e.g., January = 1 and February = 2).

Company Name	Month of Fiscal Year End*	Replacement Company	Accounting Technique Illustration
St. Jude Medical, Inc.	12		
Standard Pacific Corp.	12		
The Standard Register Company	12		7.13
Standex International Corporation	6	New	3.38
The Stanley Works	12		
Staples, Inc.	1		
Starbucks Corporation	9		2.26, 2.73
Starwood Hotels & Resorts Worldwide, Inc.	12		
Steel Dynamics, Inc.	12		
Steelcase Inc.	2		2.147
Stryker Corporation	12		
Sun Microsystems, Inc.	6		2.239
Sunoco, Inc.	12		
SuperMedia Inc.	12		
SUPERVALU INC.	2		2.49, 2.66, 2.223
Symantec Corporation	3		
SYNNEX Corporation	11		
Sysco Corporation	6		1.161, 2.270
Target Corporation	1		1.140, 2.272
Tasty Baking Company	12		
Tech Data Corporation	1		
Teleflex Incorporated	12		
Tellabs, Inc.	12		
Temple-Inland Inc.	12		
Tenet Healthcare Corporation	12		2.31, 3.19, 4.24
Tenneco Inc.	12		3.59
Terex Corporation	12		5.45
Terra Industries Inc.	12		1.153, 2.105, 2.149, 2.196
Tesoro Corporation	12		
Texas Industries, Inc.	5		1.27
Texas Instruments Incorporated	12		1.104, 4.15, 7.12
Textron Inc.	12		3.146
Thermo Fisher Scientific Inc.	12		1.120, 3.147, 4.09
Thomas & Betts Corporation	12		1.91
Thor Industries, Inc.	7		
The Timberland Company	12	New	
Time Warner Inc.	12		1.108, 3.57
The Timken Company	12		
The TJX Companies, Inc.	1		
Toll Brothers, Inc.	10		1.165
The Toro Company	10		5.24
Trinity Industries, Inc.	12		
TRW Automotive Holdings Corp.	12		
Tupperware Brands Corporation	12		
Tutor Perini Corporation	12		1.98, 3.126
Twin Disc, Incorporated	6		
Tyson Foods, Inc.	9		
Unifi, Inc.	6		
Unisys Corporation	12		
United Parcel Service, Inc.	12		2.289
United States Steel Corporation	12		
United Stationers Inc.	12		2.93
United Technologies Corporation	12		
Universal Corporation	3		
Universal Forest Products, Inc.	12		5.42, 5.55
Universal Health Services, Inc.	12		
URS Corporation	12		2.197
USG Corporation	12		
UTStarcom, Inc.	12		2.108

* Months are numbered in calendar-year sequence, January through December (e.g., January = 1 and February = 2).

Company Name	Month of Fiscal Year End*	Replacement Company	Accounting Technique Illustration
V.F. Corporation	12		2.125, 2.237
Valassis Communications, Inc.	12		1.154, 6.23
Valero Energy Corporation	12		1.155, 2.169, 2.238, 5.37
Varian Medical Systems, Inc.	9		1.57, 2.118
VeriSign, Inc.	12	New	1.89
Verizon Communications Inc.	12		2.226
Viacom Inc.	12		
Viad Corp	12		
Vishay Intertechnology, Inc.	12		1.112
Visteon Corporation	12		2.288
Vulcan Materials Company	12		1.67, 2.67, 3.113
W. R. Grace & Co.	12		
W.W. Grainger, Inc.	12		2.138, 7.32
Walgreen Co.	8		2.189
Wal-Mart Stores, Inc.	1		2.222
The Walt Disney Company	9		
Walter Energy, Inc.	12		2.274, 5.10
The Warnaco Group, Inc.	12		6.53
Warner Music Group Corp.	9		
The Washington Post Company	12		1.61
Waste Management, Inc.	12		1.169
Wausau Paper Corp.	12	New	3.95
Weis Markets, Inc.	12		
WellPoint, Inc.	12		5.19, 7.30
Wendy's/Arby's Group, Inc.	12		2.212, 3.21
Werner Enterprises, Inc.	12		
Western Digital Corporation	6		
Western Refining, Inc.	12		
The Western Union Company	12		1.171, 6.39
Weyerhaeuser Company	12		
Whirlpool Corporation	12		
Whole Foods Market, Inc.	9		1.47, 2.235, 6.50
Winn-Dixie Stores, Inc.	6		
Winnebago Industries, Inc.	8		
Wolverine World Wide, Inc.	12	New	3.39, 6.17
Worthington Industries, Inc.	5		6.16
Wyndham Worldwide Corporation	12		
Xerox Corporation	12		1.162, 2.48, 3.116
Xilinx, Inc.	3		
Yahoo! Inc.	12		
YUM! Brands, Inc.	12		
Zimmer Holdings, Inc.	12		6.54

* Months are numbered in calendar-year sequence, January through December (e.g., January = 1 and February = 2).

**COMPANIES INCLUDED IN THE 2009 EDITION
BUT NOT INCLUDED IN THIS EDITION**

Aetna Inc.
CIGNA Corporation
Circuit City Stores, Inc.
Coventry Health Care, Inc.
Embarq Corporation
Federal Screw Works
Fleetwood Enterprises, Inc.
General Motors Corporation
Humana Inc.

Longs Drug Stores Corporation
Merrimac Industries, Inc.
MPS Group, Inc.
Perot Systems Corporation
Rohm and Haas Company
Schering-Plough Corporation
UnitedHealth Group Incorporated
Wyeth

Pronouncement Index

All of the pronouncements and standards cited in the narrative portions (not in the survey company illustrations) of this edition of *Accounting Trends & Techniques* have been listed below. Titles and paragraph locations have been included for ease of use and reference.

No.	Title	Paragraph
	FASB ACCOUNTING STANDARDS UPDATE (ASU)	
2009-05	*Measuring Liabilities at Fair Value*	1.129
2009-16	*Accounting for Transfers of Financial Assets*	1.71, 2.42
2009-17	*Improvements to Financial Reporting by Enterprises Involved With Variable Interest Entities*	1.71
2010-06	*Improving Disclosures About Fair Value Measurements*	1.129, 2.17, 2.97, 2.111, 2.153, 2.175, 2.203

OTHER GUIDANCE NOT INCLUDED IN FASB ACCOUNTING STANDARDS CODIFICATION

Accounting Terminology Bulletins (AICPA)

1	*Review and Resume*	2.245

Financial Accounting Standards Board Concepts Statements

6	*Elements of Financial Statements*	3.10, 3.32

Financial Accounting Standards Board Statements

168	*The FASB Accounting Standards Codification™ and the Hierarchy of Generally Accepted Accounting Principles—a replacement of FASB Statement No. 162*	1.175

PCAOB Auditing Standards

1	*References in Auditors' Reports to the Standards of the Public Company Accounting Oversight Board*	7.15, 7.16
2	*An Audit of Internal Control Over Financial Reporting Performed in Conjunction With an Audit of Financial Statements*	7.46
5	*An Audit of Internal Control Over Financial Reporting That is Integrated With an Audit of Financial Statements*	7.46

PCAOB Rules

3100	*Compliance With Auditing and Related Professional Practice Standards*	7.02

Sarbanes-Oxley Act of 2002

Section 103 (a)	*Auditing, Quality Control, Ethics Standards*	7.02
Section 404 (a)	*Management Assessment of Internal Control—Rules Required*	7.45
Section 404 (b)	*Management Assessment of Internal Control—Internal Control Evaluation and Reporting*	7.46

SEC Regulation S-K

	Standard Instructions for Filing Forms Under the Securities Act of 1933, Securities Exchange Act of 1934 and Energy Policy and Conservation Act of 1975	1.07, 1.40

SEC Regulation S-X

	Accounting Rules—Form and Content of Financial Statements	1.40

SEC Rule 14a-3

	Information to Be Furnished to Security Holders	1.07, 1.35

Subject Index

A

Accelerated depreciation methods, 3.102–3.103

Accounting changes
  business combinations, 1.58–1.59
  defined benefit pension and postretirement plans, 1.60–1.61
  depreciation method, 1.67
  derivatives, 1.63
  earnings per share calculation, 1.64
  estimated useful lives, 1.68
  fair value measurements, 1.56–1.57
  financial instruments with debt and equity characteristics, 1.62
  inventories, 1.65
  noncontrolling interests, 1.54–1.55
  opening balance of retained earnings, 5.12–5.20
  presentation, 1.48–1.53
  presentation and disclosure excerpts, 1.54–1.68
  revenue recognition, 1.66

Accounting corrections. *See* Adjustments to opening balance of retained earnings; Prior period adjustment

Accounting estimates, 1.105–1.108

Accounting policies, disclosure, 1.43–1.47

Accounting principles, changes in, 1.48–1.68, 5.18–5.19, 7.25–7.33

Accounting Standards Codification (ASC) referencing in financial statements, 1.182–1.183

Accounts payable, 2.159–2.164

Accounts receivable, 2.27–2.51. *See also* Current receivables; Receivables sold or collateralized

Accumulated depreciation, 2.90

Accumulated other comprehensive income
  balance sheet caption, 2.267
  equity section of balance sheet, 2.273–2.274
  notes to financial statements, 2.269–2.270
  presentation, 2.263–2.266
  presentation and disclosure excerpts, 2.269–2.274
  presentation of component balances, 2.268
  statement of changes in stockholders' equity, 2.271–2.272

Acquisition method, business combinations, 1.82–1.83

Acquisitions, 1.124, 6.54

Additional paid-in capital, 2.259–2.260

Additional paid-in capital, changes in
  business combinations, 5.38
  common stock issued in connection with employee benefit plans, 5.35–5.36
  compensation recognized, 5.41
  debt conversion, 5.39
  equity component of convertible debt issuance, 5.45
  preferred stock conversion, 5.40
  presentation and disclosure excerpts, 5.29–5.49
  presentation of, 5.26–5.28, 5.33–5.34
  public offering, 5.37
  purchase of noncontrolling interest, 5.49
  reclassification of redeemable common stock, 5.44
  restricted stock, 5.48
  stock compensation tax benefit, 5.42
  stock splits, 5.29–5.32
  treasury stock issued, 5.46
  treasury stock purchased, 5.47
  warrants issued or exercised, 5.43

Additional payments related to acquisitions, 1.124

Addressee, independent auditors' report, 7.06–7.08

Adjusting events after the reporting period. *See* Subsequent events

Adjustment of gain/loss reported in prior period, 3.134

Adjustments to opening balance of retained earnings
  change in accounting principle, 5.18–5.19
  correction of an error/misstatement, 5.20
  presentation, 5.12–5.17
  presentation and disclosure excerpts, 5.18–5.20

F

Financing/support agreement, 1.122

First-in first-out inventories, 2.63–2.64

Fiscal year
  change in date of fiscal year end, 1.32
  defined, 1.33–1.34
  month of fiscal year end, 1.31
  presentation, 1.28–1.30
  presentation and disclosure excerpts, 1.32–1.34

Fixed assets. *See* Property, plant, and equipment

Foreign currency cash flows, 6.55–6.57

Foreign currency transactions, 3.23, 3.53

Format
  of balance sheet, 2.03–2.08
  of income statement, 3.03–3.09

Forward-looking information excerpt, 1.15

Franchise fees, 3.25

Franchises, 2.132

G

Gain contingencies, 1.97–1.99
  contingent receivables, 1.99
  plaintiff litigation, 1.97–1.98

Gains
  adjustment of, reported in prior period, 3.134
  business combination adjustment gain, 3.31
  change in fair value of derivatives, 3.18
  change in fair value of financial assets/liabilities, 3.28
  debt extinguishments, 3.24
  dividends, 3.21
  employee benefit-related, 3.29
  equity in earnings of investees, 3.20
  foreign currency transactions, 3.23
  franchise fees, 3.25
  insurance recoveries, 3.27
  interest, 3.17
  liability accruals reduced, 3.22
  license fees, 3.25
  litigation settlement, 3.26
  pension-related, 3.29
  presentation, 3.14
  presentation and disclosure excerpts, 3.17–3.31
  rentals, 3.30
  revenues and, 3.10–3.12
  royalties, 3.25
  sale of assets, 3.19
  unrealized, on certain investments, 4.27–4.28

General management and special purpose committee reports, 7.51–7.55

Goodwill, 2.124–2.125

Governmental investigations, 1.95

Guarantees of ESOP debt, 2.290

Guarantees/indemnifications, 1.137–1.139

H

Health care cost trend rate (2009), 3.71

Held-to-maturity securities, 2.24–2.25

I

Impairment of assets, 3.52, 6.24

In-process research and development, 6.43

Incentive compensation plans, 3.92

Income statement
  accelerated methods, 3.102–3.103
  adjustment of gain/loss reported in prior period, 3.134
  advertising, 3.44
  assumed discount rate—pensions, 3.68
  assumed rate of compensation increase—pensions, 3.69
  business combination adjustment gains/losses, 3.31, 3.63
  business component disposals, 3.132–3.133
  change in fair value of derivatives, 3.18, 3.51
  change in fair value of financial assets/liabilities, 3.28
  charges or credits shown after income tax caption, 3.135–3.139
  composite method—depreciation, 3.105
  cost of goods sold, 3.38–3.39
  cost of goods sold captions, 3.35
  debt extinguishment, 3.24, 3.55
  deferred compensation plans, 3.91
  defined benefit plans, 3.73–3.74
  defined contribution plans, 3.75
  depletion, 3.106
  depreciation expense, 3.96–3.106
  discontinuance of regulatory accounting, 3.143
  discontinued operations, 3.127–3.134
  dividend equivalent plans, 3.95
  dividends, 3.21
  earnings per share, 3.144–3.147
  employee benefit/pension related gains, 3.29
  employee compensatory plans, 3.82–3.95
  employee stock ownership plans, 3.93
  environmental clean-up, 3.58
  equity in earnings of investees, 3.20
  equity in losses of investee, 3.57
  expected rate of return—pensions, 3.70
  expense provision, income taxes, 3.110–3.112
  expenses, 3.38–3.47
  expenses other than cost of goods sold, 3.36
  extraordinary items, 3.140–3.143
  fair value adjustments, 3.62
  foreign currency transactions, 3.23, 3.53
  format, 3.03–3.09
  franchise fees, 3.25
  gains, 3.14, 3.17–3.31
  health care cost trend rate (2009), 3.71
  impairment of intangibles, 3.52
  incentive compensation plans, 3.92

O

T